View a guided tour of MyAccountingLab at
http://www.myaccountinglab.com/support/tours

For Students

Interactive Tutorial Exercises

- Homework and practice exercises with additional algorithmic–generated problems for more practice.
- Personalized interactive learning—guided solutions and learning aids for point-of-use help and immediate feedback.

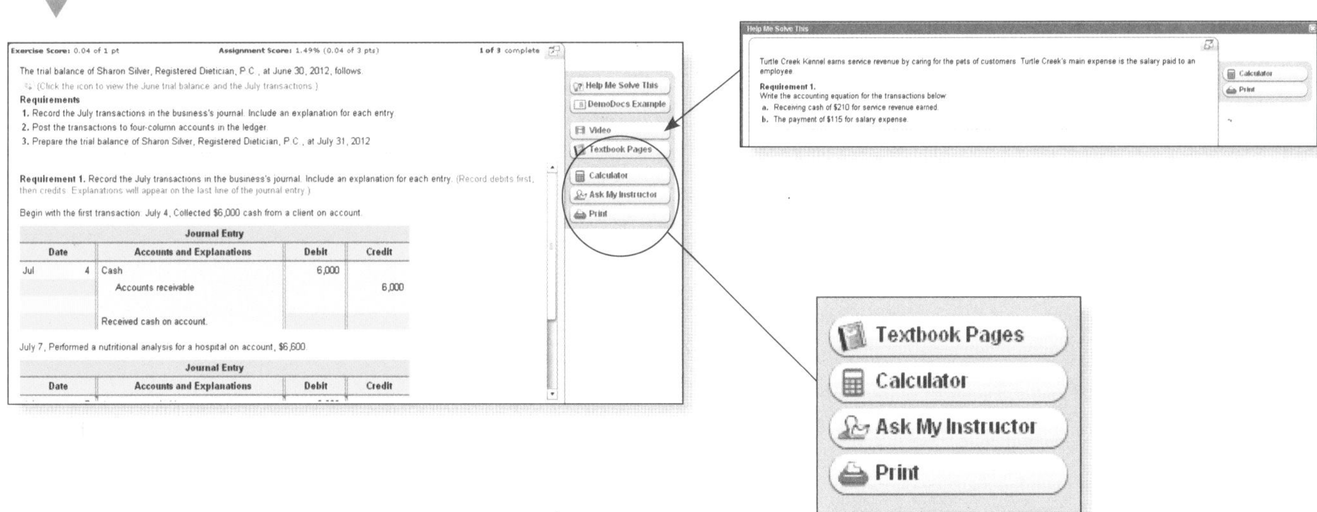

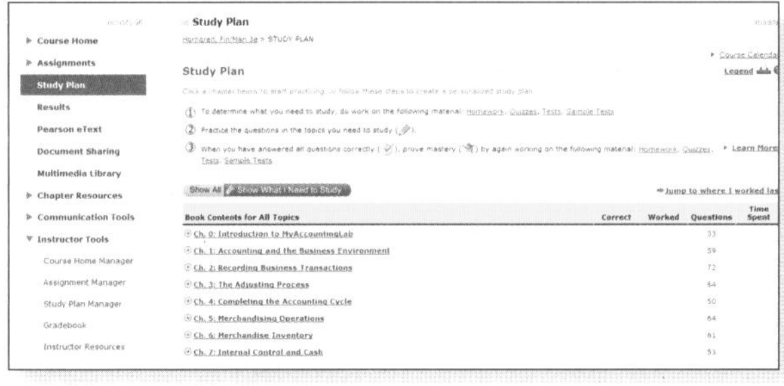

Study Plan for Self-Paced Learning

- Assists students in monitoring their own progress by offering them a customized study plan based on their test results.
- Includes regenerated exercises with new values for unlimited practice and guided multimedia learning aids for extra guidance.

Managerial Accounting

Third Edition

Karen Wilken Braun
Case Western Reserve University

Wendy M. Tietz
Kent State University

Boston Columbus Indianapolis New York San Francisco Upper Saddle River Amsterdam
Cape Town Dubai London Madrid Milan Munich Paris Montréal Toronto Delhi Mexico City
São Paulo Sydney Hong Kong Seoul Singapore Taipei Tokyo

Editorial Director: Sally Yagan
Editor in Chief: Donna Battista
Executive Editor: Stephanie Wall
Development Editor: Mignon Tucker, J.D. Brava
360° Publishing Solutions
Editorial Project Manager: Nicole Sam
Editorial Assistants: Jane Avery, Lauren Zanedis
Director of Marketing: Maggie Moylan Leen
Marketing Assistants: Ian Gold, Kimberly Lovato
Senior Managing Editors, Production: Cindy Zonneveld, Nancy Fenton
Production Project Managers: Lynne Breitfeller, Karen Carter
Manufacturing Buyer: Carol Melville
Art Director: Anthony Gemmellaro
Cover Designer: Anthony Gemmellaro
Image Lead: Karen Sanatar
Editorial Media Project Manager: Sarah Peterson
Production Media Project Manager: John Cassar
Supplements Development Editor: Jennifer Lynn
Full-Service Project Management: GEX Publishing Services
Composition: GEX Publishing Services
Printer/Binder: Courier
Cover Printer: Courier
Text Font: Sabon Roman 10/12

Library of Congress Cataloging-in-Publication Data

Braun, Karen Wilken.
Managerial accounting / Karen Wilken Braun, Wendy M. Tietz. – 3rd ed.
p. cm.
Includes index.
ISBN 978-0-13-289054-0 (casebound)
1. Managerial accounting. I. Tietz, Wendy M. II. Title.
HF5657.4.B36 2013
658.15'11–dc23
2011045840

10 9 8 7 6 5 4 3 2 1

ISBN-13: 978-0-13-289054-0
ISBN-10: 0-13-289054-2

BRIEF CONTENTS

CONTENTS

3 Job Costing 102

4 Activity-Based Costing, Lean Operations, and the Costs of Quality 178

7 Cost-Volume-Profit Analysis 394

8 Relevant Costs for Short-Term Decisions 456

11 Standard Costs and Variances 654

12 Capital Investment Decisions and the Time Value of Money 710

13 Statement of Cash Flows 776

14 Financial Statement Analysis 830

Visual Walk-Through

Sustainability

Within every chapter is a section on how sustainability applies to an accounting concept.

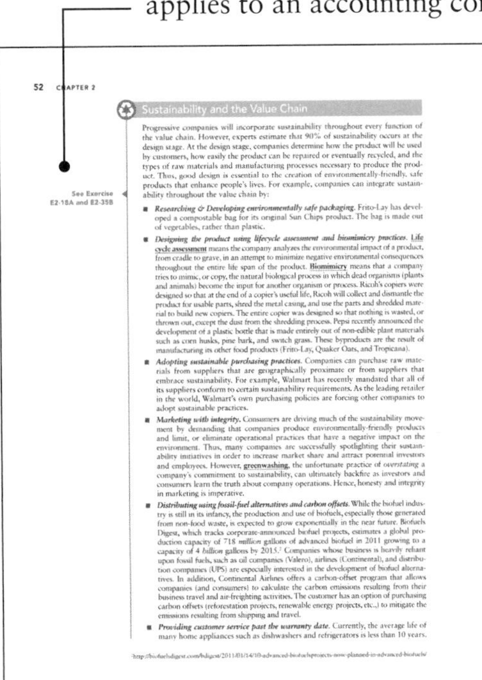

52 CHAPTER 2

Sustainability and the Value Chain

Progressive companies will incorporate sustainability throughout every function of the value chain. However, experts estimate that 90% of sustainability occurs at the design stage. At the design stage, companies determine how the product will be used by customers, how easily the product can be repaired or eventually recycled, and the types of raw materials and manufacturing processes necessary to produce the product. Thus, good design is essential to the creation of environmentally-friendly, safe products that enhance people's lives. For example, companies can integrate sustainability throughout the value chain by:

See Exercise E2-18A and E2-35B

- *Researching & Developing environmentally safe packaging.* Frito-Lay has developed a compostable bag for its original Sun Chips product. The bag is made out of vegetables, rather than plastic.
- *Designing the product using lifecycle assessment and biomimicry practices.* Life cycle assessment means the company analyzes the environmental impact of a product, from cradle to grave, in an attempt to minimize negative environmental consequences throughout the entire life span of the product. Biomimicry means that a company tries to mimic, or copy, the natural biological process in which dead organisms (plants and animals) become the input for another organism or process. Ricoh's copiers were designed so that at the end of a copier's useful life, Ricoh will collect and dismantle the product for usable parts, shred the metal casing, and use the parts and shredded material to build new copiers. The entire copier was designed so that nothing is wasted, or thrown out, except the dust from the shredding process. Pepsi recently announced the development of a plastic bottle that is made entirely out of non-edible plant materials such as corn husks, pine bark, and switch grass. These byproducts are the result of manufacturing its other food products (Frito-Lay, Quaker Oats, and Tropicana).
- *Adopting sustainable purchasing practices.* Companies can purchase raw materials from suppliers that are geographically proximate or from suppliers that embrace sustainability. For example, Walmart has recently mandated that all of its suppliers conform to certain sustainability requirements. As the leading retailer in the world, Walmart's own purchasing policies are forcing other companies to adopt sustainable practices.
- *Marketing with integrity.* Consumers are driving much of the sustainability movement by demanding that companies produce environmentally-friendly products and limit, or eliminate operational practices that have a negative impact on the environment. Thus, many companies are successfully spotlighting their sustainability initiatives in order to increase market share and attract potential investors and employees. However, greenwashing, the unfortunate practice of *overstating* a company's commitment to sustainability, can ultimately backfire as investors and consumers learn the truth about company operations. Hence, honesty and integrity in marketing is imperative.
- *Distributing using fossil-fuel alternatives and carbon offsets.* While the biofuel industry is still in its infancy, the production and use of biofuels, especially those generated from non-food waste, is expected to grow exponentially in the near future. Biofuels Digest, which tracks corporate-announced biofuel projects, estimates a global production capacity of 718 *million* gallons of advanced biofuel in 2011 growing to a capacity of 4 *billion* gallons by 2015.[2] Companies whose business is heavily reliant upon fossil fuels, such as oil companies (Valero), airlines (Continental), and distribution companies (UPS) are especially interested in the development of biofuel alternatives. In addition, Continental Airlines offers a carbon-offset program that allows companies (and consumers) to calculate the carbon emissions resulting from their business travel and air-freighting activities. The customer has an option of purchasing carbon offsets (reforestation projects, renewable energy projects, etc.,) to mitigate the emissions resulting from shipping and travel.
- *Providing customer service past the warranty date.* Currently, the average life of many home appliances such as dishwashers and refrigerators is less than 10 years.

[2]http://biofuelsdigest.com/bdigest/2011/01/14/10-advanced-biofuelsprojects-now-planned-in-advanced-biofuels/

Also included is a quick reference on which end-of-chapter problems correspond to this concept.

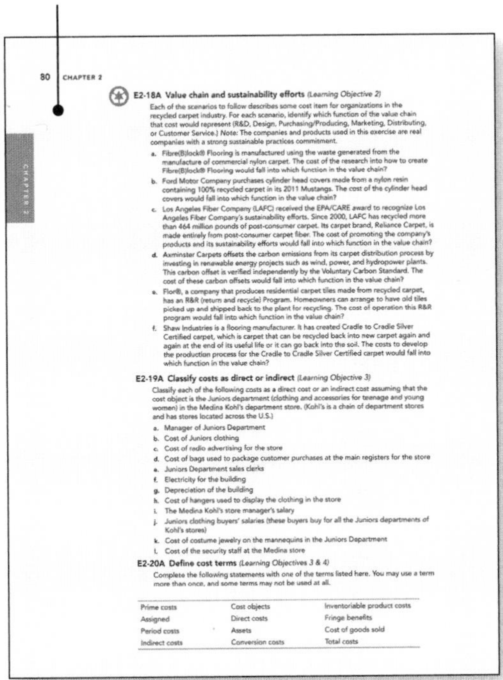

80 CHAPTER 2

E2-18A Value chain and sustainability efforts *(Learning Objective 2)*

Each of the scenarios to follow describes some cost item for organizations in the recycled carpet industry. For each scenario, identify which function of the value chain that cost would represent (R&D, Design, Purchasing/Producing, Marketing, Distributing, or Customer Service.) *Note:* The companies and products used in this exercise are real companies with a strong sustainable practices commitment.

a. Fibre(B)lock® Flooring is manufactured using the waste generated from the manufacture of commercial nylon carpet. The cost of the research into how to create Fibre(B)lock® Flooring would fall into which function in the value chain?
b. Ford Motor Company purchases cylinder head covers made from a nylon resin containing 100% recycled carpet in its 2011 Mustangs. The cost of the cylinder head covers would fall into which function in the value chain?
c. Los Angeles Fiber Company (LAFC) received the EPA/CARE award to recognize Los Angeles Fiber Company's sustainability efforts. Since 2000, LAFC has recycled more than 464 million pounds of post-consumer carpet. Its carpet brand, Reliance Carpet, is made entirely from post-consumer carpet fiber. The cost of promoting the company's products and its sustainability efforts would fall into which function in the value chain?
d. Axminster Carpets offsets the carbon emissions from its carpet distribution process by investing in renewable energy projects such as wind, power, and hydropower plants. This carbon offset is verified independently by the Voluntary Carbon Standard. The cost of these carbon offsets would fall into which function in the value chain?
e. Flor®, a company that produces residential carpet tiles made from recycled carpet, has an R&R (return and recycle) Program. Homeowners can arrange to have old tiles picked up and shipped back to the plant for recycling. The cost of operation this R&R program would fall into which function in the value chain?
f. Shaw Industries is a flooring manufacturer. It has created Cradle to Cradle Silver Certified carpet, which is carpet that can be recycled back into new carpet again and again at the end of its useful life or it can go back into the soil. The costs to develop the production process for the Cradle to Cradle Silver Certified carpet would fall into which function in the value chain?

E2-19A Classify costs as direct or indirect *(Learning Objective 3)*

Classify each of the following costs as a direct cost or an indirect cost assuming that the cost object is the Juniors department (clothing and accessories for teenage and young women) in the Medina Kohl's department store. (Kohl's is a chain of department stores and has stores located across the U.S.)

a. Manager of Juniors Department
b. Cost of Juniors clothing
c. Cost of radio advertising for the store
d. Cost of bags used to package customer purchases at the main registers for the store
e. Juniors Department sales clerks
f. Electricity for the building
g. Depreciation of the building
h. Cost of hangers used to display the clothing in the store
i. The Medina Kohl's store manager's salary
j. Juniors clothing buyers' salaries (these buyers buy for all the Juniors departments of Kohl's stores)
k. Cost of costume jewelry on the mannequins in the Juniors Department
l. Cost of the security staff at the Medina store

E2-20A Define cost terms *(Learning Objectives 3 & 4)*

Complete the following statements with one of the terms listed here. You may use a term more than once, and some terms may not be used at all.

Prime costs	Cost objects	Inventoriable product costs
Assigned	Direct costs	Fringe benefits
Period costs	Assets	Cost of goods sold
Indirect costs	Conversion costs	Total costs

Sustainability Chapter

Chapter specific to Sustainability.

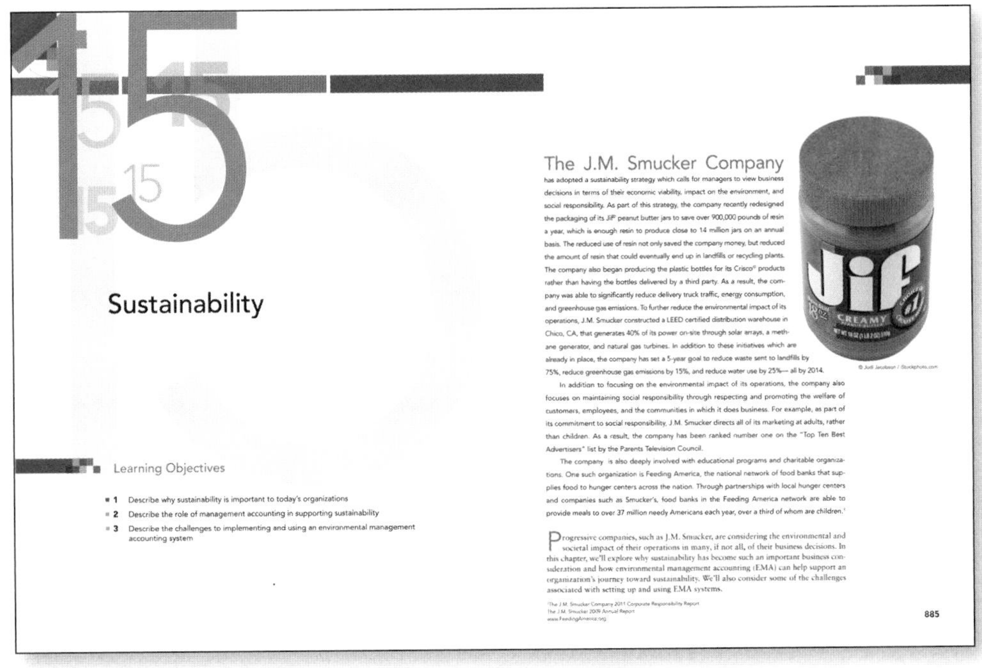

15

Sustainability

Learning Objectives

1 Describe why sustainability is important to today's organizations
2 Describe the role of management accounting in supporting sustainability
3 Describe the challenges to implementing and using an environmental management accounting system

The J.M. Smucker Company has adopted a sustainability strategy which calls for managers to view business decisions in terms of their economic viability, impact on the environment, and social responsibility. As part of this strategy, the company recently redesigned the packaging of its Jif® peanut butter jars to save over 900,000 pounds of resin a year, which is enough resin to produce close to 14 million jars on an annual basis. The reduced use of resin not only saved the company money, but reduced the amount of resin that could eventually end up in landfills or recycling plants. The company also began producing the plastic bottles for its Crisco® products rather than having the bottles delivered by a third party. As a result, the company was able to significantly reduce delivery truck traffic, energy consumption, and greenhouse gas emissions. To further reduce the environmental impact of its operations, J.M. Smucker constructed a LEED certified distribution warehouse in Chico, CA, that generates 40% of its power on-site through solar arrays, a methane generator, and natural gas turbines. In addition to these initiatives which are already in place, the company has set a 5-year goal to reduce waste sent to landfills by 75%, reduce greenhouse gas emissions by 15%, and reduce water use by 25%— all by 2014.

In addition to focusing on the environmental impact of its operations, the company also focuses on maintaining social responsibility through respecting and promoting the welfare of customers, employees, and the communities in which it does business. For example, as part of its commitment to social responsibility, J.M. Smucker directs all of its marketing at adults, rather than children. As a result, the company has been ranked number one on the "Top Ten Best Advertisers" list by the Parents Television Council.

The company is also deeply involved with educational programs and charitable organizations. One such organization is Feeding America, the national network of food banks that supplies food to hunger centers across the nation. Through partnerships with local hunger centers and companies such as Smucker's, food banks in the Feeding America network are able to provide meals to over 37 million needy Americans each year, over a third of whom are children.[1]

© Judi Jacobson / iStockphoto.com

Progressive companies, such as J.M. Smucker, are considering the environmental and societal impact of their operations in many, if not all, of their business decisions. In this chapter, we'll explore why sustainability has become such an important business consideration and how environmental management accounting (EMA) can help support an organization's journey toward sustainability. We'll also consider some of the challenges associated with setting up and using EMA systems.

[1]The J.M. Smucker Company 2011 Corporate Responsibility Report
The J.M. Smucker 2009 Annual Report
www.FeedingAmerica.org

885

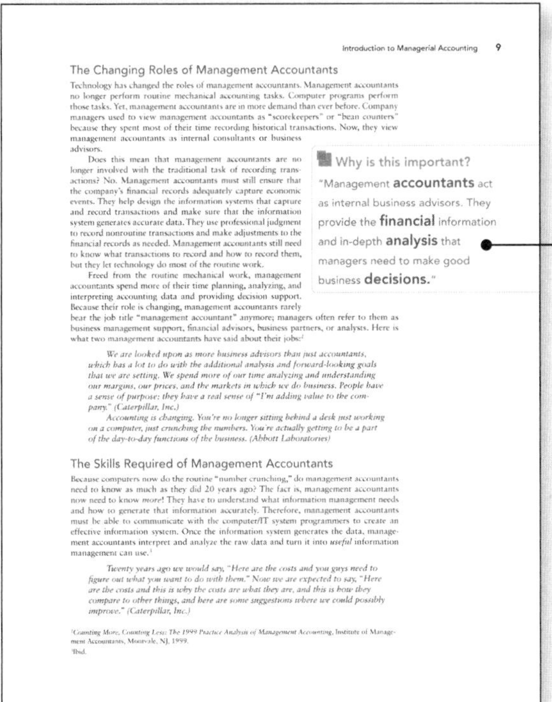

Why is this Important?

Connects accounting with the business environment so that students can better understand the business significance of managerial accounting.

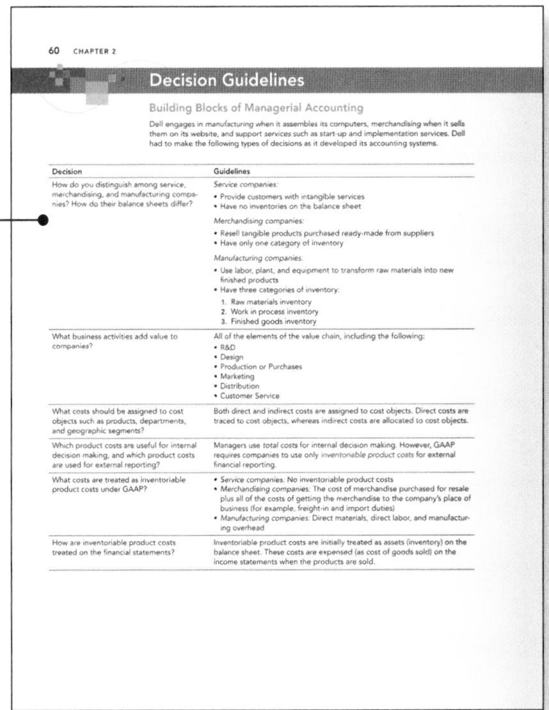

Decision Guidelines

Summarizes key terms, concepts, and formulas in the context of business decisions so that students can see how accounting is used to make decisions in business.

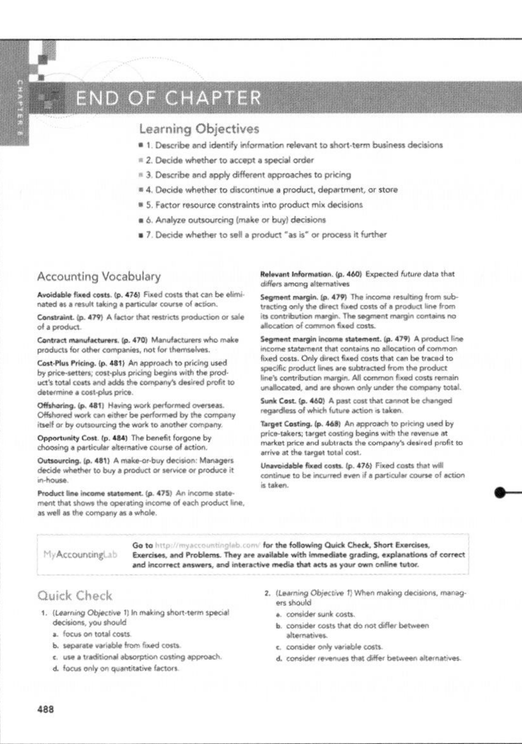

All new end-of-chapter problems

All new problems with a structure that allows students to progress from simple to more rigorous as they move from problem to problem. Also new are problems specific to sustainability that are easily identifiable with a visual cue.

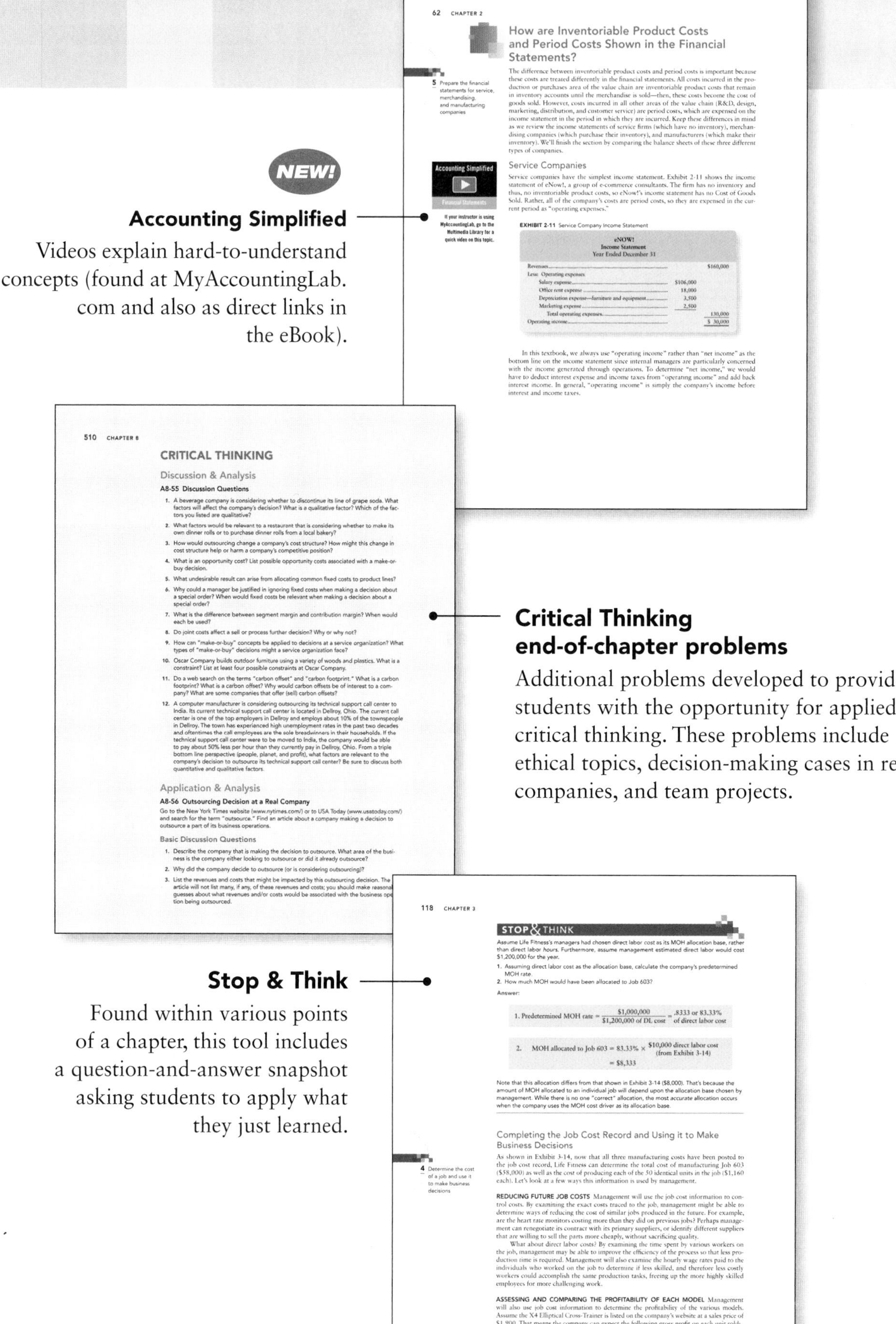

NEW!

Accounting Simplified

Videos explain hard-to-understand concepts (found at MyAccountingLab.com and also as direct links in the eBook).

62 CHAPTER 2

How are Inventoriable Product Costs and Period Costs Shown in the Financial Statements?

5 Prepare the financial statements for service, merchandising, and manufacturing companies

The difference between inventoriable product costs and period costs is important because these costs are treated differently in the financial statements. All costs incurred in the production or purchases area of the value chain are inventoriable product costs that remain in inventory accounts until the merchandise is sold—then, these costs become the cost of goods sold. However, costs incurred in all other areas of the value chain (R&D, design, marketing, distribution, and customer service) are period costs, which are expensed on the income statement in the period in which they are incurred. Keep these differences in mind as we review the income statements of service firms (which have no inventory), merchandising companies (which purchase their inventory), and manufacturers (which make their inventory). We'll finish the section by comparing the balance sheets of these three different types of companies.

Service Companies

Accounting Simplified

Financial Statements

If your instructor is using MyAccountingLab, go to the Multimedia Library for a quick video on this topic.

Service companies have the simplest income statement. Exhibit 2-11 shows the income statement of eNow!, a group of e-commerce consultants. The firm has no inventory and thus, no inventoriable product costs, so eNow!'s income statement has no Cost of Goods Sold. Rather, all of the company's costs are period costs, so they are expensed in the current period as "operating expenses."

EXHIBIT 2-11 Service Company Income Statement

eNOW!
Income Statement
Year Ended December 31

Revenues		$160,000
Less: Operating expenses		
Salary expense	$106,000	
Office rent expense	18,000	
Depreciation expense—furniture and equipment	3,500	
Marketing expense	2,500	
Total operating expenses		130,000
Operating income		$ 30,000

In this textbook, we always use "operating income" rather than "net income" as the bottom line on the income statement since internal managers are particularly concerned with the income generated through operations. To determine "net income," we would have to deduct interest expense and income taxes from "operating income" and add back interest income. In general, "operating income" is simply the company's income before interest and income taxes.

510 CHAPTER 8

CRITICAL THINKING

Discussion & Analysis

A8-55 Discussion Questions

1. A beverage company is considering whether to discontinue its line of grape soda. What factors will affect the company's decision? What is a qualitative factor? Which of the factors you listed are qualitative?
2. What factors would be relevant to a restaurant that is considering whether to make its own dinner rolls or to purchase dinner rolls from a local bakery?
3. How would outsourcing change a company's cost structure? How might this change in cost structure help or harm a company's competitive position?
4. What is an opportunity cost? List possible opportunity costs associated with a make-or-buy decision.
5. What undesirable result can arise from allocating common fixed costs to product lines?
6. Why could a manager be justified in ignoring fixed costs when making a decision about a special order? When would fixed costs be relevant when making a decision about a special order?
7. What is the difference between segment margin and contribution margin? When would each be used?
8. Do joint costs affect a sell or process further decision? Why or why not?
9. How can "make-or-buy" concepts be applied to decisions at a service organization? What types of "make-or-buy" decisions might a service organization face?
10. Oscar Company builds outdoor furniture using a variety of woods and plastics. What is a constraint? List at least four possible constraints at Oscar Company.
11. Do a web search on the terms "carbon offset" and "carbon footprint." What is a carbon footprint? What is a carbon offset? Why would carbon offsets be of interest to a company? What are some companies that offer (sell) carbon offsets?
12. A computer manufacturer is considering outsourcing its technical support call center to India. Its current technical support call center is located in Dellroy, Ohio. The current call center is one of the top employers in Dellroy and employs about 10% of the townspeople in Dellroy. The town has experienced high unemployment rates in the past two decades and oftentimes the call employees are the sole breadwinners in their households. If the technical support call center were to be moved to India, the company would be able to pay about 50% less per hour than they currently pay in Dellroy, Ohio. From a triple bottom line perspective (people, planet, and profit), what factors are relevant to the company's decision to outsource its technical support call center? Be sure to discuss both quantitative and qualitative factors.

Application & Analysis

A8-56 Outsourcing Decision at a Real Company

Go to the New York Times website (www.nytimes.com/) or to USA Today (www.usatoday.com/) and search for the term "outsource." Find an article about a company making a decision to outsource a part of its business operations.

Basic Discussion Questions

1. Describe the company that is making the decision to outsource. What area of the business is the company either looking to outsource or did it already outsource?
2. Why did the company decide to outsource (or is considering outsourcing)?
3. List the revenues and costs that might be impacted by this outsourcing decision. The article will not list many, if any, of these revenues and costs; you should make reasonal guesses about what revenues and/or costs would be associated with the business ope tion being outsourced.

Critical Thinking end-of-chapter problems

Additional problems developed to provide students with the opportunity for applied. critical thinking. These problems include ethical topics, decision-making cases in real companies, and team projects.

Stop & Think

Found within various points of a chapter, this tool includes a question-and-answer snapshot asking students to apply what they just learned.

118 CHAPTER 3

STOP & THINK

Assume Life Fitness's managers had chosen direct labor cost as its MOH allocation base, rather than direct labor *hours*. Furthermore, assume management estimated direct labor would cost $1,200,000 for the year.

1. Assuming direct labor cost as the allocation base, calculate the company's predetermined MOH rate.
2. How much MOH would have been allocated to Job 603?

Answer:

$$1.\ \text{Predetermined MOH rate} = \frac{\$1{,}000{,}000}{\$1{,}200{,}000 \text{ of DL cost}} = \begin{array}{l}.8333 \text{ or } 83.33\% \\ \text{of direct labor cost}\end{array}$$

$$2.\ \text{MOH allocated to Job 603} = 83.33\% \times \begin{array}{c}\$10{,}000 \text{ direct labor cost} \\ \text{(from Exhibit 3-14)}\end{array} = \$8{,}333$$

Note that this allocation differs from that shown in Exhibit 3-14 ($8,000). That's because the amount of MOH allocated to an individual job will depend upon the allocation base chosen by management. While there is no one "correct" allocation, the most accurate allocation occurs when the company uses the MOH cost driver as its allocation base.

Completing the Job Cost Record and Using it to Make Business Decisions

4 Determine the cost of a job and use it to make business decisions

As shown in Exhibit 3-14, now that all three manufacturing costs have been posted to the job cost record, Life Fitness can determine the total cost of manufacturing Job 603 ($58,000) as well as the cost of producing each of the 50 identical units in the job ($1,160 each). Let's look at a few ways this information is used by management.

REDUCING FUTURE JOB COSTS Management will use the job cost information to control costs. By examining the exact costs traced to the job, management might be able to determine ways of reducing the cost of similar jobs produced in the future. For example, are the heart rate monitors costing more than they did on previous jobs? Perhaps management can renegotiate its contract with its primary suppliers, or identify different suppliers that are willing to sell the parts more cheaply, without sacrificing quality.

What about direct labor costs? By examining the time spent by various workers on the job, management may be able to improve the efficiency of the process so that less production time is required. Management will also examine the hourly wage rates paid to the individuals who worked on the job to determine if less skilled, and therefore less costly workers could accomplish the same production tasks, freeing up the more highly skilled employees for more challenging work.

ASSESSING AND COMPARING THE PROFITABILITY OF EACH MODEL Management will also use job cost information to determine the profitability of the various models. Assume the X4 Elliptical Cross-Trainer is listed on the company's website at a sales price of $1,900. That means the company can expect the following gross profit on each unit sold:

Unit sales price	$1,900
Unit cost (computed on job cost record in Exhibit 3-14)	1,160
Gross profit	$ 740

EXCEL in MyAccountingLab - *Coming Spring 2012.*

- Now students can get real-world Excel practice in their classes.
- Instructors have the option to assign students end-of-chapter questions that can be completed in an Excel-simulated environment.
- Questions will be auto-graded, reported to, and visible in the grade book.
- Excel remediation will be available to students.

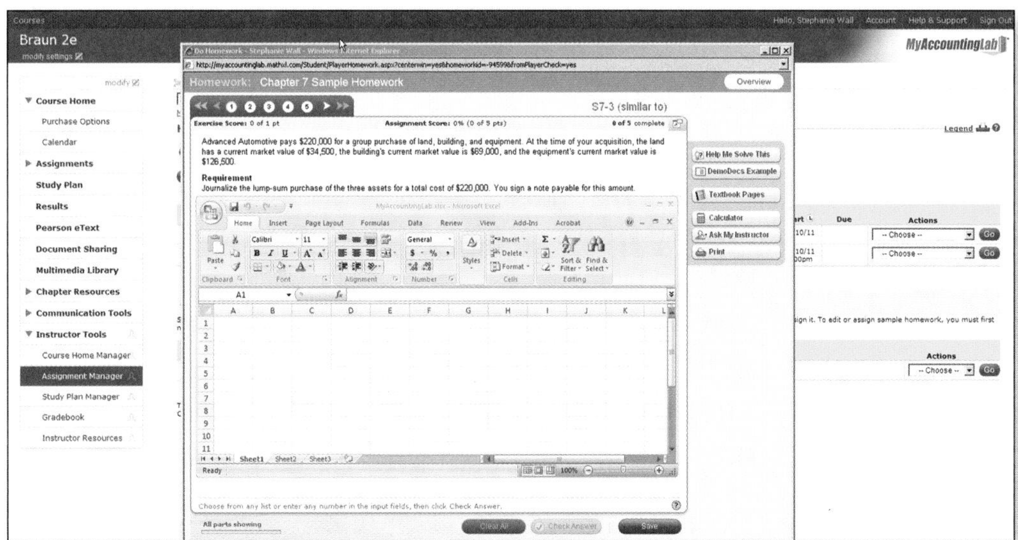

Test bank and Power Points

All rewritten and updated by the book authors. Test bank enhancements include 30% new material - new numbers in every question and about 75 new questions per chapter.

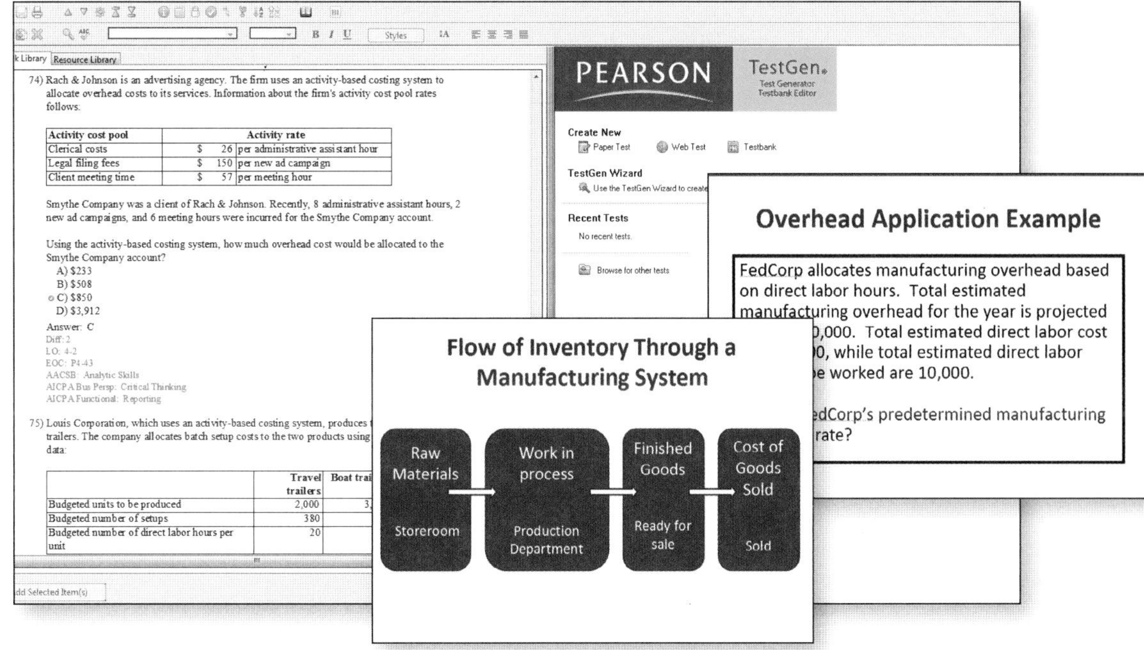

CONTENT CHANGES TO THE THIRD EDITION

Both Students and Instructors will benefit from a variety of new content in the third edition.

New and updated content enhance technical sections of the text to make them easier for students to understand:

Chapter 2	Revised section on cost of goods manufactured
Chapter 6	Revised section on variable costing
Chapter 7	New section on choosing a cost structure
Chapter 8	Revised sections on special orders, outsourcing, and deleting a product
Chapter 10	New section on transfer pricing and revised section on flexible budgeting
Chapter 11	New chapter on standard costs and variances
Chapter 15	New chapter on sustainability

Continued modernization of content:

Chapter 4	More coverage of lean operations
Chapter 6	Use of Excel for adding regression lines and equations to scatter plots
Chapter 9	Inclusion of the impact of credit and debit card transactions on budgeting
Chapter 12	Use of Excel for NPV, IRR, and time value of money calculations
Chapter 14	Use of most recent Target Corp. financial statements to illustrate topics
All Chapters	New section on how sustainability relates to the accounting topic

Consolidation and modularization of performance evaluation topics:

Chapter 10	This chapter has been completely revised to make it easier for instructors to cover or skip an assortment of performance evaluation topics

ABOUT THE AUTHORS

Karen Wilken Braun is an associate professor for the Weatherhead School of Management at Case Western Reserve University. From 1996 to 2004, Professor Braun was on the faculty of the J.M. Tull School of Accounting at the University of Georgia. She has received student-nominated Outstanding Teacher of the Year awards at both business schools.

Professor Braun has been a certified public accountant since 1985 and holds membership in both the American Accounting Association (AAA) and the Institute of Management Accountants. She is also a member of the AAA's Management Accounting Section as well as the Teaching, Learning and Curriculum Section. Her current research and teaching interests revolve around lean operations, sustainability, and corporate responsibility, while her past investigations into auditors' judgments and accounting education have been published in *Contemporary Accounting Research* and *Issues in Accounting Education*.

Dr. Braun received her Ph.D. from the University of Connecticut, where she was an AICPA Doctoral Fellow, a Deloitte & Touche Doctoral Fellow, and an AAA Doctoral Consortium Fellow. She received her B.A., summa cum laude, from Luther College, where she was a member of Phi Beta Kappa. Dr. Braun gained public accounting experience while working at Arthur Andersen & Co. and accumulated additional business and management accounting experience as Corporate Controller for Gemini Aviation, Inc.

Professor Braun has two teenage daughters, Rachel and Hannah, who are the joy of her life. In her free time she enjoys biking, gardening, hiking, skiing, and spending time with family and friends.

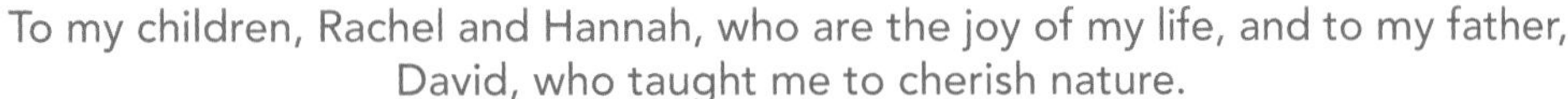

To my children, Rachel and Hannah, who are the joy of my life, and to my father, David, who taught me to cherish nature.

Karen Braun

Wendy M. Tietz is currently an associate professor in the Department of Accounting in the College of Business Administration at Kent State University, where she has taught since 2000. Prior to Kent State University, she was on the faculty at the University of Akron. She teaches in a variety of formats, including large sections, small sections, and web-based sections. She has received numerous college and university teaching awards while at Kent State University. Most recently she was named the Beta Alpha Psi Professor of the Year 2010–2011.

Dr. Tietz is a certified public accountant, a certified management accountant, and a certified information systems auditor. She is a member of the American Accounting Association (AAA), the Institute of Management Accountants, the American Institute of Certified Public Accountants, and ISACA®. She is also a member of the AAA's Teaching, Learning and Curriculum Section. She has published in *Issues in Accounting Education*, *Accounting Education: An International Journal*, and *Journal of Accounting & Public Policy*. She regularly presents at AAA regional and national meetings. She is on the editorial review board of *Accounting Education: An International Journal*.

Dr. Tietz received her Ph.D. from Kent State University. She received both her M.B.A. and B.S.A from the University of Akron. She worked in industry for several years, both as a controller for a financial institution and as the operations manager and controller for a recycled plastics manufacturer.

Dr. Tietz and her husband, Russ, have two sons who are both in college. In her spare time, she enjoys bike riding, boating, walking, running, and reading. She is also very interested in using social media in education.

To Russ, Jonathan, and Nicholas, who enrich my life through laughter and love.

Wendy Tietz

ACKNOWLEDGMENTS

We'd like to extend a special thank you to our reviewers who took the time to help us develop teaching and learning tools for Managerial Accounting courses to come. We value and appreciate their commitment, dedication, and passion for their students and the classroom:

Managerial Accounting, 3e

Arinola Adebayo, *University of South Carolina Aiken*
Dave Alldredge, *Salt Lake Community College*
Natalie Allen, *Texas A&M University*
Arnold I. Barkman, *Texas Christian University*
Gary Barnett, *Salt Lake Community College*
Scott Berube, *University of New Hampshire*
Phillip A. Blanchard, *The University of Arizona*
Ann K. Brooks, *University of New Mexico*
Molly Brown, *James Madison University*
Janet B. Butler, *Texas State University–San Marcos*
Jennifer Cainas, *University of South Florida*
Robert Clarke, *Brigham Young University–Idaho*
Jay Cohen, *Oakton Community College*
Deb Cosgrove, *University of Nebraska at Lincoln*
Kreag Danvers, *Clarion University*
Mike Deschamps, *MiraCosta College*
Kevin Dooley, *Kapiolani Community College*
Jan Duffy, *Iowa State University*
Barbara Durham, *University of Central Florida*
Robert S. Ellison, *Texas State University–San Marcos*
Jame M. Emig, *Villanova University*
Martin Epstei, *Central New Mexico Community College*
Richard Filler, *Franklin University*
Faith Fugate, *University of Nevada, Reno*
Karen Geiger, *Arizona State University*
Marina Grau, *Houston Community College*
Timothy Griffin, *Hillsborough Community College*
Michael R. Hammond, *Missouri State University*
Fei Han, *Robert Morris University*
Sheila Handy, *East Stroudsburg University*
Pamela Hopcroft, *Florida State College at Jacksonville*
Frank Ilett, *Boise State University*
Ron Jastrzebski, *Penn State University–Berks*
Catherine Jeppson, *California State University, Northridge*
Mark T. Judd, *University of San Diego*
Thomas Kam, *Hawaii Pacific University*
Emil Koren, *Saint Leo University*
Ron Lazer, *University of Houston–Bauer College*
Elliott Levy, *Bentley University*
William Lloyd, *Lock Haven University*
Lois S. Mahoney, *Eastern Michigan University*
Diane Marker, *University of Toledo*
Noel McKeon, *Florida State College at Jacksonville*
Michael Newman, *University of Houston*
Abbie Gail Parham, *Georgia Southern University*
Paige Paulsen, *Salt Lake Community College*
Letitia Pleis, *Metropolitan State College of Denver*
Will Quilliam, *Florida Southern College*
Christina M. Ritsema, *University of Northern Colorado*
Amal Said, *University of Toledo*
Lloyd Seaton, *University of Northern Colorado*
John Stancil, *Florida Southern College*
Jenny Staskey, *Northern Arizona University*
Dennis Stovall, *Grand Valley State University*
Gracelyn Stuart-Tuggle, *Palm Beach State College*
Jan Sweeney, *Baruch College, City University of New York*
Pavani Tallapally, *Slippery Rock University*
Linda Hayden Tarrago, *Hillsborough Community College*
Steven Thoede, *Texas State University*
Geoffrey Tickell, *Indiana University of Pennsylvania*
Igor Vaysman, *Baruch College*
Terri Walsh, *Seminole State*
Jeff Wong, *University of Nevada Reno*
Michael Yampuler, *University of Houston (Main Campus)*
James Zeigler, *Bowling Green State University*

Previous Editions

Nasrollah Ahadiat, *California State Polytechnic University*
Markus Ahrens, *St. Louis Community College*
Vern Allen, *Central Florida Community College*
Felix E. Amenkhienan, *Radford University*
Michael T. Blackwell, *West Liberty State College*
Charles Blumer, *St. Charles Community College*
Anna Boulware, *St. Charles Community College*
Kevin Bosner, *SUNY Genesco*
Molly Brown, *James Madison University*
Nina E. Brown, *Tarrant County College*
Helen Brubeck, *San Jose State University*
David Centers, *Grand Valley State University*
Sandra Cereola, *James Madison University*
Mike Chatham, *Radford University*
Julie Chenier, *Louisiana State University*
Thomas Clevenger, *Washburn University*
Cheryl Copeland, *California State University Fresno*
Robert Cornell, *Oklahoma State University*
Patrick Cunningham, *Dawson Community College*
Alan B. Czyzewski, *Indiana State University*

David L. Davis, *Tallahassee Community College*
Patricia A. Doherty, *Boston University School of Management*
Jimmy Dong, *Sacramento City College*
Lisa Dutchik, *Kirkwood Community College*
Darlene K. Edwards, *Bellingham Technical College*
Anita Ellzey, *Harford Community College*
Gene B. Elrod, *The University of North Texas*
Diane Eure, *Texas State University*
Robert Everett, *Lewis & Clark Community College*
Dr. Kurt Fanning, *Grand Valley State University*
Amanda Farmer, *University of Georgia*
Janice Fergusson, *University of South Carolina*
Jean Fornasieri, *Bergen Community College*
Ben Foster, *University of Louisville*
Mary Anne Gaffney, *Temple University*
Lisa Gillespie, *Loyola University–Chicago*
Shirley Glass, *Macomb Community College*
Christopher Harper, *Grand Valley State University*
Sueann Hely, *West Kentucky Community & Technical College*
Audrey S. Hunter, *Broward College*
Nancy Jones, *California State University–Chico*
Mark Judd, *University of San Diego*
David Juriga, *St. Louis Community College*
Ken Koerber, *Bucks County Community College*
Pamela Legner, *College of DuPage*
Elliott Levy, *Bentley University*
Harold T. Little, *Western Kentucky University*
D. Jordan Lowe, *Arizona State University, West Campus*
Diane Marker, *University of Toledo*
Linda Marquis, *Northern Kentucky University*
Lizbeth Matz, *University of Pittsburgh at Bradford*
David Mautz, *University of North Carolina–Wilmington*
Florence McGovern, *Bergen Community College*
Mallory McWilliams, *San Jose State University*
Robert Meyer, *Parkland College*
Kitty O'Donnell, *Onondaga Community College*
Mehmet Ozbilgin, *Baruch College, City University of New York*
Glenn Pate, *Palm Beach Community College*
Deborah Pavelka, *Roosevelt University*
Sheldon Peng, *Washburn University*
Tamara Phelan, *Northern Illinois University*
Cindy Powell, *Southern Nazarene University*
Paulette A. Ratliff-Miller, *Grand Valley State University*
Donald Reynolds, *Calvin College*
Doug Roberts, *Appalachian State University*
Anwar Salimi, *California State Polytechnic University*
Kathryn Savage, *Northern Arizona University*
Christine Schalow, *California State University–San Bernadino*
Tony Scott, *Norwalk Community College*
David Skougstad, *Metropolitan State College of Denver*
Dennis Stovall, *Grand Valley State University*
Olin Scott Stovall, *Abilene Christian University*
Gloria Stuart, *Georgia Southern University*
Gracelyn V. Stuart-Tuggle, *Palm Beach State College, Boca Raton*
Iris Stuart, *California State University, Fullerton*
Lloyd Tanlu, *University of Washington*
Diane Tanner, *University of North Florida*
Linda Tarrago, *Hillsborough Community College*
Don Trippeer, *SUNY Oneonta*
John Virchick, *Chapman University*
Andy Williams, *Edmonds Community College*
Judith Zander, *Grossmont College*

In addition, permission has been received from the Institute of Certified Management Accountants to use questions and/or unofficial answers from past CMA examinations. We appreciate their generosity.

Introduction to Managerial Accounting

Learning Objectives

1. Identify managers' three primary responsibilities
2. Distinguish financial accounting from managerial accounting
3. Describe organizational structure and the roles and skills required of management accountants within the organization
4. Describe the role of the Institute of Management Accountants (IMA) and use its ethical standards to make reasonable ethical judgments
5. Discuss and analyze the implications of regulatory and business trends

Steve Ells opened the first Chipotle Mexican Grill in 1993 on the outskirts of the University of Denver campus. Although he had never taken a business class, he was fascinated by the simple economic model he saw in place at small burrito shops in San Francisco. By putting his own spin on that simple, cost-effective business model, Steve launched what has now become a tremendously successful publicly traded restaurant chain with over 1,000 locations in 38 states. Although Steve was first drawn to the business model by the limited costs he saw—few workers, limited furnishing, food served in foil wrappers—his resulting business was not solely driven by saving money. Rather, Steve sought to run his business in a manner that would have a positive impact on all those the business touched. Chipotle's motto, "Food with Integrity," has become the driving force for every aspect of the company's operations. Chipotle is willing to spend more in order to ensure that 100% of the pork and chicken used in its restaurants has been naturally raised, and that the majority of its produce is organic and sourced from local farms when seasonably possible. It also refuses to buy dairy products from cows treated with the synthetic rBGH hormone and it uses only zero-transfat oil for frying. Chipotle uses management accounting to ensure that operating decisions, such as those above, will also provide the company with enough profit to remain a viable, strong, and growing business.

TRIPPLAAR KRISTOFFER/SIPA/
Newscom

As the Chipotle story shows, managers use accounting information for much more than preparing annual financial statements. They use managerial accounting information to guide their actions and decisions. These decisions might include opening new restaurants, adding new items to the menu, or sourcing ingredients from different suppliers. Management accounting information helps management decide whether any or all of these actions will help accomplish the company's ultimate goals. In this chapter, we'll introduce managerial accounting and discuss how managers use it to fulfill their duties. We will also explore how managerial accounting differs from financial accounting, and discuss the role of management accountants within the organization. Finally, we will discuss the regulatory and business environment in which today's managers and management accountants operate.

What is Managerial Accounting?

As you will see throughout the book, managerial accounting is very different from financial accounting. Financial accounting focuses on providing stockholders and creditors with the information they need to make investment and lending decisions. This information takes the form of financial statements: the balance sheet, income statement, statement of shareholders' equity, and statement of cash flows. On the other hand, managerial accounting focuses on providing internal management with the information it needs to run the company efficiently and effectively. This information takes many forms depending on management's needs.

To understand the kind of information managers need, let's first look at their primary responsibilities.

Managers' Three Primary Responsibilities

1 Identify managers' three primary responsibilities

Managerial accounting helps managers fulfill their three primary responsibilities, as shown in Exhibit 1-1: planning, directing, and controlling. Integrated throughout these responsibilities is **decision making** (identifying alternative courses of action and choosing among them).

EXHIBIT 1-1 Managers' Three Primary Responsibilities

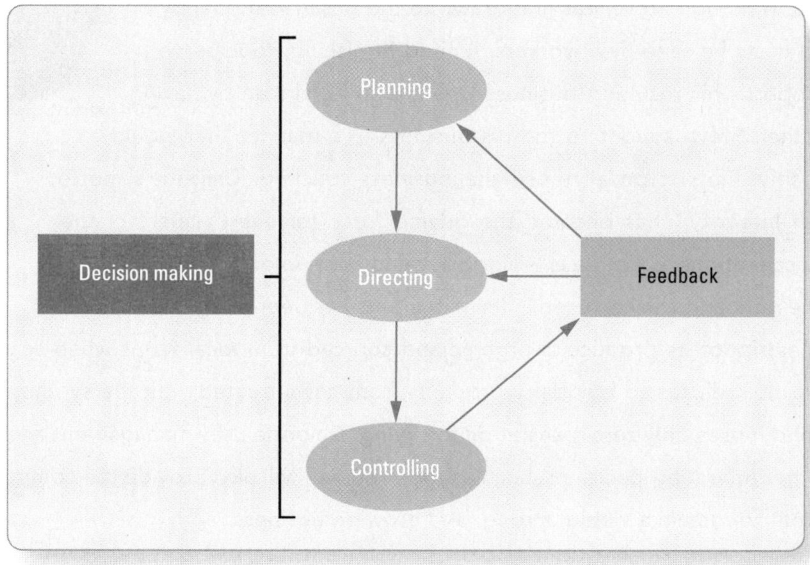

- **Planning** involves setting goals and objectives for the company and determining how to achieve them. For example, one of Chipotle's goals may be to generate more sales. One strategy to achieve this goal is to open more restaurants. For example, the company opened 129 new restaurants in 2010. Managerial accounting translates these plans into **budgets**—the quantitative expression of a plan. Management analyzes the budgets before proceeding to determine whether its expansion plans make financial sense.
- **Directing** means overseeing the company's day-to-day operations. Management uses product cost reports, product sales information, and other managerial accounting reports to run daily business operations. Chipotle would use product sales data to determine which items on the menu are generating the most sales and then uses that information to adjust menus and marketing strategies.

- **Controlling** means evaluating the results of business operations against the plan and making adjustments to keep the company pressing toward its goals. Chipotle uses performance reports to compare each restaurant's actual performance against the budget and then uses that *feedback* to take corrective actions if needed. If actual costs are higher than planned, or actual sales are lower than planned, then management may revise its plans or adjust operations. Perhaps the newly opened restaurants are not generating as much income as budgeted. As a result, management may decide to increase local advertising to increase sales.

Management is continually making decisions while it plans, directs, and controls operations. Chipotle must decide where to open new restaurants, which restaurants to refurnish, what prices to set for meals, what items to offer on its menu, and so forth. Managerial accounting gathers, summarizes, and reports on the financial impact of each of these decisions.

A Road Map: How Managerial Accounting Fits In

This book will show you how managerial accounting information helps managers fulfill their responsibilities. The rest of the text is organized around the following themes:

1. **Managerial Accounting Building Blocks** Chapter 1 helps you understand more about the management accounting profession and today's business environment. Chapter 2 teaches you some of the language that is commonly used in managerial accounting. Just as musicians must know the notes to the musical scale, management accountants *and* managers must have a common understanding of these terms in order to communicate effectively with one another.
2. **Determining Unit Cost (Product Costing)** In order to run a business profitably, managers must be able to identify the costs associated with manufacturing its products or delivering its service. For example, Chipotle's managers know the cost of producing each item on the menu as well as the cost of operating each restaurant location. Managers must have this information so that they can set prices high enough to cover costs and generate an adequate profit. Chapters 3, 4, and 5 show you how businesses determine these costs. These chapters also show how managers can effectively control costs by understanding the activities that drive costs.
3. **Making Decisions** Before Steve Ells opened the first Chipotle restaurant, he must have thought about the volume of sales needed just to break even—that is, just to cover costs. In order to do so, he had to first identify and estimate the types of costs the restaurant would incur, as well as the profit that would be generated on each meal served. These topics are covered in Chapters 6 and 7. Chapter 6 shows how managers identify different types of cost behavior, while Chapter 7 shows how managers determine the profitability of each unit sold as well as the company's breakeven point. Chapter 8 continues to use cost behavior information to walk through common business decisions, such as *outsourcing* and pricing decisions. Finally, Chapter 12 shows how managers decide whether to invest in new equipment, new projects, or new locations, such as when Chipotle decides to open a new restaurant.
4. **Planning** Budgets are management's primary tool for expressing its plans. Chapter 9 discusses all of the components of the *master budget* and the way companies like Chipotle uses the budgeting process to implement their business goals and strategies.
5. **Controlling and Evaluating** Management uses many different performance evaluation tools to determine whether individual segments of the business are reaching company goals. Chapters 10 and 11 describe these tools in detail. Chapters 13 and 14 describe how the statement of cash flows and financial statement analysis can be used to evaluate the performance of the company as a whole. Finally, Chapter 15 discusses how companies are beginning to use environmental management accounting systems to measure and minimize the negative impact of their operations on the environment. As you saw in the opening story, one of Chipotle's primary business concerns is to operate in a fashion that has minimal negative consequences for people, animals, and the planet.

Differences Between Managerial Accounting and Financial Accounting

2 Distinguish financial accounting from managerial accounting

Managerial accounting information differs from financial accounting information in many respects. Exhibit 1-2 summarizes these differences. Take a few minutes to study the exhibit and then we'll apply it to Chipotle.

EXHIBIT 1-2 Managerial Accounting Versus Financial Accounting

MANAGERIAL ACCOUNTING	ISSUE	FINANCIAL ACCOUNTING
Internal users such as managers.	Who are the primary users of the information?	External users, such as creditors, stockholders, and government regulators.
To help managers plan, direct, and control business operations and make business decisions.	What is the purpose of the information?	To help external users make investing and lending decisions.
Any internal accounting report deemed worthwhile by management.	What is the primary accounting product?	Financial statements.
Management determines what it wants in a report, and how it wants it formatted. Reports are prepared only when management believes the benefit of using the report exceeds the cost of preparing the report.	What must be included in the report, and how must it be formatted?	Generally accepted accounting principles (GAAP) determine the content and format of financial statements.
While some information is based on past transactions, managerial accounting focuses on the future. It provides information on both external and internal transactions.	What is the underlying basis of the information?	The information is based on historical transactions with external parties.
The data must be relevant.	What information characteristic is emphasized?	The data must be reliable and objective.
Segments of the business, such as products, customers, geographical regions, departments, and divisions.	What business "unit" is the report about?	The company as a whole (consolidated financial statements). Limited segment data is provided in the footnotes.
It depends on management's needs. Some reports are prepared daily, while others may be prepared only one time.	How often are the reports prepared?	Annually and quarterly.
There are no independent audits. However, the company's internal audit function may examine the procedures used in preparing the reports.	Does anyone verify the information?	Independent certified public accountants (CPAs) audit the annual financial statements of publicly traded companies and express an opinion on the fairness of the financial information they contain.
No authoritative body requires managerial accounting reports.	Is the information required by an outside group/ government agency?	Yes, the Securities and Exchange Commission (SEC) requires publicly traded companies to issue annual audited financial statements.
Management carefully considers behavioral implications when designing the managerial accounting system.	Is there any concern over how the reports will affect employee behavior?	The concern is about adequacy of disclosure; behavioral implications are secondary.

Chipotle's *financial accounting* system is geared toward producing annual and quarterly consolidated financial statements that will be used by investors and creditors to make investment and lending decisions. The financial statements, which must be prepared in accordance with Generally Accepted Accounting Principles (GAAP), objectively summarize the transactions that occurred between Chipotle and external parties during the previous period. The SEC requires that the annual financial statements of publicly traded companies, such as Chipotle, be audited by independent certified public accountants (CPAs). Chipotle's financial statements are useful to its investors and creditors, but they do not provide management with enough information to run the company effectively.

Chipotle's *managerial accounting* system is designed to provide its managers with the accounting information they need to plan, direct, and control operations. There are no GAAP-type standards or audits required for managerial accounting. Chipotle's managerial accounting system is tailored to provide the information managers need to help them make better decisions. Chipotle must weigh the benefits of the system (useful information) against the costs to develop and run the system. The costs and benefits of any particular managerial accounting system differ from one company to another. Different companies create different systems, so Chipotle's managerial accounting system will differ from Toyota's system.

In contrast to financial statements, most managerial accounting reports focus on the *future*, providing *relevant* information that helps managers make profitable business decisions. For example, before putting their plans into action, Chipotle's managers determine if their plans make sense by quantitatively expressing them in the form of budgets. Chipotle's managerial accounting reports may also plan for and reflect *internal* transactions, such as any movement of beverages and dry ingredients from central warehouses to individual restaurant locations.

To make good decisions, Chipotle's managers need information about smaller units of the company, not just the company as a whole. For example, management uses revenue and cost data on individual restaurants, geographical regions, and individual menu items to increase the company's profitability. Regional data helps Chipotle's management decide where to open more restaurants. Sales and profit reports on individual menu items help management choose menu items and decide what items to offer on a seasonal basis. Rather than preparing these reports just once a year, companies prepare and revise managerial accounting reports as often as needed.

When designing the managerial accounting system, management must carefully consider how the system will affect employees' behavior. Employees try to perform well on the parts of their jobs that the accounting system measures. If Chipotle's restaurant managers were evaluated only on their ability to control costs, they may use cheaper ingredients or hire less experienced help. Although these actions cut costs, they can hurt profits if the quality of the meals or service declines as a result. Since one of Chipotle's primary goals is to serve food that has been sourced naturally and locally, the performance measurement system needs to include more than just a focus on cost if it is to encourage managers to think beyond cost.

What Role do Management Accountants Play?

Let's look at how management accountants fit into the company's organizational structure, how their roles are changing, and the skills they need to successfully fill their roles. We'll also look at their professional association, their average salaries, and their ethical standards.

3 Describe organizational structure and the roles and skills required of management accountants within the organization

Organizational Structure

Most corporations are too large to be governed directly by their stockholders. Therefore, stockholders elect a **board of directors** to oversee the company. Exhibit 1-3 shows a typical organizational structure with the green boxes representing employees of the firm and the orange and blue boxes representing nonemployees.

The board meets only periodically, so they hire a **chief executive officer (CEO)** to manage the company on a daily basis. The CEO hires other executives to run various aspects of the organization, including the **chief operating officer (COO)** and the **chief financial officer (CFO)**. The COO is responsible for the company's operations, such as research and development (R&D), Production, and Distribution. The CFO is responsible

EXHIBIT 1-3 Typical Organizational Structure

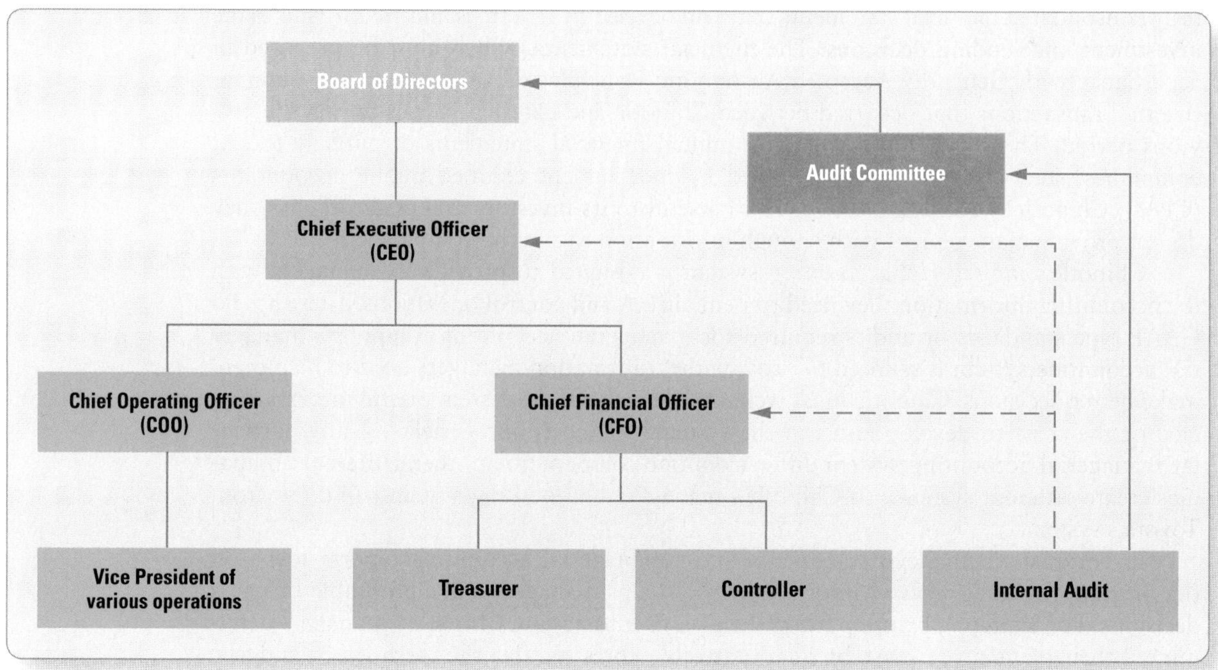

for all of the company's financial concerns. The **treasurer** and the **controller** report directly to the CFO. The treasurer is primarily responsible for raising capital (through issuing stocks and bonds) and investing funds. The controller is usually responsible for general financial accounting, managerial accounting, and tax reporting.

The New York Stock Exchange requires that listed companies have an **internal audit function**. The role of the internal audit function is to ensure that the company's internal controls and risk management policies are functioning properly. The Internal Audit Department reports directly to a subcommittee of the board of directors called the **audit committee**. The audit committee oversees the internal audit function as well as the annual audit of the financial statements by independent CPAs. Both the Internal Audit Department and the independent CPAs report directly to the audit committee for one very important reason: to ensure that management will not intimidate them or bias their work. However, since the audit committee meets only periodically, it is not practical for the audit committee to manage the internal audit function on a day-to-day basis. Therefore, the internal audit function also reports to a senior executive, such as the CFO or CEO, for administrative matters.

When you look at the organizational chart pictured in Exhibit 1-3, where do you think management accountants work? It depends on the company. Management accountants used to work in accounting departments and reported directly to the controller. Now, over half of management accountants are located throughout the company and work on cross-functional teams. **Cross-functional teams** consist of employees representing various functions of the company, such as R&D, Design, Production, Marketing, Distribution, and Customer Service. Cross-functional teams are effective because each member can address business decisions from a different viewpoint. These teams often report to various vice presidents of operations. Management accountants often take the leadership role in the teams. Here is what two managers had to say in a study about management accountants:[1]

> *Finance (the management accountant) has a unique ability and responsibility to see across all the functions and try and make sense of them. They have the neat ability to be a member of all of the different groups (functions) and yet not be a member of any of them at the same time. (U.S. West)*
>
> *Basically the role of the financial person on the team is analyzing the financial impact of the business decision and providing advice. Does this make sense financially or not? (Abbott Laboratories)*

[1]*Counting More, Counting Less: The 1999 Practice Analysis of Management Accounting*, Institute of Management Accountants, Montvale, NJ, 1999.

The Changing Roles of Management Accountants

Technology has changed the roles of management accountants. Management accountants no longer perform routine mechanical accounting tasks. Computer programs perform those tasks. Yet, management accountants are in more demand than ever before. Company managers used to view management accountants as "scorekeepers" or "bean counters" because they spent most of their time recording historical transactions. Now, they view management accountants as internal consultants or business advisors.

Does this mean that management accountants are no longer involved with the traditional task of recording transactions? No. Management accountants must still ensure that the company's financial records adequately capture economic events. They help design the information systems that capture and record transactions and make sure that the information system generates accurate data. They use professional judgment to record nonroutine transactions and make adjustments to the financial records as needed. Management accountants still need to know what transactions to record and how to record them, but they let technology do most of the routine work.

Freed from the routine mechanical work, management accountants spend more of their time planning, analyzing, and interpreting accounting data and providing decision support. Because their role is changing, management accountants rarely bear the job title "management accountant" anymore; managers often refer to them as business management support, financial advisors, business partners, or analysts. Here is what two management accountants have said about their jobs:[2]

> *We are looked upon as more business advisors than just accountants, which has a lot to do with the additional analysis and forward-looking goals that we are setting. We spend more of our time analyzing and understanding our margins, our prices, and the markets in which we do business. People have a sense of purpose; they have a real sense of "I'm adding value to the company." (Caterpillar, Inc.)*
>
> *Accounting is changing. You're no longer sitting behind a desk just working on a computer, just crunching the numbers. You're actually getting to be a part of the day-to-day functions of the business.* (Abbott Laboratories)

Why is this important?

"Management **accountants** act as internal business advisors. They provide the **financial** information and in-depth **analysis** that managers need to make good business **decisions.**"

The Skills Required of Management Accountants

Because computers now do the routine "number crunching," do management accountants need to know as much as they did 20 years ago? The fact is, management accountants now need to know *more*! They have to understand what information management needs and how to generate that information accurately. Therefore, management accountants must be able to communicate with the computer/IT system programmers to create an effective information system. Once the information system generates the data, management accountants interpret and analyze the raw data and turn it into *useful* information management can use.[3]

> *Twenty years ago we would say, "Here are the costs and you guys need to figure out what you want to do with them." Now we are expected to say, "Here are the costs and this is why the costs are what they are, and this is how they compare to other things, and here are some suggestions where we could possibly improve."* (Caterpillar, Inc.)

[2]*Counting More, Counting Less: The 1999 Practice Analysis of Management Accounting*, Institute of Management Accountants, Montvale, NJ, 1999.

[3]Ibid.

Today's management accountants need the following skills:[4]

- Solid knowledge of both financial and managerial accounting
- Analytical skills
- Knowledge of how a business functions
- Ability to work on a team
- Oral *and* written communication skills

The skills shown in Exhibit 1-4 are critical to these management accountants:

> *We're making more presentations that are seen across the division. So you have to summarize the numbers... you have to have people in sales understand what those numbers mean. If you can't communicate information to the individuals, then the information is never out there; it's lost. So, your communication skills are very important. (Abbott Laboratories)*
>
> *Usually when a nonfinancial person comes to you with financial questions, they don't really ask the right things so that you can give them the correct answer. If they ask you for cost, well, you have to work with them and say, "Well, do you want total plant cost, a variable cost, or an accountable cost?" Then, "What is the reason for those costs?" Whatever they're using this cost for determines what type of cost you will provide them with. (Caterpillar, Inc.)*

Chapter 2 explains these cost terms. The point here is that management accountants need to have a solid understanding of managerial accounting, including how different types of costs are relevant to different situations. Additionally, they must be able to communicate that information to employees from different business functions.

EXHIBIT 1-4 The Skills Required of Management Accountants

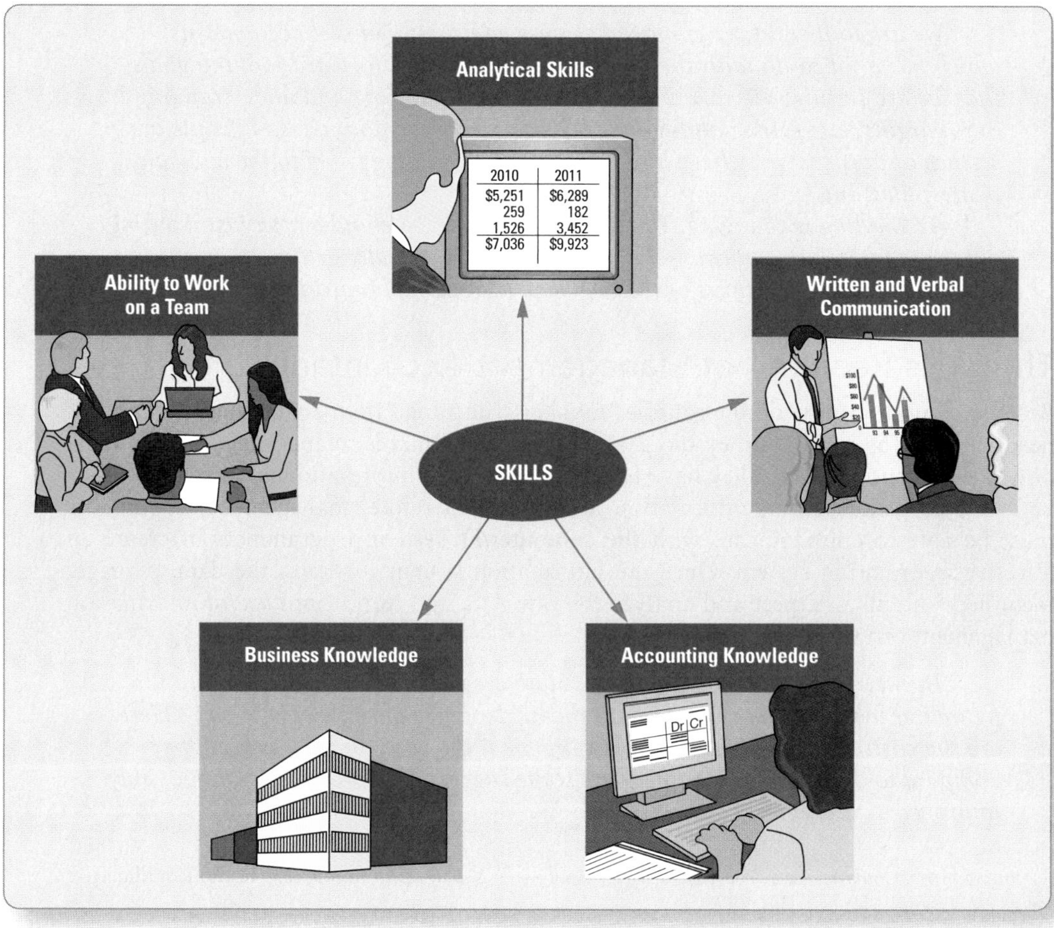

[4]Gary Siegel and James Sorenson, *What Corporate America Wants in Entry-Level Accountants*, Institute of Management Accountants, Montvale, NJ, 1994.

Professional Association

4 Describe the role of the Institute of Management Accountants (IMA) and use its ethical standards to make reasonable ethical judgments

The **Institute of Management Accountants (IMA)** is the professional association for management accountants. The mission of the IMA is to provide a forum for research, practice development, education, knowledge sharing, and advocacy of the highest ethical and best practices in management accounting and finance. The IMA also wants to educate society about the role management accountants play in organizations. According to the IMA, about 85% of accountants work in organizations, performing the roles discussed earlier. The IMA publishes a monthly journal called *Strategic Finance*. (Prior to 1999, the journal was called *Management Accounting*; but as the role of management accountants changed, so did the journal's title.) The journal addresses current topics of interest to management accountants and helps them keep abreast of recent techniques and trends.

The IMA also issues the **Certified Management Accountant (CMA)** certification. To become a CMA you must pass a rigorous examination and maintain continuing professional education. The CMA exam focuses on managerial accounting topics similar to those discussed in this book, as well as economics and business finance. While most employers do not require the CMA certification, management accountants bearing the CMA designation tend to command higher salaries and obtain higher-level positions within the company. You can find out more about the IMA and the CMA certification it offers at its website: www.imanet.org.

Average Salaries of Management Accountants

The average salaries of management accountants reflect their large skill set. Naturally, salaries will vary with the accountant's level of experience, his or her specific job responsibilities, and the size and geographical location of the company. However, to give you a general idea, in 2010, the average salary of IMA members with 1–5 years of experience was $76,228. The average salary of all IMA members was $109,265. In general, those professionals with the CMA certification earned salaries that were about 16% higher than members with no certification. You can obtain more specific salary information in the IMA's 2010 Salary Survey.[5]

Robert Half International, Inc., also publishes a free yearly guide to average salaries for all types of finance professionals. The guide also provides information on current hiring trends. To download a free copy of the *Salary Guide*, go to www.roberthalffinance.com.

Ethics

Management accountants continually face ethical challenges. The IMA has developed principles and standards to help management accountants deal with these challenges. The principles and standards remind us that society expects professional accountants to exhibit the highest level of ethical behavior. The IMA's *Statement on Ethical Professional Practice* requires management accountants to do the following:

- Maintain their professional competence
- Preserve the confidentiality of the information they handle
- Uphold their integrity
- Perform their duties with credibility

These ethical standards are summarized in Exhibit 1-5, while the full *Statement of Ethical Professional Practice* appears in Exhibit 1-6.

Why is this important?

"At the **root** of all business relationships is **trust**. Would you put your **money** in a bank that you didn't trust, invest in a company you knew was '**cooking the books**,' or loan money to someone you thought would never pay you back? As a **manager**, your trust in the other party's **ethical** behavior, and vice versa, will be a vital component to the business **decisions** you make."

[5]Lee Schiffel, K. Smith and D. Schroeder, "2010 Salary Survey," *Strategic Finance*, June 2011, pp. 26–46.

EXHIBIT 1-5 Summary of Ethical Standards

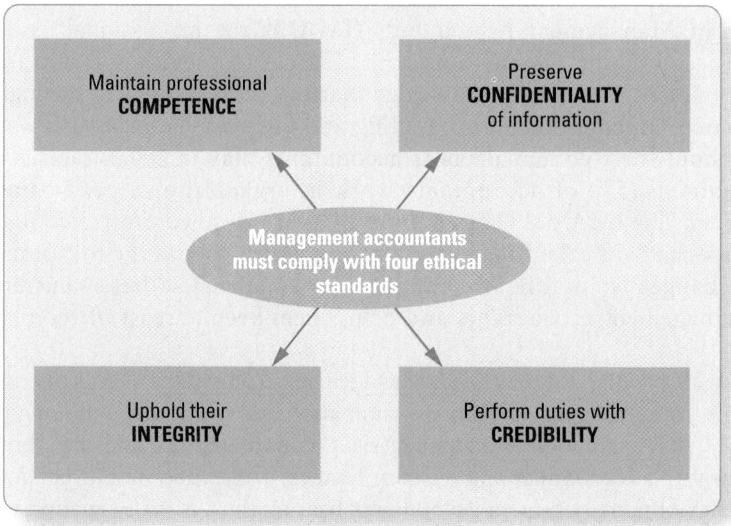

To resolve ethical dilemmas, the IMA suggests that management accountants first follow their company's established policies for reporting unethical behavior. If the conflict is not resolved through the company's procedures, the management accountant should consider the following steps:

- Discuss the unethical situation with the immediate supervisor unless the supervisor is involved in the unethical situation. If so, notify the supervisor at the next higher managerial level. If the immediate supervisor involved is the CEO, notify the audit committee or board of directors.
- Discuss the unethical situation with an objective advisor, such as an IMA ethics counselor. The IMA offers a confidential "Ethics Hotline" to its members. Members may call the hotline and discuss their ethical dilemma. The ethics counselor will not provide a specific resolution but will clarify how the dilemma relates to the IMA's *Statement of Ethical Professional Practice* shown in Exhibit 1-6.
- Consult an attorney regarding legal obligations and rights.

Examples of Ethical Dilemmas

Unfortunately, the ethical path is not always clear. You may want to act ethically and do the right thing, but the consequences can make it difficult to decide what to do. Let's consider several ethical dilemmas in light of the *Statement of Ethical Professional Practice*:

Dilemma #1

> Sarah Baker is examining the expense reports of her staff, who counted inventory at Top-Flight's warehouses in Arizona. She discovers that Mike Flinders has claimed but not included hotel receipts for over $1,000 of accommodation expenses. Other staff, who also claimed $1,000, did attach hotel receipts. When asked about the receipts, Mike admits that he stayed with an old friend, not in the hotel, but he believes that he deserves the money he saved. After all, the company would have paid his hotel bill.

By asking to be reimbursed for hotel expenses he did not incur, Flinders violated the IMA's integrity standards (conflict of interest in which he tried to enrich himself at the company's expense). Because Baker discovered the inflated expense report, she would not be fulfilling her ethical responsibilities of integrity and credibility if she allowed the reimbursement.

Dilemma #2

> As the accountant of Entreé Computer, you are aware of your company's weak financial condition. Entreé is close to signing a lucrative contract that should ensure its future. To do so, the controller states that the company must report a

profit this year (ending December 31). He suggests, "Two customers have placed orders that are really not supposed to be shipped until early January. Ask production to fill and ship those orders on December 31 so we can record them in this year's sales."

The resolution of this dilemma is less clear-cut. Many people believe that following the controller's suggestion to manipulate the company's income would violate the standards of competence, integrity, and credibility. Others would argue that because Entreé Computer already has the customer orders, shipping the goods and recording the sale in December is still ethical behavior. You might discuss the available alternatives with the next managerial level or the IMA ethics hotline counselor.

EXHIBIT 1-6 IMA Statement of Ethical Professional Practice

Members of IMA shall behave ethically. A commitment to ethical professional practice includes: overarching principles that express our values, and standards that guide our conduct.

Principles

IMA's overarching ethical principles include: Honesty, Fairness, Objectivity, and Responsibility. Members shall act in accordance with these principles and shall encourage others within their organizations to adhere to them.

Standards

A member's failure to comply with the following standards may result in disciplinary action.

I. Competence

Each member has a responsibility to:

1. Maintain an appropriate level of professional expertise by continually developing knowledge and skills.
2. Perform professional duties in accordance with relevant laws, regulations, and technical standards.
3. Provide decision support information and recommendations that are accurate, clear, concise, and timely.
4. Recognize and communicate professional limitations or other constraints that would preclude responsible judgment or successful performance of an activity.

II. Confidentiality

Each member has a responsibility to:

1. Keep information confidential except when disclosure is authorized or legally required.
2. Inform all relevant parties regarding appropriate use of confidential information. Monitor subordinates' activities to ensure compliance.
3. Refrain from using confidential information for unethical or illegal advantage.

III. Integrity

Each member has a responsibility to:

1. Mitigate actual conflicts of interest. Regularly communicate with business associates to avoid apparent conflicts of interest. Advise all parties of any potential conflicts.
2. Refrain from engaging in any conduct that would prejudice carrying out duties ethically.
3. Abstain from engaging in or supporting any activity that might discredit the profession.

IV. Credibility

Each member has a responsibility to:

1. Communicate information fairly and objectively.
2. Disclose all relevant information that could reasonably be expected to influence an intended user's understanding of the reports, analyses, or recommendations.
3. Disclose delays or deficiencies in information, timeliness, processing, or internal controls in conformance with organization policy and/or applicable law.

Institute of Management Accountants. Adapted with permission (2006).

Dilemma #3

> As a new accounting staff member at Central City Hospital, your supervisor has asked you to prepare the yearly *Medicare Cost Report*, which the government uses to determine its reimbursement to the hospital for serving Medicare patients. The report requires specialized knowledge that you don't believe you possess. The supervisor is busy planning for the coming year and cannot offer much guidance while you prepare the report.

This situation is not as rare as you might think. You may be asked to perform tasks that you don't feel qualified to perform. The competence standard requires you to perform professional duties in accordance with laws, regulations, and technical standards; but laws and regulations are always changing. For this reason, the competence standard also requires you to continually develop knowledge and skills. CPAs and CMAs are required to complete annual continuing professional education (about 40 hours per year) to fulfill this responsibility. However, even continuing professional education courses will not cover every situation you may encounter.

In the Medicare cost report situation, advise your supervisor that you currently lack the knowledge required to complete the Medicare cost report. By doing so, you are complying with the competence standard that requires you to recognize and communicate any limitations that would preclude you from fulfilling an activity. You should ask for training on the report preparation and supervision by someone experienced in preparing the report. If the supervisor denies your requests, you should ask him or her to reassign the Medicare report to a qualified staff member.

Dilemma #4

> Your company is negotiating a large multiyear sales contract that, if won, would substantially increase the company's future earnings. At a dinner party over the weekend, your friends ask you how you like your job and the company you work for. In your enthusiasm, you tell them not only about your responsibilities at work, but also about the contract negotiations. As soon as the words pop out of your mouth, you worry that you've said too much.

This situation is difficult to avoid. You may be so excited about your job and the company you work for that information unintentionally "slips out" during casual conversation with friends and family. The confidentiality standard requires you to refrain from disclosing information or using confidential information for unethical or illegal advantage. Was the contract negotiation confidential? If so, would your friends invest in company stock in hopes that the negotiations increase stock prices? Or were the negotiations public knowledge in the financial community? If so, your friends would gain no illegal advantage from the information. Recent cases, such as those involving Martha Stewart, remind us that insider trading (use of inside knowledge for illegal gain) has serious consequences. Even seemingly mundane information about company operations could give competitors an advantage. Therefore, it's best to disclose only information that is meant for public consumption.

Unethical Versus Illegal Behavior

Finally, is there a difference between unethical and illegal behavior? Not all unethical behavior is illegal, but all illegal behavior is unethical. For example, consider the competence standard. The competence standard states that management accountants have a responsibility to provide decision support information that is accurate, clear, concise, and timely. Failure to follow this standard is unethical but in most cases not illegal. Now, consider the integrity standard. It states that management accountants must abstain from any activity that might discredit the profession. A management accountant who commits an illegal act is violating this ethical standard. In other words, ethical behavior encompasses more than simply following the law. The IMA's ethical principles include honesty, fairness, objectivity, and responsibility—principles that are much broader than what is codified in the law.

Decision Guidelines

Managerial Accounting and Management Accountants

Chipotle made the following considerations in designing its managerial accounting system to provide managers with the information they need to run operations efficiently and effectively.

Decision	Guidelines
What is the primary purpose and focus of managerial accounting?	Managerial accounting provides information that helps managers plan, direct, and control operations and make better decisions; it has a • *future* orientation. • *focus on relevance* to business decisions.
How do managers design a company's managerial accounting system that is not regulated by GAAP?	Managers design the managerial accounting system so that the benefits (from helping managers make better decisions) outweigh the costs of the system.
Where should management accountants be placed within the organizational structure?	In the past, most management accountants worked in isolated departments. Now, over 50% of management accountants are deployed throughout the company and work on cross-functional teams. Management must decide which structure best suits its needs.
What skills should management accountants possess?	Because of their expanding role within the organization, most management accountants need financial and managerial accounting knowledge, analytical skills, knowledge of how a business functions, ability to work on teams, and written and oral communication skills.
By what ethical principles and standards should management accountants abide?	The IMA's overarching ethical *principles* include the following: • Honesty • Objectivity • Fairness • Responsibility The IMA's ethical *standards* include the following: • Competence • Integrity • Confidentiality • Credibility

SUMMARY PROBLEM 1

Requirements

1. Each of the following statements describes a responsibility of management. Match each statement to the management responsibility being fulfilled.

Statement	Management Responsibility
1. Identifying alternative courses of action and choosing among them	a. Planning
2. Running the company on a day-to-day basis	b. Decision making
3. Determining whether the company's units are operating according to plan	c. Directing
4. Setting goals and objectives for the company and determining strategies to achieve them	d. Controlling

2. Are the following statements more descriptive of managerial accounting or financial accounting information?
   - a. Describes historical transactions with external parties
   - b. Is not required by any authoritative body, such as the SEC
   - c. Reports on the company's subunits, such as products, geographical areas, and departments
   - d. Is intended to be used by creditors and investors
   - e. Is formatted in accordance with GAAP
3. Each of the following statements paraphrases an ethical responsibility. Match each statement to the standard of ethical professional practice being fulfilled. Each standard may be used more than once or not at all.

Responsibility	Standard of Ethical Professional Practice
1. Do not disclose company information unless authorized to do so.	a. Competence
2. Continue to develop skills and knowledge.	b. Confidentiality
3. Don't bias the information and reports presented to management.	c. Integrity
4. If you do not have the skills to complete a task correctly, do not pretend you do.	d. Credibility
5. Avoid actual *and* apparent conflicts of interest.	

SOLUTIONS

Requirement 1

1. (b) Decision making
2. (c) Directing
3. (d) Controlling
4. (a) Planning

Requirement 2

a. Financial accounting
b. Managerial accounting
c. Managerial accounting
d. Financial accounting
e. Financial accounting

Requirement 3

1. (b) Confidentiality
2. (a) Competence
3. (d) Credibility
4. (a) Competence
5. (c) Integrity

What Regulatory Issues Affect Management Accounting?

5 Discuss and analyze the implications of regulatory and business trends

The regulatory landscape is continually changing. Let's look at some of current regulations that affect managers and the managerial accounting systems that support them.

Sarbanes-Oxley Act of 2002

As a result of corporate accounting scandals, such as those at Enron and WorldCom, the U.S. Congress enacted the **Sarbanes-Oxley Act of 2002 (SOX)**. The purpose of SOX is to restore trust in publicly traded corporations, their management, their financial statements, and their auditors. SOX enhances internal control and financial reporting requirements and establishes new regulatory requirements for publicly traded companies and their independent auditors. Publicly traded companies have spent millions of dollars upgrading their internal controls and accounting systems to comply with SOX regulations.

As shown in Exhibit 1-7, SOX requires the company's CEO and CFO to assume responsibility for the financial statements and disclosures. The CEO and CFO must certify that the financial statements and disclosures fairly present, in all material respects, the operations and financial condition of the company. Additionally, they must accept responsibility for establishing and maintaining an adequate internal control structure and procedures for financial reporting. The company must have its internal controls and financial reporting procedures assessed annually.

EXHIBIT 1-7 Some Important Results of SOX

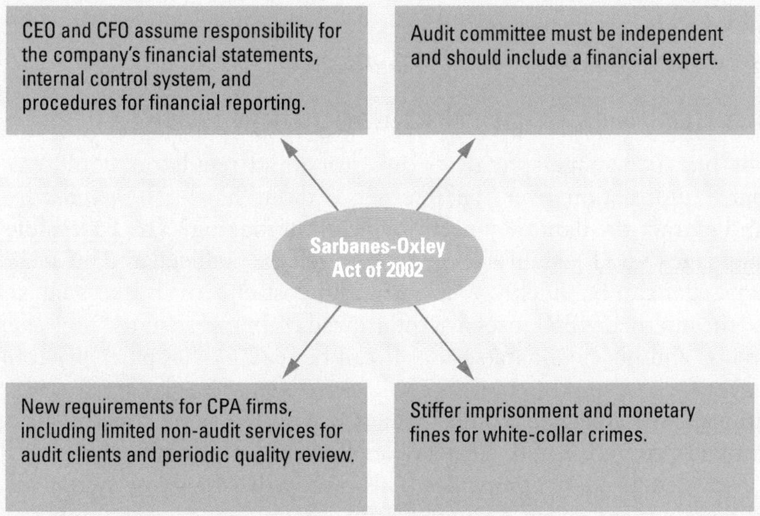

Source: Based on information from http://fmcenter.aicpa.org/Resources/Sarbanes-Oxley+Act/Summary+of+the+Provisions+of+the+Sarbanes-Oxley+Act+of+2002.htm

SOX also requires audit committee members to be independent, meaning that they may not receive any consulting or advisory fees from the company other than for their service on the board of directors. In addition, at least one of the members should be a financial expert. The audit committee oversees not only the internal audit function but also the company's audit by independent CPAs.

To ensure that CPA firms maintain independence from their client company, SOX does not allow CPA firms to provide certain non-audit services (such as bookkeeping and financial information systems design) to companies during the same period of time in which they are providing audit services. If a company wants to obtain such services from a CPA firm, it must hire a different firm to do the non-audit work. Tax services may be provided by the same CPA firm if pre-approved by the audit committee. The audit

> **Why is this important?**
> "**SOX** puts more pressure on companies, their **managers**, and their auditors to ensure that **investors** get financial information that **fairly reflects** the company's **operations.**"

partner must rotate off the audit engagement every five years, and the audit firm must undergo quality reviews every one to three years.

SOX also increases the penalties for white-collar crimes such as corporate fraud. These penalties include both monetary fines and substantial imprisonment. For example, knowingly destroying or creating documents to "impede, obstruct, or influence" any federal investigation can result in up to 20 years of imprisonment.[6] Since its enactment in 2002, SOX has significantly affected the internal operations of publicly traded corporations and their auditors. SOX will continue to play a major role in corporate management and the audit profession.

International Financial Reporting Standards (IFRS)

As a result of globalization, the need for consistent reporting standards for all companies in the world has grown. As a result, the SEC is currently considering whether to require all publicly traded companies to adopt **International Financial Reporting Standards (IFRS)** within the next few years. In many instances, IFRS vary from GAAP. While the transition to IFRS may be time consuming and expensive, in the long run it should actually save companies money and make the markets more efficient. Currently, a company operating in several different countries often must prepare several sets of financial statements using different accounting standards. As a result of IFRS, these companies will only need to prepare one set of financial statements that will be acceptable to all countries that have adopted IFRS. You can keep abreast of current IFRS developments and implications for accounting information at www.IFRS.com or www.IASB.org.

Extensible Business Reporting Language (XBRL)

Wouldn't it be nice if managers, analysts, investors, and regulators could easily access public company information over the internet without having to *manually* read pdf documents and extract the data they need for decision making? The **Extensible Business Reporting Language (XBRL)** enables companies to release financial and business information in a format that can be quickly, efficiently, and cost-effectively accessed, sorted, and analyzed over the internet. XBRL uses a standardized coding system to "tag" each piece of reported financial and business data so that it can be read by computer programs, rather than human eyes.

For example, *Sales Revenue* would be tagged with the same code by all companies so that a computer program could extract *Sales Revenue* information from an individual company or a selected group of companies. This standardized tagging system allows computers, rather than humans, to sift through financial reports and extract only the information that is needed. XBRL has several advantages:

- It decreases the need for laborious, manual searches though corporate reports for specific pieces of information.
- It decreases the time companies will spend converting their financial information into various government-prescribed formats.
- It will allow managers to easily compare their results to other companies and to industry averages.
- Investors and managers can "slice and dice" financial information however they want, to suit their decision making needs.
- It should promote the more consistent use of financial terminology since all data must be tagged using a preset, yet extensible, classification system.

[6]Go to www.AICPA.org to learn more about SOX.

Because of these benefits, the SEC is requiring that all publicly traded companies begin using XBRL for filing their financial reports for all periods after June 15, 2011. The United States joins Australia, Canada, China, Japan, the United Kingdom, and other countries in mandating the use of XBRL for publicly-traded companies. You can keep abreast of XBRL developments at www.XBRL.org and www.sec.gov.

What Business Trends Affect Management Accounting?

In this section, we'll consider some of the business trends that are currently impacting companies and the managerial accounting systems that support them.

Sustainability, Social Responsibility, and the Triple Bottom Line

In recent years, there has been an increasing awareness and growing interest in sustainability and social responsibility by both consumers and corporations. **Sustainability** is most often defined as the ability to meet the needs of the present without compromising the ability of future generations to meet their own needs.[7] Others define it as an expansion on the golden rule: "Do unto others, including future generations, as you would have them do unto you."[8] The first definition focuses more on environmental responsibility, while the second definition recognizes the additional component of social responsibility. As a result, many companies are beginning to adhere to the notion of a triple bottom line. The **triple bottom line** recognizes that a company's performance should not only be viewed in terms of its ability to generate economic profits for its owners, as has traditionally been the case, but also by its impact on people and the planet. Thus, sustainability can be viewed in terms of three interrelated factors that influence a company's ability to survive *and* thrive in the long-run: profit, people, and planet.

To move towards environmental sustainability, companies are introducing "green initiatives"—ways of doing business that have fewer negative consequences on the earth's resources. They've also recognized the need to be socially responsible—carefully considering how their business affects employees, consumers, citizens, and entire communities. Many companies have introduced means of giving back to their local communities, by monetarily supporting local schools and charities. Businesses are now viewing sustainability and social responsibility as opportunities for innovation and business development. These initiatives not only allow a company to "do the right thing," but they also can lead to economic profits by increasing demand for a company's products and services.

In every chapter of this text, you will see a special section illustrating how management accounting can help companies pursue environmentally sustainable and socially responsible business practices. These sections will be marked with a green recycle symbol, and will also point you to corresponding homework problems. In addition, Chapter 15 will introduce you to the newly emerging field of environmental management accounting.

Shifting Economy

In the last several decades, North American economies have shifted away from manufacturing toward service. Service companies provide health care, communication, transportation, banking, and other important benefits to society. Service companies now make up the largest sector of the U.S. economy. The U.S. Census Bureau expects services, especially technology and health-care services, to be among the fastest-growing industries over the next decade. Even companies that traditionally carried out manufacturing, such as General Electric (GE), are shifting toward selling more services.

Managerial accounting has its roots in the industrial age of manufacturing. Most traditional managerial accounting practices were developed to fill the needs of manufacturing

[7]1987 World Commission on Environment and Development, www.un.org/documents/ga/res/42/ares42-187.htm

[8]Gary Langenwalter, Business Sustainability: Keeping Lean but with More Green for the Company's Long Haul, 2010, AICPA, Lewisville, Texas.

firms. However, since the U.S. economy has shifted away from manufacturing, managerial accounting has shifted, too. The field of managerial accounting has *expanded* to meet the needs of service and merchandising firms as well as manufacturers. For example, consider the following:

1. Manufacturers still need to know how much each unit of their product costs to manufacture. In addition to using this information for inventory valuation and pricing decisions, manufacturers now use cost information to determine whether they should outsource production to another company or to an overseas location.
2. Service companies also need cost information to make decisions. They need to know the cost of providing a service rather than manufacturing a product. For example, banks must include the cost of servicing checking and savings accounts in the fees they charge customers. And hospitals need to know the cost of performing appendectomies to justify reimbursement from insurance companies and from Medicare.
3. Retailers need to consider importing costs when determining the cost of their merchandise. Because many goods are now produced overseas rather than domestically, determining the cost of a product is often more difficult than it was in the past. Management accountants need to consider foreign currency translation, shipping costs, and import tariffs when determining the cost of imported products.

Management accounting has expanded to meet decision-making needs for all types of businesses, including those that wish to compete globally.

Global Marketplace

The barriers to international trade have fallen over the past decades, allowing foreign companies to compete with domestic firms. Firms that are not highly efficient, innovative, and responsive to business trends will vanish from the global market. However, global markets also provide highly competitive domestic companies with great opportunities for growth.

Globalization has several implications for managerial accounting:

- Stiffer competition means managers need more accurate and timely information to make wise business decisions. Companies can no longer afford to make decisions by the "seat of their pants." Detailed, accurate, and real-time cost information has become a necessity for survival.
- Companies must decide whether to expand sales and/or production into foreign countries. To do so, managers need comprehensive estimates of the costs of running international operations and the benefits that can be reaped. They also need to be aware of regulations and laws in other countries that could impact their operations. For example, England and Europe tend to have much stricter environmental protection laws than the U.S.
- Companies can learn new management techniques by observing their international competitors. For example, the management philosophy of lean production, first developed in Japan by Toyota, is now being used by many U.S. companies to cut costs, improve quality, and speed production.

Advanced Information Systems

Many small businesses use QuickBooks or Peachtree software to track their costs and to develop the information that owners and managers need to run the business. But large companies use **enterprise resource planning (ERP)** systems that can integrate all of a company's worldwide functions, departments, and data. ERP systems such as SAP and Oracle gather company data into a centralized data warehouse. The system feeds the data into software for all of the company's business activities, from budgeting and purchasing to production and customer service.

Advantages of ERP systems include the following:

- Companies streamline their operations before mapping them into ERP software. Streamlining operations saves money.
- ERP helps companies respond quickly to changes. A change in sales instantly ripples through the ERP's purchases, production, shipping, and accounting systems.

- An ERP system can replace hundreds of separate software systems, such as different software in different regions, or different payroll, shipping, and production software.

Although ERP systems are initially expensive, they are almost a necessity for running large companies as efficiently as possible over the long run. How do managers arrive at this conclusion? They use cost benefit analysis, which weighs the expected costs of taking an action against the expected benefits of the action. The following Stop & Think illustrates a cost-benefit analysis.

STOP & THINK

Advances in technology have made electronic billing (e-billing) popular. Analysts estimate the following:

1. Companies save $7 per invoice by billing customers electronically.
2. The average large company issues 800,000 invoices a year.
3. The average cost of installing an e-billing system is $500,000. Should companies that issue 800,000 invoices a year consider e-billing?

Answer: The following one-year analysis reveals significant monetary benefit from e-billing:

Expected benefits:	
800,000 invoices × $7 savings per invoice	$5,600,000
Expected costs:	
Installation of e-billing system	(500,000)
Net expected benefits	$5,100,000

Not only does e-billing save the company money, but also it is more environmentally friendly than traditional paper-based billing. Thus, the company should strongly consider using e-billing for as many customers as possible.

Lean Operations

Lean thinking is both a philosophy and a business strategy of operating without waste. The more waste that is eliminated, the lower the company's costs will be. Why is this important? With lower costs, companies are better able to compete. One primary goal of a lean production system is to eliminate the waste of *time and money* that accompanies large inventories. Inventory takes time to store and unstore. The costs of holding inventory can add up to 25% or more of the inventory's value. Also, inventory that is held too long quickly becomes obsolete because of changing technology and consumer tastes.

Companies that advocate lean operations usually adopt the just-in-time (JIT) inventory philosophy that was first pioneered by Toyota. By manufacturing product *just in time* to fill customer orders, and no sooner, companies are able to substantially reduce the quantity of raw materials and finished product kept on hand. This, in turn, reduces storage costs (warehousing and associated security, utilities, and shrinkage costs) and handling costs (labor costs associated with storing and unstoring inventory). Since companies are making inventory *just in time* to fill customer orders, they must be able to produce a quality product very quickly. Therefore, lean companies focus on reducing throughput time, the time between buying raw materials and selling finished products, while still maintaining high quality. In Chapter 4, we'll look at some of the unique features of lean operations.

Why is this important?

"To survive in the **global marketplace**, businesses must quickly respond to customer **demand**, providing high-quality products and **services** at a reasonable price."

Total Quality Management

All companies, not just lean producers, must deliver high-quality goods and services to remain competitive. **Total quality management (TQM)** is one key to succeeding in the global economy. The goal of TQM is to delight customers by providing them with superior products and services. As part of TQM, each business function examines its own activities and works to improve performance by *continually* setting higher goals. In Chapter 4, we'll discuss how companies analyze the costs associated with their current level of quality as well as the costs of quality improvement initiatives.

ISO 9001:2008

Many firms want to demonstrate their commitment to continuous quality improvement. The International Organization for Standardization (ISO), made up of 157 member countries, has developed international quality management standards and guidelines. Firms may become **ISO 9001:2008** certified by complying with the quality management standards set forth by the ISO and undergoing extensive audits of their quality management processes. The prestigious certification gives firms a competitive advantage in the global marketplace. Many companies will purchase supplies only from firms bearing the ISO 9001 certification. To better understand the ISO's global impact, consider the following: by 2006, almost 897,000 certificates had been issued to firms in 170 countries. By 2009, the number of certifications exceeded 1,064,000.[9] The certification does not only apply to manufacturing firms. Service firms account for over 32% of all certificates issued. The American Institute of Certified Public Accountants was the first professional membership organization in the United States to earn the ISO 9001 certification.

[9]http://www.iso.org/iso/iso_catalogue/management_and_leadership_standards/certification/the_iso_survey.htm

Decision Guidelines

The Changing Regulatory and Business Environment

Successful companies have to respond to changes in the regulatory and business environment. Here are some of the decisions managers need to consider.

Decision	Guidelines
What companies need to comply with SOX?	Publicly traded companies must comply with SOX. Many of the law's specific requirements focus on implementing adequate internal controls and financial reporting procedures and maintaining independence from the company's auditors.
How will IFRS benefit international companies?	Companies that operate in more than one country will no longer be required to prepare multiple financial statements using different standards for each country in which they operate. Rather, they will prepare one set of financial statements in accordance with International Financial Reporting Standards (IFRS).
How will XBRL help managers?	XBRL will allow managers to more easily obtain and analyze publicly available financial data from their competitors, from companies they may wish to purchase, or from companies in which they may want to invest.
How do companies compete in a global economy?	They advocate sustainable and socially responsible business practices, use advanced information systems, lean operations, and TQM to compete more effectively.
How do companies decide whether to undertake new initiatives such as international expansion, ERP, lean operations, and TQM?	They use cost-benefit analysis: comparing the estimated benefits of the initiative with the estimated costs. They consider the impact of the decision not only on profits, but also on people, and the planet.

SUMMARY PROBLEM 2

EZ-Rider Motorcycles is considering whether to expand into Germany. If gas prices increase, the company expects more interest in fuel-efficient transportation such as motorcycles. As a result, the company is considering setting up a motorcycle assembly plant on the outskirts of Berlin.

EZ-Rider Motorcycles estimates it will cost $850,000 to convert an existing building to motorcycle production. Workers will need training, at a total cost of $65,000. The additional costs to organize the business and to establish relationships is estimated to be $150,000.

The CEO believes the company can earn sales profits from this expansion (before considering the costs in the preceding paragraph) of $1,624,000.

Requirement

Use cost-benefit analysis to determine whether EZ-Rider should expand into Germany.

■ SOLUTION

The following cost-benefit analysis indicates that the company should expand into Germany:

Expected Benefits:		
Expected profits from expansion sales		$ 1,624,000
Expected Costs:		
Conversion of building to manufacturing plant	$850,000	
Workforce training	65,000	
Organizing business and establishing relationships	150,000	
Total expected costs		(1,065,000)
Net expected benefits		$ 559,000

END OF CHAPTER

Learning Objectives

- 1 Identify managers' three primary responsibilities
- 2 Distinguish financial accounting from managerial accounting
- 3 Describe organizational structure and the roles and skills required of management accountants within the organization
- 4 Describe the role of the Institute of Management Accountants (IMA) and use its ethical standards to make reasonable ethical judgments
- 5 Discuss and analyze the implications of regulatory and business trends

Accounting Vocabulary

Audit Committee. (p. 8) A subcommittee of the board of directors that is responsible for overseeing both the internal audit function and the annual financial statement audit by independent CPAs.

Board of Directors. (p. 7) The body elected by shareholders to oversee the company.

Budget. (p. 4) Quantitative expression of a plan that helps managers coordinate and implement the plan.

Certified Management Accountant (CMA). (p. 11) A professional certification issued by the IMA to designate expertise in the areas of managerial accounting, economics, and business finance.

Chief Executive Officer (CEO). (p. 7) The position hired by the board of directors to oversee the company on a daily basis.

Chief Financial Officer (CFO). (p. 7) The position responsible for all of the company's financial concerns.

Chief Operating Officer (COO). (p. 7) The position responsible for overseeing the company's operations.

Controller. (p. 8) The position responsible for general financial accounting, managerial accounting, and tax reporting.

Controlling. (p. 5) One of management's primary responsibilities; evaluating the results of business operations against the plan and making adjustments to keep the company pressing toward its goals.

Cost-Benefit Analysis. (p. 21) Weighing costs against benefits to help make decisions.

Cross-Functional Teams. (p. 8) Corporate teams whose members represent various functions of the organization, such as R&D, Design, Production, Marketing, Distribution, and Customer Service.

Decision Making. (p. 4) Identifying possible courses of action and choosing among them.

Directing. (p. 4) One of management's primary responsibilities; running the company on a day-to-day basis.

Enterprise Resource Planning (ERP). (p. 20) Software systems that can integrate all of a company's worldwide functions, departments, and data into a single system.

Extensible Business Reporting Language (XBRL). (p. 18) A data tagging system that enables companies to release financial and business information in a format that can be quickly, efficiently, and cost-effectively accessed, sorted, and analyzed over the internet.

International Financial Reporting Standards (IFRS). (p. 18) The SEC has recently moved to adopt IFRS for all publicly traded companies within the next few years. In many instances, IFRS vary from GAAP.

Institute of Management Accountants (IMA). (p. 11) The professional organization that promotes the advancement of the management accounting profession.

Internal Audit Function. (p. 8) The corporate function charged with assessing the effectiveness of the company's internal controls and risk management policies.

ISO 9001:2008. (p. 22) A quality-related certification issued by the International Organization for Standardization (ISO). Firms may become ISO 9001:2008 certified by complying with the quality management standards set forth by the ISO and undergoing extensive audits of their quality management processes.

Just-in-time (JIT). (p. 21) An inventory philosophy first pioneered by Toyota in which a product is manufactured *just in time* to fill customer orders. Companies adopting JIT are able to substantially reduce the quantity of raw materials and finished product kept on hand.

Lean Thinking. (p. 21) A philosophy and business strategy of operating without waste.

Planning. (p. 4) One of management's primary responsibilities; setting goals and objectives for the company and deciding how to achieve them.

Sarbanes-Oxley Act of 2002 (SOX). (p. 17) A congressional act that enhances internal control and financial reporting requirements and establishes new regulatory requirements for publicly traded companies and their independent auditors.

Sustainability. (p. 19) The ability to meet the needs of the present without compromising the ability of future generations to meet their own needs.

Throughput Time. (p. 21) The time between buying raw materials and selling finished products.

Treasurer. (p. 8) The position responsible for raising the firm's capital and investing funds.

Triple bottom line. (p. 19) Evaluating a company's performance not only by its ability to generate economic profits, but also by its impact on people and the planet.

Total Quality Management (TQM). (p. 22) A management philosophy of delighting customers with superior products and services by continually setting higher goals and improving the performance of every business function.

MyAccountingLab **Go to http://myaccountinglab.com/ for the following Quick Check, Short Exercises, Exercises, and Problems. They are available with immediate grading, explanations of correct and incorrect answers, and interactive media that acts as your own online tutor.**

Quick Check

1. *(Learning Objective 1)* Which of the following is *not* one of the three primary responsibilities of management?
   - a. Controlling
   - b. Costing
   - c. Directing
   - d. Planning
2. *(Learning Objective 2)* Which of the following about managerial accounting is *true*?
   - a. GAAP requires managerial accounting.
   - b. Internal decision makers use managerial accounting.
   - c. CPAs audit managerial accounting reports.
   - d. Managerial accounting reports are usually prepared on an annual basis.
3. *(Learning Objective 2)* Which of the following is *not* a characteristic of managerial accounting information?
   - a. Emphasizes relevance
   - b. Focuses on the future more than the past
   - c. Provides detailed information about parts of the company, not just the company as a whole
   - d. Emphasizes reliability
4. *(Learning Objective 3)* What company position is in charge of raising the firm's capital?
   - a. Director of internal audit
   - b. Controller
   - c. COO
   - d. Treasurer
5. *(Learning Objective 3)* Which of the following statements is *true*?
   - a. The COO reports to the CFO.
   - b. The treasurer reports to the CEO.
   - c. The Internal Audit Department reports to the audit committee.
   - d. The controller reports to the internal auditor.
6. *(Learning Objective 3)* To get a job as a management accountant in most companies, you must
   - a. join the IMA.
   - b. be certified as a CMA.
   - c. be certified as a CPA.
   - d. None of the above.
7. *(Learning Objective 3)* In addition to accounting knowledge, management accountants must possess all of the following skills *except*
   - a. written communication skills.
   - b. knowledge of how a business functions.
   - c. computer programming skills.
   - d. analytical skills.
8. *(Learning Objective 4)* A management accountant who refuses an expensive gift from a software salesperson meets the ethical standard of
   - a. credibility.
   - b. confidentiality.
   - c. integrity.
   - d. competence.
9. *(Learning Objective 5)* Which of the following is *not* one of the provisions of the Sarbanes-Oxley Act of 2002?
   - a. The company's auditors assume responsibility for the financial statements.
   - b. The penalties (i.e., prison time and fines) for corporate fraud were increased.
   - c. At least one audit committee member should be a financial expert.
   - d. The CEO and CFO must certify that the financial statements fairly present the company's operations and financial condition.
10. *(Learning Objective 5)* All of the following tools help companies compete in today's market *except*
    - a. JIT.
    - b. KJD.
    - c. ERP.
    - d. TQM.

Quick Check Answers

1. b 2. b 3. d 4. d 5. c 6. d 7. c 8. c 9. a 10. b

Short Exercises

S1-1 Roles of managers *(Learning Objective 1)*

Describe the three primary roles of managers and the way they relate to one another.

S1-2 Contrast managerial and financial accounting *(Learning Objective 2)*

Managerial accounting differs from financial accounting in several areas. Specify whether each of the following characteristics relates to managerial accounting or financial accounting.

a. Focused on the future
b. Reporting is based mainly on the company as a whole
c. Reports are prepared usually quarterly and annually
d. Information is verified by external auditors
e. Focused on the past
f. Main characteristic of data is that it must be relevant
g. Reports tend to be prepared for the parts of the organization rather than the whole organization
h. Primary users are internal (for example, company managers)
i. Governed by Generally Accepted Accounting Principles (GAAP)
j. Main characteristic of data is that it must be reliable and objective
k. Reports are prepared as needed
l. Not governed by legal requirements
m. Primary users are external (i.e., creditors, investors)

S1-3 Accounting roles in the organization *(Learning Objective 3)*

The following is a list of job duties or descriptions. For each item, specify whether it would be most likely to describe the duties or responsibilities of someone working for the treasurer, the controller, or in the Internal Auditing Department.

a. Calculate the cost of a product
b. Issuing company bonds
c. Check to make sure that company risk management procedures are being followed
d. Work with various departments in preparing operating budgets for the upcoming year
e. Oversee accounts payable activities
f. Invests company funds
g. Report to the audit committee of the board of directors *and* to a senior executive, such as the CFO or CEO
h. Prepares company tax returns
i. Performing cash counts at branch offices
j. Preparing journal entries for month-end closing
k. Issuing company stock
l. Ensuring that the company's internal controls are functioning properly
m. Creating an analysis about whether to lease or buy a delivery truck

S1-4 Role of internal audit function *(Learning Objective 3)*

The following table lists several characteristics. Place a check mark next to those items that pertain directly to the internal audit function and its role within the organization.

Characteristic	Check (✓) if related to internal auditing
a. Ensures that the company achieves its profit goals	
b. Is part of the Accounting Department	
c. Usually reports to a senior executive (CFO or CEO) for administrative matters	
d. Performs the same function as independent certified public accountants	
e. External audits can be performed by the Internal Auditing Department	
f. Helps to ensure that company's internal controls are functioning properly	
g. Reports to treasurer or controller	
h. Required by the New York Stock Exchange if company stock is publicly traded on the NYSE	
i. Reports directly to the audit committee	

S1-5 Importance of ethical standards *(Learning Objective 4)*

Explain why each of the four broad ethical standards in the IMA's *Statement of Ethical Professional Practice* is necessary.

S1-6 Violations of ethical standards *(Learning Objective 4)*

The IMA's *Statement of Ethical Professional Practice* (Exhibit 1-6) requires management accountants to meet standards regarding the following:

- Competence
- Confidentiality
- Integrity
- Credibility

Consider the following situations. Which guidelines are violated in each situation?

a. You tell your brother that your company will report earnings significantly above financial analysts' estimates.

b. You see that other employees take home office supplies for personal use. As an intern, you do the same thing, assuming that this is a "perk."

c. At a conference on sustainability, you skip the afternoon session and go sightseeing.

d. You failed to read the detailed specifications of a new software package that you asked your company to purchase. After it is installed, you are surprised that it is incompatible with some of your company's older accounting software.

e. You do not provide top management with the detailed job descriptions they requested because you fear they may use this information to cut a position from your department.

S1-7 Identify current competitive tools *(Learning Objective 5)*

Companies are facing a great amount of change in every facet of their operations today. To remain competitive, companies must keep abreast of current developments in several areas. You recently got together with a group of friends who work for different companies. Your friends share information about their current challenges in adopting new tools or complying with new regulations. Excerpts from the conversation are presented in the following section. Tell whether each excerpt describes XBRL, ISO 9001:2008, sustainability, the Sarbanes-Oxley Act (SOX), or enterprise resource planning (ERP) systems.

a. Rick: My company has a new initiative at work. All employees are encouraged to recycle paper and other materials. Employees are also given one work day a year to volunteer to help local nonprofit organizations. Employees are also urged to think outside the box to find ways to reduce the company's carbon footprint. The company has also begun an internal reporting system that reports on its triple bottom line.

b. Nathan: I just started a new job in the Auditing Department. My new duties include assisting in the development of testing procedures and methods for determining internal controls effectiveness. I also oversee the testing for assurance of compliance with corporate policies. I am coordinating the review of SEC filings with our external auditors. I also am responsible for preparing periodic compliance status reports for management, the audit committee, and the external auditors.

c. Yveyue: My company is working to demonstrate its commitment to continuous quality improvement. We are currently undergoing an extensive audit of our quality management processes. We hope to gain a competitive advantage through this process.

d. Meagan: We have just installed a system at our company that integrates all of our company's data across all systems. We have one central data warehouse that contains information about our suppliers, our customers, our employees, and our financial information. The software retrieves information from this single data warehouse and all systems are integrated. The process of implementing this system has been very expensive and time-consuming, but we are reaping the benefits of being more streamlined, of being able to respond more quickly to changes in the market, and of not having several different software systems operating independently.

e. Meredith: We have been working on a system to tag all of the financial information in our quarterly and annual reports so that our financial information can be shared easily. We will be able to attach a tag to each piece of financial information. For example, we can tag our "net profits" wherever it appears in the financial reports. Any user accessing the financial reports would then be able to download the numbers for "net profits." Our stockholders and the analysts will be able to retrieve the information they need quickly, efficiently, and cost-effectively.

EXERCISES Group A

E1-8A Managers' responsibilities *(Learning Objective 1)*

Categorize each of the following activities as to which management responsibility it fulfills: planning, directing, or controlling. Some activities may fulfill more than one responsibility.

a. Management uses information on product costs to determine sales prices.
b. To lower product costs, management moves production to Mexico.
c. Management conducts variance analysis by comparing budget to actual.
d. Management reviews hourly sales reports to determine the level of staffing needed to service customers.
e. Management decides to increase sales growth by 10% next year.

E1-9A Define key terms *(Learning Objectives 1 & 2)*

Complete the following statements with one of the terms listed here. You may use a term more than once, and some terms may not be used at all.

Budget	Creditors	Managerial accounting	Planning
Controlling	Financial accounting	Managers	Shareholders

a. U.S. companies must follow GAAP or IFRS in their ________ systems.
b. Financial accounting develops reports for external parties such as ________ and ________.
c. When managers evaluate the company's performance compared to the plan, they are performing the ________ role of management.
d. ________ are decision makers inside a company.
e. ________ provides information on a company's past performance to external parties.
f. ________ systems are not restricted by GAAP or IFRS but are chosen by comparing the costs versus the benefits of the system.
g. Choosing goals and the means to achieve them is the ________ function of management.
h. ________ systems report on various segments or business units of the company.
i. ________ statements of public companies are audited annually by CPAs.

E1-10A Identify users of accounting information *(Learning Objective 3)*

For each of the following users of financial accounting information and managerial accounting information, specify whether the user would primarily use financial accounting information or managerial accounting information or both.

1. Current shareholders
2. Wall Street analyst
3. News reporter
4. Company controller
5. Board of directors
6. SEC employee
7. External auditor (public accounting firm)
8. Internal auditor
9. Potential shareholders
10. Loan officer at the company's bank
11. Manager of the Sales Department
12. Bookkeeping Department
13. Managers at regional offices
14. IRS agent

E1-11A Classify roles within the organization *(Learning Objective 3)*

Complete the following statements with one of the terms listed here. You may use a term more than once, and some terms may not be used at all.

Audit committee	Board of directors	CEO	CFO
Treasurer	Controller	Cross-functional teams	COO

a. The ________ and the ________ report to the CEO.
b. The internal audit function reports to the CFO or the ________ and the ________.
c. The ________ is directly responsible for financial accounting, managerial accounting, and tax reporting.
d. The CEO is hired by the ________.
e. The ________ is directly responsible for raising capital and investing funds.
f. The ________ is directly responsible for the company's operations.
g. Management accountants often work with ________.
h. A subcommittee of the board of directors is called the ________.

E1-12A Professional organization and certification *(Learning Objective 4)*

Complete the following sentences:

a. The ________ is a professional association for management accountants.
b. The Institute offers a professional certification called the ________, which focuses on managerial accounting topics, economics, and business finance.
c. The Institute finds that people holding the ________ certification earn, on average, more than those without the certification.
d. The Institute's monthly publication, called ________, addresses current topics of interest to management accountants.
e. The ________certification is typically aimed at those working in a company, while the ________ certification is typically aimed at those working in public accounting.

E1-13A Ethical dilemma *(Learning Objective 4)*

Mary Gonzales is the controller at Automax, a car dealership. She recently hired Cory Loftus as a bookkeeper. Loftus wanted to attend a class on Excel spreadsheets, so Gonzales temporarily took over Loftus's duties, including overseeing a fund for topping off a car's gas tank before a test drive. Gonzales found a shortage in this fund and confronted Loftus when he returned to work. Loftus admitted that he occasionally uses this fund to pay for his own gas. Gonzales estimated that the amount involved is close to $300.

Requirements

1. What should Gonzales do?
2. Would you change your answer to the previous question if Gonzales was the one recently hired as controller and Loftus was a well-liked, long-time employee who indicated that he always eventually repaid the fund?

E1-14A Classify ethical responsibilities *(Learning Objective 4)*

According to the IMA's *Statement of Ethical Professional Practice* (reproduced in the chapter), management accountants should follow four standards: competence, confidentiality, integrity, and credibility. Each of these standards contains specific responsibilities. Classify each of the following responsibilities according to the standard it addresses.

1. Inform all relevant parties regarding the appropriate use of confidential information. Monitor subordinates' activities to ensure compliance.
2. Perform professional duties in accordance with relevant laws, regulations, and technical standards.
3. Refrain from engaging in any conduct that would prejudice carrying out duties ethically.
4. Keep information confidential except when disclosure is authorized or legally required.
5. Disclose delays or deficiencies in information, timeliness, processing, or internal controls in conformance with organization policy and/or applicable law.
6. Refrain from using confidential information for unethical or illegal advantage.
7. Maintain an appropriate level of professional expertise by continually developing knowledge and skills.
8. Communicate information fairly and objectively.
9. Recognize and communicate professional limitations that would preclude responsible judgment or successful performance of an activity.
10. Mitigate actual conflicts of interest. Regularly communicate with business associates to avoid apparent conflicts of interest. Advise all parties of any potential conflicts.
11. Provide decision support information and recommendations that are accurate, clear, concise, and timely.
12. Abstain from engaging in or supporting any activity that might discredit the profession.
13. Disclose all relevant information that could reasonably be expected to influence an intended user's understanding of the reports, analyses, or recommendations.

E1-15A Define key terms *(Learning Objective 5)*

Complete the following statements with one of the terms listed here. You may use a term more than once, and some terms may not be used at all.

CEO	Internal audit	Throughput time
CFO	ISO 9001:2008	TQM
Controlling	Lean thinking	Triple bottom line
Directing	Planning	XBRL
ERP	Sarbanes-Oxley Act of 2002	
IFRS	Sustainability	

a. The SEC is expected to require the adoption of ________for all publicly traded companies within the next few years, which differs from the GAAP that companies are currently required to use.

b. ________serves the information needs of people in accounting as well as people in marketing and in the warehouse.

c. ________ is a language that utilizes a standardized coding system companies use to tag each piece of financial and business information in a format that can be quickly and efficiently accessed over the internet.

d. ________ is the management process of overseeing the company's day-to-day operations.

e. Typically, the treasurer and the controller report directly to the ________.

f. Firms acquire the ________certification to demonstrate their commitment to quality.

g. The ________ was enacted to restore trust in publicly traded corporations, their management, their financial statements, and their auditors.

h. ________ is the management process of setting goals and objectives for the company and determining how to achieve them.

i. The ________ manages the company on a daily basis.

j. ________ is the ability to meet the needs of the present without compromising the ability of future generations to meet their own needs.

k. The role of the ________ function is to ensure that the company's internal controls and risk management policies are functioning properly.

l. The goal of ________ is to delight customers by providing them with superior products and services.

m. ________ is the management process of evaluating the results of business operations against the plan and making adjustments to keep the company pressing towards its goals.

n. The ________ focuses on people, planet, and profit.

o. ________ is both a philosophy and a business strategy of operating without waste.

p. ________ is the time between buying raw materials and selling the finished products.

E1-16A Summarize the Sarbanes-Oxley Act *(Learning Objective 5)*

You just obtained an entry-level job as a management accountant. Other newly hired accountants have heard of the Sarbanes-Oxley Act of 2002 (SOX), but don't know much about it. Write a short memo to your colleagues discussing the reason for SOX, the goal of SOX, and some of the specific requirements of SOX that affect your company.

E1-17A Lean production cost-benefit analysis *(Learning Objective 5)*

Snow Rides manufactures snowboards. Richard May, the CEO, is trying to decide whether to adopt a lean thinking model. He expects that adopting lean production would save $105,000 in warehousing expenses and $51,000 in spoilage costs. Adopting lean production will require several one-time up-front expenditures: $12,750 for an employee training program, $98,000 to streamline the plant's production process, and $8,250 to identify suppliers that will guarantee zero defects and on-time delivery.

Requirements

1. What are the total costs of adopting lean production?
2. What are the total benefits of adopting lean production?
3. Should Snow Rides adopt lean production? Why or why not?

E1-18A Identify sustainability efforts as impacting people, planet, or profit *(Learning Objective 5)*

Sustainability involves more than just the impact of actions on the environment. The triple bottom line recognizes that a company has to measure its impact on people, planet, and profit for its long-term economic and social viability. To follow are examples of green initiatives recently undertaken at The J.M. Smucker Company. For each example, indicate whether this initiative would *primarily* impact people, planet, or profit.

Initiative at The J.M. Smucker Company	People, planet, or profit?
a. Achieved Silver LEED Certification on its new office building	
b. Reduced the amount of plastic used in Jif peanut butter jars by 2.2 million pounds	
c. Provided financial support to American Red Cross	
d. Submitted a report to the Carbon Disclosure Project, which is an effort to have organizations from around the world measure and disclose their greenhouse gas emissions and other sustainability efforts	
e. Generated a positive economic benefit in every community in which Smuckers has facilities	
f. Reduced delivery truck traffic and energy consumption by producing plastic bottles for *Crisco* products at its own manufacturing facility in Cincinnati rather than having the bottles shipped to them by a third party	
g. Received the Waste Reduction Awards Program Award from the State of California Waste Management Board	
h. Constructed a solar-powered warehouse	
i. Provided time off for employees to volunteer at organizations such as Boys and Girls Clubs of America and United Way	
j. Added a sustainability leader to every manufacturing facility to help to achieve established environmental goals	
k. Achieved Gold LEED Certification on its company store renovations	
l. Generated a profit for the company's shareholders	
m. Helped to establish the Heartland Education Initiative based in Orrville, Ohio, which is focused on improving education through a partnership between community organizations, parents, school, and businesses	

EXERCISES Group B

E1-19B Managers' responsibilities *(Learning Objective 1)*

Categorize each of the following activities as to which management responsibility it fulfills: planning, directing, or controlling. Some activities may fulfill more than one responsibility.

a. Management creates a sales budget for the upcoming quarter.
b. Top management selects a location for a new store.
c. Management is designing a new sales incentive program for the upcoming year.
d. The store manager posts the employee time schedule for the next week so that employees know when they are working.
e. The manager of the Service Department investigates why the actual hours spent on a recent repair job exceeded the standard for that type of repair by more than 20%.

E1-20B Define key terms *(Learning Objectives 1 & 2)*

Complete the following statements with one of the terms listed here. You may use a term more than once, and some terms may not be used at all.

Budget	Creditors	Managerial accounting	Planning
Controlling	Financial accounting	Managers	Shareholders

a. _______ systems are chosen by comparing the costs versus the benefits of the system and are not restricted by GAAP or IFRS.

b. CPAs audit the _______ statements of public companies.

c. Financial accounting develops reports for external parties such as _______ and _______.

d. Companies must follow GAAP or IFRS in their _______ systems.

e. Decision makers inside a company are the _______.

f. Choosing goals and the means to achieve them is the _______ function of management.

g. _______ systems report on various segments or business units of the company.

h. When managers evaluate the company's performance compared to the plan, they are performing the _______ role of management.

i. Information on a company's past performance is provided to external parties by _______.

E1-21B Identify users of accounting information *(Learning Objective 3)*

For each of the following users of financial accounting information and managerial accounting information, specify whether the user would primarily use financial accounting information or managerial accounting information or both.

1. Board of directors
2. Manager of the Service Department
3. Wall Street analyst
4. Internal auditor
5. Potential investors
6. Current stockholders
7. Reporter from the *Wall Street Journal*
8. Regional division managers
9. SEC examiner
10. Bookkeeping Department
11. Division controller
12. External auditor (public accounting firm)
13. Loan officer at the company's bank
14. State tax agency auditor

E1-22B Classify roles within the organization *(Learning Objective 3)*

Complete the following statements with one of the terms listed here. You may use a term more than once, and some terms may not be used at all.

Audit committee	Board of directors	CEO	CFO
Treasurer	Controller	Cross-functional teams	COO

a. Management accountants often work with _______.

b. The _______ and the _______ report to the CEO.

c. A subcommittee of the board of directors is called the _______.

d. Raising capital and investing funds are the direct responsibilities of the _______.

e. Financial accounting, managerial accounting, and tax reporting are the direct responsibilities of the _______.

f. The internal audit function reports to the CFO or the ________ and the ________.
g. The CEO is hired by the ________.
h. The company's operations are the direct responsibility of the ________.

E1-23B Professional organization and certification *(Learning Objective 4)*

Complete the following sentences:

a. The ________ is a professional association for management accountants.
b. The Institute says that more accountants work in organizations rather than at ________.
c. The Institute's monthly publication, called ________, addresses current topics of interest to management accountants.
d. The Institute offers a professional certification called the ________, which focuses on managerial accounting topics, economics, and business finance.
e. The Institute finds that people holding the ________ certification earn, on average, more than those without the certification.

E1-24B Ethical dilemma *(Learning Objective 4)*

Richard Welsh is the controller at Sangood Kitchens, a large food and kitchen store. He recently hired Helen Smith as a bookkeeper. Smith wanted to attend a class on information systems, so Welsh temporarily took over Smith's duties, including overseeing a fund for giving in-store cooking and product demonstrations. Welsh discovered a shortage in this fund and confronted Smith on it. Smith admitted that she occasionally uses the fund to pay for her own store purchases. Welsh estimated that the amount involved is close to $500.

Requirements

1. What should Welsh do?
2. Would you change your answer to the previous question if Welsh was the one recently hired as controller and Smith was a well-liked, long-time employee who indicated that she always eventually repaid the fund?

E1-25B Classify ethical responsibilities *(Learning Objective 4)*

According to the IMA's *Statement of Ethical Professional Practice* (Exhibit 1-6), management accountants should follow four standards: competence, confidentiality, integrity, and credibility. Each of these standards contains specific responsibilities. Classify each of the following responsibilities according to the standard it addresses.
Responsibility:

1. Maintain an appropriate level of professional expertise by continually developing knowledge and skills.
2. Recognize and communicate professional limitations that would preclude responsible judgment or successful performance of an activity.
3. Disclose all relevant information that could reasonably be expected to influence an intended user's understanding of the reports, analyses, or recommendations.
4. Disclose delays or deficiencies in information, timeliness, processing, or internal controls in conformance with organization policy and/or applicable law.
5. Perform professional duties in accordance with relevant laws, regulations, and technical standards.
6. Abstain from engaging in or supporting any activity that might discredit the profession.
7. Refrain from engaging in any conduct that would prejudice carrying out duties ethically.
8. Provide decision support information and recommendations that are accurate, clear, concise, and timely.
9. Keep information confidential except when disclosure is authorized or legally required.
10. Communicate information fairly and objectively.
11. Refrain from using confidential information for unethical or illegal advantage.

12. Inform all relevant parties regarding the appropriate use of confidential information. Monitor subordinates' activities to ensure compliance.
13. Mitigate actual conflicts of interest. Regularly communicate with business associates to avoid apparent conflicts of interest. Advise all parties of any potential conflicts.

E1-26B Define key terms *(Learning Objective 5)*

Complete the following statements with one of the terms listed here. You may use a term more than once, and some terms may not be used at all.

CEO	Internal audit	Throughput time
CFO	ISO 9001:2008	TQM
Controlling	Lean thinking	Triple bottom line
Directing	Planning	XBRL
ERP	Sarbanes-Oxley Act of 2002	
IFRS	Sustainability	

a. The SEC is expected to require the adoption of ________for all publicly traded companies within the next few years, which differs from the GAAP that companies are currently required to use.

b. ________is the management process of overseeing the company's day-to-day operations.

c. The________manages the company on a daily basis.

d. The ________ was enacted to restore trust in publicly traded corporations, their management, their financial statements, and their auditors.

e. Firms that acquire the ________certification to demonstrate their commitment to quality.

f. The goal of ________ is to delight the customer by providing them with superior products and services.

g. The ________ focuses on people, planet, and profit.

h. ________is the management process of setting goals and objectives for the company and determining how to achieve them.

i. The role of the ________function is to ensure that the company's internal controls and risk management policies are functioning properly.

j. ________ serves the information needs of people in accounting as well as people in marketing and in the warehouse.

k. ________ is a language that utilizes a standardized coding system companies use to tag each piece of financial and business information in a format that can be quickly and efficiently accessed over the internet.

l. ________is both a philosophy and a business strategy of operating without waste.

m. Typically, the treasurer and the controller report directly to the ________.

n. ________ is the time between buying raw materials and selling the finished products.

o. ________ is the management process of evaluating the results of business operations against the plan and making adjustments to keep the company pressing towards its goals.

p. ________ is the ability to meet the needs of the present without compromising the ability of future generations to meet their own needs.

E1-27B Summarize the Sarbanes-Oxley Act *(Learning Objective 5)*

At a family gathering, your grandmother comes to you and asks you, since you have taken many business classes, to explain the Sarbanes-Oxley Act of 2002 (SOX). She has heard about SOX on television and the internet but does not really understand it. Explain to your grandmother the reason for SOX, the goal of SOX, and some of the specific requirements of SOX.

E1-28B Lean production cost-benefit analysis *(Learning Objective 5)*

Ice Rides manufactures snowboards. Alfred Castro, the CEO, is trying to decide whether to adopt a lean thinking model. He expects that adopting lean production would save \$102,000 in warehousing expenses and \$36,500 in spoilage costs. Adopting lean production will require several one-time up-front expenditures: \$12,500 for an employee training program, \$41,500 to streamline the plant's production process, and \$8,500 to identify suppliers that will guarantee zero defects and on-time delivery.

Requirements

1. What are the total costs of adopting lean production?
2. What are the total benefits of adopting lean production?
3. Should Ice Rides adopt lean production? Why or why not?

E1-29B Identify sustainability efforts as impacting people, planet, or profit *(Learning Objective 5)*

Sustainability involves more than just the impact of actions on the environment. The triple bottom line recognizes that a company has to measure its impact on people, planet, and profit for its long-term economic and social viability. To follow are examples of green initiatives recently undertaken at The Coca-Cola Company. For each example, indicate whether this initiative would primarily impact people, planet, or profit.

Initiative at The Coca-Cola Company	People, planet, or profit?
a. Minimized the amount of water used in the manufacturing and cleaning processes resulting in a water use savings of over 2 billion liters since 2008	
b. Recruited from a wide cross section of the communities that it services so that the representation of women and minority groups in management can be improved	
c. Displayed total calorie counts on the selection buttons on company-controlled vending machines so that consumers can make informed choices	
d. Generated a profit for the company's shareholders	
e. Removed the side walls on the corrugated trays that carry products which resulted in savings of almost 2,400 metric tons of corrugated packaging in 2008 and 2009	
f. Provided training and career planning for employees to help to provide a rewarding work life	
g. Reduced the bottle cap size by .5 millimeters and shortened the bottle neck which resulted in a total plastics savings of more than 11,000 metric tons since 2007	
h. Provided on-site wellness coaching for employees in the Baltimore sales facility to help to improve employee health	
i. Diverted more than 2.5 million beverage containers from landfills by placing more than 3,000 recycling bins at NASCAR racetracks across the U.S.	
j. Generated a positive economic benefit in every community in which Coca-Cola has facilities in the United States	
k. Reduced beverage calories in U.S. schools by 88% since 2006	
l. Prohibited marketing to children under the age of 12 in its global marketing policy.	
m. Deployed hybrid electric trucks, which generate approximately one-third fewer CO_2 emissions than a regular truck, in several major U.S. cities	

PROBLEMS Group A

P1-30A Management processes and accounting information *(Learning Objectives 1 & 2)*

Allison Hopkins has her own chain of music stores, Hopkins' Music. Her stores sell musical instruments, sheet music, and other related items. Music lessons and instrument repair are also offered through the stores. Hopkins' Music also has a website that sells music merchandise. Hopkins' Music has a staff of 80 people working in six departments: Sales, Repairs, Lessons, Web Development, Accounting, and Human Resources. Each department has its own manager.

Requirements

1. For each of the six departments, describe at least one decision/action for each of the three stages of management (planning, directing, and controlling). Prepare a table similar to the following for your answer:

	Planning	Directing	Controlling
Sales			
Repairs			
Lessons			
Web Development			
Accounting			
Human Resources			

2. For each of the decisions/actions you described in Part 1, identify what information is needed for that decision/action. Specify whether that information would be generated by the financial accounting system or the managerial accounting system at Hopkins' Music.

P1-31A Ethical dilemmas *(Learning Objective 4)*

Kate Royer is the new controller for EDU Software, which develops and sells educational software. Shortly before the December 31 fiscal year-end, Matt Adams, the company president, asks Royer how things look for the year-end numbers. He is not happy to learn that earnings growth may be below 15% for the first time in the company's five-year history. Adams explains that financial analysts have again predicted a 15% earnings growth for the company and that he does not intend to disappoint them. He suggests that Royer talk to the assistant controller, who can explain how the previous controller dealt with this situation. The assistant controller suggests the following strategies:

a. Persuade suppliers to postpone billing until January 1.
b. Record as sales certain software awaiting sale that is held in a public warehouse.
c. Delay the year-end closing a few days into January of the next year so that some of next year's sales are included as this year's sales.
d. Reduce the allowance for bad debts (and bad debts expense).
e. Postpone routine monthly maintenance expenditures from December to January.

Requirement

Which of these suggested strategies are inconsistent with IMA standards? What should Royer do if Adams insists that she follow all of these suggestions?

P1-32A ERP cost-benefit analysis *(Learning Objective 5)*

As CEO of Ocean World, Dana Stuckey knows it is important to control costs and to respond quickly to changes in the highly competitive boat-building industry. When IDG Consulting proposes that Ocean World invest in an ERP system, she forms a team to evaluate the proposal: the plant engineer, the plant foreman, the systems specialist, the human resources director, the marketing director, and the management accountant.

A month later, management accountant Matt Chumura reports that the team and IDG estimate that if Ocean World implements the ERP system, it will incur the following costs:

a. $370,000 in software costs
b. $80,000 to customize the ERP software and load Ocean World's data into the new ERP system
c. $107,000 for employee training

The team estimates that the ERP system should provide several benefits:

a. More efficient order processing should lead to savings of $180,000.
b. Streamlining the manufacturing process so that it maps into the ERP system will create savings of $270,000.
c. Integrating purchasing, production, marketing, and distribution into a single system will allow Ocean World to reduce inventories, saving $230,000.
d. Higher customer satisfaction should increase sales, which, in turn, should increase profits by $145,000.

Requirements

1. If the ERP installation succeeds, what is the dollar amount of the benefits?
2. Should Ocean World install the ERP system? Why or why not? Show your calculations.
3. Why did Stuckey create a team to evaluate IDG's proposal? Consider each piece of cost-benefit information that management accountant Chumura reported. Which person on the team is most likely to have contributed each item? (*Hint:* Which team member is likely to have the most information about each cost or benefit?)

P1-33A E-commerce cost-benefit analysis *(Learning Objective 5)*

Sun Gas wants to move its sales order system to the internet. Under the proposed system, gas stations and other merchants will use a password-protected site to check the availability and current price of various products and place an order. Currently, customer service representatives take dealers' orders over the phone; they record the information on a paper form, then manually enter it into the firm's computer system.

CFO Carrie Smith believes that dealers will not adopt the new internet system unless Sun Gas provides financial assistance to help them purchase or upgrade their computer network. Smith estimates this one-time cost at $750,000. Sun Gas will also have to invest $150,000 in upgrading its own computer hardware. The cost of the software and the consulting fee for installing the system will be $230,000. The internet system will enable Sun Gas to eliminate 25 clerical positions. Smith estimates that the new system's lower labor costs will have saved the company $1,357,000.

Requirement

Use a cost-benefit analysis to recommend to Smith whether Sun Gas should proceed with the internet-based ordering system. Give your reasons, showing supporting calculations.

P1-34A Continuation of P1-33A: revised estimates *(Learning Objective 5)*

Consider the Sun Gas proposed entry into the internet-based ordering system in P1-33A. Smith revises her estimates of the benefits from the new system's lower labor costs. She now thinks the savings will be only $933,000.

Requirements

1. Compute the expected benefits of the internet-based ordering system.
2. Would you recommend that Sun Gas accept the proposal?
3. Before Smith makes a final decision, what other factors should she consider?

PROBLEMS Group B

P1-35B Management processes and accounting information

(Learning Objectives 1 & 2)

David Doors has his own electronics retail chain, Circuit Pro. His stores sell computer parts, audio-visual equipment, consumer electronics, and related items. Custom computer building and electronics repair are also offered. In addition, Circuit Pro has a website to sell its merchandise. Circuit Pro has a staff of 90 people working in six departments: Sales, Customization, Repairs, Web Development, Accounting, and Human Resources. Each department has its own manager.

Requirements

1. For each of the six departments, describe at least one decision/action for each of the three stages of management (planning, directing, and controlling). Prepare a table similar to the following for your answer:

	Planning	Directing	Controlling
Sales			
Repairs			
Customization			
Web Development			
Accounting			
Human Resources			

2. For each of the decisions/actions you described in Part 1, identify what information is needed for that decision/action. Specify whether that information would be generated by the financial accounting system or the managerial accounting system at Circuit Pro.

P1-36B Ethical dilemmas *(Learning Objective 4)*

Kara Williams is the new controller for Colors, a designer and manufacturer of sportswear. Shortly before the December 31 fiscal year-end, Lashea Lucas (the company president) asks Williams how things look for the year-end numbers. Lucas is not happy to learn that earnings growth may be below 10% for the first time in the company's five-year history. Lucas explains that financial analysts have again predicted a 12% earnings growth for the company and that she does not intend to disappoint them. She suggests that Williams talk to the assistant controller, who can explain how the previous controller dealt with this situation. The assistant controller suggests the following strategies:

a. Postpone planned advertising expenditures from December to January.
b. Do not record sales returns and allowances on the basis that they are individually immaterial.
c. Persuade retail customers to accelerate January orders to December.
d. Reduce the allowance for bad debts (and bad debts expense).
e. Colors ships finished goods to public warehouses across the country for temporary storage until it receives firm orders from customers. As Colors receives orders, it directs the warehouse to ship the goods to nearby customers. The assistant controller suggests recording goods sent to the public warehouses as sales.

Requirement

Which of these suggested strategies are inconsistent with IMA standards? What should Williams do if Lucas insists that she follow all of these suggestions?

P1-37B ERP cost-benefit analysis *(Learning Objective 5)*

As CEO of WaterSpray Marine, Sarabeth Wilson knows it is important to control costs and to respond quickly to changes in the highly competitive boat-building industry. When IDG Consulting proposes that WaterSpray Marine invest in an ERP system, she forms a team to evaluate the proposal: the plant engineer, the plant foreman, the systems specialist, the human resources director, the marketing director, and the management accountant. A month later, management accountant Matt Cook reports that the team and IDG estimate that if WaterSpray Marine implements the ERP system, it will incur the following costs:

a. $400,000 in software costs

b. $89,000 to customize the ERP software and load WaterSpray's data into the new ERP system

c. $130,000 for employee training

The team estimates that the ERP system should provide several benefits:

a. More efficient order processing should lead to savings of $118,000.

b. Streamlining the manufacturing process so that it maps into the ERP system will create savings of $120,000.

c. Integrating purchasing, production, marketing, and distribution into a single system will allow WaterSpray Marine to reduce inventories, saving $215,000.

d. Higher customer satisfaction should increase sales, which, in turn, should increase the present value of profits by $155,000.

Requirements

1. If the ERP installation succeeds, what is the dollar amount of the benefits?
2. Should WaterSpray Marine install the ERP system? Why or why not? Show your calculations.
3. Why did Wilson create a team to evaluate IDG's proposal? Consider each piece of cost-benefit information that management accountant Cook reported. Which person on the team is most likely to have contributed each item? (*Hint:* Which team member is likely to have the most information about each cost or benefit?)

P1-38B E-commerce cost-benefit analysis *(Learning Objective 5)*

Mid-West Gas wants to move its sales order system to the internet. Under the proposed system, gas stations and other merchants will use a password-protected site to check the availability and current price of various products and place an order. Currently, customer service representatives take dealers' orders over the phone; they record the information on a paper form, then manually enter it into the firm's computer system.

CFO Carrie Smith believes that dealers will not adopt the new internet system unless Mid-West Gas provides financial assistance to help them purchase or upgrade their computer systems. Smith estimates this one-time cost at $760,000. Mid-West Gas will also have to invest $155,000 in upgrading its own computer hardware. The cost of the software and the consulting fee for installing the system will be $225,000. The Web system will enable Mid-West Gas to eliminate 25 clerical positions. Smith estimates that the benefits of the new system's lower labor costs will have saved the company $1,370,000.

Requirement

Use a cost-benefit analysis to recommend to Smith whether Mid-West Gas should proceed with the internet-based ordering system. Give your reasons, showing supporting calculations.

P1-39B Continuation of P1-38B: revised estimates *(Learning Objective 5)*

Smith revises her estimates of the benefits from the new system's lower labor costs as calculated in P1-38B. She now thinks the saving will be only $925,000.

Requirements

1. Compute the expected benefits of the internet-based ordering system.
2. Would you recommend that Mid-West Gas accept the proposal?
3. Before Smith makes a final decision, what other factors should she consider?

CRITICAL THINKING

Discussion & Analysis

A1-40 Discussion Questions

1. What are the three main areas of management's responsibility? How are these three areas interrelated? How does managerial accounting support each of the responsibility areas of managers?
2. What is the Sarbanes-Oxley Act of 2002 (SOX)? How does SOX affect financial accounting? How does SOX impact managerial accounting? Is there any overlap between financial and managerial accounting in terms of the SOX impact? If so, what are the areas of overlap?
3. Why is managerial accounting more suitable for internal reporting than financial accounting?
4. A company currently has all of its managerial accountants reporting to the controller. What might be inefficient about this organizational structure? How might the company restructure? What benefits would be offered by the restructuring?
5. What skills are required of a management accountant? In what college courses are these skills taught or developed? What skills would be further developed in the workplace?
6. What is the Institute of Management Accountants (IMA)? How could being in a member of a professional organization help a person's career?
7. How might a Certified Management Accountant (CMA) certification benefit a person in his or her career? How does the CMA certification differ from the Certified Public Accountant (CPA) certification? What skills are assessed on the CMA exam?
8. What are the four ethical standards in the Institute of Management Accountants' *Statement of Ethical Professional Practice*? Describe the meaning of each of the four standards. How does each of these standards impact planning, directing, and controlling?
9. How has technology changed the work of management accountants? What other business trends are influencing managerial accounting today? How do these other trends impact management accountants' roles in the organization?
10. What significant regulatory trends are impacting accounting in general today? How do these regulatory trends affect the field of managerial accounting?
11. The effect of sustainability on the planet (environment) is probably the most visible component of the triple bottom line. For a company with which you are familiar, list two examples of its sustainability efforts related to the planet.
12. One controversial area regarding sustainability is whether organizations should use their sustainability progress and activities in their advertising. Do you think a company should publicize their sustainability efforts? Why or why not?

Application & Analysis

A1-41 Accountants and Their Jobs

Basic Discussion Questions

1. When you think of an accountant, whom do you picture? Do you personally know anyone (family member, friend, relative) whose chosen career is accounting? If so, does the person "fit" your description of an accountant or not?
2. Before reading Chapter 1, what did you picture accountants doing, day-in and day-out, at their jobs? From where did this mental picture come (e.g., movies, first accounting class, speaking with accountants, etc.)?
3. What skills are highly valued by employers? What does that tell you about "what accountants do" at their companies?

4. Chapter 1 includes several quotes from accountants at Abbott Laboratories, Caterpillar, and U.S. West. After reading these quotes and from what you know about accountants, how would you describe the role/job responsibilities of accountants?
5. Many accounting majors start their careers in public accounting. Do you think most of them stay in public accounting? Discuss what you consider to be a typical career track for accounting majors.
6. If you are not an accounting major, how do the salaries of accountants compare with your chosen field? How do the opportunities compare (i.e., demand for accountants)?

A1-42 Ethics at Enron

Watch the movie *Enron: The Smartest Guys in the Room* (Magnolia Home Entertainment, 2005, Los Angeles, California).

Basic Discussion Questions

1. Do you think such behavior is common at other companies or do you think this was a fairly isolated event?
2. How important is the "tone at the top" (the tone set by company leadership)?
3. Do you think you could be tempted to follow along if the leadership at your company had the same mentality as the leadership at Enron, or do you think you would have the courage to "just say no" or even be a "whistle-blower?"
4. Why do you think some people can so easily justify (at least to themselves) their unethical behavior?
5. In general, do you think people stop to think about how their actions will affect other people (e.g., the elderly in California who suffered due to electricity blackouts) or do they just "do their job"?
6. What was your reaction to the psychology experiment shown in the DVD? Studies have shown that unlike the traders at Enron (who received large bonuses), most employees really have very little to gain from following a superior's directive to act unethically. Why then do some people do it?
7. Do you think people weigh the potential costs of acting unethically with the potential benefits?
8. You are a business student and will someday work for company or own a business. How will watching this movie impact the way you intend to conduct yourself as an employee or owner?
9. The reporter from *Fortune* magazine asked the question, "How does Enron make its money?" Why should every employee and manager (at every company) know the answer to this question?
10. In light of the "mark-to-market" accounting that enabled Enron to basically record any profit it wished to record, can you understand why some of the cornerstones of financial accounting are "conservatism" and "recording transactions at historical cost?"
11. How did employees of Enron (and employees of the utilities company in Oregon) end up losing billions in retirement funds?

Decision Case

A1-43 Ethical standards *(Learning Objective 4)*

The IMA's *Statement of Ethical Professional Practice* (Exhibit 1-6) can be applied to more than just managerial accounting. It is also relevant to college students. Explain at least one situation that shows how each IMA standard is relevant to your experiences as a student. For example, the ethical standard of competence would suggest not cutting classes.

Ethical Issue

A1-44 Ethical dilemma *(Learning Objective 4)*

Ricardo Valencia recently resigned his position as controller for Tom White Automotive, a small, struggling foreign car dealer in Austin, Texas. Valencia has just started a new job as controller for Mueller Imports, a much larger dealer for the same car manufacturer. Demand for this particular make of car is exploding, and the manufacturer cannot produce enough cars to satisfy demand. Each manufacturer's regional sales manager is given a certain number of cars. Each regional sales manager then decides how to divide the cars among the independently owned dealerships in the region. Because most dealerships can sell every car they receive, the key is getting a large number of cars from the manufacturer's regional sales manager.

Valencia's former employer, Tom White Automotive, received only about 25 cars a month. Consequently, the dealership was not very profitable.

Valencia is surprised to learn that his new employer, Mueller Imports, receives over 200 cars a month. Valencia soon gets another surprise. Every couple of months, a local jeweler bills the dealer $5,000 for "miscellaneous services." Franz Mueller, the owner of the dealership, personally approves the payment of these invoices, noting that each invoice is a "selling expense." From casual conversations with a salesperson, Valencia learns that Mueller frequently gives Rolex watches to the manufacturer's regional sales manager and other sales executives. Before talking to anyone about this, Valencia decides to work through his ethical dilemma by answering the following questions:

1. What is the ethical issue?
2. What are my options?
3. What are the possible consequences?
4. What should I do?

Team Project

A1-45 Interviewing a local company about sustainability *(Learning Objective 5)*

In this project, you will be conducting an interview about sustainability efforts at a local organization. Find a local company or organization with which you are familiar. Arrange an interview with a manager from that organization. Before the interview, do a search on the internet about sustainability efforts of companies in that same industry so that you can ask related questions. Use the following questions to start your interview; add relevant questions related to what you discover through your internet search about sustainability efforts at similar companies. After the interview, write up a report of what you found during the interview. Conclude your report with your overall assessment of that organization's sustainability efforts.

1. What is the company's primary product or service? (*Note:* You should be able to answer this question BEFORE your interview.)
2. Does your company have a stated policy on sustainability? (Note: the company might refer to "green" practices or some other similar term rather than using the exact term of "sustainability.") What is the policy?
3. How would this manager define "sustainability?" Is the manager's definition similar to the definition of "sustainability" in the chapter?
4. Regardless of whether the company has a sustainability policy or not, what sustainability efforts does the company make with respect to the environment? For example, does the company recycle its waste? What specific types of waste are recycled? Does the company purchase recycled-content products?
5. Is the amount (or percentage) of waste that is recycled tracked in a reporting system? Who gets reports on the organization's recycling efforts?

6. How does the company measure its impact on the environment (if it does)? (For example, does it measure its carbon footprint in total? Does it measure the carbon footprint of individual projects?)
7. Does the company do any external reporting of sustainability? If so, how long has the company been reporting on its sustainability efforts? If the company does not do any sustainability reporting at the current time, does it anticipate starting to report on its sustainability efforts in the near future?
8. In the manger's opinion, is sustainability important within that organization's industry? Why or why not?

Building Blocks of Managerial Accounting

Learning Objectives

- **1** Distinguish among service, merchandising, and manufacturing companies
- **2** Describe the value chain and its elements
- **3** Distinguish between direct and indirect costs
- **4** Identify the inventoriable product costs and period costs of merchandising and manufacturing firms
- **5** Prepare the financial statements for service, merchandising, and manufacturing companies
- **6** Describe costs that are relevant and irrelevant for decision making
- **7** Classify costs as fixed or variable and calculate total and average costs at different volumes

With the introduction of the Prius,

Toyota became the front-runner in offering fuel-efficient vehicles with cutting edge technology. Ten years after the Prius's debut, Toyota is still committed to developing new environmentally friendly vehicles that "redefine what it means to be environmentally considerate." Not only has Toyota introduced award-winning vehicles, but also award-winning manufacturing plants. Toyota's use of solar energy, waste-water recycling, and improved manufacturing robotics has decreased the harmful consequences of manufacturing on the environment. At the same time, these "green" initiatives have cut plant energy costs and improved productivity.

To understand whether these and other investments were worth it, Toyota's managers needed to understand their costs across all business functions. They also needed to consider which costs should be *increased*, and which costs should be *reduced*. For example, by spending *more* money on green technologies, product quality, and safety improvements, Toyota has increased its market share and decreased warranty and liability costs. On the other hand, Toyota's cost reduction efforts in production saved the company over $1.19 billion dollars in 2008. For example, to offset rising raw material costs, Toyota's engineers have figured out ways to decrease the quantity of materials needed without sacrificing performance and quality. They also work with suppliers to help them reduce their own costs, so that the cost savings can be passed on. In this chapter, we talk about many costs: costs that both managers and management accountants must understand to successfully run a business.

Dreammediapeel | Dreamstime.com

Sources: Toyota.com, 2008 Annual Report.

So far, we have seen how managerial accounting provides information that managers use to run their businesses more efficiently. Managers must understand basic managerial accounting terms and concepts before they can use the information to make good decisions. This terminology provides the "common ground" through which managers and accountants communicate. Without a common understanding of these concepts, managers may ask for (and accountants may provide) the wrong information for making decisions. As you will see, different types of costs are useful for different purposes. Both managers and accountants must have a clear understanding of the situation and the types of costs that are relevant to the decision at hand.

What are the Most Common Business Sectors and Their Activities?

Before we talk about specific types of costs, let's consider the three most common types of companies and the business activities in which they incur costs.

Service, Merchandising, and Manufacturing Companies

1 Distinguish among service, merchandising, and manufacturing companies

Recall from Chapter 1 that many companies are beginning to adhere to the notion of a **triple bottom line**, in which the company's performance is evaluated not only in terms of profitability, but also in terms of its impact on people and the planet. Even so, for a business to flourish and grow in the long-run, it will need to generate economic profits that are sufficiently large enough to attract and retain investors, as well as fuel future expansion of operations. Companies typically generate profit through one of three basic business models: they provide a service, they sell merchandise, or they manufacture products.

Service Companies

Service companies are in business to sell intangible services—such as health care, insurance, banking, and consulting—rather than tangible products. Recall from the last chapter that service firms now make up the largest sector of the U.S. economy. Because these types of companies sell services, they generally don't have inventory. Some service providers carry a minimal amount of supplies inventory; however, this inventory is generally used for internal operations—not sold for profit. Service companies incur costs to provide services, develop new services, advertise, and provide customer service. For many service providers, salaries and benefits make up over 70% of their costs.

Merchandising Companies

Merchandising companies such as Walmart and JCPenney resell tangible products they buy from suppliers. For example, Walmart buys clothing, toys, and electronics and resells them to customers at higher prices than what it pays its own suppliers for these goods. Merchandising companies include retailers (such as Walmart) and wholesalers. **Retailers** sell to consumers like you and me. **Wholesalers**, often referred to as "middlemen," buy products in bulk from manufacturers, mark up the prices, and then sell those products to retailers.

Because merchandising companies sell tangible products, they have inventory. The cost of inventory includes the cost merchandisers pay for the goods *plus* all costs necessary to get the merchandise in place and ready to sell, such as freight-in costs and any import duties or tariffs. A merchandiser's balance sheet reports just one inventory account called "Inventory" or "Merchandise Inventory." Besides incurring inventory-related costs, merchandisers also incur costs to operate their retail stores and websites, advertise, research new products and new store locations, and to provide customer service.

Manufacturing Companies

Manufacturing companies use labor, plant, and equipment to convert raw materials into new finished products. For example, Toyota's production workers use the company's factories (production plants and equipment) to transform raw materials, such as steel, into high-performance automobiles. Manufacturers sell their products to retailers or wholesalers at a price that is high enough to cover their costs and generate a profit.

Because of their broader range of activities, manufacturers have three types of inventory (pictured in Exhibit 2-1):

1. **Raw materials inventory**: *All raw materials used in manufacturing.* Toyota's raw materials include steel, glass, tires, upholstery fabric, engines, and other automobile components. It also includes other physical materials used in the plant, such as machine lubricants and janitorial supplies.
2. **Work in process inventory**: *Goods that are partway through the manufacturing process but not yet complete.* At Toyota, the work in process inventory consists of partially completed vehicles.

3. <u>Finished goods inventory</u>: *Completed goods that have not yet been sold.* Toyota is in business to sell completed cars, not work in process. Once the vehicles are completed, they are no longer considered work in process, but rather they become part of finished goods inventory. Manufacturers sell units from finished goods inventory to merchandisers or directly to consumers.

EXHIBIT 2-1 Manufacturers' Three Types of Inventory

Exhibit 2-2 summarizes the differences among service, merchandising, and manufacturing companies.

EXHIBIT 2-2 Service, Merchandising, and Manufacturing Companies

	Service Companies	Merchandising Companies	Manufacturing Companies
Examples	Advertising agencies Banks Law firms Insurance companies	Amazon.com Kroger Walmart Wholesalers	Procter & Gamble General Mills Dell Computer Toyota
Primary Output	Intangible services	Tangible products purchased from suppliers	New tangible products made as workers and equipment convert raw materials into new finished products
Type(s) of Inventory	None	Inventory (or Merchandise Inventory)	Raw materials inventory Work in process inventory Finished goods inventory

What type of company is Outback Steakhouse, Inc.?

Answer: Some companies don't fit nicely into one of the three categories discussed previously. Restaurants are usually considered to be in the service sector. However, Outback has some elements of a service company (it serves hungry patrons), some elements of a manufacturing company (its chefs convert raw ingredients into finished meals), and some elements of a merchandising company (it sells ready-to-serve bottles of wine and beer).

As the "Stop & Think" shows, not all companies are strictly service, merchandising, or manufacturing firms. Recall from Chapter 1 that the U.S. economy is shifting more toward service. Many traditional manufacturers, such as General Electric (GE), have developed

> **Why is this important?**
> "All employees should have an **understanding** of their company's basic business model. The **Enron scandal** was finally brought to light as a **result** of someone seriously asking, "How does this company actually **make money**?" If the business model does not make **logical sense**, something fishy may be going on."

profitable service segments that provide much of their company's profits. Even merchandising firms are getting into the "service game" by selling extended warranty contracts on merchandise sold. Retailers offer extended warranties on products ranging from furniture and major appliances to sporting equipment and consumer electronics. While the merchandiser recognizes a liability for these warranties, the price charged to customers for the warranties greatly exceeds the company's cost of fulfilling its warranty obligations.

Which Business Activities Make up the Value Chain?

Many people describe Toyota, General Mills, and Dell as manufacturing companies. But it would be more accurate to say that these are companies that *do* manufacturing. Why? Because companies that do manufacturing also do many other things. Toyota also conducts research to determine what type of new technology to integrate into next year's models. Toyota designs the new models based on its research and then produces, markets, distributes, and services the cars. These activities form Toyota's <u>value chain</u>—the activities that add value to the company's products and services. The value chain is pictured in Exhibit 2-3.

EXHIBIT 2-3 The Value Chain

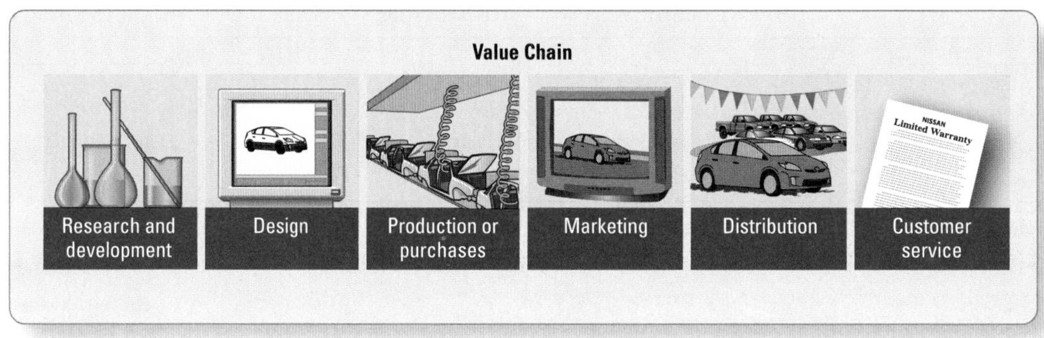

2 Describe the value chain and its elements

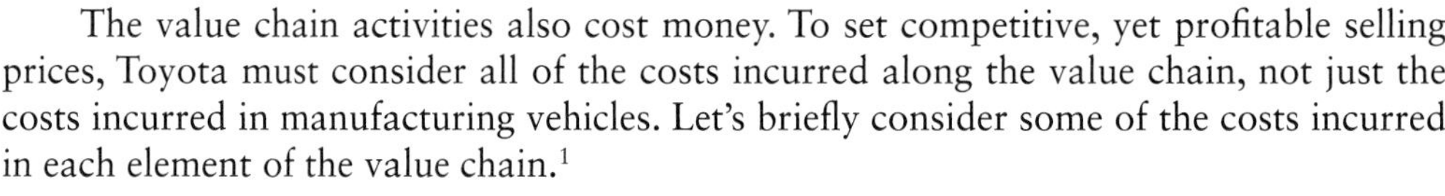

The value chain activities also cost money. To set competitive, yet profitable selling prices, Toyota must consider all of the costs incurred along the value chain, not just the costs incurred in manufacturing vehicles. Let's briefly consider some of the costs incurred in each element of the value chain.[1]

<u>Research and Development (R&D):</u> *Researching and developing new or improved products or services and the processes for producing them.* Toyota continually engages in researching and developing new technologies to incorporate in its vehicles (such as fuel cells, pre-crash safety systems, and "smart keys,") and in its manufacturing plants (such as environmentally friendly and efficient manufacturing robotics). In 2010, Toyota spent 725 million yen (approximately $8 billion dollars) on R&D.

<u>Design:</u> *Detailed engineering of products and services and the processes for producing them.* Toyota's goal is to design vehicles that create total customer satisfaction, including satisfaction with vehicle style, features, safety, and quality. As a result, Toyota updates the design of older models (such as the Corolla) and designs new prototypes (such as the new ultra-energy efficient "iQ" model) on a regular basis. Part of the design process also includes determining how to mass-produce the vehicles. Because Toyota produces nearly 7 million vehicles per year, engineers must design production plants that are efficient, yet flexible enough to allow for new features and models.

[1]Toyota Motor Corp. 2010 annual report and new.yahoo.com/s/ap/as_japan_toyota/print

Production or Purchases: *Resources used to produce a product or service or to purchase finished merchandise intended for resale.* For Toyota, the production activity includes all costs incurred to *make* the vehicles. These costs include raw materials (such as steel), plant labor (such as machine operators' wages and benefits), and manufacturing overhead (such as factory utilities and depreciation on the factory). As you can imagine, factories are very expensive to build and operate. Toyota earmarked over $1.3 billion dollars just to build and equip a new manufacturing plant in Mississippi.

For a merchandiser such as Best Buy, this value chain activity includes the cost of purchasing the inventory that the company plans to sell to customers. It also includes all costs associated with getting the inventory to the store, including freight-in costs and any import duties and tariffs that might be incurred if the merchandise was purchased from overseas.

Marketing: *Promotion and advertising of products or services.* The goal of marketing is to create consumer demand for products and services. Toyota uses print advertisements in magazines and newspapers, billboards, television commercials, and the internet to market its vehicles. Some companies use sponsorship of star athletes and sporting events to market their products. Each method of advertising costs money, but adds value by reaching different target customers.

Distribution: *Delivery of products or services to customers.* Toyota sells most of its vehicles through traditional dealerships. However, more customers are ordering "build-your-own" vehicles through Toyota's website. Toyota's distribution costs include the costs of shipping the vehicles to retailers and the costs of administering Web-based sales portals. Other industries use different distribution mechanisms. For example, Tupperware primarily sells its products through home-based parties while Amazon.com sells only through the internet. Until recently, Lands' End sold only through catalogs and the Web.

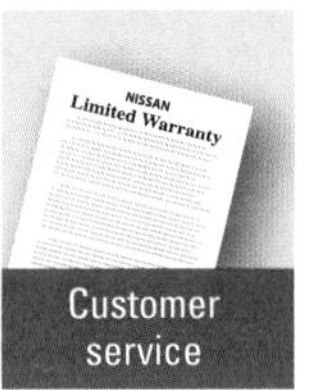

Customer Service: *Support provided for customers after the sale.* Toyota incurs substantial customer service costs, especially in connection with warranties on new car sales. Toyota generally warranties its vehicles for the first three years and/or 36,000 miles, whichever comes first. Historically, Toyota has had one of the best reputations in the auto industry for excellent quality. However, 2010 proved to be a costly and difficult year for the company, as recalls were made on over 14 million vehicles. In addition to the cost of repairing the vehicles, the company incurred millions of dollars in costs related to government fines, lawsuits, and public relations campaigns. The company has pledged its commitment to building safe and reliable vehicles.

Coordinating Activities Across the Value Chain

Many of the value chain activities occur in the order discussed here. However, managers cannot simply work on R&D and not think about customer service until after selling the car. Rather, cross-functional teams work on R&D, design, production, marketing, distribution, and customer service simultaneously. As the teams develop new model features, they also plan how to produce, market, and distribute the redesigned vehicles. They also consider how the new design will affect warranty costs. Recall from the last chapter that management accountants typically participate in these cross-functional teams. Even at the highest level of global operations, Toyota uses cross-functional teams to implement its business goals and strategy.

The value chain pictured in Exhibit 2-3 also reminds managers to control costs over the value chain as a whole. For example, Toyota spends more in R&D and product design to increase the quality of its vehicles, which, in turn, reduces customer service costs. Even though R&D and design costs are higher, the total cost of the vehicle—as measured throughout the entire value chain—is lower as a result of this trade off. Enhancing its reputation for high-quality products has also enabled Toyota to increase its market share and charge a slightly higher selling price than some of its competitors.

> **Why is this important?**
>
> "All activities in the **value chain** are important, yet each costs **money** to perform. Managers must understand how **decisions** made in one area of the value chain will **affect the costs** incurred in other areas of the value chain."

Sustainability and the Value Chain

Progressive companies will incorporate sustainability throughout every function of the value chain. However, experts estimate that 90% of sustainability occurs at the design stage. At the design stage, companies determine how the product will be used by customers, how easily the product can be repaired or eventually recycled, and the types of raw materials and manufacturing processes necessary to produce the product. Thus, good design is essential to the creation of environmentally-friendly, safe products that enhance people's lives. For example, companies can integrate sustainability throughout the value chain by:

See Exercise E2-18A and E2-35B

- ***Researching & Developing environmentally safe packaging.*** Frito-Lay has developed a compostable bag for its original Sun Chips product. The bag is made out of vegetables, rather than plastic.
- ***Designing the product using lifecycle assessment and biomimicry practices.*** **Life cycle assessment** means the company analyzes the environmental impact of a product, from cradle to grave, in an attempt to minimize negative environmental consequences throughout the entire life span of the product. **Biomimicry** means that a company tries to mimic, or copy, the natural biological process in which dead organisms (plants and animals) become the input for another organism or process. Ricoh's copiers were designed so that at the end of a copier's useful life, Ricoh will collect and dismantle the product for usable parts, shred the metal casing, and use the parts and shredded material to build new copiers. The entire copier was designed so that nothing is wasted, or thrown out, except the dust from the shredding process. Pepsi recently announced the development of a plastic bottle that is made entirely out of non-edible plant materials such as corn husks, pine bark, and switch grass. These byproducts are the result of manufacturing its other food products (Frito-Lay, Quaker Oats, and Tropicana).
- ***Adopting sustainable purchasing practices.*** Companies can purchase raw materials from suppliers that are geographically proximate or from suppliers that embrace sustainability. For example, Walmart has recently mandated that all of its suppliers conform to certain sustainability requirements. As the leading retailer in the world, Walmart's own purchasing policies are forcing other companies to adopt sustainable practices.
- ***Marketing with integrity.*** Consumers are driving much of the sustainability movement by demanding that companies produce environmentally-friendly products and limit, or eliminate operational practices that have a negative impact on the environment. Thus, many companies are successfully spotlighting their sustainability initiatives in order to increase market share and attract potential investors and employees. However, **greenwashing**, the unfortunate practice of *overstating* a company's commitment to sustainability, can ultimately backfire as investors and consumers learn the truth about company operations. Hence, honesty and integrity in marketing is imperative.
- ***Distributing using fossil-fuel alternatives and carbon offsets.*** While the biofuel industry is still in its infancy, the production and use of biofuels, especially those generated from non-food waste, is expected to grow exponentially in the near future. Biofuels Digest, which tracks corporate-announced biofuel projects, estimates a global production capacity of 718 *million* gallons of advanced biofuel in 2011 growing to a capacity of 4 *billion* gallons by 2015.[2] Companies whose business is heavily reliant upon fossil fuels, such as oil companies (Valero), airlines (Continental), and distribution companies (UPS) are especially interested in the development of biofuel alternatives. In addition, Continental Airlines offers a carbon-offset program that allows companies (and consumers) to calculate the carbon emissions resulting from their business travel and air-freighting activities. The customer has an option of purchasing carbon offsets (reforestation projects, renewable energy projects, etc.,) to mitigate the emissions resulting from shipping and travel.
- ***Providing customer service past the warranty date.*** Currently, the average life of many home appliances such as dishwashers and refrigerators is less than 10 years.

[2]http://biofuelsdigest.com/bdigest/2011/01/14/10-advanced-biofuelsprojects-now-planned-in-advanced-biofuels/

However, the original manufacturer could provide valuable customer service, prevent appliances from ending up in landfills, while at the same time creating a new revenue stream by offering reasonably-priced repair services for products that have exceeded the warranty date. For those products that are not repairable, the company could institute a policy such as Ricoh's, in which the company takes back the old product and recycles it into new products.

How do Companies Define Cost?

How do companies such as Bank of America and Toyota determine how much it costs to serve a customer or produce a Prius? Before we can answer this question, let's first consider some of the specialized language that accountants use when referring to costs.

3 Distinguish between direct and indirect costs

Cost Objects, Direct Costs, and Indirect Costs

A cost object is anything for which managers want a separate measurement of cost. Toyota's cost objects may include the following:

- Individual units (a specific, custom-ordered Prius)
- Different models (the Prius, Rav4, and Corolla)
- Alternative marketing strategies (sales through dealers versus built-to-order Web sales)
- Geographic segments of the business (United States, Europe, Japan)
- Departments (Human Resources, R&D, Legal)
- A "green" initiative (developing fuel cells)

Costs are classified as either direct or indirect with respect to the cost object. A direct cost is a cost that can be traced to the cost object. For example, say the cost object is one Prius. Toyota can trace the cost of tires to a specific Prius; therefore, the tires are a direct cost of the vehicle. An indirect cost is a cost that relates to the cost object but cannot be traced to it. For example, Toyota incurs substantial cost to run a manufacturing plant, including utilities, property taxes, and depreciation. Toyota cannot build a Prius without incurring these costs, so the costs are related to the Prius. However, it's impossible to trace a specific amount of these costs to one Prius. Therefore, these costs are considered indirect costs of a single Prius.

As shown in Exhibit 2-4, the same costs can be indirect with respect to one cost object yet direct with respect to another cost object. For example, plant depreciation, property taxes, and utilities are indirect costs of a single Prius. However, if management wants to

EXHIBIT 2-4 The Same Cost Can Be Direct or Indirect, Depending on the Cost Object

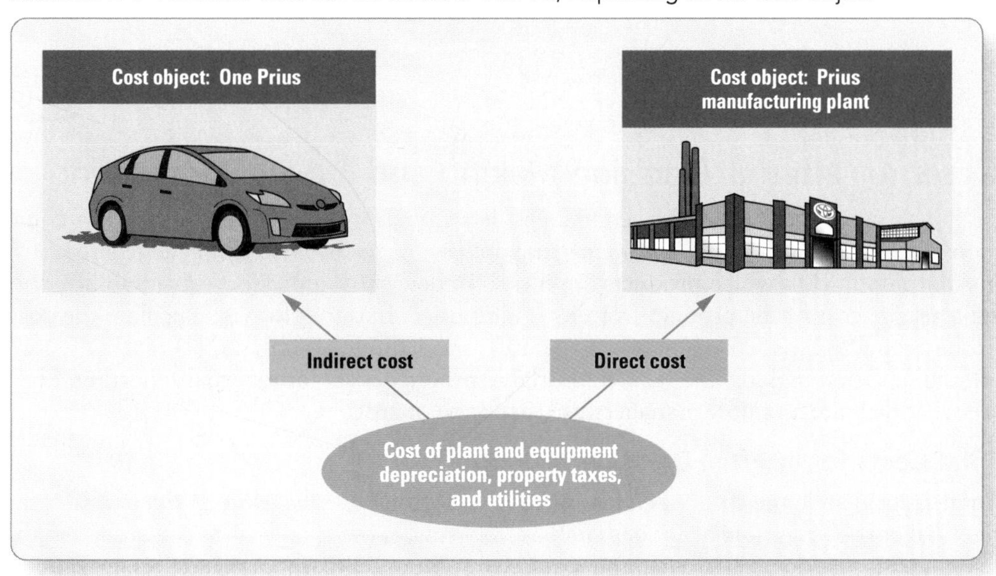

Why is this important?

"As a manager **making decisions**, you'll need different types of **cost information** for different types of decisions. To get the **information** you really want, you'll have to be able to **communicate** with the accountants using precise **definitions** of cost."

know how much it costs to operate the Prius manufacturing plant, the plant becomes the cost object; so the same depreciation, tax, and utility costs are direct costs of the manufacturing facility. Whether a cost is direct or indirect depends on the specified cost object. In this chapter, we'll be talking about a unit of product (such as one Prius) as the cost object.

If a company wants to know the *total* cost attributable to a cost object, it must assign all direct *and* indirect costs to the cost object. Assigning a cost simply means that you are "attaching" a cost to the cost object. Why? Because the cost object caused the company to incur that cost. In determining the cost of a Prius, Toyota assigns both the cost of the tires *and* the cost of running the manufacturing plant to the Priuses built at the plant.

Toyota assigns direct costs to each Prius by tracing those costs to specific vehicles. This results in a very precise cost figure, giving managers great confidence in the cost's accuracy. However, because Toyota cannot trace indirect costs to specific vehicles, it must allocate these costs between all of the vehicles produced at the plant. The allocation process results in a less precise cost figure being assigned to the cost object (one vehicle). We will discuss the allocation process in more detail in the following two chapters; but for now, think of allocation as dividing up the total indirect costs over all of the units produced, just as you might divide a pizza among friends. Exhibit 2-5 illustrates these concepts.

If your instructor is using MyAccountingLab, go to the Multimedia Library for a quick video on this topic.

EXHIBIT 2-5 Assigning Direct and Indirect Costs to Cost Objects

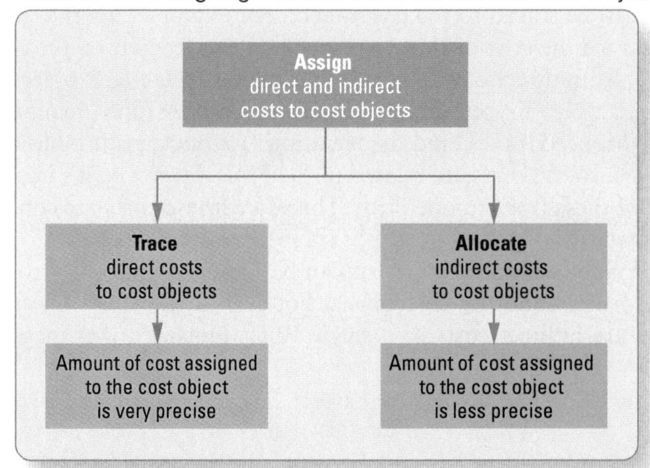

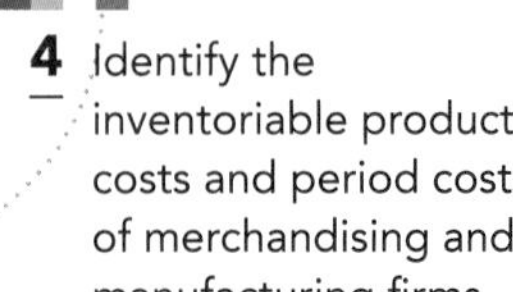

4 Identify the inventoriable product costs and period costs of merchandising and manufacturing firms

Costs for Internal Decision Making and External Reporting

Let's look more carefully at how companies determine the costs of one of the most common cost objects: products. As a manager, you'll want to focus on the products that are most profitable. But which products are these? To determine a product's profitability, you subtract the cost of the product from its selling price. But how do you calculate the cost of the product? Most companies use two different definitions of costs: (1) total costs for internal decision making and (2) inventoriable product costs for external reporting. Let's see what they are and how managers use each type of cost.

Total Costs for Internal Decision Making

Total costs include the costs of *all resources used throughout the value chain*. For Toyota, the total cost of a particular model, such as the Prius, is the total cost to research, design, manufacture, market, distribute, and service that model. Before launching a new model, managers predict the total costs of the model to set a selling price that will cover *all costs* plus return a profit. Toyota also compares each model's sale revenue to its total cost to determine which models are most profitable. Perhaps Rav4s are more profitable than Corollas. Marketing can then focus on advertising and promoting the most profitable models. We'll talk more about total costs in Chapter 8, where we discuss many common business decisions. For the next few chapters, we'll concentrate primarily on inventoriable product costs.

Inventoriable Product Costs for External Reporting

GAAP does not allow companies to use total costs to report inventory balances or Cost of Goods Sold in the financial statements. For external reporting, GAAP allows only a *portion* of the total cost to be treated as an inventoriable product cost. GAAP specifies which costs are inventoriable product costs and which costs are not. Inventoriable product costs include *only* the costs incurred during the "production or purchases" stage of the value chain. Inventoriable product costs are treated as an asset (inventory) until the product is sold. Hence, the name "inventoriable" product cost. When the product is sold, these costs are removed from inventory and expensed as cost of goods sold. Since inventoriable product costs include only costs incurred during the production or purchases stage of the value chain, all cost incurred in the *other* stages of the value chain must be expensed in the period in which they are incurred. Therefore, we refer to R&D, design, marketing, distribution, and customer service costs as period costs.

Period costs are often called "operating expenses" or "selling, general, and administrative expenses" (SG&A) on the company's income statement. Period costs are *always* expensed in the period in which they are incurred and *never* become part of an inventory account.

Exhibit 2-6 shows that a company's total cost has two components: inventoriable product costs (those costs treated as part of inventory until the product is sold) and period costs (those costs expensed in the current period regardless of when inventory is sold). GAAP requires this distinction for external financial reporting. Study the exhibit carefully to make sure you understand how the two cost components affect the income statement and balance sheet.

EXHIBIT 2-6 Total Costs, Inventoriable Product Costs, and Period Costs

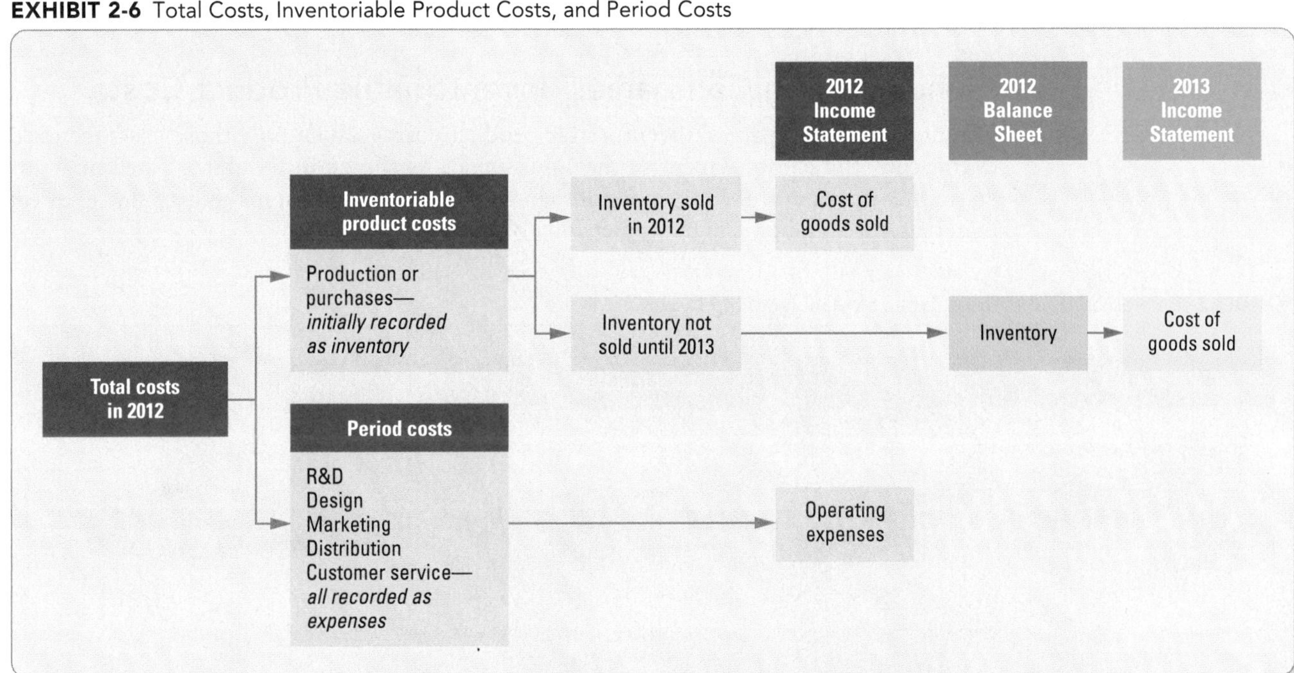

Now that you understand the difference between inventoriable product costs and period costs, let's take a closer look at the specific costs that are inventoriable in merchandising and manufacturing companies.

Merchandising Companies' Inventoriable Product Costs

Merchandising companies' inventoriable product costs include *only* the cost of purchasing the inventory from suppliers plus any costs incurred to get the merchandise to the merchandiser's place of business and ready for sale. Typically, these additional costs include freight-in costs and import duties or tariffs, if the products were purchased from overseas. Why does the cost of the inventory include freight-in charges? Think of the last time you purchased a shirt from a catalog such as L.L.Bean. The catalog may have shown the shirt's price as $30, but by the time you paid the shipping and handling charges, the shirt really cost you around $35. Likewise, merchandising companies pay freight-in charges to get the goods to their place of business (plus import duties if the goods were manufactured overseas). These charges become part of the cost of their inventory.

For instance, Home Depot's inventoriable product costs include what the company paid for its store merchandise plus freight-in and import duties. Home Depot records these costs in an asset account—Inventory—until it *sells* the merchandise. Once the merchandise sells, it belongs to the customer, not Home Depot. Therefore, Home Depot takes the cost out of its inventory account and records it as an expense—the *cost of goods sold*. Home Depot expenses costs incurred in other elements of the value chain as period costs. For example, Home Depot's period costs include store operating expenses (such as salaries, utilities, and depreciation) and advertising expenses.

Some companies, such as Pier 1 Imports, refer to their cost of goods sold as "cost of sales." However, we use the more specific term *cost of goods sold* throughout the text because it more aptly describes the actual cost being expensed in the account—the inventoriable product cost of the goods themselves.

STOP & THINK

What are the inventoriable product costs for a service firm such as H&R Block?

Answer: Service firms such as H&R Block have no inventory of products for sale. Services cannot be produced today and stored up to sell later. Because service firms have no inventory, they have no inventoriable product costs. Instead, they have only period costs that are expensed as incurred.

Manufacturing Companies' Inventoriable Product Costs

Manufacturing companies' inventoriable product costs include *only* those costs incurred during the production element of the value chain. As shown in Exhibit 2-7, manufacturers such as Toyota incur three types of manufacturing costs when making a vehicle: direct materials, direct labor, and manufacturing overhead.

EXHIBIT 2-7 Summary of the Three Types of Manufacturing Costs

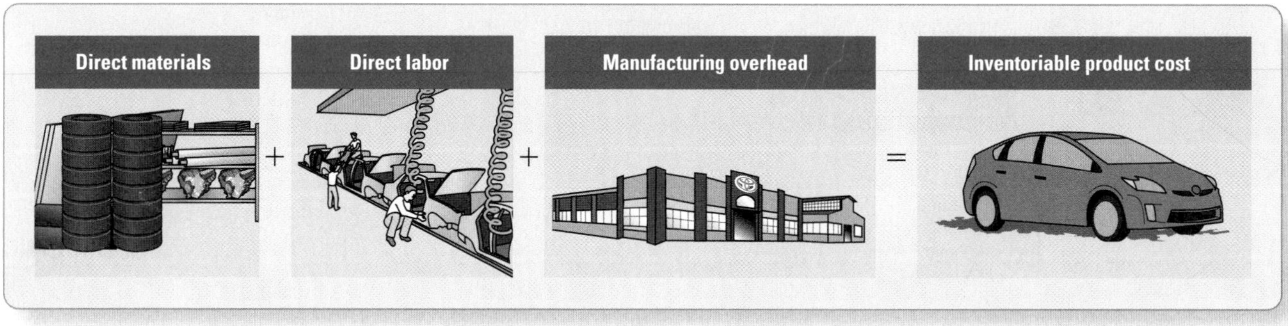

Direct Materials (DM)

Manufacturers convert raw materials into finished products. **Direct materials** are the *primary* raw materials that become a physical part of the finished product. The Prius's direct materials include steel, tires, engines, upholstery, carpet, dashboard instruments, and so forth. Toyota can trace the cost of these materials (including freight-in and import duties) to specific units or batches of vehicles; thus, they are considered direct costs of the vehicles.

Direct Labor (DL)

Although many manufacturing facilities are highly automated, most still require some direct labor to convert raw materials into a finished product. **Direct labor** is the cost of compensating employees who physically convert raw materials into the company's products. At Toyota, direct labor includes the wages and benefits of machine operators and technicians who assemble the parts and wire the electronics to build the completed vehicles. These costs are *direct* with respect to the cost object (the vehicle) because Toyota can *trace* the time each of these employees spends working on specific units or batches of vehicles.

Manufacturing Overhead (MOH)

The third production cost is manufacturing overhead. **Manufacturing overhead** *includes all manufacturing costs other than direct materials and direct labor.* In other words, manufacturing overhead includes *all indirect manufacturing costs*. Manufacturing overhead is also referred to as factory overhead because all of these costs relate to the factory. As shown in Exhibit 2-8, manufacturing overhead has three components: indirect materials, indirect labor, and other indirect manufacturing costs.

EXHIBIT 2-8 Components of Manufacturing Overhead

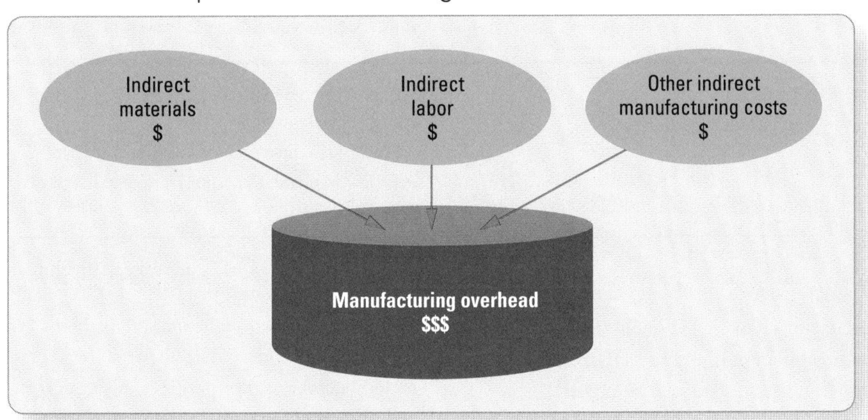

- **Indirect materials** include materials used in the plant that are not easily traced to individual units. For example, indirect materials often include janitorial supplies, oil and lubricants for the machines, and any physical components of the finished product that are very inexpensive. For example, Toyota might treat the invoice sticker placed on each vehicle's window as an indirect material rather than a direct material. Even though the cost of the sticker *could* be traced to the vehicle, it wouldn't make much sense to do so. Why? Because the cost of tracing the sticker to the vehicle outweighs the benefit management receives from the increased accuracy of the information. Therefore, Toyota treats the cost of the stickers as an indirect material, which becomes part of manufacturing overhead.
- **Indirect labor** includes the cost of all employees *in the plant* other than those employees directly converting the raw materials into the finished product. For example, at Toyota, indirect labor includes the salaries, wages, and benefits of plant forklift operators, plant security officers, plant janitors, and plant supervisors.
- **Other indirect manufacturing costs** include such plant-related costs as insurance and depreciation on the plant and plant equipment, plant property taxes, plant repairs and maintenance, and plant utilities. Indirect manufacturing costs have grown in recent years as manufacturers automate their plants with the latest technology.

If your instructor is using MyAccountingLab, go to the Multimedia Library for a quick video on this topic.

In summary, *manufacturing overhead includes all manufacturing costs other than direct materials and direct labor.*

Review: Inventoriable Product Costs or Period Costs?

Exhibit 2-9 summarizes the differences between inventoriable product costs and period costs for service, merchandising, and manufacturing companies. Study this exhibit carefully. When are such costs as depreciation, insurance, utilities, and property taxes inventoriable product costs? *Only* when those costs are related to the manufacturing plant. When those costs are related to nonmanufacturing activities such as R&D or marketing, they are treated as period costs. Service companies and merchandisers do no manufacturing, so they always treat depreciation, insurance, utilities, and property taxes as period costs. When you studied financial accounting, you studied nonmanufacturing firms. Therefore, salaries, depreciation, insurance, and taxes were always expensed.

EXHIBIT 2-9 Inventoriable Product Costs and Period Costs for Service, Merchandising, and Manufacturing Companies

	Inventoriable Product Costs	Period Costs
Accounting Treatment	• Initially recorded as inventory • Expensed as *Cost of Goods Sold* only when inventory is sold	• Always recorded as an expense • Never considered part of inventory
Type of Company:		
Service company	• None	• All costs along the value chain • For example, salaries, depreciation expense, utilities, insurance, property taxes, and advertising
Merchandising company	• Purchases of merchandise • Freight-in; customs and duties	• All costs along the value chain *except* for the purchases element • For example, salaries, depreciation expense, utilities, insurance, property taxes, advertising, and freight-out
Manufacturing company	• Direct materials • Direct labor • Manufacturing overhead (including indirect materials, indirect labor, and other indirect manufacturing costs)	• All costs along the value chain *except* for the production element • For example, R&D; freight-out; all expenses for executive headquarters (separate from plant), including depreciation, utilities, insurance, and property taxes; advertising; and CEO's salary

Prime and Conversion Costs

Managers and accountants sometimes talk about certain combinations of manufacturing costs. As shown in Exhibit 2-10, **prime costs** refer to the combination of direct materials and direct labor. Prime costs used to be the primary costs of production. However, as

EXHIBIT 2-10 Prime and Conversion Costs

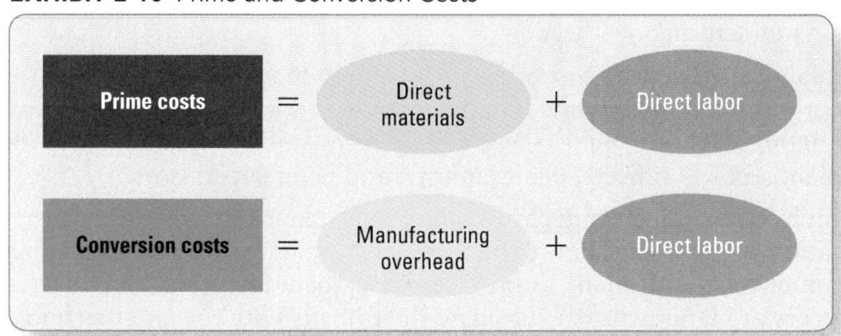

companies have automated production with expensive machinery, manufacturing overhead has become a greater cost of production. **Conversion costs** refer to the combination of direct labor and manufacturing overhead. These are the costs of *converting* direct materials into finished goods.

Additional Labor Compensation Costs

The cost of labor, in all areas of the value chain, includes more than the salaries and wages paid to employees. The cost also includes company-paid fringe benefits such as health insurance, retirement plan contributions, payroll taxes, and paid vacations. These costs are very expensive. Health insurance premiums, which have seen double-digit increases for many years, often amount to $500–$1,500 per month for *each* employee electing family coverage. Many companies also contribute an amount equal to 3% to 6% of their employees' salaries to company-sponsored retirement 401(k) plans. Employers must pay Federal Insurance Contributions Act (FICA) payroll taxes to the federal government for Social Security and Medicare, amounting to 7.65% of each employee's gross pay. In addition, most companies offer paid vacation and other benefits. Together, these fringe benefits usually cost the company an *additional* 35% beyond gross salaries and wages. Thus, an assembly-line worker who makes a $40,000 salary costs Toyota approximately another $14,000 (= $40,000 × 35%) in fringe benefits. Believe it or not, for automobiles manufactured in the United States, the cost of health care assigned to the vehicle is greater than the cost of the steel in the vehicle! Throughout the remainder of this book, any references to wages or salaries also include the cost of fringe benefits.

Decision Guidelines

Building Blocks of Managerial Accounting

Dell engages in *manufacturing* when it assembles its computers, *merchandising* when it sells them on its website, and support *services* such as start-up and implementation services. Dell had to make the following types of decisions as it developed its accounting systems.

Decision	Guidelines
How do you distinguish among service, merchandising, and manufacturing companies? How do their balance sheets differ?	*Service companies:* • Provide customers with intangible services • Have no inventories on the balance sheet *Merchandising companies:* • Resell tangible products purchased ready-made from suppliers • Have only one category of inventory *Manufacturing companies:* • Use labor, plant, and equipment to transform raw materials into new finished products • Have three categories of inventory: 1. Raw materials inventory 2. Work in process inventory 3. Finished goods inventory
What business activities add value to companies?	All of the elements of the value chain, including the following: • R&D • Design • Production or Purchases • Marketing • Distribution • Customer Service
What costs should be assigned to cost objects such as products, departments, and geographic segments?	Both direct and indirect costs are assigned to cost objects. Direct costs are traced to cost objects, whereas indirect costs are allocated to cost objects.
Which product costs are useful for internal decision making, and which product costs are used for external reporting?	Managers use *total costs* for internal decision making. However, GAAP requires companies to use only *inventoriable product costs* for external financial reporting.
What costs are treated as inventoriable product costs under GAAP?	• *Service companies:* No inventoriable product costs • *Merchandising companies:* The cost of merchandise purchased for resale plus all of the costs of getting the merchandise to the company's place of business (for example, freight-in and import duties) • *Manufacturing companies:* Direct materials, direct labor, and manufacturing overhead
How are inventoriable product costs treated on the financial statements?	Inventoriable product costs are initially treated as assets (inventory) on the balance sheet. These costs are expensed (as cost of goods sold) on the income statements when the products are sold.

SUMMARY PROBLEM 1

Requirements

1. Classify each of the following business costs into one of the six value chain elements:
   a. Costs associated with warranties and recalls
   b. Cost of shipping finished goods to overseas customers
   c. Costs a pharmaceutical company incurs to develop new drugs
   d. Cost of a 30-second commercial during the SuperBowl™
   e. Cost of making a new product prototype
   f. Cost of assembly labor used in the plant
2. For a manufacturing company, identify the following as either an inventoriable product cost or a period cost. If it is an inventoriable product cost, classify it as direct materials, direct labor, or manufacturing overhead.
   a. Depreciation on plant equipment
   b. Depreciation on salespeoples' automobiles
   c. Insurance on plant building
   d. Marketing manager's salary
   e. Cost of major components of the finished product
   f. Assembly-line workers' wages
   g. Costs of shipping finished products to customers
   h. Forklift operator's salary

SOLUTIONS

Requirement 1

a. Customer service
b. Distribution
c. Research and Development
d. Marketing
e. Design
f. Production

Requirement 2

a. Inventoriable product cost; manufacturing overhead
b. Period cost
c. Inventoriable product cost; manufacturing overhead
d. Period cost
e. Inventoriable product cost; direct materials
f. Inventoriable product cost; direct labor
g. Period cost
h. Inventoriable product cost; manufacturing overhead

How are Inventoriable Product Costs and Period Costs Shown in the Financial Statements?

5 Prepare the financial statements for service, merchandising, and manufacturing companies

The difference between inventoriable product costs and period costs is important because these costs are treated differently in the financial statements. All costs incurred in the production or purchases area of the value chain are inventoriable product costs that remain in inventory accounts until the merchandise is sold—then, these costs become the cost of goods sold. However, costs incurred in all other areas of the value chain (R&D, design, marketing, distribution, and customer service) are period costs, which are expensed on the income statement in the period in which they are incurred. Keep these differences in mind as we review the income statements of service firms (which have no inventory), merchandising companies (which purchase their inventory), and manufacturers (which make their inventory). We'll finish the section by comparing the balance sheets of these three different types of companies.

If your instructor is using MyAccountingLab, go to the Multimedia Library for a quick video on this topic.

Service Companies

Service companies have the simplest income statement. Exhibit 2-11 shows the income statement of eNow!, a group of e-commerce consultants. The firm has no inventory and thus, no inventoriable product costs, so eNow!'s income statement has no Cost of Goods Sold. Rather, all of the company's costs are period costs, so they are expensed in the current period as "operating expenses."

EXHIBIT 2-11 Service Company Income Statement

eNOW!
Income Statement
Year Ended December 31

Revenues		$160,000
Less: Operating expenses		
Salary expense	$106,000	
Office rent expense	18,000	
Depreciation expense—furniture and equipment	3,500	
Marketing expense	2,500	
Total operating expenses		130,000
Operating income		$ 30,000

In this textbook, we always use "operating income" rather than "net income" as the bottom line on the income statement since internal managers are particularly concerned with the income generated through operations. To determine "net income," we would have to deduct interest expense and income taxes from "operating income" and add back interest income. In general, "operating income" is simply the company's income before interest and income taxes.

Merchandising Companies

In contrast with service companies, merchandiser's income statements feature Cost of Goods Sold as the major expense. Exhibit 2-12 illustrates the income statement for Wholesome Foods, a regional grocery store chain. Notice how Cost of Goods Sold is deducted from Sales Revenue to yield the company's gross profit. Next, all operating expenses (*all period costs*) are deducted to arrive at the company's operating income

EXHIBIT 2-12 Merchandiser's Income Statement

Wholesome Foods
Income Statement
For the year ended December 31
(*all figures shown in thousands of dollars*)

Sales revenues		$150,000
Less: Cost of goods sold		106,500
Gross profit		$ 43,500
Less: Operating expenses		
Salaries and wages	$5,000	
Rent and utilities	3,000	
Marketing	1,000	
Total operating expenses		9,000
Operating income		$ 34,500

But how does a merchandising company calculate the Cost of Goods Sold?

- Most likely, the company uses bar coding to implement a perpetual inventory system during the year. If so, all inventory is labeled with a unique bar code that reflects 1) the sales price that will be charged to the customer, and 2) the inventoriable cost of the merchandise to the store. Every time a bar-coded product is "scanned" at the checkout counter, the company's accounting records are automatically updated to reflect 1) the sales revenue earned, 2) the cost of goods sold, and 3) the removal of the product from merchandise inventory.
- However, at the end of the period, merchandisers must also calculate Cost of Goods Sold using the periodic inventory method. Why? Because the company's accounting records only reflect those products that were scanned during checkout. Thus, the records would not reflect any breakage, theft, input errors, or obsolescence that occurred during the year. Exhibit 2-13 shows how to calculate Cost of Goods Sold using the periodic method.

EXHIBIT 2-13 Calculation of Cost of Goods Sold for a Merchandising Firm

Calculation of Cost of Goods Sold

Beginning inventory	$ 9,500
Plus: Purchases, freight-in, and any import duties	110,000
Cost of goods available for sale	119,500
Less: Ending inventory	(13,000)
Cost of goods sold	$106,500

In this calculation, we start with the beginning inventory and add to it all of the companies' *inventoriable product costs* for the period: the cost of the merchandise purchased from manufacturers or distributors, freight-in, and any import duties. The resulting total reflects the cost of all goods that were available for sale during the period. Then we subtract the cost of the products still in ending inventory to arrive at the Cost of Goods Sold.

Manufacturing Companies

Exhibit 2-14 shows the income statement for Proquest, a manufacturer of tennis balls. As you can see, the income statement for a manufacturer is essentially identical to that of a merchandising company. The only *real* difference is that the company is selling product that it has *made*, rather than merchandise that it has *purchased*. As a result, the calculation of Cost of Goods Sold is different than that shown in Exhibit 2-13.

EXHIBIT 2-14 Manufacturer's Income Statement

Proquest Income Statement For the year ended December 31 *(all figures shown in thousands of dollars)*		
Sales revenues		$65,000
Less: Cost of goods sold		40,000
Gross profit		$25,000
Less: Operating expenses		
Selling expenses	$8,000	
General and administrative expenses	2,000	
Total operating expenses		10,000
Operating income		$15,000

Calculating Cost of Goods Manufactured and Cost of Goods Sold

Exhibit 2-15 illustrates how the manufacturer's *inventoriable product costs* (direct material used, direct labor, and manufacturing overhead) flow through the three inventory accounts before they become part of Cost of Goods Sold. In order to calculate Cost of Goods Sold, a manufacturer must first figure out the amount of direct materials used and the Cost of Goods Manufactured.

EXHIBIT 2-15 Flow of Costs Through a Manufacturer's Financial Statements

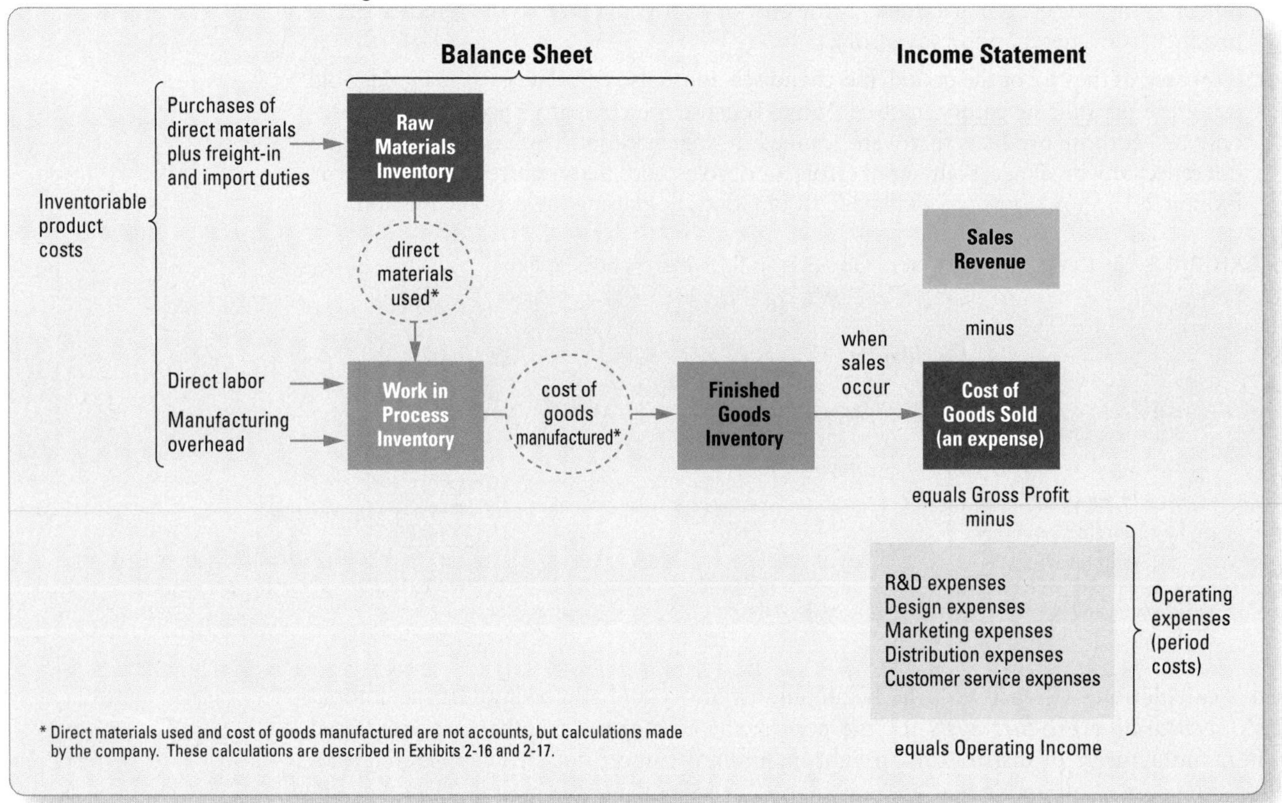

As you see in Exhibit 2-15, the **Cost of Goods Manufactured** represents the cost of those goods that were completed and moved to Finished Goods Inventory during the period.

Using Exhibit 2-15 as a guide, let's walk through the calculation of Cost of Goods Sold. We'll use three steps. Each step focuses on a different inventory account: Raw Materials, Work in Process, and Finished Goods.

Step 1: Calculate the cost of the direct materials used during the year

Step 1 simply analyzes what happened in the *Raw Materials Inventory* account during the year. As shown in Exhibit 2-16, we start with the beginning balance in the Raw Materials Inventory account and add to it all of the direct materials purchased during the year, including any freight-in and import duties. This tells us the amount of materials that were available for use during the year. Finally, by subtracting out the ending balance of Raw Materials, we are able to back into the cost of the direct materials that were used[3].

EXHIBIT 2-16 Calculation of Direct Materials Used

Calculation of Direct Materials Used (Analyze the Raw Materials Inventory account)	
Beginning Raw Materials Inventory	$ 9,000
Plus: Purchases of direct materials*, freight-in, and import duties	27,000
Materials available for use	36,000
Less: Ending Raw Material Inventory	(22,000)
Direct materials used	$ 14,000

*For simplicity, we assume that the Raw Materials Inventory account only contains direct materials.

Step 2: Calculate the cost of goods manufactured

Step 2 simply analyzes what happened in the *Work in Process Inventory* account during the year. As shown in Exhibit 2-17, we start with the beginning balance in Work in Process and then add to it all three manufacturing costs that were incurred during the year (DM used, DL, and MOH). Finally, by subtracting out the goods still being worked on at year-end (ending Work in Process Inventory) we are able to back into the Cost of Goods Manufactured. This figure represents the cost of manufacturing the units that were *completed* and sent to Finished Goods Inventory during the year.

EXHIBIT 2-17 Calculation of Cost of Goods Manufactured

Calculation of Cost of Goods Manufactured (Analyze the Work in Process Inventory account)	
Beginning Work in Process Inventory	$ 2,000
Plus: Manufacturing costs incurred	
Direct materials used	14,000
Direct labor	19,000
Manufacturing overhead	12,000
Total manufacturing costs to account for	$47,000
Less: Ending Work in Process Inventory	(5,000)
Cost of goods manufactured (CGM)	$42,000

[3]In this chapter we'll assume that the Raw Materials account only contains direct materials because the company uses indirect materials as soon as they are purchased. In Chapter 3, we expand the discussion to include manufacturers who store both direct and indirect materials in the Raw Materials Inventory account.

Step 3: Calculate the cost of goods sold

Step 3 simply analyzes what happened in the *Finished Goods Inventory* account during the year. As shown in Exhibit 2-18, we start with the beginning balance of Finished Goods Inventory and add to it the product that was manufactured during the year (CGM) to arrive at the total goods available for sale. Finally, just like a merchandiser, we subtract what was left in Finished Goods Inventory to back into the Cost of Goods Sold.

EXHIBIT 2-18 Calculation of Cost of Goods Sold

Calculation of Cost of Goods Sold (Analyze the Finished Goods Inventory account)	
Beginning Finished Goods Inventory	$ 6,000
Plus: Cost of goods manufactured (CGM)	42,000
Cost of goods available for sale	48,000
Less: Ending Finished Goods Inventory	(8,000)
Cost of goods sold	$40,000

By analyzing, step by step, what occurred in each of the three inventory accounts, we were able to calculate the Cost of Goods Sold shown on the company's Income Statement (Exhibit 2-14). Some companies combine Steps 1 and 2 into one schedule called the Schedule of Cost of Goods Manufactured. Others combine all three steps into a Schedule of Cost of Goods Sold.

You may be wondering where all of the data comes from. The beginning inventory balances were simply last year's ending balances. The purchases of direct materials, and the incurrence of direct labor and manufacturing overhead would have been captured in the company's accounting records when those costs were incurred. Finally, the ending inventory balances come from doing a physical count of inventory at the end of the year. In the coming chapters, we'll show you different systems manufacturers use to keep track of the *cost* associated with those units still in the three inventory accounts..

Comparing Balance Sheets

Now that we've looked at the income statement for each type of company, let's consider their balance sheets. The only difference relates to how inventory is shown in the current asset section:

- Service Companies show no inventory
- Merchandising companies show "inventory" or "merchandise inventory"
- Manufacturing companies show Raw Materials, Work in Process, and Finished Goods Inventory

Sometimes manufacturers just show "Inventories" on the face of the balance sheet, but disclose the breakdown of the inventory accounts (Raw Materials, Work in Process, and Finished Goods) in the footnotes to the financial statements.

What Other Cost Terms are Used by Managers?

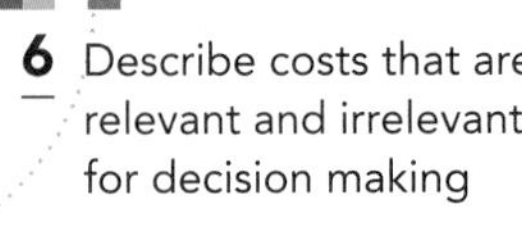

6 Describe costs that are relevant and irrelevant for decision making

So far in this chapter, we have discussed direct versus indirect costs and inventoriable product costs versus period costs. Now let's turn our attention to other cost terms that managers and accountants use when planning and making decisions.

Controllable Versus Uncontrollable Costs

When deciding to make business changes, management needs to distinguish controllable costs from uncontrollable costs. In the long run, most costs are **controllable**, meaning management is able to influence or change them. However, in the short run, companies are often "locked in" to certain costs arising from previous decisions. These are called **uncontrollable costs**. For example, Toyota has little or no control over the property tax and insurance costs of their existing plants. These costs were "locked in" when Toyota built its plants. Toyota could replace existing production facilities with different-sized plants in different areas of the world that might cost less to operate, but that would take time. To see *immediate* benefits, management must change those costs that are controllable at the present. For example, management can control costs of research and development, design, and advertising. Sometimes Toyota's management chose to *increase* rather than decrease these costs in order to successfully gain market share. However, Toyota was also able to *decrease* other controllable costs, such as the price paid for raw materials, by working with its suppliers.

Relevant and Irrelevant Costs

Decision making involves identifying various courses of action and then choosing among them. When managers make decisions, they focus on those costs and revenues that are relevant to the decision. For example, Toyota plans to build a new state-of-the-art Prius production facility in the United States. After considering alternative locations, management decided to build the facility in Blue Springs, Mississippi. The decision was based on relevant information such as the **differential cost** of building and operating the facility in Mississippi versus building and operating the facility in other potential locations. Differential cost refers to the difference in cost between two alternatives.

Say you want to buy a new car. You narrow your decision to two choices: the Nissan Sentra or the Toyota Corolla. As shown in Exhibit 2-19, the Sentra you like costs $14,480, whereas the Corolla costs $15,345. Because sales tax is based on the sales price, the Corolla's sales tax is higher. However, your insurance agent quotes you a higher price to insure the Sentra ($365 per month versus $319 per month for the Corolla). All of these costs are relevant to your decision because they differ between the two cars.

EXHIBIT 2-19 Comparison of Relevant Information

	Sentra	Corolla	Differential Cost
Car's price	$14,480	$15,345	$ (865)
Sales tax (8%) (rounded to the nearest dollar)	1,158	1,228	(70)
Insurance*	21,900	19,140	2,760
Total relevant costs	$37,538	$35,713	$1,825

*Over the five years (60 months) you plan to keep the car.

Other costs are not relevant to your decision. For example, both cars run on regular unleaded gasoline and have the same fuel economy ratings, so the cost of operating the vehicles is about the same. Likewise, you don't expect cost differences in servicing the vehicles because they both carry the same warranty and have received excellent quality ratings in *Consumer Reports*. Because you project operating and maintenance costs to be the *same* for both cars, these costs are irrelevant to your decision. In other words, they won't influence your decision either way. Based on your analysis, the differential cost is $1,825 in favor of the Corolla. Does this mean that you will choose the Corolla? Not necessarily. The Sentra may have some characteristics you like better, such as a particular paint color, more comfortable seating, or more trunk space. When making decisions, management must also consider qualitative factors (such as effect on employee morale) in addition to differential costs.

Another cost that is irrelevant to your decision is the cost you paid for the vehicle you currently own. Say you just bought a Ford F-150 pickup truck two months ago, but you've decided you need a small sedan rather than a pickup truck. The cost of the truck is a **sunk cost**. Sunk costs are costs that have already been incurred. Nothing you do now can change the fact that you already bought the truck. Thus, the cost of the truck is not relevant to your decision of whether to buy the Sentra versus the Corolla. The only thing you can do now is (1) keep your truck or (2) sell it for the best price you can get.

Management often has trouble ignoring sunk costs when making decisions, even though it should. Perhaps it invested in a factory or a computer system that no longer serves the company's needs. Many times, new technology makes management's past investments in older technology look like bad decisions, even though they weren't at the time. Management should ignore sunk costs because its decisions about the future cannot alter decisions made in the past.

Fixed and Variable Costs

7 Classify costs as fixed or variable and calculate total and average costs at different volumes

Managers cannot make good plans and decisions without first knowing how their costs behave. Costs generally behave as fixed costs or variable costs. We will spend all of Chapter 6 discussing cost behavior. For now, let's look just at the basics. **Fixed costs** stay constant in total over a wide range of activity levels. For example, let's say you decide to buy the Corolla, so your insurance cost for the year is $3,828 ($319 per month × 12 months). As shown in Exhibit 2-20, your total insurance cost stays fixed whether you drive your car 0 miles, 1,000 miles, or 10,000 miles during the year.

EXHIBIT 2-20 Fixed Cost Behavior

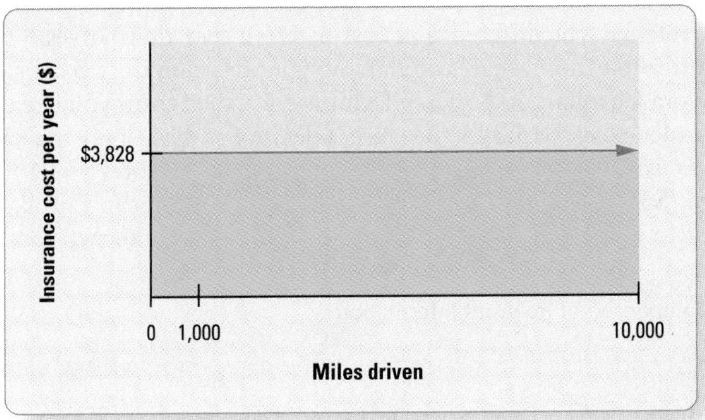

Insurance cost per year ($)
$3,828
0 1,000 10,000
Miles driven

Why is this important?
"Most **business decisions** depend on how costs are **expected** to change at different volumes of **activity**. Managers can't make good decisions without first **understanding** how their costs **behave**."

However, the total cost of gasoline to operate your car varies depending on whether you drive 0 miles, 1,000 miles, or 10,000 miles. The more miles you drive, the higher your total gasoline cost for the year. If you don't drive your car at all, you won't incur any costs for gasoline. Your gasoline costs are **variable costs**, as shown in Exhibit 2-21. Variable costs change in total in direct proportion to changes in volume. To

EXHIBIT 2-21 Variable Cost Behavior

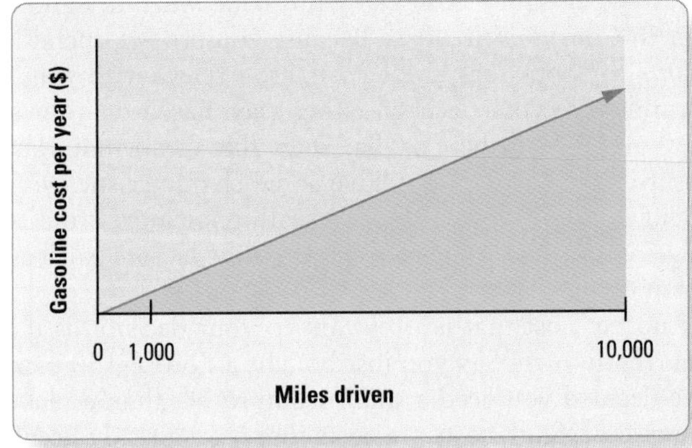

accurately forecast the total cost of operating your Corolla during the year, you need to know which operating costs are fixed and which are variable.

How Manufacturing Costs Behave

Most companies have both fixed and variable costs. Manufacturing companies know that their direct materials are variable costs. The more cars Toyota makes, the higher its total cost for tires, steel, and parts. The behavior of direct labor is harder to characterize. Salaried employees are paid a fixed amount per year. Hourly wage earners are paid only when they work. The more hours they work, the more they are paid. Nonetheless, direct labor is generally treated as a variable cost because the more cars Toyota produces, the more assembly-line workers and machine operators it must employ. Manufacturing overhead includes both variable and fixed costs. For example, the cost of indirect materials is variable, while the cost of property tax, insurance, and straight-line depreciation on the plant and equipment is fixed. The cost of utilities is partially fixed and partially variable. Factories incur a certain level of utility costs just to keep the lights on. However, when more cars are produced, more electricity is used to run the production equipment. Exhibit 2-22 summarizes the behavior of manufacturing costs.

EXHIBIT 2-22 The Behavior of Manufacturing Costs

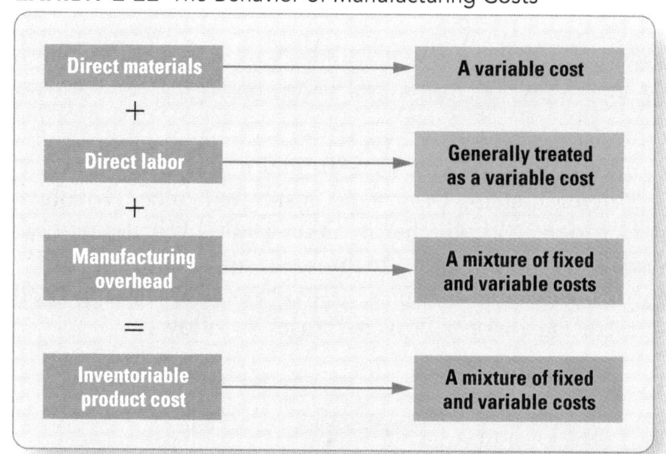

Calculating Total and Average Costs

Why is cost behavior important? Managers need to understand how costs behave to predict total costs and calculate average costs. In our example, we'll look at Toyota's total and average *manufacturing* costs; but the same principles apply to nonmanufacturing costs.

Let's say Toyota wants to estimate the total cost of manufacturing 10,000 Prius cars next year. To do so, Toyota must know 1) its total fixed manufacturing costs, and 2) the variable cost of manufacturing each vehicle. Let's assume total fixed manufacturing costs for the year at the Prius plant are $20,000,000 and the variable cost of manufacturing each Prius is $5,000.[4] How much total manufacturing cost should Toyota budget for the year? Toyota calculates it as follows:

Total fixed cost + (Variable cost per unit × Number of units) = Total cost
$20,000,000 + ($5,000 per vehicle × 10,000 vehicles) = $70,000,000

[4]All references to Toyota in this hypothetical example were created by the author solely for academic purposes and are not intended in any way to represent the actual business practices of, or costs incurred by, Toyota Motor Corporation.

What is the **average cost** of manufacturing each Prius next year? It's the total cost divided by the number of units:

$$\frac{\text{Total cost}}{\text{Number of units}} = \text{Average cost per unit}$$

$$\frac{\$70{,}000{,}000}{10{,}000 \text{ vehicles}} = \$7{,}000 \text{ per vehicle}$$

If Toyota's managers decide they need to produce 12,000 Prius cars instead, can they simply predict total costs as follows?

Average cost per unit	×	Number of units	=	Total cost???
$7,000	×	12,000	=	$84,000,000???

No! They cannot! Why? *Because the average cost per unit is NOT appropriate for predicting total costs at different levels of output.* Toyota's managers should forecast total cost based on cost behavior:

Total fixed cost	+	(Variable cost per unit	×	Number of units)	=	Total cost
$20,000,000	+	($5,000 per vehicle	×	12,000 vehicles)	=	$80,000,000

Why is the *correct* forecasted cost of $80 million less than the *faulty* prediction of $84 million? The difference stems from fixed costs. Remember, Toyota incurs $20 million of fixed manufacturing costs whether it makes 10,000 vehicles or 12,000 vehicles. As Toyota makes more Prius cars, the fixed manufacturing costs are spread over more vehicles, so the average cost per vehicle declines. If Toyota ends up making 12,000 vehicles, the new average manufacturing cost per Prius decreases as follows:

$$\frac{\text{Total cost}}{\text{Number of units}} = \text{Average cost per unit}$$

$$\frac{\$80{,}000{,}000}{12{,}000 \text{ vehicles}} = \$6{,}667 \text{ per vehicle (rounded)}$$

The average cost per unit is lower when Toyota produces more vehicles because it is using the fixed manufacturing costs more efficiently—taking the same $20 million of resources and making more vehicles with it.

The moral of the story: The average cost per unit is valid only at ONE level of output—the level used to compute the average cost per unit. Thus, NEVER use average costs to forecast costs at different output levels; if you do, you will miss the mark!

Finally, a **marginal cost** is the cost of making *one more unit.* Fixed costs will not change when Toyota makes one more Prius unless the plant is operating at 100% capacity and simply cannot make one more unit. (If that's the case, Toyota will need to incur additional costs to expand the plant.) So, the marginal cost of a unit is simply its variable cost.

As you have seen, management accountants and managers use specialized terms for discussing costs. They use different costs for different purposes. Without a solid understanding of these terms, managers are likely to make serious judgment errors.

Decision Guidelines

Building Blocks of Managerial Accounting

As a manufacturer, Dell needs to know how to calculate its inventoriable product costs for external reporting. Dell also needs to know many characteristics about its costs (that is, which are controllable, which are relevant to different decisions, which are fixed, and so forth) in order to plan and make decisions.

Decision	Guidelines
How do you compute cost of goods sold?	*Service companies:* No cost of goods sold because they don't sell tangible goods • *Merchandising companies:* Beginning inventory + Purchases plus freight-in and import duties, if any = Cost of goods available for sale − Ending inventory = Cost of goods sold • *Manufacturing companies:* Beginning finished goods inventory + Cost of goods manufactured = Cost of goods available for sale − Ending finished goods inventory = Cost of goods sold
How do you compute the cost of goods manufactured?	Beginning work in process inventory + Total manufacturing costs incurred during year (direct materials used + direct labor + manufacturing overhead) = Total manufacturing costs to account for − Ending work in process inventory = Cost of goods manufactured
How do managers decide which costs are relevant to their decisions?	Costs are relevant to a decision when they differ between alternatives and affect the future. Thus, *differential costs* are relevant, whereas *sunk costs* and costs that don't differ are not relevant.
How should managers forecast total costs for different production volumes?	Total cost = Total fixed costs + (Variable cost per unit × Number of units) Managers should *not* use a product's *average cost* to forecast total costs because it will change as production volume changes. As production increases, the average cost per unit declines (because fixed costs are spread over more units).

SUMMARY PROBLEM 2

Requirements

1. Show how to compute cost of goods manufactured. Use the following amounts: direct materials used ($24,000), direct labor ($9,000), manufacturing overhead ($17,000), beginning work in process inventory ($5,000), and ending work in process inventory ($4,000).
2. Auto-USA spent $300 million in total to produce 50,000 cars this year. The $300 million breaks down as follows: The company spent $50 million on fixed costs to run its manufacturing plants and $5,000 of variable costs to produce each car. Next year, it plans to produce 60,000 cars using the existing production facilities.
   a. What is the current *average cost* per car this year?
   b. Assuming there is no change in fixed costs or variable costs per unit, what is the *total forecasted cost* to produce 60,000 cars next year?
   c. What is the *forecasted average cost* per car next year?
   d. Why does the average cost per car vary between years?

SOLUTIONS

Requirement 1

Cost of goods manufactured:

Calculation of Cost of Goods Manufactured

Beginning Work in Process Inventory	$ 5,000
Plus: Manufacturing costs incurred	
Direct materials used	24,000
Direct labor	9,000
Manufacturing overhead	17,000
Total manufacturing costs to account for	$55,000
Less: Ending Work in Process Inventory	(4,000)
Cost of goods manufactured (CGM)	$51,000

Requirement 2

a.

Total cost ÷ Number of units = Current average cost
$300 million ÷ 50,000 cars = $6,000 per car

b.

Total fixed costs + Total variable costs = Total projected costs
$50 million + (60,000 cars × $5,000 per car) = $350 million

c.

Total cost ÷ Number of units = Projected average cost
$350 million ÷ 60,000 cars = $5,833 per car

d. The average cost per car decreases because Auto-USA will use the same fixed costs ($50 million) to produce more cars next year. Auto-USA will be using its resources more efficiently, so the average cost per unit will decrease.

END OF CHAPTER

Learning Objectives

- 1 Distinguish among service, merchandising, and manufacturing companies
- 2 Describe the value chain and its elements
- 3 Distinguish between direct and indirect costs
- 4 Identify the inventoriable product costs and period costs of merchandising and manufacturing firms
- 5 Prepare the financial statements for service, merchandising, and manufacturing companies
- 6 Describe costs that are relevant and irrelevant for decision making
- 7 Classify costs as fixed or variable and calculate total and average costs at different volumes

Accounting Vocabulary

Allocate. (p. 54) To assign an *indirect* cost to a cost object.

Assign. (p. 54) To attach a cost to a cost object.

Average cost. (p. 70) The total cost divided by the number of units.

Biomimicry. (p. 52) A means of product design in which a company tries to mimic, or copy, the natural biological process in which dead organisms (plants and animals) become the input for another organism or process.

Controllable Costs. (p. 66) Costs that can be influenced or changed by management.

Conversion Costs. (p. 59) The combination of direct labor and manufacturing overhead costs.

Cost Object. (p. 53) Anything for which managers want a separate measurement of costs.

Cost of Goods Manufactured. (p. 65) The cost of manufacturing the goods that were *finished* during the period.

Customer Service. (p. 51) Support provided for customers after the sale.

Design. (p. 50) Detailed engineering of products and services and the processes for producing them.

Differential Cost. (p. 67) The difference in cost between two alternative courses of action.

Direct Cost. (p. 53) A cost that can be traced to a cost object.

Direct Labor. (p. 57) The cost of compensating employees who physically convert raw materials into the company's products; labor costs that are directly traceable to the finished product.

Direct Materials. (p. 57) Primary raw materials that become a physical part of a finished product and whose costs are traceable to the finished product.

Distribution. (p. 51) Delivery of products or services to customers.

Finished Goods Inventory. (p. 49) Completed goods that have not yet been sold.

Fixed Costs. (p. 68) Costs that stay constant in total despite wide changes in volume.

Greenwashing. (p. 52) The unfortunate practice of *overstating* a company's commitment to sustainability.

Indirect Cost. (p. 53) A cost that relates to the cost object but cannot be traced to it.

Indirect Labor. (p. 57) Labor costs that are difficult to trace to specific products.

Indirect Materials. (p. 57) Materials whose costs are difficult to trace to specific products.

Inventoriable Product Costs. (p. 55) All costs of a product that GAAP requires companies to treat as an asset (inventory) for external financial reporting. These costs are not expensed until the product is sold.

Life cycle assessment. (p. 52) A method of product design in which the company analyzes the environmental impact of a product, from cradle to grave, in an attempt to minimize negative environmental consequences throughout the entire life span of the product.

Manufacturing Company. (p. 48) A company that uses labor, plant, and equipment to convert raw materials into new finished products.

Manufacturing Overhead. (p. 57) All manufacturing costs other than direct materials and direct labor; also called factory overhead and indirect manufacturing cost.

Marginal Cost. (p. 70) The cost of producing one more unit.

Marketing. (p. 51) Promotion and advertising of products or services.

Merchandising Company. (p. 48) A company that resells tangible products previously bought from suppliers.

Other Indirect Manufacturing Costs. (p. 57) All manufacturing overhead costs aside from indirect materials and indirect labor.

Period Costs. (p. 55) Costs that are expensed in the period in which they are incurred; often called Operating Expenses, or Selling, General, and Administrative Expenses.

Perpetual Inventory. (p. 63) An inventory system in which both Cost of Goods Sold and Inventory are updated every time a sale is made.

Periodic Inventory. (p. 63) An inventory system in which Cost of Goods Sold is calulated at the end of the period, rather than every time a sale is made.

Prime Costs. (p. 58) The combination of direct material and direct labor costs.

Production or Purchases. (p. 51) Resources used to produce a product or service, or to purchase finished merchandise intended for resale.

Raw Materials Inventory. (p. 48) All raw materials (direct materials and indirect materials) not yet used in manufacturing.

Research and Development (R&D). (p. 50) Researching and developing new or improved products or services or the processes for producing them.

Retailer. (p. 48) Merchandising company that sells to consumers.

Service Company. (p. 48) A company that sells intangible services rather than tangible products.

Sunk Cost. (p. 67) A cost that has already been incurred.

Total Costs. (p. 54) The cost of all resources used throughout the value chain.

Trace. (p. 54) To assign a *direct* cost to a cost object.

Triple bottom line. (p. 48) Evaluating a company's performance not only by its ability to generate economic profits, but also by its impact on people and the planet.

Uncontrollable Costs. (p. 67) Costs that cannot be changed or influenced in the short run by management.

Value Chain. (p. 50) The activities that add value to a firm's products and services; includes R&D, design, production or purchases, marketing, distribution, and customer service.

Variable Costs. (p. 68) Costs that change in total in direct proportion to changes in volume.

Wholesaler. (p. 48) Merchandising companies that buy in bulk from manufacturers, mark up the prices, and then sell those products to retailers.

Work in Process Inventory. (p. 48) Goods that are partway through the manufacturing process but not yet complete.

MyAccountingLab

Go to http://myaccountinglab.com/ for the following Quick Check, Short Exercises, Exercises, and Problems. They are available with immediate grading, explanations of correct and incorrect answers, and interactive media that acts as your own online tutor.

Quick Check

1. *(Learning Objective 1)* Walmart is a
   a. service company.
   b. retailer.
   c. wholesaler.
   d. manufacturer.

2. *(Learning Objective 2)* The cost of oranges at a fruit juice manufacturer is an example of a cost from which element in the value chain?
   a. Design
   b. Production
   c. Marketing
   d. Distribution

3. *(Learning Objective 2)* Which is *not* an element of Toyota's value chain?
   a. Administrative costs
   b. Cost of shipping cars to dealers
   c. Salaries of engineers who update car design
   d. Cost of print ads and television commercials

4. *(Learning Objective 3)* For Toyota, which is a direct cost with respect to the Prius?
   a. Depreciation on plant and equipment
   b. Cost of vehicle engine
   c. Salary of engineer who rearranges plant layout
   d. Cost of customer hotline

5. *(Learning Objective 3)* Which one of the following costs would be considered a direct cost of serving a particular customer at a McDonald's restaurant?
   a. The salary of the restaurant manager
   b. The depreciation on the restaurant building
   c. The cost of the hamburger patty in the sandwich the customer ordered
   d. The cost of heating the restaurant

6. *(Learning Objective 4)* Which of the following is *not* part of Toyota's manufacturing overhead?
   a. Insurance on plant and equipment
   b. Depreciation on its North American corporate headquarters
   c. Plant property taxes
   d. Plant utilities

7. *(Learning Objective 4)* The three basic components of inventoriable product costs are direct materials, direct labor, and
   a. cost of goods manufactured.
   b. manufacturing overhead.
   c. cost of goods sold.
   d. work in process.

8. *(Learning Objective 5)* In computing cost of goods sold, which of the following is the manufacturer's counterpart to the merchandiser's purchases?
   a. Direct materials used
   b. Total manufacturing costs incurred during the period
   c. Total manufacturing costs to account for
   d. Cost of goods manufactured

9. *(Learning Objective 6)* Which of the following is irrelevant to business decisions?
   a. Differential costs
   b. Sunk costs
   c. Variable costs
   d. Qualitative factors

10. *(Learning Objective 7)* Which of the following is *true*?
    a. Total fixed costs increase as production volume increases.
    b. Total fixed costs decrease as production volume decreases.
    c. Total variable costs increase as production volume increases.
    d. Total variable costs stay constant as production volume increases.

Quick Check Answers

1. b 2. b 3. a 4. b 5. c 6. b 7. b 8. d 9. b 10. c

Short Exercises

S2-1 Identify type of company from balance sheets *(Learning Objective 1)*

The current asset sections of the balance sheets of three companies follow. Which company is a service company? Which is a merchandiser? Which is a manufacturer? How can you tell?

ABC Co.		DEF Co.		GHI Co.	
Cash	$ 2,000	Cash	$ 2,500	Cash	$3,000
Accounts receivable	5,000	Accounts receivable	5,500	Accounts receivable	6,000
Raw materials inventory	1,000	Inventory	8,000	Prepaid expenses	500
Work in process inventory	800	Prepaid expenses	300	Total	$9,500
Finished goods inventory	4,000	Total	$16,300		
Total	$12,800				

S2-2 Identify types of companies and inventories *(Learning Objective 1)*

Fill in the blanks with one of the following terms: *manufacturing, service, merchandising, retailer(s), wholesaler(s), raw materials inventory, merchandise inventory, work in process inventory, finished goods inventory, freight-in, the cost of merchandise.*

a. Direct materials are stored in _______.
b. Kmart is a _______ company.
c. Manufacturers sell from their stock of _______.
d. Labor costs usually account for the highest percentage of _______ companies' costs.
e. Partially completed units are kept in the _______.
f. _______ companies generally have no inventory.
g. Intel (computer chips) is a _______ company.
h. Merchandisers' inventory consists of _______ and _______.
i. _______ companies carry three types of inventories: _______, _______, and _______.
j. H&R Block (tax preparation) is a _______ company.
k. Two types of _______ companies include _______ and _______.

S2-3 Classify costs by value chain function *(Learning Objective 2)*

Classify each of Hewlett-Packard's (HP's) costs as one of the six business functions in the value chain.

a. Depreciation on Roseville, California, plant
b. Costs of a customer support center website
c. Transportation costs to deliver laser printers to retailers such as Best Buy
d. Depreciation on research lab
e. Cost of a prime-time TV ad featuring the new HP logo
f. Salary of scientists at HP laboratories who are developing new printer technologies
g. Purchase of plastic used in printer casings
h. Salary of engineers who are redesigning the printer's on-off switch
i. Depreciation on delivery vehicles
j. Plant manager's salary

S2-4 Classify costs as direct or indirect *(Learning Objective 3)*

Classify the following as direct or indirect costs with respect to a local National Rentals equipment rental store (the store is the cost object). In addition, state whether National Rentals would trace or allocate these costs to the store.

a. The wages of store employees
b. The cost of operating the corporate payroll department
c. The cost of carpet steamers offered for rent
d. The cost of gas and oil sold at the store
e. Store utilities
f. The CEO's salary
g. The cost of the chainsaws offered for rent
h. The cost of national advertising

S2-5 Classify inventoriable product costs and period costs *(Learning Objective 4)*

Classify each of Georgia-Pacific's costs as either inventoriable product costs or period costs. Georgia-Pacific is a manufacturer of paper, lumber, and building material products.

a. Cost of new software to track inventory during production
b. Cost of electricity at one of Georgia-Pacific's paper mills
c. Salaries of Georgia-Pacific's top executives
d. Cost of chemical applied to lumber to inhibit mold from developing
e. Cost of TV ads promoting environmental awareness
f. Depreciation on the gypsum board plant
g. Purchase of lumber to be cut into boards
h. Life insurance on the CEO
i. Salaries of scientists studying ways to speed forest growth

S2-6 Classify a manufacturer's costs *(Learning Objective 4)*

Classify each of the following costs as a period cost or an inventoriable product cost. If you classify the cost as an inventoriable product cost, further classify it as direct material (DM), direct labor (DL), or manufacturing overhead (MOH).

a. Wages and benefits paid to assembly-line workers in the manufacturing plant
b. Repairs and maintenance on factory equipment
c. Lease payment on administrative headquarters
d. Salaries paid to quality control inspectors in the plant
e. Property insurance—40% of building is used for sales and administration; 60% of building is used for manufacturing
f. Standard packaging materials used to package individual units of product for sale (for example, cereal boxes in which cereal is packaged)
g. Depreciation on automated production equipment
h. Telephone bills relating to customer service call center

S2-7 Classify costs incurred by a dairy processing company

(Learning Objective 4)

Each of the following costs pertains to DairyPlains, a dairy processing company. Classify each of the company's costs as a period cost or an inventoriable product cost. Further classify inventoriable product costs as direct material (DM), direct labor (DL), or manufacturing overhead (MOH).

Cost	Period Cost or Inventoriable Product Cost?	DM, DL, or MOH?
1. Company president's annual bonus		
2. Plastic gallon containers in which milk is packaged		
3. Depreciation on Marketing Department's computers		
4. Wages and salaries paid to machine operators at dairy processing plant		
5. Research and development on improving milk pasteurization process		
6. Cost of milk purchased from local dairy farmers		
7. Lubricants used in running bottling machines		
8. Depreciation on refrigerated trucks used to collect raw milk from local dairy farmers		
9. Property tax on dairy processing plant		
10. Television advertisements for DairyPlains' products		
11. Gasoline used to operate refrigerated trucks delivering finished dairy products to grocery stores		

S2-8 Determine total manufacturing overhead *(Learning Objective 4)*

Frame Pro manufactures picture frames. Suppose the company's March records include the items described below. What is Frame Pro's total manufacturing overhead cost in March?

Company president's salary	$28,000
Plant supervisor's salary	$ 3,300
Plant janitor's salary	$ 1,500
Oil for manufacturing equipment	$ 110
Wood for frames	$48,000
Glue for picture frames	$ 450
Depreciation expense on company cars used by sales force	$ 4,100
Plant depreciation expense	$ 8,100
Interest expense	$ 3,500

S2-9 Compute Cost of Goods Sold for a merchandiser *(Learning Objective 5)*

Given the following information for a retailer, compute the cost of goods sold.

Import duties	$ 1,100
Purchases	$42,000
Ending inventory	$ 5,400
Revenues	$71,000
Marketing expenses	$10,000
Beginning inventory	$ 4,200
Website maintenance	$ 7,500
Delivery expenses	$ 1,300
Freight-in	$ 3,600

S2-10 Prepare a retailer's income statement *(Learning Objective 5)*

Gossamer Secrets is a retail chain specializing in salon-quality hair care products. During the year, Gossamer Secrets had sales of $39,300,000. The company began the year with $3,350,000 of merchandise inventory and ended the year with $4,315,000 of inventory. During the year, Gossamer Secrets purchased $23,975,000 of merchandise inventory. The company's selling, general, and administrative expenses totaled $6,150,000 for the year. Prepare Gossamer Secrets' income statement for the year.

S2-11 Calculate direct materials used *(Learning Objective 5)*

You are a new accounting intern at Allterrain Bikes. Your boss gives you the following information and asks you to compute the cost of direct materials used (assume that the company's raw materials inventory contains only direct materials).

Purchases of direct materials	$15,600
Import duties	$ 900
Freight-in	$ 600
Freight-out	$ 500
Ending raw materials inventory	$ 2,000
Beginning raw materials inventory	$ 3,900

S2-12 Compute Cost of Goods Manufactured *(Learning Objective 5)*

Robinson Manufacturing found the following information in its accounting records: $523,000 of direct materials used, $215,000 of direct labor, and $774,500 of manufacturing overhead. The Work in Process Inventory account had a beginning balance of $78,000 and an ending balance of $84,000. Compute the company's Cost of Goods Manufactured.

S2-13 Consider relevant information *(Learning Objective 6)*

You have been offered an entry-level marketing position at two highly respectable firms: one in Los Angeles, California, and one in Sioux Falls, South Dakota. What quantitative and qualitative information might be relevant to your decision? What characteristics about this information make it relevant?

S2-14 Classify costs as fixed or variable *(Learning Objective 7)*

Classify each of the following personal expenses as either fixed or variable. In some cases, your answer may depend on specific circumstances. If so, briefly explain your answer.

a. Water and sewer bill
b. Cell phone bill
c. Health club dues
d. Bus fare
e. Apartment rental
f. Internet cable service
g. Cost of groceries

EXERCISES Group A

E2-15A Identify types of companies and their inventories *(Learning Objective 1)*

Complete the following statements with one of the terms listed here. You may use a term more than once, and some terms may not be used at all.

Finished goods inventory	Inventory (merchandise)	Service companies
Manufacturing companies	Merchandising companies	Work in process inventory
Raw materials inventory	Wholesalers	

a. _______ buy products in bulk from producers, mark them up, and resell to retailers.
b. Most for-profit organizations can be described as being in one (or more) of three categories: _______, __________, and _______.
c. Honda Motors converts ______ into finished products.
d. _______ for a company such as Staples (office supplies) includes all of the costs necessary to purchase products and get them onto the store shelves.
e. Lands' End, Sears Roebuck & Co., and LL Bean are all examples of _________.
f. An insurance company, a health care provider, and a bank are all examples of _________.
g. _________ is composed of goods partially through the manufacturing process (not finished yet).
h. ______ report three types of inventory on the balance sheet.
i. _______typically do not have an inventory account.

E2-16A Classify costs along the value chain for a retailer *(Learning Objective 2)*

Suppose Radio Shack incurred the following costs at its Atlanta, Georgia, store:

Payment to consultant for advice on location of new store	$2,100	Research on whether store should sell satellite radio service	$ 600
Freight-in	$3,700	Purchases of merchandise	$39,000
Salespeople's salaries	$4,300	Rearranging store layout	$ 700
Customer Complaint Department	$ 800	Newspaper advertisements	$ 5,800
		Depreciation expense on delivery trucks	$ 1,100

Requirements

1. Classify each cost as to which category of the value chain it belongs (R&D, Design, Purchases, Marketing, Distribution, or Customer Service).
2. Compute the total costs for each value chain category.
3. How much are the total inventoriable product costs?

E2-17A Classify costs along the value chain for a manufacturer *(Learning Objectives 2 & 3)*

Suppose the cell phone manufacturer Samsung Electronics provides the following information for its costs last month (in hundreds of thousands):

Chip set	$62	Salaries of salespeople	$ 5
Rearrange production process to accommodate new robot	$ 1	Depreciation on plant and equipment	$70
Assembly-line workers' wages	$12	Exterior case for phone	$ 6
Technical customer support hotline	$ 3	Salaries of scientists who developed new model	$11
1-800 (toll-free) line for customer orders	$ 5	Delivery expense to customers via UPS	$ 8

Requirements

1. Classify each of these costs according to its place in the value chain (R&D, Design, Production, Marketing, Distribution, or Customer Service). (*Hint:* You should have at least one cost in each value chain function.)
2. Within the production category, break the costs down further into three sub-categories: Direct Materials, Direct Labor, and Manufacturing Overhead.
3. Compute the total costs for each value chain category.
4. How much are the total inventoriable product costs?
5. How much are the total prime costs?
6. How much are the total conversion costs?

E2-18A Value chain and sustainability efforts *(Learning Objective 2)*

Each of the scenarios to follow describes some cost item for organizations in the recycled carpet industry. For each scenario, identify which function of the value chain that cost would represent (R&D, Design, Purchasing/Producing, Marketing, Distributing, or Customer Service.) *Note:* The companies and products used in this exercise are real companies with a strong sustainable practices commitment.

a. Fibre(B)lock® Flooring is manufactured using the waste generated from the manufacture of commercial nylon carpet. The cost of the research into how to create Fibre(B)lock® Flooring would fall into which function in the value chain?

b. Ford Motor Company purchases cylinder head covers made from a nylon resin containing 100% recycled carpet in its 2011 Mustangs. The cost of the cylinder head covers would fall into which function in the value chain?

c. Los Angeles Fiber Company (LAFC) received the EPA/CARE award to recognize Los Angeles Fiber Company's sustainability efforts. Since 2000, LAFC has recycled more than 464 million pounds of post-consumer carpet. Its carpet brand, Reliance Carpet, is made entirely from post-consumer carpet fiber. The cost of promoting the company's products and its sustainability efforts would fall into which function in the value chain?

d. Axminster Carpets offsets the carbon emissions from its carpet distribution process by investing in renewable energy projects such as wind, power, and hydropower plants. This carbon offset is verified independently by the Voluntary Carbon Standard. The cost of these carbon offsets would fall into which function in the value chain?

e. Flor®, a company that produces residential carpet tiles made from recycled carpet, has an R&R (return and recycle) Program. Homeowners can arrange to have old tiles picked up and shipped back to the plant for recycling. The cost of operating this R&R program would fall into which function in the value chain?

f. Shaw Industries is a flooring manufacturer. It has created Cradle to Cradle Silver Certified carpet, which is carpet that can be recycled back into new carpet again and again at the end of its useful life or it can go back into the soil. The costs to develop the production process for the Cradle to Cradle Silver Certified carpet would fall into which function in the value chain?

E2-19A Classify costs as direct or indirect *(Learning Objective 3)*

Classify each of the following costs as a direct cost or an indirect cost assuming that the cost object is the Juniors department (clothing and accessories for teenage and young women) in the Medina Kohl's department store. (Kohl's is a chain of department stores and has stores located across the U.S.)

a. Manager of Juniors Department
b. Cost of Juniors clothing
c. Cost of radio advertising for the store
d. Cost of bags used to package customer purchases at the main registers for the store
e. Juniors Department sales clerks
f. Electricity for the building
g. Depreciation of the building
h. Cost of hangers used to display the clothing in the store
i. The Medina Kohl's store manager's salary
j. Juniors clothing buyers' salaries (these buyers buy for all the Juniors departments of Kohl's stores)
k. Cost of costume jewelry on the mannequins in the Juniors Department
l. Cost of the security staff at the Medina store

E2-20A Define cost terms *(Learning Objectives 3 & 4)*

Complete the following statements with one of the terms listed here. You may use a term more than once, and some terms may not be used at all.

Prime costs	Cost objects	Inventoriable product costs
Assigned	Direct costs	Fringe benefits
Period costs	Assets	Cost of goods sold
Indirect costs	Conversion costs	Total costs

a. Company-paid ______ may include health insurance, retirement plan contributions, payroll taxes, and paid vacations.
b. _______ are the costs of transforming direct materials into finished goods.
c. Direct material plus direct labor equals ___________.
d. The allocation process results in a less precise cost figure being _______ to the ___________.
e. _______ include the costs of all resources used throughout the value chain.
f. _______ are initially treated as ________ on the balance sheet.
g. Steel, tires, engines, upholstery, carpet, and dashboard instruments are used in the assembly of a car. Since the manufacturer can trace the cost of these materials (including freight-in and import duties) to specific units or batches of vehicles, they are considered _____________ of the vehicles.
h. __________ cannot be directly traced to a(n) ____________.
i. Costs that can be traced directly to a(n) ____________ are called __________.
j. When manufacturing companies sell their finished products, the costs of those finished products are removed from inventory and expensed as _____________.
k. _______ include R&D, marketing, distribution, and customer service costs.
l. GAAP requires companies to use only ______________ for external financial reporting.

E2-21A Classify and calculate a manufacturer's costs *(Learning Objectives 3 & 4)*

An airline manufacturer incurred the following costs last month (in thousands of dollars):

a. Depreciation on forklifts	$ 60
b. Property tax on corporate marketing office	$ 30
c. Cost of warranty repairs	$ 220
d. Factory janitors' wages	$ 10
e. Cost of designing new plant layout	$ 190
f. Machine operators' health insurance	$ 40
g. Airplane seats	$ 270
h. Depreciation on administrative offices	$ 70
i. Assembly workers' wages	$ 670
j. Plant utilities	$ 110
k. Production supervisors' salaries	$ 160
l. Jet engines	$1,100
m. Machine lubricants	$ 20

Requirements

1. Assuming the cost object is an airplane, classify each cost as one of the following: direct material (DM), direct labor (DL), indirect labor (IL), indirect materials (IM), other manufacturing overhead (other MOH), or period cost. (*Hint:* Set up a column for each type of cost.) What is the total for each type of cost?
2. Calculate total manufacturing overhead costs.
3. Calculate total inventoriable product costs.
4. Calculate total prime costs.
5. Calculate total conversion costs.
6. Calculate total period costs.

E2-22A Prepare the current assets section of the balance sheet

(Learning Objective 5)

Consider the following selected amounts and account balances of Knights:

Prepaid expenses	$ 6,100	Cost of goods sold	$102,000
Marketing expense	$27,000	Direct labor	$50,000
Work in process inventory	$42,000	Direct materials used	$20,100
Manufacturing overhead	$22,000	Accounts receivable	$79,000
Finished goods inventory	$59,000	Cash	$15,300
Raw materials inventory	$ 9,800	Cost of goods manufactured	$90,000

Requirement

Show how this company reports current assets on the balance sheet. Not all data are used. Is this company a service company, a merchandiser, or a manufacturer? How do you know?

E2-23A Prepare a retailer's income statement *(Learning Objective 5)*

Ron Rutland is the sole proprietor of Pampered Pets, a business specializing in the sale of high-end pet gifts and accessories. Pampered Pets' sales totaled $1,010,000 during the most recent year. During the year, the company spent $55,000 on expenses relating to website maintenance, $33,000 on marketing, and $28,000 on wrapping, boxing, and shipping the goods to customers. Pampered Pets also spent $639,000 on inventory purchases and an additional $19,900 on freight-in charges. The company started the year with $16,800 of inventory on hand and ended the year with $13,700 of inventory. Prepare Pampered Pets' income statement for the most recent year.

E2-24A Compute direct materials used and cost of goods manufactured

(Learning Objective 5)

Sharpland Industries is calculating its Cost of Goods Manufactured at year-end. Sharpland's accounting records show the following: The Raw Materials Inventory account had a beginning balance of $14,000 and an ending balance of $17,000. During the year, Sharpland purchased $58,000 of direct materials. Direct labor for the year totaled $132,000, while manufacturing overhead amounted to $164,000. The Work in Process Inventory account had a beginning balance of $22,000 and an ending balance of $18,000. Compute the Cost of Goods Manufactured for the year. (*Hint:* The first step is to calculate the direct materials used during the year.)

E2-25A Compute cost of goods manufactured and cost of goods sold

(Learning Objective 5)

Compute the cost of goods manufactured and cost of goods sold for Quality Aquatic Company for the most recent year using the amounts described next. Assume that raw materials inventory contains only direct materials.

	Beginning of Year	End of Year		End of Year
Raw materials inventory	$29,000	$31,000	Insurance on plant	$10,500
Work in process inventory	$36,000	$30,000	Depreciation—plant building and equipment	$13,000
Finished goods inventory	$22,000	$28,000	Repairs and maintenance—plant	$ 4,000
Purchases of direct materials		$73,000	Marketing expenses	$83,000
Direct labor		$89,000	General and administrative expenses	$26,500
Indirect labor		$42,000		

E2-26A Continues E2-25A: Prepare income statement *(Learning Objective 5)*

Prepare the income statement for Quality Aquatic Company in E2-25A for the most recent year. Assume that the company sold 33,000 units of its product at a price of $14 each during the year.

E2-27A Work backward to find missing amounts *(Learning Objective 5)*

JR Electronics manufactures and sells a line of smartphones. Unfortunately, JR Electronics suffered serious fire damage at its home office. As a result, the accounting records for October were partially destroyed—and completely jumbled. JR Electronics has hired you to help figure out the missing pieces of the accounting puzzle. Assume that the raw materials inventory contains only direct materials.

Work in process inventory, October 31	$ 1,800
Finished goods inventory, October 1	$ 4,200
Direct labor in October	$ 3,100
Purchases of direct materials in October	$ 9,200
Work in process inventory, October 1	0
Revenues in October	$27,300
Gross profit in October	$12,700
Direct materials used in October	$ 8,000
Raw materials inventory, October 31	$ 3,300
Manufacturing overhead in October	$ 6,300

Requirement

Find the following amounts:

a. Cost of goods sold in October
b. Beginning raw materials inventory
c. Ending finished goods inventory

E2-28A Determine whether information is relevant *(Learning Objective 6)*

Classify each of the following costs as relevant or irrelevant to the decision at hand and briefly explain your reason.

a. The type of fuel (gas or diesel) used by delivery vans when deciding which make and model of van to purchase for the company's delivery van fleet
b. Depreciation expense on old manufacturing equipment when deciding whether to replace it with newer equipment
c. The fair market value of old manufacturing equipment when deciding whether to replace it with new equipment
d. The interest rate paid on invested funds when deciding how much inventory to keep on hand
e. The cost of land purchased three years ago when deciding whether to build on the land now or wait two more years
f. The total amount of the restaurant's fixed costs when deciding whether to add additional items to the menu
g. Cost of operating automated production machinery versus the cost of direct labor when deciding whether to automate production
h. Cost of computers purchased six months ago when deciding whether to upgrade to computers with a faster processing speed
i. Cost of purchasing packaging materials from an outside vendor when deciding whether to continue manufacturing the packaging materials in-house
j. The property tax rates in different locales when deciding where to locate the company's headquarters

E2-29A Describe other cost terms *(Learning Objectives 6 & 7)*

Complete the following statements with one of the terms listed here. You may use a term more than once, and some terms may not be used at all.

Differential costs	Variable costs	Controllable costs
Marginal cost	Fixed costs	Average cost
Uncontrollable costs	Sunk costs	

a. In the long-run, most costs are ________, meaning that management is able to influence or change the amount of the cost.
b. Gasoline is one of many _______ in the operation of a motor vehicle.
c. Within the relevant range, ________ do not change in total with changes in production volume.
d. Costs that differ between alternatives are called _______.
e. The ________ per unit declines as a production facility produces more units.
f. A __________ is the cost of making one more unit.
g. A product's _______ and _______, not the product's _______, should be used to forecast total costs at different production volumes.
h. ________ are costs that have already been incurred.

E2-30A Classify costs as fixed or variable *(Learning Objective 7)*

Classify each of the following costs as fixed or variable:

a. Shipping costs for Amazon.com
b. Cost of fuel used for a national trucking company
c. Sales commissions at a car dealership
d. Cost of fabric used at a clothing manufacturer
e. Monthly office lease costs for a CPA firm
f. Cost of fruit sold at a grocery store
g. Cost of coffee used at a Starbucks' store
h. Monthly rent for a nail salon
i. Depreciation of exercise equipment at the YMCA
j. Hourly wages paid to sales clerks at Best Buy
k. Property taxes for a restaurant
l. Monthly insurance costs for the home office of a company
m. Monthly flower costs for a florist
n. Monthly depreciation of equipment for a customer service office
o. Monthly cost of French fries at a McDonald's restaurant

E2-31A Compute total and average costs *(Learning Objective 7)*

Smith Soda spends $3 on direct materials, direct labor, and variable manufacturing overhead for every unit (24-pack of soda) it produces. Fixed manufacturing overhead costs $4 million per year. The plant, which is currently operating at only 80% of capacity, produced 20 million units this year. Management plans to operate closer to full capacity next year, producing 25 million units. Management doesn't anticipate any changes in the prices it pays for materials, labor, and manufacturing overhead.

Requirements

1. What is the current total product cost (for the 20 million units), including fixed and variable costs?
2. What is the current average product cost per unit?
3. What is the current fixed cost per unit?
4. What is the forecasted total product cost next year (for the 25 million units)?
5. What is the forecasted average product cost next year?
6. What is the forecasted fixed cost per unit?
7. Why does the average product cost decrease as production increases?

EXERCISES Group B

E2-32B Identify types of companies and their inventories *(Learning Objective 1)*

Complete the following statements with one of the terms listed here. You may use a term more than once, and some terms may not be used at all.

Wholesalers	Work in process inventory	Service companies
Manufacturing companies	Raw materials inventory	Merchandising companies
Finished goods inventory	Inventory (merchandise)	

a. During production, _________ use direct labor and manufacturing overhead to convert direct materials into finished products.

b. _______ have only one category of inventory on their balance sheet.

c. During production as units are completed, they are moved out of _________ into _________.

d. _______ includes all of the costs associated with getting the goods to the store including freight-in costs and import duties if the products for resale were purchased overseas.

e. Merchandising companies can either be _______ or retailers.

f. _______ includes the wood, fasteners, and braces used in building picnic tables at a park furniture manufacturer.

g. _______ sell products to other companies (typically not to individual consumers.)

h. _______ make up the largest sector of the U.S. economy.

i. Ford Motor Company and Post Cereals can be described as __________.

E2-33B Classify costs along the value chain for a retailer *(Learning Objective 2)*

Suppose Radio Shack incurred the following costs at its Charlotte, North Carolina, store.

Payment to consultant for advice on location of new store	$2,500	Research on whether store should sell satellite radio service	$ 400
Freight-in	$3,900	Purchases of merchandise	$30,000
Salespeople's salaries	$4,000	Rearranging store layout	$ 950
Customer Complaint Department	$ 700	Newspaper advertisements	$ 5,200
		Depreciation expense on delivery trucks	$ 1,400

Requirements

1. Classify each cost as to which category of the value chain it belongs (R&D, Design, Purchases, Marketing, Distribution, Customer Service.).
2. Compute the total costs for each value chain category.
3. How much are the total inventoriable product costs?

E2-34B Classify costs along the value chain for a manufacturer *(Learning Objectives 2 & 3)*

Suppose the cell phone manufacturer Nokia provides the following information for its costs last month (in hundreds of thousands):

Chip set	$60	Salaries of salespeople	$ 7
Rearrange production process to accommodate new robot	$ 4	Depreciation on plant and equipment	$75
Assembly-line workers' wages	$12	Exterior case for phone	$ 6
Technical customer-support hotline	$ 2	Salaries of scientists who developed new model	$10
1-800 (toll-free) line for customer orders	$ 3	Delivery expense to customers via UPS	$ 5

Requirements

1. Classify each of these costs according to its place in the value chain (R&D, Design, Production, Marketing, Distribution, or Customer Service.)
2. Within the production category, break the costs down further into three sub-categories: Direct Materials, Direct Labor, and Manufacturing Overhead.
3. Compute the total costs for each value chain category.
4. How much are the total inventoriable product costs?
5. How much are the total prime costs?
6. How much are the total conversion costs?

E2-35B Value chain and sustainability efforts *(Learning Objective 2)*

Each of the scenarios to follow describes some cost item for organizations in recent years. For each scenario, identify which function of the value chain that cost would represent (R&D, Design, Purchasing/Producing, Marketing, Distributing, or Customer Service.) *Note: The companies and products used in this exercise are real companies with a strong sustainable practices commitment.*

a. GreenShipping™ is a service that companies can use to purchase carbon offsets for the carbon generated by shipments to customers. Any shipments made with UPS, FedEx, or USPS can be tracked. The GreenShipping™ calculator uses weight, distance traveled and mode of transport to calculate the carbon generated by that shipment. A carbon offset is then purchased so that the shipment becomes carbon neutral. The carbon offset helps to fund the development of renewable energy sources. The cost of these carbon offsets to the company making the shipment to their customer would fall into which function in the value chain?

b. The Red Wing Shoe Company manufactures work boots. The company has a philosophy that products should be repaired, not thrown away. After the twelve month warranty has expired on Red Wing boots, the company offers free oiling, free laces, low-cost replacement insoles, and low-cost hardware repairs. The cost of operating this shoe repair service would fall into which function in the value chain?

c. Ford Motor Company's Rouge Center in Dearborn Michigan has a "living roof" on the Dearborn Truck Plant final assembly building. It is the largest living roof in the world, encompassing 10.4 acres. The living roof is made from living grass and its primary purpose is to collect and filter rainfall as part of a natural storm water management system. It also provides cooler surroundings and offers a longer roof life than a traditional roof. The cost of promoting the company's products and its sustainability efforts would fall into which function in the value chain?

d. Nike Products, an athletic apparel and shoe manufacturer, developed the Environmental Apparel Design Tool over a period of seven years. The Environmental Apparel Design Tools helps apparel and shoe designers to make real-time choices that decrease the environmental impact of their work. With the tool, the designers can see the potential waste resulting from their design and the amount of environmentally preferred materials used by their design. When designers make changes to the preliminary product design, they can see instantly the effect of those changes on waste and input usage. The $6 million investment used to develop the Environmental Apparel Design Tool would fall into which function in the value chain?

e. Nyloboard® produces decking materials made from recycled carpet. The cost of the research into how to create Nyloboard® from recycled carpet would fall into which function in the value chain?

f. Late in 2010, the U.S. National Park Service approved the use of an erosion control system from GeoHay® for a roadway construction project in the Great Smoky Mountains National Park. GeoHay® erosion and sediment control products are produced from recycled carpet fibers. The cost of these erosion and sediment control products would fall into which function in the value chain?

E2-36B Classify costs as direct or indirect *(Learning Objective 3)*

Classify each of the following costs as a *direct cost* or an *indirect cost* assuming the cost object is the new car sales department of a local car dealership.

a. Salary of the manager of the dealership
b. Sales commissions
c. Cost of new cars
d. Cost of car detailing
e. Salary of the receptionist for the dealership
f. Depreciation on the building
g. Advertising in the local newspaper
h. Salary of the sales manager for new car sales
i. Cost of drinks provided in the reception area
j. Cost of gasoline used at the dealership
k. Utilities expense for the building
l. New car brochures provided to prospective buyers

E2-37B Define cost terms *(Learning Objectives 3 & 4)*

Complete the following statements with one of the terms listed here. You may use a term more than once, and some terms may not be used at all.

Assigned	Indirect costs	Cost objects
Assets	Fringe benefits	Total costs
Cost of goods sold	Direct costs	Prime costs
Period costs	Inventoriable product costs	Conversion costs

a. Material and labor costs that can be traced directly to particular units manufactured are _________ if the manufactured product is the _________.
b. _______ are outlays that can be identified with a specific product or department.
c. _________ include the direct costs attributable to the production of the goods.
d. In manufacturing, when goods are sold, costs are transferred from the finished goods inventory account to _________.
e. Allocation is used to _________ the _________ to a product or department.
f. _________ include direct material, direct labor, and manufacturing overhead costs.
g. _______ are the combination of direct materials and direct labor.
h. ____________ are expenditures that are not directly associated with the production of a product, such as advertising costs and general administrative costs.
i. Nearly anything of interest to a decision maker can be a __________, including products, stores, and departments.
j. Raw materials inventory, work in process inventory, and finished goods inventory are considered to be ___________ on the balance sheet.
k. ________ are those outlays that can be traced to a particular cost object.
l. _______are the cost of compensation provided employees besides the employees' salaries and wages.

E2-38B Classify and calculate a manufacturer's costs *(Learning Objectives 3 & 4)*

An airline manufacturer incurred the following costs last month (in thousands of dollars).

a. Depreciation on forklifts	$ 80
b. Property tax on corporate marketing offices	$ 35
c. Cost of warranty repairs	$ 235
d. Factory janitors' wages	$ 10
e. Cost of designing new plant layout	$ 185
f. Machine operators' health insurance	$ 70
g. Airplane seats	$ 270
h. Depreciation on administrative offices	$ 50
i. Assembly workers' wages	$ 690
j. Plant utilities	$ 140
k. Production supervisors' salaries	$ 110
l. Jet engines	$1,300
m. Machine lubricants	$ 15

Requirements

1. Assuming the cost object is an airplane, classify each cost as one of the following: direct material (DM), direct labor (DL), indirect labor (IL), indirect materials (IM), other manufacturing overhead (other MOH), or period cost. What is the total for each type of cost?
2. Calculate total manufacturing overhead costs.
3. Calculate total inventoriable product costs.
4. Calculate total prime costs.
5. Calculate total conversion costs.
6. Calculate total period costs.

E2-39B Prepare the current assets section of the balance sheet *(Learning Objective 5)*

Consider the following selected amounts and account balances of Saints:

Prepaid expenses	$ 5,900	Cost of goods sold	$106,000
Marketing expense	$29,000	Direct labor	$ 51,000
Work in process inventory	$40,000	Direct materials used	$ 23,100
Manufacturing overhead	$25,000	Accounts receivable	$ 81,000
Finished goods inventory	$61,000	Cash	$ 14,700
Raw materials inventory	$ 9,600	Cost of goods manufactured	$ 91,000

Requirement

Show how Saints reports current assets on the balance sheet. Not all data are used. Is this company a service company, a merchandiser, or a manufacturer? How do you know?

E2-40B Prepare a retailer's income statement *(Learning Objective 5)*

Roderick Thompson is the sole proprietor of Pretty Pets, a business specializing in the sale of high-end pet gifts and accessories. Pretty Pets' sales totaled $997,000 during the most recent year. During the year, the company spent $56,500 on expenses relating to website maintenance, $33,200 on marketing, and $27,500 on wrapping, boxing, and shipping the goods to customers. Pretty Pets also spent $635,000 on inventory purchases and an additional $19,500 on freight-in charges. The company started the year with $17,350 of inventory on hand, and ended the year with $13,100 of inventory. Prepare Pretty Pets' income statement for the most recent year.

E2-41B Compute direct materials used and cost of goods manufactured *(Learning Objective 5)*

Fitzcarron Industries is calculating its Cost of Goods Manufactured at year-end. The company's accounting records show the following: The Raw Materials Inventory account had a beginning balance of $17,000 and an ending balance of $18,000. During the year, the company purchased $58,000 of direct materials. Direct labor for the year totaled $128,000 while manufacturing overhead amounted to $161,000. The Work in Process Inventory account had a beginning balance of $29,000 and an ending balance of $20,000. Compute the Cost of Goods Manufactured for the year. (*Hint:* The first step is to calculate the direct materials used during the year.)

E2-42B Compute cost of goods manufactured and cost of goods sold *(Learning Objective 5)*

Compute the cost of goods manufactured and cost of goods sold for Crystal Bay Company for the most recent year using the amounts described next. Assume that raw materials inventory contains only direct materials.

	Beginning of Year	End of Year		End of Year
Raw materials inventory	$26,000	$33,000	Insurance on plant	$10,000
Work in process inventory	$35,000	$31,000	Depreciation—plant building and equipment	$13,200
Finished goods inventory	$14,000	$29,000	Repairs and maintenance—plant	$ 4,200
Purchases of direct materials		$73,000	Marketing expenses	$76,000
Direct labor		$86,000	General and administrative expenses	$27,500
Indirect labor		$40,000		

E2-43B Continues E2-42B: Prepare income statement *(Learning Objective 5)*

Prepare the income statement for Crystal Bay Company using the data in E2-42B for the most recent year. Assume that the company sold 36,000 units of its product at a price of $15 each during the year.

E2-44B Work backward to find missing amounts *(Learning Objective 5)*

LZ Electronics manufactures and sells smartphones. Unfortunately, the company recently suffered serious fire damage at its home office. As a result, the accounting records for October were partially destroyed and completely jumbled. LZ has hired you to help figure out the missing pieces of the accounting puzzle. Assume that LZ Electronics raw materials inventory contains only direct materials.

Work in process inventory, October 31	$ 1,000
Finished goods inventory, October 1	$ 4,900
Direct labor in October	$ 3,400
Purchases of direct materials in October	$ 9,600
Work in process inventory, October 1	0
Revenues in October	$27,900
Gross profit in October	$12,400
Direct materials used in October	$ 8,500
Raw materials inventory, October 31	$ 3,500
Manufacturing overhead in October	$ 6,300

Requirement

Find the following amounts:

a. Cost of goods sold in October
b. Beginning raw materials inventory
c. Ending finished goods inventory

E2-45B Determine whether information is relevant *(Learning Objective 6)*

Classify each of the following costs as relevant or irrelevant to the decision at hand and briefly explain your reason.

a. Fuel economy when purchasing new trucks for the delivery fleet.
b. Real estate property tax rates when selecting the location for a new order processing center.
c. The purchase price of the old computer when replacing it with a new computer with improved features.
d. The average cost of vehicle operation when purchasing a new delivery van.
e. The original cost of the current stove when selecting a new, more efficient stove for a restaurant.
f. The fair market value (trade-in value) of the existing forklift when deciding whether to replace it with a new, more efficient model.
g. The cost of land when determining where to build a new call center.
h. The cost of renovations when deciding whether to build a new office building or to renovate the existing office building.
i. The cost of production when determining whether to continue to manufacture the screen for a smartphone or to purchase it from an outside supplier.
j. Local tax incentives when selecting the location of a new office complex for a company's headquarters.

E2-46B Describe other cost terms *(Learning Objectives 6 & 7)*

Complete the following statements with one of the terms listed here. You may use a term more than once, and some terms may not be used at all.

Variable costs	Sunk costs	Differential costs
Marginal cost	Uncontrollable costs	Average cost
Fixed costs	Irrelevant costs	Controllable costs

a. Costs that change in total in direct proportion to changes in volume are called ________.
b. Costs and benefits that are the same for all alternatives considered and can be ignored are called __________.
c. __________ are irrelevant costs that have already been incurred and cannot be changed or recovered.
d. The __________ at any production level is the cost required to produce the next unit.
e. Research and development and advertising costs are considered to be ______________.
f. _______are costs that stay constant in total over the relevant range despite changes in volume.
g. ___________ is equal to the total costs of production divided by the number of units produced.
h. ________ are the differences in costs between two alternative courses of action.

E2-47B Classify costs as fixed or variable *(Learning Objective 7)*

Classify each of the following costs as fixed or variable:

a. Total wages paid to the hourly production workers
b. Property taxes at a manufacturer
c. Freight costs at Ford Motor Company
d. Cost of fuel for the delivery department of a home improvement store
e. Packaging costs for Crate and Barrel's web sales operations
f. Annual salary for a manager of a fast-food restaurant
g. Shipping costs for Amazon.com
h. Building lease cost for a hair care salon
i. Coffee costs for a coffee shop

j. Monthly straight-line depreciation costs for a factory
k. Monthly travel expenses for sales people
l. Property insurance costs on a warehouse
m. Cost of postage for the bills mailed by an electric company
n. Cost of produce at a grocery store
o. Monthly lawn maintenance fee for a tenant in an office building

E2-48B Compute total and average costs *(Learning Objective 7)*

Kotlan Soda spends $1 on direct materials, direct labor, and variable manufacturing overhead for every unit (12-pack of soda) it produces. Fixed manufacturing overhead costs $4 million per year. The plant, which is currently operating at only 70% of capacity, produced 20 million units this year. Management plans to operate closer to full capacity next year, producing 25 million units. Management doesn't anticipate any changes in the prices it pays for materials, labor, or manufacturing overhead.

Requirements

1. What is the current total product cost (for the 20 million units), including fixed and variable costs?
2. What is the current average product cost per unit?
3. What is the current fixed cost per unit?
4. What is the forecasted total product cost next year (for the 25 million units)?
5. What is the forecasted average product cost next year?
6. What is the forecasted fixed cost per unit?
7. Why does the average product cost decrease as production increases?

PROBLEMS Group A

P2-49A Classify costs along the value chain *(Learning Objectives 2 & 4)*

Fizz Cola produces a lemon-lime soda. The production process starts with workers mixing the lemon syrup and lime flavors in a secret recipe. The company enhances the combined syrup with caffeine. Finally, the company dilutes the mixture with carbonated water.
Fizz Cola incurs the following costs (in thousands):

Lime flavoring	$ 980
Production costs of "cents-off" store coupons for customers	$ 370
Delivery truck drivers' wages	$ 265
Bottles	$ 1,140
Sales commissions	$ 350
Plant janitors' wages	$ 1,000
Wages of workers who mix syrup	$ 7,700
Customer hotline	$ 180
Depreciation on delivery trucks	$ 300
Freight-in on materials	$ 1,500
Plant utilities	$ 850
Depreciation on plant and equipment	$ 3,100
Payment for new recipe	$ 1,140
Salt	$ 25
Replace products with expired dates upon customer complaint	$ 35
Rearranging plant layout	$ 1,400
Lemon syrup	$18,000

Requirements

1. Classify each of the listed costs according to its category in the value chain (R&D, Design, Production, Marketing, Distribution, or Customer Service.)
2. Further breakdown production costs into three subcategories: direct materials, direct labor, or manufacturing overhead.
3. Compute the total costs for each value chain category.
4. How much are the total inventoriable product costs?
5. Suppose the managers of the R&D and design functions receive year-end bonuses based on meeting their unit's target cost reductions. What are they likely to do? How might this affect costs incurred in other elements of the value chain?

P2-50A Prepare income statements *(Learning Objective 5)*

Part One: In 2010, Pam Baker opened Pam's Posies, a small retail shop selling floral arrangements. On December 31, 2011, her accounting records show the following:

Sales revenue	$55,000
Utilities for shop	$ 1,100
Inventory on December 31, 2011	$ 9,800
Inventory on January 1, 2011	$12,200
Rent for shop	$ 3,200
Sales commissions	$ 4,300
Purchases of merchandise	$37,000

Requirement

Prepare an income statement for Pam's Posies, a merchandiser, for the year ended December 31, 2011.

Part Two: Pam's Posies was so successful that Pam decided to manufacture her own brand of floral supplies: Floral Manufacturing. At the end of December 2012, her accounting records show the following:

Utilities for plant	$ 4,200
Delivery expense	$ 3,000
Sales salaries expense	$ 4,500
Plant janitorial services	$ 1,050
Work in process inventory, December 31, 2012	$ 5,000
Finished goods inventory, December 31, 2011	0
Finished goods inventory, December 31, 2012	$ 5,500
Sales revenue	$109,000
Customer service hotline expense	$ 1,600
Direct labor	$ 24,000
Direct material purchases	$ 35,000
Rent on manufacturing plant	$ 8,200
Raw materials inventory, December 31, 2011	$ 18,000
Raw materials inventory, December 31, 2012	$ 9,500
Work in process inventory, December 31, 2011	0

Requirements

1. Calculate the cost of goods manufactured for Floral Manufacturing for the year ended December 31, 2012.
2. Prepare an income statement for Floral Manufacturing for the year ended December 31, 2012.

3. How does the format of the income statement for Floral Manufacturing differ from the income statement of Pam's Posies?

Part Three: Show the ending inventories that would appear on these balance sheets:

1. Pam's Posies at December 31, 2011
2. Floral Manufacturing at December 31, 2012

P2-51A Fill in missing amounts *(Learning Objective 5)*

Certain item descriptions and amounts are missing from the monthly calculation of cost of goods manufactured and the income statement of Elly Manufacturing. Fill in the missing items.

Calculation of Cost of Goods Manufactured

Beginning ________			$ 21,000
Add: Direct ________:			
Beginning raw materials inventory	$ X		
Purchases of direct materials	53,000		
________	77,000		
Ending raw materials inventory	(23,000)		
Direct ________		$ X	
Direct ________		X	
Manufacturing overhead		45,000	
Total ________ costs ________			169,000
Total ________ costs ________			X
Less: Ending ________			(27,000)
________			$ X

ELLY MANUFACTURING COMPANY

____

________ June 30

Sales revenue		$ X
Cost of goods sold:		
Beginning ________	$116,000	
________	X	
Cost of goods ________	X	
Ending ________	X	
Cost of goods sold		210,000
Gross profit		300,000
________ expenses:		
Marketing expense	$ 94,000	
Administrative expense	X	154,000
Operating income		$ X

P2-52A Identify relevant information *(Learning Objective 6)*

You receive two job offers in the same big city. The first job is close to your parents' house, and they have offered to let you live at home for a year so you won't have to incur expenses for housing, food, or cable and internet. This job pays $44,000 per year. The second job is far from your parents' house, so you'll have to rent an apartment with parking ($12,000 per year), buy your own food ($2,500 per year), and pay for your own cable and internet ($650 per year). This job pays $49,000 per year. You still plan to do laundry at your parents' house once a week if you live in the city, and you plan to go into the city once a week to visit with friends if you live at home. Thus, the cost of operating your car will be about the same either way. In addition, your parents refuse to pay for your cell phone service ($760 per year), and you can't function without it.

Requirements

1. Based on this information alone, what is the net difference between the two alternatives (salary, net of relevant costs)?
2. What information is irrelevant? Why?
3. What qualitative information is relevant to your decision?
4. Assume that you really want to take Job #2, but you also want to live at home to cut costs. What new quantitative and qualitative information will you need to incorporate into your decision?

P2-53A Calculate the total and average costs *(Learning Objective 7)*

The owner of Riverdale Restaurant is disappointed because the restaurant has been averaging 5,000 pizza sales per month, but the restaurant and wait staff can make and serve 10,000 pizzas per month. The variable cost (for example, ingredients) of each pizza is $1.20. Monthly fixed costs (for example, depreciation, property taxes, business license, and manager's salary) are $5,000 per month. The owner wants cost information about different volumes so that some operating decisions can be made.

Requirements

1. Fill in the following chart to provide the owner with the cost information. Then use the completed chart to help you answer the remaining questions.

Monthly pizza volume	2,500	5,000	10,000
Total fixed costs	$	$	$
Total variable costs			
Total costs			
Fixed cost per pizza	$	$	$
Variable cost per pizza			
Average cost per pizza			
Selling price per pizza	$ 5.50	$ 5.50	$ 5.50
Average profit per pizza			

2. From a cost standpoint, why do companies such as Riverdale Restaurant want to operate near or at full capacity?
3. The owner has been considering ways to increase the sales volume. The owner thinks that 10,000 pizzas could be sold per month by cutting the selling price per pizza from $5.50 to $5.00. How much extra profit (above the current level) would be generated if the selling price were to be decreased? (*Hint:* Find the restaurant's current monthly profit and compare it to the restaurant's projected monthly profit at the new sales price and volume.)

PROBLEMS Group B

P2-54B Classify costs along the value chain *(Learning Objectives 2 & 4)*

Buzz Cola produces a lemon-lime soda. The production process starts with workers mixing the lemon syrup and lime flavors in a secret recipe. The company enhances the combined syrup with caffeine. Finally, the company dilutes the mixture with carbonated water. Buzz Cola incurs the following costs (in thousands):

Lime flavoring	$ 920
Production costs of "cents-off" store coupons for customers	$ 530
Delivery truck drivers' wages	$ 295
Bottles	$ 1,190
Sales commissions	$ 325
Plant janitors' wages	$ 1,000
Wages of workers who mix syrup	$ 7,700
Customer hotline	$ 190
Depreciation on delivery trucks	$ 225
Freight-in on materials	$ 1,300
Plant utilities	$ 650
Depreciation on plant and equipment	$ 3,200
Payment for new recipe	$ 1,190
Salt	$ 25
Replace products with expired dates upon customer complaint	$ 40
Rearranging plant layout	$ 1,700
Lemon syrup	$18,000

Requirements

1. Classify each of the listed costs according to its category in the value chain, (R&D, Design, Production, Marketing, Distribution, or Customer Service.)

		Production					
R&D	Design of Products or Processes	Direct Materials	Direct Labor	Manufacturing Overhead	Marketing	Distribution	Customer Service

2. Further breakdown production costs into three subcategories: Direct Materials, Direct Labor, or Manufacturing Overhead.
3. Compute the total costs for each value chain category.
4. How much are the total inventoriable product costs?
5. Suppose the managers of the R&D and design functions receive year-end bonuses based on meeting their unit's target cost reductions. What are they likely to do? How might this affect costs incurred in other elements of the value chain?

P2-55B Prepare income statements *(Learning Objective 5)*

Part One: In 2011, Lindsey Conway opened Lindsey's Blooms, a small shop selling floral arrangements. On December 31, 2011, her accounting records show the following:

Inventory on December 31, 2011	$ 9,300
Inventory on January 1, 2011	$12,000
Sales revenue	$58,000
Utilities for shop	$ 1,600
Rent for shop	$ 3,800
Sales commissions	$ 4,500
Purchases of merchandise	$38,000

Requirement

Prepare an income statement for Lindsey's Blooms, a merchandiser, for the year ended December 31, 2011.

Part Two: Lindsey's Blooms succeeded so well that Lindsey decided to manufacture her own brand of floral supplies: Floral Manufacturing. At the end of December 2012, her accounting records show the following:

Work in process inventory, December 31, 2012	$ 1,000
Finished goods inventory, December 31, 2011	0
Finished goods inventory, December 31, 2012	$ 5,000
Sales revenue	$101,000
Customer service hotline expense	$ 1,400
Utilities for plant	$ 4,100
Delivery expense	$ 3,000
Sales salaries expense	$ 4,200
Plant janitorial services	$ 1,350
Direct labor	$ 22,000
Direct material purchases	$ 39,000
Rent on manufacturing plant	$ 8,800
Raw materials inventory, December 31, 2011	$ 10,000
Raw materials inventory, December 31, 2012	$ 9,500
Work in process inventory, December 31, 2011	0

Requirements

1. Calculate the cost of goods manufactured for Floral Manufacturing for the year ended December 31, 2012.
2. Prepare an income statement for Floral Manufacturing for the year ended December 31, 2012.
3. How does the format of the income statement for Floral Manufacturing differ from the income statement of Lindsey's Blooms?

Part Three: Show the ending inventories that would appear on these balance sheets:

1. Lindsey's Blooms at December 31, 2011.
2. Floral Manufacturing at December 31, 2012.

P2-56B Fill in missing amounts *(Learning Objective 5)*

Certain item descriptions and amounts are missing from the monthly calculation of cost of goods manufactured and the income statement of Tioga Manufacturing Company. Fill in the missing items.

Calculation of the Cost of Goods Manufactured			
Beginning ________			$ 20,000
Add: Direct ________:			
Beginning raw materials inventory	$ X		
Purchases of direct materials	58,000		
________	83,000		
Ending raw materials inventory	(29,000)		
Direct ________		$ X	
Direct ________		X	
Manufacturing overhead		47,000	
Total ________ costs ________			$171,000
Total ________ costs ________			X
Less: Ending ________			(23,000)
________			$ X

Tioga Manufacturing Company ________________ ________ June 30		
Sales revenue		$ X
Cost of goods sold:		
Beginning ________	$111,000	
________	X	
Cost of goods ________	X	
Ending ________	X	
Cost of goods sold		216,000
Gross profit		264,000
________ expenses:		
Marketing expense	$100,000	
Administrative expense	X	167,000
Operating income		$ X

P2-57B Identify relevant information *(Learning Objective 6)*

You receive two job offers in the same big city. The first job is close to your parents' house, and they have offered to let you live at home for a year so you won't have to incur expenses for housing, food, or cable and internet. This job pays $41,000 per year. The second job is far away from your parents' house, so you'll have to rent an apartment with parking ($12,000 per year), buy your own food ($2,500 per year), and pay for your own cable and internet ($800 per year). This job pays $46,000 per year. You still plan to do laundry at your parents' house once a week if you live in the city and plan to go into the city once a week to visit with friends if you live at home. Thus, the cost of operating your car will be about the same either way. Additionally, your parents refuse to pay for your cell phone service ($750 per year), and you can't function without it.

Requirements

1. Based on this information alone, what is the net difference between the two alternatives (salary, net of relevant costs)?

2. What information is irrelevant? Why?
3. What qualitative information is relevant to your decision?
4. Assume you really want to take Job #2, but you also want to live at home to cut costs. What new quantitative and qualitative information will you need to incorporate in your decision?

P2-58B Calculate the total and average costs *(Learning Objective 7)*

The owner of Staten Island Restaurant is disappointed because the restaurant has been averaging 6,000 pizza sales per month but the restaurant and wait staff can make and serve 7,500 pizzas per month. The variable cost (for example, ingredients) of each pizza is $1.20. Monthly fixed costs (for example, depreciation, property taxes, business license, manager's salary) are $9,000 per month. The owner wants cost information about different volumes so that some operating decisions can be made.

Requirements

1. Fill in the chart to provide the owner with the cost information. Then use the completed chart to help you answer the remaining questions.

Monthly pizza volume	4,500	6,000	7,500
Total fixed costs			
Total variable costs			
Total costs			
Fixed cost per pizza			
Variable cost per pizza			
Average cost per pizza			
Selling price per pizza	$ 6.25	$ 6.25	$ 6.25
Average profit per pizza			

2. From a cost standpoint, why do companies such as Staten Island Restaurant want to operate near or at full capacity?
3. The owner has been considering ways to increase the sales volume. It is believed that 7,500 pizzas could be sold per month by cutting the selling price from $6.25 per pizza to $5.75. How much extra profit (above the current level) would be generated if the selling price were to be decreased? (*Hint*: Find the restaurant's current monthly profit and compare it to the restaurant's projected monthly profit at the new sales price and volume.)

CRITICAL THINKING

Discussion & Analysis

A2-59 Discussion Questions

1. Briefly describe a service company, a merchandising company, and a manufacturing company. Give an example of each type of company, but do not use the same examples as given in the chapter.
2. How do service, merchandising, and manufacturing companies differ from each other? How are service, merchandising, and manufacturing companies similar to each other? List as many similarities and differences as you can identify.
3. What is the value chain? What are the six types of business activities found in the value chain? Which type(s) of business activities in the value chain generate costs that go directly to the income statement once incurred? What type(s) of business activities in the value chain generate costs that flow into inventory on the balance sheet?
4. Compare direct costs to indirect costs. Give an example of a cost at a company that could be a direct cost at one level of the organization but would be considered an indirect cost at a different level of that organization. Explain why this same cost could be both direct and indirect (at different levels).
5. What is meant by the term "inventoriable product costs"? What is meant by the term "period costs"? Why does it matter whether a cost is an inventoriable product cost or a period cost?
6. Compare inventoriable product costs to period costs. Using a product of your choice, give examples of inventoriable product costs and period costs. Explain why you categorized your costs as you did.
7. Describe how the income statement of a merchandising company differs from the income statement of a manufacturing company. Also comment on how the income statement from a merchandising company is similar to the income statement of a manufacturing company.
8. How are the cost of goods manufactured, the cost of goods sold, the income statement, and the balance sheet related for a manufacturing company? What specific items flow from one statement or schedule to the next? Describe the flow of costs between the cost of goods manufactured, the cost of goods sold, the income statement, and the balance sheet for a manufacturing company.
9. What makes a cost relevant or irrelevant when making a decision? Suppose a company is evaluating whether to use its warehouse for storage of its own inventory or whether to rent it out to a local theater group for housing props. Describe what information might be relevant when making that decision.
10. Explain why "differential cost" and "variable cost" do *not* have the same meaning. Give an example of a situation in which there is a cost that is a differential cost but *not* a variable cost.
11. Greenwashing, the practice of overstating a company's commitment to sustainability, has been in the news over the past few years. Perform an internet search of the term "greenwashing." What examples of greenwashing can you find?
12. In the chapter, Ricoh was mentioned as a company that has designed its copiers so that at the end of the copier's life, Ricoh will collect and dismantle the product for usable parts, shred the metal casing, and use the parts and shredded material to build new copiers. This product design can be called "cradle to cradle" design. Are there any other products you are aware of that have a "cradle to cradle" design? Perform a search of the internet for "cradle to cradle design" or a related term if you need ideas.

Application & Analysis

A2-60 Costs in the Value Chain at a Real Company and Cost Objects

Choose a company with which you are familiar that manufactures a product. In this activity, you will be making reasonable assumptions about the activities involved in the value chain for this product; companies do not typically publish information about their value chain.

Basic Discussion Questions

1. Describe the product that is being produced and the company that produces it.
2. Describe the six value chain business activities that this product would pass through from its inception to its ultimate delivery to the customer.
3. List at least three costs that would be incurred in each of the six business activities in the value chain.
4. Classify each cost you identified in the value chain as either being an inventoriable product cost or a period cost. Explain your justification.
5. A cost object can be anything for which managers want a separate measurement of cost. List three different potential cost objects *other* than the product itself for the company you have selected.
6. List a direct cost and an indirect cost for each of the three different cost objects in question 5. Explain why each cost would be direct or indirect.

Decision Case

A2-61 Determine ending inventory balances *(Learning Objective 5)*

PowerBox designs and manufactures switches used in telecommunications. Serious flooding throughout North Carolina affected PowerBox's facilities. Inventory was completely ruined, and the company's computer system, including all accounting records, was destroyed.

Before the disaster recovery specialists clean the buildings, Annette Plum, the company controller, is anxious to salvage whatever records she can to support an insurance claim for the destroyed inventory. She is standing in what is left of the Accounting Department with Paul Lopez, the cost accountant.

"I didn't know mud could smell so bad," Paul says. "What should I be looking for?"

"Don't worry about beginning inventory numbers," responds Annette. "We'll get them from last year's annual report. We need first-quarter cost data."

"I was working on the first-quarter results just before the storm hit," Paul says. "Look, my report's still in my desk drawer. But all I can make out is that for the first quarter, material purchases were $476,000 and that direct labor, manufacturing overhead (other than indirect materials), and total manufacturing costs to account for were $505,000; $245,000; and $1,425,000, respectively. Wait, and cost of goods available for sale was $1,340,000."

"Great," says Annette. "I remember that sales for the period were approximately $1.7 million. Given our gross profit of 30%, that's all you should need."

Paul is not sure about that, but decides to see what he can do with this information. The beginning inventory numbers are as follows:

- Raw materials, $113,000
- Work in process, $229,000
- Finished goods, $154,000

He remembers a schedule he learned in college that may help him get started.

Requirements

1. Use exhibits in the chapter to determine the ending inventories of raw materials, work in process, and finished goods.
2. Draft an insurance claim letter for the controller, seeking reimbursement for the flood damage to inventory. PowerBox's insurance representative is Gary Streer, at Industrial Insurance, 1122 Main Street, Hartford, CT 06268. The policy number is #3454340-23. PowerBox's address is 5 Research Triangle Way, Raleigh, NC 27698.

CMA Questions

A2-62

Roberta Johnson is the manager of Sleep-Well Inn, one of a chain of motels located throughout the U.S. An example of an operating cost at Sleep-Well that is both direct and fixed is

a. Johnson's salary.
b. water.
c. toilet tissue.
d. advertising for the Sleep-Well Inn chain. *(CMA Adapted)*

A2-63

The Profit and Loss Statement of Madengrad Mining, Inc., includes the following information for the current fiscal year:

Sales	$ 160,000
Gross profit	48,000
Year-end finished good inventory	58,300
Opening finished good inventory	60,190

The cost of goods manufactured by Madengrad for the current fiscal year is

a. $46,110.
b. $49,890.
c. $110,110.
d. $113,890. *(CMA Adapted)*

A2-64

The schedule of cost of goods manufactured of Gruber Fittings, Inc., shows the following balances for its fiscal year-end:

Direct manufacturing labor	$ 280,000
Manufacturing overhead	375,000
Ending work in process inventory	230,000
Raw materials used in production	450,000
Cost of goods manufactured	1,125,000

The value of the work in process inventory at the beginning of the fiscal year was

a. $625,000.
b. $250,000.
c. $210,000.
d. $20,000. *(CMA Adapted)*

Job Costing

Learning Objectives

- ■1 Distinguish between job costing and process costing
- ■2 Understand the flow of production and how direct materials and direct labor are traced to jobs
- ■3 Compute a predetermined manufacturing overhead rate and use it to allocate MOH to jobs
- ■4 Determine the cost of a job and use it to make business decisions
- ■5 Compute and dispose of overallocated or underallocated manufacturing overhead
- ■6 Prepare journal entries for a manufacturer's job costing system
- ■7 (Appendix) Use job costing at a service firm as a basis for billing clients

Life Fitness, a division of the Brunswick

Corporation, is currently the global leader in fitness equipment. The company's roots began in the 1970s with the introduction of the world's first-ever computerized exercise bike, the Lifecycle. Since then, the company has grown to design, manufacture, and market over 300 different cardio and strength-training products, including treadmills, elliptical cross-trainers, stair climbers, and of course, exercise bikes. While the company's growth has been propelled in part by consumers' ever-increasing zeal for personal fitness, the company has also grown through carefully analyzing the profit margins on each of its products, and adjusting its operations and pricing accordingly.

How does the company figure out the profit margins on each of its 300 different models? Life Fitness would first determine how much it costs to manufacture each type of exercise machine. Each batch of identical units produced (for example, 50 units of the X4 Elliptical Cross-Trainer) is called a "job." The company's job costing system traces the direct materials and direct labor used by each job. The company then allocates some manufacturing overhead to each job. By summing the direct materials, direct labor, and manufacturing overhead assigned to each job, the company can figure out how much it costs to make each cross-trainer in the job. The company could then use this cost information to make vital business decisions, such as the following:

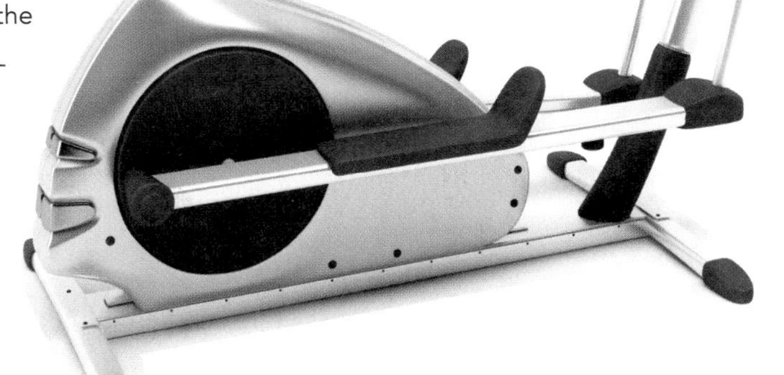

Ali Ender Birer/Shutterstock.com

Sources: Brunswick Corporation 2008 Annual Report http://us.corporate.lifefitness.com

- Setting selling prices that will lead to profits on each product
- Identifying opportunities to cut costs
- Determining which products are most profitable and therefore deserve the most marketing emphasis

Managers also need cost information on each exercise machine in order to prepare the company's financial statements. The cost is used to determine the following:

- The cost of goods sold for the income statement
- The cost of the inventory for the balance sheet

Whether you plan a career in marketing, engineering, production, general management, or accounting, you'll need to understand how much it costs to produce the company's products.

What Methods are Used to Determine the Cost of Manufacturing a Product?

1 Distinguish between job costing and process costing

Most manufacturers use one of two product costing systems in order to find the cost of producing their products:

- Process costing
- Job costing

The end goal of both product costing systems is the same: to find the cost of manufacturing one unit of product. However, the manner in which this goal is achieved differs. Management chooses the product costing system that works best for its particular manufacturing environment. Let's go over the basics of each system and identify the types of companies that would be most likely to use them.

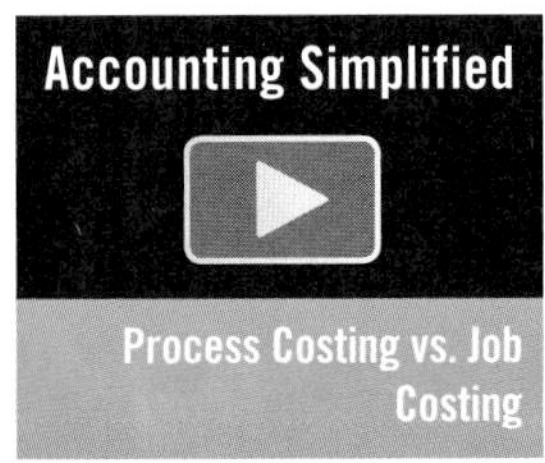

If your instructor is using MyAccountingLab, go to the Multimedia Library for a quick video on this topic.

Process Costing

Process costing is used by companies that produce extremely large numbers of identical units through a series of uniform production steps or processes. Because each unit is identical, in theory, each unit should cost the same to make. In essence, process costing averages manufacturing costs across all units produced so that each identical unit bears the same cost.

For example, let's assume Pace Foods uses two processes to make picante sauce: (1) cleaning and chopping vegetables and (2) mixing and bottling the sauce. First, Pace accumulates the costs incurred in the cleaning and chopping process over a period of time, such as a month. The costs incurred in this process include the cost of the vegetables themselves, as well as the cost of cleaning and chopping the vegetables. The company averages the total costs of this process over all units passing through the process during the same period of time.

For example, let's say Pace spends \$500,000 on purchasing, cleaning, and chopping the vegetables to make 1 million jars of picante sauce during the month. Then the average cost per jar of the cleaning and chopping process is as follows:

$$\text{Cleaning and chopping process} = \frac{\$500{,}000}{1{,}000{,}000 \text{ jars}} = \$0.50 \text{ per jar}$$

That's the unit manufacturing cost for just the first production process. Now the cleaned and chopped vegetables go through the second production process, mixing and bottling, where a similar calculation is performed to find the average cost of that process. The cost of the second process would include any raw materials used, such as the cost of the glass jars, as well as the cost of mixing the sauce and filling the jars with the sauce. Let's say the average cost to mix and bottle each jar of sauce is \$0.25.

Now Pace can determine the total cost to manufacture each jar of picante sauce:

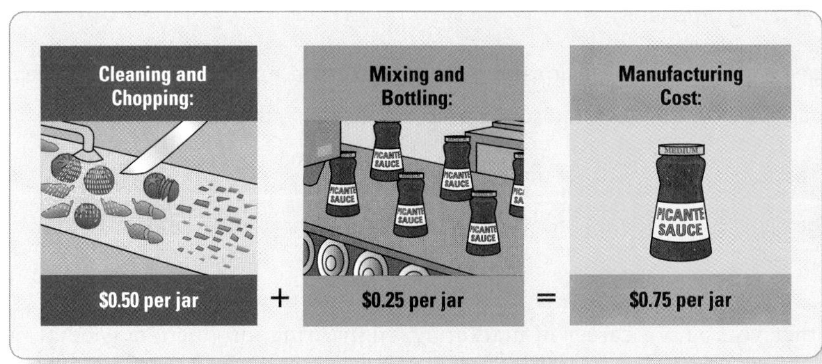

Each jar of picante sauce is identical to every other jar, so each bears the same average cost: $0.75. Once managers know the cost of manufacturing each jar, they can use that information to help set sales prices and make other business decisions. To generate a profit, the sales price will have to be high enough to cover the $0.75 per jar manufacturing cost as well as the company's operating costs incurred along other areas of the value chain (marketing, distributing, and so forth) during the period.

We'll delve more deeply into process costing in Chapter 5. For now, just remember that any company that mass-produces identical units of product will most likely use process costing to determine the cost of making each unit.

Job Costing

Whereas process costing is used by companies that mass manufacture identical units, **job costing** is used by companies that produce unique, custom-ordered products, or relatively small batches of different products. Each unique product or batch of units is considered a separate "job." Different jobs can vary considerably in direct materials, direct labor, and manufacturing overhead costs, so job costing accumulates these costs separately for each individual job. For example, Dell custom-builds each personal computer based on the exact components the customer orders. Since each PC is unique, Dell treats each order as a unique job. Life Fitness produces each of its 300 different models of exercise machines in relatively small, separate batches. Each batch of exercise machines produced is considered a separate job. Job costing would also be used by Boeing (airplanes), custom-home builders (unique houses), high-end jewelers (unique jewelry), and any other manufacturers that build custom-ordered products.

> **Why is this important?**
>
> "**Managers** need the most accurate **cost information** they can get in order to make good **business decisions.** They will choose a costing system (usually **job costing** or **process costing)** based on which system best fits their operations."

However, job costing is not limited to manufacturers. Professional service providers such as law firms, accounting firms, consulting firms, and marketing firms use job costing to determine the cost of serving each client. People working in trades such as mechanics, plumbers, and electricians also use job costing to determine the cost of performing separate jobs for clients. In both cases, the job cost is used as a basis for billing the client. In the appendix to this chapter we'll go over a complete example of how a law firm would use job costing to bill its clients.

In summary, companies use job costing when their products or services vary in terms of materials needed, time required to complete the job, and/or the complexity of the production process. Because the jobs are so different, it would not be reasonable to assign them equal costs. Therefore, the cost of each job is compiled separately. We'll spend the rest of this chapter looking at how companies compile, record, and use job costs to make important business decisions. Before moving on, take a look at Exhibit 3-1, which summarizes the key differences between job and process costing.

EXHIBIT 3-1 Differences Between Job and Process Costing

	Job Costing	Process Costing
Cost object:	Job	Process
Outputs:	Single units or small batches with large difference between jobs	Large quantities of identical units
Extent of averaging:	Less averaging—costs are averaged over the small number of units in a job (often 1 unit in a job)	More averaging—costs are averaged over the many identical units that pass through the process

STOP & THINK

Do all manufacturers use job costing or process costing systems?

Answer: Some manufacturers use a hybrid of these two costing systems if neither "pure" system mirrors their production environment very well. For example, clothing manufacturers often mass produce the same product over and over (dress shirts) but use different materials on different batches (cotton fabric on one batch and silk fabric on another). A hybrid costing system would have some elements of a process costing system (averaging labor and manufacturing overhead costs equally across all units) and some elements of a job costing system (tracing different fabric costs to different batches).

How do Manufacturers Determine a Job's Cost?

2 Understand the flow of production and how direct materials and direct labor are traced to jobs

As we've just seen, manufacturers use job costing if they produce unique products or relatively small batches of different products. Life Fitness produces each of its 300 different models in relatively small batches, so it considers each batch a separate job. In this section, we will show you how Life Fitness determines the cost of producing Job 603, a batch of 50 identical X4 Elliptical Cross-Trainers[1]. The company's market for these cross-trainers includes health and fitness clubs, college student fitness centers, professional athletic teams, city recreation departments, and direct sales to customers for home fitness gyms. As we walk through the process, keep in mind that most companies maintain the illustrated documents in electronic, rather than hard copy form. Even so, the basic information stored in the documents and the purpose for the documents remain the same.

Overview: Flow of Inventory Through a Manufacturing System

Before we delve into Life Fitness's job costing system, let's take a quick look at how the physical products, as well as costs, flow through the company. As you learned in Chapter 2, manufacturers such as Life Fitness maintain three separate types of inventory: Raw Materials, Work in Process, and Finished Goods. The cost of each of these inventories is reflected on the company's balance sheet.

As shown in Exhibit 3-2, Raw Materials (RM) Inventory is maintained in a storeroom, near the factory, until the materials are needed in production. As soon as these materials are transferred to the factory floor, they are no longer considered raw materials because they have become part of the work in process in the factory. Work in Process (WIP) Inventory consists of all products that are part-way through the production process. As soon as the manufacturing process is complete, the products are moved out of the factory and into a Finished Goods (FG) Inventory storage area, or warehouse, where they will await sale and shipment to a customer. Finally, when the products are shipped to customers, the cost of manufacturing those products becomes the Cost of Goods Sold (CGS) shown on the company's income statement.

[1]All references to Life Fitness in this hypothetical example were created by the author solely for academic purposes and are not intended, in any way, to represent the actual business practices of, or costs incurred by, Life Fitness, Inc.

EXHIBIT 3-2 Flow of Inventory Through a Manufacturing System

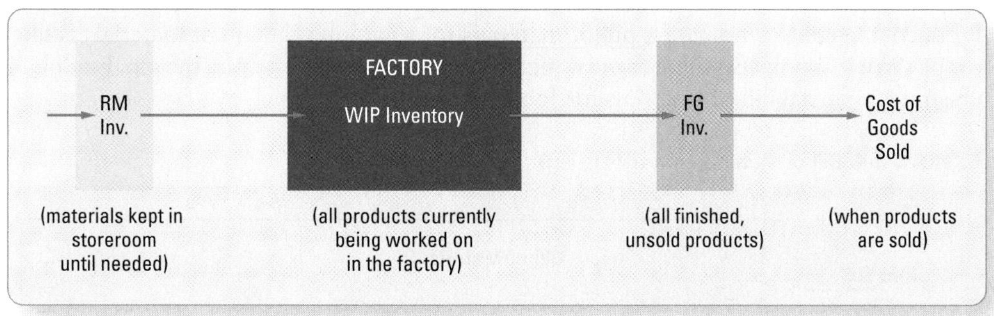

Keep this basic flow of inventory in mind as we delve into Life Fitness's job costing system.

Scheduling Production

Job costing begins with management's decision to produce a batch of units. Sometimes companies produce a batch of units just to meet a particular customer order. For example, the Chicago Bears may custom order treadmills that have characteristics not found on other models. This batch of unique treadmills would become its own job. On the other hand, most companies also produce stock inventory for products they sell on a regular basis. They want to have stock available to quickly fill customer orders. By forecasting demand for the product, the manufacturer is able to estimate the number of units that should be produced during a given time period. As shown in Exhibit 3-3, the production schedule indicates the quantity and types of inventory that are scheduled to be manufactured during the period. Depending on the company, the types of products it offers, and production time required, production schedules may cover periods of time as short as one day (Dell, producing customized laptops) or as long as one year or more (Boeing, manufacturing 737 airplanes).

EXHIBIT 3-3 Monthly Production Schedule

Production Schedule
For the Month of December

Job	Model Number	Stock or Customer	Quantity	Scheduled Start Date	Scheduled End Date
603	X4 Cross-Trainer	For stock	50	12/2	12/6
604	T5-0 Treadmill	For stock	60	12/7	12/17
605	Custom T6-C Treadmill	Chicago Bears	15	12/18	12/21
606	Custom S3-C Stair-Climber	Chicago Bears	12	12/22	12/24
	FACTORY CLOSED FOR HOLIDAYS and ANNUAL MAINTENANCE			12/25	12/31

The production schedule is very important in helping management determine the direct labor and direct materials that will be needed during the period. To complete production on time, management must make sure it will have an appropriate number of available factory workers with the specific skill-sets required for each job. Management also needs to make sure it will have all of the raw materials needed for each job. How does management do this? We'll see in the next section.

Purchasing Raw Materials

Production engineers prepare a **bill of materials** for each job. The bill of materials is like a recipe card: It simply lists all of the raw materials needed to manufacture the job. Exhibit 3-4 illustrates a partial bill of materials for Job 603:

EXHIBIT 3-4 Bill of Materials (Partial Listing)

Bill of Materials

Job: 603

Model: X4 Elliptical Cross-Trainer **Quantity:** 50 units

Part Number	Description	Quantity Needed
HRM50812	Heart rate monitor	50
LCD620	LCD entertainment screen	50
B4906	Front and rear rolling base	100
HG2567	Hand grips	100
FP689	Foot platform	100
	Etc.	

After the bill of materials has been prepared, the purchasing department checks the raw materials inventory to determine what raw materials are currently in stock, and what raw materials must be purchased. Each item has its own **raw materials record**. As shown in Exhibit 3-5, a raw materials record details information about each item in stock: the number of units received, the number of units used, and the balance of units currently in stock. Additionally, the raw materials record shows the cost of each unit purchased, the cost of each unit used, and the cost of the units still in raw materials inventory.

EXHIBIT 3-5 Raw Materials Record

Raw Materials Record

Item No.: HRM50812 **Description:** Heart rate monitor

	Received			Used				Balance		
Date	Units	Cost	Total	Requisition Number	Units	Cost	Total	Units	Cost	Total
11-25	100	$60	$6,000					100	$60	$6,000
11-30				#7235	70	$60	$4,200	30	$60	$1,800

According to the raw materials record pictured in Exhibit 3-5, only 30 heart rate monitors are currently in stock. However, the bill of materials shown in Exhibit 3-4 indicates that 50 heart rate monitors are needed for Job 603. Therefore, the purchasing department will need to buy 20 more monitors. The purchasing department also needs to consider other jobs that will be using heart rate monitors in the near future, as well as the time it takes to obtain the monitors from the company's suppliers. According to the production schedule, Job 603 is scheduled to begin production on December 2; therefore, the purchasing department needs to make sure all necessary raw materials are on hand by that date.

Life Fitness's purchasing department will issue a **purchase order** to its suppliers for the needed parts. For control purposes, incoming shipments of raw materials are counted and recorded on a **receiving report**, which is typically just a duplicate of the purchase order that does not list the quantity ordered. Life Fitness's accounting department will not pay the **invoice** (bill from the supplier) unless it agrees with the quantity of parts both ordered *and* received. By matching the purchase order, receiving report and invoice, Life Fitness ensures that it pays for only those parts that were ordered and received, *and nothing more.* This is an important control that helps companies avoid scams in which businesses are sent and billed for inventory that was not ordered.

The raw materials records also form the basis for valuing the Raw Materials Inventory account. On a given date, by adding together the balances in the individual raw materials records, the company is able to substantiate the total Raw Materials Inventory shown on the balance sheet. For example, as shown in Exhibit 3-6, on November 30, Life Fitness had $1,800 of heart rate monitors in stock, $24,000 of LCD entertainment screens, $1,200 of roller bases, and so forth. When combined, these individual balances sum to the Raw Materials Inventory balance shown on Life Fitness's November 30 balance sheet.

EXHIBIT 3-6 Individual Raw Materials Records Sum to the Raw Materials Inventory Balance

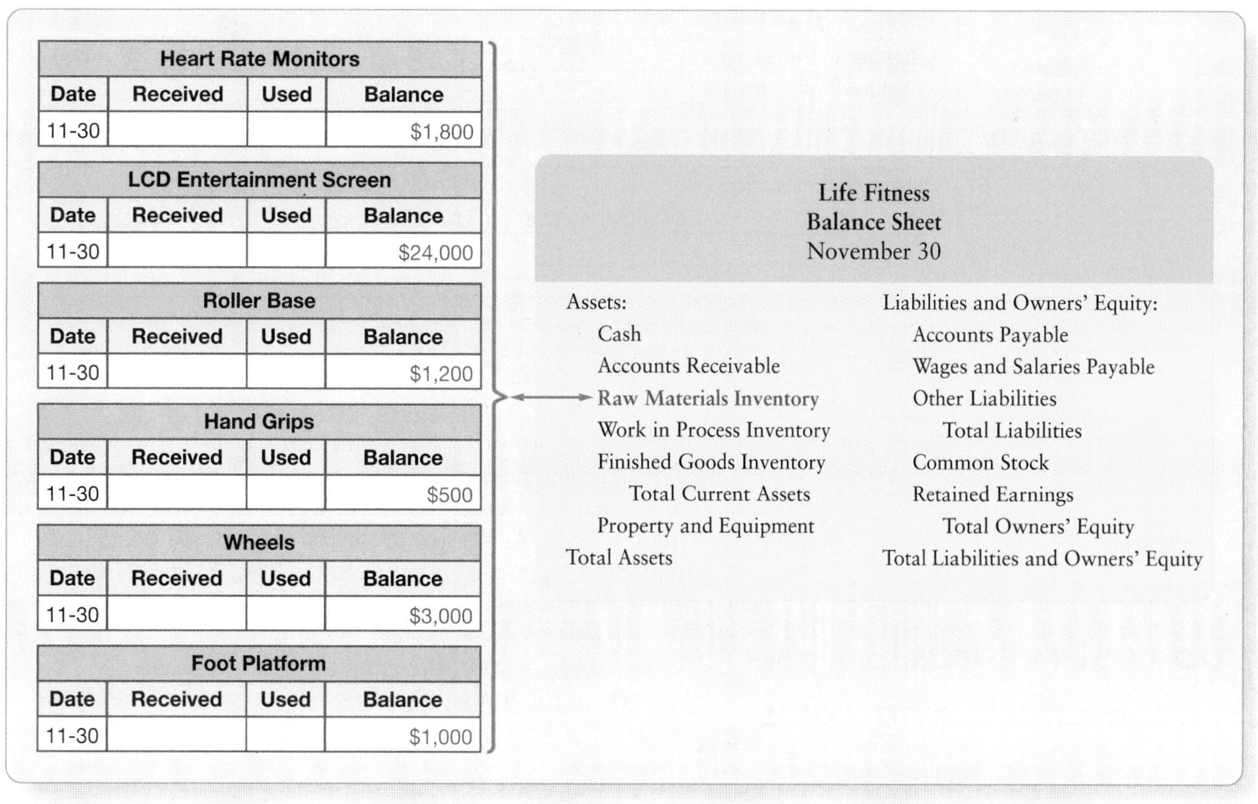

Using a Job Cost Record to Accumulate Job Costs

Once the necessary raw materials have arrived, and production is ready, Job 603 will be started. A **job cost record**, as pictured in Exhibit 3-7, will be used to accumulate all of the direct materials and direct labor used on the job, as well as the manufacturing overhead allocated to the job.

EXHIBIT 3-7 Job Cost Record

Job Cost Record

Job Number: 603

Customer: For stock

Job Description: 50 units of X4 Elliptical Cross-Trainers

Date Started: Dec. 2 **Date Completed:** ________

Manufacturing Cost Information:	**Cost Summary**
Direct Materials	$
Direct Labor	$
Manufacturing Overhead	$
Total Job Cost	$
Number of Units	÷ 50 units
Cost per Unit	$

Shipping Information:

Date	Quantity Shipped	Units Remaining	Cost Balance

Each job will have its own job cost record. Note that the job cost record is merely a form (electronic or hard copy) for keeping track of the three manufacturing costs associated with each job: direct materials, direct labor, and manufacturing overhead. As we saw in the last section, the individual raw materials records sum to the total Raw Materials Inventory shown on the balance sheet. Likewise, as shown in Exhibit 3-8, the job cost records on *incomplete* jobs sum to the total Work in Process Inventory shown on the balance sheet.

Why is this important?

"**Job cost records** keep track of **all manufacturing costs** assigned to **individual jobs** so that **managers** know how much it costs to **make** each product."

Once the job is complete, the job cost records serve as a basis for valuing Finished Goods Inventory. As shown near the bottom of Exhibit 3-7, job cost records typically listed the date and quantity of units shipped to customers, the number of units remaining in finished goods inventory, and the cost of those units. The balance of *unsold* units from *completed* job cost records sums to the total Finished Goods Inventory shown on the balance sheet.

EXHIBIT 3-8 Job Cost Records on Incomplete Jobs Sum to the WIP Inventory Balance

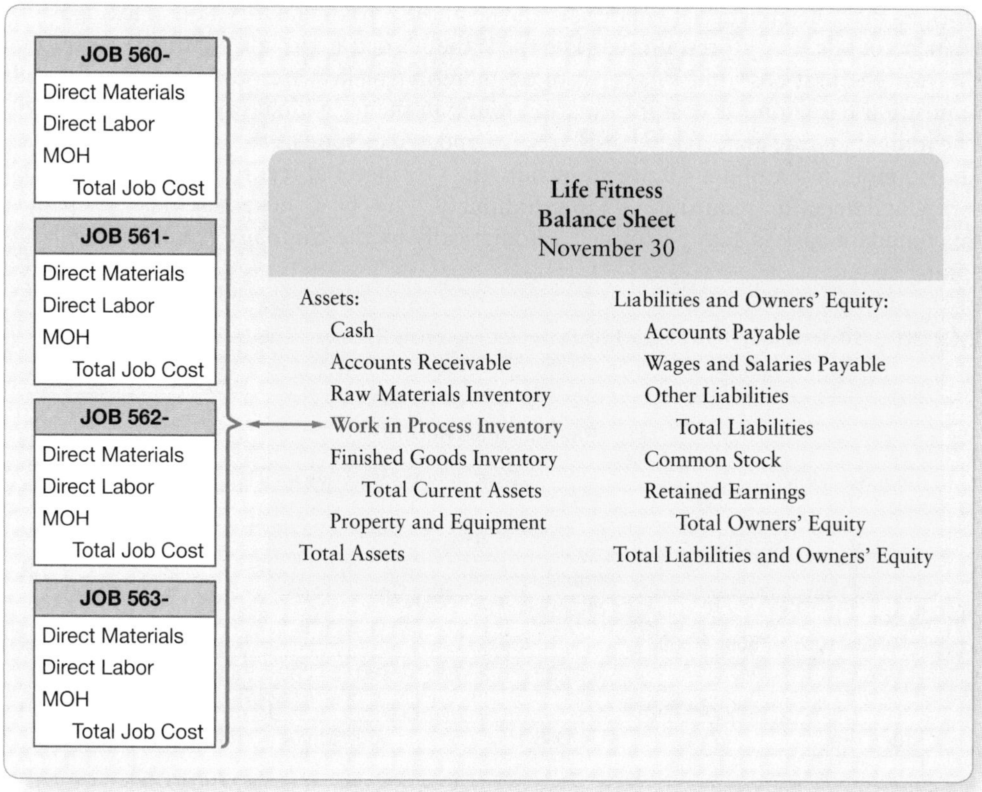

Tracing Direct Materials Cost to a Job

As you can see, the job cost records serve a vital role in a job costing system. Now let's take a look at how Life Fitness accumulates manufacturing costs on the job cost record. We'll begin by looking at how direct material costs are traced to individual jobs.

Once production is ready to begin Job 603, it will need many of the parts shown on the bill of materials (Exhibit 3-4). According to the production schedule (Exhibit 3-3) this job is scheduled to take five days to complete, so the production crew may not want all of the raw materials at once. Each time production needs some raw materials, it will fill out a <u>materials requisition</u>. As shown in Exhibit 3-9, the materials requisition is a form itemizing the raw materials currently needed from the storeroom. Again, this is normally an electronic form, but we show the hard copy here.

EXHIBIT 3-9 Materials Requisition

Materials Requisition

Date: 12/2 **Number: #7568**

Job: 603

Part Number	Description	Quantity	Unit Cost	Amount
HRM50812	Heart rate monitor	50	$60	$3,000
LCD620	LCD entertainment screen	50	$100	5,000
B4906	Front and rear rolling base	100	$5	500
	Total			**$8,500**

As soon as the materials requisition is received by the raw materials storeroom, workers **pick** the appropriate materials and send them to the factory floor. Picking is just what it sounds like: storeroom workers pick the needed materials off of the storeroom shelves. The unit cost and total cost of all materials picked are posted to the materials requisition based on the cost information found in the individual raw materials records. The individual raw materials records are also updated as soon as the materials are picked. For example, in Exhibit 3-10, we show how the raw material record for heart rate monitors is updated after requisition #7568 (Exhibit 3-9) has been picked. In most companies, this mundane task is now performed automatically by the company's computerized bar-coding system.

EXHIBIT 3-10 Raw Materials Record Updated for Materials Received and Used

Raw Materials Record

Item No.: HRM50812 **Description:** Heart rate monitor

	Received			Used				Balance		
Date	**Units**	**Cost**	**Total**	**Requisition Number**	**Units**	**Cost**	**Total**	**Units**	**Cost**	**Total**
11-25	100	$60	$6,000					100	$60	$6,000
11-30				#7235	70	$60	$4,200	30	$60	$1,800
12-1	75	$60	$4,500					105	$60	$6,300
12-2				#7568	50	$60	$3,000	55	$60	$3,300

Finally, the raw materials requisitioned for the job are posted to the job cost record. As shown in Exhibit 3-11, each time raw materials are requisitioned for Job 603, they are posted to the direct materials section of the job cost record. They are considered direct materials (rather than indirect materials), since they can be traced specifically to Job 603. By using this system to trace direct materials to specific jobs, managers know *exactly* how much direct material cost is incurred by each job.

Tracing Direct Labor Cost to a Job

Now let's look at how direct labor costs are traced to individual jobs. All direct laborers in the factory fill out **labor time records**. As shown in Exhibit 3-12, a labor time record simply records the time spent by each employee on each job he or she worked on throughout the day. Often times, these records are kept electronically. Rather than using old-fashioned time tickets and punch clocks, factory workers now "swipe" their bar-coded employee identification cards on a computer terminal and enter the appropriate job number. Based on the employee's unique hourly wage rate, the computer calculates the direct labor cost to be charged to the job.

For example, in Exhibit 3-12, we see that Hannah Smith, who is paid a wage rate of $20 per hour, worked on both Jobs 602 and 603 during the week. Hannah spent five hours working on Job 603 on December 2. Therefore, $100 of direct labor cost ($20 × 5) will be charged to Job 603 for Hannah's work on that date. On December 3, Hannah's eight hours of work on Job 603 resulted in another $160 ($20 × 8) of direct labor being charged to the job. The cost of each direct laborer's time will be computed

EXHIBIT 3-11 Posting Direct Materials Used to the Job Cost Record

Job Cost Record

Job Number: 603

Customer: For stock

Job Description: 50 units of X4 Elliptical Cross-Trainers

Date Started: Dec. 2 **Date Completed:**

Manufacturing Cost Information:	Cost Summary
Direct Materials Req. #7568: $ 8,500 (shown in Exhibit 3-9) Req. #7580: $14,000 Req. #7595: $13,500 Req. #7601: $ 4,000	$ 40,000
Direct Labor	$
Manufacturing Overhead	$
Total Job Cost	$
Number of Units	÷ 50 units
Cost per Unit	$

EXHIBIT 3-12 Labor Time Record

Labor Time Record

Employee: Hannah Smith **Week:** 12/2 – 12/9

Hourly Wage Rate: $20 **Record #:** 324

Date	Job Number	Start Time	End Time	Hours	Cost
12/2	602	8:00	11:00	3	$60
12/2	603	12:00	5:00	5	$100
12/3	603	8:00	4:00	8	$160
12/4 etc.					

using each employee's unique wage rate, just as was done with Hannah Smith's time. Then, as shown in Exhibit 3-13 (on the next page), the information from the individual labor time records is posted to the direct labor section of the job cost record. Again, this posting is normally done automatically by the company's computer system.

As you can see, by tracing direct labor cost in this fashion, jobs are charged only for the direct labor actually incurred in producing the job.

What about employee benefits, such as employee-sponsored retirement plans, health insurance, payroll taxes, and other benefits? As discussed in Chapter 2, these payroll-related benefits often add another 30% or more to the cost of gross wages and salaries. Some companies factor, or load, these costs into the hourly wage rate charged to the

EXHIBIT 3-13 Posting Direct Labor Used to the Job Cost Record

Job Cost Record

Job Number: 603

Customer: For stock

Job Description: 50 units of X4 Elliptical Cross-Trainers

Date Started: Dec. 2 **Date Completed:**

Manufacturing Cost Information:	Cost Summary
Direct Materials Req. #7568: $ 8,500 Req. #7580: $14,000 Req. #7595: $13,500 Req. #7601: $ 4,000	$ 40,000
Direct Labor No. #324 (30 hours): $100, $160, etc. (shown in Exhibit 3-12) No. #327 (40 hours): $240, $240, etc. No. #333 (36 hours): $100, $120, etc. Etc. (a total of 500 direct labor hours)	$ 10,000
Manufacturing Overhead	$
Total Job Cost	$
Number of Units	÷ 50 units
Cost per Unit	$

jobs. For example, if a factory worker earns a wage rate of $10 per hour, the job cost records would show a loaded hourly rate of about $13 per hour, which would include all benefits associated with employing the worker. However, since coming up with an *accurate* loaded hourly rate such as this is difficult, many companies treat these extra payroll-related costs as part of manufacturing overhead, rather than loading these costs into the direct labor wage rates. We'll talk about how all manufacturing overhead costs are handled in the next section.

Allocating Manufacturing Overhead to a Job

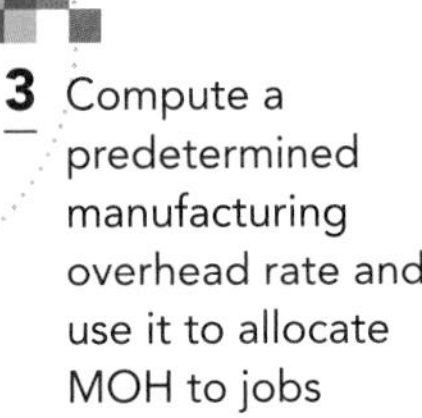

3 Compute a predetermined manufacturing overhead rate and use it to allocate MOH to jobs

So far we have traced the direct materials and direct labor costs to Job 603. Recall, however, that Life Fitness incurs many other manufacturing costs that cannot be directly traced to specific jobs. These indirect manufacturing costs, otherwise known as manufacturing overhead, include depreciation on the factory plant and equipment, utilities to run the plant, property taxes and insurance on plant, equipment maintenance, the salaries of plant janitors and supervisors, machine lubricants, and so forth. Because of the nature of these costs, we cannot tell exactly how much of these costs are attributable to producing a specific job. Therefore, we cannot trace these costs to jobs, as we did with direct materials and direct labor. Rather, we will have to allocate some reasonable amount of these costs to each job. Why bother? Generally accepted accounting principles (GAAP) mandate that manufacturing overhead *must* be treated as an inventoriable product cost for financial reporting purposes. The rationale is that these costs are a *necessary* part of the production process: Jobs could not be produced without incurring these costs. Let's now look at how companies allocate manufacturing overhead costs to jobs.

What Does Allocating Mean?

Allocating manufacturing overhead[2] to jobs simply means that we will be "splitting up" or "dividing" the total manufacturing overhead costs among the jobs we produced during the year. There are many different ways we could "split up" the total manufacturing overhead costs among jobs. For example, there are a number of different ways you could split up a pizza pie among friends: You could give equal portions to each friend, you could give larger portions to the largest friends, or you could give larger portions to the hungriest friends. All in all, you have a set amount of pizza, but you could come up with several different reasonable bases for splitting it among your friends (based on number of friends, size of friends, or hunger level of friends).

Likewise, a manufacturer has a total amount of manufacturing overhead that must be split among all of the jobs produced during the year. Since each job is unique in size and resource requirements, it wouldn't be fair to allocate an equal amount of manufacturing overhead to each job. Rather, management needs some other reasonable basis for splitting up the total manufacturing overhead costs among jobs. In this chapter, we'll discuss the most basic method of allocating manufacturing overhead to jobs. This method has traditionally been used by most manufacturers. However, more progressive companies are learning to use better, more accurate allocation systems, which we will discuss in Chapter 4. However, for now, we'll start with a basic allocation system.

Why is this important?

"Managers use the **Predetermined MOH rate** as a way to **'spread'** (allocate) **indirect** manufacturing costs, like factory utilities, **among all jobs** produced in the factory during the year."

Steps to Allocating Manufacturing Overhead

Manufacturers follow four steps to implement this basic allocation system. The first three steps are taken ***before the year begins:***

STEP 1: The company estimates its total manufacturing overhead costs for the coming year.

This is the total "pie" to be allocated. For Life Fitness, let's assume management estimates total manufacturing overhead costs for the year to be $1 million.

STEP 2: The company selects an allocation base and estimates the total amount that will be used during the year.

This is the *basis* management has chosen for "dividing up the pie." For Life Fitness, let's assume management has selected direct labor hours as the allocation base. Furthermore, management estimates that 62,500 of direct labor hours will be used during the year.

Ideally, the allocation base should be the cost driver of the manufacturing overhead costs. As the term implies, a cost driver is the primary factor that causes a cost. For example, in many companies, manufacturing overhead costs rise and fall with the amount of work performed in the factory. Because of this, most companies in the past have used either direct labor hours or direct labor cost as their allocation base. This information was also easy to gather from the labor time records or job cost records. However, for manufacturers who have automated much of their production process, machine hours is a more appropriate allocation base because the amount of time spent running the machines drives the utility, maintenance, and equipment depreciation costs in the factory. As you'll learn in Chapter 4, some companies even use multiple allocation bases to more accurately allocate manufacturing overhead costs to individual jobs. The important point is that the allocation base selected should bear a strong, positive relationship to the manufacturing overhead costs.

Accounting Simplified

Cost Drivers

If your instructor is using MyAccountingLab, go to the Multimedia Library for a quick video on this topic.

[2]The term "applying" manufacturing overhead is often used synonymously with "allocating" manufacturing overhead.

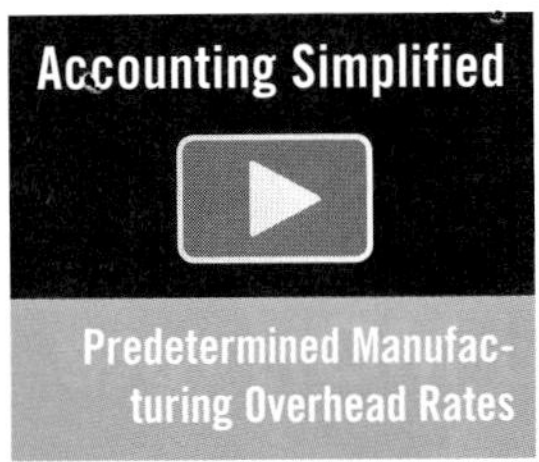

If your instructor is using MyAccountingLab, go to the Multimedia Library for a quick video on this topic.

STEP 3: The company calculates its *predetermined* manufacturing overhead (MOH) rate using the information estimated in Steps 1 and 2:

$$\text{Predetermined MOH rate} = \frac{\text{Total estimated manufacturing overhead costs}}{\text{Total estimated amount of the allocation base}}$$

For example, Life Fitness calculates its predetermined manufacturing overhead (MOH) rate as follows:

$$\text{Predetermined MOH rate} = \frac{\$1{,}000{,}000}{62{,}500 \text{ DL hours}} = \$16 \text{ per direct labor hour}$$

This rate will be used throughout the coming year. It is not revised, unless the company finds that either the manufacturing overhead costs or the total amount of the allocation base being used in the factory (direct labor hours for Life Fitness) have substantially shifted away from the estimated amounts. If this is the case, management might find it necessary to revise the rate part way through the year.

Why does the company use a *predetermined* MOH rate, based on *estimated or budgeted data*, rather than an actual MOH rate based on actual data for the year? In order to get actual data, the company would have to wait until the *end of the year* to set its MOH rate. By then, the information is too late to be useful for making pricing and other decisions related to individual jobs. Managers are willing to sacrifice some accuracy in order to get timely information on how much each job costs to produce.

Once the company has established its predetermined MOH rate, it uses that rate throughout the year to calculate the amount of manufacturing overhead to allocate to each job produced, as shown in Step 4.

STEP 4: The company allocates some manufacturing overhead to each individual job as follows:

$$\text{MOH allocated to a job} = \text{Predetermined MOH rate} \times \text{Actual amount of allocation base used by the job}$$

Let's see how this works for Life Fitness's Job 603. Since the predetermined MOH rate is based on direct labor hours ($16 per DL hour), we'll need to know how many direct labor hours were used on Job 603. From Exhibit 3-13, we see that Job 603 required a total of 500 DL hours. This information was collected from the individual labor time records and summarized on the job cost record. Therefore, we calculate the amount of manufacturing overhead to be allocated to Job 603 as follows:

$$\begin{aligned}\text{MOH to be allocated to Job 603} &= \$16 \text{ per direct labor hour} \times 500 \text{ direct labor hours}\\ &= \$8{,}000\end{aligned}$$

The $8,000 of manufacturing overhead allocated to Job 603 is now posted to the job cost record, as shown in Exhibit 3-14.

EXHIBIT 3-14 Posting Manufacturing Overhead and Completing the Job Cost Record

Job Cost Record

Job Number: 603

Customer: For stock

Job Description: 50 units of X4 Elliptical Cross-Trainers

Date Started: Dec. 2 **Date Completed:** Dec. 6

Manufacturing Cost Information:	**Cost Summary**
Direct Materials	
Req. #7568: $ 8,500	
Req. #7580: $14,000	
Req. #7595: $13,500	
Req. #7601: $ 4,000	$ 40,000
Direct Labor	
No. #324 (30 DL hours): $100, $160, etc.	
No. #327 (40 DL hours): $240, $210, etc.	
No. #333 (36 DL hours): $80, $120, etc.	
Etc.	
(a total of 500 DL hours)	$ 10,000
Manufacturing Overhead	
$16/ DL hour × 500 DL hours = $8,000	$ 8,000
Total Job Cost	$ 58,000
Number of Units	÷ 50 units
Cost per Unit	$ 1,160

When is Manufacturing Overhead Allocated to Jobs?

The point in time at which manufacturing overhead is allocated to a job depends on the sophistication of the company's computer system. In most sophisticated systems, some manufacturing overhead is allocated to a job each time some of the allocation base is posted to the job cost record. In our Life Fitness example, every time an hour of direct labor is posted to a job, $16 of manufacturing overhead would also be posted to the same job. In less sophisticated systems, manufacturing overhead is allocated only once: as soon as the job is complete and the total amount of allocation base used by the job is known (as shown in Exhibit 3-14). However, if the balance sheet date (for example, December 31) arrives before the job is complete, Life Fitness would need to allocate some manufacturing overhead to the job based on the number of direct labor hours used on the job thus far. Only by updating the job cost records will the company have the most accurate Work in Process Inventory on its balance sheet.

STOP & THINK

Assume Life Fitness's managers had chosen direct labor *cost* as its MOH allocation base, rather than direct labor *hours*. Furthermore, assume management estimated direct labor would cost \$1,200,000 for the year.

1. Assuming direct labor cost as the allocation base, calculate the company's predetermined MOH rate.
2. How much MOH would have been allocated to Job 603?

Answer:

1. Predetermined MOH rate $= \dfrac{\$1{,}000{,}000}{\$1{,}200{,}000 \text{ of DL cost}} = $ .8333 or 83.33% of direct labor cost

2. MOH allocated to Job 603 = 83.33% × \$10,000 direct labor cost (from Exhibit 3-14)
= \$8,333

Note that this allocation differs from that shown in Exhibit 3-14 (\$8,000). That's because the amount of MOH allocated to an individual job will depend upon the allocation base chosen by management. While there is no one "correct" allocation, the most *accurate* allocation occurs when the company uses the MOH cost driver as its allocation base.

Completing the Job Cost Record and Using it to Make Business Decisions

4 Determine the cost of a job and use it to make business decisions

As shown in Exhibit 3-14, now that all three manufacturing costs have been posted to the job cost record, Life Fitness can determine the total cost of manufacturing Job 603 (\$58,000) as well as the cost of producing each of the 50 identical units in the job (\$1,160 each). Let's look at a few ways this information is used by management.

REDUCING FUTURE JOB COSTS Management will use the job cost information to control costs. By examining the exact costs traced to the job, management might be able to determine ways of reducing the cost of similar jobs produced in the future. For example, are the heart rate monitors costing more than they did on previous jobs? Perhaps management can renegotiate its contract with its primary suppliers, or identify different suppliers that are willing to sell the parts more cheaply, without sacrificing quality.

What about direct labor costs? By examining the time spent by various workers on the job, management may be able to improve the efficiency of the process so that less production time is required. Management will also examine the hourly wage rates paid to the individuals who worked on the job to determine if less skilled, and therefore less costly workers could accomplish the same production tasks, freeing up the more highly skilled employees for more challenging work.

ASSESSING AND COMPARING THE PROFITABILITY OF EACH MODEL Management will also use job cost information to determine the profitability of the various models. Assume the X4 Elliptical Cross-Trainer is listed on the company's website at a sales price of \$1,900. That means the company can expect the following gross profit on each unit sold:

Unit sales price	\$1,900
Unit cost (computed on job cost record in Exhibit 3-14)	1,160
Gross profit	\$ 740

This profit analysis shows that the company would generate a gross profit of $740 on each unit sold from this job. While this may seem fairly high, keep in mind that companies incur many operating costs, outside of its manufacturing costs, that must be covered by the gross profit earned by product sales. For example, in 2010, Life Fitness spent close to $17 million on research and development for its fitness equipment![3] Managers will compare the gross profit on this model to the gross profit of other models to determine which products to emphasize selling. Obviously, management will want to concentrate on marketing those models that yield the higher profit margins.

DEALING WITH PRICING PRESSURE FROM COMPETITORS Management can also use job cost information to determine how it will deal with pricing pressure. Say a competitor drops the price of its similar elliptical cross-trainer to $1,500. The profit analysis shows that Life Fitness could drop its sales price to $1,500 and still generate $340 of gross profit on the sale ($1,500 – $1,160). In fact, Life Fitness could *undercut* the competitors by charging less than $1,500 to generate additional sales and perhaps increase its market share.

ALLOWING DISCOUNTS ON HIGH-VOLUME SALES Often times, customers will expect discounts for high-volume sales. For example, say the City of Westlake wants to order 40 of these cross-trainers for the city's recreation center and has asked for a 25% volume discount off of the regular sales price. If Life Fitness won't agree to the discount, the city will take its business to the competitor. Can Life Fitness agree to this discount and still earn a profit on the sale? Let's see:

Discounted sales price (75% of $1,900)	$1,425
Unit cost (computed on job cost record in Exhibit 3-14)	1,160
Gross profit	$ 265

These calculations show that the discounted sales price will still be profitable. We'll talk more about special orders like this in Chapter 8.

BIDDING FOR CUSTOM ORDERS Management also uses product cost information to bid for custom orders. You may recall from the production schedule (Exhibit 3-3) that the Chicago Bears placed an order for 15 custom treadmills. Management can use the job cost records from past treadmill jobs to get a good idea of how much it will cost to complete the custom order. For example, the custom treadmills may require additional components not found on the standard models. Life Fitness will factor in these additional costs to get an estimate of the total job cost before it is produced. Life Fitness will most likely use <u>cost-plus pricing</u> to determine a sales price for the custom job. When companies use cost-plus pricing, they take the cost of the job (from the estimated or actual job cost record) and add a markup to help cover operating expenses and generate a profit:

Cost plus price = Cost + Markup on cost

Usually, the markup percentage or final bid price is agreed upon in a written contract before the company

Why is this important?

"Once managers know how much it **costs** to make a **job,** they use that **information** to do the following:

- Find **cheaper** ways of producing similar jobs in the future
- Determine which products are **most profitable**
- Establish prices for **custom-ordered** jobs."

[3]Brunswick Corp 2010 10-K filing. Life Fitness is a division of Brunswick Corporation.

goes ahead with production. Let's say the Bears have agreed to pay production cost plus a 40% markup. If the job cost record shows a total job cost of $25,000 for the 15 treadmills, then the sales price is calculated as follows:

$$\text{Cost-plus price} = \$25,000 + (40\% \times \$25,000)$$
$$= \$35,000$$

PREPARING THE FINANCIAL STATEMENTS Finally, the job cost information is critical to preparing the company's financial statements. Why? Because the information is used to figure out the total Cost of Goods Sold shown on the income statement, as well as the Work in Process and Finished Goods Inventory accounts shown on the balance sheet. Every time a cross-trainer from Job 603 is sold, its cost ($1,160) becomes part of the Cost of Goods Sold during the period. Likewise, every time a cross-trainer from the job is sold, the balance in Finished Goods Inventory is reduced by $1,160. As shown earlier (Exhibit 3-8), the cost-to-date of unfinished jobs remains in the company's Work in Process Inventory.

How Can Job Costing Information be Enhanced for Decision Making?

We have just finished developing a traditional job cost record and have seen how managers use the information to make vital business decisions. With the help of today's advanced information systems, the job cost information can be further enhanced to help managers make even more informed decisions. This section describes just a few of these enhancements.

Sustainability and Job Costing

Job cost records serve a vital role for manufacturers who embrace sustainability. Since job cost records contain information about the direct materials, direct labor, and manufacturing overhead assigned to each job, they capture the essential resources required to manufacture a product. The summary information on the job cost records can be enhanced to provide management with further information about how the product or production process may affect the environment, employees involved in the manufacturing process, future consumers of the product, and future disposal of the packaging materials and product itself.

For example, the direct materials section of the job cost record can be broken down into subcategories that provide management with useful environmental information. Categories might include:

See Exercise E3-20A and E3-36B

- material inputs that are post-consumer-use or recycled materials,
- toxic versus non-toxic materials,
- packaging materials that can be recycled or composted versus those that will end up in a landfill,
- materials sourced from local suppliers versus those sourced from geographically distant suppliers (thereby increasing the company's carbon footprint),
- materials that will become waste as a result of the production process,
- materials sourced from companies that embrace fair-labor practices and environmental sustainability, and,
- materials with heavy fossil-fuel footprints.

The job cost record could also reflect the percentage of the end product that can be recycled by the consumer.

Companies embracing sustainability will also need more information about the specific resources that are treated as manufacturing overhead costs, especially those that are related to energy and water consumption. To provide better information, the accounting system should contain multiple subsidiary MOH accounts based on the types of MOH incurred. For example, the company could separately track:

- the amount (and cost) of water used (reclaimed water versus potable water),
- electricity generated from coal-burning power plants versus wind turbines,
- the amount of fossil fuel used versus biofuels used to power forklifts and equipment, and
- costs related to emission control, wastewater, and garbage disposal.

Even property taxes, property insurance, and employee training costs may be affected by a company's journey towards sustainability. Only by separately measuring these costs will management have the information it needs to adequately weigh the costs and benefits associated with environmental and social responsibility initiatives.

To provide managers with better information from which to make decisions, job cost records could also contain a section estimating the future environmental costs associated with each job. For example, **Extended Producer Responsibility (EPR)** laws, more commonly known as "take-back" laws, may create future costs associated with each job. EPR laws, which have been passed in over 25 states as well as several European countries, require manufacturers of electronic devices (such as computers and televisions) to take back their products at the end of the products' useful life. For example, the Wisconsin E-waste Law requires electronics manufacturers to take back 80% of product they have produced (by weight) in the previous 3 years[4].

The goal of EPR laws is to reduce the amount of potentially dangerous e-waste (electronic waste) in landfills by shifting the end-of-life disposal cost back to the manufacturer. By bearing the disposal cost, manufacturers should be motivated to design greener products that are repairable, more easily recyclable, and have a longer life-cycle. In addition to state EPR laws, the federal government is also considering a bill which will restrict the export of toxic e-waste to developing nations. This bill, if passed, will not only help with environmental and public health issues caused by e-waste, but also create even more incentive for manufacturers and recyclers to find alternative uses for outdated electronic equipment.

Non-Manufacturing Costs

Job costing in manufacturing companies has traditionally focused on assigning only production-related costs (direct materials, direct labor and manufacturing overhead) to jobs. The focus on manufacturing costs arises because GAAP requires that *only* inventoriable product costs be treated as assets. Costs incurred in other elements of the value chain (period costs) are not assigned to products for external financial reporting, but instead, are treated as operating expenses.

Why is this important?

"**Job cost records** can provide managers with the detailed **environmental impact** information needed to develop **greener products** and manufacturing processes."

However, for setting long-term average sales prices and making other critical decisions, manufacturers must take into account the total costs of researching and developing, designing, producing, marketing, distributing, and providing customer service for new or existing products. In other words, *they want to know the total cost of the product across the entire value chain.* But how do managers figure this out?

The same principles of tracing direct costs and allocating indirect costs apply to all costs incurred in other elements of the value chain. Managers add these non-manufacturing costs to the inventoriable job costs to build the *total cost of the product across the entire value chain.* For example, say Life Fitness spent $2 million dollars designing and marketing

[4]http://www.computertakeback.com/legislation/state_legislation.htm

the X4 Elliptical Cross-Trainer. These costs are direct costs of the X4 Elliptical product line. On the other hand, the company may have spent $3 million researching basic technology for the video screen that is used on all of its products, making it an indirect cost of the X4 Elliptical, shared with other products that use the same video screen. Life Fitness may choose to add an additional cost section to its job cost record, indicating specific operating expenses associated with each job. By adding this information to the job cost record, managers have a more complete understanding of the total job costs, not just the job's manufacturing costs.

Keep in mind that these non-manufacturing costs are assigned to products *only* for internal decision making, never for external financial reporting because GAAP does not allow it. For financial reporting, non-manufacturing costs must *always* be expenses in the period in which they are incurred as operating expenses on the balance sheet.

Direct or Variable Costing

Even though the job cost records contain information about all three manufacturing costs, managers base certain decisions on just the direct costs (direct materials and labor) or variable costs found on a job cost record. Why? For two reasons: 1) The simple allocation of MOH that we have described in this chapter results in a fairly arbitrary amount of MOH being allocated to jobs, and 2) because many MOH costs are fixed in nature, and will not be affected as a result of producing a job. Later in the book, we'll see how management accountants have addressed these issues. In Chapter 4, we'll show how managers can improve the allocation system so that the amount of manufacturing overhead assigned to the job is much more accurate. In Chapters 6 and 8, we'll discuss how direct costing (or variable costing) can be used to address the role of fixed MOH costs in the decision making process.

Decision Guidelines

Job Costing

Life Fitness uses a job costing system that assigns manufacturing costs to each batch of exercise machines that it makes. These guidelines explain some of the decisions Life Fitness made in designing its costing system.

Decision	Guidelines
Should we use job costing or process costing?	Managers use the costing system that best fits their production environment. Job costing is best suited to manufacturers that produce unique, custom-built products or relatively small batches of different products, like Life Fitness. Process costing is best suited to manufacturers that mass produce identical units in a series of uniform production processes.
How do we determine the cost of manufacturing each job?	The exact amount of direct materials and direct labor can be traced to individual jobs using materials requisitions and labor time records. However, the exact amount of manufacturing overhead attributable to each job is unknown, and therefore *cannot* be traced to individual jobs. To deal with this issue, companies *allocate* some manufacturing overhead to each job.
Should we use a predetermined manufacturing overhead rate or the actual manufacturing overhead rate?	While it would be more accurate to use the actual manufacturing overhead rate, companies would have to wait until the end of the year to have that information. Most companies are willing to sacrifice some accuracy for the sake of having timely information that will help them make decisions throughout the year. Therefore, most companies use a predetermined overhead rate to allocate manufacturing overhead to jobs as they are produced throughout the year.
How do we calculate the predetermined MOH rate?	$\text{Predetermined MOH rate} = \dfrac{\text{Total estimated manufacturing overhead cost}}{\text{Total estimated amount of the allocation base}}$
What allocation base should we use for allocating manufacturing overhead?	If possible, companies should use the cost driver of manufacturing overhead as the allocation base. The most common allocation bases are direct labor hours, direct labor cost, and machine hours. Some companies use multiple bases in order to more accurately allocate MOH. This topic will be covered in Chapter 4.
How should we allocate manufacturing overhead to individual jobs?	The MOH allocated to a job is calculated as follows: $= \text{Predetermined MOH rate} \times \text{Actual amount of allocation base used by the job}$
Can job cost records help companies in their journey towards sustainability?	Job cost records can be enhanced to provide more detail about the environmental impact of the resources used on the job. Managers can use this information to determine how their product, or production process, can become greener.
Can manufacturers also allocate operating expenses to jobs?	Operating expenses can also be assigned to jobs, but *only* for *internal decision making* purposes. Operating expenses are *never* assigned to jobs for external financial reporting purposes. Direct operating costs would be traced to jobs (such as the sales commission on a particular job or the design costs related to a particular job) while indirect operating cost (such as the R&D costs associated with several product lines) would be allocated to jobs.

SUMMARY PROBLEM 1

E-Z-Boy Furniture makes sofas, loveseats, and recliners. The company allocates manufacturing overhead based on direct labor hours. E-Z-Boy estimated a total of $2 million of manufacturing overhead and 40,000 direct labor hours for the year.

Job 310 consists of a batch of 10 recliners. The company's records show that the following direct materials were requisitioned for Job 310:

Lumber: 10 units at $30 per unit

Padding: 20 yards at $20 per yard

Upholstery fabric: 60 yards at $25 per yard

Labor time records show the following employees (direct labor) worked on Job 310:

Jesse Slothower: 10 hours at $12 per hour

Becky Wilken: 15 hours at $18 per hour

Chip Lathrop: 12 hours at $15 per hour

Requirements

1. Compute the company's predetermined manufacturing overhead rate.
2. Compute the total amount of direct materials, direct labor, and manufacturing overhead that should be shown on Job 310's job cost record.
3. Compute the total cost of Job 310, as well as the cost of each recliner produced in Job 310.

SOLUTION

1. The predetermined MOH rate is calculated as follows:

$$\text{Predetermined MOH rate} = \frac{\text{Total estimated manufacturing overhead cost}}{\text{Total estimated amount of the allocation base}}$$

For E-Z-Boy:

$$\text{Predetermined MOH rate} = \frac{\$2{,}000{,}000}{40{,}000 \text{ direct labor hours}} = \$50 \text{ per direct labor hour}$$

2. The total amount of direct materials ($2,200) and direct labor ($570) incurred on Job 310 is determined from the materials requisitions and labor time records, as shown on the following job cost record. Since the job required 37 direct labor hours, we determine the amount of manufacturing overhead to allocate to the job is as follows:

$$\begin{aligned} &= \text{Predetermined MOH rate} \times \text{Actual amount of allocation base used by the job} \\ &= \$50 \text{ per direct labor hour} \times 37 \text{ direct labor hours used on Job 310} \\ &= \$1{,}850 \end{aligned}$$

These costs are summarized on the following job cost record:

Job Cost Record

Job Number: 310

Job Description: 10 recliners

Manufacturing Cost Information:	**Cost Summary**
Direct Materials	
Lumber: 10 units × \$30 = \$300	
Padding: 20 yards × \$20 = \$400	
Fabric: 60 yards × \$25 = \$1,500	\$ 2,200
Direct Labor	
Slothower: 10 hours × \$12 = \$120	
Wilken: 15 hours × \$18 = \$270	
Lathrop: 12 hours × \$15 = \$180	
Total hours: 37 hours	\$ 570
Manufacturing Overhead	
37 direct labor hours × \$50 = \$1,850	\$ 1,850
Total Job Cost	\$ 4,620
Number of Units	÷ 10 units
Cost per Unit	\$ 462

3. The direct materials (\$2,200), direct labor (\$570), and manufacturing overhead (\$1,850) sum to a total job cost of \$4,620. When the total job cost is averaged over the 10 recliners in the job, the cost per recliner is \$462.

How do Managers Deal with Underallocated or Overallocated Manufacturing Overhead?

5 Compute and dispose of overallocated or underallocated manufacturing overhead

In the first half of the chapter, we showed how managers find the cost of producing a job. Direct materials and direct labor were traced to each job using materials requisitions and labor time records, while manufacturing overhead was allocated to each job using a predetermined overhead rate. **At the end of the period, all manufacturers will have a problem to deal with; Invariably, they will have either underallocated manufacturing overhead or overallocated manufacturing overhead to the jobs worked on during the period.**

Recall that manufacturing overhead was allocated to jobs using a *predetermined rate* which was calculated using *estimates* of the company's total annual manufacturing costs and *estimates* of the total annual allocation base (such as direct labor hours). By the end of the period, the *actual* manufacturing overhead costs incurred by the company will be known, and no doubt, will differ from the total amount allocated to jobs during the period.

For example, suppose Life Fitness incurred the following *actual* manufacturing overhead costs during the month of December:

Manufacturing Overhead Incurred	Actual MOH Costs
Indirect materials used (janitorial supplies, machine lubricants, etc.)	$ 2,000
Indirect labor (janitors' and supervisors' wages, etc.)	13,000
Other indirect manufacturing costs	
(Plant utilities, depreciation, property taxes, and insurance etc.)	10,000
Total actual manufacturing overhead costs incurred	$25,000

Now let's look at the total amount of manufacturing overhead that was *allocated* to individual jobs during the month (using the predetermined manufacturing overhead rate of $16 per direct labor hour). For simplicity, we'll assume only two jobs were worked on during December.

Job	Amount of MOH Allocated to Job
603 (from Exhibit 3-14) ($16 per DL hour × 500 DL hours)	$ 8,000
604 (not shown) ($16 per DL hour × 1,000 DL hours)	16,000
Total MOH allocated to jobs ($16 per DL hour × 1,500 DL hours)	$24,000

Notice that we don't need to have the individual job cost records available to figure out the total amount of MOH allocated to jobs during the period. Rather, we could do the following calculation to arrive at the same $24,000 figure:

Total MOH allocated = Predetermined MOH rate × Actual *total* amount of allocation base used on all jobs
= $16 per DL hour × 1,500 direct labor hours
= $24,000 total MOH allocated to jobs during the period

To determine whether manufacturing overhead had been overallocated or underallocated, we simply compare the amount of MOH actually incurred during the period with the amount of MOH that was allocated to jobs during the same period. The difference between the *actual manufacturing overhead costs incurred* and the amount of manufacturing overhead *allocated to jobs* shows that Life Fitness *underallocated* manufacturing overhead by $1,000 during December:

Actual manufacturing overhead costs **incurred**	$25,000
Manufacturing overhead **allocated** to jobs	24,000
Underallocated manufacturing overhead	$ 1,000

Accounting Simplified

Manufacturing Overhead

If your instructor is using MyAccountingLab, go to the Multimedia Library for a quick video on this topic.

By underallocating manufacturing overhead, Life Fitness *did not allocate enough* manufacturing overhead cost to the jobs worked on during the period. In other words, the jobs worked on during the period should have had a total of $1,000 more manufacturing overhead cost allocated to them than the job cost records indicated. These jobs have been undercosted, as shown in Exhibit 3-15. If, on the other hand, a manufacturer finds that the amount of manufacturing overhead allocated to jobs is *greater* than the actual amount of manufacturing overhead incurred, we would say that manufacturing overhead had been overallocated, resulting in overcosting these jobs.

EXHIBIT 3-15 Underallocated Versus Overallocated Manufacturing Overhead

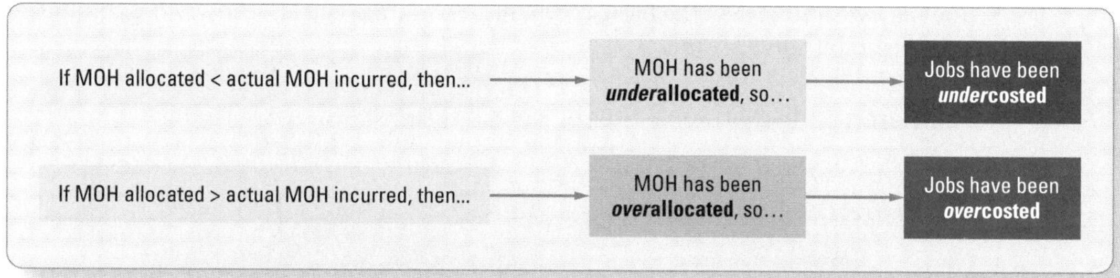

What do manufacturers do about this problem? *Assuming that the amount of under- or overallocation is immaterial, or that most of the inventory produced during the period has been sold*, manufacturers typically adjust the Cost of Goods Sold shown on the income statement for the total amount of the under- or overallocation. Why? Because the actual cost of producing these goods differed from what was initially reported on the job cost records. Since the job cost records were used as a basis for recording Cost of Goods Sold at the time the units were sold, the Cost of Goods Sold will be wrong unless it is adjusted. As shown in Exhibit 3-16, by increasing Cost of Goods Sold when manufacturing overhead has been underallocated, or by decreasing Cost of Goods Sold when manufacturing overhead has been overallocated, the company actually corrects the error that exists in Cost of Goods Sold.

EXHIBIT 3-16 Correcting Cost of Goods Sold for Underallocated or Overallocated MOH

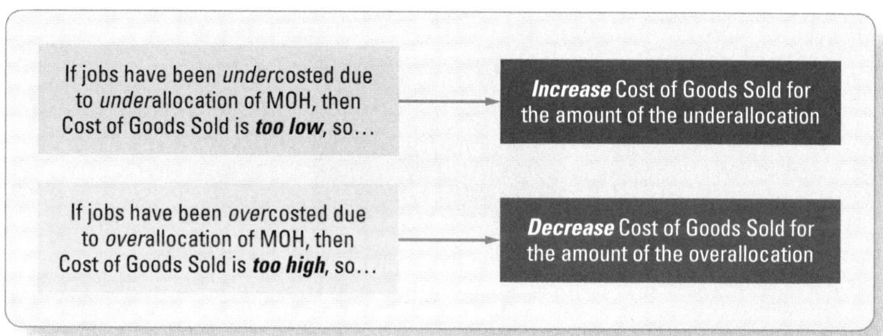

What if the amount of under- or overallocation is large, and the company has *not* sold almost all of the jobs it worked on during the period? Then the company will prorate the total amount of under- or overallocation among Work in Process Inventory, Finished Goods

Inventory, and Cost of Goods Sold based on the current status of the jobs worked on during the period. For example, if 30% of the jobs are still in Work in Process, 20% are still in Finished Goods, and 50% were sold, then the total amount of underallocation ($1,000 in the case of Life Fitness) would be roughly allocated as follows: 30% ($300) to Work in Process Inventory, 20% ($200) to Finished Goods Inventory, and 50% ($500) to Cost of Goods Sold. The exact procedure for prorating is covered in more advanced accounting textbooks.

What Journal Entries are Needed in a Manufacturer's Job Costing System?

6 Prepare the journal entries for a manufacturer's job costing system

Now that you know how manufacturers determine job costs and how those costs are used to make business decisions, let's look at how these costs are entered into the company's general ledger accounting system. We'll consider the journal entries needed to record the flow of costs through Life Fitness's accounts during the month of December. We'll use the same examples used earlier in the chapter. For the sake of simplicity, we'll continue to assume that Life Fitness only worked on two jobs during the month:

Job 603: 50 units of the X4 Elliptical Cross-Trainers

Job 604: 60 units of the T5 Treadmill

You may wish to review the basic mechanics of journal entries, shown in Exhibit 3-17, before we begin our discussion.

EXHIBIT 3-17 Review of Journal Entry and T-account Mechanics

Accounts Increased Through *Debits*:

- Assets (e.g., inventory)
- Expenses (e.g., rent expense)

Example:

WIP Inventory	
Debit	Credit
+	–

Accounts Increased Through *Credits*:

- Liabilities (e.g., wages payable)
- Revenue (e.g., sales revenue)
- Owners' Equity (e.g., retained earnings)

Example:

Wages Payable	
Debit	Credit
–	+

Additionally, keep in mind the flow of inventory that was first described in Exhibit 3-2. You may find this visual reminder helpful as we describe how the journal entries reflect the flow of inventory through the manufacturing system. Each arrow represents a journal entry that must be made to reflect activities that occur along the process: purchasing raw materials, using direct materials, using direct labor, recording actual MOH costs, allocating MOH to jobs, moving the jobs out of the factory after completion, and finally selling the units from a job.

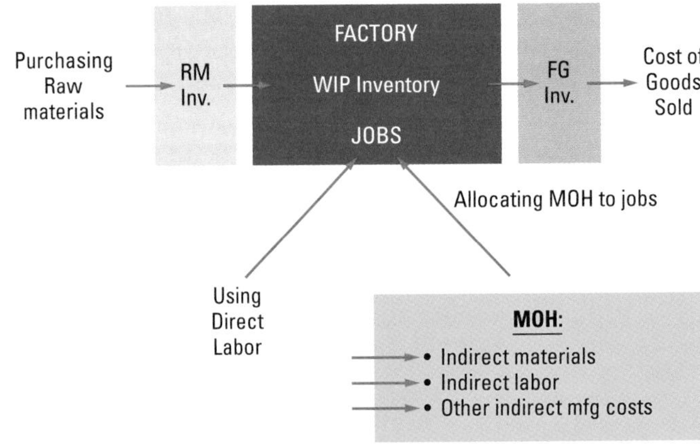

Purchase of Raw Materials

Life Fitness's purchase manager uses the bill of materials and raw materials records to determine what raw materials to purchase. Assume that Life Fitness ordered and received $90,000 of raw materials during December. Once the materials are received and verified against the purchase order and the invoice received from the supplier, the purchase is recorded as follows:

(1)	Raw Materials Inventory	90,000	
	Accounts Payable		90,000
	(to record purchases of raw materials)		

These materials will remain in the raw materials storeroom until they are needed for production. The liability in Accounts Payable will be removed when the supplier is paid.

Use of Direct Materials

Recall that direct materials are the primary physical components of the product. Each time production managers need particular direct materials for Jobs 603 and 604, they fill out a materials requisition informing the storeroom to pick the materials and send them into the manufacturing facility. Once these materials are sent into production, they become part of the work in process on Jobs 603 and 604, so their cost is added to the job cost records, as follows:

JOB 603: Cross-Trainers	
Direct Materials	$40,000
Direct Labor	
Manufacturing Overhead	
Total Job Cost	

JOB 604: Treadmills	
Direct Materials	$72,000
Direct Labor	
Manufacturing Overhead	
Total Job Cost	

From an accounting perspective, the cost of these materials must also be moved into Work in Process Inventory (through a debit) and out of Raw Materials Inventory (through a credit). The following journal entry is made:

(2)	Work in Process Inventory (40,000 + 72,000)	112,000	
	Raw Materials Inventory		112,000
	(to record the use of direct materials on jobs)		

Recall from the first half of the chapter that the individual job cost records form the underlying support for the Work in Process Inventory account shown on the Balance Sheet.[5] Therefore, the amount posted to the general ledger account ($112,000) must be identical to the sum of the amounts posted to the individual job cost records ($40,000 + $72,000 = $112,000).

Use of Indirect Materials

Indirect materials are materials used in the manufacturing plant that *cannot* be traced to individual jobs, and therefore are *not* recorded on any job cost record. Examples include janitorial supplies used in the factory and machine lubricants for the factory machines.

[5] The job cost records of unfinished jobs form the subsidiary ledger for the Work in Process Inventory account. Recall that a **subsidiary ledger** is simply the supporting detail for a general ledger account. Many other general ledger accounts (such as Accounts Receivable, Accounts Payable, and Plant & Equipment) also have subsidiary ledgers. The raw material inventory records form the subsidiary ledger for the Raw Materials Inventory account, while the job cost records on completed, unsold jobs form the subsidiary ledger for the Finished Goods Inventory account.

Once again, materials requisitions inform the raw materials storeroom to release these materials. However, instead of becoming part of the Work in Process for a particular job, the indirect materials used in the factory ($2,000) become part of the Manufacturing Overhead account. Therefore, the Manufacturing Overhead account is debited (to increase the account) and Raw Materials Inventory is credited (to decrease the account) as follows:

(3)	Manufacturing Overhead	2,000	
	Raw Materials Inventory		2,000
	(to record the use of indirect materials in the factory)		

All indirect manufacturing costs, including indirect materials, indirect labor, and other indirect manufacturing costs (such as plant insurance and depreciation) are accumulated in the Manufacturing Overhead account. The Manufacturing Overhead account is a temporary account used to "store" or "pool" indirect manufacturing costs until those costs can be allocated to individual jobs.

We can summarize the flow of materials costs through the T-accounts as follows:

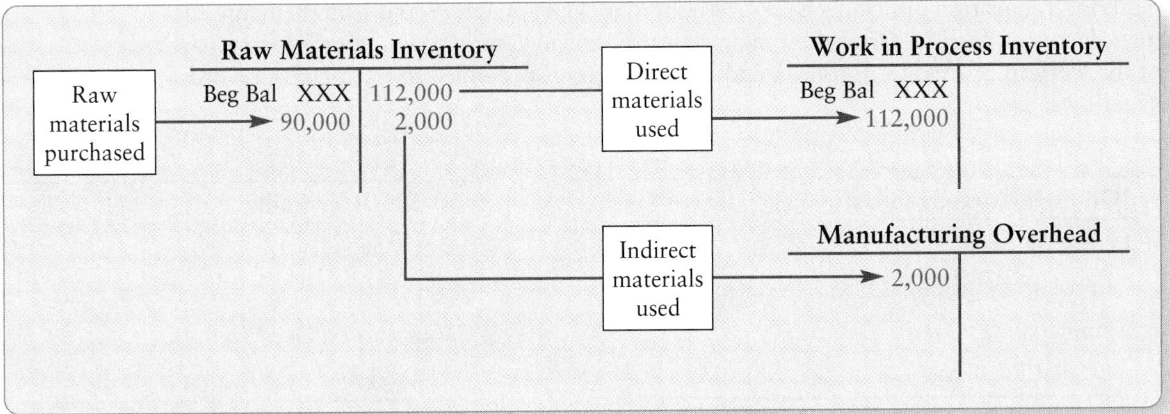

Use of Direct Labor

The labor time records of individual factory workers are used to determine exactly how much time was spent directly working on Jobs 603 and 604. The cost of this direct labor is entered on the job cost records, as shown:

JOB 603: Cross-Trainers	
Direct Materials	$40,000
Direct Labor	$10,000
Manufacturing Overhead	
Total Job Cost	

JOB 604: Treadmills	
Direct Materials	$72,000
Direct Labor	$20,000
Manufacturing Overhead	
Total Job Cost	

Again, since the job cost records form the underlying support for Work in Process Inventory, an identical amount ($10,000 + $20,000 = $30,000) must be debited to the Work in Process Inventory account. Wages Payable is credited to show that the company has a liability to pay its factory workers.

(4)	Work in Process Inventory ($10,000 + $20,000)	30,000	
	Wages Payable		30,000
	(to record the use of direct labor on jobs)		

The Wages Payable liability will be removed on payday when the workers receive their paychecks.

Use of Indirect Labor

Recall that indirect labor consists of the salary, wages, and benefits of all factory workers that are *not* directly working on individual jobs. Examples include factory janitors, supervisors, and forklift operators. Since their time cannot be traced to particular jobs, the cost of employing these factory workers during the month ($13,000) cannot be posted to individual job cost records. Thus, we record the cost of indirect labor as part of Manufacturing Overhead, *not* Work in Process Inventory:

(5)		Manufacturing Overhead	13,000	
		Wages Payable		13,000
		(to record the use of indirect labor in the factory)		

Again, the Wages Payable liability will be removed on payday when the workers receive their paychecks.

We can summarize the flow of manufacturing labor costs through the T-accounts as follows:

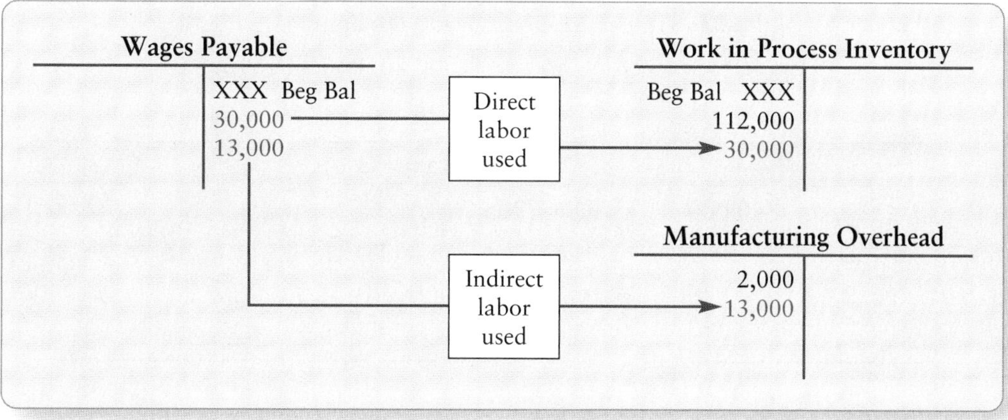

Incurring Other Manufacturing Overhead Costs

We have already recorded the indirect materials and indirect labor used in the factory during December by debiting the Manufacturing Overhead account. However, Life Fitness incurs other indirect manufacturing costs, such as plant utilities ($3,000), plant depreciation ($4,000), plant insurance ($1,000) and plant property taxes ($2,000) during the period. All of these other indirect costs of operating the manufacturing plant during the month are also accumulated in the Manufacturing Overhead account until they can be allocated to specific jobs:

(6)		Manufacturing Overhead	10,000	
		Accounts Payable *(for electric bill)*		3,000
		Accumulated Depreciation—Plant and Equipment		4,000
		Prepaid Plant Insurance *(for expiration of prepaid insurance)*		1,000
		Plant Property Taxes Payable *(for taxes to be paid)*		2,000
		(to record other indirect manufacturing costs incurred during the month)		

After recording all other indirect manufacturing costs, the Manufacturing Overhead account appears as follows:

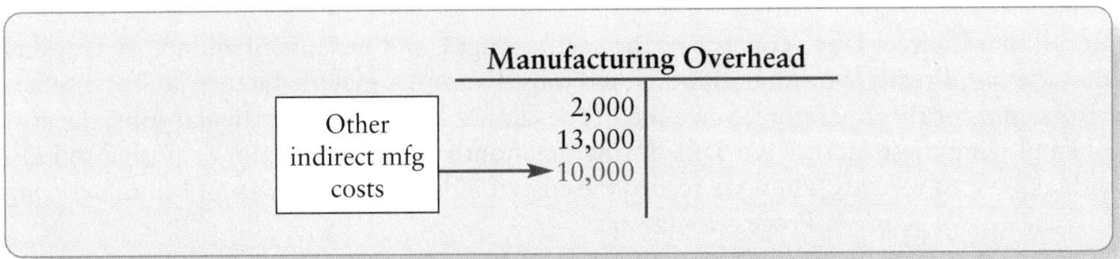

Allocating Manufacturing Overhead to Jobs

Life Fitness allocates some manufacturing overhead to each job worked on during the month using its predetermined manufacturing overhead rate, calculated in the first half of the chapter to be $16 per direct labor hour. The total direct labor hours used on each job is found on the labor time records, and is usually summarized on the job cost records. Assume Job 603 used 500 DL hours and Job 604 used 1,000 DL hours. Then the amount of manufacturing overhead allocated to each job is determined as follows:

Job 603: $16 per DL hour × 500 DL hours = $8,000
Job 604: $16 per DL hour × 1,000 DL hours = $16,000

JOB 603: Cross-Trainers	
Direct Materials	$40,000
Direct Labor (500 DL hrs)	10,000
Manufacturing Overhead	8,000
Total Job Cost	

JOB 604: Treadmills	
Direct Materials	$72,000
Direct Labor (1,000 DL hrs)	20,000
Manufacturing Overhead	16,000
Total Job Cost	

Again, since the job cost records form the underlying support for Work in Process Inventory, an identical amount ($8,000 + $16,000 = $24,000) must be debited to the Work in Process Inventory account. Since we accumulated all actual manufacturing overhead costs *into* an account called Manufacturing Overhead (through debiting the account), we now allocate manufacturing overhead costs *out* of the account by crediting it.

(7)		Work in Process Inventory ($8,000 + $16,000)	24,000	
		Manufacturing Overhead		24,000
		(to allocate manufacturing overhead to specific jobs)		

By looking at the Manufacturing Overhead T-account, you can see how actual manufacturing overhead costs are accumulated in the account through debits, while the amount of manufacturing overhead allocated to specific jobs is credited to the account:

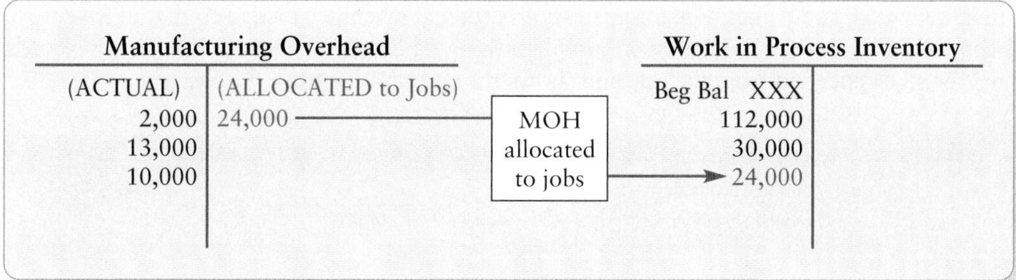

Completion of Jobs

Once the job has been completed, the three manufacturing costs shown on the job cost record are summed to find the total job cost. If the job consists of more than one unit, the total job cost is divided by the number of units to find the cost of each unit:

JOB 603: Cross-Trainers	
Direct Materials	$40,000
Direct Labor	10,000
Manufacturing Overhead	8,000
Total Job Cost	$58,000
Number of Units	÷ 50
Cost per Unit	$ 1,160

JOB 604: Treadmills	
Direct Materials	$ 72,000
Direct Labor	20,000
Manufacturing Overhead	16,000
Total Job Cost	$108,000
Number of Units	÷ 60
Cost per Unit	$ 1,800

The jobs are physically moved off of the plant floor and into the finished goods warehouse. Likewise, in the accounting records the jobs are moved out of Work in Process Inventory (through a credit) and into Finished Goods Inventory (through a debit):

(8)		Finished Goods Inventory (58,000 + 108,000)	166,000	
		Work in Process Inventory		166,000
		(to move the completed jobs out of the factory and into Finished Goods)		

The T-accounts show the movement of completed jobs off of the factory floor:

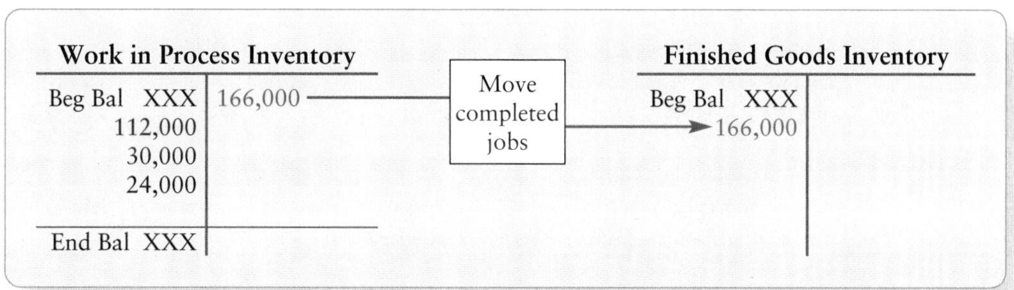

Sale of Units

For simplicity, let's assume that Life Fitness only had one sale during the month: It sold 40 cross-trainers from Job 603 and all 60 treadmills from Job 604 to the City of Westlake for its recreation centers. The sales price was $1,425 for each cross-trainer and $2,500 for each treadmill. Like most companies, Life Fitness uses a perpetual inventory system so that its inventory records are always up to date. Two journal entries are needed. The first journal entry records the revenue generated from the sale and shows the amount due from the customer:

(9)		Accounts Receivable (40 × $1,425) + (60 × $2,500)	207,000	
		Sales Revenue		207,000
		(to record the sale of 40 cross-trainers and 60 treadmills)		

The second journal entry reduces the company's Finished Goods Inventory, and records the Cost of Goods Sold. From the job cost record, we know that each cross-trainer produced in Job 603 cost $1,160 to make while each treadmill from Job 604 cost $1,800 to make. Therefore, the following entry is recorded:

(10)		Cost of Goods Sold (40 × $1,160) + (60 × $1,800)	154,400	
		Finished Goods Inventory		154,400
		(to reduce finished goods inventory and record cost of goods sold)		

The following T-accounts show the movement of the units out of Finished Goods Inventory and into Cost of Goods Sold:

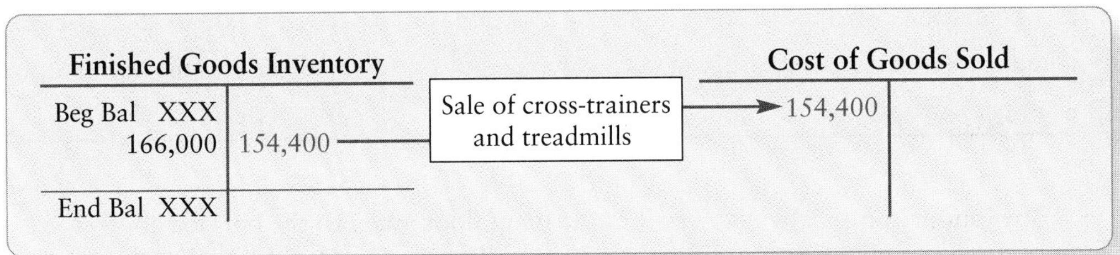

Operating Expenses

During the month, Life Fitness also incurred $32,700 of operating expenses to run its business. For example, Life Fitness incurred salaries and commissions ($20,000) for its sales people, office administrators, research and design staff, and customer service representatives. It also needs to pay rent ($3,300) for its office headquarters. The company also received a bill from its advertising agency for marketing expenses incurred during the month ($9,400). *All costs incurred outside of manufacturing function of the value chain* would be expensed in the current month as shown in the following journal entry.

(11)		Salaries and Commission Expense	20,000	
		Rent Expense	3,300	
		Marketing Expenses	9,400	
		Salaries and Commissions Payable		20,000
		Rent Payable		3,300
		Accounts Payable		9,400
		(to record all non-manufacturing costs incurred during the month)		

All non-manufacturing expenses will be shown as "operating expenses" on the company's income statement.

Closing Manufacturing Overhead

As a final step, Life Fitness must deal with the balance in the manufacturing overhead account. Since the company uses a *predetermined* manufacturing overhead rate to allocate manufacturing overhead to individual jobs, the total amount allocated to jobs will most likely differ from the amount of manufacturing overhead actually incurred.

Let's see how this plays out in the Manufacturing Overhead T-account:

1. All manufacturing overhead costs *incurred* by Life Fitness were recorded as *debits* to the Manufacturing Overhead account. These debits total $25,000 of actual manufacturing overhead incurred.
2. On the other hand, all manufacturing overhead *allocated* to specific jobs ($8,000 + $16,000) was recorded as *credits* to the Manufacturing Overhead account:

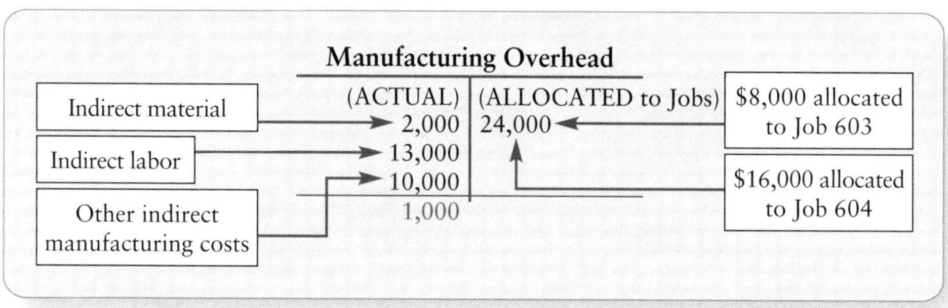

This leaves a debit balance of $1,000 in the Manufacturing Overhead account, which means that manufacturing overhead has been underallocated during the month. More manufacturing overhead costs were incurred than were allocated to jobs. Since Manufacturing Overhead is a temporary account not shown on any of the company's financial statements, it must be closed out (zeroed out) at the end of the period. Since most of the inventory produced during the period has been sold, Life Fitness will close the balance in Manufacturing Overhead to Cost of Goods Sold as follows:

(12)		Cost of Goods Sold	1,000	
		Manufacturing Overhead		1,000
		(to close the manufacturing overhead account)		

As a result of this entry, 1) the Manufacturing Overhead account now has a zero balance, and 2) the balance in Cost of Goods Sold has increased to correct for the fact that the jobs had been undercosted during the period.

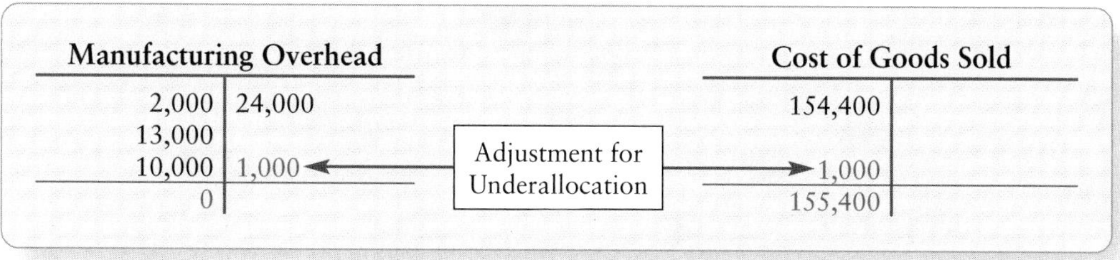

If, in some period, Life Fitness overallocates its overhead, the journal entry to close Manufacturing Overhead would be the opposite of that shown: Manufacturing Overhead would be debited to zero it out; and Cost of Goods Sold would be credited to reduce it as a result of having overcosted jobs during the period.

Now you have seen how all of the costs flow through Life Fitness's accounts during December. Exhibit 3-18 shows the company's income statement that resulted from all of the previously shown journal entries.

EXHIBIT 3-18 Income Statement After Adjusting for Underallocated Manufacturing Overhead

Life Fitness **Income Statement** December 31	
Sales Revenue	$207,000
Less: Cost of Goods Sold	155,400
Gross Profit	51,600
Less: Operating Expenses	32,700
Operating Income	$ 18,900

Decision Guidelines

Job Costing

The following decision guidelines describe the implications of over or underallocating manufacturing overhead, as well as other decisions that need to be made in a job costing environment.

Decision	Guidelines
How does overallocating or underallocating MOH affect the cost of jobs manufactured during the period?	If manufacturing overhead has been *underallocated*, it means that the jobs have been *undercosted* as a result. In other words, not enough manufacturing overhead cost was posted on the job cost records. On the other hand, if manufacturing overhead has been *overallocated*, it means that the jobs have been *overcosted*. Too much manufacturing overhead cost was posted on the job cost records.
What do we do about overallocated or underallocated manufacturing overhead?	Assuming most of the inventory produced during the period has been sold, manufacturers generally adjust the Cost of Goods Sold for the total amount of the under or overallocation. If a significant portion of the inventory is still on hand, then the adjustment will be prorated between WIP, Finished Goods, and Cost of Goods Sold.
How do we know whether to increase or decrease Cost of Goods Sold (CGS)?	If manufacturing overhead has been overallocated, then Cost of Goods Sold (CGS) is too high, and must be decreased through a credit to the CGS account. If manufacturing overhead has been underallocated, then Cost of Goods Sold is too low, and must be increased through a debit to the CGS account.
How does job costing work at a service firm (Appendix)?	Job costing at a service firm is very similar to job costing at a manufacturer. The main difference is that the company is allocating operating expenses, rather than manufacturing costs, to each client job. In addition, since there are no Inventory or Cost of Goods Sold accounts, no journal entries are needed to move costs through the system.

SUMMARY PROBLEM 2

Fashion Fabrics makes custom handbags and accessories for high-end clothing boutiques. Record summary journal entries for each of the following transactions that took place during the month of January, the *first* month of the fiscal year.

Requirements

1. $150,000 of raw materials were purchased on account.
2. During the month $140,000 of raw materials were requisitioned. Of this amount, $135,000 were traced to specific jobs, while the remaining materials were for general factory use.
3. Manufacturing labor (both direct and indirect) for the month totaled $80,000. It has not yet been paid. Of this amount, $60,000 was traced to specific jobs.
4. The company recorded $9,000 of depreciation on the plant building and machinery. In addition, $3,000 of prepaid property tax expired during the month. The company also received the plant utility bill for $6,000.
5. Manufacturing overhead was allocated to jobs using a predetermined manufacturing overhead rate of 75% of direct labor *cost*. (*Hint:* Total direct labor cost is found in Requirement 3.)
6. Several jobs were completed during the month. According to the job cost records these jobs cost $255,000 to manufacture.
7. Sales (all on credit) for the month totaled $340,000. According to the job cost records, the units sold cost $250,000 to manufacture. Assume the company uses a perpetual inventory system.
8. The company incurred operating expenses of $60,000 during the month. Assume that 80% of these were for marketing and administrative salaries and the other 20% were lease and utility bills related to the corporate headquarters.
9. In order to prepare its January financial statements, the company had to close its manufacturing overhead account.
10. Prepare the January income statement for Fashion Fabrics based on the transactions recorded in Requirements 1 through 9.

SOLUTION

1. $150,000 of raw materials were purchased on account.

	Raw Materials Inventory	150,000	
	Accounts Payable		150,000
	(to record purchases of raw materials)		

2. During the month $140,000 of raw materials were requisitioned. Of this amount, $135,000 were traced to specific jobs, while the remaining materials were for general factory use.

	Work in Process Inventory	135,000	
	Manufacturing Overhead	5,000	
	Raw Materials Inventory		140,000
	(to record the use of direct materials and indirect materials)		

3. Manufacturing labor (both direct and indirect) for the month totaled $80,000. It has not yet been paid. Of this amount, $60,000 was traced to specific jobs.

	Work in Process Inventory (*for direct labor*)	60,000	
	Manufacturing Overhead (*for indirect labor*)	20,000	
	Wages Payable		80,000
	(*to record the use of direct labor and indirect labor*)		

4. The company recorded $9,000 of depreciation on the plant building and machinery. In addition, $3,000 of prepaid property tax expired during the month. The company also received the plant utility bill for $6,000.

	Manufacturing Overhead	18,000	
	Accumulated Depreciation—Plant and Equipment		9,000
	Prepaid Plant Property Tax (*for expiration of property tax*)		3,000
	Accounts Payable (*for electric bill*)		6,000
	(*to record other indirect manufacturing costs incurred during the month*)		

5. Manufacturing overhead was allocated to jobs using a predetermined manufacturing overhead rate of 75% of direct labor cost. (*Hint:* Total direct labor cost is found in Requirement 3.)

	Work in Process Inventory (75% × $60,000 of direct labor)	45,000	
	Manufacturing Overhead		45,000
	(*to allocate manufacturing overhead to jobs*)		

6. Several jobs were completed during the month. According to the job cost records these jobs cost $255,000 to manufacture.

	Finished Goods Inventory	255,000	
	Work in Process Inventory		255,000
	(*to move the completed jobs out of the factory and into Finished Goods*)		

7. Sales (all on credit) for the month totaled $340,000. According to the job cost records, the units sold cost $250,000 to manufacture. Assume the company uses a perpetual inventory system.

	Accounts Receivable	340,000	
	Sales Revenue		340,000
	(*to record the sales and receivables*)		

	Cost of Goods Sold	250,000	
	Finished Goods Inventory		250,000
	(to reduce finished goods inventory and record cost of goods sold)		

8. The company incurred operating expenses of $60,000 during the month. Assume that 80% of these were for marketing and administrative salaries and the other 20% were lease and utility bills related to the corporate headquarters.

	Salaries Expense	48,000	
	Lease and Utilities Expense	12,000	
	Salaries and Wages Payable		48,000
	Accounts Payable		12,000
	(to record all non-manufacturing costs incurred during the month)		

9. In order to prepare its January financial statements, the company had to close its manufacturing overhead account.
An analysis of the manufacturing overhead account *prior to closing* shows the following:

Manufacturing Overhead

(ACTUAL)	(ALLOCATED)
5,000	45,000
20,000	
18,000	
	2,000

	Manufacturing Overhead	2,000	
	Cost of Goods Sold		2,000
	(to close the manufacturing overhead account to CGS)		

10. Prepare the January income statement for Fashion Fabrics based on the transactions recorded in Requirements 1 through 9.

Fashion Fabrics
Income Statement
January 31

Sales Revenue	$340,000
Less: Cost of Goods Sold**	248,000
Gross Profit	92,000
Less: Operating Expenses	60,000
Operating Income	$ 32,000

(** $250,000 − $2,000 closing adjustment)

Appendix 3A

How do Service Firms Use Job Costing to Determine the Amount to Bill Clients?

7 Use job costing at a service firm as a basis for billing clients

So far in this chapter we have illustrated job costing in a manufacturing environment. However, job costing is also used by service firms (such as law firms, accounting firms, marketing firms, and consulting firms) and by tradespeople (such as plumbers, electricians, and auto mechanics). At these firms, the work performed for each individual client is considered a separate job. Service firms need to keep track of job costs so that they have a basis for billing their clients. As shown in Exhibit 3-19, the direct costs of serving the client are traced to the job, whereas the indirect costs of serving the client are allocated to the job.

EXHIBIT 3-19 Assigning Costs to Client Jobs

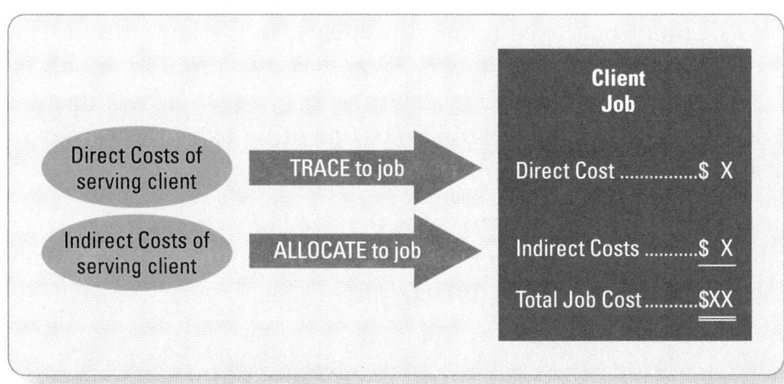

The amount billed to the client is determined by adding a profit markup to the total job cost. The main difference between job costing at a manufacturer and job costing at a service firm is that the indirect costs of serving the client are all *operating expenses*, rather than inventoriable product costs. In the next section, we will illustrate how job costing is used at Barnett & Associates law firm to determine how much to bill Client 367.

What Costs are Considered Direct Costs of Serving the Client?

The most significant direct cost at service firms is direct professional labor. In our example, direct professional labor is the attorney's time spent on clients' cases. Attorneys use labor time records to keep track of the amount of time they spend working on each client. Since most professionals are paid an annual salary rather than an hourly wage rate, firms estimate the hourly cost of employing their professionals based on the number of hours the professionals are expected to work on client jobs during the year. For example, say Attorney Theresa Fox is paid a salary of $100,000 per year. The law firm expects her to spend 2,000 hours a year performing legal work for clients (50 weeks × 40 hours per week). Therefore, for job costing purposes, the law firm converts her annual salary to an hourly cost rate as follows:

$$\frac{\$100{,}000 \text{ annual salary}}{2{,}000 \text{ hours per year}} = \$50 \text{ per hour}$$

If the labor time record indicates that Fox has spent 14 hours on Client 367, then the direct professional labor cost traced to the client is calculated as follows:

14 hours × \$50 per hour = \$700 of direct professional labor

At a law firm, very few other costs will be directly traceable to the client. Examples of other traceable costs might include travel and entertainment costs, or court filing fees related directly to specific clients. When tradespeople such as auto mechanics or plumbers use job costing, they trace their time to specific client jobs, just like attorneys do. In addition, they also trace the direct materials costs (such as the cost of new tires, an exhaust pipe, or garbage disposal) to the jobs on which those materials were used.

What Costs are Considered Indirect Costs of Serving the Client?

The law firm also incurs general operating costs, such as office rent, the salaries of office support staff, and office supplies. These are the indirect costs of serving *all* of the law firm's clients. These costs cannot be traced to specific clients, so the law firm will allocate these costs to client jobs using a *predetermined indirect cost allocation rate*. This is done using the same four basic steps as we used earlier in the chapter for a manufacturer. The only real difference is that we are allocating indirect operating expenses, rather than indirect manufacturing costs (manufacturing overhead).

STEP 1: Estimate the total indirect costs for the coming year.

Before the fiscal year begins, the law firm estimates the total indirect costs that will be incurred in the coming year:

Office rent	\$190,000
Office supplies, telephone, internet access, and copier lease	10,000
Office support staff	70,000
Maintaining and updating law library for case research	25,000
Advertising	3,000
Sponsorship of the symphony	2,000
Total indirect costs	\$300,000

STEP 2: Choose an allocation base and estimate the total amount that will be used during the year.

Next, the law firm chooses a cost allocation base. Service firms typically use professional labor hours as the cost allocation base. For example, Barnett & Associates estimates that attorneys will spend a total of 10,000 professional labor hours working on client jobs throughout the coming year.

STEP 3: Compute the predetermined indirect cost allocation rate.

The predetermined indirect cost allocation rate is found as follows:

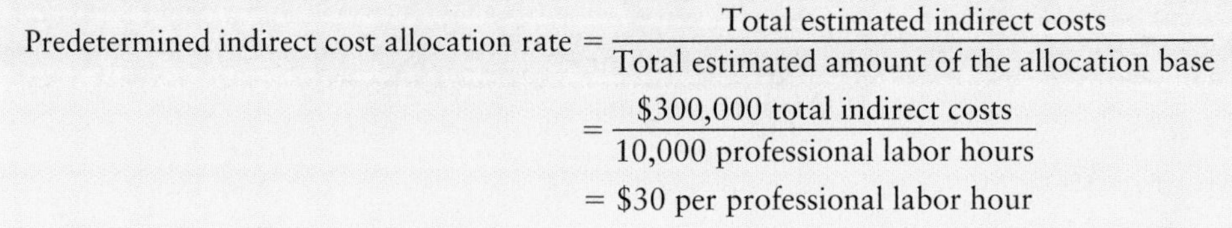

$$\text{Predetermined indirect cost allocation rate} = \frac{\text{Total estimated indirect costs}}{\text{Total estimated amount of the allocation base}}$$

$$= \frac{\$300{,}000 \text{ total indirect costs}}{10{,}000 \text{ professional labor hours}}$$

$$= \$30 \text{ per professional labor hour}$$

STEP 4: Allocate indirect costs to client jobs using the predetermined rate.

Throughout the year, indirect costs are allocated to individual client jobs using the predetermined indirect cost allocation rate. For example, assume Theresa Fox was the only attorney who worked on Client 367. Since Fox spent 14 hours working on Client 367, the amount of indirect cost allocated to the job is computed as follows:

= Predetermined indirect cost allocation rate × Actual amount of allocation base used by the job
= \$30 per professional labor hour × 14 professional labor hours
= \$420

Finding the Total Cost of the Job and Adding a Profit Markup

Barnett & Associates can now determine the total cost of serving Client 367:

Direct costs traced to Client 367 (\$50 per hour × 14 hours)	\$ 700
Indirect costs allocated to Client 367 (\$30 per hour × 14 hour)	420
Total cost of serving Client 367	\$1,120

Once the total job cost is known, Barnett & Associates can determine the amount to bill the client. Let's assume that Barnett & Associates wants to achieve a 25% profit over its costs. To achieve this profit, Barnett would bill Client 367 as follows:

Job cost + Markup for Profit = Amount to bill the client
\$1,120 + (25% × \$1,120) = \$1,400

Invoicing the Client Using a Professional Billing Rate

When service firms and tradespeople bill their clients, they rarely show the actual direct costs of providing the service, the allocation of indirect costs, or the profit they earned on the job. Rather, these figures are "hidden" from the client's view. How is this done? By incorporating these costs and profit components in the labor rate, often known as the **billing rate**, charged to the customer. Consider the last time you had your vehicle repaired. A typical mechanic billing rate exceeds \$48 per hour, yet the mechanic employed by the auto repair shop does not actually earn a \$48 per hour wage rate.

Why is this important?

"**Service** companies (such as **law firms**) and **tradespeople** (such as auto mechanics and plumbers) use **job costing** to determine how much to **bill** their clients."

Let's look at the calculations a service firm performs "behind the scenes" to determine its hourly billing rates. Barnett & Associates determines Theresa Fox's billing rate as follows:

Professional labor cost per hour	\$ 50
Plus: Indirect cost allocation rate per hour	30
Total hourly cost	\$ 80
Multiplied by the 25% profit markup	× 1.25
Hourly billing rate for Theresa Fox	\$100

Whenever Theresa Fox performs legal work for a client, her time will be billed at $100 per hour. Remember, this is the *price* Barnett & Associates charges its clients for any work performed by Theresa Fox. The actual invoice to Client 367 would look similar to Exhibit 3-20.

EXHIBIT 3-20 Invoice to Client

Barnett & Associates Law Firm
Invoice: Client 367

Work performed the week of July 23: Researching and filing patent application

Attorney Theresa Fox: 14 hours × $100 hourly billing rate $1,400

What Journal Entries are Needed in a Service Firm's Job Costing System?

The journal entries required for job costing at a service firm are much simpler than those used at a manufacturing company. That's because service firms typically have no inventory; hence, there is no need to record the movement of inventory through the system. Rather, all costs at a service company are treated as period costs, meaning they are immediately recorded as operating expenses when they are incurred (for example, salaries expense, rent expense, telephone expense, supplies expense, and so forth). The tracing of direct costs and allocation of indirect costs is performed *only* on the client's job cost record; *not* through journal entries to the company's general ledger.

END OF CHAPTER

Learning Objectives

- 1 Distinguish between job costing and process costing
- 2 Understand the flow of production and how direct materials and direct labor are traced to jobs
- 3 Compute a predetermined manufacturing overhead rate and use it to allocate MOH to jobs
- 4 Determine the cost of a job and use it to make business decisions
- 5 Compute and dispose of overallocated or underallocated manufacturing overhead
- 6 Prepare journal entries for a manufacturer's job costing system
- 7 (Appendix) Use job costing at a service firm as a basis for billing clients

Accounting Vocabulary

Bill of Materials. (p. 108) A list of all of the raw materials needed to manufacture a job.

Billing Rate. (p. 143) The labor rate charged to the customer, which includes both cost and profit components.

Cost Driver. (p. 115) The primary factor that causes a cost.

Cost-Plus Pricing. (p. 119) A pricing approach in which the company adds a desired level of profit to the product's cost.

Job Cost Record. (p. 110) A written or electronic document that lists the direct materials, direct labor, and manufacturing overhead costs assigned to each individual job.

Job Costing. (p. 105) A system for assigning costs to products or services that differ in the amount of materials, labor, and overhead required. Typically used by manufacturers that produce unique, or custom-ordered products in small batches; also used by professional service firms.

Invoice. (p. 109) Bill from a supplier.

Labor Time Record. (p. 112) A written or electronic document that identifies the employee, the amount of time spent on a particular job, and the labor cost charged to a job.

Materials Requisition. (p. 111) A written or electronic document that requests specific materials be transferred from the raw materials inventory storeroom to the production floor.

Overallocated Manufacturing Overhead. (p. 126) The amount of manufacturing overhead allocated to jobs is more than the amount of manufacturing overhead costs actually incurred; results in jobs being overcosted.

Pick. (p. 112) Storeroom workers remove items from raw materials inventory that are needed by production.

Predetermined Manufacturing Overhead Rate. (p. 116) The rate used to allocate manufacturing overhead to individual jobs; calculated before the year begins as follows: total estimated manufacturing overhead costs divided by total estimated amount of allocation base.

Process Costing. (p. 104) A system for assigning costs to a large numbers of identical units that typically pass through a series of uniform production steps. Costs are averaged over the units produced such that each unit bears the same unit cost.

Production Schedule. (p. 107) A written or electronic document indicating the quantity and types of inventory that will be manufactured during a specified time frame.

Purchase Order. (p. 109) A written or electronic document authorizing the purchase of specific raw materials from a specific supplier.

Raw Materials Record. (p. 108) A written or electronic document listing the number and cost of all units used and received, and the balance currently in stock; a separate record is maintained for each type of raw material kept in stock.

Receiving Report. (p. 109) A written or electronic document listing the quantity and type of raw materials received in an incoming shipment; the report is typically a duplicate of the purchase order without the quantity prelisted on the form.

Stock Inventory. (p. 107) Products normally kept on hand in order to quickly fill customer orders.

Subsidiary Ledger. (p. 129) Supporting detail for a general ledger account.

Underallocated Manufacturing Overhead. (p. 126) The amount of manufacturing overhead allocated to jobs is less than the amount of manufacturing overhead costs actually incurred; this results in jobs being undercosted.

Quick Check

1. *(Learning Objective 1)* Which of the following companies would be most likely to use a job costing system rather than a process costing system?
   a. Steel manufacturer
   b. CPA firm
   c. Beverage bottler
   d. Paint manufacturer

2. *(Learning Objective 1)* Would an advertising agency use job or process costing? What about a paper mill?
   a. Advertising agency—job costing
   Paper mill—job costing
   b. Advertising agency—process costing
   Paper mill—process costing
   c. Advertising agency—process costing
   Paper mill—job costing
   d. Advertising agency—job costing
   Paper mill—process costing

3. *(Learning Objective 2)* In a job costing system, all of the following statements about materials are correct *except* for which of the following?
   a. A materials requisition is used to request materials needed from the storeroom.
   b. The job cost record for a job will contain all direct material used for that particular job.
   c. Materials that cannot be traced to a particular job are treated as manufacturing overhead.
   d. All materials are always classified as direct materials.

4. *(Learning Objective 4)* How does Dell's management use product cost information?
   a. To set prices of its products
   b. To decide which products to emphasize
   c. To identify ways to cut production costs
   d. All of the above

5. *(Learning Objective 3)* The formula to calculate the amount of manufacturing overhead to allocate to jobs is
   a. predetermined overhead rate times the actual amount of the allocation base used by the specific job.
   b. predetermined overhead rate divided by the actual allocation base used by the specific job.
   c. predetermined overhead rate times the actual manufacturing overhead used on the specific job.
   d. predetermined overhead rate times the estimated amount of the allocation base used by the specific job.

6. *(Learning Objective 3)* Averaging is involved in computing unit product costs when
   a. using process costing but not when using job order costing.
   b. using job order costing but not when using process costing.
   c. using both job order costing and process costing.
   d. averaging is not involved when using either job costing or process costing.

7. *(Learning Objective 4)* For which of the following reasons would John Barnett, owner of the Barnett Associates law firm, want to know the total costs of a job (serving a particular client)?
   a. To determine the fees charged to the client
   b. For inventory valuation
   c. For external reporting
   d. All of the above

8. *(Learning Objective 5)* If the company underestimates the amount of allocation base when calculating its predetermined manufacturing overhead rate but estimates the amount of manufacturing overhead costs correctly, the amount of manufacturing overhead allocated for the year will be
   a. underallocated.
   b. overallocated.
   c. exactly equal to the actual manufacturing overhead for the year.
   d. unable to determine from the information given.

9. *(Learning Objective 5)* If manufacturing overhead is overallocated for the period by $200, then
   a. the $200 should be prorated between Work in Process Inventory, Finished Goods Inventory, and Cost of Goods Sold.
   b. actual manufacturing overhead is greater than allocated manufacturing overhead.
   c. jobs have been overcosted during the period.
   d. Cost of Goods Sold should be adjusted by an increase of $200.

10. *(Learning Objective 6)* When Dell *uses* direct labor, it *traces* the cost to the job by debiting
    a. Direct Labor.
    b. Wages Payable.
    c. Manufacturing Overhead.
    d. Work in Process Inventory.

Quick Check Answers

1. b 2. d 3. d 4. d 5. a 6. c 7. a 8. b 9. c 10. d

Short Exercises

S3-1 Decide on product costing system *(Learning Objective 1)*

Would the following companies use job costing or process costing?

a. A manufacturer of fiberglass insulation
b. A residential plumbing contractor
c. A manufacturer of fiber optic cabling
d. A custom home builder
e. A hospital

S3-2 Determine the flow of costs between inventory accounts *(Learning Objective 2)*

Parker's Wood Amenities is a manufacturing plant that makes picnic tables, benches, and other outdoor furniture. Indicate which inventory account(s) would be affected by the following actions, which occur at Parker's in the process of manufacturing its standard picnic tables. Also indicate whether the inventory account would increase or decrease as a result of the action.

a. Lumber is delivered by the supplier to the plant, where it is stored in a materials storeroom until needed.
b. Lumber is requisitioned from the storeroom to be used for tops and seats for the tables.
c. Factory workers cut the lumber for the tables.
d. Ten tables are completed and moved to the inventory storage area to await sale.
e. A customer purchases a table and takes it home.

S3-3 Compute various manufacturing overhead rates *(Learning Objective 3)*

Waldman Pools manufactures swimming pool equipment. Waldman estimates total manufacturing overhead costs next year to be $1,500,000. Waldman also estimates it will use 62,500 direct labor hours and incur $1,250,000 of direct labor cost next year. In addition, the machines are expected to be run for 50,000 hours. Compute the predetermined manufacturing overhead rate for next year under the following independent situations:

1. Assume that Waldman uses direct labor hours as its manufacturing overhead allocation base.
2. Assume that Waldman uses direct labor cost as its manufacturing overhead allocation base.
3. Assume that Waldman uses machine hours as its manufacturing overhead allocation base.

S3-4 Continuation of S3-3: compute total allocated overhead *(Learning Objective 3)*

Use your answers from S3-3 to determine the total manufacturing overhead allocated to Waldman's manufacturing jobs in the following independent situations:

1. Assume that Waldman actually used 52,300 direct labor hours.
2. Assume that Waldman actually incurred $1,025,000 of direct labor cost.
3. Assume that Waldman actually ran the machines 39,500 hours.
4. Briefly explain what you have learned about the total manufacturing overhead allocated to production.

S3-5 Continuation of S3-4: determine over- or underallocation
(Learning Objectives 3 & 5)

Use your answers from S3-4 to determine the total overallocation or underallocation of manufacturing overhead during the year. Actual manufacturing costs for the year totaled $1,225,000.

1. Assume that Waldman used direct labor hours as the allocation base.
2. Assume that Waldman used the direct labor cost as the allocation base.
3. Assume that Waldman used machine hours as the allocation base.
4. Were there any situations in which jobs were costed correctly? If not, when were they overcosted? When were they undercosted?

S3-6 Calculate rate and analyze year-end results *(Learning Objectives 3 & 5)*

Samson manufactures wooden backyard playground equipment. Samson estimated $1,800,000 of manufacturing overhead and $2,000,000 of direct labor cost for the year. After the year was over, the accounting records indicated that the company had actually incurred $1,660,000 of manufacturing overhead and $2,250,000 of direct labor cost.

1. Calculate Samson's predetermined manufacturing overhead rate assuming that the company uses direct labor cost as an allocation base.
2. How much manufacturing overhead would have been allocated to manufacturing jobs during the year?
3. At year-end, was manufacturing overhead overallocated or underallocated? By how much?

S3-7 Calculate job cost and billing *(Learning Objectives 2 & 4)*

Peter Thompson is the owner of a business that sells and installs home theater systems. He just completed a job for a builder consisting of the installation of 18 home theater systems in a new condominium complex. The installations required materials totaling $17,897 and 79 hours of direct labor hours at a wage rate of $36 per hour. Overhead is allocated to jobs using a predetermined overhead rate of $7 per direct labor hour.

1. What is the total cost of the job?
2. What is the average unit cost (per theater system installed)?
3. If Peter charges a price to the builder that is 200% of the total job cost, what price will he charge for the job?

S3-8 Calculate job cost and billing at appliance repair service
(Learning Objectives 2 & 4)

Ace Appliance provides repair services for all makes and models of home appliances. Ace Appliance charges customers for labor on each job at a rate of $47 per hour. The labor rate is high enough to cover actual technician wages of $34 per hour, to cover shop overhead (allocated at a cost of $24 per hour), and to provide a profit. Ace Appliance charges the customer "at cost" for parts and materials. A recent customer job consisted of $44 in parts and materials and 9 hours of technician time.

1. What was Ace Appliance's cost for this job? Include shop overhead in the cost calculation.
2. How much was charged to the customer for this repair job?

S3-9 Ramifications of overallocating and underallocating jobs
(Learning Objectives 2 & 5)

Answer the following questions:

1. Why do managers use a *predetermined* manufacturing overhead allocation rate rather than the *actual* rate to cost jobs?
2. Jobs will typically be overcosted or undercosted. Is one worse than the other? Explain your thoughts.

S3-10 Record purchase and use of materials *(Learning Objective 6)*

PackRite manufactures backpacks. Its plant records include the following materials-related transactions:

Purchases of canvas (on account)	$66,000
Purchases of thread (on account)	$ 600
Material requisitions:	
Canvas	$58,000
Thread	$ 100

Make the journal entries to record these transactions. Post these transactions to the Raw Materials Inventory account. If the company had $30,000 of Raw Materials Inventory at the beginning of the period, what is the ending balance of Raw Materials Inventory?

S3-11 Record manufacturing labor costs *(Learning Objective 6)*

Crystal Creations reports the following labor-related transactions at its plant in Akron, Ohio.

Plant janitor's wages	$ 560
Plant supervisor's wages	$ 860
Glassblowers' wages	$70,000

Record the journal entries for the incurrence of these wages.

S3-12 Recompute job cost at a legal firm *(Learning Objectives 3, 4, & 7)*

Barrett Associates, a law firm, hires Attorney Theresa Jodoin at an annual salary of $140,000. The law firm expects her to spend 2,000 hours per year performing legal work for clients. Indirect costs are assigned to clients based on attorney billing hours. Barrett attorneys are expected to work a total of 26,000 direct labor hours this year. Before the fiscal year begins, Barrett estimates that the total indirect costs for the upcoming year will be $390,000.

1. What would be the hourly (cost) rate to Barrett Associates of employing Jodoin?
2. If Jodoin works on Client 367 for 21 hours, what direct labor cost would be traced to Client 367?
3. What is the indirect cost allocation rate?
4. What indirect costs will be allocated to Client 367?
5. What is the total job cost for Client 367?

EXERCISES Group A

E3-13A Identify type of costing system *(Learning Objective 1)*

For each of the following companies, specify whether each company would be more likely to use job costing or process costing.

a. Nail salon
b. Doctor's office
c. Orange juice processing plant
d. Furniture manufacturer
e. Plumber
f. Architect
g. Cement plant
h. Car manufacturer
i. Home builder
j. Soft drink bottling plant
k. Television network
l. Attorney's office
m. Oil refinery
n. Appliance manufacturer

CHAPTER 3

E3-14A Describe the flow of costs in a job cost shop *(Learning Objective 2)*

Catering by Design is a company which prepares food for special occasions. The following table contains events which occur during the production of food for an occasion by Catering by Design. Put the events in the order in which they would occur by designating the step number in the Order column. Also indicate with a "+" or a "–" whether that account would increase or decrease as a result of the event.

Event	Order	Raw Materials Inventory	WIP Inventory	FG Inventory	Cost of Goods Sold	No effect on inventory or COGS
a. The meat, which is purchased raw, must be seasoned and cooked.						
b. An order was taken by phone for sandwiches and salads to be prepared for a business meeting.						
c. The customer is billed for the business luncheon.						
d. The bread, meat, cheese, and vegetables are purchased.						
e. The meat and cheeses are sliced, and the vegetables are cleaned and cut. The sandwiches and salads are prepared and packaged.						
f. The prepared food is delivered to the customer's office.						

E3-15A Understanding key document terms in a job cost shop *(Learning Objective 2)*

Listed below are several document terms. Match each term with the corresponding statement in the list provided.

Terms		
a. Bill of materials	b. Job cost record	c. Production schedule
d. Purchase orders	e. Raw materials record	f. Labor time record
g. Receiving report	h. Materials requisition	i. Invoice

1. The ________ is like a list of ingredients in a recipe, stating the materials needed to produce a product.
2. Each item in the raw materials storeroom has its own ________.
3. A(n) ________ is used to accumulate all of the costs affiliated with each job.
4. The accounting department will not pay a(n) ________ unless it agrees with the quantity of parts both ordered and received.
5. Depending on the complexity of the company and the products that it produces, the ________ may cover differing time periods.
6. The ________ is a control for the materials stored in the storeroom. In order to get direct materials, a(n) ________ must be presented.
7. Before production begins, a manufacturer's purchasing department issues ________ to its supplier for needed direct materials.
8. A(n) ________ is typically a duplicate of the purchase order but without the quantity pre-listed on the form.
9. All direct laborers in the factory fill out a(n)________.

E3-16A Understand the flow of costs in a job cost shop *(Learning Objective 2)*

Williamson Feeders manufactures bird feeders for wild bird specialty stores. In September, Williamson Feeders received an order from Wild Birds, Inc., for 20 platform bird feeders. The order from Wild Birds, Inc., became Job Number 1102 at Williamson Feeders.

A materials requisition for Job 1102 is presented in the following section. In addition to the materials requisition, the labor time records (partial) for the week that these feeders were made are presented. Other products were also being produced during that week, so not all of the labor from that week belongs to Job 1102.

Materials Requisition
Number: #1250

Date: 9/14

Job: 1102

Part Number	Description	Quantity	Unit Cost	Amount
WOCD06	Rough-hewn cedar planks	34	$2.00	
SSF0304	Stainless steel fasteners	84	$1.00	
AS222	Reinforced aluminum screens	26	$1.50	
	Total			

Labor Time Record

Employee: Greg Henderson **Week:** 9/14 – 9/20

Hourly Wage Rate: $12 **Record #:** 912

Date	Job Number	Start Time	End Time	Hours	Cost
9/14	1102	8:00	1:00		
9/14	1103	1:00	4:00		
9/15 etc.					

Labor Time Record

Employee: Andrew Peck **Week:** 9/14 – 9/20

Hourly Wage Rate: $8 **Record #:** 913

Date	Job Number	Start Time	End Time	Hours	Cost
9/14	1101	9:00	12:00		
9/14	1102	12:00	5:00		
9/15	1103	9:00	11:00		
9/15 etc.					

Job Cost Record

Job Number: 1102

Customer: Wild Birds, Inc.

Job Description: 20 Model 3F (platform bird feeders)

Date Started: Sep. 14 **Date Completed:** ________

Manufacturing Cost Information:	Cost Summary
Direct Materials Req. # :	
Direct Labor No. # No. #	
Manufacturing Overhead 9 hours × $2 per direct labor hour	$ 18
Total Job Cost	
Number of Units	÷
Cost per Unit	

Requirements

1. Calculate the total for the Materials Requisition form. Post the information (cost and requisition number) from the Materials Requisition form to the Job Cost Record in the appropriate boxes.
2. Complete the labor time records for each of the employees. Once the labor time record is completed, post the information relevant to Job 1102 to the Job Cost Record for Job Cost 1102.
3. Manufacturing overhead has already been added to the Job Cost Record. Complete the Job Cost Record by calculating the total job cost and the cost per unit. Remember that this job consisted of 20 feeders (units).

E3-17A Compute a predetermined overhead rate and calculate cost of jobs based on direct labor hours *(Learning Objectives 3 & 4)*

Leisure Heating & Cooling installs and services commercial heating and cooling systems. Leisure uses job costing to calculate the cost of its jobs. Overhead is allocated to each job based on the number of direct labor hours spent on that job. At the beginning of the current year, Leisure estimated that its overhead for the coming year would be $66,750. It also anticipated using 4,450 direct labor hours for the year. In November, Leisure started and completed the following two jobs:

	Job 101	Job 102
Direct materials used	$16,000	$10,500
Direct labor hours used..	195	72

Leisure paid a $30 per hour wage rate to the employees who worked on these two jobs.

Requirements

1. What is Leisure's predetermined overhead rate based on direct labor hours?
2. Calculate the overhead to be allocated based on direct labor hours to each of the two jobs.
3. What is the total cost of Job 101? What is the total cost of Job 102?

E3-18A Compute a predetermined overhead rate and calculate cost of job based on direct labor costs *(Learning Objectives 3 & 4)*

Raymond Restaurant Supply manufactures commercial stoves and ovens for restaurants and bakeries. Raymond uses job costing to calculate the costs of its jobs with direct labor cost as its manufacturing overhead allocation base. At the beginning of the current year, Raymond estimated that its overhead for the coming year would be $485,100. It also anticipated using 22,000 direct labor hours for the year. Raymond pays its employees an average of $35 per direct labor hour. Raymond just finished Job 371, which consisted of two large ovens for a regional bakery. The costs for Job 371 were as follows:

	Job 371
Direct materials used	$14,500
Direct labor hours used	180

Requirements

1. What is Raymond's predetermined manufacturing overhead rate based on direct labor cost?
2. Calculate the manufacturing overhead to be allocated based on direct labor cost to Job 371.
3. What is the total cost of Job 371?

E3-19A Determine the cost of a job and use it for pricing *(Learning Objectives 2 & 4)*

Jungle Jim Industries manufactures custom-designed playground equipment for schools and city parks. Jungle Jim expected to incur $707,200 of manufacturing overhead cost, 41,600 of direct labor hours, and $810,000 of direct labor cost during the year (the cost of direct labor is $36 per hour). The company allocates manufacturing overhead on the basis of direct labor hours. During May, Jungle Jim completed Job 303. The job used 155 direct labor hours and required $13,000 of direct materials. The City of Forest Hills has contracted to purchase the playground equipment at a price of 20% over manufacturing cost.

Requirements

1. Calculate the manufacturing cost of Job 303.
2. How much will the City of Forest Hills pay for this playground equipment?

E3-20A Sustainability and job costing *(Learning Objectives 2, 4, & 7)*

Lincoln Plastics manufactures custom park furniture and signage from recycled plastics (primarily shredded milk jugs.) Many of the company's customers are municipalities that are required by law to purchase goods that meet certain recycled-content guidelines. (Recycled content can include post-consumer waste materials, pre-consumer waste materials, and recovered materials.) As a result, Lincoln includes two types of direct material charges in its job cost for each job: 1) Virgin materials (non-recycled); and 2) Recycled-content materials. Lincoln also keeps track of the pounds of each type of direct material so that the final recycled-content percentage for the job can be reported to the customer. Lincoln also reports on the percentage of recycled-content as a total of total plastic used each month on its own internal reporting system to help to encourage managers to use recycled-content whenever possible.

Lincoln Plastics uses a predetermined manufacturing overhead rate of $10 per direct labor hour. Here is a summary of the materials and labor used on a recent job for Osage County:

Description	Quantity	Cost
Virgin materials	100 pounds	$ 3.50 per pound
Recycled-content materials	150 pounds	$ 3.00 per pound
Direct labor	12 hours	$15.00 per hour

Requirements

1. Calculate the total cost of the Osage County job.
2. Calculate the percentage of recycled-content used in the Osage County job (using pounds). If items purchased by Osage County are required by county charter to contain at least 50% recycled-content, does this job meet that requirement?

E3-21A Understanding key terms *(Learning Objectives 1, 2, 3, & 4)*

Listed next are several terms. Complete the following statements with one of these terms. You may use a term more than once, and some terms may not be used at all.

Cost allocation	Cost driver	Job costing	Process costing
Cost tracing	Job cost record	Materials requisition	

a. _______is used by companies that produce unique services and products.
b. Indirect costs cannot be traced to specific products, so they are divided up using a process called _______.
c. All costs for a particular job are recorded on the _______.
d. Boeing Aircraft produces commercial aircraft; it would use a(n) _______ system.
e. Raw materials are stored in a storeroom until a(n) _______is received requesting the transfer of materials to the production area.
f. The allocation base should be the _______ of the manufacturing overhead costs.
g. The _______ is used to trace the cost of direct materials to the individual job records.
h. A custom home builder would use a(n) _______ system to determine product costs.
i. _______is the assignment of direct costs to specific jobs.
j. Minute Maid produces orange juice; it would use a(n) _______system.

E3-22A Determine the cost of a job *(Learning Objectives 2, 3, & 4)*

Augustine Furniture started and finished Job 310 during May. The company's records show that the following direct materials were requisitioned for Job 310:

Lumber: 48 units at $11 per unit
Padding: 17 yards at $18 per yard
Upholstery fabric: 30 yards at $27 per yard

Labor time records show the following employees (direct labor) worked on Job 310:

Penny Rawls : 12 hours at $9 per hour
Mark Frizzell: 15 hours at $15 per hour

Augustine allocates manufacturing overhead at a rate of $8 per direct labor hour.

Requirements

1. Compute the total amount of direct materials, direct labor, and manufacturing overhead that should be shown on Job 310's job cost record.
2. Job 310 consists of nine recliners. If each recliner sells for $675, what is the gross profit per recliner?

E3-23A Compare bid prices under two different allocation bases

(Learning Objectives 3 & 4)

Streeter Recycling recycles newsprint, cardboard, and so forth, into recycled packaging materials. For the coming year, Streeter estimates total manufacturing overhead to be $350,175. The company's managers are not sure if direct labor hours (estimated to be 10,005) or machine hours (estimated to be 14,007 hours) is the best allocation base to use for allocating manufacturing overhead. Streeter bids for jobs using a 30% markup over total manufacturing cost.

After the new fiscal year began, Hollings Paper Supply asked Streeter Recycling to bid for a job that will take 1,975 machine hours and 1,600 direct labor hours to produce. The direct labor cost for this job will be $13 per hour, and the direct materials will total $25,600.

Requirements

1. Compute the total job cost and bid price if Streeter Recycling decided to use direct labor hours as the manufacturing overhead allocation base for the year.
2. Compute the total job cost and bid price if Streeter Recycling decided to use machine hours as the manufacturing overhead allocation base for the year.
3. In addition to the bid from Streeter Recycling, Hollings Paper Supply received a bid of $126,500 for this job from Cusak Recycling. What are the ramifications for Streeter Recycling?

E3-24A Analyze manufacturing overhead *(Learning Objectives 3 & 5)*

Brooks Foundry in Charleston, South Carolina, uses a predetermined manufacturing overhead rate to allocate overhead to individual jobs based on the machine hours required. At the beginning of the year, the company expected to incur the following:

Manufacturing overhead costs	$ 650,000
Direct labor cost	$1,300,000
Machine hours	81,250

At the end of the year, the company had actually incurred the following:

Direct labor cost	$1,190,000
Depreciation on manufacturing plant and equipment	$ 485,000
Property taxes on plant	$ 21,500
Sales salaries	$ 26,000
Delivery drivers' wages	$ 14,500
Plant janitors' wages	$ 11,000
Machine hours	54,500 hours

Requirements

1. Compute Brooks' predetermined manufacturing overhead rate.
2. How much manufacturing overhead was allocated to jobs during the year?
3. How much manufacturing overhead was incurred during the year? Is manufacturing overhead underallocated or overallocated at the end of the year? By how much?
4. Were the jobs overcosted or undercosted? By how much?

E3-25A Record manufacturing overhead *(Learning Objectives 5 & 6)*

Refer to the data in Exercise 3-24A. Brooks' accountant found an error in the expense records from the year reported. Depreciation on manufacturing plant and equipment was actually $401,000, not the $485,000 that had originally been reported. The unadjusted Cost of Goods Sold balance at year-end was $560,000.

Requirements

1. Prepare the journal entry(s) to record manufacturing overhead costs incurred.
2. Prepare the journal entry to record the manufacturing overhead allocated to jobs in production.

3. Use a T-account to determine whether manufacturing overhead is underallocated or overallocated and by how much.
4. Record the entry to close out the underallocated or overallocated manufacturing overhead.
5. What is the adjusted ending balance of Cost of Goods Sold?

E3-26A Record journal entries *(Learning Objectives 2, 3, 5, & 6)*

The following transactions were incurred by Nunez Fabricators during January, the first month of its fiscal year.

Requirements

1. Record the proper journal entry for each transaction.
   a. \$200,000 of materials were purchased on account.
   b. \$162,000 of materials were used in production; of this amount, \$161,000 was used on specific jobs.
   c. Manufacturing labor and salaries for the month totaled \$220,000. A total of \$210,000 of manufacturing labor and salaries was traced to specific jobs, while the remainder was indirect labor used in the factory.
   d. The company recorded \$23,000 of depreciation on the plant and plant equipment. The company also received a plant utility bill for \$14,000.
   e. \$39,000 of manufacturing overhead was allocated to specific jobs.
   f. Received bill for website services for \$5,000.
2. By the end of January, was manufacturing overhead overallocated or underallocated? By how much?

E3-27A Analyze T-accounts *(Learning Objectives 2, 3, 5, & 6)*

Touch Enterprises produces LCD touch screen products. The company reports the following information at December 31. Touch Enterprises began operations on January 31 earlier that same year.

Work in Process Inventory (Dr)	Work in Process Inventory (Cr)	Wages Payable (Dr)	Wages Payable (Cr)	Manufacturing Overhead (Dr)	Manufacturing Overhead (Cr)	Finished Goods Inventory (Dr)	Finished Goods Inventory (Cr)	Raw Materials Inventory (Dr)	Raw Materials Inventory (Cr)
31,000	126,500	72,000	72,000	1,000	46,000	126,500	114,500	57,500	32,000
61,000				11,000					
46,000		Balance 0		41,000					

Requirements

1. What is the cost of direct materials used?
2. What is the cost of indirect materials used?
3. What is the cost of direct labor?
4. What is the cost of indirect labor?
5. What is the cost of goods manufactured?
6. What is the cost of goods sold (before adjusting for any under- or overallocated manufacturing overhead)?
7. What is the actual manufacturing overhead?
8. How much manufacturing overhead was allocated to jobs?
9. What is the predetermined manufacturing overhead rate as a percentage of direct labor cost?
10. Is manufacturing overhead underallocated or overallocated? By how much?

E3-28A Job cost and bid price at a consulting firm *(Learning Objective 7)*

Chance Consulting, a real estate consulting firm, specializes in advising companies on potential new plant sites. Chance Consulting uses a job cost system with a predetermined indirect cost allocation rate computed as a percentage of expected direct labor costs.

At the beginning of the year, managing partner Sarah Chance prepared the following plan, or budget, for the year:

Direct labor hours (professionals)	19,000 hours
Direct labor costs (professionals)	$2,650,000
Office rent	$ 260,000
Support staff salaries	$ 870,000
Utilities	$ 340,000

Juda Resources is inviting several consulting firms to bid for work. Chance estimates that this job will require about 220 direct labor hours.

Requirements

1. Compute Chance Consulting's (a) hourly direct labor cost rate and (b) indirect cost allocation rate.
2. Compute the predicted cost of the Juda Resources job.
3. If Chance Consulting wants to earn a profit that equals 35% of the job's cost, how much should the company bid for the Juda Resources job?

EXERCISES Group B

E3-29B Identify type of costing system *(Learning Objective 1)*

For each of the following companies, specify whether each company would be more likely to use job costing or process costing.

a. Peanut butter processing plant
b. Custom home builder
c. Chemical producer
d. Shampoo manufacturer
e. CPA firm
f. Pest control service
g. Plywood mill
h. Auto repair shop
i. Cement plant
j. Aircraft builder
k. Dentist
l. Orange juice plant
m. House painter
n. Cleaning service

E3-30B Describe the flow of costs in a job cost shop *(Learning Objective 2)*

One of a Kind Designs is a custom dressmaker that specializes in wedding gowns. The following table contains events that occur in the manufacture and sale of gowns by One of a Kind Designs. Put the events in the order in which they would occur by designating the step number in the Order column. Also indicate with a "+" or a "–" whether that account would increase or decrease as a result of the event.

Event	Order	Raw Materials Inventory	WIP Inventory	FG Inventory	Cost of Goods Sold	No effect on inventory or COGS
a. Fabric needed for the gown is removed from the storeroom and taken to the cutting department. The pieces of fabric are then transferred to the sewing department for piecing together.						
b. A customer meets with one of the design consultants to take measurements and decide on a design for the wedding gown.						
c. The finished gown is transferred to the fitting department. They contact the customer to come in for fitting of the gown. After all of the alterations are complete the finished gown is transferred to the finished gown area to await pickup by the customer.						
d. After a final inspection the customer makes the final payment for and takes delivery of the gown.						
e. The designer places an order for the specialty fabric and trim needed to produce the gown. The materials needed for production are received and checked into the materials storeroom to be held until needed.						
f. The gown is transferred to the trim department, where the needed trim is checked out of the storeroom and applied to the gown per the design.						

E3-31B Understanding key document terms in a job cost shop

(Learning Objective 2)

Listed below are several document terms. Match each term with the corresponding statement in the list provided.

Terms		
a. Bill of materials	b. Job cost record	c. Production schedule
d. Purchase orders	e. Raw materials record	f. Labor time record
g. Receiving report	h. Materials requisition	i. Invoice

1. Each job will have its own _________.
2. Manufacturing overhead is allocated and recorded on the _________.
3. So that enough direct labor and direct materials are on hand to complete a job, the production staff prepares a(n) _________.
4. A(n) _________ is used to communicate the terms of a purchase from a supplier.
5. Often times, the _________ are kept electronically; factory workers swipe their bar-coded employee identification cards on a computer terminal and enter the appropriate job number.
6. By adding together the balances in the individual _________, the company is able to substantiate the total Raw Materials Inventory shown on the balance sheet.

7. A(n) _________ simply lists all of the raw materials needed for a job.
8. A(n) _________ is a paper or electronic form used to confirm the terms of raw materials ordered by the manufacturing company.
9. As soon as the _________ is received by the raw materials storeroom, workers pick the appropriate materials and send them to the factory floor.

E3-32B Understand the flow of costs in a job cost shop *(Learning Objective 2)*

Wilson Feeders manufactures bird feeders for wild bird specialty stores. In September, Wilson Feeders received an order from Wild Birds, Inc., for 28 platform bird feeders. The order from Wild Birds, Inc., became Job 1102 at Wilson Feeders.

A materials requisition for Job 1102 is presented in the following section. In addition to the materials requisition, the labor time records (partial) for the week that these feeders were made are presented. Other products were also being produced during that week, so not all of the labor belongs to Job 1102.

Materials Requisition
Number: #1250

Date: 9/14

Job: 1102

Part Number	Description	Quantity	Unit Cost	Amount
WOCD06	Rough-hewn cedar planks	40	$2.00	
SSF0304	Stainless steel fasteners	76	$0.50	
AS222	Reinforced aluminum screens	18	$1.50	
	Total			

Labor Time Record

Employee: Greg Henderson **Week:** 9/14 – 9/20

Hourly Wage Rate: $14 **Record #:** 912

Date	Job Number	Start Time	End Time	Hours	Cost
9/14	1102	9:00	2:00		
9/14	1103	2:00	5:00		
9/15 etc.					

CHAPTER 3

Labor Time Record

Employee: Andrew Peck **Week:** 9/14 – 9/20

Hourly Wage Rate: $6 **Record #:** 913

Date	Job Number	Start Time	End Time	Hours	Cost
9/14	1101	8:00	1:00		
9/14	1102	1:00	4:00		
9/15	1103	8:00	10:00		
9/15 etc.					

Job Cost Record

Job Number: 1102

Customer: Wild Birds, Inc.

Job Description: 28 Model 3F (platform bird feeders)

Date Started: Sep. 14 **Date Completed:** ______

Manufacturing Cost Information:	Cost Summary
Direct Materials Req. #:	
Direct Labor No. # No. #	
Manufacturing Overhead 9 hours × $2 per direct labor hour	$ 18
Total Job Cost	
Number of Units	
Cost per Unit	

Requirements

1. Calculate the total for the Materials Requisition form. Post the information (cost and requisition number) from the Materials Requisition form to the Job Cost Record in the appropriate boxes.
2. Complete the labor time records for each of the employees. Once the labor time record is completed, post the information relevant to Job 1102 to the Job Cost Record for Job Cost 1102.
3. Manufacturing overhead has already been added to the Job Cost Record. Complete the Job Cost Record by calculating the total job cost and the cost per unit. Remember that this job consisted of 28 feeders (units).

E3-33B Compute a predetermined overhead rate and calculate cost of jobs *(Learning Objectives 3 & 4)*

Mansfield Heating & Cooling installs and services commercial heating and cooling systems. Mansfield uses job costing to calculate the cost of its jobs. Overhead is allocated to each job based on the number of direct labor hours spent on that job. At the beginning of the current year, Mansfield estimated that its overhead for the coming year would be $60,000. It also anticipated using 4,000 direct labor hours for the year. In May, Mansfield started and completed the following two jobs:

	Job 101	Job 102
Direct materials used	$17,000	$13,000
Direct labor hours used	170	72

Mansfield paid a $22 per hour wage rate to the employees who worked on these two jobs.

Requirements

1. What is Mansfield's predetermined overhead rate based on direct labor hours?
2. Calculate the overhead to be allocated based on direct labor hours to each of the two jobs.
3. What is the total cost of Job 101? What is the total cost of Job 102?

E3-34B Compute a predetermined overhead rate and calculate cost of job *(Learning Objectives 3 & 4)*

Elkton Restaurant Supply manufactures commercial stove and ovens for restaurants and bakeries. Elkton uses job costing to calculate the costs of its jobs with direct labor cost as its manufacturing overhead allocation base. At the beginning of the current year, Elkton estimated that its overhead for the coming year will be $530,400. It also anticipated using 30,000 direct labor hours for the year. Elkton pays its employees an average of $40 per direct labor hour. Elkton just finished job 371, which consisted of two large ovens for a regional bakery. The costs for Job 371 were as follows:

	Job 371
Direct materials used	$16,500
Direct labor hours used	130

Requirements

1. What is Elkton's predetermined manufacturing overhead rate based on direct labor cost?
2. Calculate the manufacturing overhead to be allocated based on direct labor costs to Job 371.
3. What is the total cost of Job 371?

E3-35B Determine the cost of a job and use it for pricing *(Learning Objectives 2 & 4)*

Have Fun Industries manufactures custom-designed playground equipment for schools and city parks. Have Fun expected to incur $664,000 of manufacturing overhead cost, 41,500 of direct labor hours, and $870,000 of direct labor cost during the year (the cost of direct labor is $24 per hour). The company allocates manufacturing overhead on the basis of direct labor hours. During December, Have Fun completed Job 309. The job used 190 direct labor hours and required $15,100 of direct materials. The City of Jonestown has contracted to purchase the playground equipment at a price of 22% over manufacturing cost.

Requirements

1. Calculate the manufacturing cost of Job 309.
2. How much will the City of Jonestown pay for this playground equipment?

E3-36B Sustainability and job costing *(Learning Objectives 2, 4, & 7)*

Woodfree Plastics manufactures custom park furniture and signage from recycled plastics (primarily shredded milk jugs.) Many of the company's customers are municipalities that are required by law to purchase goods that meet certain recycled-content guidelines. (Recycled content can include post-consumer waste materials, pre-consumer waste materials, and recovered materials.) As a result, Woodfree Plastics includes two types of direct material charges in their job cost for each job: 1) Virgin materials (non-recycled); and 2) Recycled-content materials. Woodfree Plastics also keeps track of the pounds of each type of direct material so that the final recycled-content percentage for the job can be reported to the customer. The company also reports on the percentage of recycled-content as a total of plastics used each month on its own internal reporting system to help encourage managers to use recycled-content whenever possible.

Woodfree Plastics uses a predetermined manufacturing overhead rate of $15 per direct labor hour. Here is a summary of the materials and labor used on a recent job for Summit County:

Description	Quantity	Cost
Virgin materials	250 pounds	$ 3.50 per pound
Recycled-content materials	300 pounds	$ 3.00 per pound
Direct labor	12 hours	$18.00 per hour

Requirements

1. Calculate the total cost of the Summit County job.
2. Calculate the percentage of recycled-content used in the Summit County job (using pounds.) If items purchased by Summit County are required by county charter to contain at least 50% recycled-content, does the job meet that requirement?

E3-37B Understanding key terms *(Learning Objectives 1, 2, 3, & 4)*

Listed next are several terms. Complete the following statements with one of these terms. You may use a term more than once, and some terms may not be used at all.

Cost allocation	Job cost record	Materials requisition	Process costing
Cost tracing	Cost driver	Job costing	

a. A(n) _______ is any activity that causes a cost to be incurred.
b. The purpose of both _______ and _______is to determine the cost of products.
c. Kia manufactures automobiles; it uses a(n) _______ system to determine product costs.
d. _______ procedures distribute accumulated indirect costs to the programs or services that benefit from costs on the basis of percentages that represent a reasonable and equitable allocation base.
e. _______ is used by companies that produce large numbers of identical units through a series of uniform production steps or processes.
f. _______ is the process of assigning direct costs to products.
g. The _______ is used to track and accumulate all of the costs for an individual job.
h. The labor time records allow for the _______ of direct labor costs to individual jobs.
i. _______ is used by companies that produce unique, custom-ordered products, or relatively small batches of different products.
j. Simply described, _______ averages manufacturing costs across all units so that each identical unit bears the same cost.

E3-38B Determine the cost of a job *(Learning Objectives 2, 3, & 4)*

Lounge Lizard started and finished Job 310 during August. The company's records show that the following direct materials were requisitioned for Job 310:

Lumber: 47 units at $10 per unit
Padding: 13 yards at $18 per yard
Upholstery fabric: 31 yards at $27 per yard.

Labor time records show the following employees (direct labor) worked on Job 310:

Jake Schaeffer : 10 hours at $11 per hour
Jon Augustine : 18 hours at $17 per hour.

Lounge Lizard allocates manufacturing overhead at a rate of $9 per direct labor hour.

Requirements

1. Compute the total amount of direct materials, direct labor, and manufacturing overhead that should be shown on Job 310's job cost record.
2. Job 310 consists of seven recliners. If each recliner sells for $650, what is the gross profit per recliner?

E3-39B Compare bid prices under two different allocation bases *(Learning Objectives 3 & 4)*

Webster Recycling recycles newsprint, cardboard, and so forth, into recycled packaging materials. For the coming year, Webster Recycling estimates total manufacturing overhead to be $359,640. The company's managers are not sure if direct labor hours (estimated to be 9,990) or machine hours (estimated to be 17,982 hours) is the best allocation base to use for allocating manufacturing overhead. Webster Recycling bids for jobs using a 31% markup over total manufacturing cost.

After the new fiscal year began, Lundy Paper Supply asked Webster Recycling to bid for a job that will take 2,000 machine hours and 1,550 direct labor hours to produce. The direct labor cost for this job will be $12 per hour, and the direct materials will total $25,800.

Requirements

1. Compute the total job cost and bid price if Webster Recycling decided to use direct labor hours as the manufacturing overhead allocation base for the year.
2. Compute the total job cost and bid price if Webster Recycling decided to use machine hours as the manufacturing overhead allocation base for the year.
3. In addition to the bid from Webster Recycling, Lundy Paper Supply received a bid of $124,500 for this job from Kristal Recycling. What are the ramifications for Webster Recycling?

E3-40B Analyze manufacturing overhead *(Learning Objectives 3 & 5)*

Metal Foundry in Youngstown, Ohio, uses a predetermined manufacturing overhead rate to allocate overhead to individual jobs based on the machine hours required. At the beginning of the year, the company expected to incur the following:

Manufacturing overhead costs	$ 550,000
Direct labor cost	$1,550,000
Machine hours	68,750

At the end of the year, the company had actually incurred the following:

Direct labor cost	$1,230,000
Depreciation on manufacturing plant and equipment	$ 470,000
Property taxes on plant	$ 19,000
Sales salaries	$ 23,000
Delivery drivers' wages	$ 13,000
Plant janitors' wages	$ 12,000
Machine hours	57,000 hours

Requirements

1. Compute Metal Foundry's predetermined manufacturing overhead rate.
2. How much manufacturing overhead was allocated to jobs during the year?
3. How much manufacturing overhead was incurred during the year? Is manufacturing overhead underallocated or overallocated at the end of the year? By how much?
4. Were the jobs overcosted or undercosted? By how much?

E3-41B Record manufacturing overhead *(Learning Objectives 5 & 6)*

Refer to the data in Exercise E3-40B. Metal Foundry's accountant found an error in the expense records from the year reported. Depreciation on manufacturing plant and equipment was actually $415,000, not the $470,000 it had originally reported. The unadjusted Cost of Goods Sold balance at year-end was $580,000.

Requirements

1. Prepare the journal entry(s) to record manufacturing overhead costs incurred.
2. Prepare the journal entry to record the manufacturing overhead allocated to jobs in production.
3. Use a T-account to determine whether manufacturing overhead is underallocated or overallocated, and by how much.
4. Record the entry to close out the underallocated or overallocated manufacturing overhead.
5. What is the adjusted ending balance of Cost of Goods Sold?

E3-42B Record journal entries *(Learning Objectives 2, 3, 5, & 6)*

The following transactions were incurred by Whooley Fabricators during January, the first month of its fiscal year.

Requirements

1. Record the proper journal entry for each transaction.
   a. $205,000 of materials were purchased on account.
   b. $174,000 of materials were used in production; of this amount, $167,000 was used on specific jobs.
   c. Manufacturing labor and salaries for the month totaled $215,000. $180,000 of the total manufacturing labor and salaries was traced to specific jobs, while the remainder was indirect labor used in the factory.
   d. The company recorded $16,000 of depreciation on the plant and plant equipment. The company also received a plant utility bill for $12,000.
   e. $69,000 of manufacturing overhead was allocated to specific jobs.
   f. Received bill for website services for $3,000.
2. By the end of January, was manufacturing overhead overallocated or underallocated? By how much?

E3-43B Analyze T-accounts *(Learning Objectives 2, 3, 5, & 6)*

Only LCD produces LCD touch screen products. The company reports the following information at December 31. Only LCD began operations on January 31 earlier that same year.

Work in Process Inventory		Wages Payable		Manufacturing Overhead		Finished Goods Inventory		Raw Materials Inventory	
29,000	126,500	77,000	77,000	5,000	45,000	126,500	113,000	55,500	34,000
64,500				12,500					
45,000		Balance 0		38,000					

Requirements

1. What is the cost of direct materials used?
2. The cost of indirect materials used?
3. What is the cost of direct labor?
4. The cost of indirect labor?
5. What is the cost of goods manufactured?
6. What is the cost of goods sold (before adjusting for any under- or overallocated manufacturing overhead)?
7. What is the actual manufacturing overhead?
8. How much manufacturing overhead was allocated to jobs?
9. What is the predetermined manufacturing overhead rate as a percentage of direct labor cost?
10. Is manufacturing overhead underallocated or overallocated? By how much?

E3-44B Job cost and bid price at a consulting firm *(Learning Objective 7)*

White Consulting, a real estate consulting firm, specializes in advising companies on potential new plant sites. White Consulting uses a job costing system with a predetermined indirect cost allocation rate computed as a percentage of direct labor costs. At the beginning of the year, managing partner Latoya White prepared the following plan, or budget, for the year:

Direct labor hours (professionals)	20,000 hours
Direct labor costs (professionals)	$2,750,000
Office rent	$ 210,000
Support staff salaries	$ 920,000
Utilities	$ 320,000

Star Resources is inviting several consultants to bid for work. White estimates that this job will require about 240 direct labor hours.

Requirements

1. Compute White Consulting's (a) hourly direct labor cost rate and (b) indirect cost allocation rate.
2. Compute the predicted cost of the Star Resources job.
3. If White Consulting wants to earn a profit that equals 25% of the job's cost, how much should the company bid for the Star Resources job?

PROBLEMS Group A

P3-45A Analyze Manufacturing Overhead *(Learning Objectives 3 & 5)*

Premium Company produces uniforms. The company allocates manufacturing overhead based on the machine hours each job uses. Premium Company reports the following cost data for the past year:

	Budget	Actual
Direct labor hours	7,100 hours	6,500 hours
Machine hours	6,800 hours	6,800 hours
Depreciation on salespeople's autos	$23,500	$23,500
Indirect materials	$52,000	$54,500
Depreciation on trucks used to deliver uniforms to customers	$13,500	$11,000
Depreciation on plant and equipment	$64,000	$65,500
Indirect manufacturing labor	$39,500	$41,500
Customer service hotline	$21,500	$23,000
Plant utilities	$ 900	$ 1,900
Direct labor cost	$71,000	$85,000

Requirements

1. Compute the predetermined manufacturing overhead rate.
2. Calculate the allocated manufacturing overhead for the past year.
3. Compute the underallocated or overallocated manufacturing overhead. How will this underallocated or overallocated manufacturing overhead be disposed of?
4. How can managers use accounting information to help control manufacturing overhead costs?

P3-46A Use job costing at an advertising agency *(Learning Objectives 3, 4, & 7)*

Cardinal.com is an internet advertising agency. The firm uses a job cost system in which each client is a different "job." Cardinal.com traces direct labor, software licensing costs, and travel costs directly to each job (client). The company allocates indirect costs to jobs based on a predetermined indirect cost allocation rate based on direct labor hours.

At the beginning of the current year, managing partner Jon Augustine prepared a budget:

Direct labor hours (professional)	17,200 hours
Direct labor costs (professional)	$2,236,000
Support staff salaries	$ 120,000
Rent and utilities	$ 47,000
Supplies	$ 523,800
Lease payments on computer hardware	$ 66,000

During January of the current year, Cardinal.com served several clients. Records for two clients appear here:

	AllTrips.com	Port Baltimore Golf Resort
Direct labor hours	770 hours	45 hours
Software licensing costs	$ 2,700	$300
Travel costs	$10,000	$ 0

Requirements

1. Compute Cardinal.com's predetermined indirect cost allocation rate for the current year based on direct labor hours.
2. Compute the total cost of each job.
3. If Cardinal.com wants to earn profits equal to 20% of sales revenue, how much (what total fee) should it charge each of these two clients?
4. Why does Cardinal.com assign costs to jobs?

P3-47A Use job costing at a consulting firm *(Learning Objectives 3, 4, & 7)*

Bluebird Design is a website design and consulting firm. The firm uses a job cost system in which each client is a different "job." Bluebird Design traces direct labor, licensing costs, and travel costs directly to each job (client). It allocates indirect costs to jobs based on a predetermined indirect cost allocation rate computed as a percentage of direct labor costs.

At the beginning of the current year, managing partner Mary Milici prepared the following budget:

Direct labor hours (professional)	8,000 hours
Direct labor costs (professional)	$1,200,000
Support staff salaries	$ 140,000
Computer lease payments	$ 47,000
Office supplies	$ 27,000
Office rent	$ 62,000

Later that same year in November, Bluebird Design served several clients. Records for two clients appear here:

	Tasty Coop	GoGreen.com
Direct labor hours	720 hours	45 hours
Licensing costs	$2,200	$250
Travel costs	$7,000	$ 0

Requirements

1. Compute Bluebird Design's predetermined indirect cost allocation rate for the current year.
2. Compute the total cost of each of the two jobs listed.
3. If Bluebird Design wants to earn profits equal to 20% of sales revenue, how much (what total fee) should the company charge each of these two clients?
4. Why does Bluebird Design assign costs to jobs?

P3-48A Prepare job cost record *(Learning Objectives 2, 3, & 4)*

Superior Tire manufactures tires for all-terrain vehicles. Superior uses job costing and has a perpetual inventory system.

On September 22, Superior received an order for 170 TX tires from ATV Corporation at a price of $80 each. The job, assigned number 298, was promised for October 10. After purchasing the materials, Superior began production on September 30 and incurred the following direct labor and direct materials costs in completing the order:

Date	Labor Time Record No.	Description	Amount
9/30	1896	12 hours at $20	$240
10/3	1904	30 hours at $18	$540

Date	Materials Requisition No.	Description	Amount
9/30	437	60 lb. rubber at $12	$720
10/2	439	40 meters polyester fabric at $10	$400
10/3	501	100 meters steel cord at $8	$800

Superior allocates manufacturing overhead to jobs on the basis of the relation between expected overhead costs ($490,000) and expected direct labor hours (17,500). Job 298 was completed on October 3 and shipped to ATV on October 5.

Requirements

1. Prepare a job cost record for Job 298.
2. Calculate the total profit and the per-unit profit for Job 298.

P3-49A Determine and record job costs *(Learning Objectives 2, 3, 4, & 6)*

Sunset Homes manufactures prefabricated chalets in Colorado. The company uses a perpetual inventory system and a job cost system in which each chalet is a job. The following events occurred during May:

a. Purchased materials on account, $490,000.

b. Incurred total manufacturing wages of $111,000, which included both direct labor and indirect labor. Used direct labor in manufacturing as follows:

	Direct Labor
Chalet 13	$14,100
Chalet 14	$28,600
Chalet 15	$19,400
Chalet 16	$21,100

c. Requisitioned direct materials in manufacturing as follows:

	Direct Materials
Chalet 13	$41,100
Chalet 14	$56,300
Chalet 15	$62,600
Chalet 16	$66,500

d. Depreciation of manufacturing equipment used on different chalets, $6,400.

e. Other overhead costs incurred on Chalets 13–16:

Equipment rentals paid in cash	$10,900
Prepaid plant insurance expired	$ 9,000

f. Allocated overhead to jobs at the predetermined rate of 60% of direct labor cost.

g. Chalets completed: 13, 15, and 16.

h. Chalets sold on account: 13 for $95,000 and 16 for $141,000.

Requirements

1. Record the preceding events in the general journal.
2. Open T-accounts for Work in Process Inventory and Finished Goods Inventory. Post the appropriate entries to these accounts, identifying each entry by letter. Determine the ending account balances assuming that the beginning balances were zero.

3. Summarize the job costs of the unfinished chalet and show that this equals the ending balance in Work in Process Inventory.
4. Summarize the job cost of the completed chalet that has not yet been sold and show that this equals the ending balance in Finished Goods Inventory.
5. Compute the gross profit on each chalet that was sold. What costs must the gross profit cover for Sunset Homes?

P3-50A Determine flow of costs through accounts *(Learning Objectives 2 & 6)*

Best Engine reconditions engines. Its job cost records yield the following information. Best Engine uses a perpetual inventory system.

	Date			Total Cost of Job at March 31	Total Manufacturing Cost Added in April
Job No.	**Started**	**Finished**	**Sold**		
1	3/26	4/7	4/9	$1,200	
2	3/3	4/12	4/13	$1,300	
3	4/29	4/30	5/3	$1,600	
4	4/30	5/1	5/1	$ 300	$ 500
5	5/8	5/12	5/14		$ 800
6	5/23	6/6	6/9		$1,500

Requirements

1. Compute Best Engine's cost of (a) Work in Process Inventory at April 30 and May 31, (b) Finished Goods Inventory at April 30 and May 31, and (c) Cost of Goods Sold for April and May.
2. Make summary journal entries to record the transfer of completed jobs from Work in Process Inventory to Finished Goods Inventory for March and April.
3. Record the sale of Job 5 on account for $1,900.
4. Compute the gross profit for Job 5. What costs must the gross profit cover?

PROBLEMS Group B

P3-51B Analyze Manufacturing Overhead *(Learning Objectives 3 & 5)*

Weiters Company produces uniforms. The company allocates manufacturing overhead based on the machine hours each job uses. Weiters Company reports the following cost data for the past year:

	Budget	Actual
Direct labor hours	7,400 hours	6,200 hours
Machine hours	6,950 hours	6,600 hours
Depreciation on salespeople's autos	$23,500	$23,500
Indirect materials	$48,500	$53,500
Depreciation on trucks used to deliver uniforms to customers	$15,500	$13,500
Depreciation on plant and equipment	$64,500	$66,000
Indirect manufacturing labor	$39,000	$41,000
Customer service hotline	$19,500	$20,500
Plant utilities	$28,700	$31,200
Direct labor cost	$72,500	$84,000

CHAPTER 3

Requirements

1. Compute the predetermined manufacturing overhead rate.
2. Calculate the allocated manufacturing overhead for the past year.
3. Compute the underallocated or overallocated manufacturing overhead. How will this underallocated or overallocated manufacturing overhead be disposed of?
4. How can managers use accounting information to help control manufacturing overhead costs?

P3-52B Use job costing at an advertising agency *(Learning Objectives 3, 4, & 7)*

Skylark.com is an internet advertising agency. The firm uses a job cost system in which each client is a different "job." Skylark.com traces direct labor, software licensing costs, and travel costs directly to each job (client). The company allocates indirect costs to jobs based on a predetermined indirect cost allocation rate computed as a percentage of direct labor costs.

At the beginning of the current year, managing partner Ricky Beuna prepared a budget:

Direct labor hours (professional)	17,400 hours
Direct labor costs (professional)	$2,610,000
Support staff salaries	$ 140,000
Rent and utilities	$ 95,000
Supplies	$ 363,200
Lease payments on computer hardware	$ 63,000

During January of the current year, Skylark.com served several clients. Records for two clients appear here:

	DreamVacation.com	Port Greensberg Golf Resort
Direct labor hours	710 hours	40 hours
Software licensing costs	$2,200	$300
Travel costs	$7,000	$ 0

Requirements

1. Compute Skylark.com's predetermined indirect cost allocation rate for the current year based on direct labor hours.
2. Compute the total cost of each job.
3. If Skylark.com wants to earn profits equal to 20% of sales revenue, how much (what total fee) should it charge each of these two clients?
4. Why does Skylark.com assign costs to jobs?

P3-53B Use job costing at a consulting firm *(Learning Objectives 3, 4, & 7)*

Dove Design is a website design and consulting firm. The firm uses a job cost system, in which each client is a different job. Dove Design traces direct labor, licensing costs, and travel costs directly to each job (client). It allocates indirect costs to jobs based on a predetermined indirect cost allocation rate computed as a percentage of direct labor costs.

At the beginning of the current year, managing partner Mary Milici prepared the following budget:

Direct labor hours (professional)	10,000 hours
Direct labor costs (professional)	$1,400,000
Support staff salaries	$ 170,000
Computer leases	$ 49,000
Office supplies	$ 29,000
Office rent	$ 60,000

Later that same year in November, Dove Design served several clients. Records for two clients appear here:

	Dining Coop	SunNow.com
Direct labor hours	770 hours	45 hours
Software licensing costs	$ 2,300	$200
Travel costs	$ 8,000	$ 0

Requirements

1. Compute Dove Design's predetermined indirect cost allocation rate for the current year.
2. Compute the total cost of each of the two jobs listed.
3. If Dove Design wants to earn profits equal to 20% of sales revenue, how much (what total fee) should the company charge each of these two clients?
4. Why does Dove Design assign costs to jobs?

P3-54B Prepare job cost record *(Learning Objectives 2, 3, & 4)*

Best Tire manufactures tires for all-terrain vehicles. Best Tire uses job costing and has a perpetual inventory system. On November 22, Best Tire received an order for 110 TX tires from ATV Corporation at a price of $50 each. The job, assigned number 298, was promised for December 10. After purchasing the materials, Best Tire began production on November 30 and incurred the following direct labor and direct materials costs in completing the order:

Date	Labor Time Record No.	Description	Amount
11/30	1896	12 hours at $20	$240
12/3	1904	30 hours at $14	$420

Date	Materials Requisition No.	Description	Amount
11/30	437	60 lbs. rubber at $12	$ 720
12/2	439	40 meters polyester fabric at $10	$ 400
12/3	501	100 meters steel cord at $8	$ 800

Best Tire allocates manufacturing overhead to jobs on the basis of the relationship between expected overhead costs ($456,000) and expected direct labor hours (19,000). Job 298 was completed on December 3 and shipped to ATV on December 5.

Requirements

1. Prepare a job cost record for Job 298.
2. Calculate the total profit and the per-unit profit for Job 298.

P3-55B Determine and record job costs *(Learning Objectives 2, 3, 4, & 6)*

Quaint Homes manufactures prefabricated chalets in Colorado. The company uses a perpetual inventory system and a job cost system in which each chalet is a job. The following events occurred during May:

a. Purchased materials on account, $460,000.

b. Incurred total manufacturing wages of $118,000, which included both direct labor and indirect labor. Used direct labor in manufacturing as follows:

	Direct Labor
Chalet 13	$14,000
Chalet 14	$28,000
Chalet 15	$19,400
Chalet 16	$21,900

c. Requisitioned direct materials in manufacturing as follows:

	Direct Materials
Chalet 13	$41,900
Chalet 14	$56,000
Chalet 15	$62,200
Chalet 16	$66,700

d. Depreciation of manufacturing equipment used on different chalets, $6,300.

e. Other overhead costs incurred on Chalets 13–16:

Equipment rentals paid in cash	$10,000
Prepaid plant insurance expired	$ 3,000

f. Allocated overhead to jobs at the predetermined rate of 60% of direct labor cost.

g. Chalets completed: 13, 15, and 16.

h. Chalets sold on account: 13 for $96,000; 16 for $149,000.

Requirements

1. Record the events in the general journal.
2. Post the appropriate entries to the T-accounts, identifying each entry by letter. Determine the ending account balances, assuming that the beginning balances were zero.
3. Add the costs of the unfinished chalet, and show that this total amount equals the ending balance in the Work in Process Inventory account.
4. Summarize the job cost of the completed chalet that has not yet been sold and show that this equals the ending balance in Finished Goods Inventory.
5. Compute gross profit on each chalet that was sold. What costs must gross profit cover for Quaint Homes?

P3-56B Determine flow of costs through accounts *(Learning Objectives 2 & 6)*

Frugal Car reconditions engines. Its job costing records yield the following information. Frugal Car uses a perpetual inventory system.

Job No.	Date			Total Cost of Job at April 30	Total Manufacturing Cost Added in May
	Started	Finished	Sold		
1	4/26	5/7	5/9	$1,300	
2	4/3	5/12	5/13	$1,000	
3	5/29	5/31	6/3	$1,900	
4	5/31	6/1	6/1	$ 900	$ 300
5	6/8	6/12	6/14		$ 400
6	6/23	7/6	7/9		$1,400

Requirements

1. Compute Frugal Car's cost of (a) Work in Process Inventory at May 31 and June 30, (b) Finished Goods Inventory at May 31 and June 30, and (c) Cost of Goods Sold for May and June.
2. Make summary journal entries to record the transfer of completed jobs from Work in Process to Finished Goods for May and June.
3. Record the sale of Job 5 for $1,500.
4. Compute the gross profit for Job 5. What costs must the gross profit cover?

CRITICAL THINKING

Discussion & Analysis

A3-57 Discussion Questions

1. Why would it be inappropriate for a custom home builder to use process costing?
2. For what types of products is job costing appropriate? Why? For what types of products is process costing appropriate? Why?
3. What product costs must be allocated to jobs? Why must these costs be allocated rather than assigned?
4. When the predetermined manufacturing overhead rate is calculated, why are estimated costs and cost driver levels used instead of actual dollars and amounts?
5. Why should manufacturing overhead be allocated to a job even though the costs cannot be directly traced to a job? Give at least two reasons.
6. Why does management need to know the cost of a job? Discuss at least five reasons.
7. Why is it acceptable to close overallocated or underallocated manufacturing overhead to Cost of Goods Sold rather than allocating it proportionately to Work in Process Inventory, Finished Goods Inventory, and Cost of Goods Sold? Under what circumstances would it be advisable to allocate the overallocated or underallocated manufacturing overhead to Work in Process Inventory, Finished Goods Inventory, and Cost of Goods Sold?
8. Describe a situation that may cause manufacturing overhead to be overallocated in a given year. Also, describe a situation that may cause manufacturing overhead to be underallocated in a given year.
9. Explain why cost of goods sold should be lower if manufacturing overhead is overallocated. Should operating income be higher or lower if manufacturing overhead is overallocated? Why?
10. What account is credited when manufacturing overhead is allocated to jobs during the period? What account is debited when manufacturing overhead costs are incurred during the period? Would you expect these two amounts (allocated and incurred manufacturing over-head) to be the same? Why or why not?
11. How can job cost records help to promote sustainability efforts within a company?
12. Why should companies estimate the environmental costs of a given job? Why have EPR (extended producer responsibility) laws come into existence?

Application & Analysis

A3-58 *Unwrapped or How It's Made*

Product Costs and Job Costing Versus Process Costing

Go to www.YouTube.com and search for clips from the show *Unwrapped* on Food Network or *How It's Made* on the Discovery Channel. Watch a clip for a product you find interesting.

Basic Discussion Questions

1. Describe the product that is being produced and the company that makes it.
2. Summarize the production process that is used in making this product.
3. What raw materials are used to make this product?
4. What indirect materials are used to make this product?
5. Describe the jobs of the workers who would be considered "direct labor" in the making this product.

6. Describe the jobs of the workers who would be considered "indirect labor" in the making this product.
7. Define manufacturing overhead. In addition to the indirect materials and indirect labor previously described, what other manufacturing overhead costs would be incurred in this production process? Be specific and thorough. Make reasonable "guesses" if you do not know for sure.
8. Would a job-order costing system or a process costing system be used for this production process? Give specific reasons for your choice of which costing system would be most appropriate for this manufacturer.

Decision Cases

A3-59 Issues with cost of job *(Learning Objectives 2, 3, & 4)*

Hegy Chocolate is located in Cleveland. The company prepares gift boxes of chocolates for private parties and corporate promotions. Each order contains a selection of chocolates determined by the customer, and the box is designed to the customer's specifications. Accordingly, Hegy Chocolate uses a job cost system and allocates manufacturing overhead based on direct labor cost.

One of Hegy Chocolate's largest customers is the Bailey and Choi law firm. This organization sends chocolates to its clients each Christmas and also provides them to employees at the firm's gatherings. The law firm's managing partner, Peter Bailey, placed the client gift order in September for 500 boxes of cream-filled dark chocolates. But Bailey and Choi did not place its December staff-party order until the last week of November. This order was for an additional 100 boxes of chocolates identical to the ones to be distributed to clients.

Hegy Chocolate budgeted the cost per box for the original 500-box order as follows:

Chocolate, filling, wrappers, box	$14.00
Employee time to fill and wrap the box (10 min.)	2.00
Manufacturing overhead	1.00
Total manufacturing cost	$17.00

Ben Hegy, president of Hegy Chocolate, priced the order at $20 per box.

In the past few months, Hegy Chocolate has experienced price increases for both dark chocolate and direct labor. *All other costs have remained the same.* Hegy budgeted the cost per box for the second order as follows:

Chocolate, filling, wrappers, box	$15.00
Employee time to fill and wrap the box (10 min.)	2.20
Manufacturing overhead	1.10
Total manufacturing cost	$18.30

Requirements

1. Do you agree with the cost analysis for the second order? Explain your answer.
2. Should the two orders be accounted for as one or two jobs in Hegy Chocolate's system?
3. What sales price per box should Hegy set for the second order? What are the advantages and disadvantages of this price?

A3-60 Issues with the manufacturing overhead rate *(Learning Objectives 2, 3, & 4)*

All Natural manufactures organic fruit preserves sold primarily through health food stores and on the Web. The company closes for two weeks each December to allow employees to spend time with their families over the holiday season. All Natural's manufacturing overhead is mostly straight-line depreciation on its plant and air-conditioning costs for keeping the berries cool during the summer months. The company uses direct labor hours as the allocation base. President Kara Wise has just approved new accounting software and is telling Controller Melissa Powers about her decision.

"I think this new software will be great," Wise says. "It will save you time in preparing all of those reports."

"Yes, and having so much more information just a click away will help us make better decisions and help control costs," replies Powers. "We need to consider how we can use the new system to improve our business practices."

"And I know just where to start," says Wise. "You complain each year about having to predict the weather months in advance for estimating air-conditioning costs and direct labor hours for the denominator of the predetermined manufacturing overhead rate, when professional meteorologists can't even get tomorrow's forecast right! I think we should calculate the predetermined overhead rate on a monthly basis."

Controller Powers is not so sure this is a good idea.

Requirements

1. What are the advantages and disadvantages of Wise's proposal?
2. Should All Natural compute its predetermined manufacturing overhead rate on an annual basis or a monthly basis? Explain.

Team Project

A3-61 Finding the cost of flight routes *(Learning Objectives 2, 3, & 4)*

Major airlines such as American, Delta, and Continental are struggling to meet the challenges of budget carriers such as Southwest and JetBlue. Suppose Delta CFO Edward Bastian has just returned from a meeting on strategies for responding to competition from budget carriers. The vice president of operations suggests doing nothing: "We just need to wait until these new airlines run out of money. They cannot be making money with their low fares." In contrast, the vice president of marketing, not wanting to lose marketing share, suggests cutting Delta's fares to match the competition. "If JetBlue charges only $75 for that flight from New York, so must we!" Others, including CFO Bastian, emphasize the potential for cutting costs. Another possibility is starting a new budget airline within Delta. Imagine that CEO Gerald Grinstein cuts the meeting short and directs Bastian to "get some hard data."

As a start, Bastian decides to collect cost and revenue data for a typical Delta flight and then compare it to the data for a competitor. Assume that he prepares the following schedule:

	Delta	JetBlue
Route: New York to Tampa	Flight 1247	Flight 53
Distance	1,011 miles	1,011 miles
Seats per plane	142	162
One-way ticket price	$80–$621*	$75
Food and beverage	Meal	Snack

*The highest price is first-class airfare.

Excluding food and beverage, Bastian estimates that the cost per available seat mile is $0.084 for Delta, compared to $0.053 for JetBlue. (That is, the cost of flying a seat for one mile—whether or not the seat is occupied—is $0.084 for Delta and $0.053 for JetBlue.) Assume that the average cost of food and beverage is $5 per passenger for snacks and $10 for a meal.

Split your team into two groups. Group 1 should prepare its response to Requirement 1 and Group 2 should prepare its response to Requirement 2 before the entire team meets to consider Requirements 3–6.

Requirements

1. Group 1 uses the data to determine the following for Delta:
   a. The total cost of Flight 1247 assuming a full plane (100% load factor)
   b. The revenue generated by Flight 1247 assuming a 100% load factor and average revenue per one-way ticket of $102
   c. The profit per Flight 1247 given the responses to a and b

2. Group 2 uses the data to determine for JetBlue:
   a. The total cost of Flight 53 assuming a full plane (100% load factor)
   b. The revenue generated by Flight 53 assuming a 100% load factor
   c. The profit per Flight 53 given the responses to a and b
3. The entire team meets, and both groups combine their analyses. Based on the responses to Requirements 1 and 2, carefully evaluate each of the four alternative strategies discussed in Delta's executive meeting.
4. CFO Bastian wants additional data before he meets again with Delta's CEO. Each group should repeat the analyses in *both* Requirements 1 and 2 using another Delta route in Requirement 1 and a budget airline other than JetBlue in Requirement 2 (other budget airlines include America West, with a cost per available seat mile of about $0.065, and Southwest Airlines, with a cost per available seat mile of about $0.063). Information on flights, available seats, airfares, and mileage are available on airline websites.
5. The analysis in this project is based on several simplifying assumptions. As a team, brainstorm factors that your quantitative evaluation does not include but that may affect a comparison of Delta's operations against budget carriers.
6. Prepare a memo from CFO Bastian addressed to Delta CEO Grinstein summarizing the results of your analyses. Be sure to include the limitations of your analyses identified in Requirement 5.

CMA Questions

A3-62

A review of the year-end accounting records of Elk Industries discloses the following information:

Raw materials	$ 80,000
Work in process	128,000
Finished goods	272,000
Cost of goods sold	1,120,000

The company's underapplied overhead equals $133,000. On the basis of this information, Elk's cost of goods sold is most appropriately reported as

a. $987,000.
b. $1,213,100.
c. $1,218,000.
d. $1,253,000. *(CMA Adapted)*

A3-63

Wagner Corporation applies factory overhead based upon machine hours. At the beginning of the year, Wagner budgeted factory overhead at $250,000 and estimated that 100,000 machine hours would be used to make 50,000 units of product. During the year, the company produced 48,000 units, using 97,000 machine hours. Actual overhead for the year was $252,000. Under a standard cost system, the amount of factory overhead applied during the year was

a. $240,000.
b. $242,500.
c. $250,000.
d. $252,000. *(CMA Adapted)*

4

Activity-Based Costing, Lean Operations, and the Costs of Quality

Learning Objectives

1. Develop and use departmental overhead rates to allocate indirect costs
2. Develop and use activity-based costing (ABC) to allocate indirect costs
3. Understand the benefits and limitations of ABC/ABM systems
4. Describe lean operations
5. Describe and use the costs of quality framework

When Life Fitness began, it

only had one product: the Lifecycle computerized exercise bike. Since it was the first of its kind, the Lifecycle had no immediate competition. However, as the success of the company increased, other companies began to produce their own brands of fitness equipment. In addition, Life Fitness expanded its product offerings to include computerized treadmills, elliptical cross-trainers, and stair climbers.[1]

Let's suppose that, as a result of the increase in competition and product diversity, managers found they needed better, more accurate product cost information to help guide their business decisions and remain competitive.[2] A traditional job costing system would have ensured that the direct material and direct labor costs traced to each product were correct. However, the traditional method of allocating manufacturing overhead costs may not have been doing a good enough job of matching overhead costs to the products that used those overhead resources.

John Kasawa / Shutterstock.com

Life Fitness's managers may have needed a more refined cost allocation system: one that wasn't based on a single, predetermined manufacturing overhead rate. By using either *departmental overhead rates* or *activity-based costing (ABC)* to allocate manufacturing overhead, the company would be able to more accurately determine the cost of individual jobs or products. ABC could also help managers cut costs by highlighting the cost of each activity performed during production. In addition, it could help them identify the costs associated with providing high-quality products to their customers. With more accurate cost information in hand, managers would be able to secure Life Fitness's continued leadership in the market for fitness equipment.

[1]uscorporate.lifefitness.com

[2]All references to Life Fitness in this chapter are hypothetical, unless otherwise noted, and were created by the author solely for academic purposes. The examples are not intended, in any way, to represent the actual business practices of, or costs incurred by, Life Fitness, Inc.

As the chapter opening story illustrates, most companies have experienced increased competition over the past few decades. In addition, companies have sought to expand their customer base by offering a more diversified line of products. Both of these factors are good for consumers, who now enjoy more product options at very competitive prices. However, these factors also present unique challenges to business managers and the accounting systems that support them. To thrive in a globally competitive market, companies must provide value to the customer by delivering a high-quality product at an attractive price, while managing costs so the company still earns a profit. This chapter will introduce several tools that today's managers use to make their companies competitive:

- Refined costing systems
- Lean operations
- Total quality management and the costs of quality

Why and How do Companies Refine Their Cost Allocation Systems?

Organizations from Dell to Carolina Power and Light to the U.S. Marine Corps use refined cost allocation systems. Why? Because simple cost allocation systems don't always do a good job of matching the cost of overhead resources with the products that consume those resources. The following example illustrates why.

Simple Cost Allocation Systems Can Lead to Cost Distortion

David, Matt, and Marc are three college friends who share an apartment. They agree to split the following monthly costs equally:

Rent and utilities	$570
Cable TV	50
High-speed internet access	40
Groceries	240
Total monthly costs	$900

Each roommate's share is $300 ($900/3).

Things go smoothly for the first few months. But then David calls a meeting: "Since I started having dinner at Amy's each night, I shouldn't have to chip in for the groceries." Matt then pipes in: "I'm so busy studying and using the internet that I never have time to watch TV. I don't want to pay for the cable TV anymore. And Marc, since your friend Jennifer eats here most evenings, you should pay a double share of the grocery bill." Marc replies, "If that's the way you feel, Matt, then you should pay for the internet access since you're the only one around here who uses it!"

What happened? The friends originally agreed to share the costs equally. But they are not participating equally in watching cable TV, using the internet, and eating the groceries. Splitting these costs equally is not equitable.

The roommates could use a cost allocation approach that better matches costs with the people who participate in the activities that cause those costs. This means splitting the cable TV costs between David and Marc, assigning the internet access cost to Matt, and allocating the grocery bill one-third to Matt and two-thirds to Marc. Exhibit 4-1 compares the results of this refined cost allocation system with the original cost allocation system.

No wonder David called a meeting! The original cost allocation system charged him $300 a month, but the refined system shows that a more equitable share would be only $215. The new system allocates Marc $375 a month instead of $300. David was paying for resources he did not use (internet and groceries), while Marc was not paying for all of the resources (groceries) he and his guest consumed. The simple cost allocation system the roommates initially devised had ended up distorting the cost that should be charged to each roommate: David was *overcharged* by $85 while Matt and Marc were *undercharged* by an equal, but offsetting amount ($10 + $75 = $85). Notice that the total "pool" of monthly costs ($900) is the same under both allocation systems. The only difference is *how* the pool of costs is *allocated* among the three roommates.

EXHIBIT 4-1 More-Refined Versus Less-Refined Cost Allocation System

	David	Matt	Marc	Total
More-refined cost allocation system:				
Rent and utilities	$190	$190	$190	$570
Cable TV	25	0	25	50
High-speed internet access	0	40	0	40
Groceries	0	80	160	240
Total costs allocated	$215	$310	$375	$900
Less-refined original cost allocation system	$300	$300	$300	$900
Difference	$ (85)	$ 10	$ 75	$ 0

Just as the simple allocation system had resulted in overcharging David, yet undercharging Matt and Marc, many companies find that the simple overhead cost allocation system described in the last chapter results in "overcosting" some of their jobs or products while "undercosting" others. **Cost distortion** occurs when some products are overcosted while other products are undercosted by the cost allocation system. As we'll see in the following sections, companies often refine their cost allocation systems to minimize the amount of cost distortion caused by the simpler cost allocation systems. By refining their costing systems, companies can more equitably assign indirect costs (such as manufacturing overhead) to their individual jobs, products, or services. As a result, less cost distortion occurs and managers have more accurate information for making vital business decisions.

In the following section, we will be describing how refined cost allocation systems can be used to better allocate manufacturing overhead to specific products to reduce cost distortion. However, keep in mind that the same principles apply to allocating *any* indirect costs to *any* cost objects. Thus, even merchandising and service companies, as well as governmental agencies, can use these refined cost allocation systems to provide their managers with better cost information.

Why is this important?

"With better **cost information** managers are able to make more **profitable** decisions. One company reported triple sales and **five-fold increase** in profits after it implemented a **refined costing system.** By using better costs information for quoting jobs **management** was able to generate a more **profitable mix** of job contracts."[3]

[3]Hicks, Douglas. "Yes, ABC is for small business, too," *Journal of Accountancy*, Aug. 1999; p. 41.

Review: Using a Plantwide Overhead Rate to Allocate Indirect Costs

In the last chapter, we assumed that Life Fitness allocated its manufacturing overhead (MOH) costs using one predetermined MOH rate ($16 per DL hour). This rate was based on management's estimate of the total manufacturing overhead costs for the year ($1 million) and estimate of the total amount of the allocation base (62,500 DL hours) for the year.[4] The rate was calculated as follows:

$$\text{Predetermined MOH rate} = \frac{\$1{,}000{,}000}{62{,}500 \text{ DL hours}} = \$16 \text{ per direct labor hour}$$

[4]All references to Life Fitness in this hypothetical example were created by the author solely for academic purposes and are not intended, in any way, to represent the actual business practices of, or costs incurred by, Life Fitness, Inc.

This rate is also known as a **plantwide overhead rate**, because any job produced in the plant, whether it be treadmills, elliptical cross-trainers, or stair climbers, would be allocated manufacturing overhead using this single rate. It wouldn't matter whether the job was worked on in one department or many departments during the production process: The same rate would be used throughout the plant.

Let's see how this works for Life Fitness. In Chapter 3, we followed a job in which each elliptical cross-trainer required about 10 direct labor hours to make.[5] We'll continue to assume that each elliptical made by the company requires 10 direct labor hours to complete. Let's also assume that each treadmill requires 10 direct labor hours to complete. Exhibit 4-2 shows how manufacturing overhead would be allocated to a job in which one elliptical was made, and another job in which one treadmill was made, using the plantwide overhead rate.

EXHIBIT 4-2 Allocating Manufacturing Overhead Using a Plantwide Overhead Rate

	Plantwide Overhead Rate		Actual Use of Allocation Base		MOH Allocated to One Unit
Elliptical	$16 per DL hour	×	10 DL hours	=	$160
Treadmill	$16 per DL hour	×	10 DL hours	=	$160

The plantwide allocation system is illustrated in Exhibit 4-3.

EXHIBIT 4-3 Plantwide Allocation System

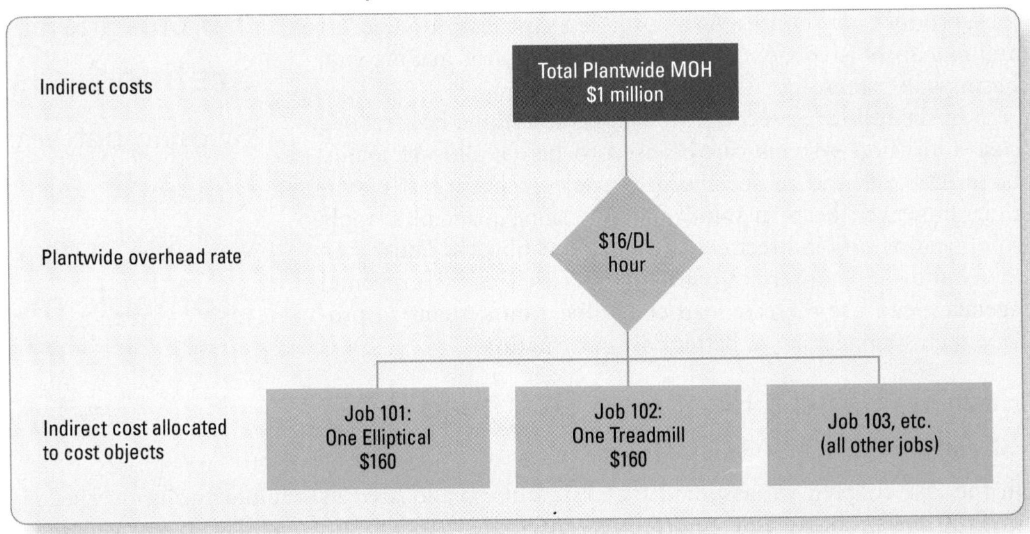

Using Departmental Overhead Rates to Allocate Indirect Costs

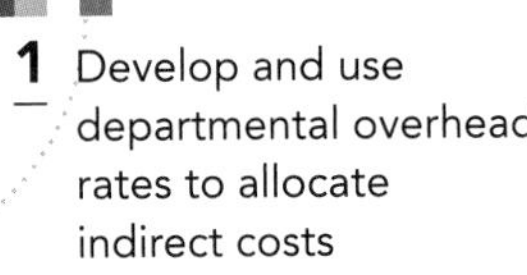

The plantwide allocation system previously described works well for some companies, but may end up distorting costs if the following conditions exist:

1. Different departments incur different amounts and types of manufacturing overhead.
2. Different jobs or products use the departments to a different extent.

If these circumstances exist, the company should strongly consider refining its cost allocation system. Let's see if these conditions exist at Life Fitness.

[5]Job 603, a batch of 50 elliptical cross-trainers, required 500 DL hours to complete. Thus, the average time spent on each unit was 10 DL hours.

CONDITION 1: DO DIFFERENT DEPARTMENTS HAVE DIFFERENT AMOUNTS AND TYPES OF MOH COSTS? As shown in Exhibit 4-4, let's assume Life Fitness has two primary production departments: Machining and Assembly. The Machining Department has a lot of machinery, which drives manufacturing overhead costs such as machine depreciation, utilities, machine lubricants, and repairs and maintenance. Let's say these overhead costs are estimated to be $400,000 for the year. On the other hand, the Assembly Department does not incur as many of these types of overhead costs. Rather, the Assembly Department's manufacturing overhead costs include more indirect labor for supervision, quality inspection, and so forth. These manufacturing overhead costs are expected to total $600,000 for the year.

Exhibit 4-4 shows that the first condition is present: Each department incurs different types and amounts of MOH. Life Fitness expects to incur a total of $1 million of manufacturing overhead: $400,000 relates to the Machining Department while $600,000 relates to the Assembly Department.

EXHIBIT 4-4 Machining and Assembly Departments' Manufacturing Overhead

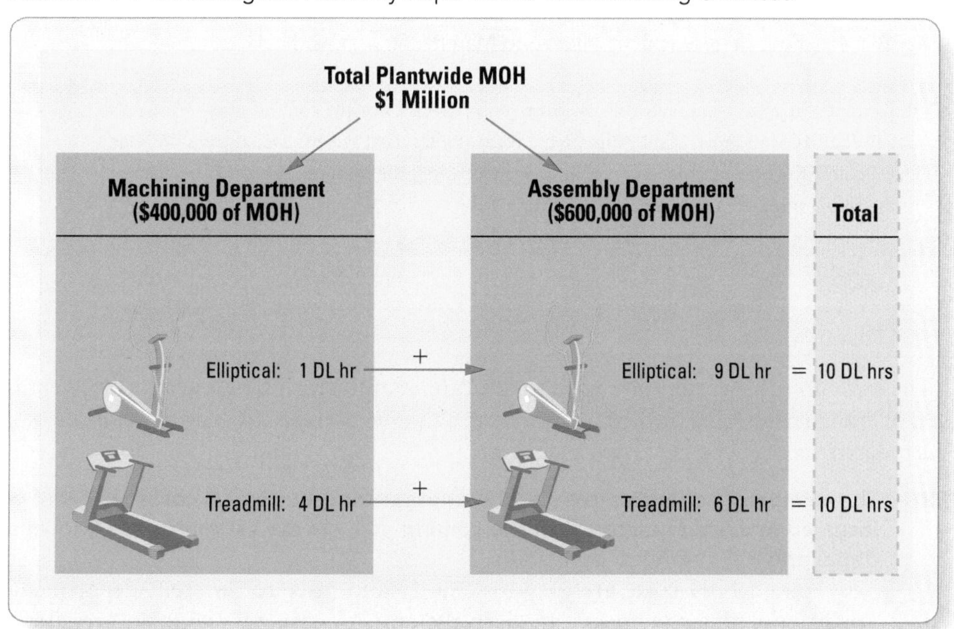

CONDITION 2: DO DIFFERENT PRODUCTS USE THE DEPARTMENTS TO A DIFFERENT EXTENT? While both ellipticals and treadmills take 10 direct labor hours in total to make, Exhibit 4-4 also shows that ellipticals and treadmills spend *different* amounts of time in each production department. Each elliptical only requires 1 DL hour in the Machining Department, but requires 9 DL hours in the Assembly Department. Contrast that with a treadmill, which spends more time in Machining to fabricate some of its components (4 DL hours) but less time in Assembly (6 DL hours). As a result of these differences, the second condition is also present. The company's cost allocation system would be much more accurate if it took these differences into account when determining how much manufacturing overhead to allocate to each product.

Since both conditions are present, the company should consider "fine-tuning" its cost allocation systems by establishing separate manufacturing overhead rates, known as departmental overhead rates, for each department. That means that Life Fitness will establish one manufacturing overhead rate for the Machining Department and another overhead rate for the Assembly Department. These rates will then be used to allocate manufacturing overhead to jobs or products based on the extent to which each product uses the different manufacturing departments.

Exhibit 4-5 shows the circumstances favoring the use of departmental overhead rates rather than a single, plantwide overhead rate.

EXHIBIT 4-5 Circumstances Favoring Departmental Overhead Rates

Departmental overhead rates increase the accuracy of job costs when....

- Each department incurs different types and amounts of manufacturing overhead.
- Each product, or job, uses the departments to a different extent.

Four Basic Steps to Computing and Using Departmental Overhead Rates

In Chapter 3, we used four steps for allocating manufacturing overhead. These steps are summarized in Exhibit 4-6.

EXHIBIT 4-6 Four Basic Steps for Allocating Manufacturing Overhead

1. Estimate the total manufacturing overhead costs (MOH) for the coming year.
2. Select an allocation base and estimate the total amount that will be used during the year.
3. Calculate the predetermined overhead rate by dividing the total estimated MOH costs by the total estimated amount of the allocation base.
4. Allocate some MOH cost to each job worked on during the year by multiplying the predetermined MOH rate by the actual amount of the allocation base used by the job.

The same four basic steps are used to allocate manufacturing overhead using departmental overhead rates. The only real difference is that we will be calculating *separate rates* for *each* department. Let's see how this is done.

STEP 1: The company estimates the total manufacturing overhead costs that will be incurred in *each department* in the coming year. These estimates are known as departmental overhead cost pools.

Some MOH costs are easy to identify and trace to different departments. For example, management can trace the cost of lease payments and repairs to the machines used in the Machining Department. Management can also trace the cost of employing supervisors and quality control inspectors to the Assembly Department. However, other overhead costs are more difficult to identify with specific departments. For example, the depreciation, property taxes, and insurance on the entire plant would have to be split, or allocated, between the individual departments, most likely based on the square footage occupied by each department in the plant.

As shown in Exhibit 4-4, Life Fitness has determined that $400,000 of its total estimated MOH relates to its Machining Department, while the remaining $600,000 relates to its Assembly Department.

Department	Total Departmental Overhead Cost Pool
Machining	$ 400,000
Assembly	$ 600,000
TOTAL MOH	$1,000,000

STEP 2: The company selects an allocation base for *each department* and estimates the total amount that will be used during the year.

The allocation base selected for each department should be the cost driver of the costs in the departmental overhead pool. Often, manufacturers will use different allocation bases for the different departments. For example, machine hours might be the best allocation base for a very automated Machining Department that uses machine robotics extensively. However, direct labor hours might be the best allocation base for an Assembly Department.

Let's assume that Life Fitness's Machining Department uses a lot of human-operated machinery, therefore the number of direct labor hours used in the department is identical to the number of hours the machines are run. While the number of machine hours is the real cost driver, direct labor hours will make an adequate surrogate. As a result, management has selected direct labor hours as the allocation base for both departments. Recall that Life Fitness estimates using a total of 62,500 direct labor hours during the year. Of this amount, management expects to use 12,500 in the Machining Department and 50,000 in the Assembly Department.

Department	Total Amount of Departmental Allocation Base
Machining	12,500 DL hours
Assembly	50,000 DL hours

STEP 3: The company calculates departmental overhead rates using the information estimated in Steps 1 and 2:

$$\text{Departmental overhead rate} = \frac{\text{Total estimated departmental overhead cost pool}}{\text{Total estimated amount of the departmental allocation base}}$$

Therefore, Life Fitness calculates its departmental overhead rates as follows:

$$\text{Machining Department overhead rate} = \frac{\$400{,}000}{12{,}500 \text{ DL hours}} = \$32 \text{ per DL hour}$$

$$\text{Assembly Department overhead rate} = \frac{\$600{,}000}{50{,}000 \text{ DL hours}} = \$12 \text{ per DL hour}$$

These first three steps are performed before the year begins, using estimated data for the year. Thus, departmental overhead rates are also "predetermined," just like the plant-wide predetermined manufacturing overhead rate discussed in Chapter 3. The first three steps, performed before the year begins, are summarized in Exhibit 4-7.

EXHIBIT 4-7 Steps to Calculating the Departmental Overhead Rates

Department	Step 1: Total Departmental Overhead Cost Pool		Step 2: Total Amount of Departmental Allocation Base		Step 3: Departmental Overhead Rate
Machining	$400,000	÷	12,500 DL hours	=	$32 per DL hour
Assembly	$600,000	÷	50,000 DL hours	=	$12 per DL hour

Once these rates have been established, the company uses them throughout the year to allocate manufacturing overhead to each job as it is produced, as shown in Step 4.

STEP 4: The company allocates some manufacturing overhead from *each* department to the individual jobs that use those departments.

The amount of MOH allocated from each department is calculated as follows:

MOH allocated to job = Departmental overhead rate × Actual amount of departmental allocation base used by job

Exhibit 4-8 shows how these departmental overhead rates would be used to allocate manufacturing to a job in which one elliptical is produced.

EXHIBIT 4-8 Allocating MOH to One Elliptical Using Departmental Overhead Rates

Department	Departmental Overhead Rate (from Exhibit 4-7)		Actual Use of Departmental Allocation Base (from Exhibit 4-4)		MOH Allocated to One Elliptical
Machining	$32 per DL hour	×	1 DL hours	=	$ 32
Assembly	$12 per DL hour	×	9 DL hours	=	108
Total					$140

Exhibit 4-9 shows how the same rates would be used to allocate manufacturing overhead to another job in which one treadmill is produced. Because the treadmill spends more time in the Machining Department, but less time in the Assembly Department, the amount of MOH allocated to the treadmill differs from the amount allocated to the elliptical in Exhibit 4-8.

EXHIBIT 4-9 Allocating MOH to One Treadmill Using Departmental Overhead Rates

Department	Departmental Overhead Rate (from Exhibit 4-7)		Actual Use of Departmental Allocation Base (from Exhibit 4-4)		MOH Allocated to One Treadmill
Machining	$32 per DL hour	×	4 DL hours	=	$128
Assembly	$12 per DL hour	×	6 DL hours	=	72
Total					$200

Exhibit 4-10 illustrates the company's departmental cost allocation system.

Had the Plantwide Overhead Rate Been Distorting Product Costs?

We have just seen that Life Fitness's refined cost allocation system allocates $140 of MOH to each elliptical, and $200 of MOH to each treadmill (Exhibits 4-8 and 4-9). Does this differ from the amount that would have been allocated to each unit using Life Fitness's original plantwide rate? Yes. Recall from Exhibit 4-2 that if Life Fitness uses a plantwide overhead rate, $160 of manufacturing overhead would be allocated to both types of equipment, simply because both types of equipment require the *same total* number of direct labor hours (10 DL hours) to produce.

The plantwide allocation system does not pick up on the nuances of how many direct labor hours are used by the products in *each* department. Therefore, it was not able to do a very good job of matching manufacturing overhead costs to the products that use those costs. As a result, the plantwide rate would have overcosted each elliptical, but undercosted each treadmill, as shown in Exhibit 4-11.

EXHIBIT 4-10 Departmental Cost Allocation System

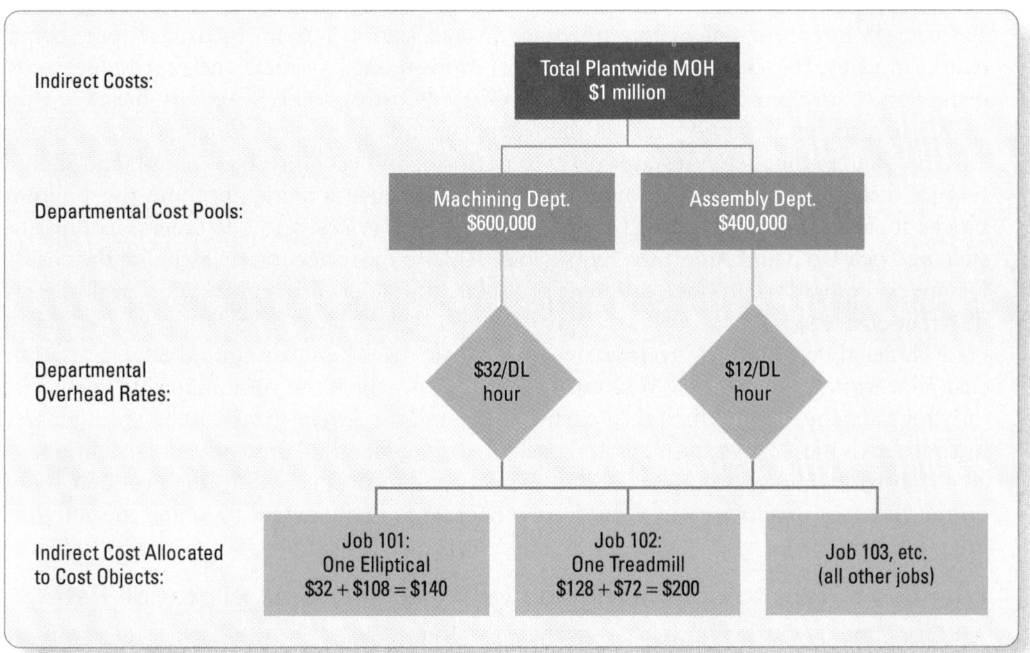

On the other hand, the refined cost allocation system recognizes the cost differences between departments and the usage difference between jobs. Therefore, the refined costing system does a *better job of matching* each department's overhead costs to the products that use the department's resources. This is the same thing we saw with the three roommates: The refined costing system did a better job of matching the cost of resources (cable, internet, groceries) to the roommates who used those resources. Because of this better matching, we can believe that the departmental overhead rates *more accurately allocate* MOH costs.

EXHIBIT 4-11 Cost Distortion Caused by Plantwide Overhead Rate

	Plantwide Overhead Rate MOH Allocation (from Exhibit 4-2)	Departmental Overhead Rates MOH Allocation (from Exhibits 4-8 and 4-9)	Amount of Cost Distortion
Elliptical......................	$160	$140	$20 *overcosted*
Treadmill	$160	$200	$40 *undercosted*

STOP & THINK

Do companies always have separate production departments, such as Machining and Assembly, for each step of the production process?

Answer: No. Rather than basing production departments on separate processing steps, some companies have separate production departments for each of their products. For example, Life Fitness could have one department for producing treadmills, another department for producing ellipticals, and yet another department for producing stair climbers. Each department would have all of the equipment necessary for producing its unique product. Departmental overhead rates would be formulated using the same four basic steps discussed above to determine a unique departmental overhead rate for each department. The only difference is that each product (for example, a treadmill) would travel through *only one* department (the Treadmill Department) rather than traveling through separate production departments (Machining and Assembly). Always keep in mind that the accounting system should reflect the actual production environment.

Using Activity-Based Costing to Allocate Indirect Costs

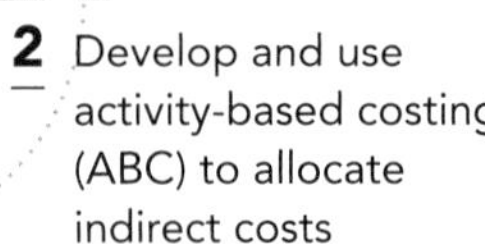

2 Develop and use activity-based costing (ABC) to allocate indirect costs

We just saw how companies can refine their cost allocation systems by using departmental overhead rates. If a company wants an even more refined system, one that reduces cost distortion to a minimum, it will use activity-based costing (ABC). **Activity-based costing (ABC)** focuses on *activities*, rather than departments, as the fundamental cost objects. ABC recognizes that activities are costly to perform, and each product manufactured may require different types and amounts of activities. Thus, activities become the building blocks for compiling the indirect costs of products, services, and customers. Companies such as Coca-Cola and American Express use ABC to more accurately estimate the cost of resources required to produce different products, to render different services, and to serve different customers.

Think about the three roommates for a moment. The most equitable and accurate cost allocation system for the roommates was one in which the roommates were charged only for the *activities* in which they participated, and the *extent* to which they participated in those activities. Likewise, activity-based costing generally causes the *least* amount of cost distortion among products because indirect costs are allocated to the products based on the (1) *types* of activities used by the product and (2) the *extent* to which the activities are used.

Four Basic Steps to Computing and Using Activity Cost Allocation Rates

ABC requires the same four basic steps listed in Exhibit 4-6. The main difference between an ABC system and a plantwide or departmental cost allocation system is that ABC systems have *separate* cost allocation rates for *each activity* identified by the company.

STEP 1: The company first identifies its primary activities and then estimates the total manufacturing overhead costs associated with *each activity*. These are known as activity cost pools.

Let's assume Life Fitness has determined that the following activities occur in its plant: First the machines must be set up to meet the particular specifications of the production run. Next, raw materials must be moved out of the storeroom and into the Machining Department, where some of the parts for the units are fabricated. Once the fabricated parts have been inspected, they are moved into the Assembly Department, along with additional raw materials that are needed from the storeroom. The units are then assembled by direct laborers, while production engineers supervise the process. All units are inspected during and after assembly. Upon passing inspection, each unit is packaged so that it is not damaged during shipment. Finally, the units are moved to the finished goods warehouse where they await shipment to customers. These activities are pictured in Exhibit 4-12.

EXHIBIT 4-12 Primary Activities Identified in the Manufacturing Plant

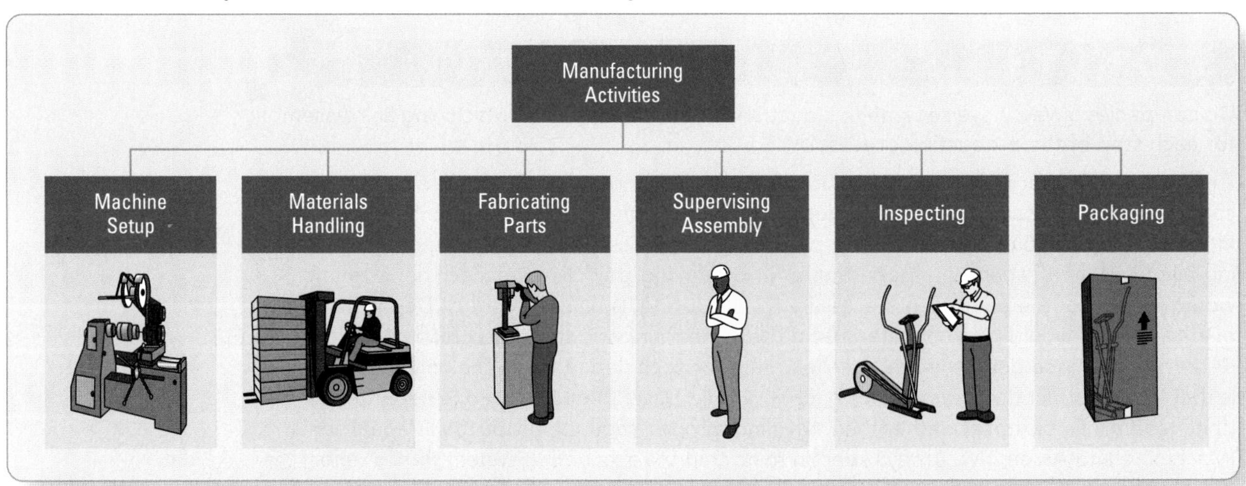

As part of this step, management must determine how much of the total estimated $1 million of MOH relates to each activity. Exhibit 4-13 shows some of the specific MOH costs that management has identified with each activity, along with the total estimated amount of each activity cost pool.

EXHIBIT 4-13 Activity Cost Pools

Activity	MOH Costs Related to the Activity	Total Activity Cost Pool
Machine Setup	Indirect labor used to set up machines	$ 80,000
Materials Handling	Forklifts, gas, operators' wages	200,000
Fabricating Parts	Machine lease payments, electricity, repairs	300,000
Supervising Assembly	Production engineers' labor	150,000
Inspecting	Testing equipment, inspection labor	170,000
Packaging	Packaging equipment	100,000
	TOTAL MOH	$1,000,000

Keep in mind that all of the costs in the activity costs pools are MOH costs; direct labor costs and direct materials costs are *not included* because they will be directly traced to specific jobs and therefore do not need to be allocated. That is why we only include supervisory labor in the overhead cost pool for the assembly activity. The machine operators and assembly-line workers are considered direct labor, so their cost will be traced to individual jobs, not allocated as part of MOH.

STEP 2: The company selects an allocation base for each activity and estimates the total amount that will be used during the year.

When selecting an allocation base for each activity, the company should keep the following in mind:

- The allocation base selected for each activity should be the *cost driver* of the costs in that particular activity cost pool.
- The company will need to keep track of how much of the allocation base each job or product uses. Therefore, the company must have the means to collect usage information about each allocation base. Thankfully, bar coding and other technological advances have helped make data collection easier and less costly in recent years.

Let's assume that Life Fitness has identified a cost driver for each activity, and has plans for how it will collect usage data. Exhibit 4-14 shows the selected allocation bases along with the total estimated amounts for the year.

EXHIBIT 4-14 Activity Allocation Bases and Total Estimated Amount of Each

Activity	Activity Allocation Base	Total Estimated Amount of Allocation Base
Machine Setup	Number of setups	8,000 setups
Materials Handling	Number of parts moved	400,000 parts
Fabricating Parts	Machine hours	12,500 machine hours
Supervising Assembly	Direct labor hours	50,000 DL hours
Inspecting	Number of inspections	34,000 inspections
Packaging	Cubic feet packaged	400,000 cubic feet

If your instructor is using MyAccountingLab, go to the Multimedia Library for a quick video on this topic.

STEP 3: The company calculates its activity cost allocation rates using the information estimated in Steps 1 and 2.

The formula for calculating the activity cost allocation rates is as follows:

$$\text{Activity cost allocation rate} = \frac{\text{Total estimated activity cost pool}}{\text{Total estimated activity allocation base}}$$

Exhibit 4-15 shows how this formula is used to compute a unique cost allocation rate for each of the company's production activities.

EXHIBIT 4-15 Computing Activity Cost Allocation Rates

Activity	Step 1: Total Activity Cost Pool (from Exhibit 4-13)		Step 2: Total Amount of Activity Allocation Base (from Exhibit 4-14)		Step 3: Activity Cost Allocation Rate
Machine Setup	$ 80,000	÷	8,000 setups	=	$10.00 per setup
Materials Handling	200,000	÷	400,000 parts	=	$ 0.50 per part
Fabricating Parts	300,000	÷	12,500 machine hours	=	$24.00 per machine hour
Supervising Assembly	150,000	÷	50,000 DL hours	=	$ 3.00 per DL hour
Inspecting	170,000	÷	34,000 inspections	=	$ 5.00 per inspection
Packaging	100,000	÷	400,000 cubic feet	=	$ 0.25 per cubic foot

Once again, these rates are calculated based on estimated, or budgeted, costs for the year. Hence, they too are "predetermined" before the year begins. Then, during the year, the company uses them to allocate manufacturing overhead to specific jobs, as shown in Step 4.

STEP 4: The company allocates some manufacturing overhead from *each* activity to the individual jobs that use the activities.

The formula is as follows:

$$\text{MOH allocated to job} = \text{Activity cost allocation rate} \times \text{Actual amount of activity allocation base used by job}$$

Exhibit 4-16 shows how these activity cost allocation rates would be used to allocate manufacturing overhead to a job in which one elliptical was produced.

EXHIBIT 4-16 Allocating MOH to One Elliptical Using ABC

Activity	Activity Cost Allocation Rate (from Exhibit 4-15)		Actual Use of Activity Allocation Base (information collected on job)		MOH Allocated to One Elliptical
Machine Setup	$10.00 per setup	×	2 setups	=	$ 20
Materials Handling	$ 0.50 per part	×	20 parts	=	10
Fabricating	$24.00 per machine hour	×	1 machine hour	=	24
Supervising Assembly	$ 3.00 per DL hour	×	9 DL hours	=	27
Inspecting	$ 5.00 per inspection	×	3 inspections	=	15
Packaging	$ 0.25 per cubic foot	×	52 cubic feet	=	13
Total					$109

Exhibit 4-17 shows how the same activity cost allocation rates are used to allocate MOH to a job in which one treadmill was produced.

EXHIBIT 4-17 Allocating MOH to One Treadmill Using ABC

Activity	Activity Cost Allocation Rate (from Exhibit 4-15)		Actual Use of Activity Allocation Base (information collected on job)		MOH Allocated to One Treadmill
Machine Setup	$10.00 per setup	×	4 setups	=	$ 40
Materials Handling	$ 0.50 per part	×	26 parts	=	13
Fabricating	$24.00 per machine hour	×	4 machine hour	=	96
Supervising Assembly	$ 3.00 per DL hour	×	6 DL hours	=	18
Inspecting	$ 5.00 per inspection	×	6 inspections	=	30
Packaging	$ 0.25 per cubic foot	×	60 cubic feet	=	15
Total					$212

Exhibit 4-18 illustrates the company's ABC system.

EXHIBIT 4-18 Illustration of the Company's ABC System

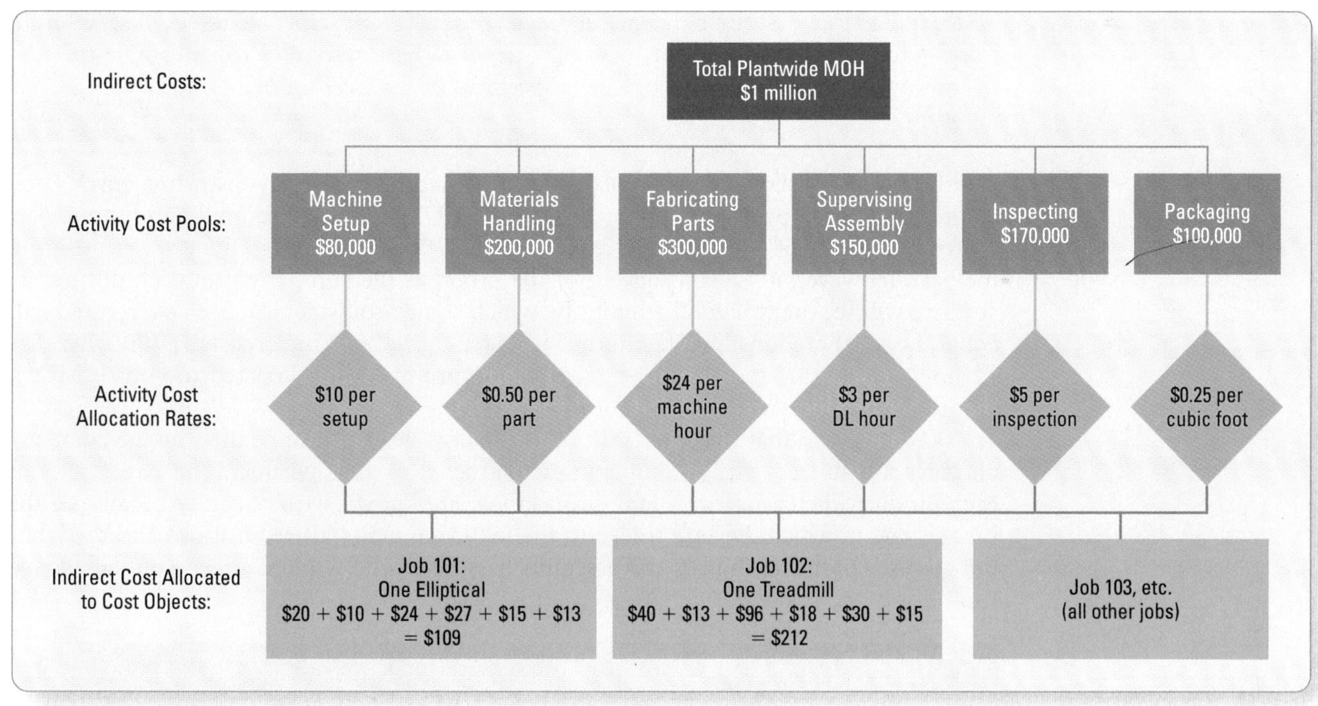

One Last Look at Cost Distortion: Comparing the Three Allocation Systems

Exhibit 4-19 compares the amount of manufacturing overhead that would have been allocated to each elliptical and each treadmill using the three cost allocation systems that we have discussed: 1) a single plantwide overhead rate, 2) departmental overhead rates, and 3) ABC.

EXHIBIT 4-19 Comparing the Three Cost Allocation Systems

	Plantwide Overhead Rate (Exhibit 4-2)	Departmental Overhead Rates (Exhibit 4-8 & 4-9)	Activity-Based Costing (Exhibit 4-16 & 4-17)
Elliptical	$160	$140	$109
Treadmill	$160	$200	$212

As you can see, each allocation system renders different answers for the amount of MOH that should be allocated to each elliptical and treadmill. Which is correct?

ABC costs are generally thought to be the most accurate because ABC takes into account 1) the *specific resources* each product uses (for example, inspecting resources) and 2) the *extent* to which they use these resources (for example three inspections of the elliptical, but six inspections of the treadmill).

Exhibit 4-19 shows that the plantwide rate had been severely distorting costs: Each elliptical had been overcosted by $51 ($160 – $109) and each treadmill had been undercosted by $52 ($160 – $212). Here, we have only looked at two units produced during the year. However, if we consider all of the products the company produced during the year, we will see that the total amount by which some products have been overcosted will equal the total amount by which other products have been undercosted. Why? Because $1 million of MOH is being allocated: If some products are allocated too much MOH, then other products are allocated too little MOH.

Keep in mind that all of this cost distortion is solely a result of the way the company allocates its indirect costs (manufacturing overhead) to each product. The direct costs of each product (direct materials and direct labor) are known with certainty because of the precise way in which they are traced to the job using materials requisitions and the labor time records of the machinists and assembly personnel who worked directly on these units.

STOP & THINK

If a company refines its costing system using departmental overhead rates or ABC, will manufacturing overhead still be overallocated or underallocated by the end of the year (as we saw in Chapter 3 when the company used a plantwide overhead rate)?

Answer: Yes. The use of *any predetermined* allocation rate will result in the over- or underallocation of manufacturing overhead. That's because *predetermined* rates are developed using *estimated* data before the actual manufacturing overhead costs and actual cost driver activity for the year are known. Refined costing systems decrease cost distortion *between* products, but do not eliminate the issue of over- or underallocating total manufacturing overhead.[6] As described in Chapter 3, Cost of Goods Sold will need to be adjusted at year-end for the *total* amount by which manufacturing overhead has been over- or underallocated.

[6]In some cases, ABC may reduce the total amount of over- or underallocation. How? Some activity cost pools may be overallocated, while others are underallocated, resulting in an offsetting total effect.

The Cost Hierarchy: A Useful Guide for Setting Up Activity Cost Pools

Some companies use a classification system, called the cost hierarchy, to establish activity cost pools. Companies often have hundreds of different activities. However, to keep the ABC system manageable, companies need to keep the system as simple as possible, yet refined enough to accurately determine product costs.[7] The cost hierarchy, pictured in Exhibit 4-20, helps managers understand the nature of each activity cost pool, and what drives it.

EXHIBIT 4-20 The Cost Hierarchy

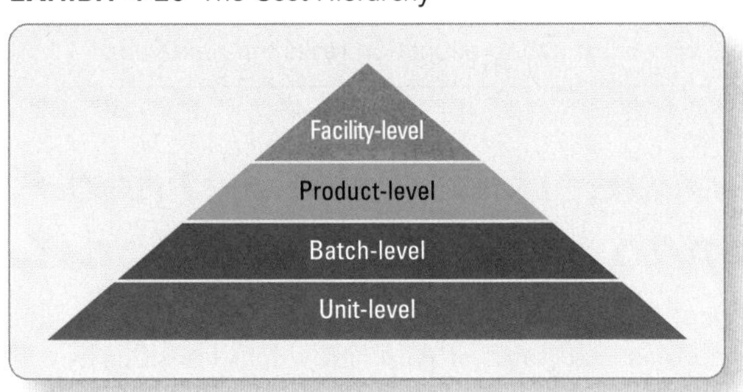

There are four categories of activity costs in this hierarchy, each determined by the underlying factor that drives its costs:

1. Unit-level activities—activities and costs incurred for every unit. Examples include inspecting and packaging *each* unit the company produces.
2. Batch-level activities—activities and costs incurred for every batch, regardless of the number of units in the batch. One example would be machine setup. Once the machines are set up for the specifications of the production run, the company could produce a batch of 1, 10, or 100 units, yet the company only incurs the machine setup cost once for the entire batch.
3. Product-level activities—activities and costs incurred for a particular product, regardless of the number of units or batches of the product produced. Examples include the cost to research, develop, design, and market new models.
4. Facility-level activities—activities and costs incurred no matter how many units, batches, or products are produced in the plant. An example is facility upkeep: the cost of depreciation, insurance, property tax, and maintenance on the entire production plant.

By considering how the costs of different activities are consumed (at the unit, batch, product, or facility level), managers are often able to maintain a relatively simple, yet accurate ABC system. After initially identifying perhaps 100 different activities, managers may be able to settle on 5–15 cost pools by combining those activities (for example, batch-level activities) that behave the same way into the same cost pools.

[7]When ABC system implementations fail, it is often due to managers' development of an overly complex system with too many cost pools and too many different cost drivers. After several redesigns of their ABC systems, Coca-Cola and Allied Signal both found that the simpler designs resulted in just as much accuracy. G. Cokins, "Learning to Love ABC," *Journal of Accountancy*, August 1999, pp. 37–39.

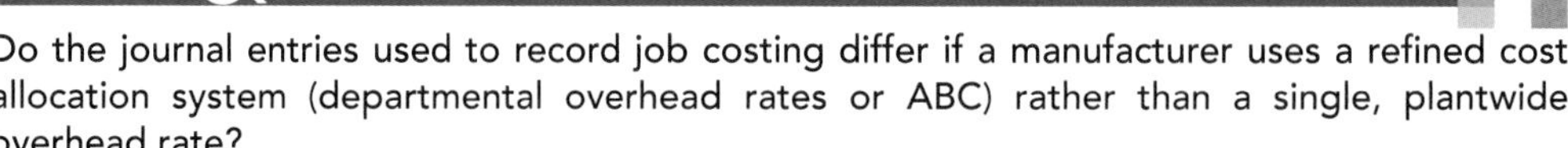

Do the journal entries used to record job costing differ if a manufacturer uses a refined cost allocation system (departmental overhead rates or ABC) rather than a single, plantwide overhead rate?

Answer: The journal entries used for a refined costing system are essentially the same as those described in Chapter 3 for a traditional job costing system. The only difference is that the company may decide to use *several* MOH accounts (one for each department or activity cost pool) rather than *one* MOH account. By using several MOH accounts, the manufacturer obtains more detailed information on each cost pool. This information may help managers make better estimates when calculating allocation rates the next year.

How do Managers Use the Refined Cost Information to Improve Operations?

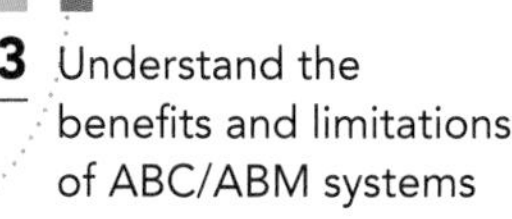

3 Understand the benefits and limitations of ABC/ABM systems

We've just seen how companies can increase the accuracy of their product costing systems by using departmental overhead rates or ABC. Now let's consider how managers use this improved cost information to run their companies more effectively and efficiently.

Activity-Based Management (ABM)

Activity-based management (ABM) refers to using activity-based cost information to make decisions that increase profits while satisfying customers' needs. Life Fitness can use ABC information for pricing and product mix decisions, for identifying opportunities to cut costs, and for routine planning and control decisions.

Pricing and Product Mix Decisions

The information provided by ABC showed Life Fitness's managers that ellipticals cost *less* to make and treadmills cost *more* to make than indicated by the original plantwide cost allocation system. As a result, managers may decide to change pricing on these products. For example, the company may be able to reduce its price on ellipticals to become more price-competitive. Or the company may decide to leave the price where it is, yet try to increase demand for this product since it is more profitable than originally assumed. On the other hand, managers will want to reevaluate the price charged for treadmills. The price must be high enough to cover the cost of producing and selling the treadmills while still being low enough to compete with other companies and earn Life Fitness a reasonable profit.

After implementing ABC, companies often realize they were overcosting their high-volume products and undercosting their low-volume products. Plantwide overhead rates based on volume-sensitive allocation bases (such as direct labor hours), end up allocating more cost to high-volume products, and less cost to low-volume products. However, ABC recognizes that not all indirect costs are driven by the number of units produced. That is to say, not all costs are unit-level costs. Rather, many costs are incurred at the batch-level or product-level where they can be spread over the number of units in the batch or in the product line. As shown in Exhibit 4-21, ABC tends to increase the unit cost of low-volume products (that have fewer units over which to spread batch-level and product-level costs), and decrease the unit cost of high-volume products.

As a result of using ABC, many companies have found that they were actually losing money on some of their products while earning much more profit than they had realized on other products! By shifting the mix of products offered away from the less profitable and towards the more profitable, companies are able to generate a higher operating income.

Cutting Costs

Most companies adopt ABC to get more accurate product costs for pricing and product mix decisions, but they often reap even *greater benefits* by using ABM to pinpoint opportunities to cut costs. For example, using ABC allowed Life Fitness to better understand what drives its manufacturing overhead costs. The plantwide allocation system failed to pinpoint what was driving manufacturing overhead costs. Hence, managers could not

EXHIBIT 4-21 Typical Result of ABC Costing

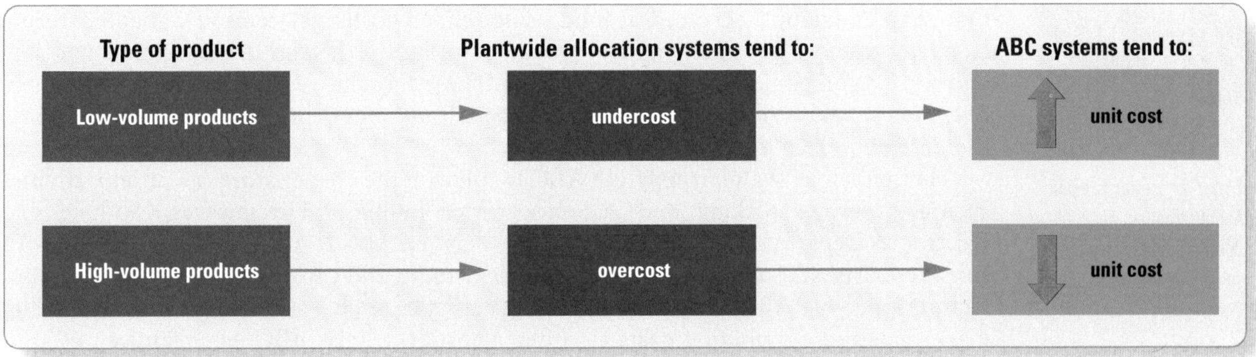

effectively determine which costs could be minimized. Once the company switched to ABC, managers realized that it costs $10 each time a machine is set up, $5 for each inspection, and so forth. Now, production managers have a "starting place" for cutting costs.

Once managers identify the company's activities and their related costs, managers can analyze whether all of the activities are really necessary. As the term suggests, value-added activities are activities for which the customer is willing to pay because these activities add value to the final product or service. In other words, these activities help satisfy the customer's expectations of the product or service. For example, fabricating component parts and assembling the units are value-added activities because they are necessary for changing raw materials into high-quality ellipticals and treadmills.

On the other hand, non-value-added activities (also referred to as waste activities), are activities that neither enhance the customer's image of the product or service nor provide a competitive advantage. These types of activities, such as storage of inventory and movement of parts from one area of the factory to another, could be reduced or removed from the process with no ill effect on the end product or service. The goal of value-engineering, as described in Exhibit 4-22, is to eliminate all waste in the system by making the company's processes as effective and efficient as possible. That means eliminating, reducing, or simplifying all non-value-added activities, and examining whether value-added activities could be improved.

EXHIBIT 4-22 The Goal of Value-Engineering

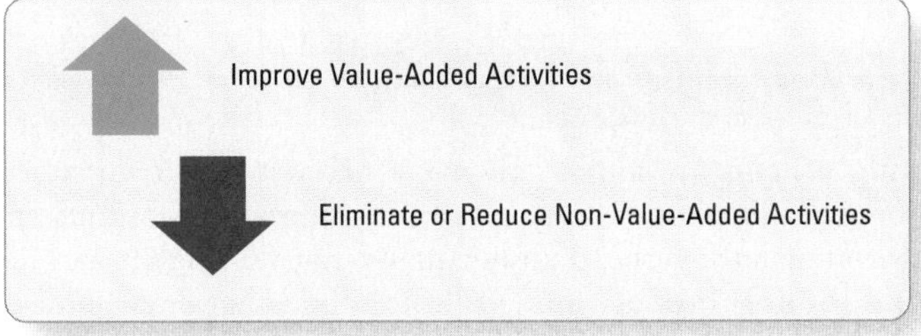

One way of determining whether an activity adds value is to ask if it could be eliminated or reduced by improving another part of the process. For example, could the movement of parts be eliminated or reduced by changing the factory layout? Could inventory storage be eliminated if the company only purchased the raw materials that were needed for each day's production run? Could inspection be reduced if more emphasis was placed on improving the production process, training employees, or using better quality inputs? In the second half of the chapter we'll discuss tools that many companies have adopted to identify and eliminate these costly non-value-added activities.

Routine Planning and Control Decisions

In addition to pricing, product mix, and cost-cutting decisions, Life Fitness can use ABC in routine planning and control. Activity-based budgeting uses the costs of activities to create budgets. Managers can compare actual activity costs to budgeted activity costs to determine how well they are achieving their goals.

If your instructor is using MyAccountingLab, go to the Multimedia Library for a quick video on this topic.

Using ABC in Service and Merchandising Companies

Our chapter example revolved around using refined costing systems at a manufacturing company to more accurately allocate manufacturing overhead. However, merchandising and service companies also find ABC useful. These firms use ABC to allocate the cost of *operating activities* (rather than production activities) among product lines or service lines to figure out which are most profitable.

For example, Walmart may use ABC to allocate the cost of store operating activities such as ordering, stocking, and customer service among its Housewares, Clothing, and Electronics Departments. An accounting firm may use ABC to allocate secretarial support, software costs, and travel costs between its tax, audit, and consulting clients. Even manufacturers may use ABC to allocate operating activities, such as research and development, marketing, and distribution costs to different product lines. ABC has also been used to determine customer profitability, not just product or service profitability. Firms use the same four basic steps discussed above, but apply them to indirect *operating* costs rather than indirect *manufacturing* costs (MOH). Once again, managers can use the data generated by ABC to determine which products or services to emphasize, to set prices, to cut costs, and to make other routine planning and control decisions.

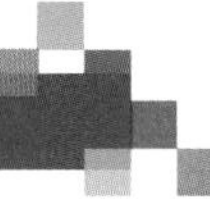

STOP & THINK

Can governmental agencies use ABC/ABM to run their operations more efficiently?

Answer: Yes. ABC/ABM is not just for private-sector companies. Several governmental agencies, including the U.S. Postal Service (USPS) and the City of Indianapolis, have successfully used ABC/ABM to run their operations more cost-effectively. For example, in the past the USPS accepted customer payments only in the form of cash or checks. After using ABC to study the cost of its revenue collection procedures (activities), the USPS found that it would be cheaper to accept debit and credit card sales. Accepting debit and credit card sales also produced higher customer satisfaction, allowing the USPS to better compete with private mail and package carriers.

The City of Indianapolis was able to save its taxpayers millions of dollars after using ABC to study the cost of providing city services (activities) to local citizens. Once the city determined the cost of its activities, it was able to obtain competitive bids for those same services from private businesses. As a result, the city outsourced many activities to private-sector firms for a lower cost.[8]

Sustainability and Refined Costing Systems

Refined costing systems are almost always a necessity for companies that wish to move toward environmental sustainability. Why? Because jobs and product lines do not drive environmental overhead costs equally. Even a smaller manufacturing company with two to three product lines will often find that environmental costs, such as solid waste disposal, water and energy consumption, hazardous material training, and so forth, are not driven equally between each product line. If a company uses a plantwide overhead rate, environmental and non-environmental overhead costs will be combined within one cost pool where they will be allocated to each of the company's product lines using the same rate. However, refined costing systems allow companies to identify and separately pool overhead costs affecting the environment and properly allocate each of those cost pools to the activities and products that drive those costs. The use of refined costing systems creates better transparency, thus giving management a clear plan for reducing their company's environmental impact.

See Exercises E4-24A and E4-37B

[8]T. Carter, "How ABC changed the Post Office," *Management Accounting*, February 1998, pp. 28–36. H. Meyer, "Indianapolis Speeds Away," *The Journal of Business Strategy*, May/June 1998, pp. 41–46.

Passing the Cost-Benefit Test

Like all other management tools, ABC/ABM must pass the cost-benefit test. The system should be refined enough to provide accurate product costs but simple enough for managers to understand. In our chapter example, ABC increased the number of allocation rates from the single plantwide allocation rate in the original system to six activity cost allocation rates. ABC systems are even more complex in real-world companies that have many more activities and cost drivers.

Circumstances Favoring ABC/ABM Systems

ABC and ABM pass the cost-benefit test when the benefits of adopting ABC/ABM exceed the costs.

The benefits of adopting ABC/ABM are higher for companies in competitive markets because

- accurate product cost information is essential for setting competitive sales prices that still allow the company to earn a profit.
- ABM can pinpoint opportunities for cost savings, which increase the company's profit or are passed on to customers through lower prices.

The benefits of adopting ABC/ABM are higher when the risk of cost distortion is high, for example, when

- the company produces many different products that use different types and amounts of resources. (If all products use similar types and amounts of resources, a simple plantwide allocation system works fine.)
- the company has high indirect costs. (If the company has relatively few indirect costs, it matters less how they are allocated.)
- the company produces high volumes of some products and low volumes of other products. (Plantwide allocation systems based on a volume-related driver, such as direct labor hours, tend to overcost high-volume products and undercost low-volume products.)

We have seen that ABC offers many benefits. However, the cost and time required to implement and maintain an ABC system are often quite high. Some companies report spending up to two to four years to design and implement their ABC systems. The larger the company, the longer it usually takes. Top management support is crucial for the success of such an expensive and time consuming initiative. Without such support, ABC implementations might easily be abandoned for an easier, less costly accounting system. Since we know ABC systems are costly to implement, how can a company judge the costs involved with setting one up?

The costs of adopting ABC/ABM are generally lower when the company has

- accounting and information system expertise to develop the system. However, even "off-the-shelf" commercial accounting packages offer ABC modules. Small companies often find that Excel spreadsheets can be used to implement ABC, rather than integrating ABC into their general ledger software.
- information technology such as bar coding, optical scanning, Web-based data collection, or data warehouse systems to record and compile cost driver data.

Are real-world companies glad they adopted ABC/ABM?

Usually, but not always. A survey shows that 89% of the companies using ABC data say that it was worth the cost.[9] However, ABC is not a cure-all. As the controller for one Midwest manufacturer said, "ABC will not reduce cost; it will only help you understand costs better to know what to correct."

[9]K. Krumwiede, "ABC: Why It's Tried and How It Succeeds," *Management Accounting*, April 1998, pp. 32–38.

Signs That the Old System May Be Distorting Costs

Broken cars or computers simply stop running. But unlike cars and computers, even broken or outdated costing systems continue to report product costs. How can you tell whether a costing system is broken and needs repair? In other words, how can you tell whether an existing costing system is distorting costs and needs to be refined by way of departmental rates or ABC?

A company's product costing system may need repair in the following situations:

Managers don't understand costs and profits:

- In bidding for jobs, managers lose bids they expected to win and win bids they expected to lose.
- Competitors with similar high-volume products price their products below the company's costs but still earn good profits.
- Employees do not believe the cost numbers reported by the accounting system.

The cost system is outdated:

- The company has diversified its product offerings since the allocation system was first developed.
- The company has reengineered its production process but has not changed its accounting system to reflect the new production environment

Decision Guidelines

Refined Costing Systems

Several years ago, Dell decided that it needed to refine its costing system. Starting with an Excel spreadsheet, Dell developed a simple ABC system that focused on the ten most critical activities. Here are some of the decisions Dell faced as it began refining its costing system.

Decision	Guidelines
How do we develop an ABC system?	**1.** Identify the activities and estimate the total MOH associated with each activity. These are known as the activity cost pools. **2.** Select a cost allocation base for each activity and estimate the total amount that will be used during the year. **3.** Calculate an activity cost allocation rate for each activity. **4.** Allocate some MOH from each activity to the individual jobs that use the activities.
How do we compute an activity cost allocation rate?	$\dfrac{\text{Total estimated activity cost pool}}{\text{Total estimated activity allocation base}}$
How do we allocate an activity's cost to a job?	**Activity cost allocation rate** × **Actual amount of activity allocation base used by job**
How can a refined costing system support environmental sustainability?	By creating separate cost pools for environmental related costs, management is better able to identify and appropriately assign costs to those activities and products driving the costs. Better transparency of information should lead to better decisions.
What types of decisions would benefit from the use of ABC?	Managers use ABC data in ABM to make the following decisions: • Pricing and product mix • Cost cutting • Routine planning and control
What are the main benefits of ABC?	• More accurate product cost information • More detailed information on costs of activities and associated cost drivers help managers control costs and eliminate non-value-added activities.
When is ABC most likely to pass the cost-benefit test?	• The company is in a competitive environment and needs accurate product costs. • The company makes different products that use different amounts of resources. • The company has high indirect costs. • The company produces high volumes of some products and lower volumes of other products. • The company has accounting and information technology expertise to implement the system.
How do we tell when a cost system needs to be refined?	• Managers lose bids they expected to win and win bids they expected to lose. • Competitors earn profits despite pricing high-volume products below our costs. • Employees do not believe cost numbers. • The company has diversified the products it manufactures. • The company has reengineered the production process but not the accounting system.

SUMMARY PROBLEM 1

Indianapolis Auto Parts (IAP) has a Seat Manufacturing Department that uses ABC. IAP's activity cost allocation rates include the following:

Activity	Allocation Base	Activity Cost Allocation Rate
Machining	Number of machine hours	\$30.00 per machine hour
Assembling	Number of parts	0.50 per part
Packaging	Number of finished seats	0.90 per finished seat

Suppose Ford has asked for a bid on 50,000 built-in baby seats that would be installed as an option on some Ford SUVs. Each seat has 20 parts and the direct materials cost per seat is \$11. The job would require 10,000 direct labor hours at a labor wage rate of \$25 per hour. In addition, IAP will use a total of 400 machine hours to fabricate some of the parts required for the seats.

Requirements

1. Compute the total cost of producing and packaging 50,000 baby seats. Also compute the average cost per seat.
2. For bidding, IAP adds a 30% markup to total cost. What price will the company bid for the Ford order?
3. Suppose that instead of an ABC system, IAP has a traditional product costing system that allocates manufacturing overhead at a plantwide overhead rate of \$65 per direct labor hour. The baby seat order will require 10,000 direct labor hours. Compute the total cost of producing the baby seats and the average cost per seat. What price will IAP bid using this system's total cost?
4. Use your answers to Requirements 2 and 3 to explain how ABC can help IAP make a better decision about the bid price it will offer Ford.

SOLUTION

Requirement 1

Total Cost of Order and Average Cost per Seat:

Direct materials: 50,000 seats × \$11.00 per seat	\$ 550,000
Direct labor: 10,000 DL hours × \$25.00 per DL hour	250,000
Manufacturing overhead:	
Machining, 400 machine hours × \$30 per machine hour	12,000
Assembling, (50,000 × 20 parts) × \$0.50 per part	500,000
Packaging, 50,000 seats × \$0.90 per seat	45,000
Total cost of order	\$1,357,000
Divide by number of seats	÷ 50,000
Average cost per seat	\$ 27.14

Requirement 2
Bid Price (ABC System):

Bid price ($1,357,000 × 130%) = $1,764,100

Requirement 3
Bid Price (Traditional System):

Direct materials: 50,000 seats × $11.00	$ 550,000
Direct labor: 10,000 DL hours × $25.00 per DL hour	250,000
Manufacturing overhead: 10,000 DL hours × $65 per DL hour	650,000
Total cost of order	$1,450,000
Divide by number of seats	÷ 50,000
Average cost per seat	$ 29.00
Bid price ($1,450,000 × 130%)	$1,885,000

Requirement 4
IAP's bid would be $120,900 higher using the plantwide overhead rate than using ABC ($1,885,000 versus $1,764,100). Assuming that the ABC system more accurately captures the costs caused by the order, the traditional plantwide overhead system overcosts the order. This leads to a higher bid price that reduces IAP's chance of winning the bid. The ABC system shows that IAP can increase its chance of winning the bid by bidding a lower price and still make a profit.

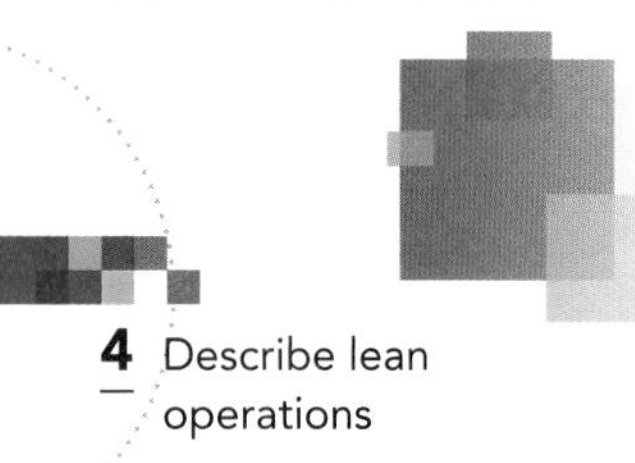

4 Describe lean operations

What is Lean Thinking?

Lean thinking is a management philosophy and strategy focused on creating value for the customer by eliminating waste. Lean is often described by the Japanese word, Kaizen, meaning "change for the better." According to the IMA, lean thinking is quickly becoming the dominant business paradigm, without which, a company has little chance of long-term survival in the global marketplace. Since management accounting systems should be designed to reflect the company's operations, it's important for you to understand the key elements of lean operations and the costs that can be reduced by eliminating waste.

One key element of creating customer value is to emphasize a short customer response time: the time that elapses between receipt of a customer order and delivery of the product or service. To shorten this time, companies need to reduce their own internal processing time. While lean thinking developed out of the manufacturing industry (and Toyota, in particular), the concepts and tools are being applied with great success to all types of companies. For example, service companies, such as hospitals, car repair shops, and fast-food restaurants, must also concern themselves with the waste imbedded in their customer response time. No matter the industry, the bottom line is clear: By eliminating wasteful activities, companies can reduce their costs and improve their customer response time.

The Eight Wastes of Traditional Operations

Advocates of lean thinking often talk about eight wastes that comprise much of the waste found in traditional organizations, including service and merchandising companies. As shown in Exhibit 4-23, these wastes are easy to remember using the acronym "DOWNTIME".[10]

EXHIBIT 4-23 The 8 wastes

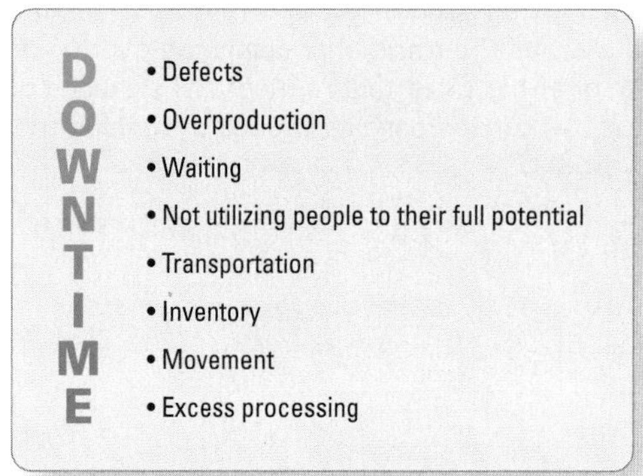

1. **Defects:** Producing defective products or services costs time and money. The product will either need to be repaired, at additional cost, or disposed of. In either case resources are wasted. The final section of this chapter is devoted to discussing the various costs associated with poor quality of product or service.
2. **Overproduction:** Overproduction means that the company is making more product than needed or making product *sooner* than it is needed. Traditional manufacturers often make products in large batches because of long and costly machine setup times and to protect themselves against higher than expected demand for the product. Also, traditional manufacturers often make extra work in process inventory so that each department will have something to continue working on in the event production stops or slows in earlier departments. For example, in Exhibit 4-24, we see the series of production steps required to produce drill bits from bar stock. If the company keeps some work in process inventory between the grinding and smoothing operations, the smoothing operation can continue even if the shaping or grinding operations slow or come to a halt as a result of machine breakdown, absence of sick workers, or other production problems.

[10]MAGNET (Manufacturing Advocacy and Growth Network), Cleveland, Ohio.

EXHIBIT 4-24 Sequence of Operations for Drill Bit Production

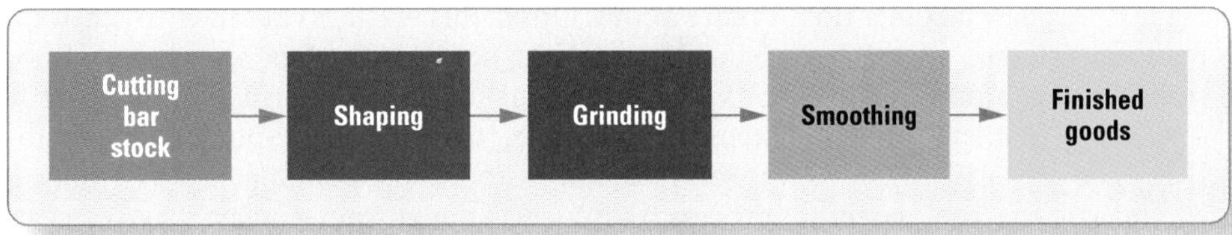

As you'll see below, overproduction can snowball into many problems, including extra wait time, extra transportation, and excess inventory build-up.

3. **Waiting:** Employees must often wait for parts, materials, information, or machine repairs before they can proceed with their tasks. In addition, because of overproduction and large batches, work in process inventory often waits in a queue for the next production process to begin. Whether it refers to people or product, wait time is wasted time. The company's customer response time could be much shorter if wait time were eliminated.
4. **Not utilizing people to their full potential:** By assuming that managers always know best, traditional companies have often underutilized their employees. In contrast, one of the key mantras of lean thinking is employee empowerment at all levels of the organization. Employees usually have excellent ideas on how their jobs could be done more efficiently and with less frustration.
5. **Transportation:** While movement of parts, inventory, and paperwork is necessary to some extent, any *excess* transportation is simply wasteful because of the equipment, manpower, and energy it requires. Excess transportation is often caused by poor plant layout, large centralized storage cribs, large batches, and long lead times that require product to be moved elsewhere until the next production process is ready to begin.
6. **Inventory:** Typically, traditional manufacturers buy more raw materials than they need "just in case" any of the materials are defective or the supplier is late with the next delivery. As noted above, they produce extra work in process inventory "just in case" something goes wrong in the production process. Also, they produce extra finished goods inventory "just in case" demand is higher than expected. In other words, large inventories are essentially a response to uncertainty. Uncertainty is a valid reason for keeping large inventories. So why are large inventories considered wasteful?
   - Inventories use cash. Companies incur interest expense from borrowing cash to finance their inventories or forgo income that could be earned from investing their cash elsewhere.
   - Large inventories hide quality problems, production bottlenecks, and obsolescence. Inventory may spoil, be broken or stolen, or become obsolete as it sits in storage and waits to be used or sold. Companies in high-tech and fashion industries are particularly susceptible to inventory obsolescence.
   - Storing and unstoring inventory is very expensive. Building space, shelving, warehouse equipment, security, computer systems, and labor are all needed to manage inventories.
7. **Movement:** In contrast to the waste of transportation, which refers to moving products and materials, the waste of movement refers to excess human motion, such as excess bending, reaching, turning, and walking. This waste is often caused by cluttered or unorganized work areas (where employees must search for the needed tools and supplies), poorly designed facilities (where employees must walk from one area of the building to another), and poorly designed work stations and work methods (where employees must continually crouch, stretch, bend, and turn to do their tasks). Not only does excess movement take time, but also it can signal unsafe work conditions that can decrease employee morale and increase the company's exposure to workman's compensation claims.

8. **Excess processing:** This waste refers to performing additional production steps or adding features the customer doesn't care about. Often, this waste is caused when customer requirements are not clearly defined, when engineering changes are made without simultaneous process changes, or when additional steps are performed to make up for shortfalls in earlier production steps. For example, to keep its price-point relatively low, IKEA flat packs all of its furniture and lets the customer perform the final assembly. By eliminating the final assembly process, IKEA gives the customer what they want at a price that is affordable. Also, IKEA saves on related transportation and warehousing costs that would be incurred on bulkier, fully-assembled furniture.

Characteristics of Lean Operations

One primary goal of a lean organization is to eliminate the waste of time and money that accompanies large inventories. Therefore, lean companies adopt a **"Just-in-Time" (JIT)** inventory philosophy. As the name suggests, JIT inventory focuses on purchasing raw materials *just in time* for production and then completing finished goods *just in time* for delivery to customers. By doing so, companies eliminate the waste of storing and unstoring raw materials and finished goods, as pictured in Exhibit 4-25.

EXHIBIT 4-25 Traditional System Versus JIT System

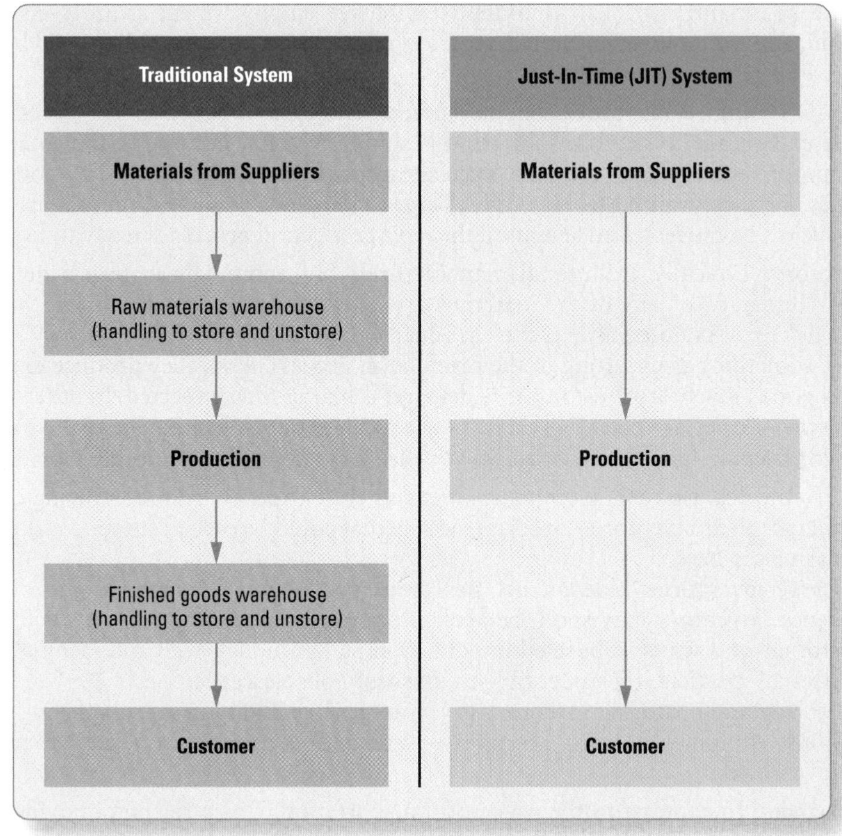

Most companies that adopt lean production have several common characteristics that help minimize the amount of inventory that is kept on hand, yet enable the company to quickly satisfy customer demand. These characteristics are described next.

Value Stream Mapping

Companies need to understand their current state of operations before they can attempt to remove waste and improve operations. Value stream maps (VSM) are used to identify and visually illustrate the flow of materials and information for each family of products or services the company offers, all the way from order receipt to final delivery. A *current state* VSM is used to illustrate the sequence of activities, communication of information, time elapsing, and build-up of inventories that is currently occurring. After identifying waste within the current state VSM, companies prepare a *future state* VSM, with waste removed, and use it as a goal for process improvement.

Production Occurs in Self-Contained Cells

One of the first wastes many companies identify on their current state VSM is the waste of time, transportation, and movement that occurs as a result of poor plant or office layout. For example, a traditional drill bit manufacturer would group all cutting machines in one area, all shaping machines in another area, all grinding machines in a third area, and all smoothing machines in a fourth area, as illustrated in Panel A of Exhibit 4-26. On the other hand, lean companies would group the machines in self-contained production cells as shown in Panel B of Exhibit 4-26. These self-contained production cells minimize the time and cost involved with physically moving parts across the factory to other departments.

EXHIBIT 4-26 Equipment Arrangement in Traditional and Lean Production Systems

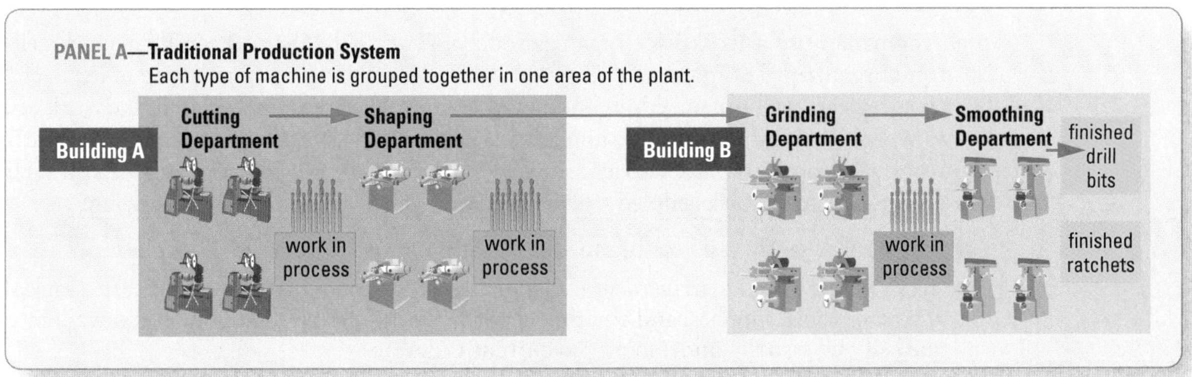

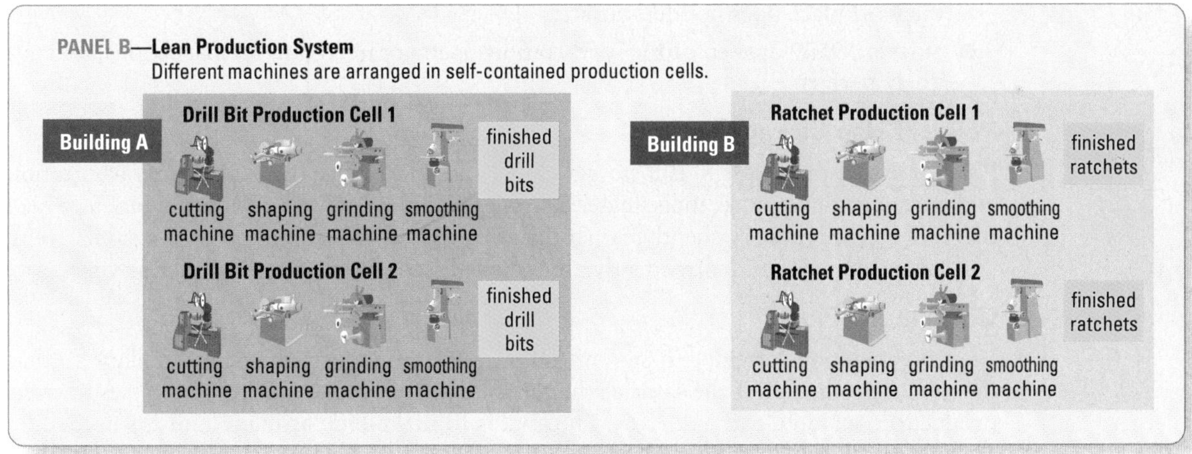

Employee Empowerment: Broad Roles and the Use of Teams

To combat the waste of not utilizing people to their full potential, lean companies focus on employee empowerment. Employees typically hold broader roles than their counterparts at traditional companies. For example, employees working in production cells do more than operate a single machine. They also conduct maintenance, perform setups, inspect their own work, and operate other machines. For example, look at Panel B of Exhibit 4-26. A worker in the Drill Bit Production Cell 1 would be cross-trained to operate all of the machines (cutting, shaping, grinding, and smoothing) in that cell. This cross-training boosts morale, lowers costs, and creates a more flexible and versatile workforce. As a result, individual workloads become much more balanced, leading to a more equitable distribution of work and a happier workforce.

Lean companies also empower employees by using small teams to identify waste and develop potential solutions to the problems identified. Problem solving at lean companies involves searching for and fixing the root cause of a problem, rather than making cosmetic changes to surface issues. To find the root cause of a problem, teams are encouraged to ask "Why?" at least five times. For example, say you received a "D" grade on an exam. Your initial response might be that you didn't understand the material. However, as you dig deeper by continually asking "Why?" you might find that the root cause was not a simple failure to understand the material, but having an overloaded schedule that didn't allow you sufficient time to study and practice the material. The solution might be to lighten your semester course load, or not to participate in so many extracurricular activities. Without fixing the root cause of the problem, you are apt to run into similar problems in the future.

Often, lean companies institute profit-sharing plans so that employees at all levels of the company are compensated for improving the company's overall performance. Because of employee empowerment, lean companies typically report higher job satisfaction and better employee morale.

5S Workplace Organization

Lean companies use a workplace organization system called "5S" to keep their work cells clean and organized. The mantra of 5S is, "a place for everything and everything in its place." By having a clean, well-organized, ergonomic workplace, every employee within the work cell knows where to find the tools and supplies they need to do each job in the cell as efficiently as possible. A clean workplace also leads to fewer defects (due to fewer contaminants), a safer work place, and fewer unscheduled machine repairs. The 5S stands for the following:

- **Sort:** Infrequently used tools and supplies are removed from the workplace.
- **Set in order:** Visual management tools, such as color-coding, are used to create a logical layout of tools, supplies, and equipment in the work cell so that anyone could walk into the cell and visually understand the current situation.
- **Shine:** All machines, floors, tools, and workstations are thoroughly cleaned.
- **Standardize:** Procedures are put in place to ensure the cleanliness and organization of the workplace does not deteriorate.
- **Sustain:** Daily upkeep of the workstations is maintained and 5S inspections are routinely performed.

Point of Use Storage

Point of use storage (POUS) is a storage system used to reduce the waste of transportation and movement. In essence, tools, materials, and equipment are stored in proximity to where they will be used most frequently, rather than in a centralized storage crib. In a similar vein, those items that are used infrequently are removed from the cells and stored elsewhere.

Continuous Flow

Lean organizations attempt to smooth the flow of production through the plant so that the rate of production is the same as the rate of demand, thus reducing the wastes of overproduction, waiting, and inventory. The goal is to make *only* as many units as needed by the next customer, whether that be the next machine operator or the final, external customer. **Takt time**, a critical concept in lean manufacturing, is the rate of production needed to meet customer demand yet avoid overproduction. The term comes from a German word for *rhythm* or *beat*. For example, if a product line has a takt time of 5 minutes, it means that one unit needs to be produced every 5 minutes. By carefully monitoring takt time, lean companies are able to identify bottlenecks, balance the workloads of different processes, avoid inventory build-up, and satisfy customer demand.

Pull System

In a traditional production system, inventory is "pushed" through production according to forecasted demand. However, in a lean production system, no inventory is made until a customer order has been received. The customer order triggers the start of the production process and "pulls" the batch through production. Even the necessary raw materials are usually not purchased until a customer order is received. Obviously, for this to work, companies must employ various tactics that will allow the company to quickly satisfy the customer's order. We discuss these tactics next.

Shorter Manufacturing Cycle Times

Since products are not started until a customer order is received, lean companies must focus on reducing their **manufacturing cycle time**: the time that elapses between the start of production and the product's completion. According to most experts, the majority of manufacturing cycle time is spent on non-value-added activities. Shorter manufacturing times also protect companies from foreign competitors whose cheaper products take longer to ship. Delivery speed has become a competitive weapon.

Reduced Setup Times

One key component of manufacturing cycle time is the time required to set up a machine that is used to manufacture more than one product. Employee training and technology helped Toyota cut setup times from several hours to just a few minutes. As a result, the company became more flexible in scheduling production to meet customer orders.

Smaller Batches

Another key component to manufacturing cycle time is batch size. Large batch sizes cause wasted wait time. Therefore, one of the key elements of lean production is the use of smaller batches. For example, assume a customer has ordered 10 units and that each unit requires three unique, sequential processes: A, B, and C. Furthermore, assume that each process takes *1 minute* to complete *on each unit*. The manufacturing cycle time is illustrated in Exhibit 4-27, where each "x" stands for one unit of the product, and the capital "X" stands for the first unit in the batch. Exhibit 4-27 shows that the entire order would take 30 minutes to complete if the manufacturer uses a batch size of 10. Exhibit 4-27 also shows that 21 minutes elapse before the first unit in the batch is completed.

EXHIBIT 4-27 Manufacturing Cycle Time with a Batch Size of 10

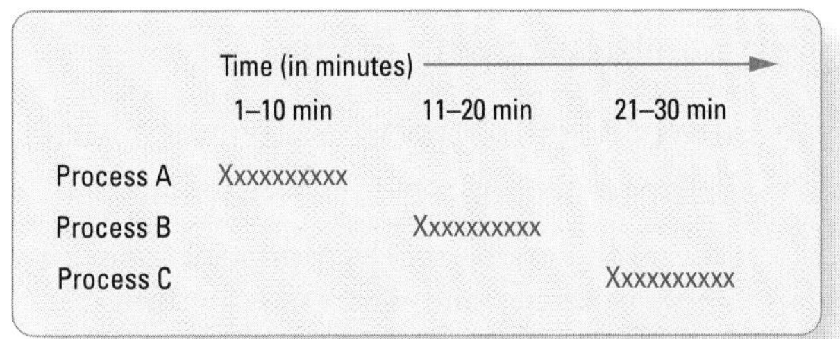

Alternatively, Exhibit 4-28 shows that the entire order could be completed in just 12 minutes if the manufacturer uses a batch size of 1. In addition, the first unit in the batch is completed after a mere 3 minutes has elapsed. Why the difference? With large batch sizes, each unit spends the bulk of the manufacturing cycle time *waiting*. Customer response time can be greatly reduced through the use of smaller batch sizes.

EXHIBIT 4-28 Manufacturing Cycle Time with a Batch Size of 1

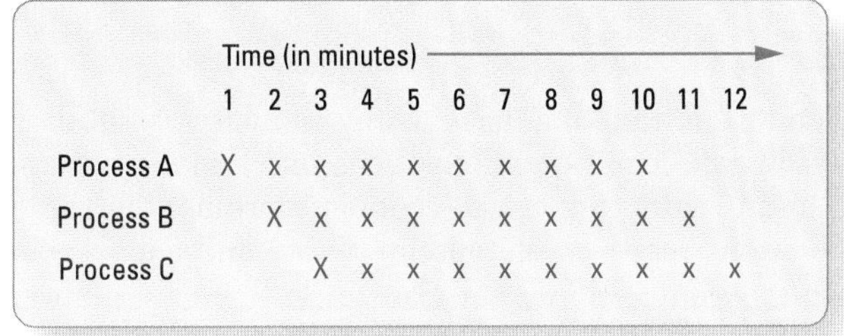

Emphasis on Quality

Lean companies focus on producing their products right the *first* time, *every* time. Why? First, they have no backup stock to give to waiting customers if they run into production problems. Second, defects in materials and workmanship can slow or shut down production. Lean companies cannot afford the time it takes to rework faulty products. Lean companies emphasize "building-in" quality rather than "inspecting-in" quality (that is, hoping to catch defective units through sample inspections). Lean companies use standardization tools, such as checklists and detailed step-by-step operating procedures, to ensure employees know how to complete each process correctly. They also use visual management and other tools to "mistake-proof" the process.

Supply-Chain Management

Because there are no inventory buffers, lean production requires close coordination with suppliers. These suppliers must guarantee *on-time delivery* of *defect-free* materials. *Supply-chain management* is the exchange of information with suppliers and customers to reduce costs, improve quality, and speed delivery of goods and services from the company's suppliers, through the company itself, and on to the company's end customers. As described in Chapter 1, suppliers that bear the ISO 9001:2008 certification have proven their ability to provide high-quality products, and thus, tend to be suppliers for lean manufacturers.

Are There Any Drawbacks to a Lean Production System?

While companies such as Toyota, Carrier, and Dell credit lean production with saving them millions of dollars, the system is not without problems. With no inventory buffers, lean producers are vulnerable when problems strike suppliers or distributors. For example, Ford cut production of its SUVs in response to the tire shortage resulting from Firestone's tire recall. It also had to shut down five of its U.S. plants when engine deliveries from Canadian suppliers were late due to security-related transportation delays in the wake of the World Trade Center attacks.

Why is this important?

"In order to **compete** and remain **profitable**, companies must cut costs by becoming as **efficient** as possible. **Lean** thinking helps **organizations** cut costs by **eliminating waste** from the system."

Lean Operations in Service and Merchandising Companies

The eight wastes and lean principles discussed previously also apply to service and merchandising firms. In fact, lean practices have become extremely popular in service companies, such as banks and hospitals, as well as merchandising companies, such as IKEA. Entire books have been written on the subject of "lean healthcare" and "lean offices." Through the use of lean tools, offices have been able to identify the waste caused by excessive document processing, layers of unnecessary authorization, unbalanced workloads, poor office layouts, and unclear communication channels. Through streamlining their internal operations, hospitals and offices have found that they are able to decrease patient and customer wait time, thereby creating higher levels of customer satisfaction while at the same time decreasing their own costs.

Sustainability and Lean Thinking

Sustainability and lean thinking have many similarities: both practices seek to reduce waste. However, lean operations focus on eliminating waste and empowering employees in an effort to increase economic profits. On the other hand, "lean and green" operations focus on eliminating waste and empowering employees not only to increase economic profits, but also to preserve the planet and improve the lives of *all* people touched by the company. While lean practices tend to center on *internal* operational waste, green practices also consider the *external* waste that may occur as a result of the product. To become greener, a lean company should be particularly cognizant of all waste that could harm the planet: packaging waste, water waste, energy waste, and emissions waste that would occur from both manufacturing the product *and* from consumers using and eventually disposing of the product.

See Exercises E4-24A and E4-37B

How do Managers Improve Quality?

5 Describe and use the cost of quality framework

Since lean companies only produce what is currently needed, it is essential that production consistently generates high-quality products. To meet this challenge, many companies adopt **total quality management (TQM)**. The goal of TQM is to provide customers with superior products and services. Each business function in the value chain continually examines its own activities to improve quality and eliminate defects.

Costs of Quality (COQ)

As part of TQM, many companies prepare cost of quality reports. **Costs of quality reports** categorize and list the costs incurred by the company related to quality. Once managers know the extent of their costs of quality, they can start to identify ways for the company to improve quality while at the same time controlling costs.

Quality-related costs generally fall into four different categories: prevention costs, appraisal costs, internal failure costs, and external failure costs. These categories form the framework for a costs of quality report. We'll briefly describe each next.

Prevention Costs

Prevention costs are costs incurred to *avoid* producing poor-quality goods or services. Often, poor quality is caused by the variability of the production process or the complexity of the product design. To reduce the variability of the production process, companies often automate as much of the process as possible. Employee training can help decrease variability in nonautomated processes. In addition, reducing the complexity of the product design or manufacturing process can prevent the potential for error: The fewer parts or processes, the fewer things that can go wrong. Frequently, companies need to literally "go back to the drawing board" (the R&D and design stages of the value chain) to make a significant difference in preventing production problems. For example, Dell reengineered its assembly process to cut in half the number of times humans touch the hard drive. As a result, the hard drive failure rate dropped 40%. Likewise, HP was able to reduce its defect rate by significantly reducing the number of parts that went into a desktop printer.

Appraisal Costs

Appraisal costs are costs incurred to *detect* poor-quality goods or services. Intel incurs appraisal costs when it tests its products. One procedure, called burn-in, heats circuits to a high temperature. A circuit that fails the burn-in test is also likely to fail in customer use. Nissan tests 100% of the vehicles that roll off the assembly lines at its plant in Canton, Mississippi. Each vehicle is put through the paces on Nissan's all-terrain test track. Any problems are identified before the vehicle leaves the plant.

Internal Failure Costs

Internal failure costs are costs incurred on defective units *before* delivery to customers. For example, if Nissan does identify a problem, the vehicle is reworked to eliminate the defect before it is allowed to leave the plant. In the worst-case scenario, a product may be so defective that it cannot be reworked and must be completely scrapped. In this case, the entire cost of manufacturing the defective unit, plus any disposal cost, would be an internal failure cost.

External Failure Costs

External failure costs are costs incurred because the defective goods or services are not detected until *after* delivery is made to customers. For example, Maytag recently recalled 250,000 washing machines because water was leaking on the electrical connections, which had the potential to cause an electrical short and ignite the circuit boards. Along with incurring substantial cost for repairing or replacing these recalled washers, the publicity of this defect could cause significant damage to the company's reputation. Damage to a company's reputation from selling defective units to end customers can considerably harm the company's future sales. Unsatisfied customers will avoid buying from the company in the future. Even worse, unsatisfied customers tend to tell their neighbors, family, and friends about any poor experiences with products or services. As a result, a company's reputation for poor quality can increase at an exponential rate. To capture the extent of this problem, external failure costs should include an estimate of how much profit the company is losing due to having a bad reputation for poor quality.

Relationship Among Costs

Exhibit 4-29 lists some common examples of the four different costs of quality. Prevention and appraisal costs are sometimes referred to as "conformance costs" since they are the costs incurred to make sure the product or service conforms to its intended design. In other words, these are the costs incurred to make sure the product is *not* defective. On the other hand, internal and external failure costs are sometimes referred to as "non-conformance costs." These are the costs incurred because the product or service *is* defective.

EXHIBIT 4-29 Four Types of Quality Costs

Prevention Costs	Appraisal Costs
Training personnel	Inspection of incoming materials
Evaluating potential suppliers	Inspection at various stages of production
Using better materials	Inspection of final products or services
Preventive maintenance	Product testing
Improved equipment	Cost of inspection equipment
Redesigning product or process	

Internal Failure Costs	External Failure Costs
Production loss caused by downtime	Lost profits from lost customers
Rework	Warranty costs
Abnormal quantities of scrap	Service costs at customer sites
Rejected product units	Sales returns and allowances due to quality problems
Disposal of rejected units	Product liability claims
Machine breakdowns	Cost of recalls

Most companies find that if they invest more in prevention costs at the front end of the value chain (R&D and design), they can generate even more savings in the back end of the value chain (production and customer service). Why? Because carefully designed products and manufacturing processes can significantly reduce the number of inspections, defects, rework, and warranty claims. Managers must make trade-offs between these costs. Companies that embrace TQM, such as Toyota, *design* and *build* quality into their products rather than having to *inspect* and *repair* later, as many traditional manufacturers do.

Costs of Quality at Service and Merchandising Companies

The costs of quality are not limited to manufacturers. Service firms and merchandising companies also incur costs of quality. For example, CPA firms spend a lot of money providing ongoing professional training to their staff. They also develop standardized audit checklists to minimize the variability of the audit procedures performed for each client. These measures help to *prevent* audit failures. Both audit managers and partners review audit work papers to *appraise* whether the audit procedures performed and evidence gathered are sufficient on each audit engagement. If audit procedures or evidence are deemed to be lacking (*internal failure*), the audit manager or partner will instruct the audit team to perform additional procedures before the firm will issue an audit opinion on the client's financial statements. This parallels the "rework" a manufacturer might perform on a product that isn't up to par. Finally, recent audit failures, such as those at Enron and WorldCom, illustrate just how expensive and devastating *external failure* can be to a CPA firm. The once prestigious international CPA firm Arthur Andersen & Co. actually went out of business because of the reputation damage caused by its audit failure at Enron.

Using Costs of Quality Reports to Aid Decisions

Now that we have examined the four costs of quality, let's see how they can be presented to management in the form of a Costs of Quality report. Let's assume Global Fitness, another manufacturer of fitness equipment, is having difficulty competing with Life Fitness because it doesn't have the reputation for high quality that Life Fitness enjoys. To examine this issue, management has prepared the Costs of Quality report shown in Exhibit 4-30.

Notice how Global Fitness identifies, categorizes, and quantifies all of the costs it incurs relating to quality. Global Fitness also calculated the percentage of total costs of quality that is incurred in each cost category. This helps company managers see just how *little* they are spending on conformance costs (prevention and appraisal). Most of their costs are internal and external failure costs. The best way to reduce these failure costs is to invest more in prevention and appraisal. Global Fitness managers can now begin to focus on how they might be able to prevent these failures from occurring.

Why is this important?

"Businesses **compete** with each other on the basis of price and quality. **Costs of Quality** reports help managers determine how they are **spending** money to ensure that consumers get the **best quality** product for the price."

EXHIBIT 4-30 Global Fitness's Costs of Quality Report

	Costs Incurred	Total Costs of Quality	Percentage of Total Costs of Quality (rounded)
Prevention Costs:			
Employee training	$ 125,000		
Total prevention costs		$ 125,000	6%*
Appraisal Costs:			
Testing	$ 175,000		
Total appraisal costs		$ 175,000	8%
Internal Failure Costs:			
Rework	$ 300,000		
Cost of rejected units	50,000		
Total internal failure costs		$ 350,000	17%
External Failure Costs:			
Lost profits from lost sales due to impaired reputation	$1,000,000		
Sales return processing	175,000		
Warranty costs	235,000		
Total external failure costs		$1,410,000	69%
Total costs of quality		$2,050,000	100%

*The percentage of total is computed as the total cost of the category divided by the total costs of quality. For example: 6% = $125,000 ÷ $2,050,000.

After analyzing the Costs of Quality report, the CEO is considering spending the following amounts on a new quality program:

Inspect raw materials	$100,000
Reengineer the production process to improve product quality	750,000
Supplier screening and certification	25,000
Preventive maintenance on plant equipment	75,000
Total costs of implementing quality programs	$950,000

Although these measures won't completely eliminate internal and external failure costs, Global Fitness expects this quality program to *reduce* costs by the following amounts:

Reduction in lost profits from lost sales due to impaired reputation	$ 800,000
Fewer sales returns to be processed	150,000
Reduction in rework costs	250,000
Reduction in warranty costs	225,000
Total cost savings	$1,425,000

According to these projections, Global Fitness's quality initiative will cost $950,000 but result in total savings of $1,425,000—for a net benefit of $475,000. In performing a cost-benefit analysis, some companies will simply compare all of the projected costs ($950,000) with all of the projected benefits ($1,425,000) as shown previously. Other companies like to organize their cost-benefit analysis by cost category so that managers have a better idea of how the quality initiative will affect each cost category. Exhibit 4-31 shows that by increasing prevention costs (by $850,000) and appraisal costs (by $100,000), Global Fitness will be able to save $250,000 in internal failure costs and $1,175,000 in external failure costs. In total, Global Fitness expects a net benefit of $475,000 if it undertakes the quality initiative. By spending more on conformance costs (prevention and appraisal costs), Global Fitness saves even more on non-conformance costs (internal and external failure costs).

The analysis shown in Exhibit 4-31 appears very straightforward. However, quality costs can be hard to measure. For example, design engineers may spend only part of their time on quality. Allocating their salaries to various activities is subjective. It is especially hard to measure external failure costs. The largest external failure cost—profits lost because of the company's reputation for poor quality—does not even appear in the accounting records. This cost must be estimated based on the experiences and judgments of the Sales Department. Because these estimates may be subjective, TQM programs also emphasize nonfinancial measures such as defect rates, number of customer complaints, and number of warranty repairs that can be objectively measured.

EXHIBIT 4-31 Cost-Benefit Analysis of Global Fitness's Proposed Quality Program

	Additional (Costs) and Cost Savings	Total New (Costs) or Cost Savings
Prevention Costs:		
Reengineer the production process	$(750,000)	
Supplier screening and certification	(25,000)	
Preventive maintenance on equipment	(75,000)	
Total additional prevention costs		$ (850,000)
Appraisal Costs:		
Inspect raw materials	$(100,000)	
Total additional appraisal costs		(100,000)
Internal Failure Costs:		
Reduction of rework costs	$ 250,000	
Total internal failure cost savings		250,000
External Failure Costs:		
Reduction of lost profits from lost sales	$ 800,000	
Reduction of sales returns	150,000	
Reduction of warranty costs	225,000	
Total external failure cost savings		1,175,000
Total savings (costs) from quality program		$ 475,000

Decision Guidelines

Lean Operations and the Costs of Quality

Dell, a worldwide leader in PC sales, is famous for its complete commitment to both the lean operations and TQM. The following are several decisions Dell's managers made when adopting these two modern management techniques.

Decision	Guidelines
How will we begin to identify waste in our organization?	Most companies find that the majority of waste occurs in eight specific areas. The "eight wastes" can be remembered as "DOWNTIME:" • Defects • Overproduction • Waiting • Not utilizing people to their full potential • Transportation • Inventory • Movement • Excess processing
What operational features will help us become more lean?	Lean operations are typically characterized by many of the following features: • Just-in-Time (JIT) inventory • Value Stream Mapping • Production in self-contained work cells • Employee empowerment through broader roles and use of small teams • 5S workplace organization • Point of use storage (POUS) • Continuous flow pull system • Shorter manufacturing cycle times • Reduced setup times • Smaller batches • Emphasis on quality • Supply-chain management
What are the four types of quality costs?	**1.** Prevention costs **2.** Appraisal costs **3.** Internal failure costs **4.** External failure costs
How do we make trade-offs among the four types of quality costs?	Investment in prevention costs and appraisal costs reduce internal and external failure costs.

SUMMARY PROBLEM 2

The CEO of IAP is concerned with the quality of its products and the amount of resources currently spent on customer returns. The CEO would like to analyze the costs incurred in conjunction with the quality of the product.

The following information was collected from various departments within the company:

Warranty returns	$120,000
Training personnel	10,000
Litigation on product liability claims	175,000
Inspecting 10% of final products	5,000
Rework	10,000
Production loss due to machine breakdowns	45,000
Inspection of raw materials	5,000

Requirements

1. Prepare a Costs of Quality report. In addition to listing the costs by category, determine the percentage of the total costs of quality incurred in each cost category.
2. Do any additional subjective costs appear to be missing from the report?
3. What can be learned from the report?

▪ SOLUTIONS

Requirement 1

	Costs Incurred	Total Costs of Quality	Percentage of Total Costs of Quality (rounded)
Prevention Costs:			
Personnel training	$ 10,000		
Total prevention costs		$ 10,000	3%*
Appraisal Costs:			
Inspecting raw materials	$ 5,000		
Inspecting 10% of final products	5,000		
Total appraisal costs		$ 10,000	3%
Internal Failure Costs:			
Rework	$ 10,000		
Production loss due to			
machine breakdown	45,000	$ 55,000	15%
Total internal failure costs			
External Failure Costs:			
Litigation costs from product			
liability claims	$175,000		
Warranty return costs	120,000		
Total external failure costs		$295,000	79%
Total costs of quality		$370,000	100%

*The percentage of total is computed as the total cost of the category divided by the total costs of quality. For example: 3% = $10,000 ÷ $370,000.

Requirement 2

Because the company has warranty returns and product liability litigation, it is very possible that the company suffers from a reputation for poor-quality products. If so, it is losing profits from losing sales. Unsatisfied customers will probably avoid buying from the company in the future. Worse yet, customers may tell their friends and family not to buy from the company. This report does not include an estimate of the lost profits arising from the company's reputation for poor-quality products.

Requirement 3

The Costs of Quality report shows that very little is being spent on prevention and appraisal, which is probably why the internal and external failure costs are so high. The CEO should use this information to develop quality initiatives in the areas of prevention and appraisal. Such initiatives should reduce future internal and external failure costs.

END OF CHAPTER

Learning Objectives

- 1 Develop and use departmental overhead rates to allocate indirect costs
- 2 Develop and use activity-based costing (ABC) to allocate indirect costs
- 3 Understand the benefits and limitations of ABC/ABM systems
- 4 Describe lean operations
- 5 Describe and use the costs of quality framework

Accounting Vocabulary

Activity-Based Costing (ABC). (p. 188) Focuses on *activities* as the fundamental cost objects. The costs of those activities become building blocks for compiling the indirect costs of products, services, and customers.

Activity-Based Management (ABM). (p. 194) Using activity-based cost information to make decisions that increase profits while satisfying customers' needs.

Appraisal Costs. (p. 209) Costs incurred to *detect* poor-quality goods or services.

Batch-Level Activities. (p. 193) Activities and costs incurred for every batch, regardless of the number of units in the batch.

Cost Distortion. (p. 181) Overcosting some products while undercosting other products.

Costs of Quality Report. (p. 209) A report that lists the costs incurred by the company related to quality. The costs are categorized as prevention costs, appraised costs, internal failure costs, and external failure costs.

Customer Response Time. (p. 202) The time that elapses between receipt of a customer order and delivery of the product or service.

Departmental Overhead Rates. (p. 183) Separate manufacturing overhead rates established for each department.

DOWNTIME. (p. 202) An acronym for the eight wastes: Defects, Overproduction, Waiting, Not utilizing people to their full potential, Transportation, Inventory, Movement, Excess processing.

Eight Wastes. (p. 202) Defects, Overproduction, Waiting, Not utilizing people to their full potential, Transportation, Inventory, Movement, Excess processing.

External Failure Costs. (p. 209) Costs incurred when the company does not detect poor-quality goods or services until *after* delivery is made to customers.

Facility-Level Activities. (p. 193) Activities and costs incurred no matter how many units, batches, or products are produced in the plant.

5S. (p. 206) A workplace organization system comprised of the following steps: Sort, Set in order, Shine, Standardize, and Sustain.

Internal Failure Costs. (p. 209) Costs incurred when the company detects and corrects poor-quality goods or services *before* making delivery to customers.

Just in Time. (p. 204) An inventory management philosophy that focuses on purchasing raw materials just in time for production and completing finished goods just in time for delivery to customers.

Kaizen. (p. 202) A Japanese work meaning "change for the better."

Lean Thinking. (p. 202) A management philosophy and strategy focused on creating value for the customer by eliminating waste.

Manufacturing Cycle Time. (p. 207) The time that elapses between the start of production and the product's completion.

Non-Value-Added Activities. (p. 195) Activities that neither enhance the customer's image of the product or service nor provide a competitive advantage; also known as *waste activities.*

Plantwide Overhead Rate. (p. 182) When overhead is allocated to every product using the same manufacturing overhead rate.

Point of Use Storage (POUS). (p. 206) A storage system used to reduce the waste of transportation and movement in which tools, materials, and equipment are stored in proximity to where they will be used most frequently.

Prevention Costs. (p. 209) Costs incurred to *avoid* poor-quality goods or services.

Product-Level Activities. (p. 193) Activities and costs incurred for a particular product, regardless of the number of units or batches of the product produced.

Takt Time. (p. 206) The rate of production needed to meet customer demand yet avoid overproduction.

Total Quality Management (TQM). (p. 209) A management philosophy of delighting customers with superior products and services by continually setting higher goals and improving the performance of every business function.

Unit-Level Activities. (p. 193) Activities and costs incurred for every unit produced.

Value Engineering. (p. 195) Eliminating waste in the system by making the company's processes as effective and efficient as possible.

Value-Added Activities. (p. 195) Activities for which the customer is willing to pay because these activities add value to the final product or service.

Waste Activities. (p. 195) Activities that neither enhance the customer's image of the product or service nor provide a competitive advantage; also known as non-value-added activities.

MyAccountingLab **Go to http://myaccountinglab.com/ for the following Quick Check, Short Exercises, Exercises, and Problems. They are available with immediate grading, explanations of correct and incorrect answers, and interactive media that acts as your own online tutor.**

Quick Check

1. *(Learning Objective 1)* Which of the following reasons would indicate that a company should consider using departmental overhead rates rather than using a single plantwide overhead rate?
   a. Each product is in each department for a different length of time.
   b. Each department spends different amounts on manufacturing overhead.
   c. Each department incurs different types of manufacturing overhead.
   d. All of the above statements are reasons why a company would choose departmental overhead rates rather than using a single plantwide overhead rate.
2. *(Learning Objective 2)* Which of the following is *not* a step in computing ABC cost allocation rates?
   a. Costs from each activity are allocated to individual jobs that use those activities.
   b. Manufacturing overhead costs associated with each primary production activity are estimated.
   c. The amounts of the allocation base to be used for each primary production activity are estimated.
   d. All of the above statements are steps in calculating ABC allocation rates.
3. *(Learning Objective 2)* Manufacturing overhead is allocated to jobs in an ABC system by using the following formula:
   a. Activity cost allocation rate × Estimated amount of activity allocation base used by the job
   b. Activity cost allocation rate ÷ Estimated amount of activity allocation base used by the job
   c. Activity cost allocation rate × Actual amount of activity allocation base used by the job
   d. Activity cost allocation rate ÷ Actual amount of activity allocation base used by the job
4. *(Learning Objective 2)* The legal costs associated with filing a patent for a new model of oven at an appliance manufacturer is an example of which type of activity?
   a. Unit-level
   b. Batch-level
   c. Product-level
   d. Facility-level
5. *(Learning Objective 3)* Which of the following is *false*?
   a. ABC focuses on allocating indirect costs.
   b. Advances in information technology have made it feasible for more companies to adopt ABC.
   c. ABC is only for manufacturing firms.
   d. A system that uses ABC is more refined than one that uses departmental overhead rates.
6. *(Learning Objective 3)* Dell can use ABC information for what decisions?
   a. Pricing
   b. Cost cutting
   c. Evaluating managers' performance
   d. All of the above
7. *(Learning Objective 3)* Which of the following is *not* a good reason for Dell to use ABC?
   a. The computer industry is highly competitive.
   b. Dell produces many more desktops than servers, and servers are more difficult to assemble.
   c. Most costs are direct; indirect costs are a small proportion of total costs.
   d. Dell has advanced information technology, including bar-coded materials and labor.
8. *(Learning Objective 4)* Lean companies use a workplace organization system called "5S" to keep their work cells clean and organized. Which of the following terms is *not* one of the 5S components?
   a. Standardize
   b. Sustain
   c. Sanitize
   d. Set in order
9. *(Learning Objective 5)* The cost of lost future sales after a customer finds flaws in a product or service is which of the following quality costs?
   a. External failure cost
   b. Internal failure cost
   c. Appraisal cost
   d. Prevention cost
10. *(Learning Objective 5)* Dell's spending on testing its computers before shipping them to customers helps *reduce* which of the following costs?
   a. Prevention cost
   b. Appraisal cost
   c. External failure cost
   d. None of the above

Quick Check Answers

1.d 2.d 3.c 4.c 5.c 6.d 7.c 8.c 9.a 10.c

Short Exercises

S4-1 Understand key terms *(Learning Objectives 1, 2, 3, 4, & 5)*

The following is a list of several terms. Complete the following statements with one of these terms. You may use a term more than once, and some terms may not be used at all.

Activity-based costing	**External failure costs**	**Manufacturing cycle time**	**TQMs**
Activity-based management	**Facility-level costs**	**POUS**	**Unit-level costs**
Appraisal costs	**Internal failure costs**	**Prevention costs**	
Appraisal costs	**Kaizen**	**Product-level costs**	
DOWNTIME	**Lean thinking**	**Takt time**	

a. The costs incurred for a particular product, regardless of the number of units or batches of the product produced, are known as ________.

b. ________ focuses on activities as fundamental building blocks in compiling the indirect costs of products, services, and customers.

c. ________ are costs incurred when defects in poor-quality goods or services are corrected before making delivery to customers.

d. ________ are incurred for every single unit of product produced.

e. Costs incurred when the company does not detect poor-quality goods or services until after delivery is made to customers are ________.

f. ________ are costs incurred no matter how many units, batches, or products are produced.

g. ________ is a Japanese word meaning "change for the better."

h. Costs incurred to detect poor-quality goods or services are ________.

i. The rate of production needed to meet customer demand yet avoid overproduction is known as ________.

j. ________ is a storage system used to reduce the waste of transportation and movement, in which tools, materials, and equipment are stored in proximity to where they will be used most frequently.

k. ________is a management philosophy of delighting customers with superior products and services by continually setting higher goals and improving every business function.

l. The time that elapses between the start of production and the product's completion is known as ________.

m. ________ is the management philosophy and strategy focused on creating value for the customer by eliminating waste.

n. The costs incurred for every batch, regardless of the number of units in the batch, are known as ________.

o. Costs incurred to avoid poor-quality goods or services are ________.

p. Using activity-based costing information to make decisions that increase profits while satisfying customers' needs is __________.

q. An acronym for the eight wastes is __________.

S4-2 Use departmental overhead rates to allocate manufacturing overhead *(Learning Objective 1)*

Maple Street Furniture uses departmental overhead rates (rather than a plantwide overhead rate) to allocate its manufacturing overhead to jobs. The company's two production departments have the following departmental overhead rates:

Cutting Department:	$12 per machine hour
Finishing Department:	$15 per direct labor hour

CHAPTER 4

Job 484 used the following direct labor hours and machine hours in the two manufacturing departments:

JOB 484	Cutting Department	Finishing Department
Direct Labor Hours	4	5
Machine Hours	9	5

1. How much manufacturing overhead should be allocated to Job 484?
2. Assume that direct labor is paid at a rate of $26 per hour and Job 484 used $2,550 of direct materials. What was the total manufacturing cost of Job 484?

S4-3 Compute departmental overhead rates *(Learning Objective 1)*

Gerbig Snacks makes potato chips, corn chips, and cheese puffs using three different production lines within the same manufacturing plant. Currently, Gerbig uses a single plantwide overhead rate to allocate its $3,762,000 of annual manufacturing overhead. Of this amount, $2,147,000 is associated with the potato chip line, $959,000 is associated with the corn chip line, and $656,000 is associated with the cheese puff line. Gerbig's plant is currently running a total of 17,100 machine hours: 11,300 in the potato chip line, 2,600 in the corn chip line, and 3,200 in the cheese puff line. Gerbig considers machine hours to be the cost driver of manufacturing overhead costs.

1. What is Gerbig's plantwide overhead rate?
2. Calculate the departmental overhead rates for Gerbig's three production lines. Round all answers to the nearest cent.
3. Which products have been overcosted by the plantwide rate? Which products have been undercosted by the plantwide rate?

S4-4 Compute activity cost allocation rates *(Learning Objective 2)*

Gerbig Snacks produces different styles of potato chips (ruffled, flat, thick-cut, gourmet) for different corporate customers. Each style of potato chip requires different preparation time, different cooking and draining times (depending on desired fat content), and different packaging (single serving versus bulk). Therefore, Gerbig has decided to try ABC to better capture the manufacturing overhead costs incurred by each style of chip. Gerbig has identified the following activities related to yearly manufacturing overhead costs and cost drivers associated with producing potato chips:

Activity	Manufacturing Overhead	Cost Driver
Preparation	$610,000	Preparation time
Cooking and draining	$972,000	Cooking and draining time
Packaging	$320,000	Units packaged

Compute the activity cost allocation rates for each activity assuming the following total estimated activity for the year: 10,000 preparation hours, 36,000 cooking and draining hours, and 4 million packages.

S4-5 Continuation of S4-4: Use ABC to allocate overhead *(Learning Objective 2)*

Gerbig Snacks just received an order to produce 15,000 single-serving bags of gourmet, fancy-cut, low-fat potato chips. The order will require 22 preparation hours and 32 cooking and draining hours. Use the activity rates you calculated in S4-4 to compute the following:

1. What is the total amount of manufacturing overhead that should be allocated to this order?
2. How much manufacturing overhead should be assigned to each bag?
3. What other costs will Gerbig need to consider to determine the total manufacturing costs of this order?

S4-6 Calculate a job cost using ABC *(Learning Objective 2)*

Wedge Industries, a family-run small manufacturer, has adopted an ABC system. The following manufacturing activities, indirect manufacturing costs, and usage of cost drivers have been estimated for the year:

Activity	Estimated Total Manufacturing Overhead Costs	Estimated Total Usage of Cost Driver
Machine setup	$150,450	3,000 setups
Machining	$999,900	5,000 machine hours
Quality control	$339,700	4,500 tests run

During May, Jim and Driscilla Wedge machined and assembled Job 557. Jim worked a total of 9 hours on the job, while Driscilla worked 7 hours on the job. Jim is paid a $25 per hour wage rate, while Driscilla is paid $32 per hour because of her additional experience level. Direct materials requisitioned for Job 557 totaled $1,350. The following additional information was collected on Job 557: the job required 2 machine setups, 5 machine hours, and 2 quality control tests.

1. Compute the activity cost allocation rates for the year.
2. Complete the following job cost record for Job 557:

Job Cost Record Job 557	Manufacturing Costs
Direct materials	?
Direct labor	?
Manufacturing overhead	?
Total job cost	$?

S4-7 Apply activity cost allocation rates *(Learning Objective 2)*

Alloy Technology uses ABC to allocate all of its manufacturing overhead. Alloy's Digital Department, which assembles and tests digital processors, reports the following data regarding processor G27:

Direct materials cost	$56.00
Direct labor cost	$49.00
Manufacturing overhead allocated	?
Manufacturing product cost	$?

The activities required to build the processors are as follows:

Activity	Allocation Base	Cost Allocated to Each Board		
Start station	Number of processor boards	6	× $ 0.70 =	$ 4.20
Dip insertion	Number of dip insertions	20	× $ 0.40 =	?
Manual insertion	Number of manual insertions	9	× $? =	5.40
Wave solder	Number of processor boards soldered	6	× $ 6.40 =	38.40
Backload	Number of backload insertions	?	× $ 0.60 =	4.20
Test	Standard time each processor board is in test activity (hr.)	0.14	× $70.00 =	?
Defect analysis	Standard time for defect analysis and repair (hr.)	0.17	× $? =	10.20
Total			$?	

1. Fill in the blanks in both the opening schedule and the list of activities.
2. Why might managers favor this ABC system instead of the older system that allocated all manufacturing overhead costs on the basis of direct labor?

S4-8 Classifying costs within the cost hierarchy *(Learning Objective 2)*

Classify each of the following costs as either unit-level, batch-level, product-level or facility-level.

a. Direct labor
b. Factory utilities
c. Direct materials
d. Product line manager salary
e. Engineering costs for new product
f. Depreciation on factory
g. CEO salary
h. Machine setup costs that are incurred whenever a new production order is started
i. Order processing
j. Patent for new product
k. Shipment of an order to a customer
l. Cost to inspect each product as it is finished

S4-9 Classifying costs within the cost hierarchy *(Learning Objective 2)*

Halliwell Manufacturing produces a variety of plastic containers using an extrusion blow molding process. The following activities are part of Halliwell Manufacturing's operating process:

1. Each container is cut from the mold once the plastic has cooled and hardened.
2. Patents are obtained for each new type of container mold.
3. Plastic resins are used as the main direct material for the containers.
4. A plant manager oversees the entire manufacturing operation.
5. The sales force incurs travel expenses to attend various trade shows throughout the country to market the containers.
6. Each container product line has a product line manager.
7. The extrusion machine is calibrated for each batch of containers made.
8. Each type of container has its own unique molds.
9. Routine maintenance is performed on the extrusion machines.
10. Rent is paid for the building that houses the manufacturing processes.

Classify each activity as either unit-level, batch-level, product-level, or facility-level.

S4-10 Determine the usefulness of refined costing systems in various situations *(Learning Objective 3)*

In each of the following situations, determine whether the company would be (1) more likely or (2) less likely to benefit from refining its costing system.

1. The company has very few indirect costs.
2. The company operates in a very competitive industry.
3. The company has reengineered its production process but has not changed its accounting system.
4. In bidding for jobs, managers lost bids they expected to win and won bids they expected to lose.
5. The company produces few products, and the products consume resources in a similar manner.
6. The company produces high volumes of some of its products and low volumes of other products.

Sunflower Inc., Data Set for S4-11 through S4-14:

Sunflower, Inc., is a technology consulting firm focused on the development and integration of cloud computing applications with client websites. President Susan Schnell's ear is ringing after an unpleasant call from client John Wilson. Wilson was irate after opening his bill for Sunflower's redesign of his company's website. Wilson said that Sunflower's major competitor, Zeta Applications, charged much lower fees to another company for which Wilson serves on the board of directors.

Schnell is puzzled for two reasons: First, she is confident that her firm knows website design and support as well as any of Sunflower's competitors. Schnell cannot understand how Zeta Applications can undercut Sunflower's rates and still make a profit. But Zeta Applications is reputed to be very profitable. Second, just yesterday Schnell received a call from client Ray Nanry. Nanry was happy with the excellent service and reasonable fees Schnell charged him for adding a database-driven-job-posting feature to his company's website. Schnell was surprised by Nanry's compliments because this was an unusual job for Sunflower that required development of complex data management and control applications, and she had felt a little uneasy accepting it.

Like most consulting firms, Sunflower traces direct labor to individual engagements (jobs). Sunflower allocates indirect costs to engagements using a budgeted rate based on direct labor hours. Schnell is happy with this system, which she has used since she established Sunflower in 1995.

Schnell expects to incur $710,500 of indirect costs this year, and she expects her firm to work 4,900 direct labor hours. Schnell and the other system consultants earn $335 per hour. Clients are billed at 160% of direct labor cost. Last month, Sunflower's consultants spent 95 hours on Wilson's engagement. They also spent 95 hours on Nanry's engagement.

S4-11 Compute and use traditional allocation rate *(Learning Objective 1)*

Refer to the Sunflower Data Set.

1. Compute Sunflower's indirect cost allocation rate.
2. Compute the total costs assigned to the Wilson and Nanry engagements.
3. Compute the operating income from the Wilson and Nanry engagements.

S4-12 Identify clues that old system is broken *(Learning Objective 3)*

Refer to the Sunflower Data Set. List all of the signals or clues indicating that Sunflower's cost system may be "broken."

S4-13 Compute activity cost allocation rates *(Learning Objective 2)*

Refer to the Sunflower Data Set. Schnell suspects that her allocation of indirect costs could be giving misleading results, so she decides to develop an ABC system. She identifies three activities: documentation preparation, information technology support, and training. Schnell figures that documentation costs are driven by the number of pages, information technology support costs are driven by the number of software applications used, and training costs are most closely associated with the number of direct labor hours worked. Estimates of the costs and quantities of the allocation bases follow:

Activity	Estimated Cost	Allocation Base	Estimated Quantity of Cost Driver
Documentation preparation	$144,500	Pages	2,890 pages
Information technology support	119,000	Applications used	700 applications
Training	447,000	Direct labor hours	4,470 hours
Total indirect costs	$710,500		

Compute the cost allocation rate for each activity.

S4-14 Continuation of S4-13: Compute job costs using ABC *(Learning Objective 2)*

Refer to the Sunflower Data Set and the activity cost allocation rates you computed in S4-13. The Wilson and Nanry engagements used the following resources last month:

Cost Driver	Wilson	Nanry
Direct labor hours	95	95
Pages	50	300
Applications used	1	78

1. Compute the cost assigned to the Wilson engagement and to the Nanry engagement using the ABC system.
2. Compute the operating income from the Wilson engagement and from the Nanry engagement using the ABC system.

S4-15 Identifying costs as value-added or non-valued-added *(Learning Objective 3)*

Identify which of the following manufacturing overhead costs are value-added and which are non-value-added.

a. Wages of the workers assembling products
b. Engineering design costs for a new product
c. Cost of moving raw materials into production
d. Salary for supervisor on the factory floor
e. Product inspection
f. Costs of reworking of defective units
g. Costs of warehousing raw materials
h. Costs arising from backlog in production

S4-16 Identifying activities as value-added or non-valued-added *(Learning Objective 3)*

Identify which of the following manufacturing overhead costs are value-added and which are non-value-added.

1. Chef cooks dinner for customer.
2. Food shipment received is recounted to make sure that the quantities ordered match the quantities received.
3. Server brings main course to customer.
4. Unused rolls are discarded at the end of the shift.

5. Server brings drink refills to a customer.
6. The manager authorizes overnight shipping for placemats since the restaurant ran out of placemats.
7. Server drops a platter of dinners.
8. Customer waits for his or her server to arrive at table to take a food order.
9. Hostess seats customer.
10. Customer receives a wilted salad. Server brings a replacement salad.

S4-17 Identify lean production characteristics *(Learning Objective 4)*

Indicate whether each of the following is characteristic of a lean production system or a traditional production system.

a. A workplace organization system called "5S" is frequently used to keep work spaces clean and organized.
b. Suppliers make frequent deliveries of small quantities of raw materials.
c. The manufacturing cycle times are longer.
d. The final operation in the production sequence "pulls" parts from the preceding operation.
e. Management works with suppliers to ensure defect-free raw materials.
f. The workflow is continuous to attempt to balance the rate of production with the rate of demand.
g. Products are produced in large batches.
h. There is an emphasis on building in quality.
i. Employees do a variety of jobs, including maintenance and setups as well as operation of machines.
j. Each employee is responsible for inspecting his or her own work.
k. Large stocks of finished goods protect against lost sales if customer demand is higher than expected.
l. Setup times are long.
m. Suppliers can access the company's intranet.

S4-18 Identifying the DOWNTIME activities at a manufacturer *(Learning Objective 4)*

The following is a list of eight waste activities found at a furniture manufacturing plant. Classify each one as a type of waste as represented by the acronym DOWNTIME (Defects, Overproductions, Waiting, Not utilizing people to their full potential, Transportation, Inventory, Movement, and Excess processing).

a. The plant manager makes all decisions in the plant; employees follow directions.
b. Furniture is shipped fully assembled to customers, incurring extra shipping costs because of the additional bulk.
c. Employees must search for tools at the beginning of each work shift since there is no standard storage spot for each tool.
d. Because the drill press is broken, the furniture assembly workers cannot do any work until it is fixed.
e. The tables made yesterday need to have new umbrella holes drilled in them because the current holes are too small.
f. Tables are made in large batches because machine setup time is costly.
g. Raw materials are delivered to materials warehousing area; when production is ready for the raw materials, tow motor drivers drive the materials to the production area.
h. Twice as much raw material as needed for current production is stocked in case defects are found in the raw material during production.

S4-19 Classifying costs of quality *(Learning Objective 5)*

Classify each of the following quality-related costs as prevention costs, appraisal costs, internal failure costs, or external failure costs.

1. Repairing defective units found
2. Legal fees from customer lawsuits
3. Inspecting products that are halfway through the production process
4. Redesigning the production process
5. Cost incurred producing and disposing of defective units
6. Incremental cost of using a higher-grade raw material
7. Training employees
8. Lost productivity due to machine break down
9. Inspecting incoming raw materials
10. Warranty repairs

S4-20 Quality initiative decision *(Learning Objective 5)*

Boatsburg manufactures high-quality speakers. Suppose Boatsburg is considering spending the following amounts on a new quality program:

Additional 20 minutes of testing for each speaker	$ 600,000
Negotiating with and training suppliers to obtain higher-quality materials and on-time delivery	$ 510,000
Redesigning the speakers to make them easier to manufacture	$1,409,000

Boatsburg expects this quality program to save costs as follows:

Reduced warranty repair costs	$202,000
Avoid inspection of raw materials	$409,000
Rework avoided because of fewer defective units	$652,000

It also expects this program to avoid lost profits from the following:

Lost sales due to disappointed customers	$855,000
Lost production time due to rework	$307,000

1. Classify each of these costs into one of the four categories of quality costs (prevention, appraisal, internal failure, external failure).
2. Should Boatsburg implement the quality program? Give your reasons.

S4-21 Categorize different costs of quality *(Learning Objective 5)*

Millan & Co. makes electronic components. Mike Millan, the president, recently instructed Vice President Steve Bensen to develop a total quality control program: "If we don't at least match the quality improvements our competitors are making," he told Bensen, "we'll soon be out of business." Bensen began by listing various "costs of quality" that Millan incurs. The first six items that came to mind were as follows:

- Costs incurred by Millan & Co.'s customer representatives traveling to customer sites to repair defective products
- Lost profits from lost sales due to reputation for less-than-perfect products
- Costs of electronic components returned by customers
- Costs of reworking defective components after discovery by company inspectors
- Costs of inspecting components in one of Millan & Co.'s production processes
- Salaries of engineers who are designing components to withstand electrical overloads

Classify each item as a prevention cost, an appraisal cost, an internal failure cost, or an external failure cost.

EXERCISES Group A

E4-22A Compare traditional and departmental cost allocations *(Learning Objective 1)*

Donovan's Fine Furnishings manufactures upscale custom furniture. Donovan's currently uses a plantwide overhead rate based on direct labor hours to allocate its $1,150,000 of manufacturing overhead to individual jobs. However, Dana Cermak, owner and CEO, is considering refining the company's costing system by using departmental overhead rates. Currently, the Machining Department incurs $825,000 of manufacturing overhead while the Finishing Department incurs $325,000 of manufacturing overhead. Dana has identified machine hours (MH) as the primary manufacturing overhead cost driver in the Machining Department and direct labor (DL) hours as the primary cost driver in the Finishing Department.

The Donovan's plant completed Jobs 450 and 455 on May 15. Both jobs incurred a total of 5 DL hours throughout the entire production process. Job 450 incurred 3 MH in the Machining Department and 4 DL hours in the Finishing Department (the other DL hour occurred in the Machining Department). Job 455 incurred 6 MH in the Machining Department and 3 DL hours in the Finishing Department (the other two DL hours occurred in the Machining Department).

Requirements

1. Compute the plantwide overhead rate assuming that Donovan's expects to incur 25,000 total DL hours during the year.
2. Compute departmental overhead rates assuming that Donovan's expects to incur 13,750 MH in the Machining Department and 13,000 DL hours in the Finishing Department during the year.
3. If Donovan's continues to use the plantwide overhead rate, how much manufacturing overhead would be allocated to Job 450 and Job 455?
4. If Donovan's uses departmental overhead rates, how much manufacturing overhead would be allocated to Job 450 and Job 455?
5. Based on your answers to Requirements 3 and 4, does the plantwide overhead rate overcost or undercost either job? Explain. If Donovan's sells its furniture at 125% of cost, will its choice of allocation systems affect product pricing? Explain.

E4-23A Compute activity rates and apply to jobs *(Learning Objective 2)*

West Horizon uses ABC to account for its chrome wheel manufacturing process. Company managers have identified four manufacturing activities that incur manufacturing overhead costs: materials handling, machine setup, insertion of parts, and finishing. The budgeted activity costs for the upcoming year and their allocation bases are as follows:

Activity	Total Budgeted Manufacturing Overhead Cost	Allocation Base
Materials handling	$ 13,200	Number of parts
Machine setup	5,200	Number of setups
Insertion of parts	49,500	Number of parts
Finishing	86,100	Finishing direct labor hours
Total	$154,000	

West Horizon expects to produce 1,000 chrome wheels during the year. The wheels are expected to use 3,300 parts, require 20 setups, and consume 2,100 hours of finishing time.

Job 420 used 100 parts, required 3 setups, and consumed 140 finishing hours.
Job 510 used 425 parts, required 6 setups, and consumed 350 finishing hours.

Requirements

1. Compute the cost allocation rate for each activity.
2. Compute the manufacturing overhead cost that should be assigned to Job 420.
3. Compute the manufacturing overhead cost that should be assigned to Job 510.

CHAPTER 4

E4-24A Apply activity cost allocation rates *(Learning Objective 2)*

Scofield Industries manufactures a variety of custom products. The company has traditionally used a plantwide manufacturing overhead rate based on machine hours to allocate manufacturing overhead to its products. The company estimates that it will incur $790,000 in total manufacturing overhead costs in the upcoming year and will use 10,000 machine hours.

Up to this point, hazardous waste disposal fees have been absorbed into the plantwide manufacturing overhead rate and allocated to all products as part of the manufacturing overhead process. Recently, the company has been experiencing significantly increased waste disposal fees for hazardous waste generated by certain products, and as a result, profit margins on all products have been negatively impacted. Company management wants to implement an activity-based costing system so that managers know the cost of each product, including its hazardous waste disposal costs.

Expected usage and costs for manufacturing overhead activities for the upcoming year are as follows:

Description of Cost Pool	Estimated Cost	Cost Driver	Estimated Activity for this Year
Machine maintenance costs	$250,000	Number of machine hours	10,000
Engineering change orders	$240,000	Number of change orders	4,000
Hazardous waste disposal	$300,000	Pounds of hazardous materials generated	1,000
Total overhead cost	$790,000		

During the year, Job 356 is started and completed. Usage for this job follows:

300 pounds of direct materials at $50 per pound
55 direct labor hours used at $20 per labor hour
100 machine hours used
6 change orders
50 pounds of hazardous waste generated

Requirements

1. Calculate the cost of Job 356 using the traditional plantwide manufacturing overhead rate based on machine hours.
2. Calculate the cost of Job 356 using activity-based costing.
3. If you were a manager, which cost estimate would provide you more useful information? How might you use this information?

E4-25A Using ABC to bill clients at a service firm *(Learning Objective 2)*

Pesarchick & Company is an architectural firm specializing in home remodeling for private clients and new office buildings for corporate clients.

Pesarchick charges customers at a billing rate equal to 120% of the client's total job cost. A client's total job cost is a combination of (1) professional time spent on the client ($63 per hour cost of employing each professional) and (2) operating overhead allocated to the client's job. Pesarchick allocates operating overhead to jobs based on professional hours spent on the job. Pesarchick estimates its five professionals will incur a total of 10,000 professional hours working on client jobs during the year.

All operating costs other than professional salaries (travel reimbursements, copy costs, secretarial salaries, office lease, and so forth) can be assigned to the three activities. Total activity costs, cost drivers, and total usage of those cost drivers are estimated as follows:

Activity	Total Activity Cost	Cost Driver	Total Usage by Corporate Clients	Total Usage by Private Clients
Transportation to clients	$ 10,500	Round-trip mileage to clients	4,500 miles	10,500 miles
Blueprint copying	37,000	Number of copies	400 copies	600 copies
Office support	186,000	Secretarial time	2,100 secretarial hours	2,900 secretarial hours
Total operating overhead	$233,500			

Lillian Yu hired Pesarchick to design her kitchen remodeling. A total of 27 professional hours were incurred on this job. In addition, Yu's remodeling job required one of the professionals to travel back and forth to her house for a total of 120 miles. The blueprints had to be copied four times because Yu changed the plans several times. In addition, 22 hours of secretarial time were used lining up the subcontractors for the job.

Requirements

1. Calculate the current indirect cost allocation rate per professional hour.
2. Calculate the amount that would be billed to Lillian Yu given the current costing structure.
3. Calculate the activity cost allocation rates that could be used to allocate operating overhead costs to client jobs.
4. Calculate the amount that would be billed to Lillian Yu using ABC costing.
5. Which type of billing system is more fair to clients? Explain.

E4-26A Compare traditional and ABC allocations at a pharmacy

(Learning Objective 2)

Wolanin Pharmacy, part of a large chain of pharmacies, fills a variety of prescriptions for customers. The complexity of prescriptions filled by Wolanin varies widely; pharmacists can spend between five minutes to six hours on a prescription order. Traditionally, the pharmacy has allocated its overhead based on the number of prescriptions in each order. For example, a customer may bring in three prescriptions in one day to be filled; the pharmacy considers this to be one order.

The pharmacy chain's controller is exploring whether activity-based costing (ABC) may better allocate the pharmacy overhead costs to pharmacy orders. The controller has gathered the following information:

Cost Pools	Total Annual Estimated Cost	Cost Driver	Total Annual Estimated Cost Driver Activity
Pharmacy occupancy costs (utilities, rent, and other costs).	$ 60,000	Technician hours	75,000
Packaging supplies (bottles, bags, and other packaging)	$ 30,000	Number of prescriptions	25,000
Professional training and insurance costs . . .	$100,000	Pharmacist hours	25,000
Total pharmacy overhead	$190,000		

The clerk for Wolanin has gathered the following information regarding two recent pharmacy orders:

Customer Order Number	Technician Hours	Number of Prescriptions	Pharmacist Hours
1247	0.5	3	1.0
1248	0.5	1	2.5

Requirements

1. What is the traditional overhead rate based on the number of prescriptions?
2. How much pharmacy overhead would be allocated to customer order number 1247 if traditional overhead allocation based on the number of prescriptions is used?
3. How much pharmacy overhead would be allocated to customer order number 1248 if traditional overhead allocation based on the number of prescriptions is used?
4. What are the following cost pool allocation rates:
   a. Pharmacy occupancy costs
   b. Packaging supplies
   c. Professional training and insurance costs
5. How much would be allocated to customer order number 1247 if activity-based costing (ABC) is used to allocate the pharmacy overhead costs?
6. How much would be allocated to customer order number 1248 if activity-based costing (ABC) is used to allocate the pharmacy overhead costs?
7. Which allocation method (traditional or activity-based costing) would produce a more accurate product cost? Explain your answer.

E4-27A Reassess product costs using ABC *(Learning Objective 2)*

Jones, Inc., manufactures only two products, Medium (42-inch) and Large (63-inch) plasma screen TVs. To generate adequate profit and cover its expenses throughout the value chain, Jones prices its TVs at 300% of manufacturing cost. The company is concerned because the Large model is facing severe pricing competition, whereas the Medium model is the low-price leader in the market. The CEO questions whether the cost numbers generated by the accounting system are correct. He has just learned about ABC and wants to reanalyze this past year's product costs using an ABC system.

Information about the company's products this past year is as follows:

Medium (42-inch) Plasma TVs
- Total direct material cost: $660,000
- Total direct labor cost: $225,000
- Production volume: 3,200 units

Large (63-inch) Plasma TVs:
- Total direct material cost: $1,227,000
- Total direct labor cost: $388,000
- Production volume: 4,000 units

Currently, the company applies manufacturing overhead on the basis of direct labor hours. The company incurred $820,000 of manufacturing overhead this year and 20,500 direct labor hours (7,875 direct labor hours making Medium TVs and 12,625 making Large TVs). The ABC team identified three primary production activities that generate manufacturing overhead costs:

- Materials Handling ($120,000); driven by number of material orders handled
- Machine Processing ($600,000); driven by machine hours
- Packaging ($100,000); driven by packaging hours

The company's only two products required the following activity levels during the year:

	Material Orders Handled	Machine Hours	Packaging Hours
Medium	350	25,000	3,000
Large	250	15,000	7,000

Requirements

1. Use the company's current costing system to find the total cost of producing all Medium (42-inch) TVs and the total cost of producing all Large (63-inch) TVs. What was the average cost of making each unit of each model? Round your answers to the nearest cent.
2. Use ABC to find the total cost of producing all Medium (42-inch) TVs and the total cost of producing all Large (63-inch) TVs. What was the average cost of making each unit of each model? Round your answers to the nearest cent.
3. How much cost distortion was occurring between Jones' two products? Calculate the cost distortion in total and on a per unit basis. Could the cost distortion explain the CEO's confusion about pricing competition? Explain.

E4-28A Use ABC to allocate manufacturing overhead *(Learning Objective 2)*

Several years after reengineering its production process, King, Corp. hired a new controller, Tammy English. She developed an ABC system very similar to the one used by King's chief rival, Risingsun. Part of the reason English developed the ABC system was because King's profits had been declining even though the company had shifted its product mix toward the product that had appeared most profitable under the old system. Before adopting the new ABC system, King had used a plantwide overhead rate based on direct labor hours that was developed years ago.

For the upcoming year, King's budgeted ABC manufacturing overhead allocation rates are as follows:

Activity	Allocation Base	Activity Cost Allocation Rate
Materials handling	Number of parts	$ 3.75 per part
Machine setup	Number of setups	$314.20 per setup
Insertion of parts	Number of parts	$ 32.00 per part
Finishing	Finishing direct labor hours	$ 54.00 per hour

The number of parts is now a feasible allocation base because King recently installed a plantwide computer system. King produces two wheel models: Standard and Deluxe. Budgeted data for the upcoming year are as follows:

	Standard	Deluxe
Parts per wheel	5.0	7.0
Setups per 1,000 wheels	15.0	15.0
Finishing direct labor hours per wheel	1.1	2.8
Total direct labor hours per wheel	2.0	3.1

The company's managers expect to produce 1,000 units of each model during the year.

Requirements

1. Compute the total budgeted manufacturing overhead cost for the upcoming year.
2. Compute the manufacturing overhead cost per wheel of each model using ABC.
3. Compute King's traditional plantwide overhead rate. Use this rate to determine the manufacturing overhead cost per wheel under the traditional system.

E4-29A Continuation of E4-28A: Determine product profitability *(Learning Objectives 2 & 3)*

Refer to your answers in E4-28A. In addition to the manufacturing overhead costs, the following data are budgeted for the company's Standard and Deluxe models for next year:

	Standard	Deluxe
Sales price per wheel	$496.00	$670.00
Direct materials per wheel	$ 32.50	$ 46.25
Direct labor per wheel	$ 45.00	$ 50.00

Requirements

1. Compute the gross profit per wheel if managers rely on the ABC unit cost data computed in E4-28A.
2. Compute the gross profit per wheel if the managers rely on the plantwide allocation cost data.
3. Which product line is more profitable for King?
4. Why might controller Tammy English have expected ABC to pass the cost-benefit test? Were there any warning signs that King's old direct-labor-based allocation system was broken?

E4-30A Work backward to determine ABC rates *(Learning Objective 2)*

Franklin Fabricators completed two jobs in June. Franklin recorded the following costs assigned to the jobs by the company's activity-based costing system:

		Allocated Cost	
Activity	**Allocation Base**	**Job 409**	**Job 622**
Materials handling	Number of parts	$ 400	$ 1,200
Lathe work	Number of lathe turns	$5,200	$15,000
Milling	Number of machine hours	$3,700	$25,000
Grinding	Number of parts	$ 360	$ 1,800
Testing	Number of output units	$ 120	$ 3,000

Job 622 required 2,500 parts, 62,500 lathe turns, and 1,000 machine hours. All 375 of the job's output units were tested. All units of Job 409 were tested.

Requirements

1. How do you know that at least one of the costs recorded for the two jobs is inaccurate?
2. Disregard materials handling costs. How many parts were used for Job 409? How many lathe turns did Job 409 require? How many machine hours? How many units were produced in Job 409?
3. A nearby company has offered to test all product units for $15 each. On the basis of ABC data, should Franklin Fabricators accept or reject the offer? Give your reason.

E4-31A Differentiate between traditional and lean operations *(Learning Objective 4)*

Briefly describe how lean production systems differ from traditional production systems along each of the following dimensions:

1. Inventory levels
2. Batch sizes
3. Setup times
4. Workplace organization
5. Roles of plant employees
6. Manufacturing cycle times
7. Quality

E4-32A Classify wastes into DOWNTIME categories *(Learning Objective 5)*

The following is a list of activities performed in an office. Classify each one as a type of waste as represented by the acronym DOWNTIME (Defect, Overproduction, Waiting, Not utilizing people to their full potential, Transportation, Inventory, Movement, and Excess processing).

a. To retrieve inventory records, clerks must click through several menus in the program to get to the record needed.
b. Sales orders are put into the computer by the sales people in the field and paper reports are generated; these sales orders are then entered into the order processing system by clerks who type the orders based on the paper reports.
c. The office is run by the office managers; employees do as they are told.
d. The computer system requires frequent restarting; restarting takes five minutes.
e. Loan approval files frequently contain errors.
f. The files needed for loan approval are carried to and from the file storage office when the files are needed.
g. Office supplies are stockpiled in the supply closet; the office manager buys in large quantities when there are sales.
h. Paperwork (for orders that might change) is printed before it is needed.
i. The office computers are slow to do the processing; the computers need to be upgraded.
j. Orders in the system are frequently missing information.
k. Employees do not have the authority and responsibility to make routine decisions.
l. Pending vacation requests must be taken to the third floor offices to get the signature of the human resources manager.
m. Approval of loans is done in batches, once a week, rather than as the loan paperwork is finished for each individual loan.
n. Each time a document needs to be notarized, someone must search for the notary seal (used to make the seal impression on the document).
o. The accounting report produces segment reports because these reports have been produced for years even though managers use other reports to manage their divisions.
p. The office manager insists that a spreadsheet program is used to store customer records, even though it would be more efficient to use a database program.

E4-33A Prepare a Cost of Quality report *(Learning Objective 5)*

The CEO of Healthy Snacks Corp. is concerned about the amount of resources currently spent on customer warranty claims. Each box of snacks is printed with the following logo: "Satisfaction guaranteed, or your money back." Since the claims are so high, she would like to evaluate what costs are being incurred to ensure the quality of the product. The following information was collected from various departments within the company:

Cost of disposing of rejected products	$ 13,000
Preventive maintenance on factory equipment	$ 7,000
Production loss due to machine breakdowns	$ 24,000
Inspection of raw materials	$ 3,000
Warranty claims	$436,000
Cost of defective products found at the inspection point	$ 93,000
Training factory personnel	$ 28,000
Recall of Batch #59374	$171,000
Inspecting products when halfway through the production process	$ 52,000

Requirements

1. Prepare a Cost of Quality report. In addition to listing the costs by category, determine the percentage of the total costs of quality incurred in each cost category.
2. Do any additional subjective costs appear to be missing from the report?
3. What can be learned from the report?

E4-34A Classify costs and make a quality-initiative decision

(Learning Objective 5)

Clarke Corp. manufactures radiation-shielding glass panels. Suppose Clarke is considering spending the following amounts on a new TQM program:

Strength-testing one item from each batch of panels	$64,000
Training employees in TQM	$29,000
Training suppliers in TQM	$33,000
Identifying preferred suppliers who commit to on-time delivery of perfect quality materials	$59,000

Clarke expects the new program to save costs through the following:

Avoid lost profits from lost sales due to disappointed customers	$92,000
Avoid rework and spoilage	$65,000
Avoid inspection of raw materials	$51,000
Avoid warranty costs	$16,000

Requirements

1. Classify each item as a prevention cost, an appraisal cost, an internal failure cost, or an external failure cost.
2. Should Clarke implement the new quality program? Give your reason.

EXERCISES Group B

E4-35B Compare traditional and departmental cost allocations *(Learning Objective 1)*

Bergeron's Fine Furnishings manufactures upscale custom furniture. Bergeron's currently uses a plantwide overhead rate, based on direct labor hours, to allocate its $1,350,000 of manufacturing overhead to individual jobs. However, Sam Bergeron, owner and CEO, is considering refining the company's costing system by using departmental overhead rates. Currently, the Machining Department incurs $900,000 of manufacturing overhead while the Finishing Department incurs $450,000 of manufacturing overhead. Bergeron has identified machine hours (MH) as the primary manufacturing overhead cost driver in the Machining Department and direct labor (DL) hours as the primary cost driver in the Finishing Department.

Bergeron's plant completed Jobs 450 and 455 on May 15. Both jobs incurred a total of 5 DL hours throughout the entire production process. Job 450 incurred 3 MH in the Machining Department and 4 DL hours in the Finishing Department (the other DL hour occurred in the Machining Department). Job 455 incurred 6 MH in the Machining Department and 3 DL hours in the Finishing Department (the other two DL hours occurred in the Machining Department).

Requirements

1. Compute the plantwide overhead rate, assuming Bergeron's expects to incur 50,000 total DL hours during the year.
2. Compute departmental overhead rates, assuming Bergeron's expects to incur 20,000 MH in the Machining Department and 25,000 DL hours in the Finishing Department during the year.
3. If Bergeron's continues to use the plantwide overhead rate, how much manufacturing overhead would be allocated to Job 450 and Job 455?
4. If Bergeron's uses departmental overhead rates, how much manufacturing overhead would be allocated to Job 450 and Job 455?
5. Based on your answers to Requirements 3 and 4, does the plantwide overhead rate overcost or undercost either of the jobs? Explain. If Bergeron's sells its furniture at 125% of cost, will its choice of allocation systems affect product pricing?

E4-36B Compute activity rates and apply to jobs *(Learning Objective 2)*

Fortunado Company uses ABC to account for its chrome wheel manufacturing process. Company managers have identified four manufacturing activities that incur manufacturing overhead costs: materials handling, machine setup, insertion of parts, and finishing. The budgeted activity costs for the upcoming year and their allocation bases are as follows:

Activity	Total Budgeted Manufacturing Overhead Cost	Allocation Base
Materials handling	$ 6,400	Number of parts
Machine setup	9,000	Number of setups
Insertion of parts	54,400	Number of parts
Finishing	89,700	Finishing direct labor hours
Total	$159,500	

Fortunado expects to produce 1,000 chrome wheels during the year. The wheels are expected to use 3,200 parts, require 25 setups, and consume 2,300 hours of finishing time.

Job 420 used 250 parts, required 3 setups, and consumed 130 finishing hours.
Job 510 used 425 parts, required 6 setups, and consumed 320 finishing hours.

Requirements

1. Compute the cost allocation rate for each activity.
2. Compute the manufacturing overhead cost that should be assigned to Job 420.
3. Compute the manufacturing overhead cost that should be assigned to Job 510.

E4-37B Apply activity cost allocation rates *(Learning Objective 2)*

Castle Industries manufactures a variety of custom products. The company has traditionally used a plantwide manufacturing overhead rate based on machine hours to allocate manufacturing overhead to its products. The company estimates that it will incur $1,310,000 in total manufacturing overhead costs in the upcoming year and will use 10,000 machine hours.

Up to this point, hazardous waste disposal fees have been absorbed into the plantwide manufacturing overhead rate and allocated to all products as part of the manufacturing overhead process. Recently the company has been experiencing significantly increased waste disposal fees for hazardous waste generated by certain products and, as a result, profit margins on all products have been negatively impacted. Company management wants to implement an activity-based costing system so that managers know the cost of each product, including its hazardous waste disposal costs.

Expected usage and costs for manufacturing overhead activities for the upcoming year are as follows:

Description of Cost Pool	Estimated Cost	Cost Driver	Estimated Activity for this Year
Machine maintenance costs	$ 350,000	Number of machine hours	10,000
Engineering change orders	360,000	Number of change orders	3,000
Hazardous waste disposal	600,000	Pounds of hazardous materials generated	1,000
Total overhead cost	$1,310,000		

During the year, Job 356 is started and completed. Usage data for this job are as follows:

400 pounds of direct materials at $50 per pound
75 direct labor hours used at $20 per labor hour
100 machine hours used
8 change orders
60 pounds of hazardous waste generated

Requirements

1. Calculate the cost of Job 356 using the traditional plantwide manufacturing overhead rate based on machine hours.
2. Calculate the cost of Job 356 using activity-based costing.
3. If you were a manager, which cost estimate would provide you more useful information? How might you use this information?

E4-38B Using ABC to bill clients at a service firm *(Learning Objective 2)*

Lambert & Company is an architectural firm specializing in home remodeling for private clients and new office buildings for corporate clients.

Lambert charges customers at a billing rate equal to 140% of the client's total job cost. A client's total job cost is a combination of (1) professional time spent on the client ($63 per hour cost of employing each professional) and (2) operating overhead allocated to the client's job. Lambert allocates operating overhead to jobs based on professional hours spent on the job. Lambert estimates its five professionals will incur a total of 10,000 professional hours working on client jobs during the year.

All operating costs other than professional salaries (travel reimbursements, copy costs, secretarial salaries, office lease, and so forth) can be assigned to the three activities. Total activity costs, cost drivers, and total usage of those cost drivers are estimated as follows:

Activity	Total Activity Cost	Cost Driver	Total Usage by Corporate Clients	Total Usage by Private Clients
Transportation to clients	$ 7,500	Round-trip mileage to clients	3,000 miles	12,000 miles
Blueprint copying	38,000	Number of copies	300 copies	700 copies
Office support	191,000	Secretarial time	2,700 secretarial hours	2,300 secretarial hours
Total operating overhead	$236,500			

Amy Lee hired Lambert & Company to design her kitchen remodeling. A total of 23 professional hours were incurred on this job. In addition, Lee's remodeling job required one of the professionals to travel back and forth to her house for a total of 124 miles. The blueprints had to be copied four times because Lee changed the plans several times. In addition, 13 hours of secretarial time were used lining up the subcontractors for the job.

Requirements

1. Calculate the current operating overhead allocation rate per professional hour.
2. Calculate the amount that would be billed to Amy Lee given the current costing structure.
3. Calculate the activity cost allocation rates that could be used to allocate operating overhead costs to client jobs.
4. Calculate the amount that would be billed to Amy Lee using ABC costing.
5. Which type of billing system is more fair to clients? Explain.

E4-39B Compare traditional and ABC cost allocations at a pharmacy *(Learning Objective 2)*

Franklin Pharmacy, part of a large chain of pharmacies, fills a variety of prescriptions for customers. The complexity of prescriptions filled by Franklin varies widely; pharmacists can spend between five minutes to six hours on a prescription order. Traditionally, the pharmacy has allocated its overhead based on the number of prescription in each order. For example, a customer may bring in three prescriptions one day to be filled; the pharmacy considers this to be one order.

The pharmacy chain's controller is exploring whether activity-based costing (ABC) may better allocate the pharmacy overhead costs to pharmacy orders. The controller has gathered the following information:

Cost Pools	Total Annual Estimated Cost	Cost Driver	Total Annual Estimated Cost Driver Activity
Pharmacy occupancy costs (utilities, rent, and other costs)	$ 80,000	Technician hours	80,000
Packaging supplies (bottles, bags, and other packaging)	30,000	Number of prescriptions	20,000
Professional training and insurance costs	110,000	Pharmacists hours	23,810
Total pharmacy overhead	$210,000		

The clerk for Franklin Pharmacy has gathered the following information regarding two recent pharmacy orders:

Customer Order Number	Technician Hours	Number of Prescriptions	Pharmacist Hours
1102	1.0	2	2.0
1103	0.5	1	4.0

Requirements

1. What is the traditional overhead rate based on the number of prescriptions?
2. How much pharmacy overhead would be allocated to customer order number 1102 if traditional overhead allocation based on the number of prescriptions is used?
3. How much pharmacy overhead would be allocated to customer order number 1103 if traditional overhead allocation based on the number of prescriptions is used?
4. What are the following cost pool allocation rates?
   a. Pharmacy occupancy costs
   b. Packing supplies
   c. Professional training and insurance costs
5. How much would be allocated to customer order number 1102 if activity-based costing (ABC) is used to allocate the pharmacy overhead costs?
6. How much would be allocated to customer order number 1103 if activity-based costing (ABC) is used to allocate the pharmacy costs?
7. Which allocation method (traditional or activity-based costing) would produce a more accurate product cost? Explain your answer.

E4-40B Reassess product costs using ABC *(Learning Objective 2)*

Jones, Inc., manufactures only two products, Medium (42-inch) and Large (63-inch) plasma screen TVs. To generate adequate profit and cover its expenses throughout the value chain, Jones prices its TVs at 300% of manufacturing cost. The company is concerned because the Large model is facing severe pricing competition, whereas the Medium model is the low-price leader in the market. The CEO questions whether the cost numbers generated by the accounting system are correct. The CEO just learned about ABC and wants to reanalyze this past year's product costs using an ABC system. Information about the company's products this past year is as follows:

Medium (42-inch) Plasma TVs

- Total direct material cost: $954,750
- Total direct labor cost: $280,000
- Production volume: 4,000 units

Large (63-inch) Plasma TVs:

- Total direct material cost: $1,520,200
- Total direct labor cost: $525,000
- Production volume: 5,000 units

Currently, the company applies manufacturing overhead on the basis of direct labor hours. The company incurred $1,020,000 of manufacturing overhead this year, and 20,400 direct labor hours (7,005 direct labor hours making Medium TVs and 13,395 making Large TVs). The ABC team identified three primary production activities that generate manufacturing overhead costs:

Materials Handling ($145,000); driven by number of material orders handled
Machine Processing ($750,000); driven by machine hours
Packaging ($125,000); driven by packaging hours

The company's only two products required the following activity levels during the year:

	Material Orders Handled	Machine Hours	Packaging Hours
Medium	225	45,000	10,000
Large	275	30,000	15,000

Requirements

1. Use the company's current costing system to find the total cost of producing all Medium (42-inch) TVs and the total cost of producing all Large (63-inch) TVs. What was the average cost of making each unit of each model? Round your answers to the nearest cent.
2. Use ABC to find the total cost of producing all Medium (42-inch) TVs and the total cost of producing all Large (63-inch) TVs. What was the average cost of making each unit of each model? Round your answers to the nearest cent.
3. How much cost distortion was occurring between the company's two products? Calculate the cost distortion in total and on a per unit basis. Could the cost distortion explain the CEO's confusion about pricing competition? Explain.

E4-41B Use ABC to allocate manufacturing overhead *(Learning Objective 2)*

Several years after reengineering its production process, Rickett Corp. hired a new controller, Jillian Harper. She developed an ABC system very similar to the one used by Rickett's chief rival. Part of the reason Harper developed the ABC system was because Rickett's profits had been declining even though the company had shifted its product mix toward the product that had appeared most profitable under the old system. Before adopting the new ABC system, Rickett had used a plantwide overhead rate, based on direct labor hours developed years ago.

For the upcoming year, the company's budgeted ABC manufacturing overhead allocation rates are as follows:

Activity	Allocation Base	Activity Cost Allocation Rate
Materials handling	Number of parts	$ 3.75 per part
Machine setup	Number of setups	$340.00 per setup
Insertion of parts	Number of parts	$ 27.00 per part
Finishing	Finishing direct labor hours	$ 53.00 per hour

The number of parts is now a feasible allocation base because Rickett recently purchased bar-coding technology. Rickett produces two wheel models: Standard and Deluxe. Budgeted data for the upcoming year are as follows:

	Standard	Deluxe
Parts per wheel	4.0	6.0
Setups per 1,000 wheels	20.0	20.0
Finishing direct labor hours per wheel	1.5	3.2
Total direct labor hours per wheel	2.0	3.0

The company's managers expect to produce 1,000 units of each model during the year.

Requirements

1. Compute the total budgeted manufacturing overhead cost for the upcoming year.
2. Compute the manufacturing overhead cost per wheel of each model using ABC.
3. Compute the company's traditional plantwide overhead rate. Use this rate to determine the manufacturing overhead cost per wheel under the traditional system.

E4-42B Continuation of E4-41B: Determine product profitability *(Learning Objectives 2 & 3)*

Refer to your answers in E4-41B. In addition to the manufacturing overhead costs, the following data are budgeted for the company's Standard and Deluxe models for next year:

	Standard	Deluxe
Sales price per wheel	$470.00	$610.00
Direct materials per wheel	$ 32.00	$ 46.25
Direct labor per wheel	$ 45.60	$ 54.00

Requirements

1. Compute the gross profit per wheel if managers rely on the ABC unit cost data.
2. Compute the gross profit per unit if the managers rely on the plantwide allocation cost data.
3. Which product line is more profitable for the company?
4. Why might the controller have expected ABC to pass the cost-benefit test? Were there any warning signs that the company's old direct-labor-based allocation system was broken?

E4-43B Work backward to determine ABC rates *(Learning Objective 2)*

Williamson Fabricators completed two jobs in June. The company recorded the following costs assigned to the jobs by the company's activity-based costing system:

		Allocated Cost	
Activity	**Allocation Base**	**Job 409**	**Job 622**
Materials handling.	Number of parts	$ 600	$ 1,800
Lathe work.	Number of lathe turns	$4,500	$14,500
Milling	Number of machine hours	$4,350	$29,000
Grinding	Number of parts	$ 312	$ 1,560
Testing.	Number of output units	$ 126	$ 2,700

Job 622 required 3,250 parts, 58,000 lathe turns, and 1,000 machine hours. All 300 of the job's output units were tested. All units of Job 409 were tested.

Requirements

1. How do you know that at least one of the costs recorded for the two jobs is inaccurate?
2. Disregard materials handling costs. How many parts were used for Job 409? How many lathe turns did Job 409 require? How many machine hours did Job 409 require? How many units were produced in Job 409?
3. A nearby company has offered to test all product units for $12 each. On the basis of ABC data, should Williamson Fabricators accept or reject the offer? Give your reason.

E4-44B Differentiate between traditional and lean production *(Learning Objective 4)*

Categorize each of the following characteristics as being either more representative of a traditional organization or a lean organization.

1. Emphasis is placed on shortening manufacturing cycle times.
2. Manufacturing plants tend to group like machinery together in different parts of the plant.
3. Setup times are shorter.
4. Produce in larger batches.
5. Strive to maintain low inventory levels.
6. Cycle time tends to be longer.
7. Quality tends to be "inspect-in" rather than "build-in."
8. Manufacturing plants tend to be organized with self-contained production cells.
9. Maintain greater quantities of raw materials, work in process, and finished goods inventories.
10. Setup times are longer.
11. High quality is stressed in every aspect of production.
12. Produce in smaller batches.

E4-45B Identifying waste activities in an office *(Learning Objective 4)*

The following is a list of waste activities found in an office. Classify each one as a type of waste as represented by the acronym DOWNTIME (Defects, Overproduction, Waiting, Not utilizing people to their full potential, Transportation, Inventory, Movement, and Excess processing).

a. The computer system requires frequent restarting; restarting takes five minutes.
b. Paperwork (that might change) is printed before it is needed.
c. The office manager insists that a spreadsheet program is used to store customer records, even though it would be more efficient to use a database program.
d. The office is run by the office manager; employees do as they are told.
e. Pending vacation requests must be taken to the third floor offices to get the signature of the human resource manager.

f. Loan approval files frequently contain errors.
g. The accounting report produces segment reports because the reports have been produced for years even though managers use other reports to manage their divisions.
h. Office supplies are stockpiled in the supply closet; the office manager buys in large quantities when there are sales.
i. Sales orders are put into the computer by the sales people in the field and paper reports are generated; these sales orders are then entered into the order processing system by clerks who type the orders based on the paper reports.
j. The office computers are slow to do the processing; the computers need to be upgraded.
k. Orders in the system are frequently missing information.
l. Employees do not have the authority and responsibility to make routine decisions.
m. The files needed for loan approval are carried to and from the file storage office when the files are needed.
n. To retrieve inventory records, clerks must click through several menus in the program to get to the record needed.
o. Approval of loans is done in batches once a week rather than as the loan paperwork is finished for each individual loan.
p. Each time a document needs to be notarized, someone must search for the notary seal (used to make the seal impression on the document).

E4-46B Prepare a Cost of Quality report *(Learning Objective 5)*

The CEO of Skinny Treats Corp. is concerned with the amounts of resources currently spent on customer warranty claims. Each box of snacks is printed with the following logo: "Satisfaction guaranteed, or your money back." Since the claims are so high, she would like to evaluate what costs are being incurred to ensure the quality of the product. The following information was collected from various departments within the company:

Warranty claims	$423,000
Cost of defective products found at the inspection point	$ 88,000
Training factory personnel	$ 32,000
Recall of Batch #59374	$175,000
Inspecting products when halfway through the production process	$ 51,000
Cost of disposing of rejected products	$ 11,000
Preventative maintenance on factory equipment	$ 8,000
Production loss due to machine breakdowns	$ 17,000
Inspection of raw materials	$ 4,000

Requirements

1. Prepare a Cost of Quality report. In addition to listing the costs by category, determine the percentage of the total costs of quality incurred in each cost category.
2. Do any additional subjective costs appear to be missing from the report?
3. What can be learned from the report?

E4-47B Classify costs and make a quality-initiative decision *(Learning Objective 5)*

Creighton Corp. manufactures radiation-shielding glass panels. Suppose the company is considering spending the following amounts on a new TQM program:

Strength-testing one item from each batch of panels	$63,000
Training employees in TQM	$23,000
Training suppliers in TQM	$35,000
Identifying preferred suppliers who commit to on-time delivery of perfect quality materials	$60,000

The company expects the new program would save costs through the following:

Avoid lost profits from lost sales due to disappointed customers	$91,000
Avoid rework and spoilage	$64,000
Avoid inspection of raw materials	$57,000
Avoid warranty costs	$17,000

Requirements

1. Classify each item as a prevention cost, an appraisal cost, an internal failure cost, or an external failure cost.
2. Should the company implement the new quality program? Give your reason.

CHAPTER 4

PROBLEMS Group A

P4-48A Implementation and analysis of departmental rates *(Learning Objective 1)*

Robillard Products manufactures its products in two separate departments: Machining and Assembly. Total manufacturing overhead costs for the year are budgeted at $1,070,000. Of this amount, the Machining Department incurs $630,000 (primarily for machine operation and depreciation) while the Assembly Department incurs $440,000. The company estimates that it will incur 10,000 machine hours (all in the Machining Department) and 17,000 direct labor hours (3,000 in the Machining Department and 14,000 in the Assembly Department) during the year.

Robillard Products currently uses a plantwide overhead rate based on direct labor hours to allocate overhead. However, the company is considering refining its overhead allocation system by using departmental overhead rates. The Machining Department would allocate its overhead using machine hours (MH), but the Assembly Department would allocate its overhead using direct labor (DL) hours.

The following chart shows the machine hours (MH) and direct labor (DL) hours incurred by Jobs 500 and 501 in each production department:

	Machining Department	Assembly Department
Job 500	9 MH	14 DL hours
	3 DL hours	
Job 501	18 MH	14 DL hours
	3 DL hours	

Both Jobs 500 and 501 used $1,800 of direct materials. Wages and benefits total $30 per direct labor hour. Robillard Products prices its products at 110% of total manufacturing costs.

Requirements

1. Compute the company's current plantwide overhead rate.
2. Compute refined departmental overhead rates.
3. Which job (Job 500 or Job 501) uses more of the company's resources? Explain.
4. Compute the total amount of overhead allocated to each job if the company uses its current plantwide overhead rate.
5. Compute the total amount of overhead allocated to each job if the company uses departmental overhead rates.
6. Do both allocation systems accurately reflect the resources that each job used? Explain.
7. Compute the total manufacturing cost and sales price of each job using the company's current plantwide overhead rate.
8. Based on the current (plantwide) allocation system, how much profit did the company *think* it earned on each job? Based on the departmental overhead rates and the sales price determined in Requirement 7, how much profit did it *really* earn on each job?
9. Compare and comment on the results you obtained in Requirements 7 and 8.

P4-49A Use ABC to compute full product costs *(Learning Objective 2)*

McKnight Corp. manufactures computer desks in its Orrville, Ohio, plant. The company uses activity-based costing to allocate all manufacturing conversion costs (direct labor and manufacturing overhead). Its activities and related data follow:

Activity	Budgeted Cost of Activity	Allocation Base	Cost Allocation Rate
Materials handling..........	$ 300,000	Number of parts	$ 0.60
Assembling...............	$2,400,000	Direct labor hours	$15.00
Painting..................	$ 180,000	Number of painted desks	$ 5.10

McKnight produced two styles of desks in March: the Standard desk and the Unpainted desk. Data for each follow:

Product	Total Units Produced	Total Direct Materials Costs	Total Number of Parts	Total Assembling Direct Labor Hours
Standard desk...............	5,000	$93,000	120,500	5,900
Unpainted desk..............	2,500	$21,000	30,500	700

Requirements

1. Compute the per-unit manufacturing product cost of Standard desks and Unpainted desks.
2. Premanufacturing activities, such as product design, were assigned to the Standard desks at $5 each and to the Unpainted desks at $4 each. Similar analyses were conducted of post-manufacturing activities, such as distribution, marketing, and customer service. The post-manufacturing costs were $22 per Standard and $21 per Unpainted desk. Compute the full product costs per desk.
3. Which product costs are reported in the external financial statements? Which costs are used for management decision making? Explain the difference.
4. What price should McKnight's managers set for Standard desks to earn a $42 profit per desk?

P4-50A Comprehensive ABC implementation *(Learning Objectives 2 & 3)*

Corbett Company develops software. The market is very competitive, and Corbett's competitors continue to introduce new products at low prices. Corbett offers a wide variety of software—from simple programs to extremely complex programs. Like most software companies, Corbett's raw material costs are insignificant.

Corbett has just hired Nicholas Wendell, a recent graduate of State University's accounting program. Wendell asks Software Department Manager Laurie Walker to join him in a pilot activity-based costing study. Wendell and Walker identify the following activities, related costs, and cost-allocation bases:

Activity	Estimated Indirect Activity Costs	Allocation Base	Estimated Quantity of Allocation Base
Applications development	$1,800,000	New applications	6 new applications
Content production	2,800,000	Lines of code	14 million lines
Testing	248,000	Testing hours	1,600 testing hours
Total indirect costs	$4,848,000		

Corbett is planning to develop the following new applications:

- X-Page
- X-Secure

X-Page requires 680,000 lines of code and 90 hours of testing, while X-Secure requires 10.2 million lines of code and 540 hours of testing. Corbett expects to produce and sell 20,000 units of X-Page and 8 units of X-Secure.

Requirements

1. Compute the cost allocation rate for each activity.
2. Use the activity-based cost allocation rates to compute the indirect cost of each unit of X-Page and X-Secure. *(Hint:* Compute the total activity costs allocated to each product line and then compute the cost per unit.)
3. The company's original single-allocation-based cost system allocated indirect costs to products at $113 per programmer hour. X-Page requires 8,000 programmer hours, while X-Secure requires 12,000 programmer hours. Compute the total indirect costs allocated to X-Page and X-Secure under the original system. Next, compute the indirect cost per unit for each product.
4. Compare the activity-based costs per unit to the costs from the simpler original system. How have the unit costs changed? Explain why the costs changed as they did.
5. What are the clues that the company's ABC system is likely to pass the cost-benefit test?

P4-51A Comprehensive ABC implementation *(Learning Objectives 2 & 3)*

Jacobson Pharmaceuticals manufactures an over-the-counter allergy medication called Breathe. Jacobson is trying to win market share from Sudafed and Tylenol. Jacobson has developed several different Breathe products tailored to specific markets. For example, the company sells large commercial containers of 1,000 capsules to health care facilities and travel packs of 20 capsules to shops in airports, train stations, and hotels.

Jacobson's controller, Sandra Dean, has just returned from a conference on ABC. She asks Keith Yeung, supervisor of the Breathe product line, to help her develop an ABC system. Dean and Yeung identify the following activities, related costs, and cost allocation bases:

Activity	Estimated Indirect Activity Costs	Allocation Base	Estimated Quantity of Allocation Base
Materials handling.	$160,000	Kilos	16,000 kilos
Packaging	430,000	Machine hours	2,300 hours
Quality assurance	113,000	Samples	2,000 samples
Total indirect costs	$703,000		

The commercial-container Breathe product line had a total weight of 8,300 kilos, used 900 machine hours, and required 240 samples. The travel-pack line had a total weight of 6,500 kilos, used 300 machine hours, and required 340 samples. Jacobson produced 2,800 commercial containers of Breathe and 20,000 travel packs.

Requirements

1. Compute the cost allocation rate for each activity.
2. Use the activity-based cost allocation rates to compute the indirect cost of each unit of the commercial containers and the travel packs. (*Hint:* Compute the total activity costs allocated to each product line and then compute the cost per unit.)
3. The company's original single-allocation-based cost system allocated indirect costs to products at $400 per machine hour. Compute the total indirect costs allocated to the commercial containers and to the travel packs under the original system. Then, compute the indirect cost per unit for each product.
4. Compare the activity-based costs per unit to the costs from the original system. How have the unit costs changed? Explain why the costs changed as they did.

P4-52A Using ABC in conjunction with quality decisions *(Learning Objectives 2 & 5)*

Creative Construction Toys Corp. is using a costs-of-quality approach to evaluate design engineering efforts for a new toy robot. The company's senior managers expect the engineering work to reduce appraisal, internal failure, and external failure activities. The predicted reductions in activities over the two-year life of the toy robot follow. Also shown is the cost allocation rate for each activity.

Activity	Predicted Reduction in Activity Units	Activity Cost Allocation Rate per Unit
Inspection of incoming materials	385	$25
Inspection of finished goods.	385	$34
Number of defective units discovered in-house.	3,400	$15
Number of defective units discovered by customers	975	$42
Lost sales to dissatisfied customers	270	$58

Requirements

1. Calculate the predicted quality cost savings from the design engineering work.
2. The company spent $75,000 on design engineering for the new toy robot. What is the net benefit of this "preventive" quality activity?
3. What major difficulty would management have had in implementing this costs-of-quality approach? What alternative approach could they use to measure quality improvement?

PROBLEMS Group B

P4-53B Implementation and analysis of departmental rates *(Learning Objective 1)*

Voisine Products manufactures its products in two separate departments: Machining and Assembly. Total manufacturing overhead costs for the year are budgeted at $1,040,000. Of this amount, the Machining Department incurs $600,000 (primarily for machine operation and depreciation) while the Assembly Department incurs $440,000. The company estimates it will incur 4,000 machines hours (all in the Machining Department) and 14,500 direct labor hours (2,500 in the Machining Department and 12,000 in the Assembly Department) during the year.

Voisine currently uses a plantwide overhead rate based on direct labor hours to allocate overhead. However, the company is considering refining its overhead allocation system by using departmental overhead rates. The Machining Department would allocate its overhead using machine hours (MH), but the Assembly Department would allocate its overhead using direct labor (DL) hours.

The following chart shows the machine hours (MH) and direct labor (DL) hours incurred by Jobs 500 and 501 in each production department.

	Machining Department	Assembly Department
Job 500	10 MH	12 DL hours
	6 DL hours	
Job 501	20 MH	12 DL hours
	6 DL hours	

Both Jobs 500 and 501 used $2,000 of direct materials. Wages and benefits total $25 per direct labor hour. Voisine prices its products at 130% of total manufacturing costs.

Requirements

1. Compute the company's current plantwide overhead rate.
2. Compute refined departmental overhead rates.
3. Which job (Job 500 or Job 501) uses more of the company's resources? Explain.
4. Compute the total amount of overhead allocated to each job if the company uses its current plantwide overhead rate.
5. Compute the total amount of overhead allocated to each job if the company uses departmental overhead rates.
6. Do both allocation systems accurately reflect the resources that each job used? Explain.
7. Compute the total manufacturing cost and sales price of each job using the company's current plantwide overhead rate.
8. Based on the current (plantwide) allocation system, how much profit did the company *think* it earned on each job? Based on the departmental overhead rates and the sales price determined in Requirement 7, how much profit did it *really* earn on each job?
9. Compare and comment on the results you obtained in Requirements 7 and 8.

P4-54B Use ABC to compute full product costs *(Learning Objective 2)*

McMillan Furniture manufactures computer desks in its Lorain, Ohio, plant. The company uses activity-based costing to allocate all manufacturing conversion costs (direct labor and manufacturing overhead). Its activities and related data follow:

Activity	Budgeted Cost of Activity	Allocation Base	Cost Allocation Rate
Materials handling.	$ 310,000	Number of parts	$ 0.70
Assembling	$2,800,000	Direct labor hours	$16.00
Painting	$ 140,000	Number of painted desks	$ 5.30

The company produced two styles of desks in March: the Standard desk and the Unpainted desk. Data for each follow:

Product	Total Units Produced	Total Direct Materials Costs	Total Number of Parts	Total Assembling Direct Labor Hours
Standard desk	7,500	$95,000	119,000	5,700
Unpainted desk.	2,500	$22,000	29,000	1,000

Requirements

1. Compute the per-unit manufacturing product cost of Standard desks and Unpainted desks.
2. Premanufacturing activities, such as product design, were assigned to the Standard desks at $7 each and to the Unpainted desks at $2 each. Similar analyses were conducted of post-manufacturing activities such as distribution, marketing, and customer service. The post-manufacturing costs were $23 per Standard and $21 per Unpainted desk. Compute the full product costs per desk.
3. Which product costs are reported in the external financial statements? Which costs are used for management decision making? Explain the difference.
4. What price should management set for Standard desks to earn a $42 profit per desk?

P4-55B Comprehensive ABC implementation *(Learning Objectives 2 & 3)*

Willitte Company develops software. The market is very competitive and Willitte's competitors continue to introduce new products at low prices. Willitte offers a wide variety of different software from simple programs to extremely complex programs. Like most software companies, Willitte's raw material costs are insignificant.

The company has just hired Ralph Smythe, a recent graduate of State University's accounting program. Smythe asks Software Department Manager Patty Bujorian to join him in a pilot activity-based costing study. Smythe and Bujorian identify the following activities, related costs, and cost-allocation bases:

Activity	Estimated Indirect Activity Costs	Allocation Base	Estimated Quantity of Allocation Base
Applications development	$2,400,000	New applications	8 new applications
Content production.	3,000,000	Lines of code	10 million lines
Testing.	350,000	Testing hours	2,000 testing hours
Total indirect costs	$5,750,000		

The company is planning to develop the following new applications:

- X-Page software
- X-Secure

X-Page requires 580,000 lines of code and 130 hours of testing, while X-Secure requires 8.7 million lines of code and 780 hours of testing. The company expects to produce and sell 35,000 units of X-Page and 13 units of X-Secure.

Requirements

1. Compute the cost allocation rate for each activity.
2. Use the activity-based cost allocation rates to compute the indirect cost of each unit of X-Page and X-Secure. (*Hint:* Compute the total activity costs allocated to each product line and then compute the cost per unit.)
3. The company's original single-allocation-base costing system allocated indirect costs to products at $134 per programmer hour. X-Page requires 10,000 programmer hours, while X-Secure requires 15,000 programmer hours. Compute the total indirect costs allocated to X-Page and X-Secure under the original system. Next, compute the indirect cost per unit for each product.
4. Compare the activity-based costs per unit to the costs from the simpler original system. How have the unit costs changed? Explain why the costs changed as they did.
5. What are the clues that the company's ABC system is likely to pass the cost-benefit test?

P4-56B Comprehensive ABC implementation *(Learning Objectives 2 & 3)*

McNeil Pharmaceuticals manufactures an over-the-counter allergy medication called Breathe. McNeil is trying to win market share from Sudafed and Tylenol. McNeil has developed several different Breathe products tailored to specific markets. For example, the company sells large commercial containers of 1,000 capsules to health care facilities and travel packs of 20 capsules to shops in airports, train stations, and hotels.

McNeil's controller, Arlene Pittinger, has just returned from a conference on ABC. She asks Gene Barr, supervisor of the Breathe product line, to help her develop an ABC system. Pittinger and Barr identify the following activities, related costs, and cost allocation bases:

Activity	Estimated Indirect Activity Costs	Allocation Base	Estimated Quantity of Allocation Base
Materials handling	$180,000	Kilos	18,000 kilos
Packaging	420,000	Machine hours	2,200 hours
Quality assurance	118,000	Samples	1,700 samples
Total indirect costs	$718,000		

The commercial-container Breathe product line had a total weight of 8,000 kilos, used 1,500 machine hours, and 270 required samples. The travel-pack line had a total weight of 6,300 kilos, used 500 machine hours, and 370 required samples. The company produced 2,600 commercial containers of Breathe and 60,000 travel packs.

Requirements

1. Compute the cost allocation rate for each activity.
2. Use the activity-based cost allocation rates to compute the indirect cost of each unit of the commercial containers and the travel packs. (*Hint:* Compute the total activity costs allocated to each product line and then compute the cost per unit.)
3. The company's original single-allocation-based cost system allocated indirect costs to products at $300 per machine hour. Compute the total indirect costs allocated to the commercial containers and to the travel packs under the original system. Then, compute the indirect cost per unit for each product.
4. Compare the activity-based costs per unit to the costs from the simpler original system. How have the unit costs changed? Explain why the costs changed as they did.

P4-57B Using ABC in conjunction with quality decisions *(Learning Objectives 2 & 5)*

Tiny Toys is using a cost-of-quality approach to evaluate design engineering efforts for a new toy robot. The company's senior managers expect the engineering work to reduce appraisal, internal failure, and external failure activities. The predicted reductions in activities over the two-year life of the toy robot follow. Also shown are the cost allocation rates for each activity.

Activity	Predicted Reduction in Activity Units	Activity Cost Allocation Rate per Unit
Inspection of incoming materials	370	$22
Inspection of finished goods	370	$29
Number of defective units discovered in-house	3,200	$13
Number of defective units discovered by customers	875	$36
Lost sales to dissatisfied customers	330	$62

Requirements

1. Calculate the predicted quality cost savings from the design engineering work.
2. The company spent $70,000 on design engineering for the new toy robot. What is the net benefit of this "preventive" quality activity?
3. What major difficulty would management have had in implementing this costs-of-quality approach? What alternative approach could they use to measure quality improvement?

CRITICAL THINKING

Discussion & Analysis

A4-58 Discussion Questions

1. Explain why departmental overhead rates might be used instead of a single plantwide overhead rate.
2. Using activity-based costing, why are indirect costs allocated while direct costs are not allocated? Discuss the difference between "allocate" and "assign."
3. How can using a single predetermined manufacturing overhead rate based on a unit-level cost driver cause a high-volume product to be overcosted?
4. Assume a company uses a plantwide predetermined manufacturing overhead rate that is calculated using direct labor hours as the cost driver. The use of this plantwide predetermined manufacturing overhead rate has resulted in cost distortion. The company's high-volume products are overcosted and its low-volume products are undercosted. What effects of this cost distortion will the company most likely be experiencing? Why might the cost distortion be harmful to the company's competitive position in the market?
5. A hospital can use activity-based costing (ABC) for costing its services. In a hospital, what activities might be considered to be value-added activities? What activities at that hospital might be considered to be non-value-added?
6. A company makes shatterproof, waterproof cases for iPhones. The company makes only one model and has been very successful in marketing its case; no other company in the market has a similar product. The only customization available to the customer is the color of the case. There is no manufacturing cost difference among the different colors of the cases. Since this company has a high-volume product, its controller thinks that the company should adopt activity-based costing. Why might activity-based costing not be as beneficial for this company as for other companies?
7. Compare a traditional production system with a lean production system. Discuss the similarities and the differences.
8. Think of a product with which you are familiar. Explain how activity-based costing could help the company that makes this product in its efforts to be "green."
9. It has been said that external failure costs can be catastrophic and much higher than the other categories. What are some examples of external failure costs? Why is it often difficult to arrive at the cost of external failures?
10. What are the four categories of quality-related costs? Name a cost in each of the four categories for each of the following types of organizations:
    a. Restaurant
    b. Hospital
    c. Law firm
    d. Bank
    e. Tire manufacturer
    f. University
11. What are the similarities between sustainability and lean thinking? What are the differences between sustainability and lean thinking?
12. Why might a company want to take lean thinking a step further by including operations and methods associated with sustainability?

Application & Analysis

A4-59 ABC in Real Companies

Choose a company in any of the following categories: airline, florist, bookstore, bank, grocery store, restaurant, college, retail clothing shop, movie theatre, or lawn service. In this activity, you will be making reasonable estimates of the types of costs and activities associated with this company; companies do not typically publish internal cost or process information. Be reasonable in your cost estimates and include your assumptions used in selecting costs.

Basic Discussion Questions

1. Describe the company selected, including its products or services.
2. List eight key activities performed at this company. Choose at least one activity in the areas of production, sales, human resources, and accounting.
3. For each of the key activities, list a potential cost driver for that activity and describe why this cost driver would be appropriate for the associated activity.

A4-60 Value-Added vs. Non-Value-Added at a Restaurant

Go to a fast-food restaurant (or think of the last time you were at a fast-food restaurant.) Observe the steps involved in providing a meal to a customer. You will be watching for value-added steps and non-value-added steps. Answer the following questions.

Basic Discussion Questions

1. Describe the steps involved with delivering the meal to the customer that you can observe.
2. Describe the "behind-the-scenes" processes that are likely in the restaurant, such as cleaning, stocking, and cooking activities.
3. With your answers for 1 and 2 list all of the possible activities, materials, and information that you think might be included on a value stream map for the restaurant. Include all of the steps you can think of (not necessarily only those you can observe).
4. Make a list of the eight wastes as denoted by the acronym DOWNTIME (Defects, Overproduction, Waiting, Not utilizing people to their full potential, Transportation, Inventory, Movement, and Excess processing.) Next to each waste category, list at least one possible non-value-added activity that might or might not be in the processes in that restaurant.
5. Go back to the list of items for the potential value stream map. Circle potential areas for improvement and explain which wastes might be involved in those areas.

Decision Cases

A4-61 Comprehensive ABC *(Learning Objectives 2 & 3)*

Axis Systems specializes in servers for work-group, e-commerce, and ERP applications. The company's original job cost system has two direct cost categories: direct materials and direct labor. Overhead is allocated to jobs at the single rate of $22 per direct labor hour.

A task force headed by Axis's CFO recently designed an ABC system with four activities. The ABC system retains the current system's two direct cost categories. Thus, it budgets only overhead costs for each activity. Pertinent data follow:

Activity	Allocation Base	Cost Allocation Rate
Materials handling	Number of parts	$ 0.85
Machine setup	Number of setups	500.00
Assembling	Assembling hours	80.00
Shipping	Number of shipments	1,500.00

Axis Systems has been awarded two new contracts that will be produced as Job A and Job B. Budget data relating to the contracts follow:

	Job A	Job B
Number of parts	15,000	2,000
Number of setups	6	4
Number of assembling hours	1,500	200
Number of shipments	1	1
Total direct labor hours	8,000	600
Number of output units	100	10
Direct materials cost	$210,000	$30,000
Direct labor cost	$160,000	$12,000

Requirements

1. Compute the product cost per unit for each job using the original costing system (with two direct cost categories and a single overhead allocation rate).
2. Suppose Axis Systems adopts the ABC system. Compute the product cost per unit for each job using ABC.
3. Which costing system more accurately assigns to jobs the costs of the resources consumed to produce them? Explain.
4. A dependable company has offered to produce both jobs for Axis for $5,400 per output unit. Axis may outsource (buy from the outside company) Job A only, Job B only, or both jobs. Which course of action will Axis's managers take if they base their decision on (a) the original system? (b) ABC system costs? Which course of action will yield more income? Explain.

A4-62 Continues A4-61: Meeting target costs

To remain competitive, Axis Systems' management believes the company must produce Job B–type servers (from A4-61) at a target cost of $5,400. Axis Systems has just joined a B2B e-market site that management believes will enable the firm to cut direct material costs by 10%. Axis's management also believes that a value-engineering team can reduce assembly time.

Requirement

Compute the assembly cost savings per Job B-type server required to meet the $5,400 target cost. (*Hint:* Begin by calculating the direct material, direct labor, and allocated activity cost per server.)

Ethical Issue

A4-63 ABC and ethical dilemma *(Learning Objective 2 & 3)*

Rachel Gambol is assistant controller at Recycled Packaging, a manufacturer of cardboard boxes and other packaging materials. Gambol has just returned from a packaging industry conference on ABC. She realizes that ABC may help Recycled Packaging meet its goal of reducing costs by 5% over each of the next three years.

The company's Order Department is a likely candidate for ABC. While orders are entered into a computer that updates the accounting records, clerks manually check customers' credit history and hand-deliver orders to shipping. This process occurs whether the sales order is for a dozen specialty boxes worth $80 or 10,000 basic boxes worth $8,000.

Gambol believes that identifying the cost of processing a sales order would justify (1) further computerizing the order process and (2) changing the way the company processes small orders. However, the significant cost savings would arise from elimination of two positions in the Order Department. The company's sales order clerks have been with the company many years. Gambol is uncomfortable with the prospect of proposing a change that will likely result in terminating these employees.

Requirement

Use the IMA *Statement of Ethical Professional Practice* (from Chapter 1) to consider Gambol's responsibility when cost savings come at the expense of employees' jobs.

CMA Problem

A4-64

SANSCOM Corporation utilized an activity-based costing system for applying costs to its two products, P and Q. In the assembly department, material handling costs vary directly with the number of parts inserted into the product. Machinery is recalibrated and oiled each weekend regardless of the number of parts inserted during the previous week. Both material handling and machinery maintenance costs are charged to the product on the basis of the number of parts inserted. Due to reengineering of the production process for Product P, the number of insertion parts per finished unit has been reduced. How will the redesign of the production process for Product P affect the activity-based cost of Product Q?

a. Material handling cost per Q unit will remain unchanged, and machinery maintenance cost per Q unit will remain unchanged.

b. Material handling cost per Q unit will increase, and machinery maintenance cost per Q unit will remain unchanged.

c. Material handling cost per Q unit will remain unchanged, and machinery maintenance cost per Q unit will increase.

d. Material handling cost per Q unit will increase, and machinery maintenance cost per Q unit will increase. *(CMA Adapted)*

5 Process Costing

Learning Objectives

- **1** Distinguish between the flow of costs in process costing and job costing
- **2** Compute equivalent units
- **3** Use process costing in the first production department
- **4** Prepare journal entries for a process costing system
- **5** Use process costing in a second or later production department

What's your favorite Jelly Belly flavor?

Chocolate Pudding? Very Cherry? Lemon Drop? Peanut Butter? Or maybe Piña Colada? Have you ever wondered how these tasty gems are made?

Each tiny Jelly Belly jelly bean spends seven to ten days going through eight different processes:

1. Cooking the centers
2. Shaping hot liquid centers into jelly beans
3. Drying
4. Sugar shower
5. Shell-building
6. Polishing
7. Stamping (name of the company on each bean)
8. Packaging

© Peter Coombs / Alamy

Source: http://jellybelly.com

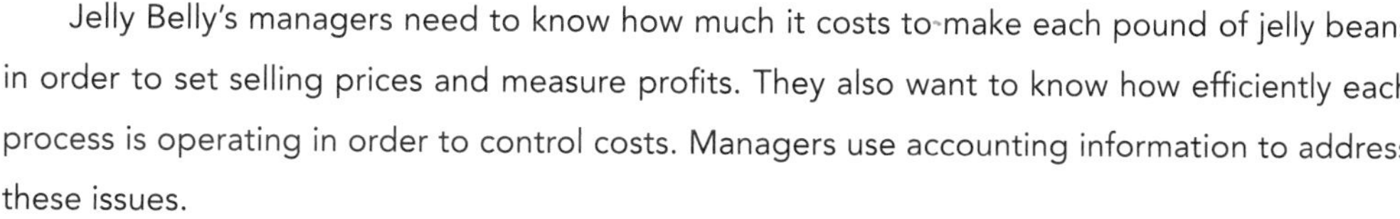

Jelly Belly's managers need to know how much it costs to make each pound of jelly beans in order to set selling prices and measure profits. They also want to know how efficiently each process is operating in order to control costs. Managers use accounting information to address these issues.

The accounting system Jelly Belly uses to find the cost of jelly beans differs from the accounting system Life Fitness uses. Why? Because Jelly Belly mass-produces its products whereas Life Fitness makes many unique models, often on a custom-ordered basis. Jelly Belly mass-produces its jelly beans in a sequence of eight production processes. Each month, Jelly Belly separately measures and accumulates the manufacturing costs incurred in each of the processes. Next, the company spreads these costs over the pounds of jelly beans that passed through each process. By doing so, Jelly Belly is able to calculate the average cost of making a pound of jelly beans in each process, as well as the average cost of making a pound of jelly beans, from start to finish.

As the chapter-opening story explains, managers need to know how much it costs to make their products. Why? So they can control costs, set selling prices, and identify their most profitable products. But finding unit cost at companies that mass manufacture requires a different approach than it does at companies that manufacture small batches of unique products. Simply put, job-costing doesn't "fit" a mass-production environment. Mass manufacturers need an accounting system that is specifically geared to match their production environment. For these types of companies, process costing is the answer. Process costing helps mass-manufacturers find the unit cost of their products, as well as the cost of each manufacturing process involved.

Process Costing: An Overview

Let's start by contrasting the two basic types of costing systems: *job costing* and *process costing*.

Two Basic Costing Systems: Job Costing and Process Costing

1 Distinguish between the flow of costs in process costing and job costing

We saw in Chapter 3 that Life Fitness and Boeing use job costing to determine the cost of producing unique goods in relatively small batches. Service companies such as law firms and hospitals also use job costing to determine the cost of serving individual clients. In contrast, companies such as Jelly Belly and Shell Oil use a series of steps (called *processes*) to make large quantities of identical units. These companies typically use *process costing* systems.

To simplify our discussion, we'll consolidate Jelly Belly's eight separate processes into three processes. We'll combine cooking, shaping, and drying the jelly bean centers into a single process called *Centers*. We'll also combine the sugar shower, shell-building, polishing, and stamping steps into a second process called *Shells*. The third and final process is *Packaging*.

Jelly Belly *accumulates* the costs of each process and then *assigns* these costs to the units (pounds of jelly beans) passing through that process.

Suppose the Centers process incurs $1,350,000 of costs to produce centers for 1,000,000 pounds of jelly beans, the Shells process incurs $800,000, and Packaging incurs $700,000. The total cost to produce a pound of jelly beans is the sum of the cost per pound for each of the three processes.

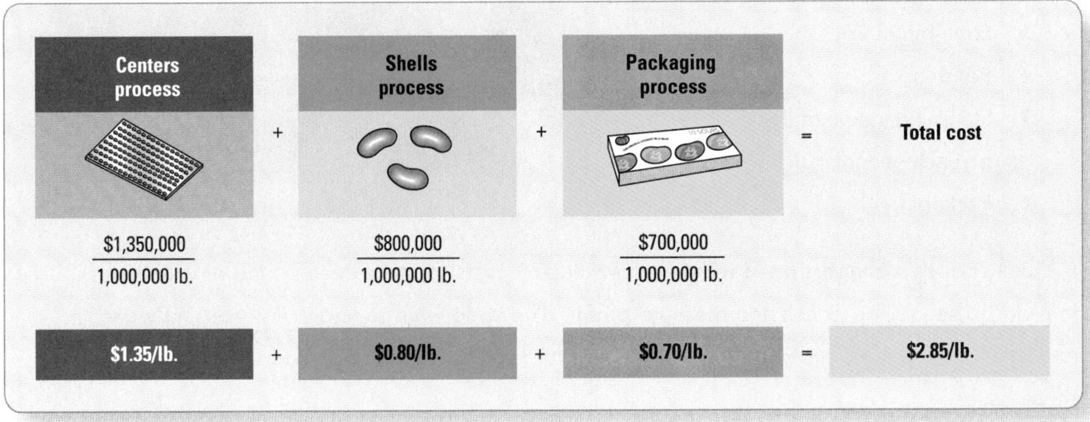

Jelly Belly's owners use the cost per pound of each process to help control costs. For example, they can compare the actual cost of producing centers for a pound of jelly beans (assumed to be $1.35 in our example) to the budget or plan. If the actual cost of the Centers process exceeds the budget, they can look for ways to cut costs in that process. Jelly Belly's owners also consider the total cost of making a pound of jelly beans (assumed to be $2.85 in our example) when setting selling prices. The price should be high enough to cover costs *and* to return a profit. Jelly Belly also uses the total cost of making a pound of jelly beans for financial reporting:

- To value the ending inventory of jelly beans for the balance sheet ($2.85 per pound still in ending inventory)
- To value cost of goods sold for the income statement ($2.85 per pound sold)

The simple computation of the cost to make a pound of jelly beans is correct *only if there are no work in process inventories*, but it takes seven to ten days to complete all of the processes. So, Jelly Belly *does* have inventories of partially complete jelly beans. These inventories make the costing more complicated. In the rest of this chapter, you'll learn how to do process costing when there are work in process inventories.

How Does the Flow of Costs Differ Between Job and Process Costing?

Exhibit 5-1 compares the flow of costs in

- a job costing system for Life Fitness (Panel A), and
- a process costing system for Jelly Belly (Panel B).

EXHIBIT 5-1 Flow of Costs in Job Costing (Panel A) and Process Costing (Panel B)

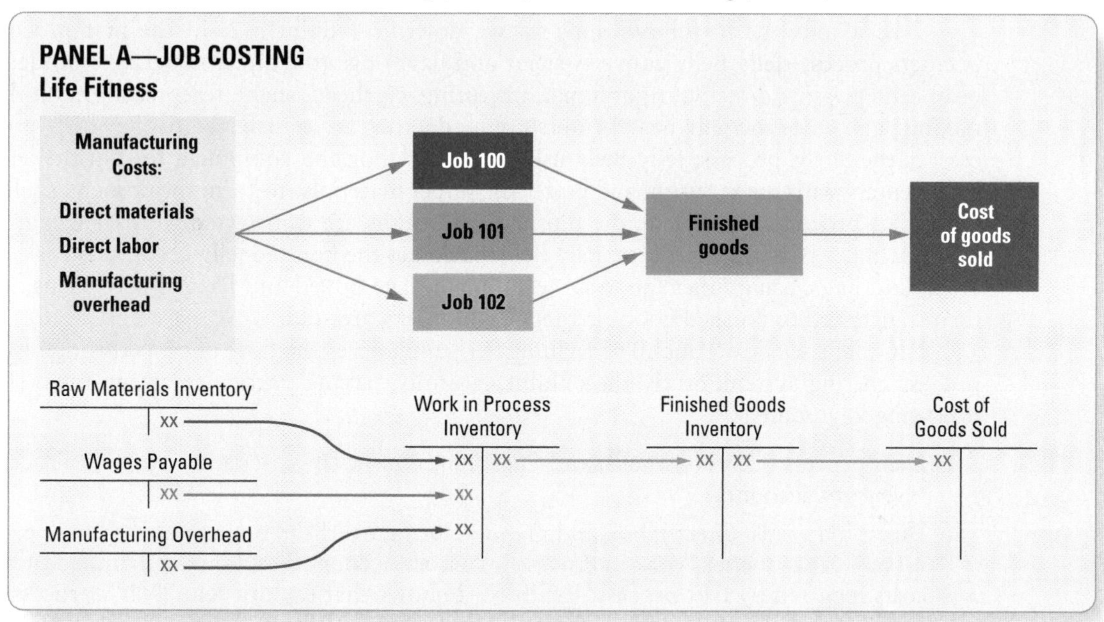

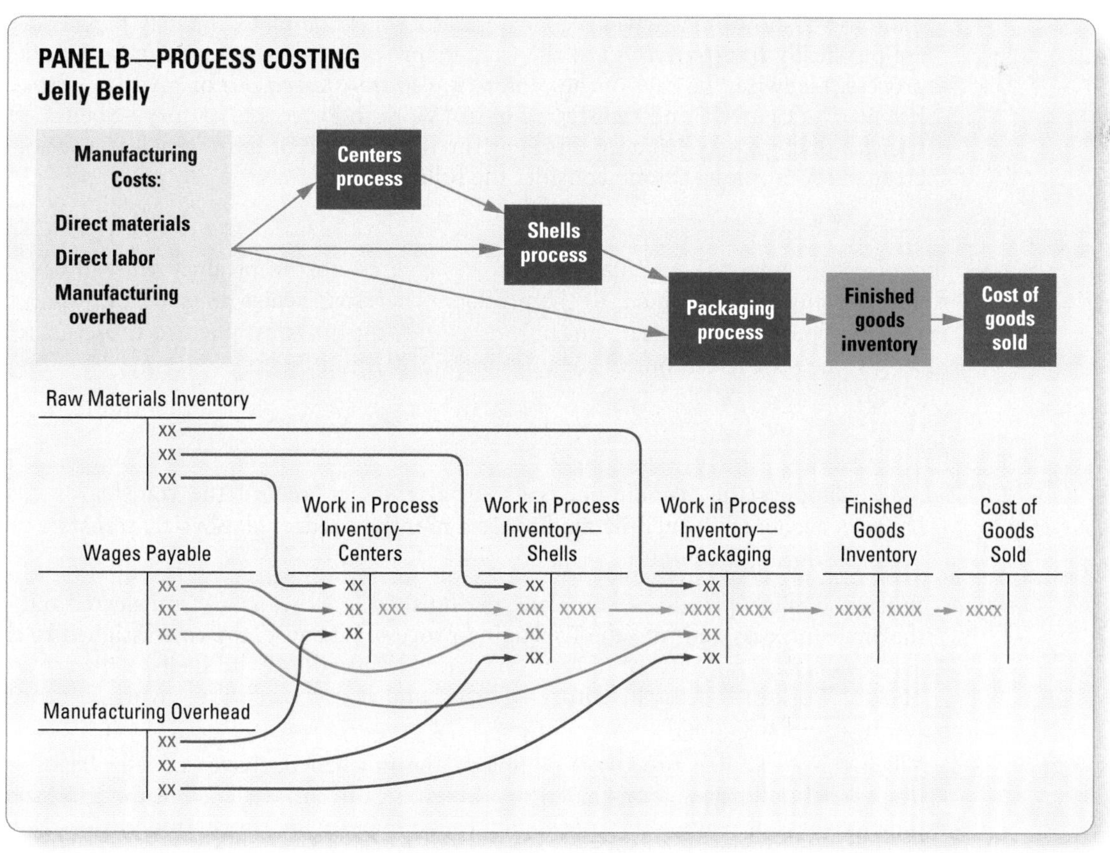

Panel A shows that Life Fitness's job costing system has a single Work in Process Inventory control account supported by individual job cost records for each job that is being worked on. Life Fitness assigns direct materials, direct labor, and manufacturing overhead to individual jobs, as explained in Chapter 3. When a job is finished, its costs flow directly into Finished Goods Inventory. When the job is sold, the cost flows out of Finished Goods Inventory and into Cost of Goods Sold.

In contrast to Life Fitness's individual jobs, Jelly Belly uses a series of three *manufacturing processes* to produce jelly beans. The movement of jelly beans through these three processes is shown in Exhibit 5-2.

Take a moment to follow along as we describe Exhibit 5-2. In the first process (Centers process) Jelly Belly converts sugar and flavorings (the direct materials) into jelly bean centers using direct labor and manufacturing overhead, such as depreciation on the mixing vats. Once the jelly bean centers are made, they are transferred to the Shells process. In the Shells process, Jelly Belly uses different labor and equipment to coat the jelly bean centers with sugar, syrup, and glaze (the direct materials) to form the crunchy shells. Once that process is complete, the finished jelly beans are transferred to the Packaging process. In the Packaging process, Jelly Belly packages the finished jelly beans into various boxes and bags, using other labor and equipment. The boxed and bagged jelly beans are then transferred to finished goods inventory until they are sold.

Now, let's see how Panel B of Exhibit 5-1 summarizes the flow of costs through this process costing system. Study the exhibit carefully, paying particular attention to the following key points:

1. Each process (Centers, Shells, and Packaging) has its own separate Work in Process Inventory account.
2. Direct materials, direct labor, and manufacturing overhead are assigned to *each* processing department's Work in Process Inventory account based on the manufacturing costs incurred by that process. Exhibit 5-2 shows that each of Jelly Belly's processes uses different direct materials, direct labor, and manufacturing overhead costs.
3. Exhibit 5-2 shows that when the Centers process is complete, the jelly bean centers are physically *transferred out* of the Centers process and *transferred in* to the Shells process. Likewise, the *cost* of the centers is also *transferred out* of "Work in Process Inventory—Centers" and *transferred in* to "Work in Process Inventory—Shells." The transfer of costs between accounts is pictured in Panel B of Exhibit 5-1 as a series of green *x*s. As a rule of thumb consider the following:

> In process costing, the manufacturing costs assigned to the product must always follow the physical movement of the product. Therefore, when units are physically transferred out of one process and into the next, the *costs* assigned to those units must *also* be transferred out of the appropriate Work in Process Inventory account and into the next.

To simplify the accounting, the journal entry to record the transfer of costs between accounts is generally made once a month to reflect *all* physical transfers that occurred during the month.

4. When the Shells process is complete, the finished jelly beans are transferred out of the Shells process and into the Packaging process. Likewise, the *cost* assigned to the jelly beans thus far (cost of making the centers and adding the shells) is *transferred out* of "Work in Process Inventory—Shells" and *transferred in* to "Work in Process Inventory—Packaging."
5. When the Packaging process is complete, the finished packages of jelly beans are transferred to finished goods inventory. Likewise, the *cost* assigned to the jelly beans thus far (cost of making and packaging the jelly beans) is transferred out of "Work in Process—Packaging" and into "Finished Goods Inventory." *In process costing, costs are transferred into Finished Goods Inventory only from the Work in Process*

EXHIBIT 5-2 Flow of Costs in Production of Jelly Beans

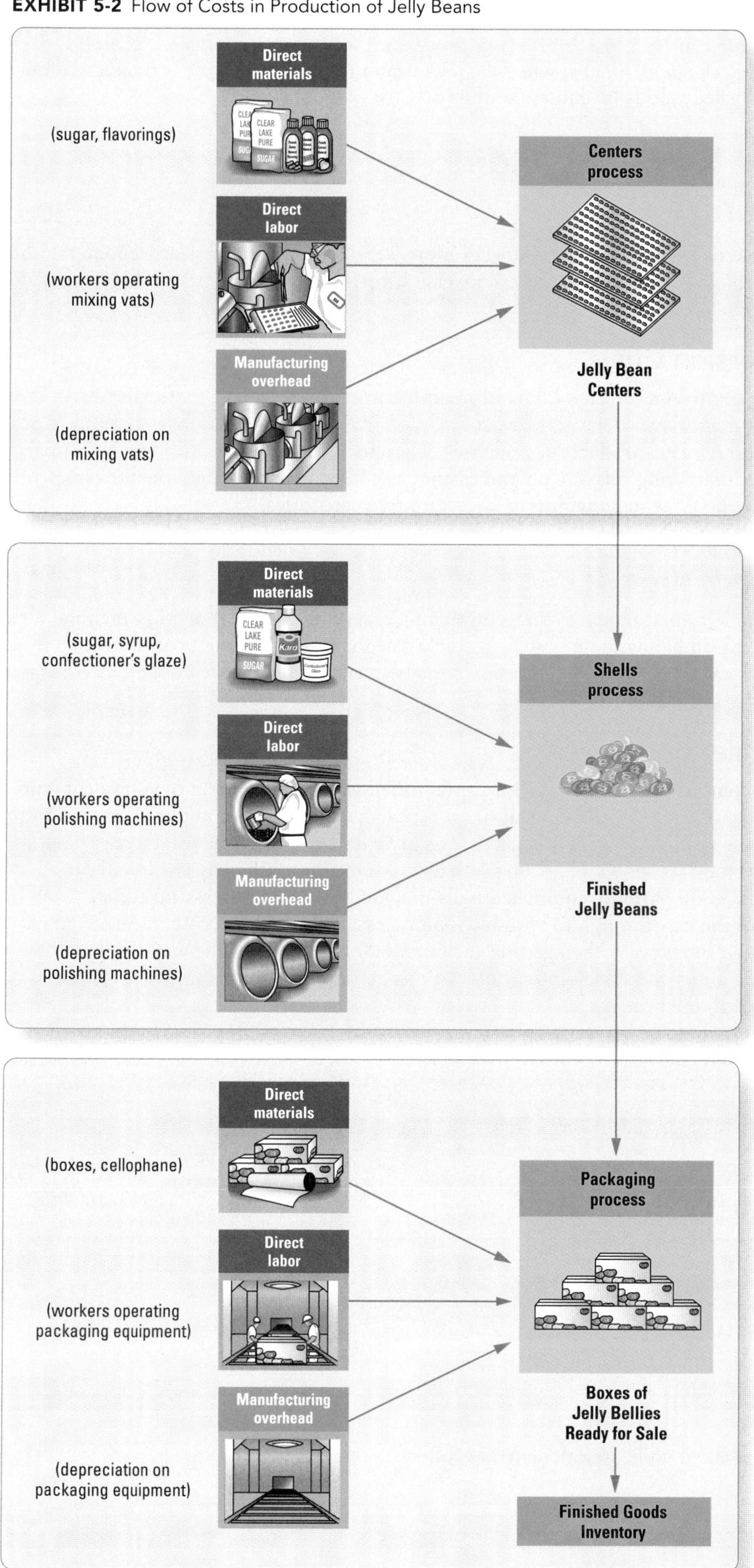

Inventory of the last manufacturing process. The transferred cost includes all costs assigned to the units from every process the units have completed (Centers, Shells, and Packaging). Finally, when the jelly beans are sold, their cost is transferred out of "Finished Goods Inventory" and into "Cost of Goods Sold."

What are the Building Blocks of Process Costing?

Before we illustrate process costing in more detail, we must first learn about the three building blocks of process costing: conversion costs, equivalent units, and inventory flow assumptions.

Conversion Costs

Chapter 2 introduced three kinds of manufacturing costs: direct materials, direct labor, and manufacturing overhead. Most companies, like Jelly Belly, that mass-produce a product use automated production processes. Therefore, direct labor is only a small part of total manufacturing costs. Companies that use automated production processes often condense the three manufacturing costs into two categories:

1. Direct materials
2. Conversion costs

Recall from Chapter 2 that conversion costs are direct labor plus manufacturing overhead. Combining these costs in a single category simplifies the process costing procedures. We call this category *conversion costs* because it is the cost to *convert* direct materials into new finished products.

Equivalent Units

2 Compute equivalent units

When a company has work in process inventories, we use the concept of **equivalent units** to express the amount of work done during a period in terms of fully completed units of output.

To illustrate equivalent units, let's look at Callaway Golf, a manufacturer of golf balls and golf clubs. As shown in Exhibit 5-3, let's assume that Callaway's golf ball production plant has 5,000 partially completed balls in ending work in process inventory. Each ball is 80% of the way through the production process. If conversion costs are incurred evenly throughout the process, then getting each of 5,000 balls 80% of the way through the process takes about the same amount of work as getting 4,000 balls (5,000 × 80%) all the way through the process.

EXHIBIT 5-3 Callaway Production Plant Time Line

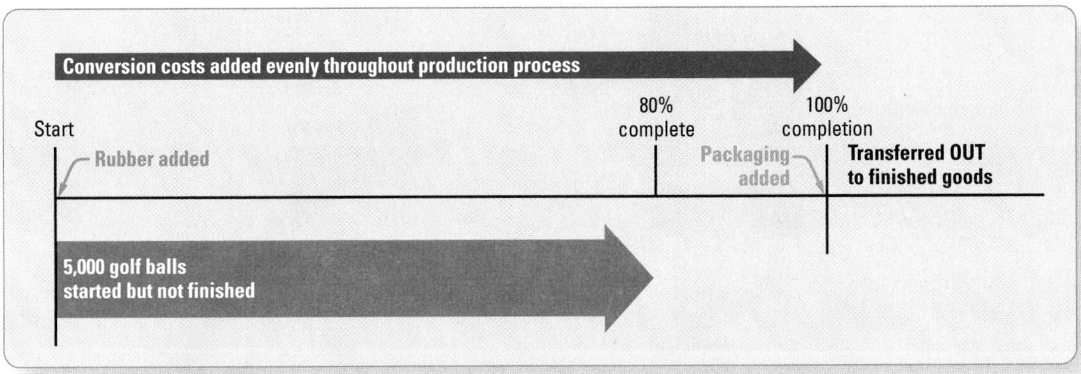

Equivalent units are calculated as follows:

Number of partially complete physical units × Percentage of process completed = Number of equivalent units

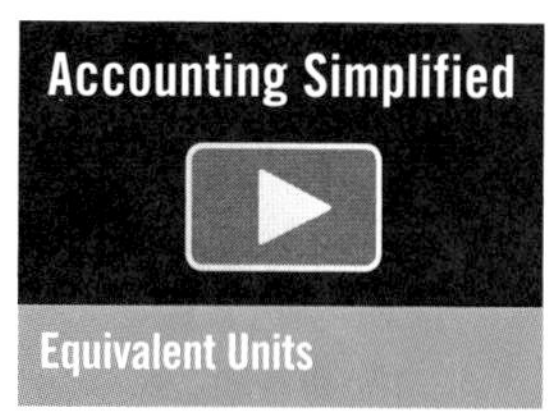

If your instructor is using MyAccountingLab, go to the Multimedia Library for a quick video on this topic.

So, the number of equivalent units of conversion costs in Callaway's ending work in process inventory is calculated as follows:

$$5{,}000 \times 80\% = 4{,}000$$

Conversion costs are usually incurred *evenly* throughout production. However, direct materials are often added at a particular point in the process. For example, Callaway adds rubber at the *beginning* of the production process, but doesn't add packaging materials until the *end*. How many equivalent units of rubber and packaging materials are in the ending inventory of 5,000 balls?

All 5,000 balls are 80% complete, so they all have passed the point at which rubber is added. Each ball has its full share of rubber (100%), so the balls have 5,000 equivalent units of rubber. In contrast, the time line in Exhibit 5-3 shows that *none* of the 5,000 balls has made it to the end of the process, where the packaging materials are added. The ending inventory, therefore, has *zero* equivalent units of packaging materials.

To summarize, the 5,000 balls in ending work in process inventory have the following:

- 5,000 equivalent units of rubber (5,000 units × 100% of rubber)
- 0 equivalent units of packaging materials (5,000 units × 0% of packaging materials)
- 4,000 equivalent units of conversion costs (5,000 units × 80% converted)

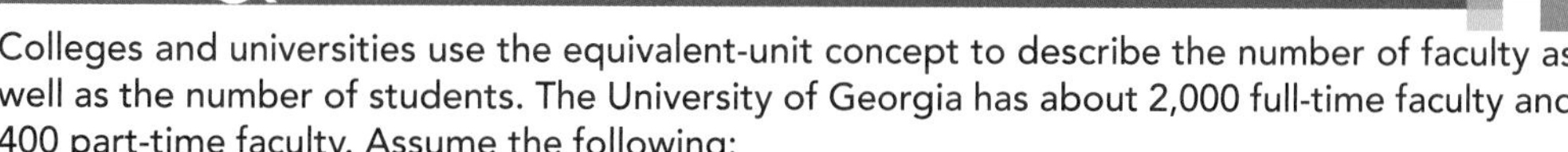

Colleges and universities use the equivalent-unit concept to describe the number of faculty as well as the number of students. The University of Georgia has about 2,000 full-time faculty and 400 part-time faculty. Assume the following:

1. A full-time faculty member teaches six courses per year.
2. 100 part-time faculty teach three courses per year.
3. 300 part-time faculty teach two courses per year.

What is the "full-time equivalent" faculty—the number of equivalent units of faculty?

Answer: Compute the full-time equivalent faculty as follows:

Full-time faculty	2,000 × 6/6 = 2,000
Half-time faculty	100 × 3/6 = 50
One-third-time faculty	300 × 2/6 = 100
Full-time equivalent faculty	2,150

Inventory Flow Assumptions

Firms compute process costing using either the weighted-average or first-in, first-out (FIFO) method. Throughout the rest of the chapter, we will use the **weighted-average method of process costing** rather than the FIFO method because it is simpler and the differences between the two methods' results are usually immaterial. *The two costing methods differ only in how they treat beginning inventory.* The FIFO method, which is explained in advanced cost accounting textbooks, requires that any units in beginning inventory be costed *separately* from any units started in the current period. The weighted-average method *combines* any beginning inventory units (and costs) with the current period's units (and costs) to get a weighted-average cost. From a cost-benefit standpoint, many firms prefer to use the weighted-average method because the extra cost of calculating the FIFO method does not justify the additional benefits they gain from using FIFO information.

How Does Process Costing Work in the First Processing Department?

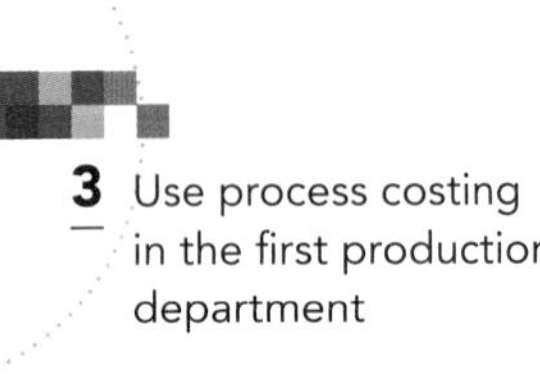

3 Use process costing in the first production department

To illustrate process costing, we'll be following SeaView, a manufacturer that mass produces swim masks. We'll see how SeaView uses the weighted-average method of process costing to measure (1) the average cost of producing each swim mask and (2) the cost of the two major processes it uses to make the masks (Shaping and Insertion).

Exhibit 5-4 illustrates SeaView's production process. The Shaping Department begins with plastic and metal fasteners (direct materials) and uses labor and equipment (conversion costs) to transform the materials into shaped masks. The direct materials are added at the *beginning* of the process, but conversion costs are incurred *evenly* throughout the

Accounting Simplified
Costing Procedure

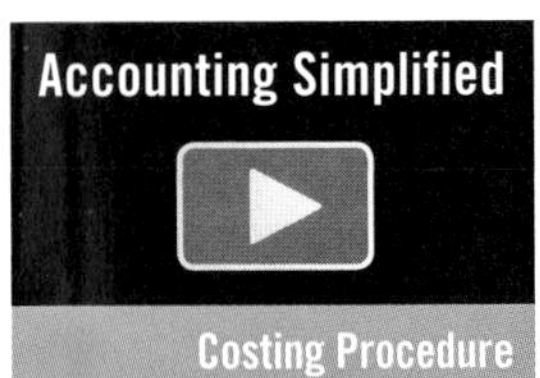

If your instructor is using MyAccountingLab, go to the Multimedia Library for a quick video on this topic.

EXHIBIT 5-4 SeaView's Production Process

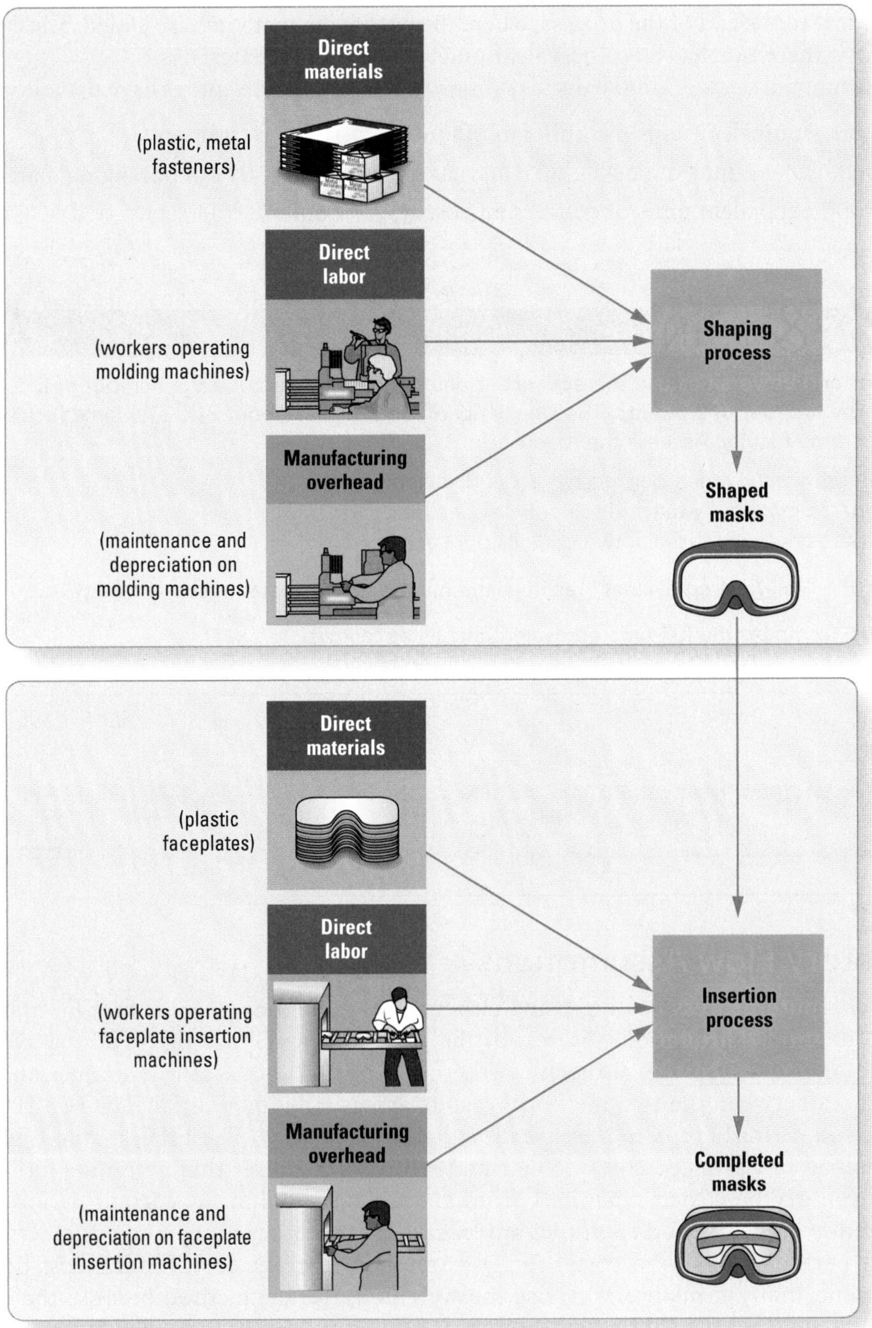
Direct materials
(plastic, metal fasteners)
Direct labor
(workers operating molding machines)
Manufacturing overhead
(maintenance and depreciation on molding machines)
Shaping process
Shaped masks
Direct materials
(plastic faceplates)
Direct labor
(workers operating faceplate insertion machines)
Manufacturing overhead
(maintenance and depreciation on faceplate insertion machines)
Insertion process
Completed masks

process. After shaping, the masks move to the Insertion Department, where the shaped masks are polished and then the clear faceplates are inserted.

Let's assume that the Shaping Department begins October with no work in process inventory. During October, the Shaping Department incurs the following costs while working on 50,000 masks:

Beginning work in process inventory		$ 0
Direct materials		140,000
Conversion costs:		
Direct labor	$21,250	
Manufacturing overhead	46,750	
Total conversion costs		68,000
Total costs to account for		$208,000

How did SeaView arrive at these costs? SeaView traces direct materials and direct labor to each processing department using materials requisitions and labor time records (just as we used these documents to trace direct materials and direct labor to individual *jobs* in Chapter 3). SeaView allocates manufacturing overhead to each processing department using a either a plantwide rate, departmental overhead rates, or ABC (just as we allocated manufacturing overhead to individual *jobs* in Chapters 3 and 4).

If, at the end of October, all 50,000 masks have been completely shaped and transferred out of the Shaping Department and into the Insertion Department, the entire $208,000 of manufacturing cost associated with these masks should *likewise* be transferred out of "Work in Process—Shaping" and into "Work in Process—Insertion." In this case, the unit cost for *just* the shaping process is $4.16 per mask ($208,000/50,000 masks).

But what if only 40,000 masks are completely through the shaping process? Let's say that at October 31, the Shaping Department still has 10,000 masks that are only one-quarter of the way through the shaping process. How do we split the $208,000 between the following?

Why is this important?

"Most food and consumer products are **mass produced.** Managers need to know 1) the **cost** of each **manufacturing** process, to make each one as **cost-efficient** as possible; and 2) the cost of **each unit,** to aid in **pricing** and other business decisions."

- 40,000 completely shaped masks transferred to the Insertion Department
- 10,000 partially shaped masks remaining in the Shaping Department's ending work in process inventory

In other words, how do we determine the cost of making the *completely* shaped masks versus the cost of making the *partially* shaped masks? We can't simply assign $4.16 to each mask because a partially shaped mask does *not* cost the same to make as a completely shaped mask. To figure out the cost of making a *completely* shaped mask versus a *partially* shaped mask, we must use the following five-step process costing procedure:

STEP 1: Summarize the flow of physical units.
STEP 2: Compute output in terms of equivalent units.
STEP 3: Summarize total costs to account for.
STEP 4: Compute the cost per equivalent unit.
STEP 5: Assign total costs to units completed and to units in ending Work in Process inventory.

We'll walk through each of these steps now.

Step 1: Summarize the Flow of Physical Units

Step 1 tracks the physical movement of swim masks into and out of the Shaping Department during the month. Follow along as we walk through this step in the first column of Exhibit 5-5. The first question addressed is this: *How many physical units did the Shaping Department work on during the month?* Recall that the Shaping Department had no masks in the beginning work in process inventory. During the month, the Shaping Department began work on 50,000 masks. Thus, the department needs to account for a *total* of 50,000 masks.

EXHIBIT 5-5 Step 1: Summarize the Flow of Physical Units
Step 2: Compute Output in Terms of Equivalent Units

SEAVIEW SHAPING DEPARTMENT
Month Ended October 31

	Step 1	Step 2 Equivalent Units	
Flow of Production	**Flow of Physical Units**	**Direct Materials**	**Conversion Costs**
Units to account for:			
Beginning work in process, October 1	0		
Started in production during October	50,000		
Total physical units to account for	50,000		
Units accounted for:			
Completed and transferred out during October	40,000	40,000	40,000
Ending work in process, October 31	10,000	10,000	2,500*
Total physical units accounted for	50,000		
Total equivalent units		50,000	42,500

*10,000 units each 25% complete = 2,500 equivalent units

The second question addressed is this: *What happened to those masks?* The Shaping Department reports that it completed and transferred out 40,000 masks to the Insertion Department during October. The remaining 10,000 partially shaped masks are still in the Shaping Department's ending work in process inventory on October 31. Notice that the *total physical units to account for* (50,000) must equal the *total physical units accounted for* (50,000). In other words, the Shaping Department must account for the whereabouts of every mask it worked on during the month.

Step 2: Compute Output in Terms of Equivalent Units

Step 2 computes all of the Shaping Department's output for the month in terms of equivalent units. Step 2 is shown in the last two columns of Exhibit 5-5. First, let's consider the 40,000 masks that were *completed and transferred out* to the Insertion Department during October. These units have been fully completed in the Shaping Department; therefore, these 40,000 completed masks have incurred 40,000 equivalent units of direct materials (40,000 masks × 100% of direct materials) and 40,000 equivalent units of conversion costs (40,000 masks × 100% of conversion costs).

Now, let's consider the 10,000 masks still in ending work in process. These masks are only 25% of the way through the shaping process on October 31. The time line in Exhibit 5-6 reminds us that all direct materials are added at the *beginning* of the shaping process. Therefore, the partially shaped masks have made it past the point where direct materials are added. As a result, these masks have incurred 10,000 equivalent units of direct materials (10,000 masks × 100% of direct materials).

Unlike direct materials, the conversion costs are added *evenly* throughout the shaping process. For these partially shaped masks, the equivalent units of conversion costs are as follows:

10,000 × 25% = 2,500 equivalent units of conversion costs

EXHIBIT 5-6 SeaView's Shaping Department Time Line

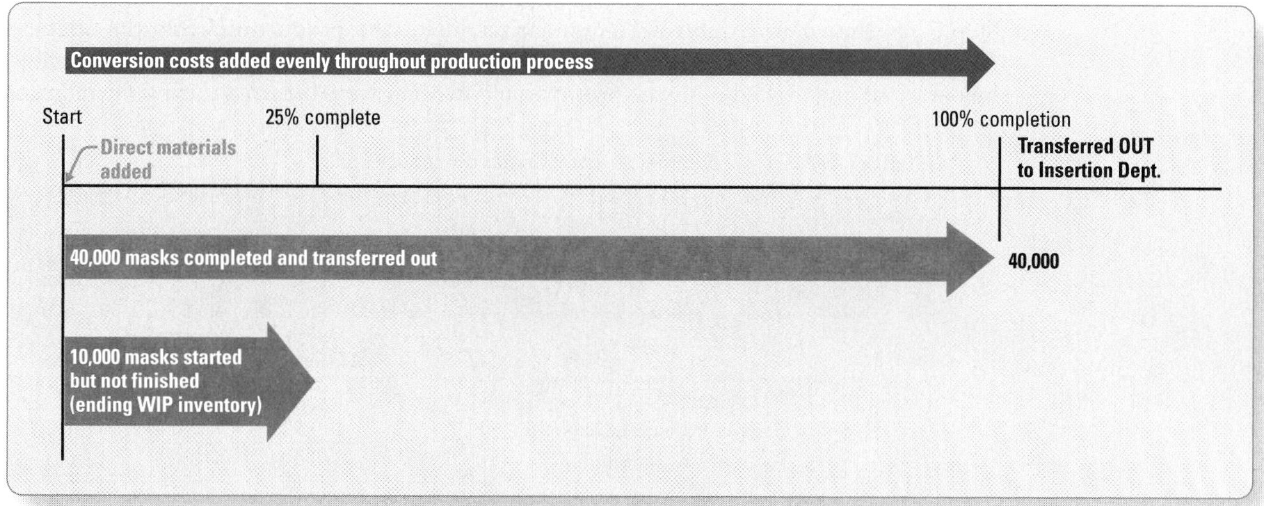

Our last step is to calculate the Shaping Department's output in terms of *total equivalent units* for the month. We must calculate totals separately for direct materials and conversion costs because they will differ in most circumstances. To find the totals, we simply add the equivalent units of all masks worked on during the month. As shown in Exhibit 5-5, the *total equivalent units of direct materials* (50,000) is simply the sum of the 40,000 equivalent units completed and transferred out *plus* the 10,000 equivalent units still in ending work in process. Likewise, the *total equivalent units of conversion costs* (42,500) is the sum of the 40,000 equivalent units completed and transferred out plus the 2,500 equivalent units still in ending work in process.

STOP & THINK

Suppose the Shaping Department adds direct materials at the *end* of the shaping process rather than at the *beginning*.

1. Draw a new time line similar to Exhibit 5-6.
2. Use the time line to determine the number of equivalent units of direct materials.

Answers

1.

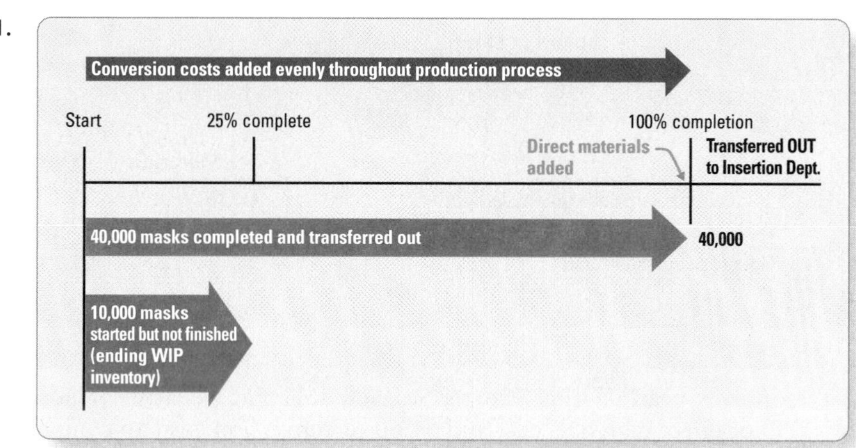

2. The time line shows that the 10,000 masks in ending work in process inventory have not made it to the end of the shaping process where materials are added. Materials have been added *only* to the 40,000 masks completed and transferred out, not to the 10,000 masks in ending work in process. Thus, there are only 40,000 total equivalent units of direct materials.

Step 3: Summarize Total Costs to Account For

Step 3, as shown in Exhibit 5-7, summarizes all of the production costs the Shaping Department must account for. These are the production costs associated with beginning inventory (if any existed) plus the production costs that were incurred during the month.[1]

EXHIBIT 5-7 Step 3: Summarize Total Costs to Account For

SEAVIEW SHAPING DEPARTMENT
Month Ended October 31

	Direct Materials	Conversion Costs	Total
Beginning work in process, October 1	$ 0	$ 0	$ 0
Costs added during October:	140,000	68,000*	208,000
Total costs to account for	$140,000	$68,000	$208,000

*21,250 of direct labor plus $46,750 of manufacturing overhead = $68,000 of conversion costs

Once again, we must show separate totals for each of the two cost categories: direct materials and conversion costs. Because the Shaping Department did not have any beginning inventory of partially shaped masks, the beginning balance in the "Work in Process Inventory—Shaping" account is zero. As shown on page 263, during the month, the Shaping Department used $140,000 of direct material and $68,000 of conversion costs ($21,250 of direct labor plus $46,750 of manufacturing overhead).

Step 4: Compute the Cost per Equivalent Unit

Remember that one of the primary goals of process costing is to average the cost of the production process over the units that pass through the process during the month. Step 4 does this by calculating the cost per equivalent unit. The word *per* means "divided by," so the *cost per equivalent unit* is the *total costs to account for* (from Step 3) divided by the *total equivalent units* (from Step 2). Because the total equivalent units for direct materials (50,000) and conversion costs (42,500) differ, we must compute a separate cost per equivalent unit for each cost category. Exhibit 5-8 shows the computations:

EXHIBIT 5-8 Step 4: Compute the Cost per Equivalent Unit

SEAVIEW SHAPING DEPARTMENT
Month Ended October 31

	Direct Materials	Conversion Costs
Total costs to account for (from Exhibit 5-7)	$140,000	$68,000
Divided by total equivalent units (from Exhibit 5-5)	÷ 50,000	÷ 42,500
Cost per equivalent unit	$ 2.80	$ 1.60

What do these figures mean? During October, SeaView's Shaping Department incurred an average of $2.80 of direct materials cost and $1.60 of conversion costs to completely shape the equivalent of one mask. In addition to using the cost per equivalent unit in the five-step process costing procedure, managers also use this information to determine how

[1]The Shaping Department did not have a beginning inventory. Summary Problem 1 illustrates a department that does have a beginning inventory. As long as we assume the weighted-average method of process costing, we include the beginning balance to arrive at total costs to account for, as shown in Exhibit 5-7.

well they have controlled costs. Managers compare the actual cost per equivalent unit to the budgeted cost per equivalent unit for both direct materials and conversion costs. If the cost per equivalent unit is the same as or lower than budgeted, the manager has successfully controlled costs.

Step 5: Assign Total Costs to Units Completed and to Units in Ending Work in Process Inventory

The goal of Step 5 (Exhibit 5-9) is to determine how much of the Shaping Department's $208,000 total costs should be assigned to (1) the 40,000 completely shaped masks transferred out to the Insertion Department and (2) the 10,000 partially shaped masks remaining in the Shaping Department's ending work in process inventory. Exhibit 5-9 shows how the equivalent units computed in Step 2 (Exhibit 5-5) are costed at the cost per equivalent unit computed in Step 4 (Exhibit 5-8).

First, consider the 40,000 masks completed and transferred out. Exhibit 5-5 shows 40,000 equivalent units for both direct materials and conversion costs. In Exhibit 5-8 we learned that the company spent $2.80 on direct materials for each equivalent unit, and $1.60 on conversion costs for each equivalent unit. Thus, the total cost of these completed masks is 40,000 × ($2.80 + $1.60) = $176,000, as shown in Exhibit 5-9. We've accomplished our first goal—now we know how much cost ($176,000) should be assigned to the completely shaped masks transferred to the Insertion Department.

EXHIBIT 5-9 Step 5: Assign Costs to Units Completed and to Units in Ending Work in Process Inventory

SEAVIEW SHAPING DEPARTMENT
Month Ended October 31

	Direct Materials	Conversion Costs		Total
Completed and transferred out (40,000)	[40,000 × ($2.80 + $1.60)]		=	$176,000
Ending work in process inventory (10,000):				
Direct materials	[10,000 × $2.80]		=	$ 28,000
Conversion costs		[2,500 × $1.60]	=	4,000
Total cost of ending work in process inventory				$ 32,000
Total costs accounted for				$208,000

Note: Equivalent units are from Exhibit 5-5; Costs per equivalent are from Exhibit 5-8.

Next, consider the 10,000 masks still in ending work in process. These masks have 10,000 equivalent units of direct materials (which cost $2.80 per equivalent unit), so the direct material cost is $28,000 (= 10,000 × $2.80). These masks also have 2,500 equivalent units of conversion costs, which cost $1.60 per equivalent unit, so the conversion costs are $4,000 (= 2,500 × $1.60). Therefore, the total cost of the 10,000 partially completed masks in the Shaping Department's ending work in process inventory is the sum of these direct material and conversion costs: $28,000 + $4,000 = $32,000. Now, we've accomplished our second goal—we know how much cost ($32,000) should be assigned to the partially shaped masks still in ending work in process inventory.

In summary, Exhibit 5-9 has accomplished our goal of splitting the $208,000 *total cost to account for* between the 40,000 masks completed and transferred out to the Insertion Department and the 10,000 partially shaped masks remaining in Work in Process Inventory.

Average Unit Costs

How does this information relate to unit costs? The average cost of making one *completely shaped* unit is $4.40 ($176,000 transferred to Insertion ÷ 40,000 completely shaped masks transferred to Insertion). This average unit cost ($4.40) is the sum of the direct material cost per equivalent unit ($2.80) and the conversion cost per equivalent unit ($1.60). The average cost of one *partially* shaped unit that is 25% of the way through the production process is \$3.20 (\$32,000 in ending inventory of Shaping ÷ 10,000 partially shaped masks). We needed the five-step process costing procedure to find these average costs per unit. If the Shaping Department manager ignored the five-step process and simply spread the entire production cost over all units worked on during the period, each unit would be assigned a cost of \$4.16 (\$208,000 ÷ 50,000 masks)—whether completely shaped or not. That would be wrong. The average cost per unit should be (and is) higher for completely shaped units transferred to the Insertion Department than it is for partially shaped units remaining in the Shaping Department's ending work in process inventory.

Recall that once the masks are shaped, they still need to have the faceplates inserted. In the second half of the chapter, we will discuss how the second process—Insertion—uses the same five-step procedure to find the *total* unit cost of making a completed mask, from start to finish.

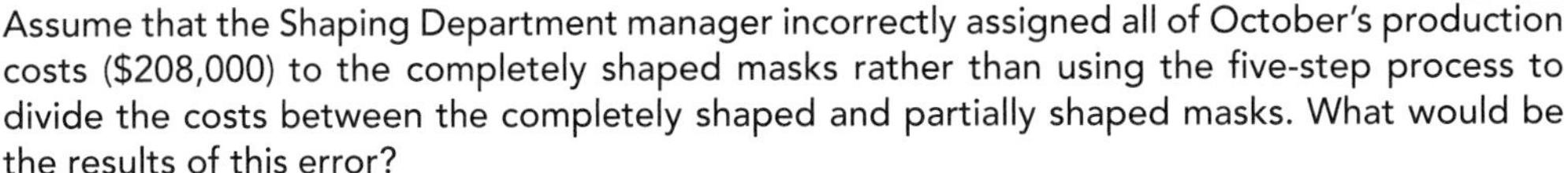

Assume that the Shaping Department manager incorrectly assigned all of October's production costs (\$208,000) to the completely shaped masks rather than using the five-step process to divide the costs between the completely shaped and partially shaped masks. What would be the results of this error?

Answer: If the manager incorrectly assigned all production costs to the completely shaped masks, the unit cost of completely shaped masks would be too high (\$208,000 ÷ 40,000 = \$5.20). In addition, the unit cost of the partially shaped masks would be too low (\$0.00). In essence, the manager would be saying that the partially shaped units were "free" to make because he or she assigned all of the production costs to the completely shaped units. To assign production costs properly, managers must use the five-step process.

Sustainability and Process Costing

As we have seen, process costing is suitable for manufacturers that produce large volumes of product using a set of standardized production processes. These manufacturing environments are conducive to employing lean practices, which eliminate economic waste from the manufacturing process, and green practices, which minimize or eliminate harmful environmental consequences.

For example, SeaView employs two standardized production processes: Shaping and Insertion. Management should be continually asking, "Are each of these production processes as efficient and environmentally friendly as they can be?" If not, then changes are warranted.

Management should study each of the production processes to discover the quantities and types of solid waste, airborne emissions, and waste water that are generated, as well as the types and quantities of energy used. Solid waste and scrap can be identified simply by studying the contents of the company's trash. These studies are known as **trash audits**, **waste audits**, or **waste sorts**. After conducting trash audits, many companies have discovered they can reclaim and repurpose the scraps into new products, or sell them to a third-party recycler. For example, Parma Plastics recovers unwanted vinyl scraps from manufacturers across North America and recycles the scraps into re-compounded vinyl.[2] Many parties benefit:

- Manufacturers reduce their waste disposal costs and generate new revenue from selling their vinyl scraps.
- Manufacturers reduce their raw material costs by buying re-compounded vinyl rather than virgin vinyl.
- Parma Plastics creates jobs and profit by manufacturing and selling the re-compounded vinyl.
- Landfills are spared from receiving vinyl scraps.

[2]http://www.iisd.org/business/viewcasestudy.aspx?id=84

Air and water discharges should also be examined to determine if any environmentally damaging substances are released into the environment.

While switching to environmentally-friendly production equipment, energy sources, and production processes may be costly in the short-run, companies may recognize long-term economic benefits as a result. For example, as carbon-trading schemes (otherwise known as "cap and trade") become more prevalent across the globe, those companies that manage to reduce their carbon emissions may be able to profit from selling their carbon credits. In searching for greener ways to manufacture and recycle their products, some companies may eventually profit from developing, patenting, and selling their own environmentally-neutral production systems and technologies.

See Exercises E5-32A and E5-45B

What Journal Entries are Needed in a Process Costing System?

4 Prepare journal entries for a process costing system

The journal entries used in a process costing system are very similar to those in a job costing system. The basic difference is that the manufacturing costs (direct materials, direct labor, and manufacturing overhead) are assigned to *processing departments*, rather than *jobs*. In addition, at the end of the month a journal entry must be made to transfer cost to the next processing department. Let's now look at the journal entries that would have been made in October for the Shaping Department.

During October, $140,000 of direct materials were requisitioned for use by the Shaping Department. In the following journal entry, notice how these costs are recorded specifically to the Shaping Department's Work in Process Inventory account. In process costing, each processing department maintains a separate Work in Process Inventory account.

	Work in Process Inventory—Shaping	140,000	
	Raw Materials Inventory		140,000
	(To record direct materials used by the Shaping Department in October.)		

Labor time records show that $21,250 of direct labor was used in the Shaping Department during October, resulting in the following journal entry:

	Work in Process Inventory—Shaping	21,250	
	Wages Payable		21,250
	(To record direct labor used in the Shaping Department in October)		

Manufacturing overhead is allocated to the Shaping Department using the company's predetermined overhead rate(s). Just as in a job costing environment, the company may use a single plantwide rate, departmental overhead rates, or ABC to allocate its manufacturing overhead costs. For example, let's say that the Shaping Department's overhead rate is $50 per machine hour and the department used 935 machine hours during the month. That means $46,750 ($50 × 935) of MOH should be allocated to the Shaping Department during October:

	Work in Process Inventory—Shaping	46,750	
	Manufacturing Overhead		46,750
	(To record manufacturing overhead allocated to the Shaping Department in October.)		

After making these journal entries during the month, the "Work in Process Inventory—Shaping" T-account appears as follows:

Work in Process Inventory—Shaping

Balance, October 1		0	
Direct materials	$208,000	140,000	
Direct labor		21,250	
Manufacturing overhead		46,750	

Notice how the sum of the costs currently in the T-account is $208,000. This is the *same total costs to* account for summarized in Exhibit 5-7. By performing the five step process at the end of the month, SeaView was able to determine how much of the $208,000 should be assigned to units still being worked on ($32,000) and how much should be assigned to the units completed and transferred out to the Insertion Department ($176,000). The company uses this information (pictured in Exhibit 5-9) to make the following journal entry:

	Work in Process Inventory—Insertion	176,000	
	Work in Process Inventory—Shaping		176,000
	(To record transfer of cost out of the Shaping Department		
	and into the Insertion Department.)		

After this journal entry is posted, the "Work in Process Inventory—Shaping" account appears as follows. Notice that the new ending balance in the account—$32,000—agrees with the amount assigned to the partially shaped masks in Exhibit 5-9.

Work in Process Inventory—Shaping

Balance, October 1	0	Transferred to Insertion	176,000
Direct materials	140,000		
Direct labor	21,250		
Manufacturing overhead	46,750		
Balance, October 31	32,000		

In the next half of the chapter, we'll look at the journal entries made by the Insertion Department to record the completion and sale of the swim masks.

Decision Guidelines

Process Costing—First Processing Department

Here are some of the key decisions SeaView made in setting up its process costing system.

Decision	Guidelines
Should SeaView use job or process costing?	SeaView mass-produces large quantities of identical swim masks using two production processes: Shaping and Insertion. It uses *process costing* to: 1. Determine the cost of each production process. 2. Determine the average direct material cost and conversion cost incurred on each unit passing through the production process.
How many Work in Process Inventory accounts does SeaView's process costing system have?	SeaView uses a separate Work in Process Inventory account for each of its two major processes: Shaping and Insertion.
How does SeaView account for partially completed units?	SeaView uses equivalent units. SeaView computes equivalent units separately for direct materials and conversion costs because it adds direct materials at a particular point in the production process but incurs conversion costs evenly throughout the process.
How does SeaView compute equivalent units of conversion costs?	SeaView's *conversion costs* are incurred evenly throughout the production process, so the equivalent units are computed as follows: $\text{Equivalent units} = \text{Number of partially complete units} \times \text{Percentage of process completed}$
How does SeaView compute equivalent units of direct materials?	SeaView's *materials* are added at specific points in the production process, so the equivalent units are computed using the following percentages: • If physical units have passed the point at which materials are added, then the units are 100% complete with respect to materials. • If physical units have not passed the point at which materials are added, then the units are 0% complete with respect to materials.
How does SeaView compute the cost per equivalent unit?	For each category (direct materials and conversion), SeaView divides the total cost to account for by the total equivalent units. The resulting information tells management the average cost of making one unit in each processing department. This information can then be compared to budget to help managers control costs.
How does SeaView split the costs of the shaping process between the following? • Swim masks completed and transferred out • Partially completed swim masks in ending work in process inventory	SeaView multiplies the cost per equivalent unit by the following: • Number of equivalent units completed and transferred out • Number of equivalent units in the ending work in process inventory

SUMMARY PROBLEM 1

Florida Tile produces ceramic tiles using two sequential production departments: Tile-Forming and Tile-Finishing. The following information was found for Florida Tile's first production process, the Tile-Forming Department.

FLORIDA TILE
TILE-FORMING DEPARTMENT
Month Ended May 31

Information about units:	
Beginning work in process, May 1	2,000 units
Started in production during May	18,000 units
Completed and transferred to Finishing Department during May	16,000 units
Ending work in process, May 31 (25% complete as to direct materials, 55% complete as to conversion cost)	4,000 units
Information about costs:	
Beginning work in process, May 1 (consists of $800 of direct materials cost and $4,000 of conversion costs)	$ 4,800
Direct materials used in May	$ 6,000
Conversion costs incurred in May	$32,400

Requirement

Use the five steps of process costing to calculate the cost that should be assigned to (1) units completed and transferred out and (2) units still in ending work in process inventory. Then prepare the journal entry needed at month-end to transfer the costs associated with the formed tiles to the next department, Tile Finishing.

▪ SOLUTION

Step 1: Summarize the flow of physical units.
Step 2: Compute output in terms of equivalent units.

FLORIDA TILE
TILE-FORMING DEPARTMENT
Month Ended May 31

	Step 1	Step 2: Equivalent Units	
Flow of Production	Flow of Physical Units	Direct Materials	Conversion Costs
Units to account for:			
Beginning work in process, May 1	2,000		
Started in production during May	18,000		
Total physical units to account for	20,000		
Units accounted for:			
Completed and transferred out in May	16,000	16,000	16,000
Ending work in process, May 31	4,000	1,000*	2,200**
Total physical units accounted for	20,000		
Total equivalent units		17,000	18,200

*Direct materials: 4,000 units each 25% complete = 1,000 equivalent units.
**Conversion costs: 4,000 units each 55% complete = 2,200 equivalent units.

Step 3: Summarize total costs to account for.

FLORIDA TILE
TILE-FORMING DEPARTMENT
Month Ended May 31

	Direct Materials	Conversion Costs	Total
Beginning work in process, May 1	$ 800	$ 4,000	$ 4,800
Costs added during May	6,000	32,400	38,400
Total costs to account for	$6,800	$36,400	$43,200

Note: All cost information is from the summary problem data set.

Step 4: Compute the cost per equivalent unit.

FLORIDA TILE
TILE-FORMING DEPARTMENT
Month Ended May 31

	Direct Materials	Conversion Costs
Total costs to account for (from Step 3)	$ 6,800	$36,400
Divided by total equivalent units (from Step 2)	÷ 17,000	÷ 18,200
Cost per equivalent unit	$ 0.40	$ 2.00

Step 5: Assign total costs to units completed and to units in ending work in process inventory.

FLORIDA TILE
TILE-FORMING DEPARTMENT
Month Ended May 31

	Direct Materials	Conversion Costs		Total
Units completed and transferred out (16,000)	[16,000 × ($0.40 + $2.00)]		=	$38,400
Units in ending work in process inventory (4,000):				
Direct materials	[1,000 × $0.40]		=	$ 400
Conversion costs		[2,200 × $2.00]	=	4,400
Total cost of ending work in process inventory				$ 4,800
Total costs accounted for				$43,200

The journal entry needed to transfer costs is as follows:

		Debit	Credit
	Work in Process Inventory—Finishing	38,400	
	Work in Process Inventory—Tile Forming		38,400

The cost of making one completely formed tile in the Forming Department is $2.40. This is the sum of the direct materials cost per equivalent unit ($0.40) and the conversion cost per equivalent unit ($2.00). The completely formed tiles must still be finished in the Finishing Department before we will know the final cost of making one tile from start to finish.

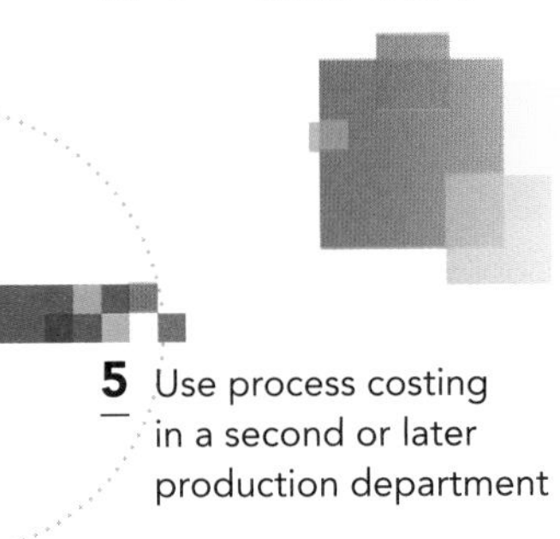

How Does Process Costing Work in a Second or Later Processing Department?

5 Use process costing in a second or later production department

Most products require a series of processing steps. Recall that Jelly Belly uses eight processing steps to make its jelly beans. In the last section, we saw how much it costs SeaView to *shape* one mask. In this section, we consider a second department, SeaView's Insertion Department. After units pass through the *final* department (Insertion, in SeaView's case), managers can determine the *entire* cost of making one unit—from start to finish. In the second or later department, we use the same five-step process costing procedure that we used for the Shaping Department, with one major difference: We separately consider the costs *transferred in* to the Insertion Department from the Shaping Department when calculating equivalent units and the cost per equivalent unit. Transferred-in costs are incurred in a previous process (the Shaping Department, in the SeaView example) and are carried forward as part of the product's cost when it moves to the next process.

To account for transferred-in costs, we will add one more column to our calculations in Steps 2–5. Let's walk through the Insertion Department's process costing to see how this is done.

Why is this important?

"Most products are **manufactured** through a **series** of production processes. To find the **total cost** of making one unit—*from* **start to finish**—managers must perform the five-step process costing procedure in **each** production department."

Process Costing in SeaView's Insertion Department

The Insertion Department receives the shaped masks and polishes them before inserting the faceplates at the end of the process. Exhibit 5-10 shows the following:

- Shaped masks are transferred in from the Shaping Department at the beginning of the Insertion Department's process.
- The Insertion Department's conversion costs are added evenly throughout the process.
- The Insertion Department's direct materials (faceplates) are not added until the *end* of the process.

EXHIBIT 5-10 SeaView's Insertion Department Time Line

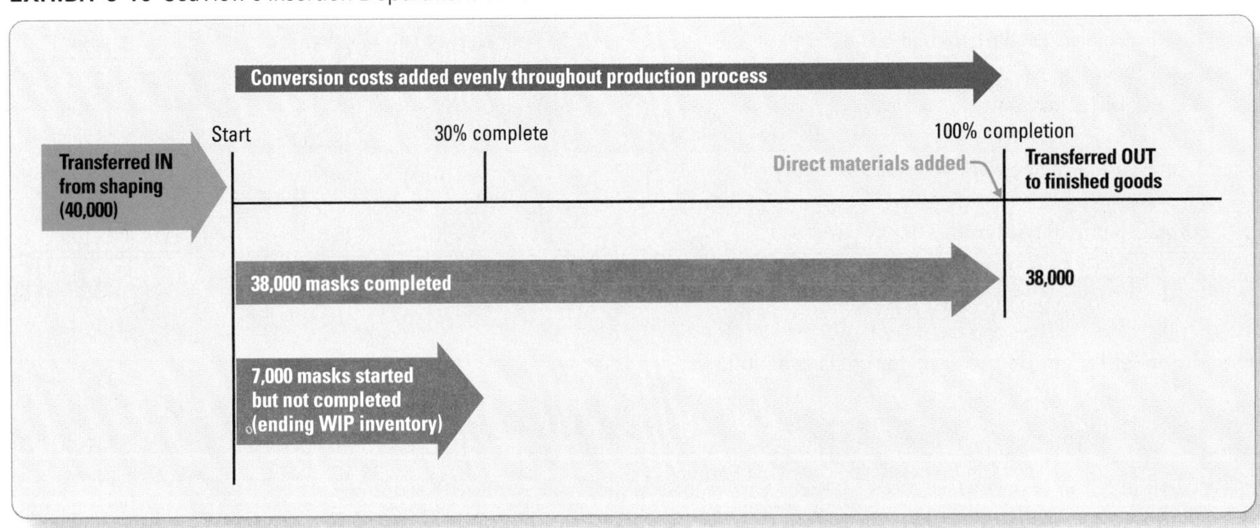

Keep in mind that *direct materials* in the Insertion Department refer *only* to the faceplates and not to the materials (the plastic and metal fasteners) added in the Shaping Department. Likewise, *conversion costs* in the Insertion Department refer to the direct labor and manufacturing overhead costs incurred *only* in the Insertion Department.

Exhibit 5-11 lists SeaView's Insertion Department data for October. The top portion of the exhibit lists the unit information, while the lower portion lists the costs. Let's walk through this information together.

EXHIBIT 5-11 SeaView's Insertion Department Data for October

Information about units:		
Beginning work in process, October 1 (0% complete as to direct materials, 60% complete as to conversion work)		5,000 masks*
Transferred in from Shaping Department during October (from Exhibit 5-6)		40,000 masks
Completed and transferred out to Finished Goods Inventory during October		38,000 masks
Ending work in process, October 31 (0% complete as to direct materials, 30% complete as to conversion work)		7,000 masks
Information about costs:		
Beginning work in process, October 1		
Transferred-in costs	$ 22,000	
Conversion costs	1,100*	
Beginning balance		$ 23,100
Transferred in from Shaping Department during October (from journal entry on page 270)		$176,000
Direct materials added during October in Insertion Department		$ 19,000
Conversion costs added during October in Insertion Department:		
Direct labor	$ 3,710	
Manufacturing overhead	9,225	
Conversion costs		$ 12,935
Total costs to account for		$231,035

*This information would have been obtained from Step 5 of the process costing procedure from September. The September 30 balance in work in process becomes the October 1 balance.

Exhibit 5-11 shows that SeaView's Insertion Department started the October period with 5,000 masks that had made it partway through the insertion process in September. During October, the Insertion Department started work on the 40,000 masks received from the Shaping Department. By the end of the month, the Insertion Department had completed 38,000 masks, while 7,000 remained partially complete.

Exhibit 5-11 also shows that the Insertion Department started October with a beginning balance of $23,100 in its Work in Process Inventory account, which is associated with the 5,000 partially completed masks in its beginning inventory. During the month, $176,000 was transferred in from the Shaping Department (recall the journal entry on page 270) for the 40,000 masks transferred into the department from Shaping. Additionally, the Insertion Department incurred $19,000 in direct material costs (faceplates) and $12,935 in conversion costs during the month.

Just as in the Shaping Department, our goal is to split the total cost in the Insertion Department ($231,035) between the following:

- The 38,000 masks that the Insertion Department completed and transferred out (this time, to Finished Goods Inventory)
- The 7,000 partially complete masks remaining in the Insertion Department's ending work in process inventory at the end of October

After splitting the total cost, we'll be able to determine the cost of making one complete mask—from start to finish. We use the same five-step process costing procedure that we used for the Shaping Department.

Steps 1 and 2: Summarize the Flow of Physical Units and Compute Output in Terms of Equivalent Units

Step 1: Summarize the Flow of Physical Units

Step 1 tracks the movement of swim masks into and out of the Insertion Department, just as we did in the Shaping Department. The data in Exhibit 5-11 shows that the Insertion Department had a beginning work in process inventory of 5,000 masks. Then, during October, the Insertion Department received 40,000 masks from the Shaping Department. Thus, Exhibit 5-12 shows that the Insertion Department has 45,000 masks to account for (5,000 + 40,000).

Where did these 45,000 masks go? Exhibit 5-11 shows that the Insertion Department completed and transferred 38,000 masks out to Finished Goods Inventory while the remaining 7,000 masks were only partway through the insertion process on October 31. Thus, Exhibit 5-12 shows that the department has accounted for all 45,000 masks.

Step 2: Compute Output in Terms of Equivalent Units

As mentioned earlier, process costing in a second or later department separately calculates equivalent units for transferred-in costs, direct materials, and conversion costs. Therefore, Step 2 in Exhibit 5-12 shows *three* columns for the Insertion Department's *three* categories

EXHIBIT 5-12 Step 1: Summarize the Flow of Physical Units
Step 2: Compute Output in Terms of Equivalent Units

SEAVIEW INSERTION DEPARTMENT
Month Ended October 31

	Step 1	Step 2: Equivalent Units		
Flow of Production	Flow of Physical Units	Transferred-in	Direct Materials	Conversion Costs
Units to account for:				
Beginning work in process, October 1	5,000			
Transferred in during October	40,000			
Total physical units to account for	45,000			
Units accounted for:				
Completed and transferred out during October	38,000	38,000*	38,000*	38,000*
Ending work in process, October 31	7,000	7,000†	0†	2,100†
Total physical units accounted for	45,000			
Total equivalent units		45,000	38,000	40,100

In the Insertion Department:
*Units completed and transferred out
Transferred-in: 38,000 units × 100% = 38,000 equivilant units
Direct materials: 38,000 units × 100% completed = 38,000 equivalent units
Conversion costs: 38,000 units × 100% completed = 38,000 equivalent units
†Ending inventory
Transferred-in: 7,000 units × 100% = 7,000 equivalent units
Direct materials: 7,000 units × 0% completed = 0 equivalent units
Conversion costs: 7,000 units × 30% completed = 2,100 equivalent units

of equivalent units: transferred-in, direct materials, and conversion costs. Let's consider each in turn.

Exhibit 5-10 shows that transferred-in masks are added at the very *beginning* of the insertion process. You might think of the shaped masks transferred in as raw materials added at the very *beginning* of the insertion process. All masks worked on in the Insertion Department—whether completed or not by the end of the month—started in the department as a shaped mask. Therefore, they are *all 100% complete with respect to transferred-in work and costs*. So, the "Transferred-in" column of Exhibit 5-12 shows 38,000 equivalent units completed and transferred out (38,000 physical units × 100%) and 7,000 equivalent units still in ending inventory (7,000 physical units × 100%).

The following rule holds: *All physical units, whether completed and transferred out or still in ending work in process, are considered 100% complete with respect to transferred-in work and costs.*

The Insertion Department calculates equivalent units of direct material the same way as in the Shaping Department. However, in the Insertion Department, the direct materials (faceplates) are added at the *end* of the process rather than at the beginning of the process. The 38,000 masks completed and transferred out contain 100% of their direct materials. On the other hand, the 7,000 masks in ending work in process inventory have *not* made it to the end of the process, so they *do not* contain faceplates. As we see in Exhibit 5-12, these unfinished masks have zero equivalent units of the Insertion Department's direct materials (7,000 physical units × 0%).

Now, consider the conversion costs. The 38,000 finished masks are 100% complete with respect to the Insertion Department's conversion costs. However, the 7,000 unfinished masks are only 30% converted (see Exhibits 5-10 and 5-11), so the equivalent units of conversion costs equal 2,100 (7,000 × 30%).

Finally, the equivalent units in each column are summed to find the *total* equivalent units for each of the three categories: transferred-in (45,000), direct materials (38,000), and conversion costs (40,100). We'll use these equivalent units in Step 4.

Steps 3 and 4: Summarize Total Costs to Account for and Compute the Cost per Equivalent Unit

Exhibit 5-13 accumulates the Insertion Department's total costs to account for based on the data in Exhibit 5-11.

EXHIBIT 5-13 Step 3: Summarize Total Costs to Account For
Step 4: Compute the Cost per Equivalent Unit

SEAVIEW INSERTION DEPARTMENT
Month Ended October 31

	Transferred-in	Direct Materials	Conversion Costs	Total
Beginning work in process, October 1 (from Exhibit 5-11)	$ 22,000	$ 0	$ 1,100	$ 23,100
Costs added during October (from Exhibit 5-11)	176,000	19,000	12,935	207,935
Total costs to account for	$198,000	$19,000	$14,035	$231,035
Divide by total equivalent units (from Exhibit 5-12)	÷ 45,000	÷ 38,000	÷ 40,100	
Cost per equivalent unit	$ 4.40	$ 0.50	$ 0.35	

In addition to direct material and conversion costs, the Insertion Department must account for transferred-in costs. Recall that transferred-in costs are incurred in a previous process (the Shaping Department, in the SeaView example) and are carried forward as part of the product's cost when the physical product is transferred to the next process.

If the Insertion Department had bought these shaped masks from an outside supplier, it would have to account for the costs of purchasing the masks. However, the Insertion Department receives the masks from an *internal* supplier—the Shaping Department. Thus, the Insertion Department must account for the costs the Shaping Department incurred to provide the shaped masks as well as the Insertion Department's own direct materials (faceplates) and conversion costs (labor and overhead to insert the faceplates).

Exhibit 5-13 shows that the Insertion Department's total costs to account for ($231,035) consists of the costs associated with beginning work in process inventory ($23,100) plus the costs added during the month ($207,935).

Exhibit 5-13 also shows Step 4: the calculation of cost per equivalent unit. For each category of cost, SeaView simply divides the total costs by the corresponding number of total equivalent units.

Step 5: Assign Total Costs to Units Completed and to Units in Ending Work in Process Inventory

Exhibit 5-14 shows how SeaView finishes the 5-step process by assigning costs to (1) units completed and transferred out to finished goods inventory and (2) units remaining in the Insertion Department's ending work in process inventory. SeaView uses the same approach as it used for the Shaping Department in Exhibit 5-9. SeaView multiplies the number of equivalent units from Step 2 (Exhibit 5-12) by the cost per equivalent unit from Step 4 (Exhibit 5-13).

EXHIBIT 5-14 Step 5: Assign Total Costs to Units Completed and to Units in Ending Work in Process Inventory

SEAVIEW INSERTION DEPARTMENT
Month Ended October 31

	Transferred-in	Direct Materials	Conversion Costs	Total
Units completed and transferred out to				
Finished Goods Inventory (38,000)	[38,000 × ($4.40 + $0.50 + $0.35)]			$199,500
Ending work in process, October 31 (7,000):				
Transferred-in costs	[7,000 × $4.40]			$ 30,800
Direct materials		[0 × $0.50]		0
Conversion costs			[2,100 × $0.35]	735
Total ending work in process, October 31				31,535
Total costs accounted for				$231,035

Exhibit 5-15 illustrates how the costs were assigned in Step 5.

EXHIBIT 5-15 Assigning Insertion Department's Costs to Units Completed and Transferred Out and to Ending Work in Process Inventory

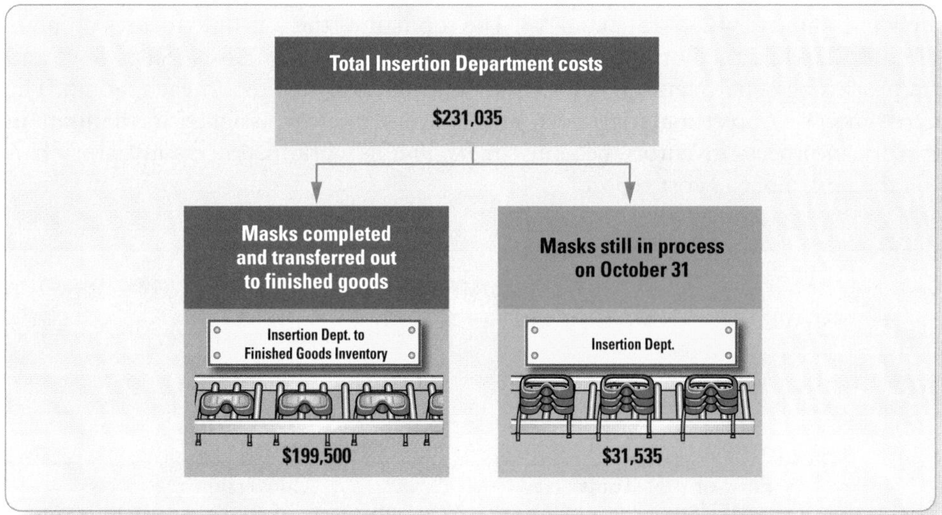

Unit Costs and Gross Profit

SeaView's managers can now compute the cost of manufacturing one swim mask, from start to finish. Step 5 shows that $199,500 should be transferred to the Finished Goods Inventory account for the 38,000 masks completed during the month. Therefore, SeaView's cost of making one completed mask is $5.25 ($199,500 ÷ 38,000 finished masks). Exhibit 5-14 shows that this cost includes the costs from both processing departments:

- $4.40 from the Shaping Department[3]
- $0.85 from the Insertion Department ($0.50 for direct materials and $0.35 for conversion costs)

SeaView's managers use this information to help control costs, set prices, and assess the profitability of the swim masks. Let's assume SeaView is able to charge customers $10 for each mask. If so, the gross profit on the sale of each of these masks will be as follows:

Sales Revenue (per mask)	$10.00
Less: Cost of Goods Sold (per mask)	5.25
Gross Profit (per mask)	$ 4.75

For SeaView to be profitable, the total gross profit (gross profit per mask × number of masks sold) will need to be high enough to cover all of SeaView's operating expenses, such as marketing and distribution expenses, incurred in non-manufacturing elements of the value chain. In addition to using the unit cost for valuing Cost of Goods Sold, SeaView will also use it to value Finished Goods Inventory ($5.25 for each mask still in finished goods inventory at the end of October).

[3]This is the same $4.40 per unit we saw the Shaping Department transfer out to the Insertion Department in the first half of the chapter. Notice how the transferred-in cost carries through from one department to the next. The weighted-average method of process costing *combines* the current period's costs ($176,000) with any costs in beginning inventory ($23,100) to yield a weighted-average cost per unit ($4.40). Therefore, the weighted average cost could be different than $4.40 if the beginning inventory had cost more or less than $4.40 per unit to make in September.

Production Cost Reports

Most companies prepare a **production cost report**, which summarizes the entire five-step process on one schedule. Notice how the production cost report for the Insertion Department shown in Exhibit 5-16 simply brings together all of the steps that we showed separately in Exhibits 5-12, 5-13, and 5-14. The top half of the schedule focuses on units (Steps 1 and 2), while the bottom half of the schedule focuses on costs (Steps 3, 4, and 5). Each processing department prepares its own production cost report each month. The transferred-in costs, direct materials cost, and conversion costs assigned to the units in *ending* work in process inventory become the *beginning* work in process inventory balances on the next month's cost report.

EXHIBIT 5-16 Production Cost Report

SEAVIEW INSERTION DEPARTMENT
Product Cost Report
Month Ended October 31

	Step 1	Step 2: Equivalent Units			
Flow of Production	**Flow of Physical Units**	**Transferred-in**	**Direct Materials**	**Conversion Costs**	
Units to account for:					
Beginning work in process, Oct. 1	5,000				
Transferred in during October	40,000				
Total physical units to account for	45,000				
Units accounted for:					
Completed and transferred out during October	38,000	38,000	38,000	38,000	
Ending work in process, Oct. 31	7,000	7,000	0	2,100	
Total physical units accounted for	45,000				
Total equivalent units		45,000	38,000	40,100	
		Steps 3, 4, and 5			
Flow of Costs		**Transferred-in**	**Direct Materials**	**Conversion Costs**	**Total**
Beginning work in process, October 1		$ 22,000	$ 0	$ 1,100	$ 23,100
Costs added during October		176,000	19,000	12,935	207,935
Total costs to account for		$198,000	$19,000	$14,035	$231,035
÷ Total equivalent units		÷ 45,000	÷ 38,000	÷ 40,100	
Cost per equivalent unit		$ 4.40	$ 0.50	$ 0.35	
Assignment of total costs:					
Units completed during October		[38,000 × ($4.40 + $0.50 + $0.35)]			$199,500
Ending work in process, October 31:					
Transferred-in costs		[7,000 × $4.40]			$ 30,800
Direct materials			[0 × $0.50]		0
Conversion costs				[2,100 × $0.35]	735
Total ending work in process, October 31					31,535
Total costs accounted for					$231,035

SeaView's managers monitor production costs by comparing the actual direct materials and conversion costs—particularly the equivalent-unit costs—with expected amounts. If actual costs are higher than expected, managers will try to uncover the reason for the increase, and look for ways to cut costs in the future without sacrificing quality.

Journal Entries in a Second Processing Department

The Insertion Department's journal entries are similar to those of the Shaping Department.

The following summary entry records the manufacturing costs incurred in the Insertion Department during the month of October (data from Exhibit 5-11):

	Account	Debit	Credit
	Work in Process Inventory—Insertion	31,935	
	Raw Materials Inventory		19,000
	Wages Payable		3,710
	Manufacturing Overhead		9,225
	(To record manufacturing costs incurred in the Insertion Department during October.)		

Next, recall the journal entry made to transfer the cost of shaped masks out of the Shaping Department and into the Insertion Department at the end of October (page 270). This journal entry would only be made *once*, but is repeated here simply as a reminder:

	Account	Debit	Credit
	Work in Process Inventory—Insertion	176,000	
	Work in Process Inventory—Shaping		176,000
	(To record the transfer cost out of the Shaping Department and into the Insertion Department.)		

The fifth step of the process costing procedure (Exhibit 5-14) showed that $199,500 should be assigned to the completed masks, while $31,535 should be assigned to the units still being worked on. Thus, the following journal entry is needed to transfer cost out of the Insertion Department and into Finished Goods Inventory:

	Account	Debit	Credit
	Finished Goods Inventory	199,500	
	Work in Process Inventory—Insertion		199,500
	(To record transfer of cost out of the Insertion Department and into Finished Goods Inventory.)		

After posting, the key accounts appear as follows:

Work in Process Inventory—Shaping

Balance, September 30	0	Transferred to Insertion	176,000
Direct materials	140,000		
Direct labor	21,250		
Manufacturing overhead	46,750		
Balance, October 31	32,000		

Work in Process Inventory—Insertion

Balance, September 30	23,100	Transferred to Finished Goods Inventory	199,500
Transferred in from Shaping	176,000		
Direct materials	19,000		
Direct labor	3,710		
Manufacturing overhead	9,225		
Balance, October 31	31,535		

Finished Goods Inventory

Balance, September 30	0		
Transferred in from Insertion	199,500		

STOP & THINK

Assume that SeaView sells 36,000 of the masks for $10 each. Assuming that SeaView uses a perpetual inventory system, what journal entries would SeaView make to record the sales transaction?

Answer: The unit cost of making one mask from start to finish is $5.25 ($199,500 transferred to Finished Goods ÷ 38,000 finished masks). SeaView will make one journal entry to record the sales revenue, and a second journal entry to record the cost of goods sold:

	Accounts Receivable (36,000 × $10.00)	360,000	
	Sales Revenue		360,000

	Cost of Goods Sold (36,000 × 5.25)	189,000	
	Finished Goods Inventory		189,000

Decision Guidelines

Process Costing—Second Process

Let's use SeaView's Insertion Department to review some of the key process costing decisions that arise in a second (or later) process.

Decision	Guidelines
At what point in the insertion process are transferred-in costs (from the shaping process) incurred?	Transferred-in costs are incurred at the *beginning* of the insertion process. The masks must be completely shaped before the insertion process begins.
What percentage of completion is used to calculate equivalent units in the "Transferred-in" column?	All units, whether completed and transferred out or still in ending work in process, are considered 100% complete with respect to transferred-in work and costs.
What checks and balances does the five-step process costing procedure provide?	The five-step procedure provides two important checks: **1.** The total units to account for (beginning inventory + units started or transferred in) *must equal* the total units accounted for (units completed and transferred out + units in ending inventory). **2.** The total costs to account for (cost of beginning inventory + costs incurred in the current period) *must equal* the total costs accounted for (cost of units completed and transferred out + cost of ending inventory).
What are the main goals of the Insertion Department's process costing?	One goal is to determine the cost of operating the department during the month. This information is by managers to control production costs. Another goal is to determine the cost of making each swim mask—from start to finish. The final goal is to split total costs between swim masks completed and transferred out to finished goods inventory and the masks that remain in the Insertion Department's ending work in process inventory.
What is a production cost report and how do managers use the information found on it?	A production cost report simply summarizes all five steps on one schedule. SeaView's managers use the cost per equivalent unit to determine the cost of producing a swim mask. These costs provide a basis for setting selling prices, performing profitability analysis to decide which products to emphasize, and so forth. These costs are also the basis for valuing inventory on the balance sheet and cost of goods sold on the income statement. Managers also use the cost per equivalent unit to control material and conversion costs and to evaluate the performance of production department managers.

SUMMARY PROBLEM 2

This problem extends the Summary Problem 1 to a second department. During May, Florida Tile Industries reports the following in its Finishing Department:

Finishing Department Data for May	
Information about units:	
Beginning work in process, May 1 (20% complete as to direct materials, 70% complete as to conversion work)	4,000 units
Transferred in from Tile-Forming Department during May	16,000 units
Completed and transferred out to Finished Goods Inventory during May	15,000 units
Ending work in process, May 31 (36% complete as to direct materials, 80% complete as to conversion work)	5,000 units
Information about costs:	
Work in process, May 1 (transferred-in costs, $10,000; direct materials costs, $488; conversion costs, $5,530)	$16,018
Transferred in from Tile-Forming Department during May (page 273)	38,400
Finishing Department direct materials added during May	6,400
Finishing Department conversion costs added during May	24,300

Requirements

1. Complete the 5-step process costing procedure to assign the Finishing Department's *total costs to account for* to units completed and to units in ending work in process inventory. (*Note*: Don't confuse the Finishing Department with finished goods inventory. The Finishing Department is Florida Tile's second process. The tiles do not become part of finished goods inventory until they have completed the second process, which happens to be called the Finishing Department.)
2. Make the journal entry to transfer the appropriate amount of cost to Finished Goods Inventory.
3. What is the cost of making one unit of product from start to finish?

▪ SOLUTION

Steps 1 and 2: Summarize the flow of physical units; compute output in terms of equivalent units.

FLORIDA TILE
FINISHING DEPARTMENT
Month Ended May 31

	Step 1	Step 2: Equivalent Units		
Flow of Production	Flow of Physical Units	Transferred-in	Direct Materials	Conversion Costs
Units to account for:				
Beginning work in process, May 1	4,000			
Transferred in from Tile-Forming Department during May	16,000			
Total physical units to account for	20,000			
Units accounted for:				
Completed and transferred out during May	15,000	15,000	15,000	15,000
Ending work in process, May 31	5,000	5,000	1,800*	4,000*
Total physical units accounted for	20,000			
Total equivalent units		20,000	16,800	19,000

*Ending inventory:
Direct materials: 5,000 units each 36% completed = 1,800 equivalent units
Converted costs: 5,000 units each 80% completed = 4,000 equivalent units

Steps 3 and 4: Summarize total costs to account for; compute the cost per equivalent unit.

FLORIDA TILE
FINISHING DEPARTMENT
Month Ended May 31

	Step 1	Step 2: Equivalent Units		
	Transferred-in	Direct Materials	Conversion Costs	Total
Beginning work in process, May 1	$10,000	$ 488	$ 5,530	$16,018
Costs added during May	38,400	6,400	24,300	69,100
Total costs to account for	$48,400	$ 6,888	$29,830	$85,118
Divide by total equivalent units	÷ 20,000	÷ 16,800	÷ 19,000	
Cost per equivalent unit	$ 2.42	$ 0.41	$ 1.57	

Step 5: Assign total costs to units completed and to units in ending work in process inventory.

FLORIDA TILE FINISHING DEPARTMENT Month Ended May 31				
Flow of Production	**Transferred-in**	**Direct Materials**	**Conversion Costs**	**Total**
Units completed and transferred out to				
Finished Goods Inventory	[15,000 × ($2.42 + $0.41 + $1.57)]			$66,000
Ending work in process, May 31:				
Transferred-in costs	[5,000 × $2.42]			12,100
Direct materials		[1,800 × $0.41]		738
Conversion costs			[4,000 × $1.57]	6,280
Total ending work in process, May 31				19,118
Total costs accounted for				$85,118

Requirement 2

Journal entry:

	Account	Debit	Credit
	Finished Goods Inventory	66,000	
	Work in Process Inventory—Finishing Department		66,000
	(To record the transfer of cost out of the Finishing Department and into Finished Goods Inventory.)		

Requirement 3

The cost of making one unit from start to finish is $4.40 ($66,000 transferred to Finished Goods Inventory divided by the 15,000 completed tiles). This consists of $2.42[4] of cost incurred in the Tile-Forming Department and $1.98 of cost incurred in the Finishing Department ($0.41 of direct materials and $1.57 of conversion costs).

[4]In Summary Problem 1, we saw that the average cost per unit in May was $2.40. The weighted-average method combines the current period's costs (May's costs) with any costs in beginning inventory to yield a weighted-average cost of $2.42 per unit.

END OF CHAPTER

Learning Objectives

- 1 Distinguish between the flow of costs in process costing and job costing
- 2 Compute equivalent units
- 3 Use process costing in the first production department
- 4 Prepare journal entries for a process costing system
- 5 Use process costing in a second or later production department

Accounting Vocabulary

Equivalent Units. (p. 260) Express the amount of work done during a period in terms of fully completed units of output.

Production Cost Report. (p. 280) Summarizes a processing department's operations for a period.

Transferred-In Costs. (p. 274) Costs incurred in a previous process that are carried forward as part of the product's cost when it moves to the next process.

Trash audit. (p. 268) Studying the contents of a company's trash in order to identify solid waste and scraps that could potentially be recycled, repurposed, or sold to create a new revenue stream. Also known as *waste audit* or *waste sort*.

Weighted-Average Method of Process Costing. (p. 261) A process costing method that *combines* any beginning inventory units (and costs) with the current period's units (and costs) to get a weighted-average cost.

Quick Check

1. *(Learning Objective 1)* Which of these companies would use process costing?
   a. Rose & Rose, an advertising agency
   b. Pace Foods, producer of Pace picante sauce
   c. Accenture management consultants
   d. Amazon.com
2. *(Learning Objective 1)* Which of these companies would use job costing?
   a. An oil refinery
   b. A dairy farm
   c. A paint manufacturer
   d. A hospital
3. *(Learning Objective 1)* All of the following statements are correct *except* for which of the following?
   a. Costs are accumulated by department when using process costing.
   b. Units produced are indistinguishable from each other in a process costing system.
   c. Process costing has the same basic purposes as job costing.
   d. Process costing would be appropriate for a custom cabinet maker.
4. *(Learning Objective 2)* Tucker Manufacturing uses weighted-average process costing. All materials at Tucker are added at the beginning of the production process. The equivalent units for materials at Tucker would be
   a. the units started plus the units in beginning work in process.
   b. the units completed and transferred out plus the units in beginning work in process.
   c. the units started plus the units in ending work in process.
   d. the units started and completed plus the units in ending work in process.
5. *(Learning Objective 2)* An equivalent unit of conversion costs is equal to
   a. an equivalent unit of material costs.
   b. the amount of conversion costs needed to produce one unit.
   c. the amount of conversion costs necessary to start a unit into work in process.
   d. half of the conversion costs necessary to produce one unit.

6. *(Learning Objective 2)* When using the weighted-average method of process costing, the computation of the cost per equivalent unit includes
   a. costs incurred during the current period only.
   b. costs incurred during the current period plus the cost of the beginning work in process inventory.
   c. costs incurred during the current period plus the cost of the ending work in process inventory.
   d. costs incurred during the current period plus all of the costs incurred in the prior period.
7. *(Learning Objective 3)* All of the following statements about process costing are true *except* for which of the following?
   a. Process costing is appropriate for those production processes where similar units are produced in a continuous flow.
   b. Equivalent units for materials and equivalent units for conversion costs are the same.
   c. Units in beginning work in process plus the units started into production should equal units in ending work in process plus units completed.
   d. Each process will have its own separate Work in Process Inventory account.
8. *(Learning Objective 3)* Which of the following statements describes Jelly Belly's process costing system?
   a. Direct materials and direct labor are traced to each specific order.
   b. Costs flow directly from a single Work in Process Inventory account to Finished Goods Inventory.
   c. Costs flow through a sequence of Work in Process Inventory accounts and then into Finished Goods Inventory from the final Work in Process Inventory account.
   d. The subsidiary Work in Process Inventory accounts consist of separate records for each individual order, detailing the materials, labor, and overhead assigned to that order.
9. *(Learning Objective 4)* The journal entry records the transfer of units from Department A to the next processing department, Department B, which includes a debit to
   a. Work in Process Inventory for Dept. B and a credit to Raw Materials Inventory.
   b. Work in Process Inventory for Dept. A and a credit to Work in Process Inventory for Dept. B.
   c. Work in Process Inventory for Dept. B and a credit to Work in Process Inventory for Dept. A.
   d. Finished Goods Inventory and a credit to Work in Process for Dept. A.
10. *(Learning Objective 5)* In general, transferred-in costs include
   a. costs incurred in the previous period.
   b. costs incurred in all prior periods.
   c. costs incurred in only the previous process.
   d. costs incurred in all prior processes.

Quick Check Answers

1. b 2. d 3. d 4. a 5. b 6. b 7. b 8. c 9. c 10. d

Short Exercises

S5-1 Compare flow of costs *(Learning Objective 1)*

Use Exhibit 5-1 to help you describe in your own words the major difference in the flow of costs between a job costing system and a process costing system.

S5-2 Flow of costs through Work in Process Inventory *(Learning Objective 1)*

Amazing Beans produces jelly beans in three sequential processing departments: Centers, Shells, and Packaging. Assume that the Shells processing department began September with $18,500 of unfinished jelly bean centers. During September, the Shells process used $42,800 of direct materials, used $12,600 of direct labor, and was allocated $17,700 of manufacturing overhead. In addition, $126,300 was transferred out of the Centers processing department during the month and $196,800 was transferred out of the Shells processing department during the month. These transfers represent the cost of the jelly beans transferred from one process to another.

1. Prepare a T-account for the "Work in Process Inventory—Shells" showing all activity that took place in the account during September.
2. What is the ending balance in the "Work in Process Inventory—Shells" on September 30? What does this figure represent?

S5-3 Recompute SeaView's equivalent units *(Learning Objective 2)*

Look at SeaView's Shaping Department's equivalent-unit computation in Exhibit 5-5. Suppose the ending work in process inventory is 30% of the way through the shaping process rather than 25% of the way through. Compute the total equivalent units of direct materials and conversion costs.

S5-4 Determine the physical flow of units (process costing Step 1) *(Learning Objective 2)*

Millson Soda's Bottling Department had 21,000 units in the beginning inventory of Work in Process on June 1. During June, 120,000 units were started into production. On June 30, 28,000 units were left in ending work in process inventory. Summarize the physical flow of units in a schedule.

S5-5 Compute equivalent units (process costing Step 2) *(Learning Objective 2)*

Quigby's Packaging Department had the following information at March 31. All direct materials are added at the *end* of the conversion process. The units in ending work in process inventory were only 28% of the way through the conversion process.

		Equivalent Units	
	Physical Units	**Direct Materials**	**Conversion Costs**
Units accounted for:			
Completed and transferred out	113,000		
Ending work in process, March 31	18,000		
Total physical units accounted for	131,000		
Total equivalent units			

Complete the schedule by computing the total equivalent units of direct materials and conversion costs for the month.

S5-6 Compute equivalent units (process costing Step 2) *(Learning Objective 2)*

The Frying Department of Crispy Potato Chips had 85,000 partially completed units in work in process at the end of August. All of the direct materials had been added to these units, but the units were only 62% of the way through the conversion process. In addition, 1,100,000 units had been completed and transferred out of the Frying Department to the Packaging Department during the month.

1. How many equivalent units of direct materials and equivalent units of conversion costs are associated with the 1,100,000 units completed and transferred out?
2. Compute the equivalent units of direct materials and the equivalent units of conversion costs associated with the 85,000 partially completed units still in ending work in process.
3. What are the total equivalent units of direct materials and the total equivalent units of conversion costs for the month?

S5-7 Summarize total costs to account for (process costing Step 3) *(Learning Objective 3)*

Romaine Company's Work in Process Inventory account had a $63,000 beginning balance on May 1 ($42,000 of this related to direct materials used during April, while $21,000 related to conversion costs incurred during April). During May, the following costs were incurred in the department:

Direct materials used	$101,000
Direct labor	$ 14,000
Manufacturing overhead allocated to the department	$158,000

Summarize the department's "Total costs to account for." Prepare a schedule that summarizes the department's total costs to account for by direct materials and conversion costs.

S5-8 Compute the cost per equivalent unit (process costing Step 4) *(Learning Objective 3)*

At the end of July, a company's mixing department had "Total costs to account for" of $755,702. Of this amount, $287,155 related to direct materials costs, while the remainder related to conversion costs. The department had 52,210 total equivalent units of direct materials and 45,490 total equivalent units of conversion costs for the month.

Compute the cost per equivalent unit for direct materials and the cost per equivalent unit for conversion costs.

S5-9 Recompute SeaView's cost per equivalent unit *(Learning Objective 3)*

Return to the original SeaView example in Exhibits 5-5 and 5-7. Suppose direct labor is $34,000 rather than $21,250. Now what is the conversion cost per equivalent unit?

S5-10 Assign costs (process costing Step 5) *(Learning Objective 3)*

Oscar Company produces its product using a *single* production process. For the month of December, Oscar Company determined its "cost per equivalent unit" to be as follows:

	Direct Materials	Conversion Costs
Cost per equivalent unit:	$5.00	$2.25

During the month, Oscar completed and transferred out 370,000 units to finished goods inventory. At month-end, 82,000 partially complete units remained in ending work in process inventory. These partially completed units were equal to 74,000 equivalent units of direct materials and 48,000 equivalent units of conversion costs.

1. Determine the total cost that should be assigned to the following:
   a. Units completed and transferred out
   b. Units in ending work in process inventory
2. What was the total costs accounted for?
3. What was Oscar's average cost of making one unit of its product?

S5-11 Flow of costs through Work in Process Inventory *(Learning Objective 4)*

Square-Tile produces its product in two processing departments: Forming and Finishing. The following T-account shows the Forming Department's Work in Process Inventory at July 31 prior to completing the five-step process costing procedure:

Work in Process Inventory—Forming Department

Beginning balance	$ 53,100	
Direct materials used	78,200	
Direct labor	14,100	
Manufacturing overhead allocated	126,000	

1. What is the Forming Department's "Total costs to account for" for the month of July?
2. Assume that after using the five-step process costing procedure, the company determines that the "cost to be assigned to units completed and transferred out" is $243,300. What journal entry is needed to record the transfer of costs to the Finishing Department?
3. After the journal entry is made, what will be the new ending balance in the Forming Department's Work in Process Inventory account?

S5-12 Assign total costs in a second processing department *(Learning Objective 5)*

After completing Steps 1–4 of the process costing procedure, Doyle Corporation arrived at the following equivalent units and costs per equivalent unit for its *final* production department for the month of August:

	Equivalent Units		
	Transferred-in	Direct Material	Conversion Costs
Units completed and transferred out	73,000	73,000	73,000
Units in ending work in process,			
August 31	9,500	8,200	3,500
Total equivalent units	82,500	81,200	76,500
Cost per equivalent unit..........	$2.94	$0.55	$1.36

1. How much cost should be assigned to the
   a. units completed and transferred out to Finished Goods Inventory during August?
   b. partially complete units still in ending work in process inventory at the end of August?
2. What was the "Total cost accounted for" during August? What other important figure must this match? What does this figure tell you?
3. What is Doyle Corporation's average cost of making *each unit* of its product from the first production department all the way through the final production department?

S5-13 Find unit cost and gross profit on a final product *(Learning Objective 5)*

Kormic Co. produces Formica countertops in two sequential production departments: Forming and Polishing. The Polishing Department calculated the following costs per equivalent unit (square feet) on its April production cost report:

	Transferred-in	Direct Materials	Conversion Costs
Cost per equivalent unit:	$2.94	$0.60	$1.16

During April, 140,000 square feet were completed and transferred out of the Polishing Department to Finished Goods Inventory. The countertops were subsequently sold for $12.50 per square foot.

1. What was the cost per square foot of the finished product?
2. Did most of the production cost occur in the Forming Department or in the Polishing Department? Explain how you can tell.
3. What was the gross profit per square foot?
4. What was the total gross profit on the countertops produced in April?

The following data set is used for S5-14 through S5-18:

Cold Springs Data Set: Filtration Department

Cold Springs produces premium bottled water. Cold Springs purchases artesian water, stores the water in large tanks, and then runs the water through two processes:

- Filtration, where workers microfilter and ozonate the water
- Bottling, where workers bottle and package the filtered water

During November, the filtration process incurs the following costs in processing 225,000 liters:

Wages of workers operating the filtration equipment	$ 12,800
Wages of workers operating ozonation equipment	$ 14,400
Manufacturing overhead allocated to filtration	$ 38,050
Water	$ 148,500

Cold Springs has no beginning inventory in the Filtration Department.

S5-14 Compute cost per liter *(Learning Objective 1)*

Refer to the Cold Springs Filtration Department Data Set.

1. Compute the November conversion costs in the Filtration Department.
2. If the Filtration Department completely processed 225,000 liters, what would be the average filtration cost per liter?
3. Now, assume that the total costs of the filtration process listed in the previous chart yield 150,000 liters that are completely filtered and ozonated, while the remaining 75,000 liters are only partway through the process at the end of November. Is the cost per completely filtered and ozonated liter higher, lower, or the same as in Requirement 2? Why?

S5-15 Summarize physical flow and compute equivalent units *(Learning Objective 2)*

Refer to the Cold Springs Filtration Department Data Set. At Cold Springs, water is added at the beginning of the filtration process. Conversion costs are added evenly throughout the process, and in November, 150,000 liters have been completed and transferred out of the Filtration Department to the Bottling Department. The 75,000 liters remaining in the Filtration Department's ending work in process inventory are 90% of the way through the filtration process. Recall that Cold Springs has no beginning inventories.

1. Draw a time line for the filtration process.
2. Complete the first two steps of the process costing procedure for the Filtration Department: summarize the physical flows of units and then compute the equivalent units of direct materials and conversion costs. Your answer should look similar to Exhibit 5-5.

S5-16 Continuation of S5-15: Summarize total costs to account for and compute cost per equivalent unit *(Learning Objective 3)*

Refer to the Cold Springs Filtration Department Data Set and your answer to S5-15. Complete Steps 3 and 4 of the process costing procedure: Summarize total costs to account for and then compute the cost per equivalent unit for both direct materials and conversion costs.

S5-17 Continuation of S5-15 and S5-16: Assign costs *(Learning Objective 3)*

Refer to the Cold Springs Filtration Department Data Set and your answer to S5-15 and S5-16. Complete Step 5 of the process costing procedure: Assign costs to units completed and to units in ending inventory. Prepare a schedule that answers the following questions.

1. What is the cost of the 150,000 liters completed and transferred out of the Filtration Department?
2. What is the cost of 75,000 liters remaining in the Filtration Department's ending work in process inventory?

S5-18 Continuation of S5-17: Record journal entry and post to T-account *(Learning Objective 4)*

Refer to the Cold Springs Filtration Department Data Set and your answer to S5-17.

1. Record the journal entry to transfer the cost of the 150,000 liters completed and transferred out of the Filtration Department and into the Bottling Department.
2. Record all of the transactions in the "Work in Process Inventory—Filtration" T-account.

The following data set is used for S5-19 through S5-22.

Fresh Springs Data Set: Bottling Department

Fresh Springs produces premium bottled water. The preceding Short Exercises considered the first process in bottling premium water — Filtration. We now consider Fresh Springs second process—Bottling. In the Bottling Department, workers bottle the filtered water and pack the bottles into boxes. Conversion costs are incurred evenly throughout the Bottling process, but packaging materials are not added until the end of the process.

February data from the Bottling Department follow:

Beginning work in process inventory (40% of the way through the process)	5,000 liters
Transferred in from Filtration	150,000 liters
Completed and transferred out to Finished Goods Inventory in February	153,000 liters
Ending work in process inventory (80% of the way through the bottling process)	2,000 liters

Costs in beginning work in process inventory		Costs added during February	
Transferred in	$750	Transferred in	$131,000
Direct materials	0	Direct materials	32,130
Direct labor	630	Direct labor	33,300
Manufacturing overhead	2,478	Manufacturing overhead	22,340
Total beginning work in process inventory as of February 1	$3,858	Total costs added during February	$218,770

The Filtration Department completed and transferred out 150,000 liters at a total cost of $131,000.

S5-19 Compute equivalent units in second department *(Learning Objectives 2 & 5)*

Refer to the Fresh Springs Bottling Department Data Set.

1. Draw a time line.
2. Complete the first two steps of the process costing procedure for the Bottling Department: summarize the physical flow of units and then compute the equivalent units of direct materials and conversion costs.

S5-20 Continuation of S5-19: Compute cost per equivalent unit in second department *(Learning Objective 5)*

Refer to the Fresh Springs Bottling Department Data Set and your answer to S5-19. Complete Steps 3 and 4 of the process costing procedure: Summarize total costs to account for and then compute the cost per equivalent unit for both direct materials and conversion costs.

S5-21 Continuation of S5-19 and S5-20: Assign costs in second department *(Learning Objective 5)*

Refer to the Fresh Springs Bottling Department Data Set and your answers to S5-19 and S5-20. Complete Step 5 of the process costing procedure: Assign costs to units completed and to units in ending inventory.

S5-22 Continuation of S5-21: Record journal entry and post to T-account *(Learning Objective 4)*

Refer to the Fresh Springs Bottling Department Data Set and your answer to S5-21.

1. Prepare the journal entry to record the cost of units completed and transferred to finished goods.
2. Post all transactions to the "Work in Process Inventory—Bottling" T-account. What is the ending balance?

EXERCISES Group A

E5-23A Diagram flow of costs *(Learning Objective 1)*

Outdoor Living produces outdoor teak furniture in a three-stage process that includes Milling, Assembling, and Finishing, in that order. Direct materials are added in the Milling and Finishing Departments. Direct labor and overhead are incurred in all three departments. The company's general ledger includes the following accounts:

Cost of Goods Sold	Materials Inventory
Wages Payable	Finished Goods Inventory
Work in Process Inventory—Milling	Manufacturing Overhead
Work in Process Inventory—Assembling	
Work in Process Inventory—Finishing	

Outline the flow of costs through the company's accounts, including a brief description of each flow. Include a T-account for each account title given.

E5-24A Analyze flow of costs through inventory T-accounts *(Learning Objective 1)*

Grandma's Bakery mass-produces bread using three sequential processing departments: Mixing, Baking, and Packaging. The following transactions occurred during January:

1. Direct materials used in the Packaging Department	$ 32,000
2. Costs assigned to units completed and transferred out of Mixing	$226,000
3. Direct labor incurred in the Mixing Department	$ 11,500
4. Beginning balance: Work in Process Inventory-Baking	$ 15,000
5. Manufacturing overhead allocated to the Baking Department	$ 79,000
6. Beginning balance: Finished Goods	$ 4,000
7. Costs assigned to units completed and transferred out of Baking	$301,000
8. Beginning balance: Work in Process Inventory-Mixing	$ 12,700
9. Direct labor incurred in the Packaging Department	$ 8,400
10. Manufacturing overhead allocated to the Mixing Department	$ 67,000
11. Direct materials used in the Mixing Department	$155,000
12. Beginning balance: Raw Materials Inventory	$ 23,900
13. Costs assigned to units completed and transferred out of Packaging	$346,500
14. Beginning balance: Work in Process Inventory-Packaging	$ 8,100
15. Purchases of Raw Materials	$173,000
16. Direct labor incurred in the Baking Department	$ 4,700
17. Manufacturing overhead allocated to the Packaging Department	$ 47,000
18. Cost of goods sold	$347,500

Note: No direct materials were used by the Baking Department.

Requirements

1. Post each of these transactions to the company's inventory T-accounts. You should set up separate T-accounts for the following:
   - Raw Materials Inventory
   - Work in Process Inventory—Mixing Department
   - Work in Process Inventory—Baking Department
   - Work in Process Inventory—Packaging Department
   - Finished Goods Inventory
2. Determine the balance at month-end in each of the inventory accounts.
3. Assume that 3,150,000 loaves of bread were completed and transferred out of the Packaging Department during the month. What was the cost per unit of making each loaf of bread (from start to finish)?

E5-25A Summarize physical units and compute equivalent units (process costing Steps 1 and 2) *(Learning Objective 2)*

Stacy's Strawberry Pies collected the following production information relating to April's baking operations:

	Physical Units	Direct Materials (% complete)	Conversion Costs (% complete)
Beginning work in process	205,000	—	—
Ending work in process	155,000	70%	90%
Units started during the month......	1,025,000		

Requirements

Complete the first two steps in the process costing procedure:

1. Summarize the flow of physical units.
2. Compute output in terms of equivalent units.

E5-26A Compute equivalent units in a second processing department *(Learning Objectives 2 & 5)*

Maynard's Mayonnaise uses a process costing system to determine its product's cost. The last of the three processes is packaging. The Packaging Department reported the following information for the month of May:

		Equivalent Units		
	Physical Units	Transferred-in	Direct Materials	Conversion Costs
Units to account for:				
Beginning work in process	27,000			
Transferred in during May	226,000			
Total units to account for.................	(a)			
Units account for:				
Completed and transferred out	(b)	(d)	(g)	(j)
Ending work in process	32,000	(e)	(h)	(k)
Total units accounted for:	(c)			
Total equivalent units.......................		(f)	(i)	(l)

The units in ending work in process inventory were 70% complete with respect to direct materials, but only 40% complete with respect to conversion.

Requirement

Summarize the flow of physical units and compute output in terms of equivalent units in order to arrive at the missing figures (a) through (l).

E5-27A Complete five-step procedure in first department *(Learning Objective 3)*

Paint by Number prepares and packages paint products. Paint by Number has two departments: (1) Blending and (2) Packaging. Direct materials are added at the beginning of the blending process (dyes) and at the end of the packaging process (cans). Conversion costs are added evenly throughout each process. Data from the month of May for the Blending Department are as follows:

Gallons:	
Beginning work in process inventory	0
Started production	9,200 gallons
Completed and transferred out to Packaging in May	6,600 gallons
Ending work in process inventory (30% of the way through the blending process)	2,600 gallons
Costs:	
Beginning work in process inventory	$ 0
Costs added during May:	
Direct materials (dyes)	5,980
Direct labor	850
Manufacturing overhead	1,733
Total costs added during May	$8,563

Requirements

1. Draw a time line.
2. Summarize the physical flow of units and compute total equivalent units for direct materials and for conversion costs.
3. Summarize total costs to account for and find the cost per equivalent unit for direct materials and conversion costs.
4. Assign total costs to units (gallons):
   a. Completed and transferred out to the Packaging Department
   b. In the Blending Department ending work in process inventory
5. What is the average cost per gallon transferred out of the Blending Department to the Packaging Department? Why would Paint by Number's managers want to know this cost?

E5-28A Continuation of E5-27A: Journal entries *(Learning Objective 4)*

Return to the Blending Department for Paint by Number in E5-27A.

Requirements

1. Present the journal entry to record the use of direct materials and direct labor and the allocation of manufacturing overhead to the Blending Department. Also, give the journal entry to record the costs of the gallons completed and transferred out to the Packaging Department.
2. Post the journal entries to the "Work in Process Inventory—Blending" T-account. What is the ending balance?

E5-29A Record journal entries *(Learning Objective 4)*

Record the following process costing transactions in the general journal:

a. Purchase of raw materials on account, $9,100
b. Requisition of direct materials to
   Assembly Department, $4,100
   Finishing Department, $2,600
c. Incurrence and payment of direct labor, $10,600
d. Incurrence of manufacturing overhead costs:
   Property taxes—plant, $1,600
   Utilities—plant, $4,800
   Insurance—plant, $1,000
   Depreciation—plant, $3,700
e. Assignment of conversion costs to the Assembly Department:
   Direct labor, $5,100
   Manufacturing overhead, $2,100
f. Assignment of conversion costs to the Finishing Department:
   Direct labor, $4,300
   Manufacturing overhead, $6,500
g. Cost of goods completed and transferred out of the Assembly Department to the Finishing Department, $10,350
h. Cost of goods completed and transferred out of the Finishing Department into Finished Goods Inventory, $15,100

E5-30A Compute equivalent units and assign costs *(Learning Objectives 2, 3, & 4)*

The Assembly Department of Value Surge Protectors began September with no work in process inventory. During the month, production that cost $44,118 (direct materials, $11,638, and conversion costs, $32,480) was started on 25,000 units. Value completed and transferred to the Testing Department a total of 19,000 units. The ending work in process inventory was 36% complete as to direct materials and 70% complete as to conversion work.

Requirements

1. Compute the equivalent units for direct materials and conversion costs.
2. Compute the cost per equivalent unit.
3. Assign the costs to units completed and transferred out and ending work in process inventory.
4. Record the journal entry for the costs transferred out of the Assembly Department to the Testing Department.
5. Post all of the transactions in the "Work in Process Inventory—Assembly" T-account. What is the ending balance?

E5-31A Complete five-step procedure in first department *(Learning Objective 3)*

Samson Winery in Kingston, New York, has two departments: Fermenting and Packaging. Direct materials are added at the beginning of the fermenting process (grapes) and at the end of the packaging process (bottles). Conversion costs are added evenly throughout each process. Data from the month of March for the Fermenting Department are as follows:

Gallons:	
Beginning work in process inventory	2,200 gallons
Started production	5,980 gallons
Completed and transferred out to Packaging in March	6,480 gallons
Ending work in process inventory (80% of the way through the fermenting process)	1,700 gallons
Costs:	
Beginning work in process inventory ($2,300 of direct materials and $2,376 of conversion cost)	$ 4,676
Costs added during March:	
Direct materials	$ 9,970
Direct labor	900
Manufacturing overhead	2,212
Total costs added during March	$13,082

Requirements

1. Draw a time line for the Fermenting Department.
2. Summarize the flow of physical units and compute the total equivalent units.
3. Summarize total costs to account for and compute the cost per equivalent unit for direct materials and conversion costs.
4. Assign total costs to units (gallons):
   a. Completed and transferred out to the Packaging Department
   b. In the Fermenting Department ending work in process inventory
5. What is the average cost per gallon transferred out of Fermenting into Packaging? Why would Samson's managers want to know this cost?

E5-32A Sustainability and process costing *(Learning Objective 3)*

Sylvan Industries manufactures plastic bottles for the food industry. On average, Sylvan pays $75 per ton for its plastics. Sylvan's waste disposal company has increased its waste disposal charge to $55 per ton for solid and inert waste. Sylvan generates a total of 500 tons of waste per month.

Sylvan's managers have been evaluating the production processes for areas to cut waste. I the process of making plastic bottles, a certain amount of machine "drool" occurs. Machine drool is the excess plastic that "drips" off the machine between molds. In the past, Sylvan has discarded the machine drool. In an average month, 150 tons of machine drool is generated.

Management has arrived at three possible courses of action for the machine drool issue:

1. Do nothing and pay the increased waste disposal charge.
2. Sell the machine drool waste to a local recycler for $10 per ton.
3. Re-engineer the production process at an annual cost of $50,000. This change in the production process would cause the amount of machine drool generated to be reduced by 50% each month. The remaining machine drool would then be sold to a local recycler for $10 per ton.

Requirements

1. What is the annual cost of the machine drool currently? Include both the original plastic cost and the waste disposal cost.
2. How much would the company save per year (net) if the machine drool were to be sold to the local recycler?

3. How much would the company save per year (net) if the production process were to be re-engineered?
4. What do you think the company should do? Explain your rationale. What do you think the company should do? Explain your rationale.

E5-33A Complete five-step procedure and journalize result

(Learning Objectives 3 & 4)

The following information was taken from the ledger of Paulson Roping:

Work in Process—Forming			
Beginning inventory, October 1	$ 37,874	Transferred to Finishing	$?
Direct materials	189,294		
Conversion costs	162,200		
Ending inventory	?		

The Forming Department had 10,250 partially complete units in beginning work in process inventory. The department started work on 74,150 units during the month and ended the month with 8,400 units still in work in process. These unfinished units were 60% complete as to direct materials but 20% complete as to conversion work. The beginning balance of $37,874 consisted of $21,410 of direct materials and $16,464 of conversion costs.

Requirement

Journalize the transfer of costs to the Finishing Department. (*Hint:* Complete the five-step process costing procedure to determine how much cost to transfer.)

E5-34A Compute equivalent units in two later departments

(Learning Objectives 2 & 5)

Selected production and cost data of Jane's Fudge follow for May:

	Flow of Physical Units	
Flow of Production	**Mixing Department**	**Heating Department**
Units to account for:		
Beginning work in process, May 1	21,000	8,000
Transferred in during May	76,000	85,000
Total physical units to account for	97,000	93,000
Units accounted for:		
Completed and transferred out during May	86,000	77,000
Ending work in process, May 31	11,000	16,000
Total physical units accounted for	97,000	93,000

On May 31, the Mixing Department's ending work in process inventory was 70% complete as to materials and 10% complete as to conversion costs.

On May 31, the Heating Department's ending work in process inventory was 55% complete as to materials and 45% complete as to conversion costs.

Requirement

Compute the equivalent units for transferred-in costs, direct materials, and conversion costs for both the Mixing and the Heating Departments.

E5-35A Complete five-step procedure in second department *(Learning Objective 5)*

Hamstein Semiconductors experienced the following activity in its Photolithography Department during December. Materials are added at the beginning of the photolithography process.

Units:	
Work in process, December 1 (80% of the way through the process)	7,000 units
Transferred in from the Polishing and Cutting Department during December	29,000 units
Completed during December	? units
Work in process, December 31 (70% of the way through the process)	11,000 units
Costs:	
Work in process, December 1 (transferred-in costs, $21,500; direct materials costs, $20,300; and conversion costs, $23,750)	$65,550
Transferred in from the Polishing and Cutting Department during December	97,300
Direct materials added during December	69,700
Conversion costs added during December	90,700

Requirements

1. Summarize flow of physical units and compute total equivalent units for three cost categories: transferred-in, direct materials, and conversion costs.
2. Summarize total costs to account for and compute the cost per equivalent unit for each cost category.
3. Assign total costs to (a) units completed and transferred to Finished Goods Inventory and (b) units in December 31 Work in Process Inventory.

EXERCISES Group B

E5-36B Diagram flow of costs *(Learning Objective 1)*

Safety Shutters produces hurricane shutters in a three-stage process that includes Cutting, Assembling, and Finishing, in that order. Direct materials are added in the Cutting and Finishing Departments. Direct labor and overhead are incurred in all three departments. The company's general ledger includes the following accounts:

Cost of Goods Sold	Materials Inventory
Wages Payable	Finished Goods Inventory
Work in Process Inventory—Cutting	Manufacturing Overhead
Work in Process Inventory—Assembling	
Work in Process Inventory—Finishing	

Outline the flow of costs through the company's accounts, including a brief description of each flow. Include a T-account for each account title given.

E5-37B Analyze flow of costs through inventory T-accounts *(Learning Objective 1)*

Early Start Bakery mass-produces bread using three sequential processing departments: Mixing, Baking, and Packaging. The following transactions occurred during May:

1. Direct materials used in the Packaging Department	$ 31,000
2. Costs assigned to units completed and transferred out of Mixing	$223,000
3. Direct labor incurred in the Mixing Department	$ 11,500
4. Beginning balance: Work in Process Inventory—Baking	$ 15,300
5. Manufactured overhead allocated to the Baking Department	$ 77,000
6. Beginning balance: Finished Goods Inventory	$ 4,500
7. Costs assigned to units completed and transferred out of Baking	$306,000
8. Beginning balance: Work in Process Inventory—Mixing	$ 12,400
9. Direct labor incurred in the Packaging Department	$ 8,700
10. Manufacturing overhead allocated to the Mixing Department	$ 61,000
11. Direct materials used in the Mixing Department	$153,000
12. Beginning balance: Raw Materials Inventory	$ 23,700
13. Costs assigned to units completed and transferred out of Packaging	$320,000
14. Beginning balance: Work in Process Inventory—Packaging	$ 8,500
15. Purchases of Raw Materials	$170,000
16. Direct labor incurred in the Baking Department	$ 4,100
17. Manufacturing overhead allocated to the Packaging Department	$ 44,000
18. Cost of goods sold	$323,000

Requirements

1. Post each of these transactions to the company's inventory T-accounts. You should set up separate T-accounts for the following:
   - Raw Materials Inventory
   - Work in Process Inventory—Mixing Department
   - Work in Process Inventory—Baking Department
   - Work in Process Inventory—Packaging Department
   - Finished Goods Inventory
2. Determine the balance at month-end in each of the inventory accounts.

3. Assume 3,200,000 loaves of bread were completed and transferred out of the Packaging Department during the month. What was the cost per unit of making each loaf of bread (from start to finish)?

E5-38B Summarize physical units and compute equivalent units (process costing Steps 1 and 2) *(Learning Objective 2)*

Patty's Pumpkin Pies collected the following production information relating to September's baking operations:

	Physical Units	Direct Materials (% complete)	Conversion Costs (% complete)
Beginning work in process............	209,000	—	—
Ending work in process.................	159,000	75%	85%
Units started during the month.....	990,000		

Requirements

Complete the first two steps in the process costing procedure:

1. Summarize the flow of physical units.
2. Compute output in terms of equivalent units.

E5-39B Compute equivalent units in a second processing department *(Learning Objectives 2 & 5)*

McGregor's Mayonnaise uses a process costing system to determine its product's cost. The last of the three processes is packaging. The Packaging Department reported the following information for the month of August:

		Equivalent Units		
	Physical Units	Transferred-in	Direct Materials	Conversion Costs
Units to account for:				
Beginning work in process	27,000			
Transferred in during July	231,000			
Total units to account for	(a)			
Units accounted for:				
Completed and transferred out	(b)	(d)	(g)	(j)
Ending work in process	32,000	(e)	(h)	(k)
Total units accounted for:	(c)			
Total Equivalent Units		(f)	(i)	(l)

The units in ending work in process inventory were 90% complete with respect to direct materials, but only 60% complete with respect to conversion.

Requirement

Summarize the flow of physical units and compute output in terms of equivalent units in order to arrive at the missing figures (a) through (l).

E5-40B Complete five-step procedure in first department *(Learning Objective 3)*

Step-by-Step Painting prepares and packages paint products. Step-by-Step has two departments: (1) Blending and (2) Packaging. Direct materials are added at the beginning of the blending process (dyes) and at the end of the packaging process (cans). Conversion costs are added evenly throughout each process. Data from the month of May for the Blending Department are as follows:

Gallons:	
Beginning work in process inventory	0
Started production	9,000 gallons
Completed and transferred out to Packaging in May	6,500 gallons
Ending work in process inventory (30% of the way through the blending process)	2,500 gallons
Costs:	
Beginning work in process inventory	$ 0
Costs added during May:	
Direct materials (dyes)	$5,670
Direct labor	800
Manufacturing overhead	2,100
Total costs added during May	$8,570

Requirements

1. Fill in the time line for the Blending Department.
2. Summarize the physical flow of units and compute total equivalent units for direct materials and for conversion costs.
3. Summarize total costs to account for and find the cost per equivalent unit for direct materials and for conversion costs.
4. Assign total costs to units (gallons):
   a. Completed and transferred out to the Packaging Department.
   b. In the Blending Department ending work in process inventory.
5. What is the average cost per gallon transferred out of the Blending Department to the Packaging Department? Why would Step-by-Step Painting's managers want to know this cost?

E5-41B Continuation of E5-40B: Journal entries *(Learning Objective 4)*

Return to the Blending Department for Step-by-Step Painting in E5-40B.

Requirements

1. Present the journal entry to record the use of direct materials and direct labor and the allocation of manufacturing overhead to the Blending Department. Also, give the journal entry to record the costs of the gallons completed and transferred out to the Packaging Department.
2. Post the journal entries to the "Work in Process Inventory—Blending" T-account. What is the ending balance?

E5-42B Record journal entries *(Learning Objective 4)*

Record the following process costing transactions in the general journal:

a. Purchase of raw materials on account, $9,500
b. Requisition of direct materials to
   Assembly Department, $4,000
   Finishing Department, $2,700
c. Incurrence and payment of manufacturing labor, $10,600
d. Incurrence of manufacturing overhead costs:
   Property taxes—plant, $1,900
   Utilities—plant, $4,100

Insurance—plant, $1,000
Depreciation—plant, $3,400

e. Assignment of conversion costs to the Assembly Department:
Direct labor, $5,200
Manufacturing overhead, $2,400

f. Assignment of conversion costs to the Finishing Department:
Direct labor, $4,600
Manufacturing overhead, $6,000

g. Cost of goods completed and transferred out of the Assembly Department to the Finishing Department, $10,250

h. Cost of goods completed and transferred out of the Finishing Department into Finished Goods Inventory, $15,700

E5-43B Compute equivalent units and assign costs *(Learning Objectives 2, 3, & 4)*

The Assembly Department of Zip Surge Protectors began September with no work in process inventory. During the month, production that cost $39,860 (direct materials, $9,900, and conversion costs, $29,960) was started on 23,000 units. Zip completed and transferred to the Testing Department a total of 15,000 units. The ending work in process inventory was 37.5% complete as to direct materials and 80% complete as to conversion work.

Requirements

1. Compute the equivalent units for direct materials and conversion costs.
2. Compute the cost per equivalent unit.
3. Assign the costs to units completed and transferred out and ending work in process inventory.
4. Record the journal entry for the costs transferred out of the Assembly Department to the Testing Department.
5. Post all of the transactions in the "Work in Process Inventory—Assembly" T-account. What is the ending balance?

E5-44B Complete five-step procedure in first department *(Learning Objective 3)*

Shelton Winery in Kingston, New York, has two departments: Fermenting and Packaging. Direct materials are added at the beginning of the fermenting process (grapes) and at the end of the packaging process (bottles). Conversion costs are added evenly throughout each process. Data from the month of March for the Fermenting Department are as follows:

Gallons:	
Beginning work in process inventory	3,000 gallons
Started production	4,840 gallons
Completed and transferred out to Packaging in March	6,490 gallons
Ending work in process inventory (80% of the way through the fermenting process)	1,350 gallons
Costs:	
Beginning work in process inventory ($2,000 of direct materials and $3,615 of conversion cost)	
Costs added during March:	$ 5,615
Direct materials	8,192
Direct labor	1,050
Manufacturing overhead	2,148
Total costs added during March	$11,390

Requirements

1. Draw a time line for the Fermenting Department.
2. Summarize the flow of physical units and compute the total equivalent units.

3. Summarize total costs to account for and compute the cost per equivalent unit for direct materials and conversion costs.
4. Assign total costs to units (gallons):
   a. Completed and transferred out to the Packaging Department.
   b. In the Fermenting Department ending work in process inventory
5. What is the average cost per gallon transferred out of Fermenting into Packaging? Why would Shelton's managers want to know this cost?

E5-45B Sustainability and process costing *(Learning Objective 3)*

Blueson Industries manufactures plastic bottles for the food industry. On average, Blueson pays $95 per ton for its plastics. Blueson's waste disposal company has increased its waste disposal charge to $65 per ton for solid and inert waste. Blueson generates a total of 1,000 tons of waste per month.

Blueson's managers have been evaluating the production processes for areas to cut waste. In the process of making plastic bottles, a certain amount of machine "drool" occurs. Machine drool is the excess plastic that "drips" off the machine between bolds. In the past, Blueson has discarded the machine drool. In an average month, 300 tons of machine drool are generated.

Management has arrived at three possible courses of action for the machine drool issue:

1. Do nothing and pay the increase waste disposal charge.
2. Sell the machine drool waste to a local recycler for $20 per ton.
3. Re-engineer the production process at an annual cost of $120,000. This change in the production process would cause the amount of machine drool generated to be reduced by 50% each month. The remaining machine drool would then be sold to a local recycler for $20 per ton.

Requirements

1. What is the annual cost of the machine drool currently? Include both the original plastics cost and the waste disposal cost.
2. How much would the company save per year (net) if the machine drool were to be sold at the local recycler?
3. How much would the company save per year (net) if the production process were to be re-engineered?
4. What do you think the company should do? Explain your rationale.

E5-46B Complete five-step procedure and journalize result *(Learning Objectives 3 & 4)*

The following information was taken from the ledger of Cleveland Roping:

Work in Process—Forming

Beginning inventory, October 1	62,618	Transferred to Finishing	?
Direct materials	214,978		
Conversion costs	162,600		
Ending inventory	?		

The Forming Department had 10,450 partially complete units in beginning work in process inventory. The department started work on 69,350 units during the month and ended the month with 8,800 units still in work in process. These unfinished units were 60% complete as to direct materials but 20% complete as to conversion work. The beginning balance of $62,618 consisted of $21,490 of direct materials and $41,128 of conversion costs.

Requirement

Journalize the transfer of costs to the Finishing Department. (*Hint*: Complete the five-step process costing procedure to determine how much cost to transfer.)

E5-47B Compute equivalent units in two later departments

(Learning Objectives 2 & 5)

Selected production and cost data of Karen's Fudge follow for May:

Flow of Production	Flow of Physical Units	
	Mixing Department	Heating Department
Units to account for:		
Beginning work in process, May 1	22,000	5,000
Transferred in during May	73,000	83,000
Total physical units to account for	95,000	88,000
Units accounted for:		
Completed and transferred out during May	83,000	78,000
Ending work in process, May 31	12,000	10,000
Total physical units accounted for	95,000	88,000

On May 31, the Mixing Department's ending work in process inventory was 80% complete as to materials and 10% complete as to conversion costs. On May 31, the Heating Department's ending work in process inventory was 75% complete as to materials and 65% complete as to conversion costs.

Requirement

Compute the equivalent units for transferred-in costs, direct materials, and conversion costs for both the Mixing and the Heating Departments.

E5-48B Complete five-step procedure in second department

(Learning Objective 5)

Brookman Semiconductors experienced the following activity in its Photolithography Department during December. Materials are added at the beginning of the photolithography process.

Units:	
Work in process, December 1 (80% of the way through the process)	5,000 units
Transferred in from the Polishing and Cutting Department during December	22,000 units
Completed during December	? units
Work in process, December 31 (70% of the way through the process)	8,000 units
Costs:	
Work in process, December 1 (transferred-in costs, $21,900; direct materials costs, $20,750; and conversion costs, $5,540)	$48,190
Transferred in from the Polishing and Cutting Department during December	96,900
Direct materials added during December	57,550
Conversion costs added during December	90,400

Requirements

1. Summarize flow of physical units and compute total equivalent units for three cost categories: transferred-in, direct materials, and conversion costs.
2. Summarize total costs to account for and compute the cost per equivalent unit for each cost category.
3. Assign total costs to (a) units completed and transferred to Finished Goods Inventory and (b) units in December 31 Work in Process Inventory.

PROBLEMS Group A

P5-49A Process costing in a single processing department

(Learning Objectives 1, 2, & 3)

Great Lips produces a lip balm used for cold-weather sports. The balm is manufactured in a single processing department. No lip balm was in process on May 31, and Great Lips started production on 20,500 lip balm tubes during June. Direct materials are added at the beginning of the process, but conversion costs are incurred evenly throughout the process. Completed production for June totaled 15,200 units. The June 30 work in process was 40% of the way through the production process. Direct materials costing $4,305 were placed in production during June, and direct labor of $3,410 and manufacturing overhead of $920 were assigned to the process.

Requirements

1. Draw a time line for Great Lips.
2. Use the time line to help you compute the total equivalent units and the cost per equivalent unit for June.
3. Assign total costs to (a) units completed and transferred to Finished Goods and (b) units still in process at June 30.
4. Prepare a T-account for Work in Process Inventory to show activity during June, including the June 30 balance.

P5-50A Process costing in a first department *(Learning Objectives 1, 3, & 4)*

The Pennsylvania Furniture Company produces dining tables in a three-stage process: Sawing, Assembly, and Staining. Costs incurred in the Sawing Department during September are summarized as follows:

Work in Process Inventory—Sawing

September 1 balance	0	
Direct materials	1,848,000	
Direct labor	142,000	
Manufacturing overhead	173,000	

Direct materials (lumber) are added at the beginning of the sawing process, while conversion costs are incurred evenly throughout the process. September activity in the Sawing Department included sawing of 14,000 meters of lumber, which were transferred to the Assembly Department. Also, work began on 2,500 meters of lumber, which on September 30 were 70% of the way through the sawing process.

Requirements

1. Draw a time line for the Sawing Department.
2. Use the time line to help you compute the number of equivalent units and the cost per equivalent unit in the Sawing Department for September.
3. Show that the sum of (a) cost of goods transferred out of the Sawing Department and (b) ending "Work in Process Inventory—Sawing" equals the total cost accumulated in the department during September.
4. Journalize all transactions affecting the company's sawing process during September, including those already posted.

P5-51A Five-step process: Materials added at different points *(Learning Objectives 1, 2, & 3)*

Tasty Chicken produces canned chicken a la king. The chicken a la king passes through three departments: (1) Mixing, (2) Retort (sterilization), and (3) Packing. In the Mixing Department, chicken and cream are added at the beginning of the process, the mixture is partly cooked, and chopped green peppers and mushrooms are added at the end of the process. Conversion costs are added evenly throughout the mixing process. November data from the Mixing Department are as follows:

Gallons		Costs	
Beginning work in process inventory	0 gallons	Beginning work in process inventory	$ 0
Started production	14,300 gallons	Costs added during November:	
Completed and transferred out to Retort in November	13,600 gallons	Chicken	21,340
		Cream	4,400
Ending work in process inventory (60% of the way through the mixing process)	700 gallons	Green peppers and mushrooms	5,440
		Direct labor	11,200
		Manufacturing overhead	9,830
		Total costs	$52,210

Requirements

1. Draw a time line for the Mixing Department.
2. Use the time line to help you summarize the flow of physical units and compute the equivalent units. (*Hint:* Each direct material added at a different point in the production process requires its own equivalent-unit computation.)
3. Compute the cost per equivalent unit for each cost category.
4. Compute the total costs of the units (gallons):
   a. Completed and transferred out to the Retort Department
   b. In the Mixing Department's ending work in process inventory

P5-52A Prepare a production cost report and journal entries *(Learning Objectives 4 & 5)*

Chrome Accessories manufactures auto roof racks in a two-stage process that includes shaping and plating. Steel alloy is the basic raw material of the shaping process. The steel is molded according to the design specifications of automobile manufacturers (Ford and General Motors). The Plating Department then adds an anodized finish.

At March 31, before recording the transfer of cost from the Plating Department to Finished Goods Inventory, the Chrome Accessories general ledger included the following account:

Work in Process Inventory—Plating		
March 1 balance	35,350	
Transferred-in from Shaping	43,200	
Direct materials	25,200	
Direct labor	22,000	
Manufacturing overhead	35,500	

The direct materials (rubber pads) are added at the end of the plating process. Conversion costs are incurred evenly throughout the process. Work in process of the Plating Department on March 1 consisted of 1,200 racks. The $35,350 beginning balance of "Work in Process—Plating" includes $21,600 of transferred-in cost and $13,750 of conversion cost. During March, 2,400 racks were transferred in from the Shaping

Department. The Plating Department transferred 2,100 racks to Finished Goods Inventory in March, and 1,500 were still in process on March 31. This ending inventory was 50% of the way through the plating process.

Requirements

1. Draw a time line for the Plating Department.
2. Prepare the March production cost report for the Plating Department.
3. Journalize all transactions affecting the Plating Department during March, including the entries that have already been posted.

P5-53A Complete five-step process in a later department *(Learning Objectives 1 & 5)*

Hamstein uses four departments to produce plastic handles for screwdrivers: Mixing, Molding, Drying, and Assembly.

Hamstein's Drying Department requires no direct materials. Conversion costs are incurred evenly throughout the drying process. Other process costing information follows:

Units:	
Beginning work in process	5,000 units
Transferred-in from the Molding Department during the period	26,000 units
Completed during the period	14,000 units
Ending work in process (20% complete as to conversion work)	17,000 units
Costs:	
Beginning work in process (transferred-in cost, $160; conversion cost, $230)	$ 390
Transferred-in from the Molding Department during the period	4,800
Conversion costs added during the period	1,858

After the drying process, the screwdrivers are completed by assembling the handles and shanks and packaging for shipment to retail outlets.

Requirements

1. Draw a time line of the Drying Department's process.
2. Use the time line to compute the number of equivalent units of work performed by the Drying Department during the period, the cost per equivalent unit, and the total costs to account for.
3. Assign total costs to (a) units completed and transferred to the assembly operation and (b) units in the Drying Department's ending work in process inventory.

PROBLEMS Group B

P5-54B Process costing in a single processing department *(Learning Objectives 1, 2, & 3)*

Grand Lips produces a lip balm used for cold-weather sports. The balm is manufactured in a single processing department. No lip balm was in process on May 31, and Grand Lips started production on 20,700 lip balm tubes during June. Direct materials are added at the beginning of the process, but conversion costs are incurred evenly throughout the process. Completed production for June totaled 15,500 units. The June 30 work in process was 30% of the way through the production process. Direct materials costing $4,761 were placed in production during June, and direct labor of $3,340 and manufacturing overhead of $925 were assigned to the process.

Requirements

1. Fill-in the time line for Grand Lips.
2. Use the time line to help you compute the total equivalent units and the cost per equivalent unit for June.
3. Assign total costs to (a) units completed and transferred to Finished Goods and (b) units still in process at June 30.
4. Prepare a T-account for Work in Process Inventory to show activity during June, including the June 30 balance.

P5-55B Process costing in a first department *(Learning Objectives 1, 3, & 4)*

The Great Northern Furniture Company produces dining tables in a three-stage process: Sawing, Assembly, and Staining. Costs incurred in the Sawing Department during September are summarized as follows:

Work in Process Inventory—Sawing		
September 1 balance	0	
Direct materials	1,830,000	
Direct labor	144,900	
Manufacturing overhead	165,300	

Direct materials (lumber) are added at the beginning of the sawing process, while conversion costs are incurred evenly throughout the process. September activity in the Sawing Department included sawing of 12,000 meters of lumber, which were transferred to the Assembly Department. Also, work began on 3,000 meters of lumber, which on September 30 were 70% of the way through the sawing process.

Requirements

1. Draw a time line for the Sawing Department.
2. Use the time line to help you compute the number of equivalent units and the cost per equivalent unit in the Sawing Department for September.
3. Show that the sum of (a) cost of goods transferred out of the Sawing Department and (b) ending "Work in Process Inventory—Sawing" equals the total cost accumulated in the department during September.
4. Journalize all transactions affecting the company's sawing process during September, including those already posted.

P5-56B Five-step process: Materials added at different points *(Learning Objectives 1, 2, & 3)*

Value World produces canned chicken a la king. The chicken a la king passes through three departments: (1) Mixing, (2) Retort (sterilization), and (3) Packing. In the Mixing Department, chicken and cream are added at the beginning of the process, the mixture is partly cooked, then chopped green peppers and mushrooms are added at the end of the process. Conversion costs are added evenly throughout the mixing process. November data from the Mixing Department are as follows:

Gallons		Costs	
Beginning work in process inventory	0 gallons	Beginning work in process inventory	$ 0
Started production	14,400 gallons	Costs added during November:	
Completed and transferred out to		Chicken	14,320
Retort in November	13,400 gallons	Cream	4,400
Ending work in process inventory (65% of the		Green peppers and mushrooms	6,700
way through the mixing process)	1,000 gallons	Direct labor	11,400
		Manufacturing overhead	3,020
		Total costs	$39,840

Requirements

1. Draw a time line for the Mixing Department.
2. Use the time line to help you summarize the flow of physical units and compute the equivalent units. (*Hint:* Each direct material added at a different point in the production process requires its own equivalent-unit computation.)
3. Compute the cost per equivalent unit for each cost category.
4. Compute the total costs of the units (gallons):
   a. Completed and transferred out to the Retort Department
   b. In the Mixing Department's ending work in process inventory

P5-57B Prepare a production cost report and journal entries *(Learning Objectives 4 & 5)*

Metal Accessories manufactures auto roof racks in a two-stage process that includes shaping and plating. Steel alloy is the basic raw material of the shaping process. The steel is molded according to the design specifications of automobile manufacturers (Ford and General Motors). The Plating Department then adds an anodized finish.

At March 31, before recording the transfer of cost from the Plating Department to Finished Goods Inventory, the Metal Accessories general ledger included the following account:

Work in Process Inventory—Plating

March 1 balance	33,900	
Transferred-in from Shaping	40,800	
Direct materials	27,600	
Direct labor	22,500	
Manufacturing overhead	34,800	

The direct materials (rubber pads) are added at the end of the plating process. Conversion costs are incurred evenly throughout the process. Work in process of the Plating Department on March 1 consisted of 1,800 racks. The $33,900 beginning balance of "Work in Process—Plating" includes $20,400 of transferred-in cost and $13,500 of conversion cost. During March, 1,800 racks were transferred in from the Shaping Department. The Plating Department transferred 2,300 racks to Finished Goods Inventory in March and 1,300 were still in process on March 31. This ending inventory was 50% of the way through the plating process.

Requirements

1. Draw a time line for the Plating Department.
2. Prepare the March production cost report for the Plating Department.
3. Journalize all transactions affecting the Plating Department during March, including the entries that have already been posted.

P5-58B Complete the five-step process in a later department *(Learning Objectives 1 & 5)*

Sidchrome uses four departments to produce plastic handles for screwdrivers: Mixing, Molding, Drying, and Assembly.

Sidchrome's Drying Department requires no direct materials. Conversion costs are incurred evenly throughout the drying process. Other process costing information follows:

Units:	
Beginning work in process	6,000 units
Transferred-in from the Molding Department during the period	27,000 units
Completed during the period	15,000 units
Ending work in process (20% complete as to conversion work)	18,000 units
Costs:	
Beginning work in process (transferred-in cost, $100; conversion cost, $220)	$ 320
Transferred-in from the Molding Department during the period	4,850
Conversion costs added during the period	2,942

After the drying process, the screwdrivers are completed by assembling the handles and shanks and packaging them for shipment to retail outlets.

Requirements

1. Draw a time line of the Drying Department's process.
2. Use the time line to compute the number of equivalent units of work performed by the Drying Department during the period, the cost per equivalent unit, and the total costs to account for.
3. Assign total costs to (a) units completed and transferred to the assembly operation and (b) units in the Drying Department's ending work in process inventory.

CRITICAL THINKING

Discussion & Analysis

A5-59 Discussion Questions

1. What characteristics of the product or manufacturing process would lead a company to use a process costing system? Give two examples of companies that are likely to be using process costing. What characteristics of the product or manufacturing process would lead a company to use a job costing system? Give two examples of companies that are likely to be using job costing.
2. How are process costing and job costing similar? How are they different?
3. What are conversion costs? In a job costing system, at least some conversion costs are assigned directly to products. Why do all conversion costs need to be assigned to processing departments in a process costing system?
4. Why not assign all costs of production during a period to only the completed units? What happens if a company does this? Why are the costs of production in any period allocated between completed units and units in work in process? Is there any situation where a company can assign all costs of production during a period to the completed units? If so, when?
5. What information generated by a process costing system can be used by management? How can management use this process costing information?
6. Why are the equivalent units for direct materials often different from the equivalent units for conversion costs in the same period?
7. Describe the flow of costs in a process costing system. List each type of journal entry that would be made and describe the purpose of that journal entry.
8. If a company has very little or no inventory, what effect does that lack of inventory have on its process costing system? What other benefits result from having very little to no inventory?
9. How does process costing differ between a first processing department and a second or later processing department?
10. "Process costing is easier to use than job costing." Do you agree or disagree with this statement? Explain your reasoning.
11. Think of a business or organization that would use process costing. What types of waste are likely to be generated during the manufacturing process? Are there ways to avoid this waste or minimize it? How might managerial accounting support the efforts to reduce waste in the production process?
12. Provide an example of how a company may change its processes to make its manufacturing more efficient or environmentally sustainable. How will the company benefit?

Application & Analysis

A5-60 Process Costing in Real Companies

Go to YouTube.com and search for clips from the show *Unwrapped* on Food Network or *How It's Made* on Discovery Channel. Watch a clip for a product that would use process costing. For some of the questions, you may need to make assumptions about the production process (i.e., companies may not publicize their entire production process). If you make any assumptions, be sure to disclose both the assumption and your rationale for that assumption.

Basic Discussion Questions

1. Describe the product selected.
2. Summarize the production process.
3. Justify why you think this production process would dictate the use of a process costing system.
4. List at least two separate processes that are performed in creating this product. What departments would house these processes?
5. Describe at least one department that would have ending work in process. What do the units look like as they are "in process"?

Decision Case

A5-61 Cost per unit and gross profit *(Learning Objective 5)*

Jimmy Jones operates Jimmy's Cricket Farm in Eatonton, Georgia. Jimmy's raises about 18 million crickets a month. Most are sold to pet stores at $12.60 for a box of 1,000 crickets. Pet stores sell the crickets for $0.05 to $0.10 each as live feed for reptiles.

Raising crickets requires a two-step process: incubation and brooding. In the first process, incubation, employees place cricket eggs on mounds of peat moss to hatch. In the second process, employees move the newly hatched crickets into large boxes filled with cardboard dividers. Depending on the desired size, the crickets spend approximately two weeks in brooding before being shipped to pet stores. In the brooding process, Jimmy's crickets consume about 16 tons of food and produce 12 tons of manure.

Jones has invested $400,000 in the cricket farm, and he had hoped to earn a 24% annual rate of return, which works out to a 2% monthly return on his investment. After looking at the farm's bank balance, Jones fears he is not achieving this return. To get more accurate information on the farm's performance, Jones bought new accounting software that provides weighted-average process cost information. After Jones input the data, the software provided the following reports. However, Jones needs help interpreting these reports.

Jones does know that a unit of production is a box of 1,000 crickets. For example, in June's report, the 7,000 physical units of beginning work in process inventory are 7,000 boxes (each one of the 7,000 boxes contains 1,000 immature crickets). The finished goods inventory is zero because the crickets ship out as soon as they reach the required size. Monthly operating expenses total $2,000 (in addition to the costs that follow).

JIMMY'S CRICKET FARM
Brooding Department
Production Cost Report (part 1 of 2)
Month Ended June 30

Flow of Production	Flow of Physical Units	Equivalent Units: Transferred-in	Equivalent Units: Direct Materials	Equivalent Units: Conversion Costs
Units to account for:				
Beginning work in process inventory, June 1	7,000			
Transferred in during June	21,000			
Total units to account for	28,000			
Units accounted for:				
Completed and shipped out during June	19,000	19,000	19,000	19,000
Ending work in process, June 30	9,000	9,000	7,200	3,600
Total physical units accounted for	28,000			
Total equivalent units		28,000	26,200	22,600

JIMMY'S CRICKET FARM
Brooding Department
Production Cost Report (part 2 of 2)
Month Ended June 30

	Transferred-in	Direct Materials	Conversion Costs	Total
Unit costs:				
Beginning work in process, June 1	$21,000	$ 39,940	$ 5,020	$ 65,960
Costs added during June	46,200	156,560	51,480	254,240
Total costs to account for	$67,200	$196,500	$56,500	$320,200
Divide by total equivalent units	÷ 28,000	÷ 26,200	÷ 22,600	
Cost per equivalent unit	$ 2.40	$ 7.50	$ 2.50	
Assignment of total cost:				
Units completed and shipped out during June	[19,000 × ($2.40 + $7.50 + $2.50)]			$235,600
Ending work in process, June 30:				
Transferred-in costs	[9,000 × $2.40]			21,600
Direct materials		[7,200 × $7.50]		54,000
Conversion costs			[3,600 × $2.50]	9,000
Total ending work in process, June 30				84,600
Total cost accounted for				$320,200

Requirements

Jimmy Jones has the following questions about the farm's performance during June:

1. What is the cost per box of crickets sold? (*Hint:* This is the cost of the boxes completed and shipped out of brooding.)
2. What is the gross profit per box?
3. How much operating income did Jimmy's Cricket Farm make in June?
4. What is the return on Jones's investment of $400,000 for the month of June? (Compute this as June's operating income divided by Jones's $400,000 investment, expressed as a percentage.)
5. What monthly operating income would provide a 2% monthly rate of return? What price per box would Jimmy's Cricket Farm have had to charge in June to achieve a 2% monthly rate of return?

Ethical Issue

A5-62 Ethical dilemma regarding percentage of completion *(Learning Objectives 2 & 5)*

Rick Penn and Joe Lopus are the plant managers for Pacific Lumber's particle board division. Pacific Lumber has adopted a just-in-time (JIT) management philosophy. Each plant combines wood chips with chemical adhesives to produce particle board to order, and all production is sold as soon as it is completed. Laura Green is Pacific Lumber's regional controller. All of Pacific Lumber's plants and divisions send Green their production and cost information. While reviewing the numbers of the two particle board plants, she is surprised that both plants estimate their ending work in process inventories at 80% complete, which is higher than usual. Green calls Lopus, whom she has known for some time. He admits that to ensure that their division met its profit goal and that both he and Penn would make their bonus (which is based on division profit), he and Penn agreed to inflate the percentage completion. Lopus explains, "Determining the percentage completion always requires judgment. Whatever the percentage completion, we'll finish the work in process inventory first thing next year."

Requirements

1. How would inflating the percentage completion of ending work in process inventory help Penn and Lopus get their bonus?
2. The particle board division is the largest of Pacific Lumber's divisions. If Green does not correct the percentage completion of this year's ending work in process inventory, how will the misstatement affect Pacific Lumber's financial statements?
3. Evaluate Lopus's justification, including the effect, if any, on next year's financial statements.
4. In considering what Green should do, answer the following questions:
    a. What is the ethical question?
    b. What are the options?
    c. What are the possible consequences?
    d. What should Green do?

Team Project

A5-63 Calculating costs for a customer order *(Learning Objective 5)*

Hermiston Food Processors in Hermiston, Oregon, processes potatoes into French fries. Production requires two processes: cutting and cooking. The cutting process begins as scalding steam explodes the potatoes' brown skin. Workers using paring knives gouge out black spots before high-pressure water blasts potatoes through a pipe and into blades arranged in a quarter-inch grid. In the cooking process, the raw shoestring fries are cooked in a bleacher, dried, partially fried at 380°F, and immediately flash-frozen at minus 75°F before being dropped into five-pound bags. Direct materials are added at the beginning of the cutting process (potatoes) and at the end of the cooking process (bags). Conversion costs are incurred evenly throughout each process.

Assume that McDonald's offers Hermiston $0.40 per pound to supply restaurants in the Far East. If Hermiston accepts McDonald's offer, the cost (per equivalent unit) that Hermiston will incur to fill the McDonald's order equals the April cost per equivalent unit. J. R. Simlott, manager of the cooking process, must prepare a report explaining whether Hermiston should accept the offer. Simlott gathers the following information from April's cooking operations:

Lola Mendez manages the cutting process. She reports the following data for her department's April operations:

HERMISTON FOOD PROCESSORS **Cooking Department** April Activity and Costs	
Beginning work in process inventory, April 1	12,000 pounds
Raw shoestring fries started in April	129,000 pounds
French fries completed and transferred out	130,000 pounds
Ending work in process inventory (30% of way through process), April 30	11,000 pounds
Costs incurred *within* the cooking department in March to start the 12,000 pounds of beginning work in process inventory	$ 576
Costs added during April:	
Direct materials	6,500
Conversion costs	15,420

Split your team into two groups. Each group should meet separately before a meeting of the entire team.

Requirements

1. The first group takes the role of Simlott, manager of the cooking production process. Before meeting with the entire team, determine the maximum transferred-in cost per pound of raw shoestring fries the cooking process can incur from the cutting process if Hermiston is to make a profit on the McDonald's order. (*Hint:* You may find it helpful to prepare a time line and to use Exhibits 5-10–5-13 as a guide for your analysis.)
2. The second group takes the role of Mendez, manager of the cutting process. Before meeting with the entire team, determine the April cost per pound of raw shoestring fries in the cutting process.
3. After each group meets, the entire team should meet to decide whether Hermiston should accept or reject the McDonald's offer.

Cost Behavior

Learning Objectives

1. Describe key characteristics and graphs of various cost behaviors
2. Use cost equations to express and predict costs
3. Use account analysis and scatter plots to analyze cost behavior
4. Use the high-low method to analyze cost behavior
5. Use regression analysis to analyze cost behavior
6. Describe variable costing and prepare a contribution margin income statement

© Profimedia International s.r.o. / Alamy

High above the rushing

waters and mist of Niagara Falls, hundreds of tourists from around the world return to the 512-room Embassy Suites[1] to enjoy a complimentary afternoon refreshment hour, relax in the hotel's pool and spa, and rest in luxurious suites overlooking the falls. A similar scene occurs across the street at the Sheraton, Marriott, and DoubleTree hotels, as well as at thousands of other travel destinations around the world.

How do hotel managers set prices high enough to cover costs and earn a profit, but low enough to fill most rooms each night? How do they plan for higher occupancy during the busy summer months and lower occupancy during the off-season? They know how their costs behave. Some hotel costs, such as the complimentary morning breakfast, rise and fall with the number of guests. But many hotel costs, such as depreciation on the building and furniture, stay the same whether 50 or 2,000 guests stay each night. In this chapter we'll learn more about how costs behave, and how managers can use that knowledge to make better business decisions.

[1]All references to Embassy Suites in this hypothetical example were created by the author solely for academic purposes and are not intended, in any way, to represent the actual business practices of, or costs incurred by, Embassy Suites.

Up to this point, we have focused our attention on product costing. We have discussed how managers use job costing or process costing to figure out the cost of making a product or providing a service. Product costs are useful for valuing inventory and calculating cost of goods sold. Product costs are also used as a starting place for setting sales prices. However, product costs are not very helpful for planning and making many business decisions. Why? Because they contain a mixture of fixed and variable costs. Some of these costs change as volume changes, but other costs do not. To make good decisions and accurate projections, managers must understand how the company's costs will react to changes in volume.

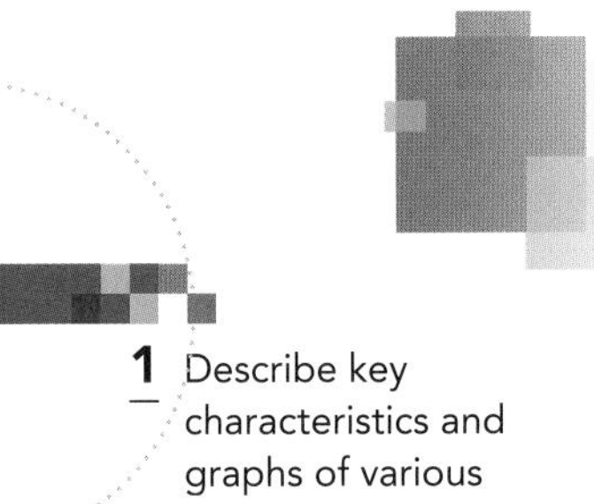

Cost Behavior: How do Changes in Volume Affect Costs?

1 Describe key characteristics and graphs of various cost behaviors

In order to make good decisions and accurate projections, managers must understand cost behavior—that is, how costs change as volume changes. Embassy Suite's managers need to understand how the hotel's costs will be affected by the number of guests staying at the hotel each night. We first consider three of the most common cost behaviors, some of which were introduced in Chapter 2 (pp. 68–69):

- Variable costs
- Fixed costs
- Mixed costs

Why is this important?

"Cost behavior is a **key** component of most **planning** and operating decisions. Without a thorough understanding of **cost behavior,** managers are apt to make less **profitable** decisions."

Variable Costs

Variable costs are costs that are incurred for every unit of volume. As a result, total variable costs change in direct proportion to changes in volume. For example, every guest at Embassy Suites is entitled to a complimentary morning breakfast and afternoon refreshment hour (drinks and snacks). Guests also receive complimentary toiletries, (shampoo, soap, lotion, and mouthwash) that they typically use or take with them. These costs are considered to be variable because they are incurred for every guest. In addition, the hotel's total cost for the complimentary breakfast and toiletries will increase as the number of guests increases.

Let's assume that the toiletries cost the hotel $3 per guest and that the breakfast and refreshment hour costs the hotel $10 per guest. Exhibit 6-1 graphs these costs in relation to the number of guests staying at the hotel. The vertical axis (y-axis) shows total variable costs, while the horizontal axis (x-axis) shows total volume of activity (thousands of guests, in this case).

EXHIBIT 6-1 Variable Costs

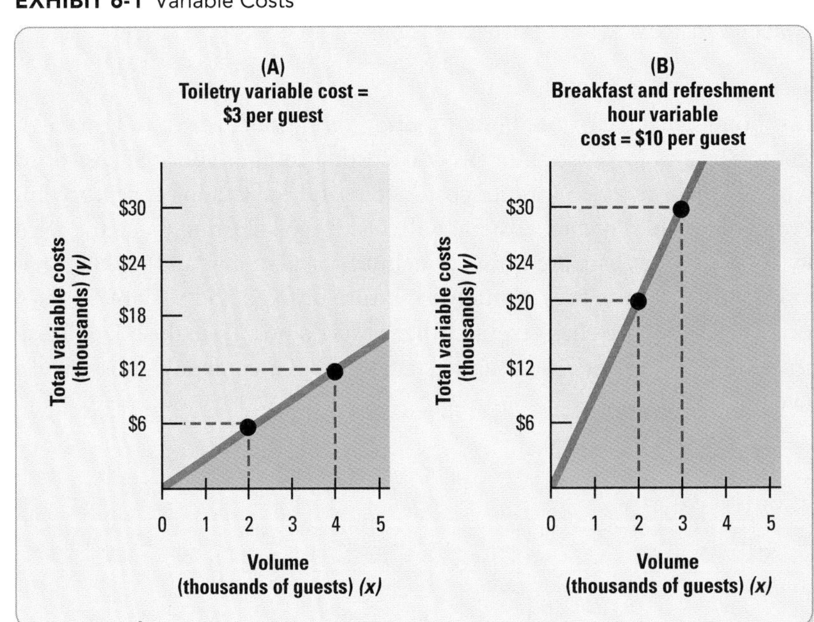

Notice a few things about these graphs:

- Graphs of variable costs always begin at the *origin*, the point that represents zero volume and zero cost. For example, if the hotel has no guests for the night, it will not incur any costs for complimentary toiletries or breakfasts.
- The *slope* of the variable cost line represents the *variable cost per unit of activity*. For example, the slope of the toiletry cost line is \$3 per guest while the slope of the breakfast cost line is \$10 per guest. As a result, the slope of the line representing the breakfast cost is steeper than that of the toiletry cost.
- Total variable costs change in *direct proportion* to changes in volume. In other words, if volume doubles, then total variable cost doubles. If volume triples then total variable cost triples. For example, Exhibit 6-1(a) shows that if the hotel serves 2,000 guests, it will spend \$6,000 on toiletries. However, doubling the number of guests to 4,000 likewise doubles the total variable cost to \$12,000.

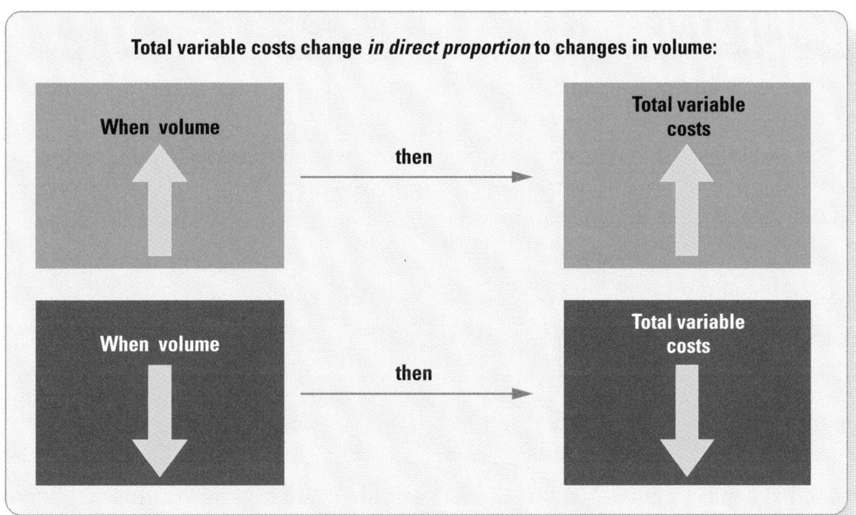

Managers do not need to rely on graphs to predict total variable costs at different volumes of activity. They can use a **cost equation**, a mathematical equation for a straight line, to express how a cost behaves. On cost graphs like the ones pictured in Exhibit 6-1, the vertical (y-axis) always shows total costs, while the horizontal axis (x-axis) shows volume of activity. Therefore, any variable cost line can be mathematically expressed as follows:

2 Use cost equations to express and predict costs

Total variable cost (y) = Variable cost per unit of activity (v) × Volume of activity (x)

Or simply:

$$y = vx$$

The hotel's total toiletry cost is as follows:

$$y = \$3x$$

where,

y = total toiletry cost
\$3 = variable cost per guest
x = number of guests

Why is this important?

"Cost **equations** help managers foresee what their **total costs** will be at **different** operating **volumes** so that they can **better** plan for the future."

We can confirm the observations made in Exhibit 6-1(a) using the cost equation. If the hotel has no guests ($x = 0$), total toiletry costs are zero, as shown in the graph. If the hotel has 2,000 guests, total toiletry costs will be as follows:

$$\begin{aligned} y &= \$3 \text{ per guest} \times 2{,}000 \text{ guests} \\ &= \$6{,}000 \end{aligned}$$

If the hotel has 4,000 guests, managers will expect total toiletry costs to be as follows:

$$\begin{aligned} y &= \$3 \text{ per guest} \times 4{,}000 \text{ guests} \\ &= \$12{,}000 \end{aligned}$$

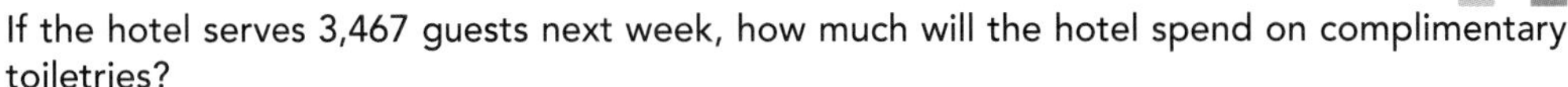

If the hotel serves 3,467 guests next week, how much will the hotel spend on complimentary toiletries?

Answer: You would have a hard time answering this question by simply looking at the graph in Exhibit 6-1(a), but cost equations can be used for any volume. We "plug in" the expected volume to our variable cost equation as follows:

$$\begin{aligned} y &= \$3 \text{ per guest} \times 3{,}467 \text{ guests} \\ &= \$10{,}401 \end{aligned}$$

Management expects complimentary toiletries next week to cost about $10,401.

Now, consider Exhibit 6-1(b), the total variable costs for the complimentary breakfast and refreshment hour. The slope of the line is $10, representing the cost of providing each guest with the complimentary breakfast and refreshments. We can express the total breakfast and refreshment hour cost as follows:

$$y = \$10x$$

where,

$$\begin{aligned} y &= \text{total breakfast and refreshment hour cost} \\ \$10 &= \text{variable cost per guest} \\ x &= \text{number of guests} \end{aligned}$$

The total cost of the breakfast and refreshment hour for 2,000 guests is as follows:

$$\begin{aligned} y &= \$10 \text{ per guest} \times 2{,}000 \text{ guests} \\ &= \$20{,}000 \end{aligned}$$

Both graphs in Exhibit 6-1 show how *total* variable costs vary with the number of guests. *But note that the variable cost per guest* (v) *remains constant in each of the graphs.* That is, Embassy Suites incurs $3 in toiletry costs and $10 in breakfast and refreshment hour costs for each guest no matter how many guests the hotel serves. Some key points to remember about variable costs are shown in Exhibit 6-2.

EXHIBIT 6-2 Key Characteristics of Variable Costs

- *Total* variable costs change in *direct proportion* to changes in volume
- The *variable cost per unit of activity* (v) remains constant and is the slope of the variable cost line
- Total variable cost graphs always begin at the origin (if volume is zero, total variable costs are zero)
- Total variable costs can be expressed as follows:

$$y = vx$$

where,

y = total variable cost
v = variable cost per unit of activity
x = volume of activity

Fixed Costs

Fixed costs are costs that do not change in total despite wide changes in volume. Many of Embassy Suites' costs are fixed because the same total cost will be incurred regardless of the number of guests that stay each month. Some of the hotel's fixed costs include the following:

- Property taxes and insurance
- Depreciation and maintenance on parking ramp, hotel, and room furnishings
- Pool, fitness room, and spa upkeep
- Cable TV and wireless internet access for all rooms
- Salaries of hotel department managers (housekeeping, food service, special events, etc.)

Most of these costs are committed fixed costs, meaning that the hotel is locked in to these costs because of previous management decisions. For example, as soon as the hotel was built, management became locked in to a certain level of property taxes and depreciation, simply because of the location and size of the hotel, and management's choice of furnishings and amenities (pool, fitness room, restaurant, and so forth). Management has little or no control over these committed fixed costs in the short run.

However, the hotel also incurs discretionary fixed costs, such as advertising expenses, that are a result of annual management decisions. Companies have more control over discretionary fixed costs in the short run.

EXHIBIT 6-3 Fixed Costs

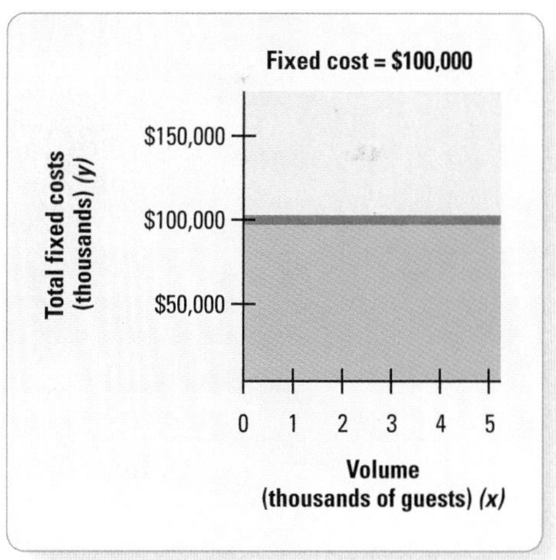

Suppose Embassy Suites incurs $100,000 of fixed costs each month. In Exhibit 6-3, the vertical axis (y-axis) shows total fixed costs while the horizontal axis (x-axis) plots volume of activity (thousands of guests). The graph shows total fixed costs as a *flat line* that intersects the y-axis at $100,000 (this is known as the vertical intercept) because the hotel will incur the same $100,000 of fixed costs regardless of the number of guests that stay during the month.

The cost equation for a fixed cost is as follows:

$$\text{Total fixed cost } (y) = \text{Fixed amount over a period of time } (f)$$

Or simply,

$$y = f$$

Embassy Suites' *monthly* fixed cost equation is as follows:

$$y = \$100,000$$

where,

$$y = \text{total fixed cost per month}$$

In contrast to the *total fixed costs* shown in Exhibit 6-3, the *fixed cost per guest* depends on the number of guests. If the hotel only serves 2,000 guests during the month, the fixed cost per guest is as follows:

$$\$100{,}000 \div 2{,}000 \text{ guests} = \$50/\text{guest}$$

If the number of guests *doubles* to 4,000, the fixed cost per guest is *cut in half*:

$$\$100{,}000 \div 4{,}000 \text{ guests} = \$25/\text{guest}$$

The fixed cost per guest is *inversely proportional* to the number of guests. When volume *increases*, the fixed cost per guest *decreases*. When volume *decreases*, the fixed cost per guest *increases*.

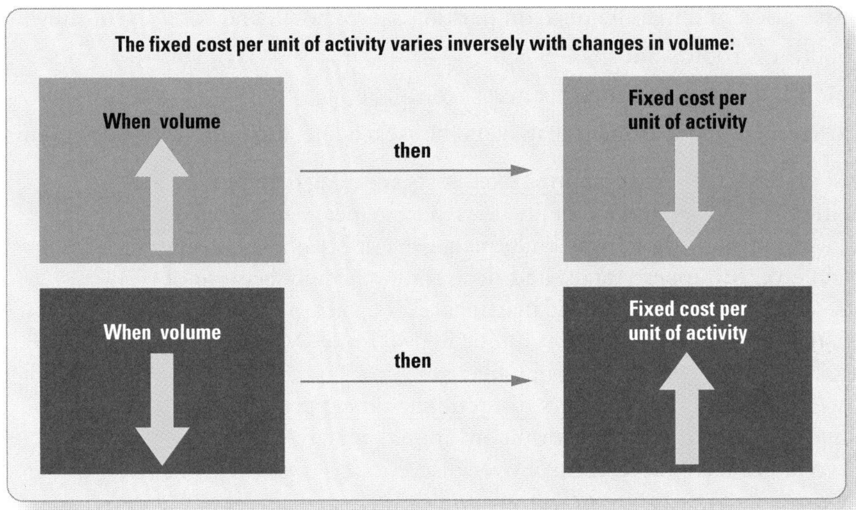

Key points to remember about fixed costs appear in Exhibit 6-4.

EXHIBIT 6-4 Key Characteristics of Fixed Costs

- *Total* fixed costs stay *constant* over a wide range of volume
- Fixed costs *per unit of activity* vary *inversely* with changes in volume:
    - Fixed cost per unit of activity *increases* when volume *decreases*
    - Fixed cost per unit of activity *decreases* when volume *increases*
- Total fixed cost graphs are always flat lines with no slope that intersect the y-axis at a level equal to total fixed costs
- Total fixed costs can be expressed as $y = f$

  where,

  y = total fixed cost

  f = fixed cost over a given period of time

STOP & THINK

Compute the (a) total fixed cost and (b) fixed cost per guest if the hotel has 16,000 guests next month. Compare the fixed cost per guest at the higher occupancy rate to the fixed cost per guest if only 2,000 guests stay during the month. Explain why hotels and other businesses like to operate near 100% capacity.

Answer:

a. Total fixed costs do not react to wide changes in volume; therefore, total fixed costs will still be $100,000.

b. Fixed costs per unit decrease as volume increases. At the higher occupancy, the fixed cost per guest is as follows:

$$\$100{,}000 \div 16{,}000 \text{ guests} = \$6.25 \text{ per guest}$$

If only 2,000 guests stay during the month, the fixed cost per guest is much higher ($50). Businesses like to operate near full capacity because it lowers their fixed cost per unit. A lower cost per unit gives businesses the flexibility to lower their prices to compete more effectively.

Mixed Costs

Mixed costs contain both variable and fixed cost components. Embassy Suites' utilities are mixed costs because the hotel requires a certain amount of utilities just to operate. However, the more guests at the hotel, the more water, electricity, and gas required. Exhibit 6-5 illustrates mixed costs.

EXHIBIT 6-5 Mixed Costs

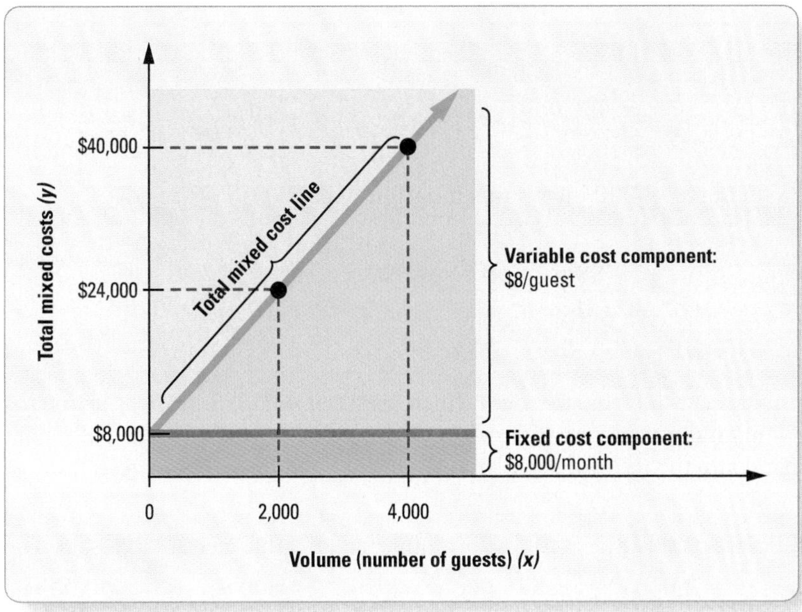

For example, let's assume that utilities for the common areas of the hotel and unoccupied rooms cost \$8,000 per month. In addition, these costs increase by \$8 per guest as each guest cools or heats his or her room, takes showers, turns on the TV and lights, and uses freshly laundered sheets and towels.

Notice the two components—variable and fixed—of the mixed cost in Exhibit 6-5. Similar to a variable cost, the total mixed cost line increases as the volume of activity increases. However, *the line does **not** begin at the origin.* Rather, it intersects the y-axis at a level equal to the fixed cost component. Even if no guests stay this month, the hotel will still incur \$8,000 of utilities cost.

Managers can once again use a cost equation to express the mixed cost line so that they can predict total mixed costs at different volumes. The mixed cost equation simply *combines* the variable cost and fixed cost equations:

Total mixed costs	=	Variable cost component	+	Fixed cost component
y	=	vx	+	f

Embassy Suites' monthly utilities cost equation is as follows:

$$y = \$8x + \$8{,}000$$

where,

y = total utilities cost per month
x = number of guests

If the hotel serves 2,000 guests this month it expects utilities to cost:

$$y = (\$8 \text{ per guest} \times 2{,}000 \text{ guests}) + \$8{,}000$$
$$= \$24{,}000$$

If the hotel serves 4,000 guests this month it expects utilities to cost:

$$y = (\$8 \text{ per guest} \times 4{,}000 \text{ guests}) + \$8{,}000$$
$$= \$40{,}000$$

Total mixed costs increase as volume increases, *but **not** in direct proportion to changes in volume*. The total mixed cost did *not* double when volume doubled. This is because of the fixed cost component. Additionally, consider the mixed cost *per guest*:

If the hotel serves 2,000 guests: \$24,000 total cost ÷ 2,000 guests = \$12.00 per guest
If the hotel serves 4,000 guests: \$40,000 total cost ÷ 4,000 guests = \$10.00 per guest

The mixed cost per guest did *not* decrease by half when the hotel served twice as many guests. This is because of the variable cost component. Mixed costs per unit decrease as volume increases, but ***not** in direct proportion* to changes in volume. Because mixed costs contain both fixed cost and variable cost components, they behave differently than purely variable costs and purely fixed costs. Key points to remember about mixed costs appear in Exhibit 6-6.

EXHIBIT 6-6 Key Characteristics of Mixed Costs

- *Total* mixed costs increase as volume increases because of the variable cost component
- Mixed costs *per unit* decrease as volume increases because of the fixed cost component
- Total mixed cost graphs slope upward but do *not* begin at the origin—they intersect the y-axis at the level of fixed costs
- Total mixed costs can be expressed as a *combination* of the variable and fixed cost equations:

Total mixed costs = variable cost component + fixed cost component

$$y = vx + f$$

where,

y = total mixed cost
v = variable cost per unit of activity (slope)
x = volume of activity
f = fixed cost over a given period of time (vertical intercept)

STOP & THINK

If your cell phone plan charges $10 per month plus $0.15 for each minute you talk, how could you express the monthly cell phone bill as a cost equation? How much will your cell phone bill be if you (a) talk 100 minutes this month or (b) talk 200 minutes this month? If you double your talk time from 100 to 200 minutes, does your total cell phone bill double? Explain.

Answer: The cost equation for the monthly cell phone bill is as follows:

$$y = \$0.15x + \$10$$

where,

y = total cell phone bill for the month
x = number of minutes used

a. At 100 minutes, the total cost is $25 [= ($0.15 per minute × 100 minutes) + $10].
b. At 200 minutes, the total cost is $40 [= ($0.15 per minute × 200 minutes) + $10].
The cell phone bill does not double when talk time doubles. The variable portion of the bill doubles from $15 ($0.15 × 100 minutes) to $30 ($0.15 × 200 minutes), but the fixed portion of the bill stays constant ($10).

Relevant Range

Managers always need to keep their **relevant range** in mind when predicting total costs. The relevant range is the band of volume where the following remain constant:

- *Total fixed costs*
- *Variable cost per unit*

A change in cost behavior means a change to a different relevant range.

Let's consider how the concept of relevant range applies to Embassy Suites. As shown in Exhibit 6-3, the hotel's current fixed costs are $100,000 per month. However, since the hotel's popularity continues to grow, room occupancy rates continue to increase.

As a result, guests are becoming dissatisfied with the amount of time they have to wait for breakfast tables and elevators. To increase customer satisfaction, management is deciding whether to expand the breakfast facilities and add a 30-passenger elevator to its existing bank of elevators. This expansion, if carried out, will increase the hotel's fixed costs to a new level. Exhibit 6-7 illustrates the hotel's current relevant range and future potential relevant range for fixed costs.

EXHIBIT 6-7 Examples of Different Relevant Ranges for Fixed Costs

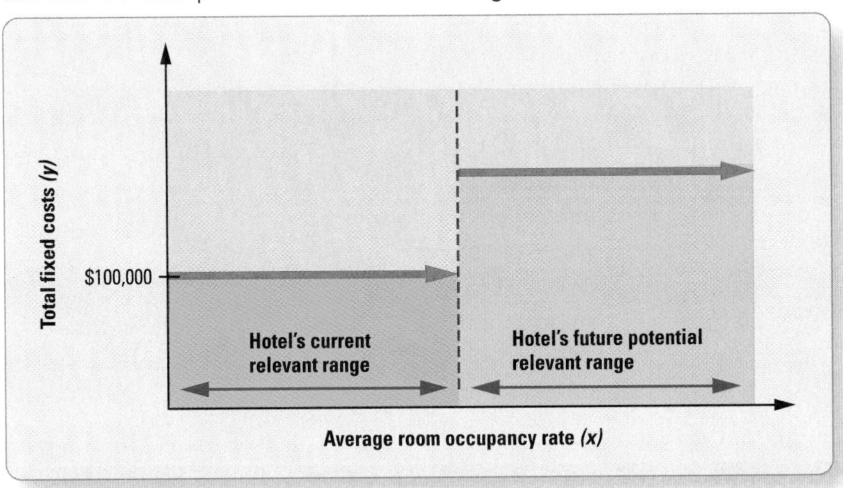

Does the concept of relevant range apply only to fixed costs? No, it also applies to variable costs. As shown in Exhibit 6-1, the hotel's current variable cost for toiletries is $3 per guest. However, as room occupancy rates continue to grow, management hopes to negotiate greater volume discounts on the toiletries from its suppliers. These volume discounts will decrease the variable toiletries cost per guest (for example, down to $2.75 per guest). Exhibit 6-8 illustrates the hotel's current relevant range and future potential relevant range for variable toiletries costs.

EXHIBIT 6-8 Examples of Different Relevant Ranges for Variable Costs

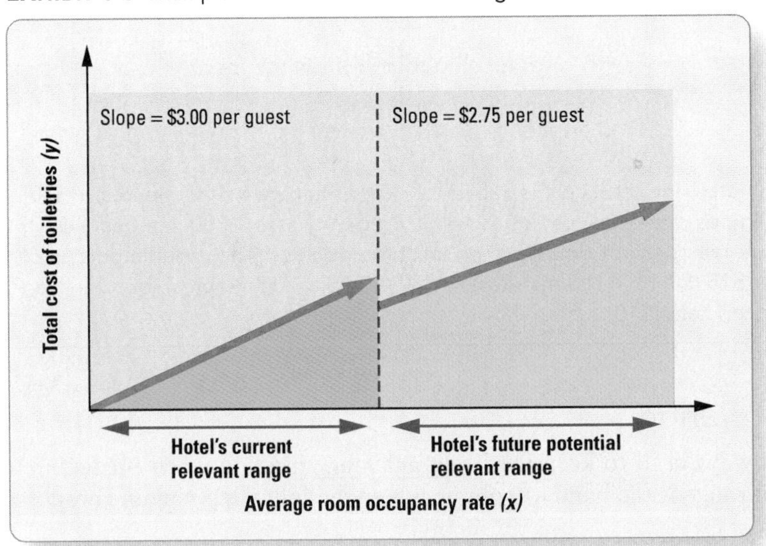

Why is the concept of relevant range important? Managers can predict costs accurately only if they use cost information for the appropriate relevant range. For example, think about your cell phone plan. Many cell phone plans offer a large block of "free" minutes for a set fee each month. If the user exceeds the allotted minutes, the cell phone company charges an additional per-minute fee. Exhibit 6-9 shows a cell phone plan in which the first 1,000 minutes of call time each month cost $50. After the 1,000 minutes are used, the user must pay an additional $0.30 per minute for every minute of call time. This cell phone plan has two relevant ranges. The first relevant range extends from 0 to 1,000 minutes. In this range, the $50 fee behaves strictly as a fixed cost. You could use 0, 100, or 975 minutes and you would still pay a flat $50 fee that month. The second relevant range starts at 1,001 minutes and extends indefinitely. In this relevant range, the cost is mixed: $50 plus $0.30 per minute. To forecast your cell phone bill each month, you need to know in which relevant range you plan to operate. The same holds true for businesses: To accurately predict costs, they need to know the relevant range in which they plan to operate.

EXHIBIT 6-9 Example of Relevant Ranges

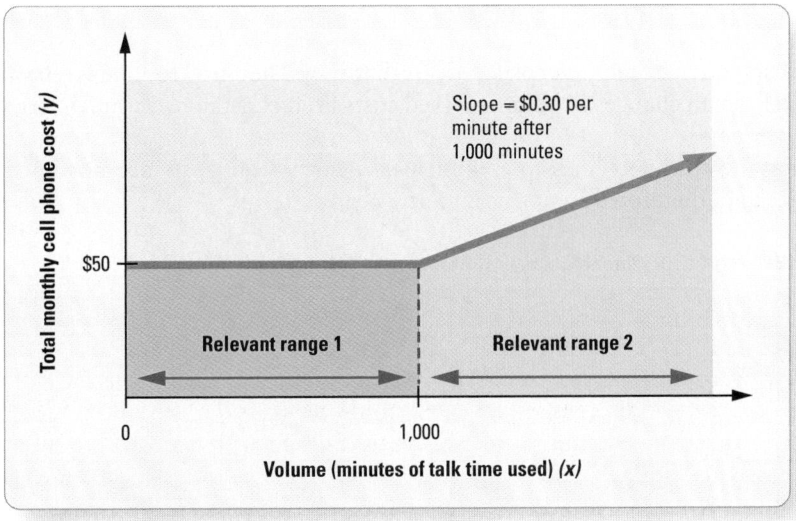

Other Cost Behaviors

While many business costs behave as variable, fixed, or mixed costs, some costs do not neatly fit these patterns. We'll briefly describe other cost behaviors you may encounter.

Step costs resemble stair steps: They are fixed over a small range of activity and then jump up to a new fixed level with moderate changes in volume. Hotels, restaurants, hospitals, and educational institutions typically experience step costs. For example, states usually require day-care centers to limit the caregiver-to-child ratio to 1:7—that is, there must be one caregiver for every seven children. As shown in Exhibit 6-10, a day-care center that takes on an eighth child must incur the cost of employing another caregiver. The new caregiver can watch the eighth through fourteenth child enrolled at the day-care center. If the day-care center takes on a fifteenth child, management will once again need to hire another caregiver, costing another $15,000 in salary. The same step cost patterns occur with hotels (maid-to-room ratio), restaurants (server-to-table ratio), hospitals (nurse-to-bed ratio), and schools (teacher-to-student ratio).

EXHIBIT 6-10 Step Costs

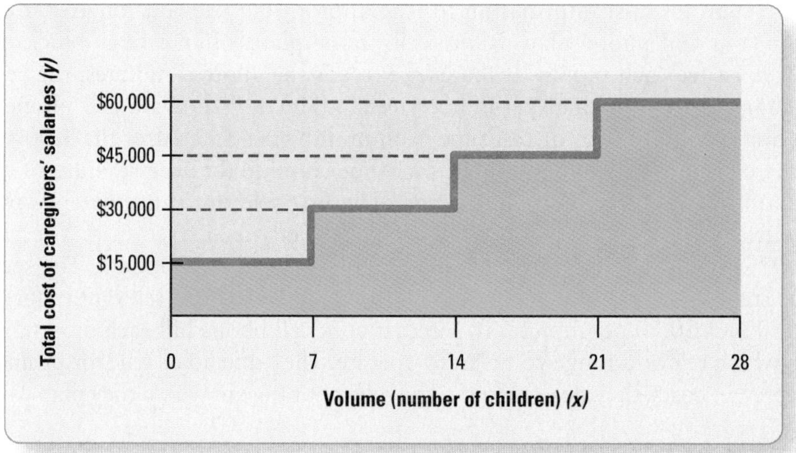

Step costs differ from fixed costs only in that they "step up" to a new relevant range with relatively small changes in volume. Fixed costs hold constant over much larger ranges of volume.

As shown by the red lines in Exhibit 6-11, curvilinear costs are not linear (not a straight line) and, therefore, do not fit into any neat pattern.

EXHIBIT 6-11 Curvilinear Costs and Straight-Line Approximations

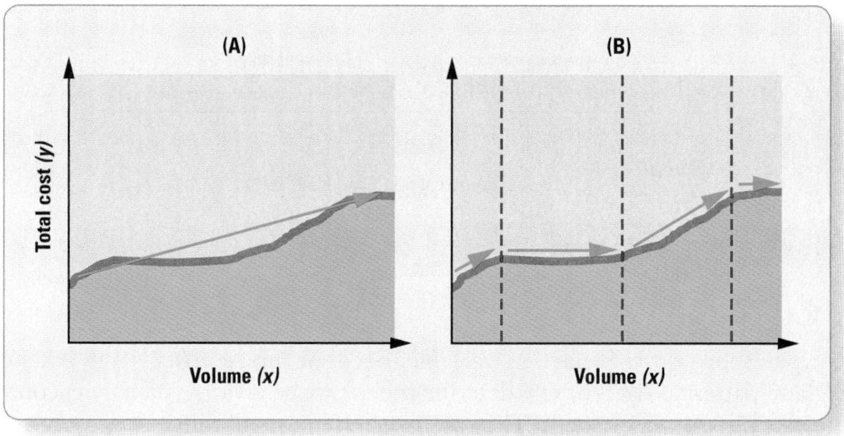

As shown by the straight green arrow in Exhibit 6-11(a), some businesses *approximate* these types of costs as mixed costs, knowing that they will have an estimation error at particular volumes. Sometimes managers also approximate step costs the same way: They simply draw a straight mixed cost line through the steps.

However, as shown in Exhibit 6-11(b), if managers need more accurate predictions, they can simply break these types of costs into smaller relevant ranges and make their predictions based on the particular relevant range. For example, the day-care center may want to predict total caregiver salaries if it enrolls 26 children. The manager knows this enrollment falls into the relevant range of 21 to 28 children, where he or she needs to employ four caregivers. The manager can then predict total caregiver salaries to be $60,000 (four caregivers × $15,000 salary per caregiver).

Sustainability and Cost Behavior

Many companies adopting sustainable business practices experience changes in the way their costs behave. For example, many banks, credit card companies, and utilities offer e-banking and e-billing services as an alternative to sending traditional paper statements and bills through the mail. E-banking and e-billing drive down a company's variable costs.

The environmental consequences of this action are tremendous if you consider the entire production and delivery cycle of the bills and statements, all of the way from the logging of the trees in the forest to the delivery of the bill at the customer's doorstep. Not only are fewer trees cut down, but also less energy is consumed in the transportation of the timber, the processing of the paper, the distribution of the paper, the delivery of the statements via the US Postal Service, and the final disposal of the paper at landfills or recycling centers. In addition, less waste-water is generated and fewer toxic air emissions are produced.

From the customer's perspective, adoption of e-billing and e-banking services provides one means for households to embrace a greener lifestyle. Charter One Bank estimates that, on an annual basis, the average household that receives e-bills and pays bills online reduces paper consumption by 6.6 pounds, saves 4.5 gallons of gasoline, saves 63 gallons of water, and cuts greenhouse gas emissions equal to the amount that would be emitted by driving 176 miles.[2] According to the US Postal Service, in 2009, 24.4 billion bills and statements (equating to 684 million pounds of paper) were delivered across the country.[3] Because of the increasing popularity of e-billing, this volume is actually down by 1.5 billion pieces since 2006. Thus, the adoption of electronic billing by the general public could have a significant positive impact on the environment.

From the company's perspective, this practice also reduces the total variable costs associated with processing, printing, and mailing statements (and cancelled checks) to each customer. In place of these variable costs, the company must incur additional fixed costs to develop secure online banking and billing websites. However, the variable cost savings generated must be substantial and cost effective. We know this because some companies offer cash incentives to customers if they switch to electronic billing. For example, Charter One Bank actually *pays* customers to go paperless: 10 cents per electronic payment made (online bill payments and debit card payments) up to $120 per year.

See Exercises 6-26A and E6-52B

[2] www.charterone.com/greensense/tips.aspx

[3] www.usps.com/householddiary/welcome.htm

We have just described the most typical cost behaviors. In the next part of the chapter, we will discuss methods managers use for determining how their costs behave.

Decision Guidelines

Cost Behavior

Suppose you manage a local fitness club. To be an effective manager, you need to know how the club's costs behave. Here are some decisions you will need to make.

Decision	Guidelines
How can you tell if a *total* cost is variable, fixed, or mixed?	• Total variable costs increase in *direct proportion* to increases in volume. • Total fixed costs stay *constant* over a wide range of volumes. • Total mixed costs increase but *not* in direct proportion to increases in volume.
How can you tell if a *per-unit* cost is variable, fixed, or mixed?	• On a per-unit basis, variable costs stay constant. • On a per-unit basis, fixed costs decrease in proportion to increases in volume (that is to say they are inversely proportional). • On a per-unit basis, mixed costs decrease, but not in direct proportion to increases in volume.
How can you tell by looking at a graph if a cost is variable, fixed, or mixed?	• Variable cost lines slope upward and begin at the origin. • Fixed cost lines are flat (no slope) and intersect the y-axis at a level equal to total fixed costs (this is known as the vertical intercept). • Mixed cost lines slope upward but do *not* begin at the origin. They intersect the y-axis at a level equal to their fixed cost component.
How can you mathematically express different cost behaviors?	• Cost equations mathematically express cost behavior using the equation for a straight line: $y = vx + f$ where, y = total cost v = variable cost per unit of activity (slope) x = volume of activity f = fixed cost (the vertical intercept) • For a variable cost, *f* is zero, leaving the following: $y = vx$ • For a fixed cost, *v* is zero, leaving the following: $y = f$ • Because a mixed cost has both a fixed cost component and a variable cost component, its cost equation is: $y = vx + f$

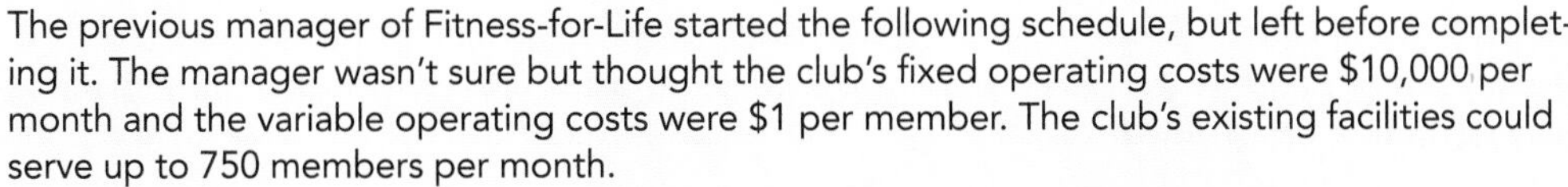

SUMMARY PROBLEM 1

The previous manager of Fitness-for-Life started the following schedule, but left before completing it. The manager wasn't sure but thought the club's fixed operating costs were $10,000 per month and the variable operating costs were $1 per member. The club's existing facilities could serve up to 750 members per month.

Requirements

1. Complete the following schedule for different levels of monthly membership assuming the previous manager's cost behavior estimates are accurate:

Monthly Operating Costs	100 Members	500 Members	750 Members
Total variable costs			
Total fixed costs			
Total operating costs			
Variable cost per member			
Fixed cost per member			
Average cost per member			

2. As the manager of the fitness club, why shouldn't you use the average cost per member to predict total costs at different levels of membership?

SOLUTIONS

Requirement 1

As volume increases, fixed costs stay constant in total but decrease on a per-unit basis. As volume increases, variable costs stay constant on a per-unit basis but increase in total in direct proportion to increases in volume:

	100 Members	500 Members	750 Members
Total variable costs	$ 100	$ 500	$ 750
Total fixed costs	10,000	10,000	10,000
Total operating costs	$10,100	$10,500	$10,750
Variable cost per member	$ 1.00	$ 1.00	$ 1.00
Fixed cost per member	100.00	20.00	13.33
Average cost per member	$101.00	$ 21.00	$ 14.33

Requirement 2

The average cost per member should not be used to predict total costs at different volumes of membership because it changes as volume changes. The average cost per member decreases as volume increases due to the fixed component of the club's operating costs. Managers should base cost predictions on cost behavior patterns, not on the average cost per member.

How do Managers Determine Cost Behavior?

In real life, managers need to figure out how their costs behave before they can make predictions and good business decisions. In this section, we discuss the most common ways of determining cost behavior.

Account Analysis

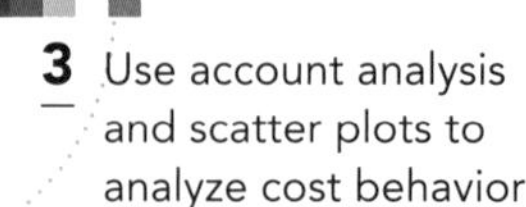

3 Use account analysis and scatter plots to analyze cost behavior

When performing <u>account analysis</u>, managers use their judgment to classify each general ledger account as a variable, fixed, or mixed cost. For example, by looking at invoices from his or her supplier, the hotel manager knows that every guest packet of toiletries costs $3. Because guests use or take these toiletries, the total toiletries cost rises in direct proportion to the number of guests. These facts allow the manager to classify the complimentary toiletries expense account as a variable cost.

Likewise, the hotel manager uses account analysis to determine how the depreciation expense accounts behave. Because the hotel uses straight-line depreciation on the parking ramp, building, and furnishings, the manager would classify the depreciation expense accounts as fixed costs. Thus, the manager can use this knowledge of cost behavior and his or her judgment to classify many accounts as variable or fixed.

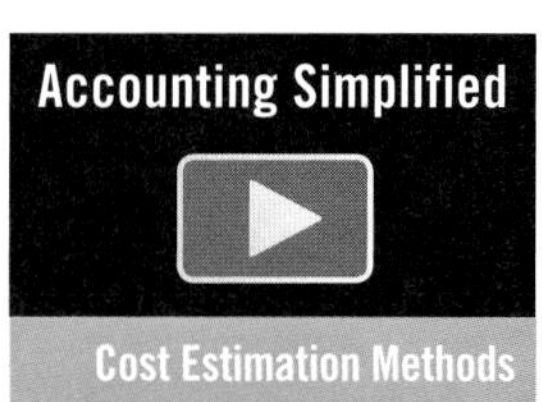

If your instructor is using MyAccountingLab, go to the Multimedia Library for a quick video on this topic.

Scatter Plots

The hotel manager also knows that many of the hotel's costs, such as utilities, are mixed. But how does the manager figure out the portion of the mixed cost that is fixed and the portion that is variable? In other words, how does the manager know from looking at the monthly utility bills that the hotel's utilities cost about $8,000 per month plus $8 more for every guest? One way of figuring this out is by collecting and analyzing historical data about costs and volume.

For example, let's assume that the hotel has collected the information shown in Exhibit 6-12 about last year's guest volume and utility costs.

EXHIBIT 6-12 Historical Information on Guest Volume and Utility Costs

Month	Guest Volume (x)	Utility Costs (y)
January	13,250	$114,000
February	15,200	136,000
March	17,600	135,000
April	18,300	157,000
May	22,900	195,400
June	24,600	207,800
July	25,200	209,600
August	24,900	208,300
September	22,600	196,000
October	20,800	176,400
November	18,300	173,600
December	15,420	142,000

As you can see, the hotel's business is seasonal. More people visit in the summer. However, special events such as the annual Festival of Lights, business conferences, and the nearby casino attract people to the hotel throughout the year.

Once the data has been collected, the manager creates a <u>scatter plot</u> of the data.

A scatter plot, which graphs the historical cost data on the y-axis and volume data on the x-axis, helps managers visualize the relationship between the cost and the volume of activity (number of guests, in our example). If there is a fairly strong relationship between the cost and volume, the data points will fall in a linear pattern, meaning they will resemble something close to a straight line. However, if there is little or no relationship between the cost and volume, the data points will appear almost random.

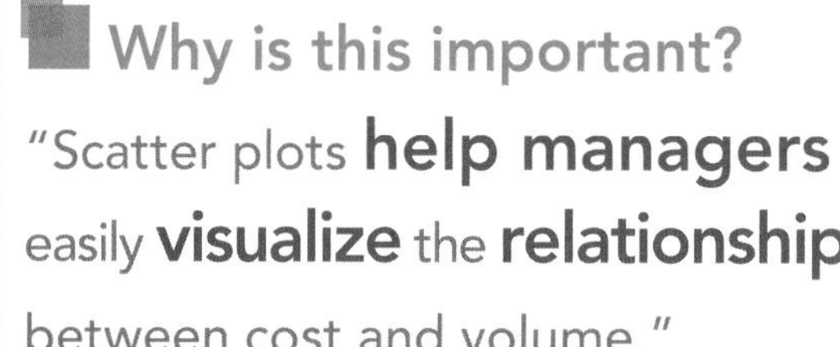

Exhibit 6-13 shows a scatter plot of the data in Exhibit 6-12. Scatter plots can be prepared by hand, but they are simpler to create using Microsoft Excel (see the "Technology Makes It Simple" feature on page 336). Notice how the data points fall in a pattern that resembles something *close* to a straight line. This shows us that there is a strong relationship between the number of guests and the hotel's utility costs. In other words, the number of guests could be considered a driver of the hotel's utilities costs (recall from our discussion of ABC in Chapter 4 that cost drivers are activities that cause costs to be incurred). On the other hand, if there were a *weaker* relationship between the number of guests and the utility costs, the data points would not fall in such a tight pattern. They would be more loosely scattered, but still in a semilinear pattern. If there were *no* relationship between the number of guests and the utility costs, the data points would appear almost random.

EXHIBIT 6-13 Scatter Plot of Monthly Data

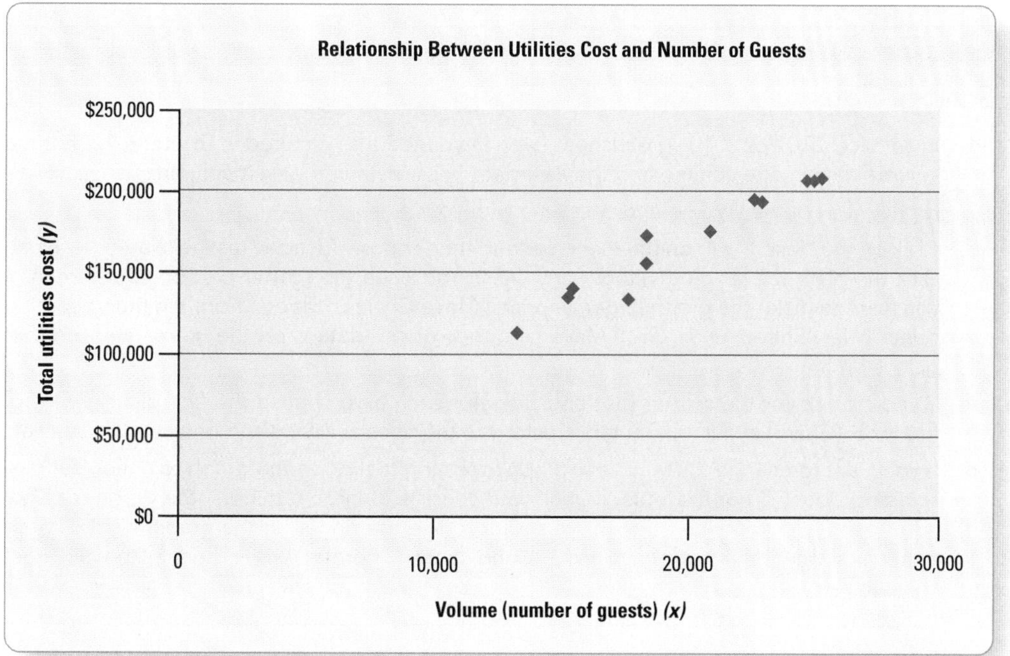

Why is this important? If the data points suggest a fairly weak relationship between the cost and the volume of the chosen activity, any cost equation based on that data will not be very useful for predicting future costs. If this is the case, the manager should consider using a different activity for modeling cost behavior. For example, many hotels use "occupancy rate" (the percentage of rooms rented) rather than number of guests as a basis for explaining and predicting variable and mixed costs.

Scatter plots are also very useful because they allow managers to identify **outliers**, or abnormal data points. Outliers are data points that do not fall in the same general pattern as the other data points. Since all data points in Exhibit 6-13 fall in the same basic pattern, no outliers appear to exist in our data. However, if a manager sees a potential outlier in the data, he or she should first determine whether the data is correct. Perhaps a clerical error was made when gathering or inputting the data. However, if the data is correct, the manager may need to consider whether to delete that data from any further analysis.

Once the scatter plot has been prepared and examined for outliers, the next step is to determine the cost behavior that best describes the historical data points pictured in the scatter plot. Take a moment and pencil in the cost behavior line that you think best represents the data points in Exhibit 6-13. Where does your line intersect the y-axis? At the origin or above it? In other words, does the utilities cost appear to be a purely variable cost or a mixed cost? If it's a mixed cost, what portion of it is fixed?

Instead of guessing, managers can use one of the following methods to estimate the cost equation that describes the data in the scatter plot:

- High-low method
- Regression analysis

The biggest difference between these methods is that the high-low method *uses only two* of the historical data points for this estimate, whereas regression analysis uses *all* of the historical data points. Therefore, regression analysis is theoretically the better of the two methods.

We'll describe both of these methods in the next sections. Before continuing, check out the "Technology Makes It Simple" feature. It shows you just how easy it is to make a scatter plot using Microsoft Excel 2007 or Excel 2010.

Technology makes it simple

Excel 2007 and Excel 2010

Scatter Plots

1. In an Excel 2007 or 2010 spreadsheet, type in your data as pictured in Exhibit 6-12. Put the volume data in one column and the associated cost data in the next column.
2. Highlight all of the volume and cost data with your cursor.
3. Click on the "Insert" tab on the menu bar and then choose "Scatter" as the chart type. Next, click the plain scatter plot (without any lines). You'll see the scatter plot on your screen. If you want to make the graph larger, choose "Move Chart Location" from the menu bar and select "New Sheet" and "OK." Make sure the volume data is on the x-axis and the cost data is on the y-axis.
4. To add labels for the scatter plot and titles for each axis, choose the first pictured layout from the "Chart Layout" menu tab. Customize the titles and labels to reflect your data set.
5. If you want to change the way your graph looks, right-click on the graph to check out customizing options. For example, if your data consists of large numbers, the graph may not automatically start at the origin. If you want to see the origin on the graph, right-click on either axis (where the number values are) and choose "Format Axis." Then, fix the minimum value at zero.

High-Low Method

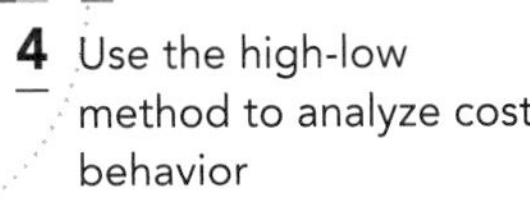

4 Use the high-low method to analyze cost behavior

The high-low method is an easy way to estimate the variable and fixed cost components of a mixed cost. The high-low method basically fits a mixed cost line through the highest and lowest *volume* data points, as shown in Exhibit 6-14, hence the name *high-low*. The high-low method produces the cost equation describing this mixed cost line.

To use the high-low method, we must first identify the months with the highest and lowest volume of activity. Looking at Exhibit 6-12, we see that the hotel served the *most* guests in July and the *fewest* guests in January. *Therefore, we use the data from only these two months in our analysis. We ignore data from all other months.* Even if a month other than July had the highest utility cost, we would still use July. Why? Because we choose the "high" data point based on the month with the highest volume of activity (number of guests)—not the highest cost. We choose the "low" data point in a similar fashion.

STEP 1: The first step is to find *the slope of the mixed cost line* that connects the January and July data points. The slope is the variable cost per unit of activity. We can determine the slope of a line as "rise over run." The *rise* is simply the

EXHIBIT 6-14 Mixed Cost Line Using High-Low Method

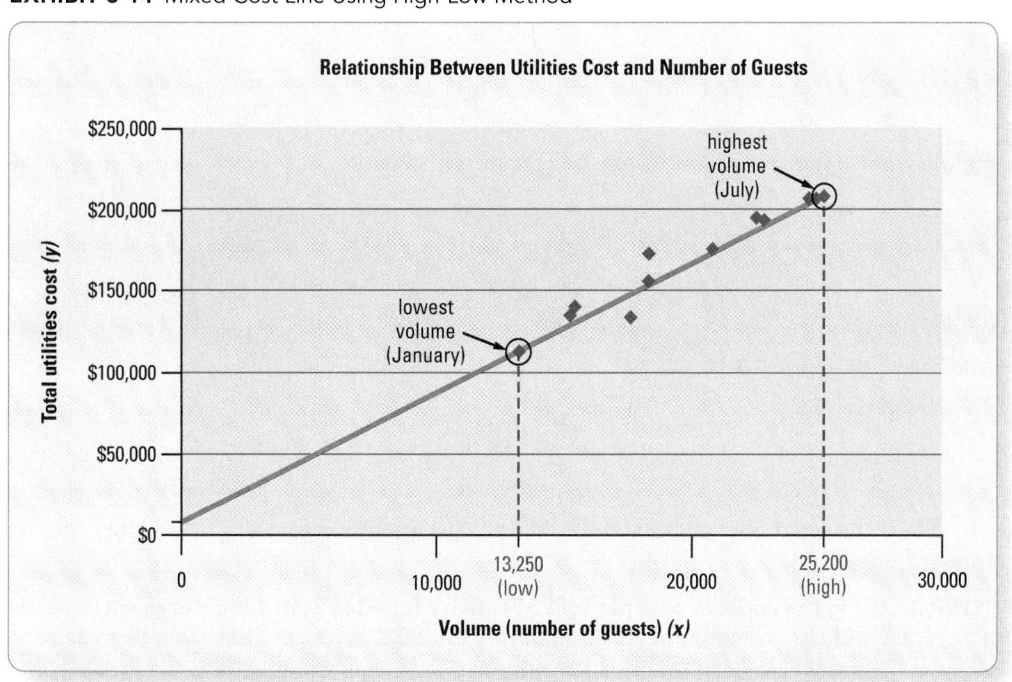

If your instructor is using MyAccountingLab, go to the Multimedia Library for a quick video on this topic.

difference in cost between the high and low data points (July and January in our case), while the *run* is the difference in *volume* between the high and low data points:

$$\text{Slope} = \text{Variable cost per unit of activity } (v) = \frac{\text{Rise}}{\text{Run}} = \frac{\text{Change in cost}}{\text{Change in volume}} = \frac{y\text{ (high)} - y\text{ (low)}}{x\text{ (high)} - x\text{ (low)}}$$

Using the data from July (as our high) and January (as our low), we calculate the slope as follows:

$$\frac{(\$209{,}600 - \$114{,}000)}{(25{,}200 \text{ guests} - 13{,}250 \text{ guests})} = \$8 \text{ per guest}$$

The slope of the mixed cost line, or variable cost per unit of activity, is $8 per guest.

STEP 2: The second step is to find the vertical intercept—the place where the line connecting the January and July data points intersects the y-axis. This is the fixed cost component of the mixed cost. We insert the slope found in Step 1 ($8 per guest) and the volume and cost data from *either* the high or low month into a mixed cost equation:

$$\begin{array}{ccccc} \text{Total mixed costs} & = & \text{Variable cost component} & + & \text{Fixed cost component} \\ y & = & vx & + & f \end{array}$$

For example, we can insert July's cost and volume data as follows:

$$\$209{,}600 = (\$8 \text{ per guest} \times 25{,}200 \text{ guests}) + f$$

And then solve for *f*:

$$f = \$8,000$$

Or we can use January's data to reach the same conclusion:

$$\begin{array}{ccc} y & = & vx + f \\ \$114,000 & = & (\$8 \text{ per guest} \times 13,250 \text{ guests}) + f \end{array}$$

And then solve for *f*:

$$f = \$8,000$$

Thus, the fixed cost component is \$8,000 per month regardless of whether we use July or January's data.

STEP 3: Using the variable cost per unit of activity found in Step 1 (\$8 per guest) and the fixed cost component found in Step 2 (\$8,000), write the equation representing the costs' behavior. This is the equation for the line connecting the January and July data points on our graph.

$$y = \$8x + \$8,000$$

where,

$$\begin{array}{l} y = \text{total monthly utilities cost} \\ x = \text{number of guests} \end{array}$$

This is the equation used by the manager in the first half of the chapter to express the hotel's utility costs.

One major drawback of the high-low method is that it uses only two data points: January and July. Because we ignored every other month, the line might not be representative of those months. In our example, the high-low line is representative of the other data points, but in other situations, it may not be. Therefore, the better method to use is regression analysis, which is explained next.

5 Use regression analysis to analyze cost behavior

Regression Analysis

<u>Regression analysis</u> is a statistical procedure for determining the line and cost equation that best fits *all of the data points, not just the high-volume and low-volume data points.* In fact, some refer to regression analysis as "the line of best fit." Since the statistical analysis considers all of the data points when forming the line, it is usually more accurate than the high-low method. A statistic (called the R-square) generated by regression analysis also tells us *how well* the line fits the data points. Regression analysis is tedious to complete by hand but simple to do using Microsoft Excel (see the "Technology Makes It Simple" feature on page 341). Many graphing calculators also perform regression analysis.

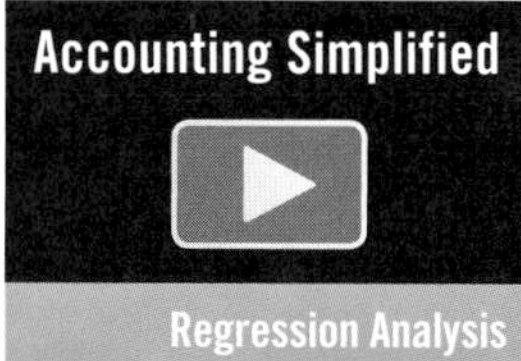

If your instructor is using MyAccountingLab, go to the Multimedia Library for a quick video on this topic.

Regression analysis using Microsoft Excel gives us the output shown in Exhibit 6-15. The output looks complicated, but for our purposes, we only need to consider the three highlighted pieces of information:

1. Intercept coefficient (this refers to the vertical intercept) = 14,538.05
2. X Variable 1 coefficient (this refers to the slope) = 7.85 (rounded)
3. The R-square value (the "goodness-of-fit" statistic) = 0.947 (rounded)

EXHIBIT 6-15 Output of Microsoft Excel Regression Analysis

	A	B	C	D	E	F	G	H	I
1	**SUMMARY OUTPUT**								
2									
3	***Regression Statistics***								
4	Multiple R		0.973273						
5	R Square		0.94726						
6	Adjusted R Square		0.941986						
7	Standard Error		8053.744						
8	Observations		12						
9									
10	**ANOVA**								
11		*df*	*SS*	*MS*	*F*	*Significance F*			
12	Regression	1	11650074512	1.17E + 10	179.6110363	1.02696E-07			
13	Residual	10	648627988.2	64862799					
14	Total	11	12298702500						
15									
16		*Coefficients*	*Standard Error*	*t Stat*	*P-value*	*Lower 95%*	*Upper 95%*	*Lower 95.0%*	*Upper 95.0%*
17	Intercept	14538.05	11898.3624	1.221853	0.249783701	-11973.15763	41049.25	-11973.16	41049.25
18	X Variable 1	7.849766	0.585720166	13.4019	1.02696E-07	6.5446997	9.154831	6.5447	9.154831

Let's look at each piece of information, starting with the highlighted information at the bottom of the output:

1. The "Intercept coefficient" is the vertical intercept of the mixed cost line. It's the fixed cost component of the mixed cost. Regression analysis tells us that the fixed component of the monthly utility bill is \$14,538 (rounded). Why is this different from the \$8,000 fixed component we found using the high-low method? It's because regression analysis considers *every* data point, not just the high- and low-volume data points, when forming the best fitting line.
2. The "X Variable 1 coefficient" is the line's slope, or our variable cost per guest. Regression analysis tells us that the hotel spends an extra \$7.85 on utilities for every guest it serves. This is slightly lower than the \$8 per guest amount we found using the high-low method.

   Using the regression output, we can write the utilities monthly cost equation as follows:

$$y = \$7.85x + \$14,538$$

where,

$$y = \text{total monthly utilities cost}$$
$$x = \text{number of guests}$$

Why is this important?

"Regression analysis is **fast** and **easy** to perform using Excel 2007 or Excel 2010. **Regression analysis** usually gives managers the most **representative** cost equations, allowing them to make the most **accurate** cost projections."

3. Now, let's look at the R-square statistic highlighted near the top of Exhibit 6-15. The R-square statistic is often referred to as a "goodness-of-fit" statistic because it tells us how well the regression line fits the data points. The R-square can range in value from zero to one, as shown in Exhibit 6-16. If there were no relationship between the number of guests and the hotel's utility costs, the data points would be scattered randomly

(rather than being in a linear pattern) and the R-square would be close to zero. If there were a *perfect* relationship between the number of guests and the hotel's utility cost, a *perfectly* straight line would run through *every* data point and the R-square would be 1.00. In our case, the R-square of 0.947 means that the regression line fits the data quite well (it's very close to 1.00). In other words, the data points *almost* fall in a straight line (as you can see in Exhibit 6-13).

EXHIBIT 6-16 Range of R-square Values

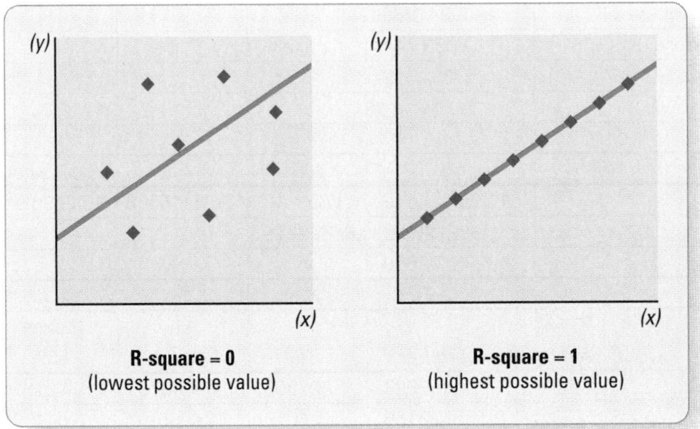

The R-square provides managers with very helpful information. The higher the R-square, the stronger the relationship between cost and volume. The stronger the relationship, the more confidence the manager would have in using the cost equation to predict costs at different volumes within the same relevant range. As a rule of thumb, an R-square over 0.80 generally indicates that the cost equation is very reliable for predicting costs at other volumes within the relevant range. An R-square between 0.50 and 0.80 means that the manager should use the cost equation with caution. However, if the R-square is fairly low (for example, less than 0.50), the manager should try using a different activity base (for example, room occupancy rate) for cost analysis because the current measure of volume is only weakly related to the costs.

Regression analysis can also help managers implement ABC. Recall from Chapter 4 that managers must choose a cost allocation base for every activity cost pool. The cost allocation base should be the primary cost driver of the costs in that pool. Management will use logic to come up with a short list of potential cost drivers for each activity cost pool. Then, management can run a regression analysis for each potential cost driver to see how strongly related it is to the activity costs in the pool. Managers compare the R-squares from each regression to see which one is highest. The regression with the highest R-square identifies the primary cost driver.

Adding a regression line to a scatter plot

Adding a regression line, the regression equation, and the R-square value to a scatter plot is very simple using Excel 2007 or Excel 2010. You'll be amazed at how quickly and easily you can create a professional-quality graph using the instructions found below.

Technology makes it simple

Excel 2007 and 2010

Adding a Regression Line, Equation, and R-square to the Scatter Plot

1. Start with the Excel Scatter plot you created using the directions found on page 336.
2. Point the cursor at any data point on your scatter plot and *right* click on the mouse.
3. Choose "Add Trendline."
4. Check the two boxes: "Display Equation on Chart" and "Display R-squared value on chart." Then "Close."
5. OPTIONAL: To force the regression line stretch back to the y-axis, point the cursor at the regression line and *right* click on the mouse. Choose "format Trendline." Then fill in the "Forecast Backward" box with the *lowest* x-value (volume) in your data set. Then "close."

Technology makes it simple

Excel 2007 and 2010

Regression Analysis

1. If you created a scatter plot, you have already done this first step. In an Excel spreadsheet, type in your data as pictured in Exhibit 6-12. Put the volume data in one column and the associated cost data in the below column.
2. Click on the "Data" tab on the menu bar.
3. Next, click on "Data Analysis." If you don't see it on your menu bar, follow the directions for add-ins given below before continuing.
4. From the list of data analysis tools, select "Regression," then "OK."
5. Follow the two instructions on the screen:
   - i. Highlight (or type in) the y-axis data range (this is your cost data).
   - ii. Highlight (or type in) the x-axis data range (this is your volume data).
   - iii. Click "OK."
6. That's all. Excel gives you the output shown in Exhibit 6-15.

DIRECTIONS FOR ADD-INs: It's easy and free to add the "Data Analysis Toolpak" if it's not already on your menu bar. You'll need to add it only once, and then it will always be on your menu bar. Simply follow these instructions:

1a. **For Excel 2007:** Click the Microsoft Office button (the colorful button in the upper-left-hand corner) and then click on the "Excel Options" box shown at the bottom.

1b. **For Excel 2010:** Click on the "File" tab on the menu bar. Then select "Options" on the left-hand side of the screen.

2. Click "Add-Ins."
3. In the "Manage" box at the bottom of the screen, select "Excel Add-ins" and click "GO."
4. In the "Add-Ins available" box, select the "Analysis Toolpak" check box and then click "OK."
5. If asked, click "Yes" to install.

Data Concerns

Cost equations are only as good as the data on which they are based. For example, if the hotel's utility bills are seasonal, management may want to develop separate cost equations for each season. For example, it might develop a winter utility bill cost equation using historical data from only the winter months. Management would do likewise for every other season. Inflation can also affect predictions. If inflation is running rampant, managers should adjust projected costs by the inflation rate. Even if the economy has generally low inflation, certain industries (such as health care) or raw material inputs may be experiencing large price changes.

Another cause for concern is outliers, or abnormal data points. Outliers can distort the results of the high-low method and regression analysis. Recall that the high-low method uses only two data points—the data points associated with the highest and lowest volumes of activity. If either of these points is an outlier, the resulting line and cost equation will be skewed. Because regression analysis uses all data points, any outlier in the data will affect the resulting line and cost equation. To find outliers, management should first plot the data like we did in Exhibit 6-13.

What are the Roles of Variable Costing and the Contribution Margin Income Statement?

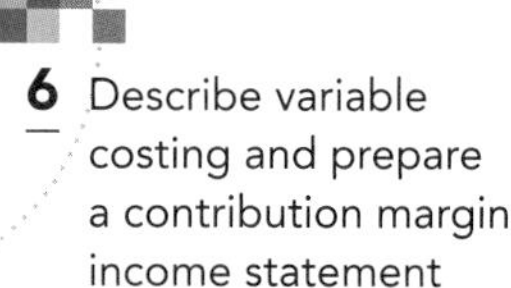

6 Describe variable costing and prepare a contribution margin income statement

You have just learned about different cost behaviors. As you'll see in the coming chapters, almost all business decisions are influenced by cost behavior. In the following sections, we'll explain how the accounting system can communicate cost behavior information to managers so that they have it readily available for planning, decision-making, and performance evaluation purposes.

Comparing Absorption Costing and Variable Costing

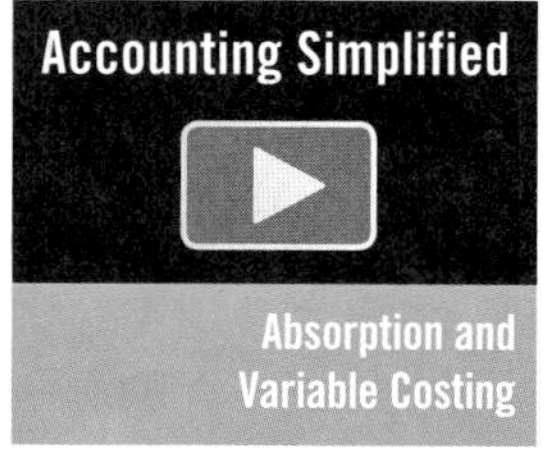

If your instructor is using MyAccountingLab, go to the Multimedia Library for a quick video on this topic.

So far in this textbook, we have used a costing concept known as absorption costing. Why? Generally Accepted Accounting Principles (GAAP) requires absorption costing for external financial reporting and the Internal Revenue Service (IRS) requires it for tax preparation. Under **absorption costing**, all manufacturing-related costs, whether fixed or variable, are "absorbed" into the cost of the product. In other words, all direct materials, direct labor, and MOH costs are treated as inventoriable product costs, as described in Chapter 2. We used absorption costing, also known as "traditional" or "full costing" when we illustrated job costing and process costing in Chapters 3, 4, and 5.

Under absorption costing, no distinction is made between manufacturing costs that rise and fall with production volume and manufacturing costs that remain fixed. As a review,

- variable manufacturing costs would include direct material, direct labor, and variable manufacturing overhead costs (MOH) such as the utilities used during the production process.
- fixed MOH costs would include property taxes and insurance on the plant, straight-line depreciation on the plant, lease payments on the production equipment and the portion of utilities that are not affected by changes in production volume.

Supporters of absorption costing argue that all of these costs—whether variable or fixed—are necessary for production to occur, so *all* of these costs should become part of the inventoriable cost of the product.

On the other hand, many accountants and managers do not agree. They argue that fixed manufacturing costs are related to the available production capacity and will be incurred *regardless* of the actual production volume which occurs during the period. Since these costs will be incurred regardless of volume, they should be treated as period costs and expensed immediately. This argument has led to the development and use of an alternative costing system known as **variable costing** (or **direct costing**) in which only *variable* manufacturing costs are treated as inventoriable product costs. Since GAAP and the IRS require absorption costing for external reporting, variable costing may only be used for internal management purposes.

One benefit of variable costing is that it often leads to better decisions. By assigning only variable manufacturing costs to each unit of product, managers can easily see how much additional manufacturing cost will be incurred every time another unit is produced. In addition, the unit cost of the product will not be affected by the number of units produced during the period, as it is when fixed manufacturing costs are absorbed into the unit cost. As we'll discuss next, another benefit of variable costing is that it provides incentives for better inventory management than does absorption costing.

Let's illustrate this concept using an example. Exhibit 6-17 provides the most recent annual data for ShredCo, a maker of electronic paper shredders.

EXHIBIT 6-17 ShredCo data

Variable costs:	
Direct material cost per unit produced	$35
Direct labor cost per unit produced	$10
Variable MOH cost per unit produced	$5
Variable operating expenses per unit sold (selling, general and administrative)	$2
Fixed costs:	
Fixed MOH	$1,000,000
Fixed operating expenses (selling, general and administrative)	$300,000
Other information:	
Units produced	40,000 units
Sales price per unit	$100

Exhibit 6-18 shows the inventoriable product cost of one unit under both absorption costing and variable costing. Notice that the only difference is the treatment of fixed MOH. Absorption costing includes fixed MOH per unit ($25) in the unit cost, whereas variable costing does not. The $75 unit cost shown in Exhibit 6-18 will be used by the company to 1) record the value of inventory on the balance sheet, and 2) record Cost of Goods Sold on the income statement when the inventory is eventually sold.

Notice how variable costing shows managers exactly how much extra cost ($50) will be incurred every time a unit is made. This transparency is not the case with absorption costing, which can easily mislead managers. To illustrate, let's assume that the company decides to produce an extra 5,000 units with its existing capacity. Using variable costing, we see the additional production cost will really be $250,000 (5,000 units × $50).

EXHIBIT 6-18 Comparing inventoriable product costs

Manufacturing Costs	Absorption Costing	Variable Costing
Direct materials	$35	$35
Direct labor	10	10
Variable MOH	5	5
Fixed MOH ($1,000,000 ÷ 40,000 units)	25	–
Unit cost	$75	$50

Why is this important?

"Variable costing **helps** manufacturers **identify** the **variable cost** of making each unit of a product. This information will be **critical** to making many of the business **decisions,** such as whether or not to outsource the product."

However, absorption costing could mislead the manager into believing that the extra cost would be $375,000 (5,000 × $75). The fallacy in this erroneous analysis stems from treating the $25 of fixed MOH in the product cost as if it were variable. In fact, the company will *not* incur an additional $25 of fixed cost with every unit produced. Rather, the company will incur $1 million of fixed cost *regardless* of the production volume, as long as the production volume stays within the company's relevant range (which in most cases is its existing production capacity). Variable costing tends be the better costing system for internal decision-making purposes because the reported unit cost is purely variable in nature.

Exhibit 6-19 illustrates period costs under both costing systems. Remember that these are often referred to as "operating expenses" in the income statement. Notice again that the only difference is the treatment of fixed MOH. Under absorption costing, *none* of the fixed MOH is expensed as a period cost. Under variable costing, *all* of the fixed MOH ($1 million) is expensed as a period cost.

EXHIBIT 6-19 Comparing period costs (operating expenses)

Operating Expenses of the Period	Absorption Costing	Variable Costing
Variable operating expenses when 40,000 units are sold (40,000 × $2)	$ 80,000	$ 80,000
Fixed operating expenses	300,000	300,000
Fixed MOH	–	1,000,000
Total period costs	$380,000	$1,380,000

Keep the following rule of thumb in mind:

The ONLY difference between absorption costing and variable costing is the treatment of Fixed MOH, and the *timing* with which it is expensed:

- Under variable costing, fixed MOH is expensed immediately as a period cost (operating expense).
- Under absorption costing, fixed MOH becomes part of the inventoriable cost of the product, which isn't expensed (as Cost of Goods Sold) until the inventory is sold.

An Alternative Income Statement Format

Now that you know the difference between absorption costing and variable costing, let's see how the information is communicated to managers in the income statement.

Comparing Income Statement Formats

Let's start with the situation in which the company sells *exactly* all of the units it produced during the period. In our example, this means that the company sells all 40,000 units it produced during the year. This situation occurs most frequently with lean producers who use Just-in-Time inventory systems. Exhibit 6-20 shows a traditional income statement, which is based on absorption costing. Notice how Cost of Goods Sold is calculated using the $75 unit cost shown in Exhibit 6-18.

EXHIBIT 6-20 Traditional Income Statement based on Absorption Costing

ShredCo **Traditional Income Statement (Absorption costing)** For the year ending December 31	
Sales revenue (40,000 × $100)	$4,000,000
Less: Cost of goods sold (40,000 × $75)	3,000,000
Gross profit	$1,000,000
Less: Operating expenses [300,000 + (40,000 × $2)]	380,000
Operating income	$ 620,000

In contrast, Exhibit 6-21 shows a **contribution margin income statement**, which is an income statement organized by cost behavior. When manufacturers use variable costing, they report income internally using a contribution margin income statement format.

EXHIBIT 6-21 Contribution Margin Income Statement using Variable Costing

ShredCo **Contribution Margin Income Statement (Variable costing)** For the year ending December 31	
Sales revenue (40,000 × $100)	$4,000,000
Less: Variable expenses	
Variable cost of goods sold (40,000 × $50)	2,000,000
Variable operating expenses (40,000 × $2)	80,000
Contribution margin	$1,920,000
Less: Fixed expenses	
Fixed MOH	1,000,000
Fixed operating expenses	300,000
Operating income	$620,000

Notice the following in Exhibit 6-21:

- The contribution margin income statement is organized by cost behavior.
- All variable costs are expensed *above* the contribution margin line. As a result, only the *variable* product cost ($50, from Exhibit 6-18) is used when calculating Variable Cost of Goods Sold.
- All fixed costs, including fixed MOH, are expensed *below* the contribution margin line.
- The **contribution margin** is equal to sales revenue minus variable expenses. It shows managers how much profit has been made on sales before considering fixed costs.
- The operating income ($620,000) is the *same* in both statements. For manufacturers, this equality will *only* occur when all of units produced during a period are also sold during that same period, resulting in no change in inventory levels.
- For service and merchandising companies, operating income will *always* be the same regardless of the income statement format used.

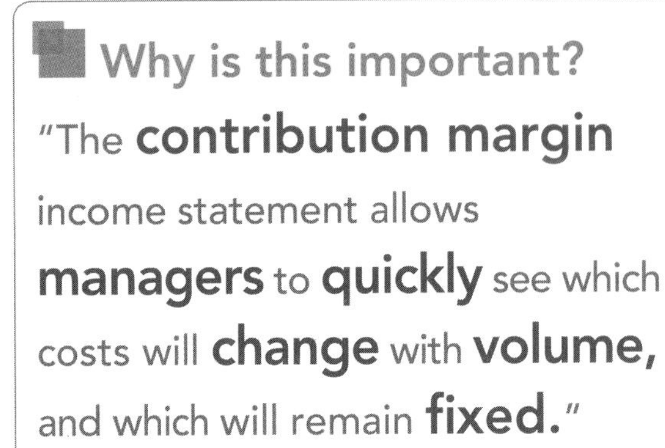

The contribution margin income statement may only be used for internal management purposes, never for external reporting. Managers like the contribution margin format because it allows them to quickly see which costs will change with fluctuations in volume, and which costs will remain the same. For example, if sales volume increases 10%, managers would expect sales revenue and variable costs to increase by 10%. As a result, the contribution margin should also increase 10%. On the other hand, all fixed costs shown below the contribution margin should not change.

Service and Merchandising Companies

Variable costing only applies to manufacturing companies since they are the only type of company that incurs manufacturing overhead costs. However, many service and merchandising companies like to use the contribution margin format of the income statement for internal management purposes. Why? Because the contribution margin income statement clearly communicates cost behavior information to managers who need this information for planning and decision making purposes. Just as shown in Exhibit 6-21, all variable expenses are deducted from revenue to arrive at the company's contribution margin. Next, all fixed expenses are subtracted from the contribution margin to arrive at operating income.

For merchandising companies, Cost of Goods Sold is considered to be a variable cost because it rises and falls with the amount of inventory sold. Service companies have no Cost of Goods Sold. Since neither of these types of companies have fixed manufacturing overhead, operating income will always be the same regardless of the income statement format used.

Comparing Operating Income: Variable versus Absorption Costing

For manufacturers, operating income will not always be the same between the two costing systems. In fact, it will *only* be the same if the manufacturer sells *exactly* what it produced during the period, as was the case in Exhibits 6-20 and 6-21. This scenario is typical of a lean producer. However, traditional manufacturers in a growing economy often produce extra safety stock, *increasing* their inventory levels to ensure against unexpected demand. On the other hand, in periods of economic recession (such as in the years 2008–2009) companies often *reduce* their inventory levels to decrease costs, build cash reserves, and adjust for lower sales demand.

We will discuss how inventory levels impact operating income, for both absorption and variable costing, under three possible scenarios:

1. Inventory levels remain constant
2. Inventory levels increase
3. Inventory levels decrease

As we discuss each scenario, keep in mind that in our example, absorption costing assigned $25 of fixed MOH to each unit of product produced by ShredCo (Exhibit 6-18).

Scenario 1: Inventory levels remain constant

As shown in Exhibits 6-20, 6-21, and 6-22, when inventory levels remain constant, both absorption costing and variable costing result in the same operating income. This scenario usually occurs at lean manufacturers since they only produce enough inventory to fill existing customer orders.

EXHIBIT 6-22 Inventory levels remain constant

In this situation, *all* fixed MOH incurred during the period ($1,000,000) is expensed under both costing systems. Under variable costing, it is expensed as a period cost ($1,000,000), as shown in Exhibit 6-21. Under absorption costing, it is first absorbed into the product's cost ($25 of the $75 unit cost), and then expensed as Cost of Goods Sold when the product is sold.

When all product is sold in the same period as it is produced, exactly $1 million of fixed MOH is expensed as part of Cost of Goods Sold (40,000 × $25) as shown in Exhibit 6-20.

Scenario 2: Inventory levels increase

As shown in Exhibit 6-23, when inventory levels increase, operating income will be greater under absorption costing than it is under variable costing. This scenario typically occurs at traditional manufacturers during times of economic growth.

EXHIBIT 6-23 Inventory levels increase

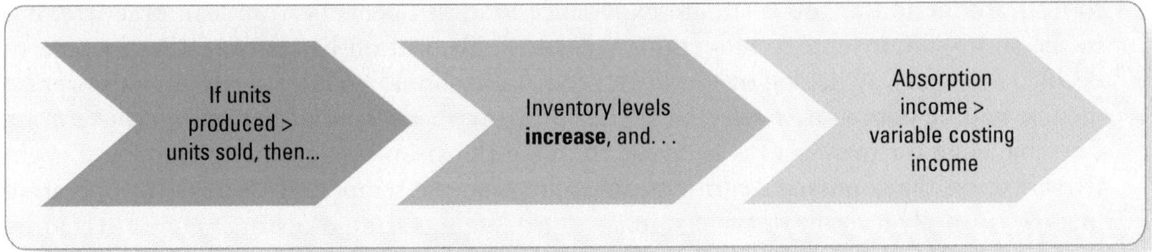

In this situation, all fixed MOH incurred during the period is expensed as a period cost under variable costing ($1,000,000). However, under absorption costing, some of the fixed MOH remains "trapped" on the balance sheet as part of the cost of inventory. For example, let's say only 30,000 of the 40,000 units are sold, leaving 10,000 units still in ending inventory. As a result, $750,000 of fixed MOH is expensed as part of Cost of Goods Sold (30,000 units × $25) while $250,000 of fixed MOH (10,000 units × $25) remains in inventory. As a result, *more* cost is expensed under variable costing than under absorption costing, leading to a higher operating income under absorption costing.

Thus, under absorption costing, managers can misuse their powers by continuing to build up unwarranted levels of inventory simply to increase operating income. The more inventory builds up, the more favorable operating income will be. Unfortunately, as we learned in Chapter 4, building unnecessary inventory is wasteful and should be avoided. Because of this drawback to absorption costing, many companies prefer to use variable costing to evaluate managers' performance. Since variable costing expenses all fixed MOH in the current period regardless of the amount of inventory produced, managers have no incentive to build unnecessary inventory.

Scenario 3: Inventory levels decrease

As shown in Exhibit 6-24, when inventory levels decrease, operating income will be greater under variable costing than it is under absorption costing. This scenario typically occurs at traditional manufacturers during times of economic recession. It also occurs when traditional manufacturers are in the process of switching to lean operations, which carry little to no inventory.

EXHIBIT 6-24 Inventory levels decrease

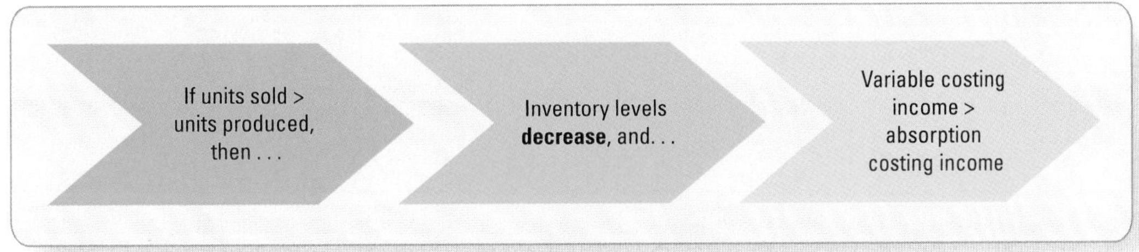

In this situation, all fixed MOH incurred during the period is expensed under variable costing ($1,000,000). However, under absorption costing, all of the fixed MOH of the period is expensed as part of Cost of Goods Sold *plus* some of the fixed MOH from the previous period. For example, let's say that 45,000 units are sold, comprised of the 40,000 units produced in the current period and 5,000 units produced in the previous period. For the sake of simplicity, we'll assume the same unit costs were incurred in the previous period. As a result of selling 45,000 units this year, \$1,125,000 of fixed MOH is expensed as Cost of Goods Sold (45,000 × \$25). This figure consists of \$1,000,000 from the current year (40,000 × \$25) and \$125,000 from the previous year (5,000 × \$25). As a result, *more* cost is expensed under absorption costing than under variable costing, leading to a lower net income under absorption costing.

Managers who are evaluated based on absorption income have every incentive to *avoid* the situation in which inventory levels decline. However, sometimes it is in the company's best interest to decrease inventory levels. For example, companies switching over to lean production methods should experience long-run benefits from lean practices, but in the short-run, inventory reductions will cause absorption-based operating income to decline. Managers switching over to lean production should be fully aware that absorption income will be temporarily affected as the company sheds itself of unnecessary inventory. The challenge for managers is to avoid thinking that lean operations are having a negative effect on the company's earnings, when, in fact, the temporary decrease in operating income is simply a result of the costing system. Again, variable costing is not affected by inventory fluctuations, making it the better costing system for evaluating performance.

Reconciling Operating Income Between the Two Costing Systems

As discussed, absorption costing is required by GAAP and the IRS, yet variable costing is preferred for internal decision-making and performance evaluation purposes. Thus, managers are often exposed to both sets of information. For manufacturers, the costing systems will yield different results for operating income when inventory levels increase or decline. Managers can easily reconcile the difference between the two income figures using the following formula:

Difference in operating income = (Change in inventory level, in units) × (Fixed MOH per unit)

We'll illustrate the use of this formula next.

Reconciling Income When Inventory Levels Increase

Let's try this formula with the example in which 40,000 units are produced, yet only 30,000 are sold. Using the formula, we predict the difference in operating income will be:

Difference in operating income = (Change in inventory level, in units) × (Fixed MOH per unit)
\$250,000 = 10,000 units × \$ 25

Since the inventory level has *grown*, we would expect operating income under absorption costing to be *greater* than it is under variable costing by \$250,000 (see Exhibit 6-23). Exhibit 6-25, which presents comparative income statements, verifies this prediction: Absorption costing income (\$390,000) is *higher* than variable costing income (\$140,000) by \$250,000.

EXHIBIT 6-25 Comparing Income when Inventory Levels Increase

Panel A: Absorption Costing:

ShredCo Traditional Income Statement (Absorption Costing) For the year ending December 31	
Sales revenue (30,000 × $100)	$3,000,000
Less: Cost of goods sold (30,000 × $75)	2,250,000
Gross profit	$ 750,000
Less: Operating expenses [300,000 + (30,000 × $2)]	360,000
Operating income	$ 390,000

Panel B: Variable Costing:

ShredCo Contribution Margin Income Statement (Variable Costing) For the year ending December 31		
Sales revenue (30,000 × $100)		$3,000,000
Less: Variable expenses		
Variable cost of goods sold (30,000 × $50)		1,500,000
Variable operating expenses (30,000 × $2)		60,000
Contribution margin		$1,440,000
Less: Fixed expenses		
Fixed MOH		1,000,000
Fixed operating expenses		300,000
Operating income		$ 140,000

Reconciling Income When Inventory Levels Decrease

Now let's briefly consider the situation in which inventory decreases, rather than increases. Let's assume that 45,000 units are sold, comprised of 40,000 that were produced in the current period plus 5,000 units that were produced in the previous period. The formula used to reconcile income suggests that operating income under absorption costing will be *lower* than it is under variable costing (see Exhibit 6-24) by $125,000:

Difference in operating income = (change in inventory level, in units) × (Fixed MOH per unit)
$125,000 = 5,000 units × $ 25

Exhibit 6-26 verifies the truth of this prediction. Operating income under absorption costing ($735,000) is $125,000 *lower* than operating income under variable costing ($860,000).

Key points to remember

You have just learned about variable costing and the contribution margin income statement. Some key points to remember are summarized in Exhibit 6-27.

EXHIBIT 6-26 Comparing Income when Inventory Levels Decrease

Panel A: Absorption Costing:

ShredCo
Traditional Income Statement (Absorption Costing)
For the year ending December 31

Sales revenue (45,000 × $100)	$4,500,000
Less: Cost of goods sold (45,000 × $75)	3,375,000
Gross profit	$1,125,000
Less: Operating expenses [300,000 + (45,000 × $2)]	390,000
Operating income	$ 735,000

Panel B: Variable Costing:

ShredCo
Contribution Margin Income Statement (Variable Costing)
For the year ending December 31

Sales revenue (45,000 × $100)	$4,500,000
Less: Variable expenses	
Variable cost of goods sold (45,000 × $50)	2,250,000
Variable operating expenses (45,000 × $2)	90,000
Contribution margin	$2,160,000
Less: Fixed expenses	
Fixed MOH	1,000,000
Fixed operating expenses	300,000
Operating income	$ 860,000

EXHIBIT 6-27 Key Points about Variable Costing and the Contribution Margin Income Statement

Variable Costing

- treats all fixed MOH costs as operating expenses in the period incurred, rather than treating fixed MOH as an inventoriable product cost.
- can only be used for internal management purposes; never for external financial reporting or tax purposes.
- is often better for decision making than absorption costing because it clearly shows managers the additional cost of making one more unit of product (the variable cost per unit).
- is often better for performance evaluation than absorption costing because it gives managers no incentive to build unnecessary inventory.
- will result in a different operating income than absorption costing for manufacturers whose inventory levels *increase* or *decrease* from the previous period.

The Contribution Margin Income Statement

- is organized by cost behavior. First, all variable expenses are deducted from sales revenue to arrive at the company's contribution margin. Next, all fixed expenses are deducted from the contribution margin to arrive at operating income.
- is often more useful than a traditional income statement for planning and decision making because it clearly distinguishes the costs that will be affected by changes in volume (the variable costs) from the costs that will be unaffected (fixed costs).
- can only be used for internal management purposes, and never for external financial reporting.
- will show the same operating income as a traditional income statement for 1) service firms, 2) merchandising companies, and 3) manufacturers *only* if their inventory levels remain stable.

Decision Guidelines

Cost Behavior

As the manager of a local fitness club, Fitness-for-Life, you'll want to plan for operating costs at various levels of membership. Before you can make forecasts, you'll need to make some of the following decisions.

Decision	Guidelines
How can I separate the fixed and the variable components of a mixed cost?	• Managers typically use the high-low method or regression analysis. • The high-low method is fast and easy but uses only two historical data points to form the cost equation and, therefore, may not be very indicative of the cost's true behavior. • Regression analysis uses every data point provided to determine the cost equation that best fits the data. It is simple to do with Excel, but tedious to do by hand.
I've used the high-low method to formulate a cost equation. Can I tell how well the cost equation fits the data?	The only way to determine how well the high-low cost equation fits the data is by (1) plotting the data, (2) drawing a line through the data points associated with the highest and lowest volume, and (3) "visually inspecting" the resulting graph to see if the line is representative of the other plotted data points.
I've used regression analysis to formulate a cost equation. Can I tell how well the cost equation fits the data?	The R-square is a "goodness-of-fit" statistic that tells how well the regression analysis cost equation fits the data. The R-square ranges from 0 to 1, with 1 being a perfect fit. When the R-square is high, the cost equation should render fairly accurate predictions.
Do I need to be concerned about anything before using the high-low method or regression analysis?	Cost equations are only as good as the data on which they are based. Managers should plot the historical data to see if a relationship between cost and volume exists. In addition, scatter plots help managers identify outliers. Managers should remove outliers before further analysis. Managers should also adjust cost equations for seasonal data, inflation, and price changes.
Can I present the club's financial statements in a manner that will help with planning and decision making?	Managers often use contribution margin income statements for internal planning and decision making. Contribution margin income statements organize costs by *behavior* (fixed versus variable) rather than by *function* (product versus period).
What is the difference between absorption and variable costing?	Fixed manufacturing costs are treated as: • inventoriable product costs under absorption costing. • period costs under variable costing.
How are inventoriable product costs calculated under absorption costing and variable costing?	*Absorption Costing*: Direct materials + Direct labor + Variable MOH + Fixed MOH = Product cost *Variable Costing*: Direct materials + Direct labor + Variable MOH = Product cost
Why is variable costing often used for internal management purposes?	• Variable costing and the contribution margin income statement help managers easily predict the cost of operating at different volumes within the relevant range. • Variable costing helps managers with decision making, because it allows them to easily see the cost of making one more unit of product. • Variable costing does not give managers incentives to build up unnecessary inventory.

Absorption Costing	*Variable Costing*
Direct materials	Direct materials
+ Direct labor	+ Direct labor
+ Variable MOH	+ Variable MOH
+ Fixed MOH	
= Product cost	= Product cost

SUMMARY PROBLEM 2

As the new manager of a local fitness club, Fitness-for-Life, you have been studying the club's financial data. You would like to determine how the club's costs behave in order to make accurate predictions for next year. Here is information from the last 6 months:

Month	Club Membership (number of members)	Total Operating Costs	Average Operating Costs per Member
July	450	$ 8,900	$19.78
August	480	$ 9,800	$20.42
September	500	$10,100	$20.20
October	550	$10,150	$18.45
November	560	$10,500	$18.75
December	525	$10,200	$19.43

Requirements

1. By looking at the "Total Operating Costs" and the "Operating Costs per Member," can you tell whether the club's operating costs are variable, fixed, or mixed? Explain your answer.
2. Use the high-low method to determine the club's monthly operating cost equation.
3. Using your answer from Requirement 2, predict total monthly operating costs if the club has 600 members.
4. Can you predict total monthly operating costs if the club has 3,000 members? Explain your answer.
5. Prepare the club's traditional income statement and its contribution margin income statement for the month of July. Assume that your cost equation from Requirement 2 accurately describes the club's cost behavior. The club charges members $30 per month for unlimited access to its facilities.
6. *Optional*: Perform regression analysis using Microsoft Excel. What is the monthly operating cost equation? What is the R-square? Why is the cost equation different from that in Requirement 2?

SOLUTIONS

Requirement 1

By looking at "Total Operating Costs," we can see that the club's operating costs are not purely fixed; otherwise, total costs would remain constant. Operating costs appear to be either variable or mixed because they increase in total as the number of members increases. By looking at the "Operating Costs per Member," we can see that the operating costs aren't purely variable; otherwise, the "per-member" cost would remain constant. Therefore, the club's operating costs are mixed.

Requirement 2

Use the high-low method to determine the club's operating cost equation:

STEP 1: The highest volume month is November, and the lowest volume month is July. Therefore, we use *only these 2 months* to determine the cost equation. The first step is to find the variable cost per unit of activity, which is the slope of the line connecting the November and July data points:

$$\frac{\text{Rise}}{\text{Run}} = \frac{\text{Change in } y}{\text{Change in } x} = \frac{y\text{ (high)} - y\text{ (low)}}{x\text{ (high)} - x\text{ (low)}} = \frac{(\$10{,}500 - \$8{,}900)}{(560 - 450\text{ members})} = \$14.55\text{ per member (rounded)}$$

STEP 2: The second step is to find the fixed cost component (vertical intercept) by plugging in the slope and either July or November data to a mixed cost equation:

$$y = vx + f$$

Using November data:

$$\$10{,}500 = (\$14.55/\text{member} \times 560\text{ guests}) + f$$

Solving for *f*:

$$f = \$2{,}352$$

Or we can use July data to reach the same conclusion:

$$\$8{,}900 = (\$14.55/\text{members} \times 450\text{ guests}) + f$$

Solving for *f*:

$$f = \$2{,}352\text{ (rounded)}$$

STEP 3: Write the monthly operating cost equation:

$$y = \$14.55x + \$2{,}352$$

where,

$$x = \text{number of members}$$
$$y = \text{total monthly operating costs}$$

Requirement 3

Predict total monthly operating costs when volume reaches 600 members:

$$y = (\$14.55 \times 600) + \$2{,}352$$
$$y = \$11{,}082$$

Requirement 4

Our current data and cost equation are based on 450 to 560 members. If membership reaches 3,000, operating costs could behave much differently. That volume falls outside our current relevant range.

Requirement 5

The club had 450 members in July and total operating costs of $8,900. Thus, its traditional income statement is as follows:

FITNESS-FOR-LIFE Income Statement Month Ended July 31	
Club membership revenue (450 × $30)	$13,500
Less: Operating expenses (given)	(8,900)
Operating income	$ 4,600

To prepare the club's contribution margin income statement, we need to know how much of the total $8,900 operating costs is fixed and how much is variable. If the cost equation from Requirement 2 accurately reflects the club's cost behavior, fixed costs will be $2,352 and variable costs will be $6,548 (= $14.55 × 450). The contribution margin income statement would look like this:

FITNESS-FOR-LIFE Contribution Margin Income Statement Month Ended July 31	
Club membership revenue (450 × $30)	$13,500
Less: Variable expenses (450 × $14.55)	(6,548)
Contribution margin	6,952
Less: Fixed expenses	(2,352)
Operating income	$ 4,600

Requirement 6

Regression analysis using Microsoft Excel results in the following cost equation and R-square:

$$y = \$11.80x + \$3,912$$

where,

x = number of members

y = total monthly operating costs

R-square = 0.8007

The regression analysis cost equation uses all of the data points, not just the data from November and July. Therefore, it better represents all of the data. The high R-square means that the regression line fits the data well and predictions based on this cost equation should be quite accurate.

END OF CHAPTER

Learning Objectives

- 1 Describe key characteristics and graphs of various cost behaviors
- 2 Use cost equations to express and predict costs
- 3 Use account analysis and scatter plots to analyze cost behavior
- 4 Use the high-low method to analyze cost behavior
- 5 Use regression analysis to analyze cost behavior
- 6 Describe variable costing and prepare a contribution margin income statement

Accounting Vocabulary

Absorption Costing. (p. 342) The costing method where products "absorb" both fixed and variable manufacturing costs.

Account Analysis. (p. 334) A method for determining cost behavior that is based on a manager's judgment in classifying each general ledger account as a variable, fixed, or mixed cost.

Committed Fixed Costs. (p. 323) Fixed costs that are locked in because of previous management decisions; management has little or no control over these costs in the short run.

Contribution Margin. (p. 345) Sales revenue minus variable expenses.

Contribution Margin Income Statement. (p. 345) Income statement that organizes costs by *behavior* (variable costs or fixed costs) rather than by *function*.

Cost Behavior. (p. 320) Describes how costs change as volume changes.

Cost Equation. (p. 321) A mathematical equation for a straight line that expresses how a cost behaves.

Curvilinear Costs. (p. 330) A cost behavior that is not linear (not a straight line).

Discretionary Fixed Costs. (p. 323) Fixed costs that are a result of annual management decisions; fixed costs that are controllable in the short run.

Fixed Costs. (p. 323) Costs that do not change in total despite wide changes in volume.

High-Low Method. (p. 336) A method for determining cost behavior that is based on two historical data points: the highest and lowest volume of activity.

Mixed Cost. (p. 325) Costs that change, but *not* in direct proportion to changes in volume. Mixed costs have both variable cost and fixed cost components.

Regression Analysis. (p. 338) A statistical procedure for determining the line that best fits the data by using *all of the historical data points, not just the high and low data points.*

Relevant Range. (p. 327) The band of volume where total fixed costs remain constant at a certain level and where the variable cost *per unit* remains constant at a certain level.

Scatter Plot. (p. 334) A graph that plots historical cost and volume data.

Step Costs. (p. 329) A cost behavior that is fixed over a small range of activity and then jumps to a different fixed level with moderate changes in volume.

Outliers. (p. 335) Abnormal data points; data points that do not fall in the same general pattern as the other data points.

Variable Costs. (p. 320) Costs incurred for every unit of activity. As a result, total variable costs change in direct proportion to changes in volume.

Variable Costing. (p. 343) The costing method that assigns only *variable* manufacturing costs to products. All fixed manufacturing costs (Fixed MOH) are expensed as period costs.

Quick Check

1. *(Learning Objective 1)* If a *per-unit* cost remains constant over a wide range of volume, the cost is most likely a
   a. variable cost.
   b. fixed cost.
   c. mixed cost.
   d. step cost.

2. *(Learning Objective 1)* The cost per unit decreases as volume increases for which of the following cost behaviors?
   a. Variable costs and fixed costs
   b. Variable costs and mixed costs
   c. Fixed costs and mixed costs
   d. Only fixed costs

3. *(Learning Objective 2)* In the following mixed cost equation, what amount represents the **total variable cost component**: $y = vx + f$?
   a. y
   b. v
   c. f
   d. vx

4. *(Learning Objective 2)* Which of the following would generally be considered a committed fixed cost for a retailing firm?
   a. Cost of a trip to Cancun given to the employee who is "Employee of the Year"
   b. Lease payments made on the store building
   c. Cost of sponsoring the local golf tournament for charity
   d. Cost of annual sales meeting for all employees

5. *(Learning Objective 3)* Which method is used to see if a relationship between the cost driver and total cost exists?
   a. Scatter plot
   b. Variance analysis
   c. Outlier
   d. Account analysis

6. *(Learning Objective 4)* When choosing the high point for the high-low method, how is the high point selected?
   a. The point with the highest total cost is chosen.
   b. The point with the highest volume of activity is chosen.
   c. The point that has the highest cost and highest volume of activity is always chosen.
   d. Both the high point and the low point are selected at random.

7. *(Learning Objective 5)* What is the advantage of using regression analysis to determine the cost equation?
   a. The method is objective.
   b. All data points are used to calculate the equation for the cost equation.
   c. It will generally be more accurate than the high-low method.
   d. All of the above statements are true about regression analysis.

8. *(Learning Objective 5)* Which of the following statements about using regression analysis is *true*?
   a. Regression analysis always ignores outliers.
   b. Regression analysis uses two points of data to arrive at the cost estimate equation.
   c. The R-square generated by the regression analysis is a measure of how well the regression analysis cost equation fits the data.
   d. Regression analysis is a subjective cost estimation method.

9. *(Learning Objective 6)* The only difference between variable costing and absorption costing lies in the treatment of
   a. fixed manufacturing overhead costs.
   b. variable manufacturing overhead costs.
   c. direct materials and direct labor costs.
   d. variable nonmanufacturing costs.

10. *(Learning Objective 6)* When inventories decline, operating income under variable costing is
   a. lower than operating income under absorption costing.
   b. the same as operating income under absorption costing.
   c. higher than operating income under absorption costing.

Quick Check Answers

1. a 2. c 3. d 4. b 5. a 6. b 7. d 8. c 9. a 10. c

Short Exercises

S6-1 Identify cost behavior *(Learning Objective 1)*

The following chart shows three different costs: Cost A, Cost B, and Cost C. For each cost, the chart shows the total cost and cost per unit at two different volumes within the same relevant range. Based on this information, identify each cost as fixed, variable, or mixed. Explain your answers.

	At 5,000 units		*At 6,000 units*	
	Total Cost	**Cost per Unit**	**Total Cost**	**Cost per Unit**
Cost A...............	$30,000	$6.00	$36,000	$6.00
Cost B...............	$30,000	$6.00	$30,000	$5.00
Cost C...............	$30,000	$6.00	$33,000	$5.50

S6-2 Sketch cost behavior graphs *(Learning Objective 1)*

Sketch graphs of the following cost behaviors. In each graph, the y-axis should be "total costs" and the x-axis should be "volume of activity."

a. Fixed
b. Step
c. Mixed
d. Curvilinear
e. Variable

S6-3 Computer fixed costs per unit *(Learning Objective 2)*

First Equipment produces high-quality basketballs. If the fixed cost per basketball is $5 when the company produces 15,000 basketballs, what is the fixed cost per basketball when it produces $18,750 basketballs? Assume that both volumes are in the same relevant range.

S6-4 Define various cost equations *(Learning Objective 2)*

Write the cost equation for each of the following cost behaviors. Define the variables in each equation.

a. Fixed
b. Mixed
c. Variable

S6-5 Predict total mixed costs *(Learning Objective 2)*

Cutting Edge Razors produces deluxe razors that compete with Gillette's Mach line of razors. Total manufacturing costs are $300,000 when 10,000 packages are produced. Of this amount, total variable costs are $20,000. What are the total production costs when 20,000 packages of razors are produced? Assume the same relevant range.

S6-6 Predict and graph total mixed costs *(Learning Objectives 1 & 2)*

Suppose T-Call offers an international calling plan that charges $5.00 per month plus $0.40 per minute for calls outside the United States.

1. Under this plan, what is your monthly international long-distance cost if you call Europe for
   a. 25 minutes?
   b. 50 minutes?
   c. 100 minutes?
2. Draw a graph illustrating your total cost under this plan. Label the axes and show your costs at 25, 50, and 100 minutes.

S6-7 Classify cost behavior *(Learning Objective 3)*

Carlson Sound builds innovative speakers for home theater systems. Identify the following costs as variable or fixed:

a. Depreciation on equipment used to cut wood enclosures
b. Wood for speaker enclosures
c. Patents on crossover relays (internal components)
d. Crossover relays
e. Grill cloth
f. Glue
g. Quality inspector's salary

S6-8 Prepare and analyze a scatter plot *(Learning Objective 3)*

Speedy Lube is a car care center specializing in ten-minute oil changes. Speedy Lube has two service bays, which limits its capacity to 3,600 oil changes per month. The following information was collected over the past six months:

Month	Number of Oil Changes	Operating Expenses
January	3,100	$36,000
February	2,500	$31,500
March	2,700	$32,500
April	2,600	$32,100
May	3,500	$36,600
June	2,800	$33,300

1. Prepare a scatter plot graphing the volume of oil changes (x-axis) against the company's monthly operating expenses (y-axis). Graph by hand or use Excel.
2. How strong of a relationship does there appear to be between the company's operating expenses and the number of oil changes performed each month? Explain. Do there appear to be any outliers in the data? Explain.
3. Based on the graph, do the company's operating costs appear to be fixed, variable, or mixed? Explain how you can tell.
4. Would you feel comfortable using this information to project operating costs for a volume of 4,000 oil changes per month? Explain.

S6-9 Use the high-low method *(Learning Objective 4)*

Refer to the Speedy Lube data in S6-8. Use the high-low method to determine the variable and fixed cost components of Speedy Lube's operating costs. Use this information to project the monthly operating costs for a month in which the company performs 3,600 oil changes.

S6-10 Use the high-low method *(Learning Objective 4)*

Two Sisters Catering uses the high-low method to predict its total overhead costs. Past records show that total overhead cost was $25,300 when 840 hours were worked and $27,500 when 940 hours were worked. If Two Sisters Catering has 865 hours scheduled for next month, what is the expected total overhead cost for next month?

S6-11 Predicting costs in a health care setting *(Learning Objective 4)*

The Surgical Care Unit of Ultra Care Health Group uses the high-low method to predict its total surgical unit supplies costs. It appears that nursing hours worked is a good predictor of surgical unit supplies costs in the unit. The supervisor for the unit has gone through the records for the past year and has found that June had the fewest nursing hours worked at 1,000 hours, while September had the most nursing hours worked at 1,500 hours. In June, total surgical unit supplies cost $30,000 and in September, total surgical unit supplies cost $38,000. If the Surgical Care Unit plans to have 1,025 nursing hours worked next month, what is the expected surgical unit supplies cost for the month?

S6-12 Critique the high-low method *(Learning Objective 4)*

You have been assigned an intern to help you forecast your firm's costs at different volumes. He thinks he will get cost and volume data from the two most recent months, plug them into the high-low method equations, and turn in the cost equation results to your boss before the hour is over. As his mentor, explain to him why the process isn't quite as simple as he thinks. Point out some of the concerns he is overlooking, including your concerns about his choice of data and method.

S6-13 Analyze a scatter plot *(Learning Objectives 3 & 4)*

The local Holiday Inn collected seven months of data on the number of room-nights rented per month and the monthly utilities cost. The data was graphed, resulting in the following scatter plot:

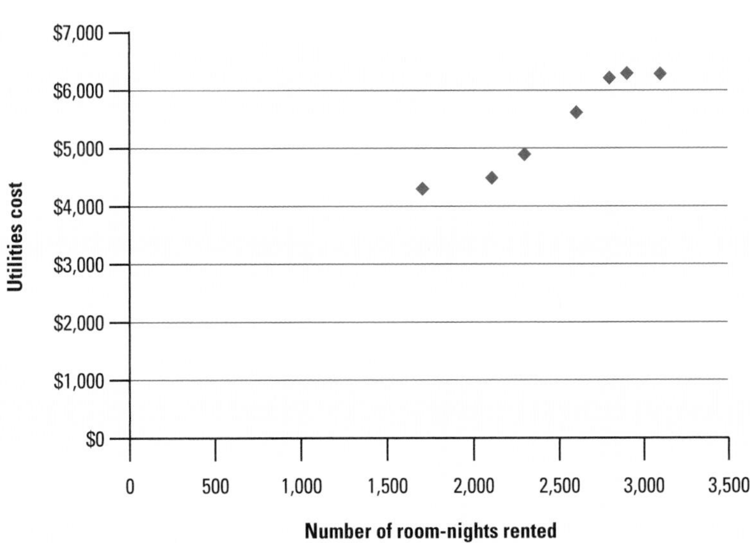

1. Based on this scatter plot, how strong of a relationship does there appear to be between the number of room-nights rented per month and the monthly utilities cost?
2. Do there appear to be any outliers in the data? Explain.
3. Suppose management performs the high-low method using this data. Do you think the resulting cost equation would be very accurate? Explain.

S6-14 Theoretical comparison of high-low and regression analysis *(Learning Objectives 4 & 5)*

Refer to the Holiday Inn scatter plot in S6-13.

1. Would the high-low method or regression analysis result in a more accurate cost equation for the data pictured in the scatter plot? Explain.
2. A regression analysis of the data revealed an R-squared figure of 0.939. Interpret this figure in light of the lowest and highest possible R-squared values.
3. As a manager, would you be confident predicting utilities costs for other room-night volumes within the same relevant range?

S6-15 Write a cost equation given regression output *(Learning Objective 5)*

An advertising agency wanted to determine the relationship between its monthly operating costs and a potential cost driver, professional hours. The output of a regression analysis performed using Excel showed the following information:

	A	B	C	D	E	F	G	H	I
1	**SUMMARY OUTPUT**								
2									
3	***Regression Statistics***								
4	Multiple R		0.85						
5	R Square		0.72						
6	Adjusted R Square		0.66						
7	Standard Error		207.23						
8	Observations		12						
9									
10	**ANOVA**								
11		*df*	*SS*	*MS*	*F*	*Significance F*			
12	Regression	1	545,878.49	545,878.49	12.71	0.02			
13	Residual	10	214,721.51	42,944.3					
14	Total	11	760,600						
15									
16		*Coefficients*	*Standard Error*	*t Stat*	*P-value*	*Lower 95%*	*Upper 95%*	*Lower 95.0%*	*Upper 95.0%*
17	Intercept	947.2	1,217.79	0.78	47.19	-2,183.23	4,077.64	-2,183.23	4,077.64
18	X Variable 1	0.27	0.08	3.57	0.02	0.02	0.08	0.02	0.08

a. Given this output, write the advertising agency's monthly cost equation.

b. Should management use this equation to predict monthly operating costs? Explain your answer.

S6-16 Prepare a contribution margin income statement *(Learning Objective 6)*

Patricia's Quilt Shoppe sells homemade Amish quilts. Patricia buys the quilts from local Amish artisans for $230 each, and her shop sells them for $380 each. Patricia also pays a sales commission of 10% of sales revenue to her sales staff. Patricia leases her country-style shop for $800 per month and pays $1,200 per month in payroll costs in addition to the sales commissions. Patricia sold 75 quilts in February. Prepare Patricia's traditional income statement and contribution margin income statement for the month.

S6-17 Prepare income statements using variable costing and absorption costing with no change in inventory levels *(Learning Objective 6)*

O'Malley's Products manufactures a single product. Cost, sales, and production information for the company and its single product is as follows:

- Selling price per unit is $60
- Variable manufacturing costs per unit manufactured (includes DM, DL & variable MOH) $32
- Variable operating expenses per unit sold $1
- Fixed manufacturing overhead (MOH) in total for the year $120,000
- Fixed operating expenses in total for the year $90,000
- Units manufactured and sold for the year 10,000 units

Requirements

1. Prepare an income statement for the upcoming year using variable costing.
2. Prepare an income statement for the upcoming year using absorption costing.

S6-18 Prepare income statements using variable costing and absorption costing when inventory units increase *(Learning Objective 6)*

Augustine Manufacturing manufactures a single product. Cost, sales, and production information for the company and its single product is as follows:

- Sales price per unit $40
- Variable manufacturing costs per unit manufactured (DM, DL & variable MOH) $23

- Variable operating expenses per unit sold $2
- Fixed manufacturing overhead (MOH) in total for the year $180,000
- Fixed operating expenses in total for the year $50,000
- Units manufactured during the year 20,000 units
- Units sold during the year 16,000 units

Requirements

1. Prepare an income statement for the upcoming year using variable costing.
2. Prepare an income statement for the upcoming year using absorption costing.
3. What causes the difference in income between the two methods?

EXERCISES Group A

E6-19A Graph specific costs *(Learning Objective 1)*

Graph these cost behavior patterns over a relevant range of 0–10,000 units:

a. Variable expenses of $10 per unit
b. Mixed expenses made up of fixed costs of $15,000 and variable costs of $3 per unit
c. Fixed expenses of $25,000

E6-20A Identify cost behavior graph *(Learning Objective 1)*

Following are a series of cost behavior graphs. The total cost is shown on the vertical (y) axis and the volume (activity) is shown on the horizontal (x) axis.

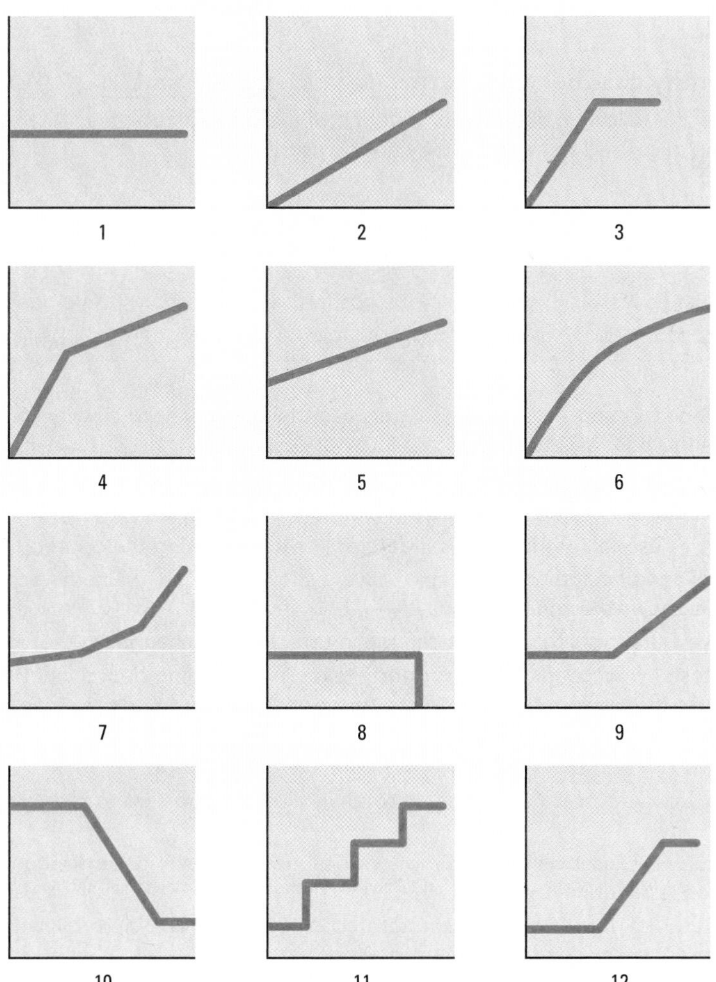

For each of the following situations, identify the graph that most closely represents the cost behavior pattern of the cost in that situation. Some graphs may be used more than once or not at all.

a. Customer service staff is paid $12.50 per hour
b. Depreciation on the company fleet of trucks (the units of production method is used with miles driven as the depreciation base)
c. Property taxes for a warehouse
d. Fuel costs for the delivery vehicles used by a local document delivery firm; assume the price per gallon is fixed at $3.10 per gallon
e. Utility costs for a production facility that is charged a fixed monthly charge of $250 by the local electrical co-op plus the following usage fees (implemented to encourage conservation):

Up to 10,000 kilowatts	$0.0020 per kilowatt
10,001–20,000 kilowatts	$0.0025 per kilowatt
More than 20,000 kilowatts	$0.0028 per kilowatt

f. Food costs for Meals on Wheels; the cost of direct materials (food) in each meal delivered is $3
g. Advertising costs for a grocery store; the store runs a four page color insert in the local newspaper once per week
h. Sales salary costs for a clothing store; each member of the sales staff is paid $400 per week plus 4% of net sales
i. Property insurance costs for an office building
j. Annual maintenance costs for the vans in a service fleet; each van is taken in for standard recommended maintenance each year. Each maintenance package is $200 per van per year.

E6-21A Identify cost behavior terms *(Learning Objectives 1, 2, 3, 4, & 5)*

Complete the following statements with one of the terms listed here. You may use a term more than once, and some terms may not be used at all.

Account analysis	Step cost(s)	High-low method
Variable cost(s)	Fixed cost(s)	Regression analysis
Curvilinear cost(s)	Total cost(s)	Average cost per unit
R-square	Mixed cost(s)	Committed fixed costs

a. When performing ________, managers use their judgment to classify each general ledger account as a ________, ________, or ________.
b. ________, when graphed, resemble stair steps.
c. Total ________ change as the cost driver volume changes.
d. ________ uses all of the historical data points in estimating the cost equation.
e. On cost graphs, the vertical (y-axis) always shows ________ while the horizontal axis (x-axis) shows the volume of activity.
f. ________ are costs that do not change in total despite changes in the level of activity.
g. The costs of occupancy (rent, property taxes, and building depreciation) are ________, because the organization is locked into these costs due to management decisions made in the past.
h. A statistic, ________, tells us how well the line fits the data.
i. A ________ is a cost that varies, in total, in direct proportion to changes in the level of activity.
j. The ________ uses only two of the historical data points in determining an estimate of the cost estimation equation.
k. The ________ should not be used to predict total costs at different levels of activity because it changes as the volume changes.
l. ________ are costs that change in total when the volume changes, but not in direct proportion to that change in volume.
m. ________ are not linear and, therefore, do not fit into a straight line.

E6-22A Forecast costs at different volumes *(Learning Objectives 1 & 2)*

Preston Drycleaners has capacity to clean up to 7,500 garments per month.

Requirements

1. Complete the following schedule for the three volumes shown.

	4,500 Garments	6,000 Garments	7,500 Garments
Total variable costs		$5,100	
Total fixed costs	____	____	____
Total operating costs	____	____	____
Variable cost per garment			
Fixed cost per garment	____	$2.40	____
Average cost per garment	____	____	____

2. Why does the average cost per garment change?
3. Suppose the owner, Dan Preston, erroneously uses the average cost per unit *at full capacity* to predict total costs at a volume of 4,500 garments. Would he overestimate or underestimate his total costs? By how much?

E6-23A Prepare income statement in two formats *(Learning Objective 6)*

Refer to the Preston Drycleaners in E6-22A. Assume that Preston charges customers $7 per garment for dry cleaning. Prepare Preston's *projected* income statement if 4,252 garments are cleaned in March. First, prepare the income statement using the traditional format; then prepare Preston's contribution margin income statement.

E6-24A Use the high-low method *(Learning Objective 4)*

Schaffer Company, which uses the high-low method to analyze cost behavior, has determined that machine hours best predict the company's total utilities cost. The company's cost and machine hour usage data for the first six months of the year follow:

Month	Total Cost	Machine Hours
January	$3,460	1,070
February	$3,760	1,170
March	$3,500	1,000
April	$3,780	1,200
May	$4,700	1,330
June	$4,200	1,400

Requirements

Using the high-low method, answer the following questions:

1. What is the variable utilities cost per machine hour?
2. What is the fixed cost of utilities each month?
3. If Schaffer Company uses 1,210 machine hours in a month, what will its total costs be?

E6-25A Use unit cost data to forecast total costs *(Learning Objective 2)*

Freedom Mailbox produces decorative mailboxes. The company's average cost per unit is $24.43 when it produces 1,300 mailboxes.

Requirements

1. What is the total cost of producing 1,300 mailboxes?
2. If $21,359 of the total costs is fixed, what is the variable cost of producing each mailbox?
3. Write Freedom Mailbox's cost equation.

4. If the plant manager uses the average cost per unit to predict total costs, what would the forecast be for 1,700 mailboxes?
5. If the plant manager uses the cost equation to predict total costs, what would the forecast be for 1,700 mailboxes?
6. What is the dollar difference between your answers to questions 4 and 5? Which approach to forecasting costs is appropriate? Why?

E6-26A Sustainability and cost estimation *(Learning Objective 4)*

Star Entertainment is a provider of cable, internet, and on-demand video services. Star currently sends monthly bills to its customers via the postal service. Because of a concern for the environment and recent increases in postal rates, Star management is considering offering an option to its customers for paperless billing. In addition to saving printing, paper, and postal costs, paperless billing will save energy and water (through reduced paper needs, reduced waste disposal, and reduced transportation needs.) While Star would like to switch to 100% paperless billing, many of its customers are not comfortable with paperless billing or may not have web access, so the paper billing option will remain regardless of whether Star adopts a paperless billing system or not.

The cost of the paperless billing system would be $140,000 per quarter with no variable costs since the costs of the system are the salaries of the clerks and the cost of leasing the computer system. The paperless billing system being proposed would be able to handle up to 900,000 bills per quarter (more than 900,000 bills per quarter would require a different computer system and is outside the scope of the current situation at Star.)

Star has gathered its cost data for the past year by quarter for paper, toner cartridges, printer maintenance costs, and postage costs for its billing department. The cost data is as follows:

	Quarter 1	Quarter 2	Quarter 3	Quarter 4
Total paper, toner, printer maintenance, and postage costs	$627,500	$635,000	$770,000	$650,000
Total number of bills mailed	575,000	605,000	725,000	625,000

Requirements

1. Calculate the variable cost per bill mailed under the current paper-based billing system.
2. Assume that the company projects that it will have a total of 700,000 bills to mail in the upcoming quarter. If enough customers choose the paperless billing option so that 25% of the mailings can be converted to paperless, how much would the company save from the paperless billing system (be sure to consider the cost of the paperless billing system)?
3. What if only 20% of the mailings are converted to the paperless option (assume a total of 700,000 bills)? Should the company still offer the paperless billing system? Explain your rationale.

E6-27A Create a scatter plot *(Learning Objective 3)*

Kelsey Gerbig, owner of Flowers 4 You, operates a local chain of floral shops. Each shop has its own delivery van. Instead of charging a flat delivery fee, Gerbig wants to set the delivery fee based on the distance driven to deliver the flowers. Gerbig wants to separate the fixed and variable portions of her van operating costs so that she has a better idea how delivery distance affects these costs. She has the following data from the past seven months:

Month	Miles Driven	Van Operating Costs
January	16,500	$5,260
February	18,500	$5,730
March	16,100	$4,960
April	17,100	$5,420
May	17,500	$5,790
June	15,800	$5,300
July	15,500	$5,040

CHAPTER 6

Requirements

1. Prepare a scatter plot of Flowers 4 You's volume (miles driven) and van operating costs.
2. Does the data appear to contain any outliers? Explain.
3. How strong of a relationship is there between miles driven and van operating costs?

E6-28A High-low method *(Learning Objective 4)*

Refer to Flowers 4 You's data in E6-27A. Use the high-low method to determine Flowers 4 You's cost equation for van operating costs. Use your results to predict van operating costs at a volume of 16,000 miles.

E6-29A Continuation of E6-27A: Regression analysis *(Learning Objective 5)*

Refer to the Flowers 4 You data in E6-27A. Use Microsoft Excel to do the following:

Requirements

1. Run a regression analysis.
2. Determine the company's cost equation (use the output from the Excel regression).
3. Determine the R-square (use the output from the Excel regression). What does Flowers 4 You's R-square indicate?
4. Predict van operating costs at a volume of 16,900 miles.

E6-30A Regression analysis using Excel output *(Learning Objective 5)*

Assume that Flowers 4 You does a regression analysis on the next year's data using Excel. The output generated by Excel is as follows:

	A	B	C	D	E	F	G	H	I
1	**SUMMARY OUTPUT**								
2									
3		***Regression Statistics***							
4	Multiple R		0.81						
5	R Square		0.65						
6	Adjusted R Square		0.58						
7	Standard Error		202.91						
8	Observations		7						
9									
10	**ANOVA**								
11		*df*	*SS*	*MS*	*F*	*Significance F*			
12	Regression	1	379,674.00	379,674.00	9.22	0.0289			
13	Residual	5	205,868.85	41,173.77					
14	Total	6	585,542.85						
15									
16		*Coefficients*	*Standard Error*	*t Stat*	*P-value*	*Lower 95%*	*Upper 95%*	*Lower 95.0%*	*Upper 95.0%*
17	Intercept	478.30	1,538.00	0.31	0.77	-3,475.25	4,431.85	-3,475.25	4,431.85
18	X Variable 1	0.30	0.10	3.04	0.03	0.05	0.55	0.05	0.55

Requirements

1. Determine the firm's cost equation (use the output from the Excel regression).
2. Determine the R-square (use the output from the Excel regression). What does Flowers 4 You's R-square indicate?
3. Predict van operating costs at a volume of 16,000 miles.

E6-31A Create a scatter plot for a hospital laboratory *(Learning Objective 3)*

The manager of the main laboratory facility at MetroHealth Center is interested in being able to predict the overhead costs each month for the lab. The manager believes that total overhead varies with the number of lab tests performed but that some costs remain the same each month regardless of the number of lab tests performed.

The lab manager collected the following data for the first seven months of the year:

Month	Number of Lab Tests Performed	Total Laboratory Overhead Costs
January	2,500	$26,800
February	2,400	$25,700
March	3,200	$25,900
April	3,650	$28,900
May	3,800	$28,500
June	1,800	$20,900
July	1,900	$19,600

Requirements

1. Prepare a scatter plot of the lab's volume (number of lab tests performed) and total laboratory overhead costs.
2. Does the data appear to contain any outliers? Explain.
3. How strong of a relationship is there between the number of lab tests performed and laboratory overhead costs?

E6-32A Using the high-low method to predict overhead for a hospital laboratory *(Learning Objective 4)*

Refer to the laboratory overhead cost and activity data for MetroHealth Center in E6-31A. Use the high-low method to determine the laboratory's cost equation for total laboratory overhead. Use your results to predict total laboratory overhead if 2,900 lab tests are performed next month.

E6-33A Using regression analysis output to predict overhead for a hospital laboratory *(Learning Objective 5)*

Using the data provided in E6-31A, the laboratory manager performed a regression analysis to predict total laboratory overhead costs. The output generated by Excel is as follows:

	A	B	C	D	E	F	G	H	I
1	**SUMMARY OUTPUT**								
2									
3	***Regression Statistics***								
4	Multiple R		0.88053406						
5	R Square		0.77534024						
6	Adjusted R Square		0.73040829						
7	Standard Error		1868.82221						
8	Observations		7						
9									
10	**ANOVA**								
11		*df*	*SS*	*MS*	*F*	*Significance F*			
12	Regression	1	60266089.17	60266089.17	17.255877	0.008875395			
13	Residual	5	17462482.26	3492496.451					
14	Total	6	77728571.43						
15									
16		*Coefficients*	*Standard Error*	*t Stat*	*P-value*	*Lower 95%*	*Upper 95%*	*Lower 95.0%*	*Upper 95.0%*
17	Intercept	14409.92	2688.512	5.359	0.003	7498.875	21320.960	7498.875	21320.960
18	X Variable 1	3.92	0.943	4.154	0.008	1.493	6.343	1.493	6.343

Requirements

1. Determine the lab's cost equation (use the output from the Excel regression).
2. Determine the R-square (use the output from the Excel regression).
3. Predict the total laboratory overhead for the month if 2,900 tests are performed.

E6-34A Performing a regression analysis to predict overhead for a hospital laboratory *(Learning Objective 5)*

The manager of the main laboratory facility at MetroHealth Center (from E6-31A) collects seven additional months of data after obtaining the regression results in E6-33A. The number of tests performed and the total monthly overhead costs for the lab follow:

Month	Number of Lab Tests Performed	Total Laboratory Overhead
August	2,900	$26,700
September	3,100	$26,200
October	2,800	$25,800
November	2,500	$24,300
December	3,600	$27,650
January	2,600	$23,700
February	3,200	$25,900

Use the Excel to do the following:

Requirements

1. Run a regression analysis.
2. Determine the lab's cost equation (use the output from the regression analysis you performed using Excel).
3. Determine the R-square using the Excel output you obtain. What does the lab's R-square indicate?
4. Predict the lab's total overhead costs for the month if 2,500 tests are performed.

E6-35A Prepare and interpret a scatter plot *(Learning Objective 3)*

Rick's Golden Pancake Restaurant features sourdough pancakes made from a strain of sourdough dating back to the Alaskan Gold Rush. To plan for the future, Rick needs to figure out his cost behavior patterns. He has the following information about his operating costs and the number of pancakes served:

Month	Number of Pancakes	Total Operating Costs
July	3,900	$2,340
August	4,200	$2,530
September	3,600	$2,440
October	3,700	$2,290
November	4,000	$2,560
December	3,850	$2,510

Requirements

1. Prepare a scatter plot of Rick's pancake volume and operating costs. (*Hint*: If you use Excel, be sure to force the vertical axis to zero.)
2. Does the data appear sound, or do there appear to be any outliers? Explain.
3. Based on the scatter plot, do operating costs appear to be variable, fixed, or mixed costs?
4. How strong of a relationship is there between pancake volume and operating costs?

E6-36A High-low method *(Learning Objective 4)*

Refer to Rick's Golden Pancake Restaurant in E6-35A.

Requirements

1. Use the high-low method to determine Rick's operating cost equation.
2. Use your answer from Requirement 1 to predict total monthly operating costs if Rick serves 4,300 pancakes in one month.
3. Can you predict total monthly operating costs if Rick serves 14,000 pancakes a month? Explain.

E6-37A Regression analysis *(Learning Objective 5)*

Refer to Rick's Golden Pancake Restaurant in E6-35A.

Requirements

1. Use Microsoft Excel to perform regression analysis on Rick's monthly data. Based on the output, write Rick's monthly operating cost equation.
2. Based on the R-square shown on the regression output, how well does this cost equation fit the data?

E6-38A Regression analysis using Excel output *(Learning Objective 5)*

Assume that Rick's Golden Pancake Restaurant does a regression analysis on the next year's data using Excel. The output generated by Excel is as follows:

	A	B	C	D	E	F	G	H	I
1	**SUMMARY OUTPUT**								
2									
3	***Regression Statistics***								
4	Multiple R		0.88						
5	R Square		0.83						
6	Adjusted R Square		0.78						
7	Standard Error		107.42						
8	Observations		6						
9									
10	**ANOVA**								
11		*df*	*SS*	*MS*	*F*	*Significance F*			
12	Regression	1	13,643.22	13,643.22	4.01	0.02			
13	Residual	4	46,156.78	11,539.19					
14	Total	5	59,800.00						
15									
16		*Coefficients*	*Standard Error*	*t Stat*	*P-value*	*Lower 95%*	*Upper 95%*	*Lower 95.0%*	*Upper 95.0%*
17	Intercept	1,787.23	574.41	3.11	0.04	192.40	3,382.06	192.40	3,382.06
18	X Variable 1	0.17	0.16	1.09	0.34	-0.26	0.60	-0.26	0.60

Requirements

1. What is the fixed cost per month?
2. What is the variable cost per pancake?
3. If Rick's Golden Pancake Restaurant serves 3,800 pancakes in a month, what would the company's total operating costs be?

E6-39A Determine cost behavior and predict operating costs

(Learning Objective 4)

Seaside Apartments is a 600-unit apartment complex. When the apartments are 90% occupied, monthly operating costs total $204,240. When occupancy dips to 80%, monthly operating costs fall to $200,880. The owner of the apartment complex is worried because many of the apartment residents work at a nearby manufacturing plant that has just announced that it will close in three months. The apartment owner fears that occupancy of her apartments will drop to 55% if residents lose their jobs and move away. Assuming the same relevant range, what can the owner expect her operating costs to be if occupancy falls to 55%?

E6-40A Prepare a contribution margin income statement *(Learning Objective 6)*

Two Turtles is a specialty pet gift store selling exotic pet-related items through its website. Two Turtles has no physical store; all sales are through its website.

Results for last year are shown next:

TWO TURTLES Income Statement Year Ended December 31		
Sales revenue		$1,011,000
Cost of goods sold		(673,000)
Gross profit		$ 338,000
Operating expenses:		
Selling and marketing expenses	$65,000	
Website maintenance expenses	60,000	
Other operating expenses	17,000	
Total operating expenses		(142,000)
Operating income		$ 196,000

For internal planning and decision-making purposes, the owner of Two Turtles would like to translate the company's income statement into the contribution margin format. Since Two Turtles is web-based, all of its cost of goods sold is variable. A large portion of the selling and marketing expenses consists of freight-out charges ($19,000), which were also variable. Only 20% of the remaining selling and marketing expenses and 25% of the website expenses were variable. Of the other operating expenses, 90% were fixed.

Based on this information, prepare Two Turtles' contribution margin income statement for last year.

E6-41A Prepare a contribution margin income statement *(Learning Objective 6)*

Cranmore Carriage Company offers guided horse-drawn carriage rides through historic Charleston, South Carolina. The carriage business is highly regulated by the city. Cranmore Carriage Company has the following operating costs during April:

Monthly depreciation expense on carriages and stable	$2,200
Fee paid to the City of Charleston	15% of ticket revenue
Cost of souvenir set of postcards given to each passenger	$0.75/set of postcards
Brokerage fee paid to independent ticket brokers (60% of tickets are issued through these brokers; 40% are sold directly by the Cranmore Carriage Company)	$1.40/ticket sold by broker
Monthly cost of leasing and boarding the horses	$46,000
Carriage drivers (tour guides) are paid on a per passenger basis	$3.20 per passenger
Monthly payroll costs of non–tour guide employees	$7,550
Marketing, website, telephone, and other monthly fixed costs	$7,100

During April (a month during peak season), Cranmore Carriage Company had 13,030 passengers. Eighty-five percent of passengers were adults ($23 fare) while 15% were children ($15 fare).

Requirements

1. Prepare the company's contribution margin income statement for the month of April. Round all figures to the nearest dollar.
2. Assume that passenger volume increases by 12% in May. Which figures on the income statement would you expect to change, and by what percentage would they change? Which figures would remain the same as in April?

E6-42A Prepare income statements using variable costing and absorption costing with changing inventory levels *(Learning Objective 6)*

Henderson Manufacturing manufactures a single product that it will sell for $80 per unit. The company is looking to project its operating income for its first two years of operations. Cost information for the single unit of its product is as follows:

- Direct material per unit produced $35
- Direct labor cost per unit produced $12
- Variable manufacturing overhead (MOH) per unit produced $6
- Variable operating expenses per unit sold $3

Fixed manufacturing overhead (MOH) for each year is $200,000, while fixed operating expenses for each year will be $85,000.

During its first year of operations, the company plans to manufacture 20,000 units and anticipates selling 15,000 of those units. During the second year of its operations, the company plans to manufacture 20,000 units and anticipates selling 24,000 units (it has units in beginning inventory for the second year from its first year of operations).

Requirements

1. Prepare an absorption costing income statement for the following:
   a. Henderson's first year of operations
   b. Henderson's second year of operations
2. Before you prepare the variable costing income statements for Henderson, predict Henderson's operating income using variable costing for both its first year and its second year without preparing the variable costing income statements. *Hint:* Calculate the variable costing operating income for a given year by taking that year's absorption costing operating income and adding or subtracting the difference in operating income as calculated using the following formula:

Difference in operating income = (Change in inventory level in units x Fixed MOH per unit)

3. Prepare a variable costing income statement for each of the following years:
   a. Henderson's first year of operations
   b. Henderson's second year of operations

E6-43A Prepare a variable costing income statement given an absorption costing income statement *(Learning Objective 6)*

Wronkovich Industries manufactures and sells a single product. The controller has prepared the following income statement for the most recent year:

Wronkovich Industries
Income Statement (Absorption costing)
For the year ending December 31

Sales revenue	$420,000
Less: Cost of goods sold	343,000
Gross profit	$ 77,000
Less: Operating expenses	67,000
Operating income	$ 10,000

The company produced 10,000 units and sold 7,000 units during the year ending December 31. Fixed manufacturing overhead (MOH) for the year was $200,000, while fixed operating expenses were $60,000. The company had no beginning inventory.

Requirements

1. Will the company's operating income under variable costing be higher, lower, or the same as its operating income under absorption costing? Why?
2. Project the company's operating income under variable costing without preparing a variable costing income statement.
3. Prepare a variable costing income statement for the year.

E6-44A Absorption and variable costing income statements

(Learning Objective 6)

The annual data that follows pertain to See Underwater, a manufacturer of swimming goggles (the company had no beginning inventories):

Sales price	$ 44
Variable manufacturing expense per unit	$ 15
Sales commission expense per unit	$ 6
Fixed manufacturing overhead	$2,475,000
Fixed operating expenses	$ 250,000
Number of goggles produced	225,000
Number of goggles sold	205,000

Requirements

1. Prepare both conventional (absorption costing) and contribution margin (variable costing) income statements for See Underwater for the year.
2. Which statement shows the higher operating income? Why?
3. The company marketing vice president believes a new sales promotion that costs $145,000 would increase sales to 225,000 goggles. Should the company go ahead with the promotion? Give your reason.

EXERCISES Group B

E6-45B Graph specific costs *(Learning Objective 1)*

Graph these cost behavior patterns over a relevant range of 0–10,000 units:

a. Variable expenses of $9 per unit
b. Mixed expenses made up of fixed costs of $15,000 and variable costs of $6 per unit
c. Fixed expenses of $20,000

E6-46B Identify cost behavior graph *(Learning Objective 1)*

Following are a series of cost behavior graphs. The total cost is shown on the vertical (y) axis and the volume (activity) is shown on the horizontal (x) axis.

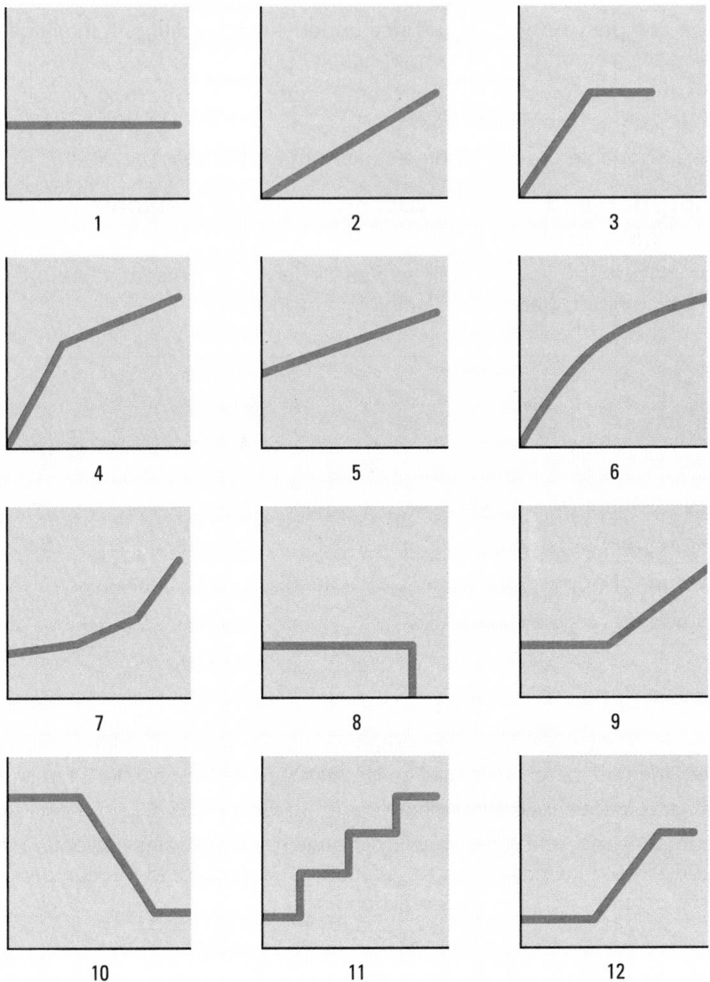

For each of the following situations, identify the graph that most closely represents the cost behavior pattern of the cost in that situation. Some graphs may be used more than once or not at all.

a. Monthly gas bill for the restaurant's delivery vehicles; cost of gas is constant at $3.10 per gallon
b. Monthly factory equipment depreciation, straight-line method is used
c. Monthly electric cost for a florist; $30 base monthly fee plus $.005 per kilowatt used
d. Total salary costs for an office; managers are paid a salary and the other workers are paid by the hour
e. Oil disposal fees for an automotive maintenance company. The oil disposal fee is based on two components: a $100 base fee plus a usage fee (to encourage reduction of waste):

Up to 10 barrels	$10 per barrel
11–25 barrels...............	$12 per barrel
More than 26 barrels....	$16 per barrel

f. Monthly cell phone expense for a mobile grooming business; the cell phones are billed at a rate of $50 for unlimited voice and text for each cell phone
g. Monthly copier costs; the lease is $350 per month with a fee of $0.02 per copy for any copies over 100,000 copies in that month

h. Wood costs for a chair manufacturer; the cost of direct materials per chair is $8.40
i. Customer service representatives are paid $13.25 per hour
j. Monthly vehicle lease costs for a company that pays $280 month plus $.11 per mile for any miles driven over 1,500 per month

E6-47B Identify cost behavior terms *(Learning Objectives 1, 2, 3, 4, & 5)*

Complete the following statements with one of the terms listed here. You may use a term more than once, and some terms may not be used at all.

R-square	Committed fixed costs	Regression analysis
Average cost per unit	Curvilinear cost(s)	Fixed cost(s)
Variable cost(s)	Total cost(s)	Mixed cost(s)
Step cost(s)	Account analysis	High-low method

a. The total ________ line increases as the volume of activity increases, but the line does not begin at the origin.
b. The slope of the total ________ line is the variable cost per unit of activity.
c. The ________ uses two data points to arrive at a cost equation to describe a mixed cost.
d. ________ is a method for determining cost behavior that is based on a manager's judgment.
e. ________ are a type of cost behavior that is fixed over a small range of activity and then jumps to a different fixed level with moderate changes in volume.
f. The ________ per unit is inversely related to the volume of activity.
g. An s-shaped line would represent a ________.
h. The ________ value is referred to as the "goodness-of-fit" statistic.
i. As the activity level rises and falls, ________ remain constant in total.
j. ________ are fixed costs that management has little or no control over in the short run.
k. ________ is equal to the sum of ________ plus ________.
l. ________ is the cost to produce a single unit of production as calculated by dividing the total cost by the total number of units produced.
m. The cost equation resulting from using ________ is described as "this line of best fit."

E6-48B Forecast costs at different volumes *(Learning Objectives 1 & 2)*

Corbin Drycleaners has the capacity to clean up to 6,000 garments per month.

Requirements

1. Complete the following schedule for the three volumes shown.

	3,000 Garments	4,500 Garments	6,000 Garments
Total variable costs		$3,825	
Total fixed costs	____	____	____
Total operating costs	____	____	____
Variable cost per garment			
Fixed cost per garment	____	$2.00	____
Average cost per garment	____	____	____

2. Why does the average cost per garment change?
3. The owner, Yvonne Corbin, uses the average cost per unit *at full capacity* to predict total costs at a volume of 3,000 garments. Would she overestimate or underestimate total costs? By how much?

E6-49B Prepare income statement in two formats *(Learning Objective 6)*

Refer to the Corbin Drycleaners in E6-48B. Assume that Corbin charges customers $7 per garment for dry cleaning. Prepare Corbin's *projected* income statement if 4,220 garments are cleaned in March. First, prepare the income statement using the traditional format; then, prepare Corbin's contribution margin income statement.

E6-50B Use the high-low method *(Learning Objective 4)*

Chen Company, which uses the high-low method to analyze cost behavior, has determined that machine hours best predict the company's total utilities cost. The company's cost and machine hour usage data for the first six months of the year follow:

Month	Total Cost	Machine Hours
January	$3,400	1,090
February	$3,730	1,170
March	$3,385	1,070
April	$3,750	1,250
May	$4,700	1,380
June	$3,985	1,470

Requirements

Using the high-low method, answer the following questions:

1. What is the variable utilities cost per machine hour?
2. What is the fixed cost of utilities each month?
3. If Chen Company uses 1,260 machine hours in a month, what will its total costs be?

E6-51B Use unit cost data to forecast total costs *(Learning Objective 2)*

Rollins Mailboxes produces decorative mailboxes. The company's average cost per unit is $20.43 when it produces 1,600 mailboxes.

Requirements

1. What is the total cost of producing 1,600 mailboxes?
2. If $24,688 of the total costs are fixed, what is the variable cost of producing each mailbox?
3. Write Rollins Mailboxes' cost equation.
4. If the plant manager uses the average cost per unit to predict total costs, what would the forecast be for 1,900 mailboxes?
5. If the plant manager uses the cost equation to predict total costs, what would the forecast be for 1,900 mailboxes?
6. What is the dollar difference between your answers to Requirements 4 and 5? Which approach to forecasting costs is appropriate? Why?

E6-52B Sustainability and cost estimation *(Learning Objective 4)*

Bright Entertainment is a provider of cable, internet, and on-demand video services. Bright currently sends monthly bills to its customers via the postal service. Because of a concern for the environment and recent increases in postal rates, Bright's management is considering offering an option to its customers for paperless billing. In addition to saving printing, paper, and postal costs, paperless billing will save energy and water (through reduced paper needs, reduced waste disposal, and reduced transportation needs.) While Bright would like to switch to 100% paperless billing, many of its customers are not comfortable with paperless billing or may not have web access, so the paper billing option will remain regardless of whether Bright adopts a paperless billing system or not.

The cost of the paperless billing system would be $125,000 per quarter with no variable costs since the costs of the system are the salaries of the clerks and the cost of leasing the computer system. The paperless billing system being proposed would be able to handle up to 900,000 bills per quarter (more than 900,000 bills per quarter would require a different computer system and is outside the scope of the current situation at Bright.)

Bright has gathered its cost data for the past year by quarter for paper, toner cartridges, printer maintenance costs, and postage costs for its billing department. The cost data is as follows:

	Quarter 1	Quarter 2	Quarter 3	Quarter 4
Total paper, toner, printer maintenance, and postage costs	$622,000	$770,000	$670,000	$642,500
Total number of bills mailed	614,000	725,000	625,000	575,000

Requirements

1. Calculate the variable cost per bill mailed under the current paper-based billing system.
2. Assume that the company projects that it will have a total of 700,000 bills to mail in the upcoming quarter. If enough customers choose the paperless billing option so that 25% of the mailing can be converted to paperless, how much would the company save from the paperless billing system (be sure to consider the cost of the paperless billing system)?
3. What if only 20% of the mailings are converted to the paperless option (assume a total of 700,000 bills)? Should the company still offer the paperless billing system? Explain your rationale.

E6-53B Create a scatter plot *(Learning Objective 3)*

Tony Long, owner of Flowers Direct, operates a local chain of floral shops. Each shop has its own delivery van. Instead of charging a flat delivery fee, Long wants to set the delivery fee based on the distance driven to deliver the flowers. Long wants to separate the fixed and variable portions of his van operating costs so that he has a better idea how delivery distance affects these costs. He has the following data from the past seven months:

Month	Miles Driven	Van Operating Costs
January	15,900	$5,430
February	17,300	$5,740
March	14,600	$4,940
April	16,300	$5,270
May	17,200	$5,820
June	15,200	$5,400
July	14,300	$4,990

Requirements

1. Prepare a scatter plot of Long's volume (miles driven) and van operating costs.
2. Do the data appear to contain any outliers? Explain.
3. How strong of a relationship is there between miles driven and van operating expenses?

E6-54B High-low method *(Learning Objective 4)*

Refer to Long's Flowers Direct data in E6-53B. Use the high-low method to determine Flowers Direct's cost equation for van operating costs. Use your results to predict van operating costs at a volume of 15,500 miles.

E6-55B Continuation of E6-53B: Regression analysis *(Learning Objective 5)*

Refer to the Flowers Direct data in E6-53B. Use Microsoft Excel to run a regression analysis, then do the following calculations:

Requirements

1. Determine the firm's cost equation (use the output from the Excel regression).
2. Determine the R-square (use the output from the Excel regression). What does Flowers Direct's R-square indicate?
3. Predict van operating costs at a volume of 15,500 miles.

E6-56B Regression analysis using Excel output *(Learning Objective 5)*

Assume that Flowers Direct does a regression analysis on the next year's data using Excel. The output generated by Excel is as follows:

	A	B	C	D	E	F	G	H	I
1									
2									
3	*Regression Statistics*								
4	Multiple R		0.96						
5	R Square		0.92						
6	Adjusted R Square		0.90						
7	Standard Error		112.91						
8	Observations		7						
9									
10	**ANOVA**								
11		*df*	*SS*	*MS*	*F*	*Significance F*			
12	Regression	1	689,408.19	689,408.19	54.08	0.0007			
13	Residual	5	63,745.52	12,749.10					
14	Total	6	753,153.71						
15									
16		*Coefficients*	*Standard Error*	*t Stat*	*P-value*	*Lower 95%*	*Upper 95%*	*Lower 95.0%*	*Upper 95.0%*
17	Intercept	826.04	629.77	1.31	0.25	-792.83	2,444.91	-792.83	2,444.91
18	X Variable 1	0.28	0.04	7.35	0.00	0.18	0.37	0.18	0.37

Requirements

1. Determine the firm's cost equation (use the output from the Excel regression).
2. Determine the R-square (use the output from the Excel regression). What does Flowers Direct's R-square indicate?
3. Predict van operating costs at a volume of 15,000 miles.

E6-57B Create a scatter plot for a hospital laboratory *(Learning Objective 3)*

The manager of the main laboratory facility at CitiHealth Center is interested in being able to predict the overhead costs each month for the lab. The manager believes that total overhead varies with the number of lab tests performed but that some costs remain the same each month regardless of the number of lab tests performed.

The lab manager collected the following data for the first seven months of the year.

Month	Number of Lab Tests Performed	Total Laboratory Overhead Costs
January	3,100	$22,800
February	2,750	$21,700
March	3,350	$23,900
April	3,750	$28,100
May	4,000	$27,500
June	2,000	$19,500
July	3,900	$27,100

Requirements

1. Prepare a scatter plot of the lab's volume (number of lab tests performed) and total laboratory overhead costs.
2. Does the data appear to contain any outliers? Explain.
3. How strong of a relationship is there between the number of lab tests performed and laboratory overhead costs?

E6-58B Using the high-low method to predict overhead for a hospital laboratory *(Learning Objective 4)*

Refer to the laboratory overhead cost and activity data for CitiHealth Center in E6-57B. Use the high-low method to determine the laboratory's cost equation for total laboratory overhead. Use your results to predict total laboratory overhead if 3,200 lab tests are performed next month.

E6-59B Using regression analysis output to predict overhead for a hospital laboratory *(Learning Objective 5)*

Using the data provided in E6-57B, the laboratory manager performed a regression analysis to predict total laboratory overhead costs. The output generated by Excel is as follows:

	A	B	C	D	E	F	G	H	I
1	**SUMMARY OUTPUT**								
2									
3	***Regression Statistics***								
4	Multiple R		0.963524797						
5	R Square		0.928380034						
6	Adjusted R Square		0.914056041						
7	Standard Error		962.6424624						
8	Observations		7						
9									
10	**ANOVA**								
11		*df*	*SS*	*MS*	*F*	*Significance F*			
12	Regression	1	60060883.16	60060883.16	64.81293443	0.000478529			
13	Residual	5	4633402.552	926680.5104					
14	Total	6	64694285.71						
15									
16		*Coefficients*	*Standard Error*	*t Stat*	*P-value*	*Lower 95%*	*Upper 95%*	*Lower 95.0%*	*Upper 95.0%*
17	Intercept	9953.28	1827.515	5.446	0.002	5255.505	14651.060	5255.505	14651.060
18	X Variable 1	4.42	0.548	8.050	0.000	3.006	5.827	3.006	5.827

Requirements

1. Determine the lab's cost equation (use the output from the Excel regression).
2. Determine the R-square (use the output from the Excel regression).
3. Predict the total laboratory overhead for the month if 2,900 tests are performed.

E6-60B Performing a regression analysis to predict overhead for a hospital laboratory *(Learning Objective 5)*

The manager of the main laboratory facility at CitiHealth Center (from E6-57B) collects seven additional months of data after obtaining the regression results in the prior period. The number of tests performed and the total monthly overhead costs for the lab follows:

Month	Number of Lab Tests Performed	Total Laboratory Overhead Costs
August	3,050	$22,300
September	2,800	$22,100
October	3,600	$25,100
November	3,800	$26,700
December	4,200	$27,300
January	2,200	$20,300
February	3,950	$28,500

Use Excel to perform the requirements.

Requirements

1. Run a regression analysis.
2. Determine the lab's cost equation (use the output from the regression analysis you perform using Excel).
3. Determine the R-square using the Excel output you obtain. What does the lab's R-square indicate?
4. Predict the lab's total overhead costs for the month if 3,000 tests are performed.

E6-61B Prepare and interpret a scatter plot *(Learning Objective 3)*

Devon's Yukon Pancake Restaurant features sourdough pancakes made from a strain of sourdough dating back to the Alaskan Gold Rush. To plan for the future, Devon needs to figure out his cost behavior patterns. He has the following information about his operating costs and the number of pancakes served:

Month	Number of Pancakes	Total Operating Costs
July	3,700	$2,330
August	4,100	$2,410
September	3,200	$2,320
October	3,400	$2,260
November	3,800	$2,520
December	3,500	$2,500

Requirements

1. Prepare a scatter plot of Devon's pancake volume and operating costs.
2. Do the data appear sound, or do there appear to be any outliers? Explain.
3. Based on the scatter plot, do operating costs appear to be variable, fixed, or mixed costs?
4. How strong of a relationship is there between pancake volume and operating costs?

E6-62B High-low method *(Learning Objective 4)*

Refer to Devon's Yukon Pancake Restaurant in E6-61B.

Requirements

1. Use the high-low method to determine Devon's operating cost equation.
2. Use your answer from Requirement 1 to predict total monthly operating costs if Devon serves 4,200 pancakes a month.
3. Can you predict total monthly operating costs if Devon serves 15,000 pancakes a month? Explain.

E6-63B Regression analysis *(Learning Objective 5)*

Refer to Devon's Yukon Pancake Restaurant in E6-61B.

Use Microsoft Excel to run a regression analysis, then perform the following calculations:

Requirements

1. Determine Devon's monthly operating cost equation (use the output from the Excel regression).
2. Based on the R-square shown on the regression output, how well does this cost equation fit the data?

E6-64B Regression analysis using Excel output *(Learning Objective 5)*

Assume that Devon's Yukon Pancake Restaurant does a regression analysis on the next year's data using Excel. The output generated by Excel is as follows:

	A	B	C	D	E	F	G	H	I
1									
2									
3	***Regression Statistics***								
4	Multiple R		0.38						
5	R Square		0.14						
6	Adjusted R Square		-0.07						
7	Standard Error		76.49						
8	Observations		6						
9									
10	**ANOVA**								
11		*df*	*SS*	*MS*	*F*	*Significance F*			
12	Regression	1	3,945.34	3,945.34	0.67	0.46			
13	Residual	4	23,404.66	5,851.16					
14	Total	5	27,350.00						
15									
16		*Coefficients*	*Standard Error*	*t Stat*	*P-value*	*Lower 95%*	*Upper 95%*	*Lower 95.0%*	*Upper 95.0%*
17	Intercept	2,116.41	316.45	6.69	0.00	1,237.80	2,995.03	1,237.80	2,995.03
18	X Variable 1	0.07	0.09	0.82	0.46	-0.17	0.32	-0.17	0.32

Requirements

1. What is the fixed cost per month?
2. What is the variable cost per pancake?
3. If Devon's Yukon Pancake Restaurant serves 3,500 pancakes in a month, what would its total operating costs be?

E6-65B Determine cost behavior and predict operating costs *(Learning Objective 4)*

SeaView Apartments is a 1000-unit apartment complex. When the apartments are 90% occupied, monthly operating costs total $228,400. When occupancy dips to 80%, monthly operating costs fall to $222,800. The owner of the apartment complex is worried because many of the apartment residents work at a nearby manufacturing plant that has just announced it will close in three months. The apartment owner fears that occupancy of her apartments will drop to 65% if residents lose their jobs and move away. Assuming the same relevant range, what should the owner expect operating costs to be if occupancy falls to 65%?

E6-66B Prepare a contribution margin income statement *(Learning Objective 6)*

Hoffwood Gifts is a specialty pet gift shop selling exotic pet-related items over the internet. Results for last year are shown next:

HOFFWOOD GIFTS
Income Statement
Year Ended December 31

Sales revenue		$ 999,000
Cost of goods sold		(670,000)
Gross profit		$ 329,000
Operating expenses:		
Selling and marketing expenses	$65,500	
Website maintenance expenses	57,500	
Other operating expenses	18,600	
Total operating expenses		(141,600)
Operating income		$ 187,400

For internal planning and decision-making purposes, the owner of Hoffwood Gifts would like to translate the company's income statement into the contribution margin format. Since Hoffwood Gifts is a web retailer and has no physical presence, all of its cost of goods sold is variable. A large portion of the selling and marketing expenses consists of freight-out charges $19,600, which were also variable. Only 20% of the remaining selling and marketing expenses and 25% of the website expenses were variable. Of the other operating expenses, 90% were fixed. Based on this information, prepare Hoffwood Gifts' contribution margin income statement for last year.

E6-67B Prepare a contribution margin income statement *(Learning Objective 6)*

Curt Carriage Company offers guided horse-drawn carriage rides through historic Charleston, South Carolina. The carriage business is highly regulated by the city. Curt Carriage Company has the following operating costs during April:

Monthly depreciation expense on carriages and stable	$2,000
Fee paid to the City of Charleston	15% of ticket revenue
Cost of souvenir set of postcards given to each passenger	$0.95/set of postcards
Brokerage fee paid to independent ticket brokers (60% of tickets are issued through these brokers; 40% are sold directly by the Curt Carriage Company)	$1.80/ticket sold by broker
Monthly cost of leasing and boarding the horses	$51,000
Carriage drivers (tour guides) are paid on a per passenger basis	$3.40 per passenger
Monthly payroll costs of non–tour guide employees	$7,600
Marketing, website, telephone, and other monthly fixed costs	$7,100

During April (a month during peak season), Curt Carriage Company had 12,960 passengers. Eighty-five percent of passengers were adults ($20 fare) while 15% were children ($12 fare).

Requirements

1. Prepare the company's contribution margin income statement for the month of April. Round all figures to the nearest dollar.
2. Assume that passenger volume increases by 17% in May. Which figures on the income statement would you expect to change and by what percentage would they change? Which figures would remain the same as in April?

E6-68B Prepare income statements using variable costing and absorption costing with changing inventory levels *(Learning Objective 6)*

Fagan Manufacturing manufactures a single product that it will sell for $120 per unit. The company is looking to project its operating income for its first two years of operations. Cost information for the single unit of its product is as follows:

- Direct material per unit produced $50
- Direct labor cost per unit produced $12
- Variable manufacturing overhead (MOH) per unit produced $10
- Variable operating expenses per unit sold $4

Fixed manufacturing overhead (MOH) for each year is $1,200,000, while fixed operating expenses for each year will be $250,000.

During its first year of operations, the company plans to manufacture 50,000 units and anticipates selling 40,000 of those units. During the second year of its operations, the company plans to manufacture 50,000 units and anticipates selling 55,000 units (it has units in beginning inventory for the second year from its first year of operations.)

Requirements

1. Prepare an absorption costing income statement for:
   a. The first year of operations
   b. The second year of operations
2. Before you prepare the variable costing income statements for Fagan, predict Fagan's operating income using variable costing for both its first year and its second year without preparing the variable costing income statements. *Hint*: Calculate the variable costing operating income for a given year by taking that year's absorption costing operating income and adding or subtracting the difference in operating income as calculated using the following formula:

   Difference in operating income = (Change in inventory level in units × Fixed MOH per unit)

3. Prepare a variable costing income statement for:
   a. The first year of operations
   b. The second year of operations

E6-69B Prepare a variable costing income statement given an absorption costing income statement *(Learning Objective 6)*

McFall Industries manufactures and sells a single product. The controller has prepared the following income statement for the most recent year:

McFall Industries Income Statement (Absorption costing) For the year ending December 31	
Sales revenue	$1,050,000
Less: Cost of goods sold	675,000
Gross profit	$ 375,000
Less: Operating expenses	260,000
Operating income	$ 115,000

The company produced 20,000 units and sold 15,000 units during the year ending December 31. Fixed manufacturing overhead (MOH) for the year was $240,000, while fixed operating expenses were $200,000. The company had no beginning inventory.

Requirements

1. Will the company's operating income under variable costing be higher, lower, or the same as its operating income under absorption costing? Why?
2. Project the company's operating income under variable costing without preparing a variable costing income statement.
3. Prepare a variable costing income statement for the year.

E6-70B Absorption and variable costing income statements *(Learning Objective 6)*

The annual data that follow pertain to Swimmerz, a manufacturer of swimming goggles (Swimmerz has no beginning inventories):

Sale price	$ 39
Variable manufacturing expense per unit	$ 16
Sales commission expense per unit	$ 7
Fixed manufacturing overhead	$2,820,000
Fixed operating expense	$ 240,000
Number of goggles produced	235,000
Number of goggles sold	225,000

Requirements

1. Prepare both conventional (absorption costing) and contribution margin (variable costing) income statements for Swimmerz for the year.
2. Which statement shows the higher operating income? Why?
3. Swimmerz's marketing vice president believes a new sales promotion that costs $150,000 would increase sales to 235,000 goggles. Should the company go ahead with the promotion? Give your reason.

PROBLEMS Group A

P6-71A Analyze cost behavior at a hospital using various cost estimation methods *(Learning Objectives 1, 2, 3, 4, & 5)*

Suzanne Spahr is the Chief Operating Officer at Union Hospital in Forest Lake, Minnesota. She is analyzing the hospital's overhead costs but is not sure whether nursing hours or the number of patient days would be the best cost driver to use for predicting the hospital's overhead. She has gathered the following information for the last six months of the most recent year:

Month	Hospital Overhead Costs	Nursing Hours	Number of Patient Days	Overhead Cost per Nursing Hour	Overhead Cost per Patient Day
July	$485,000	25,000	3,800	$19.40	$127.63
August	$540,000	26,700	4,360	$20.22	$123.85
September.........	$420,000	20,000	4,210	$21.00	$ 99.76
October	$462,000	21,900	3,450	$21.10	$133.91
November	$579,000	32,000	5,600	$18.09	$103.39
December..........	$455,000	20,400	3,270	$22.30	$139.14

Requirements

1. Are the hospital's overhead costs fixed, variable, or mixed? Explain.
2. Graph the hospital's overhead costs against nursing hours. Use Excel or graph by hand.
3. Graph the hospital's overhead costs against the number of patient days. Use Excel or graph by hand.
4. Do the data appear to be sound or do you see any potential data problems? Explain.
5. Use the high-low method to determine the hospital's cost equation using nursing hours as the cost driver. Predict total overhead costs if 26,000 nursing hours are predicted for the month.
6. Ms. Spahr runs a regression analysis using nursing hours as the cost driver to predict total hospital overhead costs. The Excel output from the regression analysis is shown next.

	A	B	C	D	E	F	G	H	I
1	**SUMMARY OUTPUT – Nursing hours as cost driver**								
2									
3	***Regression Statistics***								
4	Multiple R		0.967848203						
5	R Square		0.936730144						
6	Adjusted R Square		0.92091268						
7	Standard Error		16568.3268						
8	Observations		6						
9									
10	**ANOVA**								
11		*df*	*SS*	*MS*	*F*	*Significance F*			
12	Regression	1	16256795521	16256795521	59.2212594	0.001533989			
13	Residual	4	1098037812	274509453					
14	Total	5	17354833333						
15									
16		*Coefficients*	*Standard Error*	*t Stat*	*P-value*	*Lower 95%*	*Upper 95%*	*Lower 95.0%*	*Upper 95.0%*
17	Intercept	187378.980	39923.061	4.694	0.009	76534.789	298223.164	76534.789	298223.164
18	X Variable 1	12.440	1.617	7.696	0.002	7.954	16.933	7.954	16.993

If 26,000 nursing hours are predicted for the month, what is the total predicted hospital overhead?

CHAPTER 6

7. Ms. Spahr then ran the regression analysis using number of patient days as the cost driver. The Excel output from the regression is shown here:

	A	B	C	D	E	F	G	H	I
1	**SUMMARY OUTPUT – Using number of patient days as cost driver**								
2									
3	***Regression Statistics***								
4	Multiple R		0.75770497						
5	R Square		0.574116821						
6	Adjusted R Square		0.467646026						
7	Standard Error		42985.84532						
8	Observations		6						
9									
10	**ANOVA**								
11		*df*	*SS*	*MS*	*F*	*Significance F*			
12	Regression	1	9963701742	9963701742	5.392246976	0.08094813			
13	Residual	4	7391131591	1847782898					
14	Total	5	17354833333						
15									
16		*Coefficients*	*Standard Error*	*t Stat*	*P-value*	*Lower 95%*	*Upper 95%*	*Lower 95.0%*	*Upper 95.0%*
17	Intercept	271537.440	95772.174	2.835	0.047	5631.253	537443.620	5631.253	537443.620
18	X Variable 1	53.130	22.880	2.322	0.081	-10.395	116.655	-10.395	116.655

If 3,700 patient days are predicted for the month, what is the total predicted hospital overhead?

8. Which regression analysis (using nursing hours or using number of patient days as the cost driver) produces the best cost equation? Explain your answer.

P6-72A Analyze cost behavior *(Learning Objectives 1, 2, 3, & 4)*

Renkas Industries is in the process of analyzing its manufacturing overhead costs. Renkas Industries is not sure if the number of units produced or number of direct labor (DL) hours is the best cost driver to use for predicting manufacturing overhead (MOH) costs. The following information is available:

Month	Manufacturing Overhead Costs	Direct Labor Hours	Units Produced	MOH Cost per DL Hour	MOH Cost per Unit Produced
July	$457,000	23,200	3,580	$19.70	$127.65
August	$512,000	26,600	4,290	$19.25	$119.35
September	$421,000	19,000	4,240	$22.16	$ 99.29
October	$449,000	21,500	3,430	$20.88	$130.90
November	$571,000	31,000	5,730	$18.42	$ 99.65
December	$434,000	19,700	3,220	$22.03	$134.78

Requirements

1. Are manufacturing overhead costs fixed, variable, or mixed? Explain.
2. Graph Renkas Industries' manufacturing overhead costs against DL hours. Use Excel or graph by hand.
3. Graph Renkas Industries' manufacturing overhead costs against units produced. Use Excel or graph by hand.

4. Do the data appear to be sound, or do you see any potential data problems? Explain.
5. Use the high-low method to determine Renkas Industries' manufacturing overhead cost equation using DL hours as the cost driver. Assume that management believes all data to be accurate and wants to include all of it in the analysis.
6. Estimate manufacturing overhead costs if Renkas Industries incurs 25,000 DL hours in January.

P6-73A Continuation of P6-72A: Regression analysis *(Learning Objective 5)*

Refer to Renkas Industries in P6-72A.

Requirements

1. Use Excel regression analysis to determine Renkas Industries' manufacturing overhead cost equation using DL hours as the cost driver. Comment on the R-square. Estimate manufacturing overhead costs if Renkas Industries incurs 25,500 DL hours in January.
2. Use Excel regression analysis to determine Renkas manufacturing overhead cost equation using number of units produced as the cost driver. Use all of the data provided. Project total manufacturing overhead costs if Renkas Industries produces 4,900 units. Which cost equation is better—this one or the one from Requirement 1? Why?
3. Use Excel regression analysis to determine Renkas Industries' manufacturing overhead cost equation using number of units produced as the cost driver. This time, remove any potential outliers before performing the regression. How does this affect the R-square? Project total manufacturing overhead costs if 4,900 units are produced.
4. In which cost equation do you have the most confidence? Why?

P6-74A Prepare traditional and contribution margin income statements *(Learning Objective 6)*

The Old Tyme Ice Cream Shoppe sold 9,400 servings of ice cream during June for $4 per serving. Old Tyme purchases the ice cream in large tubs from the Golden Ice Cream Company. Each tub costs Old Tyme $11 and has enough ice cream to fill 20 ice cream cones. Old Tyme purchases the ice cream cones for $0.10 each from a local warehouse club. Old Tyme Ice Cream Shoppe is located in a local strip mall, and rent for the space is $1,900 per month. Old Tyme expenses $230 a month for the depreciation of the Shoppe's furniture and equipment. During June, Old Tyme incurred an additional $2,100 of other operating expenses (75% of these were fixed costs).

Requirements

1. Prepare Old Tyme's June income statement using a traditional format.
2. Prepare Old Tyme's June income statement using a contribution margin format.

P6-75A Determine financial statement components *(Learning Objective 6)*

Violins and More produces student-grade violins for beginning violin students. The company produced 2,300 violins in its first month of operations. At month-end, 600 finished violins remained unsold. There was no inventory in work in process. Violins were sold for $125.00 each. Total costs from the month are as follows:

Direct materials used	$99,500
Direct labor	$65,000
Variable manufacturing overhead	$31,000
Fixed manufacturing overhead	$41,400
Variable selling and administrative expenses	$10,000
Fixed selling and administrative expenses	$12,500

The company prepares traditional (absorption costing) income statements for its bankers. Violins and More would also like to prepare contribution margin income statements for management use. Compute the following amounts that would be shown on these income statements:

1. Gross profit
2. Contribution margin
3. Total expenses shown **below** the **gross profit** line
4. Total expenses shown **below** the **contribution margin** line
5. Dollar value of ending inventory under absorption costing
6. Dollar value of ending inventory under variable costing

Which income statement will have a higher operating income? By how much? Explain.

P6-76A Absorption and variable costing income statements *(Learning Objective 6)*

Owen's Foods produces frozen meals, which it sells for $9 each. The company uses the FIFO inventory costing method, and it computes a new monthly fixed manufacturing overhead rate based on the actual number of meals produced that month. All costs and production levels are exactly as planned. The following data are from the company's first two months in business:

	January	February
Sales	1,400 meals	1,600 meals
Production	2,000 meals	1,400 meals
Variable manufacturing expense per meal	$ 4	$ 4
Sales commission expense per meal	$ 1	$ 1
Total fixed manufacturing overhead	$ 700	$ 700
Total fixed marketing and administrative expenses	$ 400	$ 400

Requirements

1. Compute the product cost per meal produced under absorption costing and under variable costing. Do this first for January and then for February.
2. Prepare separate monthly income statements for January and for February, using the following:
   a. Absorption costing
   b. Variable costing
3. Is operating income higher under absorption costing or variable costing in January? In February? Explain the pattern of differences in operating income based on absorption costing versus variable costing.

PROBLEMS Group B

P6-77B Analyze cost behavior at a hospital using various cost estimation methods *(Learning Objectives 1, 2, 3, 4 & 5)*

Freida Dudley is the Chief Operating Officer at Memorial Hospital in Scandia, Minnesota. She is analyzing the hospital's overhead costs but is not sure whether nursing hours or the number of patient days would be the best cost driver to use for predicting the hospital's overhead. She has gathered the following information for the last six months of the most recent year:

Month	Hospital Overhead Costs	Nursing Hours	Number of Patient Days	Overhead Cost per Nursing Hour	Overhead Cost per Patient Day
July	$462,000	22,900	3,610	$20.17	$127.98
August	$510,000	26,300	4,330	$19.39	$117.78
September	$401,000	17,500	4,250	$22.91	$ 94.35
October	$445,000	21,700	3,460	$20.51	$128.61
November	$556,000	30,000	5,740	$18.53	$ 96.86
December	$430,000	19,000	3,230	$22.63	$133.13

Requirements

1. Are the hospital's overhead costs fixed, variable, or mixed? Explain.
2. Graph the hospital's overhead costs against nursing hours. Use Excel or graph by hand.
3. Graph the hospital's overhead costs against the number of patient days. Use Excel or graph by hand.
4. Do the data appear to be sound or do you see any potential data problems? Explain
5. Use the high-low method to determine the hospital's cost equation using nursing hours as the cost driver. Predict total overhead costs if 23,500 nursing hours are predicted for the month.
6. Ms. Dudley runs a regression analysis using nursing hours as the cost driver to predict total hospital overhead costs. The Excel output from the regression analysis is shown next:

	A	B	C	D	E	F	G	H	I
1	**SUMMARY OUTPUT**								
2									
3	***Regression Statistics***								
4	Multiple R		0.9938						
5	R Square		0.9876						
6	Adjusted R Square		0.9845						
7	Standard Error		7027.6715						
8	Observations		6						
9									
10	**ANOVA**								
11		*df*	*SS*	*MS*	*F*	*Significance F*			
12	Regression	1	1580578	1580578	320.031	3.0254			
13	Residual	4	19755	49388167.25					
14	Total	5	1600333						
15									
16		*Coefficients*	*Standard Error*	*t Stat*	*P-value*	*Lower 95%*	*Upper 95%*	*Lower 95.0%*	*Upper 95.0%*
17	Intercept	190017.690	15764.911	12.053	0.000	146247.280	233788.101	146247.280	233788.101
18	X Variable 1	12.110	0.677	17.889	0.000	10.230	13.989	10.230	13.989

If 23,500 nursing hours are predicted for the month, what is the total predicted hospital overhead?

7. Ms. Dudley then ran the regression analysis using number of patient days as the cost driver. The Excel output from the regression is shown here:

	A	B	C	D	E	F	G	H	I
1	**SUMMARY OUTPUT**								
2									
3		***Regression Statistics***							
4	Multiple R		0.75340						
5	R Square		0.5676						
6	Adjusted R Square		0.45953						
7	Standard Error		41591.550						
8	Observations		6						
9									
10	**ANOVA**								
11		*df*	*SS*	*MS*	*F*	*Significance F*			
12	Regression	1	908390	908390	5.25124	0.08371			
13	Residual	4	691942	172985					
14	Total	5	1600333						
15									
16		*Coefficients*	*Standard Error*	*t Stat*	*P-value*	*Lower 95%*	*Upper 95%*	*Lower 95.0%*	*Upper 95.0%*
17	Intercept	275852.530	85266.887	3.235	0.032	39113.700	512591.364	39113.700	512591.364
18	X Variable 1	46.660	20.364	2.292	0.084	-9.874	103.203	-9.874	103.203

If 3,300 patient days are predicted for the month, what is the total predicted hospital overhead?

8. Which regression analysis (using nursing hours or using number of patient days as the cost driver) produces the best cost equation? Explain your answer.

P6-78B Analyze cost behavior *(Learning Objectives 1, 2, 3, & 4)*

Wythe Industries is in the process of analyzing its manufacturing overhead costs. Wythe Industries is not sure if the number of units produced or the number of direct labor (DL) hours is the best cost driver to use for predicting manufacturing overhead (MOH) costs. The following information is available:

Month	Manufacturing Overhead Costs	Direct Labor Hours	Units Produced	MOH Cost per DL Hour	MOH Cost per Unit Produced
July	$470,000	22,800	3,630	$20.61	$129.48
August	$517,000	26,200	4,340	$19.73	$119.12
September	$428,000	19,000	4,190	$22.53	$102.15
October	$453,000	21,800	3,420	$20.78	$132.46
November	$557,000	29,000	5,770	$19.21	$ 96.53
December	$439,000	19,500	3,260	$22.51	$134.66

Requirements

1. Are manufacturing overhead costs fixed, variable, or mixed? Explain.
2. Graph Wythe Industries' manufacturing overhead costs against DL hours.
3. Graph Wythe Industries' manufacturing overhead costs against units produced.
4. Do the data appear to be sound or do you see any potential data problems? Explain.

5. Use the high-low method to determine Wythe Industries' manufacturing overhead cost equation using DL hours as the cost driver. Assume that management believes all the data to be accurate and wants to include all of it in the analysis.
6. Estimate manufacturing overhead costs if Wythe Industries incurs 23,000 DL hours in January.

P6-79B Continuation of P6-78B: Regression analysis *(Learning Objective 5)*

Refer to Wythe Industries in P6-78B.

Requirements

1. Use Excel regression analysis to determine Wythe Industries' manufacturing overhead cost equation using DL hours as the cost driver. Comment on the R-square. Estimate manufacturing overhead costs if Wythe Industries incurs 24,000 DL hours in January.
2. Use Excel regression analysis to determine Wythe's manufacturing overhead cost equation using number of units produced as the cost driver. Use all of the data provided. Project total manufacturing overhead costs if Wythe Industries produces 5,100 units. Which cost equation is better—this one or the one from Requirement 1? Why?
3. Use Excel regression analysis to determine Wythe Industries' manufacturing overhead cost equation using number of units produced as the cost driver. This time, remove any potential outliers before performing the regression. How does this affect the R-square? Project total manufacturing overhead costs if 5,100 units are produced.
4. In which cost equation do you have the most confidence? Why?

P6-80B Prepare traditional and contribution margin income statements *(Learning Objective 6)*

Marlo's Ice Cream Shoppe sold 9,500 servings of ice cream during June for $2 per serving. Marlo purchases the ice cream in large tubs from the Georgia Ice Cream Company. Each tub costs Marlo $11 and has enough ice cream to fill 20 ice cream cones. Marlo purchases the ice cream cones for $0.10 each from a local warehouse club. The shop is located in a local strip mall, and she pays $1,750 a month to lease the space. Marlo expenses $230 a month for the depreciation of the shop's furniture and equipment. During June, Marlo incurred an additional $2,900 of other operating expenses (75% of these were fixed costs).

Requirements

1. Prepare Marlo's June income statement using a traditional format.
2. Prepare Marlo's June income statement using a contribution margin format.

P6-81B Determine financial statement components *(Learning Objective 6)*

Violins-by-Lucy produces student-grade violins for beginning violin students. The company produced 2,400 violins in its first month of operations. At month-end, 550 finished violins remained unsold. There was no inventory in work in process. Violins were sold for $115.00 each. Total costs from the month are as follows:

Direct materials used	$139,400
Direct labor	$ 35,000
Variable manufacturing overhead	$ 32,000
Fixed manufacturing overhead	$ 52,800
Variable selling and administrative expenses	$ 9,000
Fixed selling and administrative expenses	$ 13,000

The company prepares traditional (absorption costing) income statements for its bankers.

Lucy would also like to prepare contribution margin income statements for her own management use. Compute the following amounts that would be shown on these income statements:

1. Gross profit
2. Contribution margin
3. Total expenses shown **below** the **gross profit** line
4. Total expenses shown **below** the **contribution margin** line
5. Dollar value of ending inventory under absorption costing
6. Dollar value of ending inventory under variable costing

Which income statement will have a higher operating income? By how much? Explain.

P6-82B Absorption and variable costing income statements *(Learning Objective 6)*

Jason's Meals produces frozen meals, which it sells for $10 each. The company uses the FIFO inventory costing method, and it computes a new monthly fixed manufacturing overhead rate based on the actual number of meals produced that month. All costs and production levels are exactly as planned. The following data are from the company's first two months in business:

	January	February
Sales	1,500 meals	1,900 meals
Production	2,000 meals	1,600 meals
Variable manufacturing expense per meal	$ 4	$ 4
Sales commission expense per meal	$ 1	$ 1
Total fixed manufacturing overhead	$ 800	$ 800
Total fixed marketing and administrative expenses	$ 300	$ 300

Requirements

1. Compute the product cost per meal produced under absorption costing and under variable costing. Do this first for January and then for February.
2. Prepare separate monthly income statements for January and for February, using (a) absorption costing and (b) variable costing.
3. Is operating income higher under absorption costing or variable costing in January? In February? Explain the pattern of differences in operating income based on absorption costing versus variable costing.

CRITICAL THINKING

Discussion & Analysis

A6-83 Discussion Questions

1. Briefly describe an organization with which you are familiar. Describe a situation when a manager in that organization could use cost behavior information and how the manager could use the information.
2. How are fixed costs similar to step fixed costs? How are fixed costs different from step fixed costs? Give an example of a step fixed cost and describe why that cost is not considered to be a fixed cost.
3. Describe a specific situation when a scatter plot could be useful to a manager.
4. What is a mixed cost? Give an example of a mixed cost. Sketch a graph of this example.
5. Compare discretionary fixed costs to committed fixed costs. Think of an organization with which you are familiar. Give two examples of discretionary fixed costs and two examples of committed fixed costs which that organization may have. Explain why the costs you have chosen as examples fit within the definitions of "discretionary fixed costs" and "committed fixed costs."
6. Define the terms "independent variable" and "dependent variable," as used in regression analysis. Illustrate the concepts of independent variables and dependent variables by selecting a cost a company would want to predict and what activity it might use to predict that cost. Describe the independent variable and the dependent variable in that situation.
7. Define the term "relevant range." Why is it important to managers?
8. Describe the term "R-square." If a regression analysis for predicting manufacturing overhead using direct labor hours as the dependent variable has an R-square of 0.40, why might this be a problem? Given the low R-square value, describe the options a manager has for predicting manufacturing overhead costs. Which option do you think is the best option for the manager? Defend your answer.
9. Over the past year, a company's inventory has increased significantly. The company uses absorption costing for financial statements, but internally, the company uses variable costing for financial statements. Which set of financial statements will show the highest operating income? What specifically causes the difference between the two sets of financial statements?
10. A company has adopted a lean production philosophy and, as a result, has cut its inventory levels significantly. Describe the impact on the company's external financial statements as a result of this inventory reduction. Also describe the impact of the inventory reduction on the company's internal financial statements which are prepared using variable costing.
11. What costs might a business incur by not adopting paperless services? Is paperless only profitable to large businesses or is it applicable to small businesses? Explain what factors might be involved in changing over to paperless billing.
12. How might the principles of sustainability (such as increased efficiency) affect cost behavior overall? Think of an example of a sustainable change in process or material that could impact the cost equation for that cost (i.e., the total fixed cost versus the variable cost per unit). Describe this example in detail and what might happen to total fixed costs and per unit variable costs.

Application & Analysis

A6-84 Cost Behavior in Real Companies

Choose a company with which you are familiar that manufactures a product or provides a service. In this activity, you will be making reasonable estimates of the costs and activities associated with this company; companies do not typically publish internal cost or process information.

Basic Discussion Questions

1. Describe the company you selected and the products or services it provides.
2. List ten costs that this company would incur. Include costs from a variety of departments within the company, including human resources, sales, accounting, production (if a manufacturer), service (if a service company), and others. Make sure that you have at least one cost from each of the following categories: fixed, variable, and mixed.
3. Classify each of the costs you listed as either fixed, variable, or mixed. Justify why you classified each cost as you did.
4. Describe a potential cost driver for each of the variable and mixed costs you listed. Explain why each cost driver would be appropriate for its associated cost.
5. Discuss how easy or difficult it was for you to decide whether each cost was fixed, variable, or mixed. Describe techniques a company could use to determine whether a cost is fixed, variable, or mixed.

Decision Cases

A6-85 Appendix *(Learning Objective 6)*

Suppose you serve on the board of directors of American Faucet, a manufacturer of bathroom fixtures that recently adopted a lean production philosophy. Part of your responsibility is to develop a compensation contract for Toni Moen, the vice president of manufacturing. To give her the incentive to make decisions that will increase the company's profits, the board decides to give Moen a year-end bonus if American Faucet meets a target operating income.

Write a memo to Chairperson of the Board Herbert Kohler explaining whether the bonus contract should be based on absorption costing or variable costing.

A6-86 Analyze cost behavior using a variety of methods *(Learning Objectives 1, 2, 3, 4, & 5)*

Braunhaus Microbrewery is in the process of analyzing its manufacturing overhead costs. Braunhaus Microbrewery is not sure if the number of cases or the number of processing hours is the best cost driver of manufacturing overhead (MOH) costs. The following information is available:

Month	Manufacturing Overhead Costs	Processing Hours	Cases	MOH Cost per Processing Hour	MOH Cost per Case
January	$29,500	680	8,000	$43.38	$3.69
February	27,800	575	6,750	48.35	4.12
March	24,500	500	5,500	49.00	4.45
April	29,000	600	7,250	48.33	4.00
May	28,000	650	7,800	43.08	3.59
June	29,750	710	5,600	41.90	5.31

Requirements

1. Are manufacturing overhead costs fixed, variable, or mixed? Explain.
2. Graph Braunhaus Microbrewery's manufacturing overhead costs against processing hours. Use Excel or graph by hand.
3. Graph Braunhaus Microbrewery's manufacturing overhead costs against cases produced. Use Excel or graph by hand.
4. Does the data appear to be sound, or do you see any potential data problems? Explain.

5. Use the high-low method to determine Braunhaus Microbrewery's manufacturing overhead cost equation using processing hours as the cost driver. Assume that management believes all of the data to be accurate and wants to include all of it in the analysis.
6. Estimate manufacturing overhead costs if Braunhaus Microbrewery incurs 550 processing hours in July, using the results of the high-low analysis in Requirement 5.
7. Use Excel regression analysis to determine Braunhaus Microbrewery's manufacturing overhead cost equation using processing hours as the cost driver. Comment on the R-square. Estimate manufacturing overhead costs if Braunhaus Microbrewery incurs 550 processing hours in July.
8. Use Excel regression analysis to determine Braunhaus Microbrewery's manufacturing overhead cost equation using number of cases produced as the cost driver. Use all of the data provided. Project total manufacturing overhead costs if Braunhaus Microbrewery produces 6,000 cases. Which cost equation is better—this one or the one from Requirement 7? Why?
9. Use Excel regression analysis to determine Braunhaus Microbrewery's manufacturing overhead cost equation using number of cases produced as the cost driver. This time, remove any potential outliers before performing the regression. How does this affect the R-square? Project total manufacturing overhead costs if Braunhaus Microbrewery produces 6,000 cases.
10. In which cost equation do you have the most confidence? Why?

CMA Questions

A6-87

Ace, Inc., estimates its total materials handling costs at two production levels as follows.

Cost	Gallons
$160,000	80,000
$132,000	60,000

What is the estimated total cost for handling 75,000 gallons?

a. $146,000
b. $150,000
c. $153,000
d. $165,000 *(CMA Adapted)*

A6-88

Huntington Corporation pays bonuses to its managers based on operating income, as calculated under variable costing. It is now two months before year-end, and earnings have been depressed for some time. Which one of the following should Wanda Richards, production manager, ***definitely*** implement if she desires to maximize her bonus for this year?

a. Step up production so that more manufacturing costs are deferred into inventory.
b. Cut $2.3 million of advertising and marketing costs.
c. Postpone $1.8 million of discretionary equipment maintenance until next year.
d. Implement, with the aid of the controller, an activity-based costing and activity-based management system. *(CMA Adapted)*

Cost-Volume-Profit Analysis

Learning Objectives

- **1** Calculate the unit contribution margin and the contribution margin ratio
- **2** Use CVP analysis to find breakeven points and target profit volumes
- **3** Perform sensitivity analysis in response to changing business conditions
- **4** Find breakeven and target profit volumes for multiproduct companies
- **5** Determine a firm's margin of safety, operating leverage, and most profitable cost structure

© Image Source / Alamy
© Phillip Jones / iStockphoto.com

Source: http://corporate.art.com

Art.com, Inc., has become the world's largest online retailer of fine art, photography, posters, and other wall décor. The company offers over 850,000 different products to customers ranging from budget-minded college students to professional decorators searching for high-end art. Using a domestic website, as well as 22 localized websites across five continents, the company has been able to generate sales from over 10 million customers in 120 countries. Each localized website uses the country's native language and currency, and offers local e-mail support. In addition, the company now offers free iPhone and Facebook apps that allow customers to turn personal photos into professionally-framed art, as well as preview art by importing it into a photo of their own living space. Innovations such as these continue to expand the company's marketing reach.

Even though Art.com doesn't face many of the fixed costs of traditional retail outlets, the company still incurs fixed costs related to its websites, distribution centers, and custom-framing facilities. It also incurs variable costs for each piece of art. The bottom line is, e-tail or retail, every business faces fixed and variable costs, and Art.com is no exception. Before they launched the company, how did Art.com managers figure out what sales volume they had to reach to break even? How did they forecast the volume needed to achieve their target profit? And as the company continues to operate, how do managers respond to fluctuating business conditions, changing variable and fixed costs, and pricing pressure from new competitors? Cost-volume-profit (CVP) analysis helps managers answer such questions.

In the last chapter, we discussed cost behavior patterns and the methods managers use to determine how the company's costs behave. We showed how managers use the contribution margin income statement to separately display the firm's variable and fixed costs. In this chapter, we show how managers identify the volume of sales necessary to achieve breakeven or a target profit. We also look at how changes in costs, sales price, and volume affect the firm's profit. Finally, we discuss ways to identify the firm's risk level, including ways to gauge how easily a firm's profits could turn to loss if sales volume declines.

How Does Cost-Volume-Profit Analysis Help Managers?

Cost-volume-profit analysis, or CVP, is a powerful tool that helps managers make important business decisions. Cost-volume-profit analysis expresses the relationships among costs, volume, and the company's profit. Entrepreneurs and managers use CVP analysis to determine the sales volume that will be needed just to break even, or cover costs. They also use CVP to determine the sales volume that will be needed to earn a target profit, such as $100,000 per month. And because business conditions are always changing, CVP can help managers prepare for and respond to economic changes, such as increases in costs from suppliers.

Let's begin our discussion by looking at the data needed for CVP analysis.

Data and Assumptions Required for CVP Analysis

CVP analysis relies on the interdependency of five components, or pieces of information, shown in Exhibit 7-1.

EXHIBIT 7-1 Components of CVP Analysis

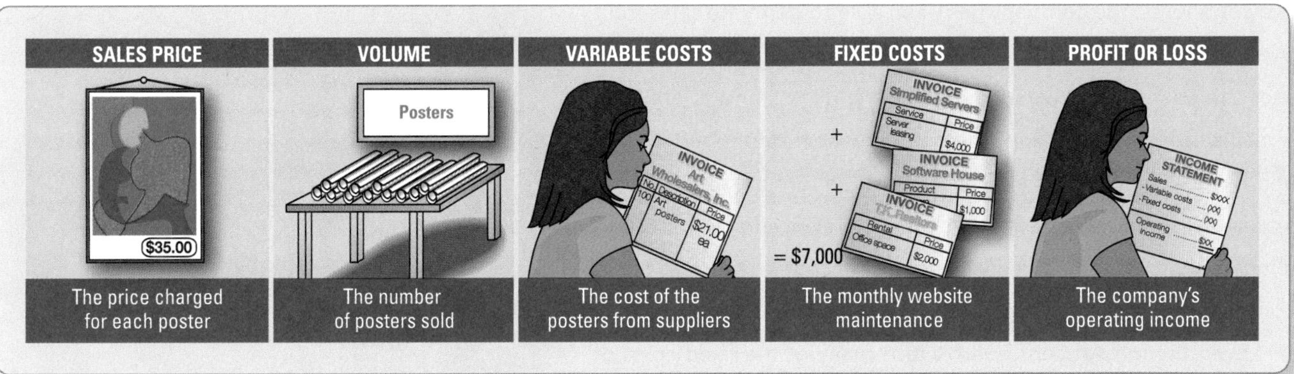

Let's examine this information in terms of a simple company example. Kay Martin, an entrepreneur, has just started an e-tail business selling art posters on the internet. Kay is a "virtual retailer" and carries no inventory. Kay's software tabulates all customer orders each day and then automatically places the order to buy posters from a wholesaler. Kay buys only what she needs to fill the prior day's sales orders. The posters cost $21 each, and Kay sells them for $35 each. Customers pay the shipping costs, so there are no other variable selling costs. Monthly fixed costs for server leasing and maintenance, software, and office rental total $7,000. Kay's relevant range extends from 0 to 2,000 posters a month. Beyond this volume, Kay will need to hire an employee and upgrade her website software in order to handle the increased volume.

Thus, we know the following:

- Sales price = $35 per poster
- Variable cost = $21 per poster
- Fixed costs = $7,000 per month

For CVP to be accurate, certain assumptions must be met. We'll itemize each of these assumptions, and discuss whether Kay's business meets the assumptions.

1. **A change in volume is the only factor that affects costs.** In Kay's business, costs are expected to increase only if volume increases. ✓
2. **Managers can classify each cost (or the components of mixed costs) as either variable or fixed. These costs are linear throughout the relevant range of volume.** In Kay's business, variable costs are $21 per poster and fixed costs are $7,000 per month. These costs are expected to remain the same unless Kay's volume exceeds 2,000 posters per month. Thus, we could draw each of these costs as straight lines on a graph. ✓

3. **Revenues are linear throughout the relevant range of volume.** In Kay's business, each poster generates $35 of sales revenue, with no volume discounts. Therefore, revenue could be graphed as a straight line beginning at the origin and sloping upwards at a rate of $35 per poster sold. ✓
4. **Inventory levels will not change.** Kay keeps no inventory. If she did, CVP analysis would still work as long as Kay did not allow her inventory levels to greatly fluctuate from one period to the next. ✓
5. **The sales mix of products will not change. Sales mix is the combination of products that make up total sales. For example, Art.com may sell 15% posters, 25% unframed photographs, and 60% framed prints. If profits differ across products, changes in sales mix will affect CVP analysis.** Kay currently offers only one size of poster, so her sales mix is 100% posters. Later in this chapter we will expand her product offerings to illustrate how sales mix impacts CVP analysis. ✓

Now that we know Kay's business meets these assumptions, we can proceed with confidence about the CVP results we will obtain. When assumptions are not met perfectly, managers should consider the results of CVP analysis to be approximations, rather than exact figures.

The Unit Contribution Margin

1 Calculate the unit contribution margin and the contribution margin ratio

The last chapter introduced the **contribution margin income statement**, which separates costs on the income statement by cost behavior rather than function. Many managers prefer the contribution margin income statement because it gives them the information for CVP analysis in a "ready-to-use" format. On these income statements, the contribution margin is the "dividing line"—all variable expenses go above the line, and all fixed expenses go below the line. The results of Kay's first month of operations is shown in Exhibit 7-2.

EXHIBIT 7-2 Contribution Margin Income Statement

KAY MARTIN POSTERS
Contribution Margin Income Statement
Month Ended August 31

Sales revenue (550 posters)	$ 19,250
Less: Variable expenses	(11,550)
Contribution margin	7,700
Less: Fixed expenses	(7,000)
Operating income	$ 700

Notice that the **contribution margin** is the excess of sales revenue over variable expenses. The contribution margin tells managers how much revenue is left—after paying variable expenses—for *contributing* toward covering fixed costs and then generating a profit. Hence the name contribution margin.

The contribution margin is stated as a *total* amount on the contribution margin income statement. However, managers often state the contribution margin on a *per unit* basis and as a *percentage*, or *ratio*. A product's **contribution margin per unit**—or unit contribution margin—is the excess of the selling price per unit over the variable cost of obtaining *and* selling each unit. Some businesses pay a sales commission on each unit or have other variable costs, such as shipping costs, for each unit sold. However, Kay's

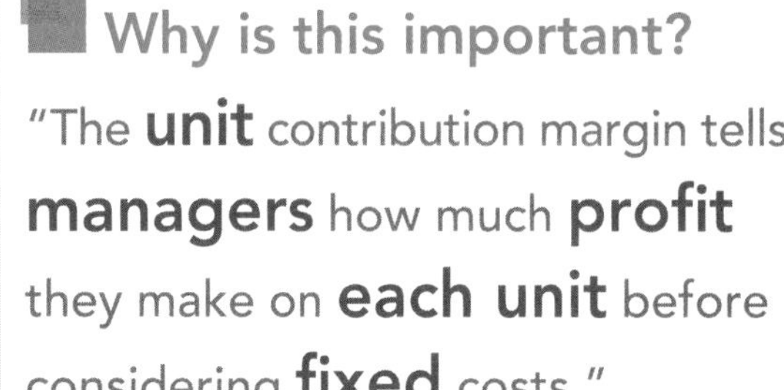

variable cost per unit is simply the price she pays for each poster. Therefore, her unit contribution margin is as follows:

Sales price per poster..................................	$ 35
Less: Variable cost per poster.......................	(21)
Contribution margin per poster....................	$ 14

The unit contribution margin indicates how much profit each unit provides *before* fixed costs are considered. Each unit *first* contributes this profit toward covering the firm's fixed costs. Once the company sells enough units to cover its fixed costs, the unit contribution margin contributes *directly* to operating income. For example, every poster Kay sells generates $14 of contribution margin that can be used to pay for the monthly $7,000 of fixed costs. After Kay sells enough posters to cover fixed costs, each additional poster she sells will generate $14 of operating income.

Managers can use the unit contribution margin to quickly forecast income at any volume within their relevant range. First, they project the total contribution margin by multiplying the unit contribution margin by the number of units they expect to sell. Then, they subtract fixed costs. For example, let's assume that Kay hopes to sell 650 posters next month. She can project her operating income as follows:

Contribution margin (650 posters × $14 per poster)....................	$ 9,100
Less: Fixed expenses..	(7,000)
Operating income..	$ 2,100

If Kay sells 650 posters next month, her operating income should be $2,100.

The Contribution Margin Ratio

In addition to computing the unit contribution margin, managers often compute the **contribution margin ratio**, which is the ratio of contribution margin to sales revenue. Kay can compute her contribution margin ratio at the unit level as follows:

$$\text{Contribution margin ratio} = \frac{\text{Unit contribution margin}}{\text{Sales price per unit}} = \frac{\$14}{\$35} = 40\%$$

Kay could also compute the contribution margin ratio using any volume of sales. Let's use her current sales volume, pictured in Exhibit 7-2:

$$\text{Contribution margin ratio} = \frac{\text{Contribution margin}}{\text{Sales revenue}} = \frac{\$7{,}700}{\$19{,}250} = 40\%$$

The contribution margin ratio is the percentage of each sales dollar that is available for covering fixed expenses and generating a profit. As shown in Exhibit 7-3, each *$1.00* of sales revenue contributes $0.40 toward fixed expenses and profit while the remaining $0.60 of each sales dollar is used to pay for variable costs.

EXHIBIT 7-3 Breakdown of $1 of Sales Revenue

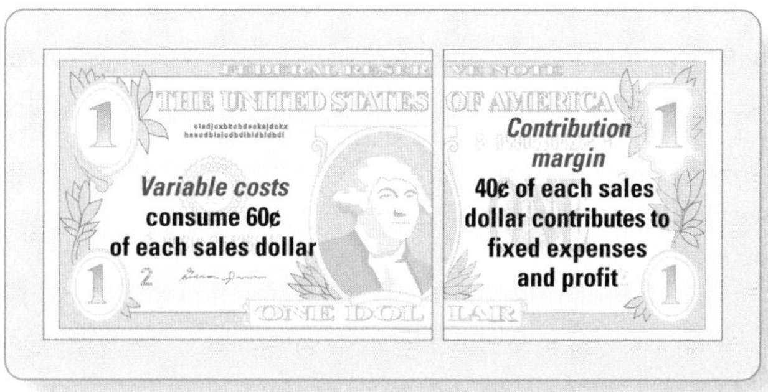

Managers can also use the contribution margin ratio to quickly forecast operating income within their relevant range. When using the contribution margin ratio, managers project income based on sales revenue (*dollars*) rather than sales *units*. For example, if Kay generates $70,000 of sales revenue one month, what operating income should she expect? To find out, Kay simply multiplies her projected sales revenue by the contribution margin ratio to arrive at the total contribution margin. Then she subtracts fixed expenses:

Contribution margin ($70,000 sales × 40%)	$28,000
Less: Fixed expenses	(7,000)
Operating income	$21,000

Let's verify. If Kay has $70,000 of sales revenue, she has sold 2,000 posters ($70,000 ÷ $35 per poster). Her complete contribution margin income statement would be calculated as follows:

Sales revenue (2,000 posters × $35/poster)	$ 70,000
Less: Variable expenses (2,000 posters × $21/poster)	(42,000)
Contribution margin (2,000 posters × $14/poster)	$ 28,000
Less: Fixed expenses	(7,000)
Operating income	$ 21,000

The contribution margin per unit and contribution margin ratio help managers quickly and easily project income at different sales volumes. However, when projecting profits, managers must keep in mind the relevant range. For instance, if Kay wants to project income at a volume of 5,000 posters, she shouldn't use the existing contribution margin and fixed costs. Her current relevant range extends to only 2,000 posters per month. At a higher volume of sales, her variable cost per unit may be lower than $21 (due to volume discounts from her suppliers) and her monthly fixed costs may be higher than $7,000 (due to upgrading her system and hiring an employee to handle the extra sales volume).

Rather than using the individual unit contribution margins on each of their products, large companies that offer hundreds or thousands of products (like Art.com) use their contribution margin *ratio* to predict profits. As long as the sales mix remains constant (one of our CVP assumptions), the contribution margin ratio will remain constant.

We've seen how managers use the contribution margin to project income; but managers use the contribution margin for other purposes too, such as motivating the sales force. Salespeople who know the contribution margin of each product can generate more profit for the company by emphasizing high-margin products. This is why many companies base sales commissions on the contribution margins produced by sales rather than on sales revenue alone.

In the next section, we'll see how managers use CVP analysis to determine the company's breakeven point.

How do Managers Find the Breakeven Point?

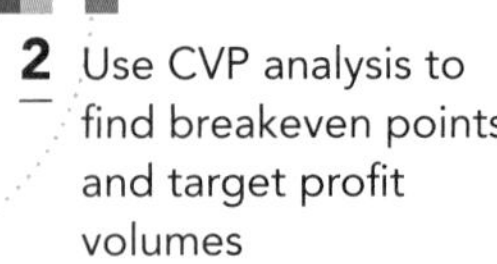

2 Use CVP analysis to find breakeven points and target profit volumes

A company's **breakeven point** is the sales level at which *operating income is zero*. Sales below the breakeven point result in a loss. Sales above the breakeven point provide a profit. Before Kay started her business, she wanted to figure out how many posters she would have to sell just to break even.

There are three ways to calculate the breakeven point. All of the approaches are based on the income statement, so they all reach the same conclusion. The first two methods find breakeven in terms of sales *units*. The last approach finds breakeven in terms of sales revenue (sales dollars).

Why is this important?

"Businesses **don't** want to operate at a **loss**. CVP analysis helps **managers** determine how many units they need to sell ***just*** to **break even.**"

1. The income statement approach
2. The shortcut approach using the *unit* contribution margin
3. The shortcut approach using the contribution margin *ratio*

Let's examine these three approaches in detail.

The Income Statement Approach

The income statement approach starts with the contribution margin income statement, and then breaks it down into smaller components:

SALES REVENUE	–	VARIABLE EXPENSES	–	FIXED EXPENSES	=	OPERATING INCOME
(Sales price per unit × Units sold)	–	(Variable cost per unit × Units sold)	–	Fixed expenses	=	Operating income

Let's use this approach to find Kay's breakeven point. Recall that Kay sells her posters for $35 each and that her variable cost is $21 per poster. Kay's fixed expenses total $7,000. At the breakeven point, operating income is zero. We use this information to solve the income statement equation for the number of posters Kay must sell to break even.

SALES REVENUE	–	VARIABLE EXPENSES	–	FIXED EXPENSES	=	OPERATING INCOME
(Sales price per unit × Units sold)	–	(Variable cost per unit × Units sold)	–	Fixed expenses	=	Operating income
($35 × Units sold)	–	($21 × Units sold)	–	$7,000	=	$ 0
($35	–	$21) × Units sold	–	$7,000	=	$ 0
		$14 × Units sold			=	$7,000
		Units sold			=	$7,000/$14
		Sales in units			=	500 posters

Kay must sell 500 posters to break even. Her breakeven point in sales revenue is $17,500 (500 posters × $35).

You can check this answer by creating a contribution margin income statement using a sales volume of 500 posters:

Sales revenue (500 posters × $35)	$ 17,500
Less: Variable expenses (500 posters × $21)	(10,500)
Contribution margin	$ 7,000
Less: Fixed expenses	(7,000)
Operating income	$ 0

Notice that at breakeven, a firm's fixed expenses ($7,000) equal its contribution margin ($7,000). In other words, the firm has generated *just* enough contribution margin to cover its fixed expenses, but *not* enough to generate a profit.

The Shortcut Approach Using the Unit Contribution Margin

To develop the shortcut approach, we start with the contribution margin income statement, and then rearrange some of its terms:

SALES REVENUE − VARIABLE EXPENSES − FIXED EXPENSES = OPERATING INCOME

Contribution margin	−	Fixed expenses	= Operating income
Contribution margin			= Fixed expenses + Operating income
(Contribution margin per unit × Units sold)			= Fixed expenses + Operating income

As a final step, we divide both sides of the equation by the contribution margin per unit. Now we have the shortcut formula:

$$\text{Sales in units} = \frac{\text{Fixed expenses} + \text{Operating income}}{\text{Contribution margin per unit}}$$

If your instructor is using MyAccountingLab, go to the Multimedia Library for a quick video on this topic.

Kay can use this shortcut approach to find her breakeven point in units. Kay's fixed expenses total $7,000, and her unit contribution margin is $14. At the breakeven point, operating income is zero. Thus, Kay's breakeven point in units is as follows:

$$\text{Sales in units} = \frac{\$7{,}000 + \$0}{\$14}$$
$$= 500 \text{ posters}$$

Why does this shortcut approach work? Recall that each poster provides $14 of contribution margin. To break even, Kay must generate enough contribution margin to cover $7,000 of fixed expenses. At the rate of $14 per poster, Kay must sell 500 posters ($7,000/$14) to cover her $7,000 of fixed expenses. Because the shortcut formula simply rearranges the income statement equation, the breakeven point is the same under both methods (500 posters).

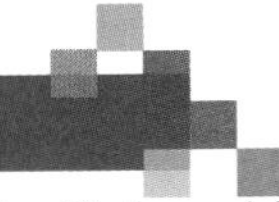

STOP & THINK

What would Kay's operating income be if she sold 501 posters? What would it be if she sold 600 posters?

Answer: Every poster sold provides $14 of contribution margin, which first contributes toward covering fixed costs, then profit. Once Kay reaches her breakeven point (500 posters), she has covered all fixed costs. Therefore, each additional poster sold after the breakeven point contributes $14 *directly to profit.* If Kay sells 501 posters, she has sold one more poster than breakeven. Her operating income is $14. If she sells 600 posters, she has sold 100 more posters than breakeven. Her operating income is $1,400 ($14 per poster × 100 posters). We can verify this as follows:

Contribution margin (600 posters × $14 per poster)	$ 8,400
Less: Fixed expenses	(7,000)
Operating income	$ 1,400

Once a company achieves breakeven, each additional unit sold contributes its unique unit contribution margin directly to profit.

The Shortcut Approach Using the Contribution Margin Ratio

It is easy to compute the breakeven point in *units* for a simple business like Kay's that has only one product. But what about companies that have thousands of products such as Art.com, Home Depot, and Amazon.com? It doesn't make sense for these companies to determine the number of each various product they need to sell to break even. Can you imagine a Home Depot manager describing breakeven as 100,000 wood screws, two million nails, 3,000 lawn mowers, 10,000 gallons of paint, and so forth? It simply doesn't make sense. Therefore, multiproduct companies usually compute breakeven in terms of *sales revenue* (dollars).

This shortcut approach differs from the other shortcut we've just seen in only one way: Fixed expenses plus operating income are divided by the contribution margin *ratio* (not by contribution margin *per unit*) to yield sales in *dollars* (not *units*):

$$\text{Sales in dollars} = \frac{\text{Fixed expenses} + \text{Operating income}}{\text{Contribution margin ratio}}$$

Recall that Kay's contribution margin ratio is 40%. At the breakeven point, operating income is $0, so Kay's breakeven point in sales revenue is as follows:

$$\text{Sales in dollars} = \frac{\$7{,}000 + \$0}{0.40}$$
$$= \$17{,}500$$

This is the same breakeven sales revenue we calculated earlier (500 posters × $35 sales price = $17,500).

Why does the contribution margin ratio formula work? Each dollar of Kay's sales contributes $0.40 to fixed expenses and profit. To break even, she must generate enough contribution margin at the rate of $0.40 per sales dollar to cover the $7,000 fixed expenses ($7,000 ÷ 0.40 = $17,500).

When determining which formula to use, keep the following rule of thumb in mind:

Dividing fixed costs by the ***unit*** *contribution margin provides breakeven in sales* ***units****. Dividing fixed costs by the contribution margin* ***ratio*** *provides breakeven in sales* ***dollars****.*

How do Managers Find the Volume Needed to Earn a Target Profit?

For established products and services, managers are more interested in the sales level needed to earn a target profit than in the breakeven point. Managers of new business ventures are also interested in the profits they can expect to earn. For example, Kay doesn't want to just break even—she wants her business to be her sole source of income. She would like the business to earn $4,900 of profit each month. How many posters must Kay sell each month to reach her target profit?

Why is this important?

"**Companies** want to make a profit. **CVP** analysis helps **managers** determine **how many** units they need to sell to earn a **target** amount of **profit.**"

How Much Must we Sell to Earn a Target Profit?

The only difference from our prior analysis is that instead of determining the sales level needed for *zero profit* (breakeven), Kay now wants to know how many posters she must sell to earn a $4,900 profit. We can use the income statement approach or the shortcut approach to find the answer. Because Kay wants to know the number of *units*, we'll use the shortcut formula based on the *unit* contribution margin. This time, instead of an operating income of zero (breakeven), we'll insert Kay's target operating income of $4,900:

$$\text{Sales in } units = \frac{\text{Fixed expenses} + \text{Operating income}}{\text{Contribution margin } per\ unit}$$

$$= \frac{\$7{,}000 + \$4{,}900}{\$14}$$

$$= \frac{\$11{,}900}{\$14}$$

$$= 850 \text{ posters}$$

This analysis shows that Kay must sell 850 posters each month to earn profits of $4,900 a month. Notice that this level of sales falls within Kay's current relevant range (0–2,000 posters per month), so the conclusion that she would earn $4,900 of income at this sales volume is valid. If the calculation resulted in a sales volume outside the current relevant range (greater than 2,000 units), we would need to reassess our cost assumptions.

Assume that Kay also wants to know how much sales revenue she needs to earn $4,900 of monthly profit. Because she already knows the number of units needed (850), she can easily translate this volume into sales revenue:

850 posters × $35 sales price/poster = $29,750 sales revenue

If Kay only wanted to know the sales revenue needed to achieve her target profit rather than the number of units needed, she could have found the answer directly by using the shortcut formula based on the contribution margin *ratio*:

$$\text{Sales in } \textit{dollars} = \frac{\text{Fixed expenses} + \text{Operating income}}{\text{Contribution margin } \textit{ratio}}$$

$$= \frac{\$7{,}000 + \$4{,}900}{0.40}$$

$$= \frac{\$11{,}900}{0.40}$$

$$= \$29{,}750$$

Finally, Kay could have used the income statement approach to find the same answers:

SALES REVENUE	−	VARIABLE EXPENSES	−	FIXED EXPENSES	=	OPERATING INCOME
($35 Units sold)	−	($21 Units sold)	−	$7,000	=	$ 4,900
($35	−	$21) Units sold	−	$7,000	=	$ 4,900
		$14 Units sold			=	$11,900
				Units sold	=	$11,900/$14
				Units sold	=	850 posters

We can prove that our answers (from any of the three approaches) are correct by preparing Kay's income statement for a sales volume of 850 units:

Sales revenue (850 posters × $35)	$ 29,750
Less: Variable expenses (850 posters × $21)	(17,850)
Contribution margin	$ 11,900
Less: Fixed expenses	(7,000)
Operating income	$ 4,900

Graphing CVP Relationships

By graphing the CVP relationships for her business, Kay can see at a glance how changes in the levels of sales will affect profits. As in the last chapter, the volume of units (posters) is placed on the horizontal x-axis, while dollars is placed on the vertical y-axis. Then, she follows five steps to graph the CVP relations for her business, as illustrated in Exhibit 7-4. This graph also shows the linear nature of Kay's costs and revenues. Recall that CVP analysis assumes costs and revenues will be linear throughout the relevant range.

EXHIBIT 7-4 Cost-Volume-Profit Graph

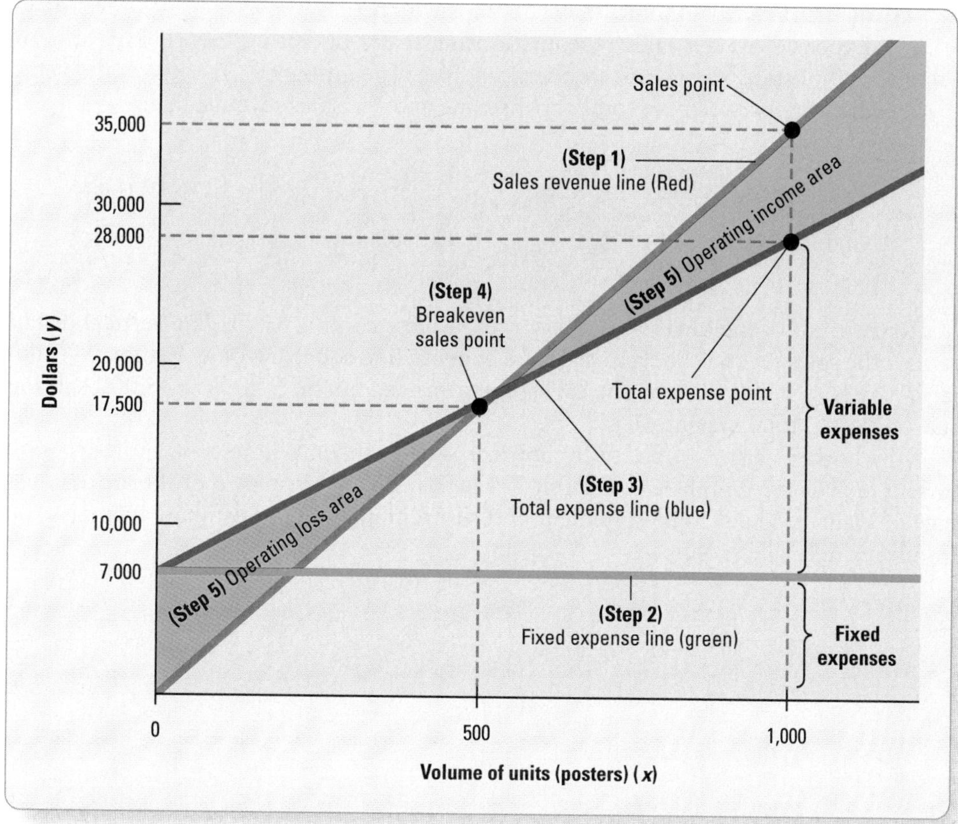

STEP 1: Choose a sales volume, such as 1,000 posters. Plot the point for total sales revenue at that volume: 1,000 posters × $35 per poster = sales of $35,000. Draw the *sales revenue line* from the origin (0) through the $35,000 point. Why does the sales revenue line start at the origin? If Kay does not sell any posters, there is no sales revenue.

STEP 2: Draw the *fixed expense line*, a horizontal line that intersects the y-axis at $7,000. Recall that the fixed expense line is flat because fixed expenses are the same ($7,000) no matter how many posters Kay sells within her relevant range (up to 2,000 posters per month).

STEP 3: Draw the *total expense line*. Total expense is the sum of variable expense plus fixed expense. Thus, total expense is a *mixed* cost. So, the total expense line follows the form of the mixed cost line. Begin by computing variable expense at the chosen sales volume: 1,000 posters × $21 per poster = variable expense of $21,000. Add variable expense to fixed expense: $21,000 + $7,000 = $28,000. Plot the total expense point ($28,000) for 1,000 units. Then, draw a line through this point from the $7,000 fixed expense intercept on the dollars axis. This is the *total expense line*. Why does the total expense line start at the fixed expense line? If Kay sells no posters, she still incurs the $7,000 fixed cost for the server leasing, software, and office rental, but she incurs no variable costs.

STEP 4: Identify the *breakeven point*. The breakeven point is the point where the sales revenue line intersects the total expense line. This is the point where sales revenue equals total expenses. Our previous analyses told us that Kay's breakeven point is 500 posters, or $17,500 in sales. The graph shows this information visually.

STEP 5: Mark the *operating income* and the *operating loss* areas on the graph. To the left of the breakeven point, the total expense line lies above the sales revenue line. Expenses exceed sales revenue, leading to an operating loss. If Kay sells only 300 posters, she incurs an operating loss. The amount of the loss is the vertical distance between the total expense line and the sales revenue line:

Sales revenue	−	Variable expenses	−	Fixed expenses	=	Operating income (Loss)
(300 × $35)	−	(300 × $21)	−	$7,000	=	$(2,800)

To the right of the breakeven point, the business earns a profit. The vertical distance between the sales revenue line and the total expense line equals income. Exhibit 7-4 shows that if Kay sells 1,000 posters, she earns operating income of $7,000 ($35,000 sales revenue – $28,000 total expenses).

Why bother with a graph? Why not just use the income statement approach or the shortcut approach? Graphs like Exhibit 7-4 help managers visualize profit or loss over a range of volume. The income statement and shortcut approaches estimate income or loss for only a single sales volume.

Decision Guidelines

CVP Analysis

Your friend wants to open her own ice cream parlor after college. She needs help making the following decisions:

Decision	Guidelines
How much will I earn on every ice cream cone I sell?	The unit contribution margin shows managers how much they earn on each unit sold after paying for variable *costs but before considering fixed expenses.* The unit contribution margin is the amount each unit earns that contributes toward covering fixed expenses and generating a profit. It is computed as follows: **Sales price per unit** **Less: Variable cost per unit** **Contribution margin per unit** The contribution margin ratio shows managers how much contribution margin is earned on every \$1 of sales. It is computed as follows: $\text{Contribution margin ratio} = \dfrac{\text{Contribution margin}}{\text{Sales revenue}}$
Can I quickly forecast my income without creating a full income statement?	The contribution margin concept allows managers to forecast income quickly at different sales volumes. First, find the total contribution margin (by multiplying the forecasted number of units by the unit contribution margin *or* by multiplying the forecasted sales revenue by the contribution margin ratio) and then subtract all fixed expenses.
How can I compute the *number of ice cream cones* I'll have to sell to break even or earn a target profit?	***Income Statement Approach:*** $\text{SALES REVENUE} - \text{VARIABLE EXPENSES} - \text{FIXED EXPENSE} = \text{OPERATING INCOME}$ $\left(\text{Sales price per unit} \times \text{Units sold}\right) - \left(\text{Variable cost per unit} \times \text{Units sold}\right) - \text{Fixed expenses} = \text{Operating income}$ ***Shortcut Unit Contribution Margin Approach:*** $\text{Sales in } \textit{units} = \dfrac{\text{Fixed expenses} + \text{Operating income}}{\text{Contribution margin } \textit{per unit}}$
How can I compute the *amount of sales revenue* (in dollars) I'll have to generate to break even or earn a target profit?	***Shortcut Contribution Margin Ratio Approach:*** $\text{Sales in } \textit{dollars} = \dfrac{\text{Fixed expenses} + \text{Operating income}}{\text{Contribution margin } \textit{ratio}}$
What will my profits look like over a range of volumes?	CVP graphs show managers, at a glance, how different sales volumes will affect profits.

SUMMARY PROBLEM 1

Fleet Foot buys hiking socks for \$6 a pair and sells them for \$10. Management budgets monthly fixed expenses of \$10,000 for sales volumes between 0 and 12,000 pairs.

Requirements

1. Use the income statement approach and the shortcut unit contribution margin approach to compute monthly breakeven sales in units.
2. Use the shortcut contribution margin ratio approach to compute the breakeven point in sales revenue (sales dollars).
3. Compute the monthly sales level (in units) required to earn a target operating income of \$14,000. Use either the income statement approach or the shortcut contribution margin approach.
4. Prepare a graph of Fleet Foot's CVP relationships, similar to Exhibit 7-4. Draw the sales revenue line, the fixed expense line, and the total expense line. Label the axes, the breakeven point, the operating income area, and the operating loss area.

SOLUTIONS

Requirement 1

Income Statement Approach:

SALES REVENUE		– VARIABLE EXPENSES		– FIXED EXPENSES	= OPERATING INCOME
(Sales price per unit	× Units sold) –	(Variable cost per unit	× Units sold) –	Fixed expenses	= Operating income
(\$10	× Units sold) –	(\$6	× Units sold) –	\$10,000	= \$ 0
(\$10	–	\$6)	× Units sold		= \$10,000
		\$4	× Units sold		= \$10,000
			Units sold		= \$10,000 ÷ \$4
			Breakeven sales in units		= 2,500 units

Shortcut Unit Contribution Margin Approach:

$$\text{Sales in units} = \frac{\text{Fixed expenses} + \text{Operating income}}{\text{Contribution margin per unit}}$$

$$= \frac{\$10{,}000 + \$0}{(\$10 - \$6)}$$

$$= \frac{\$10{,}000}{\$4}$$

$$= 2{,}500 \text{ units}$$

Requirement 2

$$\text{Sales in dollars} = \frac{\text{Fixed expenses} + \text{Operating income}}{\text{Contribution margin ratio}}$$
$$= \frac{\$10{,}000 + \$0}{0.40^*}$$
$$= \$25{,}000$$

$$^*\text{Contribution margin ratio} = \frac{\text{Contribution margin per unit}}{\text{Sales price per unit}} = \frac{\$4}{\$10} = 0.40$$

Requirement 3

Income Statement Equation Approach:

$$\text{SALES REVENUE} - \text{VARIABLE EXPENSES} - \text{FIXED EXPENSES} = \text{OPERATING INCOME}$$
$$\left(\text{Sales price per unit} \times \text{Units sold}\right) - \left(\text{Variable cost per unit} \times \text{Units sold}\right) - \text{Fixed expenses} = \text{Operating income}$$
$$(\$10 \times \text{Units sold}) - (\$6 \times \text{Units sold}) - \$10{,}000 = \$14{,}000$$
$$(\$10 - \$6) \times \text{Units sold} = \$10{,}000 + \$14{,}000$$
$$\$4 \times \text{Units sold} = \$24{,}000$$
$$\text{Units sold} = \$24{,}000 \div \$4$$
$$\text{Units sold} = 6{,}000 \text{ units}$$

Shortcut Unit Contribution Margin Approach:

$$\text{Sales in units} = \frac{\text{Fixed expenses} + \text{Operating income}}{\text{Contribution margin per unit}}$$
$$= \frac{\$10{,}000 + \$14{,}000}{(\$10 - \$6)}$$
$$= \frac{\$24{,}000}{\$4}$$
$$= 6{,}000 \text{ units}$$

Requirement 4

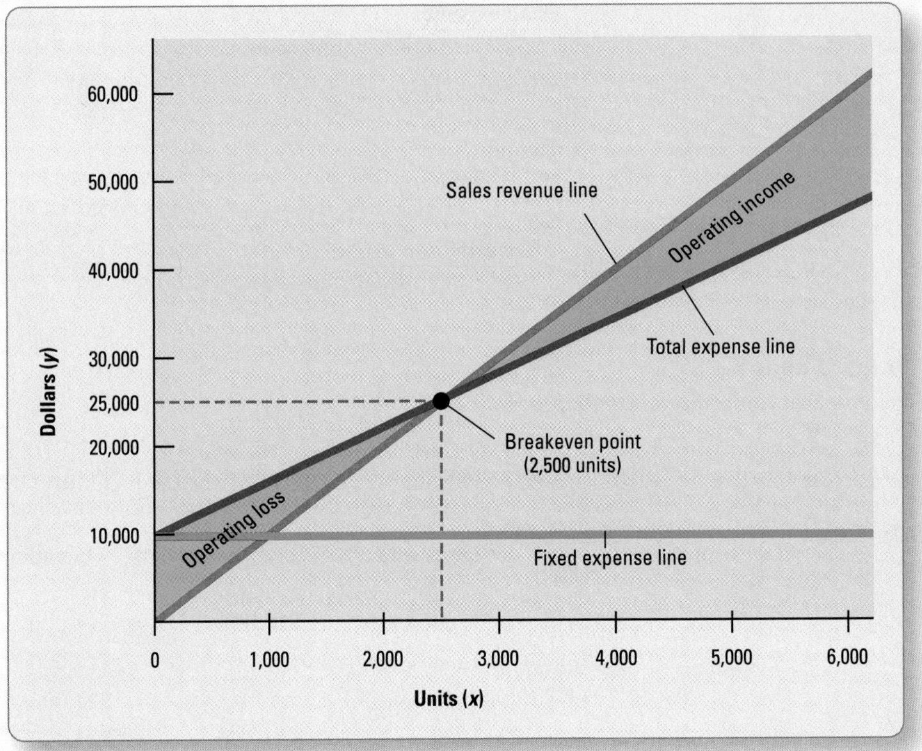

How do Managers Use CVP to Plan for Changing Business Conditions?

3 Perform sensitivity analysis in response to changing business conditions

In today's fast-changing business world, managers need to be prepared for increasing costs, pricing pressure from competitors, and other changing business conditions.

Managers use CVP analysis to conduct **sensitivity analysis**. Sensitivity analysis is a "what-if" technique that asks what results will be if actual prices or costs change or if an underlying assumption such as sales mix changes. For example, increased competition may force Kay to lower her sales price, while at the same time her suppliers increase poster costs. How will these changes affect Kay's breakeven and target profit volumes? What will happen if Kay changes her sales mix by offering posters in two different sizes? We'll tackle these issues next.

Changing the Sales Price

Let's assume that Kay has now been in business for several months. Because of competition, Kay is considering cutting her sales price to \$31 per poster. If her variable expenses remain \$21 per poster and her fixed expenses stay at \$7,000, how many posters will she need to sell to break even? To answer this question, Kay calculates a new unit contribution margin using the new sales price:

New sales price per poster	\$ 31
Less: Variable cost per poster	(21)
New contribution margin per poster	\$ 10

She then uses the new unit contribution margin to compute breakeven sales in units:

$$\text{Sales in units} = \frac{\text{Fixed expenses} + \text{Operating income}}{\text{Contribution margin per unit}}$$
$$= \frac{\$7{,}000 + \$0}{\$10}$$
$$= 700 \text{ posters}$$

With the original \$35 sale price, Kay's breakeven point was 500 posters. If Kay lowers the sales price to \$31 per poster, her breakeven point increases to 700 posters. The lower sales price means that each poster contributes *less* toward fixed expenses (\$10 versus \$14 before the price change), so Kay must sell 200 *more* posters to break even. Each dollar of sales revenue would contribute \$0.32 (\$10/\$31) rather than \$0.40 toward covering fixed expenses and generating a profit.

If Kay reduces her sales price to \$31, how many posters must she sell to achieve her \$4,900 monthly target profit? Kay again uses the new unit contribution margin to determine how many posters she will need to sell to reach her profit goals:

$$\text{Sales in units} = \frac{\$7{,}000 + \$4{,}900}{\$10}$$
$$= 1{,}190 \text{ posters}$$

Why is this important?

"**CVP analysis** helps managers prepare for and respond to **economic** changes, such as increasing costs and **pressure** to drop sales prices, so companies can remain **competitive** and **profitable**."

With the original sales price, Kay needed to sell only 850 posters per month to achieve her target profit level. If Kay cuts her sales price (and, therefore, her contribution margin), she must sell more posters to achieve her financial goals. Kay could have found the same results using the income statement approach. Exhibit 7-5 shows the effect of changes in sales price on breakeven and target profit volumes.

EXHIBIT 7-5 The Effect of Changes in Sales Price on Breakeven and Target Profit Volumes

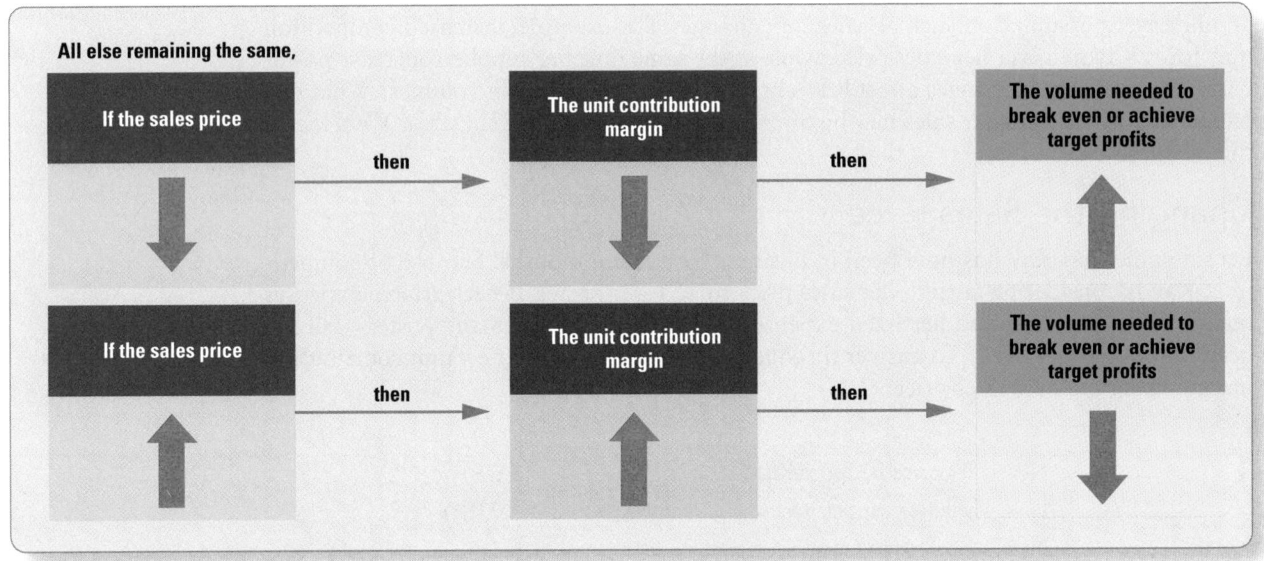

STOP & THINK

Kay believes she could dominate the e-commerce art poster business if she cut the sales price to $20. Is this a good idea?

Answer: No. The variable cost per poster is $21. If Kay sells posters for $20 each, she loses $1 on each poster. Kay will incur a loss if the sales price is less than the variable cost.

Changing Variable Costs

Let's assume that Kay does *not* lower her sales price. However, Kay's supplier raises the price for each poster to $23.80 (instead of the original $21). Kay does not want to pass this increase on to her customers, so she holds her sales price at the original $35 per poster. Her fixed costs remain $7,000. How many posters must she sell to break even after her supplier raises the prices? Kay's new contribution margin per unit drops to $11.20 ($35 sales price per poster – $23.80 variable cost per poster). So, her new breakeven point is as follows:

$$\text{Sales in units} = \frac{\text{Fixed expenses} + \text{Operating income}}{\text{Contribution margin per unit}}$$

$$= \frac{\$7{,}000 + \$0}{\$11.20}$$

$$= 625 \text{ posters}$$

Higher variable costs per unit have the same effect as lower selling prices per unit—they both reduce the product's unit contribution margin. As a result, Kay will have to sell *more* units to break even and achieve target profits. As shown in Exhibit 7-6, a *decrease* in variable costs would have just the opposite effect. Lower variable costs increase the contribution margin each poster provides and, therefore, lowers the breakeven point.

EXHIBIT 7-6 The Effect of Changes in Variable Costs on Breakeven and Target Profit Volumes

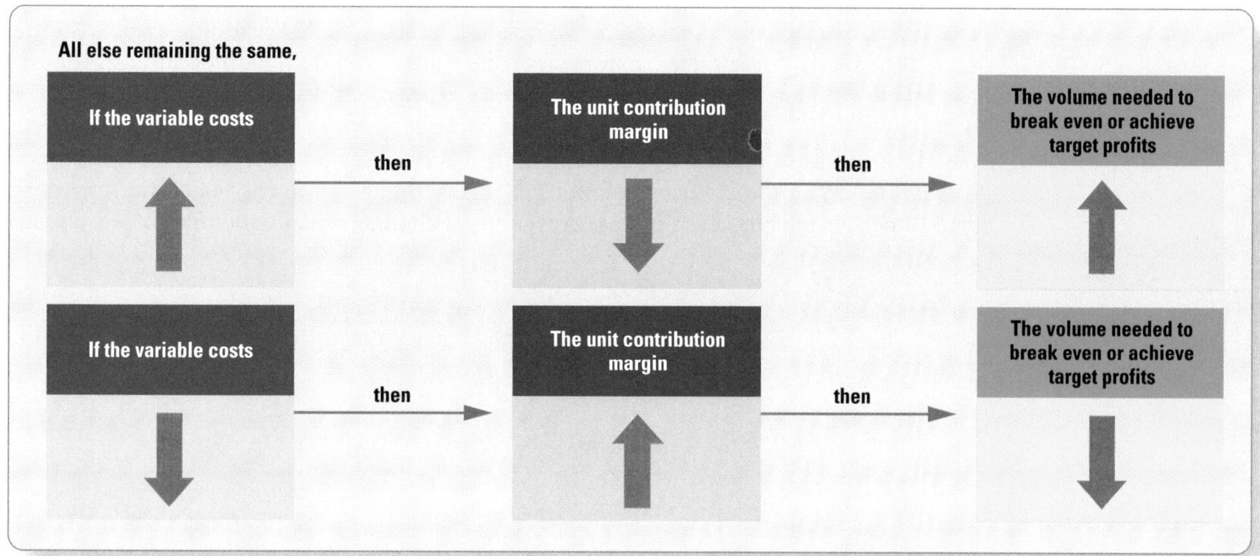

STOP & THINK

Suppose Kay is squeezed from both sides: Her supply costs have increased to $23.80 per poster, yet she must lower her price to $31 in order to compete. Under these conditions, how many posters will Kay need to sell to achieve her monthly target profit of $4,900? If Kay doesn't think she can sell that many posters, how else might she attempt to achieve her profit goals?

Answer: Kay is now in a position faced by many companies—her unit contribution margin is squeezed by both higher supply costs and lower sales prices:

New sales price per poster..................................	$ 31.00
Less: New variable cost per poster......................	(23.80)
New contribution margin per poster..................	$ 7.20

Kay's new contribution margin is about half of what it was when she started her business ($14). To achieve her target profit, her volume will have to increase dramatically (yet, it would still fall within her current relevant range for fixed costs—which extends to 2,000 posters per month):

$$\text{Sales in units} = \frac{\text{Fixed expenses} + \text{Operating income}}{\text{Contribution margin per unit}}$$

$$= \frac{\$7{,}000 + \$4{,}900}{\$7.20}$$

$$= 1{,}653 \text{ posters (rounded)}$$

Based on her current volume, Kay may not believe she can sell so many posters. To maintain a reasonable profit level, Kay may need to take other measures. For example, she may try to find a different supplier with lower poster costs. She may also attempt to lower her fixed costs. For example, perhaps she could negotiate a cheaper lease on her office space or move her business to a less expensive location. She could also try to increase her volume by spending *more* on fixed costs, such as advertising. Kay could also investigate selling other products, in addition to her regular-size posters, that would have higher unit contribution margins. We'll discuss these measures next.

Changing Fixed Costs

Let's return to Kay's original data ($35 selling price and $21 variable cost). Kay has decided she really doesn't need a storefront office at a retail strip mall because she doesn't have many walk-in customers. She could decrease her monthly fixed costs from $7,000 to $4,200 by moving her office to an industrial park.

How will this decrease in fixed costs affect Kay's breakeven point? *Changes in fixed costs do not affect the contribution margin.* Therefore, Kay's unit contribution margin is still $14 per poster. However, her breakeven point changes because her fixed costs change:

$$\text{Sales in units} = \frac{\text{Fixed expenses} + \text{Operating income}}{\text{Contribution margin per unit}}$$

$$= \frac{\$4{,}200 + \$0}{\$14.00}$$

$$= 300 \text{ posters}$$

Because of the decrease in fixed costs, Kay will need to sell only 300 posters, rather than 500 posters, to break even. The volume needed to achieve her monthly $4,900 target profit will also decline. However, if Kay's fixed costs *increase*, she will have to sell *more* units to break even. Exhibit 7-7 shows the effect of changes in fixed costs on breakeven and target profit volumes.

EXHIBIT 7-7 The Effect of Changes in Fixed Costs on Breakeven and Target Profit Volumes

All else remaining the same,

If the fixed costs ↑ **then** **The volume needed to break even or achieve target profits** ↑

If the fixed costs ↓ **then** **The volume needed to break even or achieve target profits** ↓

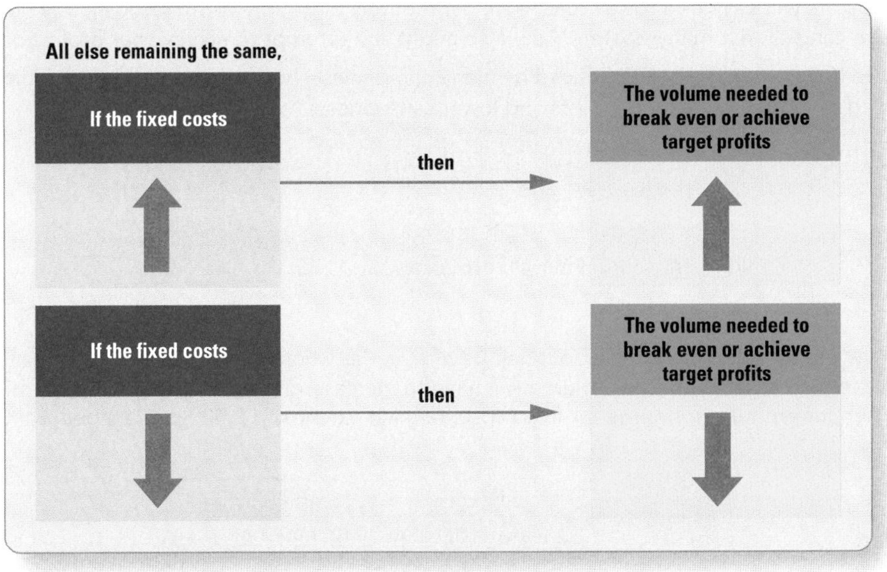

We have seen that changes in sales prices, variable costs, and fixed costs can have dramatic effects on the volume of product that companies must sell to achieve breakeven and target profits. Companies often turn to automation to decrease variable costs (direct labor); but this, in turn, increases their fixed costs (equipment depreciation). Companies often move production overseas to decrease variable and fixed production costs, feeling forced to take these measures to keep their prices as low as their competitors. For example, Charbroil, the maker of gas grills, said that if it didn't move production overseas, profits would decline, or worse yet, the company would go out of business.

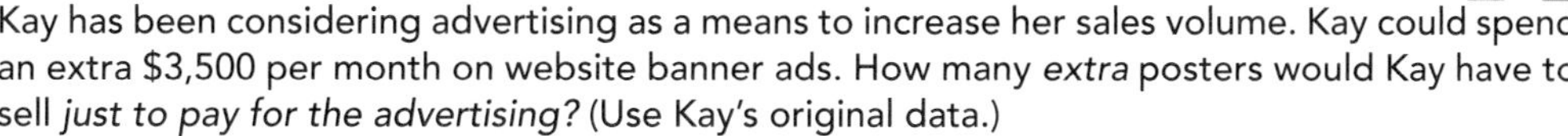

STOP & THINK

Kay has been considering advertising as a means to increase her sales volume. Kay could spend an extra $3,500 per month on website banner ads. How many *extra* posters would Kay have to sell *just to pay for the advertising?* (Use Kay's original data.)

Answer: Instead of using *all* of Kay's fixed costs, we can isolate *just* the fixed costs relating to advertising. This will allow us to figure out how many *extra* posters Kay would have to sell each month to break even on (or pay for) the advertising cost. Advertising is a fixed cost, so Kay's contribution margin remains $14 per unit.

$$\text{Sales in units} = \frac{\text{Fixed expenses} + \text{Operating income}}{\text{Contribution margin per unit}}$$

$$= \frac{\$3{,}500 + \$0}{\$14.00}$$

$$= 250 \text{ posters}$$

Kay must sell 250 *extra* posters each month just to pay for the cost of advertising. If she sells fewer than 250 extra posters, she'll increase her volume but lose money on the advertising. If she sells more than 250 extra posters, her plan will have worked—she'll increase her volume *and* her profit.

Sustainability and CVP

Sustainability initiatives can have a significant bearing on the cost information used in CVP analysis. For example, Coca-Cola[1], a recognized leader in corporate sustainability, has been able to reduce the size of the cap on its PET plastic bottles by 38%, saving 40 million pounds of plastic annually in the U.S. alone. The company has also reduced the PET in its Coke and Dasani bottles by 23% and 35%, respectively. In addition to *reducing* the PET content, the company has *increased* the percentage of recycled plastic used in these containers. The company is also working to reduce the amount of water needed for each unit of its product. As a result of these initiatives, the variable cost of packaging each unit of product has decreased. For example, the company reports that its new ultra glass contour bottle is not only 40% stronger and 20% lighter, but also 10% cheaper to produce than its traditional contour bottle.

Coca-Cola's redesign of product packaging has had favorable environmental and financial ramifications. For example, the new ultra glass contour bottle has reduced annual CO_2 emissions by an amount equivalent to planting 8,000 acres of trees. From a financial standpoint, the 10% variable cost savings on the ultra glass contour design results in a 10% increase in each bottle's contribution margin. As a result, one might assume that Coca-Cola needs to sell fewer units of product to achieve its target profit. However, keep in mind that the company had to incur many fixed costs to research, develop and design these new bottles. In addition, they probably had to invest in new production equipment to handle the new packaging design.

As the Coca-Cola example shows, sustainability initiatives often result in both cost savings *and* additional costs. These costs and cost savings may be fixed or variable in nature. Managers use CVP analysis to determine how these initiatives will impact the volume needed to achieve the company's operating income goals.

See Exercises E7-25A and E7-49B

[1]The Coca-Cola Company website. www.thecoca-colacompany.com/citizenship/package_design.html Section on Sustainable Packaging. Subsection: Reduce

Changing the Mix of Products Offered for Sale

4 Find breakeven and target profit volumes for multiproduct companies

So far, we have assumed that Kay sold only one size poster. What would happen if she offered different types of products? Companies that sell more than one product must consider their *sales mix* when performing CVP analysis. All else being equal, a company earns more income by selling high-contribution margin products than by selling an equal number of low-contribution margin products.

The same CVP formulas that are used to perform CVP analysis for a company with a single product can be used for any company that sells more than one product. However, the formulas use the *weighted-average contribution margin* of all products, rather than the contribution margin of a sole product. Each unit's contribution margin is *weighted* by the relative number of units sold. As before, the company can find the breakeven or the target profit volume in terms of units, or in terms of sales revenue. We'll consider each in turn.

Multiproduct Company: Finding Breakeven in Terms of Sales Units

Suppose Kay plans to sell two types of posters. In addition to her regular-size posters, Kay plans to sell large posters. Let's assume that none of Kay's original costs have changed. Exhibit 7-8 shows that each regular poster will continue to generate \$14 of contribution margin, while each large poster will generate \$30 of contribution margin. Kay is adding the large-poster line because it carries a higher unit contribution margin.

EXHIBIT 7-8 Calculating the Weighted-Average Contribution Margin per Unit

	Regular Posters	Large Posters	Total
Sales price per unit	\$ 35	\$ 70	
Less: Variable cost per unit	(21)	(40)	
Contribution margin per unit	\$ 14	\$ 30	
Sales mix	× 5	× 3	8
Contribution margin	\$ 70	\$ 90	\$160
Weighted-average contribution margin per unit (\$160/8)			\$ 20

For every five regular posters sold, Kay expects to sell three large posters. In other words, she expects 5/8 of the sales to be regular posters and 3/8 to be large posters. This is a 5:3 sales mix. Exhibit 7-8 shows how Kay uses this expected sales mix to find the weighted-average contribution margin per unit.

Notice that none of Kay's products actually generates \$20 of contribution margin. However, if the sales mix is 5:3, as expected, it is *as if* the contribution margin is \$20 per unit. Once Kay has computed the weighted-average contribution margin per unit, she uses it in the shortcut formula to determine the total number of posters that would need to be sold to break even:

$$\begin{aligned}\text{Sales in total units} &= \frac{\text{Fixed expenses} + \text{Operating income}}{\text{Weighted-average contribution margin per unit}}\\ &= \frac{\$7{,}000 + \$0}{\$20}\\ &= 350 \text{ posters}\end{aligned}$$

In total, Kay must sell 350 posters to breakeven. However, this is only the case if 5/8 of those sold are regular posters and 3/8 are large posters. Therefore, we must take still figure out how many of *each type* of poster must be sold to breakeven.

As a final step, Kay splits the total number of posters into the regular and large sizes using the same sales mix ratios she assumed previously:

Breakeven sales of regular posters (350 × 5/8)	218.75 regular posters
Breakeven sales of large posters (350 × 3/8)	131.25 large posters

As is often the case in real situations, these computations don't yield round numbers. Because Kay cannot sell partial posters, she must sell 219 regular posters and 132 large posters to avoid a loss. Using these rounded numbers would lead to a small rounding error in our check figures, however, so the rest of our computations will use the exact results: 218.75 regular posters and 131.25 large posters.

If Kay wants, she can now use the number of units to find her breakeven point in terms of sales revenue (amounts rounded to the nearest dollar):

218.75 regular posters at $35 each	$ 7,656
131.25 large posters at $70 each	9,188
Total revenues	$16,844

We can prove this breakeven point as follows:

	Total
Contribution margin:	
Regular posters (218.75 × $14)	$ 3,063
Large posters (131.25 × $30)	3,937
Contribution margin	$ 7,000
Less: Fixed expenses	(7,000)
Operating income	$ 0

We just found Kay's *breakeven* point, but Kay can also use the same steps to calculate the number of units she must sell to achieve a target profit. The only difference, as before, is that she would use *target profit*, rather than *zero*, as the operating income in the shortcut formula.

STOP & THINK

Suppose Kay would still like to earn a monthly profit of $4,900. Recall that she needed to sell 850 posters to achieve this profit level when she was selling only regular posters. If her sales mix is 5:3, as planned, will she need to sell *more than* or *fewer than* 850 posters to achieve her target profit? Why?

Answer: Kay will need to sell *fewer* than 850 posters because she is now selling some large posters that have a higher unit contribution margin. We can verify this as follows:

$$\text{Sales in total units} = \frac{\text{Fixed expenses} + \text{Operating income}}{\text{Weighted-average contribution margin per unit}}$$

$$= \frac{\$7{,}000 + \$0}{\$20}$$

$$= 350 \text{ posters}$$

Kay would have to sell a *total* of 595 posters—372 regular posters (595 × 5/8) and 223 large posters (595 × 3/8)—to achieve her target profit.

Multiproduct Company: Finding Breakeven in Terms of Sales Revenue

Companies that offer hundreds or thousands of products (such as WalMart and Amazon.com) will not want to find the breakeven point in terms of units. Rather, they'll want to know breakeven (or target profit volumes) in terms of sales revenue. To find this sales volume, the company needs to know, or estimate, its weighted-average contribution margin ratio. If a company prepares contribution margin income statements, it easily calculates the contribution margin ratio by dividing the total contribution margin by total sales. The contribution margin ratio is *already* weighted by the company's *actual* sales mix! The following "Stop and Think" illustrates how Amazon.com would use this approach to calculating breakeven.

STOP & THINK

Suppose Amazon.com's total sales revenue is $4.50 billion, its variable expenses total $3.15 billion, and its fixed expenses total $1.1 billion. What is the breakeven point in sales revenue?

Answer: First, Amazon computes its total contribution margin:

Sales revenue	$4.50 billion
Less: Variable expenses	3.15 billion
Contribution margin	$1.35 billion

Now Amazon is able to compute its overall contribution margin ratio, which is already weighted by the company's actual sales mix: $1.35 billion ÷ 4.50 billion = 30%.

Finally, Amazon uses the contribution margin ratio in the shortcut formula to predict the breakeven point:

$$\text{Sales in dollars} = \frac{\text{Fixed expenses} + \text{Operating income}}{\text{Contribution margin ratio}}$$

$$= \frac{\$1.1 \text{ billion} + \$0}{0.30}$$

$$= \$3.667 \text{ billion (rounded)}$$

Amazon.com must achieve sales revenue of $3.667 billion just to break even.

Unlike Amazon, Kay's business to this point has been limited to a sole product (regular posters), which had a 40% contribution margin ratio. Once Kay starts selling large posters in addition to the regular posters, her overall weighted-average contribution margin ratio will change. Recall that Kay expects to sell five regular posters for every three large posters. Exhibit 7-9 shows how Kay weights the individual contribution margins and sales revenue, using the anticipated sales mix, to arrive at her anticipated weighted-average contribution margin ratio for this particular sales mix:

EXHIBIT 7-9 Estimating the Weighted-Average Contribution Margin Ratio

Expected contribution margin:		
Regular posters (5 × $14)	$ 70	
Large posters (3 × $30)	$ 90	
Expected contribution margin		$160
Divided by expected sales revenue:		
Regular posters (5 × $35)	$175	
Large posters (3 × $70)	$210	
Expected sales revenue		÷ 385
Weighted-average contribution margin ratio		= 41.558%

Notice how Kay's weighted-average contribution margin ratio (41.558%) will be higher than it was when she sold only regular posters (40%). That's because she expects to sell some large posters that have a 42.9% contribution margin ratio ($30/$70) in addition to the regular-sized posters. Because her sales mix is changing, she now has a different contribution margin ratio.

Once Kay knows her weighted-average contribution margin ratio, she can use the shortcut formula to estimate breakeven in terms of sales revenue:

$$\text{Sales in dollars} = \frac{\text{Fixed expenses} + \text{Operating income}}{\text{Contribution margin ratio}}$$
$$= \frac{\$7{,}000 + \$0}{0.41558}$$
$$= \$16{,}844 \text{ (rounded)}$$

Notice that this is the same breakeven point in sales revenue we found earlier by first finding breakeven in *units*. Kay could also use the formula to find the total sales revenue she would need to meet her target monthly operating income of $4,900.

If Kay's actual sales mix is not five regular posters to three large posters, her actual operating income will differ from the projected amount. The sales mix greatly influences the breakeven point. When companies offer more than one product, they do not have a unique breakeven point. Every sales mix assumption leads to a different breakeven point.

STOP & THINK

Suppose Kay plans to sell 800 total posters in the 5:3 sales mix (500 regular posters and 300 large posters). She actually does sell 800 posters—375 regular and 425 large. The sale prices per poster, variable costs per poster, and fixed expenses are exactly as predicted. Without doing any computations, is Kay's actual operating income greater than, less than, or equal to her expected income?

Answer: Kay's actual sales mix did not turn out to be the 5:3 mix she expected. She actually sold more of the higher-margin large posters than the lower-margin regular posters. This favorable change in the sales mix causes her to earn a higher operating income than she expected.

Information Technology and Sensitivity Analysis

We have just seen that Kay's breakeven point and target profit volumes are very sensitive to changes in her business environment, including changes in sales prices, variable costs, fixed costs, and sales mix assumptions. Information technology allows managers to perform a wide array of sensitivity analyses before committing to decisions. Managers of small- to medium-sized companies use Excel spreadsheets to perform sensitivity analyses like those we just did for Kay. Spreadsheets allow managers to estimate how one change (or several simultaneous changes) affects business operations. Managers also use spreadsheet software to create CVP graphs like the one in Exhibit 7-4.

Many large companies use sophisticated enterprise resource planning (ERP) software such as SAP and Oracle to provide detailed data for CVP analysis. For example, after Sears stores lock their doors at 9 P.M., records for each individual transaction flow into a massive database. From a DieHard battery sold in Texas to a Trader Bay polo shirt sold in New Hampshire, the system compiles an average of 1.5 million transactions a day. With the click of a mouse, managers access sales price, variable cost, and sales volume for individual products to conduct breakeven or profit planning analyses.

What are Some Common Indicators of Risk?

A company's level of risk depends on many factors, including the general health of the economy and the specific industry in which the company operates. In addition, a firm's risk depends on its current volume of sales and the relative amount of fixed and variable costs that make up its total costs. Next, we discuss how a firm can gauge its level of risk, to some extent, by its margin of safety and its operating leverage.

Margin of Safety

5 Determine a firm's margin of safety, operating leverage, and most profitable cost structure

The **margin of safety** is the excess of actual or expected sales over breakeven sales. This is the "cushion," or drop in sales, the company can absorb without incurring a loss. The higher the margin of safety, the greater the cushion against loss and the less risky the business plan. Managers use the margin of safety to evaluate the risk of current operations as well as the risk of new plans.

Let's continue to assume that Kay has been in business for several months and that she generally sells 950 posters a month. Kay's breakeven point in our original data is 500 posters. Kay can express her margin of safety in units, as follows:

If your instructor is using MyAccountingLab, go to the Multimedia Library for a quick video on this topic.

Margin of safety in units	=	**Expected sales in units**	−	**Breakeven sales in units**
	=	950 posters	−	500 posters
	=	450 posters		

Kay can also express her margin of safety in sales revenue (sales dollars):

Margin of safety in dollars	=	**Expected sales in dollars**	−	**Breakeven sales in dollars**
	=	(950 posters × \$35)	−	(500 posters × \$35)
	=	\$33,250	−	\$17,500
	=	\$15,750		

Sales would have to drop by more than 450 posters, or \$15,750 a month, before Kay incurs a loss. This is a fairly comfortable margin.

Managers can also compute the margin of safety as a percentage of sales. Simply divide the margin of safety by sales. We obtain the same percentage whether we use units or dollars.

In units:

$$\text{Margin of safety as a percentage} = \frac{\text{Margin of safety in units}}{\text{Expected sales in units}} = \frac{450 \text{ posters}}{950 \text{ posters}} = 47.4\% \text{ (rounded)}$$

In dollars:

$$\text{Margin of safety as a percentage} = \frac{\text{Margin of safety in dollars}}{\text{Expected sales in dollars}} = \frac{\$15,750}{\$33,250} = 47.4\% \text{ (rounded)}$$

The margin of safety percentage tells Kay that sales would have to drop by more than 47.4% before she would incur a loss. If sales fall by less than 47.4%, she would still earn a profit. If sales fall exactly 47.4%, she would break even. This ratio tells Kay that her business plan is not unduly risky.

Operating Leverage

A company's operating leverage refers to the relative amount of fixed and variable costs that make up its total costs. Most companies have both fixed and variable costs. However, companies with *high* operating leverage have *relatively more fixed costs* and relatively fewer variable costs. Companies with high operating leverage include golf courses, airlines, and hotels. Because they have fewer variable costs, their contribution margin ratio is relatively high. Recall from the last chapter that Embassy Suites' variable cost of servicing each guest is low, which means that the hotel has a high contribution margin ratio and high operating leverage.

"The margin of safety and **operating leverage** help managers understand their **risk** if **volume** decreases due to a recession, **competition,** or other **changes** in the **marketplace**."

What does high operating leverage have to do with risk? If sales volume decreases, the total contribution margin will drop significantly because each sales dollar contains a high percentage of contribution margin. Yet, the high fixed costs of running the company remain. Therefore, the operating income of these companies can easily turn from profit to loss if sales volume declines. For example, airlines were financially devastated after September 11, 2001, because the number of people flying suddenly dropped, creating large reductions in contribution margin. Yet, the airlines had to continue paying their high fixed costs. High operating leverage companies are at *more* risk because their income declines drastically when sales volume declines.

What if the economy is growing and sales volume *increases*? High operating leverage companies will reap high rewards. Remember that after breakeven, each unit sold contributes its unit contribution margin directly to profit. Because high operating leverage companies have high contribution margin ratios, each additional dollar of sales will contribute more to the firm's operating income. Exhibit 7-10 summarizes these characteristics.

EXHIBIT 7-10 Characteristics of High Operating Leverage Firms

- High operating leverage companies have the following:
  - —*Higher* levels of fixed costs and *lower* levels of variable costs
  - —*Higher* contribution margin ratios
- For high operating leverage companies, changes in volume significantly affect operating income, so they face the following:
  - —*Higher* risk
  - —*Higher* potential for reward

Examples include golf courses, hotels, rental car agencies, theme parks, airlines, cruise lines, etc.

However, companies with low operating leverage have relatively *fewer* fixed costs and relatively *more* variable costs. As a result, they have much lower contribution margin ratios. For example, retailers incur significant levels of fixed costs, but more of every sales dollar is used to pay for the merchandise (a variable cost), so less ends up as contribution margin. If sales volume declines, these companies have relatively fewer fixed costs to cover, so they are at *less* risk of incurring a loss. If sales volume increases, their relatively small contribution margins ratios add to the bottom line, but in smaller increments. Therefore, they reap less reward than high operating leverage companies experiencing the same volume increases. *In other words, at low operating leverage companies, changes in sales volume do not have as much impact on operating income as they do at high operating leverage companies.* Exhibit 7-11 summarizes these characteristics.

EXHIBIT 7-11 Characteristics of Low Operating Leverage Firms

- Low operating leverage companies have the following:
  - —*Higher* levels of variable costs and *lower* levels of fixed costs
  - —*Lower* contribution margin ratios
- For low operating leverage companies, changes in volume do NOT have as significant an effect on operating income, so they face the following:
  - —*Lower* risk
  - —*Lower* potential for reward

Examples include merchandising companies and fast-food restaurants.

A company's **operating leverage factor** tells us how responsive a company's operating income is to changes in volume. The greater the operating leverage factor, the greater the impact a change in sales volume has on operating income.

The operating leverage factor, *at a given level of sales*, is calculated as follows:

$$\text{Operating leverage factor} = \frac{\text{Contribution margin}}{\text{Operating income}}$$

Why do we say, "at a given level of sales"? A company's operating leverage factor will depend, to some extent, on the sales level used to calculate the contribution margin and operating income. Most companies compute the operating leverage factor at their current or expected volume of sales, which is what we'll do in our examples.

What does the operating leverage factor tell us?

The operating leverage factor, at a given level of sales, indicates the percentage change in operating income that will occur from a 1% change in volume. In other words, it tells us how responsive a company's operating income is to changes in volume.

The *lowest* possible value for this factor is 1, which occurs only if the company has *no* fixed costs (an *extremely low* operating leverage company). *For a minute, let's assume that Kay has no fixed costs.* Given this scenario, her unit contribution margin ($14 per poster) contributes directly to profit because she has no fixed costs to cover. In addition, she has *no* risk. The worst she can do is break even, and that will occur only if she doesn't sell any posters. Let's continue to assume that she generally sells 950 posters a month, so this will be the level of sales at which we calculate the operating leverage factor:

Sales revenue (950 posters × $35/poster)	$ 33,250
Less: Variable expenses (950 posters × $21/poster)	(19,950)
Contribution margin (950 posters × $14/poster)	$ 13,300
Less: Fixed expenses	(0)
Operating income	$ 13,300

Her operating leverage factor is as follows:

$$\text{Operating leverage factor} = \frac{\$13{,}300}{\$13{,}300} = 1$$

What does this tell us?

- If Kay's volume changes by 1%, her operating income will change by 1% (= 1% × a factor of 1).
- If Kay's volume changes by 15%, her operating income will change by 15% (= 15% × a factor of 1).

Let's now see what happens if we assume, as usual, that Kay's fixed expenses are $7,000. We'll once again calculate the operating leverage factor given Kay's current level of sales (950 posters per month):

Contribution margin (950 posters × $14/poster)	$13,300
Less: Fixed expenses	(7,000)
Operating income	$ 6,300

Now that we have once again assumed that Kay's fixed expenses are $7,000, her operating leverage factor is as follows:

$$\text{Operating leverage factor} = \frac{\$13{,}300}{\$6{,}300} = 2.11 \text{ (rounded)}$$

Notice that her operating leverage factor is *higher* (2.11 versus 1) when she has *more* fixed costs ($7,000 versus $0). Kay's operating leverage factor of 2.11 tells us how responsive her income is to changes in volume.

- If Kay's volume changes by 1%, her operating income will change by 2.11% (= 1% × a factor of 2.11).
- If Kay's volume changes by 15%, her operating income will change by 31.65% (= 15% × a factor of 2.11).

Managers use the firm's operating leverage factor to determine how vulnerable their operating income is to changes in sales volume—both positive and negative.

The larger the operating leverage factor is, the greater the impact a change in sales volume has on operating income. This is true for both increases *and* decreases in volume.

Therefore, companies with higher operating leverage factors are particularly vulnerable to changes in volume. In other words, they have *both* higher risk of incurring losses if volume declines *and* higher potential reward if volume increases. Hoping to capitalize on the reward side, many companies have intentionally increased their operating leverage by lowering their variable costs while at the same time increasing their fixed costs. This strategy works well during periods of economic growth but can be detrimental when sales volume declines.

Choosing a Cost Structure

Managers often have some control over how the company's costs are structured—as fixed, variable, or a combination of the two. For example, let's assume that in addition to selling posters online, Kay has decided to lease a small retail kiosk at the local mall. To keep things simple, let's assume Kay will only be selling her regular-size posters, which sell for $35 each. Let's also assume the mall leasing agent has given Kay the following two options for leasing the space:

- Option 1: Pay $300 per month plus 10% of the sales revenue generated at the kiosk.
- Option 2: Pay $1,000 per month.

Which option should Kay choose? The answer depends on how many posters Kay thinks she will sell from the kiosk each month. As we see above, Option 1 has fewer fixed costs and more variable costs than Option 2. Thus, Kay's operating leverage would be lower under Option 1 than under Option 2. As a result, Option 1 carries less financial risk if sales volume is low, but less financial reward if sales volume is high. But how high must sales volume be to make Option 2 the better choice?

To answer this question Kay will need to figure out her **indifference point**, the point at which she would be indifferent between the two options because they both would result in the same total cost. Once Kay knows the indifference point, she can better judge which option is preferable. Let's see how this is done.

First, Kay calculates the variable and fixed costs associated with each option, as shown in Exhibit 7-12. Notice that Kay does not need to consider any of her other business expenses (such as the cost of the posters themselves or the website maintenance costs), because they will not differ between the two leasing options. In deciding which lease option to take, Kay only needs to consider those costs that are associated with the lease.

EXHIBIT 7-12 Costs associated with each leasing option

	Option 1	Option 2
Variable cost component:		
10% of sales revenue (= 10% × $35 per poster)	$3.50 per poster	-0-
Fixed Cost component:	$300	$1,000

Next, Kay develops an equation in which she sets the cost of each leasing option equal to the other. She then fills in the appropriate information and solves for number of units:

Costs under Option 1	=	**Costs under Option 2**

Variable Costs + Fixed Costs = Variable Costs + Fixed Costs

(# Units × Variable cost per unit) + Fixed Costs = (# Units × Variable cost per unit) + Fixed Costs

(# Units × $3.50) + $300 = (# Units × $0) + $1,000

(# Units × $3.50) = $700

Units = 200

Based on this analysis, Kay will be *indifferent* between the two leasing options if she sells *exactly* 200 posters per month at the kiosk. At a volume of 200 units, she would pay $1,000 for the lease under Option 1 [(200 × $3.50) + $300 = $1,000] and $1,000 for the lease under Option 2. Both options would result in the same cost.

But what if sales volume is lower or higher than 200 posters per month? As shown in Exhibit 7-13, Kay will prefer the lower operating leverage alternative (Option 1) if she sells *fewer* than 200 posters a month. However, she will prefer the higher operating leverage alternative (Option 2) if she sells *more* than 200 posters a month. Her decision will be based on whether she expect sales volume to be lower, or higher, than the indifference point.

EXHIBIT 7-13 Using an indifference point to choose the most profitable cost structure

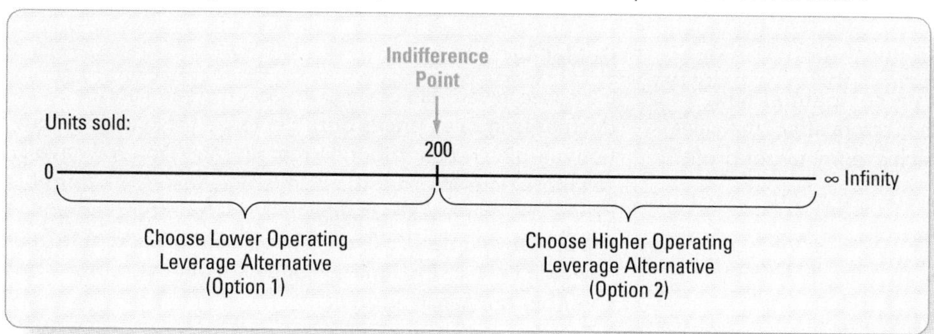

We can verify the conclusion presented in Exhibit 7-13 by calculating the lease costs at *any* volume of sales. First, let's assume that Kay expects to sell 100 posters a month at the kiosk. The lease cost under each option is calculated as follows:

Lease cost under Option 1: $300 + [10% × (100 units × $35 sales price)] = **$650**

Lease cost under Option 2: **$1,000**

As expected, when the sales volume is *lower* than the indifference point, the lease cost is lower under Option 1 than under Option 2.

Next, let's assume Kay expects to sell 500 posters a month. The lease cost is calculated as follows:

Lease cost under Option 1: $300 + [10% × (500 units × $35 sales price)] = **$2,050**

Lease cost under Option 2: **$1,000**

As expected, when the sales volume is *higher* than the indifference point, the lease cost is lower under Option 2 than under Option 1.

The following rule of thumb summarizes the conclusions presented in Exhibit 7-13:

*When faced with a choice between cost structures, choose the **lower** operating leverage option when sales volume is expected to be **lower** than the indifference point. Choose the **higher** operating leverage option when sales volume is expected to be **higher** than the indifference point.*

Managers can use this rule of thumb whenever they are faced with choices about how to structure their costs.

In this chapter, we have discussed how managers use the contribution margin and CVP analysis to predict profits, determine the volume needed to achieve breakeven or a target profit, and assess how changes in the business environment affect their profits. In the next chapter, we look at several types of short-term decisions managers must make. Cost behavior and the contribution margin will continue to play an important role in these decisions.

Decision Guidelines

CVP Analysis

Your friend opened an ice cream parlor. But now she's facing changing business conditions. She needs help making the following decisions:

Decision	Guidelines
The cost of ice cream is rising, yet my competitors have lowered their prices. How will these factors affect the sales volume I'll need to break even or achieve my target profit?	Increases in variable costs (such as ice cream) and decreases in sales prices both decrease the unit contribution margin and contribution margin ratio. You will have to sell more units in order to achieve breakeven or a target profit. You can use sensitivity analysis to better pinpoint the actual volume you'll need to sell. Simply compute your new unit contribution margin and use it in the shortcut unit contribution margin formula.
Would it help if I could renegotiate my lease with the landlord?	Decreases in fixed costs do not affect the firm's contribution margin. However, a decrease in fixed costs means that the company will have to sell fewer units to achieve breakeven or a target profit. Increases in fixed costs have the opposite effect.
I've been thinking about selling other products in addition to ice cream. Will this affect the sales volume I'll need to earn my target profit?	Your contribution margin ratio will change as a result of changing your sales mix. A company earns more income by selling higher-margin products than by selling an equal number of lower-margin products. If you can shift sales toward higher contribution margin products, you will have to sell fewer units to reach your target profit.
If the economy takes a downturn, how much risk do I face of incurring a loss?	The margin of safety indicates how far sales volume can decline before you would incur a loss: $\text{Margin of safety} = \text{Expected sales} - \text{Breakeven sales}$ The operating leverage factor indicates the percentage change in operating income that will occur from a 1% change in volume. It tells you how sensitive your company's operating income is to changes in volume. At a given level of sales, the operating leverage factor is as follows: $\text{Operating leverage factor} = \dfrac{\text{Contribution margin}}{\text{Operating income}}$
If given a choice between alternative cost structures, how do I choose the most profitable one?	Choose the *lower* operating leverage option when sales volume is expected to be *lower* than the indifference point. Choose the *higher* operating leverage option when sales volume is expected to be *higher* than the indifference point.
How do I find the indifference point?	The indifference point is found by setting the total costs of one option equal to the total costs of another option, and then solving for the volume that equates the two options.

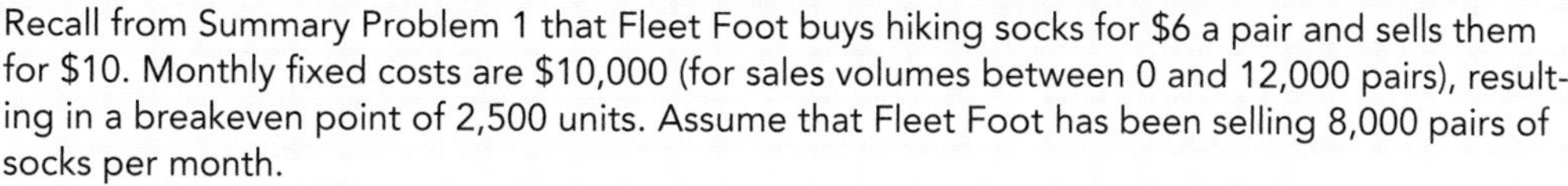

SUMMARY PROBLEM 2

Recall from Summary Problem 1 that Fleet Foot buys hiking socks for $6 a pair and sells them for $10. Monthly fixed costs are $10,000 (for sales volumes between 0 and 12,000 pairs), resulting in a breakeven point of 2,500 units. Assume that Fleet Foot has been selling 8,000 pairs of socks per month.

Requirements

1. What is Fleet Foot's current margin of safety in units, in sales dollars, and as a percentage? Explain the results.
2. At this level of sales, what is Fleet Foot's operating leverage factor? If volume declines by 25% due to increasing competition, by what percentage will the company's operating income decline?
3. Competition has forced Fleet Foot to lower its sales price to $9 a pair. How will this affect Fleet's breakeven point?
4. To compensate for the lower sales price, Fleet Foot wants to expand its product line to include men's dress socks. Each pair will sell for $7.00 and cost $2.75 from the supplier. Fixed costs will not change. Fleet expects to sell four pairs of dress socks for every one pair of hiking socks (at its new $9 sales price). What is Fleet's weighted-average contribution margin per unit? Given the 4:1 sales mix, how many of each type of sock will it need to sell to break even?

SOLUTIONS

Requirement 1

$$\begin{aligned}\text{Margin of safety in units} &= \text{Expected sales in units} - \text{Breakeven sales in units}\\ &= 8{,}000 - 2{,}500\\ &= 5{,}500 \text{ units}\end{aligned}$$

$$\begin{aligned}\text{Margin of safety in dollars} &= \text{Expected sales in dollars} - \text{Breakeven sales in dollars}\\ &= (8{,}000 \times \$10) - (2{,}500 \times \$10)\\ &= \$55{,}000\end{aligned}$$

$$\begin{aligned}\text{Margin of safety as a percentage} &= \frac{\text{Margin of safety in units}}{\text{Expected sales in units}}\\ &= \frac{5{,}500 \text{ pairs}}{8{,}000 \text{ pairs}}\\ &= 68.75\%\end{aligned}$$

Fleet Foot's margin of safety is quite high. Sales have to fall by more than 5,500 units (or $55,000) before Fleet incurs a loss. Fleet will continue to earn a profit unless sales drop by more than 68.75%.

Requirement 2

At its current level of volume, Fleet's operating income is as follows:

Contribution margin (8,000 pairs × $4/pair)	$ 32,000
Less: Fixed expenses	(10,000)
Operating income	$ 22,000

Fleet's operating leverage factor at this level of sales is computed as follows:

$$\text{Operating leverage factor} = \frac{\text{Contribution margin}}{\text{Operating income}}$$
$$= \frac{\$32{,}000}{\$22{,}000}$$
$$= 1.45 \text{ (rounded)}$$

If sales volume declines by 25%, operating income will decline by 36.25% (Fleet's operating leverage factor of 1.45 multiplied by 25%).

Requirement 3

If Fleet drops its sales price to $9 per pair, its contribution margin per pair declines to $3 (sales price of $9 – variable cost of $6). Each sale contributes less toward covering fixed costs. Fleet's new breakeven point *increases* to 3,334 pairs of socks ($10,000 fixed costs ÷ $3 unit contribution margin).

Requirement 4

	Hiking Socks	Dress Socks	Total
Sales price per unit	$ 9.00	$ 7.00	
Deduct: Variable expense per unit	(6.00)	(2.75)	
Contribution margin per unit	$ 3.00	$ 4.25	
Sales mix	× 1	× 4	5
Contribution margin	$ 3.00	$17.00	$20.00
Weighted-average contribution margin per unit ($20/5)			$ 4.00

$$\text{Sales in total units} = \frac{\text{Fixed expenses} + \text{Operating income}}{\text{Weighted-average contribution margin per unit}}$$
$$= \frac{\$10{,}000 + \$0}{\$4}$$
$$= 2{,}500 \text{ pairs of socks}$$

Breakeven sales of dress socks (2,500 × 4/5)	2,000 pairs dress socks
Breakeven sales of hiking socks (2,500 × 1/5)	500 pairs hiking socks

By expanding its product line to include higher-margin dress socks, Fleet is able to decrease its breakeven point back to its original level (2,500 pairs). However, to achieve this breakeven point, Fleet must sell the planned ratio of four pairs of dress socks to every one pair of hiking socks.

END OF CHAPTER

Learning Objectives

- 1 Calculate the unit contribution margin and the contribution margin ratio
- 2 Use CVP analysis to find breakeven points and target profit volumes
- 3 Perform sensitivity analysis in response to changing business conditions
- 4 Find breakeven and target profit volumes for multiproduct companies
- 5 Determine a firm's margin of safety, operating leverage, and most profitable cost structure

Accounting Vocabulary

Breakeven Point. (p. 400) The sales level at which operating income is zero: Total revenues = Total expenses.

Contribution Margin. (p. 397) Sales revenue minus variable expenses.

Contribution Margin Income Statement. (p. 397) An income statement that groups costs by behavior rather than function; it can be used only by internal management.

Contribution Margin Per Unit. (p. 397) The excess of the unit sales price over the variable cost per unit; also called unit contribution margin.

Contribution Margin Ratio. (p. 398) Ratio of contribution margin to sales revenue.

Cost-Volume-Profit (CVP) Analysis. (p. 396) Expresses the relationships among costs, volume, and profit or loss.

Indifference Point. (p. 424) The volume of sales at which a company would be indifferent between alternative cost structures because they would result in the same total cost.

Margin of Safety. (p. 420) Excess of expected sales over breakeven sales; the drop in sales a company can absorb without incurring an operating loss.

Operating Leverage. (p. 421) The relative amount of fixed and variable costs that make up a firm's total costs.

Operating Leverage Factor. (p. 422) At a given level of sales, the contribution margin divided by operating income; the operating leverage factor indicates the percentage change in operating income that will occur from a 1% change in sales volume.

Sales Mix. (p. 397) The combination of products that make up total sales.

Sensitivity Analysis. (p. 411) A "what-if" technique that asks what results will be if actual prices or costs change or if an underlying assumption changes.

MyAccountingLab

Go to http://myaccountinglab.com/ for the following Quick Check, Short Exercises, Exercises, and Problems. They are available with immediate grading, explanations of correct and incorrect answers, and interactive media that acts as your own online tutor.

Quick Check

1. *(Learning Objective 1)* When a company is operating at its breakeven point,
   a. its selling price will be equal to its variable expense per unit.
   b. its contribution margin will be equal to its variable expenses.
   c. its fixed expenses will be equal to its variable expenses.
   d. its total revenues will be equal to its total expenses.
2. *(Learning Objective 1)* If a company sells one unit above its breakeven sales volume, then its operating income would be equal to
   a. the unit selling price.
   b. the unit contribution margin.
   c. the fixed expenses.
   d. zero.
3. *(Learning Objective 2)* How is the unit sales volume necessary to reach a target profit calculated?
   a. Target profit / unit contribution margin
   b. Target profit / contribution margin ratio
   c. (Fixed expenses + target profit)/unit contribution margin
   d. (Fixed expenses + target profit)/contribution margin ratio
4. *(Learning Objective 2)* The number of units to be sold to reach a certain target profit is calculated as
   a. target profit / unit contribution margin.
   b. target profit / contribution margin ratio.
   c. (fixed expenses + target profit)/unit contribution margin.
   d. (fixed expenses + target profit)/contribution margin ratio.

5. *(Learning Objective 3)* The breakeven point on a CVP graph is
   a. the intersection of the sales revenue line and the total expense line.
   b. the intersection of the fixed expense line and the total expense line.
   c. the intersection of the fixed expense line and the sales revenue.
   d. the intersection of the sales revenue line and the y-axis.

6. *(Learning Objective 3)* If the sales price of a product increases while everything else remains the same, what happens to the breakeven point?
   a. The breakeven point will increase.
   b. The breakeven point will decrease.
   c. The breakeven point will remain the same.
   d. The effect cannot be determined without further information.

7. *(Learning Objective 4)* Target profit analysis is used to calculate the sales volume that is needed to
   a. cover all fixed expenses.
   b. cover all expenses.
   c. avoid a loss.
   d. earn a specific amount of net operating income.

8. *(Learning Objective 4)* A shift in the sales mix from a product with a high contribution margin ratio toward a product with a low contribution margin ratio will cause the breakeven point to
   a. increase.
   b. decrease.
   c. remain the same.
   d. increase or decrease, but the direction of change cannot be determined from the information given.

9. *(Learning Objective 5)* If the degree of operating leverage is 3, then a 2% change in the number of units sold should result in a 6% change in
   a. sales.
   b. variable expense.
   c. unit contribution margin.
   d. operating income.

10. *(Learning Objective 5)* What is the margin of safety?
    a. The amount of fixed and variable costs that make up a company's total costs
    b. The difference between the sales price per unit and the variable cost per unit
    c. The excess of expected sales over breakeven sales
    d. The sales level at which operating income is zero

Quick Check Answers

1. d 2. b 3. c 4. c 5. a 6. b 7. d 8. a 9. d 10. c

Short Exercises

Luxury Cruiseline Data Set used for S7-1 through S7-12:

Luxury Cruiseline offers nightly dinner cruises off the coast of Miami, San Francisco, and Seattle. Dinner cruise tickets sell for $120 per passenger. Luxury Cruiseline's variable cost of providing the dinner is $48 per passenger, and the fixed cost of operating the vessels (depreciation, salaries, docking fees, and other expenses) is $270,000 per month. The company's relevant range extends to 15,000 monthly passengers.

S7-1 Compute unit contribution margin and contribution margin ratio

(Learning Objective 1)

Use the information from the Luxury Cruiseline Data Set to compute the following:

a. What is the contribution margin per passenger?
b. What is the contribution margin ratio?
c. Use the unit contribution margin to project operating income if monthly sales total 10,000 passengers.
d. Use the contribution margin ratio to project operating income if monthly sales revenue totals $650,000.

S7-2 Project change in income *(Learning Objective 1)*

Use the information from the Luxury Cruiseline Data Set. If Luxury Cruiseline sells an additional 300 tickets, by what amount will its operating income increase (or operating loss decrease)?

S7-3 Find breakeven *(Learning Objective 2)*

Use the information from the Luxury Cruiseline Data Set to compute the number of dinner cruise tickets it must sell to break even and the sales dollars needed to break even.

S7-4 Find target profit volume *(Learning Objective 2)*

Use the information from the Luxury Cruiseline Data Set. If Luxury Cruiseline has a target operating income of $97,200 per month, how many dinner cruise tickets must the company sell?

S7-5 Prepare a CVP graph *(Learning Objective 2)*

Use the information from the Luxury Cruiseline Data Set. Draw a graph of Luxury Cruiseline's CVP relationships. Include the sales revenue line, the fixed expense line, and the total expense line. Label the axes, the breakeven point, the income area, and the loss area.

S7-6 Interpret a CVP graph *(Learning Objective 2)*

Describe what each letter stands for in the CVP graph.

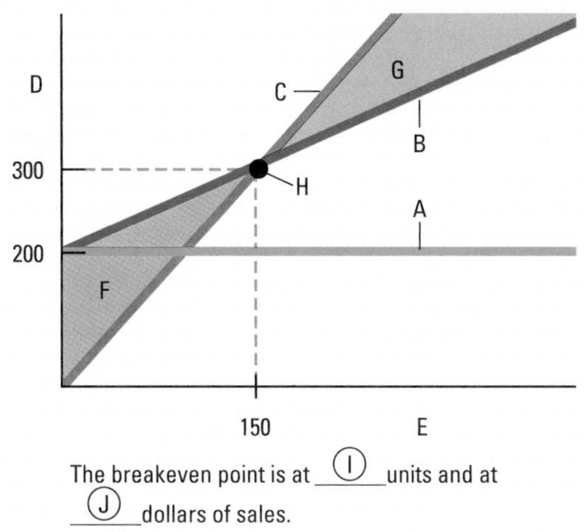

S7-7 Changes in sales price and variable costs *(Learning Objective 3)*

Use the information from the Luxury Cruiseline Data Set.

1. Suppose Luxury Cruiseline cuts its dinner cruise ticket price from $120 to $96 to increase the number of passengers. Compute the new breakeven point in units and in sales dollars. Explain how changes in sales price generally affect the breakeven point.
2. Assume that Luxury Cruiseline does *not* cut the price. Luxury Cruiseline could reduce its variable costs by no longer serving an appetizer before dinner. Suppose this operating change reduces the variable expense from $48 to $30 per passenger. Compute the new breakeven point in units and in dollars. Explain how changes in variable costs generally affect the breakeven point.

S7-8 Changes in fixed costs *(Learning Objective 3)*

Use the information from the Luxury Cruiseline Data Set. Suppose Luxury Cruiseline embarks on a cost-reduction drive and slashes fixed expenses from $270,000 per month to $180,000 per month.

1. Compute the new breakeven point in units and in sales dollars.
2. Is the breakeven point higher or lower than in S7-3? Explain how changes in fixed costs generally affect the breakeven point.

S7-9 Compute weighted-average contribution margin *(Learning Objective 4)*

Use the information from the Luxury Cruiseline Data Set. Suppose Luxury Cruiseline decides to offer two types of dinner cruises: regular cruises and executive cruises. The executive cruise includes complimentary cocktails and a five-course dinner on the upper deck. Assume that fixed expenses remain at $270,000 per month and that the following ticket prices and variable expenses apply:

	Regular Cruise	Executive Cruise
Sales price per ticket	$120	$240
Variable expense per passenger	$ 48	$180

Assuming that Luxury Cruiseline expects to sell four regular cruises for every executive cruise, compute the weighted-average contribution margin per unit. Is it higher or lower than a *simple* average contribution margin? Why? Is it higher or lower than the regular cruise contribution margin calculated in S7-1? Why? Will this new sales mix cause Luxury Cruiseline's breakeven point to increase or decrease from what it was when it sold only regular cruises?

S7-10 Continuation of S7-9: Breakeven *(Learning Objective 4)*

Refer to your answer to S7-9.

a. Compute the total number of dinner cruises that Luxury Cruiseline must sell to break even.
b. Compute the number of regular cruises and executive cruises the company must sell to break even.

S7-11 Compute margin of safety *(Learning Objective 5)*

Use the information from the Luxury Cruiseline Data Set. If Luxury Cruiseline sells 10,000 dinner cruises, compute the margin of safety

a. in units (dinner cruise tickets).
b. in sales dollars.
c. as a percentage of sales.

S7-12 Compute and use operating leverage factor *(Learning Objective 5)*

Use the information from the Luxury Cruiseline Data Set.

a. Compute the operating leverage factor when Luxury Cruiseline sells 12,000 dinner cruises.
b. If volume increases by 10%, by what percentage will operating income increase?
c. If volume decreases by 5%, by what percentage will operating income decrease?

S7-13 Compute margin of safety *(Learning Objective 5)*

Sarah has an online poster business. Suppose Sarah expects to sell 1,000 posters. Her average sales price per poster is $31 and her average cost per poster is $21. Her fixed expenses total $6,000. Compute her margin of safety

a. in units (posters).
b. in sales dollars.
c. as a percentage of expected sales.

S7-14 Compute and use operating leverage factor *(Learning Objective 5)*

Suppose Sarah sells 1,000 posters. Use the original data from S7-13 to compute her operating leverage factor. If sales volume increases 10%, by what percentage will her operating income change? Prove your answer.

S7-15 Calculating total costs under two different scenarios *(Learning Objective 5)*

The Cupcake Factory plans to open a new retail store in Medina, Ohio. The Cupcake Factory will sell specialty cupcakes for $5 per cupcake (each cupcake has a variable cost of $2.) The company is negotiating its lease for the new Medina location. The landlord has offered two leasing options: 1) a lease of $2,000 per month; or 2) a monthly lease cost of $1,000 plus 4% of the company's monthly sales revenue.

Requirements

1. If the Cupcake Factory plans to sell 1,000 cupcakes a month, which lease option would cost less each month? Why?
2. If the company plans to sell 1,800 cupcakes a month, which lease option would be more attractive? Why?

S7-16 Calculating total costs under two different scenarios
(Learning Objective 5)

Keely owns a hair salon. She gives her hairdressers two options for using her facility, equipment, and salon products: 1) they can pay Keely a flat "chair rental" of $1,200 per month or 2) they can pay her $5 per haircut plus 20% of their revenue. The hairdressers charge their customers $35 per haircut. The hairdressers incur no other expenses.

Requirements

1. At what point (number of haircuts per month) will the hairdressers be indifferent between the two payment options?
2. Because of the poor economic outlook, the hairdressers expect that people will wait longer between haircuts and start cutting their kids hair, rather than bringing them in for a trim. If volume is expected to drop below the indifference point, which payment option of the two described above will the hairdressers prefer?

EXERCISES Group A

E7-17A Prepare contribution margin income statements *(Learning Objective 1)*

Western Travel uses the contribution margin income statement internally. Western's first-quarter results are as follows:

WESTERN TRAVEL Contribution Margin Income Statement Three Months Ended March 31	
Sales revenue	$500,000
Less: Variable expenses	100,000
Contribution margin	$400,000
Less: Fixed expenses	174,000
Operating income	$226,000

Western's relevant range is sales of between $100,000 and $700,000.

Requirements

1. Prepare contribution margin income statements at sales levels of $255,000 and $363,000. (*Hint*: Use the contribution margin ratio.)
2. Compute breakeven sales in dollars.

E7-18A Work backward to find missing information *(Learning Objectives 1 & 2)*

Bentfield Dry Cleaners has determined the following about its costs: Total variable expenses are $32,000, total fixed expenses are $25,200, and the sales revenue needed to break even is $42,000. Determine the company's current 1) sales revenue and 2) operating income. (*Hint*: First, find the contribution margin ratio; then prepare the contribution margin income statement.)

E7-19A Find breakeven and target profit volume *(Learning Objectives 1 & 2)*

Happy Feet produces sports socks. The company has fixed expenses of $150,000 and variable expenses of $3.50 per package. Each package sells for $5.00.

Requirements

1. Compute the contribution margin per package and the contribution margin ratio.
2. Find the breakeven point in units and in dollars.
3. Find the number of packages Happy Feet needs to sell to earn a $22,500 operating income.

E7-20A Continuation of E7-19A: Changing costs *(Learning Objective 3)*

Refer to Happy Feet in E7-19A. If Happy Feet can decrease its variable costs to $3.00 per package by increasing its fixed costs to $160,000, how many packages will it have to sell to generate $22,500 of operating income? Is this more or less than before? Why?

E7-21A Find breakeven and target profit volume *(Learning Objectives 1 & 2)*

Owner Lei Wong is considering franchising her Global Chopsticks restaurant concept. She believes people will pay $5.75 for a large bowl of noodles. Variable costs are $2.30 a bowl. Wong estimates monthly fixed costs for franchisees at $8,400.

Requirements

1. Find a franchisee's breakeven sales in dollars.
2. Is franchising a good idea for Wong if franchisees want a minimum monthly operating income of $6,000 and Wong believes that most locations could generate $26,000 in monthly sales?

E7-22A Continuation of E7-21A: Changing business conditions *(Learning Objective 3)*

Refer to Global Chopsticks in E7-21A. Wong did franchise her restaurant concept. Because of Global Chopsticks' success, Noodles-n-More has come on the scene as a competitor. To maintain its market share, Global Chopsticks will have to lower its sales price to $5.25 per bowl. At the same time, Happy Wok hopes to increase each restaurant's volume to 6,500 bowls per month by embarking on a marketing campaign. Each franchise will have to contribute $400 per month to cover the advertising costs. Prior to these changes, most locations were selling 6,000 bowls per month.

Requirements

1. What was the average restaurant's operating income before these changes?
2. Assuming that the price cut and advertising campaign are successful at increasing volume to the projected level, will the franchisees still earn their target profit of $6,000 per month? Show your calculations.

E7-23A Compute breakeven and project income *(Learning Objectives 1 & 2)*

Stewart's Steel Parts produces parts for the automobile industry. The company has monthly fixed expenses of $640,000 and a contribution margin of 80% of revenues.

Requirements

1. Compute Stewart's Steel Parts' monthly breakeven sales in dollars.
2. Use the contribution margin ratio to project operating income (or loss) if revenues are $530,000 and if they are $1,050,000.
3. Do the results in Requirement 2 make sense given the breakeven sales you computed in Requirement 1? Explain.

E7-24A Continuation of E7-23A: Changing business conditions *(Learning Objective 3)*

Refer to Stewart's Steel Parts in E7-23A. Stewart feels like he's in a giant squeeze play: The automotive manufacturers are demanding lower prices, and the steel producers have increased raw material costs. Stewart's contribution margin has shrunk to 50% of revenues. Stewart's monthly operating income, prior to these pressures, was $200,000.

Requirements

1. To maintain this same level of profit, what sales volume (in sales revenue) must Stewart now achieve?
2. Stewart believes that his monthly sales revenue will go only as high as $1,050,000. He is thinking about moving operations overseas to cut fixed costs. If monthly sales are $1,050,000, by how much will he need to cut fixed costs to maintain his prior profit level of $200,000 per month?

E7-25A Sustainability and CVP concepts *(Learning Objective 3)*

Kingston Garage Doors manufactures a premium garage door. Currently, the price and cost data associated with the premium garage door is as follows:

Average selling price per premium garage door	$ 1,500
Average variable manufacturing cost per door	$ 600
Average variable selling cost per door	$ 150
Total annual fixed costs	$250,000

Kingston Garage Doors has undertaken several sustainability projects over the past few years. Management is currently evaluating whether to develop a comprehensive software control system for its manufacturing operations that would significantly reduce scrap and waste generated during the manufacturing process. If the company were to implement this software control system in its manufacturing operations, the use of the software control system would result in an increase of $60,000 in its annual fixed costs while the average variable manufacturing cost per door would drop by $50.

Requirements

1. What is the company's current breakeven in units and in dollars?
2. If the company expects to sell 400 premium garage doors in the upcoming year, and it does not develop the software control system, what is its expected operating income from premium garage doors?
3. If the software control system were to be developed and implemented, what would be the company's new breakeven point in units and in dollars?
4. If the company expects to sell 400 premium garage doors in the upcoming year, and it develops the software control system, what is its expected operating income from premium garage doors?
5. If the company expects to sell 400 premium garage doors in the upcoming year, do you think the company should implement the software control system? Why or why not? What factors should the company consider?

E7-26A Prepare a CVP graph *(Learning Objective 2)*

Suppose that Murray Stadium, the home of the Upstate Cardinals, earns total revenue that averages $30 for every ticket sold. Assume that annual fixed expenses are $32 million and that variable expenses are $5 per ticket.

Requirements

1. Prepare the ballpark's CVP graph under these assumptions. Label the axes, sales revenue line, fixed expense line, total expense line, operating loss area, and operating income area on the graph.
2. Show the breakeven point in dollars and in tickets.

E7-27A Work backward to find new breakeven point *(Learning Objectives 2 & 3)*

Empire Industries is planning on purchasing a new piece of equipment that will increase the quality of its production. It hopes the increased quality will generate more sales. The company's contribution margin ratio is 40%, and its current breakeven point is $400,000 in sales revenue. If the company's fixed expenses increase by $55,000 due to the equipment, what will its new breakeven point be (in sales revenue)?

E7-28A Find consequence of rising fixed costs *(Learning Objectives 1 & 3)*

Elizabeth Miller sells homemade knit scarves for $14 each at local craft shows. Her contribution margin ratio is 62.5%. Currently, the craft show entrance fees cost Elizabeth $1,400 per year. The craft shows are raising their entrance fees by 25% next year. How many *extra* scarves will Elizabeth have to sell next year just to pay for rising entrance fee costs?

E7-29A Extension of E7-28A: Multiproduct firm *(Learning Objective 4)*

John Miller admired his wife's success at selling scarves at local craft shows (E7-28A), so he decided to make two types of plant stands to sell at the shows. John makes twig stands out of downed wood from his backyard and the yards of his neighbors, so his variable cost is minimal (wood screws, glue, and so forth). However, John has to purchase wood to make his oak plant stands. His unit prices and costs are as follows:

	Twig Stands	Oak Stands
Sales price	$18.00	$38.00
Variable cost	$ 3.00	$ 8.00

The twig stands are more popular, so John sells four twig stands for every one oak stand. Elizabeth charges her husband $360 to share her booth at the craft shows (after all, she has paid the entrance fees). How many of each plant stand does John need to sell to break even? Will this affect the number of scarves Elizabeth needs to sell to break even? Explain.

E7-30A Find breakeven for a multiproduct firm *(Learning Objective 4)*

Rally Scooters plans to sell a motorized standard scooter for $50 and a motorized chrome scooter for $60. Rally Scooters purchases the standard scooter for $35 and the chrome scooter for $40. Rally Scooters expects to sell two chrome scooters for every three standard scooters. The company's monthly fixed expenses are $14,450. How many of each type of scooter must Rally Scooters sell monthly to break even? To earn $11,900?

E7-31A Work backward to find missing data *(Learning Objective 4)*

Ambrose Manufacturing manufactures two styles of watches—the Digital and the Classic. The following data pertain to the Digital:

Variable manufacturing cost	$130
Variable operating cost	$ 20
Sale price	$230

Ambrose's monthly fixed expenses total $220,000. When Digitals and Classics are sold in the mix of 6:4, respectively, the sale of 2,500 total watches results in an operating income of $90,000. Compute the contribution margin per watch for the Classic.

E7-32A Breakeven and an advertising decision at a multiproduct company *(Learning Objectives 3, 4, & 5)*

Ghent Medical Supply is a retailer of home medical equipment. Last year, Ghent's sales revenues totaled $6,300,000. Total expenses were $2,200,000. Of this amount, approximately $1,260,000 were variable, while the remainder were fixed. Since Ghent's offers thousands of different products, its managers prefer to calculate the breakeven point in terms of sales dollars rather than units.

Requirements

1. What is Ghent's current operating income?
2. What is Ghent's contribution margin ratio?
3. What is Ghent's breakeven point in sales dollars (*Hint*: The contribution margin ratio calculated in Requirement 2 is already weighted by Ghent's actual sales mix.)
4. Ghent's top management is deciding whether to embark on a $200,000 advertisement campaign. The marketing firm has projected annual sales volume to increase by 20% as a result of this campaign. Assuming that the projections are correct, what effect would this advertising campaign have on the company's annual operating income?

E7-33A Work backward through margin of safety *(Learning Objective 5)*

Bob's Bait Shop had budgeted bait sales for the season at $18,000, with a $10,500 margin of safety. However, due to unseasonable weather, bait sales reached only $17,050. Actual sales exceeded breakeven sales by what amount?

E7-34A Compute margin of safety and operating leverage *(Learning Objective 5)*

Foster's Repair Shop has a monthly target operating income of $10,500. *Variable expenses* are 50% of sales, and monthly fixed expenses are $7,000.

Requirements

1. Compute the monthly margin of safety in dollars if the shop achieves its income goal.
2. Express Foster's margin of safety as a percentage of target sales.
3. What is Foster's operating leverage factor at the target level of operating income?
4. Assume that the company reaches its target. By what percentage will the company's operating income fall if sales volume declines by 9%?

E7-35A Use operating leverage factor to find fixed costs *(Learning Objective 5)*

Guinty Manufacturing had a 1.50 operating leverage factor when sales were $50,000. Guinty Manufacturing's contribution margin ratio was 30%. What were Guinty Manufacturing's fixed expenses?

E7-36A Calculating total costs under two different scenarios *(Learning Objective 5)*

The Candle Company plans to open a new retail store in Forest Lake, Minnesota. The Candle Company will sell specialty candles for an average of $20 each. The average variable costs per candle are as follows?

- Wax $6
- Other additives $1
- Base $2

The company is negotiating its lease for the new location. The landlord has offered two leasing options:

Option A) a lease of $2,500 per month; or

Option B) a monthly lease cost of $1,200 plus 10% of the company's monthly sales revenue.

The company expects to sell approximately 900 candles per month.

Requirements

1. Which lease option is more attractive for the company under its current sales expectations? Calculate the total lease cost under:
   - Option A
   - Option B
2. At what level of sales (in units) would the company be indifferent between the two lease options? Show your proof.
3. If the company's expected sales were 500 candles instead of the projection listed in the exercise, which lease options would be more favorable for the company? Why?

E7-37A Calculating total costs under two different scenarios

(Learning Objective 5)

Hannah sells custom-ordered, fabric headbands over the internet for $10 each. The fabric and elastic used to make the headbands will cost $1 per headband. Hannah has contracted with a local seamstress to make the headbands using the seamstress's own equipment at a price of $3 per headband. Hannah has also hired an internet marketing firm to maintain the website and place banner ads on search engines and other websites. This firm charges Hannah $1,000 per month plus 20% of sales revenue. Hannah also spends $500 per month traveling to different fabric suppliers to research possible new fabrics. (Hannah's costs are expected to remain as stated, unless she sells more than 4,000 headbands per month.)

The internet firm that will be maintaining her website has offered Hannah two contract options to retain their services for the coming year. She can either pay them 1) $1,000 per month plus 20% of revenue, or 2) $2,000 per month plus 10% of revenue.

Requirements

1. Which alternative will provide her with a lower operating leverage? Briefly explain why.
2. At what level of sales (in units) will Hannah be indifferent between the two contract options?
3. If Hannah expects to sell 1,500 headbands per month during the coming year, which contract term should she choose (which would be the most profitable for her)?

E7-38A Comprehensive CVP analysis *(Learning Objectives 1, 2, 3, 4, & 5)*

Scott Cole is evaluating a business opportunity to sell grooming kits at dog shows. Scott can buy the grooming kits at a wholesale cost of $29 per set. He plans to sell the grooming kits for $84 per set. He estimates fixed costs such as travel costs, booth rental cost, and lodging to be $880 per dog show.

Requirements

1. Determine the number of grooming kits Scott must sell per show to break even.
2. Assume Scott wants to earn a profit of $1,320 per show.
   a. Determine the sales volume in units necessary to earn the desired profit.
   b. Determine the sales volume in dollars necessary to earn the desired profit.
   c. Using the contribution margin format, prepare an income statement (condensed version) to confirm your answers to parts a and b.
3. Determine the margin of safety between the sales volume at the breakeven point and the sales volume required to earn the desired profit. Determine the margin of safety in both sales dollars, units, and as a percentage.

E7-39A Comprehensive CVP analysis *(Learning Objectives 1, 2, 3, 4, & 5)*

Preston Company manufactures and sells a single product. The company's sales and expenses for last year follow:

	Total	Per Unit	%
Sales	$116,000	$40	?
Variable expenses	87,000	30	?
Contribution margin	?	?	?
Fixed expenses	11,000		
Operating income	$ 18,000		

Requirements

1. Fill in the missing numbers in the preceding table. Use the table to answer the following questions:
   a. What is the total contribution margin?
   b. What is the per unit contribution margin?
   c. What is the operating income?
   d. How many units were sold?
2. Answer the following questions about breakeven analysis:
   a. What is the breakeven point in units?
   b. What is the breakeven point in sales dollars?
3. Answer the following questions about target profit analysis and safety margin:
   a. How many units must the company sell in order to earn a profit of $55,000?
   b. What is the margin of safety in units?
   c. What is the margin of safety in sales dollars?
   d. What is the margin of safety in percentage?

E7-40A Comprehensive CVP analysis *(Learning Objectives 1, 2, 3, 4, & 5)*

Wolf Manufacturing manufactures 16 GB flash drives (jump drives). Price and cost data for a relevant range extending to 200,000 units per month are as follows:

Sales price per unit (current monthly sales volume is 120,000 units).................	$ 20.00
Variable costs per unit:	
Direct materials..	$ 6.00
Direct labor..	$ 7.00
Variable manufacturing overhead...	$ 1.80
Variable selling and administrative expenses..................................	$ 1.20
Monthly fixed expenses:	
Fixed manufacturing overhead...	$182,000
Fixed selling and administrative expenses.......................................	$267,000

Requirements

1. What is the company's contribution margin per unit? Contribution margin percentage? Total contribution margin?
2. What would the company's monthly operating income be if the company sold 150,000 units?
3. What would the company's monthly operating income be if the company had sales of $4,000,000?
4. What is the breakeven point in units? In sales dollars?
5. How many units would the company have to sell to earn a target monthly profit of $260,000?
6. Management is currently in contract negotiations with the labor union. If the negotiations fail, direct labor costs will increase by 10% and fixed costs will increase by $28,500 per month. If these costs increase, how many units will the company have to sell each month to break even?
7. Return to the original data for this question and the rest of the questions. What is the company's current operating leverage factor (round to two decimals)?
8. If sales volume increases by 5%, by what percentage will operating income increase?
9. What is the company's current margin of safety in sales dollars? What is its margin of safety as a percentage of sales?

10. Say the company adds a second line of flash drives (32 GB rather than 16 GB). A unit of the 32 GB flash drives will sell for $45 and have variable cost per unit of $21 per unit. The expected sales mix is three of the small flash drives (16 GB) for every one large flash drive (32 GB). Given this sales mix, how many of each type of flash drive will the company need to sell to reach its target monthly profit of $260,000? Is this volume higher or lower than previously needed (in Question 5) to achieve the same target profit? Why?

EXERCISES Group B

E7-41B Prepare contribution margin income statements *(Learning Objective 1)*

Worldwide Travel uses the contribution margin income statement internally. Worldwide's first quarter results are as follows:

Worldwide Travel Contribution Margin Income Statement Three Months Ended March 31	
Sales revenue	$316,500
Less: Variable expenses	126,600
Contribution margin	$189,900
Less: Fixed expenses	174,000
Operating income	$ 15,900

Worldwide's relevant range is sales of between $100,000 and $700,000.

Requirements

1. Prepare contribution margin income statements at sales levels of $220,000 and $361,000. (*Hint:* Use the contribution margin ratio.)
2. Compute breakeven sales in dollars.

E7-42B Work backward to find missing information *(Learning Objectives 1 & 2)*

Alderman's Dry Cleaners has determined the following about its costs: Total variable expenses are $37,500, total fixed expenses are $33,000, and the sales revenue needed to break even is $44,000. Determine Alderman's current 1) sales revenue and 2) operating income. (*Hint:* First, find the contribution margin ratio; then prepare the contribution margin income statement.)

E7-43B Find breakeven and target profit volume *(Learning Objectives 1 & 2)*

Trendy Toes produces sports socks. The company has fixed expenses of $85,000 and variable expenses of $1.20 per package. Each package sells for $2.00.

Requirements

1. Compute the contribution margin per package and the contribution margin ratio.
2. Find the breakeven point in units and in dollars.
3. Find the number of packages that Trendy Toes needs to sell to earn a $26,000 operating income.

E7-44B Continuation of E7-43B: Changing costs *(Learning Objective 3)*

Refer to Trendy Toes in E7-43B. If Trendy Toes can decrease its variable costs to $1.00 per package by increasing its fixed costs to $90,000, how many packages will it have to sell to generate $26,000 of operating income? Is this more or less than before? Why?

E7-45B Find breakeven and target profit volume *(Learning Objectives 1 & 2)*

Owner Jackie Long is considering franchising her Oriental Express restaurant concept. She believes people will pay $4.50 for a large bowl of noodles. Variable costs are $1.80 a bowl. Long estimates monthly fixed costs for franchisees at $9,000.

Requirements

1. Find a franchisee's breakeven sales in dollars.
2. Is franchising a good idea for Long if franchisees want a minimum monthly operating income of $7,350 and Long believes most locations could generate $23,000 in monthly sales?

E7-46B Continuation of E7-45B: Changing business conditions *(Learning Objective 3)*

Refer to Oriental Express in E7-45B. Since franchising Oriental Express, the restaurant has not been very successful due to Noodles Unlimited coming on the scene as a competitor. To increase its market share, Oriental Express will have to lower its sales price to $4.00 per bowl. At the same time, Oriental Express hopes to increase each restaurant's volume to 7,000 bowls per month by embarking on a marketing campaign. Each franchise will have to contribute $500 per month to cover the advertising costs. Prior to these changes, most locations were selling 6,500 bowls per month.

Requirements

1. What was the average restaurant's operating income before these changes?
2. Assuming the price cut and advertising campaign are successful at increasing volume to the projected level, will the franchisees earn their target profit of $7,350 per month?

E7-47B Compute breakeven and project income *(Learning Objectives 1 & 2)*

Rodger's Steel Parts produces parts for the automobile industry. The company has monthly fixed expenses of $660,000 and a contribution margin of 75% of revenues.

Requirements

1. Compute Rodger's Steel Parts' monthly breakeven sales in dollars.
2. Project operating income (or loss) if revenues are $560,000 and if they are $1,030,000.
3. Do the results in Requirement 2 make sense given the breakeven sales you computed in Requirement 1? Explain.

E7-48B Continuation of E7-47B: Changing business conditions *(Learning Objective 3)*

Refer to Rodger's Steel Parts in E7-47B. Rodger feels like he's in a giant squeeze play: The automotive manufacturers are demanding lower prices, and the steel producers have increased raw material costs. Rodger's contribution margin has shrunk to 60% of revenues. Rodger's monthly operating income, prior to these pressures, was $112,500.

Requirements

1. To maintain this same level of profit, what sales volume (in sales revenue) must Rodger now achieve?
2. Rodger believes that his monthly sales revenue will only go as high as $1,030,000. He is thinking about moving operations overseas to cut fixed costs. If monthly sales are $1,030,000, by how much will he need to cut fixed costs to maintain his prior profit level of $112,500 per month?

E7-49B Sustainability and CVP *(Learning Objective 3)*

Lopez Garage Doors manufactures a premium garage door. Currently, the price and cost data associated with the premium garage door is as follows:

Average selling price per premium garage door	$ 1,300
Average variable manufacturing cost per door	$ 550
Average variable selling cost per door	$ 150
Total annual fixed costs	$240,000

Lopez Garage Doors has undertaken several sustainability projects over the past few years. Management is currently evaluating whether to develop a comprehensive software control system for its manufacturing operations that would significantly reduce scrap and waste generated during the manufacturing process. If the company were to implement this software control system in its manufacturing operations, the use of the software control system would result in an increase of $61,000 in its annual fixed costs while the average variable manufacturing cost per door would drop by $100.

Requirements

1. What is the company's current breakeven in units and in dollars?
2. If the company expects to sell 450 premium garage doors in the upcoming year, and it does not develop the software control system, what is its expected operating income from premium garage doors?
3. If the software control system were to be developed and implemented, what would be the company's new breakeven point in units and in dollars?
4. If the company expects to sell 450 premium garage doors in the upcoming year, and it develops the software control system, what is its expected operating income from premium garage doors?
5. If the company expects to sell 450 premium garage doors in the upcoming year, do you think the company should implement the software control system? Why or why not? What factors should the company consider?

E7-50B Prepare a CVP graph *(Learning Objective 2)*

Suppose that Donovan Park, the home of the Highland Hornets, earns total revenue that averages $35 for every ticket sold. Assume that annual fixed expenses are $24 million, and that variable expenses are $5 per ticket.

Requirements

1. Prepare the ballpark's CVP graph under these assumptions. Label the axes, sales revenue line, fixed expense line, total expense line, operating loss area, and operating income area on the graph.
2. Show the breakeven point in dollars and in tickets.

E7-51B Work backward to find new breakeven point *(Learning Objectives 2 & 3)*

Edward Industries is planning on purchasing a new piece of equipment that will increase the quality of its production. It hopes the increased quality will generate more sales. The company's contribution margin ratio is 20%, and its current breakeven point is $300,000 in sales revenue. If Edward Industries' fixed expenses increase by $40,000 due to the equipment, what will its new breakeven point be (in sales revenue)?

E7-52B Find consequence of rising fixed costs *(Learning Objectives 1 & 3)*

Ramona Brown sells homemade knit scarves for $20 each at local craft shows. Her contribution margin ratio is 62.5%. Currently, the craft show entrance fees cost Ramona $500 per year. The craft shows are raising their entrance fees by 10% next year. How many *extra* scarves will Ramona have to sell next year just to pay for rising entrance fee costs?

E7-53B Extension of E7-52B: Multiproduct firm *(Learning Objective 4)*

Mike Brown admired his wife's success at selling scarves at local craft shows (E7-52B), so he decided to make two types of plant stands to sell at the shows. Mike makes twig stands out of downed wood from his backyard and the yards of his neighbors, so his variable cost is minimal (wood screws, glue, and so forth). However, Mike has to purchase wood to make his oak plant stands. His unit prices and costs are as follows.

	Twig Stands	Oak Stands
Sales price	$14.00	$40.00
Variable cost	$ 2.00	$18.00

The twig stands are more popular so Mike sells four twig stands for every one oak stand. Ramona charges her husband $350 to share her booths at the craft shows (after all, she has paid the entrance fees). How many of each plant stand does Mike need to sell to break even? Will this affect the number of scarves Ramona needs to sell to break even? Explain.

E7-54B Find breakeven for a multiproduct firm *(Learning Objective 4)*

Zippy Scooters plans to sell a motorized standard scooter for $45 and a motorized chrome scooter for $65. Zippy Scooters purchases the standard scooter for $30 and the chrome scooter for $35. Zippy Scooters expects to sell two chrome scooters for every three standard scooters. The company's monthly fixed expenses are $17,850. How many of each type of scooter must the company sell monthly to break even? To earn $14,700?

E7-55B Work backward to find missing data *(Learning Objective 4)*

Martin Timepieces manufactures two styles of watches—the Digital and the Classic. The following data pertain to the Digital:

Variable manufacturing cost	$145
Variable operating cost	$ 10
Sale price	$225

The company's monthly fixed expenses total $180,000. When Digitals and Classics are sold in the mix of 6:4, respectively, the sale of 2,500 total watches results in an operating income of $70,000. Compute the contribution margin per watch for the Classic.

E7-56B Breakeven and an advertising decision at a multiproduct company *(Learning Objectives 3, 4, & 5)*

Helton Medical Supplies is a retailer of home medical equipment. Last year, Helton's sales revenues totaled $6,500,000. Total expenses were $2,700,000. Of this amount, approximately $1,560,000 were variable, while the remainder were fixed. Since Helton offers thousands of different products, its managers prefer to calculate the breakeven point in terms of sales dollars, rather than units.

Requirements

1. What is Helton's current operating income?
2. What is Helton's contribution margin ratio?
3. What is Helton's breakeven point in sales dollars? (*Hint:* The contribution margin ratio calculated in Requirement 2 is already weighted by Helton's actual sales mix.) What does it mean?
4. Top management is deciding whether to embark on a $230,000 advertisement campaign. The marketing firm has projected annual sales volume to increase by 10% as a result of this campaign. Assuming that the projections are correct, what effect would this advertising campaign have on Helton's annual operating income?

E7-57B Work backward through margin of safety *(Learning Objective 5)*

Bennett's Bait Shop had budgeted bait sales for the season at $20,000, with a $11,700 margin of safety. However, due to unseasonable weather, bait sales only reached $18,400. Actual sales exceeded breakeven sales by what amount?

E7-58B Compute margin of safety and operating leverage *(Learning Objective 5)*

Samantha's Repair Shop has a monthly target operating income of $12,500. *Variable expenses* are 50% of sales, and monthly fixed expenses are $10,000.

Requirements

1. Compute the monthly margin of safety in dollars if the shop achieves its income goal.
2. Express Samantha's margin of safety as a percentage of target sales.
3. What is Samantha's operating leverage factor at the target level of operating income?
4. Assume that the company reaches its target. By what percentage will the company's operating income fall if sales volume declines by 8%?

E7-59B Use operating leverage factor to find fixed costs *(Learning Objective 5)*

Welch Manufacturing had a 1.25 operating leverage factor when sales were $60,000. Welch Manufacturing's contribution margin ratio was 25%. What were Welch Manufacturing's fixed expenses?

E7-60B Calculating total costs under two different scenarios *(Learning Objectives 5)*

Candles Unlimited plans to open a new retail store in White Bear Lake, Minnesota. Candles Unlimited will sell specialty candles for an average of $25 each. The average variable costs per candle are as follows:

- Wax $7
- Other additives $2
- Base $3

The company is negotiating its lease for the new location. The landlord has offered two leasing options:

Option A) a lease of $2,000 per month; or

Option B) a monthly lease cost of $1,500 plus 5% of the company's monthly sales revenue.

The company expects to sell approximately 500 candles per month.

Requirements

1. Which lease option is more attractive for the company under its current sales expectations? Calculate the total lease cost under:
   a. Option A
   b. Option B
2. At what level of sales (in units) would the company be indifferent between the two lease options? Show your proof.
3. If the company's expected sales were 300 candles instead of the projection listed in the exercise, which lease option would be more favorable for the company? Why?

E7-61B Comprehensive CVP analysis *(Learning Objectives 1, 2, 3, 4, & 5)*

Rachel sells custom-ordered, fabric headbands over the internet for $20 each. The fabric and elastic used to make the headbands will cost $4 per headband. Rachel has contracted with a local seamstress to make the headbands using the seamstress's own equipment, at a price of $8 per headband. Rachel has also hired an internet marketing firm to maintain the website and banner ads on search engines and other websites. This firm charges Rachel $1,200 per month plus 25% of sales revenue. Rachel also spends $300 per month traveling to different fabric suppliers to research possible new fabrics. (Rachel's costs are expected to remain as stated, unless she sells more than 4,000 headbands per month.)

The internet firm that will be maintaining her website has offered Rachel two contract options to retain their services for the coming year. She can either pay them 1) $1,200 per month plus 25% of revenue, or, 2) $2,400 per month plus 15% of revenue.

Requirements

1. Which alternative will provide her with a lower operating leverage? Briefly explain why.
2. At what level of sales (in units) will Rachel be indifferent between the two contract options?
3. If Rachel expects to sell 1,000 headbands per month during the coming year, which contract term should she choose (which would be the most profitable for her)?

E7-62B Comprehensive CVP analysis *(Learning Objectives 1, 2, 3, 4, & 5)*

Brett Stenback is evaluating a business opportunity to sell grooming kits at dog shows. Brett can buy the grooming kits at a wholesale cost of $37 per set. He plans to sell the grooming kits for $70 per set. He estimates fixed costs such as travel costs, booth rental cost, and lodging to be $759 per dog show.

Requirements

1. Determine the number of grooming kits Brett must sell per show to break even.
2. Assume Brett wants to earn a profit of $627 per show.
   a. Determine the sales volume in units necessary to earn the desired profit.
   b. Determine the sales volume in dollars necessary to earn the desired profit.
   c. Using the contribution margin format, prepare an income statement (condensed version) to confirm your answers to parts a and b.
3. Determine the margin of safety between the sales volume at the breakeven point and the sales volume required to earn the desired profit. Determine the margin of safety in both sales dollars, units, and as a percentage.

E7-63B Comprehensive CVP analysis *(Learning Objectives 1, 2, 3, 4, & 5)*

Gable Company manufactures and sells a single product. The company's sales and expenses for last year follow:

	Total	Per Unit	%
Sales	$110,000	$20	?
Variable expenses	82,500	15	?
Contribution margin	?	?	?
Fixed expenses	14,000		
Operating income	$ 13,500		

Requirements

1. Fill in the missing numbers in the table. Use the table to answer the following questions:
   a. What is the total contribution margin?
   b. What is the per unit contribution margin?
   c. What is the operating income?
   d. How many units were sold?
2. Answer the following questions about breakeven analysis:
   a. What is the breakeven point in units?
   b. What is the breakeven point in sales dollars?
3. Answer the following questions about target profit analysis and safety margin:
   a. How many units must the company sell in order to earn a profit of $52,000?
   b. What is the margin of safety in units?
   c. What is the margin of safety in sales dollars?
   d. What is the margin of safety in percentage?

E7-64B Comprehensive CVP analysis *(Learning Objectives 1, 2, 3, 4, & 5)*

Behr Manufacturing manufactures 16 GB flash drives (jump drives). Price and cost data for a relevant range extending to 200,000 units per month are as follows:

Sales price per unit	
(current monthly sales volume is 130,000 units)	$ 20.00
Variable costs per unit:	
Direct materials	$ 5.20
Direct labor	$ 6.00
Variable manufacturing overhead	$ 2.50
Variable selling and administrative expenses	$ 1.30
Monthly fixed expenses:	
Fixed manufacturing overhead	$191,700
Fixed selling and administrative expenses	$287,300

Requirements

1. What is the company's contribution margin per unit? Contribution margin percentage? Total contribution margin?
2. What would the company's monthly operating income be if it sold 160,000 units?
3. What would the company's monthly operating income be if it had sales of $4,000,000?
4. What is the breakeven point in units? In sales dollars?
5. How many units would the company have to sell to earn a target monthly profit of $260,000?
6. Management is currently in contract negotiations with the labor union. If the negotiations fail, direct labor costs will increase by 10% and fixed costs will increase by $27,000 per month. If these costs increase, how many units will the company have to sell each month to break even?
7. Return to the original data for this question and the rest of the questions. What is the company's current operating leverage factor (round to two decimal places)?
8. If sales volume increases by 5%, by what percentage will operating income increase?
9. What is the firm's current margin of safety in sales dollars? What is its margin of safety as a percentage of sales?
10. Say Behr Manufacturing adds a second line of flash drives (32 GB rather than 16 GB). A unit of the 32 GB flash drives will sell for $45 and have variable cost per unit of $20 per unit. The expected sales mix is six of the smaller flash drives (16 GB) for every one larger flash drive (32 GB). Given this sales mix, how many of each type of flash drive will Behr need to sell to reach its target monthly profit of $260,000? Is this volume higher or lower than previously needed (in Question 5) to achieve the same target profit? Why?

PROBLEMS Group A

P7-65A Find missing data in CVP relationships *(Learning Objectives 1 & 2)*

The budgets of four companies yield the following information:

	Company			
	Q	R	S	T
Target sales	$720,000	$328,750	$190,000	$
Variable expenses	216,000			270,000
Fixed expenses		$153,000	$ 90,000	
Operating income (loss)	$154,000	$	$	$133,000
Units sold		$131,500	12,000	18,000
Contribution margin per unit	$ 6.00		$ 9.50	$ 35.00
Contribution margin ratio		0.80		

Requirements

1. Fill in the blanks for each company.
2. Compute breakeven, in sales dollars, for each company. Which company has the lowest breakeven point in sales dollars? What causes the low breakeven point?

P7-66A Find breakeven and target profit and prepare income statements *(Learning Objectives 1 & 2)*

A traveling production of *Jersey Boys* performs each year. The average show sells 1,000 tickets at $60 a ticket. There are 120 shows each year. The show has a cast of 75, each earning an average of $300 per show. The cast is paid only after each show. The other variable expense is program printing costs of $9 per guest. Annual fixed expenses total $969,000.

Requirements

1. Compute revenue and variable expenses for each show.
2. Use the income statement equation approach to compute the number of shows needed annually to break even.
3. Use the shortcut unit contribution margin approach to compute the number of shows needed annually to earn a profit of $3,078,000. Is this goal realistic? Give your reason.
4. Prepare *Jersey Boys'* contribution margin income statement for 100 shows each year. Report only two categories of expenses: variable and fixed.

P7-67A Comprehensive CVP problem *(Learning Objectives 1, 2, & 5)*

University Calendars imprints calendars with college names. The company has fixed expenses of $1,065,000 each month plus variable expenses of $3.50 per carton of calendars. Of the variable expense, 65% is Cost of Goods Sold, while the remaining 35% relates to variable operating expenses. The company sells each carton of calendars for $13.50.

Requirements

1. Compute the number of cartons of calendars that University Calendars must sell each month to break even.
2. Compute the dollar amount of monthly sales University Calendars needs in order to earn $304,000 in operating income (round the contribution margin ratio to two decimal places).
3. Prepare the company's contribution margin income statement for June for sales of 470,000 cartons of calendars.
4. What is June's margin of safety (in dollars)? What is the operating leverage factor at this level of sales?
5. By what percentage will operating income change if July's sales volume is 12% higher? Prove your answer.

P7-68A Compute breakeven, prepare CVP graph, and respond to change *(Learning Objectives 1, 2, & 3)*

Market Time Investors is opening an office in Orlando, Florida. Fixed monthly expenses are office rent ($2,100), depreciation on office furniture ($260), utilities ($280), special telephone lines ($600), a connection with an online brokerage service ($640), and the salary of a financial planner ($5,220). Variable expenses include payments to the financial planner (14% of revenue), advertising (7% of revenue), supplies and postage (3% of revenue), and usage fees for the telephone lines and computerized brokerage service (6% of revenue).

Requirements

1. Compute the investment firm's breakeven revenue in dollars. If the average trade leads to $520 in revenue for Market Time, how many trades must it make to break even?
2. Compute dollar revenues needed to earn monthly operating income of $3,640.
3. Graph Market Time's CVP relationships. Assume that an average trade leads to $520 in revenue for the firm. Show the breakeven point, sales revenue line, fixed expense line, total expense line, operating loss area, operating income area, and sales in units (trades) and dollars when monthly operating income of $3,640 is earned. The graph should range from 0 to 40 units (trades).
4. Assume that the average revenue that Market Time Investors earns decreases to $420 per trade. How does this affect the breakeven point in number of trades?

P7-69A CVP analysis at a multiproduct firm *(Learning Objectives 4 & 5)*

The contribution margin income statement of Pepperpike Coffee for February follows:

PEPPERPIKE COFFEE Contribution Margin Income Statement For the Month Ended February 29		
Sales revenue		$103,000
Variable expenses:		
Cost of goods sold	$28,000	
Marketing expense	10,000	
General and administrative expense	3,000	41,000
Contribution margin		$62,000
Fixed expenses:		
Marketing expense	$34,650	
General and administrative expense	7,350	42,000
Operating income		$20,000

Pepperpike Coffee sells three small coffees for every large coffee. A small coffee sells for $3.00, with a variable expense of $1.50. A large coffee sells for $5.00, with a variable expense of $2.50.

Requirements

1. Determine Pepperpike Coffee's monthly breakeven point in the numbers of small coffees and large coffees. Prove your answer by preparing a summary contribution margin income statement at the breakeven level of sales. Show only two categories of expenses: variable and fixed.
2. Compute Pepperpike Coffee's margin of safety in dollars.
3. Use Pepperpike Coffee's operating leverage factor to determine its new operating income if sales volume increases 15%. Prove your results using the contribution margin income statement format. Assume that sales mix remains unchanged.

PROBLEMS Group B

P7-70B Find missing data in CVP relationships *(Learning Objectives 1 & 2)*

The budgets of four companies yield the following information:

	Company			
	Q	R	S	T
Target sales	$687,500	$480,000	$171,875	$ ______
Variable expenses	192,500	______	______	156,000
Fixed expenses	______	165,000	88,000	______
Operating income (loss)	$ 90,000	$ ______	$ ______	$131,000
Units sold	______	110,000	11,000	16,000
Contribution margin per unit	$ 6.60	______	$ 10.00	$ 39.00
Contribution margin ratio	______	0.55	______	______

Requirements

1. Fill in the blanks for each company.
2. Compute breakeven, in sales dollars, for each company. Which company has the lowest breakeven point in sales dollars? What causes the low breakeven point?

P7-71B Find breakeven and target profit and prepare income statements *(Learning Objectives 1 & 2)*

A traveling production of *Shrek* performs each year. The average show sells 1,000 tickets at $45 per ticket. There are 120 shows a year. The show has a cast of 45, each earning an average of $300 per show. The cast is paid only after each show. The other variable expense is program printing expenses of $9 per guest. Annual fixed expenses total $787,500.

Requirements

1. Compute revenue and variable expenses for each show.
2. Compute the number of shows needed annually to break even.
3. Compute the number of shows needed annually to earn a profit of $3,262,500. Is this goal realistic? Give your reason.
4. Prepare Shrek's contribution margin income statement for 120 shows each year. Report only two categories of expenses: variable and fixed.

P7-72B Comprehensive CVP problem *(Learning Objectives 1, 2, & 5)*

College Calendars imprints calendars with college names. The company has fixed expenses of $1,115,000 each month plus variable expenses of $6.00 per carton of calendars. Of the variable expense, 67% is Cost of Goods Sold, while the remaining 33% relates to variable operating expenses. College Calendars sells each carton of calendars for $18.50.

Requirements

1. Compute the number of cartons of calendars that College Calendars must sell each month to break even.
2. Compute the dollar amount of monthly sales College Calendars needs in order to earn $330,000 in operating income (round the contribution margin ratio to two decimal places).
3. Prepare College Calendar's contribution margin income statement for June for sales of 455,000 cartons of calendars.
4. What is June's margin of safety (in dollars)? What is the operating leverage factor at this level of sales?
5. By what percentage will operating income change if July's sales volume is 11% higher? Prove your answer.

P7-73B Compute breakeven, prepare CVP graph, and respond to change *(Learning Objectives 1, 2, & 3)*

Dolson Investors is opening an office in Stow, Ohio. Fixed monthly costs are office rent ($2,900), depreciation on office furniture ($330), utilities ($280), special telephone lines ($690), a connection with an online brokerage service ($700), and the salary of a financial planner ($2,700). Variable expenses include payments to the financial planner (10% of revenue), advertising (5% of revenue), supplies and postage (2% of revenue), and usage fees for the telephone lines and computerized brokerage service (3% of revenue).

Requirements

1. Compute the investment firm's breakeven revenue in dollars. If the average trade leads to $475 in revenue for Dolson Investors, how many trades must be made to break even?
2. Compute dollar revenues needed to earn monthly operating income of $3,040.
3. Graph Dolson's CVP relationships. Assume that an average trade leads to $475 in revenue for Dolson Investors. Show the breakeven point, sales revenue line, fixed expense line, total expense line, operating loss area, operating income area, and sales in units (trades) and dollars when monthly operating income of $3,040 is earned. The graph should range from 0 to 40 units (trades).
4. Assume that the average revenue Dolson Investors earns decreases to $375 per trade. How does this affect the breakeven point in number of trades?

P7-74B CVP analysis at a multiproduct firm *(Learning Objectives 4 & 5)*

The contribution margin income statement of Hemingway Coffee for February follows:

Hemingway Coffee Contribution Margin Income Statement For the Month Ended February 29		
Sales revenue		$94,000
Variable expenses:		
Cost of goods sold	$30,000	
Marketing expense	8,000	
General and administrative expense	2,000	40,000
Contribution margin		$54,000
Fixed expenses:		
Marketing expense	$24,750	
General and administrative expense	5,250	30,000
Operating income		$24,000

Hemingway Coffee sells three small coffees for every large coffee. A small coffee sells for $2.00, with a variable expense of $1.00. A large coffee sells for $4.00, with a variable expense of $2.00.

Requirements

1. Determine Hemingway Coffee's monthly breakeven point in numbers of small coffees and large coffees. Prove your answer by preparing a summary contribution margin income statement at the breakeven level of sales. Show only two categories of expenses: variable and fixed.
2. Compute Hemingway Coffee's margin of safety in dollars.
3. Use Hemingway Coffee's operating leverage factor to determine its new operating income if sales volume increases by 15%. Prove your results using the contribution margin income statement format. Assume the sales mix remains unchanged.

CRITICAL THINKING

Discussion & Analysis

A7-75 Discussion Questions

1. Define breakeven point. Why is the breakeven point important to managers?
2. Describe four different ways cost-volume-profit analysis could be useful to management.
3. The purchasing manager for Rockwell Fashion Bags has been able to purchase the material for its signature handbags for $2 less per bag. Keeping everything else the same, what effect would this reduction in material cost have on the breakeven point for Rockwell Fashion Bags? Now assume that the sales manager decides to reduce the selling price of each handbag by $2. What would the net effect of both of these changes be on the breakeven point in units for Rockwell Fashion Bags?
4. Describe three ways that cost-volume-profit concepts could be used by a service organization.
5. "Breakeven analysis isn't very useful to a company because companies need to do more than break even to survive in the long run." Explain why you agree or disagree with this statement.
6. What conditions must be met for cost-volume-profit analysis to be accurate?
7. Why is it necessary to calculate a weighted-average contribution margin ratio for a multi-product company when calculating the breakeven point for that company? Why can't all of the products' contribution margin ratios just be added together and averaged?
8. Is the contribution margin ratio of a grocery store likely to be higher or lower than that of a plastics manufacturer? Explain the difference in cost structure between a grocery store and a plastics manufacturer. How does the cost structure difference impact operating risk?
9. Alston Jewelry had sales revenues last year of $2.4 million, while its breakeven point (in dollars) was $2.2 million. What was Alston Jewelry's margin of safety in dollars? What does the term margin of safety mean? What can you discern about Alston Jewelry from its margin of safety?
10. Rondell Pharmacy is considering switching to the use of robots to fill prescriptions that consist of oral solids or medications in pill form. The robots will assist the human pharmacists and will reduce the number of human pharmacy workers needed. This change is expected to reduce the number of prescription filling errors, to reduce the customer's wait time, and to reduce the total overall costs. How does the use of the robots affect Rondell Pharmacy's cost structure? Explain the impact of this switch to robotics on Rondell Pharmacy's operating risk.
11. Suppose a company can replace the packing material it currently uses with a biodegradable packing material. The company believes this move to biodegradable packing materials will be well-received by the general public. However, the biodegradable packing materials are more expensive than the current packing materials and the contribution margin ratios of the related products will drop. What are the arguments for the company to use the biodegradable packing materials? What are the arguments for the company to not use the biodegradable materials? What do you think the company should do?
12. How can CVP techniques be used in supporting a company's sustainability efforts? Conversely, how might CVP be a barrier to sustainability efforts?

Application & Analysis

A7-76 CVP for a Product

Select one product that you could make yourself. Examples of possible products could be cookies, birdhouses, jewelry, or custom t-shirts. Assume that you have decided to start a small business producing and selling this product. You will be applying the concepts of cost-volume-profit analysis to this potential venture.

Basic Discussion Questions

1. Describe your product. What market are you targeting this product for? What price will you sell your product for? Make projections of your sales in units over each of the upcoming five years.
2. Make a detailed list of all of the materials needed to make your product. Include quantities needed of each material. Also include the cost of the material on a per-unit basis.
3. Make a list of all of the equipment you will need to make your product. Estimate the cost of each piece of equipment that you will need.
4. Make a list of all other expenses that would be needed to create your product. Examples of other expenses would be rent, utilities, and insurance. Estimate the cost of each of these expenses per year.
5. Now classify all of the expenses you have listed as being either fixed or variable. For mixed expenses, separate the expense into the fixed component and the variable component.
6. Calculate how many units of your product you will need to sell to break even in each of the five years you have projected.
7. Calculate the margin of safety in units for each of the five years in your projection.
8. Now decide how much you would like to make in before-tax operating income (target profit) in each of the upcoming five years. Calculate how many units you would need to sell in each of the upcoming years to meet these target profit levels.
9. How realistic is your potential venture? Do you think you would be able to break even in each of the projected five years? How risky is your venture (use the margin of safety to help answer this question). Do you think your target profits are achievable?

Decision Cases

A7-77 Determine the feasibility of a business plan *(Learning Objective 2)*

Brian and Nui Soon live in Macon, Georgia. Two years ago, they visited Thailand. Nui, a professional chef, was impressed with the cooking methods and the spices used in the Thai food. Macon does not have a Thai restaurant, and the Soons are contemplating opening one. Nui would supervise the cooking, and Brian would leave his current job to be the maître d'. The restaurant would serve dinner Tuesday through Saturday.

Brian has noticed a restaurant for lease. The restaurant has seven tables, each of which can seat four. Tables can be moved together for a large party. Nui is planning two seatings per evening, and the restaurant will be open 50 weeks per year.

The Soons have drawn up the following estimates:

Average revenue, including beverages and dessert	$ 40 per meal
Average cost of the food	$ 12 per meal
Chef's and dishwasher's salaries	$50,400 per *year*
Rent (premises, equipment)	$ 4,000 per month
Cleaning (linen and premises)	$ 800 per month
Replacement of dishes, cutlery, glasses	$ 300 per month
Utilities, advertising, telephone	$ 1,900 per month

Requirement

Compute *annual* breakeven number of meals and sales revenue for the restaurant. Also, compute the number of meals and the amount of sales revenue needed to earn operating income of $75,600 for the year. How many meals must the Soons serve each night to earn their target income of $75,600? Should the couple open the restaurant? Support your answer.

Ethical Issue

A7-78 Ethical dilemma with CVP analysis error *(Learning Objective 2)*

You have just begun your summer internship at Tmedic. The company supplies sterilized surgical instruments for physicians. To expand sales, Tmedic is considering paying a commission to its sales force. The controller, Jane Hewitt, asks you to compute 1) the new breakeven sales figure and 2) the operating profit if sales increase 15% under the new sales commission plan. She thinks you can handle this task because you learned CVP analysis in your accounting class.

You spend the next day collecting information from the accounting records, performing the analysis, and writing a memo to explain the results. The company president is pleased with your memo. You report that the new sales commission plan will lead to a significant increase in operating income and only a small increase in breakeven sales.

The following week, you realize that you made an error in the CVP analysis. You overlooked the sales personnel's $2,500 monthly salaries, and you did not include this fixed marketing expense in your computations. You are not sure what to do. If you tell Hewitt of your mistake, she will have to tell the president. In this case, you are afraid Tmedic might not offer you permanent employment after your internship.

Requirements

1. How would your error affect breakeven sales and operating income under the proposed sales commission plan? Could this cause the president to reject the sales commission proposal?
2. Consider your ethical responsibilities. Is there a difference between (a) initially making an error and (b) subsequently failing to inform the controller?
3. Suppose you tell Hewitt of the error in your analysis. Why might the consequences not be as bad as you fear? Should Hewitt take any responsibility for your error? What could Hewitt have done differently?
4. After considering all of the factors, should you inform Hewitt or simply keep quiet?

Team Project

A7-79 Advertising campaign and production level decisions *(Learning Objectives 1 & 3)*

EZPAK Manufacturing produces filament packaging tape. In 2012, EZPAK Manufacturing produced and sold 15 million rolls of tape. The company has recently expanded its capacity, so it can now produce up to 30 million rolls per year. EZPAK Manufacturing's accounting records show the following results from 2012:

Sale price per roll	$ 3.00
Variable manufacturing expenses per roll	$ 2.00
Variable marketing and administrative expenses per roll	$ 0.50
Total fixed manufacturing overhead costs	$8,400,000
Total fixed marketing and administrative expenses	$ 600,000
Sales	15 million rolls
Production	15 million rolls

There were no beginning or ending inventories in 2012.

In January 2013, EZPAK Manufacturing hired a new president, Kevin McDaniel. McDaniel has a one-year contract specifying that he will be paid 10% of EZPAK Manufacturing's 2013 operating income (based on traditional absorption costing) instead of a salary. In 2013, McDaniel must make two major decisions:

1. Should EZPAK Manufacturing undertake a major advertising campaign? This campaign would raise sales to 25 million rolls. This is the maximum level of sales that EZPAK Manufacturing can expect to make in the near future. The ad campaign would add an additional $3.5 million in marketing and administrative costs. Without the campaign, sales will be 15 million rolls.
2. How many rolls of tape will EZPAK Manufacturing produce?

At the end of the year, EZPAK Manufacturing's board of directors will evaluate McDaniel's performance and decide whether to offer him a contract for the following year.

Requirements

Within your group form two subgroups. The first subgroup assumes the role of Kevin McDaniel, EZPAK Manufacturing's new president. The second subgroup assumes the role of EZPAK Manufacturing's board of directors. McDaniel will meet with the board of directors shortly after the end of 2013 to decide whether he will remain at EZPAK Manufacturing. Most of your effort should be devoted to advance preparation for this meeting. Each subgroup should meet separately to prepare for the meeting between the board and McDaniel. (*Hint:* Keep computations [other than per-unit amounts] in millions.)

Kevin McDaniel should do the following:

1. Compute EZPAK Manufacturing's 2012 operating income.
2. Decide whether to adopt the advertising campaign by calculating the projected increase in operating income from the advertising campaign. Do not include the executive bonus in this calculation. Prepare a memo to the board of directors explaining this decision.

3. Assume that EZPAK Manufacturing adopts the advertising campaign. Decide how many rolls of tape to produce in 2013. Assume that no safety stock is considered necessary to EZPAK's business.
4. Given your response to Question 3, prepare an absorption costing income statement for the year ended December 31, 2013, ending with operating income before bonus. Then compute your bonus separately. The variable cost per unit and the total fixed expenses (with the exception of the advertising campaign) remain the same as in 2012. Give this income statement and your bonus computation to the board of directors as soon as possible (before your meeting with the board).
5. Decide whether you want to remain at EZPAK Manufacturing for another year. You currently have an offer from another company. The contract with the other company is identical to the one you currently have with EZPAK Manufacturing—you will be paid 10% of absorption costing operating income instead of a salary.

The board of directors should do the following:

1. Compute EZPAK Manufacturing's 2012 operating income.
2. Determine whether EZPAK Manufacturing should adopt the advertising campaign by calculating the projected increase in operating income from the advertising campaign. Do not include the executive bonus in this calculation.
3. Determine how many rolls of tape EZPAK Manufacturing should produce in 2013. Assume that no safety stock is considered necessary to EZPAK's business.
4. Evaluate McDaniel's performance based on his decisions and the information he provided to the board. (*Hint:* You may want to prepare a variable costing income statement.)
5. Evaluate the contract's bonus provision. Are you satisfied with this provision? If so, explain why. If not, recommend how it should be changed.

After McDaniel has given the board his memo and income statement and after the board has had a chance to evaluate McDaniel's performance, McDaniel and the board should meet. The purpose of the meeting is to decide whether it is in everyone's mutual interest for McDaniel to remain with EZPAK Manufacturing and, if so, the terms of the contract EZPAK Manufacturing will offer McDaniel.

Relevant Costs for Short-Term Decisions

Learning Objectives

- **1** Describe and identify information relevant to short-term business decisions
- **2** Decide whether to accept a special order
- **3** Describe and apply different approaches to pricing
- **4** Decide whether to discontinue a product, department, or store
- **5** Factor resource constraints into product mix decisions
- **6** Analyze outsourcing (make or buy) decisions
- **7** Decide whether to sell a product "as is" or process it further

Most Major Airlines, including Delta,

outsource work. Delta estimates it has been able to cut maintenance costs by $240 million over a five-year period by outsourcing much of its airplane maintenance to Miami- and Canadian-based firms. Delta also has a ten-year arrangement to outsource its European finance and accounting functions to Accenture and a seven-year contract to outsource much of its domestic human resource functions to ACS. But why would Delta outsource so much of its work? Primarily to cut costs. Due to rising fuel costs and cut-throat competition, airlines need to find ways to cut costs, and one way is through outsourcing. However, costs are not everything. Even though Delta used to save $25 million per year by outsourcing its call center work to India, customer dissatisfaction prompted Delta to bring its call center work back to the U.S. in 2009.

© Bayne Stanley / Alamy

Outsourcing also enables companies to concentrate on their core competencies—the operating activities at which they excel. When companies focus on just their core competencies, they often outsource the activities that do not give them a competitive advantage. Delta's strategy is to focus on its core competency—flying passengers—and outsource other operating activities, such as reservations, heavy airplane maintenance, finance, and human resource functions to companies that excel at those activities. By doing so, Delta not only saves money, but also makes use of the best practices offered by world-class firms.

Sources:
Harry Weber, "Delta no longer sending calls to India", *USA Today*, April 17, 2009. www.usatoday.com/travel/flights/2009-04-17-delta-outsourcing_N.htm
www.allbusiness.com, "Outsourcing of HR Functions to Regain Momentum in 2008, According to Everest Research Institute", Nov. 2, 2007
www.newratings.com, "Delta AirLines to reduce costs through maintenance outsourcing", March 30, 2005
www.accenture.com, "Helping Delta Air Lines Achieve High Performance Through Financial Outsourcing", 2006

In the last chapter, we saw how managers use cost behavior to determine the company's breakeven point and to estimate the sales volume needed to achieve target profits. In this chapter, we'll see how managers use their knowledge of cost behavior to make six special business decisions, such as whether to outsource operating activities. The decisions we'll discuss in this chapter usually pertain to short periods of time, so managers do not need to worry about the time value of money. In other words, they do not need to compute the present value of the revenues and expenses relating to the decision. In Chapter 12, we will discuss longer-term decisions (such as buying equipment and undertaking plant expansions) in which the time value of money becomes important. Before we look at the six business decisions in detail, let's consider a manager's decision-making process and the information managers need to evaluate their options.

How do Managers Make Decisions?

Exhibit 8-1 illustrates how managers decide among alternative courses of action. Management accountants help gather and analyze *relevant information* to compare alternatives. Management accountants also help with the follow-up: comparing the actual results of a decision to those originally anticipated. This feedback helps management as it faces similar types of decisions in the future. It also helps management adjust current operations if actual results of its decision are markedly different from those anticipated.

EXHIBIT 8-1 How Managers Make Decisions

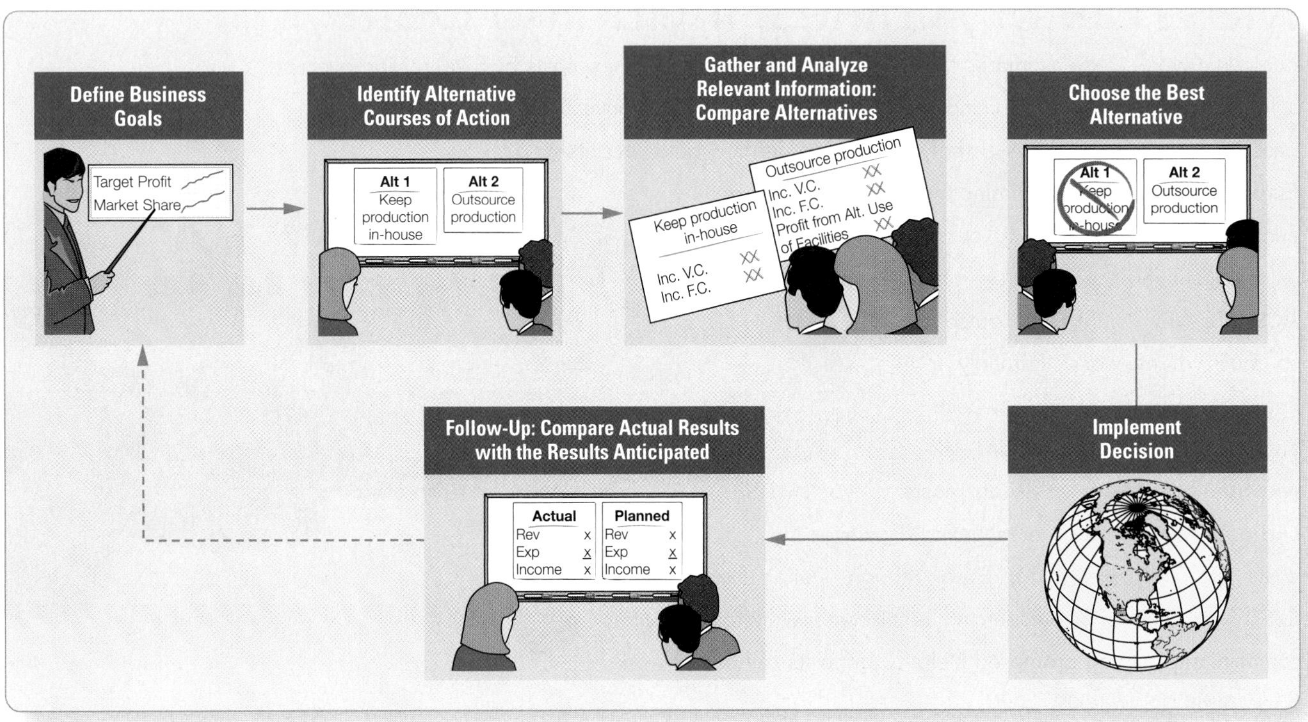

Relevant Information

1 Describe and identify information relevant to short-term business decisions

When managers make decisions, they focus on costs and revenues that are relevant to the decisions. Exhibit 8-2 shows that **relevant information**

1. is expected *future* data.
2. *differs* among alternatives.

Recall our discussion of relevant costs in Chapter 2. In deciding whether to purchase a Toyota Corolla or Nissan Sentra, the cost of the car, the sales tax, and the insurance premium are relevant because these costs

- are incurred in the *future* (after you decide to buy the car).
- *differ between alternatives* (each car has a different invoice price, sales tax, and insurance premium).

These costs are *relevant* because they affect your decision of which car to purchase.

Irrelevant costs are costs that *do not* affect your decision. For example, because the Corolla and Sentra both have similar fuel efficiency and maintenance ratings, we do not expect the car operating costs to differ between alternatives. Because these costs do not differ, they do not affect your decision. In other words, they are *irrelevant* to the decision. Similarly, the cost of a campus parking sticker is also irrelevant because the sticker costs the same whether you buy the Sentra or the Corolla.

Sunk costs are also irrelevant to your decision. Sunk costs are costs that were incurred in the *past* and cannot be changed regardless of which future action is taken. Perhaps you

EXHIBIT 8-2 Relevant Information

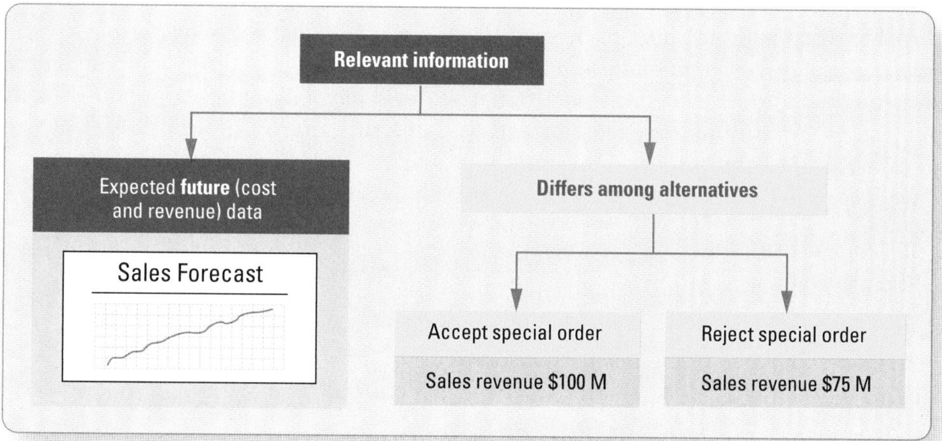

want to trade in your current truck when you buy your new car. The amount you paid for the truck—which you bought for $15,000 a year ago—is a sunk cost. In fact, it doesn't matter whether you paid $15,000 or $50,000—it's still a sunk cost. No decision made *now* can alter the past. You already bought the truck, so *the price you paid for it is a sunk cost.* All you can do *now* is keep the truck, trade it in, or sell it for the best price you can get, even if that price is substantially less than what you originally paid for the truck.

What *is* relevant is what you can get for your truck in the future. Suppose the Nissan dealership offers you $8,000 for your truck. The Toyota dealership offers you $10,000. Because the amounts differ and the transaction will take place in the future, the trade-in value is relevant to your decision.

The same principle applies to all situations—*only relevant data affect decisions.*

Relevant Nonfinancial Information

Nonfinancial, or qualitative factors, also play a role in managers' decisions. For example, closing manufacturing plants or laying off employees can seriously hurt the local community and employee morale. Outsourcing can reduce control over delivery time and product quality. Offering discounted prices to select customers can upset regular customers and tempt them to take their business elsewhere. Managers must think through the likely quantitative *and* qualitative effects of their decisions.

Managers who ignore qualitative factors can make serious mistakes. For example, the City of Nottingham, England, spent $1.6 million on 215 solar-powered parking meters after seeing how well the parking meters worked in countries along the Mediterranean Sea. However, the city did not adequately consider that British skies are typically overcast. The result? The meters didn't always work because of the lack of sunlight. The city *lost* money because people ended up parking for free! Relevant qualitative information has the same characteristics as relevant financial information: The qualitative factor occurs in the *future,* and it *differs* between alternatives. The amount of *future* sunshine required *differed* between alternatives: The mechanical meters didn't require any sunshine, but the solar-powered meters needed a great deal of sunshine.

Likewise, in deciding between the Corolla and Sentra, you will likely consider qualitative factors that differ between the cars (legroom, trunk capacity, dashboard design, and so forth) before making your final decision. Since you must live with these factors in the future, they become relevant to your decision.

Why is this important?

"The accounting information used to make **business decisions** in this chapter considers only one factor: **profitability**. However in real life, managers should consider **many** more **factors**, including the effect of the decision on **employees**, the local **community**, and the **environment**."

Keys to Making Short-Term Special Decisions

Our approach to making short-term special decisions is called the *relevant information approach* or the *incremental analysis approach*. Instead of looking at the company's *entire* income statement under each decision alternative, we'll just look at how operating income would *change or differ* under each alternative. Using this approach, we'll leave out irrelevant information—the costs and revenues that won't differ between alternatives.

We'll consider six kinds of decisions in this chapter:

1. Special sales orders
2. Pricing
3. Discontinuing products, departments, or stores
4. Product mix when resources are constrained
5. Outsourcing (make or buy)
6. Selling as is or processing further

As you study these decisions, keep in mind the two keys in analyzing short-term special business decisions shown in Exhibit 8-3:

1. **Focus on relevant revenues, costs, and profits.** Irrelevant information only clouds the picture and creates information overload. That's why we'll use the incremental analysis approach.
2. **Use a contribution margin approach that separates variable costs from fixed costs.** Because fixed costs and variable costs behave differently, they must be analyzed separately. Traditional (absorption costing) income statements, which blend fixed and variable costs, can mislead managers. Contribution margin income statements, which isolate costs by behavior (variable or fixed), help managers gather the cost-behavior information they need. Recall from Chapter 6 that unit manufacturing costs based on absorption costing are mixed costs, so they can also mislead managers. That's why variable costing is often better for decision-making purposes. If you use unit manufacturing costs in your analysis, make sure you separate the cost's fixed and variable components first.

Keep in mind that every business decision is unique. What might be a relevant cost in one decision might not be relevant in another decision. Each unique business decision needs to be assessed to determine what pieces of information are relevant. Just because a piece of information is relevant in one decision doesn't mean it will be relevant in the next. Because of this, accountants often follow the adage that different costs are used for different purposes.

EXHIBIT 8-3 Two Keys to Making Short-Term Special Decisions

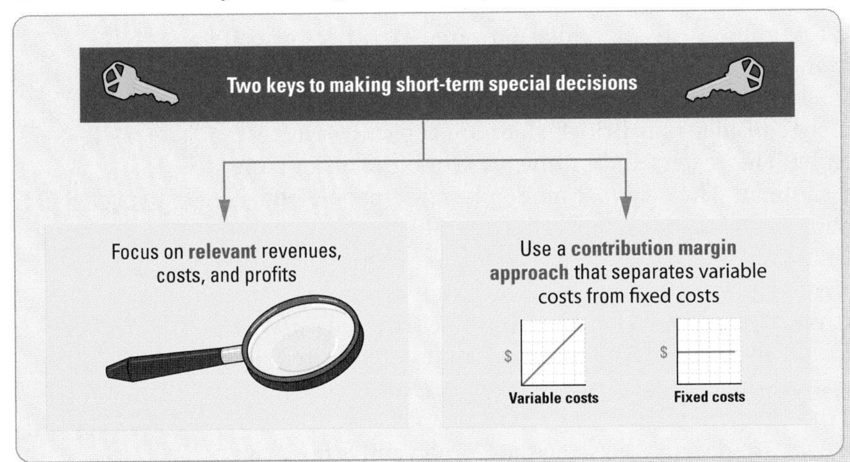

Sustainability and Short-Term Business Decisions

For companies that embrace sustainability and the triple bottom line, almost every decision will be viewed through the lens of its impact on people and the planet, as well as profitability. For example, let's look at Timberland, a company with $1.4 billion in annual revenue that specializes in outdoor shoes and clothing. Timberland is intentionally "focusing the resources, energy and profits of a publicly traded...company to combat social ills, help the environment, and improve conditions of laborers around the globe."[1]

In the words of Jeffrey Swartz, President and CEO, "Timberland believes, and has always believed, that we have a responsibility to help effect change in the communities where we work and live." The company is committed to "doing well and doing good". But how does the company work toward such lofty goals? Here are a few examples:[2]

- Employees are given up to 40 hours of paid leave each year to perform community service work.
- For the last 13 years, the company has sponsored an annual day-long employee service event. In 2010 alone, over 4,800 employees participated, generating over 35,000 hours of service to local community projects.
- The company's strict "Code of Conduct" ensures that domestic and overseas workers are employed at fair wage rates, work reasonable shifts, and work in safe factories.
- The company is committed to being environmentally conscious in the production of its products. By the end of 2012, the company hopes to label all of its footwear with a "Green Index" rating system. The index will educate consumers about the product's climate impact, chemicals used, and materials used (percentage of organic, recycled, or renewable materials used).
- The company is committed to planting 5 million trees in the next 5 years in regions of Haiti and China suffering from the effects of deforestation. Acting as carbon offsets, these trees will also help the company achieve its goal of becoming carbon neutral in all operations under its control.
- The company has earned LEED (Leadership in Energy and Environmental Design) certification on several of its retail outlets.
- The company uses solar panels on its California distribution center to provide 60% of its energy. This $3.5 million investment was made, even though cost models showed it might take 20 years for the investment to earn a return.
- In 2010, Timberland ranked #2 on Climate Count's list of companies making aggressive strides in fighting climate change.

These initiatives, as well as others, are costly. The company's financial performance, while profitable, has lagged the S&P 500 Footwear and Apparel Index over the past 5 years. However, the company does not measure its success strictly in terms of stock market returns. Rather, it adheres to the notion of the triple bottom line. Perhaps as a result, Timberland has been named one of *Fortune* magazine's "100 Best Companies to Work For" for 10 consecutive years.

See Exercises E8-17A and E8-31B

How do Managers Make Special Order and Regular Pricing Decisions?

2 Decide whether to accept a special order

We'll start our discussion on the six business decisions by looking at special sales order decisions and regular pricing decisions. In the past, managers did not consider pricing to be a short-term decision. However, product life cycles are shrinking in most industries. Companies often sell products for only a few months before replacing them with an

[1]Reingold, Jennifer, "Walking the Walk," *Fast Company*, November, 2005. http://www.fastcompany.com/magazine/100/timberland.html?page=0%2C0
[2]Timberland.com

updated model. The clothing and technology industries have always had short life cycles. Even auto and housing styles change frequently. Pricing has become a shorter-term decision than it was in the past.

Let's examine a special sales order in detail; then we will discuss regular pricing decisions.

Special Order Decisions

A special order occurs when a customer requests a one-time order at a *reduced* sales price. Often, these special orders are for large quantities. Before agreeing to the special deal, management must consider the questions shown in Exhibit 8-4.

EXHIBIT 8-4 Special Order Considerations

- Do we have excess capacity available to fill this order?
- Will the reduced sales price be high enough to cover the *incremental* costs of filling the order (the variable costs of filling the order and any additional fixed costs)?
- Will the special order affect regular sales in the long run?

First, managers must consider available capacity. If the company is already making as many units as possible and selling them all at its *regular* sales price, it wouldn't make sense to fill a special order at a *reduced* sales price. Therefore, available excess capacity is a necessity for accepting a special order. This is true for service firms (law firms, caterers, and so forth) as well as manufacturers.

Second, managers need to consider whether the special reduced sales price is high enough to cover the incremental costs of filling the order. The special price *must* exceed the variable costs of filling the order or the company will lose money on the deal. In other words, the special order must provide a positive contribution margin.

Next, the company must consider fixed costs. If the company has excess capacity, fixed costs probably won't be affected by producing more units (or delivering more service). However, in some cases, management may need to hire a consultant or incur some other fixed cost to fill the special order. If so, management will need to consider whether the special sales price is high enough to generate a positive contribution margin *and* cover the additional fixed costs.

Finally, managers need to consider whether the special order will affect regular sales in the long run. Will regular customers find out about the special order and demand a lower price or take their business elsewhere? Will the special order customer come back *again and again*, asking for the same reduced price? Will the special order price start a price war with competitors? Managers must gamble that the answers to these questions are "no" or consider how customers will respond. Managers may decide that any profit from the special sales order is not worth these risks.

Special Order Example

Let's consider a special sales order example. Suppose ACDelco sells oil filters for $3.20 each. Assume that a mail-order company has offered ACDelco $35,000 for 20,000 oil filters, or $1.75 per filter ($35,000 ÷ 20,000 = $1.75). This sale will

- use manufacturing capacity that would otherwise be idle.
- not change fixed costs.
- not require any variable marketing or administrative expenses.
- not affect regular sales.

We have addressed every consideration except one: Is the special sales price of $1.75 high enough to cover the incremental costs of filling the order. Let's take a look.

Exhibit 8-5 shows a contribution margin income statement for the current volume of oil filters sold (250,000 units). As discussed in Chapters 6 and 7, this format is much better for decision making than a traditional income statement format because it shows variable and fixed costs separately. Managers can easily see the variable cost of *manufacturing* each oil filter ($1.20) the variable cost of *selling* each oil filter ($0.30).

EXHIBIT 8-5 Contribution Margin Income Statement for Current Volume of Oil Filters

Contribution Margin Income Statement	Per Unit	Total (current volume of 250,000)
Sales revenue (at normal sales price)	$3.20	$800,000
Less variable expenses:		
Variable manufacturing costs (DM, DL, and Variable MOH)	1.20	300,000
Variable marketing and administrative costs	0.30	75,000
Contribution margin	$1.70	$425,000
Less fixed expenses:		
Fixed manufacturing costs (Fixed MOH)		200,000
Fixed marketing and administrative costs		125,000
Operating Income		$100,000

We'll use this information to determine whether ACDelco should accept the special order. Exhibit 8-6 illustrates an incremental analysis in which the revenue associated with the order is compared against the additional costs that will be incurred to fill the order. The analysis shows that the special order sales price of $1.75 is high enough to cover all incremental costs, and will provide the company with an additional $11,000 in operating income. Therefore, the order should be accepted unless managers have reason to suspect accepting the order would adversely affect regular sales in the long-run.

EXHIBIT 8-6 Incremental Analysis of Special Sales Order

Incremental Analysis for Special Order	Per Unit	Total Special Order (20,000 units)
Revenue from special order (at special order price)	$1.75	$35,000
Less variable expenses associated with the order:		
Variable manufacturing costs (DM, DL, and Variable MOH)	1.20	24,000
Contribution margin from the special order	$0.55	$11,000
Less additional fixed expenses associated with the order: (none in this example)		0
Increase in operating income from the special order		$11,000

Remember that in this particular example, ACDelco doesn't expect to incur any variable marketing or administrative costs associated with the special order. Therefore, they weren't included in Exhibit 8-6. However, this won't always be the case. Many times, companies will incur variable operating expenses on special orders, such as freight-out or sales commissions. *Only those incremental costs associated with the order should be included in the analysis.*

As shown in Exhibit 8-6, managers also need to consider any incremental fixed costs that will be incurred as a result of the order. Since the company has excess capacity with which to produce this order, fixed manufacturing overhead costs are not expected to change. Likewise, fixed selling and administrative expenses are not expected to change. Therefore, Exhibit 8-6 shows zero incremental fixed costs as a result of this order. However, if a company expects to incur a new fixed cost as a result of the order, the additional fixed cost needs to be included in the analysis.

Notice that the analysis follows the two keys to making short-term special business decisions discussed earlier: (1) focus on relevant data (revenues and costs that *will change* if ACDelco accepts the special order) and (2) use a contribution margin approach that separates variable costs from fixed costs.

To summarize, for special sales orders, the decision rule is as follows:

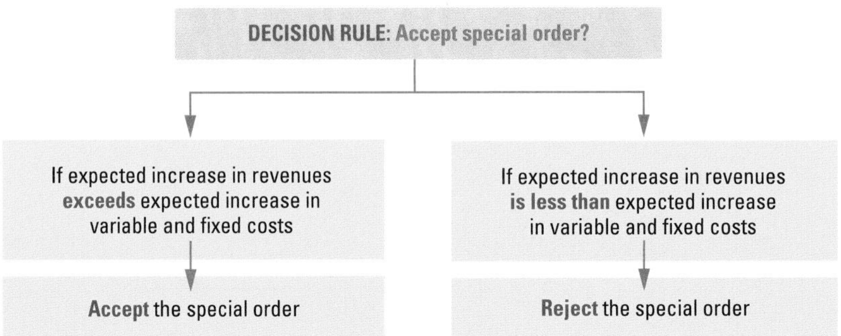

Pitfall to Avoid on Special Order Decisions

One of the most common mistakes managers make when analyzing special orders is to base their decision on the unit cost provided by absorption costing. Recall from Chapter 6 that under absorption costing, all manufacturing costs, including fixed MOH, are "absorbed" into the unit cost of the product. Absorption costing was used when we studied job costing and process costing in Chapters 3, 4, and 5 because GAAP requires it for external financial reporting purposes. Using the figures found in Exhibit 8-5, we see that the unit cost of each oil filter under absorption costing is $2.00:

Inventoriable Product Cost Using Absorption Costing	Unit Cost
Variable manufacturing costs (DM, DL, Variable MOH) per unit	$1.20
Fixed manufacturing costs (Fixed MOH) per unit at current volume	
$200,000 ÷ 250,000 units	0.80
Cost per unit using absorption costing	$2.00

The $2.00 unit cost, which GAAP mandates for inventory and cost of goods sold valuation, is *not* a good basis for making a special order decision. Why? Because it is a mixed cost, which includes both fixed and variable components. Since there is excess capacity in the plant, fixed MOH will remain $200,000 in total, regardless of whether ACDelco accepts the special order. Producing 20,000 more oil filters will *not* increase total fixed costs by $0.80 per unit. The incremental cost incurred to make each additional filter is the variable cost of $1.20 per unit, not $2.00 per unit.

STOP & THINK

In addition to the facts presented in the text, assume ACDelco will pay its sales staff a commission of $0.15 per unit on the special order. Also assume ACDelco will incur an additional $2,000 in legal fees to draw up the contract for the order. Given these additional facts, should ACDelco still accept the special order?

Answer: The special order sales price ($1.75) is still higher than the variable costs associated with filling the order ($1.20 + $0.15). As a result, the special order for 20,000 units will provide a contribution margin of $0.40 per unit, or $8,000 in total. By subtracting the incremental fixed expenses associated with the special order ($2,000) from the contribution margin, we see that the special order will increase the company's operating income by $6,000. Therefore, ACDelco should still accept the order.

Consider this: Since the special order price of $1.75 is less than the absorption cost of $2.00, a manager falling into this decision pitfall would have turned down the special order, thinking that the company would lose money on it. In reality, by not accepting the special order, this manager just cost the company $11,000 in additional profit.

Regular Pricing Decisions

3 Describe and apply different approaches to pricing

In the special order decision, ACDelco decided to sell a limited quantity of oil filters for $1.75 each even though the normal price was $3.20 per unit. But how did ACDelco decide to set its regular price at $3.20 per filter? Exhibit 8-7 shows that managers start with three basic questions when setting regular prices for their products or services.

EXHIBIT 8-7 Regular Pricing Considerations

- What is our target profit?
- How much will customers pay?
- Are we a price-taker or a price-setter for this product?

The answers to these questions are often complex and ever-changing. Stockholders expect the company to achieve certain profits. Economic conditions, historical company earnings, industry risk, competition, and new business developments all affect the level of profit that stockholders expect. Stockholders usually tie their profit expectations to the amount of assets invested in the company. For example, stockholders may expect a 10% annual return on their investment. A company's stock price tends to decline if the company does not meet target profits, so managers must keep costs low while generating enough revenue to meet target profits.

This leads to the second question: How much will customers pay? Managers cannot set prices above what customers are willing to pay or sales will decline. The amount customers will pay depends on the competition, the product's uniqueness, the effectiveness of marketing campaigns, general economic conditions, and so forth.

To address the third pricing question, imagine a continuum with price-takers at one end and price-setters at the other end. A company's products and services fall somewhere along this continuum, shown in Exhibit 8-8. Companies are price-takers when they have little or no control over the prices of their products or services. This occurs when their products and services are *not* unique or when competition is heavy. Examples include food commodities (milk and corn), natural resources (oil and lumber), and generic consumer products and services (paper towels, dry cleaning, and banking).

EXHIBIT 8-8 Price-Takers Versus Price-Setters

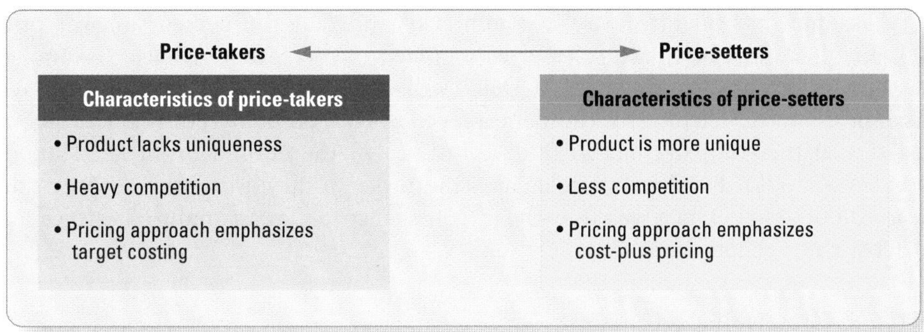

Companies are price-setters when they have more control over pricing—in other words, they can "set" prices to some extent. Companies are price-setters when their products are unique, which results in less competition. Unique products such as original art and jewelry, specially manufactured machinery, patented perfume scents, and custom-made furniture can command higher prices.

> **Why is this important?**
> "Both **branding** and product **differentiation** give managers more control over pricing. Without such features, a **company** must often settle for selling its **product** at the same price as its competitors."

Obviously, managers would rather be price-setters than price-takers. To gain more control over pricing, companies try to differentiate their products. They want to make their products unique in terms of features, service, or quality—or at least make you *think* their product is unique or somehow better even if it isn't. How do they do this? Primarily through advertising. Consider Nike's tennis shoes, Starbucks' coffee, Hallmark's wrapping paper, Nexus' shampoo, Tylenol's acetaminophen, General Mills' cereal, Capital One's credit cards, Shell's gas, Abercrombie and Fitch's jeans—the list goes on and on. Are these products really better or significantly different from their lower-priced competitors? Possibly. If these companies can make you think so, they've gained more control over their pricing because you are willing to pay *more* for their products or services. The downside? These companies must charge higher prices or sell more just to cover their advertising costs.

A company's approach to pricing depends on whether its product or service is on the price-taking or price-setting side of the spectrum. Price-takers emphasize a target costing approach. Price-setters emphasize a cost-plus pricing approach. Keep in mind that many products fall somewhere along the continuum. Therefore, managers tend to use both approaches to some extent. We'll now discuss each approach in turn.

Target Costing

When a company is a price-taker, it emphasizes a target costing approach to pricing. Target costing starts with the market price of the product (the price customers are willing to pay) and subtracts the company's desired profit to determine the product's target total cost—the *total* cost to develop, design, produce, market, deliver, and service the product. In other words, the total cost includes *every* cost incurred throughout the value chain relating to the product.

Revenue at market price
Less: Desired profit
Target total cost

In this relationship, the market price is "taken." If the product's current cost is higher than the target cost, the company must find ways to reduce costs, otherwise it will not meet its profit goals. Managers often use ABC, value engineering, and lean thinking (as discussed in Chapter 4) to find ways to cut costs. Let's look at an example of target costing.

Let's assume that oil filters are a commodity and that the current market price is \$3.00 per filter (not the \$3.20 sales price assumed in the earlier ACDelco example). Because the oil filters are a commodity, ACDelco will emphasize a target costing approach. Let's assume that ACDelco's stockholders expect a 10% annual return on the company's assets. If the company has \$1,000,000 of assets, the desired profit is \$100,000 (\$1,000,000 × 10%). Exhibit 8-9 calculates the target total cost at the current sales volume (250,000 units). Once we know the target total cost, we can analyze the fixed and variable cost components separately.

EXHIBIT 8-9 Calculating Target Full Cost

	Calculations	Total
Revenue at market price	250,000 units × \$3.00 price =	\$ 750,000
Less: Desired profit	10% × \$1,000,000 of assets	(100,000)
Target total cost		\$ 650,000

Can ACDelco make and sell 250,000 oil filters at a target total cost of $650,000 or less? We know from ACDelco's contribution margin income statement (Exhibit 8-5) that the company's variable costs are $1.50 per unit. This variable cost per unit includes both manufacturing costs ($1.20 per unit) and marketing and administrative expenses ($0.30 per unit). From Exhibit 8-5 we also know that the company incurs $325,000 in fixed costs in its current relevant range. Again, some fixed cost stems from manufacturing ($200,000) and some from marketing and administrative activities ($125,000). *In setting regular sales prices, companies must cover* ***all*** *of their costs—it doesn't matter if these costs are inventoriable product costs or period costs, or whether they are fixed or variable.*

Making and selling 250,000 filters currently costs the company $700,000 [(250,000 units × $1.50 variable cost per unit) + $325,000 of fixed costs], which is more than the target total cost of $650,000 (shown in Exhibit 8-9). So, what are ACDelco's options?

1. Accept a lower profit.
2. Cut fixed costs.
3. Cut variable costs.
4. Use other strategies. For example, ACDelco could attempt to increase sales volume. Recall that the company has excess capacity, so making and selling more units would affect only variable costs. The company could also consider changing or adding to its product mix. Finally, it could attempt to differentiate its oil filters (or strengthen its name brand) to gain more control over sales prices.

Let's look at some of these options. ACDelco may first try to cut fixed costs. As shown in Exhibit 8-10, the company would have to reduce fixed costs to $275,000 to meet its target profit. Since current fixed costs are $325,000 (Exhibit 8-5), that means the company would have to cut fixed costs by $50,000.

EXHIBIT 8-10 Calculating Target Fixed Cost

	Calculations	Total
Target total cost		$ 650,000
Less: Current variable costs	250,000 units × $1.50	(375,000)
Target fixed cost		$ 275,000

The company would start by considering whether any discretionary fixed costs could be eliminated without harming the company. Since committed fixed costs are nearly impossible to change in the short run, ACDelco will probably not be able to reduce this type of fixed cost.

If the company can't reduce its fixed costs by $50,000, it would have to lower its variable cost to $1.30 per unit, as shown in Exhibit 8-11.

EXHIBIT 8-11 Calculating Target Unit Variable Cost

	Total
Target total cost	$ 650,000
Less: Current fixed costs	(325,000)
Target total variable costs	$ 325,000
Divided by number of units	÷ 250,000
Target variable cost per unit	$ 1.30

Perhaps the company could renegotiate raw materials costs with its suppliers or find a less costly way of packaging or shipping the air filters.

However, if ACDelco can't reduce variable costs to $1.30 per unit, could it meet its target profit through a combination of lowering both fixed costs and variable costs?

STOP & THINK

Suppose ACDelco can reduce its current fixed costs, but only by $25,000. If it wants to meet its target profit, by how much will it have to reduce the variable cost of each unit? Assume that sales volume remains at 250,000 units.

Answer: Companies typically try to cut both fixed and variable costs. Because ACDelco can cut its fixed costs only by $25,000, to meet its target profit, it would have to cut its variable costs as well:

Target total cost	$ 650,000
Less: Reduced fixed costs ($325,000 − $25,000)	(300,000)
Target total variable costs	$ 350,000
Divided by number of units	÷ 250,000
Target variable cost per unit	$ 1.40

In addition to cutting its fixed costs by $25,000, the company must reduce its variable costs by $0.10 per unit ($1.50 – $1.40) to meet its target profit at the existing volume of sales.

Another strategy would be to increase sales. ACDelco's managers can use CVP analysis, as you learned in Chapter 7, to figure out how many oil filters the company would have to sell to achieve its target profit. How could the company increase demand for the oil filters? Perhaps it could reach new markets or advertise. How much would advertising cost—and how many extra oil filters would the company have to sell to cover the cost of advertising? These are only some of the questions managers must ask. As you can see, managers don't have an easy task when the current total cost exceeds the target total cost. Sometimes, companies just can't compete given the current market price. If that's the case, they may have no other choice than to exit the market for that product.

Cost-Plus Pricing

When a company is a price-setter, it emphasizes a cost-plus approach to pricing. This pricing approach is essentially the *opposite* of the target-pricing approach. **Cost-plus pricing** starts with the product's total costs (as a given) and *adds* its desired profit to determine a cost-plus price.

Total cost
Plus: Desired profit
Cost-plus price

When the product is unique, the company has more control over pricing. However, the company still needs to make sure that the cost-plus price is not higher than what customers are willing to pay. Let's go back to our original ACDelco example. This time, let's assume that the oil filters benefit from brand recognition, so the company has some control over the price it charges for its filters. Exhibit 8-12 takes a cost-plus pricing approach assuming the current level of sales.

EXHIBIT 8-12 Calculating Cost-Plus Price

	Calculations	Total
Current variable costs	250,000 units × $1.50 per unit =	$375,000
Plus: Current fixed costs		+ 325,000
Current total costs		$700,000
Plus: Desired profit	10% × $1,000,000 of assets	+ 100,000
Target revenue		$800,000
Divided by number of units		÷ 250,000
Cost-plus price per unit		$ 3.20

If the current market price for generic oil filters is $3.00, as we assumed earlier, can ACDelco sell its brand-name filters for $3.20 apiece? The answer depends on how well the company has been able to differentiate its product or brand name. The company may use focus groups or marketing surveys to find out how customers would respond to its cost-plus price. The company may find out that its cost-plus price is too high, or it may find that it could set the price even higher without jeopardizing sales.

STOP & THINK

Which costing system (job costing or process costing) do you think price-setters and price-takers typically use?

Answer: Companies tend to be price-setters when their products are unique. Unique products are produced as single items or in small batches. Therefore, these companies use job costing to determine the product's cost. However, companies are price-takers when their products are high-volume commodities. Process costing better suits this type of product.

Notice how pricing decisions used our two keys to decision making: (1) focus on relevant information and (2) use a contribution margin approach that separates variable costs from fixed costs. In pricing decisions, all cost information is relevant because the company must cover *all* costs along the value chain before it can generate a profit. However, we still needed to consider variable costs and fixed costs separately because they behave differently at different volumes.

Our pricing decision rule is as follows:

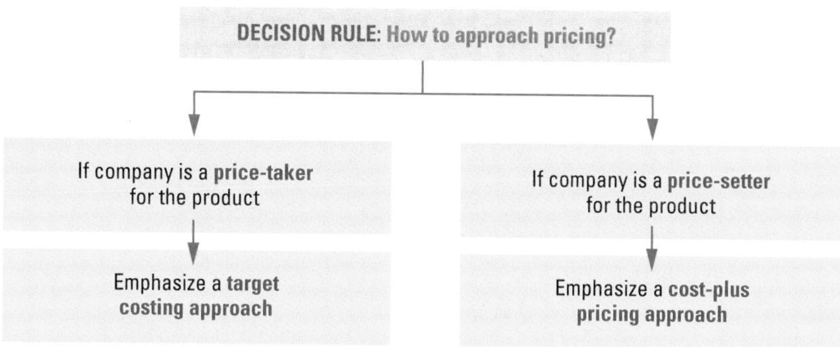

Decision Guidelines

Relevant Information for Business Decisions

Nike makes special order and regular pricing decisions. Even though it sells mass-produced tennis shoes and sports clothing, Nike has differentiated its products with advertising. Nike's managers consider both quantitative and qualitative factors as they make pricing decisions. Here are key guidelines that Nike's managers follow in making their decisions.

Decision	Guidelines
What information is relevant to a short-term special business decision?	Relevant information is as follows: 1. Pertains to the *future* 2. *Differs* between alternatives
What are two key guidelines in making short-term special business decisions?	1. Focus on *relevant* data. 2. Use a *contribution margin* approach that separates variable costs from fixed costs.
How does a company's committment to sustainability affect decision making?	Companys that are committed to sustainability will judge every decision through the lens of the triple bottom line, assessing the impact of the decision not only on company profit, but also on its consequences for people and the planet.
Should Nike accept a lower sales price than the regular price for a large order from a customer in São Paulo, Brazil?	If the revenue from the order exceeds the incremental variable and fixed costs incurred to fill the order, then accepting the order will increase operating income.
What should Nike consider in setting its regular product prices?	Nike considers the following: 1. What profit stockholders expect 2. What price customers will pay 3. Whether it is a price-setter or a price-taker
What approach should Nike take to pricing?	Nike has differentiated its products through advertising its brand name. Thus, Nike tends to be a price-setter. Nike's managers can emphasize a cost-plus approach to pricing.
What approach should discount shoe stores such as Payless ShoeSource take to pricing?	Payless ShoeSource sells generic shoes (no-name brands) at low prices. Payless is a price-taker, so managers use a target-costing approach to pricing.

SUMMARY PROBLEM 1

Linger Industries makes tennis balls. Linger's only plant can produce up to 2.5 million cans of balls per year. Current production is two million cans. Annual manufacturing, selling, and administrative fixed costs total $700,000. The variable cost of making and selling each can of balls is $1. Stockholders expect a 12% annual return on the company's $3 million of assets.

Requirements

1. What is Linger Industries' current total cost of making and selling two million cans of tennis balls? What is the current cost per unit of each can of tennis balls?
2. Assume that Linger Industries is a price-taker and the current market price is $1.45 per can of balls (this is the price at which manufacturers sell to retailers). What is the *target* total cost of producing and selling two million cans of balls? Given Linger Industries' current total costs, will the company reach stockholders' profit goals?
3. If Linger Industries cannot reduce its fixed costs, what is the target variable cost per can of balls?
4. Suppose Linger Industries could spend an extra $100,000 on advertising to differentiate its product so that it could be more of a price-setter. Assuming the original volume and costs plus the $100,000 of new advertising costs, what cost-plus price will Linger Industries want to charge for a can of balls?
5. Nike has just asked Linger Industries to supply 400,000 cans of balls at a special order price of $1.20 per can. Nike wants Linger Industries to package the balls under the Nike label (Linger will imprint the Nike logo on each ball and can). As a result, Linger Industries will have to spend $10,000 to change the packaging machinery. Assuming the original volume and costs, should Linger Industries accept this special order? (Unlike the chapter problem, assume that Linger will incur variable selling costs as well as variable manufacturing costs related to this order.)

SOLUTION

Requirement 1

The current total cost, and cost per unit are calculated as follows:

Fixed costs	$ 700,000
Plus: Total variable costs (2 million cans × $1 per unit)	+ 2,000,000
Current total costs	$2,700,000
Divided by number of units	÷ 2,000,000
Current cost per can	$ 1.35

Requirement 2

The target total cost is as follows:

Revenue at market price (2,000,000 cans × $1.45 price)	$2,900,000
Less: Desired profit (12% × $3,000,000 of assets)	(360,000)
Target total cost	$2,540,000

Linger Industries' *current* total costs ($2,700,000 from Requirement 1) are $160,000 higher than the *target* total costs ($2,540,000). If Linger Industries can't cut costs, it won't be able to meet stockholders' profit expectations.

Requirement 3

Assuming that Linger Industries cannot reduce its fixed costs, the target variable cost per can is as follows:

Target total cost (from Requirement 2)	$ 2,540,000
Less: Fixed costs...	(700,000)
Target total variable costs	$ 1,840,000
Divided by number of units.............................	÷ 2,000,000
Target variable cost per unit............................	$ 0.92

Since Linger Industries cannot reduce its fixed costs, it needs to reduce variable costs by $0.08 per can ($1.00 – $0.92) to meet its profit goals. This would require an 8% cost reduction in variable costs, which may not be possible.

Requirement 4

If Linger Industries can differentiate its tennis balls, it will gain more control over pricing. The company's new cost-plus price would be as follows:

Current total costs (from Requirement 1)............	$ 2,700,000
Plus: Additional cost of advertising	+ 100,000
Plus: Desired profit (from Requirement 2)............	+ 360,000
Target revenue...	$ 3,160,000
Divided by number of units................................	÷ 2,000,000
Cost-plus price per unit......................................	$ 1.58

Linger Industries must study the market to determine whether retailers would pay $1.58 per can of balls.

Requirement 5

First, Linger determines that it has enough extra capacity (500,000 cans) to fill this special order (400,000). Next, Linger compares the revenue from the special order with the extra costs that will be incurred to fill the order. Notice that Linger shouldn't compare the special order price ($1.20) with the current unit cost of each can ($1.35) because the unit cost contains both a fixed and variable component. Since the company has excess capacity, the existing fixed costs won't be affected by the order. The correct analysis is as follows:

Revenue from special order (400,000 × $1.20 per unit)	$ 480,000
Less: Variable cost of special order (400,000 × $1.00)	(400,000)
Contribution margin from special order..................................	$ 80,000
Less: Additional fixed costs of special order............................	(10,000)
Operating income provided by special order...........................	$ 70,000

Linger Industries should accept the special order because it will increase operating income by $70,000. However, Linger Industries also needs to consider whether its regular customers will find out about the special price and demand lower prices, too. If Linger had simply compared the special order price of $1.20 to the current unit cost of each can ($1.35), it would have rejected the special order and missed out on the opportunity to make an additional $70,000 of profit.

How do Managers Make Other Special Business Decisions?

In this part of the chapter we'll consider four more special business decisions:

- Whether to discontinue a product, department, or store
- How to factor constrained resources into product mix decisions
- Whether to make a product or outsource it (buy it)
- Whether to sell a product as is or process it further

Decisions to Discontinue Products, Departments, or Stores

4 Decide whether to discontinue a product, department, or store

Managers often must decide whether to discontinue products, departments, stores, or territories that are not as profitable as desired. Newell Rubbermaid—maker of Sharpie markers, Graco strollers, and Rubbermaid plastics—recently discontinued some of its European products lines. Home Depot closed its Expo stores. Kroger food stores replaced some in-store movie rental departments with health food departments. How do managers make these decisions? Exhibit 8-13 shows some questions managers must consider when deciding whether to discontinue a product line, department, or retail store location.

EXHIBIT 8-13 Considerations for Discontinuing Products, Departments, or Stores

- Does the product provide a positive contribution margin?
- Are there any fixed costs that can be avoided if we discontinue the product?
- Will discontinuing the product affect sales of the company's other products?
- What could we do with the freed capacity?

If your instructor is using MyAccountingLab, go to the Multimedia Library for a quick video on this topic.

In the first half of the chapter we assumed ACDelco offered only one product—oil filters. Now let's assume the company makes both oil filters and air cleaners. Exhibit 8-14 illustrates a product line income statement in contribution margin format. As you can see, a product line income statement shows the operating income of each product line, as well as the company as a whole.

EXHIBIT 8-14 Product Line Income Statement

Product Line Income Statement	Company Total (312,500 units)	Oil Filters (250,000 units)	Air Cleaners (62,500 units)
Sales revenue	$925,000	$800,000	$125,000
Less variable expenses:			
Variable manufacturing costs			
(DM, DL, and Variable MOH)	362,500	300,000	62,500
Variable marketing and			
administrative costs	87,500	75,000	12,500
Contribution margin	$475,000	$425,000	$ 50,000
Less fixed expenses:			
Fixed manufacturing costs			
(Fixed MOH)	200,000	160,000	40,000
Fixed marketing and			
administrative costs	125,000	100,000	25,000
Operating income	$150,000	$165,000	$ (15,000)

In this exhibit, notice that the contribution margin provided by oil filters ($425,000) is the same as shown in Exhibit 8-6. What differs is that the fixed costs have now been allocated between the two product lines. Since 80% of the units produced are oil filters (250,000 ÷ 312,500 total units) and since each unit takes about the same amount of time to produce, management has allocated 80% of the fixed costs to the oil filters. The remaining 20% of fixed costs have been allocated to air cleaners. Keep in mind that management could have chosen another allocation system which would have resulted in a different allocation of fixed costs.

Further notice that the air cleaner product line appears to be unprofitable. Currently, the air cleaners have an operating loss of $15,000 per period. Without this loss, management believes the company's operating income could be $15,000 higher each period. Therefore, management is considering whether to discontinue the product line. Let's now consider how management should approach this decision.

Consider the Product's Contribution Margin and Avoidable Fixed Costs

In making this decision, management should consider the questions raised in Exhibit 8-13. The first question addresses the product line's contribution margin: is it positive or negative? Exhibit 8-14 shows that the air cleaners provide $50,000 of contribution margin. This positive contribution margin means the product line is generating enough revenue to cover its own variable costs, plus provide another $50,000 that can be used to cover some of the company's fixed costs.

Had the contribution margin been negative, management would either need to raise the price of the product, if possible, cut variable costs, or discontinue the line. Management would only keep a product line with a negative contribution margin if they expected the sales of a companion product to decline as a result of discontinuing the product. For example, if customers alway buy one oil filter every time they buy an air cleaner, then sales of oil filters might decline as a result of discontinuing the air cleaners. As a result, the total contribution margin earned from the oil filters would decline. This potential loss in contribution margin on the oil filters would need to be weighed against the savings generated from eliminating the product line with a negative contribution margin.

After assessing the contribution margin, managers need to consider fixed costs. The important question is this: Can any fixed costs be eliminated if the product line is discontinued? Any fixed costs that can be eliminated as a result of discontinuing the product are known as **avoidable fixed costs**. These costs are relevant to the decision, because they will be incurred *only* if the product line is retained.

On the other hand, **unavoidable fixed costs** are those fixed costs that will continue to be incurred even if the product line is discontinued. Unavoidable fixed costs are irrelevant to the decision because they will be the same regardless of whether the product line is kept or discontinued.

Exhibit 8-15 shows the company's fixed costs in more detail. Notice that total fixed costs ($200,000 of manufacturing and $125,000 of marketing and administrative) are the same as shown in Exhibit 8-14. Managers will assess each fixed cost to determine how much, if any, is avoidable.

Exhibit 8-15 shows that management has identified $8,000 of fixed manufacturing and $10,000 of fixed marketing and administrative costs that can be eliminated if the air cleaners are discontinued. The avoidable fixed costs consist of a cancellable lease on equipment used to manufacture the air cleaners, advertisements for the air cleaners, and salaried employees who work solely on the air cleaner product line. Most of the fixed costs, such as property taxes, insurance, depreciation and so forth are unavoidable: they will continue even if the air cleaners are discontinued.

EXHIBIT 8-15 Analysis of the Company's Fixed Costs

Detailed listing of fixed expenses	Total Cost	Avoidable
Fixed manufacturing (Fixed MOH):		
Property taxes	18,000	0
Insurance	5,000	0
Depreciation on plant and production equipment	130,000	0
Fixed portion of utilities	7,000	0
Salaries of indirect labor (supervisors, janitors, etc.)	35,000	3,000
Equipment lease (cancellable)	5,000	5,000
Total fixed manufacturing costs	$200,000	$8,000
Fixed marketing and administrative:		
Building lease	17,000	0
Telephone, internet, utilities	8,000	0
Depreciation on sales vehicles and office equipment	20,000	0
Advertisements	25,000	6,000
Sales and administrative salaries	55,000	4,000
Total fixed marketing and administrative costs	$125,000	$10,000

With this information in hand, management can now determine whether or not to discontinue the air cleaner product line. Exhibit 8-16 presents management's analysis of the decision. In this analysis, managers compare the contribution margin that would be lost from discontinuing the air cleaners with the fixed cost savings that could be generated.

EXHIBIT 8-16 Incremental Analysis for Discontinuing a Product Line

Incremental Analysis—Discontinuation Decision	(Costs)/Savings
Contribution margin lost if air cleaners are discontinued (from Exhibit 8-14)	$(50,000)
Less: Cost savings from eliminating avoidable fixed costs	18,000
Decrease in company's operating income	$(32,000)

This analysis shows that the company's operating income would actually *decrease* by $32,000 if the air cleaners are discontinued. Therefore, the air cleaners should not be discontinued. The company would only eliminate the air cleaners if it could use the freed capacity to make a different product that is more profitable than the air cleaners.

Other Considerations

As noted in Exhibit 8-13, management must consider at least two other issues when making the decision to discontinue a product line, department, or store.

First, will discontinuing the product line affect sales of the company's other products? As discussed previously, some products have companion products whose sales would be hurt through discontinuing a particular product. This is also true about store departments. Can you imagine a grocery store discontinuing its produce department? Sales of every other department in the store would decline as a result of shoppers' inability to purchase fruits and vegetables at the store. On the other hand, sometimes discontinuing a product, such as one particular camera model, can increases the sales of the other company products (other camera models). The same holds true for retail stores. For example, assume two Starbucks are located close to one other. If one store is closed, then sales at the other location might increase as a result.

The second question concerns freed capacity. If a product line, department, or store is discontinued, management needs to consider what it would do with the newly freed capacity. As mentioned in the opening story, Kroger recently replaced some of its in-store movie rental departments with health food departments. Why? Managers must have determined that a health food department would be more profitable than a movie rental department. However, they could have used the space to house a sushi bar, or display other products. Management must consider which alterative use of the freed capacity will be most profitable. Finally, management should consider what to do with any newly freed labor capacity. To exercise corporate responsibility, management should do all it can to retrain employees for other areas of its operations rather than laying off employees.

Business decisions should take into account all costs affected by the choice of action.

STOP & THINK

Unlike the text example, assume that all of ACDelco's fixed costs are *unavoidable*. If the company discontinues the air cleaners, it could use the freed capacity to make spark plugs. The spark plugs are expected to provide a contribution margin of $70,000 but will require $5,000 of new fixed costs. Should ACDelco drop the air cleaners and use the freed capacity to make spark plugs?

Answer: The following incremental analysis shows that the company would be more profitable if it discontinued the air cleaners and used the freed capacity to make spark plugs.

Incremental Analysis: Product Replacement Decision	(Costs)/Savings
Contribution margin lost if air cleaners are discontinued (from Exhibit 8-14)	$(50,000)
Plus: Contribution margin gained from spark plugs	70,000
Less: New fixed costs	(5,000)
Increase in company's operating income	$ 15,000

Managers must ask what total costs—variable and fixed—will change. The key to deciding whether to discontinue products, departments, or stores is to compare the lost revenue against the costs that can be saved and to consider what would be done with the freed capacity. The decision rule is as follows:

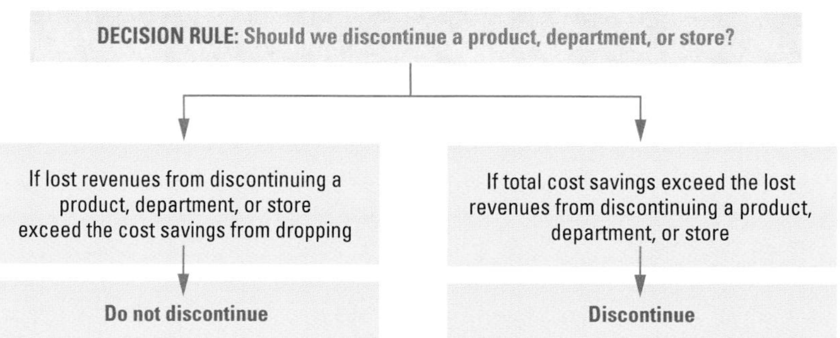

Pitfall to Avoid on Discontinuation Decisions

One of the most common mistakes managers make when analyzing whether or not to discontinue a product is to base the decision on a product line income statement that contains an allocation of common fixed expenses. Common fixed expenses are those expenses that *cannot* be traced directly to a product line. For example, in Exhibits 8-14 and 8-15, we see that fixed MOH costs such as property taxes, insurance, and depreciation are all common production costs that have been allocated between the product lines. While appropriate for product costing purposes, the allocation of common fixed costs is not appropriate for making product discontinuation decisions. Nor is the allocation of common fixed costs related to marketing and administration, such as the building lease, utilities, internet, or depreciation of office equipment.

As shown in Exhibit 8-14, the allocation of common fixed costs suggests the company's overall operating income could be $15,000 higher if the company stopped making the air cleaners. However, based on the correct analysis in Exhibit 8-16 we know the company's operating income would actually decline by $32,000 if the air cleaners were discontinued.

Since income statements with allocated common costs can potentially mislead managers, some companies prepare **segment margin income statements**, which contain no allocation of common fixed costs. Segment margin income statements look similar to Exhibit 8-14, except for two differences:

1. Only direct fixed costs that can be traced to specific product lines are deducted from the product line's contribution margin. The resulting operating income or loss for each individual product line is known as a **segment margin**.
2. All common fixed costs are shown under the company "total" column, but are not allocated among product lines.

We discuss and illustrate segment margin income statement in more detail in Chapter 10.

Product Mix Decisions when Resources are Constrained

5 Factor resource constraints into product mix decisions

Companies do not have unlimited resources. **Constraints** that restrict production or sale of a product vary from company to company. For a manufacturer, the production constraint is often the number of available machine hours. For a merchandiser such as Walmart, the primary constraint is cubic feet of display space. In order to determine which products to emphasize displaying or producing, companies facing constraints consider the questions shown in Exhibit 8-17.

EXHIBIT 8-17 Product Mix Considerations

- What constraint(s) stops us from making (or displaying) all of the units we can sell?
- Which products offer the highest contribution margin per unit of the constraint?
- Would emphasizing one product over another affect fixed costs?

Consider Union Bay, a manufacturer of shirts and jeans. Let's say the company can sell all of the shirts and jeans it produces, but it has only 2,000 machine hours of capacity. The company uses the same machines to produce both jeans and shirts. In this case, machine hours is the constraint. Note that this is a short-term decision, because in the long run, Union Bay could expand its production facilities to meet sales demand if it made financial sense to do so. The following data suggest that shirts are more profitable than jeans:

	Per Unit	
	Shirts	**Jeans**
Sale price	$ 30	$ 60
Less: Variable expenses	(12)	(48)
Contribution margin	$ 18	$ 12
Contribution margin ratio:		
Shirts—$18 ÷ $30	60%	
Jeans—$12 ÷ $60		20%

However, an important piece of information is missing—the time it takes to make each product. Let's assume that Union Bay can produce either 20 pairs of jeans *or* 10 shirts per machine hour. *The company will incur the same fixed costs either way, so fixed costs are irrelevant.* Which product should it emphasize?

To maximize profits when fixed costs are irrelevant, follow this decision rule:

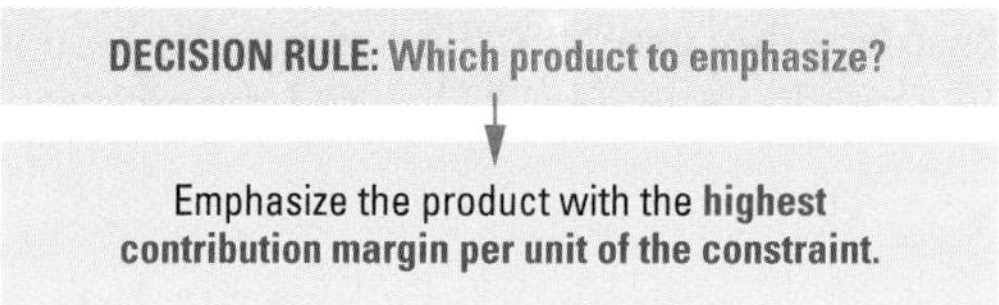

Because *machine hours* is the constraint, Union Bay needs to figure out which product has the *highest contribution margin per machine hour*. Exhibit 8-18 shows the contribution margin per machine hour for each product.

EXHIBIT 8-18 Product Mix—Which Product to Emphasize

	Shirts	Jeans
(1) Units that can be produced each machine hour	10	20
(2) Contribution margin per unit	× $18	× $12
Contribution margin per machine hour (1) × (2)	$180	$240
Available capacity—number of machine hours	× 2,000	× 2,000
Total contribution margin at full capacity	$360,000	$480,000

Jeans have a higher contribution margin per machine hour ($240) than shirts ($180). Therefore, Union Bay will earn more profit by producing jeans. Why? Because even though jeans have a lower contribution margin *per unit*, Union Bay can make twice as many jeans as shirts in the available machine hours. Exhibit 8-18 also proves that Union Bay earns more total profit by making jeans. Multiplying the contribution margin per machine hour by the available number of machine hours shows that Union Bay can earn $480,000 of contribution margin by producing jeans but only $360,000 by producing shirts.

To maximize profit, Union Bay should make 40,000 jeans (2,000 machine hours × 20 jeans per hour) and zero shirts. Why zero shirts? Because for every machine hour spent making shirts, Union Bay would *give up* $60 of contribution margin ($240 per hour for jeans versus $180 per hour for shirts).

Changing Assumptions: Product Mix When Demand is Limited

We made two assumptions about Union Bay: (1) Union Bay's sales of other products, if any, won't be hurt by this decision and (2) Union Bay can sell as many jeans and shirts as it can produce. Let's challenge these assumptions. First, how could making only jeans (and not shirts) hurt sales of the company's other products? Using other production equipment, Union Bay also makes ties and jackets that coordinate with their shirts. Tie and jacket sales might fall if Union Bay no longer offers coordinating shirts.

Let's challenge our second assumption. A new competitor has decreased the demand for Union Bay's jeans. Now, the company can sell only 30,000 pairs of jeans. Union Bay should make only as many jeans as it can sell and use the remaining machine hours to produce shirts. Let's see how this constraint in sales demand changes profitability.

Recall from Exhibit 8-18 that Union Bay will earn $480,000 of contribution margin from using all 2,000 machine hours to produce jeans. However, if Union Bay makes only 30,000 jeans, it will use only 1,500 machine hours (30,000 jeans ÷ 20 jeans per machine hour). That leaves 500 machine hours available for making shirts. Union Bay's new contribution margin will be as follows:

	Shirts	Jeans	Total
Contribution margin per machine hour (from Exhibit 8-18)	$ 180	$ 240	
Machine hours devoted to product..	× 500	× 1,500	2,000
Total contribution margin at full capacity....................................	$90,000	$360,000	$450,000

Because of the change in product mix, Union Bay's total contribution margin will fall from $480,000 to $450,000, a $30,000 decline. Union Bay had to give up $60 of contribution margin per machine hour ($240 – $180) on the 500 hours it spent producing shirts rather than jeans. However, Union Bay had no choice—the company would have incurred an *actual loss* from producing jeans that it could not sell. If Union Bay had produced 40,000 jeans but sold only 30,000, the company would have spent $480,000 to make the unsold jeans (10,000 jeans × $48 variable cost per pair of jeans) yet would have received no sales revenue from them.

What about fixed costs? In most cases, changing the product mix emphasis in the short run will not affect fixed costs, so fixed costs are irrelevant. However, fixed costs could differ when a different product mix is emphasized. What if Union Bay had a month-to-month lease on a zipper machine used only for making jeans? If Union Bay made only shirts, it could *avoid* the lease cost. However, if Union Bay makes any jeans, it needs the machine. In this case, the fixed costs become relevant because they differ between alternative product mixes (shirts only *versus* jeans only or jeans and shirts).

STOP & THINK

Would Union Bay's product mix decision change if it had a $20,000 cancelable lease on a zipper machine needed only for jean production? Assume that Union Bay can sell as many units as it makes.

Answer: We would compare the profitability as follows:

	Shirts	Jeans
Total contribution margin at full capacity (from Exhibit 8-18)	$360,000	$480,000
Less: Avoidable fixed costs	-0-	(20,000)
Net benefit	$360,000	$460,000

Even considering the zipper machine lease, producing jeans is more profitable than producing shirts. Union Bay would prefer producing jeans over shirts unless demand for jeans drops so low that the net benefit from jeans is less than $360,000 (the benefit gained from solely producing shirts).

Notice that the analysis again follows the two guidelines for special business decisions: (1) focus on relevant data (only those revenues and costs that differ) and (2) use a contribution margin approach, which separates variable from fixed costs.

Outsourcing Decisions (Make or Buy)

6 Analyze outsourcing (make or buy) decisions

Outsourcing decisions are sometimes called <u>make-or-buy</u> decisions because managers must decide whether to make a product or service in-house or buy it from another company. Sometimes people confuse the term "outsourcing" with the term "offshoring."

- <u>Outsourcing</u> refers to contracting an outside company to produce a product or perform a service. Outsourced work could be done domestically or overseas.
- <u>Offshoring</u> refers to having work performed overseas. Companies offshore work by either 1) operating their own manufacturing plants and call centers overseas or 2) outsourcing the overseas work to another company. Thus, offshored work is not necessarily outsourced work.

Outsourcing is not new. For years, companies have outsourced specialized services such as marketing, payroll processing, and legal work to firms that have expertise in those areas. More and more, brand-name companies such as Nike, IBM, and Sara Lee are outsourcing the production of their products so that they can concentrate on their core competencies of marketing and product development. In fact, so much production is outsourced that contract manufacturing has become an entire industry. **Contract manufacturers** are manufacturers who only make products for other companies, not for themselves.

Let's see how managers make outsourcing decisions. The heart of these decisions is how to best use available resources. Let's assume that Apple, the developer of iPods, is deciding whether to continue making the earbuds that are sold with the product or outsource production to Skullcandy, a company that specializes in earbuds. Let's assume Apple's cost to produce 2 million earbuds each period is as shown in Exhibit 8-19:[3]

EXHIBIT 8-19 Production Costs and Volume

Manufacturing Cost	Variable Cost per Unit	Total Cost for 2 million units
Direct materials	$4.00	8,000,000
Direct labor	0.50	1,000,000
Variable MOH	1.50	3,000,000
Total variable cost	$6.00	12,000,000
Plus: Fixed MOH		4,000,000
Total cost		$16,000,000
Divide by: Number of units		÷2,000,000
Cost per unit (absorption)		$ 8.00

Let's further assume that Skullcandy is willing to provide earbuds to Apple for $7.00 each. Should Apple make the earbuds or buy them from Skullcandy? The $7.00 price is less than the full absorption cost per unit ($8.00), but greater than Apple's variable cost per unit ($6.00). The answer isn't as easy as simply comparing unit costs. In deciding what to do, managers should consider the questions outlined in Exhibit 8-20.

Why is this important?

"Almost any **business activity** can be **outsourced** (for example, manufacturing, marketing, and payroll). **Companies** often choose to retain only their **core competencies**—things they are *really* good at doing—and **outsource** just about everything else to companies that can do it *better* for them."

EXHIBIT 8-20 Outsourcing Considerations

- How do our variable costs compare to the outsourcing cost?
- Are any fixed costs avoidable if we outsource?
- What could we do with the freed capacity?

Let's see how these considerations apply to our example:

1. **Variable costs:** The variable cost of producing each earbud ($6.00) is less than the outsourcing cost ($7.00). Based on variable costs alone, Apple should manufacture the earbuds in-house. However, managers must still consider fixed costs.
2. **Fixed costs:** Let's assume that Apple could save $500,000 of fixed costs each period by outsourcing. This savings would primarily result from laying off salaried indirect labor, such as production supervisors. However, most of the fixed manufacturing cost relates to plant capacity, and will continue to exist even if the company stops making earbuds. These costs might include property tax on the plant and non-cancellable lease payments made on the production equipment.

[3]The hypothetical cost information was created solely for academic purposes, and is not intended in any way, to represent the actual costs incurred by Apple or the price that would be charged by Skullcandy.

3. **Use of freed capacity:** We'll start by assuming that Apple has no other use for the production capacity, so it will remain idle. We will change this assumption later.

Given this information, what should Apple do? Exhibit 8-21 compares the two alternatives.

EXHIBIT 8-21 Incremental Analysis for Outsourcing Decisions

Manufacturing Costs	Make Earbuds	Outsource Earbuds	Difference: Additional Cost/ (Savings) From Outsourcing
Variable Costs:			
If Make: \$6.00 × 2,000,000 units	\$12,000,000		
If Buy: \$7.00 × 2,000,000 units		\$14,000,000	\$2,000,000
Fixed Costs	4,000,000	3,500,000	(500,000)
Total cost of producing 2,000,000 units	\$16,000,000	\$17,500,000	\$1,500,000

This analysis shows that Apple should continue to make the earbuds. Why is this the case? As shown in the last column of Exhibit 8-21, the company would spend \$2,000,000 more in variable costs to outsource the earbuds, but only save \$500,000 in fixed costs. The net result is a \$1,500,000 increase in total costs if the company outsources production.

The analysis shown in Exhibit 8-21 is partially dependent on production volume. If Apple needed fewer than 500,000 earbuds each period, then the decision would be reversed because the savings on fixed costs would outweigh the additional \$1 per unit spent on variable costs. At volumes lower than 500,000, it would be cheaper for Apple to outsource production than produce in-house.

Notice how Exhibit 8-21 uses our two keys for decision making: 1) focus on relevant data (costs that differ between alternatives), and 2) use a contribution margin approach that separates variable costs from fixed costs. Our decision rule for outsourcing is as follows:

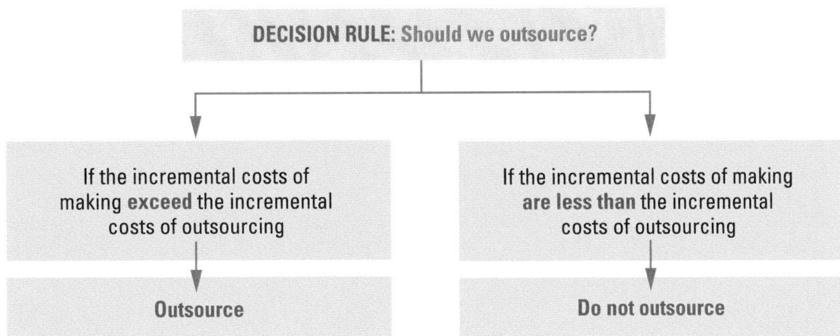

Determining an Acceptable Outsourcing Price

In Chapter 7, we used the concept of an indifference point to help managers decide how to structure costs. We can use the same concept here to determine the maximum outsourcing price Apple would be willing to pay to have another manufacturer make the earbuds. By knowing up front how much Apple would be willing to pay, the company can proactively seek bids from multiple companies, such as contract manufacturers.

Exhibit 8-22 shows how to calculate the indifference point. The exhibit begins by equating the costs of making the earbuds with the costs of outsourcing the earbuds. Next, all of the information from Exhibit 8-21 is inserted into the equations, with the exception of the variable cost per unit under the outsourcing alternative. The variable cost of outsourcing each unit is the cost we wish to solve for.

EXHIBIT 8-22 Using an Indifference Point to Find an Acceptable Outsourcing Price

Costs of making earbuds	=	Costs of outsourcing earbuds
Variable Costs + Fixed Costs	=	Variable Costs + Fixed Costs
(2,000,000 units × \$6) + \$4,000,000	=	(2,000,000 units × Variable cost per unit) + \$3,500,000
\$16,000,000	=	(2,000,000 × Variable cost per unit) + \$3,500,000
\$12,500,000	=	(2,000,000 × Variable cost per unit)
Variable cost per unit	=	\$6.25

This analysis shows that, all else being equal, Apple would be *indifferent* between making and outsourcing 2 million earbuds if the outsourcing price was exactly \$6.25 a unit. Therefore, the most Apple would be willing to pay for this volume of earbuds would be just under \$6.25 a unit.

Notice, again, that this analysis is dependent on production volume. For example, if Apple needs 3 million units, the most they would be willing to pay would be \$6.17 per unit. Why the difference? By producing more units, Apple's fixed costs are being utilized more efficiently, driving down the average cost of making each unit. As Apple's own unit cost falls, so will the price they are willing to pay some other company to make the earbuds. The opposite is also true: The fewer units Apple needs, the more they will be willing to pay another company to make the earbuds.

Alternative use of Freed Capacity

Now let's change one of our original assumptions. Instead of assuming that the production capacity will remain idle, let's assume that Apple could lease it out to another company for \$2.5 million per period. In this case, Apple must consider its **opportunity cost**, which is the benefit foregone by choosing a particular course of action. If Apple continues to make its own earbuds, it will be losing out on the opportunity to earn lease income of \$2.5 million per period.

Exhibit 8-23 incorporates this information into our analysis by showing lease income as additional income that *could be made* if the company outsources production. Thus, we show the lease income in the "Outsource Earbuds" column. This income offsets some of the cost associated with outsourcing. Alternatively, we could show the \$2.5 million as an *additional* cost (an opportunity cost) in the "Make Earbuds" column.

EXHIBIT 8-23 Incremental Analysis Incorporating Next Best Use of Freed Capacity

Manufacturing Costs	Make Earbuds	Outsource Earbuds	Difference: Additional Cost/ (Savings) from Outsourcing
Variable Costs:			
If Make: \$6.00 × 2,000,000 units	\$12,000,000		
If Buy: \$7.00 × 2,000,000 units		\$14,000,000	\$ 2,000,000
Fixed Costs	\$ 4,000,000	\$ 3,500,000	(500,000)
Total cost	\$16,000,000	\$17,500,000	\$ 1,500,000
Less: Lease income	-0-	(2.500,000)	(2,500,000)
Net Cost	\$16,000,000	15,000,000	(\$1,000,000)

This analysis shows that Apple will save \$1,000,000 each period by outsourcing production of the earbuds. This result holds regardless of whether we treat the \$2.5 million lease as income in the "outsource earbuds" column or as an opportunity cost in the "make earbuds" column. Again, notice that a different production volume could potentially result in a different outcome.

Potential Drawbacks of Outsourcing

While outsourcing often provides cost savings, it is not without drawbacks. When a company outsources, it gives up control of the production process, including control over quality and production scheduling. Rather, it must rely on the supplier to provide the product or service at an agreed-upon level of quality, at agreed-upon delivery dates. Often, one or more employees are needed just to manage the relationship with the outsourcing company to make sure that everything runs smoothly. The cost of employing any such additional personnel should also be considered when comparing the cost of outsourcing versus the cost of producing in-house.

In addition, for those companies embracing the triple bottom line, outsourcing is often not viewed as a viable alternative. Why? Because outsourcing often results in laying off employees. In addition, companies will want to thoroughly investigate and monitor the labor practices and working conditions of offshored contract work to make sure laborers are treated fairly and work in a safe environment. While overseas labor is often cheap and readily available, the exploitation of any people, in any country, is not an acceptable business practice.

Decisions to Sell As Is or Process Further

7 Decide whether to sell a product "as is" or process it further

At what point in processing should a company sell its product? Many companies, especially in the food processing and natural resource industries, face this business decision. Companies in these industries process a raw material (milk, corn, livestock, crude oil, lumber, and so forth) to a point before it is saleable. For example, Kraft pasteurizes raw milk before it is saleable. Kraft must then decide whether it should sell the pasteurized milk as is or process it further into other dairy products (reduced-fat milk, butter, sour cream, cottage cheese, yogurt, blocks of cheese, shredded cheese, and so forth). Managers consider the questions shown in Exhibit 8-24 when deciding whether to sell as is or process further.

EXHIBIT 8-24 Sell As Is or Process Further Considerations

- How much revenue will we receive if we sell the product as is?
- How much revenue will we receive if we sell the product *after* processing it further?
- How much will it cost to process the product further?

Let's consider Bertolli, the manufacturer of Italian food products. Suppose Bertolli spends $100,000 to process raw olives into 50,000 quarts of plain virgin olive oil. Should Bertolli sell the olive oil as is or should it spend more to process the olive oil into gourmet dipping oils, such as a Basil and Garlic Infused Dipping Oil? In making the decision, Bertolli's managers consider the following relevant information[2]:

- Bertolli could sell the plain olive oil for $5 per quart, for a total of $250,000 (50,000 × $5).
- Bertolli could sell the gourmet dipping oil for $7 per quart, for a total of $350,000 (50,000 × $7).
- Bertolli would have to spend $0.75 per quart, or $37,500 (50,000 × $0.75), to further process the plain olive oil into the gourmet dipping oil. This cost would include the extra direct materials required (such as basil, garlic, and the incremental cost of premium glass containers) as well as the extra conversion costs incurred (the cost of any

Why is this important?

"Some companies are able to sell their products at **different points** of completion. For example, some furniture **manufacturers** sell flat-packed bookshelves, TV stands, and home office furniture that the consumer must **finish assembling**. A **cost-benefit analysis** helps managers choose the most **profitable point** at which to sell the company's products."

[2]All references to Bertolli in this hypothetical example were created by the author solely for academic purposes and are not intended, in any way, to represent the actual business practices of, or costs incurred by Bertolli.

additional machinery and labor that the company would need to purchase in order to complete the extra processing).

By examining the incremental analysis shown in Exhibit 8-25, Bertolli's managers can see that they can increase operating income by $62,500 by further processing the plain olive oil into the gourmet dipping oil. The extra $100,000 of revenue greatly exceeds the incremental $37,500 of cost incurred to further process the olive oil.

EXHIBIT 8-25 Incremental Analysis for Sell As Is or Process Further Decision

	Sell As Is	Process Further	Difference: Additional Revenue/(Costs) from Processing Further
Expected revenue from selling 50,000 quarts of plain olive oil at $5.00 per quart	$250,000		
Expected revenue from selling 50,000 quarts of gourmet dipping oil at $7.00 per quart		$350,000	$100,000
Additional costs of $0.75 per quart to convert 50,000 quarts of plain olive oil into gourmet dipping oil		(37,500)	(37,500)
Total net benefit	$250,000	$312,500	$ 62,500

Notice that Bertolli's managers do *not* consider the $100,000 originally spent on processing the olives into olive oil. Why? It is a sunk cost. Recall from our previous discussion that a sunk cost is a past cost that cannot be changed regardless of which future action the company takes. Bertolli has incurred $100,000 regardless of whether it sells the olive oil as is or processes it further into gourmet dipping oils. Therefore, the cost is *not* relevant to the decision.

Thus, the decision rule is as follows:

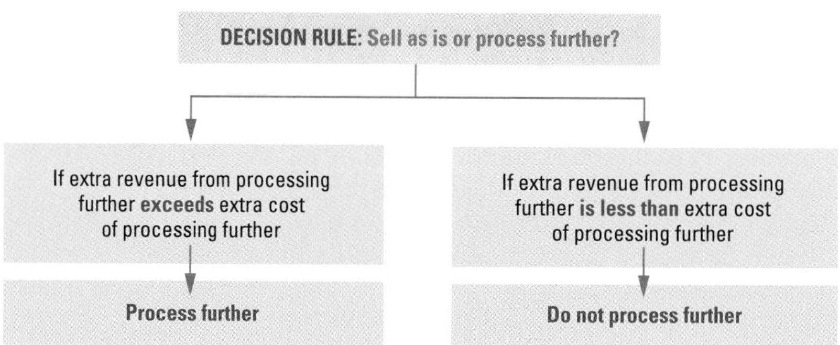

Decision Guidelines

Short-Term Special Business Decisions

Amazon.com has confronted most of the special business decisions we've covered. Here are the key guidelines Amazon.com's managers follow in making their decisions.

Decision	Guidelines
Should Amazon.com discontinue its electronics product line?	If the cost savings exceed the lost revenues from dropping the electronics product line, then dropping will increase operating income.
Given limited warehouse space, which products should Amazon.com focus on selling?	Amazon.com should focus on selling the products with the highest contribution margin per unit of the constraint, which is cubic feet of warehouse space
Should Amazon.com outsource its warehousing operations?	If the incremental costs of operating its own warehouses exceed the costs of outsourcing, then outsourcing will increase operating income.
How should a company decide whether to sell a product as is or process further?	Process further only if the extra sales revenue (from processing further) exceeds the extra costs of additional processing.

SUMMARY PROBLEM 2

Requirements

1. Aziz produces Standard and Deluxe sunglasses:

	Per Pair	
	Standard	Deluxe
Sale price	$20	$30
Variable expenses	16	21

The company has 15,000 machine hours available. In one machine hour, Aziz can produce 70 pairs of the Standard model or 30 pairs of the Deluxe model. Assuming machine hours is a constraint, which model should Aziz emphasize?

2. Just Do It! incurs the following costs for 20,000 pairs of its high-tech hiking socks:

Direct materials	$ 20,000
Direct labor	80,000
Variable manufacturing overhead	40,000
Fixed manufacturing overhead	80,000
Total manufacturing cost	$220,000
Cost per pair ($220,000 ÷ 20,000)	$ 11

Another manufacturer has offered to sell Just Do It! similar socks for $10 a pair, a total purchase cost of $200,000. If Just Do It! outsources *and* leaves its plant idle, it can save $50,000 of fixed overhead cost. Or the company can use the released facilities to make other products that will contribute $70,000 to profits. In this case, the company will not be able to avoid any fixed costs. Identify and analyze the alternatives. What is the best course of action?

SOLUTION

Requirement 1

	Style of Sunglasses	
	Standard	Deluxe
Sale price per pair	$ 20	$ 30
Variable expense per pair	(16)	(21)
Contribution margin per pair	$ 4	$ 9
Units produced each machine hour	× 70	× 30
Contribution margin per machine hour	$ 280	$ 270
Capacity—number of machine hours	× 15,000	× 15,000
Total contribution margin at full capacity	$4,200,000	$4,050,000

Decision: Emphasize the Standard model because it has the higher contribution margin per unit of the constraint—machine hours—resulting in a higher contribution margin for the company.

Requirement 2

		Outsource Socks	
	Make Socks	Facilities Idle	Make Other Products
Relevant costs:			
Direct materials	$ 20,000	—	—
Direct labor	80,000	—	—
Variable overhead	40,000	—	—
Fixed overhead	80,000	$ 30,000	$ 80,000
Outsourcing cost (20,000 × $10)	—	200,000	200,000
Total cost of obtaining socks	220,000	230,000	280,000
Profit from other products	—	—	(70,000)
Net cost of obtaining 20,000 pairs of socks	$220,000	$230,000	$210,000

Decision: Just Do It! should outsource the socks from the outside supplier and use the released facilities to make other products.

END OF CHAPTER

Learning Objectives

- 1 Describe and identify information relevant to short-term business decisions
- 2 Decide whether to accept a special order
- 3 Describe and apply different approaches to pricing
- 4 Decide whether to discontinue a product, department, or store
- 5 Factor resource constraints into product mix decisions
- 6 Analyze outsourcing (make or buy) decisions
- 7 Decide whether to sell a product "as is" or process it further

Accounting Vocabulary

Avoidable fixed costs. (p. 476) Fixed costs that can be eliminated as a result taking a particular course of action.

Constraint. (p. 479) A factor that restricts production or sale of a product.

Contract manufacturers. (p. 470) Manufacturers who make products for other companies, not for themselves.

Cost-Plus Pricing. (p. 481) An approach to pricing used by price-setters; cost-plus pricing begins with the product's total costs and adds the company's desired profit to determine a cost-plus price.

Offshoring. (p. 481) Having work performed overseas. Offshored work can either be performed by the company itself or by outsourcing the work to another company.

Opportunity Cost. (p. 484) The benefit forgone by choosing a particular alternative course of action.

Outsourcing. (p. 481) A make-or-buy decision: Managers decide whether to buy a product or service or produce it in-house.

Product line income statement. (p. 475) An income statement that shows the operating income of each product line, as well as the company as a whole.

Relevant Information. (p. 460) Expected *future* data that *differs* among alternatives

Segment margin. (p. 479) The income resulting from subtracting only the direct fixed costs of a product line from its contribution margin. The segment margin contains no allocation of common fixed costs.

Segment margin income statement. (p. 479) A product line income statement that contains no allocation of common fixed costs. Only direct fixed costs that can be traced to specific product lines are subtracted from the product line's contribution margin. All common fixed costs remain unallocated, and are shown only under the company total.

Sunk Cost. (p. 460) A past cost that cannot be changed regardless of which future action is taken.

Target Costing. (p. 468) An approach to pricing used by price-takers; target costing begins with the revenue at market price and subtracts the company's desired profit to arrive at the target total cost.

Unavoidable fixed costs. (p. 476) Fixed costs that will continue to be incurred even if a particular course of action is taken.

Quick Check

1. (*Learning Objective 1*) In making short-term special decisions, you should
   a. focus on total costs.
   b. separate variable from fixed costs.
   c. use a traditional absorption costing approach.
   d. focus only on quantitative factors.
2. (*Learning Objective 1*) When making decisions, managers should
   a. consider sunk costs.
   b. consider costs that do not differ between alternatives.
   c. consider only variable costs.
   d. consider revenues that differ between alternatives.

3. (*Learning Objective 1*) Which of the following costs are irrelevant to business decisions?
   a. Sunk costs
   b. Costs that differ between alternatives
   c. Variable costs
   d. Avoidable costs

4. (*Learning Objective 2*) Which of the following is relevant to Amazon.com's decision to accept a special order at a lower sales price from a large customer in China?
   a. The cost of Amazon.com's warehouses in the United States
   b. Amazon.com's investment in its website
   c. The cost of shipping the order to the customer
   d. Founder Jeff Bezos's salary

5. (*Learning Objective 3*) When companies are price-setters, their products and services
   a. are priced by managers using a target-pricing emphasis.
   b. tend to be unique.
   c. tend to have a great many competitors.
   d. tend to be commodities.

6. (*Learning Objective 3*) When pricing a product or service, managers must consider which of the following?
   a. Only variable costs
   b. Only period costs
   c. Only manufacturing costs
   d. All costs

7. (*Learning Objective 4*) In deciding whether to drop its electronics product line, Amazon.com would consider
   a. the costs it could save by discontinuing the product line.
   b. the revenues it would lose from discontinuing the product line.
   c. how discontinuing the electronics product line would affect sales of its other products, such as mp3s.
   d. all of the above.

8. (*Learning Objective 5*) In deciding which product lines to emphasize, Amazon.com should focus on the product line that has the highest
   a. contribution margin per unit of the constraining factor.
   b. contribution margin per unit of product.
   c. contribution margin ratio.
   d. profit per unit of product.

9. (*Learning Objective 6*) When making outsourcing decisions
   a. the manufacturing full unit cost of making the product in-house is relevant.
   b. the variable cost of producing the product in-house is relevant.
   c. avoidable fixed costs are irrelevant.
   d. expected use of the freed capacity is irrelevant.

10. (*Learning Objective 7*) When deciding whether to sell as is or process a product further, managers should ignore which of the following?
    a. The revenue if the product is processed further
    b. The cost of processing further
    c. The costs of processing the product thus far
    d. The revenue if the product is sold as is

Quick Check Answers

1. b 2. d 3. a 4. c 5. b 6. d 7. d 8. a 9. b 10. c

Short Exercises

S8-1 Determine relevance of information (*Learning Objective 1*)

You are trying to decide whether to trade in your laser printer for a more recent model. Your usage pattern will remain unchanged, but the old and new printers use different toner cartridges. Are the following items relevant or irrelevant to your decision?

a. The price of the new printer
b. The price you paid for the old printer
c. The trade-in value of the old printer
d. Paper costs
e. The difference between the cost of toner cartridges

S8-2 Special order decision (*Learning Objective 2*)

Forst Manufacturing produces and sells oil filters for $3.30 each. A retailer has offered to purchase 20,000 oil filters for $1.55 per filter. Of the total manufacturing cost per filter of $1.95, $1.50 is the variable manufacturing cost per filter. For this special order, Forst would have to buy a special stamping machine that costs $8,500 to mark the customer's logo on the special-order oil filters. The machine would be scrapped when the special order is complete. This special order would use manufacturing capacity that would otherwise be idle. No variable nonmanufacturing costs would be incurred by the special order. Regular sales would not be affected by the special order.

Would you recommend that Forst accept the special order under these conditions?

S8-3 Determine pricing approach and target price *(Learning Objective 3)*

SnowCastles operates a Rocky Mountain ski resort. The company is planning its lift ticket pricing for the coming ski season. Investors would like to earn a 14% return on the company's $100 million of assets. The company incurs primarily fixed costs to groom the runs and operate the lifts. SnowCastles projects fixed costs to be $34,000,000 for the ski season. The resort serves about 800,000 skiers and snowboarders each season. Variable costs are about $8 per guest. Currently, the resort has such a favorable reputation among skiers and snowboarders that it has some control over the lift ticket prices.

1. Would SnowCastles emphasize target costing or cost-plus pricing. Why?
2. If other resorts in the area charge $60 per day, what price should SnowCastles charge?

S8-4 Use target costing to analyze data *(Learning Objective 3)*

Consider SnowCastles from S8-3. Assume that SnowCastles' reputation has diminished and other resorts in the vicinity are charging only $60 per lift ticket. SnowCastles has become a price-taker and won't be able to charge more than its competitors. At the market price, SnowCastles' managers believe they will still serve 800,000 skiers and snowboarders each season.

1. If SnowCastles can't reduce its costs, what profit will it earn? State your answer in dollars and as a percent of assets. Will investors be happy with the profit level? Show your analysis.
2. Assume that SnowCastles has found ways to cut its fixed costs to $31 million. What is its new target variable cost per skier/snowboarder? Compare this to the current variable cost per skier/snowboarder. Comment on your results.

S8-5 Decide whether to discontinue a department *(Learning Objective 4)*

Zena Fashion in New York operates three departments: Men's, Women's, and Accessories. Zena Fashion allocates all fixed expenses (unavoidable building depreciation and utilities) based on each department's square footage. Departmental operating income data for the third quarter of the current year are as follows:

	Department			
	Men's	Women's	Accessories	Total
Sales revenue	$106,000	$54,000	$100,000	$260,000
Variable expenses	58,000	28,000	88,000	174,000
Fixed expenses	26,000	21,000	25,000	72,000
Total expenses	$ 84,000	$49,000	$113,000	$246,000
Operating income (loss)	$ 22,000	$ 5,000	$ (13,000)	$ 14,000

The store will remain in the same building regardless of whether any of the departments are discontinued. Should Zena Fashion discontinue any of the departments? Give your reason.

S8-6 Discontinue a department: Revised information *(Learning Objective 4)*

Consider Zena Fashion from S8-5. Assume that the fixed expenses assigned to each department include only direct fixed costs of the department (rather than unavoidable fixed costs as given in S8-5):

- Salary of the department's manager
- Cost of advertising directly related to that department

If Zena Fashion discontinues a department, it will not incur these fixed expenses. Under these circumstances, should Zena Fashion discontinue any of the departments? Give your reason.

S8-7 Replace a department *(Learning Objective 4)*

Consider Zena Fashion from S8-5. Assume once again that all fixed costs are unavoidable. If Zena Fashion discontinues one of the current departments, it plans to replace the discontinued department with a Shoe Department. The company expects the Shoe

Department to produce $77,000 in sales and have $47,000 of variable costs. Because the shoe business would be new to Zena Fashion, the company would have to incur an additional $7,100 of fixed costs (advertising, new shoe display racks, and so forth) per quarter related to the department. What should Zena Fashion do now?

S8-8 Product mix decision: Unlimited demand *(Learning Objective 5)*

Boxes Unlimited produces plastic storage bins for household storage needs. The company makes two sizes of bins: Large (50 gallon) and Regular (35 gallon). Demand for the product is so high that Boxes Unlimited can sell as many of each size as it can produce. The company uses the same machinery to produce both sizes. The machinery can be run for only 3,500 hours per period. The company can produce 11 Large bins every hour compared to 15 Regular bins in the same amount of time. Fixed expenses amount to $100,000 per period. Sales prices and variable costs are as follows:

	Regular	Large
Sales price per unit.	$8.50	$10.60
Variable cost per unit	$3.50	$ 4.60

1. Which product should Boxes Unlimited emphasize? Why?
2. To maximize profits, how many of each size bin should the company produce?
3. Given this product mix, what will the company's operating income be?

S8-9 Product mix decision: Limited demand *(Learning Objective 5)*

Consider Boxes Unlimited in S8-8. Assume that demand for Regular bins is limited to 30,000 units and demand for Large bins is limited to 25,000 units.

1. How many of each size bin should the company make now?
2. Given this product mix, what will be the company's operating income?
3. Explain why the operating income is less than it was when the company was producing its optimal product mix.

S8-10 Outsourcing production decision *(Learning Objectives 1 & 6)*

Suppose an Olive Garden restaurant is considering whether to (1) bake bread for its restaurant in-house or (2) buy the bread from a local bakery. The chef estimates that variable costs of making each loaf include $0.50 of ingredients, $0.20 of variable overhead (electricity to run the oven), and $0.70 of direct labor for kneading and forming the loaves. Allocating fixed overhead (depreciation on the kitchen equipment and building) based on direct labor assigns $1.00 of fixed overhead per loaf. None of the fixed costs are avoidable. The local bakery would charge Olive Garden $1.80 per loaf.

1. What is the unit cost of making the bread in-house (use absorption costing)?
2. Should Olive Garden bake the bread in-house or buy from the local bakery? Why?
3. In addition to the financial analysis, what else should Olive Garden consider when making this decision?

S8-11 Relevant information for outsourcing delivery function *(Learning Objectives 1 & 6)*

Grier Food in Lexington, Kentucky, manufactures and markets snack foods. Deela Riley manages the company's fleet of 180 delivery trucks. Riley has been charged with "reengineering" the fleet-management function. She has an important decision to make.

- Should she continue to manage the fleet in-house with the five employees reporting to her? To do so, she will have to acquire new fleet-management software to streamline Grier Food's fleet-management process.
- Should she outsource the fleet-management function to Fleet Management Services, a company that specializes in managing fleets of trucks for other companies? Fleet Management Services would take over the maintenance, repair, and scheduling of Grier Food's fleet (but Grier Food would retain ownership). This alternative would require Riley to lay off her five employees. However, her own job would be secure, as she would be Grier Food's liaison with Fleet Management Services.

Assume that Riley's records show the following data concerning Grier Food's fleet:

Book value of Grier Food's trucks, with an estimated five-year life	$3,100,000
Annual leasing fee for new fleet-management software	$ 8,600
Annual maintenance of trucks	$ 166,000
Fleet Supervisor Riley's annual salary	$ 57,000
Total annual salaries of Grier Food's five other fleet-management employees	$ 150,000

Suppose that Fleet Management Services offers to manage Grier Food's fleet for an annual fee of $280,000.

Which alternative will maximize Grier Food's short-term operating income?

S8-12 Outsourcing qualitative considerations *(Learning Objectives 1 & 6)*

Refer to Grier Food in S8-11. What qualitative factors should Riley consider before making a final decision?

S8-13 Scrap or process further decision *(Learning Objective 7)*

Paulson Auto Components has an inventory of 490 obsolete remote entry keys that are carried in inventory at a manufacturing cost of $79,870. Production Supervisor Ricky Lewis must decide to do one of the following:

- Process the inventory further at a cost of $19,000, with the expectation of selling it for $31,000
- Scrap the inventory for a sale price of $6,000

What should Lewis do? Present figures to support your decision.

S8-14 Determine most profitable final product *(Learning Objective 7)*

Cocoalicious processes cocoa beans into cocoa powder at a processing cost of $9,600 per batch. Cocoalicious can sell the cocoa powder as is, or it can process the cocoa powder further into chocolate syrup or boxed assorted chocolates. Once processed, each batch of cocoa beans would result in the following sales revenue:

Cocoa powder	$ 12,000
Chocolate syrup	$103,000
Boxed assorted chocolates	$202,000

The cost of transforming the cocoa powder into chocolate syrup would be $68,000. Likewise, the company would incur $176,000 to transform the cocoa powder into boxed assorted chocolates. The company president has decided to make boxed assorted chocolates owing to its high sales value and to the fact that the $9,600 cost of processing cocoa beans "eats up" most of the cocoa powder profits. Has the president made the right or wrong decision? Explain your answer.

EXERCISES Group A

E8-15A Determine relevant and irrelevant information *(Learning Objective 1)*

Swenson's Meats is considering whether it should replace a meat grinder patty shaper machine. The new machine will produce 25% more hamburger patties than the old machine in the same amount of time. (This machine is the bottleneck of the hamburger patty process for Swenson's.) The purchase of the new machine will cause fixed selling costs to increase, but variable selling costs will not be affected. The new machine will require installation by a specialty engineering firm. If the new machine is purchased, the old machine can be sold to an overseas meat processing company. The old machine requires frequent (quarterly) repairs and maintenance to keep it running. The new machine will require maintenance only once per year. The new machine will be paid for by signing a note payable with the bank that will cover the cost of the machine and its installation. Swenson's will have to pay interest monthly on the note payable for the new machine. The note payable that was used to purchase the old machine was fully paid off two years ago.

For each of the following costs, indicate whether each of the costs described would be relevant or not to Swenson's Meats' decision about whether to purchase the new machine or to keep the old machine.

Item	Relevant	Not Relevant
a. Cost of new machine		
b. Cost of old machine		
c. Added profits from increase in production resulting from new machine		
d. Fixed selling costs		
e. Variable selling costs		
f. Sales value of old machine		
g. Interest expense on new machine		
h. Interest expense on old machine		
i. Book value of old machine		
j. Maintenance cost of new machine		
k. Repairs and maintenance costs of old machine		
l. Installation costs of new machine		
m. Accumulated depreciation on old machine		
n. Cost per pound of hamburger		
o. Installation cost of old machine		

E8-16A Special order decisions given two scenarios *(Learning Objective 2)*

Suppose the Baseball Hall of Fame in Cooperstown, New York, has approached Collectible Cards with a special order. The Hall of Fame wants to purchase 57,000 baseball card packs for a special promotional campaign and offers $0.40 per pack, a total of $22,800. Collectible Cards' total production cost is $0.60 per pack, as follows:

Variable costs:	
Direct materials	$0.13
Direct labor	0.06
Variable overhead	0.11
Fixed overhead	0.30
Total cost	$0.60

Collectible Cards has enough excess capacity to handle the special order.

Requirements

1. Prepare an incremental analysis to determine whether Collectible Cards should accept the special sales order assuming fixed costs would not be affected by the special order.
2. Now assume that the Hall of Fame wants special hologram baseball cards. Collectible Cards must spend $5,000 to develop this hologram, which will be useless after the special order is completed. Should Collectible Cards accept the special order under these circumstances? Show your analysis.

E8-17A Sustainability and short-term decision making *(Learning Objective 2)*

Over the past several years, decommissioned U.S. warships have been turned into artificial reefs in the ocean by towing them out to sea and sinking them. The thinking was that sinking the ship would conveniently dispose of it while providing an artificial reef environment for aquatic life. In reality, some of the sunken ships have released toxin into the ocean and have been costly to decontaminate. Now the U.S. government is taking bids to instead dismantle and recycle ships that have recently been decommissioned (but have not been sunk yet.)

Assume that a recently decommissioned aircraft carrier, the USS *Forrestal*, is estimated to contain approximately 40 tons of recyclable materials able to be sold for approximately $32.3 million. The low bid for dismantling and transporting the ship materials to appropriate facilities is $33.7 million. Recycling and dismantling the ship would create about 500 jobs for about a year in the Rust Belt. This geographic area has been experiencing record-high unemployment rates in recent years.

1. Is it more financially advantageous to sink the ship (assume that it costs approximately $1.2 million to tow a ship out to sea and sink it) or to dismantle and recycle it? Show your calculations.
2. From a sustainability standpoint, what should be done with the decommissioned aircraft carrier? List some of the qualitative factors that should enter into this analysis.
3. As a taxpayer, which action would you prefer (sink or recycle)? Defend your answer.

E8-18A Special order decision and considerations *(Learning Objective 2)*

Coco Bradley Sunglasses sell for about $150 per pair. Suppose the company incurs the following average costs per pair:

Direct materials	$40
Direct labor	14
Variable manufacturing overhead	11
Variable marketing expenses	2
Fixed manufacturing overhead	16*
Total costs	$83

$*\frac{2{,}000{,}000 \text{ total fixed manufacturing overhead}}{125{,}000 \text{ pairs of sunglasses}}$

Coco Bradley has enough idle capacity to accept a one-time-only special order from Oceanside Resorts for 20,000 pairs of sunglasses at $71 per pair. Coco Bradley will not incur any variable marketing expenses for the order.

Requirements

1. How would accepting the order affect Coco Bradley's operating income? In addition to the special order's effect on profits, what other (longer-term qualitative) factors should Coco Bradley's managers consider in deciding whether to accept the order?
2. Coco Bradley's marketing manager, Jim Revo, argues against accepting the special order because the offer price of $71 is less than Coco Bradley's $83 cost to make the sunglasses. Revo asks you, as one of Coco Bradley's staff accountants, to write a memo explaining whether his analysis is correct.

E8-19A Pricing decisions given two scenarios *(Learning Objective 3)*

Smith Builders builds 1,500-square-foot starter tract homes in the fast-growing suburbs of Chicago. Land and labor are cheap, and competition among developers is fierce. The homes are "cookie-cutter," with any upgrades added by the buyer after the sale. Smith Builders' costs per developed sublot are as follows:

Land	$ 57,000
Construction	$124,000
Landscaping	$ 5,000
Variable marketing costs	$ 4,000

Smith Builders would like to earn a profit of 14% of the variable cost of each home sale. Similar homes offered by competing builders sell for $206,000 each.

Requirements

1. Which approach to pricing should Smith Builders emphasize? Why?
2. Will Smith Builders be able to achieve its target profit levels? Show your computations.

3. Bathrooms and kitchens are typically the most important selling features of a home. Smith Builders could differentiate the homes by upgrading bathrooms and kitchens. The upgrades would cost $18,000 per home but would enable Smith Builders to increase the selling prices by $31,500 per home (in general, kitchen and bathroom upgrades typically add at least 150% of their cost to the value of any home). If Smith Builders upgrades, what will the new cost-plus price per home be? Should the company differentiate its product in this manner? Show your analysis.

E8-20A Decide whether to discontinue a product line *(Learning Objective 4)*

Top managers of Entertainment Plus are alarmed by their operating losses. They are considering dropping the DVD product line. Company accountants have prepared the following analysis to help make this decision:

	Total	Blu-ray Discs	DVDs
Sales revenue	$437,000	$301,000	$136,000
Variable expenses	244,000	158,000	86,000
Contribution margin	$193,000	$143,000	$ 50,000
Fixed expenses:			
Manufacturing	134,000	77,000	57,000
Marketing and administrative	64,000	53,000	11,000
Total fixed expenses	$198,000	$130,000	$ 68,000
Operating income (loss)	$ (5,000)	$ 13,000	$ (18,000)

Total fixed costs will not change if the company stops selling DVDs.

Requirements

1. Prepare an incremental analysis to show whether Entertainment Plus should discontinue the DVD product line. Will discontinuing DVDs add $18,000 to operating income? Explain.
2. Assume that the company can avoid $20,000 of fixed expenses by discontinuing the DVD product line (these costs are direct fixed costs of the DVD product line). Prepare an incremental analysis to show whether the company should stop selling DVDs.
3. Now, assume that all $68,000 of fixed costs assigned to DVDs are direct fixed costs and can be avoided if the company stops selling DVDs. However, marketing has concluded that Blu-ray disc sales would be adversely affected by discontinuing the DVD line (retailers want to buy both from the same supplier). Blu-ray disc production and sales would decline 10%. What should the company do?

E8-21A Discontinuing a product line *(Learning Objective 4)*

Suppose General Mills is considering discontinuing its organic cereal product line. Assume that during the past year, the organic cereal's product line income statement showed the following:

Sales	$7,500,000
Cost of goods sold	6,500,000
Gross profit	$1,000,000
Operating expenses	1,250,000
Operating loss	$ (250,000)

Fixed manufacturing overhead costs account for 40% of the cost of goods, while only 30% of the operating expenses are fixed. Since the organic cereal line is only one of General Mills' breakfast cereals, only $780,000 of direct fixed costs (the majority of which is advertising) will be eliminated if the product line is discontinued. The remainder of the fixed costs will still be incurred by General Mills. If the company decides to discontinue the product line, what will happen to the company's operating income? Should General Mills discontinue the product line?

E8-22A Identify constraint, then determine product mix *(Learning Objective 5)*

Get Fit produces two types of exercise treadmills: Regular and Deluxe. The exercise craze is such that Get Fit could use all of its available machine hours producing either model. The two models are processed through the same production department.

	Per Unit	
	Deluxe	**Regular**
Sale price	$1,010	$560
Costs:		
Direct materials	$ 310	$ 90
Direct labor	88	184
Variable manufacturing overhead	264	88
Fixed manufacturing overhead*	114	38
Variable operating expenses	119	65
Total cost	$ 895	$465
Operating income	$ 115	$ 95

* *Allocated on the basis of machine hours.*

What product mix will maximize operating income? (*Hint:* Use the allocation of fixed manufacturing overhead to determine the proportion of machine hours used by each product.)

E8-23A Determine product mix for retailer *(Learning Objective 5)*

Honacker Fashions sells both designer and moderately priced fashion accessories. Top management is deciding which product line to emphasize. Accountants have provided the following data:

	Per Item	
	Designer	**Moderately Priced**
Average sale price	$205	$83
Average variable expenses	95	28
Average fixed expenses (allocated)	20	10
Average operating income	$ 90	$45

The Honacker store in Charleston, South Carolina, has 14,000 square feet of floor space. If Honacker emphasizes moderately priced goods, it can display 840 items in the store. If Honacker emphasizes designer wear, it can display only 560 designer items to create more of a boutique-like atmosphere. These numbers are also the average monthly sales in units.

Prepare an analysis to show which product to emphasize.

E8-24A Determine product mix for retailer—two stocking scenarios *(Learning Objective 5)*

Each morning, Nick Ivery stocks the drink case at Nick's Beach Hut in Newark, New Jersey. Nick's Beach Hut has 115 linear feet of refrigerated display space for cold drinks. Each linear foot can hold either five 12-ounce cans or four 20-ounce plastic or glass bottles. Nick's Beach Hut sells three types of cold drinks:

1. Cola in 12-oz. cans for $1.55 per can
2. Energy drink in 20-oz. plastic bottles for $1.80 per bottle
3. Orange soda in 20-oz. glass bottles for $2.15 per bottle

Nick's Beach Hut pays its suppliers the following:

1. $0.25 per 12-oz. can of cola
2. $0.40 per 20-oz. bottle of energy drink
3. $0.65 per 20-oz. bottle of orange soda

Nick's Beach Hut's monthly fixed expenses include the following:

Hut rental	$ 375
Refrigerator rental	75
Nick's salary	1,550
Total fixed expenses	$2,000

Nick's Beach Hut can sell all drinks stocked in the display case each morning.

Requirements

1. What is Nick's Beach Hut's constraining factor? What should Nick stock to maximize profits? What is the maximum contribution margin he could generate from refrigerated drinks each day?
2. To provide variety to customers, suppose Nick refuses to devote more than 70 linear feet and no less than 15 linear feet to any individual product. Under this condition, how many linear feet of each drink should Nick stock? How many units of each product will be available for sale each day?
3. Assuming the product mix calculated in Requirement 2, what contribution margin will Nick generate from refrigerated drinks each day?

E8-25A Make-or-buy product component *(Learning Objective 6)*

OptiSystems manufactures an optical switch that it uses in its final product. OptiSystems incurred the following manufacturing costs when it produced 72,000 units last year:

Direct materials	$ 720,000
Direct labor	180,000
Variable overhead	216,000
Fixed overhead	468,000
Total manufacturing cost for 72,000 units	$1,584,000

OptiSystems does not yet know how many switches it will need this year; however, another company has offered to sell OptiSystems the switch for $17 per unit. If OptiSystems buys the switch from the outside supplier, the manufacturing facilities that will be idle cannot be used for any other purpose, yet none of the fixed costs are avoidable.

Requirements

1. Given the same cost structure, should OptiSystems make or buy the switch? Show your analysis.
2. Now, assume that OptiSystems can avoid $100,000 of fixed costs a year by outsourcing production. In addition, because sales are increasing, OptiSystems needs 77,000 switches a year rather than 72,000. What should the company do now?
3. Given the last scenario, what is the most OptiSystems would be willing to pay to outsource the switches?

E8-26A Make-or-buy with alternative use of facilities *(Learning Objective 6)*

Refer to E8-25A. OptiSystems needs 84,000 optical switches next year (assume same relevant range). By outsourcing them, OptiSystems can use its idle facilities to manufacture another product that will contribute $120,000 to operating income, but none of the fixed costs will be avoidable. Should OptiSystems make or buy the switches? Show your analysis.

E8-27A Determine maximum outsourcing price *(Learning Objective 6)*

Henderson Containers manufactures a variety of boxes used for packaging. Sales of its Model A20 box have increased significantly to a total of 420,000 A20 boxes. Henderson has enough existing production capacity to make all of the boxes it needs. The variable cost of making each A20 box is $0.70. By outsourcing the manufacture of these A20 boxes, Henderson can reduce its current fixed costs by $84,000. There is no alternative use for the factory space freed up through outsourcing, so it will just remain idle.

What is the maximum Henderson will pay per Model A20 box to outsource production of this box?

E8-28A Sell as is or process further *(Learning Objective 7)*

Naturalmaid processes organic milk into plain yogurt. Naturalmaid sells plain yogurt to hospitals, nursing homes, and restaurants in bulk, one-gallon containers. Each batch, processed at a cost of $800, yields 600 gallons of plain yogurt. The company sells the one-gallon tubs for $6.00 each and spends $0.10 for each plastic tub. Naturalmaid has recently begun to reconsider its strategy. Management wonders if it would be more profitable to sell individual-sized portions of fruited organic yogurt at local food stores. Naturalmaid could further process each batch of plain yogurt into 12,800 individual portions (3/4 cup each) of fruited yogurt. A recent market analysis indicates that demand for the product exists. Naturalmaid would sell each individual portion for $0.50. Packaging would cost $0.05 per portion, and fruit would cost $0.15 per portion. Fixed costs would not change. Should Naturalmaid continue to sell only the gallon-sized plain yogurt (sell as is) or convert the plain yogurt into individual-sized portions of fruited yogurt (process further)? Why?

EXERCISES Group B

E8-29B Determine relevant and irrelevant information *(Learning Objective 1)*

Zippy Frozen Foods purchased new computer-controlled production machinery last year from Advanced Design. The equipment was purchased for $4.1 million and was paid for with cash. A representative from Advanced Design recently contacted Zippy management because Advanced Design has an even more efficient piece of machinery available. The new design would double the production output of the equipment purchased last year but would cost Zippy another $5.0 million. The old machinery was installed by an engineering firm; the same firm would be required to install the new machinery. Fixed selling costs would not change if the new machinery were to be purchased. The variance selling cost per unit would decrease. Raw material costs (i.e., food ingredients) would remain the same with either machine. The new machinery would be purchased by signing a note payable at the bank and interest would be paid monthly on the note payable. Maintenance costs on the new machine would be the same as the maintenance costs on the machinery purchased last year. Advanced Design is offering a trade-in on the machinery purchased last year against the purchase price of the new machinery.

For each of the following costs, indicate whether each of the costs described would be relevant or not to Zippy Frozen Foods' decision about whether to purchase the new machinery or not.

Item	Relevant	Not Relevant
a. Book value of old machine		
b. Maintenance cost of new machine		
c. Maintenance cost of old machine		
d. Installation cost of new machine		
e. Accumulated depreciation on old machine		
f. Cost per pound of pizza dough		
g. Installation cost of old machine		
h. Cost of the new machine		
i. Cost of the old machine		
j. Added profits from the increase in production resulting from the new machine		
k. Fixed selling costs		
l. Variable selling costs		
m. Trade-in value of old machine		
n. Interest expense on new machine		
o. Sales tax paid on old machine		

E8-30B Special order decisions given two scenarios *(Learning Objective 2)*

Suppose the Baseball Hall of Fame in Cooperstown, New York, has approached SportCardz with a special order. The Hall of Fame wishes to purchase 50,000 baseball card packs for a special promotional campaign and offers $0.35 per pack, a total of $17,500. SportCardz total production cost is $0.55 per pack, as follows:

Variable costs:	
Direct materials	$0.12
Direct labor	0.07
Variable overhead	0.11
Fixed overhead	0.25
Total cost	$0.55

SportCardz has enough excess capacity to handle the special order.

Requirements

1. Prepare an incremental analysis to determine whether SportCardz should accept the special sales order assuming fixed costs would not be affected by the special order.
2. Now assume that the Hall of Fame wants special hologram baseball cards. SportCardz will spend $5,400 to develop this hologram, which will be useless after the special order is completed. Should SportCardz accept the special order under these circumstances? Show your analysis.

E8-31B Sustainability and short-term decision making *(Learning Objective 2)*

Over the past several years, decommissioned U.S. warships have been turned into artificial reefs in the ocean by towing them out to sea and sinking them. The thinking was that sinking the ship would conveniently dispose of it while providing an artificial reef environment for aquatic life. In reality, some of the sunken ships have released toxins into the ocean and have been costly to decontaminate. Now the U.S. government is taking bids to instead dismantle and recycle ships that have recently been decommissioned (but have not been sunk yet.)

Assume that a recently decommissioned aircraft carrier, the USS *Independence*, is estimated to contain approximately 40 tons of recyclable materials able to be sold for approximately $30.8 million. The low bid for dismantling and transporting the ship materials to appropriate facilities is $32.3 million. Recycling and dismantling the ship would create about 500 jobs for about a year in the Rust Belt. This geographic area has been experiencing record-high unemployment rates in recent years.

Requirements

1. Is it more financially advantageous to sink the ship (assume that it costs approximately $1.2 million to tow a ship out to sea and sink it) or to dismantle and recycle it? Show your calculations.
2. From a sustainability standpoint, what should be done with the decommissioned aircraft carrier? List some of the qualitative factors that should enter into this analysis.
3. As a taxpayer, which action would you prefer (sink or recycle)? Defend your answer.

E8-32B Special order decision and considerations *(Learning Objective 2)*

Sera Shade Sunglasses sell for about $151 per pair. Suppose the company incurs the following average costs per pair:

Direct materials	$40
Direct labor	12
Variable manufacturing overhead	7
Variable marketing expenses	4
Fixed manufacturing overhead	16*
Total costs	$79

*$2,100,000 total fixed manufacturing overhead / 131,250 pairs of sunglasses

Sera Shade has enough idle capacity to accept a one-time-only special order from Oceanview Hotels for 23,000 pairs of sunglasses at $64 per pair. Sera Shade will not incur any variable marketing expenses for the order.

Requirements

1. How would accepting the order affect Sera Shade's operating income? In addition to the special order's effect on profits, what other (longer-term, qualitative) factors should the company's managers consider in deciding whether to accept the order?
2. Sera Shade's marketing manager argues against accepting the special order because the offer price of $64 is less than the cost to make the sunglasses. The marketing manager asks you, as one of Sera Shades' staff accountants, to explain whether this analysis is correct.

E8-33B Pricing decisions given two scenarios *(Learning Objective 3)*

Johnson Builders builds 1,500-square-foot starter tract homes in the fast-growing suburbs of Atlanta. Land and labor are cheap, and competition among developers is fierce. The homes are "cookie-cutter," with any upgrades added by the buyer after the sale. Johnson Builders' costs per developed sublot are as follows:

Land	$ 53,000
Construction	$125,000
Landscaping	$ 6,000
Variable marketing costs	$ 1,000

Johnson Builders would like to earn a profit of 16% of the variable cost of each home sale. Similar homes offered by competing builders sell for $201,000 each.

Requirements

1. Which approach to pricing should Johnson Builders emphasize? Why?
2. Will Johnson Builders be able to achieve its target profit levels? Show your computations.
3. Bathrooms and kitchens are typically the most important selling features of a home. Johnson Builders could differentiate the homes by upgrading bathrooms and kitchens. The upgrades would cost $24,000 per home but would enable Johnson Builders to increase the selling prices by $42,000 per home (in general, kitchen and bathroom upgrades typically add at least 150% of their cost to the value of any home.) If Johnson Builders upgrades, what will the new cost-plus price per home be? Should the company differentiate its product in this manner? Show your analysis.

E8-34B Decide whether to discontinue a product line *(Learning Objective 4)*

Top managers of Movies Plus are alarmed by their operating losses. They are considering discontinuing the DVD product line. Company accountants have prepared the following analysis to help make this decision:

	Total	Blu-ray Discs	DVDs
Sales revenue	$429,000	$305,000	$124,000
Variable expenses	240,000	152,000	88,000
Contribution margin	$189,000	$153,000	$ 36,000
Fixed expenses:			
Manufacturing	128,000	73,000	55,000
Marketing and administrative	64,000	53,000	11,000
Total fixed expenses	$192,000	126,000	$ 66,000
Operating income (loss)	$ (3,000)	$ 27,000	$ (30,000)

Total fixed costs will not change if the company stops selling DVDs.

Requirements

1. Prepare an incremental analysis to show whether Movie Plus should discontinue the DVD product line. Will discontinuing the DVDs add $30,000 to operating income? Explain.
2. Assume that Movies Plus can avoid $32,000 of fixed expenses by discontinuing the DVD product line (these costs are direct fixed costs of the DVD product line). Prepare an incremental analysis to show whether Movies Plus should stop selling DVDs.
3. Now, assume that all $66,000 of fixed costs assigned to DVDs are direct fixed costs and can be avoided if the company stops selling DVDs. However, marketing has concluded that Blu-ray disc sales would be adversely affected by discontinuing the DVD line (retailers want to buy both from the same supplier). Blu-ray disc production and sales would decline 10%. What should the company do?

E8-35B Discontinuing a product line *(Learning Objective 4)*

Suppose Post Cereals is considering discontinuing its maple cereal product line. Assume that during the past year, the maple cereal product line income statement showed the following:

Sales	$ 5,200,000
Cost of goods sold	6,350,000
Gross profit	$ (1,150,000)
Operating expenses	1,500,000
Operating loss	$ (2,650,000)

Fixed manufacturing overhead costs account for 40% of the cost of goods, while only 30% of the operating expenses are fixed. Since the maple cereal line is only one of Post Cereals' breakfast cereals, only $755,000 of direct fixed costs (the majority of which is advertising) will be eliminated if the product line is discontinued. The remainder of the fixed costs will still be incurred by Post Cereals. If the company decides to discontinue the product line, what will happen to the company's operating income? Should Post Cereals discontinue the maple cereal product line?

E8-36B Identify constraint, then determine product mix *(Learning Objective 5)*

TreadMile produces two types of exercise treadmills: Regular and Deluxe. The exercise craze is such that TreadMile could use all of its available machine hours producing either model. The two models are processed through the same production department.

	Per Unit	
	Deluxe	**Regular**
Sale price	$990	$550
Costs:		
Direct materials	$300	$100
Direct labor	82	182
Variable manufacturing overhead	252	84
Fixed manufacturing overhead*	126	42
Variable operating expenses	115	67
Total cost	$875	$475
Operating income	$115	$ 75

**Allocated on the basis of machine hours.*

What product mix will maximize operating income? (*Hint*: Use the allocation of fixed manufacturing overhead to determine the proportion of machine hours used by each product.)

E8-37B Determine product mix for retailer *(Learning Objective 5)*

Melanie Fashions sells both designer and moderately priced fashion accessories. Top management is deciding which product line to emphasize. Accountants have provided the following data:

	Per Item	
	Designer	**Moderately Priced**
Average sale price	$210	$85
Average variable expenses	75	25
Average fixed expenses (allocated)	15	10
Average operating income	$120	$50

The Melanie Fashions store in Reno, Nevada, has 15,000 square feet of floor space. If Melanie emphasizes moderately priced goods, it can display 900 items in the store. If Melanie emphasizes designer wear, it can display only 600 designer items to create more of a boutique-like atmosphere. These numbers also are the average monthly sales in units. Prepare an analysis to show which product to emphasize.

E8-38B Determine product mix for retailer—two stocking scenarios *(Learning Objective 5)*

Each morning, Mark Johnston stocks the drink case at Mark's Beach Hut in Myrtle Beach, South Carolina. Mark's Beach Hut has 120 linear feet of refrigerated display space for cold drinks. Each linear foot can hold either five 12-ounce cans or three 20-ounce plastic or glass bottles.

Mark's Beach Hut sells three types of cold drinks:

1. Cola in 12-oz. cans, for $1.50 per can
2. Juice in 20-oz. plastic bottles, for $1.65 per bottle
3. Diet cola in 20-oz. glass bottles, for $2.15 per bottle

Mark's Beach Hut pays its suppliers the following:

1. $0.10 per 12-oz. can of cola
2. $0.45 per 20-oz. bottle of juice
3. $0.65 per 20-oz. bottle of diet cola

Mark's Beach Hut's monthly fixed expenses include the following:

Hut rental	$ 370
Refrigerator rental	85
Mark's salary	1,400
Total fixed expenses	$1,855

Mark's Beach Hut can sell all the drinks stocked in the display case each morning.

Requirements

1. What is Mark's Beach Hut's constraining factor? What should Mark stock to maximize profits? What is the maximum contribution margin he could generate from refrigerated drinks each day?
2. To provide variety to customers, suppose Mark refuses to devote more than 70 linear feet and no less than 20 linear feet to any individual product. Under this condition, how many linear feet of each drink should Mark stock? How many units of each product will be available for sale each day?
3. Assuming the product mix calculated in Requirement 2, what contribution margin will Mark generate from refrigerated drinks each day?

E8-39B Make-or-buy product component *(Learning Objective 6)*

World Systems manufactures an optical switch that it uses in its final product. World Systems incurred the following manufacturing costs when it produced 66,000 units last year:

Direct materials	$ 726,000
Direct labor	99,000
Variable overhead	132,000
Fixed overhead	363,000
Total manufacturing cost for 66,000 units	$1,320,000

World Systems does not yet know how many switches it will need this year; however, another company has offered to sell World Systems the switch for $12.50 per unit. If World Systems buys the switch from the outside supplier, the manufacturing facilities that will be idle cannot be used for any other purpose, yet none of the fixed costs are avoidable.

Requirements

1. Given the same cost structure, should World Systems make or buy the switch? Show your analysis.
2. Now, assume that World Systems can avoid $99,000 of fixed costs a year by outsourcing production. In addition, because sales are increasing, World Systems needs 71,000 switches a year rather than 66,000. What should World Systems do now?
3. Given the last scenario, what is the most World Systems would be willing to pay to outsource the switches?

E8-40B Make-or-buy with alternative use of facilities *(Learning Objective 6)*

Refer to E8-39B. World Systems needs 80,000 optical switches next year (assume same relevant range). By outsourcing them, World Systems can use its idle facilities to manufacture another product that will contribute $120,000 to operating income, but none of the fixed costs will be avoidable. Should World Systems make or buy the switches? Show your analysis.

E8-41B Determine maximum outsourcing price *(Learning Objective 6)*

Augustine Containers manufactures a variety of boxes used for packaging. Sales of its Model A30 box have increased significantly to a total of 360,000 A30 boxes. Augustine has enough existing production capacity to make all of the boxes it needs. The variable cost of making each A30 box is $0.80. By outsourcing the manufacture of these A30 boxes, Augustine can reduce its current fixed costs by $54,000. There is no alternative use for the factory space freed up through outsourcing, so it will just remain idle.

What is the maximum Augustine will pay per Model A30 box to outsource production of this box?

E8-42B Sell as is or process further *(Learning Objective 7)*

Dairyfood processes organic milk into plain yogurt. Dairyfood sells plain yogurt to hospitals, nursing homes, and restaurants in bulk, one-gallon containers. Each batch, processed at a cost of $800, yields 570 gallons of plain yogurt. Dairyfood sells the one-gallon tubs for $6.00 each, and spends $0.10 for each plastic tub. Management has recently begun to reconsider its strategy. Dairyfood wonders if it would be more profitable to sell individual-sized portions of fruited organic yogurt at local food stores. Dairyfood could further process each batch of plain yogurt into 12,160 individual portions (3/4 cup each) of fruited yogurt. A recent market analysis indicates that demand for the product exists. Dairyfood would sell each individual portion for $0.50. Packaging would cost $0.08 per portion, and fruit would cost $0.12 per portion. Fixed costs would not change. Should Dairyfood continue to sell only the gallon-sized plain yogurt (sell as is) or convert the plain yogurt into individual-sized portions of fruited yogurt (process further)? Why?

PROBLEMS Group A

P8-43A Special order decision and considerations *(Learning Objective 2)*

Summer Fun manufactures flotation vests in Atlanta, Georgia. Summer Fun's contribution margin income statement for the most recent month contains the following data:

Sales in units	31,000
Sales revenue	$496,000
Variable expenses:	
Manufacturing	$ 93,000
Marketing and administrative	104,000
Total variable expenses	197,000
Contribution margin	$299,000
Fixed expenses:	
Manufacturing	130,000
Marketing and administrative	87,000
Total fixed expenses	$217,000
Operating income	$ 82,000

Suppose Luxury Cruiselines wants to buy 5,700 vests from Summer Fun. Acceptance of the order will not increase Summer Fun's variable marketing and administrative expenses or any of its fixed expenses. The Summer Fun plant has enough unused capacity to manufacture the additional vests. Luxury Cruiseline has offered $10 per vest, which is below the normal sale price of $16.

Requirements

1. Prepare an incremental analysis to determine whether Summer Fun should accept this special sales order.
2. Identify long-term factors Summer Fun should consider in deciding whether to accept the special sales order.

P8-44A Pricing of nursery plants *(Learning Objective 3)*

Nature House operates a commercial plant nursery where it propagates plants for garden centers throughout the region. Nature House has $4.9 million in assets. Its yearly fixed costs are $682,000, and the variable costs for the potting soil, container, label, seedling, and labor for each gallon-sized plant total $1.30. Nature House's volume is currently 480,000 units. Competitors offer the same quality plants to garden centers for $4.00 each. Garden centers then mark them up to sell to the public for $9 to $11, depending on the type of plant.

Requirements

1. Nature House's owners want to earn a 14% return on the company's assets. What is Nature House's target full cost?
2. Given Nature House's current costs, will its owners be able to achieve their target profit? Show your analysis.
3. Assume that Nature House has identified ways to cut its variable costs to $1.15 per unit. What is its new target fixed cost? Will this decrease in variable costs allow the company to achieve its target profit? Show your analysis.
4. Nature House started an aggressive advertising campaign strategy to differentiate its plants from those grown by other nurseries. Nature House doesn't expect volume to be affected, but it hopes to gain more control over pricing. If Nature House has to spend $110,400 this year to advertise and its variable costs continue to be $1.15 per unit, what will its cost-plus price be? Do you think Nature House will be able to sell its plants to garden centers at the cost-plus price? Why or why not?

P8-45A Prepare and use contribution margin statements for discontinuing a line decision *(Learning Objective 4)*

Members of the board of directors of Security One have received the following operating income data for the year just ended:

	Product Line		
	Industrial Systems	**Household Systems**	**Total**
Sales revenue	$320,000	$330,000	$650,000
Cost of goods sold:			
Variable	$ 39,000	$ 42,000	$ 81,000
Fixed	220,000	67,000	287,000
Total cost of goods sold	$259,000	$109,000	$368,000
Gross profit	$ 61,000	$221,000	$282,000
Marketing and administrative expenses:			
Variable	65,000	73,000	138,000
Fixed	40,000	22,000	62,000
Total marketing and administrative expenses	$105,000	$95,000	$200,000
Operating income (loss)	$ (44,000)	$126,000	$ 82,000

Members of the board are surprised that the industrial systems product line is losing money. They commission a study to determine whether the company should discontinue the line. Company accountants estimate that discontinuing industrial systems will decrease fixed cost of goods sold by $83,000 and decrease fixed marketing and administrative expenses by $13,000.

Requirements

1. Prepare an incremental analysis to show whether Security One should discontinue the industrial systems product line.
2. Prepare contribution margin income statements to show Security One's total operating income under the two alternatives: (a) with the industrial systems line and (b) without the line. Compare the *difference* between the two alternatives' income numbers to your answer to Requirement 1. What have you learned from this comparison?

P8-46A Product mix decision under constraint *(Learning Objective 5)*

Brett Products, located in Buffalo, New York, produces two lines of electric toothbrushes: Deluxe and Standard. Because Brett can sell all of the toothbrushes it produces, the owners are expanding the plant. They are deciding which product line to emphasize. To make this decision, they assemble the following data:

	Per Unit	
	Deluxe Toothbrush	Standard Toothbrush
Sale price	$92	$45
Variable expenses	23	18
Contribution margin	$69	$27
Contribution margin ratio	75%	60%

After expansion, the factory will have a production capacity of 4,700 machine hours per month. The plant can manufacture either 56 Standard electric toothbrushes or 25 Deluxe electric toothbrushes per machine hour.

Requirements

1. Identify the constraining factor for Brett.
2. Prepare an analysis to show which product line to emphasize.

P8-47A Outsourcing decision given alternative use of capacity *(Learning Objective 6)*

Outdoor Life manufactures snowboards. Its cost of making 1,890 bindings is as follows:

Direct materials	$18,000
Direct labor	3,200
Variable manufacturing overhead	2,340
Fixed manufacturing overhead	6,700
Total manufacturing costs	$30,240
Cost per pair ($30,240 ÷ 1,890)	$ 16.00

Suppose an outside supplier will sell bindings to Outdoor Life for $13 each. Outdoor Life will pay $2.00 per unit to transport the bindings to its manufacturing plant, where it will add its own logo at a cost of $0.40 per binding.

Requirements

1. Outdoor Life's accountants predict that purchasing the bindings from the outside supplier will enable the company to avoid $2,000 of fixed overhead. Prepare an analysis to show whether Outdoor Life should make or buy the bindings.
2. The facilities freed by purchasing bindings from the outside supplier can be used to manufacture another product that will contribute $3,300 to profit. Total fixed costs will be the same as if Outdoor Life had produced the bindings. Show which alternative makes the best use of Outdoor Life's facilities: (a) make bindings, (b) buy bindings and leave facilities idle, or (c) buy bindings and make another product.

P8-48A Sell or process further decisions *(Learning Objective 7)*

Root Chemical has spent $244,000 to refine 70,000 gallons of acetone, which can be sold for $2.30 a gallon. Alternatively, Root Chemical can process the acetone further. This processing will yield a total of 60,000 gallons of lacquer thinner that can be sold for $3.00 a gallon. The additional processing will cost $0.60 per gallon of lacquer thinner. To sell the lacquer thinner, Root Chemical must pay shipping of $0.19 a gallon and administrative expenses of $0.11 a gallon on the thinner.

Requirements

1. Diagram Root's decision.
2. Identify the sunk cost. Is the sunk cost relevant to Root's decision? Why or why not?
3. Should Root sell the acetone or process it into lacquer thinner? Show the expected net revenue difference between the two alternatives.

PROBLEMS Group B

P8-49B Special order decision and considerations *(Learning Objective 2)*

Nautical Products, Inc., manufactures flotation vests in San Diego, California. Nautical Products' contribution margin income statement for the most recent month contains the following data:

Sales in units	29,000
Sales revenue	$435,000
Variable expenses:	
Manufacturing	$ 87,000
Marketing and administrative	102,000
Total variable expenses	$189,000
Contribution margin	$246,000
Fixed expenses:	
Manufacturing	124,000
Marketing and administrative	88,000
Total fixed expenses	$212,000
Operating income (loss)	$ 34,000

Suppose Royal Cruiselines wishes to buy 5,600 vests from Nautical Products. Acceptance of the order will not increase Nautical Products' variable marketing and administrative expenses. The Nautical Products plant has enough unused capacity to manufacture the additional vests. Royal Cruiselines has offered $6 per vest, which is below the normal sale price of $15.

Requirements

1. Prepare an incremental analysis to determine whether Nautical Products should accept this special sales order.
2. Identify long-term factors Nautical Products should consider in deciding whether to accept the special sales order.

P8-50B Pricing of nursery plants *(Learning Objective 3)*

Garden House operates a commercial plant nursery where it propagates plants for garden centers throughout the region. Garden House has $4.4 million in assets. Its yearly fixed costs are $580,000, and the variable costs for the potting soil, container, label, seedling, and labor for each gallon-sized plant total $1.15. Garden House's volume is currently 480,000 units. Competitors offer the same quality plants to garden centers for $3.40 each. Garden centers then mark them up to sell to the public for $8 to $10, depending on the type of plant.

Requirements

1. Garden House's owners want to earn a 13% return on the company's assets. What is Garden House's target full cost?
2. Given Garden House's current costs, will its owners be able to achieve their target profit? Show your analysis.
3. Assume that Garden House has identified ways to cut its variable costs to $1.00 per unit. What is its new target fixed cost? Will this decrease in variable costs allow the company to achieve its target profit? Show your analysis.

4. Garden House started an aggressive advertising campaign strategy to differentiate its plants from those grown by other nurseries. Garden House doesn't expect volume to be affected, but it hopes to gain more control over pricing. If Garden House has to spend $120,000 this year to advertise and its variable costs continue to be $1.00 per unit, what will its cost-plus price be? Do you think Garden House will be able to sell its plants to garden centers at the cost-plus price? Why or why not?

P8-51B Prepare and use contribution margin statements for discontinuing a line decision *(Learning Objective 4)*

Members of the board of directors of Safety Systems have received the following operating income data for the year just ended:

	Product Line		
	Industrial Systems	**Household Systems**	**Total**
Sales revenue	$330,000	$360,000	$690,000
Cost of goods sold:			
Variable	$ 35,000	$ 44,000	$ 79,000
Fixed	250,000	67,000	317,000
Total cost of goods sold	$285,000	$111,000	$396,000
Gross profit	$ 45,000	$249,000	$294,000
Marketing and administrative expenses:			
Variable	62,000	76,000	138,000
Fixed	39,000	23,000	62,000
Total marketing and administrative expenses	$101,000	$ 99,000	$200,000
Operating income (loss)	$ (56,000)	$150,000	$ 94,000

Members of the board are surprised that the industrial systems product line is losing money. They commission a study to determine whether the company should discontinue the line. Company accountants estimate that discontinuing industrial systems will decrease fixed cost of goods sold by $81,000 and decrease fixed marketing and administrative expenses by $14,000.

Requirements

1. Prepare an incremental analysis to show whether Safety Systems should discontinue the industrial systems product line.
2. Prepare contribution margin income statements to show Safety Systems' total operating income under the two alternatives: (a) with the industrial systems line and (b) without the line. Compare the *difference* between the two alternatives' income numbers to your answer to Requirement 1. What have you learned from this comparison?

P8-52B Product mix decision under constraint *(Learning Objective 5)*

Branson Products, Inc., located in Orlando, Florida, produces two lines of electric toothbrushes: Deluxe and Standard. Because Branson can sell all the toothbrushes it can produce, the owners are expanding the plant. They are deciding which product line to emphasize. To make this decision, they assemble the following data:

	Per Unit	
	Deluxe Toothbrush	**Regular Toothbrush**
Sale price	$80	$50
Variable expenses	22	16
Contribution margin	$58	$34
Contribution margin ratio	72.5%	68%

After expansion, the factory will have a production capacity of 4,600 machine hours per month. The plant can manufacture either 68 Standard electric toothbrushes or 28 Deluxe electric toothbrushes per machine hour.

Requirements

1. Identify the constraining factor for Branson.
2. Prepare an analysis to show which product line to emphasize.

P8-53B Outsourcing decision given alternative use of capacity *(Learning Objective 6)*

Snowtime Sports manufactures snowboards. Its cost of making 20,000 bindings is as follows:

Direct materials	$ 20,000
Direct labor	80,000
Variable manufacturing overhead	40,000
Fixed manufacturing overhead	80,000
Total manufacturing costs	$220,000
Cost per pair ($220,000 / 20,000)	$ 11.00

Suppose an outside supplier will sell bindings to Snowtime Sports for $9 each. Snowtime Sports would pay $1.00 per unit to transport the bindings to its manufacturing plant, where it would add its own logo at a cost $0.20 of per binding.

Requirements

1. Snowtime Sports' accountants predict that purchasing the bindings from an outside supplier will enable the company to avoid $2,100 of fixed overhead. Prepare an analysis to show whether Snowtime Sports should make or buy the bindings.
2. The facilities freed by purchasing bindings from the outside supplier can be used to manufacture another product that will contribute $2,900 to profit. Total fixed costs will be the same as if Snowtime Sports had produced the bindings. Show which alternative makes the best use of Snowtime Sports' facilities: (a) make bindings, (b) buy bindings and leave facilities idle, or (c) buy bindings and make another product.

P8-54B Sell or process further decisions *(Learning Objective 7)*

Stenbeck Chemical has spent $244,000 to refine 71,000 gallons of acetone, which can be sold for $2.00 a gallon. Alternatively, Stenbeck Chemical can process the acetone further. This processing will yield a total of 60,000 gallons of lacquer thinner that can be sold for $3.40 a gallon. The additional processing will cost $0.85 per gallon of lacquer thinner. To sell the lacquer thinner, Stenbeck Chemical must pay shipping of $0.19 a gallon and administrative expenses of $0.11 a gallon on the thinner.

Requirements

1. Diagram Stenbeck's decision.
2. Identify the sunk cost. Is the sunk cost relevant to Stenbeck's decision? Why or why not?
3. Should Stenbeck sell the acetone or process it into lacquer thinner? Show the expected net revenue difference between the two alternatives.

CRITICAL THINKING

Discussion & Analysis

A8-55 Discussion Questions

1. A beverage company is considering whether to discontinue its line of grape soda. What factors will affect the company's decision? What is a qualitative factor? Which of the factors you listed are qualitative?
2. What factors would be relevant to a restaurant that is considering whether to make its own dinner rolls or to purchase dinner rolls from a local bakery?
3. How would outsourcing change a company's cost structure? How might this change in cost structure help or harm a company's competitive position?
4. What is an opportunity cost? List possible opportunity costs associated with a make-or-buy decision.
5. What undesirable result can arise from allocating common fixed costs to product lines?
6. Why could a manager be justified in ignoring fixed costs when making a decision about a special order? When would fixed costs be relevant when making a decision about a special order?
7. What is the difference between segment margin and contribution margin? When would each be used?
8. Do joint costs affect a sell or process further decision? Why or why not?
9. How can "make-or-buy" concepts be applied to decisions at a service organization? What types of "make-or-buy" decisions might a service organization face?
10. Oscar Company builds outdoor furniture using a variety of woods and plastics. What is a constraint? List at least four possible constraints at Oscar Company.
11. Do a web search on the terms "carbon offset" and "carbon footprint." What is a carbon footprint? What is a carbon offset? Why would carbon offsets be of interest to a company? What are some companies that offer (sell) carbon offsets?
12. A computer manufacturer is considering outsourcing its technical support call center to India. Its current technical support call center is located in Dellroy, Ohio. The current call center is one of the top employers in Dellroy and employs about 10% of the townspeople in Dellroy. The town has experienced high unemployment rates in the past two decades and oftentimes the call employees are the sole breadwinners in their households. If the technical support call center were to be moved to India, the company would be able to pay about 50% less per hour than they currently pay in Dellroy, Ohio. From a triple bottom line perspective (people, planet, and profit), what factors are relevant to the company's decision to outsource its technical support call center? Be sure to discuss both quantitative and qualitative factors.

Application & Analysis

A8-56 Outsourcing Decision at a Real Company

Go to the New York Times website (www.nytimes.com/) or to USA Today (www.usatoday.com/) and search for the term "outsource." Find an article about a company making a decision to outsource a part of its business operations.

Basic Discussion Questions

1. Describe the company that is making the decision to outsource. What area of the business is the company either looking to outsource or did it already outsource?
2. Why did the company decide to outsource (or is considering outsourcing)?
3. List the revenues and costs that might be impacted by this outsourcing decision. The article will not list many, if any, of these revenues and costs; you should make reasonable guesses about what revenues and/or costs would be associated with the business operation being outsourced.

4. List the qualitative factors that could influence the company's decision whether to outsource this business operation or not. Again, you need to make reasonable guesses about the qualitative factors that might influence the company's decision to outsource or not.

Decision Case

A8-57 Outsourcing e-mail *(Learning Objective 6)*

AI Banking provides banks web access to sophisticated financial information and analysis systems. The company combines these tools w ith benchmarking data access, including e-mail and wireless communications, so that banks can instantly evaluate individual loan applications and entire loan portfolios. All information is encrypted and is available 24/7.

AI Banking's CEO, Amanda Duncan, is happy with the company's growth. To better focus on client service, Duncan is considering outsourcing some functions. CFO Sarabeth Miracle suggests that the company's e-mail may be the place to start. She recently attended a conference and learned that companies such as Continental Airlines, DellNet, GTE, and NBC were outsourcing their e-mail function. Duncan asks Miracle to identify costs related to AI Banking's in-house Microsoft Exchange e-mail application, which has 2,400 mailboxes. This information follows:

Variable costs:	
E-mail license	$7 per mailbox per month
Virus protection license	$1 per mailbox per month
Other variable costs	$4 per mailbox per month
Fixed costs:	
Computer hardware costs	$94,300 per month
$8,050 monthly salary for two information technology staff members who work only on e-mail	$16,100 per month

Requirements

1. Compute the *total cost* per mailbox per month of AI Banking's current e-mail function.
2. Suppose Mail.com, a leading provider of email services, offers to host AI Banking's e-mail function for $7 per mailbox per month. If AI Banking outsources its e-mail to Mail.com, AI Banking will still need the virus protection software; its computer hardware; and one information technology staff member who would be responsible for maintaining virus protection, quarantining suspicious e-mail, and managing content (e.g., screening e-mail for objectionable content). Should CEO Duncan accept Mail.com's offer? Why or why not?
3. Suppose for an additional $5 per mailbox per month, Mail.com will also provide virus protection, quarantine, and content-management services. Outsourcing these additional functions would mean that AI Banking would not need an e-mail information technology staff member or the separate virus protection license. Should CEO Duncan outsource these extra services to Mail.com? Why or why not?

Ethical Issue

A8-58 Outsourcing and ethics *(Learning Objective 6)*

Mary Tan is the controller for Duck Associates, a property management company in Portland, Oregon. Each year, Tan and payroll clerk Toby Stock meet with the external auditors about payroll accounting. This year, the auditors suggest that Tan consider outsourcing Duck Associates' payroll accounting to a company specializing in payroll processing services. This would allow Tan and her staff to focus on their primary responsibility: accounting for the properties under management. At present, payroll requires 1.5 employee positions—payroll clerk Toby Stock and a bookkeeper who spends half her time entering payroll data in the system.

Tan considers this suggestion and she lists the following items relating to outsourcing payroll accounting:

a. The current payroll software that was purchased for $4,000 three years ago would not be needed if payroll processing were outsourced.
b. Duck Associates' bookkeeper would spend half her time preparing the weekly payroll input form that is given to the payroll processing service. She is paid $450 a week.
c. Duck Associates would no longer need payroll clerk Toby Stock, whose annual salary is $42,000.
d. The payroll processing service would charge $2,000 a month.

Requirements

1. Would outsourcing the payroll function increase or decrease Duck Associates' operating income?
2. Tan believes that outsourcing payroll would simplify her job, but she does not like the prospect of having to lay off Stock, who has become a close personal friend. She does not believe there is another position available for Stock at his current salary. Can you think of other factors that might support keeping Stock rather than outsourcing payroll processing? How should each of the factors affect Tan's decision if she wants to do what is best for Duck Associates and act ethically?

Team Project

A8-59 Relevant information to outsourcing decision *(Learning Objective 6)*

John Menard is the founder and sole owner of Menards. Analysts have estimated that his chain of home improvement stores scattered around nine midwestern states generate about $3 billion in annual sales. But how can Menards compete with giant Home Depot?

Suppose Menard is trying to decide whether to invest $45 million in a state-of-the-art manufacturing plant in Eau Claire, Wisconsin. Menard expects the plant would operate for 15 years, after which it would have no residual value. The plant would produce Menards's own line of Formica countertops, cabinets, and picnic tables.

Suppose Menards would incur the following unit costs in producing its own product lines:

	Per Unit		
	Countertops	**Cabinets**	**Picnic Tables**
Direct materials	$15	$10	$25
Direct labor	10	5	15
Variable manufacturing overhead	5	2	6

Rather than Menard making these products, assume that he can buy them from outside suppliers. Suppliers would charge Menards $40 per countertop, $25 per cabinet, and $65 per picnic table.

Whether Menard makes or buys these products, assume that he expects the following annual sales:

- Countertops—487,200 at $130 each
- Picnic tables—100,000 at $225 each
- Cabinets—150,000 at $75 each

If "making" is sufficiently more profitable than outsourcing, Menard will build the new plant. John Menard has asked your consulting group for a recommendation. Menard uses the straight-line depreciation method.

Requirements

1. Are the following items relevant or irrelevant in Menard's decision to build a new plant that will manufacture his own products?
   a. The unit sale prices of the countertops, cabinets, and picnic tables (the sale prices that Menards charges its customers)
   b. The prices that outside suppliers would charge Menards for the three products if Menards decides to outsource the products rather than make them
   c. The $45 million to build the new plant
   d. The direct materials, direct labor, and variable overhead that Menards would incur to manufacture the three product lines
   e. Menard's salary
2. Determine whether Menards should make or outsource the countertops, cabinets, and picnic tables assuming that the company has already built the plant and, therefore, has the manufacturing capacity to produce these products. In other words, *what is the annual difference in cash flows* if Menards decides to make rather than outsource each of these three products?
3. Write a memo giving your recommendation to Menard. The memo should clearly state your recommendation and briefly summarize the reasons for your recommendation.

A8-60 CMA Question

Breegle Company produces three products (B-40, J-60, and H-102) from a single process. Breegle uses the physical volume method to allocate joint costs of $22,500 per batch to the products. Based on the following information, which product(s) should Breegle continue to process after the split-off point in order to maximize profit?

	B-40	J-60	H-102
Physical units produced per batch	1,500	2,000	3,200
Sales value per unit at splitoff	$10.00	$4.00	$7.25
Cost per unit of further processing after splitoff	3.05	1.00	2.50
Sales value per unit after further processing	12.25	5.70	9.75

a. B-40 only.
b. J-60 only.
c. H-102 only.
d. B-40 and H-102 only.

(CMA Adapted)

The Master Budget

Learning Objectives

- **1** Describe how and why managers use budgets
- **2** Prepare the operating budgets
- **3** Prepare the financial budgets
- **4** Prepare budgets for a merchandiser

© Profimedia International s.r.o. / Alamy

Campbell Soup Company's

goal is "to win with integrity in the workplace, the marketplace, and the community as the world's most extraordinary food company." How will the company attain this goal? First, it identifies key strategies. Some of Campbell's key strategies include expanding its icon brands (such as Campbell's Soup, V8 Juice, and Pepperidge Farms Snacks), increasing margins through improving productivity, and advancing its commitment to organizational excellence and social responsibility. These strategies require detailed plans be put into place. The company's managers express these plans, in financial terms, through budgets. The company's budgets reflect and support each of these key strategies. For example, management has budgeted millions of dollars toward researching new products in order to expand its iconic brands. Management has also budgeted millions of dollars towards new, more productive manufacturing equipment and an ERP information system that should improve profit margins and increase organizational excellence. Is the company on track for reaching its goal of winning in the workplace, marketplace and community? In 2010, Campbell became a four-time winner of Gallup's "Great Workplace Award," for creating an extraordinary workplace environment for its employees. This prestigious award is only given to 25 companies a year, worldwide. For the past five years, Campbell's total shareowner return has exceeded the Standard & Poor's 500 Stock Index and Standard & Poor's Packaged Foods Index. And in 2010, Campbell ranked as one of the 10 most socially responsible U.S. companies and 100 Best Corporate Citizens. The company's budget is a vital tool in making it all happen.

Sources: Campbell Soup Company, 2010 Annual Report www.gallup.com/consulting/25312/gallup-great-workplace-award.aspx

Budgeting is perhaps the most widely used management accounting tool employed by companies, organizations, and governments throughout the world. Even individuals, such as you and I, can benefit from creating a personal budget that shows how we plan to use our resources and to make sure our spending does not get out of control. For example, if your goal is to buy a car directly after college or a house five years after college, then you need to plan for those goals. Your budget should include saving enough money each year to accumulate the down payments you'll need. By carefully planning how you'll spend and save your resources, you'll have a better chance of reaching your goals.

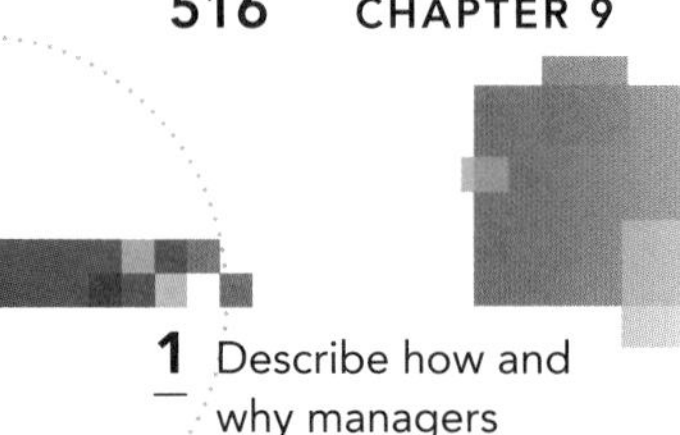

1 Describe how and why managers use budgets

How and Why do Managers Use Budgets?

As you'll see throughout this chapter, management uses budgeting to express its plans and to assess how well it's reaching its goals. In this section, we'll take a closer look at how budgets are used and developed, the benefits of budgeting, and the particular budgets that are prepared as part of the company's master budget.

How are Budgets Used?

All companies and organizations use budgets for the same reasons you would in your personal life—to plan for the future and control the revenues and expenses related to those plans. Exhibit 9-1 shows how managers use budgets in fulfilling their major responsibilities of planning, directing, and controlling operations. Budgeting is an on-going cycle: Company strategies lead to detailed plans, which in turn lead to actions. Results are then compared to the budget to provide managers feedback. This feedback allows managers to take corrective actions and if necessary, revise strategies, which starts the cycle over.

EXHIBIT 9-1 Managers Use Budgets to Plan and Control Business Activities

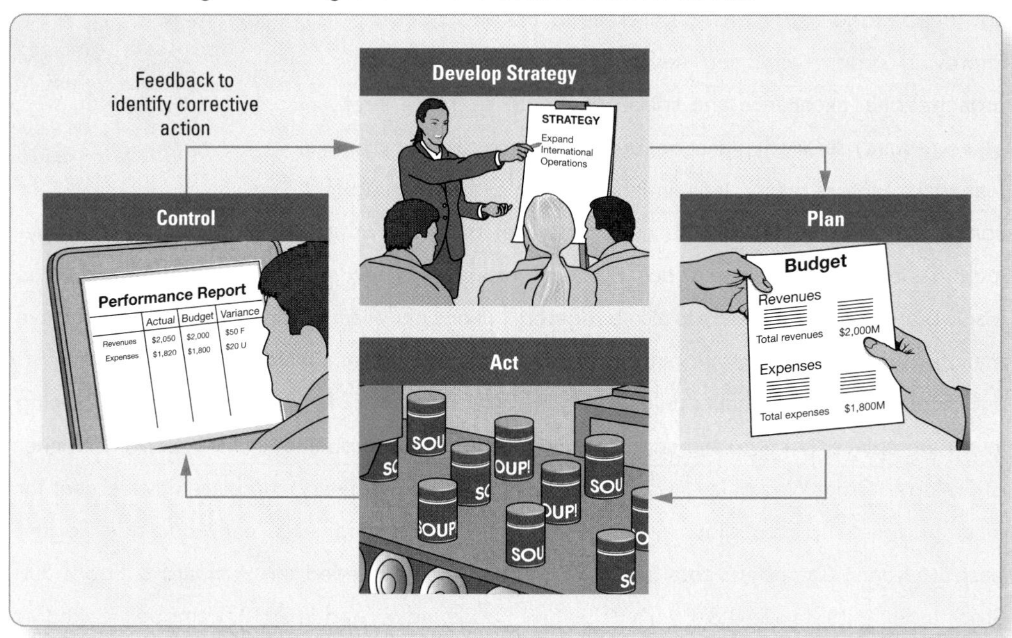

How are Budgets Developed?

A few years ago Campbell was not performing up to expectations. The first step toward getting the company back on track was management's decision to create long-term strategic goals. **Strategic planning** involves setting long-term goals that may extend 5–10 years into the future. Long-term, loosely-detailed budgets are often created to reflect expectations for these long-term goals.

Once the goals are set, management designs key strategies for attaining the goals. These strategies, such as Campbell's expansion of its iconic brands and improvements to production efficiency, are then put into place through the use of shorter-term budgets for an entire fiscal year. However, even a yearly budget is not detailed enough to guide many management decisions. For example, Campbell's soup production managers must know what month of the year they expect to receive and start using new production machinery. They must also decide how much of each raw material (vegetables, chicken, and so forth) to purchase each month to meet production requirements for both existing and new products. In turn, this will affect monthly cash needs. Therefore, companies usually prepare a budget for every month of the fiscal year.

Many companies set aside time during the last two quarters of the fiscal year to create their budget for the upcoming fiscal year. Other companies prepare rolling, or continuous budgets. A **rolling budget** is a budget that is continuously updated so that the next 12 months of operations are always budgeted. For example, as soon as January is over, the next January is added to the budget. The benefit of a rolling budget is that managers always have a budget for the next 12 months.

Who is Involved in the Budgeting Process?

Rather than using a "top-down" approach in which top management determines the budget, most companies use some degree of participative budgeting. As the term implies, **participative budgeting** involves the participation of many levels of management. Participative budgeting is beneficial for the following reasons:

- Lower level managers are closer to the action, and should have a more detailed knowledge for creating realistic budgets.
- Managers are more likely to accept, and be motivated by budgets they helped to create.

However, participative budgeting also has disadvantages:

- The budget process can become much more complex and time consuming as more people participate in the process.
- Managers may intentionally build **slack** into the budget for their area of operation by overbudgeting expenses or underbudgeting revenue. Why would they do this? They would do so for three possible reasons: 1) because of uncertainty about the future, 2) to make their performance look better when actual results are compared against budgeted amounts at the end of the period, and 3) to have the resources they need in the event of budget cuts.

Even with participative budgeting, someone must still have the "final say" on the budget. Often, companies use a **budget committee** to review the submitted budgets, remove unwarranted slack, and revise and approve the final budget. The budget committee often includes upper management, such as the CEO and CFO, as well as managers from every area of the value chain (such as Research and Development, Marketing, Distribution, and so forth). By using a cross-functional budget committee, the final budget is more likely to reflect a comprehensive view of the organization and be accepted by managers than if the budget were prepared by one person or department for the entire organization. The budget committee is often supported by full-time staff personnel devoted to updating and analyzing the budgets.

What is the Starting Point for Developing the Budgets?

Many companies use the prior year's budgeted figures, or actual results, as the *starting point* for creating the budget for the coming year. Of course, those figures will then be modified to reflect

- new products, customers, or geographical areas;
- changes in the marketplace caused by competitors;
- changes in labor contracts, raw material, and fuel costs;
- general inflation;
- and any new strategies.

However, this approach to budgeting may cause year-after-year increases that after time, grow out of control. To prevent perpetual increases in budgeted expenses, many companies intermittently use zero-based budgeting. When a company implements **zero-based budgeting**, all managers begin with a budget of zero and must justify *every dollar* they put in the budget. This budgeting approach is very time-consuming and labor intensive. Therefore, companies only use it from time to time in order to keep their expenses in check.

What are the Benefits of Budgeting?

Exhibit 9-2 summarizes three key benefits of budgeting. Budgeting forces managers to plan, promotes coordination and communication, and provides a benchmark for motivating employees and evaluating actual performance.

EXHIBIT 9-2 Benefits of Budgeting

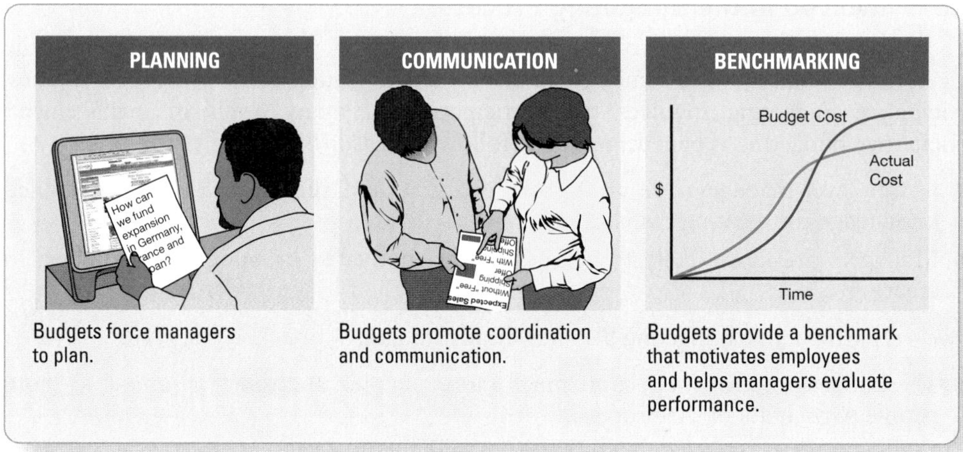

Budgets force managers to plan.

Budgets promote coordination and communication.

Budgets provide a benchmark that motivates employees and helps managers evaluate performance.

Planning

Business managers are extremely busy directing the day-to-day operations of the company. The budgeting process forces managers to spend time planning for the future, rather than only concerning themselves with daily operations. The sooner companies develop a plan and have time to act on the plan, the more likely they will achieve their goals.

Coordination and Communication

The budget coordinates a company's activities. It forces managers to consider relations among operations across the entire value chain. For example, Campbell's decision to expand its iconic brands will first affect the research and development function. However, once new products are developed, the design and production teams will need to focus on how and where the products will be mass produced. The marketing team will need to develop attractive labeling and create a successful advertising campaign. The distribution team may need to alter its current distribution system to accommodate the new products. And customer service will need to be ready to handle any complaints or warranty issues. All areas of the value chain are ultimately affected by management's plans. The budget process helps to communicate and coordinate the effects of the plan.

Benchmarking

Budgets provide a benchmark that motivates employees and helps managers evaluate performance. The budget provides a target that most managers will try to achieve, especially if they participated in the budgeting process and the budget has been set at a realistic level. Budgets should be achievable with effort. Budgets that are too "tight" (too hard to achieve) or too "loose" (too easy to achieve) do not provide managers with much motivation.

Think about exams for a moment. Some professors have a reputation for giving "impossible" exams while others may be known for giving "easy" exams. In either of these cases, students are rarely motivated to put much effort into learning the material because they feel they won't be rewarded for their additional efforts. However, if students feel that a professor's exam can be achieved with effort, they will be more likely to devote themselves to learning the material. In other words, the perceived "fairness" of the exam affects how well the exam motivates students to study. Likewise, if a budget is perceived to be "fair," employees are likely to be motivated by it.

Budgets also provide a benchmark for evaluating performance. At the end of the period, companies use performance reports, such as the one pictured in Exhibit 9-3, to compare "actual" revenues and expenses against "budgeted" revenues and expenses. The variance, or difference between actual and budgeted figures, is used to evaluate how well the manager controlled operations and to determine whether the plan needs to be revised. The use of budgets for performance evaluation will be discussed in more detail in Chapters 10 and 11. In this chapter, we'll focus primarily on the use of budgets for planning purposes.

EXHIBIT 9-3 Summary Performance Report

	Actual	Budget	Variance (Actual − Budget)
Sales revenue	$550	$600	$(50)
Less: Total expenses	90	68	(22)
Net income	$460	$532	$(72)

What is the Master Budget?

The master budget is the comprehensive planning document for the entire organization. It consists of all of the supporting budgets needed to create the company's budgeted financial statements. Exhibit 9-4 shows all of the components of the master budget for a manufacturer, and the order in which they are usually prepared. The master budgets of service and merchandising firms are less complex, and will be discussed in the final section of the chapter.

EXHIBIT 9-4 Master Budget for a Manufacturing Company

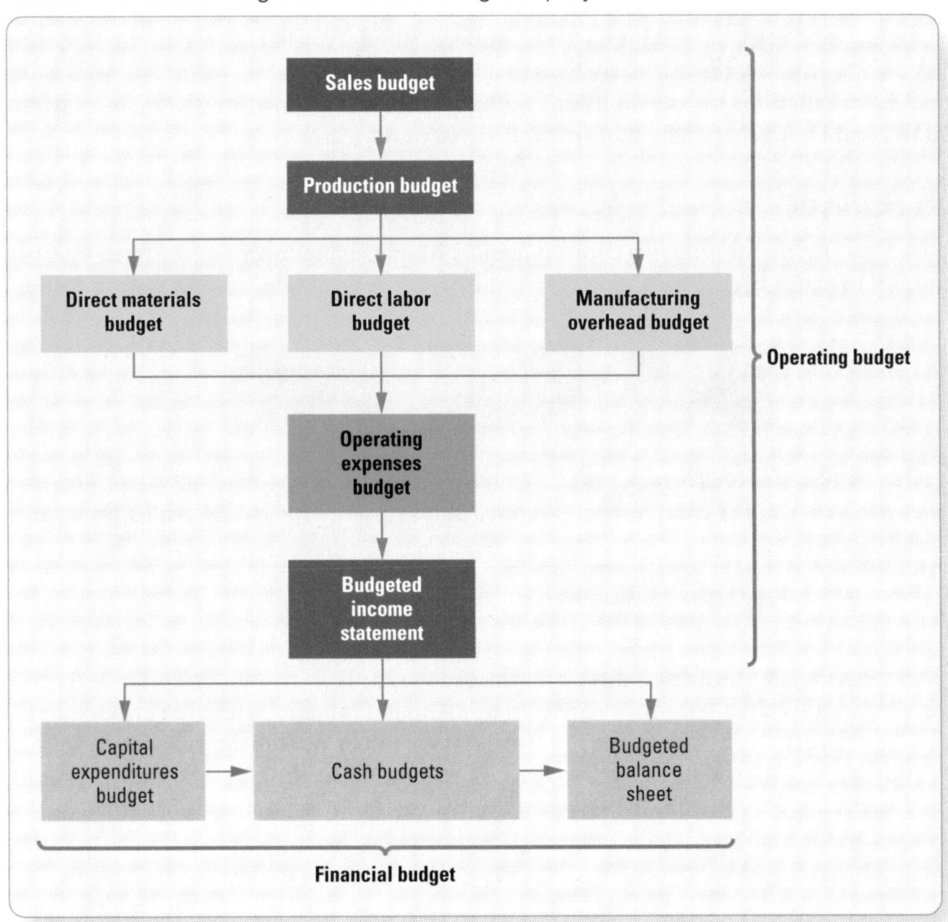

The operating budgets are the budgets needed to run the daily operations of the company. The operating budgets culminate in a budgeted income statement. As Exhibit 9-4 shows, the starting point of the operating budgets is the sales budget because it affects most other components of the master budget. After estimating sales, manufacturers prepare the production budget, which determines how many units need to be produced. Once production volume is established, managers prepare the budgets determining the amounts of direct materials, direct labor, and manufacturing overhead that will be needed to meet production. Next, managers prepare the operating expenses budget. After all of these budgets are prepared, management will be able to prepare the budgeted income statement.

As you'll see throughout the chapter, cost behavior will be an important factor in developing many of the operating budgets. Total fixed costs will not change as volume changes within the relevant range. However, total variable costs will fluctuate as volume fluctuates.

The financial budgets project the collection and payment of cash, as well as forecast the company's budgeted balance sheet. The capital expenditure budget shows the company's plan for purchasing property, plant, and equipment. The cash budget projects the cash that will be available to run the company's operations and determines whether the company will have extra funds to invest or whether the company will need to borrow cash. Finally, the budgeted balance sheet forecasts the company's position at the end of the budget period.

How are the Operating Budgets Prepared?

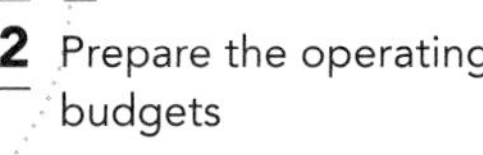

2 Prepare the operating budgets

We will be following the budget process for Tucson Tortilla, a fairly small, independently owned manufacturer of tortilla chips. The company sells its product, by the case, to restaurants, grocery stores, and convenience stores. To keep our example simple, we will just show the budgets for the first three months of the fiscal year, rather than all 12 months. Since many companies prepare quarterly budgets (budgets that cover a three-month period), we'll also show the quarterly figures on each budget. For every budget, we'll walk through the calculations for the month of January. Then we'll show how the same pattern is used to create budgets for the months of February and March.

Sales Budget

The sales budget is the starting place for budgeting. Managers multiply the expected number of unit sales by the expected sales price per unit to arrive at the expected total sales revenue.

For example, Tucson Tortilla expects to sell 30,000 cases of tortilla chips in January, at a sales price of $20 per case, so the estimated sales revenue for January is as follows:

$$30,000 \text{ cases} \times \$20 \text{ per case} = \$600,000$$

The sales budget for the first three months of the year is shown in Exhibit 9-5. As you can see, the monthly sales volume is expected to fluctuate. January sales are expected to be higher than February sales due to the extraordinary number of chips purchased for Super Bowl™ parties. Also, since more tortillas chips are sold when the weather warms up, the company expects sales to begin their seasonal upward climb beginning in March.

As shown in the lower portion of Exhibit 9-5, managers may also choose to indicate the type of sale that will be made. Tucson Tortilla expects 20% of its sales to be cash (COD) sales. Companies often use COD ("collect on delivery"[1]) collection terms if the customer is new, has a poor credit rating, or has not paid on time in the past. Tucson Tortilla will still sell to these customers, but will demand payment immediately when the inventory is delivered.

EXHIBIT 9-5 Sales Budget

Tucson Tortilla
Sales Budget
For the Quarter Ended March 31

	Month			
	January	February	March	1st Quarter
Unit sales (cases)	30,000	20,000	25,000	75,000
Unit selling price	× $ 20	× $ 20	× $ 20	× $ 20
Total sales revenue	$600,000	$400,000	$500,000	$1,500,000
Type of Sale:				
Cash sales (20%)	$120,000	$ 80,000	$100,000	$ 300,000
Credit sales (80%)	480,000	320,000	400,000	1,200,000
Total sales revenue	$600,000	$400,000	$500,000	$1,500,000

The remaining 80% of sales will be made on credit. Tucson Tortilla's credit terms are "net 30," meaning the customer has up to 30 days to pay for its purchases. Having this information available on the sales budget will help managers prepare the cash collections budget later.

Why is this important?

"The **sales budget** is the **basis** for every other budget. If sales are not projected as **accurately** as possible, all other budgets will be **off target**."

Production Budget

Once managers have estimated how many units they expect to sell, they can figure out how many units they need to produce. Most manufacturers maintain some ending finished goods inventory, or safety stock, which is inventory kept on hand in case demand is higher than predicted, or the problems in the factory slow production (such as machine breakdown, employees out sick, and so forth). As a result, managers need to factor in the desired level of ending inventory when deciding how much inventory to produce. They do so as follows:

[1]In the past, COD meant "cash on delivery." However, as other forms of payment (such as checks, credit cards, and debit cards) have become more common, the word "cash" has been replaced with the word "collect" to incorporate these additional types of payments.

Let's walk through this calculation step-by-step:

- First, managers figure out how many total units they need. To do this, they add the number of units they plan to sell to the number of units they want on hand at the end of the month. *Let's assume Tucson Tortilla wants to maintain an ending inventory equal to 10% of the next month's expected sales (20,000 cases in February). Thus, the total number of cases needed in January is as follows:*

30,000 cases for January sales + (10% × 20,000) = 32,000 total cases needed

- Next, managers calculate the amount of inventory they expect to have on hand at the beginning of the month. *Since Tucson Tortilla desires ending inventory to be 10% of the next month's sales, managers expect to have 10% of January's sales on hand on December 31, which becomes the beginning balance on January 1st:*

10% × 30,000 cases = 3,000 cases in beginning inventory on January 1

- Finally, by subtracting what the company already has in stock at the beginning of the month from the total units needed, the company is able to calculate how many units to produce:

32,000 cases needed − 3,000 cases in beginning inventory = 29,000 cases to produce

Exhibit 9-6 shows Tucson Tortilla's Production Budget for the first three months of the year. As the red arrows show, the ending inventory from one month (January 31) always becomes the beginning inventory for the next month (February 1).

If your instructor is using MyAccountingLab, go to the Multimedia Library for a quick video on this topic.

EXHIBIT 9-6 Production Budget

Tucson Tortilla
Production Budget
For the Quarter Ended March 31

	Month			
	January	**February**	**March**	**1st Quarter**
Unit sales (from Sales Budget)	30,000	20,000	25,000	75,000
Plus: Desired end inventory	2,000	2,500	3,200*	3,200**
Total needed	32,000	22,500	28,200	78,200
Less: Beginning inventory	(3,000)	(2,000)	(2,500)	(3,000)**
Units to produce	**29,000**	**20,500**	**25,700**	**75,200**

* April sales are projected to be 32,000 units.
** Since the quarter begins January 1 and ends March 31, the beginning inventory for the quarter is the balance on January 1 and the ending inventory for the quarter is the balance on March 31.

Now that the company knows how many units it plans to produce every month, it can figure out the amount of direct materials, direct labor, and manufacturing overhead that will be needed. As shown in the following sections, the company will create separate budgets for each of these three manufacturing costs. Each budget will be driven by the number of units to be produced each month.

Direct Materials Budget

The format of the direct materials budget is quite similar to the production budget:

Let's walk through the process using January as an example:

- First, the company figures out the quantity of direct materials (DM) needed for production. *Let's assume Tucson Tortilla's only direct material is masa harina, the special corn flour used to make tortilla chips. Each case of tortilla chips requires 5 pounds of this corn flour. Therefore, the quantity of direct materials needed for January production is as follows:*

  29,000 cases to be produced × 5 pounds per case = 145,000 pounds

- Next, the company adds in the desired ending inventory of direct materials. Some amount of direct materials safety stock is usually needed in case suppliers do not deliver all of the direct materials needed on time. *Let's assume that Tucson Tortilla wants to maintain an ending inventory of direct materials equal to 10% of the materials needed for next month's production (102,500 required in February, as shown in Exhibit 9-7):*

  145,000 pounds + (10% × 102,500) = 155,250 total pounds needed

- Next, managers determine the direct material inventory they expect to have on hand at the beginning of the month. *Tucson Tortilla expects to have 10% of the materials needed for January's production in stock on December 31, which becomes the opening balance on January 1:*

  10% × 145,000 pounds = 14,500 pounds in beginning inventory

  Finally, by subtracting what the company already has in stock at the beginning of the month from the total quantity needed, the company is able to calculate the quantity of direct materials they need to purchase:

  155,250 pounds needed − 14,500 pounds in beginning inventory = 140,750 pounds to purchase

- Finally, the company calculates the expected cost of purchasing those direct materials. *Let's say Tucson Tortilla can buy the masa harina corn flour in bulk for $1.50 per pound.*

  140,750 pounds × $1.50 = $211,125

Exhibit 9-7 shows Tucson Tortilla's direct materials budget for the first three months of the year.

EXHIBIT 9-7 Direct Materials Budget

Tucson Tortilla
Direct Materials Budget for Masa Harina Corn Flour
For the Quarter Ended March 31

	Month			
	January	February	March	1st Quarter
Unit to be produced (from Production Budget)	29,000	20,500	25,700	75,200
× Quantity (pounds) of DM needed per unit	× 5 lbs	× 5 lbs	× 5 lbs	× 5 lbs
Quantity (pounds) needed for production	145,000	102,500	128,500	376,000
Plus: Desired end inventory of DM	10,250	12,850	16,150*	16,150**
Total quantity (pounds) needed	155,250	115,350	144,650	392,150
Less: Beginning inventory of DM	(14,500)	(10,250)	(12,850)	(14,500)**
Quantity (pounds) to purchase	140,750	105,100	131,800	377,650
× Cost per pound	× $1.50	× $1.50	× $1.50	× $1.50
Total cost of DM purchases	$211,125	$157,650	$197,700	$566,475

* 161,500 pounds are needed for production in April.
** Since the quarter begins January 1 and ends March 31, the beginning inventory for the quarter is the balance on January 1 and the ending inventory for the quarter is the balance on March 31.

Direct Labor Budget

The direct labor (DL) budget is determined as follows:

Units to be Produced × DL Hours per Unit = Total DL Hours Required × DL Cost per Hour = Total Direct Labor Cost

Tucson Tortilla's factory is fairly automated, so very little direct labor is required. *Let's assume that each case requires only 0.05 of an hour. Direct laborers are paid $22 per hour. Thus, the direct labor cost for January is projected to be as follows:*

29,000 cases × 0.05 hours per case = 1,450 hours required × $22 per hour = $31,900

The Direct Labor budget for the first three months of the year is shown in Exhibit 9-8:

EXHIBIT 9-8 Direct Labor Budget

Tucson Tortilla
Direct Labor Budget
For the Quarter Ended March 31

	Month			
	January	February	March	1st Quarter
Units to be produced (from Production Budget)	29,000	20,500	25,700	75,200
× Direct labor hours per unit	× 0.05	× 0.05	× 0.05	× 0.05
Total hours required	1,450	1,025	1,285	3,760
× Direct labor cost per hour	× $ 22	× $ 22	× $ 22	× $ 22
Total Direct labor cost	$31,900	$22,550	$28,270	$82,720

Manufacturing Overhead Budget

The manufacturing overhead budget is highly dependent on cost behavior. Some overhead costs, such as indirect materials, are variable. For example, Tucson Tortilla considers the oil used for frying the tortilla chips to be an indirect material. Since a portion of the oil is absorbed into the chips, the amount of oil required increases as production volume increases. Thus, the cost is variable. The company also considers salt and cellophane packaging to be variable indirect materials. *Tucson Tortilla expects to spend $1.25 on indirect materials for each case of tortilla chips produced, so January's budget for indirect materials is as follows:*

29,000 cases × $1.25 = $36,250 of indirect materials

Costs such as utilities and indirect labor are mixed costs. Mixed costs are usually separated into their variable and fixed components using one of the cost behavior estimation methods already discussed in Chapter 6. *Based on engineering and cost studies, Tucson Tortilla has determined that each case of chips requires $0.75 of variable indirect labor, and $0.50 of variable utility costs as a result of running the production machinery. These variable costs are budgeted as follows for January:*

29,000 cases × $0.75 = $21,750 of variable indirect labor
29,000 cases × $0.50 = $14,500 of variable factory utilities

Finally, many manufacturing overhead costs are fixed. *Tucson Tortilla's fixed costs include depreciation, insurance, and property taxes on the factory. The company also incurs some fixed indirect labor (salaried production engineers that oversee the daily manufacturing operation) and a fixed amount of utilities just to keep the lights, heat, or air conditioning on in the plant regardless of the production volume.*

Exhibit 9-9 shows that the manufacturing overhead budget usually has separate sections for variable and fixed overhead costs so that managers can easily see which costs will change as production volume changes.

Now that we have completed budgets for each of the three manufacturing costs (direct materials, direct labor, and manufacturing overhead), we turn our attention to operating expenses.

EXHIBIT 9-9 Manufacturing Overhead Budget

Tucson Tortilla
Manufacturing Overhead Budget
For the Quarter Ended March 31

	Month			
	January	February	March	1st Quarter
Units to be Produced (from Production Budget)	29,000	20,500	25,700	75,200
Variable Costs:				
Indirect materials ($1.25 per case)	$ 36,250	$25,625	$32,125	$ 94,000
Indirect labor—variable portion ($0.75 per case)	21,750	15,375	19,275	56,400
Utilities—variable portion ($0.50 per case)	14,500	10,250	12,850	37,600
Total variable MOH	$ 72,500	$51,250	$64,250	$188,000
Fixed MOH Costs:				
Depreciation on factory and production equipment	$ 10,000	$10,000	$10,000	$ 30,000
Insurance and property taxes on the factory	3,000	3,000	3,000	9,000
Indirect labor—fixed portion	15,000	15,000	15,000	45,000
Utilities—fixed portion	2,000	2,000	2,000	6,000
Total fixed MOH	$ 30,000	$30,000	$30,000	$ 90,000
Total manufacturing overhead	$102,500	$81,250	$94,250	$278,000

Operating Expenses Budget

Recall that all costs incurred in every area of the value chain, except production, must be expensed as operating expenses in the period in which they are incurred. Thus all research and development, design, marketing, distribution, and customer service costs will be shown on the operating expenses budget.

Some operating expenses are variable, based on how many units will be *sold* (not produced). *For example, to motivate its sales force to generate sales, Tucson Tortilla pays its sales representatives a $1.50 sales commission for every case they sell.*

30,000 sales units × $1.50 = $45,000 sales commission expense in January

The company also incurs $2.00 of shipping costs on every case sold.

30,000 sales units × $2.00 = $60,000 shipping expense in January

Finally, the company knows that not all of the sales made on credit will eventually be collected. Based on experience, Tucson Tortilla expects monthly bad debt expense to be 1% of its credit sales. Since January credit sales are expected to be $480,000 (from Sales Budget, Exhibit 9-5), the company's bad debt expense for January is as follows:

$480,000 of credit sales in January × 1% = $4,800 bad debt expense for January

Other operating expenses are fixed: They will stay the same each month even though sales volume fluctuates. *For example, Tucson Tortilla's fixed expenses include salaries, office rent, depreciation on office equipment and the company's vehicles, advertising, telephone, and internet service.*

As shown in Exhibit 9-10, operating expenses are usually shown according to their cost behavior.

EXHIBIT 9-10 Operating Expenses Budget

Tucson Tortilla
Operating Expenses Budget
For the Quarter Ended March 31

	Month			
	January	February	March	1st Quarter
Sales units (from Sales Budget)	30,000	20,000	25,000	75,000
Variable Operating Expenses:				
Sales commissions expense ($1.50 per case sold)	$ 45,000	$ 30,000	$ 37,500	$112,500
Shipping expense ($2.00 per case sold)	60,000	40,000	50,000	150,000
Bad debt expense (1% of credit sales)	4,800	3,200	4,000	12,000
Variable operating expenses	$109,800	$ 73,200	$ 91,500	$274,500
Fixed Operating Expenses:				
Salaries	$ 20,000	$ 20,000	$ 20,000	$ 60,000
Office rent	4,000	4,000	4,000	12,000
Depreciation	6,000	6,000	6,000	18,000
Advertising	2,000	2,000	2,000	6,000
Telephone and internet	1,000	1,000	1,000	3,000
Fixed operating expenses	$ 33,000	$ 33,000	$ 33,000	$ 99,000
Total operating expenses	$142,800	$106,200	$124,500	$373,500

Budgeted Income Statement

A budgeted income statement looks just like a regular income statement, except for the fact that it uses budgeted data. Recall the general format for an income statement:

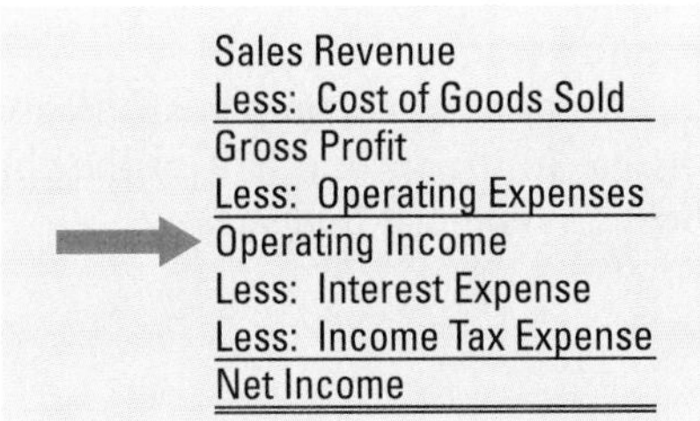

This textbook has focused on a company's operating income, rather than net income. However, a complete income statement would include any interest expense (and/or interest income) as well as a provision for income taxes. These additional costs are subtracted from operating income to arrive at net income.

We have already computed the budgeted sales revenue and operating expenses on separate budgets. But we still need to calculate the Cost of Goods Sold before we can prepare the income statement.

Tucson Tortilla computes its Cost of Goods Sold as follows:

This will be relatively simple for Tucson Tortilla since the company produces only one product.

The cost of manufacturing each case of tortilla chips is shown in Exhibit 9-11. Almost all of the information presented has already been presented and used to prepare the budgets for direct materials, direct labor, and manufacturing overhead. The only new piece of information is the total production volume for the year, budgeted to be 400,000 cases.

EXHIBIT 9-11 Budgeted Manufacturing Cost per Unit

Tucson Tortilla Budgeted Manufacturing Cost per Unit	
Direct materials (5 pounds of corn flour per case × \$1.50 per pound)[a]	\$ 7.50
Direct labor (0.05 hours per case × \$22 per hour)[b]	1.10
Manufacturing overhead[c]:	
Variable—indirect materials (\$1.25 per case), variable indirect labor (\$0.75 per case), and variable utilities (\$0.50 per case)	2.50
Fixed—\$30,000 per month × 12 months = \$360,000 for the year	
So, the fixed cost per unit is \$360,000 ÷ 400,000[d] cases	0.90
Cost of manufacturing each case	\$12.00

[a] From Exhibit 9-7
[b] From Exhibit 9-8
[c] From Exhibit 9-9
[d] Recall that companies base their predetermined MOH rate on the total estimated cost and volume for the *entire year*, rather than on monthly costs and volumes that will fluctuate.

Why is this important?

"The **budgeted income statement** helps managers know in advance whether their plans will result in an **acceptable** level of **income**. If not, **management** will need to consider how it can cut expenses or increase **sales revenues**."

Exhibit 9-12 shows the company's budgeted income statement for January. Interest expense is budgeted to be zero since the company has no outstanding debt. The income tax expense is budgeted to be 35% of income before taxes. The company will prepare budgeted income statements for each month and quarter, as well as for the entire year.

We have now completed the operating budgets for Tucson Tortilla. In the second half of the chapter, we'll prepare Tucson Tortilla's financial budgets.

EXHIBIT 9-12 Budgeted Income Statement

Tucson Tortilla Budgeted Income Statement For the month ended January 31	
Sales (30,000 cases × $20 per case, from Exhibit 9-5)	$600,000
Less: Cost of goods sold (30,000 cases × $12.00 per case, from Exhibit 9-11)	360,000
Gross profit	240,000
Less: Operating expenses (from Exhibit 9-10)	142,800
Operating income	$ 97,200
Less: Interest expense (or add interest income)	0
Less: Income tax expense*	34,020
Net income	$ 63,180

*The corporate income tax rate for most companies is currently 35% of income before tax ($97,200 × 35% = $34,020).

Decision Guidelines

The Master Budget

Let's consider some of the decisions Campbell Soup Company made as it set up its budgeting process.

Decision	Guidelines
What should be the driving force behind the budgeting process?	The company's long-term goals and strategies drive the budgeting of the company's resources.
What are budgets used for?	Managers use budgets to help them fulfill their primary responsibilities: planning, directing, and controlling operations. Managers use feedback from the budgeting process to take corrective actions and, if necessary, revise strategies.
Who should be involved in the budgeting process?	Budgets tend to be more realistic and more motivational if lower level managers, as well as upper level managers, are allowed to participate in the budgeting process. The budgeting process tends to encompass a more comprehensive view when managers from all areas of the value chain participate in the process and serve on the budget committee.
What period of time should the budgets cover?	Long-term, strategic planning often results in forecasts of revenues and expenses 5–10 years into the future. Monthly and yearly budgets provide much more detailed information to aid management's shorter-term decisions.
How tough should the budget be to achieve?	Budgets are more useful for motivating employees and evaluating performance if they can be achieved with effort. Budgets that are too tight (too hard to achieve) or too loose (too easy to achieve) are not as beneficial.
What benefits should a company expect to obtain from developing a budget?	Benefits include the following: • Planning • Coordination and Communication • Benchmarking (used for both motivation and performance evaluation)
What budgets should be included in a manufacturer's master budget?	The *operating budgets* includes all budgets necessary to create a budgeted income statement. For a manufacturer, this includes the following: • Sales Budget • Production Budget • Direct Materials Budget • Direct Labor Budget • Manufacturing Overhead Budget • Operating Expenses Budget • Budgeted Income Statement The *financial budgets* include the capital expenditures budget, the cash budgets, and the budgeted balance sheet.

SUMMARY PROBLEM 1

Pillows Unlimited makes decorative throw pillows for home use. The company sells the pillows to home décor retailers for $14 per pillow. Each pillow requires 1.25 yards of fabric, which the company obtains at a cost of $6 per yard. The company would like to maintain an ending stock of fabric equal to 10% of the next month's production requirements. The company would also like to maintain an ending stock of finished pillows equal to 20% of the next month's sales. Sales (in units) are projected to be as follows for the first 3 months of the year:

January	100,000
February	110,000
March	115,000

Requirements

Prepare the following budgets for the first three months of the year, as well as a summary budget for the quarter:

1. Prepare the sales budget, including a separate section that details the type of sales made. For this section, assume that 10% of the company's pillows are cash sales, while the remaining 90% are sold on credit terms.
2. Prepare the production budget. Assume that the company anticipates selling 120,000 units in April.
3. Prepare the direct materials purchases budget. Assume the company needs 150,000 yards of fabric for production in April.

SOLUTIONS

Requirement 1

Pillows Unlimited
Sales Budget
For the Quarter ended March 31

	Month			
	January	February	March	1st Quarter
Unit sales	100,000	110,000	115,000	325,000
Unit selling price	×$ 14	×$ 14	×$ 14	×$ 14
Total sales revenue	$1,400,000	$1,540,000	$1,610,000	$4,550,000
Type of Sale:				
Cash sales (10%)	$ 140,000	$ 154,000	$ 161,000	$ 455,000
Credit sales (90%)	1,260,000	1,386,000	1,449,000	4,095,000
Total sales revenue	$1,400,000	$1,540,000	$1,610,000	$4,550,000

Requirement 2

Pillows Unlimited Production Budget For the Quarter ended March 31				
	Month			
	January	February	March	1st Quarter
Unit sales	100,000	110,000	115,000	325,000
Plus: Desired end inventory (20% of next month's unit sales)	22,000	23,000	24,000	24,000
Total needed	122,000	133,000	139,000	349,000
Less: Beginning inventory	(20,000)*	(22,000)	(23,000)	(20,000)
Units to produce	102,000	111,000	116,000	329,000

*January 1 balance (equal to December 31 balance) is 20% of the projected unit sales in January (100,000).

Requirement 3

Pillows Unlimited Direct Materials Budget For the Quarter ended March 31				
	Month			
	January	February	March	1st Quarter
Units to be produced (from Production Budget)	102,000	111,000	116,000	329,000
× Quantity (yards) of DM needed per unit	× 1.25	× 1.25	× 1.25	× 1.25
Quantity (yards) needed for production	127,500	138,750	145,000	411,250
Plus: Desired end inventory of DM (10% of the amount needed for next month's production)	13,875	14,500	15,000	15,000
Total quantity (yards) needed	141,375	153,250	160,000	426,250
Less: Beginning inventory of DM	(12,750)*	(13,875)	(14,500)	(12,750)
Quantity (yards) to purchase	128,625	139,375	145,500	413,500
× Cost per pound	× $ 6.00	× $ 6.00	× $ 6.00	× $ 6.00
Total cost of DM purchases	$771,750	$836,250	$873,000	$2,481,000

*January 1 balance (equal to December 31 balance) is 10% of the quantity needed for January's production (127,500).

How are the Financial Budgets Prepared?

3 Prepare the financial budgets

In the first half of the chapter, we prepared Tucson Tortilla's operating budgets, culminating with the company's budgeted income statement. In this part of the chapter we turn our attention to Tucson Tortilla's financial budgets. Managers typically prepare a capital expenditures budget as well as three separate cash budgets:

1. Cash collections (or receipts) budget
2. Cash payments (or disbursements) budget
3. Combined cash budget, complete with financing arrangements

Finally, managers prepare the budgeted balance sheet. Each of these budgets is illustrated next.

Capital Expenditure Budget

The capital expenditure budget shows the company's intentions to invest in new property, plant, or equipment (capital investments). When planned capital investments are significant, this budget must be developed early in the process because the additional investments may affect depreciation expense, interest expense (if funds are borrowed to pay for the investments), or dividend payments (if stock is issued to pay for the investments). Chapter 12 contains a detailed discussion of the capital budgeting process, including the techniques managers use in deciding whether to make additional investments.

Exhibit 9-13 shows Tucson Tortilla's capital expenditure budget for the first three months of the year. *Tucson Tortilla expects to invest in new computers, delivery vans, and production equipment in January. The depreciation expense shown in the operating budget and the depreciation shown in the MOH budget reflect these anticipated investments. No other capital investments are planned in the first quarter of the year.*

EXHIBIT 9-13 Capital Expenditure Budget

Tucson Tortilla
Capital Expenditure Budget
For the Quarter Ended March 31

	Month			
	January	**February**	**March**	**1st Quarter**
Computers and Printers	$ 15,000			
Delivery Vans	35,000			
Production Equipment	75,000			
Total new investments in property, plant and equipment	$125,000	0	0	$125,000

Cash Collections Budget

The cash collections budget is all about timing: *When* does Tucson Tortilla expect to receive cash from its sales? Of course, Tucson Tortilla will receive cash immediately on its cash (COD) sales. From the Sales Budget (Exhibit 9-5) we see that the company expects the following cash sales in January:

Cash (COD) sales = $120,000

However, most of the company's sales are made on credit. Recall that Tucson Tortilla's credit terms are "net 30 days," meaning customers have 30 days to pay. Therefore, most customers will wait nearly 30 days (a full month) before paying. However, some companies may be experiencing cash flow difficulties and may not be able to pay Tucson Tortilla on time. Because of this, Tucson Tortilla doesn't expect to receive payment on all of its credit sales the month after the sale.

Based on collection history, Tucson Tortilla expects 85% of its credit sales to be collected in the month after sale, and 14% to be collected two months after the sale. Tucson Tortilla expects that 1% of credit sales will never be collected, and therefore, has recognized a 1% bad debt expense in its operating expenses budget. Furthermore, assume that December credit sales were $500,000 and November credit sales were $480,000.

Anticipated January Collections of Credit Sales:

85% × $500,000 (December credit sales) = $425,000

14% × $480,000 (November credit sales) = $ 67,200

Exhibit 9-14 shows Tucson Tortilla's expected cash collections for the first three months of the year:

EXHIBIT 9-14 Cash Collections Budget

Tucson Tortilla
Cash Collections Budget
For the Quarter Ended March 31

	Month			
	January	**February**	**March**	**1st Quarter**
Cash sales (from Sales Budget)	$120,000	$ 80,000	$100,000	$ 300,000
Collections on Credit Sales:				
85% of credit sales made one month ago	425,000	408,000[a]	272,000[c]	1,105,000
14% of credit sales made two months ago	67,200	70,000[b]	67,200[d]	204,400
Total cash collections	$612,200	$558,000	$439,200	$1,609,400

[a] 85% × $480,000 (January credit sales, Exhibit 9-5) = $408,000
[b] 14% × $500,000 (December credit sales, Exhibit 9-5) = $70,000
[c] 85% × $320,000 (February credit sales, Exhibit 9-5) = $272,000
[d] 14% × $480,000 (January credit sales, Exhibit 9-5) = $67,200

Cash Payments Budget

The cash payments budget is also about timing: *When* will Tucson Tortilla pay for its direct materials purchases, direct labor costs, manufacturing overhead costs, operating expenses, capital expenditures, and income taxes? Let's tackle each cost, one at a time.

DIRECT MATERIALS PURCHASES *Tucson Tortilla has been given "net 30 days" payment terms from its suppliers of the corn flour used to make the tortilla chips. Therefore, Tucson Tortilla waits a month before it pays for the direct material purchases shown in the Direct Materials Budget (Exhibit 9-7). So, the company will pay for its December purchases (projected to be $231,845) in January, its January purchases of $211,125 (Exhibit 9-7) in February, its February purchases of $157,650 (Exhibit 9-7) in March, and so forth:*

	January	February	March	1st Quarter
Cash payments for DM purchases	$231,845	$211,125	$157,650	$600,620

DIRECT LABOR *Tucson Tortilla's factory employees are paid twice a month for the work they perform during the month. Therefore, January's direct labor cost of $31,900 (Exhibit 9-8) will be paid in January, and likewise, for each month.*

	January	February	March	1st Quarter
Cash payments for direct labor	$31,900	$22,550	$28,270	$82,720

MANUFACTURING OVERHEAD Tucson Tortilla must consider when it pays for its manufacturing overhead costs. *Let's assume that the company pays for all manufacturing overhead costs except for depreciation, insurance, and property taxes* ***in the month in which they are incurred.*** *Depreciation is a non-cash expense, so it never appears on the cash payments budget. Insurance and property taxes are typically paid on a semiannual basis. While Tucson Tortilla budgets a cost of $3,000 per month for factory insurance and property tax, it doesn't actually pay these costs on a monthly basis. Rather, Tucson Tortilla prepays its insurance and property tax twice a year, in January and July. The amount of these semiannual payments is calculated as shown:*

$3,000 monthly cost × 12 months = $36,000 ÷ 2 = $18,000 payments in January and July

So, the cash payments for manufacturing overhead costs are expected to be as follows:

	January	February	March	1st Quarter
Total manufacturing overhead (from Exhibit 9-9)	$102,500	$ 81,250	$ 94,250	$278,000
Less: Depreciation (not a cash expense)	(10,000)	(10,000)	(10,000)	(30,000)
Less: Property tax and insurance (paid twice a year, not monthly)	(3,000)	(3,000)	(3,000)	(9,000)
Plus: Semiannual payments for property taxes and insurance	18,000	0	0	18,000
Cash payments for MOH costs	$107,500	$ 68,250	$ 81,250	$257,000

OPERATING EXPENSES *Let's assume that the company pays for all operating expenses, except depreciation and bad debt expense,* ***in the month in which they are incurred.*** *Both depreciation and bad debt expense are non-cash expenses, so they never appear on the cash payments budget. Bad debt expense simply recognizes the sales revenue that will never be collected. Therefore, these non-cash expenses need to be deducted from the total operating expenses to arrive at* ***cash*** *payments for operating expenses:*

	January	February	March	1st Quarter
Total operating expenses (from Exhibit 9-10)	$142,800	$106,200	$124,500	$373,500
Less: Depreciation expense	(6,000)	(6,000)	(6,000)	(18,000)
Less: Bad debt expense	(4,800)	(3,200)	(4,000)	(12,000)
Cash payments for operating expenses	$132,000	$ 97,000	$114,500	$343,500

CAPITAL EXPENDITURES The timing of these cash payments have already been scheduled on the Capital Expenditures Budget in Exhibit 9-13.

INCOME TAXES Corporations must make quarterly income tax payments for their estimated income tax liability. For corporations like Tucson Tortilla that have a December 31 fiscal year-end, the first income tax payment is not due until April 15. The remaining payments are due June 15, September 15, and December 15. *As a result, Tucson Tortilla will not show any income tax payments in the first quarter of the year.*

DIVIDENDS Like many corporations, Tucson Tortilla pays dividends to its shareholders on a quarterly basis. Tucson Tortilla plans to pay $25,000 in cash dividends in January for the company's earnings in the fourth quarter of the previous year.

Finally, we pull all of these cash payments together onto a single budget, as shown in Exhibit 9-15.

EXHIBIT 9-15 Cash Payments Budget

Tucson Tortilla
Cash Payments Budget
For the Quarter Ended March 31

	Month			
	January	February	March	1st Quarter
Cash payments for direct materials purchases	$231,845	$211,125	$157,650	$ 600,620
Cash payments for direct labor	31,900	22,550	28,270	82,720
Cash payments for manufacturing overhead	107,500	68,250	81,250	257,000
Cash payments for operating expenses	132,000	97,000	114,500	343,500
Cash payments for capital investments	125,000	0	0	125,000
Cash payments for income taxes	0	0	0	0
Cash dividends	25,000	0	0	25,000
Total cash payments	$653,245	$398,925	$381,670	$1,433,840

Combined Cash Budget

The combined cash budget simply merges the budgeted cash collections and cash payments to project the company's ending cash position. Exhibit 9-16 shows the following:

- Budgeted cash collections for the month are added to the beginning cash balance to determine the total cash available.
- Budgeted cash payments are then subtracted to determine the ending cash balance before financing.
- Based on the ending cash balance before financing, the company knows whether it needs to borrow money or whether it has excess funds with which to repay debt or invest.

By looking at Exhibit 9-16, we see that Tucson Tortilla expects to begin the month with $36,100 of cash. However, by the end of the month, it will be short of cash. Therefore, the company's managers must plan for how they will handle this shortage. One strategy would be to delay the purchase of equipment planned for January. Another strategy would be to borrow money. Let's say Tucson Tortilla has prearranged a line of credit that carries an interest rate of prime plus 1%. A line of credit is a lending arrangement from a bank in which a company is allowed to borrow money as needed, up to a specified maximum amount, yet only pay interest on the portion that is actually borrowed until it is repaid.

EXHIBIT 9-16 Combined Cash Budget

Tucson Tortilla
Combined Cash Budget
For the Quarter Ended March 31

	Month			
	January	February	March	1st Quarter
Beginning balance of cash	$ 36,100	$ 15,055	$ 153,980	$ 36,100
Cash collections (Exhibit 9-14)	612,200	558,000	439,200	1,609,400
Total cash available	648,300	573,055	593,180	1,645,500
Less: Cash payments (Exhibit 9-15)	(653,245)	(398,925)	(381,670)	(1,433,840)
Ending cash balance before financing	(4,945)	174,130	211,510	211,660
Financing:				
Borrowings	20,000	0	0	20,000
Repayments	0	(20,000)	0	(20,000)
Interest payments	0	(150)	0	(150)
End cash balance	$ 15,055	$ 153,980	$ 211,510	$ 211,510

The line of credit will enable Tucson Tortilla to borrow funds to meet its short-term cash deficiencies. Let's say that Tucson Tortilla wants to maintain an ending cash balance of at least $15,000. By borrowing $20,000 on its line of credit at the end of January, the company will have slightly more ($15,055) than its minimum desired balance.

The cash budget also shows that Tucson Tortilla will be able to repay this borrowing, along with the accrued interest, in February. Assuming Tucson Tortilla borrows the $20,000 for a full month at an interest rate of 9%, February's interest payment would be calculated as follows:

$$\$20{,}000 \text{ loan} \times 1/12 \text{ of the year} \times 9\% \text{ interest rate} = \$150$$

Exhibit 9-16 also shows that Tucson Tortilla expects to have a fairly substantial cash balance at the end of both February and March. The company's managers use the cash budgets to determine when this cash will be needed and to decide how to invest it accordingly. Since the first quarterly income tax payment is due April 15, management will want to invest most of this excess cash in a safe, short-term investment, such as a money market fund or short-term certificate of deposit. The company will also need cash in April to pay shareholders a quarterly dividend. Any cash not needed in the short run can be invested in longer-term investments. Managers exercising good cash management should have a plan in place for both cash deficiencies and cash excesses.

Why is this important?

"The combined **cash budget** lets managers know in **advance** when they will be **short** on cash and need to **borrow** money, or when they may have **extra funds** to invest."

Budgeted Balance Sheet

Exhibit 9-17, shows Tucson Tortilla's budgeted balance sheet as of January 31. The company will prepare a budgeted balance sheet for each month of the year.

EXHIBIT 9-17 Budgeted Balance Sheet

Tucson Tortilla Budgeted Balance Sheet January 31		
Assets		
Cash (from Cash Budget, Exhibit 9-16)	$ 15,055	
Accounts receivable, net of allowance[A]	549,450	
Raw materials inventory (from Direct Materials Budget: 10,250 lbs end inventory × $1.50)	15,375	
Finished goods inventory (from Production Budget: 2,000 cases × $12.00 unit cost)	24,000	
Prepaid property taxes and insurance[B]	15,000	
Total current assets		$ 618,880
Property, plant, and equipment[C]	6,350,000	
Less: Accumulated depreciation[D]	(1,920,000)	
Property, plant, and equipment, net		4,430,000
Total assets		$5,048,880
Liabilities and Stockholders' Equity		
Accounts payable[E]	$ 211,125	
Income tax liability (from income statement, Exhibit 9-12)	34,020	
Other current liabilities (line of credit) (from Cash Budget, Exhibit 9-16)	20,000	
Total liabilities		$ 265,145
Stockholders' equity[F]		4,783,735
Total liabilities and stockholders' equity		$5,048,880

[A] **Accounts Receivable, Net of Allowance**	
January credit sales (from Sales Budget, Exhibit 9-5)	$480,000
15% of December's credit sales ($500,000) yet to be collected	75,000
Accounts receivable, January 31	$555,000
Less: Allowance for uncollectible accounts (Assume $750 balance prior to additional $4,800 bad debt expense, Exhibit 9-10)	(5,550)
Accounts receivable, net of allowance for uncollectible accounts	$549,450

[B] **Prepaid Property Tax and Insurance**	
Semiannual payment made in January (cash payments for MOH, p. 534)	$18,000
Less: January cost (MOH Budget, Exhibit 9-9)	3,000
Prepaid property tax and insurance, January 31	$15,000

^C **Property, Plant, and Equipment**	
December 31 balance (assumed)	$6,225,000
Plus: January's investment in new equipment (Capital Expenditure Budget, Exhibit 9-13)	125,000
Property, plant, and equipment, January 31	$6,350,000

^D **Accumulated Depreciation**	
December 31 balance (assumed)	$1,904,000
Plus: January's depreciation from Manufacturing Overhead Budget, Exhibit 9-9	10,000
Plus: January's depreciation from Operating Expenses Budget, Exhibit 9-10	6,000
Accumulated depreciation, January 31	$1,920,000

^E **Accounts Payable**	
January's DM purchases to be paid in February (p. 533 and Exhibit 9-15)	211,125
Accounts payable, January 31	$211,125

^F **Stockholders' Equity**	
December 31 balance of common stock and retained earnings (assumed)	$4,720,555
Plus: January's net income (Budgeted Income Statement, Exhibit 9-12)	63,180
Stockholders' equity, January 31	$4,783,735

Sensitivity Analysis and Flexible Budgeting

The master budget models the company's *planned* activities. Managers try to use the best estimates possible when creating budgets. However, managers do not have a crystal ball for making predictions. Some of the key assumptions (such sales volume) used to create the budgets may turn out to be different than originally predicted. How do managers prepare themselves for potentially different scenarios? They use sensitivity analysis and flexible budgeting.

As shown in Exhibit 9-18, **sensitivity analysis** is a *what if* technique that asks *what* a result will be *if* a predicted amount is not achieved or *if* an underlying assumption changes. For example, *what if* shipping costs increase due to increases in gasoline prices? *What if* the cost of the corn flour increases or union workers negotiate a wage increase? *What if* sales are 15% cash and 85% credit, rather than 20% cash and 80% credit? How will any

EXHIBIT 9-18 Sensitivity Analysis

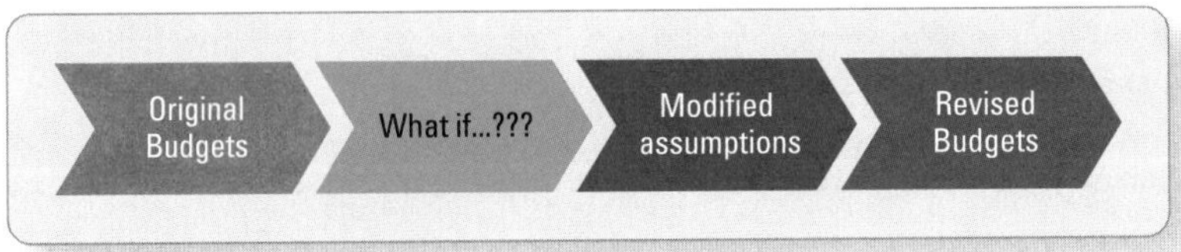

or all of these changes in key assumptions affect Tucson Tortilla's budgeted income and budgeted cash position?

In addition to these "what if" scenarios, management is particularly concerned with sales projections. Why? Because the sales budget is the driving force behind most of the other budgets. If the budgeted sales figures change, then most other budgets will also change. To address this concern, managers often prepare **flexible budgets**, which are budgets prepared for different volumes of activity. Cost behavior is much of the driving force behind flexible budgets. Recall that as volume changes within the relevant range, only total variable costs should change. Fixed costs should remain unaffected. We'll discuss flexible budgets again in Chapter 10, where we show how flexible budgets are often used at the end of the period as the best basis for performance evaluation.

Technology makes it cost-effective to perform comprehensive sensitivity analyses and flexible budgets. Most companies use computer spreadsheet programs or special budget software to prepare the master budget and all of its components. Managers perform sensitivity analysis by simply changing one or several of the underlying assumptions in the budgets, such as sales volume, direct material cost, and collection terms. The budget software automatically computes a complete set of revised budgets based on the changes.

Armed with a better understanding of how changes in key assumption will affect the company's bottom line and cash position, today's managers can be prepared to lead the company when business conditions change.

Sustainability and Budgeting

Budgets reflect and communicate management's goals and objectives. Managers leading their companies towards more sustainable practices will want to reflect those goals in the company's budgets. For example, Campbell Soup Company has set long-term environmental goals for 2020 which include:[1]

- Cutting water use and greenhouse gas emissions in half per ton of food produced
- Recycling 95% of waste generated
- Delivering 75% of packaging from sustainable materials
- Sourcing 40% of energy used from renewable or alternative energy sources

The adoption of these long-term goals will affect most, if not all of the company's shorter-term budgets. For example, the operating expense budget should reflect additional resources devoted to researching and developing more sustainable packaging materials. Once developed, the new packaging will impact the direct materials budget. The operating expense budget should also include additional resources for marketing the sustainably packaged products, which should in turn create additional sales to be included in the sales budget. The capital expenditures budget will reflect plans to purchase new energy saving production equipment, such as the $15.1 million of environmentally related capital investments that Campbell made in 2009. The company's MOH budget will in turn be affected by depreciation of the new equipment, as well as the reduction of water cost, the recycling of waste, and the use of alternative forms of energy. All of these measures will impact the cash budget, as well as the company's projected income statement and balance sheet.

See Exercises E9-15A and E9-35B

Recall that budgets also serve as benchmarks for judging performance. By developing strategic environmental goals that span several years, and then tracking yearly performance, Campbell can see how well it is working towards achieving those longer-term goals. For example, in 2009, Campbell was able to reduce water use per ton of food produced by 9.5% from what it had been in 2008. In 2009, Campbell also recycled 84% of waste generated (up from 64% for US operations in 2008). These key metrics indicate that Campbell is well on its way towards achieving its longer-term environmental goals.

[1]Campbell Soup Company 2010 Corporate Social Responsibility Report

How do the Budgets for Service and Merchandising Companies Differ?

4 Prepare budgets for a merchandiser

Earlier in this chapter we presented the master budget for a manufacturing company. The components of the master budget for a manufacturing company were summarized in Exhibit 9-4. The master budgets for service companies and merchandising companies are somewhat less complex, and will be described next.

Service Companies

Recall that service companies have no merchandise inventory. Therefore, their operating budgets only include the Sales Budget, the Operating Expenses Budget, and the Budgeted Income Statement, as shown in Exhibit 9-19. Notice that the financial budgets are the same as those a manufacturer would prepare.

EXHIBIT 9-19 Master Budget for a Service Company

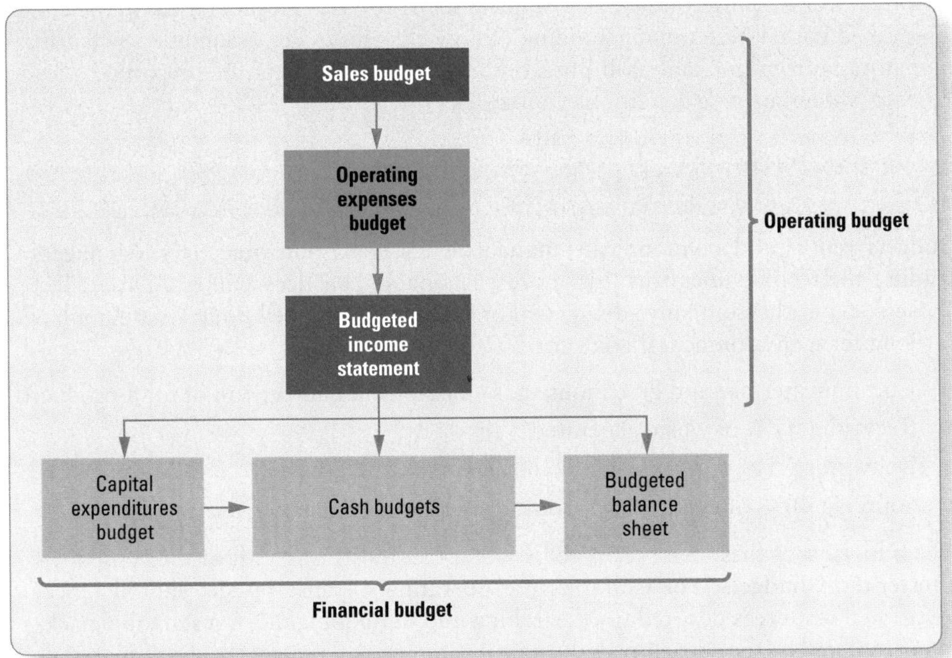

Merchandising Companies

Since merchandising companies purchase ready-made products, they do not need to prepare the Production, Direct Materials, Direct Labor, or Manufacturing Overhead Budgets. Replacing these budgets is a combined <u>Cost of Goods Sold, Inventory, and Purchases Budget</u>, as shown in Exhibit 9-20.

The Cost of Goods Sold, Inventory, and Purchases budget follows the same general format as the manufacturer's production budget except that it is calculated at cost (in dollars) rather than in units:[2]

Cost of Goods Sold	(the inventory we plan to sell during the month, at cost)
Plus: Desired Ending Inventory	(the amount of inventory we want on hand at month's end)
Total Inventory Needed	(the total amount of inventory needed)
Less: Beginning Inventory	(the amount of inventory we have on hand)
Purchases of Inventory	(the amount of inventory we need to purchase)

[2]A merchandiser could first prepare this budget in units, and then convert it to dollars. However, merchandisers usually have hundreds or thousands of products for sale, so it is often simpler to directly state it in dollars.

EXHIBIT 9-20 Master Budget for a Merchandising Company

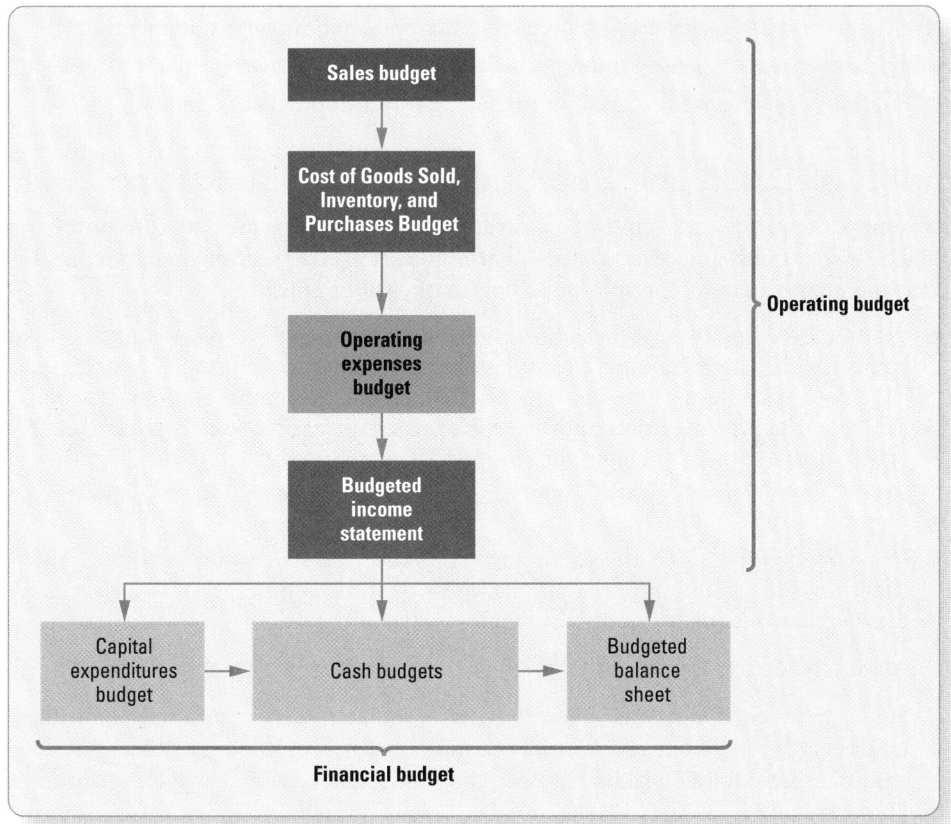

Notice that the format of the budget is easy to remember because it follows the name of the budget: We start with *Cost of Goods Sold*, then consider *inventory* levels, and finally arrive at the amount of *purchases* to be made. Let's try an example:

Let's say one Circle J convenience store expects sales of $500,000 in January, $520,000 in February, $530,000 in March, and $550,000 in April. Let's also assume that management sets its prices to achieve an overall 40% gross profit. As a result, Cost of Goods Sold is 60% of the sales revenue (100% – 40%). Finally, management wishes to have ending inventory equal to 10% of the next month's Cost of Goods Sold. Exhibit 9-21 shows the Cost of Goods Sold, Inventory, and Purchases budget for the first three months of the year. Keep in mind that all figures (other than Sales Revenue) are shown at cost.

EXHIBIT 9-21 Merchandiser's Cost of Goods Sold, Inventory, and Purchases Budget

Circle J Convenience Store
Cost of Goods Sold, Inventory, and Purchases Budget
For the months of January and February

	Month		
	January	February	March
Sales revenue (from Sales Budget)	$500,000	$520,000	$530,000
Cost of goods sold (60% of sales revenue)	$300,000	$312,000	$318,000
Plus: Desired ending inventory 10% of next month's cost of goods sold)	31,200	31,800	33,000[b]
Total inventory required	331,200	343,800	351,000
Less: Beginning inventory	(30,000)[a]	(31,200)	(31,800)
Purchases of inventory	$301,200	$312,600	$319,200

[a] December 31 balance (equal to January 1 balance) is 10% of January's Cost of Goods Sold.
[b] April sales of $550,000 × 60% = $330,000; April Cost of Goods Sold × 10% = $33,000

Figures from this budget are then used as follows:

- *Cost of Goods Sold* is used in preparing the budgeted income statement.
- *Ending Inventory* is used in preparing the budgeted balance sheet.
- *Purchases of Inventory* is used in preparing the cash payments budget.

Impact of Credit and Debit Card Sales on Budgeting

Consumers often use credit and debit cards to pay for online and in-store purchases at retailers, gas stations, and restaurants. What implications do these payment methods have on the merchants that accept "plastic" in place of cash or checks?

- Credit card companies (MasterCard, Visa, and American Express)[3] and their issuing banks charge the merchant a transaction fee for each purchase made using plastic. The fee is usually a fixed amount *plus* a percentage of the amount charged. For example, the typical transaction fee for each credit card sale is between $0.25 and $0.50, *plus* 1–5% of the amount charged.[4] The actual fee will depend on the credit card brand and the merchant. Reward cards, such as those tied to frequent flyer miles, typically charge higher fees.
- In exchange for the fee, the credit card company and its issuing bank pays the merchant the entire amount of the purchase *less* the transaction fee. A deposit is made to the merchant's bank account within a few days of the sale.

Debit card transaction fees are usually lower than credit card transaction fees. Why?

1. Since debit card purchases require an associated PIN (personal identification number), the risk of fraud is lower than it is with a credit card. Thus, the issuing credit card company will have lower costs associated with stolen and fraudulently used cards.
2. Debit card sales are paid to the merchant using money that is in the customer's bank account, rather than money that is in essence loaned to the customer by the credit card company. Since the cash used for the deposit is not subject to credit risk, it is made with "cheaper" funds.
3. Beginning October 1, 2011, the Federal Reserve set a cap on the debit card transaction fees that banks can charge merchants. The new limit is as follows:

Limit on *debit* card fees = $0.22 per transaction + 0.05% of the amount of the transaction

Notice that the amount charged on the value of the transaction (0.0005) is substantially less than it is for a typical credit card transaction.[5]

Although credit and debit card transaction fees are costly to merchants, the acceptance of plastic payment methods also has benefits:

- Merchants would lose potential sales if they did not allow customers to pay with credit and debit cards.
- The acceptance of credit cards decreases the costs associated with bounced checks, misappropriation of cash, and the activities associated with preparing and transporting cash deposits (sometimes via armored vehicle collection services).
- Merchants receive the cash quickly, which may improve their cash flow.

[3]These three credit card companies control approximately 93% of the credit card transactions in the United States. By 2008, $48 billion in transaction fees were assessed by credit card issuers. www.newrules.org/retail/news/soaring-credit-card-transaction-fees-squeeze-independent-businesses

[4]www.allbusiness.com/sales/internet-e-commerce/3930-1.html

[5]www.federalreserve.gov/newsevents/press/bcreg/20110629a.htm. Banks with less than $10 billion in assets are exempt from the new cap. In addition, if a bank does not have fraud prevention policies and procedures in place, the cap is $0.21 per transaction rather than $0.22 per transaction.

Let's try an example:

Say a customer purchases some clothes at Aeropostale for \$50 and uses a MasterCard to pay for the purchase. Let's also assume that MasterCard charges Aeropostale a transaction fee equal to \$0.25 + 2% of the amount charged. The transaction fee on this sale would be:

$$\text{Transaction Fee} = \$0.25 + (2\% \times \text{Amount Charged})$$
$$\$1.25 = \$0.25 + (2\% \times \$50)$$

Within a few days, MasterCard would deposit the following amount in Aeropostale's bank account:

$$\text{Cash Deposited} = \text{Amount Charged on Credit Card} - \text{Transaction Fee}$$
$$\$48.75 = \$50.00 - \$1.25$$

The anticipation of this credit card sale would be shown in the budgets as follows:

- The \$50 sale would be shown in the Sales Budget, *in the month of sale*.
- The \$1.25 transaction fee would be shown in the Operating Expense Budget, *in the month of sale*.
- The \$48.75 would be shown as a cash receipt on the Cash Collections Budget, *in the month of collection* (which is typically within one to seven days of the actual sale).

When preparing the master budget, merchants need to consider:

- The percentage of sales that will be made using debit cards and credit cards
- The different transaction fees charged for debit and credit card transactions
- The length of time between the sale and the deposit.

Retail Credit Cards

Many retailers, such as Target, Kohl's, and Old Navy issue their own credit cards in addition to accepting credit cards such as Visa and MasterCard. When a customer uses a store-based credit card, no transaction fee is incurred. However, the risk of collection falls back on the merchant, rather than on a third-party credit card company. The merchant must wait for the customer to make payments on the credit card bill. The cash collection may occur over several months, several years, or never. The cash collections budget will take into account the aging of these receivables. Likewise, the operating expense budget will need to take into consideration possible bad debts. Finally, the company will need to budget for interest income assessed on unpaid balances and any fees charged to the customer for late payments.

Decision Guidelines

The Master Budget

Let's consider some additional decisions with respect to budgeting.

Decision	Guidelines
What is the key to preparing the cash collections and cash payments budgets?	The key to preparing the cash budgets is *timing*. *When* will cash be received, and *when* will cash be paid? The timing of cash collections and cash payments often differs from the period in which the related revenues and expenses are recognized on the income statement.
What can be done to prepare for possible changes in key, underlying budget assumptions?	Management uses sensitivity analysis to understand how changes in key, underlying assumptions might affect the company's financial results. This awareness helps managers cope with changing business conditions when they occur.
How does sustainability impact budgeting?	Companies that are planning on adopting any sustainable practice will want to capture those plans in their budgets. Any or all of the budgets could be impacted by plans to adopt sustainable practices.
How does the master budget of a service company differ from that of a manufacturer?	Service companies have no inventory to make or sell, thus their operating budgets are less complex. The operating budgets include the: • Sales Budget • Operating Expense Budget • Budgeted Income Statement
How does the master budget of a merchandising company differ from that of a manufacturer?	Merchandising companies buy their inventory, rather than make it. In place of the Production budget, they use a "Cost of Goods Sold, Inventory, and Purchases" budget. This budget follows the same basic format as the Production budget. The amounts on the budget are calculated at cost, rather than in units. The operating budgets include the: • Sales budget • Cost of Goods Sold, Inventory, and Purchases budget • Operating Expense budget • Budgeted Income statement
How does the acceptance of debit and credit card payments affect a merchant's budgets?	Merchants must budget for the transaction fees charged by the credit card companies and their issuing banks. The transaction fee needs to be shown on the operating expense budget. The amount of credit and debit card sales, net of the transaction fee, will be shown on the cash receipts budget.
How are credit and debit card transaction fees calculated?	The transaction fee is typically a set dollar amount per transaction, plus a percentage of the amount of sale charged on a credit or debit card. For example: Transaction Fee = \$0.25 + (2% × Amount Charged)
How does the acceptance of debit and credit cards affect the cash collection budget?	The amount of cash shown on the cash collections budget will be the net amount deposited: Cash Deposited = Amount Charged on Credit Card − Transaction Fee

SUMMARY PROBLEM 2

The following information was taken from Pillows Unlimited Sales Budget, found in Summary Problem 1 on page 530:

Pillows Unlimited
Sales Budget—Type of Sale
For the Quarter Ended March 31

	Month			
Type of Sale:	January	February	March	1st Quarter
Cash sales (10%)	$ 140,000	$ 154,000	$ 161,000	$ 455,000
Credit sales (90%)	1,260,000	1,386,000	1,449,000	4,095,000
Total sales revenue	$1,400,000	$1,540,000	$1,610,000	$4,550,000

The company's collection history indicates that 75% of credit sales are collected in the month after the sale, 15% are collected two months after the sale, 8% are collected three months after the sale, and the remaining 2% are never collected.

Assume the following additional information was gathered about the types of sales made in the fourth quarter (October through December) of the previous year:

Pillows Unlimited
Sales Budget—Type of Sale
For the Quarter Ended December 31

	Month			
Type of Sale:	October	November	December	4th Quarter
Cash sales (10%)	$ 142,800	$ 151,200	$ 137,200	$ 431,200
Credit sales (90%)	1,285,200	1,360,800	1,234,800	3,880,800
Total sales revenue	$1,428,000	$1,512,000	$1,372,000	$4,312,000

The following information was taken from Pillows Unlimited Direct Materials Budget, found in Summary Problem 1 on page 530:

	January	February	March	1st Quarter
Total cost of DM purchases	$771,750	$836,250	$873,000	$2,481,000

Assume that the total cost of direct materials purchases in December was $725,000. The company pays 40% of its direct materials purchases in the month of purchase, and pays the remaining 60% in the month after purchase.

Requirements

1. Prepare the Cash Collections Budget for January, February, and March, as well as a summary for the first quarter.
2. Prepare the Cash Disbursements Budget for Direct Materials purchases for the months of January, February, and March, as well as a summary for the quarter.

■ SOLUTIONS

Requirement 1

Pillows Unlimited
Cash Collections Budget
For the Quarter Ended March 31

	Month			
	January	February	March	1st Quarter
Cash sales	$ 140,000	$ 154,000	$ 161,000	$ 455,000
Collections on credit sales:				
75% of credit sales made last month	926,100[A]	945,000[D]	1,039,500[G]	2,910,600
15% of credit sales made two months ago	204,120[B]	185,220[E]	189,000[H]	578,340
8% of credit sales made two months ago	102,816[C]	108,864[F]	98,784[I]	310,464
Total cash collections	$1,373,036	$1,393,084	$1,488,284	$4,254,404

[A]December credit sales ($1,234,800) × 75% = $ 926,100
[B]November credit sales ($1,360,800) × 15% = $ 204,120
[C]October credit sales ($1,285,200) × 8% = $ 102,816

[D]January credit sales ($1,260,000) × 75% = $ 945,000
[E]December credit sales ($1,234,800) × 15% = $ 185,220
[F]November credit sales ($1,360,800) × 8% = $ 108,864

[G]February credit sales ($1,386,000) × 75% = $1,039,500
[H]January credit sales ($1,260,000) × 15% = $ 189,000
[I]December credit sales ($1,234,800) × 8% = $ 98,784

Requirement 2

Pillows Unlimited
Cash Payments Budget—Direct Materials
For the Quarter Ended March 31

	Month			
	January	February	March	1st Quarter
40% of current month DM purchases	$308,700[A]	$334,500[C]	$349,200[E]	$ 992,400
60% of last month's DM purchases	435,000[B]	463,050[D]	501,750[F]	1,399,800
Total cash payments for DM	$743,700	$797,550	$850,950	$2,392,200

[A]January DM purchases ($771,750) × 40% = $308,700
[B]December DM purchases ($725,000) × 60% = $435,000

[C]February DM purchases ($836,250) × 40% = $334,500
[D]January DM purchases ($771,750) × 60% = $463,050

[E]March DM purchases ($873,000) × 40% = $349,200
[F]February DM purchases ($836,250) × 60% = $501,750

END OF CHAPTER

Learning Objectives

- 1 Describe how and why managers use budgets
- 2 Prepare the operating budgets
- 3 Prepare the financial budgets
- 4 Prepare budgets for a merchandiser

Accounting Vocabulary

Budget Committee. (p. 517) A committee comprised of upper management, as well as cross-functional managers, who review, revise, and approve the final budget.

COD. (p. 521) Collect on Delivery, or Cash on Delivery. A sales term indicating that the inventory must be paid for at the time of delivery.

Cost of Goods Sold, Inventory, and Purchases Budget. (p. 540) A merchandiser's budget that computes the Cost of Goods Sold, the amount of desired ending inventory, and amount of merchandise to be purchased.

Financial Budgets. (p. 520) The budgets that project the collection and payment of cash, as well as forecast the company's budgeted balance sheet.

Flexible Budgets. (p. 539) Budgets prepared for different volumes of activity.

Line of Credit. (p. 536) A lending arrangement from a bank in which a company is allowed to borrow money as needed, up to a specified maximum amount, yet only pay interest on the portion that is actually borrowed until it is repaid.

Master Budget. (p. 519) The comprehensive planning document for the entire organization. The master budget includes the operating budgets and the financial budgets.

Operating Budgets. (p. 520) The budgets needed to run the daily operations of the company. The operation budgets culminate in a budgeted income statement.

Participative Budgeting. (p. 517) Budgeting that involves the participation of many levels of management.

Rolling Budget. (p. 517) A budget that is continuously updated so that the next 12 months of operations are always budgeted; also known as a continuous budget.

Safety Stock. (p. 521) Extra inventory kept on hand in case demand is higher than expected or problems in the factory slow production.

Sensitivity Analysis. (p. 538) A *what if* technique that asks what a result will be if a predicted amount is not achieved or if an underlying assumption changes.

Slack. (p. 517) Intentionally overstating budgeted expenses or understating budgeted revenues in order to cope with uncertainty, make performance appear better, or make room for potential budget cuts.

Strategic Planning. (p. 516) Setting long-term goals that may extend 5–10 years into the future.

Variance. (p. 519) The difference between actual and budgeted figures (revenues and expenses).

Zero-Based Budgeting. (p. 517) A budgeting approach in which managers begin with a budget of zero and must justify every dollar put into the budget.

MyAccountingLab

Go to http://myaccountinglab.com/ for the following Quick Check, Short Exercises, Exercises, and Problems. They are available with immediate grading, explanations of correct and incorrect answers, and interactive media that acts as your own online tutor.

Quick Check

1. *(Learning Objective 1)* Amazon.com expects to receive which of the following benefits when it uses its budgeting process?
   a. The planning required to develop the budget helps managers foresee and avoid potential problems before they occur.
   b. The budget helps motivate employees to achieve Amazon.com's sales growth and cost reduction goals.
   c. The budget provides Amazon.com's managers with a benchmark against which to compare actual results for performance evaluation.
   d. All of the above.

2. *(Learning Objective 1)* Budgets are
   a. required by Generally Accepted Accounting Principles (GAAP).
   b. future-oriented.
   c. only used by large corporations.
   d. prepared by the controller for the entire company.

3. *(Learning Objective 1)* Technology has made it easier for managers to perform all of the following tasks *except*
   a. sensitivity analyses.
   b. combining individual units' budgets to create the companywide budget.
   c. removing slack from the budget.
   d. preparing responsibility center performance reports that identify variances between actual and budgeted revenues and costs.
4. *(Learning Objective 2)* Which of the following is the starting point for the master budget?
   a. The sales budget
   b. The direct materials budget
   c. The production budget
   d. The operating expenses budget
5. *(Learning Objective 2)* The income statement is part of which element of a company's master budget?
   a. The operating budgets
   b. The capital expenditures budget
   c. The financial budgets
   d. The cash budgets
6. *(Learning Objective 2)* The usual starting point for a direct labor budget for a manufacturer is the
   a. direct materials budget.
   b. sales budget.
   c. cash budget.
   d. production budget.
7. *(Learning Objective 3)* The following budgets are all financial budgets *except* for the
   a. combined cash budget.
   b. budgeted balance sheet.
   c. budgeted income statement.
   d. capital expenditures budget.
8. *(Learning Objective 3)* Which of the following expenses would *not* appear in a cash budget?
   a. Depreciation expense
   b. Wages expense
   c. Interest expense
   d. Marketing expense
9. *(Learning Objective 4)* Which of the following budgets would ordinarily *not* be prepared by a service company?
   a. Sales budget
   b. Operating expense budget
   c. Production budget
   d. Budgeted income statement
10. *(Learning Objective 4)* For a merchandising company, the Cost of Goods Sold, Inventory, and Purchases budget replaces all of the following budgets *except* the:
   a. Production budget
   b. Sales budget
   c. Direct labor budget
   d. Direct materials budget

Quick Check Answers

1. d 2. b 3. c 4. a 5. a 6. d 7. c 8. a 9. c 10. b

Short Exercises

S9-1 Order of preparation and components of master budget
(Learning Objective 1)

Identify the order in which a manufacturer would prepare the following budgets. Also note whether each budget is an operating budget or a financial budget.

a. Budgeted income statement
b. Combined cash budget
c. Sales budget
d. Budgeted balance sheet
e. Cash payments budget
f. Direct materials budget
g. Production budget

S9-2 Understand key terms and definitions *(Learning Objectives 1 & 2)*

Listed next are several terms. Complete the following statements with one of these terms. You may use a term more than once, and some terms may not be used at all.

Operating budgets	Production budget	Master budget	Participative budgeting
Financial budgets	Slack	Zero-based budgeting	Strategic planning
Safety stock	Variance	Budget committee	Rolling budget

a. Managers will sometimes build ________ into their budgets to protect themselves against unanticipated expenses or lower revenues.
b. The ________ is the difference between actual and budgeted figures and is used to evaluate how well the manager controlled operations during the period.
c. ________ are often used by companies to review submitted budgets, make revisions as needed, and approve the final budgets.
d. ________ is extra inventory of finished goods that is kept on hand in case demand is higher than predicted or problems in the factory slow production.
e. The sales budget and production budget are examples of ________.
f. ________ is a budgeting process that begins with departmental managers and flows up through middle management to top management.
g. ________ is a budget that is continuously updated by adding months to the end of the budgeting period.
h. ________ is the comprehensive planning document for the entire organization.
i. These budgets, ________, project both the collection and payment of cash and forecast the company's budgeted balance sheet.
j. The ________ is used to forecast how many units should be made to meet the sales projects.
k. When an organization builds its budgets from the ground up, it is using ________.
l. ________ is the process of setting long-term goals that may extend several years into the future.

S9-3 Prepare a Sales Budget *(Learning Objective 2)*

Sport Physicians, Inc., offers two types of physical exams for students: the basic physical and the extended physical. The charge for the basic physical is $75, while the charge for the extended physical is $140. Sport Physicians expects to perform 200 basic physicals and 160 extended physicals in July, 220 basic and 190 extended in August, and 100 basic and 80 extended in September. Prepare the sales budget for the second quarter (July through September), with a column for each month and for the quarter in total.

S9-4 Production budget *(Learning Objective 2)*

Thomas Cycles manufactures chainless bicycles. On March 31, Thomas Cycles had 280 bikes in inventory. The company has a policy that the ending inventory in any month must be 10% of the following month's expected sales. Thomas Cycles expects to sell the following number of bikes in each of next four months:

April	1,050 bikes
May	1,190 bikes
June	1,360 bikes
July	1,240 bikes

Prepare a production budget for the second quarter, with a column for each month and for the quarter.

S9-5 Direct materials budget *(Learning Objective 2)*

The Bakery on the Riverbank produces organic bread that is sold by the loaf. Each loaf requires 1/2 of a pound of flour. The bakery pays $3.00 per pound of the organic flour used in its loaves. The bakery expects to produce the following number of loaves in each of the upcoming four months:

July	1,480 loaves
August	1,940 loaves
September	1,720 loaves
October	1,400 loaves

The bakery has a policy that it will have 20% of the following month's flour needs on hand at the end of each month. At the end of June, there were 75 pounds of flour on hand. Prepare the direct materials budget for the third quarter, with a column for each month and for the quarter.

S9-6 Direct labor budget *(Learning Objective 2)*

The Production Department of Carrington Manufacturing has prepared the following schedule of units to be produced over the first quarter of the upcoming year:

	January	February	March
Units to be produced	550	640	800

Each unit requires 5.0 hours of direct labor. Direct labor workers are paid an average of $20 per hour. How many hours will be required in January? In February? In March?

S9-7 Manufacturing overhead budget *(Learning Objective 2)*

Poppy Corporation is preparing its manufacturing overhead budget. The direct labor budget for the upcoming quarter is as follows:

	April	May	June
Budgeted direct labor hours	410	730	680

The company's variable manufacturing overhead rate is $1.20 per direct labor hour and the company's fixed manufacturing overhead is $3,100 per month. How much manufacturing overhead will be budgeted for April? For May? For June?

S9-8 Operating expenses budget *(Learning Objective 2)*

Hyannisport Corporation is preparing its operating expenses budget. The budgeted unit sales for the upcoming quarter are as follows:

	July	August	September
Budgeted unit sales	1,290	1,420	1,730

The company's variable operating expenses are $4.00 per unit. Fixed monthly operating expenses include $5,200 for salaries, $3,800 for office rent, and depreciation of $2,800. How much operating expenses will be budgeted for July? For August? For September?

S9-9 Budgeted income statement *(Learning Objective 2)*

Scandia Scales manufactures a specialty precision scale. For January, Scandia expects to sell 1,400 scales at an average price of $2,360 per unit. Scandia's average manufacturing cost of each unit sold is $1,490. Variable operating expenses for Scandia Scales will be $1.50 per unit sold and fixed operating expenses are expected to be $7,300 for the month. Monthly interest expense is $3,200. Scandia Scales has a tax rate of 40% of income before taxes. Prepare Scandia Scales' budgeted income statement for January.

S9-10 Cash collections budget *(Learning Objective 3)*

Keystone Service anticipates the following sales revenue over a five-month period:

	November	December	January	February	March
Sales revenue	$16,100	$10,900	$15,800	$12,900	$14,200

Keystone Service's sales are 40% cash and 60% credit. Keystone Service's collection history indicates that credit sales are collected as follows:

25% in the month of the sale
50% in the month after the sale
15% two months after the sale
10% are never collected

How much cash will be collected in January? In February? In March?

S9-11 Cash payments budget *(Learning Objective 3)*

Centennial Corporation is preparing its cash payments budget for next month. The following information pertains to the cash payments:

a. Centennial Corporation pays for 50% of its direct materials purchases in the month of purchase and the remainder the following month. Last month's direct material purchases were $75,000, while the company anticipates $87,000 of direct material purchases next month.
b. Direct labor for the upcoming month is budgeted to be $36,000 and will be paid at the end of the upcoming month.
c. Manufacturing overhead is estimated to be 130% of direct labor cost each month and is paid in the month in which it is incurred. This monthly estimate includes $13,000 of depreciation on the plant and equipment.
d. Monthly operating expenses for next month are expected to be $41,000, which includes $2,500 of depreciation on office equipment and $1,600 of bad debt expense. These monthly operating expenses are paid during the month in which they are incurred.
e. Centennial Corporation will be making an estimated tax payment of $7,800 next month. How much cash will be paid out next month?

S9-12 Cash budget *(Learning Objective 3)*

Henderson Services, Inc., has $8,300 cash on hand on January 1. The company requires a minimum cash balance of $7,300. January cash collections are $548,430. Total cash payments for January are $575,160. Prepare a cash budget for January. How much cash, if any, will Henderson need to borrow by the end of January?

S9-13 Estimate credit card fees *(Learning Objective 4)*

The local grocery store expects that customers will use credit cards to pay for a total of 60,000 sales transactions during the month of April. These transactions are expected to amount to $3,000,000 in total sales revenue. The credit card issuers charge the store a transaction fee equal to $0.30 per transaction plus 2% of the amount charged. When budgeting for operating expenses in April, how much should the store expect to incur for credit card transaction fees?

S9-14 Inventory, purchases, and cost of goods sold *(Learning Objective 4)*

Heisler Company sells its smartphone worldwide. Heisler expects to sell 4,600 smartphones for $160 each in January and 4,000 smartphones for $225 each in February. All sales are cash only. Heisler expects cost of goods sold to average 60% of sales revenue and the company expects to sell 4,300 smartphones in March for $300 each. Heisler's target ending inventory is $10,000 plus 50% of the next month's cost of goods sold.

1. Prepare the sales budget for January and February.
2. Prepare Heisler's inventory, purchases, and cost of goods sold budget for January and February.

EXERCISES Group A

E9-15A Budgeting and sustainability *(Learning Objective 1)*

Dudley Beverages manufactures its own soda pop bottles. The bottles are made from polyethylene terephthalate (PET), a lightweight yet strong plastic. Dudley uses as much PET recycled resin pellets in its bottles as it can, both because using recycled PET helps Dudley to meet its sustainability goals and because recycled PET is less expensive than virgin PET.

Dudley is continuing to search for ways to reduce its costs and its impact on the environment. PET plastic is melted and blown over soda bottle molds to produce the bottles. One idea Dudley's engineers have suggested is to retrofit the soda bottle molds and change the plastic formulation slightly so that 20% less PET plastic is used for each bottle. The average kilograms of PET per soda bottle before any redesign is 0.005 kg. The cost of retrofitting the soda bottle molds will result in a one-time charge of $18,000, while the plastic reformulation will cause the average cost per kilogram of PET plastic to change from $2.00 to $2.20.

Dudley's management is analyzing whether the change to the bottle molds to reduce PET plastic usage should be made. Management expects the following number of soda bottles to be used in the upcoming year:

	Quarter 1	Quarter 2	Quarter 3	Quarter 4
Number of soda pop bottles to be produced	2,500,000	2,900,000	3,200,000	2,300,000

For the upcoming year, management expects the beginning inventory of PET to be 1,250 kilograms, while ending inventory is expected to be 1,700 kilograms. During the first three quarters of the year, management wants to keep the ending inventory of PET at the end of each quarter equal to 10% of the following quarter's PET needs.

Requirements

1. Using the original data (before any redesign of soda bottles), prepare a direct materials budget to calculate the cost of PET purchases in each quarter for the upcoming year and for the year in total.
2. Assume that the company retrofits the soda bottle molds and changes the plastic formulation slightly so that less PET plastic is used in each bottle. Now prepare a direct materials budget to calculate the cost of PET purchases in each quarter for the upcoming year and for the year in total for this possible scenario.
3. Compare the cost of PET plastic for Requirement 1 (original data) and for Requirement 2 (making change to using less PET.) What is the direct material cost savings from making the change to using less PET? Compare the total of those savings to the cost of retrofitting the soda bottle molds. Should the company make the change? Explain your rationale.

E9-16A Prepare a sales budget for a retail organization *(Learning Objective 2)*

Upstate College Bookstore is the bookstore on campus for students and faculty. Upstate College Bookstore shows the following sales projections in units by quarter for the upcoming year:

Quarter	Books	School Supplies	Apparel	Miscellaneous
1st	1,590	200	510	690
2nd	850	140	350	580
3rd	1,760	250	880	870
4th	680	120	540	480

The average price of an item in each of the departments is as follows:

	Average sales per unit
Books	$88
School supplies	$10
Apparel	$25
Miscellaneous	$ 8

Requirement

Prepare a sales budget for the upcoming year by quarter for the Upstate College Bookstore, with sales categorized by the four product groupings (books, school supplies, apparel, and miscellaneous).

E9-17A Prepare a sales budget for a not-for-profit organization

(Learning Objective 2)

Copley Preschool operates a not-for-profit morning preschool. Each family pays a non-refundable registration fee of $115 per child per school year. Monthly tuition for the nine-month school year varies depending on the number of days per week that the child attends preschool. The monthly tuition is $125 for the two-day program, $145 for the three-day program, $170 for the four-day program, and $185 for the five-day program. The following enrollment has been projected for the coming year:

Two-day program:	80 children
Three-day program:	36 children
Four-day program:	52 children
Five-day program:	12 children

In addition to the morning preschool, Copley Preschool offers a Lunch Bunch program where kids have the option of staying an extra hour for lunch and playtime. Copley Preschool charges an additional $2 per child for every Lunch Bunch attended. Historically, half the children stay for Lunch Bunch an average of 15 times a month.

Requirement

Calculate Copley Preschool's budgeted revenue for the school year.

E9-18A Production budget *(Learning Objective 2)*

Wolanin Foods produces specialty soup sold in jars. The projected sales in dollars and jars for each quarter of the upcoming year are as follows:

	Total sales revenue	Number of jars sold
1st quarter	$180,000	153,000
2nd quarter	$214,000	184,000
3rd quarter	$257,000	211,000
4th quarter	$196,000	163,500

Wolanin anticipates selling 226,000 jars with total sales revenue of $266,000 in the first quarter of the year *following* the year given in the preceding table. Wolanin has a policy that the ending inventory of jars must be 30% of the following quarter's sales. Prepare a production budget for the year that shows the number of jars to be produced each quarter and for the year in total.

E9-19A Direct materials budget *(Learning Objective 2)*

Milford Industries manufactures a popular interactive stuffed animal for children that requires two computer chips inside each toy. Milford Industries pays $1 for each computer chip. To help to guard against stockouts of the computer chip, Milford Industries has a policy that states that the ending inventory of computer chips should be at least 30% of the following month's production needs. The production schedule for the first four months of the year is as follows:

	Stuffed animals to be produced
January	5,200
February	4,700
March	4,000
April	4,600

Requirement

Prepare a direct materials budget for the first quarter that shows both the number of computer chips needed and the dollar amount of the purchases in the budget.

E9-20A Production and direct materials budgets *(Learning Objective 2)*

Osborne Manufacturing produces self-watering planters for use in upscale retail establishments. Sales projections for the first five months of the upcoming year show the estimated unit sales of the planters each month to be as follows:

	Number of planters to be sold
January	3,900
February	3,200
March	3,700
April	4,400
May	4,900

Inventory at the start of the year was 975 planters. The desired inventory of planters at the end of each month should be equal to 25% of the following month's budgeted sales. Each planter requires 4 pounds of polypropylene (a type of plastic). The company wants to have 30% of the polypropylene required for next month's production on hand at the end of each month. The polypropylene costs $0.20 per pound.

Requirements

1. Prepare a production budget for each month in the first quarter of the year, including production in units for each month and for the quarter.
2. Prepare a direct materials budget for the polypropylene for each month in the first quarter of the year, including the pounds of polypropylene required, and the total cost of the polypropylene to be purchased.

E9-21A Direct labor budget *(Learning Objective 2)*

Valentine Industries manufactures three models of a product in a single plant with two departments: Cutting and Assembly. The company has estimated costs for each of the three product models: the Flash, the Royal, and the Zip models. The company is currently analyzing direct labor hour requirements for the upcoming year.

	Cutting	Assembly
Estimated hours per unit:		
Flashes	1.6	2.0
Royals	1.1	2.6
Zips	1.2	2.7
Direct labor hour rate	$9	$10

Budgeted unit production for each of the products is as follows:

	Number of units to be produced
Product model:	
Flashes	590
Royals	730
Zips	810

Requirement

Prepare a direct labor budget for the upcoming year that shows the budgeted direct labor costs for each department and for the company as a whole.

E9-22A Manufacturing overhead budget *(Learning Objective 2)*

The Donaldson Company is in the process of preparing its manufacturing overhead budget for the upcoming year. Sales are projected to be 40,000 units. Information about the various manufacturing overhead costs follows:

	Variable rate per unit	Total fixed costs
Indirect materials	$1.40	
Supplies	$1.00	
Indirect labor	$0.40	$68,000
Plant utilities	$0.10	$35,000
Repairs and maintenance	$0.60	$14,000
Depreciation on plant and equipment		$42,000
Insurance on plant and equipment		$20,000
Plant supervision		$66,000

Requirement

Prepare the manufacturing overhead budget for the Donaldson Company for the upcoming year.

E9-23A Prepare an operating expenses budget and an income statement *(Learning Objective 2)*

Fairlawn Preschool operates a not-for-profit morning preschool that operates nine months of the year. Fairlawn Preschool has 160 kids enrolled in its various programs. The preschool's primary expense is payroll. Teachers are paid a flat salary each of the nine months as follows:

Teachers of two-day program:	$ 430 per month
Teachers of three-day program:	$ 660 per month
Teachers of four-day program:	$ 880 per month
Teachers of five-day program:	$1,050 per month
Preschool director's salary:	$1,980 per month

Fairlawn Preschool has 8 two-day program teachers, 3 three-day program teachers, 5 four-day program teachers, and 4 five-day program teachers. The preschool also has a director.

In addition to the salary expense, the preschool must pay federal payroll taxes (FICA taxes) in the amount of 7.65% of salary expense. The preschool leases its facilities from a local church, paying $5,000 every month it operates. Fixed operating expenses (telephone, internet access, bookkeeping services, and so forth) amount to $900 per month over the nine-month school year. Variable monthly expenses (over the nine-month school year) for art supplies and other miscellaneous supplies are $12 per child. Revenue for the entire nine-month school year from tuition, registration fees, and the lunch program is projected to be $233,400.

Requirements

1. Prepare Fairlawn Preschool's monthly operating budget. Round all amounts to the nearest dollar.
2. Using your answer from Requirement 1, create Fairlawn Preschool's budgeted income statement for the entire nine-month school year. You may group all operating expenses together.
3. Fairlawn Preschool is a not-for-profit preschool. What might the preschool do with its projected income for the year?

E9-24A Budgeted income statement *(Learning Objective 2)*

Irvin Labs performs a specialty lab test for local companies for $50 per test. For the upcoming quarter, Irvin Labs is projecting the following sales:

	January	February	March
Number of lab tests	5,800	4,100	5,700

The budgeted cost of performing each test is $22. Operating expenses are projected to be $60,000 in January, $52,000 in February, and $65,000 in March. Irvin Labs is subject to a corporate tax rate of 30%.

Requirement

Prepare a budgeted income statement for the first quarter, with a column for each month and for the quarter.

E9-25A Prepare a budgeted income statement *(Learning Objective 2)*

Klaben Motors is a chain of car dealerships. Sales in the fourth quarter of last year were $6,000,000. Suppose management projects that its current year's quarterly sales will increase by 3% in quarter 1, by another 4% in quarter 2, by another 6% in quarter 3, and by another 5% in quarter 4. Management expects cost of goods sold to be 50% of revenues every quarter, while operating expenses should be 30% of revenues during each of the first two quarters, 25% of revenues during the third quarter, and 35% during the fourth quarter.

Requirement

Prepare a budgeted income statement for each of the four quarters and for the entire year.

E9-26A Cash collections budget *(Learning Objective 3)*

Grisham Corporation has found that 80% of its sales in any given month are credit sales, while the remainder are cash sales. Of the credit sales, Grisham Corporation has experienced the following collection pattern:

25% paid in the month of the sale
50% paid in the month after the sale
22% paid two months after the sale
3% of the sales are never collected

November sales for last year were $105,000, while December sales were $125,000. Projected sales for the next three months are as follows:

January sales	$165,000
February sales	$130,000
March sales	$180,000

Requirement

Prepare a cash collections budget for the first quarter, with a column for each month and for the quarter.

E9-27A Cash payments budget *(Learning Objective 3)*

The St. Germaine Company is preparing its cash payments budget. The following items relate to cash payments the company anticipates making during the second quarter of the upcoming year.

a. The company pays for 45% of its direct materials purchases in the month of purchase and the remainder the following month. The company's direct material purchases for March through June are anticipated to be as follows:

March	April	May	June
$116,000	$132,000	$120,000	$146,000

b. Direct labor is paid in the month in which it is incurred. Direct labor for each month of the second quarter is budgeted as follows:

April	May	June
$46,000	$56,000	$71,000

c. Manufacturing overhead is estimated to be 140% of direct labor cost each month. This monthly estimate includes $33,000 of depreciation on the plant and equipment. All manufacturing overhead (excluding depreciation) is paid in the month in which it is incurred.

d. Monthly operating expenses for March through June are projected to be as follows:

March	April	May	June
$77,000	$86,000	$89,000	$92,000

Monthly operating expenses are paid in the month after they are incurred. Monthly operating expenses include $9,000 for monthly depreciation on administrative offices and equipment, and $3,400 for bad debt expense.

e. The company plans to pay $3,000 (cash) for a new server in May.

f. The company must make an estimated tax payment of $11,500 on June 15.

Requirement

Prepare a cash payments budget for April, May, and June and for the quarter.

E9-28A Combined cash budget *(Learning Objective 3)*

Brimfield Health Center provides a variety of medical services. The company is preparing its cash budget for the upcoming third quarter. The following transactions are expected to occur:

a. Cash collections from services in July, August, and September are projected to be $99,000, $152,000, and $121,000 respectively.

b. Cash payments for the upcoming third quarter are projected to be $148,000 in July, $109,000 in August, and $135,000 in September.

c. The cash balance as of the first day of the third quarter is projected to be $36,000.

d. The health center has a policy that it must maintain a minimum cash balance of $27,000.

The health center has a line of credit with the local bank that allows it to borrow funds in months that it would not otherwise have its minimum balance. If the company has more than its minimum balance at the end of any given month, it uses the excess funds to pay off any outstanding line of credit balance. Each month, Brimfield Health Center pays interest on the prior month's line of credit ending balance. The actual interest rate that the health center will pay floats since it is tied to the prime rate. However, the interest rate paid during the budget period is expected to be 1% of the prior month's line of credit ending balance (if the company did not have an outstanding balance at the end of the prior month, then Brimfield Health Center does not have to pay any interest). All line of credit borrowings are taken or paid off on the first day of the month. As of the first day of the third quarter, Brimfield Health Center did not have a balance on its line of credit.

Requirement

Prepare a combined cash budget for Brimfield Health Center for the third quarter, with a column for each month and for the quarter total.

E9-29A Estimate debit and credit card fees *(Learning Objective 4)*

The local drug store expects to have 30,000 sales transactions in November, amounting to $900,000 in sales revenue. The store expects that 60% of the sales transactions will be made using credit or debit cards. Although customers use credit cards and debit cards with differing transaction fees, the average transaction fee charged to the store amounts to $0.20 per transaction plus 3% of the amount charged.

1. How many sales transactions does the store expect will be paid by customers using credit or debit cards?
2. How much of November's sales revenue is expected to be paid by customers using credit or debit cards?
3. When budgeting for November's operating expenses, how much should the store expect to incur in credit and debit card transaction fees?
4. Assuming the credit and debit card companies process the deposit the same day as the transaction, how much cash does the store expect the credit and debit card companies to deposit in the store's bank account during the month of November?

E9-30A Prepare sales and cash collections budgets *(Learning Objectives 2 & 3)*

Augustine Reeds, a manufacturer of saxophone, oboe, and clarinet reeds, has projected sales to be $900,000 in October, $964,000 in November, $1,040,000 in December, and $922,000 in January. Augustine's sales are 25% cash and 75% credit. Augustine's collection history indicates that credit sales are collected as follows:

20% in the month of the sale
70% in the month after the sale
8% two months after the sale
2% are never collected

Requirements

1. Prepare a sales budget for all four months, showing the breakdown between cash and credit sales.
2. Prepare a cash collections budget for December and January. Round all answers up to the nearest dollar.

E9-31A Prepare a budgeted balance sheet *(Learning Objective 3)*

Use the following information to prepare a budgeted balance sheet for Zucca Corporation at March 31. Show computations for the cash and stockholders' equity amounts.

a. March 31 inventory balance, $13,405.
b. March payments for inventory, $4,300.
c. March payments of accounts payable and accrued liabilities, $8,500.
d. March 31 accounts payable balance, $2,100.
e. February 28 furniture and fixtures balance, $34,600; accumulated depreciation balance, $29,860.
f. February 28 stockholders' equity, $28,520.
g. March depreciation expense, $700.
h. Cost of goods sold, 70% of sales.
i. Other March expenses, including income tax, total $8,000; paid in cash.

j. February 28 cash balance, $11,500.
k. March budgeted sales, $12,500.
l. March 31 accounts receivable balance, one-fourth of March sales.
m. March cash receipts, $14,400.

E9-32A Prepare a cash budget *(Learning Objective 3)*

Helton Medical Supply began October with $10,600 cash. Management forecasts that collections from credit customers will be $12,200 in October and $15,800 in November. The business is scheduled to receive $5,000 cash on a business note receivable in October. Projected cash payments include inventory purchases ($13,200 in October and $13,300 in November) and operating expenses ($3,600 each month).

Helton Medical Supply's bank requires a $10,000 minimum balance in the business' checking account. At the end of any month when the account balance dips below $10,000, the bank automatically extends credit to the business in multiples of $1,000. Helton Medical Supply borrows as little as possible and pays back loans in quarterly installments of $2,000 plus 4% interest on the entire unpaid principal. The first payment occurs three months after the loan.

Requirement

Prepare Helton Medical Supply's cash budget for October and November.

E9-33A Finish an incomplete cash budget *(Learning Objective 3)*

You recently began a job as an accounting intern at Mountain Adventures. Your first task was to help prepare the cash budget for February and March. Unfortunately, the computer with the budget file crashed, and you did not have a backup or even a hard copy. You ran a program to salvage bits of data from the budget file. After entering the following data in the budget, you may have just enough information to reconstruct the budget.

Mountain Adventures eliminates any cash deficiency by borrowing the exact amount needed from State Street Bank, where the current interest rate is 6%. Mountain Adventures pays interest on its outstanding debt at the end of each month. The company also repays all borrowed amounts at the end of the month as cash becomes available.

Requirement

Complete the following cash budget:

MOUNTAIN ADVENTURES
Cash Budget
February and March

	February	March
Beginning cash balance	$ 16,200	$?
Cash collections	?	79,800
Cash from sale of plant assets	0	1,900
Cash available	$106,200	$?
Cash payments:		
Purchase of inventory	$?	$41,000
Operating expenses	47,200	?
Total payments	$ 98,000	$?
(1) Ending cash balance before financing	$?	$27,400
Minimum cash balance desired	23,000	23,000
Cash excess (deficiency)	$?	$?
Financing of cash deficiency:		
Borrowing (at end of month)	$?	$?
Principal repayments (at end of month)	?	?
Interest expense	?	?
(2) Total effects of financing	$?	$?
Ending cash balance (1) + (2)	$?	$?

E9-34A Prepare an inventory, purchases, and cost of goods sold budget *(Learning Objective 4)*

Lightning Readers sells eReaders. Its sales budget for the nine months ended September 30 follows:

	Quarter Ended			
	Mar 31	Jun 30	Sep 30	Nine-Month Total
Cash sales, 30%	$ 37,500	$ 52,500	$ 45,000	$135,000
Credit sales, 70%	87,500	122,500	105,000	315,000
Total sales, 100%	$125,000	$175,000	$150,000	$450,000

In the past, cost of goods sold has been 70% of total sales. The director of marketing and the financial vice president agree that each quarter's ending inventory should not be below $30,000 plus 20% of cost of goods sold for the following quarter. The marketing director expects sales of $225,000 during the fourth quarter. The January 1 inventory was $15,000.

Requirement

Prepare an inventory, purchases, and cost of goods sold budget for each of the first three quarters of the year. Compute cost of goods sold for the entire nine-month period.

EXERCISES Group B

E9-35B Budgeting and Sustainability *(Learning Objective 1)*

Crawford Beverages manufactures its own soda pop bottles. The bottles are made from polyethylene terephthalate (PET), a lightweight yet strong plastic. Crawford uses as much PET recycled resin pellets in its bottles as it can, both because using recycled PET helps Crawford to meet its sustainability goals and because recycled PET is less expensive than virgin PET.

Crawford is continuing to search for ways to reduce its costs and its impact on the environment. PET plastic is melted and blown over soda bottle molds to produce the bottles. One idea Crawford's engineers have suggested is to retrofit the soda bottle molds and change the plastic formulation slightly so that 20% less PET plastic is used for each bottle. The average kilograms of PET per soda bottle before any redesign is 0.005 kg. The cost of retrofitting the soda bottle molds will result in a one-time charge of $24,000, while the plastic reformulation will cause the average cost per kilogram of PET plastic to change from $2.50 to $2.60.

Crawford's management is analyzing whether the change to the bottle molds to reduce PET plastic usage should be made. Management expects the following number of soda bottles to be used in the upcoming year:

	Quarter 1	Quarter 2	Quarter 3	Quarter 4
Number of soda pop bottles to be produced	2,000,000	3,000,000	2,700,000	2,500,000

For the upcoming year, management expects the beginning inventory of PET to be 1,000 kilograms, while ending inventory is expected to be 1,700 kilograms. During the first three quarters of the year, management wants to keep the ending inventory of PET at the end of each quarter's PET needs.

Requirements

1. Using the original date (before any redesign of soda bottles), prepare a direct materials budget to calculate the cost of PET purchases in each quarter for the upcoming year and for the year in total.
2. Assume that the company retrofits the soda bottle molds and changes the plastic formulation slightly so that less PET plastic is used in each bottle. Now prepare a direct materials budget to calculate the cost of PET purchases in each quarter for the upcoming year and for the year in total for this possible scenario.
3. Compare the cost of PET plastic for Requirement 1 (original data) and for Requirement 2 (making the change to using less PET.) What is the direct material cost saving from making the change to using less PET? Compare the total of those savings to the cost of retrofitting the soda bottle molds. Should the company make the change? Explain your rationale.

E9-36B Prepare a sales budget for a retail organization *(Learning Objective 2)*

Parma College Bookstore is the bookstore on campus for students and faculty. Parma College Bookstore shows the following sales projections in units by quarter for the upcoming year:

Quarter	Books	School Supplies	Apparel	Miscellaneous
1st	1,580	280	550	630
2nd	840	120	390	560
3rd	1,760	290	820	820
4th	680	100	540	490

The average price of an item in each of the departments is as follows:

	Average sales per unit
Books	$87
School supplies	$18
Apparel	$28
Miscellaneous	$ 4

Requirement

Prepare a sales budget for the upcoming year by quarter for the Parma College Bookstore, with sales categorized by the four product groupings (books, school supplies, apparel, and miscellaneous).

E9-37B Prepare a sales budget for a not-for-profit organization *(Learning Objective 2)*

Wadsworth Preschool operates a not-for-profit morning preschool. Each family pays a nonrefundable registration fee of $140 per child per school year. Monthly tuition for the eight-month school year varies depending on the number of days per week that the child attends preschool. The monthly tuition is $130 for the two-day program, $155 for the three-day program, $180 for the four-day program, and $195 for the five-day program. The following enrollment has been projected for the coming year:

Two-day program: 88 children	Four-day program: 54 children
Three-day program: 34 children	Five-day program: 28 children

In addition to the morning preschool, Wadsworth Preschool offers a Lunch Bunch program where kids have the option of staying an extra hour for lunch and playtime. The preschool charges an additional $2 per child for every Lunch Bunch attended. Historically, half the children stay for Lunch Bunch an average of 10 times a month.

Requirement

Calculate Wadsworth Preschool's budgeted revenue for the school year.

E9-38B Production budget *(Learning Objective 2)*

Gable Foods produces specialty soup sold in jars. The projected sales in dollars and jars for each quarter of the upcoming year are as follows:

	Total sales revenue	Number of jars sold
1st quarter	$187,000	150,500
2nd quarter	$216,000	184,000
3rd quarter	$253,000	210,000
4th quarter	$191,000	160,000

Gable anticipates selling 220,000 jars with total sales revenue of $261,000 in the first quarter of the year following the year given in the preceding table. Gable has a policy that the ending inventory of jars must be 30% of the following quarter's sales. Prepare a production budget for the year that shows the number of jars to be produced each quarter and for the year in total.

E9-39B Direct materials budget *(Learning Objective 2)*

Schaeffer Industries manufactures a popular interactive stuffed animal for children that requires three computer chips inside each toy. Schaeffer Industries pays $2 for each computer chip. To help to guard against stockouts of the computer chip, Schaeffer Industries has a policy that states that the ending inventory of computer chips should be at least 30% of the following month's production needs. The production schedule for the first four months of the year is as follows:

	Stuffed animals to be produced
January	5,100
February	4,500
March	4,100
April	4,000

Requirement

Prepare a direct materials budget for the first quarter that shows both the number of computer chips needed and the dollar amount of the purchases in the budget.

E9-40B Production and direct materials budgets *(Learning Objective 2)*

Snyder Manufacturing produces self-watering planters for use in upscale retail establishments. Sales projections for the first five months of the upcoming year show the estimated unit sales of the planters each month to be as follows:

	Number of planters to be sold
January	3,400
February	3,800
March	3,300
April	4,900
May	4,600

Inventory at the start of the year was 850 planters. The desired inventory of planters at the end of each month should be equal to 25% of the following month's budgeted sales. Each planter requires 3 pounds of polypropylene (a type of plastic). The company wants to have 20% of the polypropylene required for next month's production on hand at the end of each month. The polypropylene costs $0.20 per pound.

Requirements

1. Prepare a production budget for each month in the first quarter of the year, including production in units for each month and for the quarter.
2. Prepare a direct materials budget for the polypropylene for each month in the first quarter of the year, including the pounds of polypropylene required, and the total cost of the polypropylene to be purchased.

E9-41B Direct labor budget *(Learning Objective 2)*

Laughton Industries manufactures three models of a product in a single plant with two departments: Cutting and Assembly. The company has estimated costs for each of the three product models, which are the Flash, the Regal, and the Imperial models.

The company is currently analyzing direct labor hour requirements for the upcoming year.

	Cutting	Assembly
Estimated hours per unit:		
Flashes	1.6	2.4
Regals	1.1	2.1
Imperials	1.0	2.0
Direct labor hour rate	$10	$12

Budgeted unit production for each of the products is as follows:

	Number of units to be produced
Product model:	
Flashes	590
Regals	760
Imperials	810

Requirement

Prepare a direct labor budget for the upcoming year that shows the budgeted direct labor costs for each department and for the company as a whole.

E9-42B Manufacturing overhead budget *(Learning Objective 2)*

The Robbins Company is in the process of preparing its manufacturing overhead budget for the upcoming year. Sales are projected to be 44,000 units. Information about the various manufacturing overhead costs follows:

	Variable rate per unit	Total fixed costs
Indirect materials	$0.90	
Supplies	$0.80	
Indirect labor	$0.30	$65,000
Plant utilities	$0.20	$38,000
Repairs and maintenance	$0.40	$14,000
Depreciation on plant and equipment		$40,000
Insurance on plant and equipment		$22,000
Plant supervision		$62,000

Requirement

Prepare the manufacturing overhead budget for the Robbins Company for the upcoming year.

E9-43B Prepare an operating expenses budget and an income statement *(Learning Objective 2)*

Hinkley Preschool operates a not-for-profit morning preschool that operates nine months of the year. The preschool has 160 kids enrolled in its various programs. The preschool's primary expense is payroll. Teachers are paid a flat salary each of the nine months as follows:

Salary data	
Teachers of two-day program:	\$ 400 per month
Teachers of three-day program:	\$ 600 per month
Teachers of four-day program:	\$ 800 per month
Teachers of five-day program:	\$ 900 per month
Preschool director's salary:	\$1,400 per month

Hinkley Preschool has 8 two-day program teachers, 5 three-day program teachers, 7 four-day program teachers, and 3 five-day program teachers. Hinkley Preschool also has a director.

In addition to the salary expense, Hinkley Preschool must pay federal payroll taxes (FICA taxes) in the amount of 7.65% of salary expense. The preschool leases its facilities from a local church, paying \$4,000 per month. Fixed operating expenses (telephone, internet access, bookkeeping services, and so forth) amount to \$700 per month over the nine-month school year. Variable monthly expenses (over the nine-month school year) for art supplies and other miscellaneous supplies are \$12 per child. Revenue for the entire nine-month school year from tuition, registration fees, and the lunch program is projected to be \$233,400.

Requirements

1. Prepare Hinkley Preschool's monthly operating budget. Round all amounts to the nearest dollar.
2. Using your answer from Requirement 1, create Hinkley Preschool's budgeted income statement for the entire nine-month school year. You may group all operating expenses together.
3. Hinkley Preschool is a not-for-profit preschool. What might the preschool do with its projected income for the year?

E9-44B Budgeted income statement *(Learning Objective 2)*

Engleman Labs performs a specialty lab test for local companies for \$45 per test. For the upcoming quarter, Engleman Labs is projecting the following sales:

	January	February	March
Number of tests	5,600	4,000	5,700

The budgeted cost of performing each test is \$20. Operating expenses are projected to be \$59,000 in January, \$56,000 in February, and \$61,000 in March. Engleman Labs is subject to a corporate tax rate of 30%.

Requirement

Prepare a budgeted income statement for the first quarter, with a column for each month and for the quarter in total.

E9-45B Prepare a budgeted income statement *(Learning Objective 2)*

Chesrown Motors is a chain of car dealerships. Sales in the fourth quarter of last year were \$8,000,000. Suppose its management projects that its current year's quarterly sales will increase by 4% in quarter 1, by another 5% in quarter 2, by another 5% in quarter 3, and by another 3% in quarter 4. Management expects cost of goods sold to be 50% of revenues every quarter, while operating expenses should be 30% of revenues during each of the first two quarters, 20% of revenues during the third quarter, and 25% during the fourth quarter.

Requirement

Prepare a budgeted income statement for each of the four quarters and for the entire year.

E9-46B Cash collections budget *(Learning Objective 3)*

Majestic Corporation has found that 70% of its sales in any given month are credit sales, while the remainder are cash sales. Of the credit sales, the company has experienced the following collection pattern:

25% paid in the month of the sale
50% paid in the month after the sale
16% paid two months after the sale
9% of the sales are never collected

November sales for last year were $80,000, while December sales were $125,000. Projected sales for the next three months are as follows:

January sales	$150,000
February sales	$130,000
March sales	$170,000

Requirement

Prepare a cash collections budget for the first quarter, with a column for each month and for the quarter.

E9-47B Cash payments budget *(Learning Objective 3)*

Kobe Corporation is preparing its cash payments budget. The following items relate to cash payments Kobe Corporation anticipates making during the second quarter of the upcoming year.

a. Kobe Corporation pays for 50% of its direct materials purchases in the month of purchase and the remainder the following month. The company direct material purchases for March through June are anticipated to be as follows:

March	April	May	June
$116,000	$133,000	$122,000	$147,000

b. Direct labor is paid in the month in which it is incurred. Direct labor for each month of the second quarter is budgeted as follows:

April	May	June
$44,000	$54,000	$69,000

c. Manufacturing overhead is estimated to be 140% of direct labor cost each month. This monthly estimate includes $31,000 of depreciation on the plant and equipment. All manufacturing overhead (excluding depreciation) is paid in the month in which it is incurred.

d. Monthly operating expenses for March through June are projected to be as follows:

March	April	May	June
$74,000	$88,000	$83,000	$93,000

Monthly operating expenses are paid in the month after they are incurred. Monthly operating expenses include $15,000 for monthly depreciation on administrative offices and equipment, and $3,100 for bad debt expense.

e. Kobe Corporation plans to pay $4,000 (cash) for a new server in May.

f. Kobe Corporation must make an estimated tax payment of $11,000 on June 15.

Requirement

Prepare a cash payments budget for April, May, and June and for the quarter.

E9-48B Combined cash budget *(Learning Objective 3)*

Streetsboro Health Center provides a variety of medical services. The company is preparing its cash budget for the upcoming third quarter. The following transactions are expected to occur:

a. Cash collections from services in July, August, and September are projected to be $99,000, $150,000, and $120,000, respectively.
b. Cash payments for the upcoming third quarter are projected to be $146,000 in July, $103,000 in August, and $130,000 in September.
c. The cash balance as of the first day of the third quarter is projected to be $32,000.

Streetsboro Health Center has a policy that it must maintain a minimum cash balance of $25,000. The company has a line of credit with the local bank that allows it to borrow funds in months that it would not otherwise have the minimum balance. If the company has more than the minimum balance at the end of any given month, it uses the excess funds to pay off any outstanding line of credit balance. Each month, Streetsboro Health Center pays interest on the prior month's line of credit ending balance. The actual interest rate that Streetsboro Health Center will pay floats since it is tied to the prime rate. However, the interest rate paid during the budget period is expected to be 1% of the prior month's line of credit ending balance (if it did not have an outstanding balance at the end of the prior month, then the company does not have to pay any interest). All line of credit borrowings are taken or paid off on the first day of the month. As of the first day of the third quarter, Streetsboro Health Center did not have a balance on its line of credit.

Requirement

Prepare a combined cash budget for Streetsboro Health Center for the third quarter, with a column for each month and for the quarter total.

E9-49B Estimate debit and credit card fees *(Learning Objective 4)*

The local hardware store expects to have 40,000 in total sales transactions in November, amounting to $700,000 in sales revenue. The store expects that 60% of the sales transactions will be made using credit or debit cards. Although customers use credit cards and debit cards with differing transaction fees, the average transaction fee charged to the store amounts to $0.30 per transaction plus 2% of the amount charged.

1. How many sales transactions does the store expect will be paid by customers using credit or debit cards?
2. How much of November's sales revenue is expected to be paid by customers using credit or debit cards?
3. When budgeting for November's operating expenses, how much should the store expect to incur in credit and debit card transaction fees?
4. Assuming the credit and debit card companies process the deposit the same day as the transaction, how much cash does the store expect the credit and debit card companies to deposit in the store's bank account during the month of November?

E9-50B Prepare sales and cash collections budgets *(Learning Objectives 2 & 3)*

Goodman Reeds, a manufacturer of saxophone, oboe, and clarinet reeds, has projected sales to be $890,000 in October, $960,000 in November, $1,030,000 in December, and $932,000 in January. Goodman's sales are 30% cash and 70% on credit. Goodman's collection history indicates that credit sales are collected as follows:

20% in the month of the sale
60% in the month after the sale
14% two months after the sale
6% are never collected

Requirements

1. Prepare a sales budget for all four months, showing the breakdown between cash and credit sales.
2. Prepare a cash collection budget for December and January. Round all answers up to the nearest dollar.

E9-51B Prepare a budgeted balance sheet *(Learning Objective 3)*

Use the following information to prepare a budgeted balance sheet for Grimm Corporation at March 31. Show computations for the cash and owners' equity amounts.

a. March 31 inventory balance, $17,965.
b. March payments for inventory, $4,700.
c. March payments of accounts payable and accrued liabilities, $8,500.
d. March 31 accounts payable balance, $2,200.
e. February 28 furniture and fixtures balance,$34,700; accumulated depreciation balance, $29,830.
f. February 28 owners' equity, $28,890.
g. March depreciation expense, $400.
h. Cost of goods sold, 40% of sales.
i. Other March expenses, including income tax, total $6,000; paid in cash.
j. February 28 cash balance, $11,800.
k. March budgeted sales, $12,700.
l. March 31 accounts receivable balance, one-fourth of March sales.
m. March cash receipts, $14,100.

E9-52B Prepare a cash budget, then revise *(Learning Objective 3)*

Donovan Medical Supply began October with $11,200 cash.

Management forecasts that collections from credit customers will be $12,000 in October and $14,800 in November. The business is scheduled to receive $5,000 cash on a business note receivable in October. Projected cash payments include inventory purchases ($13,200 in October and $12,400 in November) and operating expenses ($4,000 each month).

Donovan's bank requires a $10,000 minimum balance in the business's checking account. At the end of any month when the account balance dips below the minimum balance, the bank automatically extends credit to the business in multiples of $1,000. Donovan's borrows as little as possible and pays back loans in quarterly installments of $2,000, plus 2% interest on the entire unpaid principal. The first payment occurs three months after the loan.

Requirement

Prepare Donovan Medical Supply's cash budget for October and November.

E9-53B Finish an incomplete cash budget *(Learning Objective 3)*

You recently began a job as an accounting intern at Rocky Adventures. Your first task was to help prepare the cash budget for February and March. Unfortunately, the computer with the budget file crashed, and you did not have a backup or even a hard copy. You ran a program to salvage bits of data from the budget file. After entering the following data in the budget, you may have just enough information to reconstruct the budget.

Rocky Adventures eliminates any cash deficiency by borrowing the exact amount needed from State Street Bank, where the current interest rate is 6%. Rocky Adventures pays interest on its outstanding debt at the end of each month. The company also repays all borrowed amounts at the end of the month, as cash becomes available.

CHAPTER 9

Requirement

Complete the following cash budget:

Rocky Adventures Cash Budget February and March		
	February	March
Beginning cash balance	$ 16,400	$?
Cash collections	?	79,600
Cash from sale of plant assets	0	2,100
Cash available	$106,500	?
Cash payments:		
Purchase of inventory	$?	$ 41,400
Operating expenses	47,300	?
Total payments	$ 97,900	?
(1) Ending cash balance before financing	?	$ 25,000
Minimum cash balance desired	(20,000)	(20,000)
Cash excess (deficiency)	$?	$?
Financing of cash deficiency:		
Borrowing (at end of month)	$?	$?
Principal repayments (at end of month)	?	?
Interest expense	?	?
(2) Total effects of financing	$?	$?
Ending cash balance (1) + (2)	$?	$?

E9-54B Prepare an inventory, purchases, and cost of goods sold budget

(Learning Objective 4)

Clear Readers sells eReaders. Its sales budget for the nine months ended September 30 follows:

	Quarter Ended			Nine-Month
	Mar 31	Jun 30	Sep 30	Total
Cash sales, 30%	$ 36,000	$ 51,000	$ 43,500	$130,500
Credit sales, 70%	84,000	119,000	101,500	304,500
Total sales, 100%	$120,000	$170,000	$145,000	$435,000

In the past, cost of goods sold has been 70% of total sales. The director of marketing and the financial vice president agree that each quarter's ending inventory should not be below $25,000 plus 20% of cost of goods sold for the following quarter. The marketing director expects sales of $220,000 during the fourth quarter. The January 1 inventory was $19,000.

Requirement

Prepare an inventory, purchases, and cost of goods sold budget for each of the first three quarters of the year. Compute cost of goods sold for the entire nine-month period.

PROBLEMS Group A

P9-55A Comprehensive budgeting problem *(Learning Objectives 2 & 3)*

Dudley Manufacturing is preparing its master budget for the first quarter of the upcoming year. The following data pertain to Dudley Manufacturing's operations:

Current Assets as of December 31 (prior year):	
Cash	$ 4,500
Accounts receivable, net	$ 50,000
Inventory	$ 15,000
Property, plant, and equipment, net	$122,500
Accounts payable	$ 42,400
Capital stock	$126,000
Retained earnings	$ 22,920

a. Actual sales in December were $70,000. Selling price per unit is projected to remain stable at $10 per unit throughout the budget period. Sales for the first five months of the upcoming year are budgeted to be as follows:

January	$83,000
February	$92,000
March	$94,000
April	$97,000
May	$89,000

b. Sales are 30% cash and 70% credit. All credit sales are collected in the month following the sale.

c. Dudley Manufacturing has a policy that states that each month's ending inventory of finished goods should be 25% of the following month's sales (in units).

d. Of each month's direct material purchases, 10% are paid for in the month of purchase, while the remainder is paid for in the month following purchase. Two pounds of direct material is needed per unit at $2 per pound. Ending inventory of direct materials should be 10% of next month's production needs.

e. Most of the labor at the manufacturing facility is indirect, but there is some direct labor incurred. The direct labor hours per unit is 0.02. The direct labor rate per hour is $10 per hour. All direct labor is paid for in the month in which the work is performed. The direct labor total cost for each of the upcoming three months is as follows:

   January $1,705
   February $1,850
   March $1,895

f. Monthly manufacturing overhead costs are $5,000 for factory rent, $3,000 for other fixed manufacturing expenses, and $1.20 per unit for variable manufacturing overhead. No depreciation is included in these figures. All expenses are paid in the month in which they are incurred.

g. Computer equipment for the administrative offices will be purchased in the upcoming quarter. In January, Dudley Manufacturing will purchase equipment for $6,200 (cash), while February's cash expenditure will be $12,000 and March's cash expenditure will be $16,800.

h. Operating expenses are budgeted to be $1 per unit sold plus fixed operating expenses of $1,400 per month. All operating expenses are paid in the month in which they are incurred.

i. Depreciation on the building and equipment for the general and administrative offices is budgeted to be $4,700 for the entire quarter, which includes depreciation on new acquisitions.

j. Dudley Manufacturing has a policy that the ending cash balance in each month must be at least $4,000. It has a line of credit with a local bank. The company can borrow in increments of $1,000 at the beginning of each month, up to a total outstanding loan balance of $160,000. The interest rate on these loans is 2% per month simple interest (not compounded). Dudley Manufacturing would pay down on the line of credit balance if it has excess funds at the end of the quarter. The company would also pay the accumulated interest at the end of the quarter on the funds borrowed during the quarter.

k. The company's income tax rate is projected to be 30% of operating income less interest expense. The company pays $11,000 cash at the end of February in estimated taxes.

Requirements

1. Prepare a schedule of cash collections for January, February, and March, and for the quarter in total. Use the following format:

Cash Collections Budget

	January	February	March	Quarter
Cash sales				
Credit sales				
Total cash collections				

2. Prepare a production budget, using the following format:

Production Budget

	January	February	March	Quarter
Unit sales*				
Plus: Desired ending inventory				
Total needed				
Less: Beginning inventory				
Units to be produced				

*Hint: Unit sales = Sales in dollars + Selling price per unit

3. Prepare a direct materials budget, using the following format:

Direct Materials Budget				
	January	February	March	Quarter
Units to be produced				
× Pounds of DM needed per unit				
Quantity (pounds) needed for production				
Plus: Desired ending inventory of DM				
Total quantity (pounds) needed				
Less: Beginning inventory of DM				
Quantity (pounds) to purchase				
× Cost per pound				
Total cost of DM purchases				

4. Prepare a cash payments budget for the direct material purchases from Requirement 3, using the following format:

Cash Payments for Direct Material Purchases Budget				
	January	February	March	Quarter
December purchases (from Accounts Payable)				
January purchases				
February purchases				
March purchases				
Total cash payments for direct material purchases				

5. Prepare a cash payments budget for direct labor, using the following format:

Cash Payments for Direct Labor Budget				
	January	February	March	Quarter
Direct labor				

6. Prepare a cash payments budget for manufacturing overhead costs, using the following format:

Cash Payments for Manufacturing Overhead Budget

	January	February	March	Quarter
Variable manufacturing overhead costs				
Rent (fixed)				
Other fixed MOH				
Total payments for MOH costs				

7. Prepare a cash payments budget for operating expenses, using the following format:

Cash Payments for Operating Expenses Budget

	January	February	March	Quarter
Variable operating expenses				
Fixed operating expenses				
Total payments for operating expenses				

8. Prepare a combined cash budget, using the following format:

Combined Cash Budget

	January	February	March	Quarter
Cash balance, beginning				
Add cash collections				
Total cash available				
Less cash payments:				
Direct material purchases				
Direct labor				
Manufacturing overhead costs				
Operating expenses				
Tax payment				
Equipment purchases				
Total cash payments				
Ending cash balance before financing				
Financing:				
Borrowings				
Repayments				
Interest payments				
Cash balance, ending				

9. Calculate the budgeted manufacturing cost per unit, using the following format (assume that fixed manufacturing overhead is budgeted to be $0.70 per unit for the year):

Budgeted Manufacturing Cost per Unit	
Direct materials cost per unit	
Direct labor cost per unit	
Variable manufacturing overhead costs per unit	
Fixed manufacturing overhead per unit	
Budgeted cost of manufacturing each unit	

10. Prepare a budgeted income statement for the quarter ending March 31, using the following format:

Budgeted Income Statement For the Quarter Ending March 31	
Sales	
Cost of goods sold*	
Gross profit	
Operating expenses	
Depreciation	
Operating income	
Less interest expense	
Less provision for income taxes	
Net income	

*Cost of goods sold = Budgeted cost of manufacturing each unit × Number of units sold

P9-56A Prepare a budgeted income statement *(Learning Objective 2)*

The budget committee of Greta Fashions, an upscale women's clothing retailer, has assembled the following data. As the business manager, you must prepare the budgeted income statements for May and June.

a. Sales in April were $60,000. You forecast that monthly sales will increase 10% in May and 5% in June.

b. Greta Fashions maintains inventory of $10,000 plus 10% of sales revenues budgeted for the following month. Monthly purchases average 50% of sales revenues in that same month. Actual inventory on April 30 is $16,600. Sales budgeted for July are $70,000.

c. Monthly salaries amount to $7,000. Sales commissions equal 5% of sales for that month. Combine salaries and commissions into a single figure.

d. Other monthly expenses are as follows:

Rent expense	$3,000, paid as incurred
Depreciation expense	$ 300
Insurance expense	$ 200, expiration of prepaid amount
Income tax	20% of operating income

Requirement

Prepare Greta Fashions' budgeted income statements for May and June. Show cost of goods sold computations.

CHAPTER 9

P9-57A Cash budgets *(Learning Objective 3)*

Wendell's Restaurant Supply is preparing its cash budgets for the first two months of the upcoming year. Here is the information about the company's upcoming cash receipts and cash disbursements:

a. Sales are 60% cash and 40% credit. Credit sales are collected 30% in the month of sale and the remainder in the month after sale. Actual sales in December were $57,000. Schedules of budgeted sales for the two months of the upcoming year are as follows:

	Budgeted Sales Revenue
January	$61,000
February	$71,000

b. Actual purchases of direct materials in December were $25,500. The company's purchases of direct materials in January are budgeted to be $22,500 and $27,000 in February. All purchases are paid 40% in the month of purchase and 60% the following month.

c. Salaries and sales commissions are also paid half in the month earned and half the next month. Actual salaries were $7,500 in December. Budgeted salaries in January are $8,500 and February budgeted salaries are $10,000. Sales commissions each month are 10% of that month's sales.

d. Rent expense is $2,700 per month.

e. Depreciation is $2,800 per month.

f. Estimated income tax payments are made at the end of January. The estimated tax payment is projected to be $12,500.

g. The cash balance at the end of the prior year was $21,000.

Requirements

1. Prepare schedules of (a) budgeted cash collections, (b) budgeted cash payments for purchases, and (c) budgeted cash payments for operating expenses. Show amounts for each month and totals for January and February.
2. Prepare a combined cash budget similar to exhibits in the chapter. If no financing activity took place, what is the budgeted cash balance on February 28?

P9-58A Prepare a combined cash budget and a budgeted balance sheet *(Learning Objective 3)*

Towson Medical Supply has applied for a loan. First National Bank has requested a budgeted balance sheet as of April 30, and a combined cash budget for April. As Towson Medical Supply's controller, you have assembled the following information:

a. March 31 equipment balance, $52,400; accumulated depreciation, $41,300.

b. April capital expenditures of $42,800 budgeted for cash purchase of equipment.

c. April depreciation expense, $900.

d. Cost of goods sold, 60% of sales.

e. Other April operating expenses, including income tax, total $13,200, 25% of which will be paid in cash and the remainder accrued at April 30.

f. March 31 owners' equity, $93,700.

g. March 31 cash balance, $40,600.

h. April budgeted sales, $90,000, 70% of which is for cash. Of the remaining 30%, half will be collected in April and half in May.

i. April cash collections on March sales, $29,700.

j. April cash payments of March 31 liabilities incurred for March purchases of inventory, $17,300.

k. March 31 inventory balance, $29,600.

l. April purchases of inventory, $10,000 for cash and $36,800 on credit. Half of the credit purchases will be paid in April and half in May.

Requirements

1. Prepare the budgeted balance sheet for Towson Medical Supply at April 30. Show separate computations for cash, inventory, and owners' equity balances.
2. Prepare the combined cash budget for April.
3. Suppose Towson Medical Supply has become aware of more efficient (and more expensive) equipment than it budgeted for purchase in April. What is the total amount of cash available for equipment purchases in April, before financing, if the minimum desired ending cash balance is $21,000? (For this requirement, disregard the $42,800 initially budgeted for equipment purchases.)
4. Before granting a loan to Towson Medical Supply, First National Bank asks for a sensitivity analysis assuming that April sales are only $60,000 rather than the $90,000 originally budgeted. (While the cost of goods sold will change, assume that purchases, depreciation, and the other operating expenses will remain the same as in the earlier requirements.)
   a. Prepare a revised budgeted balance sheet for Towson Medical Supply, showing separate computations for cash, inventory, and owners' equity balances.
   b. Suppose Towson Medical Supply has a minimum desired cash balance of $23,000. Will the company need to borrow cash in April?
   c. In this sensitivity analysis, sales declined by 33 1/3% ($30,000 ÷ $90,000). Is the decline in expenses and income more or less than 33 1/3%? Explain.

P9-59A Prepare an inventory, purchases, and cost of goods sold budget *(Learning Objective 4)*

Radical Logos buys logo-imprinted merchandise and then sells it to university bookstores. Sales are expected to be $2,001,000 in September, $2,230,000 in October, $2,385,000 in November, and $2,570,000 in December. Radical Logos sets its prices to earn an average 40% gross profit on sales revenue. The company does not want inventory to fall below $415,000 plus 20% of the next month's cost of goods sold.

Requirement

Prepare an inventory, purchases, and cost of goods sold budget for the months of October and November.

P9-60A Estimate debit and credit card fees *(Learning Objective 4)*

The local Thai restaurant expects sales to be $500,000 in January. The average restaurant bill is $40. Only 20% of restaurant bills are paid in cash, while 70% are paid with credit cards and 10% are paid with debit cards. The transaction fees charged by the credit and debit card issuers are as follows:

- Credit cards: $0.50 per transaction + 2% of the amount charged
- Debit cards: $0.22 per transaction + 0.05% of the amount charged

Requirements

a. How much of the total sales revenue is expected to be paid with cash?
b. How many customer transactions does the company expect in January?
c. How much of the total sales revenue is expected to be paid with credit cards?
d. How many customer transactions will be paid for by customers using credit cards?
e. When budgeting for January's operating expenses, how much should the restaurant expect to incur in credit card transaction fees?
f. How much of the total sales revenue is expected to be paid with debit cards?
g. How many customer transactions will be paid for by customers using debit cards?
h. When budgeting for January's operating expenses, how much should the restaurant expect to incur in debit card transaction fees?
i. How much money will be deposited in the restaurant's bank account during the month of January related to credit and debit card sales? Assume the credit and debit card issuers deposit the funds on the same day the transactions occur at the restaurant (there is no processing delay).

PROBLEMS Group B

P9-61B Comprehensive budgeting problem *(Learning Objectives 2 & 3)*

Ravenna Manufacturing is preparing its master budget for the first quarter of the upcoming year. The following data pertain to Ravenna Manufacturing's operations:

Current assets as of December 31 (prior year):	
Cash	$ 4,500
Accounts receivable, net	$ 46,000
Inventory	$ 15,000
Property, plant, and equipment, net	$122,000
Accounts payable	$ 42,400
Capital stock	$125,000
Retained earnings	$ 22,920

a. Actual sales in December were $70,000. Selling price per unit is projected to remain stable at $10 per unit throughout the budget period. Sales for the first five months of the upcoming year are budgeted to be as follows:

January	$83,000
February	$99,000
March	$96,000
April	$90,000
May	$86,000

b. Sales are 30% cash and 70% credit. All credit sales are collected in the month following the sale.

c. Ravenna Manufacturing has a policy that states that each month's ending inventory of finished goods should be 25% of the following month's sales (in units).

d. Of each month's direct material purchases, 20% are paid for in the month of purchase, while the remainder is paid for in the month following purchase. Two pounds of direct material is needed per unit at $2.00 per pound. Ending inventory of direct materials should be 10% of next month's production needs.

e. Most of the labor at the manufacturing facility is indirect, but there is some direct labor incurred. The direct labor hours per unit is 0.03. The direct labor rate per hour is $8 per hour. All direct labor is paid for in the month in which the work is performed. The direct labor total cost for each of the upcoming three months is as follows:

January	$2,088
February	$2,358
March	$2,268

f. Monthly manufacturing overhead costs are $5,000 for factory rent, $3,000 for other fixed manufacturing expenses, and $1.20 per unit for variable manufacturing overhead. No depreciation is included in these figures. All expenses are paid in the month in which they are incurred.

g. Computer equipment for the administrative offices will be purchased in the upcoming quarter. In January, the company will purchase equipment for $5,000 (cash), while February's cash expenditure will be $12,000 and March's cash expenditure will be $16,000.

h. Operating expenses are budgeted to be $1.00 per unit sold plus fixed operating expenses of $1,000 per month. All operating expenses are paid in the month in which they are incurred.

i. Depreciation on the building and equipment for the general and administrative offices is budgeted to be $4,900 for the entire quarter, which includes depreciation on new acquisitions.

j. Ravenna Manufacturing has a policy that the ending cash balance in each month must be at least $4,000. The company has a line of credit with a local bank. It can borrow in increments of $1,000 at the beginning of each month, up to a total outstanding loan balance of $125,000. The interest rate on these loans is 1% per month simple interest (not compounded). Ravenna Manufacturing would pay down on the line of credit balance if it has excess funds at the end of the quarter. The company would also pay the accumulated interest at the end of the quarter on the funds borrowed during the quarter.

k. The company's income tax rate is projected to be 30% of operating income less interest expense. The company pays $10,000 cash at the end of February in estimated taxes.

Requirements

1. Prepare a schedule of cash collections for January, February, and March, and for the quarter in total.

Cash Collections Budget

	January	February	March	Quarter
Cash sales				
Credit sales				
Total cash collections				

2. Prepare a production budget. (Hint: Unit sales = Sales in dollars / Selling price per unit.)

Production Budget

	January	February	March	Quarter
Unit sales				
Plus: Desired ending inventory				
Total needed				
Less: Beginning inventory				
Units to be produced				

3. Prepare a direct materials budget.

Direct Materials Budget

	January	February	March	Quarter
Units to be produced				
× Pounds of DM needed per unit				
Quantity (pounds) needed for production				
Plus: Desired ending inventory of DM				
Total quantity (pounds) needed				
Less: Beginning inventory of DM				
Quantity (pounds) to purchase				
× Cost per pound				
Total cost of DM purchases				

4. Prepare a cash payments budget for the direct material purchases from Requirement 3.

Cash Payments for Direct Material Purchases Budget

	January	February	March	Quarter
December purchases (from Accounts Payable)				
January purchases				
February purchases				
March purchases				
Total cash payments for DM purchases				

5. Prepare a cash payments budget for direct labor, using the following format:

Cash Payments for Direct Labor Budget

	January	February	March	Quarter
Direct labor				

6. Prepare a cash payments budget for manufacturing overhead costs.

Cash Payments for Manufacturing Overhead Costs Budget

	January	February	March	Quarter
Variable manufacturing overhead costs				
Rent (fixed)				
Other fixed MOH				
Total payments for MOH costs				

7. Prepare a cash payments budget for operating expenses.

Cash Payments for Operating Expenses Budget

	January	February	March	Quarter
Variable operating expenses				
Fixed operating expenses				
Total payments for operating expenses				

8. Prepare a combined cash budget.

Combined Cash Budget

	January	February	March	Quarter
Cash balance, beginning				
Add cash collections				
Total cash available				
Less cash payments:				
Direct material purchases				
Direct labor costs				
Manufacturing overhead costs				
Operating expenses				
Tax payment				
Equipment purchases				
Total disbursements				
Ending cash balance before financing				
Financing:				
Borrowings				
Repayments				
Interest payments				
Total financing				
Cash balance, ending				

9. Calculate the budgeted manufacturing cost per unit (assume that fixed manufacturing overhead is budgeted to be $0.70 per unit for the year).

Budgeted Manufacturing Cost per Unit	
Direct materials cost per unit	
Direct labor cost per unit	
Variable manufacturing overhead costs per unit	
Fixed manufacturing overhead per unit	
Budgeted cost of manufacturing each unit	

10. Prepare a budgeted income statement for the quarter ending March 31. (Hint: Cost of goods sold = Budgeted cost of manufacturing each unit × Number of units sold)

Budgeted Income Statement For the Quarter Ended March 31	
Sales	
Cost of goods sold	
Gross profit	
Operating expenses	
Depreciation expense	
Operating income	
Less interest expense	
Less provision for income taxes	
Net income	

P9-62B Prepare budgeted income statement *(Learning Objective 2)*

The budget committee of Soventino Fashions, an upscale women's clothing retailer, has assembled the following data. As the business manager, you must prepare the budgeted income statements for May and June.

a. Sales in April were $40,000. You forecast that monthly sales will increase 10% in May and 5% in June.

b. The company maintains inventory of $10,000 plus 10% of the sales revenue budgeted for the following month. Monthly purchases average 50% of sales revenue in that same month. Actual inventory on April 30 is $13,000. Sales budgeted for July are $70,000.

c. Monthly salaries amount to $5,000. Sales commissions equal 5% of sales for that month. Combine salaries and commissions into a single figure.

d. Other monthly expenses are as follows:

Rent expense	$2,000, paid as incurred
Depreciation expense	$ 500
Insurance expense	$ 100, expiration of prepaid amount
Income tax	20% of operating income

Requirement

Prepare Soventino Fashions' budgeted income statements for May and June. Show cost of goods sold computations.

P9-63B Cash budgets *(Learning Objective 3)*

Omega's Restaurant Supply is preparing its cash budgets for the first two months of the upcoming year. Here is the information about the company's upcoming cash receipts and cash disbursements:

a. Sales are 70% cash and 30% credit. Credit sales are collected 30% in the month of sale and the remainder in the month after sale. Actual sales in December were $51,000. Schedules of budgeted sales for the two months of the upcoming year are as follows:

	Budgeted sales revenue
January	$59,000
February	$69,000

b. Actual purchases of materials in December were $24,000. The company's purchases of direct materials in January are budgeted to be $23,000 and $25,500 in February. All purchases are paid 30% in the month of purchase and 70% the following month.

c. Salaries and sales commissions are also paid half in the month earned and half the next month. Actual salaries were $8,000 in December. Budgeted salaries in January are $9,000 and February budgeted salaries are $10,500. Sales commissions each month are 8% of that month's sales.

d. Rent expense is $3,200 per month.

e. Depreciation is $2,900 per month.

f. Estimated income tax payments are made at the end of January. The estimated tax payment is projected to be $13,500.

g. The cash balance at the end of the prior year was $25,000.

Requirements

1. Prepare schedules of (a) budgeted cash collections, (b) budgeted cash payments for purchases, and (c) budgeted cash payments for operating expenses. Show amounts for each month and totals for January and February.
2. Prepare a combined cash budget. If no financing activity took place, what is the budgeted cash balance on February 28?

P9-64B Prepare a combined cash budget and a budgeted balance sheet *(Learning Objective 3)*

Hastings Medical Supply has applied for a loan. First National Bank has requested a budgeted balance sheet at April 30 and a combined cash budget for April. As Hastings Medical Supply's controller, you have assembled the following information:

a. March 31 equipment balance, $52,800; accumulated depreciation, $41,900.

b. April capital expenditures of $42,400 budgeted for cash purchase of equipment.

c. April depreciation expense, $800.

d. Cost of goods sold, 45% of sales.

e. Other April operating expenses, including income tax, total $14,000, 35% of which will be paid in cash and the remainder accrued at April 30.

f. March 31 owners' equity, $93,800.

g. March 31 cash balance, $40,900.

h. April budgeted sales, $90,000, 60% of which is for cash; of the remaining 40%, half will be collected in April and half in May.

i. April cash collections on March sales, $29,900.

j. April cash payments of March 31 liabilities incurred for March purchases of inventory, $17,100.

k. March 31 inventory balance, $29,200.

l. April purchases of inventory, $10,300 for cash and $37,000 on credit. Half of the credit purchases will be paid in April and half in May.

Requirements

1. Prepare the budgeted balance sheet for Hastings Medical Supply at April 30. Show separate computations for cash, inventory, and stockholders' equity balances.
2. Prepare the combined cash budget for April.
3. Suppose Hastings Medical Supply has become aware of more efficient (and more expensive) equipment than it budgeted for purchase in April. What is the total amount of cash available for equipment purchases in April, before financing, if the minimum desired ending cash balance is $19,000? (For this requirement, disregard the $42,400 initially budgeted for equipment purchases.)
4. Before granting a loan to Hastings, First National Bank asks for a sensitivity analysis assuming that April sales are only $60,000 rather than the $90,000 originally budgeted. (While the cost of goods sold will change, assume that purchases, depreciation, and the other operating expenses will remain the same as in the earlier requirements.)
   a. Prepare a revised budgeted balance sheet for the company, showing separate computations for cash, inventory, and stockholders' equity balances.
   b. Suppose Hastings has a minimum desired cash balance of $23,000. Will the company need to borrow cash in April?
   c. In this sensitivity analysis, sales declined by 33 1/3% ($30,000/$90,000). Is the decline in expenses and income more or less than 33 1/3%? Explain.

P9-65B Prepare an inventory, purchases, and cost of goods sold budget *(Learning Objective 4)*

University Logos buys logo-imprinted merchandise and then sells it to university bookstores. Sales are expected to be $2,004,000 in September, $2,180,000 in October, $2,380,000 in November, and $2,550,000 in December. University Logos sets its prices to earn an average 30% gross profit on sales revenue. The company does not want inventory to fall below $405,000 plus 10% of the next month's cost of goods sold.

Requirement

Prepare an inventory, purchases, and cost of goods sold budget for the months of October and November.

P9-66B Estimate debit and credit card fees *(Learning Objective 4)*

The local Japanese-style steakhouse expects sales to be $500,000 in January. The average restaurant bill is $50. Only 25% of restaurant bills are paid in cash, while 70% are paid with credit cards and 5% are paid with debit cards. The transaction fees charged by the credit and debit card issuers are as follows:

- Credit cards: $0.50 per transaction + 2% of the amount charged
- Debit cards: $0.22 per transaction + 0.05% of the amount charged

Requirements

a. How much of the total sales revenue is expected to be paid with cash?
b. How many customer transactions does the company expect in January?
c. How much of the total sales revenue is expected to be paid with credit cards?
d. How many customer transactions will be paid for by customers using credit cards?
e. When budgeting for January's operating expenses, how much should the restaurant expect to incur in credit card transaction fees?
f. How much of the total sales revenue is expected to be paid with debit cards?
g. How many customer transactions will be paid for by customers using debit cards?
h. When budgeting for January's operating expenses, how much should the restaurant expect to incur in debit card transaction fees?
i. How much money will be deposited in the restaurant's bank account during the month of January related to credit and debit card sales? Assume the credit and debit card issuers deposit the funds on the same day the transactions occur at the restaurant (there is no processing delay).

CRITICAL THINKING

Discussion & Analysis

A9-67 Discussion Questions

1. "The sales budget is the most important budget." Do you agree or disagree? Explain your answer.
2. List at least four reasons why a company would use budgeting.
3. Describe the difference between an operating budget and a capital budget.
4. Describe the process for developing a budget.
5. Compare and contrast "participative budgeting" with "top-down" budgeting.
6. What is a budget committee? What is the budget committee's role in the budgeting process?
7. What are operating budgets? List at least four operating budgets.
8. What are financial budgets? List at least three financial budgets.
9. Managers may build slack into their budgets so that their target numbers are easier to attain. What might be some drawbacks to building slack into the budgets?
10. How does the master budget for a service company differ from a master budget for a manufacturing company? Which (if any) operating budgets differ and how specifically do they differ? Which (if any) financial budgets differ and how specifically do they differ?
11. Give an example of a sustainable practice, if adopted that would affect a company's budget. How might this sustainable practice, if adopted, impact the company's budget in both the short-term and in the long-term?
12. Why might a company want to state environmental goals for increased sustainability in its budgets? Explain.

Application & Analysis

A9-68 Budgeting for a Single Product

In this activity, you will be creating budgets for a single product for each of the months in an upcoming quarter. Select a product that you could purchase in large quantities (at a Sam's Club or other warehouse retail chain) and repackage into smaller quantities to offer for sale at a sidewalk café, a sporting event, a flea market, or other similar venue. Investigate the price and quantity at which this product is available at the warehouse. Choose a selling price for the smaller (repackaged) package. Make reasonable assumptions about how many of the smaller units you can sell in each of the next four months (you will need the fourth month's sales in units for the operating budgets).

Basic Discussion Questions

1. Describe your product. What is your cost of this product? What size (quantity) will you purchase? At what price will you sell your repackaged product? Make projections of your sales in units in each of the upcoming three months.
2. Estimate how many hours you will spend in each of the upcoming three months doing the purchasing, repackaging, and selling. Select a reasonable wage rate for yourself. What will your total labor costs be in each of the upcoming three months?
3. Prepare a sales budget for each of the upcoming three months.
4. Prepare the direct material budgets for the upcoming three months, assuming that you need to keep 10% of the direct materials needed for next month's sales on hand at the end of each month (this requirement is why you needed to estimate unit sales for four months).
5. Prepare a direct labor budget (for your labor) for each of the upcoming three months.
6. Think about any other expenses you are likely to have (i.e., booth rental at a flea market

or a vendor license). Prepare the operating expenses budget for each of the upcoming three months.

7. Prepare a budgeted income statement that reflects the budgets you prepared, including the sales budget, direct materials budget, direct labor budget, and the operating expenses budget. This budgeted income statement should include one column for each of the three months in the quarter and it should also include a total column that represents the totals of the three months. What is your projected profit by month and for the quarter?

Decision Case

A9-69 Suggest performance improvements *(Learning Objective 1)*

Angie Hughes recently joined Cycle World, a bicycle store in St. Louis, as an assistant manager. She recently finished her accounting courses. Cycle World's manager and owner, Loretta Harland, asks Hughes to prepare a budgeted income statement for the upcoming year based on the information she has collected. Hughes' budget follows:

CYCLE WORLD **Budgeted Income Statement** For the Year Ending July 31		
Sales revenue		$244,000
Cost of goods sold		177,000
Gross profit		$ 67,000
Operating expenses:		
Salary and commission expense	$46,000	
Rent expense	8,000	
Depreciation expense	2,000	
Insurance expense	800	
Miscellaneous expenses	12,000	68,800
Operating loss		$ (1,800)
Interest expense		225
Net loss		$ (2,025)

Requirement

Hughes does not want to give Harland this budget without making constructive suggestions for steps Harland could take to improve expected performance. Write a memo to Harland outlining your suggestions.

A9-70 Prepare cash budgets under two alternatives *(Learning Objectives 2 & 3)*

Each autumn, as a hobby, Pauline Spahr weaves cotton place mats to sell at a local craft shop. The mats sell for $20 per set of four mats. The shop charges a 10% commission and remits the net proceeds to Spahr at the end of December. Spahr has woven and sold 25 sets in each of the last two years. She has enough cotton in inventory to make another 25 sets. She paid $7 per set for the cotton. Spahr uses a four-harness loom that she purchased for cash exactly two years ago. It is depreciated at the rate of $10 per month. The accounts payable relate to the cotton inventory and are payable by September 30.

Spahr is considering buying an eight-harness loom so that she can weave more intricate patterns in linen. The new loom costs $1,000; it would be depreciated at $20 per month. Her bank has agreed to lend her $1,000 at 18% interest, with $200 principal plus accrued interest payable each December 31. Spahr believes she can weave 15 linen place mat sets in time for the Christmas rush if she does not weave any cotton mats. She predicts that each linen set will sell for $50. Linen costs $18 per set. Spahr's supplier will sell her linen on credit, payable December 31.

Spahr plans to keep her old loom whether or not she buys the new loom. The balance sheet for her weaving business at August 31 is as follows:

PAULINE SPAHR, WEAVER Balance Sheet August 31			
Current assets:		Current liabilities:	
Cash	$ 25	Accounts payable	$ 74
Inventory of cotton	175		
	$ 200		
Fixed assets:			
Loom	500	Stockholders' equity	386
Accumulated depreciation	(240)		
	$ 260		
Total assets	$ 460	Total liabilities and stockholders' equity	$460

Requirements

1. Prepare a combined cash budget for the four months ending December 31, for two alternatives: weaving the place mats in cotton using the existing loom and weaving the place mats in linen using the new loom. For each alternative, prepare a budgeted income statement for the four months ending December 31 and a budgeted balance sheet at December 31.
2. On the basis of financial considerations only, what should Spahr do? Give your reason.
3. What nonfinancial factors might Spahr consider in her decision?

Ethical Issue

A9-71 Ethical considerations for padded budgets *(Learning Objectives 1 & 4)*

Residence Suites operates a regional hotel chain. Each hotel is operated by a manager and an assistant manager/controller. Many of the staff who run the front desk, clean the rooms, and prepare the breakfast buffet work part-time or have a second job, so turnover is high.

Assistant manager/controller John Rach asked the new bookkeeper to help prepare the hotel's master budget. The master budget is prepared once a year and submitted to company headquarters for approval. Once approved, the master budget is used to evaluate the hotel's performance. These performance evaluations affect hotel managers' bonuses; they also affect company decisions about which hotels deserve extra funds for capital improvements.

When the budget was almost complete, Rach asked the bookkeeper to increase amounts budgeted for labor and supplies by 15%. When asked why, Rach responded that hotel manager Lauren Romick told him to do this when he began working at the hotel. Romick explained that this budgetary cushion gave her flexibility in running the hotel. For example, because company headquarters tightly controls capital improvement funds, Romick can use the extra money budgeted for labor and supplies to replace broken televisions or to pay "bonuses" to keep valued employees. Rach initially accepted this explanation because he had observed similar behavior at his previous place of employment.

Put yourself in Rach's position. In deciding how to deal with the situation, answer the following questions:

1. What is the ethical issue?
2. What are my options?
3. What are the possible consequences?
4. What should I do?

Team Project

A9-72 Analyzing and discussing budget concerns *(Learning Objectives 1, 2, & 3)*

PharmSys provides enterprise and information technology consulting services to the pharmaceuticals industry. PharmSys is organized into several divisions. A companywide planning committee sets general strategy and goals for the company and its divisions, but each division develops its own budget.

Rick Watson is the new division manager of wireless communications software. His division has two departments: Development and Sales. Carrie Pronai manages the 20 or so programmers and systems specialists typically employed in the Development Department to create and update the division's software applications. Liz Smith manages the Sales Department.

PharmSys considers the divisions to be investment centers. To earn his bonus next year, Watson must achieve a 30% return on the $3 million invested in his division. This amounts to $900,000 of income (30% × $3 million). Within the wireless division, development is a cost center, while sales are a revenue center.

Budgeting is in progress. Pronai met with her staff and is now struggling with two sets of numbers. Alternative A is her best estimate of next year's costs. However, unexpected problems can arise in the writing of software, and finding competent programmers is an ongoing challenge. She knows that Watson was a programmer before he earned an MBA, so he should be sensitive to this uncertainty. Consequently, she is thinking of increasing her budgeted costs (Alternative B). Her department's bonuses largely depend on whether the department meets its budgeted costs.

PHARMSYS
Wireless Division
Development Budget

	Alternative A	Alternative B
Salaries expense (including overtime and part-time)	$2,400,000	$2,640,000
Software expense	120,000	132,000
Travel expense	65,000	71,500
Depreciation expense	255,000	255,000
Miscellaneous expense	100,000	110,000
Total expense	$2,940,000	$3,208,500

Liz Smith is also struggling with her sales budget. Companies have made their initial investments in communications software, so it is harder to win new customers. If things go well, she believes her sales team can maintain the level of growth achieved over the last few years. This is Alternative A in the sales budget. However, if Smith is too optimistic, sales may fall short of the budget. If this happens, her team will not receive bonuses. Therefore, Smith is considering reducing the sales numbers and submitting Alternative B.

PHARMSYS
Wireless Division
Sales Budget

	Alternative A	Alternative B
Sales revenue	$5,000,000	$4,500,000
Salaries expense	360,000	360,000
Travel expense	240,000	210,500

Split your team into three groups. Each group should meet separately before the entire team meets.

Requirements

1. The first group plays the role of Development Manager Carrie Pronai. Before meeting with the entire team, determine which set of budget numbers you are going to present to Rick Watson. Write a memo supporting your decision. Give this memo to the third group before the team meeting.
2. The second group plays the role of Sales Manager Liz Smith. Before meeting with the entire team, determine which set of budget numbers you are going to present to Rick Watson. Write a memo supporting your decision. Give this memo to the third group before the team meeting.
3. The third group plays the role of Division Manager Rick Watson. Before meeting with the entire team, use the memos that Pronai and Smith provided to prepare a division budget based on the sales and development budgets. Your divisional overhead costs (additional costs beyond those incurred by the Development and Sales Departments) are approximately $390,000. Determine whether the wireless division can meet its targeted 30% return on assets given the budgeted alternatives submitted by your department managers.

During the meeting of the entire team, the group playing Watson presents the division budget and considers its implications. Each group should take turns discussing its concerns with the proposed budget. The team as a whole should consider whether the division budget must be revised. The team should prepare a report that includes the division budget and a summary of the issues covered in the team meeting.

A9-73 CMA-1 Crisper, Inc. plans to sell 80,000 bags of potato chips in June, and each of these bags requires five potatoes. Pertinent data includes:

	Bags of potato chips	Potatoes
Actual June inventory	15,000 bags	27,000 potatoes
Desired June 30 inventory	18,000 bags	23,000 potatoes

What number of units of raw material should Crisper plan to purchase?

a. 381,000
b. 389,000
c. 411,000
d. 419,000

A9-74 CMA-2 Holland Company is in the process of projecting its cash position at the end of the second quarter. Shown below is pertinent information from Holland's records.

Cash balance at end of 1st quarter	$ 36,000
Cash collections from customers for 2nd quarter	1,300,000
Accounts payable at end of 1st quarter	100,000
Accounts payable at end of 2nd quarter	75,000
All 2nd quarter costs and expenses (accrual basis)	1,200,000
Depreciation (accrued expense included above)	60,000
Purchases of equipment (for cash)	50,000
Gain on sale of asset (for cash)	5,000
Net book value of asset sold	35,000
Repayment of notes payable	66,000

From the data above, determine Holland's projected cash balance at the end of the second quarter.

a. Zero
b. $25,000
c. $60,000
d. $95,000

(CMA Adapted)

Performance Evaluation

Learning Objectives

1 Understand decentralization and describe different types of responsibility centers

2 Develop performance reports

3 Calculate ROI, sales margin, and capital turnover

4 Prepare and evaluate flexible budget performance reports

5 Describe the balanced scorecard and identify KPIs for each perspective

United Parcel Service (UPS) delivers over 5.4 billion packages a year in over 200 countries. To achieve such astonishing volume, UPS employs over 425,000 people and flies more than 1,900 flight segments each day into 800 airports around the world. How does management successfully guide the actions of all of these employees? First, it divides—or decentralizes—the company into three segments: domestic packaging, international packaging, and nonpackaging services (such as supply chain and logistics). It further breaks each packaging segment into geographic regions and each region into districts. Management gives each district manager authority to make decisions for his or her district. Because top management wants *every* employee to know how his or her day-to-day job contributes to the company's goals, it implemented a system, called the balanced scorecard, for communicating strategy to all district managers and employees. Management can also use the balanced scorecard to measure whether each district is meeting its goals and to assess where changes should be made. According to one UPS executive, "The balanced scorecard provided a road map—the shared vision of our future goals—with action elements that let *everyone* contribute to our success."

Tim Boyle/Bloomberg via Getty Images

Sources: Robert Kaplan and David Norton, *The Strategy-Focused Organization: How Balanced Scorecard Companies Thrive in the New Business Environment*, Harvard Business School Press, Boston, 2001, pp. 21–22, 239–241; www.ups.com (2009).

Has the balanced scorecard helped UPS become an industry leader? In 2008, Fortune rated UPS as the "World's Most Admired Company in its Industry" for the tenth consecutive year. Year after year, UPS continues to win awards in the areas of E-commerce, technology, business excellence, and corporate citizenship.

In Chapter 9 we saw how businesses such as Campbell Soup Company and Tucson Tortilla set strategic goals and then develop planning budgets to help reach those goals. In this chapter, we'll see how companies use budgets and other tools, such as the balanced scorecard, to evaluate performance and control operations.

How Does Decentralization Affect Performance Evaluation?

1 Understand decentralization and describe different types of responsibility centers

In a small company, such as Tucson Tortilla (discussed in Chapter 9), the owner or top manager often makes all planning and operating decisions. Small companies can use **centralized** decision making because of the smaller scope of their operations. However, when a company grows, it is impossible for a single person to manage the entire organization's operations. Therefore, most companies, like Campbell Soup Company, decentralize as they grow.

Companies that **decentralize** split their operations into different operating segments. Top management delegates decision-making responsibility to the segment managers. Top management determines the type of decentralization that best suits the company's strategy. For example, decentralization may be based on

- geographic area
- product line
- distribution channel (such as retail sales versus online sales)
- customer base
- business function or some other business characteristic.

For example, UPS decentralizes its company by geographic area (domestic and international). Sherwin-Williams decentralizes its operations by customer base (commercial and consumer paint divisions). Campbell Soup Company decentralizes its company by type of product *and* geographical location (Baking and Snacking; U.S. Soup, Sauces and Beverages; and International Soup, Sauces and Beverages).

Advantages and Disadvantages of Decentralization

Before we look at specific types of business segments, let's consider some of the advantages and disadvantages of decentralization.

Advantages

Most growing companies decentralize out of necessity. However, decentralization provides many potential benefits.

FREES TOP MANAGEMENT'S TIME By delegating responsibility for daily operations to segment managers, top management can concentrate on long-term strategic planning and higher-level decisions that affect the entire company.

ENCOURAGES USE OF EXPERT KNOWLEDGE Decentralization allows top management to hire the expertise each business segment needs to excel in its specific operations. Specialized knowledge often helps segment managers make better decisions than the top company managers could make.

IMPROVES CUSTOMER RELATIONS Segment managers focus on just one segment of the company, allowing them to maintain close contact with important customers and suppliers. Thus, decentralization often leads to improved customer and supplier relations, which can result in quicker customer response times.

PROVIDES TRAINING Decentralization also provides segment managers with training and experience necessary to become effective top managers. Companies often groom their lower-level managers to move up through the company, taking on additional responsibility and gaining more knowledge of the company with each step.

IMPROVES MOTIVATION AND RETENTION Empowering segment managers to make decisions increases managers' motivation and job satisfaction, which often improves job performance and retention.

Disadvantages

The many advantages of decentralization usually outweigh the disadvantages. However, decentralization can cause potential problems, including those outlined below.

POTENTIAL DUPLICATION OF COSTS Decentralization may cause a company to duplicate certain costs or assets. For example, several business segments could maintain their own payroll and human resource departments. Companies can often avoid such duplications by providing centralized services. For example, Marriott segments its hotels by property type (limited service, full-service, luxury), yet each hotel property shares one centralized reservations website.

POTENTIAL PROBLEMS ACHIEVING GOAL CONGRUENCE Goal Congruence occurs when the goals of the segment managers align with the goals of top management. Decentralized companies often struggle to achieve goal congruence. Segment managers may not fully understand the big picture, or the ultimate goals that upper management is trying to achieve. They may make decisions that are good for their segment but may be detrimental to another segment of the company or the company as a whole. For example, in order to control costs, one division may decide to offshore production to an overseas factory with poor working conditions. However, top management may embrace, promote, and market social responsibility and the use of fair labor practices. If so, the division is not acting in accordance with top management's goals.

Performance Evaluation Systems

Once a company decentralizes operations, top management is no longer involved in running the day-to-day operations of the segments. Performance evaluation systems provide upper management with the feedback it needs to maintain control over the entire organization, even though it has delegated responsibility and decision-making authority to segment managers. To be effective, performance evaluation systems should

- clearly communicate expectations,
- provide benchmarks that promote goal congruence and coordination between segments, and
- motivate segment managers (possibly through paying bonus incentives to managers who achieve performance targets).

Responsibility accounting, discussed next, is an integral part of most companies' performance evaluation systems.

What is Responsibility Accounting?

A responsibility center is a part of an organization whose manager is accountable for planning and controlling certain activities. Lower-level managers are often responsible for budgeting and controlling costs of a single value chain function. For example, at Campbell's, one manager is responsible for planning and controlling the *production* of Campbell's soup at a single plant, while another is responsible for planning and controlling the *distribution* of the product to customers. Lower-level managers report to higher-level managers, who have broader responsibilities. For example, managers in charge of production and distribution report to senior managers responsible for profits earned by an entire product line.

Responsibility accounting is a system for evaluating the performance of each responsibility center and its manager. Responsibility accounting performance reports compare plans (budgets) with actual results for each center. Superiors then evaluate how well each manager controlled the operations for which he or she was responsible.

Types of Responsibility Centers

Exhibit 10-1 illustrates four types of responsibility centers. We'll briefly describe each type of responsibility center.

EXHIBIT 10-1 Four types of responsibility centers

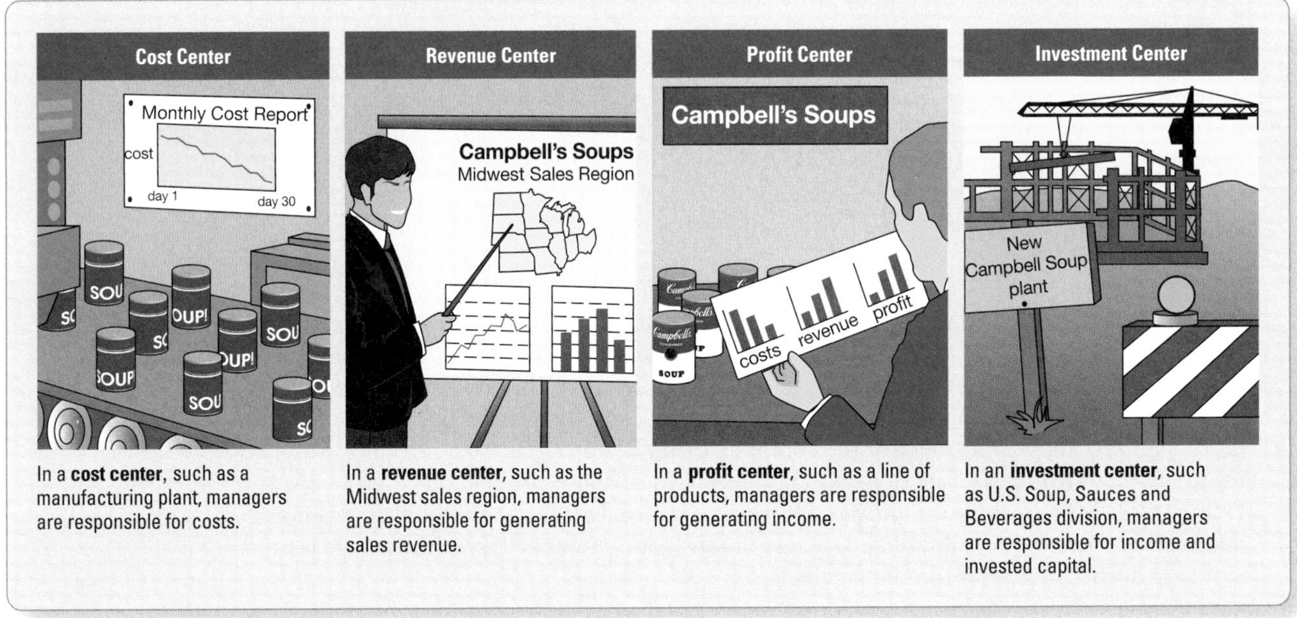

Cost Center

In a cost center, managers are accountable for costs only. Manufacturing operations, such as the Campbell's Chicken Noodle Soup manufacturing plant, are cost centers. The plant manager controls costs by ensuring that the entire production process runs efficiently. The plant manager is *not* responsible for generating revenues because he or she is not involved in selling the product. The plant manager is evaluated on his or her ability to control *costs* by comparing actual costs to budgeted costs.

Revenue Center

In a revenue center, managers are accountable primarily for revenues. Many times, revenue centers are sales territories, such as Campbell's Soups Midwest and Southeast sales regions. Managers of revenue centers may also be responsible for the costs of their own sales operations. Revenue center performance reports compare actual revenues to budgeted revenues.

Profit Center

In a profit center, managers are accountable for both revenues and costs and, therefore, profits. For example, at Campbell's, a manager is responsible for the entire line of Campbell's ready-to-serve and condensed soup products. This manager is accountable for increasing sales revenue *and* controlling costs to achieve profit goals for the entire line of soups. Superiors evaluate the manager's performance by comparing actual revenues, expenses, and profits to the budget.

Investment Center

In an investment center, managers are responsible for (1) generating revenues, (2) controlling costs, and (3) efficiently managing the division's assets. Investment centers are generally large divisions of a corporation. For example, the Campbell Soup Company has four different divisions:

- U.S. Soup, Sauces and Beverages;
- Baking and Snacking;

- International Soup, Sauces and Beverages; and
- U.S. Foodservice.

Investment centers are treated almost as if they were stand-alone companies. Division managers generally have broad responsibility, including deciding how to use assets. As a result, managers are held responsible for generating as much profit as they can with those assets.

Organization Chart

Exhibit 10-2 shows a partial organization chart for Campbell Soup Company.

- At the top level, the CEO oversees each of the four divisions (*investment centers*).
- The manager of each division overseas all of the product lines (*profit centers*) in that division. For example, the VP of U.S. Soup, Sauces and Beverages oversees the *Prego* pasta sauces, *Pace* Mexican sauces, *V8* juice and juice drinks, *Campbell's* soups, and *Swanson* broths.[1]
- The manager of each product line is responsible for evaluating lower-level managers of *cost centers* (such as plants that make Pace products) and *revenue centers* (such as managers responsible for selling Pace products).

EXHIBIT 10-2 Partial Organization Chart

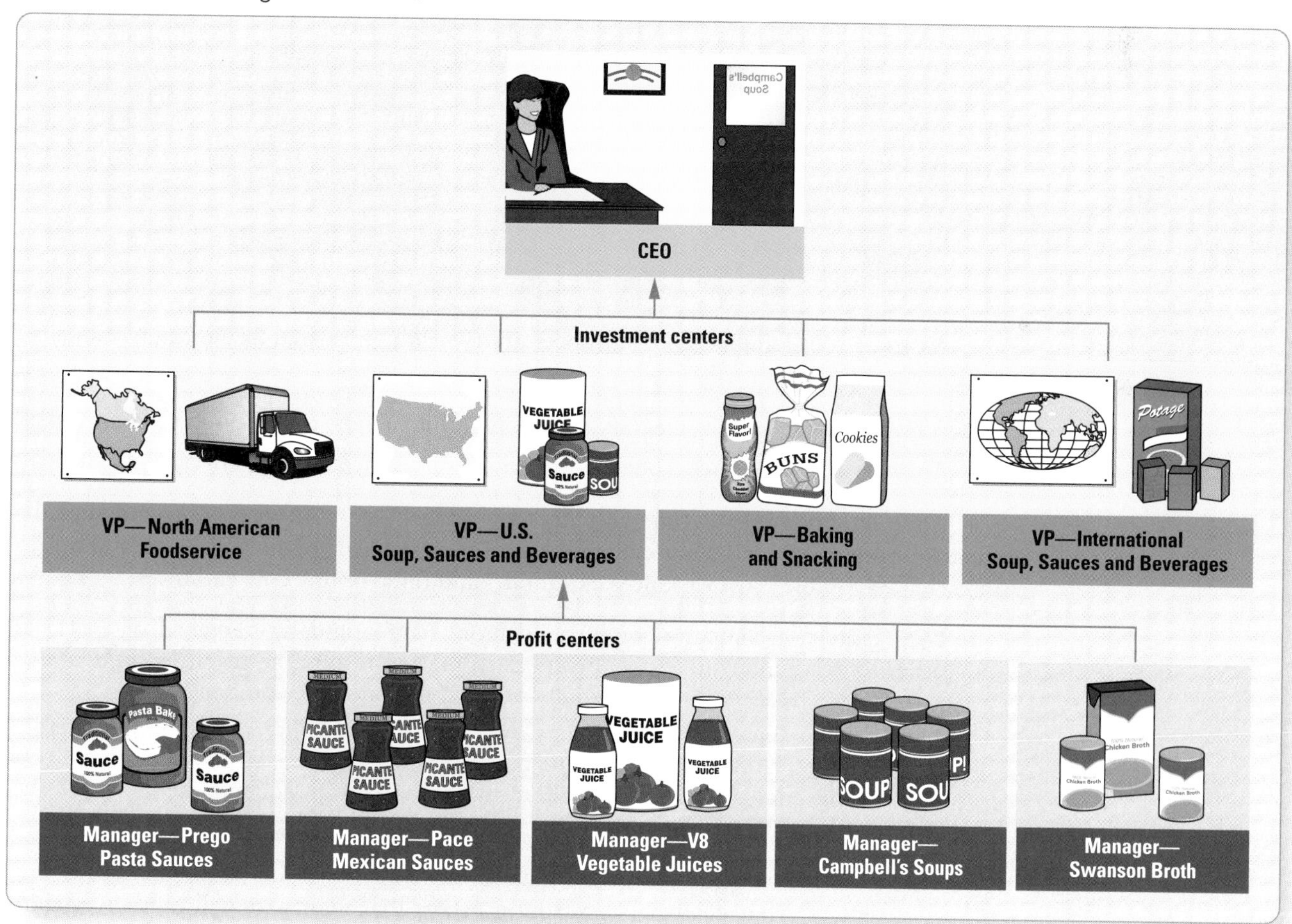

[1]For the sake of simplicity, we only illustrate five of the nine product lines that actually fall under the U.S. Soup, Sauces and Beverages segment.

Responsibility Center Performance Reports

2 Develop performance reports for different responsibility centers

As introduced in Chapter 9, a **performance report** compares actual revenues and expenses against budgeted figures. The difference between actual and budget is known as a **variance**. The specific figures included on each performance report will depend on the type of responsibility center being evaluated. For example,

- the performance reports of cost centers will only include *costs* incurred within the center.
- the performance reports of revenue centers will only include the *revenues* generated by the center.

Exhibit 10-3 illustrates a partial performance report for a revenue center—the Midwest Sales Region of Campbell's condensed soups. Since the manager is only responsible for generating sales revenue, only revenues are included in the report.

EXHIBIT 10-3 Partial Performance Report for a Revenue Center

Performance Report
Midwest Sales Region—Sales Revenue for Condensed Soups*
For the month ending March 31

Product	Actual Sales	Budgeted Sales	Variance	Variance %**
Beef Barley Soup	$ 2,367,200	$ 2,400,000	$ 32,800 U	1.37% U
Chicken Noodle Soup	15,896,000	15,000,000	896,000 F	5.97% F
Cream of Mushroom	9,325,500	9,000,000	325,500 F	3.62% F
Minestrone	1,374,300	1,500,000	125,700 U	8.38% U
Tomato	13,678,400	13,500,000	178,400 F	1.32% F
Vegetable Soup	4,683,100	4,500,000	183,100 F	4.1% F

* All figures in this report are hypothetical.
** Calculated as the variance divided by the budgeted amount.

As you see in Exhibit 10-3, variances are typically presented as either favorable (F) or unfavorable (U).

- A **favorable variance** is one that causes operating income to be higher than budgeted.
- An **unfavorable variance** is one that causes operating income to be lower than budgeted.

Although favorable *revenue* variances are typically good news for the company, the same interpretation can be misleading when it comes to *cost* variances. Be careful *not* to interpret "favorable" cost variances as "good," and unfavorable cost variances as "bad."

- For example, a company could spend more than originally budgeted on R&D in order to bring innovative new products to market faster. The resulting *unfavorable* variance for R&D costs may actually be *good* news for the company.
- On the other hand, a manager may purchase lower-quality materials to generate cost savings. The resulting *favorable* materials cost variance would actually be *bad* news for the company, since it would most likely result in reducing the quality of the end product.

Managers use a technique called **management by exception** when analyzing performance reports. Management by exception means that managers will only investigate budget variances that are relatively large. Let's use a personal example to illustrate this concept. Consider your monthly cell phone bill. You probably have an expectation of how large your monthly cell phone bill will be. If the actual bill is close to your expectation, you'll just pay the bill without giving it too much additional thought. However, if the actual bill is much higher or much lower than you expected, you probably will look at the detailed charges for calls, texts, and data usage to determine why the bill was so much different than what you expected.

Managers do the same thing. If the actual costs or revenues are close to budget, they assume operations are in control. However, if the variance between budget and actual is relatively large, they'll investigate the cause of the variance. Managers often have a decision rule for variance investigation that is expressed as a percentage, dollar amount, or a combination of the two. For example, the manager of the Midwest Sales Region may decide to investigate only those variances that are greater than 5% *and* $150,000. Exhibit 10-3 shows that the variance for both Chicken Noodle Soup and Minestrone exceeds 5%. However, of the two, only the Chicken Noodle Soup variance exceeds $150,000. Therefore, the manager would only investigate the Chicken Noodle Soup variance.

Segment Margin

The performance reports of profit and investment centers include both revenues and expenses. Performance reports are often presented in the contribution margin format rather than the traditional income statement format. These reports often include a line called "segment margin." A segment margin is the operating income generated by a profit or investment center *before* subtracting common fixed costs that have been allocated to the center. For example, Exhibit 10-4 illustrates a hypothetical performance report for Pace Mexican Sauces.

EXHIBIT 10-4 Performance report highlighting the profit center's segment margin

Performance Report
Pace Mexican Sauces—Performance Report*
For Fiscal Year 2010
(In millions of dollars)

	Actual	Budgeted	Variance	Variance %
Sales	$1,280	$1,300	$20 U	1.54% U
Less: Variable expenses				
Variable cost of goods sold	660	657	3 U	0.46% U
Variable operating expenses	110	123	13 F	10.57% F
Contribution Margin	510	520	10 U	1.92% U
Less: Direct fixed expenses				
Fixed manufacturing overhead	200	204	4 F	1.96% F
Fixed operating expenses	65	61	4 U	6.56% U
Segment margin	245	255	10 U	3.92% U
Less: Common fixed expenses allocated to the profit center	20	21	1 F	4.76% F
Operating income	$ 225	$ 234	$ 9 U	3.85%

* All figures are hypothetical.

As you look at Exhibit 10-4, notice that fixed expenses are separated into two categories:

- Direct fixed expenses include those fixed expenses that can be traced to the profit center. An example might include advertisements for Pace Mexican Sauces.
- Common fixed expenses include those fixed expenses that *cannot* be traced to the profit center. Rather, these are fixed expenses incurred by the overarching investment center (the U.S. Soup, Sauces and Beverages division) that have been allocated among the different profit centers in the division. For example, these allocated costs may include the division's cost of providing a common computer information system, human resources department, payroll department, and legal department. By sharing these services, the different product lines avoid duplication of the costs and assets that would otherwise need to be maintained by the individual profit centers.

Since the manager of the profit center has little to no control over the allocation of the common fixed expenses, he or she should not be held. responsible for them.[2] Therefore, the manager is typically held responsible for the center's segment margin, not its operating income.

[2]The various methods used to allocate centralized service expenses and other common fixed expenses are covered in more advanced cost accounting textbooks.

Organization-wide Performance Reports

Exhibit 10-5 illustrates how the performance reports for each level of management shown in Exhibit 10-2 flow *up* to the top of the company. Notice the following in the exhibit:

- The operating income from each profit center, such as Pace Mexican Sauces (at the bottom of the exhibit), flows into the performance report for an investment center (in the middle of the exhibit).
- Likewise, the operating income from each investment center, such as U.S. Soup, Sauces and Beverages, flows into the performance report for the entire company (at the top of the exhibit).
- Costs incurred by corporate headquarters (shown in the top of the exhibit) are treated as a cost center and are typically not allocated to any of the divisions.
- In addition to those performance reports pictured, performance reports related to the cost and revenue centers under each profit center would exist and flow up to the profit centers.

EXHIBIT 10-5 Organization-wide performance reports

Corporate
Performance Report for Fiscal Year 2010
(In millions of dollars)

	Actual	Budget	Variance	Variance %
U.S. Soups, Sauces and Beverages	$ 943	$ 916	$27 F	2.95%
Baking and Snacking	322	327	5 U	1.53%
International Soups, Sauces and Beverages	161	150	11 F	7.33%
North American Foodservice	$ 43	44	1 U	2.27%
Corporate	(121)	(125)	4 F	3.20%
Operating Income	$1,348	$1,312	$36 F	2.74%

U.S. Soup, Sauces, and Beverages
Performance Report for Fiscal Year 2010
(In millions of dollars)

	Actual	Budget	Variance	Variance %
Prego Pasta	$198	$190	$ 8 F	4.21%
Pace Mexican	225	234	9 U	3.85%
V8 Vegetable	65	60	5 F	8.33%
Campbell's Soups	325	312	13 F	4.17%
Swanson Broth	130	120	10 F	8.33%
Operating Income	$943	$916	$27 F	2.95%

Pace Mexican Sauces
Performance Report for Fiscal Year 2010

Revenue and Expenses	Actual	Budget	Variance	Variance %
Sales	$1,280	$1,300	$20 U	1.54%
Less: Variable Expenses	770	780	10 F	1.29%
Contribution Margin	510	520	10 U	1.92%
Less: Direct Fixed Costs	265	265	0	0
Segment Margin	245	255	10 U	3.92%
Less: Common Fixed Costs	20	21	1 F	4.76%
Operating Income	$ 225	$ 234	$ 9 U	3.85%

* All information presented in this exhibit is hypothetical, and was created by the author solely for academic purposes, except the actual operating income of the corporate divisions (shown in the top table).

Responsibility accounting assigns managers responsibility for their segment's performance. But superiors should not misuse the system to erroneously find fault or place blame. Some variances are controllable, while others are not.

For example, managers have no control over the general economic conditions of the country that may reduce sales. Nor do they have control over droughts, floods, and frosts that increase the cost of the agricultural materials in their products. Likewise, they have little or no control over the cost of electricity and gas used to power plants and deliver products. Managers need to carefully consider the causes of large variances so that they can focus on improving those that are controllable, while developing strategies for minimizing the risk associated with uncontrollable variances.

Evaluation of Investment Centers

3 Calculate ROI, Sales Margin, and Capital Turnover

As discussed above, investment centers are typically large divisions of a company. The duties of an investment center manager are similar to those of a CEO of an entire company. Investment center managers are responsible for *both* generating profit *and* making the best use of the investment center's assets. For example, an investment center manager has the authority to decide how much inventory to hold, what types of investments to make, how aggressively to collect accounts receivable, and whether to open new stores or close old ones. In this section, we'll look at the two performance measures most commonly used to assess the performance of investment centers: 1) Return on Investment and 2) Residual Income. To do this, we'll first need some financial data.

Exhibit 10-6 shows actual 2010 data for two of Campbell's divisions.[3] Statement of Financial Accounting Standards Number 131 (SFAS 131) requires publically traded companies to disclose this type of segment information in the footnotes to its financial statements.[4]

EXHIBIT 10-6 Division Information for Campbell Soup Company

2010 Data (All figures are in millions of dollars)	Operating Income	Assets	Sales Revenue
U.S. Soups, Sauces and Beverages..................	$ 943	$2,146	$3,700
Baking and Snacking	322	1,710	1,975

The Exhibit 10-6 shows that the U.S. Soup, Sauces and Beverages division (henceforth referred to as U.S. Soup) is providing more profit to the company than is the Baking and Snacking division. However, a simple comparison between the operating income of each division is misleading because it does not consider the size of each division. Based on its assets, the U.S. Soup division is larger than the Baking and Snacking division. Therefore, we would expect the U.S. Soup division to generate more income. To adequately evaluate an investment center's financial performance, top managers assess each division's operating income *in relationship to its assets*. They typically do so by calculating the division's return on investment or residual income.

Return on Investment (ROI)

Return on Investment (ROI) measures the amount of income an investment center earns relative to the size of its assets. Companies typically define ROI as follows:

$$\text{ROI} = \frac{\text{Operating income}}{\text{Total assets}}$$

[3]Campbell Soup Company 2010 Annual Report

[4]SFAS 131, "Disclosures about Segments of an Enterprise and Related Information," June 1997, Financial Accounting Standards Board, Norwalk, CT.

Let's calculate the ROI for both the U.S. Soup and Baking and Snacking divisions, using the income and assets of each division found in Exhibit 10-6:

$$\text{U.S Soup Division ROI} = \frac{943}{2{,}146} = 44\% \text{ (rounded)}$$

$$\text{Baking and Snacking Division ROI} = \frac{322}{1{,}710} = 19\% \text{ (rounded)}$$

The resulting ROI indicates that the U.S. Soup division is generating much more income for every dollar of its assets than is the Baking and Snacking division:

- The U.S. Soup division earns $0.44 on every $1.00 of assets.
- The Baking and Snacking division earns $0.19 on every $1.00 of assets.

If you had $1,000 to invest, would you rather invest it in the U.S. Soup division or the Baking and Snacking division? Management would much rather have a 44% return on its investment than a 19% return. When top management decides how to invest excess funds, they often consider each division's ROI. A division with a higher ROI is more likely to receive extra funds because it has a track record of providing a higher return with the investment.

In addition to comparing ROI across divisions, management also compares a division's ROI across time to determine whether the division is becoming more or less profitable. For example, Exhibit 10-7 shows the actual ROI of the two divisions over the past six years.

EXHIBIT 10-7 Actual Division ROI Over Time

ROI (rounded)	2010	2009	2008	2007	2006	2005
U.S. Soup	44%	43%	44%	39%	39%	36%
Baking & Snacking	19%	16%	7%	14%	11%	12%

The ROI of the both divisions has been trending upwards slightly, except for a lower-than-normal ROI in the 2008 Baking and Snacking division. The 2008 setback was caused when the division divested itself of certain international food brands.

In addition to benchmarking ROI over time, management often benchmarks divisional ROI with other companies in the same industry to determine how each division is performing compared to its competitors.

Sales Margin and Capital Turnover

To determine what is driving a division's ROI, management often restates the ROI equation in its expanded form:

$$\text{ROI} = \frac{\text{Operating income}}{\text{Sales}} \times \frac{\text{Sales}}{\text{Total assets}} = \frac{\text{Operating income}}{\text{Total assets}}$$

Notice that sales, or sales revenue, is incorporated in the denominator of the first term and in the numerator of the second term. When the two terms are multiplied together, Sales revenue cancels out, leaving the original ROI formula.

Why do managers rewrite the ROI formula this way? Because it helps them better understand how they can improve their ROI. The first term in the expanded equation is the sales margin, which focuses on profitability by showing how much operating income the division earns on every $1 of sales revenue. Sales margin is defined as:

$$\text{Sales margin} = \frac{\text{Operating income}}{\text{Sales}}$$

Let's calculate each division's sales margin using the information in Exhibit 10-6:

$$\text{U.S Soup Division Sales Margin} = \frac{943}{3{,}700} = 25.5\%\ \text{(rounded)}$$

$$\text{Baking and Snacking Division Sales Margin} = \frac{322}{1{,}975} = 16.3\%\ \text{(rounded)}$$

The U.S. Soup division is earning $0.25 on every $1.00 of sales revenue, whereas the Baking and Snacking division is only earning $0.16 on every $1.00 of sales revenue. Overall, the products in the U.S. Soup division are more profitable than the products in the Baking and Snacking division. To improve this statistic, the division manager needs to focus on cutting costs so that more operating income can be earned for every dollar of sales revenue. However, they'll need to be careful in cutting costs, so as not to jeopardize the long-term success of the division.

Next, let's consider each division's **capital turnover**, which focuses on how efficiently the division uses its assets to generate sales revenue. Capital turnover is defined as:

$$\text{Capital turnover} = \frac{\text{Sales}}{\text{Total assets}}$$

Let's calculate each division's capital turnover using the information from Exhibit 10-6:

$$\text{U.S Soup Division Capital Turnover} = \frac{3{,}700}{2{,}146} = 1.72\ \text{(rounded)}$$

$$\text{Baking and Snacking Division Capital Turnover} = \frac{1{,}975}{1{,}710} = 1.15\ \text{(rounded)}$$

The U.S. Soup division has a capital turnover of 1.72, which means the division generates $1.72 of sales revenue with every $1 of assets. The Baking and Snacking division generates only $1.15 of sales revenue with every $1.00 of assets. The U.S. Soup division uses its assets more efficiently in generating sales than does the Baking and Snacking division. To improve this statistic, the division manager should try to reduce or eliminate nonproductive assets—for example, by collecting accounts receivables more aggressively or decreasing inventory levels.

As the following table shows, the ROI of the U.S. Soup division is higher than the Baking and Snacking Division because 1) the division is earning more profit on every dollar of sales, *and* 2) the division is generating more sales revenue with every dollar of assets:

	Sales Margin	×	Capital Turnover	=	ROI
U.S. Soup	25.5%	×	1.72	=	44%
Baking and Snacking	16.3%	×	1.15	=	19%

Residual Income (RI)

Rather than using ROI to evaluate the performance of their investment centers, many companies use the concept of residual income. Similar to ROI, the residual income calculation is based on both the division's operating income and its assets, thereby measuring the division's profitability with respect to the size of its assets. However, the residual income calculation incorporates one more important piece of information: management's target rate of return. The target rate of return is the minimum acceptable rate of return that top management expects a division to earn with its assets. Management's target rate of return is based on many factors. Some of these factors include

- the risk level of the division's business
- interest rates
- investor's expectations
- return being earned by other divisions
- general economic conditions.

As these factors change over time, management's target rate of return will also change.

Residual income (RI) determines whether the division has created any excess (or residual) income above and beyond management's expectations. Residual income is calculated as follows:

RI = Operating income − Minimum acceptable income

The minimum acceptable income is defined as top management's target rate of return multiplied by the division's total assets. Thus,

RI = Operating income − (Target rate of return × Total assets)

Notice in this equation that the RI compares the division's actual operating income with the minimum operating income that top management expects *given the size of the division's assets*. A positive RI means that the division's operating income exceeds top management's target rate of return. A negative RI means the division is not meeting the target rate of return.

Let's calculate the residual income for the U.S. Soup division, assuming a 25% target rate of return:[5]

U.S Soup division RI = \$943 − (25% × \$2,146) = \$406.5

The positive RI indicates that the U.S. Soup division exceeded top management's 25% target return expectations. The RI calculation also confirms what we learned about the U.S. Soup division's ROI. Recall that the U.S. Soup division's ROI was 44%, which is higher than the targeted 25%.

Let's also calculate the RI for the Baking and Snacking division:

Baking and Snacking division RI = \$322 − (25% × \$1,710) = (\$105.5)

The Baking and Snacking division's RI is negative. This means that the Baking and Snacking division did not use its assets as effectively as top management expected, and was therefore unable to achieve the minimum acceptable rate of return of 25%. Recall that the Baking and Snacking division's ROI was 19%.

Exhibit 10-8 summarizes the performance measures we have just discussed.

[5]Management's actual target rate of return is unknown. 25% is used simply for illustrative purposes.

EXHIBIT 10-8 Summary of Investment Center Performance Measures

Performance Measure	Formula
ROI	$\text{ROI} = \dfrac{\text{Operating income}}{\text{Total assets}}$
Sales Margin	$\text{Sales margin} = \dfrac{\text{Operating income}}{\text{Sales}}$
Capital Turnover	$\text{Capital turnover} = \dfrac{\text{Sales}}{\text{Total assets}}$
Residual Income	$\text{RI} = \text{Operating income} - (\text{Target rate of return} \times \text{Total assets})$

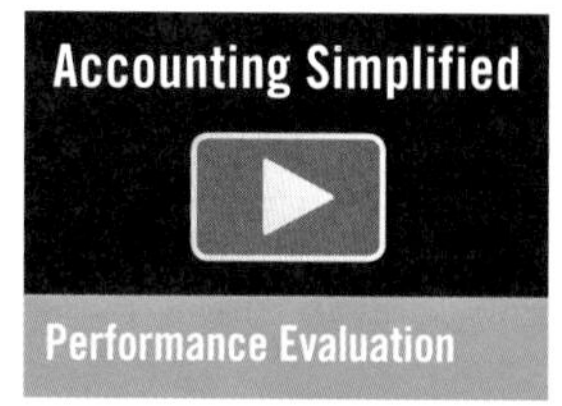

If your instructor is using MyAccountingLab, go to the Multimedia Library for a quick video on this topic.

Goal Congruence

Since the ROI calculation already shows managers whether or not the division has reached the target rate of return, why do some companies prefer using residual income rather than ROI? The answer is that residual income often leads to better goal congruence. For example, say a manager is considering investing in a new $100,000 piece of equipment that would provide $30,000 of annual income. Upper management would want the divisions to invest in this equipment because its return (30%) exceeds the target rate (25%). But what will the division managers do?

- If evaluated based on residual income, division managers will invest in the equipment because it will increase the division's residual income by $5,000 [=$30,000 – (25% × $100,000)].
- If evaluated based on ROI, the division manager's decision may depend on its current ROI. If the division's current ROI is *less than* 30%, the manager has an incentive to invest in the equipment in order to *increase* the division's overall ROI. However, if the division's current ROI is *greater than* 30%, investing in the equipment would *decrease* the division's ROI. In this case, the manager would probably *not* invest in the equipment.

Thus, residual income enhances goal congruence, whereas ROI may or may not.

Measurement Issues

The ROI and RI calculations appear to be very straightforward; however, management must make some decisions before these calculations can be made. Most of these decisions involve how to measure the assets used in the ROI and RI calculations.

- ***Which balance sheet date should we use?*** Because total assets will differ between the beginning of the period and the end of the period, companies must choose a particular point in time for measuring assets. In the Campbell's example, we chose to use total assets at the *end* of the year. Some companies use the average of the beginning of the year and end of the year.
- ***Should we include all assets?*** Management must also decide if it wants to include *all* assets in the total asset figure. Many firms, such as Kohl's and ALDI, are continually buying land on which to build future retail outlets. Until those stores are built and opened, the land (including any construction in progress) is a nonproductive asset, which is not generating any operating income. Including nonproductive assets in the total asset figure will drive down ROI and RI. Therefore, some firms do not include nonproductive assets in these calculations.
- ***Should we use the gross book value or net book value of the assets?*** The gross book value is the historical cost of the assets. The net book value is the historical cost of the assets *less* accumulated depreciation. Using the net book value of assets has a

definite drawback. Because of depreciation, the net book value of assets continues to decrease over time until the assets are fully depreciated. As a result, ROI and RI get *larger over time simply because of depreciation* rather than from actual improvements in operations.

In general, calculating ROI based on the net book value of assets gives managers incentive to continue using old, outdated equipment because the net book value of the asset keeps decreasing. However, top management may want the division to invest in new technology to create operational efficiency. The long-term effects of using outdated equipment may be devastating as competitors use new technology to produce cheaper products and sell at lower prices. Thus, to create goal congruence, some firms prefer calculating ROI based on the gross book value of assets or even based on the assets' current replacement cost, rather than the assets' net book value.

- ***Should we make other adjustments to income or assets?*** Some companies use a modified residual income calculation referred to as economic value added (EVA®). To arrive at EVA, managers make several adjustments to the way income and assets are measured in the residual income formula. For example, research and development expenses are often added back to income (not viewed as expenses) while total assets are usually reduced by the company's current liabilities. EVA calculations are covered in more advanced accounting and finance textbooks.

Limitations of Financial Performance Evaluation

Since companies have traditionally existed to generate profit for their owners, performance evaluation has historically revolved around financial performance. However, financial performance measurement has limitations. For example, one serious drawback of financial performance measures is their short-term focus. Companies usually prepare performance reports and calculate ROI and RI using a time frame of one year or less. If upper management uses a short time frame, division managers have an incentive to take actions that will lead to an immediate increase in these measures, even if such actions may not be in the company's long-term interest (such as cutting back on R&D or advertising).

On the other hand, many potentially positive actions may take longer than one year to generate income at the targeted level. Many **product life cycles** start slow, even incurring losses in the early stages, before generating profit. If managers are evaluated on short-term financial performance only, they may be hesitant to introduce new products that may take time to generate acceptable profits.

As a potential remedy, management can measure financial performance using a longer time horizon, such as three to five years. Extending the time frame gives segment managers the incentive to think long term rather than short term and make decisions that will positively impact the company over the next several years.

As discussed earlier in this book, many companies are incorporating the triple bottom line (People, Planet, and Profit) into their performance evaluation systems. The second half of this chapter describes how the inclusion of non-financial performance metrics, including environmental metrics, can give managers a more "balanced" view of the company's performance.

Transfer Pricing

In large, diversified companies, one division will often buy products or components from another division rather than buying them from an outside supplier. For example, one division of General Electric may purchase some of the parts it needs to produce wind turbines from another division that makes those parts. The price charged for the internal sale of product between two different divisions of the same company is known as the **transfer price**.

The transfer price becomes sales revenue for the selling division, and a cost for the buying division. Therefore, the operating income, ROI, sales margin, and residual income of each division will be affected by the transfer price that is used. Setting a fair transfer price is often difficult since each division will want to maximize its own profits. The selling division will want the price to be as high as possible, while the buying division will want the price to be as low as possible.

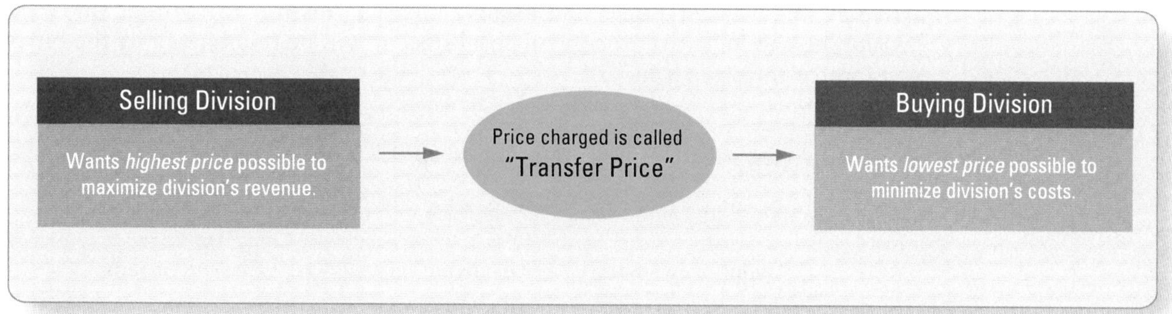

In selecting the transfer price, management's ultimate goal should be to optimize the company's *overall* profitability by encouraging a transfer to take place *only* if the company would benefit by the exchange. This benefit is usually a result of cost savings. For example, if excess capacity exists, the incremental cost of manufacturing additional product for an internal sale is the variable cost of production. Furthermore, the selling division can often avoid certain marketing or distribution costs on internal sales. **Vertical integration**, the practice of purchasing other companies within one's supply chain, is predicated by the notion that a company's profits can be maximized by owning one's supplier.

Strategies for Determining a Transfer Price

The following strategies are often used to determine the transfer price.

1. **Market price**: If an outside market for the product exists, the market price is often viewed as the fairest price to use. The selling division will obtain the sales revenue it would have received on an outside sale, and the buying division will pay what it would have paid for product from an outside supplier. If the selling division can save on marketing or distribution costs, the market price could be reduced by all or a portion of the cost savings in arriving at the transfer price.
2. **Negotiated price**: Division managers negotiate until they reach agreement on a transfer price. The negotiated transfer price will usually be somewhere between the variable cost and the market price. The *lowest* acceptable price to the selling division will be the variable cost of producing and selling the product. Any lower price would result in a negative contribution margin to the selling division. The *highest* acceptable price to the buying division will be the market price. Any higher price would result in additional cost to the buying division. The disadvantage of this method is that negotiation takes time and effort, and may cause friction between company managers.

Why is this important?

"Each division's **profits** will be affected by the **transfer price** that is used. The **selling division** will want the price to be as **high** as possible, whereas the **buying division** will want it to be as **low** as possible."

3. **Cost:** If no outside market for the product exists, then some definition of cost is often used to set the transfer price. As noted above, variable cost would be the lowest fair price to use if excess capacity exists whereas full absorption cost (including fixed manufacturing overhead) is also often viewed as a reasonable price. Additionally, a profit markup can be added to either definition of cost to arrive at fair transfer price. The disadvantage of this method is that the selling division has no incentive to control costs since it will be reimbursed by the buying division for the costs it incurs.

These strategies are summarized in Exhibit 10-9.

EXHIBIT 10-9 Strategies for Determining Transfer Price

	Advantages	Disadvantages	Considerations
Market Price	Usually viewed as fair by both parties.	Can only be used if an outside market exists.	The market price could be reduced by any cost savings occurring from the internal sale (e.g., marketing costs).
Negotiated Price	Allows division managers to act autonomously rather than being dictated a transfer price by top management.	Takes time and effort. May lead to friction (or better understanding) between division managers.	Negotiated transfer price will generally fall in the range between: • Variable cost (low end) • Market price (high end)
Cost or Cost-plus a markup	Useful if a market price is not available.	Selling division has no incentive to control costs. A "fair" markup may be difficult to determine.	Several definitions of cost could be used, ranging from variable cost to full absorption cost.

Global Considerations

In addition to these strategies for setting the transfer price, management should consider the following factors if the divisions operate in different areas of the globe:

- Do the divisions operate under different taxing authorities such that income tax rates are higher for one division than the other?
- Would the amount paid for customs and duties be impacted by the transfer price used?

If either of these situations exist, then management will want to carefully craft the transfer price to avoid as much income tax, customs, and duties as legally possible.

As you can see, setting an optimal transfer price involves careful analysis. Keep in mind that internal sales should only be encouraged if the company, overall, would profit by the exchange taking place. This additional profit is usually the result of cost savings that occur from producing the product internally rather than buying it on the open market. Any transfer price selected is simply a mechanism for dividing this additional profit between the selling and the buying divisions.

In the next half of the chapter, we'll explain flexible budgeting and the balanced scorecard. These are two additional tools that companies often use to extend the way they evaluate performance.

Decision Guidelines

Performance Evaluation

Let's consider some issues regarding performance evaluation.

Decision	Guidelines
How do companies decentralize?	Managers determine the type of segmentation that best suits the company's strategy. Companies often decentralize by geographic area, product line, distribution channel, customer base, or business function.
What should managers be held responsible for?	**Cost center:** Manager is responsible for costs. **Revenue center:** Manager is responsible for revenues. **Profit center:** Manager is responsible for both revenues and costs and, therefore, profits. **Investment center:** Manager is responsible for revenues, costs, and the efficient use of the assets invested in the division.
How should upper management evaluate the performance of the responsibility centers and their managers?	Actual performance should be compared with the budget. Using management by exception, any large variances should be investigated, with an emphasis on uncovering information, rather than placing blame.
How are variances interpreted?	Favorable (F) variances increase income from what was budgeted while Unfavorable (U) variances decrease income. Favorable cost variances are not necessarily "good" and unfavorable cost variances are not necessarily "bad."
What is a segment margin?	A segment margin is the operating income achieved by the segment *before* subtracting any common fixed costs that have been allocated to the segment.
What additional measures are used to evaluate investment centers?	ROI and Residual Income. Both performance measures evaluate the division in terms of how profitable the division is relative to the size of its assets.
How is ROI calculated?	$\text{ROI} = \dfrac{\text{Operating income}}{\text{Total assets}}$ ROI can also be calculated as: $\text{Sales margin} \times \text{Capital turnover}$
How is sales margin calculated?	$\text{Sales margin} = \dfrac{\text{Operating income}}{\text{Sales}}$ The sales margin tells managers how much operating income is earned on every $1 of sales revenue.
How is capital turnover calculated?	$\text{Capital turnover} = \dfrac{\text{Sales}}{\text{Total assets}}$ The capital turnover tells managers how much sales revenue is generated for every $1 of assets invested in the division.
How is residual income calculated?	$\text{RI} = \text{Operating income} - (\text{Target rate of return} \times \text{Total assets})$ If residual income is positive, it means the division has earned income in excess of upper management's target rate of return. If it is negative, then the division has not met management's expectations.
What is a transfer price and how is it determined?	A transfer price is the price charged between divisions for the internal sale of a product. The transfer price is often based on the following: • Market price of product • Negotiated price (usually between variable cost and market price) • Cost (variable or absorption) or cost plus a markup

SUMMARY PROBLEM 1

The following table contains actual segment data for Campbell Soup Company's other two divisions: 1) International Soup, Sauces, and Beverages, and 2) North American Foodservice.

2010 Data (All figures are in millions of dollars)	Operating Income	Assets	Sales Revenue
International Soup, Sauces, and Beverages	$161	$1,396	$1,423
North American Foodservice................................	43	360	578

Requirements

1. Compute each division's ROI.
2. Compute each division's sales margin.
3. Compute each division's capital turnover.
4. Comment on the results of the preceding calculations.
5. Compute each division's residual income, assuming upper management desires a 25% minimum rate of return.
6. How does the financial performance of these two divisions compare to the two divisions, U.S. Soup and Snacking and Baking divisions, discussed in the chapter?

SOLUTIONS

1. ROI

$$\text{International Soup ROI} = \frac{161}{1,396} = 11.5\% \text{ (rounded)}$$

$$\text{North American Foodservice ROI} = \frac{43}{360} = 11.9\% \text{ (rounded)}$$

2. Sales Margin

$$\text{International Soup sales margin} = \frac{161}{1,423} = 11.3\% \text{ (rounded)}$$

$$\text{North American Foodservice sales margin} = \frac{43}{578} = 7.4\% \text{ (rounded)}$$

3. Capital Turnover

$$\text{International Soup capital turnover} = \frac{1{,}423}{1{,}396} = 1.02 \text{ (rounded)}$$

$$\text{North American Foodservice capital turnover} = \frac{578}{360} = 1.61 \text{ (rounded)}$$

4. Both divisions are earning about the same ROI (11.5% versus 11.9%). However, the reasons for their ROI differ. The International Soup division is earning a higher profit on every dollar sold (11.3% versus 7.4%), but generating less sales revenue with every dollar of assets ($1.02 versus $1.61). To increase ROI, the International Soup division needs to concentrate on becoming more efficient with its assets in order to increase its capital turnover. The Foodservice division needs to concentrate on cutting costs in order to increase its sales margin.

5. Residual Income

$$\text{International Soup RI} = \$161 - (25\% \times \$1{,}396) = (\$188)$$

$$\text{North American Foodservice RI} = \$43 - (25\% \times \$360) = (\$47)$$

Assuming management's minimum acceptable rate of return is 25%, the negative residual income means that neither division is generating income at an acceptable level.

6. The ROI provided by the US Soup division (44%) and Baking and Snacking division (19%) are both higher than the ROI provided by the International division (11.5%) and Foodservice division (11.9%).

How do Managers Use Flexible Budgets to Evaluate Performance?

4 Prepare and evaluate Flexible Budget Performance Reports

In the first part of this chapter we looked at performance reports that compared actual costs with budgeted amounts. There is nothing wrong with comparing actual results against the master planning budget. Many companies do so. However, managers usually gain better insights by comparing actual results against a **flexible budget**, which is a budget prepared for a different level of volume than that which was originally anticipated.

To illustrate this concept, let's return to Tucson Tortilla, the company we used in Chapter 9 to illustrate budgeting. Exhibit 10-10 shows a performance report for sales revenue and operating expenses that compares actual results against the master (planning) budget. The budgeted information was taken from the Sales Budget (see Exhibit 9-5) and Operating Expenses Budget (see Exhibit 9-10), while the actual results were gathered from the company's general ledger.

EXHIBIT 10-10 Master Budget Performance Report

Tucson Tortilla
Master Budget Performance Report—Sales and Operating Expenses
For the month ended March 31

	Actual 28,724 cases	Master Budget 25,000 cases	Master Budget Variance 3,724F	Variance % 14.9%F
Sales revenue				
($20 per case)	$603,225	$500,000	$103,225 F	20.6% F
Variable operating expenses:				
Sales commission expense				
($1.50 per case sold)	$ 45,960	$37,500	$8,460 U	22.5% U
Shipping expense				
($2.00 per case sold)	54,578	50,000	4,578 U	9.2% U
Bad debt expense				
(1% of credit sales*)	5,127	4,000	1,127 U	28.2% U
Fixed operating expenses:				
Salaries	21,000	20,000	1,000 U	5% U
Office rent	4,000	4,000	0	0%
Depreciation	6,000	6,000	0	0%
Advertising	2,800	2,000	800 U	40% U
Telephone and internet	980	1,000	20 F	2% F
Total operating expenses	$140,445	$124,500	$15,945 U	12.8% U

* The company assumed 80% of sales would be made on credit terms.

The difference between the actual revenues and expenses and the master budget is known as a **master budget variance**. This variance is really the result of an "apples-to-oranges" comparison. Why is this the case? Notice how the comparison is made between actual results for one volume (28,724 cases) and the budgeted revenues and costs for the planning volume (25,000). Of course, we would expect the actual revenues and variable expenses to be higher than budgeted simply because sales volume was 14.9% higher than budgeted. However, we wouldn't expect fixed costs to change as long as the actual volume was still within the relevant range of operations. But notice that actual expenses were 0% to 40% higher than expected. Management will want to understand why these variances occurred.

To provide more of an "apples-to-apples" comparison, many companies compare actual results to a flexible budget prepared *for the actual volume achieved*. This flexible budget will be used strictly for evaluating performance. Notice the distinction between the purposes of the two budgets:

- The original master budget for 25,000 cases was used for *planning purposes at the beginning of the period.*
- The new flexible budget for 28,724 cases will be used for *performance evaluation purposes at the end of the period.*

In essence, the flexible budget is the budget managers *would have* prepared at the beginning of the period if they had a crystal ball telling them the correct volume. The flexible budget allows managers to compare actual revenues and expenses with what they would have expected them to be given the actual volume. By creating a flexible budget, managers will be able to determine the portion of the master budget variance that is due to unanticipated volume and the portion of the master budget variance that is due to causes other than volume.

Creating a Flexible Budget Performance Report

To create a flexible budget like the one shown in Exhibit 10-11, managers simply use the actual volume achieved (28,724 cases) and the original budget assumptions (shown in parentheses). For example, the flexible budget shown in Exhibit 10-11 (in boldface) includes the following calculations:

- Sales Revenue: 28,724 cases × $20 per case = $574,480
- Sales Commission: 28,724 cases × $1.50 per case = $43,086
- Shipping Expense: 28,724 cases × $2.00 per case = $57,448
- Bad Debt Expense: $574,480 of flexible budget sales revenue × 80% credit × 1% = $4,596
- Fixed Operating Expense: should not be affected by changes in volume. Therefore, the flexible budget amounts are the same as originally budgeted in the master budget.

EXHIBIT 10-11 Creating a Flexible Budget Performance Report

Tucson Tortilla
Flexible Budget Performance Report—Sales and Operating Expenses
For the month ended March 31

	Actual 28,724 cases	Flexible Budget Variance	Flexible Budget 28,724 cases	Volume Variance	Master Budget 25,000 cases
Sales revenue					
($20 per case)	$603,225		**$574,480**		$500,000
Variable operating expenses:					
Sales commission expense					
($1.50 per case sold)	$ 45,960		**$ 43,086**		$ 37,500
Shipping expense					
($2.00 per case sold)	54,578		**57,448**		50,000
Bad debt expense					
(1% of credit sales*)	5,127		**4,596**		4,000
Fixed operating expenses:					
Salaries	21,000		**20,000**		20,000
Office rent	4,000		**4,000**		4,000
Depreciation	6,000		**6,000**		6,000
Advertising	2,800		**2,000**		2,000
Telephone & internet	980		**1,000**		1,000
Total operating expenses	$140,445		**$138,130**		$124,500

* The company assumed 80% of sales would be made on credit terms.

Notice how this performance report includes the same actual costs and master budget figures shown in Exhibit 10-10. In addition, the flexible budget is placed in the middle column of the performance report. Two columns flank the middle column: Volume Variance and the Flexible Budget Variance.

Volume Variance

Accounting Simplified

Volume and Flexible-Budget Variances

If your instructor is using MyAccountingLab, go to the Multimedia Library for a quick video on this topic.

The volume variance is the difference between the master budget and the flexible budget. Recall that the only difference between these two budgets is the *volume* of units on which they are based. They both use the *same* budget assumptions, but a different volume. The master budget is based on 25,000 cases. The flexible budget is based on 28,724 cases. The volume variance arises *only* because the volume of cases actually sold differs from the volume originally anticipated in the master budget, hence the name *volume variance*. The volume variances are shown in blue ink in Exhibit 10-12.

EXHIBIT 10-12 Volume Variances

Tucson Tortilla
Flexible Budget Performance Report—Sales and Operating Expenses
For the month ended March 31

	Actual 28,724 cases	Flexible Budget Variance	Flexible Budget 28,724 cases	Volume Variance	Master Budget 25,000 cases
Sales revenue					
($20 per case)	$603,225		$574,480	$74,480 F	$500,000
Variable operating expenses:					
Sales commission expense					
($1.50 per case sold)	$ 45,960		$ 43,086	$ 5,586 U	$ 37,500
Shipping expense					
($2.00 per case sold)	54,578		57,448	7,448 U	50,000
Bad debt expense					
(1% of credit sales*)	5,127		4,596	596 U	4,000
Fixed operating expenses:					
Salaries	21,000		20,000	0	20,000
Office rent	4,000		4,000	0	4,000
Depreciation	6,000		6,000	0	6,000
Advertising	2,800		2,000	0	2,000
Telephone & internet	980		1,000	0	1,000
Total operating expenses	$140,445		$138,130	$13,630 U	$124,500

The volume variance represents the portion of the master budget variance in Exhibit 10-10 that management would expect considering that 3,724 more cases were sold than originally anticipated. For example, because of the increase in sales volume, the volume variance shows that

- sales revenue *should be* $74,480 higher than originally budgeted, and
- total operating expenses *should be* $13,630 higher than originally budgeted.

However, the master budget variance in Exhibit 10-10 revealed that

- sales revenue is *actually* $103,225 higher than budgeted, and
- total operating expenses are *actually* $15,985 higher than budgeted.

So, why are actual revenues and expenses still higher than they should be, even considering the volume increase? The answers can be found in the flexible budget variance.

Flexible Budget Variance

The flexible budget variance is the difference between the flexible budget and actual results. The flexible budget variances are shown in dark orange ink in Exhibit 10-13.

EXHIBIT 10-13 Flexible Budget Variances and Volume Variances

Tucson Tortilla
Flexible Budget Performance Report—Sales and Operating Expenses
For the month ended March 31

	Actual 28,724 cases	Flexible Budget Variance	Flexible Budget 28,724 cases	Volume Variance	Master Budget 25,000 cases
Sales revenue					
($20 per case)	$603,225	$28,745 F	$574,480	$74,480 F	$500,000
Variable operating expenses:					
Sales commission expense					
($1.50 per case sold)	$ 45,960	$ 2,874 U	$ 43,086	$ 5,586 U	$ 37,500
Shipping expense					
($2.00 per case sold)	54,578	2,870 F	57,448	7,448 U	50,000
Bad debt expense					
(1% of credit sales*)	5,127	531 U	4,596	596 U	4,000
Fixed operating expenses:					
Salaries	21,000	1,000 U	20,000	0	20,000
Office rent	4,000	0	4,000	0	4,000
Depreciation	6,000	0	6,000	0	6,000
Advertising	2,800	800 U	2,000	0	2,000
Telephone & internet	980	20 F	1,000	0	1,000
Total operating expenses	$140,445	$ 2,315 U	$138,130	$13,630 U	$124,500

Since all variances related to volume have already been accounted for through the volume variance, the flexible budget variance highlights *causes other than volume*. For example:

- The $28,745 F variance for sales revenue must mean that the cases were sold at an average price *higher* than $20 per case.
- The $2,874 U variance for commission expense must mean that the commissions were paid at a rate *higher* than $1.50 per case.
- The $2,870 F variance for shipping expense must mean that the shipping costs were *lower* than $2.00 per case.
- The $531 U variance for bad debt expense must mean that either more than 80% of sales were made on credit or bad debts were expensed at a rate greater than 1%.

Underlying Causes of the Variances

As discussed in the first half of the chapter, managers will use *management by exception* to determine which variances to investigate. Upper management will rely on the managers of each responsibility center to provide answers to their inquiries. At other times, upper management already knows the reasons for the variances, yet needs the performance report to understand how their operational decisions affected the company's finances.

For example, let's assume that upper management decided to modify its sales strategy beginning in March from the original plan found in the master budget. In order to increase sales, upper management decided to

- spend more on advertising
- increase the salaries of the sales staff
- pay a higher sales commission per case, and
- ease credit terms so that more sales qualified for credit, rather than COD terms.

The unfavorable *flexible budget cost variances* shown in Exhibit 10-13 reflect these operational changes. However, the *sales volume variances* in Exhibit 10-13 also show the positive effect of these changes: the additional sales revenue was more than enough to offset the increased costs. Not only was extra sales volume generated, but sales were also made at a higher price per case than budgeted (as shown by the flexible budget variance for sales revenue). Finally, as a result of the increased volume, management was able to negotiate a lower shipping cost per case, resulting in a favorable flexible budget variance for shipping. All in all, management's strategy paid off.

Master Budget Variance: A Combination of Variances

Now that we have prepared a flexible budget performance report, it's easy to see how the master budget variance can be viewed as a combination of two separate variances, the 1) volume variance and 2) flexible budget variance. This combination is summarized in Exhibit 10-14.

EXHIBIT 10-14 Master Budget Variance

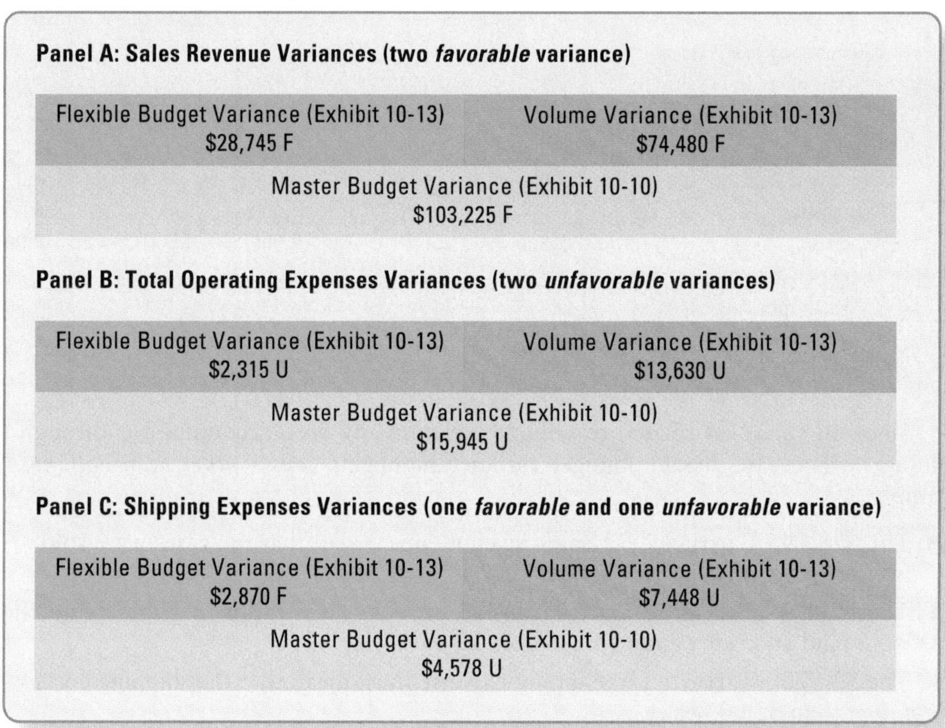

In Exhibit 10-14, notice how the master budget variance could be a combination of *favorable* variances (as in Panel A), a combination of *unfavorable* variances (as in Panel B) or a combination of one favorable variance *and* one unfavorable variance (as in Panel C).

For example, in Panel C we see the variances for Shipping Expenses consist of a *favorable* flexible budget variance ($2,870 F) and an *unfavorable* volume variance ($7,448 U). Together, these two variances *net* to an unfavorable master budget variance of $4,578 U. This example illustrates why it's important to separate the overall master budget variance into its two components. Only by separating the variances would a manager know that the shipping expenses were actually lower per case than anticipated, but higher overall due to the volume of cases shipped.

Decomposing the Flexible Budget Variance

We have just seen how the master budget variance can be decomposed into a volume variance and a flexible budget variance. If managers want, they can decompose the *flexible budget variance* into two additional variances (a price variance and an efficiency variance) to better understand what is causing the flexible budget variance. Manufacturers often do this for their direct materials, direct labor, and manufacturing overhead costs. All of Chapter 11 is devoted to calculating these more detailed manufacturing variances.

How do Companies Incorporate Nonfinancial Performance Measurement?

5 Describe the balanced scorecard and identify KPIs for each perspective

In the past, performance evaluation systems revolved almost entirely around *financial* performance. On the one hand, this focus makes sense because one of the primary goals of any company, even those that adhere to the notion of a triple bottom line (profit, people, and planet), is to generate profit for its owners. On the other hand, *current* financial performance tends to reveal the results of *past* decisions and actions rather than indicate *future* performance of the company. As a result, financial performance measures are known as **lag indicators**. Management also needs **lead indicators**, which are performance measures that predict future performance.

The Balanced Scorecard

In the early 1990s, Robert Kaplan and David Norton introduced the **balanced scorecard**.[6] The balanced scorecard recognizes that management must consider *both* financial performance measures *and* operational performance measures when judging the performance of a company and its segments. These measures should be linked with the company's goals and its strategy for achieving those goals. The balanced scorecard represents a major shift in corporate performance measurement: Financial indicators are no longer the sole measure of performance; they are now only *one* measure among a broader set of performance measures. Keeping score of operational performance measures *and* traditional financial performance measures gives management a "balanced," comprehensive view of the organization.

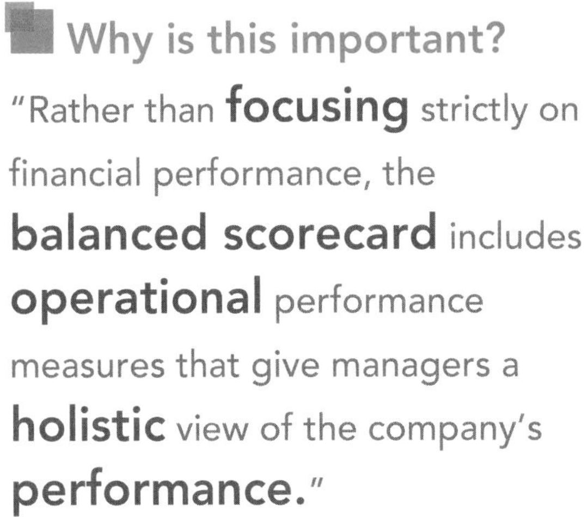

The Four Perspectives of the Balanced Scorecard

The balanced scorecard views the company from four different perspectives, each of which evaluates a specific aspect of organizational performance:

1. Financial perspective
2. Customer perspective
3. Internal business perspective
4. Learning and growth perspective

If your instructor is using MyAccountingLab, go to the Multimedia Library for a quick video on this topic.

Exhibit 10-15 (on the next page) illustrates how the company's strategy affects, and, in turn, is affected by all four perspectives. In addition, it shows the cause-and-effect relationship linking the four perspectives.

Companies that adopt the balanced scorecard develop specific objectives they want to achieve within each of the four perspectives. These objectives are critical to the company's overall success. As shown in Exhibit 10-16, company's use **key performance indicators (KPIs)**, which are summary performance metrics, to assess how well a company is achieving its goals. For example, the company could use "*average customer satisfaction rating*" as a KPI to measure the company's ability to please customers. "*Number of warranty claims*" could be used to measure the company's ability to produce quality products.

KPIs are continually measured, and are reported on a **performance scorecard** or **performance dashboard**, a report that allows managers to visually monitor and focus on managing the company's key activities and strategies as well as business risks.[7] Short-term and long-term targets for each KPI should also be displayed on the dashboard or scorecard

[6] Robert Kaplan and David Norton, "The Balanced Scorecard—Measures That Drive Performance," *Harvard Business Review on Measuring Corporate Performance*, Boston, 1991, pp. 123-145; Robert Kaplan and David Norton, *Translating Strategy into Action: The Balanced Scorecard*, Boston, Harvard Business School Press, 1996.
[7] Wayne Eckerson. Performance Dashboards: Measuring, monitoring and managing your business. John Wiley & Sons. 2006. Brian Ballou, Dan Heitger, and Laura Donnell, "Creating Effective Dashboards," *Strategic Finance*, March 2010.

EXHIBIT 10-15 The four perspectives of the Balanced Scorecard

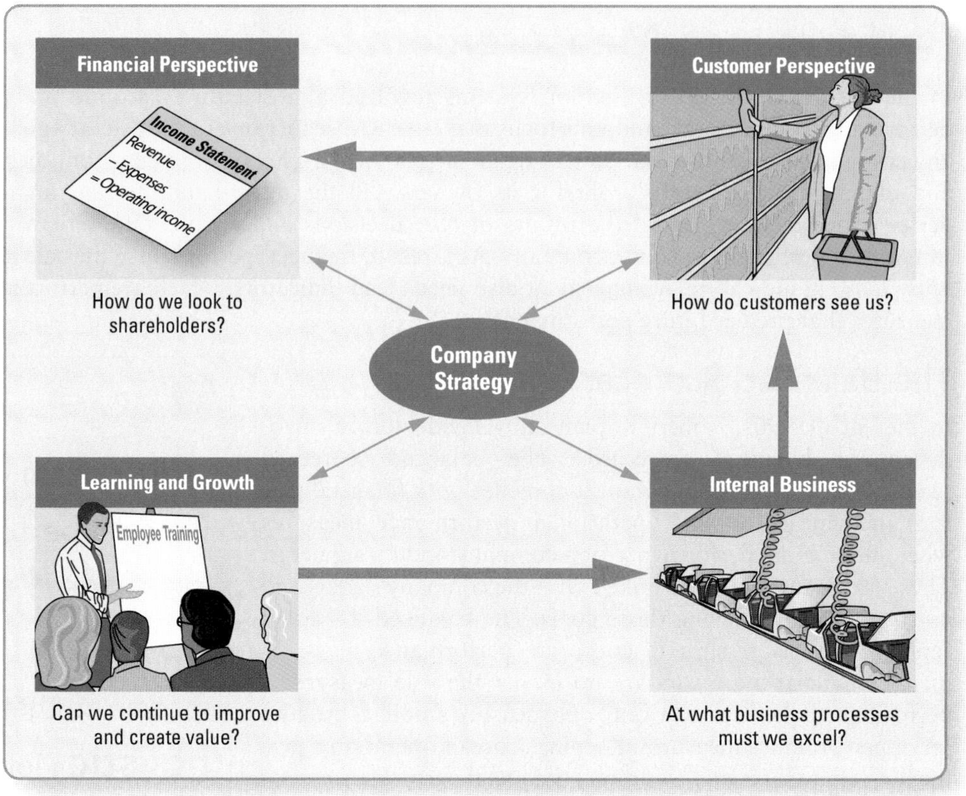

Financial Perspective
Income Statement
Revenue
− Expenses
= Operating income
How do we look to shareholders?
Customer Perspective
How do customers see us?
Company Strategy
Learning and Growth
Employee Training
Can we continue to improve and create value?
Internal Business
At what business processes must we excel?

EXHIBIT 10-16 Linking Company Goals to Key Performance Indicators

COMPANY GOALS
Examples of Critical Factors and Corresponding KPIs
CRITICAL FACTORS
customer satisfaction
operational efficiency
employee excellence
financial profitability
KEY PERFORMANCE INDICATORS (KPIs)
market share
yield rate
employee training hours
revenue growth

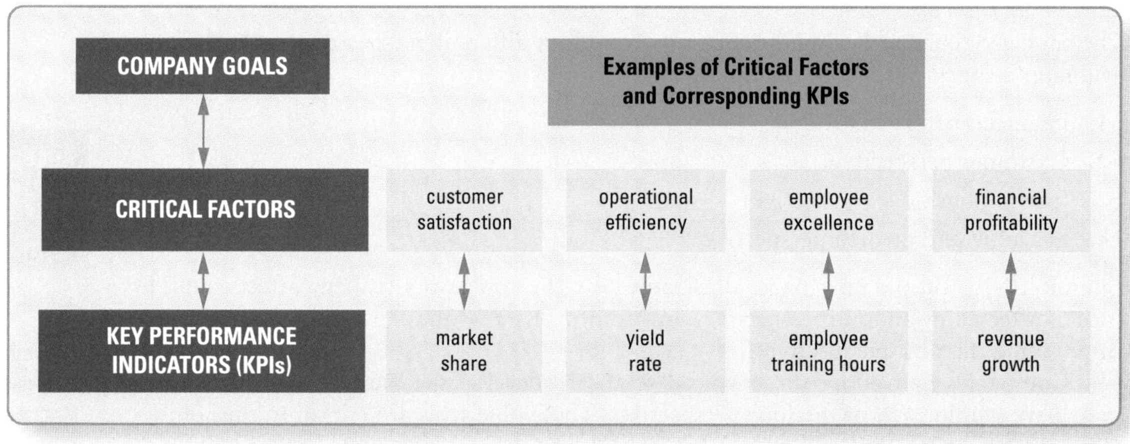

so that managers can determine whether the company is improving and moving towards each objective, or whether new strategies need to be developed. To focus attention on the most critical elements to success and to prevent information overload, management should use only a few KPIs for each balanced scorecard perspective.

Let's now consider each of the perspectives and how they are linked together. We'll also present some of the more commonly used KPIs.

Financial Perspective

The financial perspective helps managers answer the question, "*How do we look to shareholders?*" Shareholders are primarily concerned with the company's profitability. As shown in Exhibit 10-17, managers must continually attempt to increase profits through the following:

1. **increasing revenue:** introducing new products, gaining new customers, expanding into new markets
2. **controlling costs:** seeking to minimize costs without jeopardizing quality or long-run success, eliminating costs associated with wasteful activities
3. **increasing productivity:** using existing assets as efficiently as possible

EXHIBIT 10-17 Financial Perspective

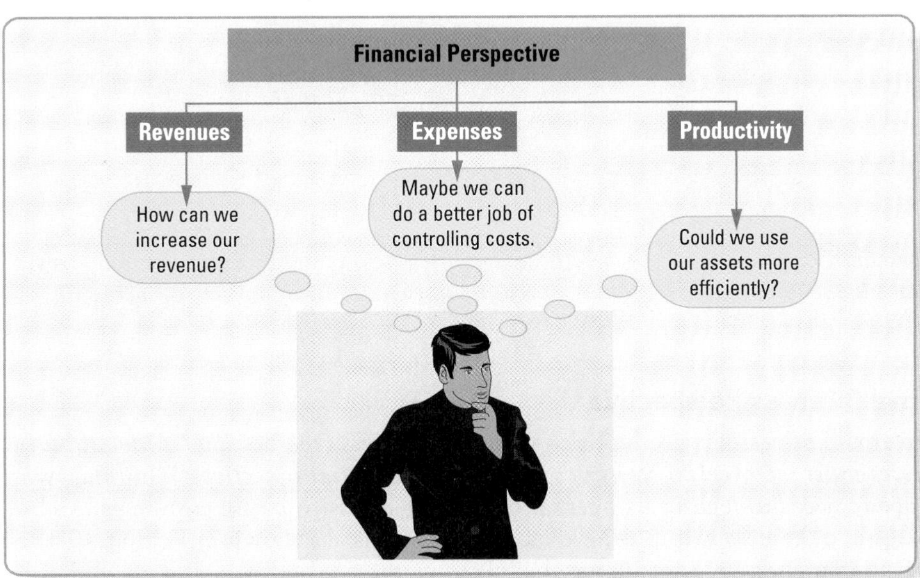

Common KPIs: *sales revenue growth, sales margin, gross margin percentage, capital turnover, ROI, Residual income, earnings per share*

Customer Perspective

The customer perspective helps managers evaluate the question, "*How do customers see us?*" Customer satisfaction is a top priority for long-term success. If customers aren't happy, they won't come back. Therefore, customer satisfaction is critical for the company to achieve its financial goals.

As shown in Exhibit 10-18, customers are typically concerned with four product or service attributes:

1. **price:** the lower the better
2. **quality:** the higher, the better
3. **sales service:** importance of knowledgeable and helpful salespeople
4. **delivery time:** the shorter the better

EXHIBIT 10-18 Customer Perspective

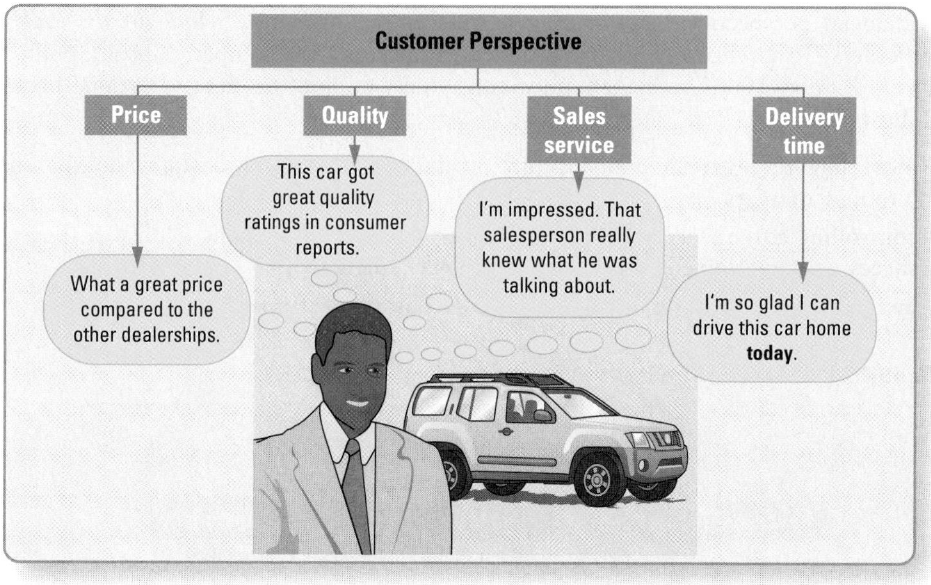

Common KPIs: *average customer satisfaction rating, percentage of market share, increase in the number of customers, number of repeat customers, rate of on-time deliveries.*

Internal Business Perspective

The internal business perspective helps managers address the question, "***At what business processes must we excel to satisfy customer and financial objectives?***" In other words, a company needs to tend to its internal operations if it is to please customers. And only by pleasing customers will it achieve its financial goals. As shown in Exhibit 10-19, the answer to that question incorporates the following three factors:

1. **innovation:** developing new products, such as the iPad and Wii
2. **operations:** using lean operating techniques, as discussed in Chapter 4, to increase efficiency
3. **post-sales support:** providing excellent customer service after the sale

Learning and Growth Perspective

The learning and growth perspective helps managers assess the question, "***Can we continue to improve and create value?***" Much of a company's success boils down to its people. A company cannot be successful in the other perspectives (financial, customer, internal operations) if it does not have the right people in the right positions, a solid and ethical leadership team, and the information systems that employees need. Therefore, the learning and growth perspective lays the foundation needed for success in the other perspectives. As shown in Exhibit 10-20, the learning and growth perspective focuses on the following three factors:

1. **employee capabilities:** critical and creative thinkers, skilled, knowledgeable, motivated
2. **information system capabilities:** a system that provides timely and accurate data
3. **the company's "climate for action:"** corporate culture supports communication, teamwork, change, and employee growth

EXHIBIT 10-19 Internal Business Perspective

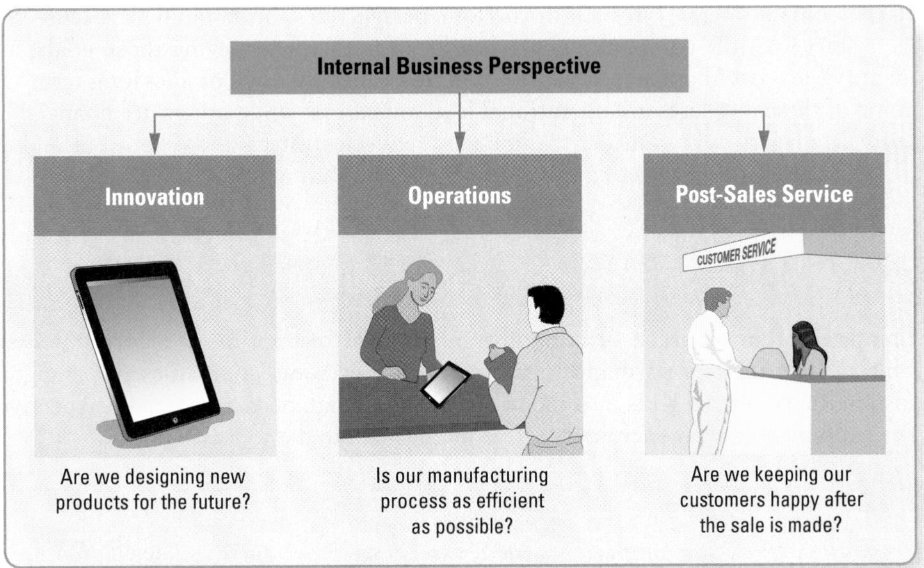

Common KPIs: *number of new products developed, new product development time, defect rate, manufacturing lead time, yield rate, number of warranty claims received, average customer wait time for customer service, average repair time*

EXHIBIT 10-20 Learning and Growth Perspective

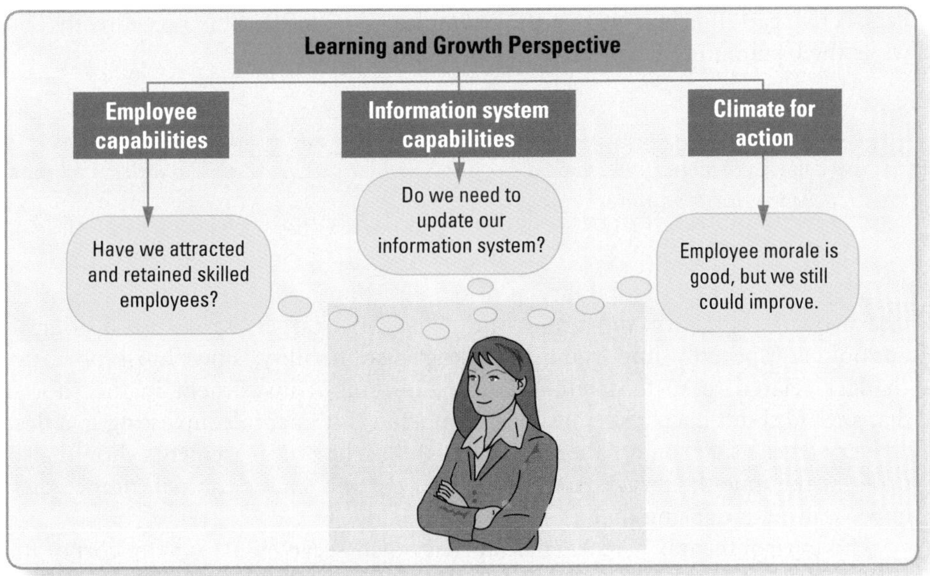

Common KPIs: *hours of employee training, employee satisfaction, employee turnover, percentage of processes with real-time feedback, percentage of employees with access to real-time data, number of employee suggestions implemented, percentage of employees involved in problem solving teams, employee rating of communication and corporate culture*

In summary, the balanced scorecard focuses performance measurement on progress toward the company's goals in each of the four perspectives. In designing the scorecard, managers start with the company's goals and its strategy for achieving those goals, and then identify the *most* important measures of performance that will predict long-term success. Some of these measures are operational lead indicators, while others are financial lag indicators. Managers must consider the linkages between strategy and operations and the way those operations will affect finances now and in the future.

Sustainability and Performance Evaluation

Companies that embrace sustainability and social responsibility incorporate relevant KPIs in their performance evaluation system. Some companies will integrate sustainability-related KPIs into the four traditional balanced scorecard perspectives. For example, KPIs for each perspective might include the following:[8]

- Financial: *water cost, recycling revenues, waste disposal costs*
- Customer: *number of green products, percentage of products reclaimed after use*
- Internal Business: *energy consumption, water consumption, greenhouse gas emissions*
- Learning and Growth: *number of functions with environmental responsibilities, management attention to environmental issues*

Other companies add a fifth perspective, "Sustainability," or even add a sixth perspective, "Community," to reflect triple bottom line goals. The Sustainability Perspective could include any of the examples given in the blue box directly above, while the Community Perspective might include:

- Community: *percentage of profit donated to local schools and organizations, percentage of materials sourced locally, product safety ratings, number of hours devoted to local volunteering*

KPIs relating to sustainability and social responsibility should be objective and measurable, with both short-term and long-term targets specified. A long-term outlook is especially important regarding sustainability, since most operational changes related to sustainability require substantial investment in the short-run that should result in cost savings in the long-run (for example, investing in a fleet of delivery trucks that run on alternative fuels). Baseline measurements should also be taken at the time the targets are adopted, so that managers can determine whether improvements are being made.

The environmental performance metrics also serve as a way for corporations to report their journey towards sustainability to stakeholders. For example, many companies, including Campbell Soup Company, now publish an annual Corporate Responsibility Report in addition to their annual financial report. This report details the company's environmental goals and summarizes the company's progress towards them.

See Exercises E10-32A and E10-49B

[8]M.J. Epstein and P.S. Wisner. "Using a Balanced Scorecard to Implement Sustainability," *Environmental Quality Management*, 2001.

Decision Guidelines

Performance Evaluation and the Balanced Scorecard

Decision	Guidelines
How can flexible budgets aid in performance evaluation?	There is nothing wrong with comparing actual results against the master planning budget. However, managers usually gain additional insights by comparing actual results against a flexible budget, which is a budget prepared for the actual volume achieved, rather than the volume originally used for planning purposes.
What is the master budget variance?	The master budget variance is the difference between the actual results and the master planning budget. This variance can be decomposed into two separate variances: 1) a volume variance, and 2) a flexible budget variance, by first creating a flexible budget.
How is a flexible budget prepared?	A flexible budget is prepared by multiplying the budgeted revenue per unit and variable cost per unit by the actual volume achieved. Since total fixed costs are not affected by changes in volume, they are the same on the flexible budget as they were on the original master budget. The flexible budget presents the revenues and expenses that management would have expected, given the actual volume achieved.
What is the volume variance?	The volume variance is the difference between the master planning budget and the flexible budget. It represents the portion of the master budget variance that was caused by actual volume being different than originally budgeted.
What is the flexible budget variance?	The flexible budget variance is the difference between actual costs and the flexible budget. It represents the portion of the master budget variance that was caused by factors *other than* volume differences.
Should the performance evaluation system include lag or lead measures?	Better performance evaluation systems include *both* lag and lead measures. Lag measures reveal the results of past actions, while lead measures project future performance.
What are the four balanced scorecard perspectives?	1. Financial perspective 2. Customer perspective 3. Internal business perspective 4. Learning and growth perspective
How do companies include sustainability-related KPIs in their balanced scorecards?	Companies either include sustainability-related KPIs within each of the four perspectives, or they add separate perspectives for sustainability and/or corporate responsibility.

SUMMARY PROBLEM 2

Requirements

1. Each of the following describes a key performance indicator. Determine which of the balanced scorecard perspectives is being addressed (financial, customer, internal business, or learning and growth).
   a. Employee turnover
   b. Earnings per share
   c. Percentage of on-time deliveries
   d. Revenue growth rate
   e. Percentage of defects discovered during manufacturing
   f. Number of warranties claimed
   g. New product development time
   h. Number of repeat customers
   i. Number of employee suggestions implemented
2. Read the following company initiatives and determine which of the balanced scorecard perspectives is being addressed (financial, customer, internal business, or learning and growth).
   a. Purchasing efficient production equipment
   b. Providing employee training
   c. Updating retail store lighting
   d. Paying quarterly dividends
   e. Updating the company's information system

SOLUTIONS

Requirement 1

a. Learning and growth
b. Financial
c. Customer
d. Financial
e. Internal business
f. Internal business
g. Internal business
h. Customer
i. Learning and growth

Requirement 2

a. Internal business
b. Learning and growth
c. Customer
d. Financial
e. Learning and growth

END OF CHAPTER

Learning Objectives

- 1 Understand decentralization and describe different types of responsibility centers
- 2 Develop performance reports
- 3 Calculate ROI, sales margin, and capital turnover
- 4 Prepare and evaluate flexible budget performance reports
- 5 Describe the balanced scorecard and identify KPIs for each perspective

Accounting Vocabulary

Balanced Scorecard. (p. 613) A performance evaluation system designed by Kaplan and Norton that integrates financial and operational performance measures along four perspectives: financial, customer, internal business, and learning and growth.

Capital Turnover. (p. 599) Sales revenue divided by total assets. The capital turnover shows how much sales revenue is generated with every $1.00 of assets.

Common fixed expenses. (p. 595) Fixed expenses that *cannot* be traced to the segment. Rather, these are fixed expenses incurred by a higher level segment that have been allocated to the underlying segments.

Cost center. (p. 592) A responsibility center in which managers are responsible for controlling costs.

Decentralize. (p. 590) Companies that split their operations into different operating segments.

Direct fixed expenses. (p. 595) Fixed expenses that can be traced to the segment.

Favorable variance. (p. 594) A variance that causes operating income to be higher than budgeted.

Flexible budget. (p. 608) A summarized budget prepared for different levels of volume.

Flexible Budget Variance. (p. 610) The difference between the flexible budget and actual results. The flexible budget variances are due to *something other than volume.*

Goal Congruence. (p. 591) When the goals of the segment managers align with the goals of top management.

Gross Book Value. (p. 601) Historical cost of assets.

Investment center. (p. 592) A responsibility center in which managers are responsible for generating revenues, controlling costs, and efficiently managing the division's assets.

Key performance indicators (KPIs). (p. 613) Summary performance metrics that allow managers to assess how well the company's objectives are being met.

Lag indicators. (p. 613) Performance indicators that reveal the results of past actions and decisions.

Lead indicators. (p. 613) Performance measures that predict future performance.

Management by exception. (p. 594) A management technique in which managers only investigate budget variances that are relatively large.

Master Budget variance. (p. 608) The difference between actual results and the master budget.

Net Book Value. (p. 601) Historical cost of assets less accumulated depreciation.

Performance reports. (p. 594) Reports that compare actual results against budgeted figures.

Performance scorecard or dashboard. (p. 613) A report displaying the measurement of KPIs, as well as their short-term and long-term targets. The report allows managers to visually monitor and focus on managing the company's key activities and strategies as well as business risks.

Profit center. (p. 592) A responsibility center in which managers are responsible for both revenues and costs, therefore, profits.

Residual income. (p. 600) Operating income minus the minimum acceptable operating income given the size of the division's assets. Residual income shows whether the division is earning income above or below management's expectations.

Responsibility accounting. (p. 591) A system for evaluating the performance of each responsibility center and its manager.

Responsibility Center. (p. 591) A part of an organization whose manager is accountable for planning and controlling certain activities.

Return on Investment (ROI). (p. 597) Operating income divided by total assets. The ROI measures the profitability of a division relative to the size of its assets.

Revenue center. (p. 592) A responsibility center in which managers are responsible for generating revenue.

Sales margin. (p. 598) Operating income divided by sales revenue. The sales margin shows how much income is generated for every $1.00 of sales.

Segment margin. (p. 595) The operating income generated by a profit or investment center *before* subtracting the common fixed costs that have been allocated to the center.

Unfavorable variance. (p. 594) A variance that causes operating income to be lower than budgeted.

Variance. (p. 594) The difference between an actual amount and the budget.

Volume variance. (p. 610) The difference between the master budget and the flexible budget. The volume variance arises *only* because the volume of cases actually sold differs from the volume originally anticipated in the master budget.

Quick Check

1. *(Learning Objective 1)* Which is not one of the potential advantages of decentralization?
   a. Improves customer relations
   b. Increases goal congruence
   c. Improves motivation and retention
   d. Supports use of expert knowledge

2. *(Learning Objective 1)* The McDonald's Division of The Coca-Cola Company is *most likely* treated as a
   a. cost center.
   b. revenue center.
   c. profit center.
   d. investment center.

3. *(Learning Objective 2)* When management only investigates budget variances that are large, this is an example of
   a. management by principles.
   b. management by exception.
   c. management by objectives.
   d. management by reasonability.

4. *(Learning Objective 3)* Which of the following is a disadvantage of financial performance measures such as Return on Investment (ROI) and residual income?
   a. not readily understood by managers
   b. focus on short-term performance
   c. cannot be used in a balanced scorecard
   d. cannot be used to evaluate division performance

5. *(Learning Objective 3)* For which type of responsibility center would it be appropriate to measure performance using Return on Investment (ROI)?
   a. Cost center
   b. Revenue center
   c. Profit center
   d. Investment center

6. *(Learning Objective 3)* The following are all common strategies to determine the transfer price between divisions *except* for
   a. competitor cost.
   b. cost.
   c. market price.
   d. negotiated price.

7. *(Learning Objective 4)* A flexible budget
   a. is used for planning purposes at only the beginning of the period.
   b. contains only variable costs but does not include fixed costs since fixed costs do not change.
   c. contains a plan for a range of activity levels so that the plan can be adjusted to reflect changes in activity level.
   d. is the plan for one level of activity and cannot be adjusted for changes in the level of activity.

8. *(Learning Objective 4)* The volume variance on a flexible budget report is the difference between the
   a. actual results and the static budget.
   b. actual results and the flexible budget.
   c. master budget and the actual results.
   d. master budget and the flexible budget.

9. *(Learning Objective 5)* Average repair time on products returned for service would be a typical measure for which of the following balanced scorecard perspectives?
   a. financial
   b. customer
   c. internal business
   d. learning and growth

10. *(Learning Objective 5)* Which of the following balanced scorecard perspectives essentially asks the question, "Can we continue to improve and create value?"
   a. financial
   b. customer
   c. internal business
   d. learning and growth

Quick Check Answers

1. b 2. d 3. b 4. b 5. d 6. a 7. c 8. d 9. c 10. d

Short Exercises

S10-1 Identify responsibility centers *(Learning Objective 1)*

Fill in the blanks with the phrase that best completes the sentence. Not all phrases are used and some phrases may be used more than once.

A cost center	**A responsibility center**	**Lower**
An investment center	**A revenue center**	**Higher**
A profit center	**The same**	

a. The Shoe Department at Target Stores, which is responsible for buying and selling merchandise, is ________.

b. ________ is any segment of the business whose manager is accountable for specific activities.

c. Managers of cost and revenue centers are at ________ levels of the organization than are managers of profit and investment centers.

d. The sales manager in charge of Nike's Northeast sales territory oversees ________.

e. The Pharmacy Department of the Green Township Giant Eagle grocery store is ________.

f. The Accounting Department at Macy's, Inc. (a retailer with stores across the United States), is ________.

g. HP's Imaging and Printing Group (IPG), a division of the Hewlett-Packard Company, produces and sells printing and scanning equipment; IPG would be ________.

h. The production line at the Ford Rouge plant in Dearborn, Michigan, where Ford F-150 trucks are manufactured, is considered ________.

i. Honda North America, a division of The Honda Motor Company, is ________.

j. The North Canton location of the chain Damon's Grill and Sports Bar is ________.

S10-2 Identify types of responsibility centers *(Learning Objective 1)*

Identify each responsibility center as a cost center, a revenue center, a profit center, or an investment center.

a. Coca-Cola's investor relations website provides operating and financial information to investors and other interested parties.

b. The manager of the Speedway, a gasoline and convenience store located in Forest Lake, Minnesota, is evaluated based on the station's revenues and expenses.

c. A charter airline records revenues and expenses for each airplane each month. Each airplane's performance report shows its ratio of operating income to average book value.

d. The manager of the southwest sales territory is evaluated based on a comparison of current period sales against budgeted sales.

e. The Pharmacy Department of an Acme supermarket reports income for the current year.

f. Speedway is a subsidiary of Marathon Oil Corporation; Speedway owns and operates approximately 1,350 gasoline and convenience stores in the United States.

g. The Human Resources Department of the Progressive Group of Insurance Companies prepares its budget and subsequent performance report on the basis of its expected expenses for the year.

h. The shopping section of Burpee.com reports both revenues and expenses.

S10-3 Give advice about decentralization *(Learning Objective 1)*

Grandma Jones's Cookie Company sells homemade cookies made with organic ingredients. Her sales are strictly web-based. The business is exceeding Grandma Jones's expectations, with orders coming in from consumers and corporate event planners across the country. Even by employing a full-time baker and a web designer, Grandma Jones can no longer handle the business on her own. She wants your advice on whether she should decentralize and, if so, how she should do it. Explain some of the advantages and disadvantages of decentralization and offer her three ways she might decentralize her company.

S10-4 Classify types of subunits *(Learning Objective 1)*

Each of the following managers has been given certain decision-making authority. Classify each manager according to the type of responsibility center he or she manages.

1. Manager of Holiday Inn's central reservation office
2. Manager of various corporate-owned Holiday Inn locations
3. Manager of the Holiday Inn corporate division
4. Manager of the Housekeeping Department at the Holiday Inn
5. Manager of the Holiday Inn Express corporate division
6. Manager of the complimentary breakfast buffet at the Holiday Inn Express

S10-5 Calculate performance report variances *(Learning Objective 2)*

The following is a partial performance report for a revenue center for Shasta's Restaurants, Midwest Division.

Midwest Division—Sales Revenue for Shasta Restaurants
For the Month Ending June 30

Product	Actual Sales	Budgeted Sales	Variance	Variance %
Food	$156,000	$150,000	?	?
Dessert	$ 18,200	$ 20,000	?	?
Bar	$ 65,720	$ 62,000	?	?
Catering	$ 48,960	$ 48,000	?	?

Fill in the missing amounts. Indicate whether each variance is favorable (F) or unfavorable (U).

S10-6 Calculate ROI, capital turnover, and sales margin *(Learning Objectives 3)*

Rollins Chemical Corporation has three divisions. To follow is division information from the most recent year.

Division Information for Rollins Chemical
For the Year Ending December 31

(All information is in millions of dollars)	Operating Income	Assets	Sales Revenue
Functional Ingredients	$5,445	$12,100	$21,780
Consumer Markets	$2,075	$ 8,300	$20,750
Performance Materials	$3,000	$10,000	$15,000

For each of the three divisions, calculate sales margin, capital turnover, and Return on Investment (ROI).

Extreme Sports Data Set used for S10-7 through S10-9:

Extreme Sports Company makes snowboards, downhill skis, cross-country skis, skateboards, surfboards, and in-line skates. The company has found it beneficial to split operations into two divisions based on the climate required for the sport: Snow Sports and Non-Snow Sports. The following divisional information is available for the past year:

	Sales	Operating Income	Total Assets	Current Liabilities
Snow Sports......	$5,200,000	$1,040,000	$4,000,000	$470,000
Non-Snow Sports...	$8,400,000	$1,680,000	$6,000,000	$770,000

Extreme's management has specified a target 16% rate of return. The company's weighted average cost of capital (WACC) is 10%, and its effective tax rate is 37%.

S10-7 Calculate ROI *(Learning Objective 3)*

Refer to Extreme Sports Data Set.

1. Calculate each division's ROI.
2. Top management has extra funds to invest. Which division will most likely receive those funds? Why?
3. Can you explain why one division's ROI is higher? How could management gain more insight?

S10-8 Compute sales margin and capital margin turnover *(Learning Objective 3)*

Refer to the Extreme Sports Data Set.

1. Compute each division's sales margin. Interpret your results.
2. Compute each division's capital turnover (round to two decimal places). Interpret your results.
3. Use your answers to Question 2 along with your answers to Question 1 to recalculate ROI using the expanded formula. Do your answers agree with your ROI calculations in S10-7?

S10-9 Compute RI *(Learning Objective 3)*

Refer to the Extreme Sports Data Set. Compute each division's RI. Interpret your results. Are your results consistent with each division's ROI?

S10-10 Determine transfer price range *(Learning Objective 3)*

KitchenAid makes a variety of products, including stand mixers. KitchenAid's Stand Mixer Division can use a component, K32, manufactured by KitchenAid's Electrical Division. The market price for K32 is $18 per unit. The variable cost per unit for K32 in the Electrical Division is $13, while the absorption cost per unit is $16. The divisions at KitchenAid use a negotiated price strategy to set transfer prices between divisions.

What is the lowest acceptable transfer price to the Electrical Division? What is the highest acceptable transfer price that the Stand Mixer Division would pay? Explain your answer.

S10-11 Interpret a performance report *(Learning Objective 4)*

The following is a partially completed performance report for Sunshine Pools.

SUNSHINE POOLS
Income Statement Performance Report
Year Ended April 30

	Actual Results at Actual Prices	Flexible Budget Variance	Flexible Budget for Actual Number of Output Units	Volume Variance	Master Budget
Output units (pools installed)	6	?	?	?	5
Sales revenue	$102,000	?	$108,000	?	$90,000
Variable expenses	57,000	?	60,000	?	50,000
Fixed expenses	21,000	?	25,000	?	25,000
Total expenses	78,000	?	85,000	?	75,000
Operating income	$ 24,000	?	$ 23,000	?	$15,000

1. How many pools did Sunshine originally think it would install in April?
2. How many pools did Sunshine actually install in April?
3. How many pools is the flexible budget based on? Why?
4. What was the budgeted sales price per pool?
5. What was the budgeted variable cost per pool?
6. Define the flexible budget variance. What causes it?
7. Define the volume variance. What causes it?
8. Fill in the missing numbers in the Performance Report.

S10-12 Complete a master budget performance report *(Learning Objective 4)*

The following table contains a partial master budget performance report for Decadent Chocolates. Fill in the missing amounts. Be sure to indicate whether variances are favorable (F) or unfavorable (U).

DECADENT CHOCOLATES
Master Budget Performance Report—Sales and Operating Expenses
For Year Ended December 31

	Actual 12,700 batches	Flexible Budget Variance	Flexible Budget 12,700 batches	Volume Variance	Master Budget 11,600 batches
Sales Revenue ($30 per batch)	$376,500	?	$ 381,000	?	$348,000
Variable Operating Expenses:					
Sales Expense ($2 per batch sold)	$ 23,400	?	$ 25,400	?	$ 23,200
Shipping Expense ($3 per batch sold)	36,500	?	38,100	?	34,800
Fixed Operating Expenses:					
Salaries	9,500	?	8,700	?	8,700
Office rent	2,500	?	2,500	?	2,500
Total Operating Expenses	$ 71,900	?	$ 74,700	?	$ 69,200
Operating Income (Revenue less Expenses)	$304,600	?	$ 306,300	?	$278,800

S10-13 Classify KPIs by balanced scorecard perspective *(Learning Objective 5)*

Classify each of the following key performance indicators according to the balanced scorecard perspective it addresses. Choose from financial perspective, customer perspective, internal business perspective, or learning and growth perspective.

a. Customer satisfaction ratings
b. Number of defects found during manufacturing
c. Number of warranty claims received
d. ROI
e. Number of employee suggestions implemented
f. Revenue growth
g. Rate of on-time deliveries
h. Percentage of sales force with access to real-time inventory levels

S10-14 Classify KPIs by balanced scorecard perspective *(Learning Objective 5)*

Classify each of the following key performance indicators according to the balanced scorecard perspective it addresses. Choose from financial perspective, customer perspective, internal business perspective, or learning and growth perspective.

a. Yield rate (number of units produced per hour)
b. Average repair time
c. Employee satisfaction
d. Number of repeat customers
e. Variable cost per unit
f. Percentage of market share
g. Number of hours of employee training
h. Number of new products developed

S10-15 Use vocabulary terms *(Learning Objective 1, 2, 3, 4, & 5)*

Complete the following statements with one of the terms listed here. You may use a term more than once. Some terms may not be used at all.

Capital turnover	**Common fixed expenses**	**Cost center**
Direct fixed expenses	**Favorable variance**	**Flexible budget**
Flexible budget variance	**Goal congruence**	**Investment center**
Key performance indicators (KPIs)	**Management by exception**	**Master budget variance**
Profit center	**Return on Investment (ROI)**	**Revenue center**
Sales margin	**Unfavorable variance**	**Volume variance**

a. The headquarters for an international consulting firm is considered to be a(n) ________.
b. Fixed expenses that can be traced to the segment are called ________.
c. ________ shows how much income is generated for every $1.00 of sales.
d. ________ are included on balanced scorecards and help managers assess how well the company's objectives are being met.
e. The difference between actual results and the master budget is called the ________.
f. When the goals of the segments managers in a company are the same, then ________ is achieved.
g. The local branch office of a national bank is considered to be a(n) ________.
h. Fixed expenses that cannot be traced to the segment are called ________.
i. A(n) ________ is a budget prepared for a different volume level than that which was originally anticipated.
j. The difference between the flexible budget and actual results is called the ________.
k. ________ measures the profitability of a division relative to the size of its assets.
l. If budgeted salary expense is higher than the actual salary expense, then a(n) ________ will result.
m. A(n) ________ manager is responsible for generating revenue.

n. The ________ arises only because the actual volume sold differs from the volume originally anticipated in the master budget.

o. ________ shows how much sales revenue is generated with every $1.00 of assets.

p. If budgeted sales revenue is greater than the actual sales revenue, then a(n) ________ will result.

q. ________ is a management technique in which managers only investigate budget variances that are relatively large.

r. The legal department of a manufacturer is considered to be a(n) ________.

EXERCISES Group A

E10-16A Identify centralized and decentralized organizations

(Learning Objective 1)

The following table lists a series of descriptions of decentralized organizations or centralized organizations. For each description, indicate whether that scenario is more typical of a decentralized organization or a centralized organization.

Characteristic	Decentralized (D) or Centralized (C)
a. Specialty Motors Inc., wants to empower its managers to make decisions so that the managers' motivation is increased and retention of managers increases.	
b. The duplication of services caused the Rondell Company to "flatten" its organization structure. The Rondell Company now has a single payroll department, a single human resources department and a single administrative headquarters.	
c. The Plastic Lumber Company, Inc., is managed by its owner, who oversees production, sales, engineering, and the other administrative functions.	
d. Wasick Company has a policy that it promotes from within the company whenever possible. It has formal training programs for lower-level managers.	
e. Krampf Corporation is divided into several operating units.	
f. Two Turtles is a small independent pet shop in Akron, Ohio. The owner is also the manager of the store.	
g. The managers at Shroath Company have the authority to make decisions about product offerings and pricing because Shroath Company wants its managers to be able to respond quickly to changes in local market demand.	

E10-17A Identify type of responsibility center *(Learning Objective 1)*

Each of the following situations describes an organizational unit. Identify which type of responsibility center each underlined item is (cost, revenue, profit, or investment center).

Organization	Type of Responsibility Center (Cost, Revenue, Profit, or Investment)
a. Trek Bicycle Corporation manufactures and distributes bicycles and cycling products under the Trek, Gary Fisher, Bontrager, and Klein brand names.	
b. The Hershey Company is one of the oldest chocolate companies in the United States. Its product lines include the Mauna Loa Macadamia Nuts, Dagoba Organic Chocolates, and Joseph Schmidt Confections.	
c. The Human Resources Department is responsible for recruiting and training for the Kohl's Corporation.	
d. The reservation office for BlueSky Airlines, Inc., is responsible for both web sales and counter sales.	
e. The Disney Store at Spring Hill Mall in West Dundee, Illinois, is owned by The Walt Disney Company.	
f. H & R Block Tax Services, H & R Block Bank, and RSM McGlandrey are all divisions of their parent corporation, H & R Block.	
g. Sherwin-Williams Store #1933 is located in Copley, Ohio. The store sells paints, wallpapers, and supplies to do-it-yourself customers and to professional wall covering installers.	
h. The Accounting Research and Compliance Department at FirstEnergy is responsible for researching how new accounting pronouncements and rules will impact FirstEnergy's financial statements.	
i. The Southwestern Sales Region of McDermott Foods is responsible for selling the various product lines of McDermott.	
j. The Taxation Department at Verizon Communications, Inc., is responsible for preparing the federal, state, and local income and franchise tax returns for the corporation.	
k. The Roseville Chipotle restaurant in Minnesota, is owned by its parent Chipotle Mexican Grill, Inc. The Roseville Chipotle, like other Chipotle restaurants, serves burritos, fajitas, and tacos and competes in the "fast-casual" dining category.	

E10-18A Complete and analyze a performance report *(Learning Objective 2)*

One subunit of Hazelton Sports Company has the following financial results last month:

Hazelton Water Sports Subunit	Actual	Budget	Budget Variance (U or F)	Variance %* (U or F)
Direct materials	$16,140	$15,000		
Direct labor	19,020	20,000		
Indirect labor	29,300	25,000		
Utilities	13,110	12,000		
Depreciation	19,000	19,000		
Repairs and maintenance	3,370	4,000		
Total	$99,940	$95,000		

**Flexible budget variance ÷ Flexible budget*

Requirements

1. Complete the performance evaluation report for this subunit (round to four decimals).
2. Based on the data presented, what type of responsibility center is the subunit?
3. Which items should be investigated if part of the management's decision criteria is to investigate all variances exceeding $2,800 or 10.5%?
4. Should only unfavorable variances be investigated? Explain.

E10-19A Create a performance report for a revenue center *(Learning Objective 2)*

Irvin Chemical Corporation has several segments within its Northern Division. To follow are the actual and budgeted sales revenues for the most recent year ending June 30. All dollar amounts are in millions.

Segment	Actual Sales	Budgeted Sales
Plastics	$11,845	$11,500
Chemicals and Energy	$ 3,710	$ 3,500
Hydrocarbons	$ 5,184	$ 5,400
Coatings	$11,250	$12,500
Health Sciences	$11,088	$ 9,900

Prepare a performance report for the Northern Division revenue center. Include each of the segments as an individual line item (rather than adding all to show just one sales revenue line.)

E10-20A Prepare a segment margin performance report *(Learning Objective 2)*

Caldrone Industries has gathered the following information about the actual sales revenues and expenses for its pharmaceuticals segment for the most recent year.

Sales	$880,000
Variable Cost of Goods Sold	$204,000
Variable Operating Expenses	$153,600
Direct Fixed Manufacturing Overhead	$ 86,400
Direct Fixed Operating Expenses	$ 22,050
Common Fixed Expenses	$ 19,080

Budgeted data for the same time period for the pharmaceutical segment are as follows (all data is in millions):

Budgeted sales in units	8,000
Budgeted average selling price per unit	$ 100
Variable Cost of Goods Sold per unit	$ 25
Variable Operating Expenses per unit	$ 20
Direct Fixed Manufacturing Overhead (in total)	$80,000
Direct Fixed Operating Expenses (in total)	$21,000
Common Fixed Expenses Allocated to the Pharmaceutical Segment	$18,000

Prepare a segment margin performance report for the pharmaceutical segment. In this report, be sure to include lines for the contribution margin, the segment margin, and operating income. Use Exhibit 10-4 in the chapter as a guide. Calculate a variance and a variance percentage for each line in the report. Round to the nearest hundredth for the variance percentages (for example, if your answer is 16.2384%, round it to 16.24%).

E10-21A Compute and interpret the expanded ROI equation *(Learning Objective 3)*

Toro, a national manufacturer of lawn-mowing and snow-blowing equipment, segments its business according to customer type: Professional and Residential. Assume the following divisional information was available for the past year (in thousands of dollars):

	Sales	Operating Income	Total Assets
Residential	$ 850,000	$ 68,000	$200,000
Professional	$1,095,000	$153,300	$365,000

Assume that management has a 25% target rate of return for each division. (All data in this exercise is hypothetical.)

Requirements

Round all of your answers to four decimal places.

1. Calculate each division's ROI.
2. Calculate each division's sales margin. Interpret your results.
3. Calculate each division's capital turnover. Interpret your results.
4. Use the expanded ROI formula to confirm your results from Requirement 1. What can you conclude?
5. Calculate each division's residual income (RI). Interpret your results.

E10-22A Relationship between ROI and residual income *(Learning Objective 3)*

Data on three unrelated companies are given in the following table.

	Anderson Company	Beatty Industries	Carmen, Inc.
Sales	$102,000	?	$490,000
Operating income	$ 35,700	$114,100	?
Total assets	$ 85,000	?	?
Sales margin	?	14%	8%
Capital turnover	?	5.00	?
Return on investment (ROI)	?	?	20%
Target rate of return	11%	18%	?
Residual income	?	?	$ 1,960

Requirement

Fill in the missing information in the preceding table.

E10-23A Compute ROI, residual income, and EVA *(Learning Objective 3)*

Results from Pioneer Corporation's most recent year of operations is presented in the following table.

Operating income	$ 9,240
Total assets	$14,000
Current liabilities	$ 4,400
Sales	$38,500
Target rate of return	14%

Requirements

1. Calculate the sales margin, capital turnover, and return on investment (ROI).
2. Calculate the residual income.

E10-24A Comparison of ROI and residual income *(Learning Objective 3)*

Sinclair Ceramics, a division of Heisler Corporation, has an operating income of $82,000 and total assets of $410,000. The required rate of return for the company is 11%. The company is evaluating whether it should use return on investment (ROI) or residual income (RI) as a measurement of performance for its division managers.

The manager of Sinclair Ceramics has the opportunity to undertake a new project that will require an investment of $164,000. This investment would earn $21,320 for Sinclair Ceramics.

Requirements

1. What is the original return on investment (ROI) for Sinclair Ceramics (before making any additional investment)?
2. What would the ROI be for Sinclair Ceramics if this investment opportunity were undertaken? Would the manager of the Sinclair Ceramics division want to make this investment if she were evaluated based on ROI? Why or why not?
3. What is the ROI of the investment opportunity? Would the investment be desirable from the standpoint of Heisler Corporation? Why or why not?

4. What would the residual income (RI) be for Sinclair Ceramics if this investment opportunity were to be undertaken? Would the manager of the Sinclair Ceramics division want to make this investment if she were evaluated based on RI? Why or why not?
5. What is the RI of the investment opportunity? Would the investment be desirable from the standpoint of Heisler Corporation? Why or why not?
6. Which performance measurement method, ROI or RI, promotes goal congruence? Why?

E10-25A Determine transfer price range *(Learning Objective 3)*

Greene Motors manufactures specialty tractors. It has two divisions: a Tractor Division and a Tire Division. The Tractor Division can use the tires produced by the Tire Division. The market price per tire is $55.

The Tractor Division has the following costs per tire:
Direct material cost per tire $25
Conversion costs per tire $3

Fixed manufacturing overhead cost for the year is expected to total $100,000. The Tractor Division expects to manufacture 50,000 tires this year. The fixed manufacturing overhead per tire is $2 ($100,000 divided by 50,000 tires).

Requirements

1. Assume that the Tire Division has excess capacity, meaning that it can produce tires for the Tractor Division without giving up any of its current tire sales to outsiders. If Greene Motors has a negotiated transfer price policy, what is the lowest acceptable transfer price? What is the highest acceptable transfer price?
2. If Greene Motors has a cost-plus transfer price policy of full absorption cost plus 20%, what would the transfer price be?
3. If the Tire Division is currently producing at capacity (meaning that it is selling every single tire it has the capacity to produce), what would likely be the most fair transfer price strategy to use? What would be the transfer price in this case?

E10-26A Prepare a flexible budget performance report *(Learning Objective 4)*

Main Street Muffins sells its muffins to restaurants and coffee houses for an average selling price of $25 per case. The following information relates to the budget for Main Street Muffins for this year:

Budgeted sales in cases	8,000 cases
Packaging cost per case	$ 1
Shipping expense per case	$ 3
Sales commission expense	2% of sales price
Salaries expense (total)	$6,200
Office rent (total)	$3,500
Depreciation (total)	$2,500
Insurance expense (total)	$1,900
Office supplies expense (total)	$ 900

During the year, Main Street Muffins actually sold 8,300 cases resulting in total sales revenue of $215,400. Actual expenses (in total) from this year are as follows:

Packaging cost (total)	$ 8,700
Shipping expense (total)	$25,900
Sales commission expense (total)	$ 4,308
Salaries expense (total)	$ 6,900
Office rent (total)	$ 3,500
Depreciation (total)	$ 2,500
Insurance expense (total)	$ 1,800
Office supplies expense (total)	$ 1,200

Requirement

Construct a flexible budget performance report for Main Street Muffins for the year. Be sure to indicate whether each variance is favorable (F) or unfavorable (U).

E10-27A Complete and analyze a performance report *(Learning Objective 4)*

The accountant for a subunit of Landeau Sports Company went on vacation before completing the subunit's monthly performance report. This is as far as she got:

Landeau Subunit X Revenue by Product	Actual	Flexible Budget Variance	Flexible Budget	Volume Variance	Master Budget
Downhill Model RI	$ 328,000			$16,000 F	$ 304,000
Downhill Model RII	157,000		$171,000		151,000
Cross-Country Model EXI	280,000	$2,000 U	282,000		300,000
Cross-Country Model EXII	253,000		245,000	18,500 U	263,500
Snowboard Model LXI	422,000	1,000 F			402,000
Total	$1,440,000				$1,420,500

Requirements

1. Complete the performance evaluation report for this subunit.
2. Based on the data presented, what type of responsibility center is this subunit?
3. Which items should be investigated if part of the management's decision criteria is to investigate all variances exceeding $15,500? Interpret your results. (What could cause these variances? What impact might these variances have on company inventory levels and operations?)

E10-28A Work backward to find missing values *(Learning Objective 4)*

Mission Industries has a relevant range extending to 30,500 units each month. The following performance report provides information about Mission's budget and actual performance for November:

MISSION INDUSTRIES
Income Statement Performance Report
Month Ended November 30

	Actual Results at Actual Prices	(A)	Flexible Budget for Actual Number of Output Units	(B)	Master Budget
Output units	28,000		(C)		30,500
Sales revenue	$252,000	$5,600 F	(D)		
Variable cost			(E)		$189,100
Fixed cost	$ 18,500	(F)			$ 25,000
Operating income					(G)

Requirement

Find the missing data for letters A–G. Be sure to label any variances as favorable or unfavorable. (*Hint:* A and B are titles.)

E10-29A Differentiate between lag and lead indicators *(Learning Objective 5)*

Explain the difference between lag and lead indicators. Are financial performance measures typically referred to as lag or lead indicators? Explain, using The Ford Motor Company (an automobile manufacturer) as an example. Are operational measures (such as customer satisfaction ratings, defect rate, and number of on-time deliveries) typically referred to as lag or lead indicators?

E10-30A Construct a balanced scorecard *(Learning Objective 5)*

Cardinal Corporation is preparing its balanced scorecard for the past quarter. The balanced scorecard contains four perspectives: financial, customer, internal business process, and learning and growth. Through its strategic management planning process, Cardinal Corporation has selected two specific objectives for each of the four perspectives; these specific objectives are listed in the following table.

Specific Objective
Increase sales of core product line.
Develop new core products.
Improve employee product knowledge.
Increase customer satisfaction.
Improve post-sales service.
Increase market share.
Increase profitability of core product line.
Improve employee job satisfaction.

Cardinal Corporation has collected key performance indicators (KPIs) to measure progress toward achieving its specific objectives. The following table contains the KPIs and corresponding data that Cardinal Corporation has collected for the past quarter.

KPI	Goal	Actual
Hours of employee training provided	2,400	2,350
Average repair time (number of days)	1.0	1.6
Sales revenue growth—Core product line	$2,000,000	$2,200,000
Employee turnover rate (number of employees leaving company/number of total employees)	3%	6%
Core product line profit as a percentage of core product line sales	12%	17%
Market share percentage	19%	18%
Number of new core products	26	24
Customer satisfaction rating (1–5, with 1 being most satisfied)	1.3	1.2

Requirement

Prepare a balanced scorecard report for Cardinal Corporation, using the following format.

Cardinal Corporation
Balanced Scorecard Report
For Quarter Ended December 31

Perspective	Objective	KPI	Goal	Actual	Goal Achieved? (✓ if met)
Financial					
Customer					
Internal Business Process					
Learning and Growth					

For each of the specific objectives listed, place that objective under the appropriate perspective heading in the report. Select a KPI from the list of KPIs that would be appropriate to measure progress towards each objective. (There are two specific objectives for each perspective and one KPI for each of the specific objectives.) In the last column in the Balanced Scorecard Report, place a checkmark if the associated KPI goal has been achieved.

E10-31A Classify KPIs by balanced scorecard perspective *(Learning Objective 5)*

Classify each of the following key performance indicators according to the balanced scorecard perspective it addresses. Choose from financial perspective, customer perspective, internal business perspective, or learning and growth perspective.

a. Downtime (the amount of time service is not available)
b. Percentage of orders filled each week
c. Gross margin growth
d. Number of new patents
e. Employee satisfaction ratings
f. Number of customer complaints
g. Number of information system upgrades completed
h. Return on Investment (ROI)
i. New product development time
j. Employee turnover rate
k. Percentage of products with online help manuals
l. Customer satisfaction survey ratings

E10-32A Sustainability and the balanced scorecard *(Learning Objective 5)*

Classify each of the following sustainability key performance indicators (KPIs) according to the balanced scorecard perspective it addresses. Choose from the following five perspectives:

- Financial perspective
- Customer perspective
- Internal business perspective
- Learning and growth perspective
- Community perspective

KPI

a. Revenue from recycling packaging materials
b. Total liters of water used
c. Number of sustainability training hours
d. Number of employee hours devoted to local volunteering
e. Charitable contributions as a percent of income
f. Customer survey rating company's green reputation
g. Number of employees on sustainability teams
h. Cubic meters of natural gas used for heating facilities
i. Total megawatt hours of electricity purchased
j. Percent of bottles and cans sold recovered through company-supported recovery programs
k. Cost of water used
l. Indirect greenhouse gas emissions from electricity purchased and consumed
m. Number of functions with environmental responsibilities
n. Number of green products
o. Percentage of profit donated to local schools
p. Volume of Global Greenhouse Gas (GHG) emissions
q. Waste disposal costs
r. Percentage of products reclaimed after customer use

E10-33A Identify centralized and decentralized organizations

(Learning Objective 1)

The following table lists a series of descriptions of decentralized organizations or centralized organizations. For each description, indicate whether that scenario is more typical of a decentralized organization or a centralized organization.

Characteristic	Decentralized (D) or Centralized (C)
a. Smythe Resorts and Hotels, Inc., wants to empower its managers to make decisions so that the managers' motivation is increased and retention of managers increases.	
b. Philips Corporation has formal training programs for lower-level managers and has a policy that it promotes from within the company whenever possible.	
c. The Plastic Lumber Company, Inc., is managed by its owner, who oversees production, sales, engineering, and the other administrative functions.	
d. Daniels Furniture, Inc., is divided into several operating units.	
e. Fulton Holdings wants its managers to be able to respond quickly to changes in local market demand so the managers have the authority to make decisions about product offerings and pricing.	
f. Craft Supplies & More is a small independent craft shop and is managed by its owner.	
g. Mayflower Corporation now has a single payroll department, a single human resource department, and a single administrative headquarters since Mayflower Corporation "flattened" its organization structure.	

EXERCISES Group B

E10-34B Identify type of responsibility center *(Learning Objective 1)*

Each of the following situations describes an organizational unit. Identify which type of responsibility center each underlined item is (cost, revenue, profit, or investment center).

Organization	Type of Responsibility Center (Cost, Revenue, Profit, or Investment)
a. The Barnes & Noble bookstore in Asheville, North Carolina, is owned by its parent, Barnes & Noble, Inc.	
b. The Human Resources Department at American Greetings is responsible for hiring and training new associates.	
c. The JCPenney store in the Oakpark Shopping Center in Kansas City is owned by the JCPenney Company, Inc.	
d. The Information System Department is responsible for designing, installing, and servicing the information systems throughout Kohl's Corporation.	
e. The reservation office for CharterNow Airlines, Inc., is responsible for both website sales and counter sales.	
f. In addition to other accounting duties, the Financial Reporting and Control & Analysis Department at Progressive Insurance is responsible for performing a monthly analysis of general ledger accounts and fluctuations as a control mechanism.	
g. The Goodyear Tire & Rubber Company is one of the oldest tire companies in the world. Its geographic regions include North America, Europe, Africa, South America, Asia, and Australia.	
h. The Dairy Group Account team of the Dean Foods Company is responsible for sales and servicing for the SUPERVAU, Target, and Costco accounts.	
i. The Fairmont Chicago, The Fairmont Royal York in Toronto, and The Fairmont Orchid in Hawaii are all hotels owned by their parent corporation, Fairmont Hotels & Resorts.	
j. The J.M. Smucker Company Store and Café is located in Wooster, Ohio. The store sells a variety of company products, while the café offers items made with ingredients from the Smucker's brands.	
k. The 3M Company manufactures and distributes products under the Post-it, Scotch, Nexcare, and Thinsulate brand names.	

E10-35B Complete and analyze a performance report *(Learning Objective 2)*

One subunit of River Sports Company has the following financial results last month:

RiverSports Subunit X	Actual	Flexible Budget	Flexible Budget Variance (U or F)	Variance %* (U or F)
Direct materials	$ 26,925	$ 25,000		
Direct labor	14,235	15,000		
Indirect labor	29,275	26,000		
Utilities	13,170	12,000		
Depreciation	15,500	15,500		
Repairs and maintenance	6,315	7,500		
Total	$105,420	$101,000		

**Flexible budget variance ÷ Flexible budget*

Requirements

1. Complete the performance evaluation report for this subunit (round to four decimals).
2. Based on the data presented, what type of responsibility center is this subunit?
3. Which items should be investigated if part of management's decision criteria is to investigate all variances exceeding $3,100 or 11%?
4. Should only unfavorable variances be investigated? Explain.

E10-36B Create a performance report for a revenue center *(Learning Objective 2)*

Wendell Chemical Corporation has several segments within its Northern Division. To follow are the actual and budgeted sales revenues for the most recent year ending June 30. All dollar amounts are in millions.

Segment	Actual Sales	Budgeted Sales
Plastics	$14,872	$14,300
Chemicals and Energy	$ 4,116	$ 4,200
Hydrocarbons	$ 7,420	$ 7,000
Coatings	$10,580	$11,500
Health Sciences	$ 9,570	$ 8,700

Prepare a performance report for the Northern Division revenue center. Include each of the segments as an individual line item (rather than adding all to show just one sales revenue line.)

E10-37B Prepare a segment margin performance report *(Learning Objective 2)*

Noble Industries has gathered the following information about the actual sales revenues and expenses for its pharmaceuticals segment for the most recent year (all data is in millions).

Sales	$1,248,000
Variable Cost of Goods Sold	$ 652,800
Variable Operating Expenses	$ 225,600
Direct Fixed Manufacturing Overhead	$ 156,600
Direct Fixed Operating Expenses	$ 26,250
Common Fixed Expenses	$ 15,450

Budgeted data for the same time period for the pharmaceutical segment are as follows (all data is in millions):

Budgeted sales in units	8,000
Budgeted average selling price per unit	$ 150
Variable Cost of Goods Sold per unit	$ 80
Variable Operating Expenses per unit	$ 30
Direct Fixed Manufacturing Overhead (in total)	$145,000
Direct Fixed Operating Expenses (in total)	$ 25,000
Common Fixed Expenses Allocated to the Pharmaceutical Segment	$ 15,000

Prepare a segment margin performance report for the pharmaceutical segment. In this report, be sure to include lines for the contribution margin, the segment margin, and operating income. Use Exhibit 10-4 in the chapter as a guide. Calculate a variance and a variance percentage for each line in the report. Round to the nearest hundredth for the variance percentages (for example, if your answer is 16.2384%, round it to 16.24%).

E10-38B Compute and interpret the expanded ROI equation
(Learning Objective 3)

Toro, a national manufacturer of lawn-mowing and snow-blowing equipment, segments its business according to customer type: Professional and Residential. Assume that the following divisional information was available for the past year (in thousands of dollars):

	Sales	Operating Income	Total Assets
Residential	$420,000	$ 58,800	$210,000
Professional	$608,000	$152,000	$380,000

Management has a 25% target rate of return for each division. (All data in this exercise is hypothetical.)

Requirements

1. Calculate each division's ROI. Round all of your answers to four decimal places.
2. Calculate each division's sales margin. Interpret your results.
3. Calculate each division's capital turnover. Interpret your results.
4. Use the expanded ROI formula to confirm your results from Requirement 1. What can you conclude?
5. Calculate each division's residual income (RI). Interpret your results.

E10-39B Relationship between ROI and residual income *(Learning Objective 3)*

Data on three unrelated companies are given in the following table.

	Abercrombie Company	Benson Industries	Cappela, Inc.
Sales	$114,000	?	$484,000
Operating income	$ 39,900	$117,000	?
Total assets	$ 71,250	?	?
Sales margin	?	15%	10%
Capital turnover	?	5.20	?
Return on investment (ROI)	?	?	22%
Target rate of return	10%	22%	?
Residual income	?	?	$ 4,400

Requirement

Fill in the missing information.

E10-40B Compute ROI and residual income *(Learning Objective 3)*

Results from Quinn Corporation's most recent year of operations is presented in the following table:

Operating income	$ 8,800
Total assets	$16,000
Current liabilities	$ 3,600
Sales	$35,200
Target rate of return	14%

Requirements

1. Calculate the sales margin, capital turnover, and return on investment (ROI).
2. Calculate the residual income.

E10-41B Comparison of ROI and residual income *(Learning Objective 3)*

McKnight Ceramics, a division of Piper Corporation, has an operating income of $63,000 and total assets of $420,000. The required rate of return for the company is 9%. The company is evaluating whether it should use return on investment (ROI) or residual income (RI) as a measurement of performance for its division managers.

The manager of McKnight Ceramics has the opportunity to undertake a new project that will require an investment of $140,000. This investment would earn $18,200 for McKnight Ceramics.

Requirements

1. What is the original return on investment (ROI) for McKnight Ceramics (before making any additional investment)?
2. What would the ROI be for McKnight Ceramics if this investment opportunity were undertaken? Would the manager of the McKnight Ceramics division want to make this investment if she were evaluated based on ROI? Why or why not?
3. What is the ROI of the investment opportunity? Would the investment be desirable from the standpoint of Piper Corporation? Why or why not?
4. What would the residual income (RI) be for McKnight Ceramics if this investment opportunity were to be undertaken? Would the manager of the McKnight Ceramics division want to make this investment if she were evaluated based on RI? Why or why not?
5. What is the RI of the investment opportunity? Would the investment be desirable from the standpoint of Piper Corporation? Why or why not?
6. Which performance measurement method, ROI or RI, promotes goal congruence? Why?

E10-42B Determine transfer price range *(Learning Objective 3)*

Phelps Motors manufactures specialty tractors. It has two divisions: a Tractor Division and a Tire Division. The Tractor Division can use the tires produced by the Tire Division. The market price per tire is $49.

The Tractor Division has the following costs per tire:
Direct material cost per tire $22
Conversion costs per tire $4

Fixed manufacturing overhead cost for the year is expected to total $120,000. The Tractor Division expects to manufacture 60,000 tires this year. The fixed manufacturing overhead per tire is $2 ($120,000 divided by 60,000 tires).

Requirements

1. Assume that the Tire Division has excess capacity, meaning that it can produce tires for the Tractor Division without giving up any of its current tire sales to outsiders. If Phelps Motors has a negotiated transfer price policy, what is the lowest acceptable transfer price? What is the highest acceptable transfer price?
2. If Phelps Motors has a cost-plus transfer price policy of full absorption cost plus 20%, what would the transfer price be?

3. If the Tire Division is currently producing at capacity (meaning that it is selling every single tire it has the capacity to produce), what would likely be the most fair transfer price strategy to use? What would be the transfer price in this case?

E10-43B Prepare a flexible budget performance report *(Learning Objective 4)*

Fourth Street Muffins sells its muffins to restaurants and coffee houses for an average selling price of $30 per case. The following information relates to the budget for Fourth Street Muffins for this year:

Budgeted sales in cases	8,000 cases
Packaging cost per case	$ 2.00
Shipping expense per case	$ 3.50
Sales commission expense	2% of sales price
Salaries expense (total)	$5,900
Office rent (total)	$3,800
Depreciation (total)	$2,000
Insurance expense (total)	$1,500
Office supplies expense (total)	$ 800

During the year, Fourth Street Muffins actually sold 8,100 cases resulting in total sales revenue of $251,400. Actual expenses (in total) from this year are as follows:

Packaging cost (total)	$ 17,800
Shipping expense (total)	$ 28,100
Sales commission expense (total)	$ 5,028
Salaries expense (total)	$ 6,300
Office rent (total)	$ 3,200
Depreciation (total)	$ 2,000
Insurance expense (total)	$ 2,100
Office supplies expense (total)	$ 600

Requirement

Construct a flexible budget performance report for Fourth Street Muffins for the year. Use Exhibit 10-12 as a guide. Be sure to indicate whether each variance is favorable (F) or unfavorable (U).

E10-44B Complete and analyze a performance report *(Learning Objective 4)*

The accountant for a subunit of Gutierrez Sports Company went on vacation before completing the subunit's monthly performance report. This is as far as she got:

Gutierrez Sports—Subunit X Revenue by Product	Actual	Flexible Budget Variance	Flexible Budget	Volume Variance	Master Budget
Downhill Model RI	$ 321,000			$17,000 F	$ 298,000
Downhill Model RII	158,000		$168,000		150,000
Cross-Country Model EXI	289,000	$1,000 U	290,000		307,000
Cross-Country Model EXII	254,000		248,000	19,500 U	267,500
Snowboard Model LXI	423,000	7,000 F			398,000
Total	$1,445,000				$1,420,500

Requirements

1. Complete the performance evaluation report for this subunit.
2. Based on the data presented, what type of responsibility center is this subunit?
3. Which items should be investigated if part of the management's decision criteria is to investigate all variances exceeding $17,000? Interpret your results. (What could cause these variances? What impact might these variances have on company inventory levels and operations?)

E10-45B Work backward to find missing values *(Learning Objective 4)*

Golden Corporation has a relevant range extending to 30,800 units each month. The following performance report provides information about Golden's budget and actual performance for June.

	Actual Results at Actual Prices	(A)	Flexible Budget for Actual Number of Output Units	(B)	Master Budget
Output units	27,000		(C)		30,800
Sales revenue	$253,500	$5,100 F	(D)		
Variable cost			(E)		$189,420
Fixed cost	$ 17,500	(F)			$ 22,500
Operating income					(G)

Requirement

Find the missing data for letters A through G. Be sure to label any variances as favorable or unfavorable. (*Hint*: A and B are titles.)

E10-46B Differentiate between lag and lead indicators *(Learning Objective 5)*

Explain the difference between lag and lead indicators. Are financial performance measures typically referred to as lag and lead indicators? Explain, using iTunes (an online store selling audio and video content for computers and mobile devices) as an example. Are operational measures (such as customer satisfaction ratings, number of subscribers, and number of time-out errors) typically referred to as lag or lead indicators?

E10-47B Construct a balanced scorecard *(Learning Objective 5)*

Royal Corporation is preparing its balanced scorecard for the past quarter. The balanced scorecard contains four perspectives: financial, customer, internal business process, and learning and growth. Through its strategic management planning process, Royal Corporation has selected two specific objectives for each of the four perspectives; these specific objectives are listed in the following table.

Specific Objective
1. Improve post-sales service.
2. Increase number of customers.
3. Increase gross margin.
4. Improve employee morale.
5. Increase profitability of core product line.
6. Increase plant safety.
7. Improve employee job satisfaction.
8. Increase customer retention.

Royal Corporation has collected key performance indicators (KPIs) to measure progress towards achieving its specific objectives. The following table contains the KPIs and corresponding data that Royal Corporation has collected for the past quarter.

KPI	Goal	Actual
Employee turnover rate (number of employees leaving/number of total employees)	2%	3%
Average repair time (number of days)	1.0	0.9
Core product line profit as a percentage of core product line sales	17%	13%
Employee satisfaction rating (1-5, with 1 being most satisfied)	1.0	1.2
Gross margin growth percentage	25%	26%
Number of customers	210,000	212,000
Number of plant accidents	0	2
Percentage of repeat customers	85%	82%

Requirement

Prepare a balanced scorecard report for Royal Corporation, using the following format.

Royal Corporation
Balanced Scorecard Report
For Quarter Ended December 31

Perspective	Objective	KPI	Goal	Actual	Goal Achieved? (✓ if met)
Financial					
Customer					
Internal Business Process					
Learning and Growth					

For each of the specific objectives listed, place that objective under the appropriate perspective heading in the report. Select a KPI from the list of KPIs that would be appropriate to measure progress towards each objective. (There are two specific objectives for each perspective and one KPI for each of the specific objectives.) In the last column in the Balanced Scorecard Report, place a checkmark if the associated KPI goal has been achieved.

E10-48B Classify KPIs by balanced scorecard perspective *(Learning Objective 5)*

Classify each of the following key performance indicators according to the balanced scorecard perspective it addresses. Choose from financial perspective, customer perspective, internal business perspective, or learning and growth perspective.

a. Customer satisfaction ratings
b. Machine downtime as a percent of total work hours
c. Pounds processed per hour
d. Percentage of employees with access to upgraded information system
e. Wait time per order prior to start of production
f. Sales margin
g. Manufacturing cycle time (average length of production process)
h. Earning growth
i. Average machine setup time
j. Number of new customers
k. Employee promotion rate
l. Cash flow from operations

E10-49B Sustainability and the balanced scorecard *(Learning Objective 5)*

Classify each of the following sustainability key performance indicators (KPIs) according to the balanced scorecard perspective it addresses. Choose from the following five perspectives:

- Financial perspective
- Customer perspective

- Internal business perspective
- Learning and growth perspective
- Community perspective

KPI

a. Product safety ratings
b. Total mega joules of energy used
c. Number of functions with environmental responsibilities
d. Percentage of recycled content in products
e. Revenue from recycling packaging materials
f. Cost of water used
g. Direct greenhouse gas emissions
h. Waste disposal costs
i. Number of employee hours devoted to volunteering at Habitat for Humanity
j. Percent of bottles and cans sold recovered through company-supported recovery programs
k. Percentage of products sourced locally
l. Percent of plants in compliance with internal wastewater treatment standards
m. Number of sustainability training hours
n. Number of employees on sustainability teams
o. Percentage of products reclaimed after customer use
p. Number of green products
q. Packaging use ratio defined as grams of materials used per liter of product produced
r. Customer survey rating company's green reputation

PROBLEMS Group A

P10-50A Evaluate subunit performance *(Learning Objective 4)*

One subunit of Keener Sports Company had the following financial results last month:

Keener Sports Subunit X	Actual	Flexible Budget	Flexible Budget Variance (U or F)	Variance % (U or F)*
Sales	$430,000	$400,000		
Cost of goods sold	325,000	312,500		
Gross margin	$105,000	$ 87,500		
Operating expenses	38,850	37,500		
Operating income before service department charges	$ 66,150	$ 50,000		
Service department charges (allocated)	37,500	25,000		
Operating income	$ 28,650	$ 25,000		

**Flexible budget variance ÷ Flexible budget*

Requirements

1. Compute the performance evaluation report for this subunit (round to three decimal places).
2. Based on the data presented, what type of responsibility center is this subunit?
3. Which items should be investigated if part of the management's decision criteria is to investigate all variances equal to or exceeding $12,500 and exceeding 14% (both criteria must be met)?
4. Should only unfavorable variances be investigated? Explain.

5. Is it possible that the variances are due to a higher-than-expected sales volume? Explain.
6. Do you think management will place equal weight on each of the $12,500 variances? Explain.
7. Which balanced scorecard perspective is being addressed through this performance report? In your opinion, is this performance report a lead or lag indicator? Explain.
8. Give one key performance indicator for the other three balanced scorecard perspectives. Indicate which perspective is being addressed by the indicator you list. Are they lead or lag indicators? Explain.

P10-51A Prepare a flexible budget for planning *(Learning Objective 2)*

Great Bubbles, Inc., produces multicolored bubble solution used for weddings and other events. The company's static budget income statement for March follows. It is based on expected sales volume of 65,000 bubble kits.

GREAT BUBBLES, INC.
Master Budget Income Statement
Month Ended March 31

Sales revenue	$188,500
Variable expenses:	
Cost of goods sold	$ 81,250
Sales commissions	19,500
Utility expense	3,250
Fixed expenses:	
Salary expense	30,000
Depreciation expense	20,000
Rent expense	8,000
Utility expense	6,000
Total expenses	$168,000
Operating income	$ 20,500

Great Bubbles' plant capacity is 72,500 kits. If actual volume exceeds 72,500 kits, the company must expand the plant. In that case, salaries will increase by 10%, depreciation by 15%, and rent by $4,000. Fixed utilities will be unchanged by any volume increase.

Requirements

1. Prepare flexible budget income statements for the company, showing output levels of 65,000, 70,000, and 75,000 kits.
2. Graph the behavior of the company's total costs.
3. Why might Great Bubbles' managers want to see the graph you prepared in Requirement 2 as well as the columnar format analysis in Requirement 1? What is the disadvantage of the graphic approach?

P10-52A Prepare and interpret a performance report *(Learning Objective 2)*

Refer to the Great Bubbles data in P10-51A. The company sold 70,000 bubble kits during March, and its actual operating income was as follows:

GREAT BUBBLES, INC. Master Budget Income Statement Month Ended March 31	
Sales revenue	$208,000
Variable expenses:	
Cost of goods sold	$ 88,000
Sales commissions	24,000
Utility expense	3,500
Fixed expenses:	
Salary expense	32,300
Depreciation expense	20,000
Rent expense	7,000
Utility expense	6,000
Total expenses	$180,800
Operating income	$ 27,200

Requirements

1. Prepare an income statement performance report for March in a format similar to Exhibit 10-12.
2. What accounts for most of the difference between actual operating income and master budget operating income?
3. What is Great Bubbles' master budget variance? Explain why the income statement performance report provides Great Bubbles' managers with more useful information than the simple master budget variance. What insights can Great Bubbles' managers draw from this performance report?

P10-53A Evaluate divisional performance *(Learning Objective 3)*

Sherwin-Williams is a national paint manufacturer and retailer. The company is segmented into five divisions: Paint Stores (branded retail location), Consumer (paint sold through stores such as Sears, Home Depot, and Lowe's), Automotive (sales to auto manufacturers), International, and Administration. The following is selected hypothetical divisional information for the company's two largest divisions: Paint Stores and Consumer (in thousands of dollars).

	Sales	Operating Income	Total Assets
Paint stores....	$3,900,000	$507,000	$1,500,000
Consumer......	$1,250,000	$175,000	$1,562,500

Assume that management has specified a 20% target rate of return.

Requirements

Round all calculations to two decimal places.

1. Calculate each division's ROI.
2. Calculate each division's sales margin. Interpret your results.
3. Calculate each division's capital turnover. Interpret your results.
4. Use the expanded ROI formula to confirm your results from Requirement 1. Interpret your results.
5. Calculate each division's RI. Interpret your results and offer recommendations for any divisions with negative RI.

6. Total asset data were provided in this problem. If you were to gather this information from an annual report, how would you measure total assets? Describe your measurement choices and some of the pros and cons of those choices.
7. Describe some of the factors that management considers when setting its minimum target rate of return. Describe some of the factors that management considers when setting its minimum target rate of return.
8. Explain why some firms prefer to use RI rather than ROI for performance measurement.
9. Explain why budget versus actual performance reports are insufficient for evaluating the performance of investment centers.

P10-54A Collect and analyze division data from an annual report

(Learning Objective 4)

QuickCo segments its company into four distinct divisions. The net revenues, operating profit, and total assets for these divisions are disclosed in the footnotes to QuickCo's consolidated financial statements and the following presented information:

Notes to Consolidated Financial Statements

Note 1-Basis of Presentation and Our Divisions:

We manufacture, market, and sell a variety of products through our divisions, including furniture and fixtures for the home, office, stores, and health-care facilities. The accounting policies are the same for each division, as indicated in Note 2. There is, however, one exception. QuickCo centrally manages commodity derivatives and does not allocate any gains and losses incurred by these contracts to individual divisions. These derivatives are used to hedge the underlying price risk to the commodities used in production. The resulting gains and losses from these contracts are recorded under corporate expenses rather than allocated to specific divisions.

	Net Revenue			Operating Profit		
	2012	2011	2010	2012	2011	2010
Home furnishings	$11,250	$10,150	$9,750	$3,150	$2,875	$2,325
Office furniture	9,000	8,100	7,800	1,710	1,530	1,470
Store displays	12,500	11,300	10,800	1,500	1,360	1,300
Health-care furnishings	2,250	2,100	2,000	765	740	720
Total division............	35,000	31,650	30,350	7,125	6,505	5,815
Corporate				(270)	(230)	(185)
Total	$35,000	$31,650	$30,350	$6,855	$6,275	$5,630

Corporate includes the costs of our corporate headquarters, centrally-managed initiatives, and certain gains and losses that cannot be accurately allocated to specific divisions, such as derivative gains and losses.

	Amortization of Intangible Assets			Depreciation and Other Amortization		
	2012	2011	2010	2012	2011	2010
Home furnishings	$ 16	$ 11	$ 11	$ 420	$ 410	$ 415
Office furniture	76	71	71	280	260	255
Store displays	74	69	67	490	435	395
Health-care furnishings....			4	30	35	32
Total division....................	166	151	153	1,220	1,140	1,097
Corporate				15	20	19
Total	$166	$151	$153	$1,235	$1,160	$1,116

	Total Assets			Capital Spending		
	2012	2011	2010	2012	2011	2010
Home furnishings	$ 7,500	$ 6,250	$ 5,750	$ 505	$ 515	$ 475
Office furniture	7,500	6,900	6,700	490	320	265
Store displays	15,625	14,425	14,025	845	675	540
Health-care furnishings	1,250	1,050	1,000	25	25	30
Total division	31,875	28,625	27,475	1,865	1,535	1,310
Corporate	1,700	5,260	3,460	220	225	110
Total	$33,575	$33,885	$30,935	$2,085	$1,760	$1,420

Corporate Assets consist of cash, short-term investments, and property, plant, and equipment. The corporate property, plant, and equipment includes the headquarters building, equipment within, and the surrounding property.

Requirements

1. What are QuickCo's four business divisions? Make a table listing each division, its net revenues, operating profit, and total assets.
2. Use the data you collected in Requirement 1 to calculate each division's sales margin. Interpret your results.
3. Use the data you collected in Requirement 1 to calculate each division's capital turnover. Interpret your results.
4. Use the data you collected in Requirement 1 to calculate each division's ROI. Interpret your results.
5. Can you calculate RI using the data presented? Why or why not?

PROBLEMS Group B

P10-55B Evaluate subunit performance *(Learning Objective 4)*

One subunit of Charles Sports Company had the following financial results last month:

Charles Sports–Subunit X	Actual	Flexible Budget	Flexible Budget Variance (U or F)	Variance % (U or F)*
Sales	$490,500	$450,000		
Cost of goods sold	261,500	250,000		
Gross margin	$229,000	$200,000		
Operating expenses	83,440	80,000		
Operating income before service Department charges	$145,560	$120,000		
Service department charges (allocated)	57,500	46,000		
Operating income	$ 88,060	$ 74,000		

**Flexible budget variance ÷ Flexible budget*

CHAPTER 10

Requirements

1. Complete the performance evaluation report for the subunit (round to three decimal places).
2. Based on the data presented, what type of responsibility center is this subunit?
3. Which items should be investigated if part of management's decision criteria is to investigate all variances equal to or exceeding $11,500 and exceeding 14% (both criteria must be met)?
4. Should only unfavorable variances be investigated? Explain.
5. Is it possible that the variances are due to a higher-than-expected sales volume? Explain.
6. Do you think management will place equal weight on each of the $11,500 variances? Explain.
7. Which balanced scorecard perspective is being addressed through this performance report? In your opinion, is this performance report a lead or lag indicator? Explain.
8. List one key performance indicator for the other three balanced scorecard perspectives. Indicate which perspective is being addressed by the indicators you list. Are they lead or lag indicators? Explain.

P10-56B Prepare a flexible budget for planning *(Learning Objective 2)*

Everlasting Bubbles produces multicolored bubble solution used for weddings and other events.

Everlasting Bubbles' plant capacity is 62,500 kits. If actual volume exceeds 62,500 kits, the company must expand the plant. In that case, salaries will increase by 10%, depreciation by 15%, and rent by $4,000. Fixed utilities will be unchanged by any volume increase.

The company's master budget income statement for January follows. It is based on expected sales volume of 55,000 bubble kits.

EVERLASTING BUBBLES, INC. Master Budget Income Statement Month Ended January 31	
Sales revenue	$170,500
Variable expenses:	
Cost of goods sold	68,750
Sales commissions	13,750
Utility expense	5,500
Fixed expenses:	
Salary expense	30,000
Depreciation expense	20,000
Rent expense	15,000
Utility expense	7,000
Total expenses	$160,000
Operating income	$ 10,500

Requirements

1. Prepare flexible budget income statements for the company, showing output levels of 55,000, 60,000, and 65,000 kits.
2. Graph the behavior of the company's total costs.
3. Why might Everlasting Bubbles' managers want to see the graph you prepared in Requirement 2 as well as the columnar format analysis in Requirement 1? What is the disadvantage of the graphic approach?

P10-57B Prepare and interpret a performance report *(Learning Objective 2)*

Refer to the Everlasting Bottles Data in P10-56B. The company sold 60,000 bubble kits during January and its actual operating income was as follows:

EVERLASTING BUBBLES, INC. Master Budget Income Statement Month Ended January 31	
Sales revenue	$191,000
Variable expenses:	
Cost of goods sold	$ 75,500
Sales commissions	18,000
Utility expense	6,000
Fixed expenses:	
Salary expense	32,200
Depreciation expense	20,000
Rent expense	14,000
Utility expense	7,000
Total expenses	$172,700
Operating income	$ 18,300

Requirements

1. Prepare an income statement performance report for January.
2. What accounts for most of the difference between actual operating income and master budget operating income?
3. What is Everlasting Bubbles' master budget variance? Explain why the income statement performance report provides Everlasting Bubbles' managers with more useful information than the simple master budget variance. What insights can Everlasting Bubbles' managers draw from this performance report?

P10-58B Evaluate divisional performance *(Learning Objective 3)*

Sherwin-Williams Paints is a national paint manufacturer and retailer. The company is segmented into five divisions: Paint Stores (branded retail locations), Consumer (paint sold through stores like Sears, Home Depot, and Lowe's), Automotive (sales to auto manufacturers), International, and Administration. The following is selected hypothetical divisional information for its two largest divisions: Paint Stores and Consumer (in thousands of dollars).

	Sales	Operating Income	Total Assets
Paint stores	$3,750,000	$480,000	$1,500,000
Consumer	$1,000,000	$150,000	$1,250,000

Assume that management has specified a 20% target rate of return.

Requirements

Round all calculations to four decimal places.

1. Calculate each division's ROI.
2. Calculate each division's sales margin. Interpret your results.
3. Calculate each division's capital turnover. Interpret your results.
4. Use the expanded ROI formula to confirm your results from Requirement 1. Interpret your results.
5. Calculate each division's RI. Interpret your results and offer recommendations for any division with negative RI.

6. Total asset data was provided in this problem. If you were to gather this information from an annual report, how would you measure total assets? Describe your measurement choices and some of the pros and cons of those choices.
7. Describe some of the factors that management considers when setting its minimum target rate of return.
8. Explain why some firms prefer to use RI rather than ROI for performance measurement.
9. Explain why budget versus actual performance reports are insufficient for evaluating the performance of investment centers.

P10-59B Collect and analyze division data from an annual report

(Learning Objective 3)

BarnaCo segments its company into four distinctive divisions. The net revenues, operating profit, and total assets for these divisions are disclosed in the footnotes to BarnaCo consolidated financial statements and presented here.

	Net Revenue			Operating Profit		
	2012	2011	2010	2012	2011	2010
Home furnishings	$11,000	$ 9,900	$ 9,500	$2,530	$2,255	$1,705
Office furniture	9,100	8,200	7,900	1,820	1,640	1,580
Store displays	12,100	10,900	10,400	1,210	1,070	1,010
Health-care furnishings	1,500	1,350	1,250	495	470	450
Total division........	33,700	30,350	29,050	6,055	5,435	4,745
Corporate...........				(290)	(250)	(205)
Total....................	$33,700	$30,350	$29,050	$5,765	$5,185	$4,540

	Amortization of Intangible Assets			Depreciation and Other Amortization		
	2012	2011	2010	2012	2011	2010
Home furnishings	$ 12	$ 7	$ 7	$ 415	$ 405	$ 410
Office furniture	80	75	75	280	260	255
Store displays	76	71	69	475	420	380
Health-care furnishings			6	45	50	47
Total division..................	168	153	157	1,215	1,135	1,092
Corporate......................				35	40	39
Total..............................	$168	$153	$157	$1,250	$1,175	$1,131

	Total Assets			Capital Spending		
	2012	2011	2010	2012	2011	2010
Home furnishings	$ 6,875	$ 5,625	$ 5,125	$ 510	$ 520	$ 480
Office furniture	6,500	5,900	5,700	490	320	265
Store displays	11,000	9,800	9,400	825	655	520
Health-care furnishings...	625	425	375	30	30	35
Total division..................	25,000	21,750	20,600	1,855	1,525	1,300
Corporate......................	1,700	5,260	3,460	185	190	75
Total..............................	$26,700	$27,010	$24,060	$2,040	$1,715	$1,375

CHAPTER 10

Notes to Consolidated Financial Statements

Note 1-Basis of Presentation and Our Divisions:

We manufacture, market, and sell a variety of products through our divisions, including furniture and fixtures for the home, office, stores, and health-care facilities. The accounting policies are the same for each division, as indicated in Note 2. There is, however, one exception. BarnaCo centrally manages commodity derivatives and does not allocate any gains and losses incurred by these contracts to individual divisions. These derivatives are used to hedge the underlying price risk to the commodities used in production. The resulting gains and losses from these contracts are recorded under corporate expenses rather than allocated to specific divisions.

Corporate includes the costs of our corporate headquarters, centrally-managed initiatives, and certain gains and losses that cannot be accurately allocated to specific divisions, such as derivative gains and losses.

Corporate Assets consist of cash, short-term investments, and property, plant, and equipment. The corporate property, plant and equipment includes the headquarters building, equipment within, and the surrounding property.

Requirements

1. What are BarnaCo's four business divisions? Make a table listing each division, its net revenues, operating profit, and total assets.
2. Use the data you collected in Requirement 1 to calculate each division's sales margin. Interpret your results.
3. Use the data you collected in Requirement 1 to calculate each division's capital turnover. Interpret your results.
4. Use the data you collected in Requirement 1 to calculate each division's ROI. Interpret your results.
5. Can you calculate RI using the data presented? Why or why not?

CRITICAL THINKING

Discussion & Analysis

A10-60 Discussion Questions

1. Describe at least four advantages of decentralization. Also describe at least two disadvantages to decentralization.
2. Compare and contrast a cost center, a revenue center, a profit center, and an investment center. List a specific example of each type of responsibility center. How is the performance of managers evaluated in each type of responsibility center?
3. Explain the potential problem which could arise from using ROI as the incentive measure for managers. What are some specific actions a company might take to resolve this potential problem?
4. Describe at least two specific actions that a company could take to improve its ROI.
5. Define residual income. How is it calculated? Describe the major weakness of residual income.
6. Compare and contrast a master budget and a flexible budget.
7. Describe two ways managers can use flexible budgets.
8. Define key performance indicator (KPI). What is the relationship between KPIs and a company's objectives? Select a company of any size with which you are familiar. List at least four examples of specific objectives that company might have and one potential KPI for each of those specific objectives.
9. List and describe the four perspectives found on a balanced scorecard. For each perspective, list at least two examples of KPIs which might be used to measure performance on that perspective.
10. Contrast lag indicators with lead indicators. Provide an example of each type of indicator.
11. Some companies integrate sustainability measures into the traditional four perspectives in their balanced scorecards. Other companies create a new perspective (or two) for sustainability. Which method do you think would result in better supporting sustainability efforts throughout the organization? Explain your viewpoint.
12. Find an annual report for a publicly held company (go to the company's website and look for "Investor Relations" or a similar link). How many sustainability initiatives can you find in the annual report? What internal balanced scorecard measures do you think they might use to measure progress on each sustainability initiative? (You will have to use your imagination, since typically most balanced scorecard measures are not publicly disclosed.)

Application & Analysis

A10-61 Segmented Financial Information

Select a company you are interested in and obtain its annual reports by going to the company's website. Download the annual report for the most recent year. (On many companies' websites, you will need to visit the Investor Relations section to obtain the company's financial statements.) You may also collect the information from the company's Form 10-K, which can be found at http://sec.gov/idea/searchidea/companysearch_idea.html.

Basic Discussion Questions

1. Locate the company's annual report as outlined previously. Find the company's segment information; it should be in the "Notes to Consolidated Financial Statements" or another, similarly named section. Look for the word "Segment" in a heading; that is usually the section you need.
2. List the segments as reported in the annual report. Make a table listing each operating segment, its revenues, income, and assets.
3. Use the data you collected in Requirement 2 to calculate each segment's sales margin. Interpret your results.
4. Use the data you collected in Requirement 2 to calculate each segment's capital turnover. Interpret your results.
5. Use the data you collected in Requirement 2 to calculate each segment's ROI. Interpret your results.
6. Can you calculate RI using the data presented? Why or why not?
7. The rules for how segments should be presented in the annual report are governed by external financial accounting rules. The information you gathered for the previous

requirements would be used by investors and other external stakeholders in their analysis of the company and its stock. Internally, the company most likely has many segments. Based on what you know about the company and its products or services, list at least five potential segments that the company might use for internal reporting. Explain why this way of segmenting the company for internal reporting could be useful to managers.

Decision Cases

A10-62 Collect and analyze divisional data *(Learning Objective 3)*

Colgate-Palmolive operates two product segments. Using the company's website, locate segment information for 2010 in the company's 2010 annual report. (*Hint:* Look under investor relations.) Then, look in the financial statement footnotes.

Requirements

1. What are two segments (ignore geographical subsets of the one product segment)? Gather data about each segment's net sales, operating income, and identifiable assets.
2. Calculate ROI for each segment.
3. Which segment has the highest ROI? Explain why.
4. If you were on the top management team and could allocate extra funds to only one division, which division would you choose? Why?

A10-63 Compute flexible budget and volume variances *(Learning Objective 2)*

Roland Films distributes DVDs to retailers. Roland's top management meets monthly to evaluate the company's performance. Controller Sabrina Ecton prepared the following performance report for the meeting.

Ecton also revealed that the actual sales price of $10 per movie was equal to the budgeted sales price and that there were no changes in inventories for the month.

Management is disappointed by the operating income results. CEO Karen Jensen exclaims, "How can actual operating income be roughly 12% of the static budget amount when there are so many favorable variances?"

Roland Films, Inc.
Income Statement Performance Report
Month Ended March 31

	Actual Results	Master Budget	Variance
Sales revenue	$1,640,000	$1,960,000	$320,000 U
Variable expenses:			
Cost of goods sold	773,750	980,000	206,250 F
Sales commissions	77,375	107,800	30,425 F
Shipping expense	42,850	53,900	11,050 F
Fixed expenses:			
Salary expense	311,450	300,500	10,950 U
Depreciation expense	208,750	214,000	5,250 F
Rent expense	128,250	108,250	20,000 U
Advertising expense	81,100	68,500	12,600 U
Total expenses	1,623,525	1,832,950	209,425 F
Operating income	$ 16,475	$ 127,050	$110,575 U

Requirements

1. Prepare a more informative performance report. Be sure to include a flexible budget for the actual number of DVDs bought and sold.
2. As a member of Roland's management team, which variances would you want to investigate? Why?
3. Jensen believes that many consumers are postponing purchases of new movies until after the introduction of a new video format. In light of this information, how would you rate the company's performance?

11

Standard Costs and Variances

Learning Objectives

- **1** Explain how and why standard costs are developed
- **2** Compute and evaluate direct material variances
- **3** Compute and evaluate direct labor variances
- **4** Explain the advantages and disadvantages of using standard costs and variances
- **5** Compute and evaluate variable overhead variances
- **6** Compute and evaluate fixed overhead variances
- **7** (Appendix) Record standard costing journal entries

When Apple introduced its legendary iPad in 2010, the direct material cost for a 16GB model was estimated to be $259.60 while the cost of the 32GB model was only 11% higher at $289.10. Although Apple never released its actual costs, a market intelligence company by the name of iSuppli performed "tear down" research to determine the cost of each direct material component found within the iPad: $95 for the touch screen, $26.80 for the processor, $10.50 for the aluminum casing, and so forth. By adding up all of the component costs, iSuppli was able to estimate the total direct material cost of the iPad. In addition to direct materials, manufacturing conversion costs were estimated at $9 per unit.

What iSuppli did was very similar to what many manufacturers do: They figure out how much it *should* cost, in terms of direct materials, direct labor, and manufacturing overhead, to produce their products. These estimates, known as **standard costs**, are used as performance benchmarks against which actual production costs are evaluated. The finance and accounting professionals at Apple's WW Product Cost group are responsible for creating standard costs and analyzing actual costs in relation to the standards. As production costs change due to factors such as technological advances, product redesign (for example, the iPad 2), and sustainability initiatives, standard costs are revised to provide management with realistic cost targets. The variances between standard and actual costs guide managers' attention toward areas of operation that may need their attention. Standard costs also help managers set budgets, such as the total direct material budget for the 20.1 million iPads that are expected to be shipped in 2012.

Sources: http://www.businessweek.com/technology/content/apr2010/tc2010046_788280.htm
http://www.computerworld.com/s/article/9175020/iPad_costs_more_to_make_than_first_thought_says_iSuppli
http://www.isuppli.com/Teardowns/MarketWatch/Pages/iPad-andImitators-Set-to-Shake-up-Electronics-Supply-Chain.aspx
http://jobs.apple.com/index.ajs?BID=1&method=mExternal.showJob&RID=79010&CurrentPage=1

In Chapter 9 we described how managers of Tucson Tortilla planned for the coming year by preparing a master budget. In Chapter 10, we saw how its managers could evaluate performance by comparing actual to budgeted revenues and costs. To gain a better understanding of the master budget variance, managers created a flexible budget to separate the master budget variance into two components: 1) a volume variance and 2) a flexible budget variance. In this chapter, we'll see how the managers of Tucson Tortilla can deepen their analysis by further separating the flexible budget variance into two additional variances: 1) a price variance and 2) a quantity or efficiency variance. To do this, we'll first need to discuss standard costs.

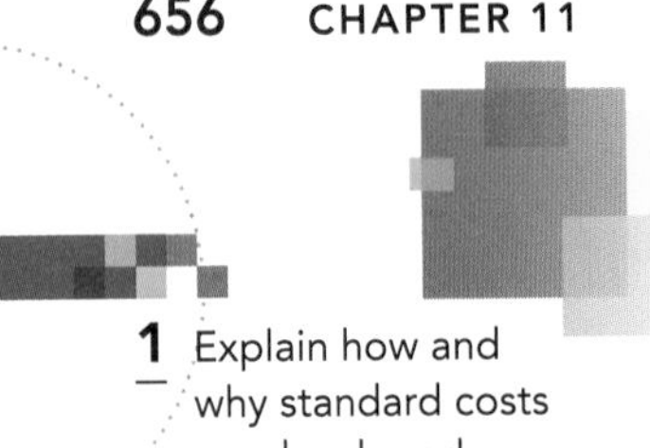

What are Standard Costs?

1 Explain how and why standard costs are developed

Think of a **standard cost** as a budget for a single unit of product. For Tucson Tortilla, a single unit of product is one case of tortilla chips. If a company produces many different products, it will develop a standard cost for each type of product. For example, Colgate-Palmolive will develop a standard cost for each type of toothpaste, soap, and laundry detergent it produces. Even service companies develop standard costs. For example, many hospitals develop standard costs for routine procedures, such as tonsillectomies. The standard cost becomes the benchmark for evaluating actual costs.

For example, let's say the standard cost of producing one case of tortilla chips is $12.00, yet the company actually incurred $12.10 to produce each case during July. The company's managers will want to know why the difference, or variance, of $0.10 per case occurred. Although $0.10 per case may not seem like much, it really is a lot when you consider that the company produces thousands of cases per month. Companies like Coca-Cola, who sold 25.5 billion of cases of product in 2010,[1] are eager to control every penny of cost associated with each unit of product. In highly competitive markets, the company will not be able to pass along cost increases to consumers in the form of price increases. That means that the company's profit margin will shrink with every additional penny of cost incurred. Managers' ability to understand the reasons behind cost variances is a critical factor in controlling future costs.

In our example, why did Tucson Tortilla spend more than anticipated? Perhaps the price of flour increased. Or perhaps more labor was needed than originally expected. On the other hand, extraordinarily hot weather could have driven up the cost of air conditioning used in manufacturing facility. As you can see, the variance in cost could have been due to direct materials, direct labor, manufacturing overhead, or any combination of the three. Managers will only be able to understand the reasons for this unfavorable variance by investigating further.

Why is this important?

"Managers use **standard costs** as a **benchmark** against which to **evaluate** actual costs. If actual costs are **substantially different** than standard costs, **managers** will want to know why so that they have a basis for **improving operations**."

Types of Standards

When managers develop standard costs (often simply referred to as **standards**), they must first determine what type of standard they want to create. **Ideal standards** are standards based on perfect or ideal conditions. These types of standards, which are also known as **perfection standards**, do not allow for any poor quality raw materials, waste in the production process, machine-breakdown, or other inefficiencies. This type of standard is best suited for companies that strive for perfection, such as those that implement lean production systems described in Chapter 4.[2]

Rather than using ideal standards, many companies use **practical (or attainable) standards** that are based on currently attainable conditions. Practical standards include allowances for *normal* amounts of waste and inefficiency. Many managers believe that practical standards make the best cost benchmarks and provide the most employee motivation since they can be attained with a reasonable amount of effort.

Information Used to Develop and Update Standards

Managers draw on many sources of information when setting standards. They consider the amount of material and labor used on each unit produced in the *past*. They also consider the *current* cost of inputs, such as negotiated labor rates and raw materials prices.

[1]The Coca-Cola Company 2010 10-K.

[2]In fact, many lean producers do not advocate the use of standards at all. Since one of the primary goals of lean production is continuous improvement, advocates argue that no standard is ideal enough. Improvements can always be made.

Finally, they estimate how *future* changes in the economy or in the manufacturing process might affect the standards being developed. Engineering studies help determine the amount of time and quantity of material that *should be* needed to produce each unit.

In order to serve as realistic benchmarks, once developed, standards need to be kept up to date. Standards should be adjusted whenever a long-term change in costs or inputs is anticipated. For example, standards should be adjusted when:

- a new labor contract is negotiated with union workers,
- a non-temporary change in raw material costs occurs, or
- a part of the production process is reengineered.

Using outdated standards defeats the entire purpose of using standards in the first place.

Computing Standard Costs

Manufacturers typically prepare standard costs for the direct material, direct labor, and manufacturing overhead required for each unit of product. With respect to manufacturing overhead (MOH), some manufacturers only set standards for the variable MOH per unit since the fixed MOH per unit will fluctuate with changes in volume. Many companies also prepare standards for operating costs. For simplicity, we'll limit our discussion to the three manufacturing costs. We will also assume that Tucson Tortilla has decided to develop practical, rather than ideal, standards.

Standard Cost of Direct Materials

In Chapter 9, we learned that Tucson Tortilla's only direct material (DM) is *masa harina*, corn flour. Engineering studies show that each case of chips requires five pounds of flour, including allowances for normal amounts of spoilage and waste. The company can purchase the flour, including freight-in and purchase discounts, for $1.50 per pound. Therefore, the standard direct material cost per case of tortilla chips is calculated as follows:

Standard Quantity of DM	×	Standard Price of DM	=	Standard cost of DM per case
5 lbs	×	$1.50/pound	=	$7.50

This calculation reveals that Tucson Tortilla expects to spend $7.50 on the direct materials for each case of tortilla chips produced.

Standard Cost of Direct Labor

Companies compute the standard cost of direct labor (DL) in a similar fashion. In Chapter 9, we learned that each case of tortilla chips requires only 0.05 hours of direct labor. This time requirement includes allowances for cleanup, breaks, and so forth since employees are paid for that time as well as actual work time. Furthermore, direct laborers are paid $22 per hour, including payroll taxes and employee benefits. Therefore, the standard direct labor cost per case of tortilla chips is:

Standard Quantity of DL	×	Standard Price of DL	=	Standard cost of DL per case
0.05 DL hours	×	$22.00/DL hour	=	$1.10

Since the production process is fairly automated, the company only anticipates spending $1.10 of direct labor on each case.

Standard Cost of Manufacturing Overhead

Since most of Tucson Tortilla's production process is automated, the company allocates its manufacturing overhead (MOH) using machine hours (MH) as its allocation base. Engineering studies indicate that each case of chips requires 0.10 machine hours to produce. In Chapter 9, we learned that the company expects to produce 400,000 cases of chips during the year. Therefore, the total allocation base is 40,000 machine hours.

Rather than using one predetermined overhead rate as discussed in Chapter 3, some manufacturers split their manufacturing overhead into two rates: a fixed MOH rate and a variable MOH rate. Let's see how this is done.

At a volume of 400,000 cases, Tucson Tortilla expects total variable overhead to be $1,000,000. Using this information, Tucson Tortilla calculates its predetermined *variable* MOH rate as follows:

Total estimated variable MOH	÷	Total estimated amount of the allocation base	=	Variable MOH rate
$1,000,000	÷	40,000 machine hours	=	$25/machine hour

Using the variable MOH rate, Tucson Tortilla can compute the standard cost of variable manufacturing overhead per case as follows:

Standard Quantity of MH	× Variable MOH rate	=	Standard Variable MOH per case
0.10 machine hours	× $25/machine hours	=	$2.50

In Chapter 9, we learned that the company expects to incur $30,000 of fixed overhead each month, resulting in a total of $360,000 for the year. Therefore, the fixed MOH rate can be calculated as follows:

Total estimated fixed MOH	÷	Total estimated amount of the allocation base	=	Fixed MOH rate
$360,000	÷	40,000 machine hours	=	$9/machine hour

The standard cost of *fixed* manufacturing overhead *per case* is calculated as follows:

Standard Quantity of MH	× Fixed MOH rate	=	Standard Fixed MOH per case
0.10 machine hours	× $9/machine hour	=	$0.90

Standard Cost of One Unit

Exhibit 11-1 shows how Tucson Tortilla adds together the standard cost of direct materials, direct labor and manufacturing overhead to determine the standard cost of producing one case of tortilla chips.

EXHIBIT 11-1 Standard cost of producing one unit of product

Manufacturing Cost	Standard Quantity (SQ) × Standard Price (SP)	Standard Cost per Case
Direct materials	5 lbs × $1.50/lb =	$ 7.50
Direct labor	0.05 DL hours × $22/DL hour =	1.10
Variable MOH	0.10 machine hours × $25/machine hour =	2.50
Fixed MOH	0.10 machine hours × $9/machine hour =	0.90
Total		$12.00

The $12 per case figure shown in Exhibit 11-1 may look familiar to you. Indeed, it is the same budgeted unit cost that we used in Chapter 9 when we calculated cost of goods sold for the budgeted Income Statement (Exhibit 9-12). Although we presented the budgeting chapter prior to this chapter, many companies develop standard costs *first*, and *then* use that information to help develop their planning budgets. Standard costs ease the budgeting process by providing a basis for calculating many figures in the master budget.

Sustainability and Standard Costs

In order to advance environmental sustainability, many companies are reengineering their products and packaging. For example, in 2009, J.M. Smucker reduced the amount of resin in its JIF peanut butter jars by 2.2 million pounds—enough resin to produce 34 million jars! Likewise, Kraft reduced the amount of plastic in the lids of its salad dressing bottles and Coca-Cola reduced the amount of plastic in its beverage bottles. These packaging changes not only reduced the amount of plastic that will eventually end up in landfills or recycling plants, but also saved the companies millions of dollars.

Sustainability initiatives such as these will also require management to rethink their direct material quantity and price standards, as less plastic and different types of plastic are used. Reengineering the production process may also result in changes to manufacturing overhead standards, as new equipment is installed and production time is decreased. Operating standards, such as the transportation cost of distributing the product, will also decrease, as the lighter products and smaller containers reduce trucking costs.

Companies may also find themselves creating standards for the amount of waste that leaves the production process in the form of air pollution, scrap, or waste water. Government regulations are forcing companies to cap, or limit, the amount of CO_2 and other pollutants that result from the production process. Therefore, companies will have standards for the maximum pollutants allowed to leave their plants.

See Exercises E11-22A and E11-41B

How do Managers Use Standard Costs to Compute DM and DL Variances?

We just showed how managers develop standard costs. Managers use standards at the beginning of the period to help with the budgeting planning process. Managers also use standards at the end of the period, to evaluate performance and help control future costs. Let's see how this is done.

Using Standard Costs to Develop the Flexible Budget

As we saw in the last chapter, managers often compare actual costs against a flexible budget, rather than directly against the planning budget. Recall that the flexible budget reflects the total cost that *should have been incurred, given the actual volume achieved.*

For example, let's assume that Tucson Tortilla actually produced 31,000 cases of chips during the month of January, even though the company originally planned to produce 29,000 cases. Exhibit 11-2 shows the flexible budget for variable production costs. To generate the flexible budget, managers multiplied the standard costs per unit by the *actual number of units produced.*

EXHIBIT 11-2 Comparing Variable Production Costs with the Flexible Budget

Variable Production Costs (standard cost from Exhibit 11-1)	Actual Costs of Producing 31,000 cases	Flexible Budget for 31,000 cases*	Flexible Budget Variance
Direct Material ($7.50 per case)	$224,000	$232,500	$8,500 F
Direct Labor ($1.10 per case)	34,875	34,100	775 U
Variable MOH ($2.50 per case)	85,200	77,500	7,700 U

*Actual volume of 31,000 cases multiplied by the standard costs per case shown in Exhibit 11-1.

Notice the mixture of favorable and unfavorable flexible budget variances. We'll refer back to this exhibit quite often as we explore the reasons for these variances in the next sections.

Direct Material Variances

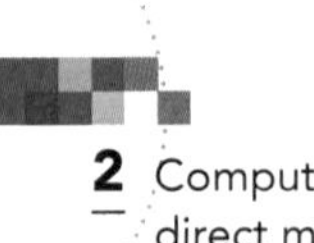

2 Compute and evaluate direct material variances

From Exhibit 10-2 we know that Tucson Tortilla spent $8,500 less on direct materials than standards indicated would be spent to make 31,000 cases. Was this because the company *paid* less for the material than expected, *used* less material than expected, or a combination of the two?

When the amount of materials purchased is the same as the amount used (our example here), we can split the flexible budget variance for direct materials into two separate variances: a price variance and a quantity variance, as shown in Exhibit 11-3.

EXHIBIT 11-3 Splitting the Flexible Budget Variance into Two Components

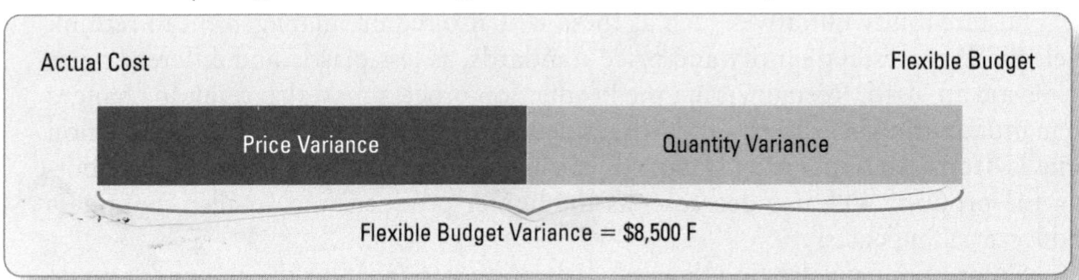

The way we do this is illustrated in Exhibit 11-4. In this model, notice that the company's actual costs are on the top-left side and are stated at Actual Quantity (AQ) × Actual Price (AP). The company's flexible budget is shown on the top-right side and is stated as the standard cost allowed *for the actual volume of output*. It is computed as the Standard Quantity Allowed (SQA) for the actual output × Standard Price (SP). As shown at the bottom in orange, the difference between the two outside terms is the total flexible budget variance.

EXHIBIT 11-4 Direct Materials Variances if DM purchased equals DM used

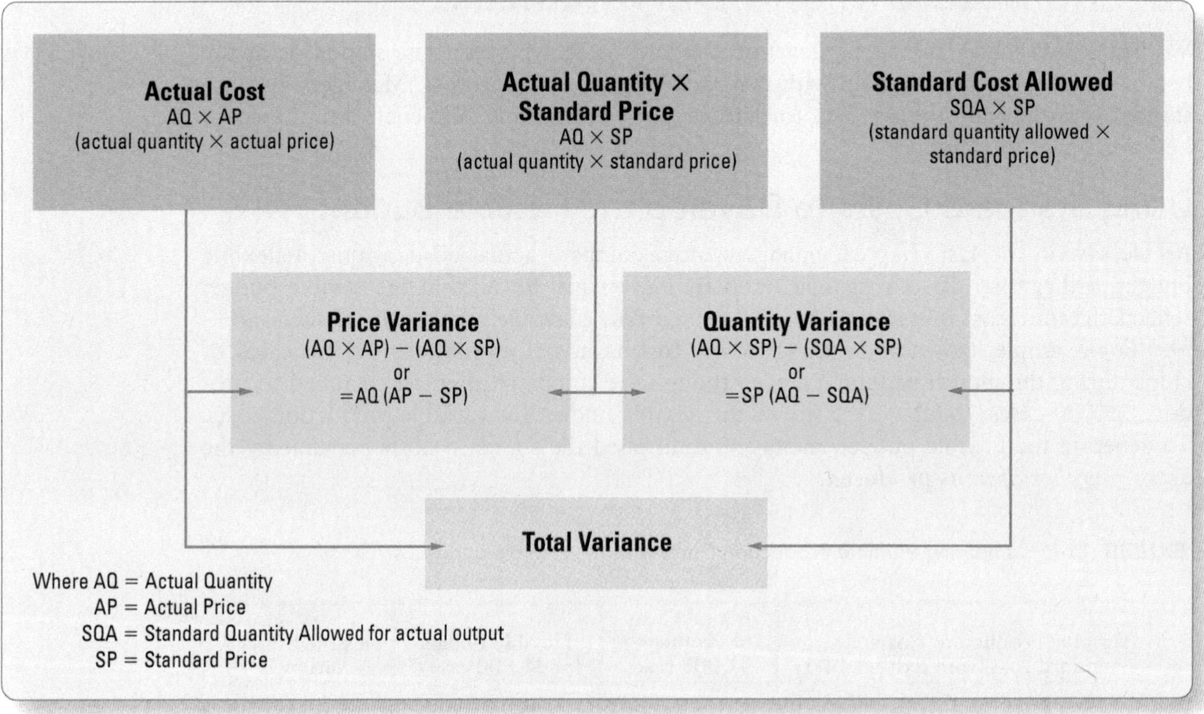

Next, we insert a middle term in the exhibit. The middle term is a mixture of the two outside terms and is defined as: Actual Quantity (AQ) × Standard Price (SP). This middle

term will help us separate the total flexible budget variance into two components: a price variance and a quantity variance.

The direct materials price variance tells managers how much of the total variance is due to paying a higher or lower price than expected for the direct materials it purchased. The direct materials quantity variance tells managers how much of the total variance is due to using a larger or smaller quantity of direct materials than expected. The formulas for these variances are shown in the middle row of Exhibit 11-4.

Let's see how this works for Tucson Tortilla. First, we'll need the following information:

Actual data for January:	
Number of cases produced	31,000 cases
Direct materials purchased	160,000 pounds at $1.40 per pound
Direct materials used	160,000 pounds

Next, we'll insert our company-specific data into the basic model, as shown in Exhibit 11-5. Notice how the "Actual Cost" of $224,000 is the same as what we showed in Exhibit 11-2. Also, the "Standard Cost Allowed" of $232,500 and the total favorable variance of $8,500 are the same as the figures shown in Exhibit 11-2.

EXHIBIT 11-5 Tucson Tortilla's Direct Materials Variances

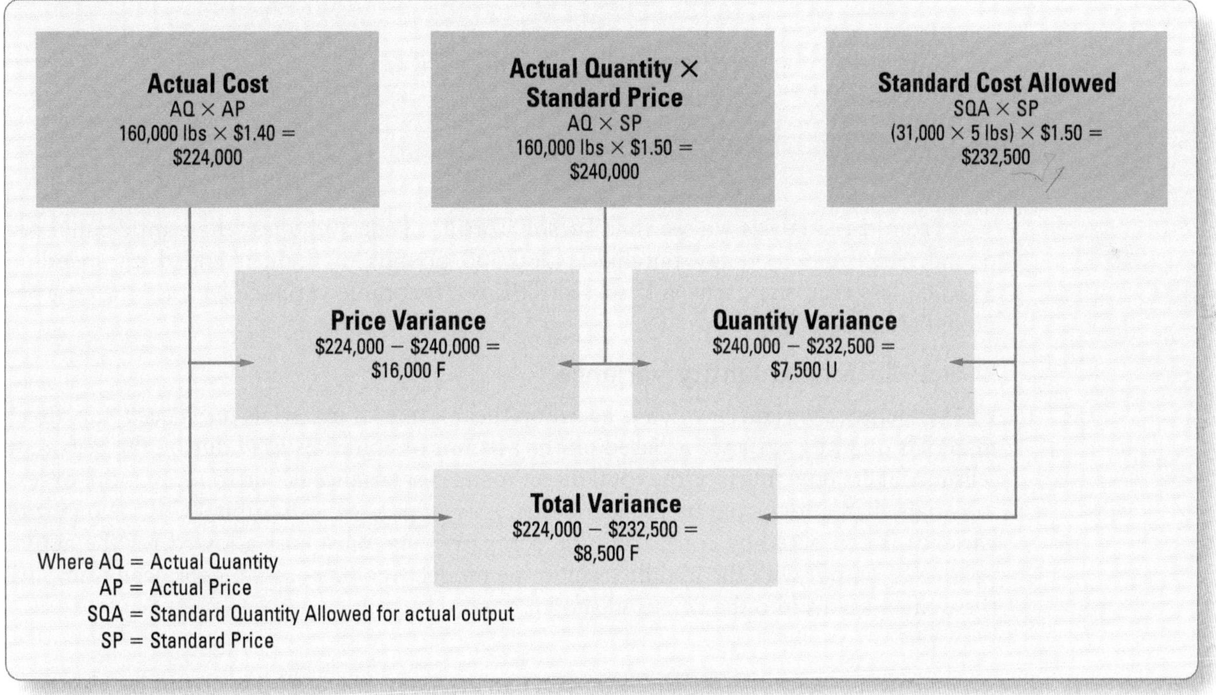

The calculations in Exhibit 11-5 show us that the total direct materials variance of $8,500 is in fact the result of two causes: 1) a favorable price variance of $16,000 and 2) an unfavorable quantity variance of $7,500. The two variances net together to equal the total flexible budget variance of $8,500.

In the next sections we'll explain these variances in more detail and show how formulas can be used as an alternative to creating the diagrams illustrated in Exhibits 11-4 and 11-5.

Direct Material Price Variance

The direct materials prices variance tells managers how much of the overall variance is due to paying a higher or lower price than expected for the quantity of materials it *purchased*. As you can see in Exhibit 11-4, the price variance is computed by comparing the company's actual costs on the left side of the model with the middle term in the model. The lavender boxes in the middle row show that we can simplify the calculations by factoring out the actual quantity (AQ) purchased from both terms in the model as follows:

$$
\begin{aligned}
\text{DM price variance} &= (\text{AQ} \times \text{AP}) - (\text{AQ} \times \text{SP}) \\
&= \text{AQ}\ (\text{AP} - \text{SP})
\end{aligned}
$$

The simplified equation should make sense: it simply calculates the price differential between what was paid for the direct material input (pounds of flour, in our case) and the price anticipated by the standards. The price differential is then multiplied by the quantity of direct materials *purchased*.

Since the amount of materials purchased may be different than the amount of materials used, we will henceforth use the notation AQP to denote the "Actual Quantity Purchased" and AQU to denote the "Actual Quantity Used." In our current example, Tucson Tortilla both purchased and used the same amount of direct materials during January. However, this more specific notation will help us later when we encounter a situation in which the amount of material *purchased* differs from the amount of material *used*.

Let's use the simplified equation to calculate Tucson Tortilla's DM price variance:

$$
\begin{aligned}
\text{DM price variance} &= \text{Actual Quantity Purchased} \times (\text{Actual Price} - \text{Standard Price}) \\
&= \text{AQP} \times (\text{AP} - \text{SP}) \\
&= 160{,}000 \text{ lbs} \times (\$1.40 - \$1.50) \\
&= 160{,}000 \text{ lbs} \times (\$0.10) \\
&= \$16{,}000 \text{ Favorable}
\end{aligned}
$$

From this analysis we see that Tucson Tortilla spent $0.10 *less* than anticipated per pound. Since the company purchased 160,000 pounds of flour, it ended up spending $16,000 less than standards anticipated. This is a favorable variance because the cost per pound is *less* than expected.

Direct Material Quantity Variance

Unlike the price variance, which is based on the amount of materials *purchased*, the direct materials quantity variance is based on the amount of materials *used* during the period. It tells managers how much of the total direct materials variance is due to *using* more or less materials than anticipated by the standards. As you can see in Exhibit 11-4, the quantity variance is computed by comparing the company's standard cost allowed for the actual volume of output with the middle term in the model. Again, we can algebraically simplify these calculations into the equation shown next.

$$
\begin{aligned}
\text{DM quantity variance} &= \text{Standard Price} \times (\text{Actual Quantity Used} - \text{Standard Quantity Allowed}) \\
&= \text{SP} \times (\text{AQU} - \text{SQA}) \\
&= \$1.50 \times [160{,}000 \text{ lbs} - (31{,}000 \text{ cases} \times 5 \text{ lbs/case})] \\
&= \$1.50 \times (160{,}000 \text{ lbs} - 155{,}000 \text{ lbs}) \\
&= \$1.50 \times 5{,}000 \text{ lbs} \\
&= \$7{,}500 \text{ U}
\end{aligned}
$$

Note the following:

1. Since this variance addresses the efficiency with which materials were used, the calculation involves the quantity of direct materials *used* during the period (AQU), *not* the quantity *purchased* (AQP).

2. To calculate the standard quantity of materials allowed (SQA), we start with the number of units actually produced (31,000 cases) and then multiply it by the standard quantity of material allowed per unit (5 lbs per case). The result (155,000 lbs) tells us how much direct material the company expected to use given the actual volume of output.

From this analysis, we see that the company used 5,000 more pounds of corn flour during the period than standards indicated should be used. At a standard price of $1.50 per pound, the excess use of flour cost the company an unanticipated $7,500. This variance is unfavorable, because the company used more direct materials than they should have.

Evaluating Direct Material Variances

Exhibit 11-6 shows us that the favorable flexible budget variance for direct material of $8,500 resulted from

1. purchasing the corn flour at a better-than-expected price, resulting in a savings of $16,000, and
2. using more corn flour than expected, resulting in an additional cost of $7,500.

EXHIBIT 11-6 Summary of Direct Materials Variances

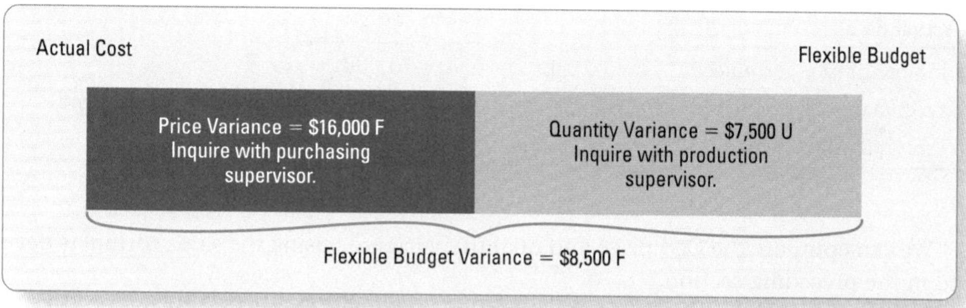

Management will want to know why both of these variances occurred. The best source of information about the price variance is the purchasing supervisor. The supervisor should know why the company was able to purchase the materials at a better-than-expected price. Perhaps alternative suppliers entered the market. Or, a bumper crop of corn pushed down flour prices at all suppliers. On the other hand, perhaps the company was able to make use of faster payment terms, and as a result was able to obtain the flour at a greater discount. Maybe the purchasing agent bought lower grade corn flour. Many possibilities exist.

Note that while the variance is referred to as "favorable," the result may not necessarily be a "good" thing. For example, if the company bought lower grade corn flour, did it have a detrimental impact on the taste of the tortilla chips? Or did it cause additional waste or spoilage that might account for the unfavorable quantity variance?

Management will learn more about the quantity variance by talking with the production supervisor. The production supervisor is in the best position to know why extra corn flour was used. Was something wrong with the corn flour when it arrived (torn bags, inadequate moisture content, and so forth)? Did an accident occur in transporting the flour from the raw material storage area to the production area? Was a batch of chips ruined by adding too much salt? Again, many possibilities exist.

Management will want to uncover the root cause of the variance to determine whether the extra cost was controllable or not. For example, if the corn flour was in poor condition when it arrived, Tucson Tortilla may be able to receive a credit from its supplier or the transportation company that trucked in the flour. Additionally, Tucson Tortilla may want to search for a new supplier. If the cause was a human error in the factory, precautionary measures might be developed that would prevent such errors in the future.

Computing DM Variances when the Quantity of DM Purchased Differs from the Quantity of DM Used

In the example just illustrated, we assumed that the quantity of direct materials purchased was the same as the quantity of direct materials used. This is often the case with lean producers since they buy inventory "just in time" to use it in production. However, traditional manufacturers often buy extra safety stock to ensure they have enough raw materials on hand to meet production if sales demand exceeds the forecast. Recall that we took safety stock into consideration in Chapter 9 when we budgeted the amount of direct materials to purchase (see Exhibit 9-7). As a result, manufacturers often buy slightly more than they immediately need. On the other hand, if raw materials inventory has grown too large, companies will intentionally buy less than the amount required for production in order to shrink their inventory. In either case, the quantity of direct materials purchased may differ from the quantity of direct materials used.

When this occurs, managers still compute the price and quantity variances, but keep the following important points in mind:

1. The DM price variance will be based on the quantity of DM *purchased* (AQP).
2. The DM quantity variance will be based on the quantity of DM *used* (AQU).
3. The DM price and quantity variances will no longer sum (or net) to the total flexible budget variance.

Let's try an example. Assume that the following activity took place in February.

Actual data for February:	
Number of cases produced	20,000 cases
Direct materials purchased	105,000 pounds at $1.45 per pound
Direct materials used	98,000 pounds

We can compute the DM price and quantity variances using the same formulas developed in the preceding section.

The price variance is based on the actual quantity *purchased* (AQP):

$$\begin{aligned}\text{DM price variance} &= \text{AQP} \times (\text{AP} - \text{SP})\\ &= 105{,}000 \text{ lbs} \times (\$1.45 - \$1.50)\\ &= 105{,}000 \text{ lbs} \times (\$0.05)\\ &= \$5{,}250 \text{ F}\end{aligned}$$

By purchasing 105,000 pounds of corn flour at a price that was $0.05 less than standard, the company saved $5,250.

The quantity variance is based on the actual quantity of materials *used* (AQU):

$$\begin{aligned}\text{DM quantity variance} &= \text{SP} \times (\text{AQU} - \text{SQA})\\ &= \$1.50 \times [98{,}000 \text{ lbs} - (20{,}000 \text{ cases} \times 5 \text{ lbs/case})]\\ &= \$1.50 \times (98{,}000 \text{ lbs} - 100{,}000 \text{ lbs})\\ &= \$1.50 \times (2{,}000 \text{ lbs})\\ &= \$3{,}000 \text{ F}\end{aligned}$$

This analysis reveals that the company used 2,000 fewer pounds of corn flour than standards projected, resulting in a cost savings of $3,000.

Direct Labor Variances

3 Compute DL variances

From Exhibit 11-2 we know that Tucson Tortilla only spent $775 more than anticipated on direct labor. Because this is such a small variance, some managers might not consider investigating it. However, it's possible that the total variance is made up of large, but offsetting individual variances, similar to what we saw with the direct materials variances.

By splitting the total direct labor variance into two separate variances, a rate variance and an efficiency variance, we can find out whether the company *paid a higher wage rate* to the factory workers than expected, *used* more time in making the chips than expected, or some combination of these two factors.

Let's assume the following information about Tucson Tortilla's January operations:

Actual data for January:	
Number of cases produced	31,000 cases
Direct labor hours	1,500 hours
Direct labor cost	\$34,875 (resulting in an average wage rate of \$23.25/hr*)

* \$34,875/1,500 hours = \$23.25/hr

Exhibit 11-7 shows the general model for direct labor (DL) variances is almost identical to the model used for direct materials variances. The only real difference is in the names of the variances. For example, instead of a DM *price* variance, we have a DL *rate* variance. The **direct labor rate variance** tells managers how much of the total labor variance is due to paying a higher or lower hourly wage rate than anticipated.

Likewise, instead of the DM *quantity* variance, we have a DL *efficiency* variance. The quantity of time used in production tells management how efficiently employees were working. Therefore, the **direct labor efficiency variance** tells managers how much of the total labor variance is due to using a greater or lesser amount of time than anticipated.

While the terminology for DL variances is slightly different than it was for DM variances, the calculations are essentially the same.

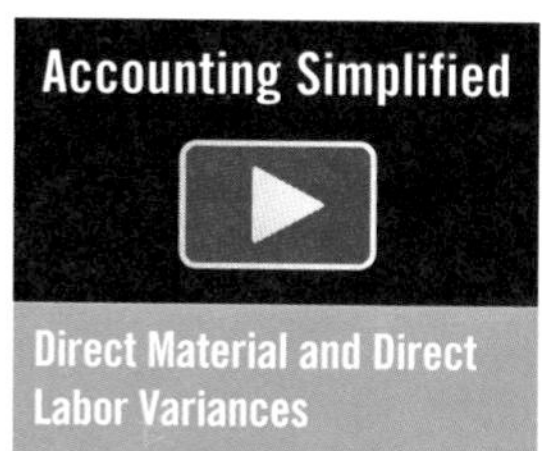

If your instructor is using MyAccountingLab, go to the Multimedia Library for a quick video on this topic.

EXHIBIT 11-7 Calculation of Tuscon Tortilla's Direct Labor Variances

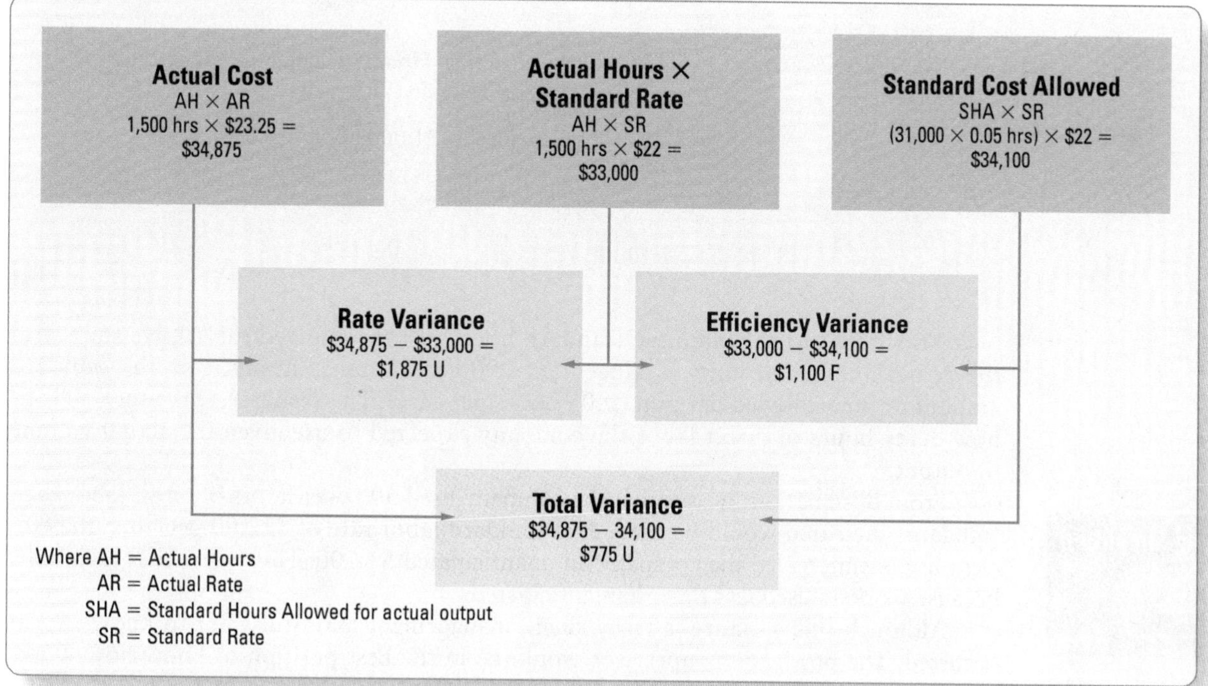

Although the total direct labor variance is small (\$775), Exhibit 11-7 shows us the importance of digging down deeper: the total variance is made up of 1) an unfavorable rate variance of \$1,875 and 2) an offsetting favorable efficiency variance of \$1,100. In the next sections we'll go over these variances in more detail.

Direct Labor Rate Variance

As shown in Exhibit 11-7, the direct labor rate variance is computed on the left side of the model by comparing the company's actual costs with the middle term in the model. Alternatively, we can algebraically simplify the equation, just like we did for the direct material variances. The resulting simplified equation is as follows:

$$
\begin{aligned}
\text{DL rate variance} &= \text{Actual Hours} \times (\text{Actual Rate} - \text{Standard Rate}) \\
&= \text{AH} \times (\text{AR} - \text{SR}) \\
&= 1{,}500 \text{ hrs} \times (\$23.25 - \$22.00) \\
&= 1{,}500 \text{ hrs} \times \$1.25 \\
&= \$1{,}875 \text{ U}
\end{aligned}
$$

This analysis shows management the overall dollar impact of paying an average wage rate that was higher than anticipated. The human resources supervisor and the plant supervisor should be able to explain why this happened. Several possibilities exist. For example, perhaps some lower paid employees were sick or on vacation, and higher paid employees filled in during their absence. Perhaps a wage premium was offered to workers during January to keep morale up during this peak production month. Even though the variance was "unfavorable," neither of these possible explanations suggest poor management. Rather, they simply explain why the average wage rate paid was higher than expected, resulting in an unanticipated additional cost of $1,875.

Direct Labor Efficiency Variance

As you can see in Exhibit 11-7, the efficiency variance is computed on the right side of the model by comparing the company's standard cost allowed with the middle term in the model. Again, we can algebraically simplify these calculations into the equation shown next.

$$
\begin{aligned}
\text{DL efficiency variance} &= \text{Standard Rate} \times (\text{Actual Hours} - \text{Standard Hours Allowed}) \\
&= \text{SR} \times (\text{AH} - \text{SHA}) \\
&= \$22.00 \times [1{,}500 \text{ hrs} - (31{,}000 \text{ cases} \times 0.05 \text{ hrs/case})] \\
&= \$22.00 \times (1{,}500 \text{ hrs} - 1{,}550 \text{ hrs}) \\
&= \$22.00 \times (50 \text{ hrs}) \\
&= \$1{,}100 \text{ F}
\end{aligned}
$$

Notice that to calculate the standard hours of time allowed (SHA), we start with the actual number of units produced (31,000 cases) and multiply it by the standard amount of time allowed per unit (0.05 hours per case). The result (1,550 hours) tells us how many hours of direct labor the company expected to use given the actual volume of output.

From this analysis, we see that the company used 50 fewer hours of direct labor than standards indicated would be used. At a standard labor rate of $22.00 per hour, the efficient use of time saved the company an unanticipated $1,100. This variance is favorable, because workers used *less* time than anticipated.

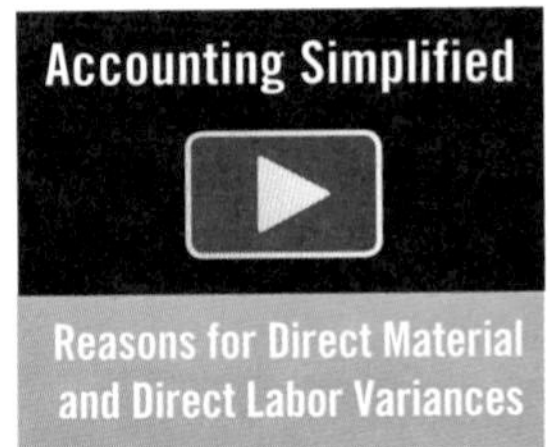

If your instructor is using MyAccountingLab, go to the Multimedia Library for a quick video on this topic.

Although this variance is fairly small, management may still want to know why it occurred. The production supervisor would be in the best position to know how workers were able to produce the actual volume of output faster than expected. Perhaps by using higher-skilled, higher-paid individuals, the work was performed at a faster speed. By searching out the reason for the favorable variance, management may gain a better understanding of how the efficiency occurred and whether similar efficiencies might be replicated in the future or in other areas of operations. Exhibit 11-8 summarizes Tucson Tortilla's direct labor variances for January.

EXHIBIT 11-8 Summary of Direct Labor Variances

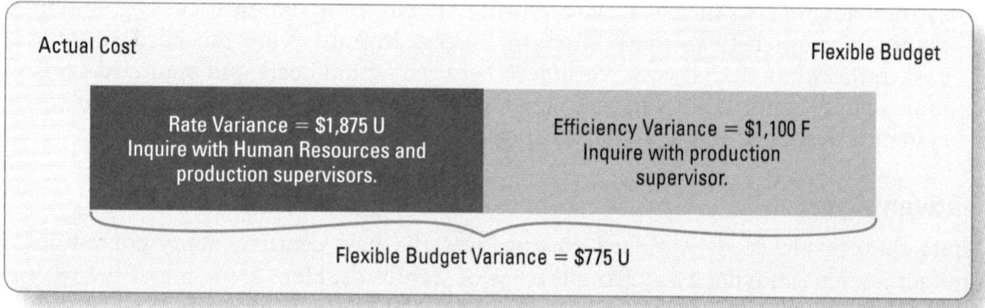

Summary of Direct Material and Direct Labor Variances

Exhibit 11-9 summarizes the formulas for the direct material and direct labor variances, as well as the party responsible for best explaining why the variance occurred.

EXHIBIT 11-9 Summary of DM and DL Variance Formulas

Variance	Formula	Inquire with...
Direct Material Price Variance	= Actual Quantity Purchased × (Actual Price − Standard Price) = AQP × (AP − SP)	Purchasing Supervisor
Direct Material Quantity Variance	= Standard Price × (Actual Quantity Used − Standard Quantity Allowed) = SP × (AQU − SQA)	Production Supervisor
Direct Labor Rate Variance	= Actual Hours × (Actual Rate − Standard Rate) = AH × (AR − SR)	Human Resources and Production Supervisors
Direct Labor Efficiency Variance	= Standard Rate × (Actual Hours − Standard Hours Allowed) = SR × (AH − SHA)	Production Supervisor

Advantages and Disadvantages of Using Standard Costs and Variances

4 Explain the advantages and disadvantages of using standard costs and variances

The practice of using standard costs and variances was developed in the early twentieth century, during the advent and growth of mass manufacturing. Although many manufacturers continue to use standard costs and variances, others do not. Management must weigh the costs against the benefits to decide whether they want to use standard costs and perform detailed variance analysis. Even if management uncovers variances, they will want to use management by exception to determine which variances are significant enough to warrant investigation.

Advantages

- **Cost benchmarks:** One of the greatest advantages of using standard costs is having a benchmark by which to judge actual costs. However, this benchmark is only valid if the standards are kept up to date.
- **Usefulness in budgeting:** Standards are often used as the basis for many components in the master budget, such as the direct materials, direct labor, and manufacturing overhead budgets.
- **Motivation:** The use of practical, or attainable, standards should increase employee motivation because it gives employees a reasonable goal to achieve.

- **Standard costing systems simplify bookkeeping:** Many manufacturers use standards as the backbone to their standard costing system. In a standard costing system, all manufacturing costs entering Work in Process Inventory are recorded at standard cost, rather than actual cost. Variances between actual costs and standard costs are immediately captured in variance accounts in the general ledger. This type of costing system is described in the appendix to this chapter.

Disadvantages

Despite the prevalence of standard costing over the past century, many contemporary manufacturers are moving away from the use of standards. Here are some of the reasons:

- **Outdated or inaccurate standards:** As mentioned previously, standard costs can quickly become outdated or inaccurate as the cost of inputs or the production process changes. Standards should be reviewed an updated at least yearly. They should also be updated whenever a change in process or input costs is considered to be non-temporary in nature. Keeping standards up to date is costly.
- **Lack of timeliness:** In the past, variances were often computed once a month. In today's fast-paced world, such information is often too old to be useful. As a result, some companies are moving towards the daily calculations of variances.
- **Focus on operational performance measures and visual management:** Because of the need for timely data, many lean producers are placing greater emphasis on operational performance measures that are collected daily, or even hourly, and visually displayed where front-line workers can immediately see performance levels. They find such visual reminders much more effective for motivating front-line employees than relying on price and efficiency variances.
- **Lean thinking:** As discussed in Chapter 4, lean companies strive for continual improvement. That means that current standards are not "good enough." Rather than focusing on whether or not production has met current standards, lean producers focus on finding new ways to decrease waste, increase efficiency, and increase quality. They concentrate on looking forward rather than looking at the past.
- **Increase in automation and decrease in direct labor:** Most manufacturers have shifted toward automated production processes. For many manufacturers, direct labor is no longer a primary component of production or a driver of overhead costs. In addition, for companies that pay employees a salary rather than an hourly-wage rate, direct labor is a fixed cost, rather than a variable cost. Finally, at lean companies, employees tend to be multiskilled and cross-trained to perform a number of duties, rather than a single, repetitive task. These front-line workers are held in high esteem by management, and considered to be part of a team effort, rather than a labor force to be controlled. To these companies, direct labor standards are no longer relevant or helpful.
- **Unintended behavioral consequences:** Use of traditional standards can cause unintended behavioral consequences. For example, to obtain a favorable price variance, the purchasing supervisor may buy larger quantities of raw materials than needed. Likewise, a production manager may overproduce to obtain a favorable fixed overhead volume variance (discussed in the second half of the chapter). However, as we learned in Chapter 4, holding or producing excess quantities of inventories is wasteful and costly, and should be avoided.

Decision Guidelines

Standard Costs and Variances

Let's consider some decisions management must make with regards to standard costs and variances.

Decision	Guidelines
What is a standard cost and how can it be used?	A standard cost is a budget for a single unit of product. Standards costs are used as performance benchmarks against which to evaluate actual costs.
Should we use ideal (perfection) standards or practical (attainable) standards?	Since ideal standards are only achievable under flawless conditions, they are best suited for lean producers who strive for perfection. Practical standards, which are attainable with effort, are typically used by traditional manufacturers who want to use motivational, yet realistic, benchmarks.
What information is used to develop standards?	Companies use a combination of historical, current, and projected data to develop standards. Managers often use engineering time and motion studies to determine the quantity of time and materials needed to produce each unit.
How often should standard costs be updated?	Standard costs should be reviewed at least once a year and updated whenever a non-temporary change in costs, inputs, or processes occurs.
How is the direct material price variance computed?	$= \text{Actual Quantity Purchased} \times (\text{Actual Price} - \text{Standard Price})$ $= \text{AQP} \times (\text{AP} - \text{SP})$
How is the direct material quantity variance computed?	$= \text{Standard Price} \times (\text{Actual Quantity Used} - \text{Standard Quantity Allowed})$ $= \text{SP} \times (\text{AQU} - \text{SQA})$
How is the direct labor rate variance computed?	$= \text{Actual Hours} \times (\text{Actual Rate} - \text{Standard Rate})$ $= \text{AH} \times (\text{AR} - \text{SR})$
How is the direct labor efficiency variance computed?	$= \text{Standard rate} \times (\text{Actual Hours} - \text{Standard Hours Allowed})$ $= \text{SR} \times (\text{AH} - \text{SHA})$
Who is usually in the best position to explain why the variances occurred?	DM price variance: Purchasing Supervisor DM quantity variance: Production Supervisor DL rate variance: Production and Human Resources Supervisors DL efficiency variance: Production Supervisor

SUMMARY PROBLEM 1

Memoirs, Inc., produces several different styles and sizes of picture frames. The collage frame consists of 12 interconnected matted picture slots, each surrounded by a wood frame. Engineering studies indicate that each collage frame will require the following direct materials and direct labor:

Materials and Labor:	Quantity of Input	Price of Input
Wood trim for frame borders	18 feet	$ 0.35 per foot
Mattes for individual pictures	12 mattes	$ 0.05 per matte
Sheet glass top	4 square feet	$ 4.00 per square foot
Pressboard frame backing	4 square feet	$ 0.25 per square foot
Direct Labor	0.25 hours	$16 per hour

The following activity regarding direct labor and wood trim occurred during March.

Number of frames produced	25,000 frames
Wood trim purchased	450,000 feet at $0.37 per foot
Wood trim used	455,000 feet
Direct labor hours	6,500 hours
Direct labor cost	$100,750 (resulting in an average wage rate of $15.50/hr*)

* $100,750/6,500 hours = $15.50/hr

Requirements

1. Calculate the standard direct materials cost and standard direct labor cost for each collage frame.
2. Calculate the wood trim direct materials price and efficiency variances for the month of March.
3. Calculate the direct labor rate and efficiency variances for the month of March.

SOLUTIONS

Requirement 1

The standard cost of direct materials and direct labor is calculated by multiplying the standard quantity of input needed for each collage frame by the standard price of the input:

Materials and Labor:	Quantity of Input (a)	Price of Input (b)	Standard Cost (a × b)
Wood trim for frame borders	18 feet	$ 0.35 per foot	$ 6.30
Mattes for individual pictures	12 mattes	$ 0.05 per matte	0.60
Sheet glass top	4 square feet	$ 4.00 per square foot	16.00
Pressboard frame backing	4 square feet	$ 0.25 per square foot	1.00
Direct material cost per unit			$23.90
Direct Labor	0.25 hours	$16 per hour	$ 4.00

Requirement 2

The direct material price variance is based on the quantity of materials (wood trim) *purchased*:

$$\begin{aligned} \text{DM price variance} &= \text{AQP} \times (\text{AP} - \text{SP}) \\ &= 450{,}000 \text{ ft} \times (\$0.37 - \$0.35) \\ &= 450{,}000 \text{ ft} \times \$0.02 \\ &= \$9{,}000 \text{ U} \end{aligned}$$

The company spent $0.02 per foot more than anticipated on the 450,000 feet of wood trim that it purchased, resulting in an unfavorable price variance of $9,000.

The direct materials quantity variance is based on the quantity of materials (wood trim) *used*:

$$\begin{aligned} \text{DM quantity variance} &= \text{SP} \times (\text{AQU} - \text{SQA}) \\ &= \$0.35 \times [455{,}000 \text{ ft} - (25{,}000 \text{ frames} \times 18 \text{ ft/frame})] \\ &= \$0.35 \times (455{,}000 \text{ ft} - 450{,}000 \text{ ft}) \\ &= \$0.35 \times 5{,}000 \text{ ft} \\ &= \$1{,}750 \text{ U} \end{aligned}$$

This analysis reveals that using 5,000 more feet of wood trim than anticipated resulted in an unanticipated additional cost of $1,750.

Requirement 3

The direct labor rate variance is computed as follows:

$$\begin{aligned} \text{DL rate variance} &= \text{AH} \times (\text{AR} - \text{SR}) \\ &= 6{,}500 \text{ hrs} \times (\$15.50 - \$16.00) \\ &= 6{,}500 \text{ hrs} \times (\$0.50) \\ &= \$3{,}250 \text{ F} \end{aligned}$$

The company spent $0.50 less per hour than anticipated, resulting in a $3,250 F variance over the 6,500 hours that were worked.

The direct labor efficiency variance is calculated as follows:

$$\begin{aligned} \text{DL efficiency variance} &= \text{SR} \times (\text{AH} - \text{SHA}) \\ &= \$16.00 \times [6{,}500 - (25{,}000 \text{ frames} \times 0.25 \text{ hrs/frame})] \\ &= \$16.00 \times (6{,}500 - 6{,}250 \text{ hrs}) \\ &= \$16.00 \times 250 \text{ hrs} \\ &= \$4{,}000 \text{ U} \end{aligned}$$

At a standard labor rate of $16.00 per hour, the extra use of time cost the company an unanticipated $4,000.

How do Managers Use Standard Costs to Compute MOH Variances?

In the first half of the chapter we learned how Tucson Tortilla developed standard costs and then used those standards to evaluate their direct material and direct labor costs. In this half of the chapter, we'll look at the four manufacturing overhead (MOH) variances that are typically computed: two related to variable MOH costs and two related to fixed MOH costs.

Variable Manufacturing Overhead Variances

5 Compute and evaluate variable overhead variances

From Exhibit 11-2, we learned that Tucson Tortilla had an unfavorable flexible budget variance of $7,700. But why did this unexpected additional cost occur?

Manufacturers usually split the total variable MOH variance into rate and efficiency variances, just as they do for direct labor. Exhibit 11-10 shows the general model for calculating variable MOH rate and efficiency variances is almost identical to the model used for direct labor rate and efficiency variances. The only real difference in the calculations is the rate that is used: we use the *variable manufacturing overhead rate*, not the direct labor wage rate. And since Tucson Tortilla allocates its overhead using machine hours, the hours refer to machine hours rather than direct labor hours.[3] Here is the information from January's operations:

Data for January	
Number of cases produced	31,000 cases
Standard variable MOH rate	$ 25 per machine hour
Standard hours required per case	0.10 machine hours
Actual machine hours	3,000 machine hours
Actual variable MOH costs	$85,200 (resulting in an *actual* variable MOH rate of $28.40* per machine hour)

* $85,200/3,000 hours = $28.40/machine hour

Variable Overhead Rate Variance

As shown in Exhibit 11-10, the **variable overhead rate variance** is the difference between the actual variable MOH costs incurred during the period ($85,200) and the amount of variable MOH expected ($75,000) considering the actual hours worked. It tells managers whether more or less was spent on variable overhead than expected given the actual machine hours run. Because of this, the variable overhead rate variance is also sometimes called the **variable overhead spending variance**. The variance formula can be algebraically simplified into the following formula:

$$\begin{aligned}\text{Variable MOH rate variance} &= \text{Actual Hours} \times (\text{Actual Rate} - \text{Standard Rate})\\ &= AH \times (AR - SR)\\ &= 3{,}000 \text{ machine hrs} \times (\$28.40 - \$25.00)\\ &= 3{,}000 \text{ machine hrs} \times (\$3.40)\\ &= \$10{,}200 \text{ U}\end{aligned}$$

The interpretation of this variance is not quite as straight-forward as the interpretation of the direct labor rate variance. For one, variable MOH is made up of a number of different

[3]Many companies allocate manufacturing overhead using direct labor hours rather than machine hours. For these companies, the hours used in calculating the manufacturing overhead variances will be *identical* to the hours used in calculating the direct labor variances.

EXHIBIT 11-10 Calculation of Variable Overhead Variances

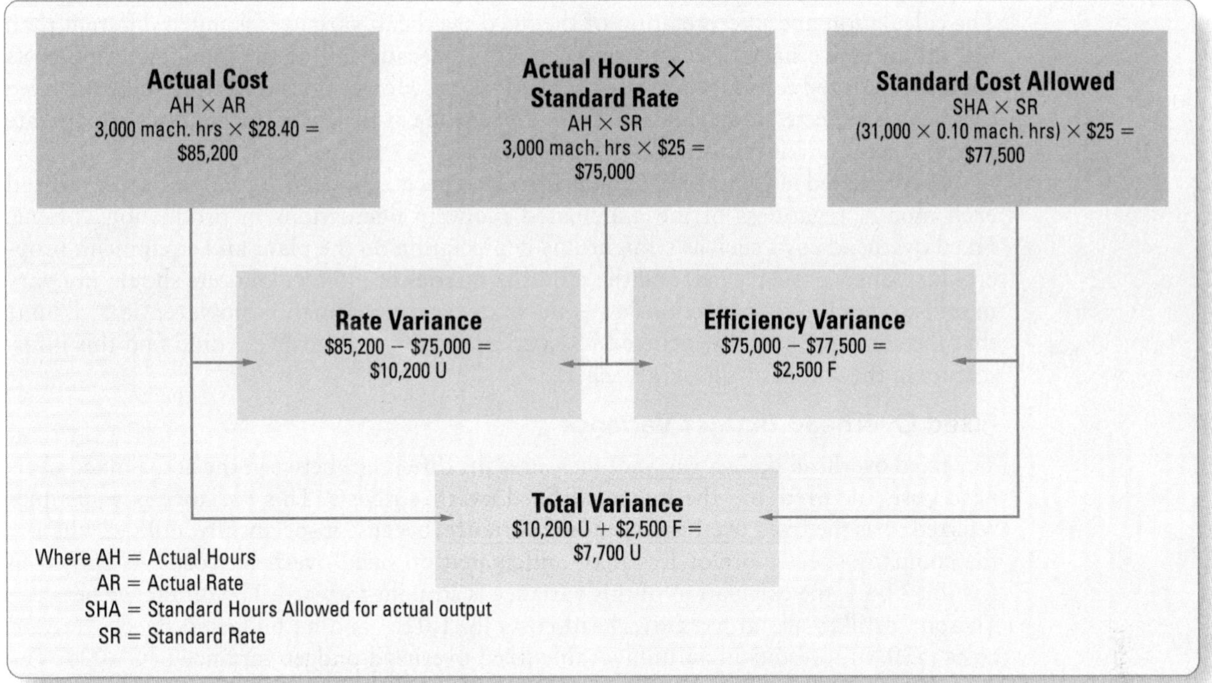

costs, including indirect materials, indirect labor, and other variable overhead costs such as the variable portion of the utility bill. One particular cost (for example, indirect materials) could be higher than expected, yet another cost (for example, indirect labor) could be less than expected. As a result, the variance could be due to more than one input.

Secondly, we don't know if the variance is due to *using* more of the input than expected (for example, using more indirect materials than expected) or because the input *cost more* than expected from the suppliers. On average, management expected variable overhead to cost $25 per machine hour. However, we see that the actual rate ($28.40 per machine hour) turned out to be quite a bit higher. The production supervisor is usually in the best position to help management understand why this variance occurred.

Variable Overhead Efficiency Variance

As shown in Exhibit 11-10, the variable overhead efficiency variance is the difference between the actual machine hours run and the standard machine hours allowed for the actual production volume, calculated at the variable MOH rate. Again, it can be algebraically simplified into the following formula:

Variable MOH efficiency variance = Standard Rate × (Actual Hours − Standard Hours Allowed)
= SR × (AH − SHA)
= $25 × [3,000 mch hrs − (31,000 cases × 0.10 mch hrs/case)]
= $25 × (3,000 mch hrs − 3,100 mch hrs)
= $25 × (100 mch hrs)
= $2,500 F

The efficiency variance does not tell management anything with regards to how efficiently variable manufacturing overhead was used. Rather, it is directly tied to the efficiency with which the machine hours were used. It tells managers how much of the total variable MOH variance is due to using more or fewer machine hours than anticipated for the actual volume of output. The production supervisor would be in the best position to explain why this variance occurred.

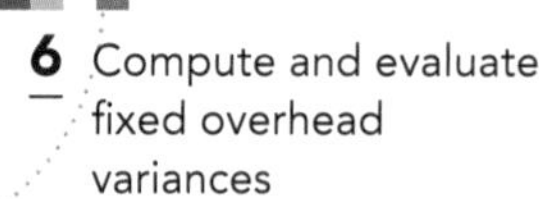

6 Compute and evaluate fixed overhead variances

Fixed Manufacturing Overhead Variances

The calculation and interpretation of the fixed overhead variances is much different than the variances we have discussed thus far. Why? Because all of the manufacturing costs we have analyzed thus far have been *variable* costs. However, as the name suggests, fixed overhead is expected to remain at a *fixed* level as long as the company continues to operate within a certain (relevant) range of production.

As discussed in Chapter 9, Tucson Tortilla expects to incur $30,000 of fixed overhead each month, regardless of the anticipated monthly fluctuations in production volume. Fixed overhead costs such as straight-line depreciation on the plant and equipment, property insurance, property tax, and the monthly salaries of indirect laborers should not vary month-to-month as production levels fluctuate to meet demand. However, let's assume that the company actually incurred $31,025 of fixed overhead. We would find this information in the company's general ledger.

Fixed Overhead Budget Variance

The <u>fixed overhead budget variance</u> measures the difference between the actual fixed overhead costs incurred and the budgeted fixed overhead costs. This variance is sometimes referred to as the <u>fixed overhead spending variance</u>, because it specifically looks at whether the company spent more or less than anticipated on fixed overhead costs. As shown in Exhibit 11-11, the calculation of this variance is straight forward. The difference between Tucson Tortilla's actual fixed overhead costs ($31,025) and its budgeted fixed overhead costs ($30,000) results in an unfavorable fixed overhead budget variance of $1,025. The variance is unfavorable if actual fixed overhead costs are more than budgeted, and favorable if actual costs are lower than budgeted.

EXHIBIT 11-11 Calculation of Fixed Overhead Variances

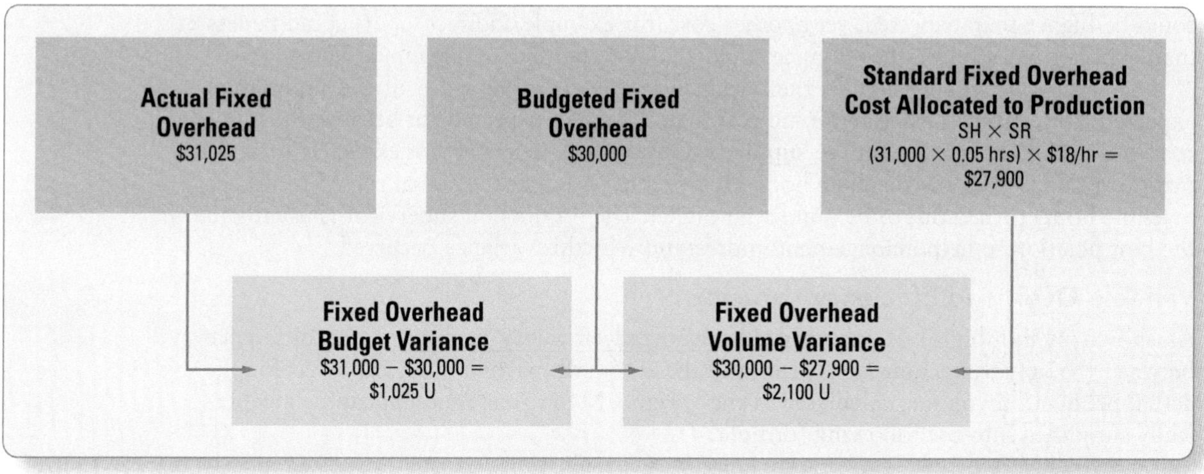

The best way to uncover the cause of the fixed overhead budget variance is to compare each fixed overhead cost component against the budgeted amount. Perhaps indirect laborers received a raise that was not foreseen when the budget was prepared. Perhaps the insurance company increased its premiums, or the city increased property taxes. Although the variance is labeled "unfavorable," the reason for the variance may not be a bad thing. Nor may it be controllable. For example, let's say the unfavorable variance was caused by a raise in salary given to certain indirect laborers in the plant. The raise may result in a boost to employee morale, leading to better productivity. On the other hand, if the unfavorable variance was caused by an increase in city property taxes, management may have little recourse. If however, the variance was caused by an increase in insurance premiums, management may decide to shop around for a different insurance carrier.

Fixed Overhead Volume Variance

As shown in Exhibit 11-11, the **fixed overhead volume variance** is the difference between the budgeted fixed overhead and the *standard fixed overhead cost* allocated to production.[4] The standard cost is calculated the same way as we calculated earlier standard costs: we start with the actual volume produced (31,000 cases) then multiply it by the standard hours allowed per case (0.10 machine hrs) to get the standard hours allowed. Finally, we multiply the standard hours allowed by the fixed MOH rate ($9/DL hr) to get the standard fixed overhead cost allocated to production:

$$\begin{aligned}\text{Standard Fixed Overhead Cost Allocated to Production} &= (\text{Standard Hours Allowed} \times \text{Standard Rate})\\ &= (31{,}000 \text{ cases} \times 0.10 \text{ mach. hrs/case}) \times \$9/\text{hr}\\ &= 3{,}100 \text{ hrs} \times \$9/\text{machine hr}\\ &= \$27{,}900\end{aligned}$$

The fixed overhead volume variance results from two causes:

1. Treating fixed overhead costs *as if* they were variable in order to allocate the costs to individuals units of product; and
2. Incorrectly estimating the level of activity when calculating the predetermined fixed MOH rate.

For example, Tucson Tortilla calculated its predetermined fixed MOH rate ($9/machine hour) based on an estimated yearly production volume of 400,000 cases. Recall from Chapter 6 that fixed costs per unit of activity vary inversely with changes in volume. Had the production estimate been higher than 400,000 cases, the predetermined fixed overhead rate would have been lower than $9 per machine hour. On the other hand, had the production estimate been lower than 400,000 cases, the fixed overhead rate would have been higher than $9 per machine hour. Since production volume was not the same as anticipated, we expect a difference between what was budgeted for fixed overhead and the amount of fixed overhead allocated to production.

In essence, the fixed overhead volume variance measures the utilization of the fixed capacity costs. If volume is higher than originally anticipated, the variance will be favorable, because more units were produced with the same amount of fixed resources. In essence, the company used those fixed resources more efficiently. In this situation, the standard fixed overhead cost allocated to production is *greater* than the amount budgeted. In other words, the company *overallocated* fixed overhead to production, as shown in Exhibit 11-12.

EXHIBIT 11-12 Favorable Fixed Overhead Volume Variance

On the other hand, if production volume is lower than anticipated, the variance is denoted as unfavorable due to the fact that fixed costs were not used to produce as many units as anticipated. Since the number of units produced was less than anticipated,

[4]In Chapter 3 we learned about a *normal* costing system in which manufacturing overhead is allocated to production using a predetermined MOH rate multiplied by the actual quantity of the allocation base used (such as actual machine hours used by the job). In a *standard* costing system, companies allocate manufacturing overhead to production differently: they multiply the predetermined manufacturing overhead rate by the *standard quantity of the allocation base allowed,* rather than the *actual quantity of the allocation base used.*

production capacity was used less efficiently than anticipated, leading to an unfavorable volume variance. In this situation, the standard fixed overhead cost allocated to production is less than the amount budgeted. In other words, the company *underallocated* fixed overhead, as shown in Exhibit 11-13.

EXHIBIT 11-13 Unfavorable Fixed Overhead Volume Variance

Extreme caution should be used when interpreting the volume variance. Again, favorable does not equate with "good," nor does unfavorable equate with "bad." For companies striving to create lean production environments, inventory levels will naturally fall, leading to an unfavorable volume variance. Has a "bad" decision been made? Absolutely not! The lean producer will generally be much more efficient in the long run than its traditional counterpart. The challenge during the transition phase will be for management to determine how to best use the newly freed capacity, and not be misled by the resulting temporary unfavorable volume variances that may occur.

Standard Costing Systems

As we have just seen, many manufacturers use standard costs independent of the general ledger accounting system to evaluate performance through variance analysis. However, other companies integrate standards directly into their general ledger accounting. This method of accounting, called standard costing, is discussed in the Appendix to this chapter.

Decision Guidelines

Standard Costs and Variances

Let's consider some of management's decisions related to overhead variances.

Decision	Guidelines
Should we calculate and interpret all manufacturing overhead variances the same way?	Variable overhead costs are expected to change in total as production volume changes. However, fixed overhead costs should stay constant within a relevant range of production. Therefore, management will want to analyze variable and fixed MOH variances separately.
What variable overhead variances should we compute?	Two variable overhead variances are typically computed: • Rate (or spending) variance tells managers if they spent more or less than anticipated on variable MOH costs considering the actual hours of work used. • Efficiency variance tells managers nothing about the efficiency with which variable overhead costs were used. Rather, it is tied directly to the efficiency with which machine hours or labor hours were used.
How is the variable overhead *rate* (or *spending*) variance computed?	= Actual Hours × (Actual Rate − Standard Rate) = AH × (AR − SR)
How is the variable overhead *efficiency* variance computed?	= Standard Rate × (Actual hours − Standard Hours Allowed) = SR × (AH − SHA)
What fixed overhead variances should we compute?	Two fixed overhead variances are typically computed: • Budget (or spending) variance tells managers if they spent more or less than anticipated on fixed overhead costs. • Volume variance tells managers if too much or too little fixed overhead was allocated to production due to the actual volume of production being different than the volume used to calculate the predetermined fixed MOH rate.
How is the fixed overhead *budget* variance computed?	= Actual fixed overhead − Budgeted fixed overhead
How is the fixed overhead *volume* variance computed?	= Budgeted fixed overhead − Standard fixed overhead cost allocated to production = Budgeted fixed overhead − (SHA × SR)
Who is usually in the best position to explain why variances occurred?	Management will want to compare the actual cost of individual MOH components (such as indirect labor, utilities, property taxes) against the budgets for those same components. The purchasing and production supervisors may also be able to offer insights.
How should the fixed overhead volume variance be interpreted?	A favorable variance means that more units were produced than originally anticipated, leading to an overallocation of fixed MOH. An unfavorable variance means that fewer units were produced than originally anticipated, leading to an underallocation of fixed MOH.

SUMMARY PROBLEM 2

Memoirs, Inc., produces several different styles and sizes of picture frames. The following activity describes Memoirs' overhead costs during March:

Number of frames produced	25,000 frames
Predetermined variable MOH rate	$ 6.00 per DL hour
Predetermined fixed MOH rate	$ 12.00 per DL hour
Budgeted fixed manufacturing overhead	$70,000
Actual direct labor hours	6,500 hours
Actual variable manufacturing overhead	$40,625, resulting in an actual rate of $6.25* per DL hour
Actual fixed manufacturing overhead	$68,000
Standard direct labor allowed per unit	0.25 hours per frame

*$40,625/6,500 hours

Requirements

1. Calculate the variable overhead rate and efficiency variances for the month of March.
2. Calculate the fixed overhead budget and volume variances for the month of March.

SOLUTIONS

Requirement 1

Variable MOH rate variance = Actual Hours × (Actual Rate − Standard Rate)
= AH × (AR − SR)
= 6,500 hrs × ($6.25 − $6.00)
= 6,500 hrs × ($0.25)
= $1,625 U

Variable MOH efficiency variance = Standard Rate × (Actual Hours − Standard Hours Allowed)
= SR × (AH − SHA)
= $6.00 × [6,500 − (25,000 frames × 0.25 hrs/frame)]
= $6.00 × (6,500 − 6,250 hrs)
= $6.00 × 250 hrs
= $1,500 U

Requirement 2

The fixed overhead variances are calculated as follows:

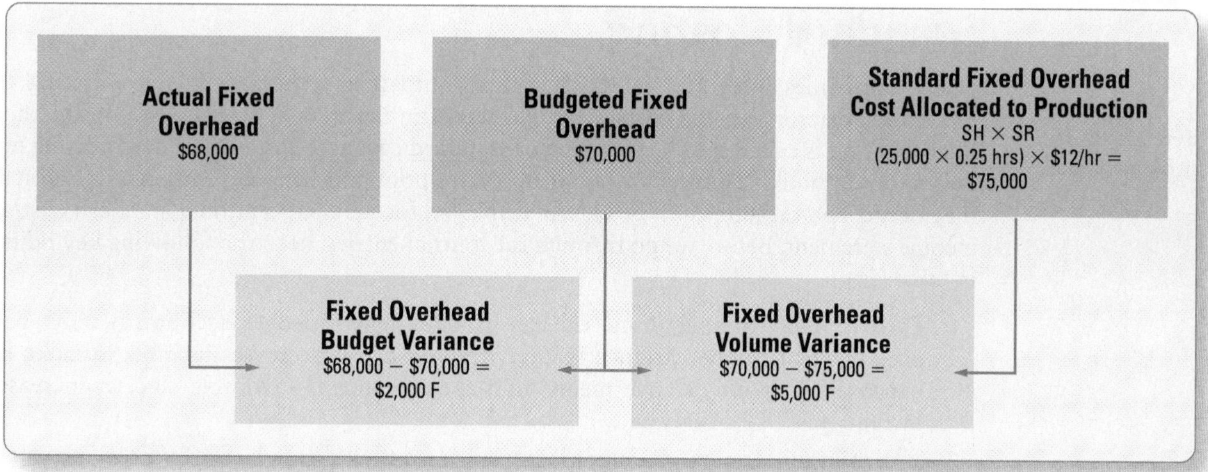

- The budget variance is favorable since less was spent on fixed overhead than budgeted.
- The volume variance is favorable since more was allocated to production than was budgeted. This means that more units were produced than budgeted.

Appendix 11A

Standard Costing

7 Record standard costing journal entries

Many companies integrate standards directly into their general ledger accounting by recording inventory-related costs at standard cost rather than at actual cost. This method of accounting is called **standard costing** or **standard cost accounting**. Standard costing not only saves on bookkeeping costs but also isolates price and efficiency variances as soon as they occur. The variances will be clearly displayed for management on a standard costing income statement. Before we go through the journal entries, keep the following key points in mind:

1. Each type of variance discussed has its own general ledger account. A debit balance means that the variance is unfavorable since it decreases income (just like an expense). A credit balance means that the variance is favorable since it increases income (just like a revenue).
2. Just as in job costing, the manufacturing costs flow through the inventory accounts in the following order: raw materials → work in process → finished goods → cost of goods sold. The difference is that *standard costs* rather than actual costs are used to record the manufacturing costs entered into the inventory accounts.
3. At the end of the period, the variance accounts are closed to Cost of Goods Sold to correct for the fact that the standard costs recorded in the accounts were different from actual costs. Assuming that most inventory worked on during the period has been sold, any error from using standard costs rather than actual costs is contained in Cost of Goods Sold. Closing the variances to Cost of Goods Sold corrects the account balance.

Journal Entries

We use Tucson Tortilla's *January* transactions, just as we did in the chapter, to demonstrate standard costing.

1. **Recording Raw Materials Purchases**—Tucson Tortilla debits Raw Materials Inventory for the *actual quantity* of corn flour purchased (160,000 pounds) recorded at the *standard price* ($1.50 per pound). It credits Accounts Payable for the *actual quantity* of corn flour purchased (160,000 pounds) recorded at the *actual price* ($1.40 per pound) because this is the amount owed to Tucson Tortilla's suppliers. The difference is the direct material *price* variance.

	Raw Materials Inventory (160,000 × $1.50)	240,000	
	Accounts Payable (160,000 × $1.40)		224,000
	DM Price Variance		16,000
	(to record purchase of raw materials)		

The favorable price variance is the same shown as in Exhibit 11-5. Since it is favorable, it has a credit balance which increases Tucson Tortilla's January profits.

2. **Recording Use of Direct Materials**—When Tucson Tortilla *uses* direct materials, it debits Work in Process Inventory at standard: *standard price* ($1.50) × *standard quantity* of direct materials that should have been used (31,000 cases × 5 lbs per case = 155,000 pounds). *This maintains Work in Process Inventory at a purely standard cost.* Raw Materials Inventory is credited for the *actual quantity* of materials used in production (160,000 pounds) recorded at the *standard price* ($1.50) since this is the price at which the materials were entered into Raw Materials Inventory in the

previous journal entry. The difference is the direct materials *quantity* variance. The direct materials quantity variance is recorded when Tucson Tortilla records the *use* of direct materials:

	Work in Process Inventory (155,000 × $1.50)	232,500	
	DM Quantity Variance	7,500	
	Raw Materials Inventory (160,000 × $1.50)		240,000
	(to record use of direct materials)		

The unfavorable quantity price variance is the same as shown in Exhibit 11-5. Since it is unfavorable, it has a debit balance, which decreases Tucson Tortilla's January profits.

3. **Recording Direct Labor Costs**—Since Work in Process Inventory is maintained at standard cost, Tucson Tortilla debits Work in Process Inventory for the *standard rate* for direct labor ($22 per hour) × *standard hours* of direct labor that should have been (31,000 cases × 0.05 hours per case = 1,550 hours). Tucson Tortilla credits Wages Payable for the *actual* hours worked at the *actual* wage rate since this is the amount owed to employees. At the same time, Tucson Tortilla records the direct labor price and efficiency variances calculated in Exhibit 11-7. The *unfavorable* DL Rate Variance is recorded as a *debit*, while the *favorable DL* Efficiency Variance is recorded as a *credit.*

	Work in Process Inventory (1,550 hrs × $22)	34,100	
	DL Rate Variance (Exhibit 11-7)	1,875	
	DL Efficiency Variance (Exhibit 11-7)		1,100
	Wages Payable (1,500 hrs × $23.25)		34,875
	(to record use of direct labor)		

4. **Recording Manufacturing Overhead Costs Incurred**—Tucson Tortilla records manufacturing overhead costs as usual, debiting the manufacturing overhead account and crediting various accounts. The actual costs can be found in Exhibits 11-10 and Exhibit 11-11:

	Variable Manufacturing Overhead (Exhibit 11-10)	85,200	
	Fixed Manufacturing Overhead (Exhibit 11-11)	31,025	
	Various Accounts		116,225
	(to record actual overhead costs incurred)		

5. **Allocating Overhead**—In standard costing, the overhead allocated to Work in Process Inventory is computed using the standard overhead rates ($25/MH for variable MOH and $9/MH for fixed overhead) × standard quantity of the allocation base allowed for the actual output (31,000 cases × 0.10 MH per case = 3,100 MH). As usual, the Manufacturing Overhead account is credited when allocating overhead:

	Work in Process Inventory	105,400	
	Variable Manufacturing Overhead		
	(3,100 MH × $25/MH)		77,500
	Fixed Manufacturing Overhead		
	(3,100 MH × $9/MH)		27,900

This journal entry corresponds with our calculations in Exhibits 11-10 and Exhibit 11-11.

6. **Recording the Completion**—So far, Work in Process has been debited with $372,000 of manufacturing cost ($232,500 of direct materials + $34,100 of direct labor + $105,400 of MOH). Does this make sense? According to Exhibit 11-1, the standard cost of manufacturing one case is $12.00. If we take the $372,000 of cost and divide it by 31,000 cases, we get $12.00 per case! This is how it should be—through the standard costing journal entries, Tucson Tortilla has successfully recorded each case at its standard cost of $12. In addition, it has captured all of the variances in separate variance accounts on the general ledger. As the units are completed, the standard cost of each case is transferred out of Work in Process and into Finished Goods:

	Finished Goods Inventory (31,000 × $12.00)	372,000	
	Work in Process Inventory (31,000 × $12.00)		372,000
	(to record completion of the 31,000 cases)		

7. **Recording the Sale and Release of Inventory**—When the cases are sold, *Sales Revenue* is recorded at the standard, or budgeted sales price ($20 per case, from Exhibit 9-5), but Accounts Receivable (and Cash, for COD sales) is recorded at the actual sales price. Let's assume the company actually sold 32,000 cases at an average price of $20.25 per unit, resulting in a favorable flexible budget sales revenue variance of $8,000.

	Accounts Receivable and Cash (32,000 × $20.25)	648,000	
	Flexible Budget Sales Revenue Variance		8,000
	Sales Revenue (32,000 × $20.00)		640,000
	(to record the sale of 32,000 cases)		

Under a perpetual inventory system, Tucson Tortilla must also release inventory for the cases it has sold. Since these cases were recorded at standard cost ($12.00 each), they must be removed from Finished Goods Inventory and be entered into Cost of Goods Sold at the same standard cost:

	Cost of Goods Sold (32,000 × $12.00)	384,000	
	Finished Goods Inventory (32,000 × $12.00)		384,000
	(to record cost of goods sold for the 32,000 cases)		

8. **Closing Manufacturing Overhead**—Tucson Tortilla must close its temporary MOH accounts. Rather than closing them directly to Cost of Goods Sold, as we did in Chapter 3, in a standard costing system the accounts are closed to variance accounts. The company closes the Variable Manufacturing Overhead account to the variable MOH variances shown in Exhibit 11-10:

	Variable overhead rate variance	10,200	
	Variable overhead efficiency variance		2,500
	Variable manufacturing overhead		7,700
	(to close the Variable MOH account)		

Likewise, it closes the Fixed Manufacturing Overhead account to the fixed MOH variances shown in Exhibit 11-11:

	Fixed Overhead Budget Variance	1,025	
	Fixed Overhead Volume Variance	2,100	
	Fixed Manufacturing Overhead		3,125
	(to close the Fixed MOH account)		

These two journal entries zero out the two manufacturing overhead accounts.

Standard Costing Income Statement

Exhibit 11-14 shows a standard costing income statement that highlights the variances for Tucson Tortilla's management (we only show down to the gross profit line). It shows revenues and cost of goods sold, first at standard and then at actual. Although the overall effect of the variances was minimal ($3,100 U), the report clearly shows management the size of each variance. Managers will use management by exception to determine which variances, if any, they wish to investigate.

EXHIBIT 11-14 Standard Costing Income Statement

Tucson Tortilla Standard Cost Income Statement For the month ended January 31		
Sales revenue at standard cost (32,000 × $20)		$ 640,000
Flexible budget sales revenue variance (favorable)		8,000 F
Sales revenue at actual		648,000
Cost of goods sold at standard cost (32,000 × $12)		384,000
Manufacturing cost variances: U/ (F)		
DM price variance	$(16,000) F	
DM quantity variance	7,500 U	
DL rate variance	1,875 U	
DL efficiency variance	(1,100) F	
Variable MOH rate variance	10,200 U	
Variable MOH efficiency variance	(2,500) F	
Fixed MOH budget variance	1,025 U	
Fixed MOH volume variance	2,100 U	
Total manufacturing variances		3,100 U
Cost of Goods Sold (at actual)		387,100
Gross Profit (actual)		$260,900

At the end of the period, all of the cost variance accounts are closed to zero-out their balances. Why? For two reasons: (1) The financial statements prepared for *external* users never show variances (variances are only for internal management's use) and (2) the general ledger must be corrected for the fact that standard costs, rather than actual costs, were used to record manufacturing costs. Since all of the cases were sold, the error in costing currently exists in the cost of goods sold account. Therefore, each cost variance account will be closed to Cost of Goods Sold. Likewise, the flexible budget sales revenue variance will be closed to Sales Revenue.

END OF CHAPTER

Learning Objectives

- 1 Explain how and why standard costs are developed
- 2 Compute and evaluate direct material variances
- 3 Compute and evaluate direct labor variances
- 4 Explain the advantages and disadvantages of using standard costs and variances
- 5 Compute and evaluate variable overhead variances
- 6 Compute and evaluate fixed overhead variances
- 7 (Appendix) Record standard costing journal entries

Accounting Vocabulary

Attainable standards. (p. 656) Standards based on currently attainable conditions that include allowances for normal amounts of waste and inefficiency. Also known as practical standards.

Direct labor efficiency variance. (p. 665) This variance tells managers how much of the total labor variance is due to using a greater or lesser amount of time than anticipated. It is calculated as follows: SR × (AH – SHA).

Direct labor rate variance. (p. 665) This variance tells managers how much of the total labor variance is due to paying a higher or lower hourly wage rate than anticipated. It is calculated as follows: AH × (AR – SR).

Direct materials price variance. (p. 661) This variance tells managers how much of the total direct materials variance is due to paying a higher or lower price than expected for the direct materials it purchased. It is calculated as follows: AQP × (AP – SP).

Direct materials quantity variance. (p. 661) This variance tells managers how much of the total direct materials variance is due to using a larger or smaller quantity of direct materials than expected. It is calculated as follows: SP × (AQU – SQA).

Fixed overhead budget variance. (p. 674) This variance measures the difference between the actual fixed overhead costs incurred and the budgeted fixed overhead costs. This variance is sometimes referred to as the **fixed overhead spending variance**, because it specifically looks at whether the company spent more or less than anticipated on fixed overhead costs.

Fixed overhead volume variance. (p. 675) This variance is the difference between the budgeted fixed overhead and the *standard fixed overhead cost* allocated to production. In essence, the fixed overhead volume variance measures the utilization of the fixed capacity costs. If volume is higher than originally anticipated, the variance will be favorable. If volume is lower than originally anticipated, the variance will be unfavorable.

Ideal standards. (p. 656) Standards based on perfect or ideal conditions that do not allow for any waste in the production process, machine breakdown, or other inefficiencies. Also known as perfection standards.

Perfection standards. (p. 656) Standards based on perfect or ideal conditions that do not allow for any waste in the production process, machine breakdown, or other inefficiencies. Also known as ideal standards.

Practical standards. (p. 656) Standards based on currently attainable conditions that include allowances for normal amounts of waste and inefficiency. Also known as attainable standards.

Standard cost. (p. 656) The budget for a single unit of product. Also simply referred to as standards.

Standard cost accounting. (p. 680) Another common name for Standard Costing.

Standard costing. (p. 680) Also known as standard cost accounting. A method of accounting in which product costs are entered into the general ledger inventory accounts at standard cost, rather than actual cost. The variances are captured in their own general ledger accounts and displayed on a standard costing income statement prior to being closed out at the end of the period.

Standards (p. 656) Another common name for standard costs.

Variable overhead efficiency variance. (p. 673) This variance tells managers how much of the total variable MOH variance is due to using more or fewer hours of the allocation base (usually machine hours or DL hours) than anticipated for the actual volume of output. It is calculated as follows: SR × (AH – SHA).

Variable overhead rate variance. (p. 672) Also called the variable overhead spending variance. This variance tells managers whether more or less was spent on variable overhead than they expected would be spent for the hours worked. It is calculated as follows: AH × (AR – SR).

Variable overhead spending variance. (p. 672) Another common name for variable overhead rate variance.

MyAccountingLab **Go to http://myaccountinglab.com/ for the following Quick Check, Short Exercises, Exercises, and Problems. They are available with immediate grading, explanations of correct and incorrect answers, and interactive media that acts as your own online tutor.**

Quick Check

1. *(Learning Objective 1)* Which of the following would be *least* likely to cause a direct material quantity standard to be outdated?
   a. The company has adopted lean practices throughout its facilities and has reduced waste throughout the manufacturing process.
   b. The price of a main direct material has increased significantly, causing the company to use a substitute material that cannot be used as efficiently as the original material.
   c. Demand for the product has increased steadily over the past two years in spite of a worsening economy.
   d. A new machine is installed that will reduce the amount of scrap being generated in the manufacturing process.
2. *(Learning Objective 2)* The direct materials price variance is calculated using
   a. the budgeted quantity of materials to be purchased
   b. the actual quantity of materials purchased.
   c. the actual quantity of materials used.
   d. the budgeted quantity of materials to be used.
3. *(Learning Objective 2)* All of the following could cause an unfavorable direct materials quantity variance *except:*
   a. lower quality materials.
   b. an increase in selling price.
   c. an outdated direct material standard.
   d. something else.
4. *(Learning Objective 3)* The direct labor efficiency variance is calculated using
   a. the standard labor rate per hour
   b. the actual labor rate per hour
   c. the standard material price
   d. the actual material price
5. *(Learning Objective 3)* Of the following choices, which would be the most likely to be the cause of an unfavorable direct labor rate variance?
   a. Using lower paid, less skilled workers
   b. Performing the work more efficiently
   c. Selling fewer units than originally budgeted
   d. Using highly paid, skilled workers for routine jobs normally performed by minimum wage workers
6. *(Learning Objective 4)* Advantages of using standard costs include all of the following *except* that
   a. standard costing provides benchmarks by which to evaluate actual costs.
   b. managers can evaluate the efficiency of production workers.
   c. the price sensitivity of customers can be analyzed.
   d. standard costing simplifies the bookkeeping.
7. *(Learning Objective 5)* The variable overhead spending variance is calculated using the following formula:
   a. Standard Rate × (Actual Hours − Standard Hours).
   b. Actual Hours × (Actual Rate − Standard Rate).
   c. Standard Hours × (Actual Rate − Standard Rate).
   d. Actual Rate × (Actual Hours − Standard Hours).
8. *(Learning Objective 6)* The fixed overhead variances are
   a. the spending variance and the efficiency variance.
   b. the rate variance and the efficiency variance.
   c. the price variance and the quantity variance.
   d. the budget variance and the volume variance.
9. *(Learning Objective 6)* The production volume variance is favorable whenever
   a. actual output exceeds expected input.
   b. the standard variable overhead rate exceeds the actual variable overhead rate.
   c. expected output exceeds actual input.
   d. the actual variable overhead rate exceeds the standard variable overhead rate.
10. *(Learning Objective 7)* When a company uses direct materials, the amount of the debit to Work in Process Inventory is based on the
    a. actual quantity of the materials used × actual price per unit of the materials.
    b. standard quantity of the materials allowed for the actual production quantity × actual price per unit of the materials.
    c. standard quantity of the materials allowed for the actual production quantity × standard price per unit of the materials.
    d. actual quantity of the materials used × standard price per unit of the materials.

Quick Check Answers

1. c 2. b 3. b 4. a 5. d 6. c 7. b 8. d 9. a 10. c

Short Exercises

S11-1 Compute the standard cost of direct materials *(Learning Objective 1)*

Spahr Confections is known for its creamy milk chocolate fudge. Spahr sells its fudge to local retailers. A "unit" of fudge is a ten pound batch. The standard quantities of ingredients for a batch include 9.5 cups of sugar, 20 ounces of chocolate chips, 18 ounces of butter, and 24 ounces of evaporated milk. The standard costs for each of the ingredients are as follows: $0.20 per cup of sugar, $0.15 per ounce of chocolate chips, $0.12 per ounce of butter, and $0.08 per ounce of evaporated milk. Calculate the standard direct material cost per batch of fudge.

S11-2 Compute the standard cost of direct labor *(Learning Objective 1)*

Spahr Confections produces fudge in ten pound batches. Each batch takes 0.2 hours of direct labor, which includes allowances for breaks, cleanup, and other downtime. Spahr pays its direct labor workers an average of $18.00 per hour. Calculate the standard direct labor cost per batch of fudge.

S11-3 Calculate direct material variances when the quantity purchased equals the quantity used *(Learning Objective 2)*

Bellweather Ceramics produces large planters to be used in urban landscaping projects. A special earth clay is used to make the planters. The standard quantity of clay used for each planter is 31 pounds. Bellweather uses a standard cost of $2.15 per pound of the clay. Bellweather produced 2,500 planters in May. In that month, 80,000 pounds of clay were purchased and used at the total cost of $164,000.

Requirements

1. Calculate the direct materials price variance.
2. Calculate the direct materials quantity variance.

S11-4 Calculate direct material variances when the quantity purchased differs from the quantity used *(Learning Objective 2)*

Brooke Landscaping produces faux boulders to be used in various landscaping applications. A special resin is used to make the planters. The standard quantity of resin used for each boulder is 9 pounds. Brooke uses a standard cost of $1.80 per pound for the resin. Brooke produced 1,500 boulders in June. In that month, 16,000 pounds of resin were purchased at a total cost of $32,000. A total of 13,400 pounds were used in producing the boulders in June.

Requirements

1. Calculate the direct materials price variance.
2. Calculate the direct materials quantity variance.

S11-5 Calculate direct labor variances *(Learning Objective 3)*

Speedy Oil performs oil changes. The standard wage rate for oil change technicians is $15 per hour. By analyzing its past records of time spent on oil changes, Speedy Oil has developed a standard of 15 minutes (or 0.25 hours) per oil change.

In July, 1,200 oil changes were performed at Speedy Oil. Oil change technicians worked a total of 280 direct labor hours at an average rate of $16 per hour.

Requirement

Calculate the direct labor efficiency variance.

S11-6 Identify advantages and disadvantages of standard costs and variance analysis *(Learning Objective 4)*

In the following list, identify whether the situation would indicate that a company should use standard costs and variance analysis or if the company should move away from standard costs and variance analysis.

Situation	Use standard costs	Move away from standard costs
1. Need timely reports about production results		
2. Would like to simplify the bookkeeping process		
3. Want benchmarks by which to judge actual costs		
4. There has been an increase in automation in the manufacturing process and a corresponding decrease in direct labor		
5. Would like to increase employee motivation levels		
6. Would like to facilitate the budgeting process		
7. Will be implementing lean practices throughout the organization		
8. Would like to use operational performance measures and visual management cues		

S11-7 Calculate variable overhead variances *(Learning Objective 5)*

Silla Industries produces 3,000 tables last month. The standard variable manufacturing overhead (MOH) rate used by Silla is $20 per machine hour. Each table requires 0.2 machine hours. Actual machine hours used last month were 620 and the actual variable MOH rate last month was $19.50.

Requirements

1. Calculate the variable overhead rate variance.
2. Calculate the variable overhead efficiency variance.

S11-8 Calculate fixed overhead variances *(Learning Objective 6)*

Bauer Manufacturing produces premium dog houses. Each dog house requires 2.0 hours of machine time for its elaborate trim and finishing. For the current year, Bauer calculated its predetermined fixed manufacturing overhead (MOH) rate to be $24 per machine hour. Bauer budgets its fixed MOH to be $50,000 per month. Last month, Bauer produced 1,200 dog houses and incurred $53,000 (actual) of fixed MOH.

Requirements

1. Calculate the fixed overhead budget variance.
2. Calculate the fixed overhead volume variance.

S11-9 Calculate and interpret fixed overhead variances *(Learning Objective 5 & 6)*

Miracle Industries produces high-end flutes for professional musicians across the globe. Actual fixed manufacturing overhead for the year was $1,200,000, while the budgeted fixed manufacturing overhead was $1,220,000. Using a standard costing system, the company allocated $1,190,000 of overhead to production.

Requirements

1. Calculate the total fixed overhead variance. What does this tell managers?
2. Determine the fixed overhead budget variance. What does this tell managers?
3. Determine the fixed overhead production volume variance. What does this tell managers?

S11-10 Calculate overhead rates *(Learning Objective 5 & 6)*

The Vittorio Restaurant Group supplies its franchise restaurants with many pre-manufactured ingredients (such as bags of frozen French fries), while other ingredients (such as lettuce and tomatoes) are obtained from local suppliers. Assume that the manufacturing plant processing the fries anticipated incurring a total of $3,220,000 of manufacturing overhead during the year. Of this amount, $1,380,000 is fixed. Manufacturing overhead is allocated based on machine hours. The plant anticipates running the machines 230,000 hours next year.

Requirements

1. Compute the standard variable overhead rate.
2. Compute the predetermined fixed manufacturing overhead rate.

S11-11 Calculate and interpret overhead variances *(Learning Objective 6)*

Assume that the Heese Corporation's manufacturing facility actually incurred $2,978,000 of manufacturing overhead for the year. Total fixed manufacturing overhead was budgeted at $3,040,000. Using a standard costing system, the company allocated $2,947,000 of manufacturing overhead to production.

Requirements

1. Calculate the total fixed manufacturing overhead variance. What does this tell managers?
2. Determine the fixed overhead budget variance. What does this tell managers?
3. Determine the fixed overhead volume variance. What does this tell managers?
4. Doublecheck: Do the two variances (computed in Requirements 2 and 3) sum to the total overhead variance computed in Requirement 1?

S11-12 Record costing transactions *(Learning Objective 7)*

During the week, the Vittorio Restaurant Group's French fry manufacturing facility purchased 10,200 pounds of potatoes at a price of $1.08 per pound. The standard price per pound is $1.00. During the week, 9,860 pounds of potatoes were used. The standard quantity of potatoes that should have been used for the actual volume of output was 9,800 pounds.

Requirements

1. Record the following transactions using a standard cost accounting system:
   a. The purchase of potatoes
   b. The use of potatoes
2. Are the variances favorable or unfavorable? Explain.

S11-13 Record standard costing transactions *(Learning Objective 7)*

During the week, the Vittorio Restaurant Group's French fry manufacturing facility incurred 2,000 hours of direct labor. Direct laborers were paid $12.25 per hour. The standard hourly labor rate is $12. Standards indicate that for the volume of output actually achieved, the factory should have used 2,100 hours.

Requirements

1. Record the labor transactions using a standard costs accounting system.
2. Are the variances favorable or unfavorable? Explain.

EXERCISES Group A

E11-14A Calculate standard cost and gross profit per unit *(Learning Objective 1)*

Rocco's Bakery makes desserts for local restaurants. Each pan of gourmet brownies requires 2 cups flour, ½ cup chopped pecans, ¼ cup cocoa, 1 cup sugar, ½ cup chocolate chips, 3 eggs, and ⅓ cup oil. Each pan requires 20 minutes of direct labor for mixing, cutting, and packaging. Each pan must bake for 30 minutes. Restaurants purchase the gourmet brownies by the pan, not by the individual serving. Each pan is currently sold for $10. Standard costs are $2.08 per bag of flour (16 cups in a bag), $4.00 per bag of pecans (3 cups per bag), $2.40 per tin of cocoa (2 cups per tin), $2.08 per 5-pound bag of sugar (16 cups in a bag), $1.80 per bag of chocolate chips (2 cups per bag), $1.56 per dozen eggs, $2.16 per bottle of oil (6 cups per bottle), and $0.40 for packaging materials. The standard wage rate is $12 per hour. Rocco allocates bakery overhead at $5.00 per oven hour.

Requirements

1. What is the standard cost per pan of gourmet brownies?
2. What is the standard gross profit per pan of gourmet brownies?
3. How often should Rocco reassess standard quantities and standard prices for inputs?

E11-15A Calculate standard cost per unit *(Learning Objective 1)*

FlowerMate is a manufacturer of large flower pots for urban settings. The company has these standards:

Direct materials (resin)	10 pounds per pot at a cost of $4.00 per pound
Direct labor	2.0 hours at a cost of $16.00 per hour
Standard variable manufacturing overhead rate	$3.00 per direct labor hour
Predetermined fixed manufacturing overhead rate	$7.00 per direct labor hour

FlowerMate allocates fixed manufacturing overhead to production based on standard direct labor hours.

Requirements

1. Compute the standard cost of each of the following inputs per pot: direct materials, direct labor, variable manufacturing overhead, and fixed manufacturing overhead.
2. Determine the standard cost of one flower pot.

E11-16A Calculate and explain direct material variances *(Learning Objective 2)*

University Rings produces class rings. Its best-selling model has a direct materials standard of 12 grams of a special alloy per ring. This special alloy has a standard cost of $65.00 per gram. In the past month, University Rings purchased 12,300 grams of this alloy at a total cost of $797,040. A total of 12,100 grams were used last month to produce 1,000 rings.

Requirements

1. What is the actual cost per gram of the special alloy that University Rings paid last month?
2. What is the direct materials price variance?
3. What is the direct materials quantity variance?
4. How might the direct materials price variance for University Rings last month be causing the direct materials quantity variance?

E11-17A Calculate missing direct materials variables *(Learning Objective 2)*

Last month, Banner Corporation purchased and used the same quantity of material in producing its product, speed bumps for traffic control. Complete the following table.

Direct materials information	Medium speed bump	Large speed bump
Standard pounds per unit	12	?
Standard price per pound	$ 2.00	$ 2.50
Actual quantity purchased and used per unit	?	16.75
Actual price paid for material per pound	$ 2.50	$ 2.80
Price variance	$1,000 U	$2,010 U
Quantity variance	$ 800 F	?
Total direct material variance	?	$1,260 U
Number of units produced	200	400

E11-18A Calculate and explain direct labor variances *(Learning Objective 3)*

Secaur Tax Services prepares tax returns for senior citizens. The standard in terms of (direct labor) time spent on each return is 2 hours. The direct labor standard wage rate at Secaur is $16.00 per hour. Last month, 1,590 direct labor hours were used to prepare 800 tax returns. Total wages totaled $26,235.

Requirements

1. What is the actual (direct labor) wage rate per hour paid last month?
2. What is the direct labor rate variance?
3. What is the direct labor efficiency variance?
4. How might the direct labor rate variance for Secaur last month be causing the direct labor efficiency variance?

E11-19A Calculate and interpret direct material and direct labor variances *(Learning Objective 2 & 3)*

The Vittorio Restaurant Group manufactures the bags of frozen French fries used at its franchised restaurants. Last week, Vittorio's purchased and used 102,000 pounds of potatoes at a price of $0.85 per pound. During the week, 1,600 direct labor hours were incurred in the plant at a rate of $12.50 per hour. The standard price per pound of potatoes is $0.95, and the standard direct labor rate is $12.25 per hour. Standards indicate that for the number of bags of frozen fries produced, the factory should have used 99,000 pounds of potatoes and 1,500 hours of direct labor.

Requirements

1. Determine the direct materials price and quantity variances. Be sure to label each variance as favorable or unfavorable.
2. Think of a plausible explanation for the variances found in Requirement 1.
3. Determine the direct labor rate and efficiency variances. Be sure to label each variance as favorable or unfavorable.
4. Could the explanation for the labor variances be tied to the material variances? Explain.

E11-20A Calculate the materials and labor variances *(Learning Objective 2 & 3)*

Boat Guard, which used a standard cost accounting system, manufactured 210,000 boat fenders during the year, using 1,310,000 feet of extruded vinyl purchased at $1.45 per foot. Production required 4,700 direct labor hours that cost $16 per hour. The materials standard was 6 feet of vinyl per fender at a standard cost of $1.55 per foot. The labor standard was 0.025 direct labor hour per fender at a standard cost of $15 per hour.

Requirements

1. Compute the price and quantity variances for direct materials. Compute the rate and efficiency variances for direct labor.
2. Does the pattern of variances suggest that Boat Guard's managers have been making trade-offs? Explain.

E11-21A Record materials and labor transactions *(Learning Objective 7)*

Refer to the data in E11-20A.

Requirements

1. Make the journal entries to record the purchase and use of direct materials.
2. Make the journal entries to record the direct labor.

E11-22A Calculate the standard cost of a product before and after proposed sustainability effort changes *(Learning Objective 1 & 4)*

Wolanin Containers currently uses a recycled plastic to make bottles for the food industry.

Current bottle production information:

The cost and time standards per batch of 10,000 bottles are as follows:

Plastic 300 kilograms at $6.00 per kg
Direct labor 2.0 hours at $20.00 per hour

The variable manufacturing overhead rate is based on total estimated variable manufacturing overhead of $500,000 and estimated total DLH of 10,000. Wolanin allocates its variable manufacturing overhead based on direct labor hours (DLH).

Proposed changes to bottle design and production process:

The container division manager is considering having both the bottle redesigned and the bottle production process reengineered so that the plastic usage would drop by 20% overall due both to generating less scrap in the manufacturing process and using less plastic in each bottle. In addition to decreasing the amount of plastic used in producing the bottles, the additional following benefits would be realized:

a. Direct labor hours would be reduced by 10% because less scrap would be handled in the production process.
b. Total estimated variable manufacturing overhead would be reduced by 5% because less scrap would need to be hauled away, less electricity would be used in the production process, and less inventory would need to be stocked.

Requirements

1. Calculate the standard cost per batch of 10,000 bottles using the current data (before the company makes any changes). Include direct materials, direct labor, and variable manufacturing overhead in the standard cost per unit.
2. Calculate the standard cost per batch of 10,000 bottles if the company makes the changes to the bottle design and production process so that less plastic is used. Include direct materials, direct labor, and variable manufacturing overhead in the standard cost per unit.
3. Calculate the cost savings per batch by comparing the standard cost per batch under each scenario (current versus proposed change). Assume that the total cost to implement the changes would be $114,390. How many batches of bottles would need to be produced after the changes to have the cost savings total equal the cost to make these changes?
4. What other benefits might arise from making this change to using less plastic in the manufacture of the bottles? Are there any risks? What would you recommend the company do?

E11-23A Recognize advantages and disadvantages of standard cost and variance analysis in various situations *(Learning Objective 4)*

The following scenarios describe situations currently facing companies. For each scenario, indicate whether a standard costing system would be beneficial in that situation or not and explain why or why not. Each scenario is independent of the other scenarios.

a. The company has recently begun manufacturing a new type of computer chip. The company has very little experience with this type of product or with the manufacturing process used for manufacturing the chips. Managers want to be able to have cost benchmarks so that they can judge whether the actual costs are reasonable for this product.
b. Lean practices are being implemented throughout the organization at all levels and in all departments. One of the goals of the lean movement is to eliminate inventories if at all possible. Another goal is to strive for continuous improvement in both the time spent in the manufacturing process and the amount of materials used in the product.
c. As the company grows, the bookkeeping for actual direct material purchases, actual payroll costs, and actual manufacturing overhead is becoming increasingly complex; the number of transactions to be recorded has significantly increased. Much time is being spent by both managers and accountants in the company recording all of the actual transaction data.
d. An exercise equipment manufacturer has recently installed a robotic manufacturing system. This robotic system will be used for most of the welding, painting, assembly, and testing processes in its facility. The workers who used to do these tasks (welding, painting, assembly, and testing) will be retrained and will instead oversee various production lines rather than working directly on the products.
e. Management wants to design an incentive system that would pay out monthly incentives to factory workers if certain cost and time standards are achieved (or beaten). The goal of this program would be to increase employee motivation levels.
f. A rare and expensive chemical is used in the production of the company's main product. The cost of this material fluctuates wildly on a day-to-day basis, depending on market conditions. In addition, company engineers are continually working to redesign the product to use less of this material. Small incremental decreases in the material usage are being achieved on an ongoing basis.
g. The company has started using several real-time operating performance metrics to manage operations. Examples of metrics being used include manufacturing lead time in days, manufacturing volume by day, downtime in hours, material cost by day, and several other measures. These performance metrics are available to management in a dashboard that is updated hourly.

E11-24A Compute and interpret overhead variances *(Learning Objective 5 & 6)*

Faucher Foods processes bags of organic frozen vegetables sold at specialty grocery stores. Faucher allocates manufacturing overhead based on direct labor hours. Faucher has budgeted fixed manufacturing overhead for the year to be $630,000. The predetermined fixed manufacturing overhead rate is $16 per direct labor hour, while the standard variable manufacturing overhead rate is $0.75 per direct labor hour. The direct labor standard for each case is one-quarter (0.25) of an hour.

The company actually processed 160,000 cases of frozen organic vegetables during each year and incurred $679,080 of manufacturing overhead. Of this amount, $640,000 was fixed. The company also incurred a total of 41,200 direct labor hours.

Requirements

1. How much variable overhead would have been allocated to production? How much fixed overhead would have been allocated to production?
2. Compute the variable MOH rate variance and the variable MOH efficiency variance. What do these variances tell managers?
3. Compute the fixed MOH budget variance and the fixed overhead volume variance. What do these variances tell managers?

E11-25A Vocabulary *(Learning Objective 1, 2, 3, 4, 5 & 6)*

Match the term on the left with the definition on the right.

Term	Definition
1. Direct materials price variance	a. Measures the difference between the actual fixed MOH costs incurred and the budgeted fixed MOH costs
2. Fixed overhead budget variance	b. Also called the variable overhead spending variance
3. Direct labor efficiency variance	c. Tells managers how much of the total variance is due to paying a different hourly wage rate than anticipated
4. Standard cost	d. Standards based on conditions that do not allow for any waste in the production process
5. Variable overhead rate variance	e. Tells managers how much of the total variance is due to using a difference quantity of direct materials than expected
6. Direct materials quantity variance	f. Measures the difference between the budgeted fixed MOH costs and the standard allocated MOH costs
7. Ideal standards	g. Also known as attainable standards
8. Variable overhead efficiency variance	h. Tells managers how much of the total variance is due to paying a different price than expected for direct materials
9. Practical standards	i. Tells managers how much of the total variance is due to using a greater or lesser amount of time than anticipated
10. Direct labor rate variance	j. Tells managers how much of the total variable MOH variance is due to using more or less of the allocation base than anticipated for the actual volume of output
11. Fixed overhead volume variance	k. The budget for a single unit of product

Data Set for E11-26A through E11-30A

FlowerMate is a manufacturer of large flower pots for urban settings. The company has these standards:

Direct materials (resin)...	10 pounds per pot at a cost of $4.00 per pound
Direct labor	2.0 hours at a cost of $16.00 per hour
Standard variable manufacturing overhead rate	$3.00 per direct labor hour
Budgeted fixed manufacturing overhead	$10,000
Standard fixed MOH rate..	$7.00 per direct labor hour (DLH)

CHAPTER 11

FlowerMate allocated fixed manufacturing overhead to production based on standard direct labor hours. Last month, FlowerMate reported the following actual results for the production of 1,000 flower pots:

Direct materials	Purchased 11,200 pounds at a cost of \$4.20 per pound; Used 10,500 pounds to produce 1,000 pots
Direct labor	Worked 2.2 hours per flower pot (2,200 total DLH) at a cost of \$15.00 per hour
Actual variable manufacturing overhead	\$3.40 per direct labor hour for total actual variable manufacturing overhead of \$7,480
Actual fixed manufacturing overhead..............	\$9,800
Standard fixed manufacturing overhead allocated based on actual production	\$14,000

E11-26A Calculate and interpret direct material variances *(Learning Objective 2)*

Refer to the FlowerMate data set.

Requirements

1. Compute the direct materials price variance and the direct materials quantity variance.
2. What is the total variance for direct materials?
3. Who is *generally* responsible for each variance?
4. Interpret the variances.

E11-27A Calculate and interpret direct labor variances *(Learning Objective 3)*

Refer to the FlowerMate data set.

Requirements

1. Compute the direct labor rate variance and the direct labor efficiency variance.
2. What is the total variance for direct labor?
3. Who is *generally* responsible for each variance?
4. Interpret the variances.

E11-28A Calculate and interpret overhead variances *(Learning Objective 5 & 6)*

Refer to the FlowerMate data set.

Requirements

1. Compute the variable manufacturing overhead variances. What do each of these variances tell management?
2. Compute the fixed manufacturing overhead variances. What do each of these variances tell management?

E11-29A Make journal entries in a standard costing system *(Learning Objective 7)*

Refer to the FlowerMate data set. Assume the company uses a standard cost accounting system.

Requirements

1. Record FlowerMate's direct materials and direct labor journal entries.
2. Record FlowerMate's journal entries for manufacturing overhead, including the entry that records the overhead variances and closes the Manufacturing Overhead account.
3. Record the journal entries for the completion and sale of the 1,000 flower pots, assuming FlowerMate sold (on account) all of the flower pots at a sales price of \$480 each (there were no beginning or ending inventories.)

E11-30A Prepare a standard cost income statement *(Learning Objective 7)*

Refer to the FlowerMate data set. Prepare a standard cost income statement for the company's management. Assume that sales were \$480,000 and actual marketing and administrative expenses were \$76,500.

E11-31A Interpret a standard cost income statement *(Learning Objective 7)*

The managers of Kerwin Co., a contract manufacturer of computer monitors, are seeking explanations for the variances in the following report. Explain the meaning of each of the company's materials, labor and overhead variances.

Kerwin Co. Standard Cost Income Statement Year Ended December 31		
Sales revenue at standard cost		$1,205,000
Flexible budget sales revenue variance		5,000
Sales revenue at actual		$1,210,000
Cost of goods sold at standard cost		710,000
Manufacturing cost variances:		
Direct materials price variance	$32,000 U	
Direct materials quantity variance	8,000 F	
Direct labor rate variance	9,000 U	
Direct labor efficiency variance	25,000 F	
Variable overhead rate variance	21,000 U	
Variable overhead efficiency variance	3,000 F	
Fixed overhead budget variance	6,000 U	
Fixed overhead volume variance	9,000 F	
Total manufacturing variances		23,000
Cost of goods sold at actual cost		$ 733,000
Gross profit		$ 477,000
Marketing and administrative expenses		418,000
Operating income		$ 59,000

E11-32A Prepare a standard cost income statement *(Learning Objective 7)*

Eastern Outfitters' revenue and expense information for April follows:

Sales revenue at standard cost	$558,000
Flexible budget sales revenue variance	$ 3,500
Sales revenue at actual	$561,500
Cost of goods sold (standard)	$344,500
Direct materials price variance	$ 2,800 F
Direct materials quantity variance	$ 6,100 F
Direct labor rate variance	$4,400 U
Direct labor efficiency variance	$ 2,200 F
Variable overhead rate variance	$2,000 U
Variable overhead efficiency variance	$ 3,000 F
Fixed overhead budget variance	$1,800 U
Fixed overhead volume variance	$ 5,000 F

Requirement

Prepare a standard cost income statement for management through gross profit. Report all standard cost variances for management's use. Has management done a good or poor job of controlling costs? Explain.

EXERCISES Group B

E11-33B Calculate standard costs *(Learning Objective 1)*

Danno's Bakery makes desserts for local restaurants. Each pan of gourmet bars requires 2 cups of flour, ½ cup chopped pecans, ¼ cup cocoa, 1 cup sugar, ½ cup chocolate chips, 3 eggs, and ⅓ cup oil. Each pan requires 20 minutes of direct labor for mixing, cutting, and packaging. Each pan must bake for 30 minutes. Restaurants purchase the gourmet bars by the pan, not by the individual serving. Each pan is currently sold for $13. Standard costs are as follows: $3.36 per bag of flour (24 cups in a bag), $12.00 per bag of pecans (4 cups per bag), $3.72 per tin of cocoa (3 cups per tin), $2.40 per 5-pound bag of sugar (16 cups in a bag), $2.40 per bag of chocolate chips (3 cups per bag), $0.84 per dozen eggs, $2.16 per bottle of oil (8 cups per bottle), and $0.60 for packaging materials. The standard wage rate is $15 per hour. Danno allocates bakery overhead at $5.20 per oven hour.

Requirements

1. What is the standard cost per pan of gourmet bars?
2. What is the standard gross profit per pan of gourmet bars?
3. How often should Danno reassess standard quantities and standard prices for inputs?

E11-34B Calculate the standard cost per unit *(Learning Objective 1)*

DaisyMate is a manufacturer of large flower pots for urban settings. The company has these standards:

Direct materials (resin)..........	5 pounds per pot at a cost of $3.00 per pound
Direct labor	2.0 hours at a cost of $18.00 per hour
Standard variable manufacturing overhead..........	$10.00 per direct labor hour

DaisyMate allocates fixed manufacturing overhead to production based on standard direct labor hours.

Requirements

1. Compute the standard cost of each of the following inputs per bottle: direct materials, direct labor, variable manufacturing overhead, and fixed manufacturing overhead.
2. Determine the standard cost of one flower pot.

E11-35B Calculate and explain direct material variances *(Learning Objective 2)*

Varsity Rings produces class rings. Its best-selling model has a direct material standard of 13 grams of a special alloy per ring. This special alloy has a standard cost of $75.00 per gram. In the past month, Varsity Rings purchased 28,500 grams of this alloy at a total cost of $2,128,950. A total of 26,100 grams were used last month to produce 2,000 rings.

Requirements

1. What is the actual cost per gram of the special alloy that Varsity Rings paid last month?
2. What is the direct materials price variance?
3. What is the direct materials quantity variance?
4. How might the direct materials price variance for Varsity Rings last month be causing the direct materials quantity variance?

E11-36B Calculate missing direct material variables *(Learning Objective 2)*

Last month, Russell Corporation purchased and used the same quantity of material in producing its speed bumps, a traffic control product. Complete the following table:

Direct materials information	Medium speed bump	Large speed bump
Standard pounds per unit	10	20
Standard price per pound	$ 4.00	?
Actual quantity purchased and used per unit	?	19
Actual price paid for material	$ 4.25	$ 6.00
Price variance	$1,950 U	$ 1,216 F
Quantity variance	$ 800 F	?
Total direct material variance	?	$10,808 F
Number of units produced	800	1,600

E11-37B Calculate and explain direct labor variances *(Learning Objective 3)*

Pettigrew Tax Services prepares tax returns for senior citizens. The standard in terms of (direct labor) time spent on each return is 1.5 hours. The direct labor standard wage rate at Pettigrew is $15.00 per hour. Last month, 1,630 direct labor hours were used to prepare 1,000 tax returns. Total wages totaled $22,820.

Requirements

1. What is the actual (direct labor) wage rate per hour paid last month?
2. What is the direct labor rate variance?
3. What is the direct labor efficiency variance?
4. How might the direct labor rate variance for Pettigrew last month be causing the direct labor efficiency variance?

E11-38B Calculate and interpret direct material variances *(Learning Objective 2 & 3)*

The Morgan Restaurant Group manufactures the bags of frozen French fries used at its franchised restaurants. Last week, Morgan's purchased and used 103,000 pounds of potatoes at a price of $0.70 per pound. During the week, 2,200 direct labor hours were incurred in the plant at a rate of $12.45 per hour. The standard price per pound of potatoes is $0.80, and the standard direct labor rate is $12.20 per hour. Standards indicate that for the number of bags of frozen fries produced, the factory should have used 100,000 pounds of potatoes and 2,100 hours of direct labor.

Requirements

1. Determine the direct materials price and quantity variances. Be sure to label each variance as favorable or unfavorable.
2. Think of a plausible explanation for the variances found in Requirement 1.
3. Determine the direct labor rate and efficiency variances. Be sure to label each variance as favorable or unfavorable.
4. Could the explanation for the labor variances be tied to the material variances? Explain.

E11-39B Complete and analyze a performance report *(Learning Objective 2 & 3)*

Wave Guard, which uses a standard cost accounting system, manufactured 230,000 boat fenders during the year, using 1,890,000 feet of extruded vinyl purchased at $1.20 per foot. Production required 4,600 direct labor hours that cost $15.50 per hour. The materials standard was 8 feet of vinyl per fender at a standard cost of $1.35 per foot. The labor standard was 0.026 direct labor hour per fender at a standard cost of $15 per hour.

Requirements

1. Compute the price and quantity variances for direct materials. Compute the rate and efficiency variances for direct labor.
2. Does the pattern of variances suggest that Wave Guard's managers have been making trade-offs? Explain.

E11-40B Record materials and labor transactions *(Learning Objective 7)*

Refer to the data in E11-39B.

Requirements

1. Make journal entries to record the purchase and use of direct materials.
2. Make journal entries to record the direct labor.

E11-41B Calculate the standard cost of a product before and after proposed sustainability effort changes *(Learning Objective 1 & 4)*

Gerbig Containers currently uses a recycled plastic to make bottles for the food industry.

Current bottle production information:

The cost and time standards per batch of 10,000 bottles are as follows:

Plastic 300 kilograms at $5.00 per kg
Direct labor 2.0 hours at $20.00 per hour

The variable manufacturing overhead rate is based on total estimated variable manufacturing overhead of $400,000 and estimated total DLH of 40,000. Gerbig allocates its variable manufacturing overhead based on direct labor hours (DLH).

Proposed changes to bottle design and production process:

The container division manager is considering having both the bottle redesigned and the bottle production process reengineered so that the plastic usage would drop by 30% overall due both to generating less scrap in the manufacturing process and using less plastic in each bottle. In addition to decreasing the amount of plastic used in producing the bottles, the additional following benefits would be realized:

a. Direct labor hours would be reduced by 10% because less scrap would be handled in the production process.
b. Total estimated variable manufacturing overhead would be reduced by 20% because less scrap would need to be hauled away, less electricity would be used in the production process, and less inventory would need to be stocked.

Requirements

1. Calculate the standard cost per batch of 10,000 bottles using the current data (before the company makes any changes). Include direct materials, direct labor, and variable manufacturing overhead in the standard cost per unit.
2. Calculate the standard cost per batch of 10,000 bottles if the company makes the changes to the bottle design and production process so that less plastic is used. Include direct materials, direct labor, and variable manufacturing overhead in the standard cost per unit.
3. Calculate the cost savings per batch by comparing the standard cost per batch under each scenario (current versus proposed change). Assume that the total cost to implement the changes would be $141,980. How many batches of bottles would need to be produced after the change to have the cost savings total equal the cost to make the changes?
4. What other benefits might arise from making this change to using less plastic in the manufacture of the bottles? Are there any risks? What would you recommend the company do?

E11-42B Recognize advantages and disadvantages of standard cost and variance analysis in various situations *(Learning Objective 4)*

The following scenarios describe situations currently facing companies. For each scenario, indicate whether a standard costing system would be beneficial in that situation or not and explain why or why not. Each scenario is independent of the other scenarios.

a. Management wants to design an incentive system that would pay out monthly incentives to factory workers if certain cost and time standards are achieved (or beaten). The goal of this program would be to increase employee motivation levels.
b. The company has started using several real-time operating performance metrics to manage operations. Examples of metrics being used include manufacturing lead time

in days, manufacturing volume by day, downtime in hours, material cost by day, and several other measures. These performance metrics are available to management in a dashboard that is updated hourly.

c. The company has recently begun manufacturing a new type of computer chip. The company has very little experience with this type of product or the manufacturing process used for manufacturing the chips. Managers want to be able to have cost benchmarks so that they can judge whether the actual costs are reasonable for this product.

d. Lean practices are being implemented throughout the organization at all levels and in all departments. One of the goals of the lean movement is to eliminate inventories if at all possible. Another goal is to strive for continuous improvement in both the time spent in the manufacturing process and the amount of materials used in the product.

e. A rare and expensive chemical is used in the production of the company's main product. The cost of this material fluctuates wildly on a day to day basis, depending on market conditions. In addition, company engineers are continually working to redesign the product to use less of this material. Small incremental decreases in the material usage are being achieved on an ongoing basis.

f. As the company grows, the bookkeeping for actual direct material purchases, actual payroll costs, and actual manufacturing overhead is becoming increasingly complex; the number of transactions to be recorded has significantly increased. Much time is being spent by both managers and accountants in the company recording all of the actual transaction data.

g. An exercise equipment manufacturer has recently installed a robotic manufacturing system. This robotic system will be used for most of the welding, painting, assembly, and testing processes in its facility. The workers who used to do these tasks (welding, painting, assembly, and testing) will be retrained and will instead oversee various production lines rather than working directly on the products.

E11-43B Calculate and interpret overhead variances *(Learning Objectives 5 & 6)*

Dorsey Foods processes bags of organic frozen vegetables sold at specialty grocery stores. Dorsey allocates manufacturing overhead based on direct labor hours. The company has budgeted fixed manufacturing for the year to be $630,000. The predetermined fixed manufacturing overhead rate is $15.50 per direct labor hour, while the standard variable manufacturing overhead rate is $0.85 per direct labor hour. The direct labor standards for each case is one-quarter of an hour.

The company actually processed 160,000 cases of frozen organic vegetables during the year and incurred $665,080 of manufacturing overhead. Of this amount, $628,000 was fixed. The company also incurred a total of 41,200 direct labor hours.

Requirements

1. How much variable overhead would have been allocated to production? How much fixed overhead would have been allocated to production?
2. Compute the variable MOH rate variance and the variable MOH efficiency variance. What do these variances tell managers?
3. Compute the fixed MOH budget variance and the fixed overhead volume variance. What do these variances tell managers?

E11-44B Vocabulary *(Learning Objectives 1, 2, 3, 4, 5 & 6)*

Match the term on the left with the definition on the right.

Term	Definition
1. Fixed overhead volume variance	a. Tells managers how much of the total variance is due to paying a different hourly wage rate than anticipated
2. Direct labor efficiency variance	b. Tells managers how much of the total variance is due to using a greater or lesser amount of time being worked than anticipated
3. Practical standards	c. Tells managers how much of the total variance is due to using a difference quantity of direct materials than expected
4. Standard cost	d. Tells managers how much of the total variable MOH variance is due to using more or less hours of the allocation base than anticipated for the actual volume of output
5. Direct materials quantity variance	e. Measures the difference between the budgeted fixed MOH costs and the standard allocated MOH costs
6. Direct labor rate variance	f. Tells managers how much of the total variance is due to paying a different price than expected for direct materials
7. Variable overhead rate variance	g. The budget for a single unit of product
8. Fixed overhead budget variance	h. Also called the variable overhead spending variance
9. Ideal standards	i. Also known as attainable standards
10. Direct materials price variance	j. Standards based on conditions that do not allow for any waste in the production process
11. Variable overhead efficiency variance	k. Measures the difference between the actual fixed MOH costs incurred and the budgeted fixed MOH costs

Data Set for E11-45B through E11-49B

DaisyMate is a manufacturer of large flower pots for urban settings. The company has these standards:

Direct materials (resin)..	5 pounds per pot at a cost of $3.00 per pound
Direct labor	2.0 hours at a cost of $18.00 per hour
Standard variable manufacturing overhead rate	$10.00 per direct labor hour
Budgeted fixed manufacturing overhead............	$8,800
Standard fixed MOH rate....................................	$2.50 per direct labor hour (DLH)

DaisyMate allocates fixed manufacturing overhead to production based on standard direct labor hours. Last month, DaisyMate reported the following actual results for the production of 2,000 flower pots:

Direct materials	Purchased 10,800 pounds at a cost of $4.00 per pound; Used 10,300 pounds to produce 2,000 pots
Direct labor	Worked 2.1 hours per unit (4,200 total DLH) at a cost of $18.60 per hour
Actual variable manufacturing overhead	$10.50 per direct labor hour for total actual variable manufacturing overhead of $44,100
Actual fixed manufacturing overhead.........	$10,200
Standard fixed manufacturing overhead allocated based on actual production	$10,000

E11-45B Calculate and interpret direct materials variances *(Learning Objective 2)*

Refer to the DaisyMate data set.

Requirements

1. Compute the direct materials price variance and the direct materials quantity variance.
2. What is the total variance for direct materials?
3. Who is generally responsible for each variance?
4. Interpret the variances.

E11-46B Calculate and interpret direct labor variances *(Learning Objective 2)*

Refer to the DaisyMate data set.

Requirements

1. Compute the direct labor rate variance and the direct labor efficiency variance.
2. What is the total variance for direct labor?
3. Who is generally responsible for each variance?
4. Interpret the variances.

E11-47B Calculate and interpret overhead variances *(Learning Objectives 5 & 6)*

Refer to the DaisyMate data set. Calculate and interpret overhead variances.

Requirements

1. Compute the variable manufacturing overhead variances. What do each of these variances tell management?
2. Compute the fixed manufacturing overhead variances. What do each of these variances tell management?

E11-48B Make journal entries in a standard costing system *(Learning Objective 7)*

Refer to the DaisyMate data set. Assume the company uses a standard cost accounting system.

Requirements

1. Record DaisyMate's direct materials and direct labor journal entries.
2. Record DaisyMate's journal entries for manufacturing overhead, including the entry that records the overhead variances and closes the Manufacturing Overhead account.
3. Record the journal entries for the completion and sale of the 2,000 flower pots, assuming DaisyMate's sold (on account) all of the flower pots at a sales price of $240 each (there were no beginning or ending inventories).

E11-49B Prepare a standard cost income statement *(Learning Objective 7)*

Refer to the DaisyMate data set. Prepare a standard cost income statement for the company's management. Assume that sales were $480,000 and actual marketing and administrative expenses were $76,500.

E11-50B Interpret a standard cost income statement *(Learning Objective 7)*

The managers of Sesnie Co., a contract manufacturer of computer monitors, are seeking explanations for the variances in the following report. Explain the meaning of each of the company's material, labor, and overhead variances.

Sesnie Co.
Standard Cost Income Statement
Year Ended December 31

Sales revenue at standard cost		$1,208,000
Flexible budget sales revenue variance		2,000
Sales revenue at actual		$1,210,000
Cost of goods sold at standard cost		710,000
Manufacturing cost variances:		
Direct materials price variance	$10,000 F	
Direct materials quantity variance	34,000 U	
Direct labor rate variance	10,000 U	
Direct labor efficiency variance	24,000 F	
Variable overhead rate variance	16,000 U	
Variable overhead efficiency variance	3,000 F	
Fixed overhead budget variance	11,000 U	
Fixed overhead volume variance	9,000 F	
Total manufacturing variances		25,000
Cost of goods sold at actual cost		$ 735,000
Gross profit		$ 475,000
Marketing and administrative expenses		416,000
Operating income		$ 59,000

E11-51B Prepare a standard cost income statement *(Learning Objective 7)*
Western Outfitters' revenue and expense information for April follows:

Sales revenue at standard cost	$555,000
Flexible budget sales revenue variance	$ 6,000
Sales revenue at actual	$561,000
Cost of goods sold (standard)	$342,000
Direct materials price variance	$ 2,800 F
Direct materials quantity variance	$ 6,400 F
Direct labor rate variance	$ 4,250 U
Direct labor efficiency variance	$ 2,450 F
Variable overhead rate variance	$ 1,600 U
Variable overhead efficiency variance	$ 1,000 F
Fixed overhead budget variance	$ 2,050 U
Fixed overhead volume variance	$ 7,050 F

Requirement

Prepare a standard cost income statement for management through gross profit. Report all standard cost variances for management's use. Has management done a good or poor job of controlling costs? Explain.

PROBLEMS Group A

P11-52A Calculate and explain direct material and direct labor variances

(Learning Objectives 1, 2, 3 & 4)

Kelly Fabrics manufactures a specialty monogrammed blanket. To follow are the cost standards for this blanket:

Direct materials (fabric)	2.0 yards per blanket at $9.50 per yard
Direct labor	0.5 direct labor hours per blanket at $13.00 per hour

Actual results from last month's production of 2,000 blankets follows:

Actual cost of 4,800 yards of direct material (fabric) purchased	$42,240
Actual yards of direct material (fabric) used	4,150
Actual wages for 1,100 direct labor hours worked...	$13,420

Requirements

1. What is the standard direct material cost for one blanket?
2. What is the actual cost per yard of fabric purchased?
3. Calculate the direct material price and quantity variances.
4. What is the standard direct labor cost for one blanket?
5. What is the actual direct labor cost per hour?
6. Calculate the direct labor rate and efficiency variances.
7. Analyze each variance and speculate as to what may have caused that variance.
8. Look at all four variances together (the big picture). How might they all be related? What variance is very likely to have caused the other variances?

P11-53A Comprehensive standards and variances problem

(Learning Objectives 2, 3, 4, 5 & 6)

Peterson Awning manufactures awnings and uses a standard cost system. Peterson allocates overhead based on the number of direct labor hours. To follow are the company's cost and standards data:

Standards:
Direct materials 22.0 yards per awning at $15.00 per yard
Direct labor 3.0 hours per awning at $16.00 per hour
Variable MOH standard rate $5.00 per direct labor hour
Predetermined fixed MOH standard rate $8.00 per direct labor hour
Total budgeted fixed MOH cost $48,000

Actual cost and operating data from the most recent month follows:
Purchased 49,200 yards at a total cost of $728,160
Used 45,100 yards in producing 2,100 awnings
Actual direct labor cost of $96,985 for a total of 5,950 hours
Actual variable MOH $31,238
Actual fixed MOH $53,000

All manufacturing overhead is allocated on the basis of direct labor hours.

Requirements

1. Calculate the standard cost of one awning.
2. Calculate the following variances:
   a. The direct material variances.

b. The direct labor variances.

c. The variable manufacturing overhead variances.

d. The fixed manufacturing overhead variances.

3. Explain what each of the variances you calculated means and give at least one possible explanation for each of those variances. Are any of the variances likely to be interrelated?

P11-54A Comprehensive standards and variances problem

(Learning Objectives 1, 2, 3, 4, 5 & 6)

Arvind Manufacturing produces ceramic teapots. Arvind allocates overhead based on the number of direct labor hours. The company is looking into using a standard cost system and has developed the following standards (one "unit" is a batch of 100 teapots).

Standards:
Direct material 50 pounds per batch at $2.00 per pound
Direct labor 3.0 hours per batch at $14.00 per hour
Variable MOH standard rate $2.00 per direct labor hour
Predetermined fixed MOH standard rate $3.00 per direct labor hour
Total budgeted fixed MOH cost $1,000

Actual cost and operating data from the most recent month follows:
Purchased 2,600 pounds at a cost of $1.90 per pound
Used 2,200 pounds in producing 40 batches
Actual direct labor cost of $2,030 at an average direct labor cost per hour of $14.50
Actual variable MOH $322
Actual fixed MOH $1,300

All manufacturing overhead is allocated on the basis of direct labor hours.

Requirements

1. Calculate the standard cost of one batch.
2. Calculate the following variances:
   a. The direct material variances.
   b. The direct labor variances.
   c. The variable manufacturing overhead variances.
   d. The fixed manufacturing overhead.
3. Have the company's managers done a good job or a poor job controlling materials, labor and overhead costs? Why or why not?
4. Describe how the company's managers can benefit from the standard costing system. Do you think the company should continue with the standard cost system?

P11-55A Work backward through labor variances *(Learning Objective 3)*

Christine's Music manufactures harmonicas. Christine uses standard costs to judge performance. Recently, a clerk mistakenly threw away some of the records, and only partial data for October exists. Christine knows that the total direct labor variance for the month was $390 F and that the standard labor rate was $9 per hour. A recent pay cut caused a favorable labor price variance of $0.50 per hour. The standard direct labor hours for actual October outputs were 5,200.

Requirements

1. Find the actual number of direct labor hours worked during October. First, find the actual direct labor rate her hour. Then, determine the actual number of direct labor hours worked by setting up the computation of the total direct labor variance as given.
2. Compute the direct labor rate and efficiency variances. Do these variances suggest that the manager may have made trade-offs? Explain.

P11-56A Determine all variances and make journal entries

(Learning Objectives 2, 3, 4, 5, 6 & 7)

Garnett manufactures embroidered jackets. The company uses a standard cost system to control manufacturing costs. The following data represents the standard unit cost of a jacket:

Direct materials (3.0 sq. ft × $4.00 per sq. ft)........		$12.00
Direct labor (2.0 hours × $9.40 per hour)........		18.80
Manufacturing overhead:		
Variable (2.0 hours × $0.65 per hour)........	$1.30	
Fixed (2.0 hours × $2.20 per hour)........	4.40	$ 5.70
Total standard cost per jacket........		$ 36.50

Fixed overhead in total was budgeted to be $63,360 for each month.

Actual data for November of the current year include the following:

a. Actual production was 14,000 jackets.
b. Actual direct material used was 2.50 square feet per jacket at an actual cost of $4.10 per square foot.
c. Actual direct labor usage of 25,400 hours for a total cost of $241,300.
d. Actual fixed overhead cost was $57,500, while actual variable overhead cost was $17,780.

Requirements

1. Compute the price and quantity variances for direct materials.
2. Compute the rate and efficiency variances for direct labor.
3. Compute the rate and efficiency variances for variable overhead.
4. Compute the fixed overhead budget variance and the fixed overhead volume variance.
5. Garnett's management intentionally purchased superior materials for November production. How did this decision affect the other cost variances? Overall, was the decision wise? Explain.
6. Journalize the usage of direct materials and the assignment of direct labor, including the related variances.

PROBLEMS Group B

P11-57B Calculate and explain direct material and direct labor variances

(Learning Objectives 1, 2, 3 & 4)

Royal Fabrics manufacturers a specialty monogrammed blanket. To follow are the cost and labor standards for this blanket:

Direct material (fabric): 2.5 yards per blanket at $10.00 per yard

Direct labor: 0.5 direct labor hours per blanket at $14.00 per hour

Actual results from last month's production of 2,000 blankets follows:

Actual cost of 4,100 yards of direct material (fabric) purchased: $39,360

Actual yards of direct material (fabric) used: 3,900

Actual wages for 1,100 direct labor hours worked: $10,800

Requirements

1. What is the standard direct material cost for one blanket?
2. What is the actual cost per yard of fabric purchased?
3. Calculate the direct material price and quantity variances.
4. What is the standard direct labor cost for one blanket?
5. What is the actual direct labor cost per hour?
6. Calculate the direct labor rate and efficiency variances.
7. Analyze each variance and speculate as to what may have caused that variance.
8. Look at all four variances together (the big picture). How might they all be related? What variance is very likely to have caused the other variances?

P11-58B Comprehensive standards and variances problem

(Learning Objectives 2, 3, 4, 5 & 6)

Johnson Awnings manufactures awning and uses a standard cost system. Johnson allocates overhead based on the number of direct labor hours. To follow are the company's cost and standards data:

Standards:
Direct material 21.0 yards per awning at $14.00 per yard
Direct labor 4.0 hours per awning at $16.00 per hour
Variable MOH standard rate $6.00 per direct labor hour
Predetermined fixed MOH standard rate $7.00 per direct labor hour
Total budgeted fixed MOH cost $52,000

Actual cost and operating data from the most recent month follows:
Purchased 53,500 yards at a total cost of $754,350
Used 47,200 yards in producing 2,200 awnings
Actual direct labor cost of $138,330 for a total of 8,700 hours
Actual variable MOH cost $54,810
Actual fixed MOH cost $56,000

All manufacturing overhead is allocated on the basis of direct labor hours.

Requirements

1. Calculate the standard cost of one awning.
2. Calculate the following variances:
   a. The direct material variances.
   b. The direct labor variances.
   c. The variable manufacturing overhead variances.
   d. The fixed manufacturing overhead variances.
3. Explain what each of the variances you calculated means and give at least one possible explanation for each of those variances. Are any of the variances likely to be interrelated?

P11-59B Comprehensive standards and variances problem

(Learning Objectives 1, 2, 3, 4, 5 & 6)

Mikhail Manufacturing produces ceramic teapots. Mikhail allocates overhead based on the number of direct labor hours. The company is looking into using a standard cost system and has developed the following standards (one "unit" is a batch of 100 teapots).

Standards:
Direct material 100 pounds per batch at $3.00 per pound
Direct labor 4.0 hours per batch at $15.00 per hour
Variable MOH standard rate $6.00 per direct labor hour
Predetermined fixed MOH standard rate $8.00 per direct labor hour
Total budgeted fixed MOH cost $5,000

Actual cost and operating data from the most recent month follows:
Purchased 8,600 pounds at a cost of $3.40 per pound
Used 8,400 pounds in producing 80 batches
Actual direct labor cost of $6,090 at an average direct labor cost per hour of $14.50
Actual variable MOH cost $2,100
Actual fixed MOH cost $5,200

All manufacturing overhead is allocated on the basis of direct labor hours.

Requirements

1. Calculate the standard cost of one batch.
2. Calculate the following variances:
   a. The direct material variances.
   b. The direct labor variances.
   c. The variable manufacturing overhead variances.
   d. The fixed manufacturing overhead variances.
3. Have the company's managers done a good job or a poor job controlling materials, labor, and overhead costs? Why or why not?
4. Describe how the company's managers can benefit from the standard costing system. Do you think the company should continue with the standard cost system?

P11-60B Work backward through labor variances *(Learning Objective 3)*

Carol's Music manufactures harmonicas. Carol uses standard costs to judge performance. Recently, a clerk mistakenly threw away some of the records, and only partial data for October exists. Carol knows that the total direct labor variance for the month was $300 F and that the standard labor rate was $11 per hour. A recent pay cut caused a favorable labor price variance of $0.60 per hour. The standard direct labor hours for actual October outputs were 5,700.

Requirements

1. Find the actual number of direct labor hours worked during October. First, find the actual direct labor rate per hour. Then, determine the actual number of direct labor hours worked by setting up the computation of the total direct labor variance as given.
2. Compute the direct labor rate and efficiency variances. Do these variances suggest that the manager may have made trade-offs? Explain.

P11-61B Determine all variances and make journal entries *(Learning Objectives 2, 3, 4, 5, 6 & 7)*

Huntsman manufactures embroidered jackets. The company uses a standard cost system to control manufacturing costs. The following data represents the standard unit cost of a jacket:

Direct materials (3.0 sq. ft × $8.00 per sq. ft)		$24.00
Direct labor (2.0 hours × $11.00 per hour)		22.00
Manufacturing overhead:		
Variable (2.0 hours × $0.75 per hour)	$1.50	
Fixed (2.0 hours × $2.40 per hour)	4.80	6.30
Total standard cost per jacket		$52.30

Fixed overhead in total was budgeted to be $61,500 for each month.

Actual data for November of the current year include the following:

a. Actual production was 12,000 jackets.
b. Actual direct materials usage was 3.1 square feet per jacket at an actual cost of $7.50 per square foot.
c. Actual direct labor usage of 25,100 hours for a total cost of $271,080.
d. Actual fixed overhead cost was $59,800, while actual variable overhead cost was $17,570.

Requirements

1. Compute the price and quantity variances for direct materials.
2. Compute the rate and efficiency variances for direct labor.
3. Compute the rate and efficiency variances for variable overhead.
4. Compute the fixed overhead budget variance and the fixed overhead volume variance.
5. Huntsman's management intentionally purchased superior materials for November production. How did this decision affect the other cost variances? Overall, was the decision wise? Explain.
6. Journalize the usage of direct materials and the assignment of direct labor, including the related variances.

CRITICAL THINKING

Discussion & Analysis

A11-62 Discussion Questions

1. Suppose a company is implementing lean accounting throughout the organization. Why might standard costing *not* be beneficial for that company?
2. What advantages might be experienced by a company if it adopts ideal standards for its direct material standards and direct labor standards? What advantages are there to using practical standards? As an employee, which would you prefer and why? Does your answer change if you are the manager in charge of production? Why or why not?
3. Select a product with which you are familiar. Describe what type of standards (direct material and direct labor) might be in effect for that product wherever it is produced. For each of these standards, discuss how those standards may become outdated. How frequently would you think the company would need to evaluate each of the standards?
4. Service organization also use standards. Describe what types of standards might be in effect at each of the following types of organizations:
    - Hospitals.
    - Law firms.
    - Accounting firms.
    - Auto repair shops.
    - Fast-food restaurants.
5. What does the direct materials price variance measure? Who is generally responsible for the direct materials price variance? Describe two situations that could result in a favorable materials price variance. Describe two situations that could result in an unfavorable materials price variance.
6. What does the direct materials efficiency variance measure? Who is generally responsible for the direct materials efficiency variance? Describe two situations that could result in a favorable direct materials efficiency variance. Describe two situations that could result in an unfavorable direct materials efficiency variance.
7. What does the direct labor price variance measure? Who is generally responsible for direct labor price variance? Describe two situations that could result in a favorable labor price variance. Describe two situations that could result in an unfavorable direct labor variance.
8. What does the direct labor efficiency variance measure? Who is generally responsible for the direct labor efficiency variance? Describe two situations that could result in a favorable direct labor efficiency variance. Describe two situations that could result in an unfavorable direct labor efficiency variance.
9. Describe at least four ways a company could use standard costing and variance analysis.
10. What are the two manufacturing overhead variances? What does each measure? Who within the organization would be responsible for each of these variances?
11. Suppose a company that makes and sells spaghetti sauce in plastic jars makes a change to its bottle that allows it to use significantly less plastic in each bottle. Describe at least four ways this change could help the company and its sustainability efforts.
12. Think of a company that manufactures a product. What type of standards do you think that company might have regarding its sustainability efforts? Do you think sustainability standards would be beneficial for the company? Why or why not?

Application & Analysis

A11-63 Analyzing Variances and Potential Causes

Go to YouTube.com and search for clips from the show "Unwrapped" on Food Network or "How It's Made" on Discovery Channel. Watch a clip for a product you find interesting. Companies are not likely to disclose everything about their production process and other trade secrets. When you answer the following questions, you may have to make reasonable assumptions or guesses about the manufacturing process, materials, and labor.

Basic Discussion Questions

1. Describe the product that is being produced. Briefly outline the production process.
2. What direct materials are used to make this product? In general, what has happened to the cost of these materials over the past year? To find information about the price of materials, you might try one of these sources (or a combination of these sources):
   a. Go to the New York Times website (http://nytimes.com/) or to USA Today (http://www.usatoday.com/) and search for each of the materials.
   b. Find the company's annual report on its website and read its discussion about its cost of production.
3. Given what you have discovered about the cost of materials for this product, were the price variances for each material likely to be favorable or unfavorable (answer separately for each individual material)?
4. In general, what has probably occurred to the cost of direct labor for this company? Again, to find clues about its labor costs, you might try one of the options listed in Question 2. If you cannot find anything specific about this company, then discuss what has happened to the cost of labor in general over the past year.
5. Given what you have discovered about the cost of labor, was the labor rate variance likely to be favorable or unfavorable?
6. It is unlikely that the company has released information about its quantity (efficiency) variances. In general, though, what could cause this company's material quantity variances to be favorable? What could cause these material quantity variances to be unfavorable?
7. In general, what could cause this company's labor efficiency variances to be favorable? What could cause these labor efficiency variances to be unfavorable?

Ethical Issues

A11-64 Ethical dilemmas relating to standards *(Learning Objective 3)*

Austin Landers is the accountant for Sun Coast, a manufacturer of outdoor furniture that is sold through specialty stores and internet companies. Annually, Landers is responsible for reviewing the standard costs for the following year. While reviewing the standard costs for the coming year, two ethical issues arise. Use the IMA's *Statement of Ethical Professional Practice* (in Chapter 1) to identify the ethical dilemma in each situation. Identify the relevant factors in each situation and suggest what Landers should recommend to the controller.

Issue 1: Landers has been approached by Dara Willis, a former colleague who worked with Landers when they were both employed by a public accounting firm. Willis recently started her own firm, Willis Benchmarking Associates, which collects and sells data on industry benchmarks. She offers to provide Landers with benchmarks for the outdoor furniture industry free of charge if he will provide her with the last three years of Sun Coast's standard and actual costs. Willis explains that this is how she obtains most of her firm's benchmarking data. Landers always has a difficult time with the standard-setting process and believes that the benchmark data would be very useful.

Issue 2: Sun Coast's management is starting a continuous improvement policy that requires a 10% reduction in standard costs each year for the next three years. Dan Jones, manufacturing supervisor of the Teak furniture line, asks Landers to set loose standard costs this year before the continuous improvement policy is implemented. Jones argues that there is no other way to meet the tightening standards while maintaining the high quality of the Teak line.

Team Project

A11-65 Evaluate standard setting approaches *(Learning Objective 3)*

Pella is the world's second largest manufacturer of wood windows and doors. In 1992, Pella entered the national retail market with its ProLine windows and doors, manufactured in Carroll, Iowa. Since then, Pella has introduced many new product lines with manufacturing facilities in several states.

Suppose Pella has been using a standard cost system that bases price and quantity standards on Pella's historical long-run average performance. Assume Pella should use some basis other than historical performance for setting standards.

Requirements

1. List the types of variances you recommend that Pella compute (for example, direct materials price variance for glass). For each variance, what specific standards would Pella need to develop? In addition to cost standards, do you recommend that Pella develop any nonfinancial standards? Explain.
2. There are many approaches to setting standards other than simply using long-run average historical prices and quantities.
   a. List three alternative approaches that Pella could use to set standards and explain how Pella could implement each alternative.
   b. Evaluate each alternative method of setting standards, including the pros and cons of each method.
   c. Write a memo to Pella's controller detailing your recommendations. First, should Pella retain its historical data-based standard cost approach? If not, which alternative approach should it adopt?

12

Capital Investment Decisions and the Time Value of Money

Learning Objectives

1. Describe the importance of capital investments and the capital budgeting process
2. Use the payback and accounting rate of return methods to make capital investment decisions
3. Use the time value of money to compute the present and future values of single lump sums and annuities
4. Use discounted cash flow models to make capital investment decisions
5. Compare and contrast the four capital budgeting methods

Cedar Fair Entertainment

Company is the leading operator of amusement parks in the United States and Canada, entertaining over 22 million guests each year. The company's flagship park, Cedar Point, in Sandusky, Ohio, is known as the "Roller Coaster Capital of the World." The park has a world-record breaking collection of 17 roller coasters, as well as an abundance of non-coaster rides and activities. These roller coasters include some of the *fastest* and *tallest* roller coasters in North America. The newest roller coaster, "Maverick," cost over $21 million to build. The company doesn't mind paying that kind of money for a new ride, as long as it is expected to generate handsome returns in years to come. According to Cedar Fair's chief executive officer, the company "remains committed to investing in new rides and attractions...on an annual basis." The CEO views these "strategic investments" as one of the keys to the company's success. In the eyes of customers, the strategy has worked: Cedar Point has been voted the "Best Amusement Park in the World" for 13 consecutive years, by *Amusement Today's* international survey.

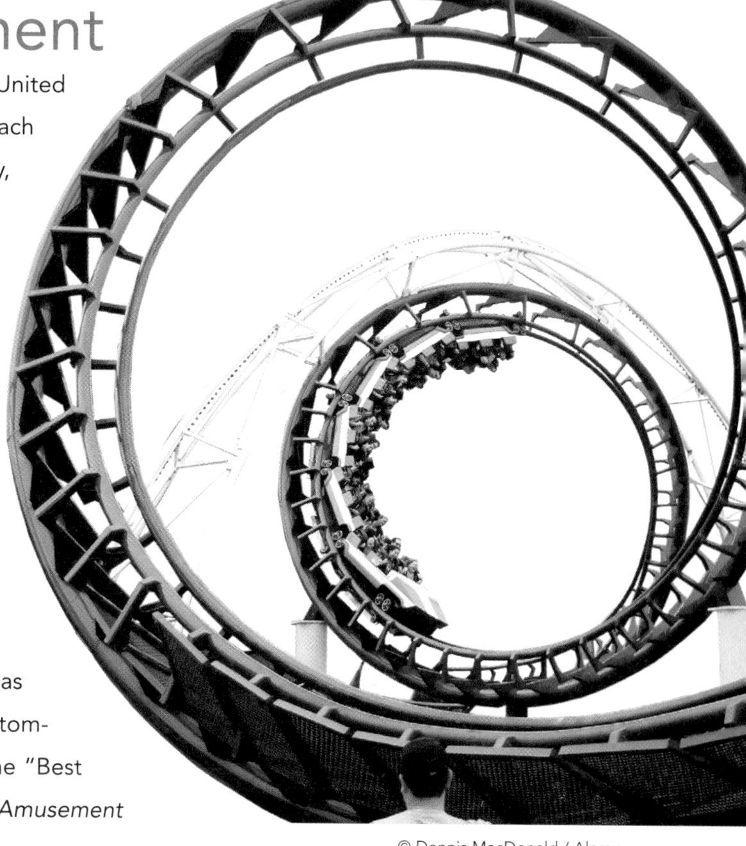

Source: Cedarpoint.com

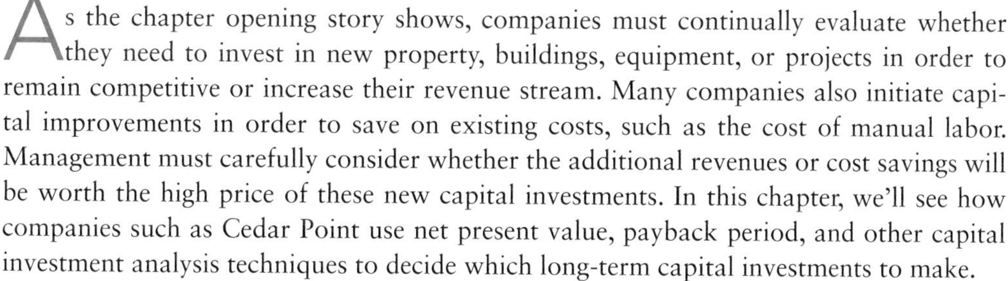

As the chapter opening story shows, companies must continually evaluate whether they need to invest in new property, buildings, equipment, or projects in order to remain competitive or increase their revenue stream. Many companies also initiate capital improvements in order to save on existing costs, such as the cost of manual labor. Management must carefully consider whether the additional revenues or cost savings will be worth the high price of these new capital investments. In this chapter, we'll see how companies such as Cedar Point use net present value, payback period, and other capital investment analysis techniques to decide which long-term capital investments to make.

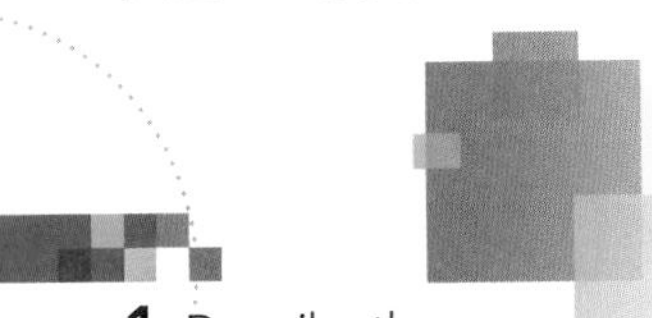

What is Capital Budgeting?

1 Describe the importance of capital investments and the capital budgeting process

The process of making capital investment decisions is often referred to as **capital budgeting**. Companies make capital investments when they acquire *capital assets*—assets used for a long period of time. Capital investments include buying new equipment, building new plants, automating production, and developing major commercial websites. In addition to affecting operations for many years, capital investments usually require large sums of money. Cedar Point's decision to spend $21 million on the Maverick roller coaster will tie up resources for years to come—as will Marriott's decision to spend $187 million to renovate its Marco Island Marriott Beach Resort, Golf Club, and Spa.

Capital investment decisions affect all types of businesses as they try to become more efficient by automating production and implementing new technologies. Grocers and retailers such as Walmart have invested in expensive self-scan check-out machines, while airlines such as Delta and Continental have invested in self-check-in kiosks. These new technologies cost money. How do managers decide whether these expansions in plant and equipment will be good investments? They use capital budgeting analysis. Some companies, such as Georgia Pacific, employ staff dedicated solely to capital budgeting analysis. They spend thousands of hours a year determining which capital investments to pursue.

> **Why is this important?**
>
> "Each of these **four methods** help managers **decide** whether it would be wise to **invest** large sums of money in **new projects**, buildings, or equipment."

Four Popular Methods of Capital Budgeting Analysis

In this chapter, we discuss four popular methods of analyzing potential capital investments:

1. Payback period
2. Accounting rate of return (ARR)
3. Net present value (NPV)
4. Internal rate of return (IRR)

The first two methods, payback period and accounting rate of return, are fairly quick and easy to calculate and work well for capital investments that have a relatively short life span, such as computer equipment and software that may have a useful life of only two to three years. Management often uses the payback period and accounting rate of return to screen potential investments from those that are less desirable. The payback period provides management with valuable information on how fast the cash invested will be recouped. The accounting rate of return shows the effect of the investment on the company's accrual-based income. However, these two methods are inadequate if the capital investments have a longer life span. Why? Because these methods do not consider the time value of money. The last two methods, net present value and internal rate of return, factor in the time value of money, so they are more appropriate for longer-term capital investments such as Cedar Point's new roller coasters and rides. Management often uses a combination of methods to make final capital investment decisions.

Capital budgeting is not an exact science. Although the calculations these methods require may appear precise, remember that they are based on predictions about an uncertain future. These predictions must consider many unknown factors, such as changing consumer preferences, competition, and government regulations. The further into the future the decision extends, the more likely actual results will differ from predictions. Long-term decisions are riskier than short-term decisions.

Focus on Cash Flows

Generally Accepted Accounting Principles (GAAP) are based on accrual accounting, but capital budgeting focuses on cash flows. The desirability of a capital asset depends on its ability to generate *net cash inflows*—that is, inflows in excess of outflows—over the asset's useful life. Recall that operating income based on accrual accounting contains noncash expenses such as depreciation expense and bad-debt expense. The capital investment's *net cash inflows,* therefore, will differ from its operating income. Of the four capital budgeting methods covered in this chapter, only the accounting rate of return method uses accrual-based accounting income. The other three methods use the investment's projected *net cash inflows*.

What do the projected net cash inflows include? Cash *inflows* include future cash revenue generated from the investment, any future savings in ongoing cash operating costs resulting from the investment, and any future residual value of the asset. To determine the investment's *net* cash inflows, the inflows are *netted* against the investment's future cash *outflows*, such as the investment's ongoing cash operating costs and refurbishment, repairs, and maintenance costs. The initial investment itself is also a significant cash outflow. However, in our calculations, *we refer to the amount of the investment separately from all other cash flows related to the investment.* The projected net cash inflows are "given" in our examples and in the assignment material. In reality, much of capital investment analysis revolves around projecting these figures as accurately as possible using input from employees throughout the organization.

Capital Budgeting Process

As shown in Exhibit 12-1, the first step in the capital budgeting process is to identify potential investments—for example, new technology and equipment that may make the company more efficient, competitive, and profitable. Employees, consultants, and outside sales vendors often offer capital investment proposals to management. After identifying potential capital investments, managers next estimate the investments' net cash inflows. As discussed previously, this step can be very time-consuming and difficult. However, managers make the best projections possible given the information they have. The third step is to analyze the investments using one or more of the four methods listed previously. Sometimes the analysis involves a two-stage process. In the first stage, managers screen the investments using one or both of the methods that do *not* incorporate the time value of money: payback period or accounting rate of return. These simple methods quickly weed out undesirable investments. Potential investments that "pass the initial test" go on to a second stage of analysis. In the second stage, managers further analyze the potential investments using the net present value or internal rate of return method. Because these methods consider the time value of money, they provide more accurate information about the potential investment's profitability. Since each method evaluates the potential investment from a different angle, some companies use all four methods to get the most "complete picture" they can about the investment.

Some companies can pursue all of the potential investments that meet or exceed their decision criteria. However, because of limited resources, other companies must engage in **capital rationing** and choose among alternative capital investments. This is the fourth step pictured in Exhibit 12-1. Based on the availability of funds, managers determine if and when to make specific capital investments. For example, management may decide to wait three years to buy a certain piece of equipment because it considers other investments to be more important. In the intervening three years, the company will reassess whether it should still invest in the equipment. Perhaps technology has changed and even better equipment is available. Perhaps consumer tastes have changed, so the company no longer needs the equipment. Because of changing factors, long-term capital budgets are rarely set in stone.

As a final step, most companies perform **post-audits** of their capital investments. After investing in the assets, they compare the actual net cash inflows generated from the investment to the projected net cash inflows. Post-audits help companies determine whether the investments are going as planned and deserve continued support or whether

EXHIBIT 12-1 Capital Budgeting Process

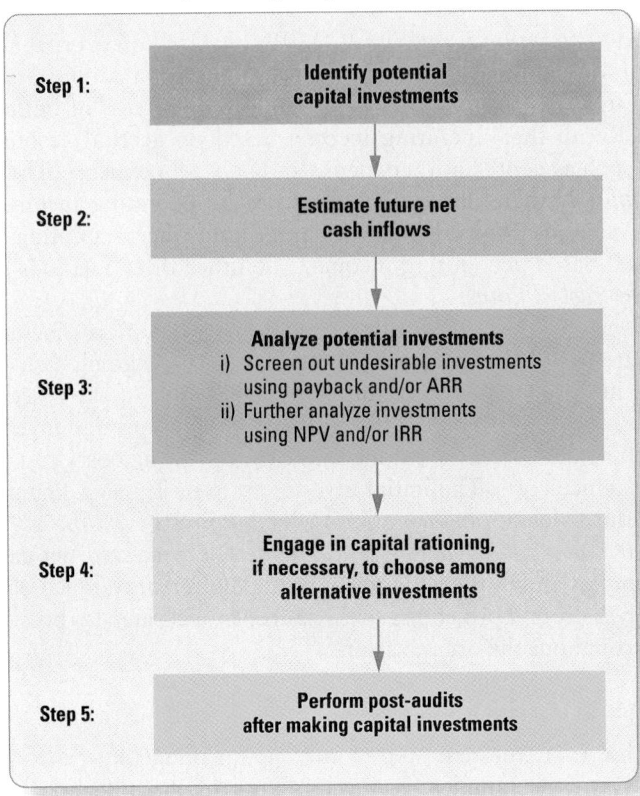

they should abandon the project and sell the assets (if possible). Managers also use feedback from post-audits to better estimate net cash inflow projections for future projects. If managers expect routine post-audits, they will more likely submit realistic net cash inflow estimates with their capital investment proposals.

Sustainability and Capital Investments

Investments in "green" technologies often require large capital outlays that are subject to capital investment analysis. Investments in clean energy have risen dramatically in recent years, especially with respect to wind and solar power projects. In 2010 alone, $243 billion was invested globally in clean energy.[1] Companies deciding whether to invest in solar paneling on retail outlets (Target)[2], a fleet of electric vehicles (Continental Airlines)[3], or LEED certified buildings (Best Buy)[4] will want to assess how quickly payback will occur and how prudent the investment will be. Their analysis should consider all of the future revenues and cost savings that may occur as a result of using greener technology.

See Exercises E12-22A and E12-42B

For example, companies need to be aware of grants and tax breaks offered by governmental agencies for investing in green technology. These government-sponsored incentives should be treated as reductions in the initial cost of the investment or as periodic cost savings, depending on how the incentive is structured and when it is received. Companies should also factor in future cost savings from having fewer lawsuits, regulatory fines, and clean-up costs as a result of investing in green technology. Furthermore, as the supply of fossil fuels decreases and the cost of it rises, greener technology may also result in lower annual operating costs.

[1] "China leads in clean-energy investing," Christopher Martin, Plain Dealer, March 30, 2011.
[2] http://www.environmentalleader.com/2007/04/30/target-begins-solar-power-rollout/
[3] https://www.continental.com/web/en-US/content/company/globalcitizenship/environment.aspx
[4] http://www.jetsongreen.com/2007/08/best-buy-to-bui.html

When renovating existing facilities, or constructing new facilities, LEED certification should be considered. LEED, which stands for "Leadership in Energy and Environmental Design," is a certification system developed by the U.S. Green Building Council as a way of promoting and evaluating environmentally friendly construction projects. Five factors are assessed as part of the certification process:[5]

1. Site development
2. Water efficiency
3. Energy efficiency
4. Materials selection
5. Indoor environmental quality

Why do companies care about LEED certification? Besides being better for the planet and the people who work in the buildings, LEED certified buildings typically have lower operating costs which often result in higher returns on the investment. Additionally, LEED certified buildings have a competitive advantage over non-certified buildings. As a result, LEED certified buildings often attract more potential buyers and command higher lease prices.

How do Managers Calculate the Payback Period and Accounting Rate of Return?

Payback Period

2 Use the payback and accounting rate of return methods to make capital investment decisions

Payback is the length of time it takes to recover, in net cash inflows, the cost of the capital outlay. The payback model measures how quickly managers expect to recover their investment dollars. The shorter the payback period, the more attractive the asset, *all else being equal*. Why? The quicker an investment pays itself back, the less inherent risk that the investment will become unprofitable. Computing the payback period depends on whether net cash inflows are equal each year or whether they differ over time. We consider each in turn.

Payback with Equal Annual Net Cash Inflows

Tierra Firma makes camping gear. The company is considering investing $240,000 in hardware and software to develop a business-to-business (B2B) portal. Employees throughout the company will use the B2B portal to access company-approved suppliers. Tierra Firma expects the portal to save $60,000 each year for the six years of its useful life. The savings will arise from a reduction in the number of purchasing personnel the company employs and from lower prices on the goods and services purchased. Net cash inflows arise from an increase in revenues, a decrease in expenses, or both. In Tierra Firma's case, the net cash inflows result from lower expenses.

When net cash inflows are equal each year, managers compute the payback period as follows:

Why is this important?

"Companies want to **recover their cash** as quickly as possible. The **payback period** tells managers **how long** it will take before the investment is **recouped.**"

$$\text{Payback period} = \frac{\text{Amount invested}}{\text{Expected annual net cash inflow}}$$

Tierra Firma computes the investment's payback as follows:

$$\text{Payback period for B2B portal} = \frac{\$240{,}000}{\$60{,}000} = 4 \text{ years}$$

[5] http://www.usgbc.org

The left side of Exhibit 12-2 verifies that Tierra Firma expects to recoup the $240,000 investment in the B2B portal by the end of Year 4, when the accumulated net cash inflows total $240,000.

EXHIBIT 12-2 Payback—Equal Annual Net Cash Inflows

		Net Cash Inflows			
		B2B Portal		Website Development	
Year	Amount Invested	Annual	Accumulated	Annual	Accumulated
0	$240,000	—	—	—	—
1	—	$60,000	$ 60,000	$80,000	$ 80,000
2	—	60,000	120,000	80,000	160,000
3	—	60,000	180,000	80,000	240,000
4	—	60,000	240,000		
5	—	60,000	300,000		
6	—	60,000	360,000		

Useful Life

Useful Life

Tierra Firma is also considering investing $240,000 to develop a website. The company expects the website to generate $80,000 in net cash inflows each year of its three-year life. The payback period is computed as follows:

$$\text{Payback period for website development} = \frac{\$240{,}000}{\$80{,}000} = 3 \text{ years}$$

The right side of Exhibit 12-2 verifies that Tierra Firma will recoup the $240,000 investment for website development by the end of Year 3, when the accumulated net cash inflows total $240,000.

Payback with Unequal Net Cash Inflows

The payback equation works only when net cash inflows are the same each period. When periodic cash flows are unequal, you must accumulate net cash inflows until the amount invested is recovered. Assume that Tierra Firma is considering an alternate investment, the Z80 portal. The Z80 portal differs from the B2B portal and website in two respects: (1) it has *unequal* net cash inflows during its life, and (2) it has a $30,000 residual value at the end of its life. The Z80 portal will generate net cash inflows of $100,000 in Year 1, $80,000 in Year 2, $50,000 each year in Years 3–5, $30,000 in Year 6, and $30,000 when it is sold at the end of its life. Exhibit 12-3 shows the payback schedule for these unequal annual net cash inflows.

By the end of Year 3, the company has recovered $230,000 of the $240,000 initially invested and is only $10,000 short of payback. Because the expected net cash inflow in Year 4 is $50,000, by the end of Year 4, the company will have recovered *more* than the initial investment. Therefore, the payback period is somewhere between three and four years. Assuming that the cash flow occurs evenly throughout the fourth year, the payback period is calculated as follows:

$$\text{Payback} = 3 \text{ years} + \frac{\$10{,}000 \text{ (amount needed to complete recovery in Year 4)}}{\$50{,}000 \text{ (projected net cash inflow in Year 4)}}$$

$$= 3.2 \text{ years}$$

EXHIBIT 12-3 Payback—Unequal Annual Net Cash Inflows

		Net Cash Inflows Z80 Portal	
Year	**Amount Invested**	**Annual**	**Accumulated**
0	$240,000	—	—
1	—	100,000	$100,000
2	—	80,000	180,000
3	—	50,000	230,000
4	—	50,000	280,000
5	—	50,000	330,000
6	—	30,000	360,000
Residual Value		30,000	390,000

Useful Life (years 1–6)

Criticism of the Payback Period Method

A major criticism of the payback method is that it focuses only on time, not on profitability. The payback period considers only those cash flows that occur *during* the payback period. This method ignores any cash flows that occur *after* that period, including any residual value. For example, Exhibit 12-2 shows that the B2B portal will continue to generate net cash inflows for two years after its payback period. These additional net cash inflows amount to $120,000 ($60,000 × 2 years), yet the payback method ignores this extra cash. A similar situation occurs with the Z80 portal. As shown in Exhibit 12-3, the Z80 portal will provide an additional $150,000 of net cash inflows, including residual value, after its payback period of 3.2 years. In contrast, the website's useful life, as shown in Exhibit 12-2, is the *same* as its payback period (three years). Since no additional cash flows occur after the payback period, the website will merely cover its cost and provide no profit. Because this is the case, the company has little or no reason to invest in the website even though its payback period is the shortest of all three investments.

Exhibit 12-4 compares the payback period of the three investments. As the exhibit illustrates, the payback method does not consider the asset's profitability. *The method only tells management how quickly it will recover its cash.* Even though the website has the shortest payback period, both the B2B portal and the Z80 portal are better investments because they provide profit. The key point is that the investment with the shortest payback period is best *only when all other factors are the same*. Therefore, managers usually use the payback method as a screening device to "weed out" investments that will take too long to recoup. They rarely use payback period as the sole method for deciding whether to invest in the asset.

EXHIBIT 12-4 Comparing Payback Periods Between Investments

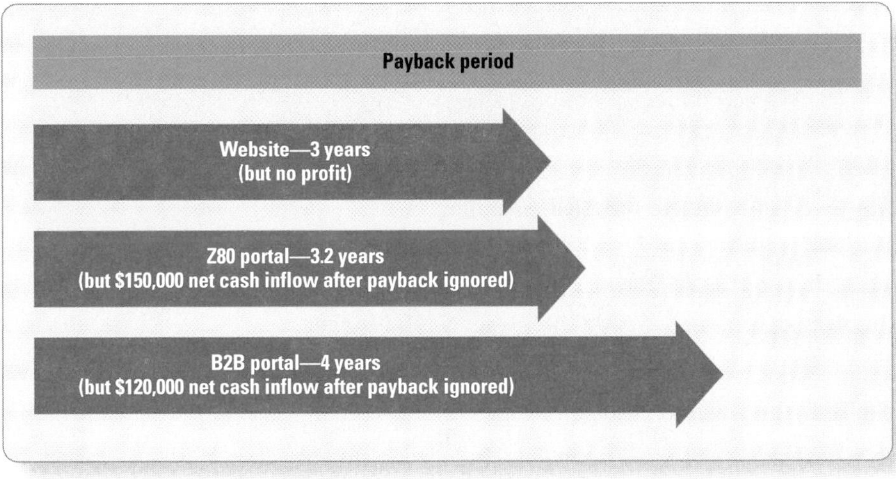

When using the payback period method, managers are guided by the following decision rule:

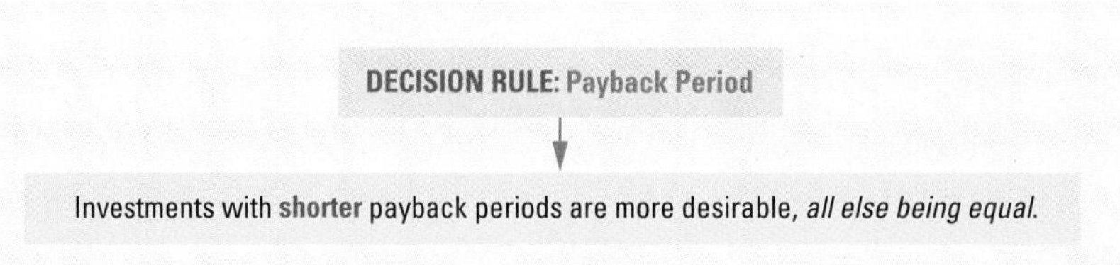

Accounting Rate of Return (ARR)

Companies are in business to earn profits. One measure of profitability is the **accounting rate of return (ARR)** on an asset:[6]

$$\text{Accounting rate of return} = \frac{\text{Average annual operating income from asset}}{\text{Initial investment}}$$

The ARR focuses on the *operating income, not the net cash inflow*, that an asset generates. The ARR measures the average annual rate of return over the asset's life. Recall that operating income is based on *accrual accounting*. Therefore, any noncash expenses such as depreciation expense must be subtracted from the asset's net cash inflows to arrive at its operating income. Assuming that depreciation expense is the only noncash expense relating to the investment, we can rewrite the ARR formula as follows:

$$\text{ARR} = \frac{\text{Average annual net cash flow} - \text{Annual depreciation expense}}{\text{Initial investment}}$$

Exhibit 12-5 reviews how to calculate annual depreciation expense using the straight-line method.

EXHIBIT 12-5 Review of Straight-Line Depreciation Expense Calculation

$$\text{Annual depreciation expense} = \frac{\text{Initial cost of asset} - \text{Residual value}}{\text{Useful life of asset (in years)}}$$

Investments with Equal Annual Net Cash Inflows

Recall that the B2B portal, which costs \$240,000, has equal annual net cash inflows of \$60,000, a six-year useful life, and no residual value.

First, we must find the B2B portal's annual depreciation expense:

$$\text{Annual depreciation expense} = \frac{\$240{,}000 - 0}{6 \text{ years}} = \$40{,}000$$

Now, we can complete the ARR formula:

$$\text{ARR} = \frac{\$60{,}000 - \$40{,}000}{\$240{,}000} = \frac{\$20{,}000}{\$240{,}000} = 8.33\% \text{ (rounded)}$$

The B2B portal will provide an average annual accounting rate of return of 8.33%.

[6]Some managers prefer to use the average investment, rather than the initial investment, as the denominator. For simplicity, we will use the initial investment.

Investments with Unequal Net Cash Inflows

Now, consider the Z80 portal. Recall that the Z80 portal would also cost $240,000 but it had unequal net cash inflows during its life (as pictured in Exhibit 12-3) and a $30,000 residual value at the end of its life. Since the yearly cash inflows vary in size, we need to first calculate the Z80's *average* annual net cash inflows:[7]

Total net cash inflows *during* operating life of asset (does not include the residual value at the end of life)[7] (Year 1 + Year 2, and so forth) from Exhibit 12-3	$360,000
Divide by: Asset's operating life (in years)	÷ 6 years
Average annual net cash inflow from asset	$ 60,000

Now, let's calculate the asset's annual depreciation expense:

$$\text{Annual depreciation expense} = \frac{\$240{,}000 - \$30{,}000}{6 \text{ years}} = \$35{,}000$$

Finally, we can complete the ARR calculation:

$$\text{ARR} = \frac{\$60{,}000 - \$35{,}000}{\$240{,}000} = \frac{\$25{,}000}{\$240{,}000} = 10.42\% \text{ (rounded)}$$

Notice that the Z80 portal's average annual operating income ($25,000) is higher than the B2B portal's average operating income ($20,000). Since the Z80 asset has a residual value at the end of its life, less depreciation is expensed each year, leading to a higher average annual operating income and a higher ARR.

Companies that use the ARR model set a minimum required accounting rate of return. If Tierra Firma required an ARR of at least 10%, its managers would not approve an investment in the B2B portal but would approve an investment in the Z80 portal.

The decision rule is as follows:

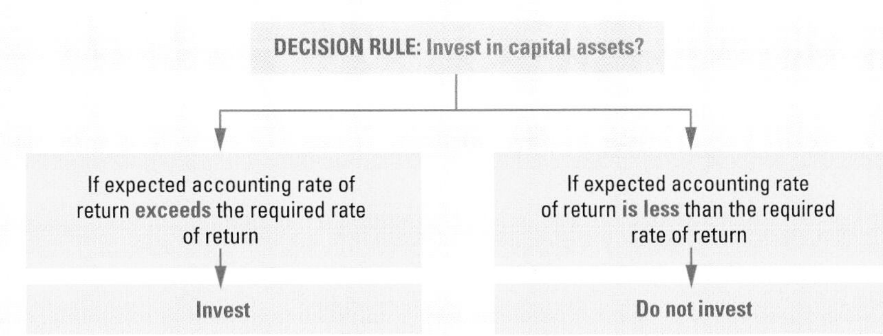

In summary, the payback period focuses on the time it takes for the company to

[7]The residual value is not included in the net cash inflows *during* the asset's operating life because we are trying to find the asset's average *annual operating* income. We assume that the asset will be sold for its expected residual value ($30,000) at the *end* of its life, resulting in no additional accounting gain or loss.

recoup its cash investment but ignores all cash flows occurring after the payback period. Because it ignores any additional cash flows (including any residual value), the method does not consider the profitability of the project.

The ARR, however, measures the profitability of the asset over its entire life using accrual accounting figures. It is the only method that uses accrual accounting rather than net cash inflows in its computations. As discussed in Chapter 10, company divisions are often evaluated based on accounting income. Therefore, the investment's ARR helps managers see how the investment will impact their division's profitability. The payback period and ARR methods are simple and quick to compute, so managers often use them to screen out undesirable investments and to gain a more complete picture of the investment's desirability. However, both methods ignore the time value of money.

Decision Guidelines

Capital Budgeting

Amazon.com started as a virtual retailer. It held no inventory. Instead, it bought books and CDs only as needed to fill customer orders. As the company grew, its managers decided to invest in their own warehouse facilities. Why? Owning warehouse facilities allows Amazon.com to save money by buying in bulk. Also, shipping all items in the customer's order in one package from one location saves shipping costs. Here are some of the guidelines Amazon.com's managers used as they made the major capital budgeting decision to invest in building warehouses.

Decision	Guidelines
Why is this decision important?	Capital budgeting decisions typically require large investments and affect operations for years to come.
What method shows us how soon we will recoup our cash investment?	The payback method shows how quickly managers will recoup their investment. The method highlights investments that are too risky due to long payback periods. However, it doesn't reveal any information about the investment's profitability.
Does any method consider the impact of the investment on accrual-based accounting income?	The accounting rate of return is the only capital budgeting method that shows how the investment will affect accrual-based accounting income, which is important to financial statement users. All other methods of capital investment analysis focus on the investment's net cash inflows.
How do we compute the payback period if cash flows are *equal*?	$\text{Payback period} = \dfrac{\text{Amount invested}}{\text{Expected annual net cash inflow}}$
How do we compute the payback period if cash flows are *unequal*?	Accumulate net cash inflows until the amount invested is recovered.
How do we compute the ARR?	$\text{Accounting rate of return} = \dfrac{\text{Average annual operating income from asset}}{\text{Initial investment}}$ We can also write this formula as follows: $\text{ARR} = \dfrac{\text{Average annual net cash flow} - \text{Annual depreciation expense}}{\text{Initial investment}}$

SUMMARY PROBLEM 1

Zetamax is considering buying a new bar-coding machine for its Austin, Texas plant. The company screens its potential capital investments using the payback period and accounting rate of return methods. If a potential investment has a payback period of less than four years and a minimum 7% accounting rate of return, it will be considered further. The data for the machine follow:

Cost of machine	\$48,000
Estimated residual value	\$ 0
Estimated annual net cash inflow (each year for five years)	\$13,000
Estimated useful life	5 years

Requirements

1. Compute the bar-coding machine's payback period.
2. Compute the bar-coding machine's ARR.
3. Should Zetamax turn down this investment proposal or consider it further?

SOLUTIONS

Requirement 1

$$\text{Payback period} = \frac{\text{Amount invested}}{\text{Expected annual net cash inflow}} = \frac{\$48{,}000}{\$13{,}000} = 3.7 \text{ years (rounded)}$$

Requirement 2

$$\text{Accounting rate of return} = \frac{\text{Average annual net cash inflow} - \text{Annual depreciation expense}}{\text{Initial investment}}$$

$$= \frac{\$13{,}000 - \$9{,}600^{*}}{\$48{,}000}$$

$$= \frac{\$3{,}400}{\$48{,}000}$$

$$= 7.08\%$$

*Depreciation expense = \$48,000 ÷ 5 years = \$9,600

Requirement 3

The bar-coding machine proposal passes both initial screening tests. The payback period is slightly less than four years, and the accounting rate of return is slightly higher than 7%. Zetamax should further analyze the proposal using a method that incorporates the time value of money.

How do Managers Compute the Time Value of Money?

3 Use the time value of money to compute the present and future values of single lump sums and annuities

A dollar received today is worth more than a dollar to be received in the future. Why? Because you can invest today's dollar and earn extra income. The fact that invested money earns income over time is called the **time value of money**, and this explains why we would prefer to receive cash sooner rather than later. The time value of money means that the timing of capital investments' net cash inflows is important. Two methods of capital investment analysis incorporate the time value of money: the NPV and IRR. This section reviews time value of money concepts to make sure you have a firm foundation for discussing these two methods.

Why is this important?

"The **time value of money** is a critical factor in many management **decisions**. In addition to its use in capital investment analysis, it's also used for **personal financial planning** (such as retirement planning), **business valuation** (for purchasing businesses), and financing decisions **(borrowing and lending)**."

Factors Affecting the Time Value of Money

The time value of money depends on several key factors:

1. The principal amount (p)
2. The number of periods (n)
3. The interest rate (i)

The principal (p) refers to the amount of the investment or borrowing. Because this chapter deals with capital investments, we'll primarily discuss the principal in terms of investments. However, the same concepts apply to borrowings (which you probably discussed in your financial accounting course when you studied bonds payable). We state the principal as either a single lump sum or an annuity. For example, if you want to save money for a new car after college, you may decide to invest a single lump sum of $10,000 in a certificate of deposit (CD). However, you may not currently have $10,000 to invest. Instead, you may invest funds as an annuity, depositing $2,000 at the end of each year in a bank savings account. An **annuity** is a stream of *equal installments* made at *equal time intervals*. An *ordinary annuity* is an annuity in which the installments occur at the *end* of each period.[8]

The number of periods (n) is the length of time from the beginning of the investment until termination. All else being equal, the shorter the investment period, the lower the total amount of interest earned. If you withdraw your savings after four years rather than five years, you will earn less interest. If you begin to save for retirement at age 22 rather than age 45, you will earn more interest before you retire. In this chapter, the number of periods is stated in years.[9]

The interest rate (i) is the annual percentage earned on the investment. **Simple interest** means that interest is calculated *only* on the principal amount. **Compound interest** means that interest is calculated on the principal *and* on all interest earned to date. *Compound interest assumes that all interest earned will remain invested at the same interest rate, not withdrawn and spent.* Exhibit 12-6 compares simple interest (6%) on a five-year, $10,000 CD with interest compounded yearly. As you can see, the amount of compound interest earned each year grows as the base on which it is calculated (principal plus cumulative interest to date) grows. Over the life of this particular investment, the total amount of compound interest is about 13% more than the total amount of simple interest. Most investments yield compound interest, so we assume compound interest rather than simple interest for the rest of this chapter.

[8] In contrast to an *ordinary annuity*, an *annuity due* is an annuity in which the installments occur at the *beginning* of each period. Throughout this chapter we use ordinary annuities since they are better suited to capital budgeting cash flow assumptions.

[9] The number of periods can also be stated in days, months, or quarters. If so, the interest rate needs to be adjusted to reflect the number of time periods in the year.

EXHIBIT 12-6 Simple Versus Compound Interest for a Principal Amount of $10,000 at 6% over Five Years

Year	Simple Interest Calculation	Simple Interest	Compound Interest Calculation	Compound Interest*
1	$10,000 × 6% =	$ 600	$10,000 × 6% =	$ 600
2	$10,000 × 6% =	600	($10,000 + 600) × 6% =	636
3	$10,000 × 6% =	600	($10,000 + 600 + 636) × 6% =	674
4	$10,000 × 6% =	600	($10,000 + 600 + 636 + 674) × 6% =	715
5	$10,000 × 6% =	600	($10,000 + 600 + 636 + 674 + 715) × 6% =	758
	Total interest	$3,000	Total interest	$3,383

*Rounded

Fortunately, time value calculations involving compound interest do not have to be as tedious as shown in Exhibit 12-6. Formulas and tables (or proper use of business calculators or Excel applications) simplify the calculations. In the next sections, we will discuss how to use these tools to perform time value of money calculations.

Future Values and Present Values: Points Along the Time Continuum

Consider the time line in Exhibit 12-7. The future value or present value of an investment simply refers to the value of an investment at different points in time.

EXHIBIT 12-7 Present Value and Future Value Along the Time Continuum

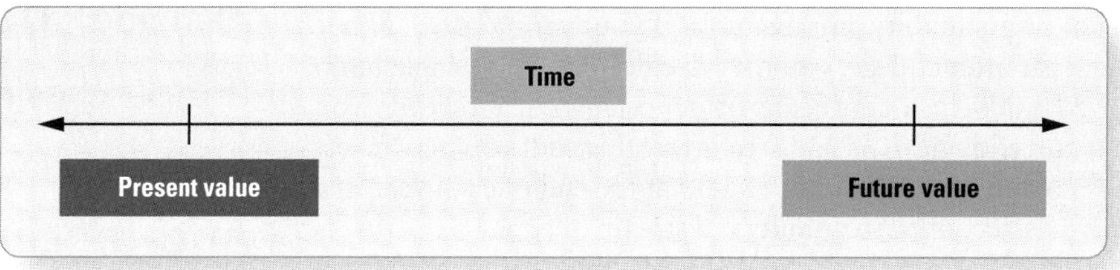

We can calculate the future value or the present value of any investment by knowing (or assuming) information about the three factors listed earlier: (1) the principal amount, (2) the period of time, and (3) the interest rate. For example, in Exhibit 12-6, we calculated the interest that would be earned on (1) a $10,000 principal (2) invested for five years (3) at 6% interest. The future value of the investment is its worth at the end of the five-year time frame—the original principal *plus* the interest earned. In our example, the future value of the investment is as follows:

$$\begin{aligned}\text{Future value} &= \text{Principal} + \text{Interest earned}\\ &= \$10{,}000 + \$3{,}383\\ &= \$13{,}383\end{aligned}$$

If we invest $10,000 *today*, its *present value* is simply the $10,000 principal amount. So, another way of stating the future value is as follows:

$$\text{Future value} = \text{Present value} + \text{Interest earned}$$

We can rearrange the equation as follows:

Present value	=	Future value	−	Interest earned
$10,000	=	$13,383	−	$3,383

The only difference between present value and future value is the amount of interest that is earned in the intervening time span.

Future Value and Present Value Factors

Calculating each period's compound interest, as we did in Exhibit 12-6, and then adding it to the present value to determine the future value (or subtracting it from the future value to determine the present value) is tedious. Fortunately, mathematical formulas simplify future value and present value calculations. Mathematical formulas have been developed that specify future values and present values for unlimited combinations of interest rates (i) and time periods (n). Separate formulas exist for single lump-sum investments and annuities.

The formulas have been calculated using various interest rates and time periods. The results are displayed in tables. The formulas and resulting tables are shown in Appendix 12A at the end of this chapter:

1. Present Value of $1 (Table A, p. 741)—*used for lump-sum amounts*
2. Present Value of Annuity of $1 (Table B, p. 742)—*used for annuities*
3. Future Value of $1 (Table C, p. 743)—*used for lump-sum amounts*
4. Future Value of Annuity of $1 (Table D, p. 744)—*used for annuities*

Take a moment to look at these tables because we are going to use them throughout the rest of the chapter. Note that the columns are interest rates (i) and the rows are periods (n).

The data in each table, known as future value factors (FV factors) and present value factors (PV factors), are for an investment (or loan) of $1. To find the future value of an amount other than $1, you simply multiply the FV factor found in the table by the principal amount. To find the present value of an amount other than $1, you multiply the PV factor found in the table by the principal amount.

Rather than using these tables, you may want to use a business calculator that has been programmed with time value of money functions or Microsoft Excel. Business calculators and Excel make time value of money computations much easier because you do not need to find the correct PV and FV factors in the tables. Rather, you simply enter the principal amount, interest rate, and number of time periods and instruct the calculator or Excel to solve for the present or future value.

Appendix 12B shows how to use the TI-83(Plus) and TI-84 (Plus) to perform basic time value of money computations as well as NPV and IRR computations. Appendix 12C shows how to use Excel for present value, future value, NPV and IRR calculations. Instructions for operating other programmed calculators can usually be found on the manufacturer's website.

Appendix 12B and 12C also show how to compute every problem illustrated throughout the rest of the chapter using either a programmed calculator or Excel. As you will see in Appendix 12B and 12C, using a programmed calculator or Excel results in slightly different answers than those presented in the text when using the tables. The differences are due to the fact that the PV and FV factors found in the tables have been rounded to three digits. Finally, all end-of-chapter material has been solved using the tables, Excel, and programmed calculators so that you will have the exact solution for the method you choose to use.

Calculating Future Values of Single Sums and Annuities Using FV Factors

Let's go back to our $10,000 lump-sum investment. If we want to know the future value of the investment five years from now at an interest rate of 6%, we determine the FV factor from the table labeled Future Value of $1 (Appendix 12A, Table C). We use this table for lump-sum amounts. We look down the 6% column and across the 5 periods row and find that the future value factor is 1.338. We finish our calculations as follows:

Future value = Principal amount × (FV factor for i = 6%, n = 5)
= \$10,000 × (1.338)
= \$13,380

This figure agrees with our earlier calculation of the investment's future value (\$13,383) in Exhibit 12-6. (The difference of \$3 is due to two facts: (1) the tables round the FV and PV factors to three decimal places, and (2) we rounded our earlier yearly interest calculations in Exhibit 12-6 to the nearest dollar.)

Let's also consider our alternative investment strategy: investing \$2,000 at the end of each year for five years. The procedure for calculating the future value of an annuity is similar to calculating the future value of a lump-sum amount. This time, we use the Future Value of Annuity of \$1 table (Appendix 12A, Table D). Assuming 6% interest, we once again look down the 6% column. Because we will be making five annual installments, we look across the row marked 5 periods. The Annuity FV factor is 5.637. We finish the calculation as follows:

Future value = Amount of each cash installment × (Annuity FV factor for i = 6%, n = 5)
= \$2,000 × (5.637)
= \$11,274

This is considerably less than the future value (\$13,380) of the lump sum of \$10,000 even though we invested \$10,000 out of pocket either way.

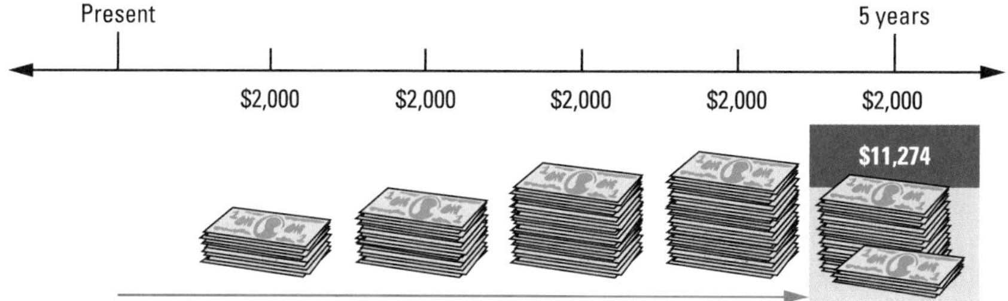

STOP & THINK

Explain why the future value of the annuity ($11,274) is less than the future value of the lump sum ($13,380). Prove that the $11,274 future value is correct by calculating interest using the "longhand" method shown earlier.

Answer: Even though you invested $10,000 out of pocket under both investments, the timing of the investment significantly affects the amount of interest earned. The $10,000 lump sum invested immediately earns interest for the full five years. However, the annuity doesn't begin earning interest until Year 2 (because the first installment isn't made until the *end* of Year 1). In addition, the amount invested begins at $2,000 and doesn't reach a full $10,000 until the end of Year 5. Therefore, the base on which the interest is earned is smaller than the lump-sum investment for the entire five-year period. As shown here, the $11,274 future value of a $2,000 annuity for five years is correct.

Year	Interest Earned During Year (6%) (rounded)	Investment Installment (end of year)	Cumulative Balance at End of Year (investments plus interest earned to date)*
1	$ 0	$2,000	$ 2,000
2	120	2,000	4,120
3	247	2,000	6,367
4	382	2,000	8,749
5	525	2,000	11,274

*This is the base on which the interest is earned the next year.

Calculating Present Values of Single Sums and Annuities Using PV Factors

The process for calculating present values—often called discounting cash flows—is similar to the process for calculating future values. The difference is the point in time at which you are assessing the investment's worth. Rather than determining its value at a future date, you are determining its value at an earlier point in time (today). For our example, let's assume that you've just won the lottery after purchasing one $5 lottery ticket. The state offers you three payout options for your after-tax prize money:

Option #1: $1,000,000 now
Option #2: $150,000 at the end of each year for the next 10 years
Option #3: $2,000,000 10 years from now

Which alternative should you take? You might be tempted to wait 10 years to "double" your winnings. You may be tempted to take the money now and spend it. However, let's assume that you plan to prudently invest all money received—no matter when you receive it—so that you have financial flexibility in the future (for example, for buying a house, retiring early, and taking vacations). How can you choose among the three payment alternatives when the *total amount* of each option varies ($1,000,000 versus $1,500,000 versus $2,000,000) and the *timing* of the cash flows varies (now versus some each year versus later)? Comparing these three options is like comparing apples to oranges—we just can't do it—unless we find some common basis for comparison. Our common basis for comparison will be the prize money's worth at a certain point in time—namely, today. In other words, if we convert each payment option to its *present value*, we can compare apples to apples.

We already know the principal amount and timing of each payment option, so the only assumption we'll have to make is the interest rate. The interest rate will vary depending on the amount of risk you are willing to take with your investment. Riskier investments (such as stock investments) command higher interest rates; safer investments (such as FDIC-insured bank deposits) yield lower interest rates. Let's assume that after investigating possible investment alternatives, you choose an investment contract with an 8% annual return.

We already know that the present value of Option #1 is $1,000,000. Let's convert the other two payment options to their present values so that we can compare them. We'll need to use the Present Value of Annuity of $1 table (Appendix 12A, Table B) to convert payment Option #2 (since it's an annuity) and the Present Value of $1 table (Appendix 12A, Table A) to convert payment Option #3 (since it's a single lump sum). To obtain the PV factors, we look down the 8% column and across the 10 period row. Then, we finish the calculations as follows:

Option #1

Present value = $1,000,000

Option #2

Present value = Amount of each cash installment × (Annuity PV factor for i = 8%, n = 10)
Present value = $150,000 × (6.710)
Present value = $1,006,500

Option #3

Present value = Principal amount × (PV factor for i = 8%, n = 10)
Present value = $2,000,000 × (0.463)
Present value = $926,000

Exhibit 12-8 shows that we have converted each payout option to a common basis—its worth today—so we can make a valid comparison of the options. Based on this comparison, we should choose Option #2 because its worth, in today's dollars, is the highest of the three options.

Now that we have studied time value of money concepts, we will discuss the two capital budgeting methods that incorporate the time value of money: net present value (NPV) and internal rate of return (IRR).

EXHIBIT 12-8 Comparing Present Values of Lottery Payout Options at i = 8%

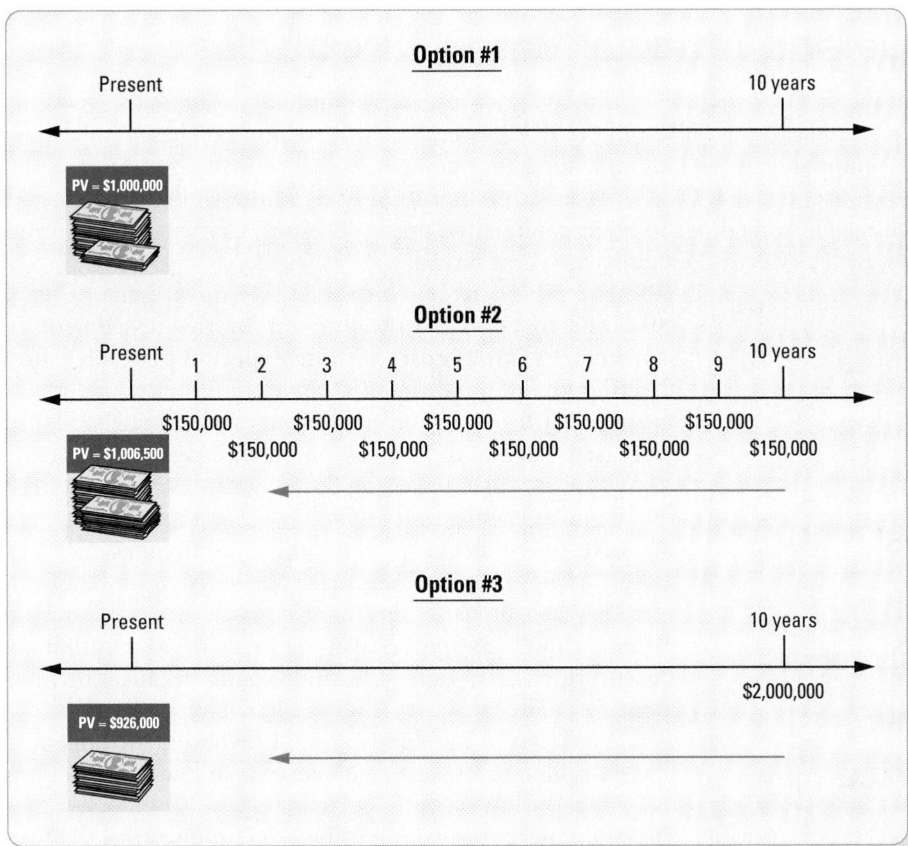

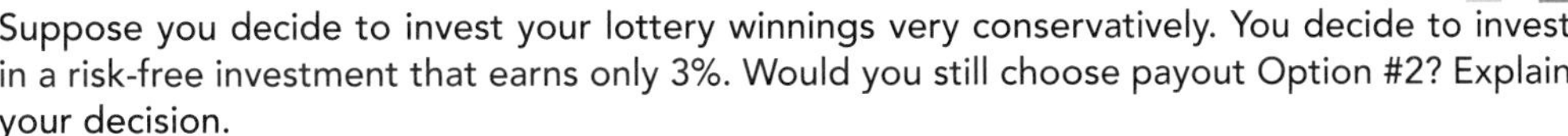

Suppose you decide to invest your lottery winnings very conservatively. You decide to invest in a risk-free investment that earns only 3%. Would you still choose payout Option #2? Explain your decision.

Answer: Using a 3% interest rate, the present values of the payout options are as follows:

Payment Options	Present Value of Lottery Payout (Present value calculation, i = 3%, n = 10)
Option #1	$1,000,000 (already stated at its present value)
Option #2	$1,279,500 (= $150,000 × 8.530)
Option #3	$1,488,000 (= $2,000,000 × .744)

When the lottery payout is invested at 3% rather than 8%, the present values change. Option #3 is now the best alternative because its present value is the highest. Present values and future values are extremely sensitive to changes in interest rate assumptions, especially when the investment period is relatively long.

How do Managers Calculate the Net Present Value and Internal Rate of Return?

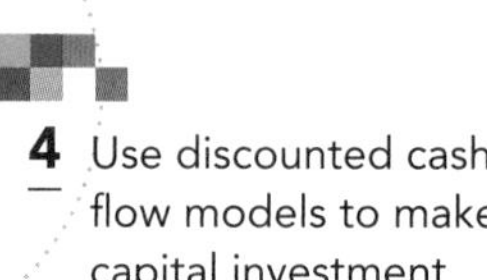

4 Use discounted cash flow models to make capital investment decisions

Neither the payback period nor the ARR incorporate the time value of money. *Discounted cash flow models*—the NPV and the IRR—overcome this weakness. These models incorporate compound interest by assuming that companies will reinvest future cash flows when they are received. Over 85% of large industrial firms in the United States use discounted cash flow methods to make capital investment decisions. Companies that provide services, such as Cedar Point, also use these models.

The NPV and IRR methods rely on present value calculations to *compare* the amount of the investment (the investment's initial cost) with its expected net cash inflows. Recall that an investment's *net cash inflows* includes all *future* cash flows related to the investment, such as future increased sales and cost savings netted against the investment's future cash operating costs. Because the cash outflow for the investment occurs *now* but the net cash inflows from the investment occur in the *future*, companies can make valid "apple-to-apple" comparisons only when they convert the cash flows to the *same point in time*—namely, the present value. Companies use the present value rather than the future value to make the comparison because the investment's initial cost is already stated at its present value.[10]

As shown in Exhibit 12-9, in a favorable investment, the present value of the investment's net cash inflows exceeds the initial cost of the investment. In terms of our earlier lottery example, the lottery ticket turned out to be a "good investment" because the present value of its net cash inflows (the present value of the lottery payout under *any* of the three payout options) exceeded the cost of the investment (the $5 lottery ticket). Let's begin our discussion by taking a closer look at the NPV method.

EXHIBIT 12-9 Comparing the Present Value of an Investment's Net Cash Inflows Against the Investment's Initial Cost

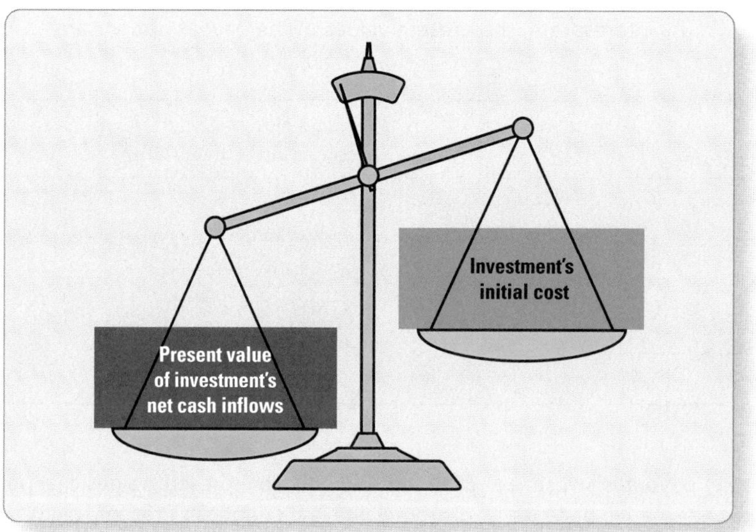

[10]If the investment is to be purchased through lease payments, rather than a current cash outlay, we would still use the current cash price of the investment as its initial cost. If no current cash price is available, we would discount the future lease payments back to their present value to estimate the investment's current cash price.

Net Present Value (NPV)

Allegra is considering producing MP3 players and digital video recorders (DVRs). The products require different specialized machines, each costing $1 million. Each machine has a five-year life and zero residual value. The two products have different patterns of predicted net cash inflows:

	Annual Net Cash Inflows	
Year	**MP3 Players**	**DVRs**
1	$ 305,450	$ 500,000
2	305,450	350,000
3	305,450	300,000
4	305,450	250,000
5	305,450	40,000
Total	$1,527,250	$1,440,000

The MP3 project generates more net cash inflows, but the DVR project brings in cash sooner. To decide how attractive each investment is, we find its **net present value (NPV)**. The NPV is the *difference* between the present value of the investment's net cash inflows and the investment's cost. We *discount* the net cash inflows to their present value—just as we did in the lottery example—using Allegra's minimum desired rate of return. This rate is called the **discount rate** because it is the interest rate used for the present value calculations. It's also called the **required rate of return** or **hurdle rate** because the investment must meet or exceed this rate to be acceptable. The discount rate depends on the riskiness of investments. The higher the risk, the higher the discount rate. Allegra's discount rate for these investments is 14%.

We compare the present value of the net cash inflows to the investment's initial cost to decide which projects meet or exceed management's minimum desired rate of return. In other words, management is deciding whether the $1 million is worth more (because the company would have to give it up now to invest in the project) or whether the project's future net cash inflows are worth more. Managers can make a valid comparison between the two sums of money only by comparing them at the *same* point in time—namely at their present value.

NPV with Equal Annual Net Cash Inflows (Annuity)

Allegra expects the MP3 project to generate $305,450 of net cash inflows each year for five years. Because these cash flows are equal in amount and occur every year, they are an annuity. Therefore, we use the Present Value of Annuity of $1 table (Appendix 12A, Table B) to find the appropriate Annuity PV factor for $i = 14\%$, $n = 5$.

The present value of the net cash inflows from Allegra's MP3 project is as follows:

$$\begin{aligned}\text{Present value} &= \text{Amount of each cash inflow} \times (\text{Annuity PV factor for } i = 14\%, n = 5)\\ &= \$305{,}450 \times (3.433)\\ &= \$1{,}048{,}610\end{aligned}$$

Next, we subtract the investment's initial cost ($1 million) from the present value of the net cash inflows ($1,048,610). The difference of $48,610 is the net present value (NPV), as shown in Exhibit 12-10 (on the next page).

EXHIBIT 12-10 NPV of Equal Net Cash Inflows—MP3 Project

	Annuity PV Factor (i = 14%, n = 5)	Net Cash Inflow	Present Value
Present value of annuity of equal annual net cash inflows for 5 years at 14%	3.433* ×	$305,450 =	$ 1,048,610
Investment			(1,000,000)
Net present value of the MP3 project			$ 48,610

*Annuity PV factor is found in Appendix 12A, Table B.

A *positive* NPV means that the project earns *more* than the required rate of return. A *negative* NPV means that the project fails to earn the required rate of return. This leads to the following decision rule:

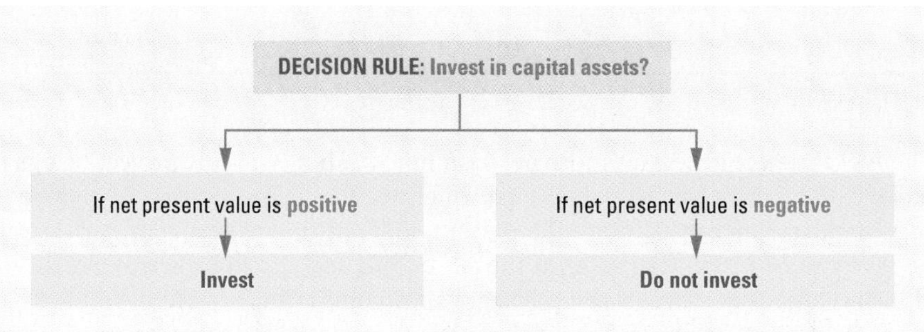

In Allegra's case, the MP3 project is an attractive investment. The $48,610 positive NPV means that the MP3 project earns *more than* Allegra's 14% target rate of return. In other words, management would prefer to give up $1 million today to receive the MP3 project's future net cash inflows. Why? Because those future net cash inflows are worth more than $1 million in today's dollars (they are worth $1,048,610).

Another way managers can use present value analysis is to start the capital budgeting process by computing the total present value of the net cash inflows from the project to determine the *maximum* the company can invest in the project and still earn the target rate of return. For Allegra, the present value of the net cash inflows is $1,048,610. This means that Allegra can invest a maximum of $1,048,610 and still earn the 14% target rate of return. Because Allegra's managers believe they can undertake the project for $1 million, the project is an attractive investment.

NPV with Unequal Annual Net Cash Inflows

In contrast to the MP3 project, the net cash inflows of the DVR project are unequal—$500,000 in Year 1, $350,000 in Year 2, and so forth. Because these amounts vary by year, Allegra's managers *cannot* use the annuity table to compute the present value of the DVR project. They must compute the present value of each individual year's net cash inflows *separately, as separate lump sums received in different years,* using the Present Value of $1 table (Appendix 12A, Table A).

Exhibit 12-11 shows that the $500,000 net cash inflow received in Year 1 is discounted using a PV factor of i = 14%, n = 1, while the $350,000 net cash inflow received in Year 2 is discounted using a PV factor of i = 14%, n = 2, and so forth. After separately discounting each of the five year's net cash inflows, we find that the *total* present value of the DVR project's net cash inflows is $1,078,910. Finally, we subtract the investment's cost ($1 million) to arrive at the DVR project's NPV: $78,910.

Because the NPV is positive, Allegra expects the DVR project to earn more than the 14% target rate of return, making this an attractive investment.

EXHIBIT 12-11 NPV with Unequal Net Cash Inflows—DVR Project

	PV Factor (i = 14%)		Net Cash Inflow		Present Value
Present value of each year's net cash inflows discounted at 14%:					
Year 1 (n = 1)	0.877*	×	$500,000	=	$ 438,500
Year 2 (n = 2)	0.769	×	350,000	=	269,150
Year 3 (n = 3)	0.675	×	300,000	=	202,500
Year 4 (n = 4)	0.592	×	250,000	=	148,000
Year 5 (n = 5)	0.519	×	40,000	=	20,760
Total present value of net cash inflows					1,078,910
Investment					(1,000,000)
Net present value of the DVR project					$ 78,910

*PV factors are found in Appendix 12A, Table A.

Capital Rationing and the Profitability Index

Exhibits 12-10 and 12-11 show that both the MP3 and DVR projects have positive NPVs. Therefore, both are attractive investments. Because resources are limited, companies are not always able to invest in all capital assets that meet their investment criteria. For example, Allegra may not have the funds to invest in both the DVR and MP3 projects at this time. In this case, Allegra should choose the DVR project because it yields a higher NPV. The DVR project should earn an additional $78,910 beyond the 14% required rate of return, while the MP3 project returns an additional $48,610.

> **Why is this important?**
> "The **profitability index** allows managers to **compare** potential investments of **different sizes** so that they can choose the **most profitable** investment."

This example illustrates an important point. The MP3 project promises more *total* net cash inflows. But the *timing* of the DVR cash flows—loaded near the beginning of the project—gives the DVR investment a higher NPV. The DVR project is more attractive because of the time value of money. Its dollars, which are received sooner, are worth more now than the more distant dollars of the MP3 project.

If Allegra had to choose between the MP3 and DVR project, it would choose the DVR project because that project yields a higher NPV ($78,910). However, comparing the NPV of the two projects is valid *only* because both projects require the same initial cost—$1 million.

In contrast, Exhibit 12-12 summarizes three capital investment options that Raycor, a sporting goods manufacturer, faces. Each capital project requires a different initial investment. All three projects are attractive because each yields a positive NPV. Assuming that Raycor can invest in only one project at this time, which one should it choose? Project B yields the highest NPV, but it also requires a larger initial investment than the alternatives.

EXHIBIT 12-12 Raycor's Capital Investment Options

	Project A	Project B	Project C
Present value of net cash inflows	$150,000	$238,000	$182,000
Investment	(125,000)	(200,000)	(150,000)
Net present value (NPV)	$ 25,000	$ 38,000	$ 32,000

To choose among the projects, Raycor computes the **profitability index** (also known as the **present value index**). The profitability index is computed as follows:

Profitability index = Present value of net cash inflows ÷ Investment

The profitability index computes the number of dollars returned for every dollar invested, *with all calculations performed in present value dollars*. It allows us to compare alternative investments in present value terms, like the NPV method, but also considers differences in the investments' initial cost. Let's compute the profitability index for all three alternatives.

	Present value of net cash inflows	÷ Investment	=	Profitability index
Project A:	$150,000	÷ $125,000	=	1.20
Project B:	$238,000	÷ $200,000	=	1.19
Project C:	$182,000	÷ $150,000	=	1.21

The profitability index shows that Project C is the best of the three alternatives because it returns $1.21 in present value dollars for every $1.00 invested. Projects A and B return slightly less.

Let's also compute the profitability index for Allegra's MP3 and DVR projects:

	Present value of net cash inflows	÷ Investment	=	Profitability index
MP3:	$1,048,610	÷ $1,000,000	=	1.049
DVR:	$1,078,910	÷ $1,000,000	=	1.079

The profitability index confirms our prior conclusion that the DVR project is more profitable than the MP3 project. The DVR project returns $1.079 (in present value dollars) for every $1.00 invested. This return is beyond the 14% return already used to discount the cash flows. We did not need the profitability index to determine that the DVR project was preferable because both projects required the same investment ($1 million).

NPV of a Project with Residual Value

Many assets yield cash inflows at the end of their useful lives because they have residual value. Companies discount an investment's residual value to its present value when determining the *total* present value of the project's net cash inflows. The residual value is discounted as a single lump sum—not an annuity—because it will be received only once, when the asset is sold.

Suppose Allegra expects the MP3 project equipment to be worth $100,000 at the end of its five-year life. This represents an additional *lump sum* future cash inflow from the MP3 project. To determine the MP3 project's NPV, we discount the residual value ($100,000) using the Present Value of $1 table ($i$ = 14%, n = 5) (see Appendix 12A, Table A). We then *add* its present value ($51,900) to the present value of the MP3 project's other net cash inflows ($1,048,610) as shown in Exhibit 12-13:

EXHIBIT 12-13 NPV of a Project with Residual Value

	PV Factor (i = 14%, n = 5)		Net Cash Inflow		Present Value
Present value of annuity	3.433	×	$305,450	=	$ 1,048,610
Present value of residual value (single lump sum)	0.519	×	100,000	=	51,900
Total present value of net cash inflows					$ 1,100,510
Investment					$(1,000,000)
Net present value (NPV)					$ 100,510

Because of the expected residual value, the MP3 project is now more attractive than the DVR project. If Allegra could pursue only the MP3 or DVR project, it would now choose the MP3 project because its NPV ($100,510) is higher than the DVR project ($78,910) and both projects require the same investment ($1 million).

Sensitivity Analysis

Capital budgeting decisions affect cash flows far into the future. Allegra's managers might want to know whether their decision would be affected by any of their major assumptions. For example consider the following:

- Changing the discount rate from 14% to 12% or to 16%
- Changing the net cash flows by 10%
- Changing an expected residual value

Managers can use spreadsheet software or programmed calculators to quickly perform sensitivity analysis.

Internal Rate of Return (IRR)

The NPV method only tells management whether the investment exceeds the hurdle rate. Since both the MP3 player and DVR projects yield positive NPVs, we know they provide *more* than a 14% rate of return. But what exact rate of return would these investments provide? The IRR method answers that question.

The **internal rate of return (IRR)** is the rate of return, based on discounted cash flows, that a company can expect to earn by investing in the project. *It is the interest rate that makes the NPV of the investment equal to zero:*

$$\text{NPV} = 0$$

Let's look at this concept in another light by inserting the definition of NPV:

$$\text{Present value of the investment's net cash inflows} - \text{Investment's cost} = 0$$

Or if we rearrange the equation:

$$\text{Investment's cost} = \text{Present value of the investment's net cash inflows}$$

In other words, the IRR is the *interest rate* that makes the cost of the investment equal to the present value of the investment's net cash inflows. The higher the IRR, the more desirable the project. Like the profitability index, the IRR can be used in the capital rationing process.

IRR computations are very easy to perform on programmed calculators and Microsoft Excel (see Appendix 12B and 12C). However, IRR computations are much more cumbersome to perform using the tables.

IRR with Equal Annual Net Cash Inflows (Annuity)

When the investment is an annuity, we can develop a formula that will tell us the Annuity PV factor associated with the investment's IRR. We start with the equation given previously and then substitute in as follows:

Investment's cost = Present value of the investment's net cash inflows

Investment's cost = Amount of each equal net cash inflow × Annuity PV factor (i = ?, n = given)

Finally, we rearrange the equation to obtain the following formula:

$$\frac{\text{Investment's cost}}{\text{Amount of each equal net cash inflow}} = \text{Annuity PV factor } (i = ?, n = \text{given})$$

Let's use this formula to find the Annuity PV factor associated with Allegra's MP3 project. Recall that the project would cost $1 million and result in five equal yearly cash inflows of $305,450:

$$\frac{\$1{,}000{,}000}{\$305{,}450} = \text{Annuity PV factor } (i = ?, n = 5)$$

$$3.274 = \text{Annuity PV factor } (i = ?, n = 5)$$

Next, we find the interest rate that corresponds to this Annuity PV factor. Turn to the Present Value of Annuity of $1 table (Appendix 12A, Table B). Scan the row corresponding to the project's expected life—five years, in our example. Choose the column(s) with the number closest to the Annuity PV factor you calculated using the formula. The 3.274 annuity factor is in the 16% column.

Therefore, the IRR of the MP3 project is 16%.

Allegra expects the project to earn an internal rate of return of 16% over its life. Exhibit 12-14 confirms this result: Using a 16% discount rate, the project's NPV is zero. In other words, 16% is the discount rate that makes the investment cost equal to the present value of the investment's net cash inflows.

EXHIBIT 12-14 IRR–MP3 Project

	Annuity PV Factor (i = 16%, n = 5)		Net Cash Inflow		Total Present Value
Present value of annuity of equal annual net cash inflows for 5 years at 16%	3.274	×	$305,450	=	$ 1,000,000†
Investment					(1,000,000)
Net present value of the MP3 project					$ 0‡

†Slight rounding error.
‡The zero difference proves that the IRR is 16%.

To decide whether the project is acceptable, compare the IRR with the minimum desired rate of return. The decision rule is as follows:

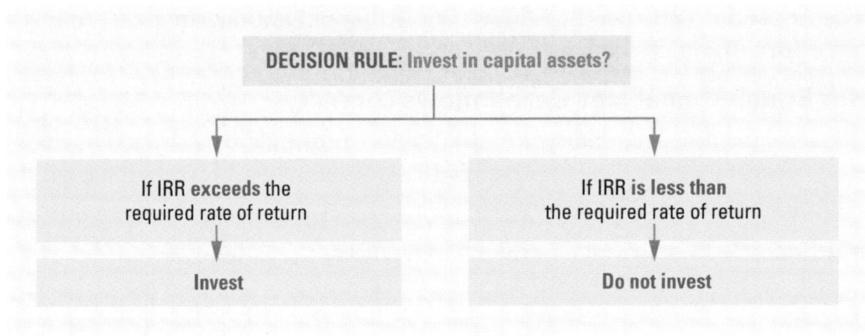

Recall that Allegra's hurdle rate is 14%. Because the MP3 project's IRR (16%) is higher than the hurdle rate (14%), Allegra would invest in the project.

In the MP3 project, the exact Annuity PV factor (3.274) appears in the Present Value of an Annuity of $1 table (Appendix 12A, Table B). Many times, the exact factor will not appear in the table. For example, let's find the IRR of Tierra Firma's B2B Portal. Recall that the B2B portal had a six-year life with annual net cash inflows of $60,000. The investment cost $240,000. We find its Annuity PV factor using the formula given previously:

$$\frac{\text{Investment's cost}}{\text{Amount of each equal net cash inflow}} = \text{Annuity PV factor } (i = ?, n = \text{given})$$

$$\frac{\$240{,}000}{\$60{,}000} = \text{Annuity PV factor } (i = ?, n = 6)$$

$$4.00 = \text{Annuity PV factor } (i = ?, n = 6)$$

Now, look in the Present Value of Annuity of $1 table in the row marked 6 periods (Appendix 12A, Table B). You will not see 4.00 under any column. The closest two factors are 3.889 (at 14%) and 4.111 (at 12%).

Thus, the B2B portal's IRR is somewhere between 12% and 14%.

If we used a calculator programmed with the IRR function, we would find the exact IRR is 12.98%. If Tierra Firma had a 14% hurdle rate, it would *not* invest in the B2B portal because the portal's IRR is less than 14%.

IRR with Unequal Annual Net Cash Inflows

Because the DVR project has unequal cash inflows, Allegra cannot use the Present Value of Annuity of $1 table to find the asset's IRR. Rather, Allegra must use a trial-and-error procedure to determine the discount rate that makes the project's NPV equal to zero. Recall from Exhibit 12-11 that the DVR's NPV using a 14% discount rate is $78,910. Since the NPV is *positive*, the IRR must be *higher* than 14%. Allegra performs the trial-and-error process using *higher* discount rates until it finds the rate that brings the net present value of the DVR project to *zero*. Exhibit 12-15 shows that at 16%, the DVR has an NPV of $40,390; therefore, the IRR must be higher than 16%. At 18%, the NPV is $3,980, which is very close to zero. Thus, the IRR must be slightly higher than 18%. If we use a calculator programmed with the IRR function rather than the trial-and-error procedure, we would find that the IRR is 18.23%.

EXHIBIT 12-15 Finding the DVR's IRR Through Trial and Error

	Net Cash Inflow		PV Factor (for i = 16%)		Present Value at 16%	Net Cash Inflow		PV Factor (for i = 18%)		Present Value at 18%
Year 1 (n = 1)	$500,000	×	0.862*	=	$ 431,000	$500,000	×	0.847*	=	$ 423,500
Year 2 (n = 2)	350,000	×	0.743	=	260,050	350,000	×	0.718	=	251,300
Year 3 (n = 3)	300,000	×	0.641	=	192,300	300,000	×	0.609	=	182,700
Year 4 (n = 4)	250,000	×	0.552	=	138,000	250,000	×	0.516	=	129,000
Year 5 (n = 5)	40,000	×	0.476	=	19,040	40,000	×	0.437	=	17,480
Total present value of net cash inflows					$ 1,040,390					$ 1,003,980
Investment					(1,000,000)					(1,000,000)
Net present value (NPV)					$ 40,390					$ 3,980

*PV factors are found in Appendix 12A, Table A.

The DVR's internal rate of return is higher than Allegra's 14% hurdle rate, so the DVR project is attractive.

How do the Capital Budgeting Methods Compare?

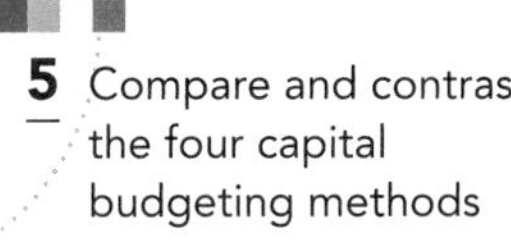

5 Compare and contrast the four capital budgeting methods

If your instructor is using MyAccountingLab, go to the Multimedia Library for a quick video on this topic.

We have discussed four capital budgeting methods commonly used by companies to make capital investment decisions—two that ignore the time value of money (payback period and ARR) and two that incorporate the time value of money (NPV and IRR). Exhibit 12-16 summarizes the similarities and differences between the two methods that ignore the time value of money.

EXHIBIT 12-16 Capital Budgeting Methods That *Ignore* the Time Value of Money

Payback Period	ARR
• Simple to compute • Focuses on the time it takes to recover the company's cash investment • Ignores any cash flows occurring after the payback period, including any residual value • Highlights risks of investments with longer cash recovery periods • Ignores the time value of money	• The only method that uses accrual accounting figures • Shows how the investment will affect operating income, which is important to financial statement users • Measures the average profitability of the asset over its entire life • Ignores the time value of money

Exhibit 12-17 considers the similarities and differences between the two methods that incorporate the time value of money.

EXHIBIT 12-17 Capital Budgeting Methods That *Incorporate* the Time Value of Money

NPV	IRR
• Incorporates the time value of money and the asset's net cash flows over its entire life • Indicates whether the asset will earn the company's minimum required rate of return • Shows the excess or deficiency of the asset's present value of net cash inflows over its initial investment cost • The profitability index should be computed for capital rationing decisions when the assets require different initial investments	• Incorporates the time value of money and the asset's net cash flows over its entire life • Computes the project's unique rate of return • No additional steps needed for capital rationing decisions

Keep in mind that managers often use more than one method to gain different perspectives on the risks and returns of potential capital investments.

STOP & THINK

A pharmaceutical company is considering two research projects that require the same initial investment. Project A has an NPV of $232,000 and a 3-year payback period. Project B has an NPV of $237,000 and a payback period of 4.5 years. Which project would you choose?

Answer: Many managers would choose Project A even though it has a slightly lower NPV. Why? The NPV is only $5,000 lower, yet the payback period is significantly shorter. The uncertainty of receiving operating cash flows increases with each passing year. Managers often forgo small differences in expected cash inflows to decrease the risk of investments.

Decision Guidelines

Capital Budgeting

Here are more of the guidelines Amazon.com's managers used as they made the major capital budgeting decision to invest in building warehouses.

Decision	Guidelines
Which capital budgeting methods are best?	No one method is best. Each method provides a different perspective on the investment decision.
Why do the NPV and IRR models calculate the present value of an investment's net cash flows?	Because an investment's cash inflows occur in the future, yet the cash outlay for the investment occurs now, all of the cash flows must be converted to a common point in time. These methods use the *present* value as the common point in time.
How do we know if investing in warehouse facilities will be worthwhile?	Investment in warehouse facilities may be worthwhile if the NPV is positive or the IRR exceeds the required rate of return.
How do we compute the net present value (NPV) if the investment has equal annual cash inflows?	Compute the present value of the investment's net cash inflows using the Present Value of an Annuity of $1 table and then subtract the investment's cost.
How do we compute the net present value (NPV) if the investment has unequal annual cash inflows?	Compute the present value of each year's net cash inflows using the Present Value of $1 (lump sum) table, sum the present value of the inflows, and then subtract the investment's cost.
How do we compute the internal rate of return (IRR) if the investment has equal annual cash inflows?	Find the interest rate that yields the following Annuity PV factor: $\text{Annuity PV factor} = \dfrac{\text{Investment's cost}}{\text{Amount of each equal net cash inflow}}$
How do we compute the internal rate of return (IRR) if the investment has unequal annual cash inflows?	Use trial and error, a business calculator, or spreadsheet software to find the IRR. See Appendix 12B and 12C for instructions.

SUMMARY PROBLEM 2

Recall from Summary Problem 1 that Zetamax is considering buying a new bar-coding machine. The investment proposal passed the initial screening tests (payback period and accounting rate of return), so the company now wants to analyze the proposal using the discounted cash flow methods. Recall that the bar-coding machine costs $48,000, has a five-year life, and has no residual value. The estimated net cash inflows are $13,000 per year over its life. The company's hurdle rate is 16%.

Requirements

1. Compute the bar-coding machine's NPV.
2. Find the bar-coding machine's IRR (exact percentage not required).
3. Should Zetamax buy the bar-coding machine? Why or why not?

SOLUTIONS

Requirement 1

Present value of annuity of equal annual net cash inflows at 16% ($13,000 × 3.274*)	$ 42,562
Investment	(48,000)
Net present value	$ (5,438)

*Annuity PV factor (i = 16%, n = 5).

Requirement 2

$$\frac{\text{Investment's cost}}{\text{Amount of each equal net cash inflow}} = \text{Annuity PV factor } (i = ?, n = \text{given})$$

$$\frac{\$48{,}000}{\$13{,}000} = \text{Annuity PV factor } (i = ?, n = 5)$$

$$3.692 = \text{Annuity PV factor } (i = ?, n = 5)$$

Because the cash inflows occur for five years, we look for the PV factor 3.692 in the row marked n = 5 on the Present Value of Annuity of $1 table (Appendix 12A, Table B). The PV factor is 3.605 at 12% and 3.791 at 10%. Therefore, the bar-coding machine has an IRR that falls between 10% and 12%. (*Optional:* Using a programmed calculator, we find an 11.038% internal rate of return.)

Requirement 3

Decision: Do not buy the bar-coding machine. It has a negative NPV and its IRR falls below the company's required rate of return. Both methods show that this investment does not meet management's minimum requirements for investments of this nature.

Appendix 12A

Present Value Tables and Future Value Tables

Table A Present Value of $1

Present Value of $1													
Periods	1%	2%	3%	4%	5%	6%	8%	10%	12%	14%	16%	18%	20%
1	0.990	0.980	0.971	0.962	0.952	0.943	0.926	0.909	0.893	0.877	0.862	0.847	0.833
2	0.980	0.961	0.943	0.925	0.907	0.890	0.857	0.826	0.797	0.769	0.743	0.718	0.694
3	0.971	0.942	0.915	0.889	0.864	0.840	0.794	0.751	0.712	0.675	0.641	0.609	0.579
4	0.961	0.924	0.888	0.855	0.823	0.792	0.735	0.683	0.636	0.592	0.552	0.516	0.482
5	0.951	0.906	0.863	0.822	0.784	0.747	0.681	0.621	0.567	0.519	0.476	0.437	0.402
6	0.942	0.888	0.837	0.790	0.746	0.705	0.630	0.564	0.507	0.456	0.410	0.370	0.335
7	0.933	0.871	0.813	0.760	0.711	0.665	0.583	0.513	0.452	0.400	0.354	0.314	0.279
8	0.923	0.853	0.789	0.731	0.677	0.627	0.540	0.467	0.404	0.351	0.305	0.266	0.233
9	0.914	0.837	0.766	0.703	0.645	0.592	0.500	0.424	0.361	0.308	0.263	0.225	0.194
10	0.905	0.820	0.744	0.676	0.614	0.558	0.463	0.386	0.322	0.270	0.227	0.191	0.162
11	0.896	0.804	0.722	0.650	0.585	0.527	0.429	0.350	0.287	0.237	0.195	0.162	0.135
12	0.887	0.788	0.701	0.625	0.557	0.497	0.397	0.319	0.257	0.208	0.168	0.137	0.112
13	0.879	0.773	0.681	0.601	0.530	0.469	0.368	0.290	0.229	0.182	0.145	0.116	0.093
14	0.870	0.758	0.661	0.577	0.505	0.442	0.340	0.263	0.205	0.160	0.125	0.099	0.078
15	0.861	0.743	0.642	0.555	0.481	0.417	0.315	0.239	0.183	0.140	0.108	0.084	0.065
20	0.820	0.673	0.554	0.456	0.377	0.312	0.215	0.149	0.104	0.073	0.051	0.037	0.026
25	0.780	0.610	0.478	0.375	0.295	0.233	0.146	0.092	0.059	0.038	0.024	0.016	0.010
30	0.742	0.552	0.412	0.308	0.231	0.174	0.099	0.057	0.033	0.020	0.012	0.007	0.004
40	0.672	0.453	0.307	0.208	0.142	0.097	0.046	0.022	0.011	0.005	0.003	0.001	0.001

The factors in the table were generated using the following formula:

$$\text{Present Value of \$1} = \frac{1}{(1 + i)^n}$$

where:

i = annual interest rate

n = number of periods

Table B Present Value of Annuity of $1

Present Value of Annuity of $1													
Periods	1%	2%	3%	4%	5%	6%	8%	10%	12%	14%	16%	18%	20%
1	0.990	0.980	0.971	0.962	0.952	0.943	0.926	0.909	0.893	0.877	0.862	0.847	0.833
2	1.970	1.942	1.913	1.886	1.859	1.833	1.783	1.736	1.690	1.647	1.605	1.566	1.528
3	2.941	2.884	2.829	2.775	2.723	2.673	2.577	2.487	2.402	2.322	2.246	2.174	2.106
4	3.902	3.808	3.717	3.630	3.546	3.465	3.312	3.170	3.037	2.914	2.798	2.690	2.589
5	4.853	4.713	4.580	4.452	4.329	4.212	3.993	3.791	3.605	3.433	3.274	3.127	2.991
6	5.795	5.601	5.417	5.242	5.076	4.917	4.623	4.355	4.111	3.889	3.685	3.498	3.326
7	6.728	6.472	6.230	6.002	5.786	5.582	5.206	4.868	4.564	4.288	4.039	3.812	3.605
8	7.652	7.325	7.020	6.733	6.463	6.210	5.747	5.335	4.968	4.639	4.344	4.078	3.837
9	8.566	8.162	7.786	7.435	7.108	6.802	6.247	5.759	5.328	4.946	4.607	4.303	4.031
10	9.471	8.983	8.530	8.111	7.722	7.360	6.710	6.145	5.650	5.216	4.833	4.494	4.192
11	10.368	9.787	9.253	8.760	8.306	7.887	7.139	6.495	5.938	5.553	5.029	4.656	4.327
12	11.255	10.575	9.954	9.385	8.863	8.384	7.536	6.814	6.194	5.660	5.197	4.793	4.439
13	12.134	11.348	10.635	9.986	9.394	8.853	7.904	7.103	6.424	5.842	5.342	4.910	4.533
14	13.004	12.106	11.296	10.563	9.899	9.295	8.244	7.367	6.628	6.002	5.468	5.008	4.611
15	13.865	12.849	11.938	11.118	10.380	9.712	8.559	7.606	6.811	6.142	5.575	5.092	4.675
20	18.046	16.351	14.878	13.590	12.462	11.470	9.818	8.514	7.469	6.623	5.929	5.353	4.870
25	22.023	19.523	17.413	15.622	14.094	12.783	10.675	9.077	7.843	6.873	6.097	5.467	4.948
30	25.808	22.396	19.600	17.292	15.373	13.765	11.258	9.427	8.055	7.003	6.177	5.517	4.979
40	32.835	27.355	23.115	19.793	17.159	15.046	11.925	9.779	8.244	7.105	6.234	5.548	4.997

The factors in the table were generated using the following formula:

$$\text{Present value of annuity of \$1} = \frac{1}{i}\left[1 - \frac{1}{(1+i)^n}\right]$$

where:

i = annual interest rate

n = number of periods

Table C Future Value of $1

Future Value of $1													
Periods	1%	2%	3%	4%	5%	6%	8%	10%	12%	14%	16%	18%	20%
1	1.010	1.020	1.030	1.040	1.050	1.060	1.080	1.100	1.120	1.140	1.160	1.180	1.200
2	1.020	1.040	1.061	1.082	1.103	1.124	1.166	1.210	1.254	1.300	1.346	1.392	1.440
3	1.030	1.061	1.093	1.125	1.158	1.191	1.260	1.331	1.405	1.482	1.561	1.643	1.728
4	1.041	1.082	1.126	1.170	1.216	1.262	1.360	1.464	1.574	1.689	1.811	1.939	2.074
5	1.051	1.104	1.159	1.217	1.276	1.338	1.469	1.611	1.762	1.925	2.100	2.288	2.488
6	1.062	1.126	1.194	1.265	1.340	1.419	1.587	1.772	1.974	2.195	2.436	2.700	2.986
7	1.072	1.149	1.230	1.316	1.407	1.504	1.714	1.949	2.211	2.502	2.826	3.185	3.583
8	1.083	1.172	1.267	1.369	1.477	1.594	1.851	2.144	2.476	2.853	3.278	3.759	4.300
9	1.094	1.195	1.305	1.423	1.551	1.689	1.999	2.358	2.773	3.252	3.803	4.435	5.160
10	1.105	1.219	1.344	1.480	1.629	1.791	2.159	2.594	3.106	3.707	4.411	5.234	6.192
11	1.116	1.243	1.384	1.539	1.710	1.898	2.332	2.853	3.479	4.226	5.117	6.176	7.430
12	1.127	1.268	1.426	1.601	1.796	2.012	2.518	3.138	3.896	4.818	5.936	7.288	8.916
13	1.138	1.294	1.469	1.665	1.886	2.133	2.720	3.452	4.363	5.492	6.886	8.599	10.669
14	1.149	1.319	1.513	1.732	1.980	2.261	2.937	3.798	4.887	6.261	7.988	10.147	12.839
15	1.161	1.346	1.558	1.801	2.079	2.397	3.172	4.177	5.474	7.138	9.266	11.974	15.407
20	1.220	1.486	1.806	2.191	2.653	3.207	4.661	6.728	9.646	13.743	19.461	27.393	38.338
25	1.282	1.641	2.094	2.666	3.386	4.292	6.848	10.835	17.000	26.462	40.874	62.669	95.396
30	1.348	1.811	2.427	3.243	4.322	5.743	10.063	17.449	29.960	50.950	85.850	143.371	237.376
40	1.489	2.208	3.262	4.801	7.040	10.286	21.725	45.259	93.051	188.884	378.721	750.378	1,469.772

The factors in the table were generated using the following formula:

$$\text{Future Value of } \$1 = (1 + i)^n$$

where:

i = annual interest rate
n = number of periods

Table D Future Value of Annuity of $1

Future Value of Annuity of $1

Periods	1%	2%	3%	4%	5%	6%	8%	10%	12%	14%	16%	18%	20%
1	1.000	1.000	1.000	1.000	1.000	1.000	1.000	1.000	1.000	1.000	1.000	1.000	1.000
2	2.010	2.020	2.030	2.040	2.050	2.060	2.080	2.100	2.120	2.140	2.160	2.180	2.200
3	3.030	3.060	3.091	3.122	3.153	3.184	3.246	3.310	3.374	3.440	3.506	3.572	3.640
4	4.060	4.122	4.184	4.246	4.310	4.375	4.506	4.641	4.779	4.921	5.066	5.215	5.368
5	5.101	5.204	5.309	5.416	5.526	5.637	5.867	6.105	6.353	6.610	6.877	7.154	7.442
6	6.152	6.308	6.468	6.633	6.802	6.975	7.336	7.716	8.115	8.536	8.977	9.442	9.930
7	7.214	7.434	7.662	7.898	8.142	8.394	8.923	9.487	10.089	10.730	11.414	12.142	12.916
8	8.286	8.583	8.892	9.214	9.549	9.897	10.637	11.436	12.300	13.233	14.240	15.327	16.499
9	9.369	9.755	10.159	10.583	11.027	11.491	12.488	13.579	14.776	16.085	17.519	19.086	20.799
10	10.462	10.950	11.464	12.006	12.578	13.181	14.487	15.937	17.549	19.337	21.321	23.521	25.959
11	11.567	12.169	12.808	13.486	14.207	14.972	16.645	18.531	20.655	23.045	25.733	28.755	32.150
12	12.683	13.412	14.192	15.026	15.917	16.870	18.977	21.384	24.133	27.271	30.850	34.931	39.581
13	13.809	14.680	15.618	16.627	17.713	18.882	21.495	24.523	28.029	32.089	36.786	42.219	48.497
14	14.947	15.974	17.086	18.292	19.599	21.015	24.215	27.975	32.393	37.581	43.672	50.818	59.196
15	16.097	17.293	18.599	20.024	21.579	23.276	27.152	31.772	37.280	43.842	51.660	60.965	72.035
20	22.019	24.297	26.870	29.778	33.066	36.786	45.762	57.275	72.052	91.025	115.380	146.630	186.690
25	28.243	32.030	36.459	41.646	47.727	54.865	73.106	98.347	133.330	181.870	249.210	342.600	471.980
30	34.785	40.568	47.575	56.085	66.439	79.058	113.280	164.490	241.330	356.790	530.310	790.950	1,181.900
40	48.886	60.402	75.401	95.026	120.800	154.760	259.060	442.590	767.090	1,342.000	2,360.800	4,163.200	7,343.900

The factors in the table were generated using the following formula:

$$\text{Future Value of Annuity of \$1} = \frac{(1 + i)^n - 1}{i}$$

where:

i = annual interest rate

n = number of periods

Appendix 12B

Using a TI-83, TI-83 Plus, TI-84, or TI-84 Plus Calculator to Perform Time Value of Money Calculations

Technology makes it simple

Time Value of Money Calculations

Using a TI-83, TI-83 Plus, TI-84, or TI-84 Plus Calculator to Perform Time Value of Money Calculations

Steps to perform basic present value and future value calculations:

1. On the TI-83 Plus or TI-84 Plus: Press [APPS] *to show the applications menu.*

   On the TI-83 or TI-84: Press [2nd] [X^{-1}] [ENTER] *to show the applications menu.*
2. Choose **Finance** *to see the finance applications menu.*
3. Choose **TVM solver** *to obtain the list of time value of money (TVM) variables:*

   N = *number of periods (years)*

   I% = *interest rate per year* (**do not convert percentage to a decimal**)

   PV = *present value*

   PMT = *amount of each annuity installment*

   FV = *future value*

   P/Y = *number of compounding periods per year* **(leave setting at 1)**

   C/Y = *number of coupons per year* **(leave setting at 1)**

   PMT: **End** or Begin *(leave setting on* **End** *to denote an ordinary annuity)*
4. **Enter the known variables** and **set all unknown variables to zero** (except P/Y and C/Y, which need to be left set at 1).
5. To compute the unknown variable, scroll to the line for the variable you want to solve and then press [ALPHA] [ENTER].
6. The answer will now appear on the calculator.
7. Press [2nd] [QUIT] *to exit the TVM solver when you are finished.* **If you would like to do more TVM calculations, you do not need to exit. Simply repeat Steps 4 and 5 using the new data.**

Comments:

i. The order in which you input the variables does not matter.

ii. The answer will be shown as a negative number unless you input the original cash flow data as a negative number. **Use the [(-)] key to enter a negative number, not the minus key; otherwise you will get an error message.** The calculator follows a cash flow sign convention that assumes that all positive figures are cash inflows and all negative figures are cash outflows.

iii. The answers you get will vary slightly from those found using the PV and FV tables in Appendix A. Why? Because the PV and FV factors in the tables have been rounded to three digits.

Example 1: Future Value of a Lump Sum

Let's use our lump-sum investment example from the text. Assume that you invest $10,000 for five years at an interest rate of 6%. Use the following procedure to find its future value five years from now:

1. On the TI-83 Plus or TI-84 Plus: Press [APPS] *to show the applications menu.*

   On the TI-83 or TI-84: Press [2nd] [X^{-1}] [ENTER] *to show the applications menu.*

2. Choose **Finance** *to see the finance applications menu.*
3. Choose **TVM solver** *to obtain the list of time value of money (TVM) variables.*
4. Fill in the variables as follows:

   N = **5**

   I% = **6**

   PV = **–10000** *(Be sure to use the negative number (-) key, not the minus sign.)*

   PMT = **0**

   FV = **0**

   P/Y = 1

   C/Y = 1

   PMT: **End** or Begin
5. To compute the unknown future value, scroll down to **FV** and press [ALPHA] [ENTER].
6. The answer will now appear as **FV** = **13,382.26** (rounded).

If you forgot to enter the $10,000 principal as a negative number (in Step 4), the FV will be displayed as a negative.

Example 2: Future Value of an Annuity

Let's use the annuity investment example from the text. Assume that you invest $2,000 at the end of each year for five years. The investment earns 6% interest. Use the following procedure to find the investment's future value five years from now:

1. On the TI-83 Plus or TI-84 Plus: Press [APPS] *to show the applications menu.*

   On the TI-83 or TI-84: Press [2nd] [X^{-1}] [ENTER] *to show the applications menu.*
2. Choose **Finance** *to see the finance applications menu.*
3. Choose **TVM solver** *to obtain the list of time value of money (TVM) variables.*
4. Fill in the variables as follows:

   N = **5**

   I%= **6**

   PV = **0**

   PMT = **–2000** *(Be sure to use the negative number (-) key, not the minus sign.)*

   FV = **0**

   P/Y = 1

   C/Y = 1

   PMT: **End** or Begin
5. To compute the unknown future value, scroll down to **FV** and press [ALPHA] [ENTER].
6. The answer will now appear as **FV** = **11,274.19 (rounded)**.

If you forgot to enter the $2,000 annuity as a negative number (in Step 4), the FV will be displayed as a negative.

Example 3: Present Value of an Annuity—Lottery Option #2

Let's use the lottery payout Option #2 from the text for our example. Option #2 was to receive $150,000 at the end of each year for the next ten years. The interest rate was assumed to be 8%. Use the following procedure to find the present value of this payout option:

1. On the TI-83 Plus or TI-84 Plus: Press [APPS] *to show the applications menu.*

   On the TI-83 or TI-84: Press [2nd] [X^{-1}] [ENTER] *to show the applications menu.*
2. Choose **Finance** *to see the finance applications menu.*
3. Choose **TVM solver** *to obtain the list of time value of money (TVM) variables.*
4. Fill in the variables as follows:

N = **10**

I%= **8**

PV = **0**

PMT = **–150000** *(Be sure to use the negative number (-) key, not the minus sign.)*

FV = **0**

P/Y = 1

C/Y = 1

PMT: **End** or Begin

5. To compute the unknown future value, scroll down to **PV** and press [ALPHA] [ENTER].
6. The answer will now appear as **PV = 1,006,512.21** (rounded).

Had we not entered the annuity as a negative figure, the present value would have been shown as a negative.

Example 4: Present Value of a Lump Sum—Lottery Option #3

Let's use the lottery payout Option #3 from the text as our example. Option #3 was to receive $2 million ten years from now. The interest rate was assumed to be 8%. Use the following procedure to find the present value of this payout option:

1. On the TI-83 Plus or TI-84 Plus: Press [APPS] *to show the applications menu.*

   On the TI-83 or TI-84: Press [2nd] [X^{-1}] [ENTER] *to show the applications menu.*
2. Choose **Finance** *to see the finance applications menu.*
3. Choose **TVM solver** *to obtain the list of time value of money (TVM) variables.*
4. Fill in the variables as follows:

   N = **10**

   I%= **8**

   PV = **0**

   PMT = **0**

   FV = **–2000000** *(Be sure to use the negative number (-) key, not the minus sign.)*

   P/Y = 1

   C/Y = 1
5. PMT: **End** or Begin
6. To compute the unknown future value, scroll down to **PV** and press [ALPHA] [ENTER].
7. The answer will now appear as **PV = 926,386.98** (rounded).

Had we not entered the $2 million future cash flow as a negative, the present value would have been shown as a negative.

Technology makes it simple

NPV Calculations

Using a TI-83, TI-83 Plus, TI-84, or TI-84 Plus calculator to perform NPV calculations

Steps to performing NPV calculations:

If you are currently in the TVM solver mode, exit by pressing [2nd] [Quit].

1. On the TI-83 Plus or TI-84 Plus: Press [APPS] *to show the applications menu.*

   On the TI-83 or TI-84: Press [2nd] [X^{-1}] [ENTER] *to show the applications menu.*
2. Choose **Finance** *to see the finance applications menu.*
3. Choose **npv** *to obtain the NPV prompt:* **npv(**.

4. Fill in the following information, paying close attention to using the correct symbols: **npv (hurdle rate, initial investment*, {cash flow in Year 1, cash flow in Year 2, etc.})**
5. To compute the NPV, press [ENTER].
6. The answer will now appear on the calculator.
7. To exit the worksheet, press [CLEAR]. Alternatively, if you would like to change any of the assumptions for sensitivity analysis, you may press [2nd] [ENTER] to recall the formula, edit any of the values, and then recompute the new NPV by pressing [ENTER].

Note: If you would like to find just the present value (not the NPV) of a stream of unequal cash flows, use a zero (0) for the initial investment.

Example 1: NPV of Allegra's MP3 Project—An Annuity

Recall that the MP3 project required an investment of $1 million and was expected to generate equal net cash inflows of $305,450 each year for five years. The company's discount, or hurdle rate, was 14%.

1. On the TI-83 Plus or TI-84 Plus: Press [APPS] *to show the applications menu.*
   On the TI-83 or TI-84: Press [2nd] [X^{-1}] [ENTER] *to show the applications menu.*
2. Choose **Finance** *to see the finance applications menu.*
3. Choose **npv** *to obtain the NPV prompt:* **npv(**.
4. Fill in the following information, paying close attention to using the correct symbols:
   npv (14, –1000000, {305450, 305450, 305450, 305450, 305450}) *(Be sure to use the negative number (-) key, not the minus sign.)*
5. To compute the NPV, press [ENTER].
6. The answer will now appear on the calculator: **48,634.58** (rounded).
7. [CLEAR] the worksheet or recall it [2nd] [ENTER] for sensitivity analysis.

Example 2: NPV of Allegra's DVR Project—Unequal Cash Flows

Recall that the DVR project required an investment of $1 million and was expected to generate the unequal periodic cash inflows shown in Exhibit 12-11.

1. On the TI-83 Plus or TI-84 Plus: Press [APPS] *to show the applications menu.*
   On the TI-83 or TI-84: Press [2nd] [X^{-1}] [ENTER] *to show the applications menu.*
2. Choose **Finance** *to see the finance applications menu.*
3. Choose **npv** *to obtain the NPV prompt:* **npv(**.
4. Fill in the following information, paying close attention to using the correct symbols:
   npv (14, –1000000, {500000, 350000, 300000, 250000, 40000}) *(Be sure to use the negative number (-) key, not the minus sign.)*
5. To compute the NPV, press [ENTER].
6. The answer will now appear on the calculator: **79,196.40** (rounded).
7. [CLEAR] the worksheet or recall it [2nd] [ENTER] for sensitivity analysis.

Example 3: Investment with a Residual Value

If an investment has a residual value, simply add the residual value as an additional cash inflow in the year in which it is to be received. For example, assume as we did in Exhibit 12-13 that the MP3 project equipment will be worth $100,000 at the end of its five-year life. This represents an additional expected cash inflow to the company in Year 5, so we'll show the cash inflow in Year 5 to be $405,450 (= $305,450 + $100,000).

1. On the TI-83 Plus or TI-84 Plus: Press [APPS] *to show the applications menu.*
   On the TI-83 or TI-84: Press [2nd] [X^{-1}] [ENTER] *to show the applications menu.*
2. Choose **Finance** *to see the finance applications menu.*
3. Choose **npv** *to obtain the NPV prompt:* **npv(**.

**The initial investment must be entered as a negative number.*

4. Fill in the following information, paying close attention to using the correct symbols:

   npv (14, –1000000, {305450, 305450, 305450, 305450, 405450}) *(Be sure to use the negative number (-) key, not the minus sign.)*
5. To compute the NPV, press [ENTER].
6. The answer will now appear on the calculator: **100,571.45** (rounded).
7. [CLEAR] the worksheet or recall it [2nd] [ENTER] for sensitivity analysis.

Technology makes it simple

IRR Calculations

Using a TI-83, TI-83 Plus, TI-84, or TI-84 Plus calculator to perform IRR calculations

The procedure for finding the IRR is virtually identical to the procedure used to find the NPV. The only differences are that we choose IRR rather than NPV from the Finance menu and we don't insert a given hurdle rate.

Steps to performing IRR calculations:

If you are currently in the TVM solver mode, exit by pressing [2nd] [Quit].

1. On the TI-83 Plus or TI-84 Plus: Press [APPS] *to show the applications menu.*

   On the TI-83 or TI-84: Press [2nd] [X^{-1}] [ENTER] *to show the applications menu.*
2. Choose **Finance** *to see the finance applications menu.*
3. Choose **irr** *to obtain the IRR prompt:* **irr(**.
4. Fill in the following information, paying close attention to using the correct symbols: **irr (initial investment*, {cash flow in Year 1, cash flow in Year 2, etc.})**
5. To compute the IRR press [ENTER].
6. The answer will now appear on the calculator.
7. To exit the worksheet, press [CLEAR]. Alternatively, if you would like to change any of the assumptions for sensitivity analysis, you may press [2nd] [ENTER] to recall the formula, edit any of the values, and then recompute the new IRR by pressing [ENTER].

Example 1: IRR of Allegra's MP3 Project—An Annuity

Recall that the MP3 project required an investment of $1 million and was expected to generate equal net cash inflows of $305,450 each year for five years. Use the following procedure to find the investment's IRR:

1. On the TI-83 Plus or TI-84 Plus: Press [APPS] *to show the applications menu.*

   On the TI-83 or TI-84: Press [2nd] [X^{-1}] [ENTER] *to show the applications menu.*
2. Choose **Finance** *to see the finance applications menu.*
3. Choose **irr** *to obtain the IRR prompt:* **irr(**.
4. Fill in the following information, paying close attention to using the correct symbols:

   irr (–1000000, {305450, 305450, 305450, 305450, 305450}) *(Be sure to use the negative number (-) key, not the minus sign.)*
5. To compute the IRR, press [ENTER].
6. The answer will now appear on the calculator: **16.01** (rounded).
7. [CLEAR] the worksheet or recall it [2nd] [ENTER] for sensitivity analysis.

**The initial investment must be entered as a negative number.*

Example 2: IRR of Allegra's DVR Project—Unequal Cash Flows

Recall that the DVR project required an investment of $1 million and was expected to generate the unequal periodic cash inflows shown in Exhibit 12-11. Use the following procedures to find the investment's IRR:

1. On the TI-83 Plus or TI-84 Plus: Press [APPS] *to show the applications menu.*

   On the TI-83 or TI-84: Press [2nd] [X^{-1}] [ENTER] *to show the applications menu.*
2. Choose **Finance** *to see the finance applications menu.*
3. Choose **irr** *to obtain the IRR prompt:* **irr(**.
4. Fill in the following information, paying close attention to using the correct symbols:

   irr (–1000000, {500000, 350000, 300000, 250000, 40000}) *(Be sure to use the negative number (-) key, not the minus sign.)*
5. To compute the IRR, press [ENTER].
6. The answer will now appear on the calculator: **18.23** (rounded).
7. [CLEAR] the worksheet or recall it [2nd] [ENTER] for sensitivity analysis.

Example 3: Investment with a Residual Value

If an investment has a residual value, simply add the residual value as an additional cash inflow in the year in which it is to be received. For example, assume as we did in Exhibit 12-13 that the MP3 project equipment will be worth $100,000 at the end of its five-year life. This represents an additional expected cash inflow to the company in Year 5, so we'll show the cash inflow in Year 5 to be $405,450 (= $305,450 + $100,000).

1. On the TI-83 Plus or TI-84 Plus: Press [APPS] *to show the applications menu.*

   On the TI-83 or TI-84: Press [2nd] [X^{-1}] [ENTER] *to show the applications menu.*
2. Choose **Finance** *to see the finance applications menu.*
3. Choose **irr** *to obtain the IRR prompt:* **irr(**.
4. Fill in the following information, paying close attention to using the correct symbols:

   irr (–1000000, {305450, 305450, 305450, 305450, 405450}) *(Be sure to use the negative number (-) key, not the minus sign.)*
5. To compute the IRR, press [ENTER].
6. The answer will now appear on the calculator: **17.95** (rounded).
7. [CLEAR] the worksheet or recall it [2nd] [ENTER] for sensitivity analysis.

Appendix 12C

Using Microsoft Excel (2007 and 2010) to Perform Time Value of Money Calculations

Technology makes it simple

Future Value Computations

1. In an Excel spreadsheet click on **Formulas**.
2. Click on **Financial**.
3. Choose **FV** from the drop down list. The following will appear as a dialog box:

   Rate

   Nper

   Pmt

   Pv

   Type
4. Fill in the interest **Rate**, in decimal format (for example 14% would be input as .14).
5. Fill in the number of periods (for example, five years would be input as 5 in the space by **Nper**).
6. If the amount is an annuity, fill in the yearly installment as negative number in the space by **Pmt.**
7. If the amount is a lump sum, fill in the lump sum as a negative number in the space by **Pv**.
8. Leave the space by **Type** blank.
9. The future value is shown under the dialog box.

Example 1: Future Value of a Lump Sum

Let's use our lump-sum investment example from page 724 of the text. Assume that you invest $10,000 for five years at an interest rate of 6%. Use the following procedure to find its future value five years from now:

1. In an Excel spreadsheet click on **Formulas**.
2. Click on **Financial**.
3. Choose **FV** from the drop down list. The following will appear as a dialog box. Fill in the variables as follows:

   Rate = **.06**

   Nper = **5**

   Pmt = (leave blank since this is used for annuities)

   PV = -**10000** (the negative sign indicates that the amount is a cash outflow, not inflow)

   Type = (leave blank)
4. The future value now appears under the dialog box as = $13,382.26 (rounded).

Example 2: Future Value of an Annuity

Let's use the annuity investment example from page 724 of the text. Assume that you invest $2,000 at the end of each year for five years. The investment earns 6% interest. Use the following procedures to find the investment's future value five years from now.

1. In an Excel spreadsheet click on **Formulas**.
2. Click on **Financial**.

3. Choose **FV** from the drop down list. The following will appear as a dialog box. Fill in the variables as follows:

   Rate = **.06**

   Nper = **5**

   Pmt = -**2000** (the negative sign indicates that the amount is a cash outflow, not inflow)

   PV = (leave blank since this is used for lump-sum amounts)

   Type = (leave blank)
4. The future value now appears under the dialog box as = $11,274.19 (rounded).

Technology makes it simple

Present Value Computations

1. In an Excel spreadsheet click on **Formulas**.
2. Click on **Financial**.
3. Choose **PV** from the drop down list. The following will appear as a dialog box:

   Rate

   Nper

   Pmt

   FV

   Type
4. Fill in the interest **Rate**, in decimal format (for example, 14% would be input as .14).
5. Fill in the number of periods (for example, five years would be input as 5).
6. If the amount is an annuity, fill in the yearly installment as negative number in the space by **Pmt**.
7. If the amount is a lump sum, fill in the lump sum as a negative number in the space by **FV**.
8. Leave the space by **Type** blank.
9. The present value is shown under the dialog box.

Example 1: Present Value of an Annuity-Lottery Option #2

Let's use the lottery payout Option #2 from page 727–728 of the text for our example. Option #2 was to receive $150,000 at the end of each year for the next ten years. The interest rate was assumed to be 8%. Use the following procedures to find the present value of the payout option:

1. In an Excel spreadsheet click on **Formulas**.
2. Click on **Financial**.
3. Choose **PV** from the drop down list. The following will appear as a dialog box. Fill in the variables as follows:

   Rate = **.08**

   Nper = **10**

   Pmt = -**150000**

   Fv = (leave blank since this is used for lump sums)

   Type = (leave blank)
4. The present value answer now appears under the dialog box as= $1,006,512.21 **(**rounded**)**.

Example 2: Present Value of a Lump Sum-Lottery Option #3

Let's use the lottery payout Option #3 from page 727–728 of the text for our example. Option #3 was to receive $2 million ten years from now. The interest rate was assumed to be 8%. Use the following procedures to find the present value of the payout option:

1. In an Excel spreadsheet click on **Formulas**.
2. Click on **Financial**.
3. Choose **PV** from the drop down list. The following will appear as a dialog box. Fill in the variables as follows:

   Rate = **.08**

   Nper = **10**

   Pmt = (leave blank since this is used for annuities)

   FV= -**2000000**

   Type = (leave blank)
4. The present value answer now appears under the dialog box as = $926,386.98 (rounded).

Technology makes it simple

Net Present Value (NPV) Calculations

1. In an Excel spreadsheet, type in the future cash flows expected from the investment. Begin with the cash flow expected in Year 1. In the next cell type in the cash flow expected in Year 2. Continue in the same fashion until all future cash flows are shown in separate cells, in the order in which they are expected to be received.
2. Click on **Formulas**.
3. Click on **Financial.**
4. Choose **NPV** from the drop down list. The following will appear as a dialog box:

   Rate

   Value 1
5. Fill in the interest **Rate**, in decimal format (for example, 14% would be input as .14)
6. Next to **Value 1**, highlight the array of cells containing the cash flow data from Step 1.
7. The **"Formula result"** will appear at the bottom of the dialog box. The result is the present value of the future cash flows.
8. Finally, subtract the initial cost of the investment to obtain the NPV.

Example 1: NPV of Allegra's MP3 Project—An annuity

Recall from pages 731–732 of the text that the MP3 project required an investment of $1 million and was expected to generate equal net cash inflows of $305,450 each year for five years. The company's discount rate was 14%.

1. In an Excel spreadsheet, type in the future cash flows expected from the investment in the order in which they are expected to be received. Your spreadsheet should show five consecutive cells as follows: 305450, 305450, 305450, 305450, 305450.
2. Click on **Formulas**.

3. Click on **Financial**.
4. Choose **NPV** from the drop down list. The following will appear as a dialog box. Fill in the variables as follows:

   Rate = .14

   Value 1 = (Highlight array of cells containing the cash flow data from Step 1)
5. The present value of the cash flows appears at the bottom of the dialog box as = **1,048,634.58.**
6. Finally, subtract the initial cost of the investment ($1 million) to obtain the NPV = $48,634.58.

Example 2: NPV of Allegra's DVR Project-Unequal Cash Flows

Recall from pages 731–733 of the text that the DVR project required an investment of $1 million and was expected to generate the unequal periodic cash inflows shown in Exhibit 12-11. The company's discount rate was 14%.

1. In an Excel spreadsheet, type in the future cash flows expected from the investment in the order in which they are expected to be received. Your spreadsheet should show five consecutive cells with the following values in them: 500000, 350000, 300000, 250000, 40000.
2. Click on **Formulas**.
3. Click on **Financial.**
4. Choose **NPV** from the drop down list. The following will appear as a dialog box. Fill in the variables as follows:

   Rate = .14

   Value 1 = (Highlight array of cells containing the cash flow data from Step 1)
5. The present value of the cash flows appears at the bottom of the dialog box as = **1,079,196.40 (rounded)**.
6. Finally, subtract the initial cost of the investment ($1 million) to obtain the NPV = $79,196.40 (rounded).

Example 3: Investment with a residual value

If an investment has a residual value, simply add the residual value as an additional cash inflow in the year in which it is to be received. For example, assume as we did in Exhibit 12-13 on page 734 that the MP3 project equipment will be worth $100,000 at the end of its five-year life. This represents an additional expected cash inflow to the company in Year 5.

1. In an Excel spreadsheet, type in the future cash flows expected from the investment in the order in which they are expected to be received. Your spreadsheet should show five consecutive cells with the following values in them: 305450, 305450, 305450, 305450, 405350
2. Click on **Formulas**.
3. Click on **Financial**.
4. Choose **NPV** from the drop down list. The following will appear as a dialog box. Fill in the variables as follows:

   Rate = .14

   Value 1 = (Highlight array of cells containing the cash flow data from Step 1)
5. The present value of the cash flows appears at the bottom of the dialog box as = **1,100,571.45 (rounded)**.
6. Finally, subtract the initial cost of the investment ($1 million) to obtain the NPV = $100,571.45 (rounded).

Technology makes it simple

Internal Rate of Return (IRR) Calculations

1. In an Excel spreadsheet, first type in the initial investment as a negative number. For example, -1000000 for a $1 million investment. In the next cell, type in the cash flow expected in Year 1. In the following cell type in the cash flow expected in Year 2. Continue in the same fashion until all future cash flows are shown in separate cells, in the order in which they are expected to be received.
2. Click on **Formulas**.
3. Click on **Financial**.
4. Choose **IRR** from the drop down list. The following will appear as a dialog box:

   Value 1
5. Next to **Value 1**, highlight the array of cells containing the data from Step 1.
6. The **"Formula result"** will appear at the bottom of the dialog box. The result is the Internal Rate of Return (IRR).

Example 1: IRR of Allegra's MP3 Project-An annuity

Recall that the MP3 project required an investment of $1 million and was expected to generate equal net cash inflows of $305,450 each year for five years.

1. In an Excel spreadsheet, first type in the initial investment as a negative number and then type in the future cash flows expected from the investment in the order in which they are expected to be received. Your spreadsheet should show the following consecutive cells: **-1000000, 305450, 305450, 305450, 305450, 305450.**
2. Click on **Formulas**.
3. Click on **Financial**.
4. Choose **IRR** from the drop down list. The following will appear as a dialog box. Fill in the variables as follows:

   Value 1 = (Highlight array of cells containing the data from Step 1)
5. The IRR appears at the bottom of the dialog box as = 16.01% (rounded).

Example 2: IRR of Allegra's DVR Project-Unequal Cash Flows

Recall that the DVR project required an investment of $1 million and was expected to generate the unequal periodic cash inflows shown in Exhibit 12-11.

1. In an Excel spreadsheet, first type in the initial investment as a negative number and then type in the future cash flows expected from the investment in the order in which they are expected to be received. Your spreadsheet should show the following consecutive cells: **-1000000, 500000, 350000, 300000, 250000, 40000.**
2. Click on **Formulas**.
3. Click on **Financial**.
4. Choose **IRR** from the drop down list. The following will appear as a dialog box. Fill in the variables as follows:

   Value 1 = (Highlight array of cells containing the data from Step 1)
5. The IRR appears at the bottom of the dialog box as = **18.23% (rounded).**

Example 3: Investment with a residual value

If an investment has a residual value, simply add the residual value as an additional cash inflow in the year in which it is to be received. For example, assume as we did in Exhibit 12-13 that the MP3 project equipment will be worth $100,000 at the end of its five-year life. This represents an additional expected cash inflow to the company in Year 5.

1. In an Excel spreadsheet, type in the future cash flows expected from the investment in the order in which they are expected to be received. Your spreadsheet should show six consecutive cells with the following values in them: **-1000000, 305450, 305450, 305450, 305450, 405350.**
2. Click on **Formulas**.
3. Click on **Financial**.
4. Choose **IRR** from the drop down list. The following will appear as a dialog box. Fill in the variables as follows:

   Value 1 = (Highlight array of cells containing the data from Step 1)
5. The IRR appears at the bottom of the dialog box as = **17.95% (rounded)**.

END OF CHAPTER

Learning Objectives

- 1 Describe the importance of capital investments and the capital budgeting process
- 2 Use the payback and accounting rate of return methods to make capital investment decisions
- 3 Use the time value of money to compute the present and future values of single lump sums and annuities
- 4 Use discounted cash flow models to make capital investment decisions
- 5 Compare and contrast the four capital budgeting methods

Accounting Vocabulary

Accounting Rate of Return. (p. 718) A measure of profitability computed by dividing the average annual operating income from an asset by the initial investment in the asset.

Annuity. (p. 723) A stream of equal installments made at equal time intervals.

Capital Budgeting. (p. 712) The process of making capital investment decisions. Companies make capital investments when they acquire *capital assets*—assets used for a long period of time.

Capital Rationing. (p. 713) Choosing among alternative capital investments due to limited funds.

Compound Interest. (p. 723) Interest computed on the principal *and* all interest earned to date.

Discount Rate. (p. 731) Management's minimum desired rate of return on an investment; also called the hurdle rate and required rate of return.

Hurdle Rate. (p. 731) Management's minimum desired rate of return on an investment; also called the discount rate and required rate of return.

Internal Rate of Return (IRR). (p. 735) The rate of return (based on discounted cash flows) that a company can expect to earn by investing in a capital asset. The interest rate that makes the NPV of the investment equal to zero.

LEED certification. (p.715) LEED, which stands for "Leadership in Energy and Environmental Design," is a certification system developed by the U.S. Green Building Council as a way of promoting and evaluating environmentally friendly construction projects.

Net Present Value (NPV). (p. 731) The *difference* between the present value of the investment's net cash inflows and the investment's cost.

Payback. (p. 715) The length of time it takes to recover, in net cash inflows, the cost of a capital outlay.

Post-Audits. (p. 713) Comparing a capital investment's actual net cash inflows to its projected net cash inflows.

Present Value Index. (p. 733) An index that computes the number of dollars returned for every dollar invested, *with all calculations performed in present value dollars.* It is computed as present value of net cash inflows divided by investment; also called profitability index.

Profitability Index. (p. 733) An index that computes the number of dollars returned for every dollar invested, *with all calculations performed in present value dollars.* Computed as present value of net cash inflows divided by investment; also called present value index.

Required Rate of Return. (p. 731) Management's minimum desired rate of return on an investment; also called the discount rate and hurdle rate.

Simple Interest. (p. 723) Interest computed *only* on the principal amount.

Time Value of Money. (p. 723) The fact that money can be invested to earn income over time.

MyAccountingLab **Go to http://myaccountinglab.com/ for the following Quick Check, Short Exercises, Exercises, and Problems. They are available with immediate grading, explanations of correct and incorrect answers, and interactive media that acts as your own online tutor.**

Quick Check

1. *(Learning Objective 1)* Examples of capital budgeting investments could include all of the following *except*
   a. building a new store.
   b. installing a new computer system.
   c. paying bonuses to the sales force.
   d. developing a new website.

2. *(Learning Objective 2)* Suppose Amazon.com is considering investing in warehouse-management software that costs $500,000, has $50,000 residual value, and should lead to cost savings of $120,000 per year for its five-year life. In calculating the ARR, which of the following figures should be used as the equation's denominator?
   a. $225,000
   b. $500,000
   c. $250,000
   d. $275,000

3. *(Learning Objective 2)* Using the information from Question 2, which of the following figures should be used in the equation's numerator (average annual operating income)?
   a. $120,000
   b. $20,000
   c. $30,000
   d. $10,000

4. *(Learning Objective 3)* Which of the following affects the present value of an investment?
   a. The interest rate
   b. The number of time periods (length of the investment)
   c. The type of investment (annuity versus single lump sum)
   d. All of the above

5. *(Learning Objective 5)* When making capital rationing decisions, the size of the initial investment required may differ between alternative investments. The profitability index can be used in conjunction with which of the following methods to help managers choose between alternatives?
   a. IRR
   b. ARR
   c. Payback Period
   d. NPV

6. *(Learning Objective 4)* The IRR is
   a. the same as the ARR.
   b. the firm's hurdle rate.
   c. the interest rate at which the NPV of the investment is zero.
   d. none of the above.

7. *(Learning Objective 5)* Which of the following methods uses accrual accounting rather than net cash flows as a basis for calculations?
   a. Payback
   b. ARR
   c. NPV
   d. IRR

8. *(Learning Objective 5)* Which of the following methods does not consider the investment's profitability?
   a. Payback
   b. ARR
   c. NPV
   d. IRR

9. *(Learning Objective 4)* Which of the following is *true* regarding capital rationing decisions?
   a. Companies should always choose the investment with the shortest payback period.
   b. Companies should always choose the investment with the highest NPV.
   c. Companies should always choose the investment with the highest ARR.
   d. None of the above

10. *(Learning Objective 4)* Which of the following is the most reliable method for making capital budgeting decisions?
    a. NPV method
    b. ARR method
    c. Payback method
    d. Post-audit method

Quick Check Answers

1. c 2. b 3. c 4. d 5. d 6. c 7. b 8. a 9. d 10. a

Short Exercises

S12-1 Order the capital budgeting process *(Learning Objective 1)*

Place the following activities in order from first to last to illustrate the capital budgeting process:

a. Budget capital investments
b. Project investments' cash flows
c. Perform post-audits
d. Make investments
e. Use feedback to reassess investments already made
f. Identify potential capital investments
g. Screen/analyze investments using one or more of the methods discussed

Medley Products Data Set used for S12-2 through S12-5:

Medley Products is considering producing MP3 players and digital video recorders (DVRs). The products require different specialized machines, each costing $1 million. Each machine has a five-year life and zero residual value. The two products have different patterns of predicted net cash inflows:

	Annual Net Cash Inflows	
Year	**MP3 Players**	**DVRs**
1	$ 332,000	$ 500,000
2	332,000	380,000
3	332,000	320,000
4	332,000	280,000
5	332,000	25,000
Total	$1,660,000	$1,505,000

Medley will consider making capital investments only if the payback period of the project is less than 3.5 years and the ARR exceeds 8%.

S12-2 Compute payback period—equal cash inflows *(Learning Objective 2)*

Refer to the Medley Products Data Set. Calculate the MP3-player project's payback period. If the MP3 project had a residual value of $125,000, would the payback period change? Explain and recalculate if necessary. Does this investment pass Medley's payback period screening rule?

S12-3 Compute payback period—unequal cash inflows *(Learning Objective 2)*

Refer to the Medley Products Data Set. Calculate the DVR project's payback period. If the DVR project had a residual value of $125,000, would the payback period change? Explain and recalculate if necessary. Does this investment pass Medley's payback period screening rule?

S12-4 Compute ARR—equal cash inflows *(Learning Objective 2)*

Refer to the Medley Products Data Set. Calculate the MP3-player project's ARR. If the MP3 project had a residual value of $125,000, would the ARR change? Explain and recalculate if necessary. Does this investment pass Medley's ARR screening rule?

S12-5 Compute ARR—unequal cash inflows *(Learning Objective 2)*

Refer to the Medley Products Data Set. Calculate the DVR project's ARR. If the DVR project had a residual value of $125,000, would the ARR change? Explain and recalculate if necessary. Does this investment pass Medley's ARR screening rule?

S12-6 Compute annual cash savings *(Learning Objective 2)*

Suppose Medley Products is deciding whether to invest in a DVD-HD project. The payback period for the $10 million investment is two years, and the project's expected life is seven years. What equal annual net cash inflows are expected from this project?

S12-7 Find the present values of future cash flows *(Learning Objective 3)*

Your grandmother would like to share some of her fortune with you. She offers to give you money under one of the following scenarios (you get to choose):

1. $7,000 a year at the end of each of the next eight years
2. $45,000 (lump sum) now
3. $75,000 (lump sum) eight years from now

Calculate the present value of each scenario using a 6% interest rate. Which scenario yields the highest present value? Would your preference change if you used a 12% interest rate?

S12-8 Show how timing affects future values *(Learning Objective 3)*

Assume that you make the following investments:

a. You invest a lump sum of $8,000 for four years at 14% interest. What is the investment's value at the end of four years?
b. In a different account earning 14% interest, you invest $2,000 at the end of each year for four years. What is the investment's value at the end of four years?
c. What general rule of thumb explains the difference in the investments' future values?

S12-9 Compare payout options at their future values *(Learning Objective 3)*

Listed below are three lottery payout options.

Option 1: $1,000,000 now
Option 2: $150,000 at the end of each year for the next ten years
Option 3: $2,000,000 ten years from now

Rather than compare the payout options at their present values (as is done in the chapter), compare the payout options at their future value ten years from now.

a. Using an 8% interest rate, what is the future value of each payout option?
b. Rank your preference of payout options.
c. Does computing the future value rather than the present value of the options change your preference of payout options? Explain.

S12-10 Relationship between the PV tables *(Learning Objective 3)*

Use the Present Value of $1 table (Appendix 12A, Table A) to determine the present value of $1 received one year from now. Assume a 14% interest rate. Use the same table to find the present value of $1 received two years from now. Continue this process for a total of five years.

a. What is the *total* present value of the cash flows received over the five-year period?
b. Could you characterize this stream of cash flows as an annuity? Why or why not?
c. Use the Present Value of Annuity of $1 table (Appendix 12A, Table B) to determine the present value of the same stream of cash flows. Compare your results to your answer in Part A.
d. Explain your findings.

S12-11 Compute NPV—equal net cash inflows *(Learning Objective 4)*

Munyon Music is considering investing $675,000 in private lesson studios that will have no residual value. The studios are expected to result in annual net cash inflows of $100,000 per year for the next nine years. Assuming that Munyon Music uses an 8% hurdle rate, what is net present value (NPV) of the studio investment? Is this a favorable investment?

S12-12 Compute IRR—equal net cash inflows *(Learning Objective 4)*

Refer to Munyon Music in S12-11. What is the approximate internal rate of return (IRR) of the studio investment?

S12-13 Compute NPV—unequal net cash inflows *(Learning Objective 4)*

The local Red Owl supermarket is considering investing in self-checkout kiosks for its customers. The self-checkout kiosks will cost $47,000 and have no residual value. Management expects the equipment to result in net cash savings over three years as customers grow accustomed to using the new technology: $17,000 the first year; $22,000 the second year; $24,000 the third year. Assuming a 14% discount rate, what is the NPV of the kiosk investment? Is this a favorable investment? Why or why not?

S12-14 Compute IRR—unequal net cash inflows *(Learning Objective 4)*

Refer to Red Owl in S12-13. What is the approximate internal rate of return (IRR) of the kiosk investment?

S12-15 Compare the capital budgeting methods *(Learning Objective 5)*

Fill in each statement with the appropriate capital budgeting method: payback period, ARR, NPV, or IRR.

a. In capital rationing decisions, the profitability index must be computed to compare investments requiring different initial investments when the _______ method is used.
b. _______ ignores salvage value.
c. _______ uses discounted cash flows to determine the asset's unique rate of return.
d. _______ highlights risky investments.
e. _______ measures profitability but ignores the time value of money.
f. _______ and _______ incorporate the time value of money.
g. _______ focuses on time, not profitability.
h. _______ uses accrual accounting income.
i. _______ finds the discount rate that brings the investment's NPV to zero.

EXERCISES Group A

E12-16A Identify capital investments *(Learning Objective 1)*

Which of the following purchases would be considered to be capital investments?

Purchase Item	Capital Investment?
a. The construction of a new office complex for $1,850,000.	
b. The projected cost of productivity bonuses for the coming year is $900,000.	
c. The advertising campaign to launch a new product is estimated at $400,000.	
d. Purchase and installation of new manufacturing equipment for $4,500,000.	
e. The installation of new computer terminals and software in all retail outlets is estimated to cost $1,400,000.	
f. The purchase and customization of a new production facility for $2,650,000.	
g. The new customer service training is budgeted to cost $450,000.	
h. New tablet computers for the sales force will cost $300,000.	
i. New telecommunication software for the customer response center will cost $890,000.	
j. The cost of the quality program for the upcoming year is estimated at $250,000.	

E12-17A Compute payback period—equal cash inflows *(Learning Objective 2)*

Lodi Products is considering acquiring a manufacturing plant. The purchase price is $2,320,000. The owners believe the plant will generate net cash inflows of $290,000 annually. It will have to be replaced in seven years. To be profitable, the investment payback must occur before the investment's replacement date. Use the payback method to determine whether Lodi Products should purchase this plant.

E12-18A Compute payback period—unequal cash inflows *(Learning Objective 2)*

West Hill Hardware is adding a new product line that will require an investment of $1,500,000. Managers estimate that this investment will have a 10-year life and generate net cash inflows of $310,000 the first year, $300,000 the second year, and $250,000 each year thereafter for eight years. The investment has no residual value. Compute the payback period.

E12-19A ARR with unequal cash inflows *(Learning Objective 2)*

Refer to the West Hill Hardware information in E12-18A. Compute the ARR for the investment.

E12-20A Compute and compare ARR *(Learning Objective 2)*

Donofrio Products is considering whether to upgrade its equipment. Managers are considering two options. Equipment manufactured by Smith costs $850,000 and will last six years and have no residual value. The Smith equipment will generate annual operating income of $161,500. Equipment manufactured by Kyler costs $1,375,000 and will remain useful for seven years. It promises annual operating income of $247,500, and its expected residual value is $100,000.

Which equipment offers the higher ARR?

E12-21A Compare retirement savings plans *(Learning Objective 3)*

Assume that you want to retire early at age 54. You plan to save using one of the following two strategies: (1) save $4,200 a year in an IRA beginning when you are 24 and ending when you are 54 (30 years) or (2) wait until you are 39 to start saving and then save $8,400 per year for the next 15 years. Assume that you will earn the historic stock market average of 10% per year.

Requirements

1. How much out-of-pocket cash will you invest under the two options?
2. How much savings will you have accumulated at age 54 under the two options?
3. Explain the results.
4. If you let the savings continue to grow for eight more years (with no further out-of-pocket investments), under each scenario, what will the investment be worth when you are age 62?

E12-22A Calculate the payback and NPV for a sustainable energy project *(Learning Objective 1 and 3)*

Terra Industries is evaluating investing in solar panels to provide some of the electrical needs of its main office building in Tempe, Arizona. The solar panel project would cost $540,000 and would provide cost savings in its utility bills of $60,000 per year. It is anticipated that the solar panels would have a life of 20 years and would have no residual value.

Requirements

1. Calculate the payback period in years of the solar panel project.
2. If the company uses a discount rate of 10%, what is the net present value of this project?
3. If the company has a rule that no projects will be undertaken that have a payback period of more than five years, would this investment be accepted? If not, what arguments could the energy manager make to try to obtain approval for the solar panel project?
4. What would you do if you were in charge of approving capital investment proposals?

E12-23A Fund future cash flows *(Learning Objective 3)*

Lily wants to take the next five years off work to travel around the world. She estimates her annual cash needs at $40,000 (if she needs more, she'll work odd jobs). Lily believes she can invest her savings at 8% until she depletes her funds.

Requirements

1. How much money does Lily need now to fund her travels?
2. After speaking with a number of banks, Lily learns she'll be able to invest her funds only at 6%. How much does she need now to fund her travels?

E12-24A Choosing a lottery payout option *(Learning Objective 3)*

Congratulations! You've won a state lotto! The state lottery offers you the following (after-tax) payout options:

Option #1: $14,500,000 five years from now

Option #2: $2,050,000 at the end of each year for the next five years

Option #3: $13,000,000 three years from now

Requirement

Assuming that you can earn 8% on your funds, which option would you prefer?

E12-25A Solve various time value of money scenarios *(Learning Objective 3)*

1. Suppose you invest a sum of $3,000 in an account bearing interest at the rate of 14% per year. What will the investment be worth six years from now?
2. How much would you need to invest now to be able to withdraw $6,000 at the end of every year for the next 20 years? Assume a 12% interest rate.
3. Assume that you want to have $160,000 saved seven years from now. If you can invest your funds at a 6% interest rate, how much do you currently need to invest?
4. Your aunt Betty plans to give you $2,000 at the end of every year for the next ten years. If you invest each of her yearly gifts at a 12% interest rate, how much will they be worth at the end of the ten-year period?
5. Suppose you want to buy a small cabin in the mountains four years from now. You estimate that the property will cost $61,250 at that time. How much money do you need to invest each year in an account bearing interest at the rate of 6% per year to accumulate the $61,250 purchase price?

E12-26A Calculate NPV—equal annual cash inflows *(Learning Objective 4)*

Use the NPV method to determine whether Princeton Products should invest in the following projects:

- *Project A* costs $280,000 and offers eight annual net cash inflows of $64,000. Princeton Products requires an annual return of 12% on projects like A.
- *Project B* costs $385,000 and offers nine annual net cash inflows of $74,000. Princeton Products demands an annual return of 14% on investments of this nature.

Requirement

What is the NPV of each project? What is the maximum acceptable price to pay for each project?

E12-27A Calculate IRR—equal cash inflows *(Learning Objective 4)*

Refer to Princeton Products in E12-26A. Compute the IRR of each project and use this information to identify the better investment.

E12-28A Calculate NPV—unequal cash flows *(Learning Objective 4)*

Monette Industries is deciding whether to automate one phase of its production process. The manufacturing equipment has a six-year life and will cost $900,000. Projected net cash inflows are as follows:

Year 1	$260,000
Year 2	$253,000
Year 3	$225,000
Year 4	$215,000
Year 5	$204,000
Year 6	$178,000

Requirements

1. Compute this project's NPV using Monette Industries' 14% hurdle rate. Should Monette Industries invest in the equipment? Why or why not?
2. Monette Industries could refurbish the equipment at the end of six years for $100,000. The refurbished equipment could be used one more year, providing $76,000 of net cash inflows in Year 7. In addition, the refurbished equipment would have a $52,000 residual value at the end of Year 7. Should Monette Industries invest in the equipment and refurbish it after six years? Why or why not? (*Hint*: In addition to your answer to Requirement 1, discount the additional cash outflow and inflows back to the present value.)

E12-29A Compute IRR—unequal cash flows *(Learning Objective 4)*

Baskette Products is considering an equipment investment that will cost $920,000. Projected net cash inflows over the equipment's three-year life are as follows: Year 1: $492,000; Year 2: $402,000; and Year 3: $290,000. Baskette wants to know the equipment's IRR.

Requirement

Use trial and error to find the IRR within a 2% range. (*Hint*: Use Baskette's hurdle rate of 12% to begin the trial-and-error process.)

Optional: Use a business calculator spreadsheet to compute the exact IRR.

E12-30A Capital rationing decision *(Learning Objective 4)*

Liverpool Manufacturing is considering three capital investment proposals. At this time, Liverpool Manufacturing has funds available to pursue only one of the three investments.

	Equipment A	Equipment B	Equipment C
Present value of net cash inflows	$1,700,000	$1,950,000	$2,200,000
Investment	($1,360,000)	($1,875,000)	($2,000,000)
NPV	$ 340,000	$ 75,000	$ 200,000

Requirement

Which investment should Liverpool Manufacturing pursue at this time? Why?

Frost Valley Expansion Data Set used for E12-31A through E12-34A:

Assume that Frost Valley's managers developed the following estimates concerning a planned expansion to its Waterfall Park Lodge (all numbers assumed):

Number of additional skiers per day	100
Average number of days per year that weather conditions allow skiing at Flint Valley	150
Useful life of expansion (in years)	8
Average cash spent by each skier per day	$ 250
Average variable cost of serving each skier per day	$ 150
Cost of expansion	$6,000,000
Discount rate	12%

Assume that Frost Valley uses the straight-line depreciation method and expects the lodge expansion to have a residual value of $600,000 at the end of its eight-year life.

E12-31A Compute payback and ARR with residual value *(Learning Objective 2)*

Consider how Frost Valley, a popular ski resort, could use capital budgeting to decide whether the $6 million Waterfall Park Lodge expansion would be a good investment.

Requirements

1. Compute the average annual net cash inflow from the expansion.
2. Compute the average annual operating income from the expansion.
3. Compute the payback period.
4. Compute the ARR.

E12-32A Continuation of E12-31A: Compute payback and ARR with no residual value *(Learning Objective 2)*

Refer to the Frost Valley Expansion Data Set. *Assume that the expansion has zero residual value.*

Requirements

1. Will the payback period change? Explain and recalculate if necessary.
2. Will the project's ARR change? Explain and recalculate if necessary.
3. Assume that Frost Valley screens its potential capital investments using the following decision criteria: Maximum payback period = 5 years and minimum accounting rate of return = 10%.
   Will Frost Valley consider this project further or reject it?

E12-33A Calculate NPV with and without residual value *(Learning Objective 4)*

Refer to the Frost Valley Expansion Data Set.

Requirements

1. What is the project's NPV? Is the investment attractive? Why or why not?
2. Assume that the expansion has no residual value. What is the project's NPV? Is the investment still attractive? Why or why not?

E12-34A Calculate IRR with no residual value *(Learning Objective 4)*

Refer to the Frost Valley Expansion Data Set. Assume that the expansion has no residual value. What is the project's IRR? Is the investment attractive? Why or why not?

E12-35A Comparing capital budgeting methods *(Learning Objective 5)*

The following table contains information about four projects in which Rhodes Corporation has the opportunity to invest. This information is based on estimates that different managers have prepared about their potential project.

Project	Investment Required	Net Present Value	Life of Project	Internal Rate of Return	Profitability Index	Payback Period in Years	Accounting Rate of Return
A	$ 220,000	$ 61,190	5	23%	1.28	2.82	18%
B	$ 410,000	$ 37,744	6	22%	1.09	3.20	14%
C	$1,030,000	$191,498	3	18%	1.19	2.17	13%
D	$1,545,000	$ 52,680	4	12%	1.03	3.07	23%

Requirements

1. Rank the four projects in order of preference by using the
   a. net present value.
   b. project profitability index.
   c. internal rate of return.
   d. payback period.
   e. accounting rate of return.
2. Which method(s) do you think is best for evaluating capital investment projects in general? Why?

EXERCISES Group B

E12-36B Identify capital investments *(Learning Objective 1)*

Which of the following purchases would be considered capital investments?

Purchase Item	Capital Investment?
a. The replacement of the engine on one of the company's aircraft is $190,000 (this will not increase the useful life of the plane).	
b. The delivered, installed cost of a new production line is $140,000.	
c. The cost of raw materials for the year is estimated at $980,000.	
d. All of the computers at the help desk are being upgraded at a cost of $123,000.	
e. To support the launch of the new product line, staff training costs are $100,000.	
f. The cost to develop and implement the new Facebook retail app is $565,000.	
g. The upgrade of the customer service fleet to new fuel-efficient vehicles has a cost of $300,000.	
h. The total cost of the management succession program for the coming year is projected to be $230,000.	
i. The cost to retrofit one of a company's closed retail outlets into a customer service center is projected to be $100,000.	
j. The cost of workers' compensation insurance for the coming year is projected to be $200,000.	

E12-37B Compute payback period—equal cash inflows *(Learning Objective 2)*

Preston Products is considering acquiring a manufacturing plant. The purchase price is $1,890,000. The owners believe the plant will generate net cash inflows of $315,000 annually. It will have to be replaced in nine years. To be profitable, the investment payback must occur before the investment's replacement date. Use the payback method to determine whether Preston should purchase this plant.

E12-38B Compute payback period—unequal cash inflows *(Learning Objective 2)*

Archer Hardware is adding a new product line that will require an investment of $2,000,000. Managers estimate that this investment will have a 10-year life and generate net cash inflows of $650,000 the first year, $490,000 the second year, and $250,000 each year thereafter for eight years. The investment has no residual value. Compute the payback period.

E12-39B ARR with unequal cash inflows *(Learning Objective 2)*

Refer to the Archer Hardware information in E12-38B. Compute the ARR for the investment.

E12-40B Compute and compare ARR *(Learning Objective 2)*

Miguel Products is considering whether to upgrade its manufacturing equipment. Managers are considering two options. Equipment manufactured by McKnight costs $940,000 and will last for four years with no residual value. The McKnight equipment will generate annual operating income of $141,000. Equipment manufactured by Logan costs $1,125,000 and will remain useful for five years. It promises annual operating income of $236,250, and its expected residual value is $105,000. Which equipment offers the higher ARR?

E12-41B Compare retirement savings plans *(Learning Objective 3)*

Assume you want to retire early at age 52. You plan to save using one of the following two strategies: (1) save $3,000 a year in an IRA beginning when you are 27 and ending when you are 52 (25 years) or (2) wait until you are 37 to start saving and then save $5,000 per year for the next 15 years. Assume you will earn the historic stock market average of 10% per year.

Requirements

1. How much out-of-pocket cash will you invest under the two options?
2. How much savings will you have accumulated at age 52 under the two options?

3. Explain the results.
4. If you were to let the savings continue to grow for 10 more years (with no further out-of-pocket investments), under each scenario, what will the investments be worth when you are age 62?

E12-42B Calculate the payback and NPV for a sustainable energy project *(Learning Objectives 1 & 3)*

Terra Industries is evaluating investing in solar panels to provide some of the electrical needs of its main building in Tempe, Arizona. The solar panel project would cost $540,000 and would provide cost savings in its utility bills of $67,500 per year. It is anticipated that the solar panels would have a life of 20 years and would have no residual value.

Requirements

1. Calculate the payback period in years of the solar panel project.
2. If the company uses a discount rate of 8%, what is the net present value of this project?
3. If the company has a rule that no projects will be undertaken that would have a payback period of more than five years, would this investment be accepted? If not, what arguments could the energy manager make to try to obtain approval for the solar panel project?
4. What would you do if you were in charge of approving capital investment proposals?

E12-43B Fund future cash flows *(Learning Objective 3)*

Rachel wants to take the next four years off work to travel around the world. She estimates her annual cash needs at $29,000 (if she needs more, she'll work odd jobs). Rachel believes she can invest her savings at 10% until she depletes her funds.

Requirements

1. How much money does Rachel need now to fund her travels?
2. After speaking with a number of banks, Rachel learns she'll only be able to invest her funds at 4%. How much does she need now to fund her travels?

E12-44B Choosing a lottery payout option *(Learning Objective 3)*

Congratulations! You've won a state lotto! The state lottery offers you the following (after-tax) payout options:

Option #1: $12,000,000 six years from now
Option #2: $2,250,000 at the end of each year for the next six years
Option #3: $10,500,000 three years from now

Requirement

Assuming that you can earn 8% on your funds, which option would you prefer?

E12-45B Solve various time value of money scenarios *(Learning Objective 3)*

Solve these various time value of money scenarios.

1. Suppose you invest a sum of $5,000 in an account bearing interest at the rate of 10% per year. What will the investment be worth six years from now?
2. How much would you need to invest now to be able to withdraw $10,000 at the end of every year for the next 20 years? Assume a 12% interest rate.
3. Assume that you want to have $170,000 saved seven years from now. If you can invest your funds at an 8% interest rate, how much do you currently need to invest?
4. Your aunt Betty plans to give you $2,000 at the end of every year for the next 10 years. If you invest each of her yearly gifts at a 12% interest rate, how much will they be worth at the end of the 10-year period?
5. Suppose you would like to buy a small cabin in the mountains four years from now. You estimate that the property will cost $56,875 at that time. How much money would you need to invest each year in an account bearing interest at the rate of 6% per year in order to accumulate the $56,875 purchase price?

E12-46B Calculate NPV—equal annual cash inflows *(Learning Objective 4)*

Use the NPV method to determine whether Gendron Products should invest in the following projects:

- *Project A* costs $285,000 and offers eight annual net cash inflows of $60,000. Gendrons Products requires an annual return of 14% on projects like A.
- *Project B* costs $385,000 and offers nine annual net cash inflows of $70,000. Gendron Products demands an annual return of 12% on investments of this nature.

Requirement

What is the NPV of each project? What is the maximum acceptable price to pay for each project?

E12-47B Calculate IRR—equal cash inflows *(Learning Objective 4)*

Refer to Gendron Products in E12-46B. Compute the IRR of each project and use this information to identify the better investment.

E12-48B Calculate NPV—unequal cash flows *(Learning Objective 4)*

Bobbin Industries is deciding whether to automate one phase of its production process. The manufacturing equipment has a six-year life and will cost $920,000.

Projected net cash inflows are as follows:	
Year 1	$265,000
Year 2	$254,000
Year 3	$222,000
Year 4	$211,000
Year 5	$205,000
Year 6	$174,000

Requirements

1. Compute this project's NPV using Bobbin Industries' 14% hurdle rate. Should Bobbin Industries invest in the equipment? Why or why not?
2. Bobbin Industries could refurbish the equipment at the end of six years for $100,000. The refurbished equipment could be used for one more year, providing $73,000 of net cash inflows in Year 7. Additionally, the refurbished equipment would have a $52,000 residual value at the end of Year 7. Should Bobbin Industries invest in the equipment and refurbish it after six years? Why or why not? (*Hint:* In addition to your answer to Requirement 1, discount the additional cash outflows and inflows back to the present value.)

E12-49B Compute IRR—unequal cash flows *(Learning Objective 4)*

Chandler Chairs is considering an equipment investment that will cost $955,000. Projected net cash inflows over the equipment's three-year life are as follows: Year 1: $494,000; Year 2: $390,000; and Year 3: $304,000. Chandler wants to know the equipment's IRR.

Requirement

Use trial and error to find the IRR within a 2% range. (*Hint*: Use Chandler's hurdle rate of 10% to begin the trial-and-error process.)

E12-50B Capital rationing decision *(Learning Objective 4)*

Whiston Manufacturing is considering three capital investment proposals. At this time, Whiston Manufacturing only has funds available to pursue one of the three investments.

	Equipment A	Equipment B	Equipment C
Present value of net cash inflows	$1,710,000	$1,960,000	$2,210,000
Investment	($1,425,000)	($1,750,000)	($2,125,000)
NPV	$ 285,000	$ 210,000	$ 85,000

Requirement

Which investment should Whiston Manufacturing pursue at this time? Why?

Hope Valley Data Set used for E12-51B–E12-54B.

Assume that Hope Valley's managers developed the following estimates concerning a planned expansion of its Blizzard Park Lodge (all numbers assumed):

Number of additional skiers per day	110
Average number of days per year that weather conditions allow skiing at Hope Valley	125
Useful life of expansion (in years)	8
Average cash spent by each skier per day	$ 230
Average variable cost of serving each skier per day	$ 130
Cost of expansion	$5,500,000
Discount rate	12%

E12-51B Compute payback and ARR with residual value *(Learning Objective 2)*

Consider how Hope Valley, a popular ski resort, could use capital budgeting to decide whether the $10 million Blizzard Park Lodge expansion would be a good investment.

Requirements

1. Compute the average annual net cash inflow from the expansion.
2. Compute the average annual operating income from the expansion.
3. Compute the payback period.
4. Compute the ARR.

E12-52B Continuation of E12-51B: Compute payback and ARR with no residual value *(Learning Objective 2)*

Refer to the Hope Valley data in E12-51B. Now assume the expansion has zero residual value.

Requirements

1. Will the payback period change? Explain and recalculate if necessary.
2. Will the project's ARR change? Explain and recalculate if necessary.
3. Assume Hope Valley screens its potential capital investments using the following decision criteria: maximum payback period of five years, minimum accounting rate of return of 10%. Will Hope Valley consider this project further or reject it?

E12-53B Calculate NPV with and without residual value *(Learning Objective 4)*

Refer to the Hope Valley data in E12-51B. Assume that Hope Valley uses the straight-line depreciation method and expects the lodge expansion to have a residual value of $1,100,000 at the end of its eight-year life. It has already calculated the average annual net cash inflow per year to be $1,375,000.

Requirements

1. What is the project's NPV? Is the investment attractive? Why or why not?
2. *Assume the expansion has no residual value.* What is the project's NPV? Is the investment still attractive? Why or why not?

E12-54B Calculate IRR with no residual value *(Learning Objective 4)*

Refer to the Hope Valley data in E12-51B. Assume that Hope uses the straight-line depreciation method and expects the lodge expansion to have no residual value at the end of its eight-year life. The company has already calculated the average annual net cash inflow per year to be $1,375,000 and the NPV of the expansion to be $1,775,400. What is the project's IRR? Is the investment attractive? Why?

E12-55B Comparing capital budgeting methods *(Learning Objective 5)*

The following table contains information about four projects in which Morales Corporation has the opportunity to invest. This information is based on estimates that different managers have prepared about the company's potential project.

Project	Investment Required	Net Present Value	Life of Project	Internal Rate of Return	Profitability Index	Payback Period in Years	Accounting Rate of Return
A	$ 225,000	$ 35,908	5	20%	1.16	2.96	19%
B	$ 405,000	$ 49,740	6	23%	1.12	3.12	14%
C	$1,030,000	$151,325	3	18%	1.15	2.17	13%
D	$1,530,000	$ 18,870	4	13%	1.01	3.00	22%

Requirements

1. Rank the four projects in order of preference by using the
   a. net present value.
   b. project profitability index.
   c. internal rate of return.
   d. payback period.
   e. accounting rate of return.
2. Which method(s) do you think is best for evaluating capital investment projects in general? Why?

PROBLEMS Group A

P12-56A Solve various time value of money scenarios *(Learning Objectives 3 & 4)*

1. Irving just hit the jackpot in Las Vegas and won $45,000! If he invests it now at a 14% interest rate, how much will it be worth in 20 years?
2. Forrest would like to have $4,000,000 saved by the time he retires in 30 years. How much does he need to invest now at a 10% interest rate to fund his retirement goal?
3. Assume that Vivian accumulates savings of $2 million by the time she retires. If she invests this savings at 12%, how much money will she be able to withdraw at the end of each year for 20 years?
4. Donna plans to invest $3,000 at the end of each year for the next eight years. Assuming a 10% interest rate, what will her investment be worth eight years from now?
5. Assuming a 6% interest rate, how much would Vanna have to invest now to be able to withdraw $13,000 at the end of each year for the next ten years?

6. Ray is considering a capital investment that costs $510,000 and will provide the following net cash inflows:

Year	Net Cash Inflow
1	$308,000
2	$200,000
3	$102,000

Using a hurdle rate of 10%, find the NPV of the investment.

7. What is the IRR of the capital investment described in Question 6?

P12-57A Retirement planning in two stages *(Learning Objective 3)*

You are planning for a very early retirement. You would like to retire at age 40 and have enough money saved to be able to draw $230,000 per year for the next 45 years (based on family history, you think you'll live to age 85). You plan to save for retirement by making 20 equal annual installments (from age 20 to age 40) into a fairly risky investment fund that you expect will earn 14% per year. You will leave the money in this fund until it is completely depleted when you are 85 years old. To make your plan work, answer the following:

1. How much money must you accumulate by retirement? (*Hint:* Find the present value of the $230,000 withdrawals. You may want to draw a time line showing the savings period and the retirement period.)
2. How does this amount compare to the total amount you will draw out of the investment during retirement? How can these numbers be so different?
3. How much must you pay into the investment each year for the first 20 years? (*Hint:* Your answer from Requirement 1 becomes the future value of this annuity.)
4. How does the total out-of-pocket savings compare to the investment's value at the end of the 20-year savings period and the withdrawals you will make during retirement?

P12-58A Evaluate an investment using all four methods *(Learning Objectives 2 & 4)*

Ocean World is considering purchasing a water park in San Antonio, Texas for $2,400,000. The new facility will generate annual net cash inflows of $600,000 for eight years. Engineers estimate that the facility will remain useful for eight years and have no residual value. The company uses straight-line depreciation. Its owners want payback in less than five years and an ARR of 10% or more. Management uses a 12% hurdle rate on investments of this nature.

Requirements

1. Compute the payback period, the ARR, the NPV, and the approximate IRR of this investment. (If you use the tables to compute the IRR, answer with the closest interest rate shown in the tables.)
2. Recommend whether the company should invest in this project.

P12-59A Compare investments with different cash flows and residual values *(Learning Objectives 2 & 4)*

Abrahms operates a chain of sandwich shops. The company is considering two possible expansion plans. Plan A would open eight smaller shops at a cost of $9,450,000. Expected annual net cash inflows are $1,890,000 with zero residual value at the end of 10 years. Under Plan B, Abrahms would open three larger shops at a cost of $9,400,000. This plan is expected to generate net cash inflows of $1,175,000 per year for 10 years, the estimated life of the properties. Estimated residual value is $1,880,000. Abrahms uses straight-line depreciation and requires an annual return of 8%.

Requirements

1. Compute the payback period, the ARR, and the NPV of these two plans. What are the strengths and weaknesses of these capital budgeting models?
2. Which expansion plan should Abrahms choose? Why?
3. Estimate Plan A's IRR. How does the IRR compare with the company's required rate of return?

PROBLEMS Group B

P12-60B Solve various time value of money scenarios *(Learning Objectives 3 & 4)*

1. Harold just hit the jackpot in Las Vegas and won $25,000! If he invests it now, at a 10% interest rate, how much will it be worth 15 years from now?
2. Curtis would like to have $3,000,000 saved by the time he retires 40 years from now. How much does he need to invest now at a 12% interest rate to fund his retirement goal?
3. Assume that Ramona accumulates savings of $1.0 million by the time she retires. If she invests this savings at 12%, how much money will she be able to withdraw at the end of each year for 15 years?
4. Ivana plans to invest $3,000 at the end of each year for the next eight years. Assuming a 12% interest rate, what will her investment be worth eight years from now?
5. Assuming a 12% interest rate, how much would Amanda have to invest now to be able to withdraw $13,000 at the end of every year for the next nine years?
6. Chuck is considering a capital investment that costs $510,000 and will provide the following net cash inflows:

Year	Net Cash Inflow
1	$300,000
2	$198,000
3	$106,000

   Using a hurdle rate of 10%, find the NPV of the investment.
7. What is the IRR of the capital investment described in Question 6?

P12-61B Retirement planning in two stages *(Learning Objective 3)*

You are planning for an early retirement. You would like to retire at age 40 and have enough money saved to be able to draw $225,000 per year for the next 35 years (based on family history, you think you'll live to age 75). You plan to save by making 10 equal annual installments (from age 30 to age 40) into a fairly risky investment fund that you expect will earn 10% per year. You will leave the money in this fund until it is completely depleted when you are 75 years old.

To make your plan work, answer the following:

1. How much money must you accumulate by retirement? (*Hint*: Find the present value of the $225,000 withdrawals. You may want to draw a time line showing the savings period and the retirement period.)
2. How does this amount compare to the total amount you will draw out of the investment during retirement? How can these numbers be so different?
3. How much must you pay into the investment each year for the first 10 years? (*Hint*: Your answer from Requirement 1 becomes the future value of this annuity.)
4. How does the total out-of-pocket savings compare to the investment's value at the end of the 10-year savings period and the withdrawals you will make during retirement?

P12-62B Evaluate an investment using all four methods *(Learning Objectives 2 & 4)*

Aquatic Fun is considering purchasing a water park in Cleveland, Ohio for $2,500,000. The new facility will generate annual net cash inflows of $625,000 for ten years. Engineers estimate that the facility will remain useful for ten years and have no residual value. The company uses straight-line depreciation. Its owners want payback in less than five years and an ARR of 10% or more. Management uses a 12% hurdle rate on investments of this nature.

Requirements

1. Compute the payback period, the ARR, the NPV, and the approximate IRR of this investment.
2. Recommend whether the company should invest in this project.

E12-63B Compare investments with different cash flows and residual values

(Learning Objectives 2 & 4)

Martinson Restaurant Group operates a chain of sub shops. The company is considering two possible expansion plans. Plan A would involve opening eight smaller shops at a cost of $7,500,000. Expected annual net cash inflows are $1,500,000, with zero residual value at the end of ten years. Under Plan B, Martinson would open three larger shops at a cost of $7,425,000. This plan is expected to generate net cash inflows of $1,237,500 per year for ten years, the estimated life of the properties. Estimated residual value for Plan B is $990,000. Martinson uses straight-line depreciation and requires an annual return of 8%.

Requirements

1. Compute the payback period, the ARR, and the NPV of these two plans. What are the strengths and weaknesses of these capital budgeting models?
2. Which expansion plan should Martinson choose? Why?
3. Estimate Plan A's IRR. How does the IRR compare with the company's required rate of return?

CRITICAL THINKING

Discussion & Analysis

A12-64 Discussion Questions

1. Describe the capital budgeting process in your own words.
2. Define capital investment. List at least three examples of capital investments other than the examples provided in the chapter.
3. "As the required rate of return increases, the net present value of a project also increases." Explain why you agree or disagree with this statement.
4. Summarize the net present value method for evaluating a capital investment opportunity. Describe the circumstances that create a positive net present value. Describe the circumstances that may cause the net present value of a project to be negative. Describe the advantages and disadvantages of the net present value method.
5. Net cash inflows and net cash outflows are used in the net present value method and in the internal rate of return method. Explain why accounting net income is not used instead of cash flows.
6. Suppose you are a manager and you have three potential capital investment projects from which to choose. Funds are limited, so you can only choose one of the three projects. Describe at least three methods you can use to select the one project in which to invest.
7. The net present value method assumes that future cash inflows are immediately reinvested at the required rate of return, while the internal rate of return method assumes that future cash inflows are immediately invested at the internal rate of return rate. Which assumption is better? Explain your answer.
8. The decision rule for NPV analysis states that the project with the highest NPV should be selected. Describe at least two situations when the project with the highest NPV may not necessarily be the best project to select.
9. List and describe the advantages and disadvantages of the internal rate of return method.
10. List and describe the advantages and disadvantages of the payback method.
11. Oftentimes, investments in sustainability projects do not meet traditional investment selection criteria. Suppose you are a manager and have prepared a proposal to install solar panels to provide lighting for the office. The payback period for the project is longer than the company's required payback period and the project's net present value is slightly negative. What arguments could you offer to the capital budgeting committee for accepting the solar energy project in spite of it not meeting the capital selection criteria?
12. Think of a company with which you are familiar. What are some examples of possible sustainable investments that company may be able to undertake? How might the company management justify these possible investments?

Application & Analysis

A12-65 Evaluating the Purchase of an Asset with Various Capital Budgeting Methods

In this activity, you will be evaluating whether you should purchase a hybrid car or its gasoline-engine counterpart. Select two car models that are similar, with one being a hybrid model and one being the non-hybrid model. (For example, the Honda Civic is available as a hybrid or a gasoline-engine model.) Assume that you plan on keeping your car for 10 years and that at the end of the 10 years, the resale value of both models will be negligible.

Basic Discussion Questions

1. Research the cost of each model (include taxes and title costs). Also, obtain an estimate of the miles per gallon fuel efficiency of each model.
2. Estimate the number of miles you drive each year. Also estimate the cost of a gallon of fuel.

3. Given your previous estimates from 1 and 2, estimate the total cost of driving the hybrid model for one year. Also estimate the total cost of driving the non-hybrid model for one year. Calculate the savings offered by the hybrid model over the non-hybrid model.
4. Calculate the NPV of the hybrid model, using the annual fuel savings as the annual cash inflow for the 10 years you would own the car.
5. Compare the NPV of the hybrid model with the cost of the gasoline-engine model. Which model has the lowest cost (the lowest NPV)? From a purely financial standpoint, does the hybrid model make sense?
6. Now look at the payback period of the hybrid model. Use the difference between the cost of the hybrid model and the gasoline-engine model as the investment. Use the annual fuel savings as the expected annual net cash inflow. Ignoring the time value of money, how long does it take for the additional cost of the hybrid model to pay for itself through fuel savings?
7. What qualitative factors might affect your decision about which model to purchase?

Decision Case

A12-66 Apply time value of money to a personal decision *(Learning Objective 3)*

Kelsey Gerbig, a second-year business student at the University of Utah, will graduate in two years with an accounting major and a Spanish minor. Gerbig is trying to decide where to work this summer. She has two choices: work full-time for a bottling plant or work part-time in the accounting department of a meat-packing plant. She probably will work at the same place next summer as well. She is able to work twelve weeks during the summer.

The bottling plant would pay Gerbig $380 per week this year and 7% more next summer. At the meat-packing plant, she would work 20 hours per week at $8.75 per hour. By working only part-time, she could take two accounting courses this summer. Tuition is $225 per hour for each of the four-hour courses. Gerbig believes that the experience she gains this summer will qualify her for a full-time accounting position with the meat-packing plant next summer. That position will pay $550 per week.

Gerbig sees two additional benefits of working part-time this summer. First, she could reduce her studying workload during the fall and spring semesters by one course each term. Second, she would have the time to work as a grader in the university's accounting department during the fifteen-week fall term. Grading pays $50 per week.

Requirements

1. Suppose that Gerbig ignores the time value of money in decisions that cover this short of a time period. Suppose also that her sole goal is to make as much money as possible between now and the end of next summer. What should she do? What non-quantitative factors might Gerbig consider? What would *you* do if you were faced with these alternatives?
2. Now, suppose that Gerbig considers the time value of money for all cash flows that she expects to receive one year or more in the future. Which alternative does this consideration favor? Why?

13

Statement of Cash Flows

Learning Objectives

- **1** Classify cash flows as operating, investing, or financing activities
- **2** Prepare the statement of cash flows using the indirect method
- **3** Prepare the statement of cash flows using the direct method

Digital Vision/Getty Images

Source: www.money-zine.com/Financial-Planning/Debt-Consolidation/Credit-Card-Debt-statistics/

In the past 25 years the

United States has seen the proliferation of credit card debt. From 1985 to 2010, total consumer debt grew from $355 billion to $2.4 trillion. As a result, the average American citizen owes $7,800 in credit card debt. Why do people use credit cards? Some people use credit cards simply as a matter of convenience, so they don't have to carry cash or personal checks. But many people use credit cards because they do not have enough funds to pay for the things they need or want. In other words, the cash they generate from their salary or wages is not high enough to cover their expenses (such as food, clothing, housing, and entertainment) and make necessary debt payments (such as monthly car and student loan payments). In the end, credit card debt is incurred because cash inflows are not high enough to cover cash outflows.

Just as cash flows are important to personal finances, they are equally important to a company's finances. To better understand the financial health of a company, we must understand how the company generates cash, and how the cash is being used. That's exactly the kind of information that is presented in the statement of cash flows.

As the opening story shows, good cash management is critical to individuals and companies, alike. Managers use cash budgets, as discussed in Chapter 9, to plan for their cash needs. But investors and creditors, who want to understand how the company is generating and using cash, do not have access to internal cash budgets. Rather, they must rely on the company's financial statements to provide them with information on whether the company's cash increased or decreased over the course of the year, and the reasons for the change. In this chapter, we'll discuss how the statement of cash flows presents investors, creditors, and managers with important information on how a company generated and used cash over a given period of time.

What is the Statement of Cash Flows?

Companies prepare four basic financial statements:

1. Income statement
2. Balance sheet
3. Statement of stockholders' equity
4. Statement of cash flows[1]

You are already familiar with the first three statements from your financial accounting course. These statements do not present much information about the company's cash. For example, the balance sheet gives a "snapshot" of the company's ending cash balance, but it does not report *whether* cash increased or decreased during the period or *why*. The **statement of cash flows** is an important and necessary statement because it shows the overall increase or decrease in cash during the period, as well as *how* the company *generated* and *used* cash during the period. Exhibit 13-1 shows the basic format of a statement of cash flows.

EXHIBIT 13-1 Basic Format of the Statement of Cash Flows

SportsTime, Inc. Statement of Cash Flows For the Year Ending December 31, 2012	
Cash provided (or used) by operating activities (itemized list)	$XXX
Cash provided (or used) by investing activities (itemized list)	XX
Cash provided (or used) by financing activities (itemized list)	XX
Net increase (or decrease) in cash	XXX
Cash, beginning of the period	XX
Cash, end of the period	$XXX

Why is cash so important? It is important because anyone involved with the company has certain expectations regarding the company's cash:

- Employees expect payment of their salaries and wages.
- Suppliers expect payment for their products and services.
- Creditors expect to be repaid loans and interest payments.
- Investors expect dividends.
- Governmental taxing authorities expect payment of income and property taxes.

Why is this important?

"The statement of cash flows shows how the company **generated** and **used cash** during the year, enabling **managers, investors, and creditors** to predict whether the company can meet its cash **obligations** in the future."

The statement of cash flows helps all of these stakeholders evaluate how the company has generated and used cash in the past, which in turn helps them predict whether the company will be able meet its cash obligations in the future. It also helps managers understand if the company is generating sufficient cash from its day-to-day operating activities to enable investments in new equipment, new stores, or new businesses. If insufficient cash is being generated from the day-to-day operations of the company to fund these investments, then the company may need to cut back on expenses or planned investments, or consider raising more capital through selling stocks or taking out loans.

[1]Statement of Accounting Standards No. 95 governs cash flow reporting. The standard was produced by the Financial Accounting Standards Board in 1987.

Typically, the statement of cash flows defines "cash" as all cash and cash equivalents. Cash generally includes petty cash, checking, and savings accounts. Cash equivalents include very safe, highly liquid assets that are readily convertible into cash, such as money market funds, certificates of deposit that mature in less than three months, and U.S. treasury bills. Throughout this chapter, any references to cash will include cash and cash equivalents.

Three Types of Activities That Generate and Use Cash

1 Classify cash flows as operating, investing, or financing activities

As Exhibit 13-1 illustrates, the statement of cash flows classifies all business transactions into three different types of activities. These activities are presented on the statement of cash flows in the following order:

1. Operating activities
2. Investing activities
3. Financing activities

Let's take a look at the kind of transactions that would fall under each category.

Why is this important?

"Financial statement readers want to know how much of the company's cash was generated from **day-to-day** company **operations** versus how much was raised by **selling investments** or company stock, or by **borrowing money.** A company that doesn't raise sufficient **cash** from operations won't be able to **survive** in the long-run."

Operating Activities

Operating activities primarily consist of the day-to-day profit-making activities of the company. These activities include such transactions as making or buying inventory, selling inventory, selling services, paying employees, advertising, and so forth. These activities typically affect current asset accounts such as inventory and accounts receivable, as well as current liability accounts such as salaries payable and accounts payable. Operating activities also include *any other activity that affects net income* (not just operating income). Therefore, this category also includes receiving interest income and paying interest expense; receiving dividend income; and paying for income tax expense. Keep the following rule of thumb in mind when deciding if an activity should be classified as an operating activity:[2]

Transactions that affect net income, current assets, and current liabilities are classified as operating activities on the statement of cash flows.

Investing Activities

Investing activities include transactions that involve buying or selling long-term assets. These activities include buying or selling property, plant, or equipment; buying or selling stock in other companies (if the stock is meant to be held for the long term); or loaning money to other companies with the goal of earning interest income from the loan. Keep the following rule of thumb in mind when deciding if an activity should be classified as an investing activity:

Transactions that affect long-term assets are classified as investing activities on the statement of cash flows.

[2]Since the entire statement of cash flows, including cash flows from operating, investing, and financing activities is needed to explain the change in the company's cash account during the year, the change in the cash account is the only current asset account excluded from this rule of thumb.

Financing Activities

Financing activities include transactions that either generate capital for the company or pay it back. These activities include selling company stock, issuing long-term debt (such as notes or bonds), buying back company stock (also known as treasury stock), paying dividends to stockholders, and repaying the principal amount on loans. Keep the following rule of thumb in mind when deciding whether an activity should be classified as a financing activity:

> *Transactions that affect long-term liabilities and stockholders' equity are classified as financing activities on the statement of cash flows.*

Exhibit 13-2 presents a list of common sources and uses of cash and shows how they are classified on the statement of cash flows. We have italicized those items that you may have difficulty remembering because they are not completely intuitive.

EXHIBIT 13-2 Classification of Activities on the Statement of Cash Flows

Operating Activities
(Cash flows related to the primary, day-to-day profit making activities of the company; these activities affect net income, current assets, and current liabilities)

- Cash received from sale of services or merchandise
- ***Cash received from interest income***
- ***Cash received from dividend income***
- Cash paid to purchase inventory
- Cash paid for selling, general, and administrative expenses
- ***Cash paid for interest expense***
- Cash paid for income taxes

Non-cash adjustments to net income (indirect method):

- Depreciation and amortization expense
- Gain or loss on sale of property, plant, or equipment

Investing Activities
(Cash flows related to buying and selling investments; these activities affect long-term assets)

- Cash received from sale of property, plant, or equipment
- Cash received from collection of long-term loans
- Cash received from sale of long-term equity (stock) investments
- Cash paid to purchase property, plant, or equipment
- Cash paid for purchasing long-term equity (stock) investments

Financing Activities
(Cash flows related to generating and repaying capital; these activities affect long-term liabilities and stockholders' equity accounts)

- Cash received from issuing long-term debt (such as notes and bonds)
- Cash received from issuing stock
- Cash received from using a line of credit
- Cash used to pay back long-term debt
- ***Cash used to pay dividends***
- Cash used to buy back company stock (treasury stock)

For example, consider the following:

- Even though interest income and dividend income is earned from investments, they are both classified as cash flows from operating activities because they *affect (increase) net income.*
- Interest expense occurs because the company has borrowed money, so you might think this is a financing activity. However, it is classified as an operating activity because it *affects (decreases) net income.*
- Certain revenues and expenses (such as depreciation) affect net income, yet do not generate or use cash. Under the indirect method, they are used in the operating section of the statement of cash flows to reconcile accrual basis net income back to the cash basis.
- The *payment* of dividends is a distribution of the company's equity (not an expense on the income statement); therefore, it is classified as a financing activity.

Noncash Investing and Financing Activities

Sometimes companies have significant investing or financing activities that do not involve cash. For example, a company may purchase property, plant, or equipment by issuing common stock to the seller, rather than paying cash. Liabilities, such as bonds or notes payable, may be extinguished by converting them to common stock.

Any significant noncash investing or financing activity must be disclosed in a supplementary schedule to the statement of cash flows or in a footnote to the financial statements. Why? Because these activities will affect *future* cash flows, such as the future payment of dividends and interest. Since financial statement readers use the statement of cash flows to make predictions about future cash flows, they need to be made aware of any noncash investing or financing transactions that took place during the year.

Two Methods of Presenting Operating Activities

The operating activities section of the statement of cash flows may be presented using either the direct or indirect method. These different methods only affect the *format* of the presentation. Both methods result in the *same* dollar figure for the total cash provided by operating activities. Keep in mind that these methods only affect the operating activities section and have no bearing on the investing or financing sections of the statement.

Direct Method

The **direct method** lists the receipt and payment of cash for specific operating activities. For example, the operating activities would list such line items as the following:

- Cash receipts from customers
- Cash payments for inventory
- Cash payments for salaries and wages
- Cash payments for insurance

In essence, the direct method lists many of the same items shown on the income statement, but calculates them on a cash basis, rather than accrual basis. Recall that the **accrual basis of accounting** requires that revenues are recorded when they are earned (when the sale takes place), rather than when cash is received on the sale. Likewise, expenses are recorded when they are incurred, rather than when they are paid. These timing differences give rise to current assets such as accounts receivable and current liabilities such as wages payable. Thus, accrual based net income almost always differs from the cash basis.

Indirect Method

The **indirect method** begins with the company's net income, which is prepared on an accrual basis, and then reconciles it back to the cash basis through a series of adjustments. This method reconciles net income to the cash basis by adjusting for 1) noncash revenues (such as gains on the sale of property, plant and equipment) or expenses (such as depreciation or amortization), and 2) changes in the current asset and current liability accounts. For example, an increase in accounts receivable indicates that more sales were made than were collected. Therefore, an adjustment would be made to net income to reflect this increase in accounts receivable.

Which Method is Most Commonly Used?

Recent surveys show that over 98% of companies currently use the indirect method.[3] Why? Because it is easier and, therefore, less costly to prepare. Furthermore, if a company chooses to use the direct method, it must also provide a supplementary schedule reconciling net income to the cash basis. In essence, a company that chooses to use the direct method must also perform the indirect method for a supplementary disclosure.

Currently, the Financial Accounting Standards Board (FASB) and International Accounting Standards Board (IASB) *encourage* companies to use the direct method. However, the boards have jointly proposed that companies be *required* to use the direct method in the future.[4] The outcome of this proposal is uncertain at this time. The second half of the chapter will illustrate both the indirect and direct methods.

Sustainability and the Statement of Cash Flows

You've just learned that *all* business transactions must be classified into one of three different types of activities for the statement of cash flows. A company's sustainability initiatives will also fall into the same three categories. Some examples are listed next.

Operating Activities—affect net income, current assets and current liabilities

- Expenses related to researching and developing sustainable products and packaging
- Income generated from selling scrap and recyclable materials
- Income and expenses related to producing, marketing, and distributing new "green" products

Investing Activities—affect long-term assets

See Exercises E13-20A and E13-30A

- Investments in solar paneling or wind turbines
- Investments in environmentally-friendly production equipment
- Investments in LEED certified buildings

Financing Activities—affect long-term liabilities and owner's equity

- Stocks issued to raise capital for projects involving biofuel production
- Bonds issued to raise capital for investing in a fleet of hybrid delivery vehicles

Historically, "green" activities such as those listed, have not been shown as separate line items in the statement of cash flows. Rather, they have been presented combined with other similar activities. For example, all capital investments, whether environmentally friendly or not, have been presented as "investments in plant and equipment." However, to provide more detailed information to both internal and external users, management may want to consider separately disclosing cash flows related to significant green activities. The disclosures could be made as separate line items on the statement of cash flows (such as the examples listed previously), or as footnotes to the financial statements.

---

[3]American Institute of Certified Public Accountants, *Accounting Trends and Techniques: 2004*, Jersey City, NJ, 2004.

[4]Financial Accounting Standards Board, *Financial Accounting Series Discussion Paper Number 1630-100: Preliminary Views on Financial Statement Presentation*, Norwalk, CT, October 16, 2008, Paragraph 3.70–3.83.

Decision Guidelines

Statement of Cash Flows

The following guidelines present some decisions that need to be made before preparing the statement of cash flows.

Decision	Guidelines
What financial statements should my company prepare?	A set of financial statements includes the 1) income statement, 2) balance sheet, 3) statement of stockholders' equity, and 4) statement of cash flows.
How should my company define "cash" for the statement of cash flows?	The statement of cash flows usually explains changes in both cash and cash equivalents. Cash and cash equivalents include petty cash, checking and savings account deposits, money markets, short-term certificates of deposit, and U.S. treasury bills.
What types of cash flows should be presented on the statement of cash flows?	All cash flows must be classified into one of the following three categories: 1. Cash flows from operating activities 2. Cash flows from investing activities 3. Cash flows from financing activities
How can I tell if a cash transaction should be classified as an operating activity?	Cash flows from operating activities include the day-to-day profit-making activities of the firm. These activities include any transactions that affect net income (including interest income and expense, and dividend income), current assets, or current liabilities.
How can I tell if a cash transaction should be classified as an investing activity?	Cash flows from investing activities include all transactions that affect long-term assets.
How can I tell if a cash transaction should be classified as a financing activity?	Cash flows from financing activities include transactions that generate capital for the company or pay it back. These transactions affect long-term liabilities and stockholders' equity.
My company purchased a piece of land in exchange for company stock. Since the transaction didn't affect cash, do we include it on the statement of cash flows?	Even though the transaction didn't affect cash this year, it needs to be disclosed because it will affect *future* cash flows. All significant non-cash investing or financing transactions need to be disclosed in either a supplementary schedule to the statement of cash flows or in a footnote to the financial statements.
Should my company use the direct or indirect method for presenting the cash flows from operating activities?	Either method is *currently* acceptable. However, if you use the direct method, you must also present a supplementary schedule that is much like the information presented using the indirect method.

SUMMARY PROBLEM 1

Classify each of the following transactions as an operating, investing, or financing activity.

1. Payment of salaries
2. Purchase of land
3. Issuance of stock
4. Repayment of long-term notes
5. Payment of rent
6. Collection of sales revenue
7. Conversions of bonds payable to common stock
8. Loss on the sale of equipment
9. Purchase of another company's stock (to be held for more than one year)
10. Purchase of merchandise inventory
11. Proceeds from the sale of a building
12. Payment of dividends
13. Collection of interest income
14. Purchase of treasury stock (company buys back its own stock)
15. Payment of interest on long-term debt

SOLUTION

Transaction	Type of Activity
1. Payment of salaries	Operating
2. Purchase of land	Investing
3. Issuance of stock	Financing
4. Repayment of long-term notes	Financing
5. Payment of rent	Operating
6. Collection of sales revenue	Operating
7. Conversion of bonds payable to common stock	Noncash Financing and Investing; must be disclosed even though it doesn't use cash
8. Loss on the sale of equipment	Operating
9. Purchase of another company's stock (to be held for more than one year)	Investing
10. Purchase of merchandise inventory	Operating
11. Proceeds from the sale of a building	Investing
12. Payment of dividends	Financing
13. Collection of interest income	Operating
14. Purchase of treasury stock (company buys back its own stock)	Financing
15. Payment of interest on long-term debt	Operating

How is the Statement of Cash Flows Prepared Using the Indirect Method?

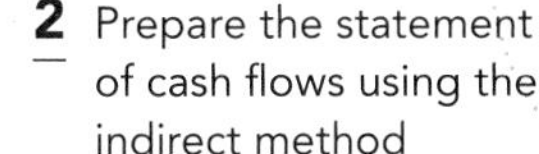

2 Prepare the statement of cash flows using the indirect method

In this section, we'll use the indirect method to prepare the statement of cash flows for SportsTime, Inc., a regional retailer of sporting goods equipment.

Information Needed to Prepare the Statement of Cash Flows

In order to prepare the statement of cash flows, the following company information is needed:

1. Income statement for the current year
2. Comparative balance sheets (balance sheets for the end of the current year and prior year)
3. Miscellaneous additional information relating to investing and financing transactions

Exhibit 13-3 presents SportsTime's income statement while Exhibit 13-4 presents the company's comparative balance sheets. Additional information about the company's investing and financing transactions will be presented as needed throughout the remainder of the chapter.

Why is this important?

"**Most companies** currently use the **indirect method**, so understanding how it is prepared and **interpreted** is crucial. This method highlights the **differences** between accrual based net income and the **cash basis**."

EXHIBIT 13-3 Income Statement

SportsTime, Inc.
Income Statement
For the Year Ended December 31, 2012

Sales revenue		$9,500,000
Cost of goods sold		7,125,000
Gross profit		2,375,000
Operating expenses:		
Salaries and wages expense	$580,000	
Insurance expense	25,000	
Depreciation expense	142,000	
Other operating expenses	230,000	977,000
Operating income		1,398,000
Other income and expenses:		
Interest expense	60,000	
Gain on sale of PP&E	1,000	59,000
Income before taxes		1,339,000
Income tax expense		401,700
Net income		$ 937,300

Preparing the Cash Flows from Operating Activities

The indirect method requires that we begin the operating activities section with the company's accrual based net income, which is found on the income statement. Then, we make all adjustments needed to convert, or reconcile net income back to a cash basis. These adjustments will include the following:

- Noncash expenses and revenues (found on the income statement)
- Changes in the current asset accounts (found on the comparative balance sheets)
- Changes in the current liability accounts (found on the comparative balance sheets)

EXHIBIT 13-4 Comparative Balance Sheets

SportsTime, Inc.
Balance Sheets
December 31, 2012 and 2011

	2012	2011	Change Increase/ (Decrease)
Assets			
Current assets:			
Cash	$ 203,500	$ 125,000	$ 78,500
Accounts receivable	365,000	330,000	35,000
Inventory	632,000	657,000	(25,000)
Prepaid insurance	20,000	15,000	5,000
Total current assets	1,220,500	1,127,000	
Property, plant, and equipment	3,415,000	2,900,000	515,000
Less accumulated depreciation	(499,000)	(380,000)	119,000
Investments	285,000	185,000	100,000
Total assets	$4,421,500	$3,832,000	
Liabilities			
Current liabilities:			
Accounts payable	$ 245,000	$ 285,000	(40,000)
Wages payable	57,000	48,500	8,500
Interest payable	3,000	8,000	(5,000)
Income taxes payable	146,700	120,000	26,700
Other accrued expenses payable	15,500	28,500	(13,000)
Total current liabilities	467,200	490,000	
Long-term liabilities	550,000	750,000	(200,000)
Total liabilities	1,017,200	1,240,000	
Stockholders' equity			
Common stock	1,100,000	1,100,000	0
Retained earnings	2,304,300	1,492,000	812,300
Total stockholders' equity	3,404,300	2,592,000	
Total liabilities and equity	$4,421,500	$3,832,000	

Noncash Expenses

Depreciation expense is perhaps the most common noncash expense found on the income statement. Depreciation is simply the systematic write-off of the cost of plant and equipment over time. No cash actually trades hands when depreciation expense is recorded. Since depreciation expense reduced net income by $142,000 (Exhibit 13-3), but didn't use cash, we must *add it back* to net income in order to convert net income back to the cash basis. Therefore, we begin our statement of cash flows by adding back depreciation expense, as shown (in blue) in Exhibit 13-5.

We would also add back any amortization of intangible assets or depletion of natural resources for the same reason. SportsTime's income statement does not show any amortization or depletion expense, so these adjustments are not needed.

Noncash Revenues

The income statement in Exhibit 13-3 shows a $1,000 gain on the sale of property, plant, and equipment (PP&E). A gain on the sale arises when the equipment is sold for *more* than its net book value. The **net book value** is the original cost of the equipment less its accumulated depreciation. Let's assume that SportsTime sold some old display shelves and dressing room chairs for $3,000. Company records indicate that this equipment originally

EXHIBIT 13-5 Adjusting Net Income for Depreciation Expense

SportsTime, Inc. Statement of Cash Flows—Indirect Method For the Year Ended December 31, 2012		
Operating Activities		
Net income		$937,300
Adjustments to reconcile net income to cash basis:		
Depreciation expense	$142,000	

cost $25,000 and that at the time of sale, accumulated depreciation on this equipment totaled $23,000. The gain on sale would have been calculated as follows:

Sale price of equipment		$3,000
Original cost of the equipment	$25,000	
Less: Accumulated depreciation	23,000	
Net book value of equipment		2,000
Gain on sale		$1,000

The actual cash received on the sale, $3,000, will be reported as a source of cash in the investing section of the statement of cash flows. But the $1,000 gain, which increased accrual based net income, does not actually represent cash received. Therefore, the $1,000 gain must be *deducted* from net income to convert it back to the cash basis. Exhibit 13-6 incorporates this gain (in blue) on our developing statement of cash flows.

EXHIBIT 13-6 Adjusting Net Income for Gain on Sale

SportsTime, Inc. Statement of Cash Flows—Indirect Method For the Year Ended December 31, 2012		
Operating Activities:		
Net income		$937,300
Adjustments to reconcile net income to cash basis:		
Depreciation expense	$142,000	
Gain on sale of equipment	(1,000)	

Conversely, a loss on the sale of equipment would have occurred if the equipment was sold for *less* than the equipment's net book value. Since a loss doesn't represent a payout of cash (in fact, cash is received for the sale) we would *add back the loss* to net income to convert it back to the cash basis.

Changes in Current Asset Accounts

The next step in preparing the statement of cash flows is to adjust net income for any changes in current asset accounts. The comparative balance sheets in Exhibit 13-4 shows that the balance in all current asset accounts changed over the year. Remember, the entire statement of cash flows is attempting to explain the change in the cash account. So, we will need to analyze the changes to all current asset accounts *except* for cash.

Let's first look at those accounts that had *increases* over the course of the year: accounts receivable and prepaid insurance.

ACCOUNTS RECEIVABLE Exhibit 13-4 shows a $35,000 increase in accounts receivable. An *increase* in accounts receivable indicates that *more* sales were made than were collected. To reconcile net income back to the cash basis, we need to subtract any sales that were not yet collected in cash. To do so, we *subtract* the $35,000 *increase* in accounts receivable from net income.

PREPAID INSURANCE Exhibit 13-4 shows a $5,000 increase in prepaid insurance. An *increase* in prepaid insurance indicates that the company *paid more* for insurance than was recorded as insurance expense. To reconcile net income to the cash basis, we need to subtract more than was expensed. To do so, we *subtract* the $5,000 *increase* in prepaid insurance from net income.

Exhibit 13-7 illustrates the general rule for reconciling net income to cash for *increases* in any current asset accounts.

EXHIBIT 13-7 General Rule for Increases in Current Asset Accounts

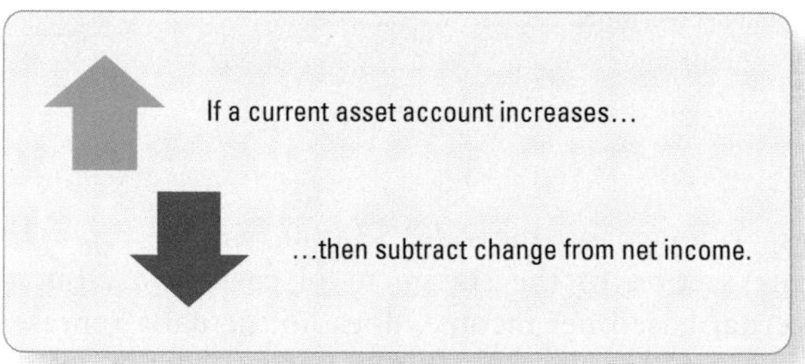

Now let's look at an example of a current asset account that decreased over the course of the year.

INVENTORY Exhibit 13-4 shows a $25,000 *decrease* in inventory. The *decrease* in inventory indicates that the company sold more merchandise inventory than it purchased. Its inventory level shrunk. So the Cost of Goods Sold expensed on the income statement is greater than the cash paid to purchase the merchandise from the company's suppliers. To reconcile net income back to the cash basis, we need to subtract less than the amount expensed. To do so, we *add back* the $25,000 *decrease* in inventory to net income.

Exhibit 13-8 illustrates the general rule for reconciling net income to cash for *decreases* in any current asset accounts.

EXHIBIT 13-8 General Rule for Decreases in Current Asset Accounts

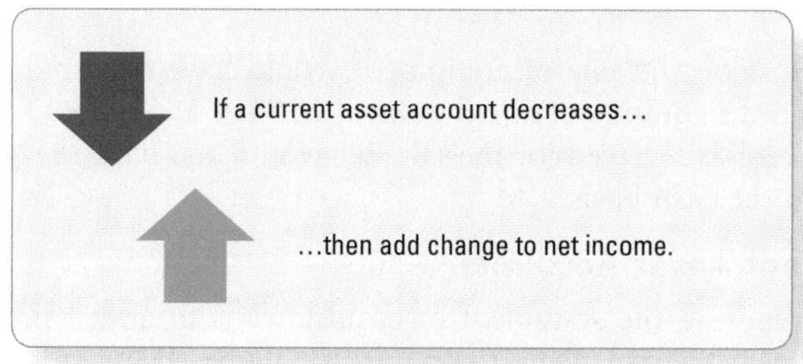

The general rule of thumb for current asset accounts is as follows:

- *If a current asset account* ***increases,*** *then* ***subtract*** *the change from net income.*
- *If a current asset account* ***decreases,*** *then* ***add*** *the change to net income.*

Notice that for changes in current assets, we reconcile net income back to the cash basis by adjusting in the *opposite* direction.

Exhibit 13-9 illustrates our developing statement of cash flows after incorporating changes in the current asset accounts (in blue).

EXHIBIT 13-9 Adjusting Net Income for Changes in Current Asset Accounts

SportsTime, Inc.
Statement of Cash Flows—Indirect Method
For the Year Ended December 31, 2012

Operating Activities:		
Net income		$937,300
Adjustments to reconcile net income to cash basis:		
Depreciation expense	$142,000	
Gain on sale of equipment	(1,000)	
Increase in accounts receivable	(35,000)	
Decrease in inventory	25,000	
Increase in prepaid insurance	(5,000)	

Changes in Current Liability Accounts

Now let's take a look at one current liability account that decreased over the course of the year (interest payable), and another that increased (wages payable).

INTEREST PAYABLE Exhibit 13-4 shows a $5,000 *decrease* in interest payable. A *decrease* in interest payable indicates that the company paid out more than it expensed for interest expense during the year. Therefore, to reconcile net income to the cash basis, we need to subtract *more* than was expensed. To do so, we subtract the $5,000 decrease in interest payable from net income.

The general rule of thumb for *decreases* in current liabilities is pictured in Exhibit 13-10.

EXHIBIT 13-10 General Rule for Decreases in Current Liability Accounts

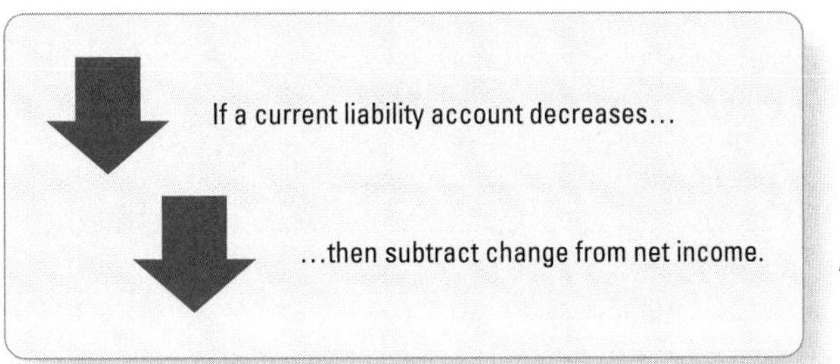

WAGES PAYABLE Exhibit 13-4 shows a $8,500 *increase* in wages payable. An *increase* in wages payable indicates that more wage expense was incurred than was paid. To reconcile net income to the cash basis, we need to subtract *less* than was expensed. Therefore, we need to add back the $8,500 increase in wages payable to net income.

The general rule of thumb for *increases* in current liabilities is pictured in Exhibit 13-11.

EXHIBIT 13-11 General Rule for Increases in Current Liability Accounts

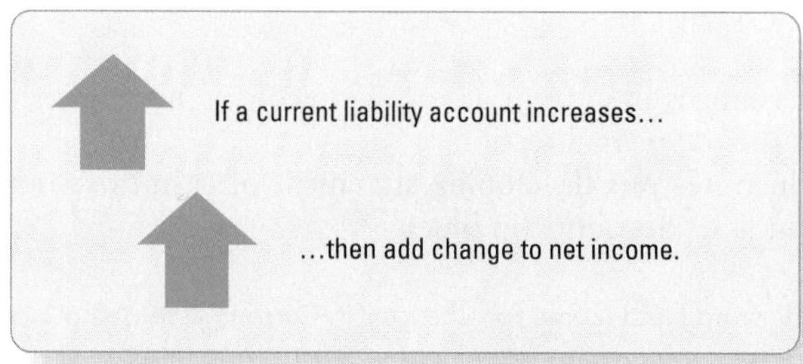

The general rule of thumb for current liability accounts is as follows:

- *If a current liability account* ***increases,*** *then* ***add*** *the change to net income.*
- *If a current liability account* ***decreases,*** *then* ***subtract*** *the change from net income.*

Notice that for changes in current liabilities, we reconcile net income back to the cash basis by adjusting in the *same* direction. The adjustments for changes in current liability accounts are pictured in blue in Exhibit 13-12.

Interpreting Cash Flows from Operating Activities

Exhibit 13-12 shows the completed operating activities section of the statement of cash flows. As you can see, the day-to-day profit making activities of the company have generated over $1 million in cash during the year. That's a positive sign—a company that is not providing cash from operating activities can't survive in the long-run. It also shows that cash was drained by allowing accounts receivable to increase and by paying down many of the company's current liabilities (such as accounts payable, interest payable, and other accrued expenses). Finally, this reconciliation shows that cash provided by operations was $103,200 higher than net income, once again showing that accrual based net income differs from the cash basis.

EXHIBIT 13-12 Cash Flows from Operating Activities (Indirect Method)

SportsTime, Inc.
Statement of Cash Flows—Operating Activities (Indirect Method)
For the Year Ended December 31, 2012

Operating Activities:		
Net income		$937,300
Adjustments to reconcile net income to cash basis:		
Depreciation expense	$142,000	
Gain on sale of equipment	(1,000)	
Increase in accounts receivable	(35,000)	
Decrease in inventory	25,000	
Increase in prepaid insurance	(5,000)	
Decrease in accounts payable	(40,000)	
Increase in wages payable	8,500	
Decrease in interest payable	(5,000)	
Increase in income taxes payable	26,700	
Decrease in other accrued expenses payable	(13,000)	103,200
Net cash provided by operating activities		1,040,500

Now that we have prepared the operating section (using the indirect method), let's take a look at how we prepare the investing and financing sections.

Preparing the Cash Flows from Investing Activities

Recall that transactions affecting long-term asset accounts are classified as investing activities. So the first step in preparing the investing section is to determine whether any changes occurred in the long-term assets accounts during the year. The comparative balance sheets presented in Exhibit 13-4 show changes in three long-term asset accounts:

1. Property, Plant, and Equipment—increase of $515,000
2. Accumulated Depreciation (a contra asset to Property, Plant, and Equipment)—increase of $119,000
3. Investments—increase of $100,000

After noting these changes, we would need to delve into the company's records (such as the general journal) to find more information about these investing activities. The following additional information was found:

a. Equipment originally costing $25,000 was sold for $3,000. The equipment had accumulated depreciation of $23,000, resulting in a gain of $1,000.

b. The company purchased $100,000 of stock in XYZ company. No stock investments were sold during the year.

Now let's see how we use this information to sort out investment activities that took place during the year.

Property, Plant, and Equipment

By analyzing the change in this account, we can figure out how much cash the company paid for new property, plant, and equipment (PP&E) during the year:

Beginning balance, PP&E (from Exhibit 13-4)	$2,900,000
Plus: Purchases of PP&E	?
Less: Original cost of equipment sold (from the additional information given)	(25,000)
Ending balance, PP&E (from Exhibit 13-4)	$3,415,000

We can illustrate this relationship in the form of an equation, and then solve for the unknown amount:

Beginning PP&E	+	Purchases of PP&E	−	PPE sold	=	Ending PP&E
$2,900,000	+	???		− $25,000	=	$3,415,000

We can rearrange the equation as follows:

Purchases of PP&E = $3,415,000 + $25,000 − $2,900,000

Solving the equation yields the following:

Purchases of PP&E = $540,000

On the statement of cash flows, we will show that $540,000 was used to purchase new property, plant, and equipment. Additionally, the sale of the old equipment for $3,000 will be shown as a *receipt* of cash. Notice that the statement of cash flows doesn't just show the net change in the Property, Plant, and Equipment account. Rather, the company needs to show separate line items for new investments purchased and old investments sold.

Accumulated Depreciation

This account is reconciled as follows:

Beginning balance, Accumulated depreciation (Exhibit 13-4)	$380,000
Plus: Depreciation expense (Exhibit 13-3)	142,000
Less: Accumulated depreciation on sold equipment (from the additional information given)	(23,000)
Ending balance, Accumulated depreciation (Exhibit 13-4)	$499,000

We already accounted for the depreciation expense as an adjustment to net income in the operating activities section of the statement of cash flows. Likewise, the accumulated depreciation on the sold equipment was taken into account in calculating the gain on sale. This too, became an adjustment to net income in the operating activities section. Since we have completely reconciled the change in this account and have already made the necessary adjustments, no other adjustments are needed.

Investments

Changes in long-term investments are analyzed as follows:

Beginning balance, Investments (Exhibit 13-4)	$185,000
Plus: Purchases of stock investments (from the additional information given)	?
Less: Sale of stock investments	?
Ending balance, Investments (Exhibit 13-4)	$285,000

According to the additional information given, SportsTime purchased $100,000 of new stock investments during the year, and did not sell any. Therefore, the investment account is completely reconciled as follows:

Beginning investments	+	Purchases of investments	−	Investments sold	=	Ending investments
$185,000	+	$100,000	−	$0	=	$285,000

Any purchase or sale of long-term investments needs to be listed *separately* on the statement of cash flows. Keep in mind that if the company had sold some investments for an amount that differed from the original purchase price, a gain or loss would have resulted. This gain or loss would be shown as an adjustment to net income in the operating section of the statement, much like a gain or loss on the sale of property, plant, or equipment.

Now that we have analyzed the changes in each long-term asset account, we can prepare the investing section of the statement of cash flows. Exhibit 13-13 shows that the company used much of the cash it generated from operations ($1,040,500, from Exhibit 13-12) to pay for new investments in property, plant, and equipment ($540,000) and new stock investments ($100,000).

EXHIBIT 13-13 Investing Activities Section of the Statement of Cash Flows

SportsTime, Inc.
Statement of Cash Flows—Investing Activities Section
For the Year Ended December 31, 2012

Investing Activities:		
Cash used to purchase property, plant, and equipment	$(540,000)	
Proceeds from the sale of equipment	3,000	
Cash used to purchase investments in stock	(100,000)	
Net cash used by investing activities		(637,000)

Preparing the Cash Flows from Financing Activities

Financing activities include transactions that either generate capital for the company or pay it back. Financing activities affect long-term liabilities and owner's equity accounts. The comparative balance sheets shown in Exhibit 13-4 show changes in the company's long-term liabilities, common stock, and retained earnings accounts. We'll have to analyze the changes in each of these accounts to determine the cash provided and used by financing activities. We'll also need the following information obtained from company records.

a. $100,000 of new bonds were issued during the year.
b. $300,000 of bonds were repaid during the year.
c. The board of directors declared cash dividends of $125,000 during the year.

Long-Term Liabilities

Any change in long-term liabilities can be explained either by new borrowings (issuance of notes or bonds payable) or the repayment of principal on existing debt:

Beginning balance, Long-term liabilities (Exhibit 13-4)	$750,000
Plus: Cash proceeds from new bond issuance	?
Less: Repayment of principal on existing debt	?
End balance, Long-term liabilities (Exhibit 13-4)	$550,000

The additional information provided reconciles this account as follows:

Beginning long-term liabilities	+	Bond issuance	−	Repayments of principal	=	Ending long-term liabilities
$750,000	+	$100,000	−	$300,000	=	$550,000

We'll need to show the issuance and repayments separately on the statement of cash flows.

Common Stock

There was no change in the common stock account on the balance sheet (Exhibit 13-4); therefore, we can conclude that no transactions involving common stock took place during the year.

Retained Earnings

Retained earnings represents the cumulative earnings of a company, less distributions to the company's owners. We analyze the retained earnings account as follows:

Beginning balance, Retained earnings (Exhibit 13-4)	$1,492,000
Plus: Net income (Exhibit 13-3)	937,300
Less: Dividends declared during the year (from the additional information given)	(125,000)
Ending balance, Retained earnings (Exhibit 13-4)	$2,304,300

Since there was no dividends payable shown on the balance sheet, we can conclude that all dividends declared during the year ($125,000) were also paid out to stockholders. Remember, dividends are a distribution of capital back to the owners; not an expense on the income statement. Therefore, the dividends paid will be shown as a use of cash in the financing section of the statement of cash flows.

Exhibit 13-14 shows the completed statement of cash flows for SportsTime, prepared using the indirect method. The information provided in the financing section shows that the company used $300,000 for paying down long-term debt, but obtained $100,000 of new debt (perhaps at a lower interest rate). The company used an additional $125,000 to pay dividends to its owners.

EXHIBIT 13-14 Statement of Cash Flows (Indirect Method)

SportsTime, Inc.
Statement of Cash Flows—Indirect Method
For the Year Ended December 31, 2012

Operating Activities:		
Net income		$ 937,300
Adjustments to reconcile net income to cash basis:		
Depreciation expense	$142,000	
Gain on sale of equipment	(1,000)	
Increase in accounts receivable	(35,000)	
Decrease in inventory	25,000	
Increase in prepaid insurance	(5,000)	
Decrease in accounts payable	(40,000)	
Increase in wages payable	8,500	
Decrease in interest payable	(5,000)	
Increase in income taxes payable	26,700	
Decrease in other accrued expenses payable	(13,000)	103,200
Net cash provided by operating activities		1,040,500
Investing Activities:		
Cash used to purchase property, plant, and equipment	(540,000)	
Proceeds from the sale of equipment	3,000	
Cash used to purchase investments in stock	(100,000)	
Net cash used by investing activities		(637,000)
Financing Activities:		
Proceeds from bond issuance	100,000	
Repayment of long-term debt	(300,000)	
Cash payments for dividends	(125,000)	
Net cash used by investing activities		(325,000)
Net increase in cash		78,500
Cash at the beginning of the year		125,000
Cash at the end of the year		$ 203,500

Interpreting the Statement of Cash Flows

The statement of cash flows shown in Exhibit 13-14 presents a detailed explanation of how SportsTime generated and used cash during the year. In summary, we see that a little over \$1 million in cash was generated by the company's day-to-day operating activities. Roughly 61% of this cash was used to purchase new, long-term investments, while 31% was used to decrease company debt and pay dividends. The remaining 8% was added to the company's cash balance, leaving cash \$78,500 higher than it was at the beginning of the year.

Free Cash Flow

Many potential investors calculate the company's free cash flow using the information provided on the statement of cash flows. **Free cash flow** represents the amount of excess cash a business generates after taking into consideration the capital expenditures necessary to maintain its business. This cash can then be used for expansion, to pay dividends, pay down debt, or for any other business purpose (which is why it is called "free"). Essentially, it is the cash generated from the company's core business that is "left over" after paying bills and making capital expenditures. Free cash flow is calculated as follows:

Free cash flow = Cash flow from operating activities − Capital expenditures

Using the information provided in Exhibit 13-14, we can calculate SportsTime's free cash flow as follows:

= \$1,040,500 − \$540,000
= \$500,500

The presence of free cash flow means that SportsTime has the ability to expand, produce new products, pay dividends, buy back treasury stock, or reduce its debt. Potential investors place high value on a company's ability to generate free cash flow and often use it as a means of valuing stock.

Recap: Steps to Preparing the Statement of Cash Flows Using the Indirect Method

Exhibit 13-15 summarizes the steps used to create a statement of cash flows using the indirect method.

EXHIBIT 13-15 Steps for Using the Indirect Method

Step 1. Begin the operating section with the company's net income and add back any noncash expenses (such as depreciation or losses on the sale of property, plant, and equipment) and subtract any noncash revenues (such as gains on the sale of property, plant, or equipment). This information is found on the company's income statement.

Step 2. Adjust net income for all changes in current asset and current liability accounts (other than the Cash account) that are found on the company's comparative balance sheet:

- **Add back** decreases in current asset accounts and increases in current liability accounts.
- **Subtract** increases in current asset accounts and decreases in current liability accounts.

Step 3. Prepare the investing section by analyzing the changes in all long-term asset accounts found on the company's comparative balance sheet. Separately list all cash transactions that took place during the year affecting these accounts (such as buying and selling property). Any gains or losses on sales, depreciation, or amortization of these assets has already been accounted for in the operating section.

Step 4. Prepare the financing section by analyzing the changes in all long-term liability and equity accounts found on the company's comparative balance sheet. Separately list all cash transactions that took place during the year affecting these accounts (such as issuing new debt or paying down existing debt, selling stock, buying treasury stock, or paying dividends).

Step 5. Present a subtotal of the amount of cash provided or used by each of the three types of activities (operating, investing, and financing). Use the subtotals to find the overall increase or decrease in cash during the year. Then add the increase to (or subtract the decrease from) the company's beginning cash balance to arrive at the ending cash balance shown on the company's balance sheet.

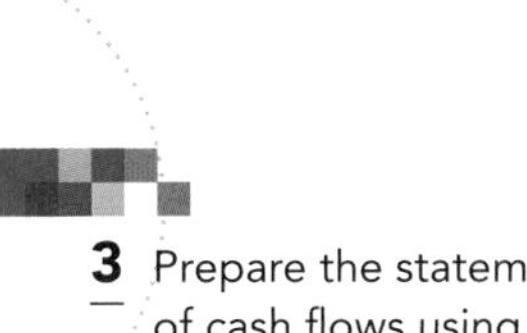

How is the Statement of Cash Flows Prepared Using the Direct Method?

3 Prepare the statement of cash flows using the direct method

In this section, we'll prepare the statement of cash flows using the direct method. Keep in mind that the choice of method (indirect versus direct) only affects the operating activities section of the statement of cash flows. The investing and financing sections are the same regardless of the method used.

Overview

The direct method lists the receipt and payment of cash for specific operating activities. For example, the operating activities would list such line items as follows:

- Cash receipts from customers
- Cash payments (to suppliers) for purchase of inventory
- Cash payments (to employees) for salaries and wages

In essence, the direct method lists many of the same items shown on the income statement, but calculates them on a cash, rather than accrual basis. Exhibit 13-16 shows SportsTime's statement of cash flow using the direct method. Notice the reference numbers (1–7) provided on the right-hand side of the schedule. These reference numbers are only provided for the sake of instruction, and are never included on an actual statement of cash flows. In the following section, we'll show the supporting calculations for each referenced line item on the statement.

Why is this important?

"In the **future**, the **FASB** and **IASB** may require companies to use the **direct method**. This method shows, in a straightforward manner, what the company **received and paid cash** for during the year."

EXHIBIT 13-16 Statement of Cash Flows (Direct Method)

SportsTime, Inc.
Statement of Cash Flows—Direct Method
For the Year Ended December 31, 2012

Operating Activities:			***Ref.**
Cash receipts from customers	$ 9,465,000		(1)
Cash payments for inventory	(7,140,000)		(2)
Cash payments for insurance	(30,000)		(3)
Cash payments for salaries and wages	(571,500)		(4)
Cash payments for interest expense	(65,000)		(5)
Cash payments for income taxes	(375,000)		(6)
Cash payments for other operating expenses	(243,000)		(7)
Net cash provided by operating activities		$1,040,500	
Investing Activities:			
Cash used to purchase property, plant, and equipment	(540,000)		
Proceeds from the sale of equipment	3,000		
Cash used to purchase investments in stock	(100,000)		
Net cash used by investing activities		(637,000)	
Financing Activities:			
Proceeds from bond issuance	100,000		
Repayment of long-term debt	(300,000)		
Cash payments for dividends	(125,000)		
Net cash used by investing activities		(325,000)	
Net increase in cash and cash equivalents		78,500	
Cash and cash equivalents at the beginning of the year		125,000	
Cash and cash equivalents at the end of the year		$ 203,500	

*Reference numbers are provided for the sake of instruction only, and are never actually shown on the statement of cash flows.

Notice that the cash provided by operating activities ($1,040,500) is the *same* as we found using the indirect method (shown in Exhibit 13-14).

Determining Cash Payments and Receipts

The best way to make sure you've captured all cash transactions from operating activities is to analyze *every* current asset and current liability account shown on the balance sheet (Exhibit 13-4), and incorporate related information from the income statement (Exhibit 13-3) as necessary. Let's start with current assets.

(1) Cash Receipts from Customers

To determine the amount of cash received from customers we must analyze accounts receivable. Accounts receivable increases when sales are made and decreases when cash is collected:

Beginning balance, Accounts receivable (Exhibit 13-4)	$ 330,000
Plus: Sales revenue (from income statement)	9,500,000
Less: Cash collections of accounts receivable	?
Ending balance, Accounts receivable (Exhibit 13-4)	$ 365,000

Solving for the unknown, we determine that cash collections of sales must be $9,465,000.

(2) Cash Payments for Inventory

The next current asset account on the balance sheet is inventory. We'll use this account, along with accounts payable (current liability), to figure out how much cash was used to purchase inventory. First let's think about what affects the inventory account: The account increases for the purchase of inventory, and decreases for the cost of goods sold. Therefore, we can establish the following relationship:

Beginning balance, Inventory (Exhibit 13-4)	$ 657,000
Plus: Purchases of inventory	?
Less: Cost of goods sold (Exhibit 13-3)	(7,125,000)
Ending balance, Inventory (Exhibit 13-4)	$ 632,000

Solving for the unknown, we determine that purchases of inventory must have been $7,100,000.

However, did the company pay for all of these purchases during the year? We'll only know by investigating the changes in accounts payable (we assume SportsTime uses accounts payable only for inventory purchases):

Beginning balance, Accounts payable (Exhibit 13-4)	$ 285,000
Plus: Purchases of inventory	7,100,000
Less: Cash payments for inventory	(?)
Ending balance, Accounts payable (Exhibit 13-4)	$ 245,000

Solving for the unknown, we determine that payments for inventory must have been $7,140,000.

(3) Cash Payments for Insurance

The next current asset on the balance sheet is prepaid insurance. This account will increase for purchases of insurance, and decrease as a result of recording insurance expense:

Beginning balance, Prepaid insurance (Exhibit 13-4)	$ 15,000
Plus: Payments for insurance	?
Less: Insurance expense (Exhibit 13-3)	(25,000)
Ending balance, Prepaid insurance (Exhibit 13-4)	$ 20,000

Solving for the unknown, we determine that payments for insurance must have been $30,000.

We've analyzed all of the current asset accounts found on the company's balance sheet, so now we turn our attention to the current liability accounts shown in Exhibit 13-4. The first current liability shown is accounts payable. We've already analyzed that account when calculating the amount of inventory purchased. The remaining current liability accounts include wages payable, interest payable, income taxes payable, and other accrued expenses payable. We'll examine each of these next.

(4) Cash Payments for Salaries and Wages

Wages payable increases when we record salaries and wages expense, and decreases when the company pays its employees:

Beginning balance, Wages payable (Exhibit 13-4)	$ 48,500
Plus: Salaries and wages expense (Exhibit 13-3)	580,000
Less: Payments for salaries and wages	(?)
Ending balance, Wages payable (Exhibit 13-4)	$ 57,000

Solving for the unknown, we determine that payments for salaries and wages must have been $571,500.

(5) Cash Payments for Interest Expense

Interest payable increases when we record interest expense, and decreases when the company pays interest:

Beginning balance, Interest payable (Exhibit 13-4)	$ 8,000
Plus: Interest expense (Exhibit 13-3)	60,000
Less: Payments for interest	(?)
Ending balance, Interest payable (Exhibit 13-4)	$ 3,000

Solving for the unknown, we determine that payments for interest expense must have been $65,000.

(6) Cash Payments for Income Taxes

Income taxes payable increases when we record income tax expense, and decreases when the company pays income taxes:

Beginning balance, Income taxes payable (Exhibit 13-4)	$120,000
Plus: Income tax expense (Exhibit 13-3)	401,700
Less: Payments for income taxes	(?)
Ending balance, Income taxes payable (Exhibit 13-4)	$146,700

Solving for the unknown, we determine that payments for income taxes must have been $375,000.

(7) Cash Payments for Other Operating Expenses

SportsTime's income statement lists many of their operating expenses separately: salaries and wages expense, insurance expense, and depreciation expense. It then lumps together its remaining operating expenses, as shown in Exhibit 13-3. "Other operating expenses" would include such expenses as rent, utilities, telephone and internet, supplies, and so forth. SportsTime records liabilities for these expenses as "other accrued expenses payable":

Beginning balance, Other accrued expenses payable (Exhibit 13-4)	$ 28,500
Plus: Other operating expenses (Exhibit 13-3)	230,000
Less: Payments for other operating expenses	(?)
Ending balance, Other accrued expenses payable (Exhibit 13-4)	$ 15,500

Solving for the unknown, we determine that payments for other operating expenses must have been $243,000.

Cash Flows from Operating Activities

By analyzing each current asset and current liability account, we have figured out the actual cash receipts and cash payments made for each operating activity during the year. After listing each transaction separately (Exhibit 13-16), we see that the cash flows from operating activities totals $1,040,500, just as it did using the indirect method.

Comparing the Direct and Indirect Methods

As you can see, the direct method requires much more analysis than the indirect method. As a result, most companies currently use the indirect method. However, the FASB and IASB have jointly recommended that companies use the direct method because it shows cash receipts and cash payments in a much more straightforward manner. Nonetheless, both methods result in the same *total* amount of cash provided by operating activities (for SportsTime, $1,040,500).

Decision Guidelines

Statement of Cash Flows

Companies have a choice of using the indirect method or direct method. The following decision guidelines provide general guidance for preparing the statement of cash flows using either method.

Decision	Guidelines
What kind of information is needed in order to prepare the statement of cash flows?	The following information is needed: 1. Income statement for the year 2. Balance sheets for the current and prior year (comparative balance sheets) 3. Additional information about investing and financing activities that occurred during the year
If my company uses the indirect method, what adjustments should be shown when reconciling net income to the cash basis?	1. All noncash expenses are ***added back*** to net income. 2. All noncash revenues are ***deducted*** from net income. 3. All changes in current asset and current liability accounts will either be added, or deducted from net income (as indicated below).
To reconcile net income to the cash basis, do we add or subtract changes in current asset accounts? (indirect method)	• *If a current asset account* ***increases****, then* ***subtract*** *the change from net income.* • *If a current asset account* ***decreases****, then* ***add*** *the change to net income.*
To reconcile net income to the cash basis, do we add or subtract changes in current liability accounts? (indirect method)	• *If a current liability account* ***increases****, then* ***add*** *the change to net income.* • *If a current liability account* ***decreases****, then* ***subtract*** *the change from net income.*
What process should be used to prepare the investing section of the statement of cash flows?	You will need to analyze the change in every long-term asset account found on the balance sheet. Purchases and sales of investments need to be disclosed separately on the statement of cash flows. (You can't just show the net change in each account.)
What process should be used to prepare the financing section of the statement of cash flows?	You will need to analyze the change in every long-term liability and owner's equity account found on the balance sheet to determine the financing transactions that took place during the year.
My company has decided to use the direct method. What process should be used to prepare the operating section of the statement of cash flows?	Each current asset and current liability account will need to be analyzed to determine the cash transactions underlying the change in the account. These transactions typically include the following: • Receipts from customers • Payments for inventory • Payments for salaries and wages • Payments for other operating expenses (listed separately, or grouped together, depending on the presentation of expenses in the income statement)

SUMMARY PROBLEM 2

Today's Fashion is a local retailer of trend-setting clothing. The company's income statement and comparative balance sheets are presented below. In addition, the following information was gathered from the company's records:

a. No new debt was issued during the year.
b. Dividends of $200,000 were declared by the board of directors.
c. Equipment with an original cost of $20,000 was sold for $9,000.
The equipment had accumulated depreciation of $15,000 at the time of sale.

Requirement

Prepare the company's statement of cash flows using the indirect method.

Today's Fashion Income Statement For the Year Ended December 31, 2012		
Sales revenue		$4,750,000
Cost of goods sold		3,562,500
Gross profit		1,187,500
Operating expenses:		
Salaries and wages expense	$340,000	
Insurance expense	10,000	
Depreciation expense	75,000	
Other operating expenses	125,000	550,000
Operating income		637,500
Other income and expenses:		
Interest expense	8,000	
Gain on sale of PP&E	4,000	4,000
Income before taxes		633,500
Income tax expense		190,050
Net income		$ 443,450

Today's Fashion
Balance Sheets
December 31, 2012 and 2011

	2012	2011	Change Increase/ (Decrease)
Assets			
Current assets:			
Cash and cash equivalents	$ 187,000	$ 85,000	$102,000
Accounts receivable	37,000	57,000	(20,000)
Inventory	337,500	350,000	(12,500)
Prepaid insurance	5,000	3,000	2,000
Total current assets	566,500	495,000	
Property, plant, and equipment	1,860,000	1,660,000	200,000
Less accumulated depreciation	(310,000)	(250,000)	60,000
Investments	50,000	50,000	0
Total assets	$2,166,500	1,955,000	
Liabilities			
Current liabilities:			
Accounts payable	$ 65,000	$ 85,000	(20,000)
Wages payable	29,000	25,000	4,000
Interest payable	2,000	8,000	(6,000)
Income taxes payable	100,050	85,000	15,050
Other accrued expenses payable	13,000	18,000	(5,000)
Total current liabilities	209,050	221,000	
Long-term liabilities	80,000	100,000	(20,000)
Total liabilities	289,050	321,000	
Stockholders' equity			
Common stock	850,000	850,000	0
Retained earnings	1,027,450	784,000	243,450
Total stockholders' equity	1,877,450	1,634,000	
Total liabilities and equity	$2,166,500	$1,955,000	

SOLUTION

The following steps are taken to prepare the statement of cash flows using the indirect method:

1. We begin the operating section with the company's net income, and add back any noncash expenses (depreciation) and then subtract any noncash revenues (gains on the sale of property, plant, or equipment).
2. We then adjust net income for all changes in current asset and current liability accounts (other than the cash account):
   - We *add* decreases in current asset accounts and increases in current liability accounts.
   - We *subtract* increases in current asset accounts and decreases in current liability accounts.
3. To prepare the investing section, we analyze the changes in all long-term asset accounts. We separately list all cash transactions that took place during the year

(for example, buying and selling property, plant, and equipment or long-term investments). Any gains, losses, depreciation, or amortization of these assets has already been accounted for in the operating section.

4. To prepare the financing section, we analyze the changes in all long-term liability and equity accounts. We separately list all cash transactions that took place during the year (for example, issuing new debt or paying down existing debt, selling stock, buying treasury stock, or paying dividends).

Today's Fashion
Statement of Cash Flows—Indirect Method
For the Year Ended December 31, 2012

Operating Activities:		
Net income		$ 443,450
Adjustments to reconcile net income to cash basis:		
Depreciation expense	$75,000	
Gain on sale of equipment	(4,000)	
Decrease in accounts receivable	20,000	
Decrease in inventory	12,500	
Increase in prepaid insurance	(2,000)	
Decrease in accounts payable	(20,000)	
Increase in wages payable	4,000	
Decrease in interest payable	(6,000)	
Increase in income taxes payable	15,050	
Decrease in other accrued expenses payable	(5,000)	89,550
Net cash provided by operating activities		533,000
Investing Activities:		
Cash used to purchase property, plant, and equipment	(220,000)	
Proceeds from the sale of equipment	9,000	
Net cash used by investing activities		(211,000)
Financing Activities:		
Repayment of long-term debt	(20,000)	
Cash payments for dividends	(200,000)	
Net cash used by investing activities		(220,000)
Net increase in cash		102,000
Cash, beginning of the year		85,000
Cash, end of the year		$ 187,000

Analysis of Investing and Financing Activities:
Property, Plant, and Equipment:

Beginning balance, PP&E	$1,660,000
Plus: Purchases of PP&E	?
Less: Original cost of equipment sold (given)	(20,000)
Ending balance, PP&E	$1,860,000

Solving for the unknown, the company must have purchases of $220,000 of property, plant, and equipment. This will be shown as an investing activity.

Accumulated Depreciation:

Beginning balance, Accumulated depreciation	$250,000
Plus: Depreciation expense	75,000
Less: Accumulated depreciation on sold equipment (given)	(15,000)
Ending balance, Accumulated depreciation	$310,000

The depreciation expense will be shown as an operating activity.

Gain on Sale of Equipment

Sale price of equipment (given)		$9,000
Original cost of the equipment	$20,000	
Less: Accumulated depreciation	15,000	
Net book value of equipment		5,000
Gain on sale		$4,000

The $4,000 gain on sale will be shown as an adjustment to net income in the operating section while the $9,000 cash received will be shown as an investing activity.

Long-Term Liabilities:

Beginning balance, Long-term liabilities	$100,000
Plus: Cash proceeds from new bond issuance (given)	0
Less: Repayment of principal on existing debt	?
End balance, Long-term liabilities	$ 80,000

Solving for the unknown, the company must have repaid $20,000 of principal on the existing long-term debt. This will be shown as an investing activity.

Retained Earnings:

Beginning balance, Retained earnings	$ 784,000
Plus: Net income	443,450
Less: Dividends declared during the year (given)	(200,000)
Ending balance, Retained earnings	$1,027,450

The payment of dividends will be shown as a financing activity.

END OF CHAPTER

Learning Objectives

- 1 Classify cash flows as operating, investing, or financing activities
- 2 Prepare the statement of cash flows using the indirect method
- 3 Prepare the statement of cash flows using the direct method

Accounting Vocabulary

Accrual Basis of Accounting. (p. 781) Revenues are recorded when they are earned (when the sale takes place), rather than when cash is received on the sale. Likewise, expenses are recorded when they are incurred, rather than when they are paid.

Cash Equivalents. (p. 779) Very safe, highly liquid assets that are readily convertible into cash, such as money market funds, certificates of deposit that mature in less than three months, and U.S. treasury bills.

Comparative Balance Sheets. (p. 785) A comparison of the balance sheets from the end of two fiscal periods; usually highlighting the changes in each account.

Direct Method. (p. 781) A method of presenting cash flows from operating activities that separately lists the receipt and payment of cash for specific operating activities.

Financing Activities. (p. 780) Activities that either generate capital for the company or pay it back, such as issuing stock or long-term debt, paying dividends, and repaying principal amounts on loans; this includes all activities that affect long-term liabilities and owner's equity.

Free Cash Flow. (p. 795) The amount of excess cash a business generates after taking into consideration the capital expenditures necessary to maintain its business. It is calculated as cash flows from operating activities minus capital expenditures.

Indirect Method. (p. 781) A method of presenting the cash flows from operating activities that begins with the company's net income, which is prepared on an accrual basis, and then reconciles it back to the cash basis through a series of adjustments.

Investing Activities. (p. 779) Activities that involve buying or selling long-term assets, such as buying or selling property, plant, or equipment; buying or selling stock in other companies (if the stock is meant to be held for the long term); or loaning money to other companies with the goal of earning interest income from the loan.

Net Book Value. (p. 786) The original cost of plant or equipment less its accumulated depreciation.

Operating Activities. (p. 779) The day-to-day profit-making activities of the company, such as making or buying inventory, selling inventory, selling services, paying employees, advertising, and so forth; This also includes *any other activity that affects net income* (not just operating income), current assets, or current liabilities.

Statement of Cash Flows. (p. 778) One of the four basic financial statements; the statement shows the overall increase or decrease in cash during the period as well as how the company generated and used cash during the period.

MyAccountingLab

Go to http://myaccountinglab.com/ **for the following Quick Check, Short Exercises, Exercises, and Problems. They are available with immediate grading, explanations of correct and incorrect answers, and interactive media that acts as your own online tutor.**

Quick Check

1. (*Learning Objective 1*) Dividends paid to a company's stockholders would appear on the statement of cash flows as a(n)
   a. increase in the investing section.
   b. decrease in the investing section.
   c. increase in the financing section.
   d. decrease in the financing section.
2. (*Learning Objective 1*) Which of the following would be classified as a decrease in the financing section of the statement of cash flows?
   a. Purchase of new equipment
   b. Issuance of common stock
   c. Retirement of long-term bonds payable
   d. Sale of a building
3. (*Learning Objective 1*) The cash proceeds from a sale of a plant asset would appear on the statement of cash flows as a(n)
   a. increase in the investing section.
   b. decrease in the investing section.
   c. increase in the financing section.
   d. decrease in the financing section.
4. (*Learning Objective 2*) Poppins Corporation prepares its statement of cash flow using the indirect method. Which of the following items would be deducted from net income when calculating the net cash from operations?
   a. A loss on sale of land
   b. A gain on sale of property, plant, and equipment
   c. An increase in salaries payable
   d. A decrease in accounts receivable

5. (*Learning Objective 2*) When preparing the cash provided by operations section of the statement of cash flows using the indirect method, which of the following would provide cash?
   a. A decrease in salaries payable
   b. An increase in accounts receivable
   c. A decrease in long-term investments
   d. An increase in accounts payable

6. (*Learning Objective 2*) When preparing the cash provided by operations section of the statement of cash flows using the indirect method, which of the following would be shown as a use of cash?
   a. A decrease in prepaid insurance
   b. An increase in accounts receivable
   c. An increase in salaries payable
   d. A decrease in property, plant, and equipment

7. (*Learning Objective 2*) An increase in the Taxes Payable account from the beginning of the year to the end of year would be what type of adjustment to "net cash provided by operations" if the company uses the indirect method when preparing its statement of cash flows?
   a. Would not affect "net cash provided by operations"
   b. A decrease to "net cash provided by operations"
   c. An increase to "net cash provided by operations"
   d. Unable to determine without the amount of the cash paid for taxes

8. (*Learning Objective 3*) Allyson Corporation uses the indirect method to prepare its statement of cash flows. If the "net cash provided by operations" on its statement was $37,500, what would the net cash provided by operations using the direct method be?
   a. Less than $37,500
   b. $37,500
   c. More than $37,500
   d. Cannot be determined from the information provided

9. (*Learning Objective 3*) Sacco Pretzel Company uses the direct method to prepare its statement of cash flows. When calculating the net cash provided (used) by operations, which of the following items would be deducted from net income?
   a. Cash paid for income taxes
   b. Gain on sale of land
   c. Depreciation expense
   d. Cash paid for dividends

10. (*Learning Objective 3*) Which of the following sections will be prepared differently if the direct method is used to prepare the statement of cash flows instead of the indirect method?
   a. Operating activities
   b. Investing activities
   c. Financing activities
   d. All of the sections will be different

Quick Check Answers

1. d 2. c 3. a 4. b 5. d 6. b 7. c 8. b 9. a 10. a

Short Exercises

S13-1 Classifying cash flows (*Learning Objective 1*)

Rolling Hills Corporation is preparing its statement of cash flows (indirect method) for the past year. Listed below are items used in preparing the company's statement of cash flows. Specify how each item would be treated on Rolling Hills Corporation's statement of cash flows by using the following abbreviations:

1. Operating activity—addition to net income (O+)
2. Operating activity—subtraction from net income (O–)
3. Financing activity (F)
4. Investing activity (I)
5. Activity that is not on the statement of cash flows (NA)

Items to Classify in Operating Section of Statement of Cash Flows (Indirect Method)			
a. Depreciation expense	—	h. Decrease in inventory	—
b. Retained earnings	—	i. Decrease in accounts payable	—
c. Increase in prepaid expense	—	j. Collection of cash from customers	—
d. Loss on sale of building	—	k. Gain on sale of land	—
e. Payment of dividends	—	l. Issuance of common stock	—
f. Increase in accounts receivable	—	m. Purchase of equipment	—
g. Net income	—	n. Increase in accrued liabilities	—

S13-2 Identifying activities for the statement of cash flows—indirect method *(Learning Objectives 1 & 2)*

Identify each of McCloud Industries' transactions listed below as operating (O), investing (I), financing (F), noncash investing and financing (NIF), or a transaction that is not reported on the statement of cash flows (NA). Also indicate whether the transaction increases (+) or decreases (–) cash. The indirect method is used for operating activities.

a. Decrease in accrued liabilities	—	i. Depreciation of equipment	—
b. Loss on sale of equipment	—	j. Acquisition of building by cash payment	—
c. Payment of long-term debt	—	k. Net income	—
d Issuance of common stock for cash	—	l. Decrease in raw materials inventory	—
e. Purchase of long-term investment	—	m. Payment of cash dividend	—
f. Acquisition of equipment by issuance of note payable	—	n. Increase in prepaid expenses	—
g. Sale of long-term investment	—	o. Purchase of treasury stock	—
h. Accrual of salary expense	—	p. Cash sale of land	—

S13-3 Preparing the operation cash flows section (indirect method) *(Learning Objective 2)*

Baxter Corporation began the year with accounts receivable, inventory, and prepaid expenses totaling $64,000. At the end of the year, Baxter had a total of $76,000 for these current assets. At the beginning of the year, it owed current liabilities of $45,000, and at year-end, current liabilities totaled $38,000.

Net income for the year was $85,000. Included in net income was a $4,000 gain on the sale of land and depreciation expense of $9,000.

Show how Baxter should report cash flows from operating activities for the year. Baxter uses the indirect method.

S13-4 Classify cash flows as operating, investing, or financing *(Learning Objectives 1 & 2)*

For each of the following situations, identify whether the activity is an operating, investing, or financing activity and compute the cash provided or used by the activity.

	Activity	Operating (O) Investing (I) Financing (F)	Amount of Cash Flow	Increase (+) Decrease (–)
a.	Bonds payable were retired for their face value of $68,000 (cash paid). Cash dividends of $10,000 were also paid. A new note payable was signed for cash proceeds of $26,000.			
b.	A plant asset with a cost of $67,000 and accumulated depreciation of $13,000 was sold for a $20,000 loss.			
c.	Current assets (not including cash) increased by $2,000 and current liabilities decreased by $9,000. There was no depreciation. Net income was $53,000 for the year.			
d.	Common stock was issued for $300,000 cash. Dividends of $24,000 were paid in cash.			
e.	Noncash current assets decreased by $1,000 and current liabilities decreased by $12,000. Depreciation was $16,000 for the year, while net income was $50,000.			
f.	A building with a cost of $184,000 and accumulated depreciation of $44,000 was sold for a $16,000 gain.			
g.	Net income for last year was $114,000. The accumulated depreciation balance increased by $20,000. There were no changes in noncash current assets or liabilities. There were also no sales of plant assets.			
h.	Net income was $22,000 for the year. Accounts receivable increased by $3,000 and accounts payable increased by $4,000. There were no other changes in the noncash current assets and current liabilities. There was no depreciation for the year.			
i.	Bonds payable with a face value of $56,000 were retired with a cash payment for their face value. New bonds were issued later in the year for $38,000.			

S13-5 Calculate investing cash flows *(Learning Objectives 1, 2, & 3)*

Martin Company reported the following financial statements for 2011 and 2012:

Martin Company Income Statement For Year Ended December 31, 2012		
Sales revenue		$4,830,000
Cost of goods sold		2,840,000
Gross profit		$1,990,000
Operating expenses:		
Salaries and wage expense	$330,000	
Insurance expense	15,000	
Depreciation expense	74,000	
Other operating expenses	123,000	542,000
Operating income		$1,448,000
Other income and expenses:		
Interest expense		6,900
Income before taxes		$1,441,100
Income tax expense		403,000
Net income		$1,038,100

Martin Company Balance Sheets As of December 31, 2012 and 2011	2012	2011
Assets		
Current assets:		
Cash and cash equivalents	$ 582,000	$ 468,000
Accounts receivable	75,000	16,000
Inventory	930,000	250,000
Prepaid insurance	4,700	4,700
Total current assets	$1,591,700	$ 738,700
Property, plant, and equipment	1,220,000	1,110,000
Less: Accumulated depreciation	(275,000)	(201,000)
Investments	45,000	69,000
Total assets	$2,581,700	$1,716,700
Liabilities		
Current liabilities:		
Accounts payable (inventory purchases)	$ 29,000	$ 44,000
Salaries payable	14,000	15,000
Interest payable	2,800	5,500
Taxes payable	270,000	33,000
Other accrued operating expenses	28,000	17,000
Total current liabilities	$ 343,800	$ 114,500
Bonds payable	64,000	80,000
Total liabilities	$ 407,800	$ 194,500
Stockholders' equity		
Common stock	$ 722,000	$ 779,000
Retained earnings	1,451,900	743,200
Total stockholders' equity	$2,173,900	$1,522,200
Total liabilities and equity	$2,581,700	$1,716,700

Compute the following investing cash flows:

a. Purchases of plant assets (all were for cash). There were no sales of plant assets.

b. Proceeds from the sale of investments. There were no purchases of investments.

S13-6 Calculate financing cash flows *(Learning Objectives 2 & 3)*

Use the data given in S13-5 for the Martin Company to compute the following financing cash flows:

a. New borrowing or payment of long-term notes payable. Martin Company had only one long-term note payable transaction during the year.

b. Issuance of common stock or retirement of common stock. The company had only one common stock transaction during the year.

c. Payment of cash dividends (same as dividends declared).

S13-7 Classify cash flows as operating, investing, or financing *(Learning Objectives 1, 2, & 3)*

The items in the following table may or may not appear in a statement of cash flows.

	Operating (O) Investing (I) Financing (F)	Direct (D) Indirect (I) Both (B)	Increase (+) Decrease (–)
1. Increase in taxes payable			
2. Principal payments on long-term note payable			
3. Purchase of plant assets			
4. Depreciation expense			
5. Cash paid for taxes			
6. Dividends paid			
7. Issuance of stock			
8. Decrease in accounts receivable			
9. Increase in wages payable			
10. Cash paid to suppliers			
11. Cash received from customers			
12. Purchase of treasury stock			

For each of the items in the table, indicate the following:

1. Would the item appear on the statement of cash flows under operating activities (O), investing activities (I), or financing activities (F)?
2. Would the item appear on the statement of cash flows using the direct method (D), indirect method (I), or both (B)?
3. Would the item result in an increase (+) or a decrease (–) when computing cash flow?

S13-8 Prepare statement of cash flows (indirect method)

(Learning Objective 2)

Duncan Corporation uses the indirect method to prepare its statement of cash flows. Data related to cash activities for last year appears next.

Net income	$ 92,600
Dividends paid (cash)	$ 50,500
Depreciation expense	$ 12,000
Net decrease in current assets	$ 21,400
Issued new notes payable for cash	$ 61,200
Paid cash for building	$279,000
Net decrease in current liabilities	$ 5,300
Sold investment for cash	$350,000

Answer the following questions:

1. What was the net cash flow from operating activities for the year?
2. What was the cash flow from (or used for) investing activities for the year?
3. What was the cash flow from (or used for) financing activities for the year?
4. What was the net change in cash for the year?
5. If the beginning balance of cash for the year was $151,000, what was the balance of cash at the end of the year?

S13-9 Calculate increase or decrease in current assets and liabilities *(Learning Objective 3)*

A recent statement of cash flows for NewArt Company reported the following information:

Net income	$452,700
Depreciation	68,000
Cash effect of changes in:	
Accounts receivable	23,000
Inventory	(15,500)
Other current assets	(8,800)
Accounts payable	20,000
Other current liabilities	(197,000)
Net cash provided by operations	$342,400

Based on the information presented in the statement of cash flows for NewArt Company, determine whether the following accounts increased or decreased during the period: Accounts Receivable, Inventory, Other Current Assets, Accounts Payable, and Other Current Liabilities.

S13-10 Prepare statement of cash flows (direct method) *(Learning Objective 3)*

Audrey Corporation uses the direct method to prepare its statement of cash flows. Data related to cash activities for last year appears next.

Paid for equipment	$16,000	Paid for interest	$ 4,500
Paid to suppliers	$33,000	Paid for utilities	$13,000
Paid for insurance	$ 9,000	Paid dividends	$ 7,200
Depreciation expense	$ 3,200	Received from customers	$59,000
Paid for advertising	$ 7,300	Paid for taxes	$ 5,700
Received from sale of land	$17,000	Received from issuing long-term note payable	$22,000
Received from sale of plant assets	$ 6,600	Paid to employees	$15,000

Answer the following questions:

1. What was the net cash flow from operating activities for the year?
2. What was the net cash flow from investing activities for the year?
3. What was the net cash flow from financing activities for the year?
4. What was the net change in cash for the year?
5. If the beginning balance of cash for the year was $350,000, what was the balance of cash at the end of the year?

EXERCISES Group A

E13-11A Prepare operating cash flows section (indirect method) *(Learning Objective 2)*

The comparative balance sheet for Waterfall Travel Services, Inc., for December 31, 2012 and 2011, is as follows:

Waterfall Travel Services, Inc. Balance Sheets As of December 31, 2012 and 2011		
	2012	**2011**
Assets		
Cash	$ 44,000	$ 15,000
Accounts receivable (net)	77,000	86,000
Inventories	58,000	19,000
Prepaid insurance	9,000	11,000
Land	106,000	119,000
Equipment	77,000	58,000
Accumulated depreciation—equipment	(20,000)	(14,000)
Total	$351,000	$294,000
Liabilities and Stockholders' equity		
Accounts payable	$ 26,000	$ 31,000
Wages payable	30,000	21,000
Interest payable	16,000	14,000
Income taxes payable	12,000	10,000
Note payable (long-term)	94,000	85,000
Total liabilities	$178,000	$161,000
Common stock	136,000	123,000
Retained earnings	37,000	10,000
Total stockholders' equity	$173,000	$133,000
Total liabilities and stockholders' equity	$351,000	$294,000

The following information is taken from the records of Waterfall Travel Services, Inc.:

a. Land was sold for $9,700.
b. Equipment was purchased for cash.
c. There were no disposals of equipment during the year.
d. The common stock was issued for cash.
e. Net income for 2012 was $39,000.
f. Cash dividends paid during the year were $12,000.

Waterfall Travel Services, Inc., uses the indirect method for preparing the statement of cash flows. Prepare the operating section of the statement of cash flows for 2012.

E13-12A Prepare statement of cash flow preparation (indirect method) *(Learning Objective 2)*

Using the data given in E13-11A, prepare the statement of cash flows (indirect method) for Waterfall Travel Services, Inc., for 2012.

E13-13A Calculate cash flows from operating, investing, and financing activities (direct method) *(Learning Objectives 2 & 3)*

Compute the following cash flows for Star Media Services Company for the past year:

1. The beginning balance of Retained Earnings was $138,000, while the end of the year balance of Retained Earnings was $177,000. Net income for the year was $61,000. No dividends payable were on the balance sheet. How much was paid in cash dividends during the year?

2. The beginning and ending balances of the Common Stock account were $213,000 and $277,000, respectively. Where would the increase in Common Stock appear on the statement of cash flows?
3. The beginning and ending balances of the Treasury Stock account were $57,000 and $75,000, respectively. Where would the increase in Treasury Stock appear on the statement of cash flows?
4. The Property, Plant, & Equipment (net) increased by $8,000 during the year to have a balance of $153,000 at the end of the year. Depreciation for the year was $15,000. Acquisitions of new plant assets during the year totaled $41,000. Plant assets were sold at a loss of $2,000.
   a. What were the cash proceeds from the sale of plant assets?
   b. What amount would be reported on the investing section of the statement of cash flows? Would it be a source of cash or a use of cash?
   c. What amount, if any, would be reported on the operating section of the statement of cash flows?

E13-14A Calculate operating cash flows (indirect method)

(Learning Objective 2)

Springtown Corporation has the following activities for the past year:

Net income	$?	Cost of goods sold	$44,000
Payment of dividends	$ 6,000	Other operating expenses	$11,000
Proceeds from issuance of stock	$ 79,000	Depreciation expense	$16,000
Purchase of treasury stock	$ 13,000	Purchase of equipment	$23,000
Sales revenue	$123,000	Proceeds from sale of land	$21,000
Payment of note payable	$ 18,000	Increase in current assets other than cash	$ 4,000
Decrease in current liabilities	$ 9,000		

Requirement

Prepare the operating activities section of Springtown Corporation's statement of cash flows for the year ended December 31st, using the indirect method for operating cash flows.

E13-15A Prepare statement of cash flows (indirect method) *(Learning Objective 2)*

Using the data given in E13-14A, prepare statement of cash flows for Springtown Corporation for the year. Springtown Corporation uses the indirect method for operating activities.

E13-16A Prepare statement of cash flows (indirect method) *(Learning Objective 2)*

Winder Corporation is preparing its statement of cash flows for the past year. The company has gathered the following information about the past year just ended on December 31st.

Retire bond payable (long-term)	$10,000	Decrease in accounts receivable	$11,000
Paid dividends in cash	$33,000	Increase in salaries payable	$ 9,000
Decrease in inventory	$ 9,000	Depreciation expense	$17,000
Decrease in accounts payable	$ 6,000	Increase in prepaid insurance	$ 300
Sold land (investment)	$22,000	Decrease in other short-term liabilities	$ 4,000
Increase in interest payable	$ 900	Increase in taxes payable	$ 1,000
Cash balance, beginning of year	$87,000	Purchase of new computer system	$12,000
		Net income	$89,000

Requirement

Prepare a statement of cash flows for the past year using the indirect method.

E13-17A Compute operating cash flows using direct method *(Learning Objective 3)*

Sugarcreek Spas provides the following data for the year just ended December 31st.

Payment of note payable	$ 4,500	Payments to employees	$ 65,500
Depreciation expense	$ 4,900	Proceeds from sale of land	$ 40,000
Purchase of equipment	$ 9,000	Payment of dividends	$ 10,000
Purchase of treasury stock	$ 12,500	Payments to suppliers	$ 69,000
Gain on sale of land	$ 1,000	Increase in salaries payable	$ 10,500
Cost of goods sold	$111,000	Payment of income tax	$ 11,500
Proceeds from issuance of common stock	$ 14,500	Collections from customers	$154,000
Beginning balance, cash	$ 12,500	Sales revenue	$166,000

Requirement

Prepare the operating activities section of Sugarcreek Spas' statement of cash flows for the year just ended, using the direct method for operating cash flows.

E13-18A Prepare statement of cash flows (direct method) *(Learning Objective 3)*

Using the data from E13-17A, prepare the statement of cash flows using the direct method.

E13-19A Prepare statement of cash flows (direct method) *(Learning Objective 3)*

Sedlak Interiors began the year with cash of $51,000. During the year, Sedlak Interiors earned service revenue of $410,000. Cash collections for the year were $380,000. Expenses for the year were $360,000, with $345,000 of that total paid in cash. Sedlak Interiors also used cash to purchase equipment for $75,000 and to pay a cash dividend to stockholders of $35,000. During the year, Sedlak Interiors also borrowed $42,000 cash by issuing a note payable.

Requirement

Prepare the company's statement of cash flows using the direct method.

E13-20A Classify sustainable activities' effect on cash flows *(Learning Objectives 1, 2, and 3)*

The Plastic Lumber Company, Inc., (PLC) is a manufacturer that takes in post-consumer plastics (i.e., empty milk jugs) and recycles those plastics into a "plastic lumber" that can be used to build furniture, decking, and a variety of other items. Because Plastic Lumber has a strong focus on sustainability, the company managers try, whenever possible, to use recycled materials and to invest in sustainable projects.

Last year, the company engaged in several sustainable practices that have an impact on its cash flows. For each of the transactions listed below, indicate whether the transaction would have affected the operating, investing, or financing cash flows of the company. Additionally, indicate whether each transaction would have increased (+) or decreased (−) cash.

Transactions:

1. PLC built a new building for its manufacturing facility. The new building is LEED certified and was paid for with cash.
2. Engineers and scientists at PLC performed research into whether another kind of post-consumer plastic not currently used in its plastics extrusion process could be used.
3. Solar panels were installed on PLC's administrative offices to supply part of the electricity needed for its operations.
4. PLC issued common stock during the year to help finance growth.
5. New production equipment that is 50% more energy efficient than the old equipment was purchased for cash.

6. Six Honda Civic Hybrid automobiles were purchased for the use of the sales staff.
7. PLC became a minority partner in a wind-turbine project by investing $1 million in cash in the project.
8. PLC sold plastic scrap generated by its manufacturing process.
9. Throughout the year, PLC participated in several trade shows that featured green products for use by parks and recreation facilities. For each trade show, PLC incurred cash expenses for transportation, registration, meals and lodging, and booth setup.
10. A new delivery truck that uses biofuel was purchased for cash.

EXERCISES Group B

E13-21B Prepare operating cash flows section (indirect method) *(Learning Objective 2)*

The comparative balance sheet for Anderson Travel Services, Inc., for December 31, 2012 and 2011, is as follows:

Anderson Travel Services, Inc.
Balance Sheet
As of December 31, 2012 and 2011

	2012	2011
Assets		
Cash	$ 44,000	$ 18,000
Accounts receivable (net)	79,000	82,000
Inventories	57,000	16,000
Prepaid insurance	9,000	14,000
Land	104,000	121,000
Equipment, net	84,000	53,000
Accumulated depreciation—equipment	(20,000)	(15,000)
Total	$357,000	$289,000
Liabilities and Stockholders' equity		
Accounts payable	$ 28,000	$ 32,000
Wages payable	26,000	23,000
Interest payable	15,000	13,000
Income tax payable	10,000	7,000
Notes payable, long-term	99,000	89,000
Total liabilities	$178,000	$164,000
Common stock	142,000	115,000
Retained earnings	37,000	10,000
Total stockholders' equity	$179,000	$125,000
Total liabilities and stockholders' equity	$357,000	$289,000

The following information is taken from the records of Anderson Travel Services, Inc.:

a. Land was sold for $13,200.
b. Equipment was purchased for cash.
c. There were no disposals of equipment during the year.
d. The common stock was issued for cash.
e. Net income for 2012 was $32,000.
f. Cash dividends paid during the year were $5,000.

Anderson Travel Services, Inc., uses the indirect method for preparing the statement of cash flows. Prepare the operating section of the statement of cash flows for 2012.

E13-22B Prepare statement of cash flow preparation (indirect method) *(Learning Objective 2)*

Using the data given in E13-21B, prepare the statement of cash flows (indirect method) for Anderson Travel Services, Inc., for 2012.

E13-23B Calculate cash flows from operating, investing, and financing activities (direct method) *(Learning Objectives 2 & 3)*

Compute the following cash flows for Moulton Flooring Company for the past year:

1. The beginning balance of Retained Earning was $135,000, while the end of the year balance of Retained Earnings was $180,000. Net income for the year was $63,000. No dividends payable were on the balance sheet. How much was paid in cash dividends during the year?
2. The beginning and ending balances of the Common Stock account were $214,000 and $275,000, respectively. Where would the increase in Common Stock appear on the statement of cash flows?
3. The beginning and ending balances of the Treasury Stock account were $55,000 and $79,000, respectively. Where would the increase in Treasury Stock appear on the statement of cash flows?
4. The Property, Plant, & Equipment (net) increased by $8,000 during the year to have a balance of $147,000 at the end of the year. Depreciation for the year was $16,000. Acquisitions of new plant assets during the year totaled $37,000. Plant assets were sold at a loss of $3,000.
   a. What were the cash proceeds from the sale of plant assets?
   b. What amount would be reported on the investing section of the statement of cash flows? Would it be a source of cash or a use of cash?
   c. What amount would be reported on the operating section of the statement of cash flows? How would it be presented?

E13-24B Calculate operating cash flows (indirect method) *(Learning Objective 2)*

Brooklyn Corporation has the following activities for the past year:

Net income	$?	Cost of goods sold	$47,000
Payment of dividends	$ 6,000	Other operating expenses	$15,000
Proceeds from issuance of stock	$ 75,000	Depreciation expense	$17,000
Purchase of treasury stock	$ 10,000	Purchase of equipment	$28,000
Sales revenue	$120,000	Proceeds from sale of land	$26,000
Payment of note payable	$ 12,000	Increase in current assets other than cash	$ 7,000
Decrease in current liabilities	$ 10,000		

Requirement

Prepare the operating activities section of Brooklyn Corporation's statement of cash flows for the year ended December 31st, using the indirect method for operating cash flows.

E13-25B Prepare statement of cash flows (indirect method) *(Learning Objective 2)*

Using the data given in E13-24B, prepare the statement of cash flows for Brooklyn Corporation for the year. Brooklyn Corporation uses the indirect method for operating activities.

E13-26B Prepare statement of cash flows (indirect method) *(Learning Objective 3)*

Festival Corporation is preparing its statement of cash flows for the past year just ended on December 31st. The controller has gathered the following information about the past year.

Retire bond payable (long-term)	$16,000	Decrease in accounts receivable	$ 8,000
Paid dividends in cash	$35,000	Increase in salaries payable	$ 9,000
Decrease in inventory	$ 7,000	Depreciation expense	$10,000
Decrease in accounts payable	$ 6,000	Increase in prepaid insurance	$ 700
Sold land (investment)	$26,000	Decrease in other short-term liabilities	$ 5,000
Increase in interest payable	$ 900	Increase in taxes payable	$ 2,000
Cash balance, beginning of year	$87,000	Purchase of new computer system	$17,000
Net income	$91,000		

Requirement

Prepare a statement of cash flows for the past year using the indirect method.

E13-27B Compute operating cash flows using the direct method *(Learning Objective 3)*

Maplebrook Spas provides the following data for the year just ended December 31st.

Payment of note payable	$ 6,500	Payments to employees	$ 63,500
Depreciation expense	$ 4,100	Proceeds from sale of land	$ 44,500
Purchase of equipment	$ 8,000	Payment of dividends	$ 11,500
Purchase of treasury stock	$ 12,500	Payments to suppliers	$ 69,000
Gain on sale of land	$ 1,500	Increase in salaries payable	$ 12,000
Cost of goods sold	$109,000	Payment of income tax	$ 9,000
Proceeds from issuance of common stock	$ 14,500	Collections from customers	$147,000
Beginning balance, cash	$ 12,000	Sales revenue	$171,000

Requirement

Prepare the operating activities section of Maplebrook Spas' statement of cash flows for the year ended December 31st using the direct method for operating cash flows.

E13-28B Prepare statement of cash flows (direct method) *(Learning Objective 3)*

Using the data for E13-27B, prepare the statement of cash flows using the direct method.

E13-29B Prepare statement of cash flows (direct method) *(Learning Objective 3)*

Marcus Interiors began the year with cash of $50,000. During the year, Marcus Interiors earned service revenue of $402,000. Cash collections for the year were $385,000. Expenses for the year were $375,000, with $360,000 of that total paid in cash. Marcus Interiors also used cash to purchase equipment for $70,000 and to pay a cash dividend to stockholders of $28,000. During the year, Marcus Interiors borrowed $54,000 cash by issuing a note payable.

Requirement

Prepare the company's statement of cash flows using the direct method.

E13-30B Classify sustainable activities' effect on cash flows *(Learning Objectives 1, 2 and 3)*

The Plastic Lumber Company, Inc., (PLC) is a manufacturer that takes in post-consumer plastics (i.e., empty milk jugs) and recycles those plastics into a "plastic lumber" that can be used to build furniture, decking, and a variety of other items. Because Plastic Lumber has a strong focus on sustainability, the company managers try, whenever possible, to use recycled materials and to invest in sustainable projects.

Last year, the company engaged in several sustainable practices that have an impact on its cash flows. For each of the transactions listed below, indicate whether the transaction would have affected the operating, investing, or financing cash flows of the company. Additionally, indicate whether each transaction would have increased (+) or decreased (−) cash.

Transactions:

1. Engineers at PLC performed research into a new process that injects tiny air bubbles into the plastic to reduce the usage of raw materials (plastics) and to reduce the weight of the finished products.
2. A Honda Civic Hybrid automobile was purchased for use by the CEO of PLC.
3. PLC became a minority partner in a solar-panel electricity generation project by investing $1 million in cash in the project
4. Throughout the year, PLC participated in several trade shows that featured green products for use by parks and recreation facilities. For each trade show, PLC incurred cash expenses for transportation, registration, meals and lodging, and booth setup.
5. A fleet of plug-in electric cars was purchased for sales staff.
6. PLC installed a "living roof" on its manufacturing facility. This roof is made mostly from sedum, runoff and doubles the expected life of the roof over a conventional roof. The plants also reduce heating and cooling needs by providing an extra layer of insulation. Additionally, the plants absorb carbon dioxide to help to reduce greenhouse gases. The living roof was paid for with cash.
7. When the plastic wood is cut into lengths needed to build picnic tables, the end pieces cut off are scrap. PLC sold this cutting scrap to another recycler.
8. A wind-turbine was built to power part of PLC's operations.
9. PLC issues long-term bonds during the year to help to finance growth.
10. New production equipment that is 40% more energy efficient than the old equipment was purchased for cash.

PROBLEMS Group A

P13-31A Prepare statement of cash flows (indirect method) *(Learning Objective 2)*

Prepare statement of cash flows using the indirect method. The income statement for 2012 and the balance sheets for 2012 and 2011 are presented for Gibson Industries, Inc.

Gibson Industries, Inc. Income Statement For Year Ended December 31, 2012		
Sales revenue		$958,000
Cost of goods sold		386,000
Gross profit		$572,000
Operating expenses:		
Salaries and wage expense	$184,000	
Insurance expense	11,500	
Depreciation expense	46,200	
Other operating expenses	88,000	329,700
Operating income		$242,300
Other income and expenses:		
Gain on sale of equipment	2,500	
Interest expense	5,100	$ 2,600
Income before taxes		239,700
Income tax expense		71,910
Net income		$167,790

Gibson Industries, Inc.
Balance Sheets
As of December 31, 2012 and 2011

	2012	2011
Assets		
Current assets:		
Cash and cash equivalents	$ 477,000	$ 288,000
Accounts receivable	77,000	129,000
Inventory	326,000	213,000
Prepaid insurance	9,500	5,500
Total current assets	$ 889,500	$ 635,500
Property, plant, and equipment	625,000	595,000
Less: Accumulated depreciation	(149,000)	(112,000)
Investments	93,000	73,000
Total assets	$1,458,500	$1,191,500
Liabilities		
Current liabilities:		
Accounts payable (inventory purchases)	$ 59,000	$ 39,000
Salaries payable	16,100	17,400
Interest payable	1,500	800
Taxes payable	62,910	13,000
Other accrued operating expenses	6,100	3,000
Total current liabilities	145,610	73,200
Bonds payable	65,000	23,000
Total liabilities	210,610	96,200
Stockholders' equity		
Common stock	601,000	601,000
Retained earnings	646,890	494,300
Total stockholders' equity	1,247,890	1,095,300
Total liabilities and equity	$1,458,500	$1,191,500

Additional information follows:

a. Sold plant asset for $4,100. Original cost of this plant asset was $10,800 and it had $9,200 of accumulated depreciation associated with it.
b. Paid $5,500 on the bonds payable; issued $47,500 of new bonds payable.
c. Declared and paid cash dividends of $15,200.
d. Purchased new investment for $20,000.
e. Purchased new equipment for $40,800.

Requirement

Prepare a statement of cash flows for Gibson Industries, Inc., for the year ended December 31, 2012, using the indirect method.

P13-32A Prepare statement of cash flows (indirect method) *(Learning Objectives 1 & 2)*

The 2012 and 2011 balance sheets of West Corporation follow. The 2012 income statement is also provided. West had no noncash investing and financing transactions during 2012. During the year, West sold equipment for $15,100, which had originally cost $12,700 and had a book value of $10,700. West did not issue any notes payable during the year but did issue common stock for $30,000.

Requirements

1. Prepare the statement of cash flows for West Corporation for 2012 using the indirect method.
2. Evaluate West's cash flows for the year. Discuss each of the categories of cash flows in your response.

West Corporation
Income Statement
As of December 31, 2012

Sales revenue		$347,000
Cost of goods sold		78,000
Gross profit		$269,000
Operating expenses:		
Salaries and wage expense	$26,500	
Depreciation expense	4,900	
Other operating expenses	12,500	43,900
Operating income		$225,100
Other income and expenses:		
Gain on sale of equipment	$ 4,400	
Interest expense	9,900	5,500
Income before taxes		$219,600
Income tax expense		36,600
Net income		$183,000

West Corporation
Balance Sheets
For Years Ended December 31, 2012 and 2011

	2012	2011
Assets		
Current assets:		
Cash and cash equivalents	$ 50,000	$ 23,500
Accounts receivable	32,100	29,100
Inventory	86,000	93,300
Prepaid insurance	3,300	2,800
Total current assets	$171,400	$148,700
Property, plant, and equipment	153,000	136,000
Less: Accumulated depreciation	(30,000)	(27,100)
Investments	113,000	0
Total assets	$407,400	$257,600
Liabilities		
Current liabilities:		
Accounts payable (inventory purchases)	$ 33,200	$ 36,500
Salaries payable	2,900	7,400
Interest payable	2,400	0
Taxes payable	5,300	0
Other accrued operating expenses	18,800	22,100
Total current liabilities	$ 62,600	$66,000
Bonds payable	78,000	113,000
Total liabilities	$140,600	$179,000
Stockholders' equity		
Common stock	$107,000	$ 77,000
Retained earnings	159,800	1,600
Total stockholders' equity	$266,800	$ 78,600
Total liabilities and equity	$407,400	$257,600

P13-33A Prepare a statement of cash flows (direct method) *(Learning Objectives 1 & 3)*

Crayton Digital Services, Inc., has provided the following data from the company's records for the year just ended December 31st:

a.	Collection of interest	$ 5,900
b.	Cash sales	$ 251,500
c.	Credit sales	$ 675,500
d.	Proceeds from sale of investment	$ 12,900
e.	Gain on sale of investment	$ 2,100
f.	Payments to suppliers	$ 572,500
g.	Cash payments to purchase plant assets	$ 52,900
h.	Depreciation expense	$ 63,700
i.	Salaries expense	$ 77,500
j.	Payment of short-term note payable by issuing common stock	$ 71,800
k.	Cost of goods sold	$ 568,000
l.	Proceeds from issuance of note payable	$ 24,900
m.	Income tax expense and payment	$ 38,100
n.	Proceeds from issuance of common stock	$ 21,000
o.	Receipt of cash dividends	$ 6,800
p.	Interest revenue	$ 6,200
q.	Payment of cash dividends	$ 28,900
r.	Collections of accounts receivable	$ 574,500
s.	Amortization expense	$ 3,800
t.	Payments on long-term notes payable	$ 47,500
u.	Interest expense and payments	$ 12,100
v.	Purchase of equipment by issuing common stock to seller	$ 17,700
w.	Payment of salaries	$ 74,400
x.	Proceeds from sale of plant assets	$ 24,500
y.	Loss on sale of plant assets	$ 3,000
z.	Cash and cash equivalents balance, beginning of year	$ 25,100

Requirements

1. Prepare the statement of cash flows for Crayton Digital Services, Inc., using the direct method for cash flows from operations. Note that you will need to calculate the ending balance of cash and cash equivalents. Include a schedule of noncash investing and financing activities.
2. Evaluate Crayton's cash flows for the year. Discuss each of the categories of cash flows in your response.

P13-34A Prepare statements of cash flows (indirect and direct method)

(Learning objectives 1, 2, & 3)

Douglas Graphics Company, Inc., has the following comparative balance sheet as of March 31, 2012.

Douglas Graphics Company, Inc.
Balance Sheet
As of March 31, 2012 and 2011

	2012	2011	Increase (Decrease)
Current assets:			
Cash	$ 55,400	$ 14,600	$ 40,800
Accounts receivable	51,000	53,800	(2,800)
Inventories	64,800	59,800	5,000
Prepaid expenses	3,500	5,400	(1,900)
Long-term investment	10,000	6,700	3,300
Equipment, net	71,800	70,300	1,500
Land	34,500	95,000	(60,500)
Total assets	$291,000	$305,600	$ (14,600)
Current liabilities:			
Note payable, short-term	$ 43,400	$ 48,900	$ (5,500)
Accounts payable	4,500	3,000	1,500
Income tax payable	14,000	15,200	(1,200)
Salary payable	9,200	12,100	(2,900)
Interest payable	8,200	6,900	1,300
Accrued liabilities	1,400	3,200	(1,800)
Long-term note payable	48,700	93,200	(44,500)
Common stock	69,000	61,200	7,800
Retained earnings	92,600	61,900	30,700
Total liabilities and equity	$291,000	$305,600	$ (14,600)

Selected transaction data for the year ended March 31, 2012, include the following:

a.	Net income	$ 76,500
b.	Paid long-term note payable with cash	$ 59,900
c.	Cash payments to employees	$ 42,100
d.	Loss on sale of land	$ 9,900
e.	Acquired equipment by issuing long-term note payable	$ 15,400
f.	Cash payments to suppliers	$145,200
g.	Cash paid for interest	$ 3,300
h.	Depreciation expense on equipment	$ 13,900
i.	Paid short-term note payable by issuing common stock	$ 5,500
j.	Paid cash dividends	$ 45,800
k.	Received cash for issuance of common stock	$ 2,300
l.	Cash received from customers	$297,800
m.	Cash paid for income taxes	$ 11,900
n.	Sold land for cash	$ 50,600
o.	Interest received (in cash)	$ 1,600
p.	Purchased long-term investment for cash	$ 3,300

Requirements

1. Prepare the statement of cash flows for Douglas Graphics Company, Inc., for the year ended March 31, 2012, using the indirect method for operating cash flows. Include a schedule of noncash investing and financing activities. All of the current accounts, except short-term notes payable, result from operating transactions.
2. Also prepare a supplementary schedule of cash flows from operations using the direct method.

PROBLEMS Group B

P13-35B Prepare statement of cash flows (indirect method) *(Learning Objective 2)*

Prepare the statement of cash flows using the indirect method. The income statement for 2012 and the balance sheets for 2012 and 2011 are presented for Henderson Industries.

Henderson Industries, Inc. Income Statement For Year Ended December 31, 2012		
Sales revenue		$952,000
Cost of goods sold		386,000
Gross profit		$566,000
Operating expenses:		
Salary and wage expense	$189,000	
Insurance expense	11,000	
Depreciation expense	46,900	
Other operating expense	82,000	328,900
Operating income		$237,100
Other income and expense:		
Gain on sale of equipment	$ 3,500	
Interest expense	5,100	1,600
Income before taxes		$235,500
Income tax expense		70,650
Net income		$164,850

Henderson Industries, Inc.
Comparative Balance Sheet
As of December 31, 2012 and 2011

	2012	2011
Assets		
Current assets:		
Cash and cash equivalents	$ 478,000	$ 292,000
Accounts receivable	77,000	121,000
Inventory	335,000	214,000
Prepaid expenses	6,000	5,500
Total current assets	$ 896,000	$ 632,500
Property, plant, and equipment	600,000	595,000
Less: Accumulated depreciation	(150,000)	(113,000)
Investments	90,000	76,000
Total assets	$1,436,000	$1,190,500
Liabilities		
Current liabilities:		
Accounts payable (inventory purchases)	$ 60,000	$ 40,000
Salaries payable	16,000	17,300
Interest payable	1,700	800
Taxes payable	61,650	10,000
Other accrued operating expenses	6,200	3,500
Total current liabilities	$ 145,550	$ 71,600
Bonds payable	66,000	26,000
Total liabilities	$ 211,550	$ 97,600
Stockholders' equity		
Common stock	$ 609,000	$ 609,000
Retained earnings	615,450	483,900
Total stockholders' equity	$1,224,450	$1,092,900
Total liabilities and stockholders' equity	$1,436,000	$1,190,500

Additional information follows:

a. Sold plant asset for $3,900. Original cost of this plant asset was $10,300 and it had $9,900 of accumulated depreciation associated with it.
b. Paid $4,500 on the bonds payable; issued $44,500 of new bonds payable.
c. Declared and paid cash dividends of $33,300.
d. Purchased new investment for $14,000.
e. Purchased new equipment for $15,300.

Requirement

Prepare a statement of cash flows for Henderson Industries, Inc., for the year ended December 31, 2012, using the indirect method.

P13-36B Prepare statement of cash flows (indirect method) *(Learning Objectives 1 & 2)*

The 2012 and 2011 balance sheets of Wallace Corporation follow. The 2012 income statement is also provided. Wallace had no noncash investing and financing transactions during 2012. During the year, Wallace sold equipment for $15,400, which had originally cost $13,600 and had a book value of $11,100. Wallace did not issue any notes payable during the year but did issue common stock for $31,000.

Requirements

1. Prepare the statement of cash flows for Wallace Corporation for 2012 using the indirect method.
2. Evaluate Wallace's cash flows for the year. Discuss each of the categories of cash flows in your response.

Wallace Corporation Income Statement For Year Ended December 31, 2012		
Sales revenue		$348,000
Cost of goods sold		72,000
Gross profit		$276,000
Operating expenses:		
Salary and wage expense	$25,500	
Depreciation expense	5,400	
Other operating expense	15,000	45,900
Operating income		$230,100
Other income and expense:		
Gain on sale of equipment	$ 4,300	
Interest expense	9,700	5,400
Income before taxes		$224,700
Income tax expense		37,400
Net income		$187,300

Wallace Corporation Comparative Balance Sheet As of December 31, 2012 and 2011		
	2012	**2011**
Assets		
Current assets:		
Cash and cash equivalents	$ 47,500	$ 23,500
Accounts receivable	31,700	29,900
Inventory	86,200	93,200
Prepaid expenses	3,400	2,400
Total current assets	$168,800	$149,000
Property, plant, and equipment	153,000	138,000
Less: Accumulated depreciation	(30,200)	(27,300)
Investments	116,000	0
Total assets	$407,600	$259,700
Liabilities		
Current liabilities:		
Accounts payable (inventory purchases)	$ 33,600	$ 36,700
Salaries payable	2,700	7,200
Interest payable	2,200	0
Taxes payable	5,700	0
Other accrued operating expenses	18,900	22,700
Total current liabilities	$ 63,100	$ 66,600
Bonds payable	77,000	115,000
Total liabilities	$140,100	$181,600
Stockholders' equity		
Common stock	107,000	76,000
Retained earnings	160,500	2,100
Total stockholders' equity	$267,500	$ 78,100
Total liabilities and equity	$407,600	$259,700

P13-37B Prepare a statement of cash flows (direct method) *(Learning Objectives 1 & 3)*

Freedom Digital Services, Inc., has provided the following data from the company's records for the year just ended December 31st:

a.	Collection of interest	$ 5,900
b.	Cash sales	$252,000
c.	Credit sales	$674,000
d.	Proceeds from sale of investment	$ 12,100
e.	Gain on sale of investment	$ 2,500
f.	Payments to suppliers	$573,500
g.	Cash payments to purchase plant assets	$ 52,100
h.	Depreciation expense	$ 63,100
i.	Salaries expense	$ 77,800
j.	Payment of short-term note payable by issuing common stock	$ 72,300
k.	Cost of goods sold	$566,500
l.	Proceeds from issuance of note payable	$ 24,600
m.	Income tax expense and payment	$ 38,000
n.	Proceeds from issuance of common stock	$ 22,500
o.	Cash receipt of dividend revenue	$ 6,500
p.	Interest revenue	$ 6,200
q.	Payment of cash dividends	$ 28,700
r.	Collections of accounts receivable	$575,500
s.	Amortization expense	$ 3,800
t.	Payments on long-term notes payable	$ 44,000
u.	Interest expense and payments	$ 12,700
v.	Purchase of equipment by issuing common stock to seller	$ 17,800
w.	Payment of salaries	$ 74,200
x.	Proceeds from sale of plant assets	$ 24,400
y.	Loss on sale of plant assets	$ 3,100
z.	Cash and cash equivalents balance, beginning of year	$ 25,000

Requirements

1. Prepare the statement of cash flows for Freedom Digital Services, Inc., using the direct method for cash flows from operations. Note that you will need to calculate the ending balance of cash and cash equivalents. Include a schedule of noncash investing and financing activities.
2. Evaluate Freedom's cash flows for the year. Discuss each of the categories of cash flows in your response.

P13-38B Prepare statements of cash flows (indirect and direct method) *(Learning Objectives 1, 2, & 3)*

Riley Company, Inc., has the following comparative balance sheet as of March 31, 2012.

Riley Company, Inc. Balance Sheet As of March 31, 2012 and 2011			
	2012	2011	Increase (Decrease)
Current assets:			
Cash	$ 55,300	$ 14,200	$ 41,100
Accounts receivable	51,200	53,500	(2,300)
Inventories	65,400	60,500	4,900
Prepaid expenses	4,100	5,400	(1,300)
Long-term investment	9,700	7,100	2,600
Equipment, net	71,000	70,800	200
Land	35,000	96,000	(61,000)
Total assets	$291,700	$307,500	$(15,800)
Current liabilities:			
Note payable, short-term	$ 43,200	$ 48,600	$ (5,400)
Accounts payable	4,300	3,200	1,100
Income tax payable	13,800	15,400	(1,600)
Salary payable	9,800	12,200	(2,400)
Interest payable	8,700	7,500	1,200
Accrued liabilities	1,300	3,300	(2,000)
Long-term note payable	47,300	93,400	(46,100)
Common stock	69,300	61,400	7,900
Retained earnings	94,000	62,500	31,500
Total liabilities and equity	$291,700	$307,500	$(15,800)

Selected transaction data for the year ended March 31, 2012, include the following:

a. Net income, $76,300
b. Paid long-term note payable with cash, $59,600
c. Cash payments to employees, $42,200
d. Loss on sale of land, $9,300
e. Acquired equipment by issuing long-term note payable, $13,500
f. Cash payments to suppliers, $147,300
g. Cash paid for interest, $3,400
h. Depreciation expense on equipment, $13,300
i. Paid short-term note payable by issuing common stock, $5,400
j. Paid cash dividends, $44,800
k. Received cash for issuance of common stock, $2,500
l. Cash received from customers, $297,300
m. Cash paid for income taxes, $12,300
n. Sold land for cash, $51,700
o. Interest received (in cash), $1,800
p. Purchased long-term investment for cash, $2,600

Requirements

1. Prepare the statement of cash flows for Riley Company, Inc., for the year ended March 31, 2012, using the indirect method for operating cash flows. Include a schedule of noncash investing and financing activities. All of the current accounts except short-term notes payable result from operating transactions.
2. Also prepare a supplementary schedule of cash flows from operations using the direct method.

CRITICAL THINKING

Discussion & Analysis

A13-39 Discussion Questions

1. How do managers use the statement of cash flows?
2. Describe at least four needs for cash within a business.
3. Define an "operating activity." List two examples of an operating activity on the statement of cash flows that would *increase* cash. List two examples of an operating activity that would *decrease* cash.
4. Define an "investing activity." List two examples of an investing activity on the statement of cash flows that would *increase* cash. List two examples of an investing activity that would *decrease* cash.
5. Define a "financing activity." List two examples of a financing activity on the statement of cash flows that would *increase* cash. List two examples of a financing activity that would *decrease* cash.
6. Define a "noncash investing or financing" activity. Describe an activity that would need to be disclosed as a noncash investing or financing activity.
7. Describe the difference between the direct and the indirect methods of preparing the operating section of the statement of cash flows.
8. Describe the process for reconciling net income to the cash basis. What items are added to net income? What items are subtracted from net income?
9. When preparing a statement of cash flows using the indirect method, what information is needed? What documents or statements would be used?
10. Summarize the process for preparing the operations section of the statement of cash flows when using the direct method.
11. Provide an example of an operating cash inflow that could result from sustainability activities. Also provide an example of an operating cash outflow that would support sustainability.
12. Think of a company with which you are familiar. Describe an investing activity related to a company's sustainability efforts that would be classified as a use of cash on a company's statement of cash flows. Describe a financing activity related to a company's sustainability efforts that would be classified as a use of cash on a company's statement of cash flows.

Application & Analysis

A13-40 Comparing Cash Flow Statements from Companies in the Same Industry

Select an industry in which you are interested and select two companies within that industry. Obtain their annual reports by going to each company's website and downloading the report for the most recent year. (On many company websites, you will need to visit the Investor Relations section or other similarly named link to obtain the company's financial statements.)

Basic Discussion Questions

For each of the companies you selected, answer the following:

1. Which method is used to calculate the cash provided or used by operations?
2. What items increased cash provided by operations?
3. What items decreased cash provided by operations?
4. Overall, was cash increased or decreased by operating activities?
5. Did investing activities in total increase cash or decrease cash during the year? What were the major uses or sources of cash related to investing?

6. Did financing activities in total increase cash or decrease cash during the year? What were the major uses or sources of cash related to financing?
7. What items (if any) are disclosed as significant noncash financing or investing activities?

Now that you have looked at each company's cash flow statements individually, compare the two companies. What can you tell about each company from its statement of cash flows? Can you tell if one company is stronger than the other from their statements of cash flows? What clues do you have?

Decision Cases

A13-41 Use cash flow data to evaluate potential investments *(Learning Objectives 1 & 2)*

Your company has some excess cash and would like to invest it in the stock of another company. You investigate several different stocks and are trying to decide which stock would be the best investment for your company. One factor you investigate is each company's cash flow. The summaries of the cash flow statements for your three top stock choices follow:

(000s omitted)	**Baxter Corp.**		**Meredith Enterprises**		**Rollyson, Inc.**	
Net cash provided by (used for) operating activities		$ (20,000)		$ 28,100		$ 16,000
Cash provided by (used for) investing activities:						
Cash used to purchase plant or equipment			$ (12,100)		$ (25,000)	
Proceeds from the sale of equipment	$ 8,000					
Cash used to purchase investments in stock	—		(5,000)		—	
Net cash provided by (used for) investing activities		8,000		(17,100)		$ (25,000)
Cash provided by (used for) financing activities:						
Proceeds from bond issuance	23,500		4,000		5,000	
Repayment of long-term debt	(1,000)		(2,000)			
Cash proceeds from issuance of stock					12,000	
Cash payments for dividends	(2,500)		(5,000)		—	
Net cash provided by (used for) financing activities		20,000		(3,000)		17,000
Net increase in cash		$ 8,000		$ 8,000		$ 8,000

Although you will look at many other criteria in your stock purchase recommendation, what can you tell about each of the three companies listed? Based solely on cash flow, which stock appears to be better?

14

Financial Statement Analysis

Learning Objectives

1. Perform a horizontal analysis of financial statements
2. Perform a vertical analysis of financial statements
3. Prepare and use common-size financial statements
4. Compute the standard financial ratios

With over $66 billion in annual

sales, Target Corporation is currently the third largest retailer in the United States. Its trademark symbol, the bull's-eye, is recognized by 97% of people surveyed. Target has a reputation for being one of the largest supporters of corporate social responsibility. Ever since 1962, Target has committed 5% of its yearly income to support local communities. In addition, Target is committed to integrating environmental sustainability throughout its business operations. As a result of these corporate practices, *Fortune* magazine has ranked Target Corporation as one of "America's Most Admired Companies" and *Newsweek* ranked Target in the top 15% of the country's largest public companies in its Green ratings.

All of these accolades might lead one to believe that Target must be highly profitable. Indeed, Target *has* earned a profit in each of the past ten years. But, net income alone does not tell the whole story. Has revenue grown steadily, or have there been large fluctuations—ups and downs—over the course recent years? How big was each year's profit in relation to sales? For every dollar sold, how much of it ended up as gross profit, and how much of it went to pay for operating expenses? What kind of return has the company been providing to shareholders? And how quickly has Target been able to sell its highly seasonable and fashion-trended merchandise?

Financial statement analysis can help us answer these questions.

© Presselect / Alamy

Sources: www.target.com, www.stores.org/2010/Top-100-Retailers, www.mghus.com/blog/2011/01/21/whats-a-logo-without-a-name/

Investors and creditors can't evaluate a company very well by examining the financial statements from only one year. Performance is better judged by comparing financial statement data:

- From year to year
- With a competitor, such as Walmart
- With industry averages

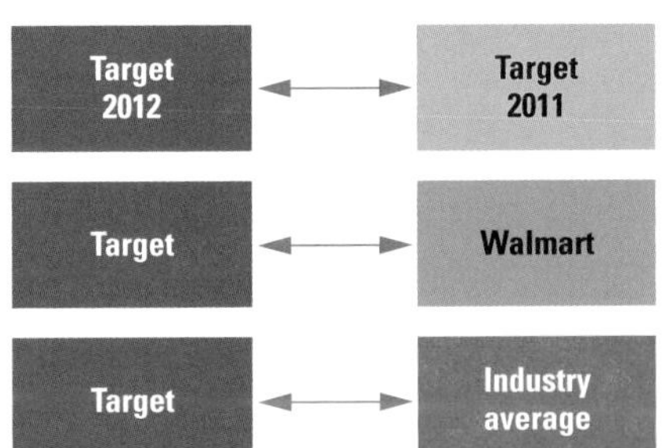

In this chapter, we'll examine several analytical tools that are frequently used to judge the financial performance of a company as a whole. To illustrate, we'll apply these tools to Supermart, a regional retailer of general merchandise that is similar to, but much smaller than Target. Then we will apply these analytical tools directly to Target Corporation's financial statements in the mid-chapter and end-of-chapter summary problems.

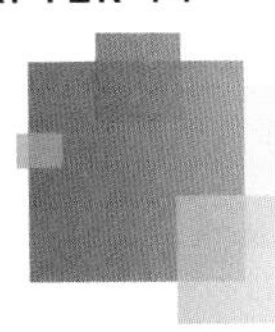

What are the Most Common Methods of Analysis?

> **Why is this important?**
> "Evaluating the **performance** of a company is difficult without some type of **benchmark** for **comparison**. Therefore, managers typically benchmark **financial performance** over time, against other companies, or against **industry averages**."

There are three ways to analyze financial statements:

- Horizontal analysis provides a year-to-year comparison of a company's performance in different periods.
- Vertical analysis provides a means of evaluating the relative size of each line item in the financial statements. It also allows us to compare companies of different size.
- Ratio analysis provides a means of evaluating the relationships between key components of the financial statements.

We'll explain the first two methods in this half of the chapter, and then devote the entire second half of the chapter to ratio analysis.

To use these tools, we must begin with the company's financial statements. Exhibit 14-1 presents Supermart's income statement for the last two years, while Exhibit 14-2 presents the company's balance sheet for the last two years.

EXHIBIT 14-1 Supermart Income Statement

Supermart
Income Statement
For the Years Ended December 31, 2012 and 2011

(amounts in thousands)	2012	2011
Sales revenue	$858,000	$803,000
Cost of goods sold	513,000	509,000
Gross profit	345,000	294,000
Operating expenses	244,000	237,000
Operating income	101,000	57,000
Interest expense	20,000	14,000
Income before income taxes	81,000	43,000
Income tax expense	33,000	17,000
Net income	$ 48,000	$ 26,000

Horizontal Analysis

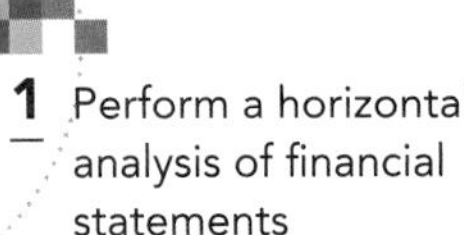

1 Perform a horizontal analysis of financial statements

Many decisions hinge on whether sales, expenses, and net income are increasing or decreasing. Have sales and other revenues risen from last year? By how much? Sales may have increased by $20,000, but considered alone, this fact is not very helpful. The *percentage change* in sales over time is more helpful. It is better to know that sales increased by 20% than to know that sales increased by $20,000.

The study of percentage changes in comparative statements is called **horizontal analysis**. Computing a percentage change in comparative statements requires two steps:

1. Compute the dollar amount of the change from the earlier period to the later period.
2. Divide the dollar amount of change by the earlier period amount. We call the earlier period the base period.

EXHIBIT 14-2 Supermart Balance Sheet

Supermart
Balance Sheet
December 31, 2012 and 2011

(amounts in thousands)	2012	2011
Assets		
Current assets:		
Cash	$ 29,000	$ 32,000
Accounts receivables, net	114,000	85,000
Inventory	113,000	111,000
Other current assets	6,000	8,000
Total current assets	262,000	236,000
Property, plant, and equipment, net	507,000	399,000
Other noncurrent assets	18,000	9,000
Total assets	$787,000	$644,000
Liabilities		
Current liabilities:		
Accounts payable	$ 73,000	$ 68,000
Notes payable	42,000	27,000
Accrued liabilities	27,000	31,000
Total current liabilities	142,000	126,000
Long-term liabilities	289,000	198,000
Total liabilities	431,000	324,000
Stockholders' Equity		
Common stock, no par	186,000	186,000
Retained earnings	170,000	134,000
Total stockholders' equity	356,000	320,000
Total liabilities and equity	$787,000	$644,000

Let's illustrate with Supermart's sales revenue, shown in Exhibit 14-1:

STEP 1: Compute the dollar amount of change in sales revenue from 2011 to 2012:

2012		2011		Increase
$858,000	−	$803,000	=	$55,000

STEP 2: Divide the dollar amount of change by the base-period amount. This computes the percentage change for the period:

$$\text{Percentage change} = \frac{\text{Dollar amount of change}}{\text{Base-year amount}}$$

$$= \frac{\$55,000}{\$803,000} = 0.068 \text{ (rounded)} = 6.8\%$$

We now see that Supermart's sales revenue increased by $55,000, or 6.8%, over the previous year.

Horizontal Analysis of the Income Statement

Exhibit 14-3 shows a complete horizontal analysis of Supermart's income statement.

EXHIBIT 14-3 Supermart Comparative Income Statement—Horizontal Analysis

Supermart
Comparative Income Statements
For the Years Ended December 31, 2012 and 2011

			Increase (Decrease)	
(amounts in thousands)	2012	2011	Change	Percentage*
Sales revenue	$858,000	$803,000	$55,000	6.8%
Cost of goods sold	513,000	509,000	4,000	0.8%
Gross profit	345,000	294,000	51,000	17.3%
Operating expenses	244,000	237,000	7,000	3.0%
Operating income	101,000	57,000	44,000	77.2%
Interest expense	20,000	14,000	6,000	42.9%
Income before income taxes	81,000	43,000	38,000	88.4%
Income tax expense	33,000	17,000	16,000	94.1%
Net income	$ 48,000	$ 26,000	$22,000	84.6%

*rounded

The horizontal analysis shows that sales increased by almost 7%, yet the cost of goods sold increased by less than 1%. Supermart was either able to raise its prices, find cheaper suppliers, or sell products with higher margins. As a result, gross profit was about 17% higher than the previous year. Supermart was also able to hold its operating expenses to a 3% increase. These factors all contributed to increasing operating income by 77% over the previous year! Interest expense increased 42%, either as a result of a higher interest rate, more debt, or a combination of the two. Finally, as a result of the increased income, income taxes also increased substantially. The end result was an 84% increase in net income over the previous year.

Horizontal Analysis of the Balance Sheet

Exhibit 14-4 shows a complete horizontal analysis of Supermart's balance sheet.

The horizontal analysis shows that Supermart's accounts receivable grew substantially over the year (34%), while its cash decreased about 9%. The company may have relaxed its credit terms to generate more sales. The company also has taken on more short- and long-term debt, which may have been used to finance the significant additions to property, plant, and equipment and the increase in noncurrent assets that occurred during the year.

Trend Percentages

Trend percentages are a form of horizontal analysis. Trends indicate the direction a business is taking over a longer period of time, such as three, five, or ten years. For example, in Exhibit 14-3, we saw that Supermart's net income increased a whopping 84% over the previous year. Has income always been increasing at such a significant rate? Or was that an isolated growth spurt limited to a one-year period? Investors typically like to see smooth growth trends over time, rather than large, sporadic fluctuations in sales and net income.

Trend percentages are computed by selecting a base year. The base-year amounts are set equal to 100%. The amounts for each following year are expressed as a percentage of the base amount. To compute trend percentages, divide each item in the following years by the base-year amount.

$$\text{Trend \%} = \frac{\text{Any year \$}}{\text{Base year \$}}$$

EXHIBIT 14-4 Comparative Balance Sheet—Horizontal Analysis

Supermart
Comparative Balance Sheet
December 31, 2012 and 2011

			Increase (Decrease)	
(amounts in thousands)	2012	2011	Change	Percentage*
Assets				
Current assets:				
Cash	$ 29,000	$ 32,000	$ (3,000)	(9.4%)
Accounts receivables, net	114,000	85,000	29,000	34.1%
Inventory	113,000	111,000	2,000	1.8%
Other current assets	6,000	8,000	(2,000)	(25.0%)
Total current assets	262,000	236,000	26,000	11.0%
Property, plant, and equipment, net	507,000	399,000	108,000	27.1%
Other noncurrent assets	18,000	9,000	9,000	100.0%
Total assets	$787,000	$644,000	$143,000	22.2%
Liabilities				
Current liabilities:				
Accounts payable	$ 73,000	$ 68,000	$ 5,000	7.4%
Notes payable	42,000	27,000	15,000	55.6%
Accrued liabilities	27,000	31,000	(4,000)	(12.9%)
Total current liabilities	142,000	126,000	16,000	12.7%
Long-term liabilities	289,000	198,000	91,000	46.0%
Total liabilities	431,000	324,000	107,000	33.0%
Stockholders' Equity				
Common stock, no par	186,000	186,000	0	0.0%
Retained earnings	170,000	134,000	36,000	26.9%
Total stockholders' equity	356,000	320,000	36,000	11.3%
Total liabilities and equity	$787,000	$644,000	$143,000	22.2%

*rounded

Supermart's sales revenue, and trend percentages from 2007 to 2012, are pictured in Exhibit 14-5. We selected 2007 as the base, so that year's percentage is set equal to 100.

EXHIBIT 14-5 Supermart's Sales Trend

	2012	2011	2010	2009	2008	Base Year 2007
Sales revenue	$858,000	$780,000	$690,000	$648,000	$618,000	$600,000
Trend percentage	143%	130%	115%	108%	103%	100%

From the percentages, we see that sales increased at a fairly slow, even rate in the earlier years (2007–2010). However, the rate of increase picked up in the later years (2011 and 2012). Supermart is obviously experiencing growth, either in existing store sales, or by adding new retail locations. Trend data is often pictured using line graphs. In fact, publically traded companies show the trend of their stock returns in the 10-K filings required by the Securities and Exchange Commission (SEC). Exhibit 14-6 shows Supermart's sales trends. As you can see, sales have increased every year, but the rate of increase has been larger in recent years (as shown by the steeper incline of the line from 2011–2012).

EXHIBIT 14-6 Line Graph of Sales Trend

Sales Trend

Net Sales Revenue

$1,000,000
$900,000
$800,000
$700,000
$600,000
$500,000
$400,000
$300,000
$200,000
$100,000
$0

2007 2008 2009 2010 2011 2012

You can perform a trend analysis on any item you consider important. Trend analysis is widely used to predict the future.

Vertical Analysis

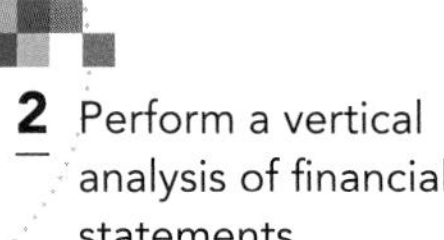

2 Perform a vertical analysis of financial statements

As we have seen, horizontal analysis and trend percentages highlight changes in an item over time. But no single technique gives a complete picture of a business, so we also need vertical analysis.

Vertical analysis of a financial statement shows the relationship of each item to a base amount, which is the 100% figure. Every other item on the statement is then reported as a percentage of that base. When performing vertical analysis of an income statement, sales revenue is usually considered the base (100%).

$$\text{Vertical analysis \% for income statement} = \frac{\text{Each income statement item}}{\text{Revenue (net sales)}}$$

Exhibit 14-7 shows the vertical analysis of Supermart's 2012 income statement. The vertical analysis shows that the Supermart's gross profit is 40% of sales revenue. Operating expenses use up 28% of each dollar sold, while income taxes and interest use up another 6%. As a result of all of these expenses, only 5.6% of every sales dollar ends up as net income (for every $1.00 of sales revenue, a little less than $0.06 ends up as net income).

When performing vertical analysis of a balance sheet, total assets is usually considered the base (100%).

$$\text{Vertical analysis \% for balance sheet} = \frac{\text{Each balance sheet line item}}{\text{Total assets}}$$

Exhibit 14-8 shows the vertical analysis of Supermart's 2012 balance sheet. The base amount (100%) is total assets.

EXHIBIT 14-7 Income Statement—Vertical Analysis

Supermart
Income Statement
For the Year Ended December 31, 2012

(amounts in thousands)	Amount	Percentage*
Sales revenue	$858,000	100.0%
Cost of goods sold	513,000	59.8%
Gross profit	345,000	40.2%
Operating expenses	244,000	28.4%
Operating income	101,000	11.8%
Interest expense	20,000	2.4%
Income before income taxes	81,000	9.4%
Income tax expense	33,000	3.8%
Net income	$ 48,000	5.6%

*rounded

EXHIBIT 14-8 Balance Sheet—Vertical Analysis

Supermart
Balance Sheet
December 31, 2012

(amounts in thousands)	Amount	Percentage*
Assets		
Current assets:		
Cash	$ 29,000	3.7%
Accounts receivables, net	114,000	14.5%
Inventory	113,000	14.4%
Other current assets	6,000	0.8%
Total current assets	262,000	33.3%
Property, plant, and equipment, net	507,000	64.4%
Other noncurrent assets	18,000	2.3%
Total assets	$787,000	100.0%
Liabilities		
Current liabilities:		
Accounts payable	$ 73,000	9.3%
Notes payable	42,000	5.3%
Accrued liabilities	27,000	3.4%
Total current liabilities	142,000	18.0%
Long-term liabilities	289,000	36.7%
Total liabilities	431,000	54.8%
Stockholders' Equity		
Common stock, no par	186,000	23.6%
Retained earnings	170,000	21.6%
Total stockholders' equity	356,000	45.2%
Total liabilities and equity	$787,000	100.0%

*rounded

The vertical analysis of Supermart's balance sheet reveals that most of the company's assets (64%) consist of property, plant, and equipment. Inventory and receivables together make up about 29% of the company's assets. While the company is in the business of selling merchandise and, therefore, needs a fair amount of inventory, the receivables balance may be higher than desirable. Current liabilities is only 18% of total assets, but long-term debt is double that amount. Finally, stockholders' equity makes up a significant portion of assets (45%).

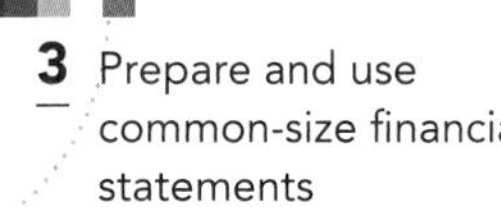

3 Prepare and use common-size financial statements

How do we Compare One Company with Another?

Horizontal analysis and vertical analysis provide a great deal of useful data about a company. But the Supermart data apply to only one business. Many times we want to **benchmark**, or compare, a company against either 1) its competitor, or 2) industry averages.

To compare Supermart to another company, we can use a common-size statement. A **common-size statement** reports only percentages—the same percentages that appear in a vertical analysis. By using only the percentages, rather than gross dollar amounts, we are able to compare companies that vary in terms of size. For example, in Exhibit 14-9 we use common-size income statements to compare Supermart, a smaller regional retailer, to Target, a large national retailer.

EXHIBIT 14-9 Common-Size Income Statement

Supermart
Common-Size Income Statement
Supermart Versus Target

	Supermart	Target*
Sales revenue	100.0%	100.0%
Cost of goods sold	59.8%	69.0%
Gross profit	40.2%	31.0%
Operating expenses	28.4%	23.7%
Operating income	11.8%	7.3%
Interest expense	2.4%	1.3%
Income before income taxes	9.4%	6.0%
Income tax expense	3.8%	2.2%
Net income	5.6%	3.8%

*Adapted from Target's 2010 income statement

Exhibit 14-9 shows that Supermart is actually more profitable, on each dollar of sales revenue (5.6%), than Target (3.8%). Supermart's gross margin (40.2%) is about 9 percentage points higher than Target's (31.0%), but its operating expenses use up more of each sales dollar (28.4%) than do Target's operating expenses (23.7%). Likewise, Supermart's income taxes and interest expense also use up a slightly larger percentage of sales revenue. Despite these small differences, none of the line item percentages are drastically different than Target's.

We could also compare Supermart against industry averages, using the same type of anlaysis. However, since Target is the third largest retailer in the country, it accounts for a large portion of the industry average. Therefore, we wouldn't expect the results to be much different.

Before going on, be sure to review the decision guidelines. Then practice what you have learned in Summary Problem 1 by performing vertical and horizontal analysis on Target Corporation's financial statements.

Decision Guidelines

Horizontal and Vertical Analysis

In order to make well-informed financial decisions, investors, creditors, and managers need to determine how well the company is performing. The following guidelines help these decision makers judge the financial performance of a company.

Decision	Guidelines
What methods are generally used to evaluate a company's performance?	• Horizontal analysis • Vertical analysis • Ratio analysis
How does trend analysis differ from horizontal analysis?	Horizontal analysis performed over a longer period of time (3–10 years) is usually called trend analysis. When performing trend analysis, a base year is chosen, and set to 100%. All years after the base year are calculated as a percentage of the base year.
What line item on the income statement is used as the base amount (100%) for vertical analysis?	Net sales revenue is generally used as the base (100%) for vertical analysis of the income statement.
What line item on the balance sheet is used as the base amount (100%) for vertical analysis?	Total assets are generally used as the base (100%) for vertical analysis of the balance sheet.
How can I compare two companies that differ in size?	Common-size income statements and balance sheets are generally used to compare companies that differ in size. Common-size financial statements present the vertical analysis percentages of different companies, side-by-side.

SUMMARY PROBLEM 1

Target Corporation's annual sales and net income data for the years 2000–2010 are presented next. Also shown are Target Corporation's 2010 and 2009 comparative income statements (adapted).[1] Keep in mind that the latest recession began in the United States in December 2007 and technically ended in the summer of 2009. This recession had a far-reaching impact on most sectors of the economy, including retailers.

(in millions)	2010	2009	2008	2007	2006	2005	2004	2003	2002	2001	2000
Sales*	$66,530	$63,836	$63,339	$62,530	$58,783	$51,844	$46,102	$41,303	$43,152	$39,363	$36,561
Net income	$ 2,920	$ 2,488	$ 2,214	$ 2,849	$ 2,787	$ 2,408	$ 3,198	$ 1,809	$ 1,654	$ 1,368	$ 1,264

* Includes the company's credit card operations, including credit card revenue, net of credit card expense.

Target Corporation
Income Statement (Adapted)
For the Fiscal Year 2010 and 2009*

(Dollars in millions)	2010	2009
Sales revenue**	$66,530	$63,836
Cost of goods sold	45,725	44,062
Gross profit	20,805	19,774
Operating expenses:		
Selling, general, and administrative	13,469	13,078
Depreciation	2,084	2,023
Operating income	5,252	4,673
Interest expense, net	757	801
Income tax expense	1,575	1,384
Net income	$ 2,920	$ 2,488

*Because of the busy holiday season, retailers rarely end their fiscal year at December 31. Target's 2010 fiscal year ended January 29, 2011, and its 2009 fiscal year ended January 30, 2010.
**Includes the company's credit card operations including credit card revenue, net of credit card expenses.

Requirements

1. Perform a trend analysis for the years 2000–2010, using 2000 as the base year. Comment on the results.
2. Perform a horizontal analysis for the years 2009–2010 and comment on the results.
3. Perform a vertical analysis for the years 2009–2010 and comment on the results.

[1]Target Corporation 10-K, 2011

▪ SOLUTIONS

Requirement 1

(in millions)	2010	2009	2008	2007	2006	2005	2004	2003	2002	2001	2000
Sales revenue	$66,530	$63,836	$63,339	$62,530	$58,783	$51,844	$46,102	$41,303	$43,152	$39,363	$36,561
Trend percentage*	182%	175%	173%	171%	161%	142%	126%	113%	118%	108%	100%
Net income	$ 2,920	$ 2,488	$ 2,214	$ 2,849	$ 2,787	$ 2,408	$ 3,198	$ 1,809	$ 1,654	$ 1,368	$ 1,264
Trend percentage*	231%	197%	175%	225%	220%	191%	253%	143%	131%	108%	100%

*rounded

Sales revenue has gradually increased over time. Current sales revenue is 231% of what it had been in the base year, 2000. Likewise, current net income is 182% of what it had been in the base year. However, the increase in net income was not as gradual as the increase in sales. In fact, net income has had significant yearly variations that do not correspond directly with the increase in sales. Operations, other than sales, must have significantly influenced net income in certain years.

Requirement 2

Target Corporation
Horizontal Analysis of Comparative Income Statements
For the Fiscal Years 2010 and 2009

(Dollars in millions)	2010	2009	Increase (Decrease) Amount	Increase (Decrease) Percentage*
Sales revenue	$66,530	$63,836	$2,694	4.2%
Cost of goods sold	45,725	44,062	1,663	3.8%
Gross profit	20,805	19,774	1,031	5.2%
Operating expenses:				
Selling, general, and administrative	13,469	13,078	391	3.0%
Depreciation	2,084	2,023	61	3.0%
Operating income	5,252	4,673	579	12.4%
Interest expense, net	757	801	(44)	-5.5%
Income tax expense	1,575	1,384	191	13.8%
Net income	$ 2,920	$ 2,488	$ 432	17.4%

*rounded

Sales revenue increased at a greater rate (4.2%) than Cost of Goods Sold, leading to an increase in gross profit of 5.2%. Operating expenses only increased by 3%, which, combined with the increase in gross profit, led to an increase of 12.4% in operating income. As expected, income tax increased at a similar rate (13.8%). Finally, interest expense declined by 5.5% leading to an overall increase in net income of 17.4%.

Requirement 3

Target Corporation Vertical Analysis of Comparative Income Statements For the Fiscal Years 2010 and 2009				
	2010		2009	
	Amount	Percent*	Amount	Percent*
Sales revenue	$66,530	100.0%	$63,836	100.0%
Cost of goods sold	45,725	68.7%	44,062	69.0%
Gross profit	20,805	31.3%	19,774	31.0%
Operating expenses:				
Selling, general, and administrative	13,469	20.2%	13,078	20.5%
Depreciation	2,084	3.1%	2,023	3.2%
Operating income	5,252	7.9%	4,673	7.3%
Interest expense, net	757	1.1%	801	1.3%
Income tax expense	1,575	2.4%	1,384	2.2%
Net income	$ 2,920	4.4%	$ 2,488	3.9%

*rounded

The vertical analysis shows that Target's gross profit is roughly 31% of sales. Selling, general, and administrative expenses use up about 20% of the company's sales revenue, while depreciation accounts for about 3% of sales revenue. Interest and income taxes, combined, use up another 3.5% of sales revenue. As a result, net income is approximately 4% of sales revenue. That means, for every dollar of sales revenue generated by the company, only about four cents ends up as net income.

What are Some of the Most Common Financial Ratios?

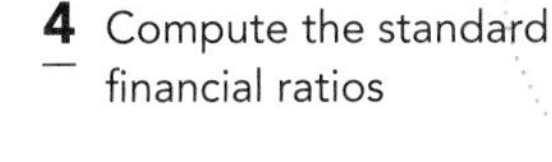

4 Compute the standard financial ratios

In this half of the chapter, we'll discuss many different financial ratios that managers, investors, and creditors use when analyzing a company's financial statements. Most of the information needed for these ratios can be found in the company's financial statements (refer to Supermart's income statement and balance sheet in Exhibits 14-1 and 14-2). A few of the ratios require the knowledge of the company's closing market price, which can be found in the *Wall Street Journal*. Other ratios require knowledge of the number of shares outstanding. This information can be obtained in the company's 10-K filing.

The ratios we'll discuss in this chapter may be classified as follows:

1. Measuring ability to pay current liabilities
2. Measuring ability to sell inventory and collect receivables
3. Measuring ability to pay long-term debt
4. Measuring profitability
5. Analyzing stock investments

Measuring Ability to Pay Current Liabilities

Working capital is defined as follows:

Working capital = Current assets − Current liabilities

Working capital measures the ability to meet short-term obligations with current assets. Supermart's 2012 working capital is calculated as follows:

$262,000 − $142,000 = $120,000

This shows that Supermart has ample current assets to meet its current obligations. Rather than measuring working capital alone, managers often measure the company's ability to meet current obligations by calculating two common ratios: the *current ratio* and the *acid-test*, or *quick ratio*.

Why is this important?

"Managers use different **financial ratios** to evaluate a company's performance, depending on the underlying **need**. For example, if a manager wants to know how **quickly inventory** is selling, he or she will calculate inventory **turnover**. If a manager wants to know how easily the **company** will be able to meet its current **obligations,** he or she will calculate the current ratio or **current ratio**."

Current Ratio

The most widely used ratio is the current ratio, which is current assets divided by current liabilities. The current ratio measures the ability to pay current liabilities with current assets.

Supermart's current ratio at December 31, 2012 and 2011 is calculated as follows:[2]

Formula	Supermart's Current Ratio 2012	2011
Current ratio = $\frac{\text{Current assets}}{\text{Current liabilities}}$	$\frac{\$262,000}{\$142,000} = 1.85$	$\frac{\$236,000}{\$126,000} = 1.87$

[2]The solutions to all ratio calculations in this chapter have been rounded.

What is an acceptable current ratio? The answer depends on the industry, however a current ratio of 2.0 is generally considered fairly strong. Compare Supermart's current ratio of 1.85 with the current ratios of some well-known companies in the same industry:[3]

Company	Current Ratio
Walmart	0.89
JCPenney	2.41
Kohl's	2.08

Acid-Test Ratio

The **acid-test ratio**, or **quick ratio**, tells us whether the entity could pay all of its current liabilities if they came due *immediately*. That is, could the company pass this *acid test*?

To compute the acid-test ratio, we add cash, short-term investments, and net current receivables (accounts and notes receivable, net of allowances) and divide this sum by current liabilities. Inventory and prepaid expenses are *not* included in the acid test because they are the least liquid current assets. Supermart's acid-test ratios for 2012 and 2011 follow:

Formula	Supermart's Acid-Test Ratio 2012	2011
$\text{Acid-test ratio} = \dfrac{\text{Cash} + \text{Short-term investments} + \text{Net current receivables}}{\text{Current liabilities}}$	$\dfrac{\$29{,}000 + \$0 + \$114{,}000}{\$142{,}000} = 1.01$	$\dfrac{\$32{,}000 + \$0 + \$85{,}000}{\$126{,}000} = 0.93$

An acid-test ratio of 0.90 to 1.00 is acceptable in most industries. We do not present comparative statistics for Walmart, JCPenney, and Kohl's, since their balance sheets do not identify short-term investments separately.

Measuring Ability to Sell Inventory and Collect Receivables

The ability to sell inventory and collect receivables is fundamental to business. In this section, we discuss three ratios that measure the company's ability to sell inventory and collect receivables.

Inventory Turnover

Inventory turnover measures the number of times a company sells its average level of inventory during a year. A high rate of turnover indicates ease in selling inventory; a low rate indicates difficulty. A value of "6" means that the company sold its average level of inventory six times—every two months—during the year.

To compute inventory turnover, we divide cost of goods sold by the average inventory for the period. We use the cost of goods sold—not sales—because both cost of goods sold and inventory are stated *at cost*. Sales at *retail prices* are not comparable with inventory *at cost*.

Supermart's inventory turnover for 2012 is as follows:

Formula	Supermart's 2012 Inventory Turnover
$\text{Inventory turnover} = \dfrac{\text{Cost of goods sold}}{\text{Average inventory}}$	$\dfrac{\$513{,}000}{(\$111{,}000 + \$113{,}000)/2} = 4.6$

[3]All information given for Walmart Stores, Inc., JCPenney, and Kohl's Corporation, was calculated using the companies' financial statements reported for fiscal year 2010 (fiscal year ended January 29, 2011), as found in each company's SEC 10-K filing.

Notice that average inventory is calculated by adding the beginning inventory ($111,000) and ending inventory ($113,000) for the period, and then dividing by two.

Inventory turnover varies widely with the nature of the business. Because of product innovation, some industries (for example, high-technology industries), must turn their inventory very quickly to avoid inventory obsolescence. However, in other industries, the risk of obsolescence is not so great.

Compare Supermart's inventory turnover with that of some well-known companies in the same industry:

Company	Inventory Turnover
Walmart	9.13
JCPenney	3.46
Kohl's	3.81

Accounts Receivable Turnover

Accounts receivable turnover measures the ability to collect cash from credit customers. This means that the higher the ratio, the faster the cash collections. But a receivable turnover that's too high may indicate that credit is too tight, causing the loss of sales to good customers.

For illustrative purposes we'll assume that all of Supermart's sales were made on account. The accounts receivable turnover is computed by dividing net credit sales by average net accounts receivable. Supermart's accounts receivable turnover ratio for 2012 is computed as follows:

Formula	Supermart's 2012 Accounts Receivable Turnover
$\text{Accounts receivable turnover} = \dfrac{\text{Net credit sales}}{\text{Average net accounts receivable}}$	$\dfrac{\$858{,}000}{(\$85{,}000 + \$114{,}000)/2} = 8.6$

We don't show comparative statistics for Walmart, JCPenney, or Kohl's since their balance sheets do not show any receivables (most customers pay with cash, debit, or credit cards).

Days' Sales in Receivables

The **days' sales in receivables** ratio also measures the ability to collect receivables. Days' sales in receivables tell us how many days' sales remain in Accounts Receivable. To compute the ratio, we can follow a logical two-step process:

1. Divide net sales by 365 days to figure average sales for one day.
2. Divide this average day's sales amount into average net accounts receivable.

This two-step process is illustrated using Supermart's 2012 data as follows:

Formula	Supermart's 2012 Days' Sales in Accounts Receivable
Days' sales in *average* Accounts receivable:	
1. $\text{One day's sales} = \dfrac{\text{Net sales}}{\text{365 days}}$	$\dfrac{\$858{,}000}{\text{365 days}} = \$2{,}351$
2. $\dfrac{\text{Day's sales in average}}{\text{accounts receivable}} = \dfrac{\text{Average net accounts receivable}}{\text{One day's sales}}$	$\dfrac{(\$85{,}000 + \$114{,}000)/2}{\$2{,}351} = \text{42 days}$

Supermart's ratio tells us that 42 average days' sales remain in accounts receivable and need to be collected. Let's assume that like many companies, Supermart gives its customers 30 days to pay. Supermart's ratio shows that on average, customers are taking longer—about 45 days—to pay. This could be a result of general economic conditions (such as a recession), or Supermart's particular customer base. In either event, Supermart may need to increase its efforts to collect receivables more quickly if it expects to be paid within 30 days of sale.

Measuring Ability to Pay Long-Term Debt

The ratios discussed so far yield insight into current assets and current liabilities. They help us measure ability to sell inventory, collect receivables, and pay current liabilities. Most businesses also have long-term debt. Two key indicators of a business's ability to pay long-term liabilities are the *debt ratio* and the *times-interest-earned ratio*.

Debt Ratio

A loan officer at Metro Bank is evaluating loan applications from two companies. Both companies have asked to borrow $500,000 and have agreed to repay the loan over a five-year period. The first firm already owes $600,000 to another bank. The second owes only $100,000. Other things equal, you are more likely to lend money to Company 2 because that company owes less than Company 1.

The relationship between total liabilities and total assets—called the **debt ratio**—shows the proportion of assets financed with debt. When the debt ratio is 1, all of the assets are financed with debt. A debt ratio of 0.50 means that debt finances half the assets; the owners of the business have financed the other half. The higher the debt ratio, the higher the company's financial risk. The debt ratios for Supermart at the end of 2010 and 2009 follow:

Formula	Supermart's Debt Ratio 2012	Supermart's Debt Ratio 2011
$\text{Debt ratio} = \dfrac{\text{Total liabilities}}{\text{Total assets}}$	$\dfrac{\$431,000}{\$787,000} = 0.55$	$\dfrac{\$324,000}{\$644,000} = 0.50$

Supermart's debt ratio increased slightly in 2012. Let's look at the debt ratios of some well-known companies in the same industry:

Company	Debt Ratio
Walmart	0.61
JCPenney	0.58
Kohl's	0.40

Times-Interest-Earned Ratio

The debt ratio says nothing about ability to pay interest expense. Analysts use the **times-interest-earned ratio** to relate income to interest expense. This ratio is also called the **interest-coverage ratio**. It measures the number of times operating income can cover interest expense. A high interest-coverage ratio indicates ease in paying interest expense; a low ratio suggests difficulty.

To compute this ratio, we divide operating income by interest expense. Calculation of Supermart's times-interest-earned ratio follows:

Formula	Supermart's Times-Interest-Earned Ratio 2012	Supermart's Times-Interest-Earned Ratio 2011
$\text{Times-interest-earned ratio} = \dfrac{\text{Income from operations}}{\text{Interest expense}}$	$\dfrac{\$101,000}{\$20,000} = 5.05$	$\dfrac{\$57,000}{\$14,000} = 4.07$

The company's times-interest-earned ratio shows that in 2012, the company could pay its interest about five times over with the amount of operating income it earned. Therefore, Supermart should have little trouble paying the interest expense it owes to creditors. Compare Supermart's times-interest-earned ratio with other companies in the same industry:

Company	Times-Interest-Earned Ratio
Walmart	11.58
JCPenney	3.60
Kohl's	13.57

Measuring Profitability

The fundamental goal of business is to earn a profit. Ratios that measure profitability are often reported in the business press. We examine four profitability measures.

Rate of Return on Net Sales

In business, the term *return* is used broadly as a measure of profitability. Consider a ratio called the rate of return on net sales, or simply return on sales. This ratio shows the percentage of each sales dollar earned as net income. Supermart's rate of return on sales follows:

Formula	Supermart's Rate of Return on Sales 2012	2011
$\text{Rate of return on sales} = \dfrac{\text{Net income}}{\text{Net sales}}$	$\dfrac{\$48{,}000}{\$858{,}000} = 5.6\%$	$\dfrac{\$26{,}000}{\$803{,}000} = 3.2\%$

Companies strive for a high rate of return on sales. The higher the rate of return, the more sales dollars end up as profit. Supermart experienced a significant increase in its return on sales in the last year. Return on sales varies greatly depending on the industry. General merchandise retailers typically have a very low return on sales. Compare Supermart's rate of return on sales to the rates of return for some leading companies in the same industry:

Company	Rate of Return on Sales
Walmart	3.91%
JCPenney	2.19%
Kohl's	6.06%

Rate of Return on Total Assets

The rate of return on total assets, or simply return on assets, measures success in using assets to earn a profit. Two groups finance a company's assets:

1. Creditors have loaned money to the company, and they earn interest.
2. Shareholders have invested in stock, and their return is net income.

The sum of interest expense and net income is the return to the two groups that have financed the company's assets. Computation of the return-on-assets ratio for Supermart follows:

Formula	Supermart's 2012 Rate of Return on Total Assets
$\text{Rate of return on assets} = \dfrac{\text{Net income} + \text{Interest expense}}{\text{Average total assets}}$	$\dfrac{\$48{,}000 + \$20{,}000}{(\$644{,}000 + \$787{,}000)/2} = 9.5\%$

Compare Supermart's rate of return on assets with the rates of some other companies:

Company	Rate of Return on Assets
Walmart	10.59%
JCPenney	4.84%
Kohl's	9.39%

Rate of Return on Common Stockholders' Equity

A popular measure of profitability is **rate of return on common stockholders' equity**, often shortened to **return on equity**. This ratio shows the relationship between net income and common stockholders' equity—how much income is earned for each $1 invested by the common shareholders.

To compute this ratio, we subtract preferred dividends from net income to get net income available to the common stockholders. Then, we divide net income available to common stockholders by average common equity during the year. Common equity is total stockholders' equity minus preferred equity. The 2012 rate of return on common stockholders' equity for Supermart follows:

	Formula	Supermart's 2012 Rate of Return on Common Stockholders' Equity
Rate of return on common stockholders' equity	$= \dfrac{\text{Net income} - \text{Preferred dividends}}{\text{Average common stockholders' equity}}$	$\dfrac{\$48{,}000 - \$0}{(\$320{,}000 + \$356{,}000)/2} = 14.2\%$

Supermart's return on equity (14.2%) is higher than its return on assets (9.5%). This difference results from borrowing at one rate—for example, 8%—and investing the money to earn a higher rate, such as the firm's 14.2% return on equity.

This practice is called **trading on the equity**, or using **leverage**. It is directly related to the debt ratio. The higher the debt ratio reaches, the higher the leverage. Companies that finance operations with debt are said to *leverage* their positions.

During good times, leverage increases profitability. But leverage can have a negative impact on profitability. Therefore, leverage is a double-edged sword, increasing profits during good times but compounding losses during bad times. Compare Supermart's return on equity with the rates of some leading companies in the same industry.

Company	Rate of Return on Common Stockholders' Equity
Walmart	22.78%
JCPenney	7.60%
Kohl's	13.96%

Earnings per Share of Common Stock

Earnings per share of common stock, or simply **earnings per share (EPS)**, is perhaps the most widely quoted of all financial statistics. EPS is the only ratio that must appear on the face of the income statement. EPS is the amount of net income earned for each share of the company's outstanding *common* stock. Recall the following:

Outstanding stock = Issued stock − Treasury stock

Earnings per share is computed by dividing net income available to common stockholders by the number of common shares outstanding during the year. Preferred dividends are subtracted from net income because the preferred stockholders have a prior claim to dividends.

Let's assume Supermart has no preferred stock outstanding and no preferred dividends. Let's also assume that Supermart had 10,000 shares of common stock outstanding throughout 2011 and 2012. Given this information, we calculate the company's EPS as follows:

Formula	Supermart's Earnings per Share 2012	Supermart's Earnings per Share 2011
Earnings per share of common stock $= \frac{\text{Net income} - \text{Preferred dividends}}{\text{Number of shares of common stock outstanding}}$	$\frac{\$48{,}000 - \$0}{10{,}000} = \$4.80$	$\frac{\$26{,}000 - \$0}{10{,}000} = \$2.60$

Supermart's EPS increased significantly. Most companies strive to increase EPS each year, but general economic conditions, such as a recession, can prevent companies from doing so. Other leading companies in the same industry reported the following earnings per share on their income statements:

Company	Earnings Per Share
Walmart	$4.48
JCPenney	$1.64
Kohl's	$3.67

Analyzing Stock Investments

Investors purchase stock to earn a return on their investment. This return consists of two parts: (1) gains (or losses) from selling the stock at a price above (or below) the purchase price and (2) dividends. The ratios we examine in this section help analysts evaluate stock investments.

Price/Earnings Ratio

The price/earnings ratio is the ratio of the market price of a share of common stock to the company's earnings per share. It shows the market price of $1 of earnings. This ratio, abbreviated P/E, appears in the stock listings of the *Wall Street Journal*. The daily closing price of all publicly traded stocks can also be found in the *Wall Street Journal*.

Let's say the market price of Supermart's common stock was $60 at the end of 2012 and $35 at the end of 2011. Supermart's P/E ratio is calculated as follows:

Formula	Supermart's Price/Earnings Ratio 2012	Supermart's Price/Earnings Ratio 2011
P/E ratio $= \frac{\text{Market price per share of common stock}}{\text{Earnings per share}}$	$\frac{\$60.00}{\$4.80} = 12.5$	$\frac{\$35.00}{\$2.60} = 13.5$

Supermart's P/E ratio of 12.5 means that the company's stock is selling at 12.5 times earnings. The P/E ratio of other firms in the same industry follows:

Company	Price/Earnings Ratio
Walmart	12.52
JCPenney	19.69
Kohl's	13.95

Dividend Yield

Dividend yield is the ratio of dividends per share to the stock's market price per share. This ratio measures the percentage of a stock's market value that is returned annually as dividends. *Preferred* stockholders, who invest primarily to receive dividends, pay special attention to dividend yield.

Supermart paid annual cash dividends of $1.20 per share of common stock in 2012 and $1.00 in 2011, and market prices of the company's common stock were $60 in 2012 and $35 in 2011. The firm's dividend yield on common stock follows:

Formula	Dividend Yield on Supermart's Common Stock 2012	2011
Dividend yield on common stock* $= \dfrac{\text{Dividend per share of common stock}}{\text{Market price per share of common stock}}$	$\dfrac{\$1.20}{\$60.00} = 2.0\%$	$\dfrac{\$1.00}{\$35.00} = 2.9\%$

*Dividend yields may also be calculated for preferred stock.

An investor who buys Supermart common stock for $60 can expect to receive 2% of the investment annually in the form of cash dividends.

The dividends paid by companies varies substantially. Notice that Kohl's Corporation doesn't pay dividends:

Company	Dividend Yield
Walmart	2.16%
JCPenney	2.48%
Kohl's	0%

Book Value per Share of Common Stock

Book value per share of common stock is common equity divided by the number of common shares outstanding. Common equity equals total stockholders' equity less preferred equity. Supermart has no preferred stock outstanding. Its book-value-per-share-of- common-stock ratios follow (10,000 shares of common stock were outstanding).

Formula	Book Value per Share of Supermart's Common Stock 2012	2011
Book value per share of common stock $= \dfrac{\text{Total stockholders' equity} - \text{Preferred equity}}{\text{Number of shares of common stock outstanding}}$	$\dfrac{\$356{,}000 - \$0}{10{,}000} = \$35.60$	$\dfrac{\$320{,}000 - \$0}{10{,}000} = \$32.00$

Many experts argue that book value is not useful for investment analysis. It bears no relationship to market value and provides little information beyond stockholders' equity reported on the balance sheet. But some investors base their investment decisions on book value. For example, some investors rank stocks on the basis of the ratio of market price to book value. To these investors, the lower the ratio, the more attractive the stock, as this implies that the stock might be undervalued.

Red Flags in Financial Statement Analysis

Analysts look for *red flags* that may signal financial trouble. Recent accounting scandals highlight the importance of these red flags. The following conditions may reveal that the company is too risky.

- **Movement of Sales, Inventory, and Receivables.** Sales, receivables, and inventory generally move together. Increased sales lead to higher receivables and require more inventory to meet demand. Strange movements among sales, inventory, and receivables make the financial statements look suspect.
- **Earnings Problems.** Has net income decreased significantly for several years in a row? Has income turned into a loss? Most companies cannot survive years of consecutive loss.
- **Decreased Cash Flow.** Cash flow validates net income. Is cash flow from operations consistently lower than net income? If so, the company is in trouble. Are the sales of plant assets a major source of cash? If so, the company may face a cash shortage.
- **Too Much Debt.** How does the company's debt ratio compare to that of major competitors? If the debt ratio is too high, the company may be unable to pay its debts.
- **Inability to Collect Receivables.** Are days' sales in receivables growing faster than those of competitors? A cash shortage may be looming.
- **Buildup of Inventories.** Is inventory turnover too slow? If so, the company may be unable to sell goods or it may be overstating inventory.

Sustainability and Financial Statement Analysis

The financial statements present a high-level overview of the company's financial performance. As a result, a company's journey towards sustainability will not be readily apparent from the traditional type of financial statement analysis discussed in this chapter. Rather, management should consider disclosing the company's sustainability targets and achievements in the footnotes to the financial statements or in the management discussion and analysis section of the company's annual report. Alternatively, the company can disclose this type of information in a separate Corporate Social Responsibility report, otherwise known as a CSR report.

For example, the front end of PepsiCo's 2010 annual report is steeped in disclosure with respect to the company's emphasis on a triple bottom line: *people, profit,* and *planet*. The company discloses goals in each of the following areas:

1. Performance—*providing financial performance to shareholders*
2. Human sustainability—*improving nutritional impact of products on consumers*
3. Environmental sustainability—*minimizing negative consequences of operations on the planet*
4. Talent sustainability—*creating a work environment that supports employees' health, satisfaction, and dignity.*

For each goal, PepsiCo briefly discusses the company's progress and achievements. As a result, the financial statement reader gains a perspective on how various sustainability initiatives are being integrated into the company's operations. The reader can then compare goals and achievements over time or against other companies in the same industry, just as they do with financial data.

See Exercises E14-23A and E14-35B

Decision Guidelines

Using Ratios in Financial Statement Analysis

How can investors, creditors, and managers measure a company's ability to pay bills, sell inventory, collect receivables, pay long-term debt and so forth? How can they evaluate stock investments? The decision guidelines summarize the ratios that help to answer these questions.

Ratio	Computation	Information Provided
Measuring ability to pay current liabilities:		
1. Current ratio	$\dfrac{\text{Current assets}}{\text{Current liabilities}}$	Measures ability to pay current liabilities with current assets
2. Acid-test (quick) ratio	$\dfrac{\text{Cash} + \text{Short-term investments} + \text{Net current receivables}}{\text{Current liabilities}}$	Shows ability to pay all current liabilities if they come due immediately
Measuring ability to sell inventory and collect receivables:		
3. Inventory turnover	$\dfrac{\text{Cost of goods sold}}{\text{Average inventory}}$	Indicates salability of inventory—the number of times a company sells its average inventory during a year
4. Accounts receivable turnover	$\dfrac{\text{Net credit sales}}{\text{Average net accounts receivable}}$	Measures ability to collect cash from customers
5. Days' sales in receivables	$\dfrac{\text{Average net accounts receivable}}{\text{One day's sales}}$	Shows how many days' sales remain in Accounts Receivable—how many days it takes to collect the average level of receivables
Measuring ability to pay long-term debt:		
6. Debt ratio	$\dfrac{\text{Total liabilities}}{\text{Total assets}}$	Indicates percentage of assets financed with debt
7. Times-interest-earned ratio	$\dfrac{\text{Income from operations}}{\text{Interest expense}}$	Measures the number of times operating income can cover interest expense

Ratio	Computation	Information Provided
Measuring profitability:		
8. Rate of return on net sales	$\dfrac{\text{Net income}}{\text{Net sales}}$	Shows the percentage of each sales dollar earned as net income
9. Rate of return on total assets	$\dfrac{\text{Net income} + \text{Interest expense}}{\text{Average total assets}}$	Measures how profitably a company uses its assets
10. Rate of return on common stockholders' equity	$\dfrac{\text{Net income} - \text{Preferred dividends}}{\text{Average common stockholders' equity}}$	Gauges how much income is earned for each dollar invested by common shareholders
11. Earnings per share of common stock	$\dfrac{\text{Net income} - \text{Preferred dividends}}{\text{Number of shares of common stock outstanding}}$	Gives the amount of net income earned for each share of the company's common stock
Analyzing stock as an investment:		
12. Price/earnings ratio	$\dfrac{\text{Market price per share of common stock}}{\text{Earnings per share}}$	Indicates the market price of $1 of earnings
13. Dividend yield	$\dfrac{\text{Annual dividend per share of common (or preferred) stock}}{\text{Market price per share of common (or preferred) stock}}$	Shows the percentage of a stock's market value returned as dividends to stockholders each year
14. Book value per share of common stock	$\dfrac{\text{Total stockholders equity} - \text{Preferred equity}}{\text{Number of shares of common stock outstanding}}$	Indicates the recorded accounting amount for each share of common stock outstanding.

SUMMARY PROBLEM 2

Target Corporation's income statement was presented in Summary Problem 1 on page 840. The company's balance sheet (adapted), at the end of fiscal year 2010 and 2009 is presented below.[4]

Target Corporation
Balance Sheet (Adapted)
End of Fiscal Year*

(Dollars in millions)	2010	2009
Assets		
Current assets:		
Cash and cash equivalents	$ 1,712	$ 2,200
Credit card receivables, net of allowance	6,153	6,966
Inventory	7,596	7,179
Other current assets	1,752	2,079
Total current assets	17,213	18,424
Property, plant, and equipment, net	25,493	25,280
Other noncurrent assets	999	829
Total assets	$43,705	$44,533
Liabilities		
Current liabilities:		
Accounts payable	$ 6,625	$ 6,511
Other current liabilities	3,445	4,816
Total current liabilities	10,070	11,327
Long-term liabilities	18,148	17,859
Total liabilities	28,218	29,186
Stockholders' Equity		
Common stock and Additional paid-in capital	3,370	2,981
Retained earnings*	12,117	12,366
Total stockholders' equity	15,487	15,347
Total liabilities and stockholders' equity	$43,705	$44,533

*January 29, 2011 (fiscal year 2010) and January 31, 2010 (fiscal year 2009)

Other company information follows:

- Target has no preferred stock issued or outstanding.
- There were 704,038,218 common shares issued and outstanding at the end of fiscal year 2010.
- Cash dividends of $0.84 per share were declared during fiscal year 2010.
- The closing market price per share was $54.35 on Friday, January 29, 2011 (the end of fiscal year 2010).[5]

Requirement 1

Calculate the following ratios for fiscal year 2010:

1. Current ratio
2. Acid-test ratio
3. Inventory turnover

[4]Target Corporation 2011 10-K
[5]http://bigcharts.marketwatch.com.

4. Days' sales in receivables
5. Debt ratio
6. Times-interest-earned ratio
7. Rate of return on net sales
8. Rate of return on total assets
9. Rate of return on common stockholders' equity
10. Earnings per share of common stock
11. Price/earnings ratio
12. Dividend yield
13. Book value per share of common stock

Requirement 2

Compare Target's ratios to the ratios presented in the chapter for Walmart, JCPenney, and Kohl's. Do any of Target's ratios differ dramatically?

SOLUTIONS

Requirement 1

$$1)\ \text{Current ratio} = \frac{\textit{Current assets}}{\textit{Current liabilities}} = \frac{\$17{,}213}{\$10{,}070} = 1.71$$

$$2)\ \text{Acid-test ratio} = \frac{\textit{Cash + ST investments + Net current receivables}}{\textit{Current liabilities}} = \frac{\$1{,}712 + 0^{*} + \$6{,}153}{\$10{,}070} = 0.78$$

*No short-term investments are listed separately on the balance sheet. However, they may be a part of "other current assets." We also assume that all net receivables are current.

$$3)\ \text{Inventory turnover} = \frac{\textit{Cost of goods sold}}{\textit{Average inventory}} = \frac{\$45{,}725}{(\$7{,}179 + \$7{,}596)/2} = 6.19$$

$$4)\ \text{Days' sales in receivables} = \frac{\textit{Average net accounts receivable}}{\textit{One day's sales}} = \frac{(\$6{,}966 + \$6{,}153)/2}{(\$66{,}530)/365} = 35.98\ \text{days}$$

$$5)\ \text{Debt ratio} = \frac{\textit{Total liabilities}}{\textit{Total assets}} = \frac{\$28{,}218}{\$43{,}705} = 0.65$$

$$6)\ \text{Times-interest-earned ratio} = \frac{\textit{Income from operations}}{\textit{Interest expense}} = \frac{\$5{,}252}{\$757} = 6.94$$

$$7)\ \text{Rate of return on net sales} = \frac{\textit{Net income}}{\textit{Sales revenue}} = \frac{\$2{,}920}{\$66{,}530} = 4.39\%$$

$$8)\ \text{Rate of return on total assets} = \frac{\textit{Net income + Interest expense}}{\textit{Average total assets}} = \frac{\$2{,}920 + \$757}{(\$43{,}705 + \$44{,}533)/2} = 8.33\%$$

$$9)\ \text{Rate of return on common stockholders' equity} = \frac{\textit{Net income} - \textit{Preferred dividends}}{\textit{Average common stockholder's equity}} = \frac{\$2{,}920 - \$0}{(\$15{,}347 + 15{,}487)/2} = 18.94\%$$

$$10)\ \text{Earnings per share of common stock} = \frac{\textit{Net income} - \textit{Preferred dividends}}{\textit{Number of shares of common stock outstanding}} = \frac{\$2{,}920\ \textit{million}}{704{,}038{,}218} = \$4.15$$

$$11)\ \text{Price/earnings ratio} = \frac{\textit{Market price per share of common stock}}{\textit{Earnings per share}} = \frac{\$54.35}{\$4.15} = 13.09$$

$$12)\ \text{Dividend yield} = \frac{\textit{Dividend per share of common stock}}{\textit{Market price per share of common stock}} = \frac{\$0.84}{\$54.35} = 1.55\%$$

$$13)\ \text{Book value per share of common stock} = \frac{\textit{Total stockholders' equity} - \textit{Preferred equity}}{\textit{Number of shares of common stock outstanding}} = \frac{\$15{,}487\ \textit{million} - 0}{704{,}038{,}218} = \$22.00$$

Requirement 2

All of Target Corporation's ratios are in the same general range as those presented for Walmart, JCPenney, and Kohl's. For example, let's look at one ratio from each of the five categories of ratios discussed earlier:

1. Measuring ability to pay current liabilities

   Current Ratio—Target's current ratio (1.71) is better than Walmart's (0.89), but not as high as JCPenney's (2.41) or Kohl's (2.08). This means Target should have be able to meet its current obligations, using current assets, much easier than Walmart has the ability to do.

2. Measuring ability to sell inventory and collect receivables

   Inventory Turnover—Target's inventory turnover (6.19) is much better than JCPenney's (3.46) and Kohl's (3.81) but not as high as Walmart's (9.13). This means that Target is able to sell its inventory much more quickly than JCPenney and Kohl's can.

3. Measuring ability to pay long-term debt

   Debt ratio—Target's debt ratio (0.65) is only slightly higher than Walmart's (0.61) and JCPenney's (0.58) but much higher than Kohl's (0.40). This means that more of Target's assets were funded through debt than Kohl's assets were.

4. Measuring profitability

   Return on equity—Target's return on equity (18.94%) is better than JCPenney's (7.60%) and Kohl's (13.96%), but worse than Walmart's (22.78%). This means that Target is providing a return to its common stockholders of almost 19 cents on every dollar of stock invested in the company.

5. Analyzing stock investments

   Dividend yield—Target's dividend yield (1.55%) is much better than Kohl's (0%), but less than Walmart's (2.16%), and JCPenney's (2.48%). This means that Target is paying shareholders dividends at a rate of 1.5% of what one share of common stock would have cost investors if they had bought the stock at closing balance sheet date.

END OF CHAPTER

Learning Objectives

- 1 Perform a horizontal analysis of financial statements
- 2 Perform a vertical analysis of financial statements
- 3 Prepare and use common-size financial statements
- 4 Compute the standard financial ratios

Accounting Vocabulary

Accounts Receivable Turnover. (p. 845) Measures a company's ability to collect cash from credit customers. To compute accounts receivable turnover, divide net credit sales by average net accounts receivable.

Acid-Test Ratio. (p. 844) Ratio of the sum of cash plus short-term investments plus net current receivables to total current liabilities. It tells whether the entity can pay all of its current liabilities if they come due immediately; also called the *quick ratio*.

Benchmarking. (p. 838) The practice of comparing a company with other companies or industry averages.

Book Value per Share of Common Stock. (p. 850) Common stockholders' equity divided by the number of shares of common stock outstanding. It is the recorded amount for each share of common stock outstanding.

Common-Size Statement. (p. 838) A financial statement that reports only percentages (no dollar amounts).

Current Ratio. (p. 843) Current assets divided by current liabilities. It measures the ability to pay current liabilities with current assets.

Days' Sales in Receivables. (p. 845) Ratio of average net accounts receivable to one day's sale. It indicates how many days' sales remain in Accounts Receivable awaiting collection.

Debt Ratio. (p. 846) Ratio of total liabilities to total assets. It shows the proportion of a company's assets that is financed with debt.

Dividend Yield. (p. 850) Ratio of dividends per share of stock to the stock's market price per share. It tells the percentage of a stock's market value that the company returns to stockholders annually as dividends.

Earnings per Share (EPS). (p. 848) Amount of a company's net income for each share of its outstanding common stock.

Horizontal Analysis. (p. 832) Study of percentage changes in comparative financial statements.

Interest-Coverage Ratio. (p. 846) Ratio of income from operations to interest expense. It measures the number of times that operating income can cover interest expense; also called the *times-interest earned ratio*.

Inventory Turnover. (p. 844) Ratio of cost of goods sold to average inventory. It indicates how rapidly inventory is sold.

Leverage. (p. 848) Earning more income on borrowed money than the related interest expense, thereby increasing the earnings for the owners of the business; also called *trading on equity*.

Price/Earnings (P/E) Ratio. (p. 849) Ratio of the market price of a share of common stock to the company's earnings per share. It measures the value that the stock market places on $1 of a company's earnings.

Quick Ratio. (p. 844) Ratio of the sum of cash plus short-term investments plus net current receivables to total current liabilities. It tells whether the entity can pay all its current liabilities if they come due immediately; also called the *acid-test ratio*.

Rate of Return on Common Stockholders' Equity. (p. 848) Net income minus preferred dividends divided by average common stockholders' equity. It is a measure of profitability; also called *return on equity*.

Rate of Return on Net Sales. (p. 847) Ratio of net income to net sales. It is a measure of profitability; also called *return on sales*.

Rate of Return on Total Assets. (p. 847) Net income plus interest expense divided by average total assets. This ratio measures a company's success in using its assets to earn income for the people who finance the business; also called *return on assets*.

Ratio Analysis. (p. 832) Evaluating the relationships between two or more key components of the financial statements.

Return on Assets. (p. 847) Net income plus interest expense, divided by average total assets. This ratio measures a company's success in using its assets to earn income for the people who finance the business; also called *rate of return on total assets*.

Return on Equity. (p. 848) Net income minus preferred dividends, divided by average common stockholders' equity. It is a measure of profitability; also called *rate of return on common stockholders' equity*.

Return on Sales. (p. 847) Ratio of net income to net sales. It is a measure of profitability; also called *rate of return on net sales*.

Times-Interest-Earned Ratio. (p. 846) Ratio of income from operations to interest expense. It measures the number of times operating income can cover interest expense; also called the *interest-coverage ratio*.

Trading on Equity. (p. 848) Earning more income on borrowed money than the related interest expense, thereby increasing the earnings for the owners of the business; also called *leverage*.

Trend Percentages. (p. 834) A form of horizontal analysis in which percentages are computed by selecting a base year as 100% and expressing amounts for following years as a percentage of the base amount.

Vertical Analysis. (p. 832) Analysis of a financial statement that reveals the relationship of each statement item to a specified base, which is the 100% figure.

Working Capital. (p. 843) Current assets minus current liabilities; measures a business's ability to meet its short-term obligations with its current assets.

MyAccountingLab **Go to http://myaccountinglab.com/ for the following Quick Check, Short Exercises, Exercises, and Problems. They are available with immediate grading, explanations of correct and incorrect answers, and interactive media that acts as your own online tutor.**

Quick Check

1. *(Learning Objective 1)* Analyzing the percentage changes in comparative financial statements from year to year is known as
   - a. horizontal analysis.
   - b. benchmarking.
   - c. trend analysis.
   - d. vertical analysis.
2. *(Learning Objective 1)* What technique would you use to help predict future revenues and expenses of a company?
   - a. Capital analysis
   - b. Benchmarking
   - c. Trend analysis
   - d. Vertical analysis
3. *(Learning Objective 2)* Showing each item on the income statement as a percentage of sales is an example of
   - a. horizontal analysis.
   - b. benchmarking.
   - c. trend analysis.
   - d. vertical analysis.
4. *(Learning Objective 2)* Which of the following amounts is usually used as the base amount when performing a vertical analysis of a balance sheet?
   - a. Current assets
   - b. Current liabilities
   - c. Total liabilities
   - d. Total liabilities and stockholders' equity
5. *(Learning Objective 3)* Analysts can use common-size financial statements to
   - a. compare the relative proportion of assets, liabilities, equity, revenues, and expenses within a company over time or between companies of different sizes.
   - b. evaluate the financial statements of companies in different industries of the same size.
   - c. determine whether a company is in stable financial condition.
   - d. determine which company's stock should be purchased.
6. *(Learning Objective 4)* Which of the following ratios is a measure of a company's ability to pay long-term debt?
   - a. Times-interest-earned ratio
   - b. Rate of return on total assets
   - c. Current ratio
   - d. Accounts receivable turnover
7. *(Learning Objective 4)* Which of the following ratios is a measure of a company's ability to sell inventory and collect receivables?
   - a. Acid-test ratio
   - b. Debt ratio
   - c. Days' sales in receivables
   - d. Times-interest-earned ratio
8. *(Learning Objective 4)* Of the following ratios, which would not be effective in judging a company's ability to pay its current bills?
   - a. Quick ratio
   - b. Price-earnings ratio
   - c. Acid-test ratio
   - d. Current ratio
9. *(Learning Objective 4)* (Cash + short-term investments + net current receivables) divided by current liabilities is the formula for
   - a. return on assets.
   - b. current ratio.
   - c. working capital ratio.
   - d. acid-test ratio.
10. *(Learning Objective 4)* If Sarhan Corporation has a current ratio of 2.0, which transaction will normally increase Sarhan's current ratio?
    - a. Making a sale to a customer on account
    - b. Paying a long-term note payable off with cash
    - c. Receiving cash from customers on accounts receivables
    - d. Purchasing new equipment by issuing a long-term notes payable

Quick Check Answers

1. a 2. c 3. d 4. d 5. a 6. a 7. c 8. b 9. d 10. a

Short Exercises

S14-1 Horizontal analysis of revenue and cost of sales *(Learning Objective 1)*

Plantson reported the following on its comparative income statement:

(in millions)	2012	2011	2010
Revenue	$12,852	$12,240	$12,000
Cost of sales	$ 5,100	$ 4,640	$ 4,000

Perform a horizontal analysis of revenues and gross profit—both in dollar amounts and in percentages—for 2012 and 2011.

S14-2 Find trend percentages *(Learning Objective 2)*

Williams Group reported the following revenues and net income amounts:

(in millions)	2012	2011	2010	2009
Revenue..................................	$10,300	$9,600	$9,300	$10,000
Net income.............................	$ 648	$ 582	$ 552	$ 600

a. Show Williams Group's trend percentages for revenues and net income. Use 2009 as the base year and round to the nearest percent.

b. Which measure increased faster during 2010–2012?

S14-3 Vertical analysis of assets *(Learning Objective 2)*

McCormick Optical Company reported the following amounts on its balance sheet at December 31:

Cash and receivables..	$ 51,870
Inventory	39,710
Property, plant, and equipment, net..	98,420
Total assets...	$190,000

Perform a vertical analysis of McCormick Optical Company's assets at year end.

S14-4 Prepare common-size income statements *(Learning Objective 3)*

Compare Ramirez and Azul by converting their income statements to common size.

	Ramirez	Azul
Net sales..	$10,500	$21,000
Cost of goods sold...	6,510	14,805
Other expense	3,150	5,040
Net income..	$ 840	$ 1,155

Which company earns more net income? Which company's net income is a higher percentage of its net sales?

Hajjar's Data Set used for S14-5 through S14-9:

Hajjar's, a home-improvement store chain, reported these summarized figures (in billions):

Hajjar's
Income Statement
For the Year Ended December 31, 2012

Net sales	$42,522,500
Cost of goods sold	29,900,000
Interest expense	405,820
All other expenses	9,665,300
Net income	$ 2,551,380

Hajjar's
Balance Sheet
December 31, 2012 and 2011

	2012	2011		2012	2011
Cash	$ 1,300,000	$ 900,000	Total current liabilities	$ 4,800,000	$ 3,250,000
Short-term investments	250,000	275,000	Long-term liabilities	4,529,000	4,760,000
Accounts receivable	200,000	219,400	Total liabilities	9,329,000	8,010,000
Inventory	4,870,000	4,330,000			
Other current assets	600,000	455,600	Common stock	3,520,000	2,500,000
Total current assets	7,220,000	6,180,000	Retained earnings	7,431,000	6,175,000
All other assets	13,060,000	10,505,000	Total equity	10,951,000	8,675,000
Total assets	$20,280,000	$16,685,000	Total liabilities and equity	$20,280,000	$16,685,000

S14-5 Find current ratio *(Learning Objective 4)*

Refer to the Hajjar's Data Set.

a. Compute Hajjar's current ratio at December 31, 2012 and 2011.
b. Did Hajjar's current ratio improve, deteriorate, or hold steady during 2012?

S14-6 Analyze inventory and receivables *(Learning Objective 4)*

Use the Hajjar's Data Set to compute the following:

a. The rate of inventory turnover for 2012.
b. Days' sales in average receivables during 2012.

S14-7 Compute and interpret debt ratio *(Learning Objective 4)*

Refer to the Hajjar's Data Set.

a. Compute the debt ratio at December 31, 2012.
b. Is Hajjar's ability to pay its liabilities strong or weak? Explain your reasoning.

S14-8 Compute profitability ratios *(Learning Objective 4)*

Use the Hajjar's Data Set to compute these profitability measures for 2012:

a. Rate of return on net sales
b. Rate of return on total assets (interest expense for 2012 was $405,820)
c. Rate of return on common stockholders' equity

Are these rates of return strong or weak?

S14-9 Determine earnings per share *(Learning Objective 4)*

Use the Hajjar's Data Set when making the following calculations:

a. Compute earnings per share (EPS) for Hajjar's. The number of shares outstanding was 392,520.

b. Compute Hajjar's price/earnings ratio. The price of a share of Hajjar's is $70.20.

S14-10 Find missing values on income statement *(Learning Objective 4)*

A skeleton of Hollister Mills' income statement appears as follows (amounts in thousands):

HOLLISTER MILLS Income Statement Year Ended December 31	
Net sales	$7,200
Cost of goods sold	(a)
Selling and administrative expenses	1,830
Interest expense	(b)
Other expenses	175
Income before taxes	$1,400
Income tax expense	(c)
Net income	$ (d)

Use the following ratio data to complete Hollister Mills' income statement:

a. Inventory turnover was 13.0 (beginning inventory was $750; ending inventory was $720).

b. Rate of return on sales is 0.09.

S14-11 Find missing values on balance sheet *(Learning Objective 4)*

A skeleton of Hollister Mills' balance sheet appears as follows (amounts in thousands):

HOLLISTER MILLS Balance Sheet December 31			
Cash	$ 85	Total current liabilities	$2,000
Receivables	(a)	Long-term note payable	(e)
Inventories	650	Other long-term liabilities	800
Prepaid expenses	(b)		
Total current assets	(c)		
Plant assets, net	(d)		
Other assets	2,150	Stockholders' equity	2,250
Total assets	$6,800	Total liabilities and equity	$ (f)

Use the following ratio data to complete Hollister Mills' balance sheet:

a. The current ratio is 0.80.

b. The acid-test ratio is 0.40.

EXERCISES Group A

E14-12A Trend analysis of working capital *(Learning Objective 1)*

Compute the dollar amount of change and the percentage of change in Weekly News Group's working capital each year during 2011 and 2012. Is this trend favorable or unfavorable?

	2012	2011	2010
Total current assets	$275,640	$254,000	$214,500
Total current liabilities	$195,000	$182,000	$152,000

E14-13A Horizontal analysis *(Learning Objective 1)*

Prepare a horizontal analysis of the following comparative income statement of Spellbound Designs.

Spellbound Designs
Comparative Income Statements
Years Ended December 31, 2012 and 2011

	2012	2011
Net sales revenue	$504,000	$420,000
Expenses:		
Cost of goods sold	$241,920	$210,000
Selling and general expenses	$120,960	$105,000
Other expense	$ 30,240	$ 21,000
Total expenses	$393,120	$336,000
Net income	$110,880	$ 84,000

Why did net income increase by a higher percentage than net sales revenue during 2012?

E14-14A Compute trend percentages *(Learning Objective 1)*

Compute trend percentages for Harmond Realtors net revenue and net income for the following five-year period using 2008 as the base year.

(in thousands)	2012	2011	2010	2009	2008
Net revenue	$1,632	$1,428	$1,377	$1,122	$1,275
Net income	$ 182	$ 169	$ 117	$ 104	$ 130

Which grew faster during the period, net revenue or net income?

E14-15A Perform vertical analysis *(Learning Objective 2)*

Ruby Designs has requested that you perform a vertical analysis of its balance sheet.

Ruby Designs, Inc. Balance Sheet As of December 31	
Assets	
Total current assets	$ 51,675
Property, plant, and equipment, net	232,375
Other assets	40,950
Total assets	$325,000
Liabilities	
Total current liabilities	$ 58,500
Long-term debt	125,450
Total liabilities	$183,950
Stockholders' equity	
Total stockholders' equity	$141,050
Total liabilities and stockholders' equity	$325,000

E14-16A Prepare common-size income statement *(Learning Objective 3)*

Prepare a comparative common-size income statement for Spellbound Designs using the 2012 and 2011 data of Exercise 14-13A. To an investor, how does 2012 compare with 2011? Explain your reasoning.

E14-17A Calculate ratios *(Learning Objective 4)*

Balance sheet:	Current year	Preceding year
Cash	$ 14,200	$ 20,000
Short-term investments	$ 5,320	$ 23,000
Net receivables	$ 56,000	$ 74,000
Inventory	$ 80,000	$ 68,000
Prepaid expenses	$ 10,860	$ 9,200
Total current assets	$166,380	$194,200
Total current liabilities	$118,000	$ 88,000
Income statement:		
Net credit sales	$456,250	
Cost of goods sold	$321,900	

Requirement

Compute the following ratios for the current year:

a. Current ratio

b. Acid-test ratio

c. Inventory turnover

d. Days' sales in average receivables

E14-18A More ratio analysis *(Learning Objective 4)*

Nature Frames has asked you to determine whether the company's ability to pay current liabilities and total liabilities improved or deteriorated during 2012. To answer that question, compute these ratios for 2012 and 2011, using the following data:

	2012	2011
Cash	$ 62,500	$ 49,000
Short-term receivables	$ 29,000	—
Net receivables	$128,460	$128,160
Inventory	$245,340	$261,620
Total assets	$565,000	$496,000
Total current liabilities	$282,000	$206,000
Long-term note payable	$ 45,700	$ 71,760
Income from operations	$158,700	$161,190
Interest expense	$ 46,000	$ 40,500

a. Current ratio
b. Acid-test ratio
c. Debt ratio
d. Times-interest-earned ratio

E14-19A Compute profitability ratios *(Learning Objective 4)*

Compute four ratios that measure Lansbury's ability to earn profits. The company's comparative income statement follows. The data for 2010 are given as needed.

Lansbury
Comparative Income Statement
Years Ended December 31, 2012, 2011, and 2010

(Dollars in thousands)	2012	2011	2010
Net sales	$116,650	$139,250	
Cost of goods sold	65,000	58,000	
Selling and administrative expenses	21,000	24,000	
Interest expense	10,000	11,000	
Income tax expense	4,319	35,110	
Net income	$ 16,331	$ 11,140	
Additional data:			
Total assets	$202,000	$191,000	$178,000
Common stockholders' equity	$ 89,000	$ 89,000	$ 61,000
Preferred dividends	$ 3,070	$ 3,070	$ —
Common shares outstanding during the year	14,900	14,900	14,000

Did the company's operating performance improve or deteriorate during 2012?

E14-20A Compute stock ratios *(Learning Objective 4)*

Evaluate the common stock of Nelson State Bank as an investment. Specifically, use the three stock ratios to determine whether the common stock has increased or decreased in attractiveness during the past year.

	Current year	Last year
Net income	$ 80,400	$ 47,200
Dividends—common	$ 21,580	$ 21,580
Dividends—preferred	$ 14,000	$ 14,000
Total stockholders' equity at year end (includes 80,000 shares of common stock)	$809,300	$639,150
Preferred stock, 6%	$220,000	$220,000
Market price per share of common	$ 20.00	$ 8.00

E14-21A Find missing values *(Learning Objective 4)*

The following data (dollar amounts in millions) are adapted from the financial statements of Best Value Stores, Inc.

Total current assets	$11,700
Accumulated depreciation	$ 2,000
Total liabilities	$15,000
Preferred stock	$ 0
Debt ratio	60 %
Current ratio	1.44

Requirement

Complete Best Value's condensed balance sheet.

Current assets	$?
Property, plant, and equipment	$?
Less: Accumulated depreciation	(?)
Total assets	$?
Current liabilities	$?
Long-term liabilities	?
Stockholders' equity	?
Total liabilities and stockholders' equity	$?

E14-22A Calculate ratios *(Learning Objective 4)*

River Rock Corporation reported these figures:

Balance sheet	2012	2011	Income statement	2012
Cash and equivalents	$ 5,120	$ 2,800	Sales	$14,235
Receivables	2,300	1,600	Cost of sales	4,350
Inventory	1,800	1,200	Operating expenses	885
Prepaid expenses	3,240	2,800	Operating income	$ 9,000
Total current assets	$12,460	$ 8,400	Interest expense	400
Other assets	22,000	18,500	Other expense	6,200
Total assets	$34,460	$26,900	Net income	$ 2,400
Total current liabilities	$14,000	$13,000		
Long-term liabilities	4,960	5,400		
Common equity	15,500	8,500		
Total liabilities and equity	$34,460	$26,900		

River Rock has 3,200 shares of common stock outstanding. Its stock has traded recently at $27.00 per share. You would like to gain a better understanding of River Rock's financial position. Calculate the following ratios for 2012 and interpret the results:

a. Inventory turnover
b. Days' sales in receivables
c. Acid-test ratio
d. Times-interest-earned
e. Return on stockholders' equity
f. Earnings per share
g. Price/earnings ratio

E14-23A Classify company sustainability measurements into triple bottom line components *(Learning Objective 4)*

In its 2010 Annual Report, PepsiCo lists several sustainability goals and commitments it has made. In the following list from PepsiCo's 2010 Annual Report, categorize each goal (or measurement) as to whether it is oriented towards the people, planet, or profit component or the triple bottom line.

	Excerpts of Goals and Commitments from PepsiCo, Inc.'s 2010 Annual Report	People, Profit, or Planet?
a.	Expand PepsiCo Foundation and PepsiCo corporate contribution initiatives to promote healthier communities, including enhancing diet and physical activity programs.	
b.	Continue to lead the industry by incorporating at least 10 percent recycled polyethylene terephthalate (rPET) in our primary soft drink containers in the U.S., and broadly expand the use of rPET across key international markets.	
c.	Ensure a safe workplace by continuing to reduce lost-time injury rates, while striving to improve other occupational health and safety metrics through best practices.	
d.	Improve our electricity-use efficiency by 20 percent per unit of production by 2015.	
e.	Match eligible associate charitable contributions globally, dollar-for-dollar, through the PepsiCo Foundation.	
f.	Deliver total shareholder returns in the top quartile of our industry group.	
g.	Increase cash flow in proportion to net income growth over three-year windows.	
h.	Reduce the average amount of saturated fat per serving in key global food brands, in key countries, by 15 percent by 2020, compared to a 2006 baseline.	

	Excerpts of Goals and Commitments from PepsiCo, Inc.'s 2010 Annual Report	People, Profit, or Planet?
i.	Reduce packaging weight by 350 million pounds—avoiding the creation of one billion pounds of landfill waste by 2012.	
j.	Reduce the average amount of added sugar per serving in key global beverage brands, in key countries, by 25 percent by 2020, compared to a 2006 baseline.	

Source: PepsiCo 2010 Annual report (retrieved from http://www.pepsico.com/Download/PepsiCo_Annual_Report_2010_Full_Annual_Report.pdf on May 24, 2011)

EXERCISES Group B

E14-24B Trend analysis of working capital *(Learning Objective 1)*

Compute the dollar amount of change and the percentage of change in DuBois Enterprises' working capital each year during 2011 and 2012. Is this trend favorable or unfavorable?

	2012	2011	2010
Total current assets	$380,080	$348,000	$313,000
Total current liabilities	$184,000	$176,000	$153,000

E14-25B Horizontal analysis *(Learning Objective 1)*

Prepare a horizontal analysis of the following comparative income statement of Sunny Day Designs.

Sunny Day Designs
Comparative Income Statement
Years Ended December 31, 2012 and 2011

	2012	2011
Net sales revenue	$540,000	$450,000
Expenses:		
Cost of goods sold	$243,000	$225,000
Selling and general expenses	97,200	90,000
Other expense	32,400	22,500
Total expenses	372,600	337,500
Net income	$167,400	$112,500

Why did net income increase by a higher percentage than net sales revenue during 2012?

E14-26B Compute trend percentages *(Learning Objective 1)*

Compute trend percentages for Rolling Hills Realtors' net revenue and net income for the following five-year period, using 2008 as the base year.

(in thousands)	2012	2011	2010	2009	2008
Net revenue	$1,404	$1,188	$1,026	$972	$1,080
Net income	$ 170	$ 160	$ 120	$100	$ 125

Which grew faster during the period, net revenue or net income?

E14-27B Perform vertical analysis *(Learning Objective 2)*

National Graphics has requested that you perform a vertical analysis of its balance sheet.

National Graphics, Inc. Balance Sheet As of December 31	
Assets	
Total current assets	$ 42,050
Property, plant, and equipment, net	209,380
Other assets	38,570
Total assets	$290,000
Liabilities	
Total current liabilities	$ 53,940
Long-term debt	110,490
Total liabilities	$164,430
Stockholders' equity	
Total stockholders' equity	$125,570
Total liabilities and stockholders' equity	$290,000

E14-28B Prepare common-size income statement *(Learning Objective 3)*

Prepare a comparative common-size income statement for Sunny Day Designs using the 2012 and 2011 data of Exercise 14-25B. To an investor, how does 2012 compare with 2011? Explain your reasoning.

E14-29B Calculate ratios *(Learning Objective 4)*

The financial statements of a company include the following items:

Balance sheet:	Current year	Preceding year
Cash	$ 14,000	$ 24,000
Short-term investments	$ 7,020	$ 27,500
Net receivables	$ 54,000	$ 65,560
Inventory	$ 76,000	$ 74,000
Prepaid expenses	$ 20,800	$ 7,700
Total current assets	$171,820	$198,760
Total current liabilities	$121,000	$ 85,000
Income statement:		
Net credit sales	$445,300	
Cost of goods sold	$315,000	

Requirement

Compute the following ratios for the current year:

a. Current ratio
b. Acid-test ratio
c. Inventory turnover
d. Days' sales in average receivables

E14-30B More ratio analysis *(Learning Objective 4)*

Scenic Frames has asked you to determine whether the company's ability to pay current liabilities and total liabilities improved or deteriorated during 2012. To answer this question, compute these ratios for 2012 and 2011, using the following data:

	2012	2011
Cash	$ 59,000	$ 47,000
Short-term investments	$ 29,500	—
Net receivables	$110,060	$118,240
Inventory	$247,520	$271,320
Total assets	$566,000	$492,000
Total current liabilities	$272,000	$204,000
Long-term note payable	$ 61,940	$ 46,920
Income from operations	$168,295	$159,580
Interest expense	$ 48,500	$ 39,500

a. Current ratio
b. Acid-test ratio
c. Debt ratio
d. Times-interest-earned ratio

E14-31B Compute profitability ratios *(Learning Objective 4)*

Compute four ratios that measure Sudbury Industries ability to earn profits. The company's comparative income statement follows. The data for 2010 are given as needed.

Sudbury Industries
Comparative Income Statement
Years Ended December 31, 2012, 2011, and 2010

(Dollars in thousands)	2012	2011	2010
Net sales	$198,830	$160,625	
Cost of goods sold	106,000	98,000	
Selling and administrative expenses	44,000	36,000	
Interest expense	7,500	8,500	
Income tax expense	21,447	2,705	
Net income	$ 19,883	$ 15,420	
Additional data:			
Total assets	$204,000	$190,000	$178,000
Common stockholders' equity	$ 88,000	$ 81,430	$ 78,570
Preferred dividends	$ 2,940	$ 2,940	$ 0
Common shares outstanding during the year	16,943	16,943	14,500

Did the company's operating performance improve or deteriorate during 2012?

E14-32B Compute stock ratios *(Learning Objective 4)*

Evaluate the common stock of Webster State Bank as an investment. Specifically, use the three stock ratios to determine whether the common stock has increased or decreased in attractiveness during the past year.

	Current year	Last year
Net income	$ 66,500	$ 64,300
Dividends—common	$ 22,440	$ 22,440
Dividends—preferred	$ 11,500	$ 11,500
Total stockholders' equity at year-end (includes 88,000 shares of common stock)	$885,600	$683,200
Preferred stock (6%)	$230,000	$230,000
Market price per share of common stock	$ 17.00	$ 15.00

E14-33B Find missing values *(Learning Objective 4)*

The following data (dollar amounts in millions) are adapted from the financial statements of Superior Value Stores, Inc.

Total current assets	$11,700
Accumulated depreciation	$ 1,600
Total liabilities	$18,000
Preferred stock	$ 0
Debt ratio	45%
Current ratio	1.44

Requirement

Complete Superior Value's condensed balance sheet.

Current assets	$?
Property, plant, and equipment	$?
Less: Accumulated depreciation	(?)
Total assets	$?
Current liabilities	$?
Long-term liabilities	?
Stockholders' equity	?
Total liabilities and stockholders' equity	$?

E14-34B Calculate ratios *(Learning Objective 4)*

Blue Stone Corporation reported these figures:

Balance sheet	2012	2011	Income statement	2012
Cash and equivalents	$ 1,720	$ 1,500	Sales	$13,505
Receivables	2,700	1,740	Cost of sales	5,600
Inventory	2,300	1,700	Operating expenses	3,005
Prepaid expenses	760	3,210	Operating income	$ 4,900
Total current assets	$ 7,480	$ 8,150	Interest expense	200
Other assets	19,500	17,500	Other expense	2,150
Total assets	$26,980	$25,650	Net income	$ 2,550
Total current liabilities	8,500	7,500		
Long-term liabilities	3,980	2,650		
Common equity	14,500	15,500		
Total liabilities and equity	$26,980	$25,650		

Blue Stone has 3,000 shares of common stock outstanding. Its stock has traded recently at $28.90 per share. You would like to gain a better understanding of Blue Stone's financial position. Calculate the following ratios for 2012 and interpret the results:

a. Inventory turnover
b. Days' sales in receivables
c. Acid-test ratio
d. Times-interest-earned
e. Return on stockholders' equity
f. Earnings per share
g. Price/earnings ratio

E14-35B Classify company sustainability measurements into triple bottom line components *(Learning Objective 4)*

In its 2010 Annual Report, PepsiCo lists several sustainability goals and commitments it has made. In the following list from PepsiCo's 2010 Annual Report, categorize each goal (or measurement) as to whether it is oriented towards the *people*, *planet*, or *profit* component of the triple bottom line.

	Excerpts of Goals and Commitments from PepsiCo, Inc.'s 2010 Annual Report	People, Profit, or Planet?
a.	Foster diversity and inclusion by developing a workforce that reflects local communities.	
b.	Rank among the top two suppliers in customer (retail partner) surveys where third-party measures exist.	
c.	Work to eliminate all solid waste to landfills from our production facilities.	
d.	Sustain or improve brand equity scores for PepsiCo's 19 billion-dollar brands in the top 10 markets.	
e.	Increase the amount of whole grains, fruits, vegetables, nuts, seeds and low-fat dairy in our global product portfolio.	
f.	Reduce our fuel-use intensity by 25 percent per unit of production by 2015.	
g.	Reduce the average amount of sodium per serving in key global food brands, in key countries, by 25 percent by 2015, compared to a 2006 baseline.	
h.	Improve our water-use efficiency by 20 percent per unit of production by 2015.	
i.	Grow international revenues at two times real global GDP growth rate.	
j.	Grow savory snack and liquid refreshment beverage market share in the top 20 markets.	

Source: PepsiCo 2010 Annual report (retrieved from http://www.pepsico.com/Download/PepsiCo_Annual_Report_2010_Full_Annual_Report.pdf on May 24, 2011)

PROBLEMS Group A

P14-36A Prepare trend analysis *(Learning Objectives 1 & 4)*

Net sales revenue, net income, and common stockholders' equity for Clear Optical Corporation, a manufacturer of contact lenses, follow for a four-year period.

(in thousands)	2012	2011	2010	2009
Net sales revenue	$7,437	$7,035	$6,499	$6,700
Net income	$ 700	$ 476	$ 420	$ 560
Ending common stockholders' equity	$5,525	$3,225	$5,275	$3,125

Requirements

1. Compute trend percentages for each item for 2009 through 2012. Use 2009 as the base year.
2. Compute the rate of return on common stockholders' equity for 2010 through 2012.

P14-37A Comprehensive analysis *(Learning Objectives 2, 3, & 4)*

Franklin Department Stores' chief executive officer (CEO) has asked you to compare the company's profit performance and financial position with the average for the industry. The CEO has given you the company's income statement and balance sheet, as well as the industry average data for retailers.

Franklin Department Stores, Inc.
Income Statement Compared with Industry Average
For Year Ended December 31

	Franklin	Industry Average
Net sales	$779,000	100.0%
Cost of goods sold	527,383	65.8%
Gross profit	$251,617	34.2%
Operating expenses	161,253	19.6%
Operating income	$ 90,364	14.6%
Other expenses	7,011	0.6%
Net income	$ 83,353	14.0%

Franklin Department Stores, Inc.
Balance Sheet Compared with Industry Average
As of December 31

	Franklin	Industry Average
Current assets	$332,220	71.0%
Fixed assets, net	128,380	23.7%
Intangible assets, net	5,880	0.8%
Other assets	23,520	4.5%
Total assets	$490,000	100.0%
Current liabilities	$227,360	48.2%
Long-term liabilities	110,740	16.6%
Stockholders' equity	151,900	35.2%
Total liabilities and stockholders' equity	$490,000	100.0%

Requirements

1. Prepare a common-size income statement and balance sheet for Franklin Department Stores. The first column of each statement should present Franklin Department Stores' common-size statement, while the second column should present the industry averages.
2. For the profitability analysis, compute Franklin Department Stores' (a) ratio of gross profit to net sales, (b) ratio of operating income to net sales, and (c) ratio of net income to net sales. Compare these figures with the industry averages. Is Franklin Department Stores' profit performance better or worse than the industry average?
3. For the analysis of financial position, compute Franklin Department Stores' (a) ratio of current assets to total assets and (b) ratio of stockholders' equity to total assets. Compare these ratios with the industry averages. Is Franklin Department Stores' financial position better or worse than the industry averages?

P14-38A Effect of transactions on ratios *(Learning Objective 4)*

Financial statement data of *American Traveler* magazine include the following items (dollars in thousands):

Cash	$ 25,000
Accounts receivable, net	$ 83,500
Inventories	$169,500
Total assets	$680,000
Short-term notes payable	$ 51,500
Accounts payable	$105,000
Accrued liabilities	$ 43,500
Long-term liabilities	$208,000
Net income	$ 73,440
Common shares outstanding	48,000

Requirements

1. Compute *American Traveler*'s current ratio, debt ratio, and earnings per share. Round all ratios to two decimal places.
2. Compute the three ratios after evaluating the effect of each transaction that follows. Consider each transaction *separately*.
   a. Purchased inventory on account, $60,000
   b. Borrowed $170,000 on a long-term note payable
   c. Issued 6,000 shares of common stock, receiving cash of $136,000
   d. Received cash on account, $21,500

P14-39A Ratio analysis over two years *(Learning Objective 4)*

Comparative financial statement data of Danfield, Inc., follow:

Danfield, Inc.
Comparative Income Statement
Years Ended December 31, 2012 and 2011

	2012	2011
Net sales	$466,840	$419,560
Cost of goods sold	250,000	210,000
Gross profit	$216,840	$209,560
Operating expenses	134,000	127,000
Income from operations	$ 82,840	$ 82,560
Interest expense	10,900	12,800
Income before income tax	$ 71,940	$ 69,760
Income tax expense	25,940	33,760
Net income	$ 46,000	$ 36,000

Danfield, Inc.
Comparative Balance Sheet
December 31, 2012 and 2011

	2012	2011	2010*
Current assets:			
Cash	$ 91,000	$ 92,000	
Current receivables, net	106,000	180,000	$130,000
Inventories	140,000	110,000	226,000
Prepaid expenses	9,500	5,000	
Total current assets	$346,500	$387,000	
Property, plant, and equipment, net	201,000	172,000	
Total assets	$547,500	$559,000	
Total current liabilities	$192,500	$225,000	
Long-term liabilities	95,000	119,000	
Total liabilities	$287,500	$344,000	
Preferred stock, 8%	125,000	125,000	
Common stockholders' equity, no par	135,000	90,000	110,000
Total liabilities and stockholders' equity	$547,500	$559,000	

**Selected 2010 amounts*

1. Market price of Danfield's common stock: $40.14 at December 31, 2012, and $25.87 at December 31, 2011
2. Common shares outstanding: 10,000 during 2012 and 10,000 during 2011
3. All sales are credit sales

Requirements

1. Compute the following ratios for 2012 and 2011:
   a. Current ratio
   b. Times-interest-earned ratio
   c. Inventory turnover
   d. Return on common stockholders' equity
   e. Earnings per share of common stock
   f. Price/earnings ratio

2. Decide (a) whether Danfield's ability to pay debts and to sell inventory improved or deteriorated during 2012 and (b) whether the investment attractiveness of its common stock appears to have increased or decreased.

P14-40A Make an investment decision *(Learning Objective 4)*

Assume that you are purchasing an investment and have decided to invest in a company in the smartphone business. You have narrowed the choice to JT Electronics or Zylo Electronics and have assembled the following data.

Selected income statement data for the current year follows:

	JT	Zylo
Net sales (all on credit)	$452,600	$511,000
Cost of goods sold	$209,000	$255,000
Interest expense	—	$ 18,500
Net income	$ 56,100	$ 64,400

Selected balance sheet data at the *beginning* of the current year follows:

	JT	Zylo
Current receivables, net	$ 40,880	$ 40,700
Inventories	$ 82,000	$ 82,500
Total assets	$260,000	$273,000
Common stock:		
$1 par, (10,000 shares)	$ 11,000	
$1 par, (15,000 shares)		$ 14,000

Selected balance sheet and market-price data at the *end* of the current year follows:

	JT	Zylo
Current assets:		
Cash	$ 29,000	$ 20,500
Short-term investments	$ 46,300	$ 22,200
Current receivables, net	$ 36,000	$ 44,000
Inventories	$ 70,000	$105,000
Prepaid expenses	$ 2,700	$ 4,300
Total current assets	$184,000	$196,000
Total assets	$265,000	$272,000
Total current liabilities	$106,000	$102,000
Total liabilities	$106,000	$136,000
Common stock:		
$1 par, (10,000 shares)	$ 11,000	
$1 par, (15,000 shares)		$ 14,000
Total stockholders' equity	$159,000	$136,000
Market price per share of common stock	$ 86.70	$ 85.10

Your strategy is to invest in companies that have low price/earnings ratios but appear to be in good shape financially. Assume that you have analyzed all other factors and that your decision depends on the results of ratio analysis.

Requirement

Compute the following ratios for both companies for the current year and decide which company's stock better fits your investment strategy.

a. Acid-test ratio
b. Inventory turnover
c. Days' sales in average receivables
d. Debt ratio
e. Earnings per share of common stock
f. Price/earnings ratio

PROBLEMS Group B

P14-41B Prepare trend analysis *(Learning Objectives 1 & 4)*

Net sales revenue, net income, and common stockholders' equity for Crystal Vision Corporation, a manufacturer of contact lenses, follow for a four-year period.

(in thousands)	2012	2011	2010	2009
Net sales revenue	$7,293	$6,838	$6,305	$6,500
Net income	$ 682	$ 473	$ 418	$ 550
Ending common stockholders' equity	$3,558	$4,192	$2,688	$4,000

Requirements

1. Compute trend percentages for each item for 2009 through 2012. Use 2009 as the base year.
2. Compute the rate of return on common stockholders' equity for 2010 through 2012.

P14-42B Comprehensive analysis *(Learning Objectives 2, 3, & 4)*

Ambrose Department Stores' chief executive officer (CEO) has asked you to compare the company's profit performance and financial position with the average for the industry. The CEO has given you the company's income statement and balance sheet, as well as the industry average data for retailers.

Ambrose Department Stores, Inc.
Income Statement Compared with Industry Average
For Year Ended December 31

	Ambrose	Industry Average
Net sales	$783,000	100.0%
Cost of goods sold	530,091	65.8%
Gross profit	$252,909	34.2%
Operating expenses	161,298	19.9%
Operating income	$91,611	14.3%
Other expenses	7,047	0.4%
Net income	$ 84,564	13.9%

Ambrose Department Stores, Inc.
Balance Sheet Compared with Industry Average
As of December 31

	Ambrose	Industry Average
Current assets	$284,340	71.7%
Fixed assets, net	110,040	23.7%
Intangible assets, net	4,200	0.6%
Other assets	21,420	4.6%
Total assets	$420,000	100.0%
Current liabilities	$192,360	48.3%
Long-term liabilities	92,400	16.5%
Stockholders' equity	135,240	35.2%
Total liabilities and stockholders' equity	$420,000	100.0%

Requirements

1. Prepare a common-size income statement and balance sheet for Ambrose Department Stores. The first column of each statement should present Ambrose Department Stores' common-size statement, while the second column should present the industry averages.
2. For the profitability analysis, compute Ambrose Department Stores' (a) ratio of gross profit to net sales, (b) ratio of operating income to net sales, and (c) ratio of net income to net sales. Compare these figures with the industry averages. Is Ambrose Department Stores' profit performance better or worse than the average for the industry?
3. For the analysis of financial position, compute Ambrose Department Stores' (a) ratios of current assets to total assets and (b) ratio of stockholders' equity to total assets. Compare these ratios with the industry averages. Is Ambrose Department Stores' financial position better or worse than the industry averages?

P14-43B Effect of transactions on ratios *(Learning Objective 4)*

Financial statement data of *Road Trip* magazine include the following information (dollars in thousands):

Cash	$ 23,500
Accounts receivable, net	$ 79,000
Inventories	$197,800
Total assets	$630,000
Short-term notes payable	$ 50,500
Accounts payable	$100,000
Accrued liabilities	$ 59,500
Long-term liabilities	$193,200
Net income	$ 78,300
Common shares outstanding	58,000

Requirements

1. Compute *Road Trip*'s current ratio, debt ratio, and earnings per share. Round all ratios to two decimal places.
2. Compute the three ratios after evaluating the effect of each transaction that follows. Consider each transaction *separately*.
   a. Purchased inventory on account, $48,000
   b. Borrowed $210,000 on a long-term note payable
   c. Issued 7,250 shares of common stock, receiving cash of $176,400
   d. Received cash on account, $19,500

P14-44B Ratio analysis over two years *(Learning Objective 4)*
Comparative financial statement data of Topsfield, Inc., follow:

Topsfield, Inc.
Comparative Income Statement
Years Ended December 31, 2012 and 2011

	2012	2011
Net sales	$463,560	$410,600
Cost of goods sold	248,000	212,000
Gross profit	$215,560	$198,600
Operating expenses	131,000	125,000
Income from operations	$ 84,560	$ 73,600
Interest expense	11,200	11,500
Income before income tax	$ 73,360	$ 62,100
Income tax expense	6,760	8,500
Net income	$ 66,600	$ 53,600

Topsfield, Inc.
Comparative Balance Sheet
December 31, 2012 and 2011

	2012	2011	2010*
Current assets:			
Cash	$ 99,000	$100,000	
Current receivables, net	100,500	107,500	$ 99,000
Inventories	139,000	181,000	158,200
Prepaid expenses	10,000	6,500	
Total current assets	$348,500	$395,000	
Property, plant, and equipment, net	207,000	179,000	
Total assets	$555,500	$574,000	
Total current liabilities	$212,500	$250,000	
Long-term liabilities	131,000	67,000	
Total liabilities	$343,500	$317,000	
Preferred stock, 8%	85,000	85,000	
Common stockholders' equity, no par	127,000	172,000	188,000
Total liabilities and stockholders' equity	$555,500	$574,000	

**Selected 2010 amounts*

1. Market price of Topfield's common stock: $53.13 at December 31, 2012, and $35.64 at December 31, 2011
2. Common shares outstanding: 13,000 during 2012 and 13,000 during 2011
3. All sales are credit sales

Requirements

1. Compute the following ratios for 2012 and 2011:
   a. Current ratio
   b. Times-interest-earned ratio
   c. Inventory turnover
   d. Return on common stockholders' equity
   e. Earnings per share of common stock
   f. Price/earnings ratio
2. Decide (a) whether Topfield's ability to pay debts and to sell inventory improved or deteriorated during 2012 and (b) whether the investment attractiveness of its common stock appears to have increased or decreased.

P14-45B Make an investment decision *(Learning Objective 4)*

Assume that you are purchasing an investment and have decided to invest in a company in the smartphone business. You have narrowed the choice to NT Electronics or Xoom Corporation and have assembled the following data.

Selected income statement data for the current year follows:

	NT	Xoom
Net sales (all on credit)	$401,500	$554,800
Cost of goods sold	$209,000	$231,000
Interest expense	—	$ 16,500
Net income	$ 49,000	$ 63,000

Selected balance sheet data at the *beginning* of the current year follows:

	NT	Xoom
Current receivables, net	$ 34,300	$ 53,480
Inventories	$ 86,000	$ 77,000
Total assets	$259,000	$271,000
Common stock:		
$1 par (13,000 shares)	$ 10,000	
$1 par (16,000 shares)		$ 14,000

Selected balance sheet and market-price data at the *end* of the current year follows:

	NT	Xoom
Current assets:		
Cash	$ 30,500	$ 22,000
Short-term investments	52,220	21,200
Current receivables, net	35,000	40,000
Inventories	66,000	98,000
Prepaid expenses	2,280	6,800
Total current assets	$186,000	$188,000
Total assets	$436,000	$434,375
Total current liabilities	$109,000	$104,000
Total liabilities	$109,000	$139,000
Common stock:		
$1 par (13,000 shares)	$ 10,000	
$1 par (16,000 shares)		$ 14,000
Total stockholders' equity	$372,000	$295,375
Market price per share of common stock	$ 73.50	$ 81.90

Your strategy is to invest in companies that have low price/earnings ratios but appear to be in good shape financially. Assume that you have analyzed all other factors and that your decision depends on the results of ratio analysis.

Requirement

Compute the following ratios for both companies for the current year and decide which company's stock better fits your investment strategy.

a. Acid-test ratio
b. Inventory turnover
c. Days' sales in average receivables
d. Debt ratio
e. Earnings per share of common stock
f. Price/earnings ratio

CRITICAL THINKING

Discussion & Analysis

A14-46 Discussion & Questions

1. Describe horizontal analysis. Describe vertical analysis. What is each technique used for? How are the two methods similar? How are they different?
2. How is the current ratio calculated? What is it used to measure? How is it interpreted?
3. Assume a company has a current ratio of 2.0. List two examples of transactions that could cause the current ratio to increase. Also list two examples of transactions that could cause the current ratio to decrease.
4. What does the accounts receivable turnover measure? What does a relatively high accounts receivable turnover indicate about a company?
5. Describe the set of circumstances that could result in net income increasing while ROI decreases.
6. Suppose a company has a relatively high inventory turnover. What does the high inventory turnover indicate about the company's short-term liquidity?
7. Describe at least four financial conditions that may signal financial trouble.
8. Describe at least two reasons that a company's ratios might not be comparable over time.
9. Compare and contrast the current ratio and the quick ratio.
10. Describe why book value per share of common stock may not be useful for investment analysis.
11. Find a recent annual report for a publically held company in which you are interested. Summarize what sustainability information is provided in that annual report. Based on the sustainability information provided in the annual report, what measurements do you think the company might use to track its sustainability efforts? (You can use your imagination here; the actual sustainability measures are unlikely to be in the annual report.)
12. There are three components in the triple bottom line; *people*, *planet*, and *profit*. Which component do you think is most important? Why?

Application & Analysis

A14-47 Calculating Ratios for Companies Within the Same Industry

Select an industry you are interested in and select three companies within that industry. Obtain their annual reports by going to each company's website and downloading the report for the most recent year. (On many companies' websites, you will need to visit the Investor Relations section to obtain the company's financial statements.) You may also collect the information from the company's Form 10-K, which can be found at www.sec.gov/idea/searchidea/companysearch_idea.html.

Basic Discussion Questions

For each of the three companies you selected, answer the following:

1. Calculate two ratios that measure the ability to pay current liabilities.
2. Calculate at least two ratios that measure the ability to sell inventory and collect receivables.
3. Calculate at least two ratios that measure the ability to pay long-term debt.
4. Calculate at least two ratios that measure profitability.
5. Calculate at least two ratios that help to analyze the stock as an investment.

Now that you have crunched the numbers, interpret the ratios. What can you tell about each company and its financial position? Is one company clearly better than the others in terms of its financial position, or are all three companies similar to each other?

Decision Cases

A14-48 Investment recommendation *(Learning Objective 4)*

Assume you are an investment analyst at a brokerage firm. It is your job to recommend investments for your clients. The only information you have are some ratio values for two companies in the pharmaceuticals industry.

Ratio	PharmaKurtz	Harvan-Smith
Return on equity	21.5%	32.3%
Return on assets	16.4%	17.1%
Days' sales in receivables	42	36
Inventory turnover	8	6
Gross profit percentage	51%	53%
Net income as a percentage of sales	8.3%	7.2%
Times interest earned	9	16

Write a report to the brokerage firm's investment committee. Recommend one company's stock over the other. State the reasons for your recommendation.

A14-49 Effect of transactions on ratios *(Learning Objective 4)*

General Allied Conglomerates (GAC) and First Star Corporation (FSC) both had a bad year in 2012; the companies' auto parts units suffered net losses. The loss pushed some return measures into the negative column, and the companies' ratios deteriorated. Assume that top management of GAC and FSC are pondering ways to improve their ratios. In particular, management is considering the following transactions:

1. Borrow $100 million on long-term debt
2. Purchase treasury stock for $500 million cash
3. Expense one-fourth of the goodwill carried on the books
4. Create a new auto design division at a cash cost of $300 million
5. **Purchase patents from another manufacturer, paying $20 million cash**

Requirement

Top management wants to know the effects of these transactions (increase, decrease, or no effect) on the following ratios:

a. **Current ratio**
b. **Debt ratio**
c. **Return on equity**

A14-50 Identify affected ratios *(Learning Objective 4)*

Cathy Wolanin is the controller of Saturn, a dance club whose year-end is December 31. Wolanin prepares checks for suppliers in December and posts them to the appropriate accounts in that month. However, she holds on to the checks and mails them to the suppliers in January. What financial ratio(s) are most affected by the action? What is Wolanin's purpose in undertaking this activity?

Ethical Issue

A14-51 Effect of decisions on ratios *(Learning Objective 4)*

Betsy Ross Flag Company's long-term debt agreements make certain demands on the business. For example, Ross may not purchase treasury stock in excess of the balance of retained earnings. Also, long-term debt may not exceed stockholders' equity, and the current ratio may not fall below 1.50. If Ross fails to meet any of those requirements, the company's lenders have the authority to take over management of the company.

Changes in consumer demand have made it hard for Ross to attract customers. Current liabilities have mounted faster than current assets, causing the current ratio to fall to 1.47. Before releasing financial statements, Ross's management is scrambling to improve the current ratio. The controller points out that an investment can be classified as either long-term or short-term, depending on management's intention. By deciding to convert an investment to cash within one year, Ross can classify the investment as short-term—a current asset. On the controller's recommendation, Ross's board of directors votes to reclassify long-term investments as short-term.

Requirements

1. What effect will reclassifying the investments have on the current ratio? Is Ross's true financial position stronger as a result of reclassifying the investments?
2. Shortly after the financial statements are released, sales improve and so, too, does the current ratio. As a result, Ross's management decides not to sell the investments it had reclassified as short-term. Accordingly, the company reclassifies the investments as long-term. Has management behaved unethically? Give the reasoning underlying your answer.

Team Project

A14-52 Comparison of common-size financials *(Learning Objective 3)*

Select a company and obtain its financial statements. Convert the income statement and the balance sheet to common size and compare the company you selected to the industry average. Discuss how the company you selected measures up to the industry averages and form an opinion as to whether this company is above average, average, or below average. Use Google to find resources for identifying industry averages and common-size statements by industry. Clearly identify your sources and discuss why the source(s) you have used are likely to be reliable sources.

15

Sustainability

Learning Objectives

1. Describe why sustainability is important to today's organizations
2. Describe the role of management accounting in supporting sustainability
3. Describe the challenges to implementing and using an environmental management accounting system

© Jodi Jacobson / iStockphoto.com

The J.M. Smucker Company

has adopted a sustainability strategy which calls for managers to view business decisions in terms of their economic viability, impact on the environment, and social responsibility. As part of this strategy, the company recently redesigned the packaging of its Jif© peanut butter jars to save over 900,000 pounds of resin a year, which is enough resin to produce close to 14 million jars on an annual basis. The reduced use of resin not only saved the company money, but reduced the amount of resin that could eventually end up in landfills or recycling plants. The company also began producing the plastic bottles for its Crisco© products rather than having the bottles delivered by a third party. As a result, the company was able to significantly reduce delivery truck traffic, energy consumption, and greenhouse gas emissions. To further reduce the environmental impact of its operations, J.M. Smucker constructed a LEED certified distribution warehouse in Chico, CA, that generates 40% of its power on-site through solar arrays, a methane generator, and natural gas turbines. In addition to these initiatives which are already in place, the company has set a 5-year goal to reduce waste sent to landfills by 75%, reduce greenhouse gas emissions by 15%, and reduce water use by 25%— all by 2014.

In addition to focusing on the environmental impact of its operations, the company also focuses on maintaining social responsibility through respecting and promoting the welfare of customers, employees, and the communities in which it does business. For example, as part of its commitment to social responsibility, J.M. Smucker directs all of its marketing at adults, rather than children. As a result, the company has been ranked number one on the "Top Ten Best Advertisers" list by the Parents Television Council.

The company is also deeply involved with educational programs and charitable organizations. One such organization is Feeding America, the national network of food banks that supplies food to hunger centers across the nation. Through partnerships with local hunger centers and companies such as Smucker's, food banks in the Feeding America network are able to provide meals to over 37 million needy Americans each year, over a third of whom are children.[1]

Progressive companies, such as J.M. Smucker, are considering the environmental and societal impact of their operations in many, if not all, of their business decisions. In this chapter, we'll explore why sustainability has become such an important business consideration and how environmental management accounting (EMA) can help support an organization's journey toward sustainability. We'll also consider some of the challenges associated with setting up and using EMA systems.

[1]The J.M. Smucker Company 2011 Corporate Responsibility Report.
The J.M. Smucker 2009 Annual Report
www.FeedingAmerica.org.

Why is Sustainability Important?

By definition, anything, including an activity, business, culture, or life, is sustainable if it can be maintained on an ongoing, indefinite basis. The most widely-used definition of **sustainability** with respect to business traces its roots to a report developed by the United Nations in 1987 in which sustainable development was defined as development that meets the needs of the present without compromising the ability of future generations to meet their own needs.[2]

At its 2005 World Summit, the United Nations reaffirmed the interdependence of economic, societal, and environmental factors with respect to global development.[3] As a result, businesses, such as the J.M. Smucker Company, are assessing their own practices from a "triple bottom line" viewpoint. As first discussed in Chapter 1, the **triple bottom line** recognizes that a company's performance should not only be viewed in terms of its ability to generate economic profits for its owners, as has traditionally been the case, but also be viewed by its impact on people and the planet. Thus, sustainability can be viewed in terms of three interrelated factors that influence a company's ability to survive *and* thrive in the long-run: profit, people, and planet.

From a sustainability standpoint, the world is a system connected by space and time. Air pollution in North America, for example, affects air quality in Europe (space connections). Choices we make about our energy sources today will impact future generations (time connections). Because of these connections, companies that do not incorporate sustainability into their core business values put their own long-term success and the world itself at risk.

Reasons to Embed Sustainability in the Organization

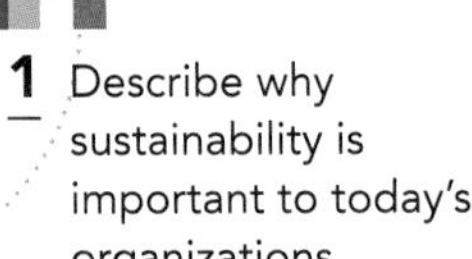

1 Describe why sustainability is important to today's organizations

Business is at a tipping point. The twentieth-century business model which often gravitated towards the exploitation of nature and people in pursuit of profit, through a "take-make-waste" mentality, is metamorphosing into a life-sustaining business model. Because of the global reach and the economic power they wield, large corporations are recognizing they are in a better position to affect positive world change, from both a societal and environmental standpoint, than are many national governments and non-profit agencies. As a result, businesses are beginning to embed sustainability into their core business functions, rather than simply "tacking on" isolated and temporary solutions to environmental and social issues brought to their attention by activists.

Rather than taking a defensive stance as many companies did during the twentieth century, businesses are going on the offensive by making sustainability a driving force in every aspect of their value chain. Businesses have and are continuing to evolve: They are now realizing they can act as positive agents of change while at the same time uphold their fiduciary responsibility to provide value to their stockholders. The tension between profit creation and social responsibility is evaporating, as corporations recognize the business opportunity and value created through imbedding sustainability in all that they do.

Even though sustainability initiatives can be expensive initially, research shows that these initiatives, when implemented properly, can actually increase profits for corporations. For example, Johnson Controls has won several awards for its sustainable practices over the past several years. Between 2001 and 2006, Johnson Controls experienced market growth that was 25 times the Dow Jones Industrial Average.[4]

Sustainability should be the concern of every organization, regardless of sector, location, or size. While "doing the right thing" for the planet, society, and future generations should be reason enough to adopt sustainable practices, companies are finding that embedding sustainability throughout the organization simply makes good business sense. Some compelling business reasons for adopting sustainable practices include the following:

1. Cost reduction
2. Regulatory compliance
3. Stakeholder influence
4. Competitive strategy

[2]Brundtland Report, World Commission on Environment and Development (WCED), 1987.
[3]www.un.org/summit2005/documents.html
[4]Accenture Case Study on Johnson Controls, "Pursuing Sustainability at Johnson Controls," retrieved at https://microsite.accenture.com/sustainability/Documents/Pursuing_Sustainability_at_Johnson_Controls.pdf on July 7, 2010.

Exhibit 15-1 pictures how these forces act upon an organization, compelling it to adopt sustainable business practices.

EXHIBIT 15-1 Business Reasons for Adopting Sustainable Practices

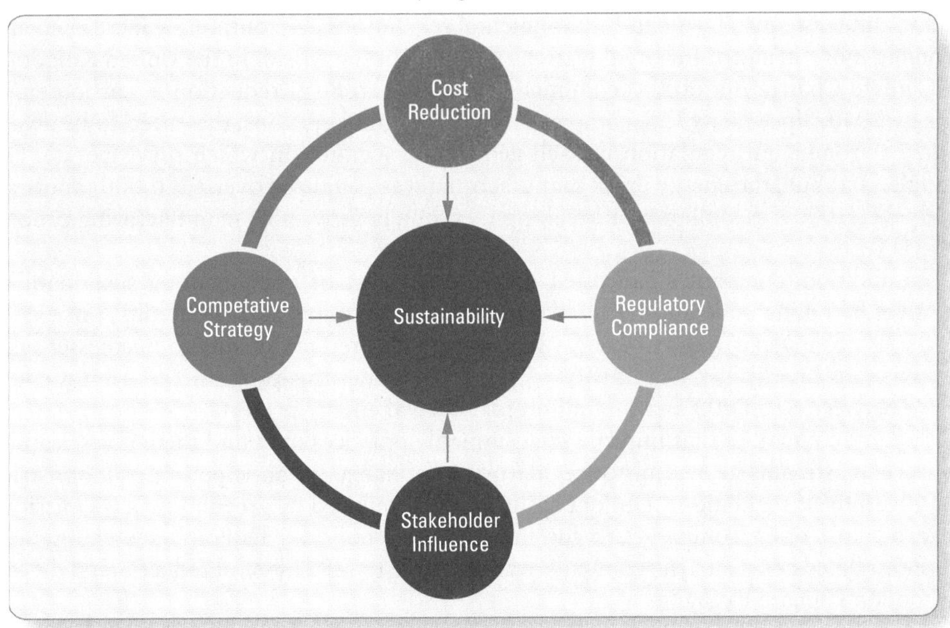

Cost Reduction

In many cases, implementing programs to support environmental sustainability will reduce an organization's costs. For example, the staff at the DoubleTree Hotel in Portland, Oregon, wanted the hotel to go "green." As an experiment on one floor of the hotel, they put placards in each room which gave guests the choice of reusing their sheets and towels if they were staying more than one day. They installed dispensers for high-quality soap and shampoo in each room instead of providing the traditional small disposable bottles. They also put signs up encouraging guests to turn off the heating/air conditioning and lighting when they were not in their room. On the "green" floor, housekeeping costs (time spent by maids cleaning the rooms) were lower, laundry costs (including water, energy, and sewer charges) were lower, and the cost of personal consumables (shampoo and soap) was significantly reduced. Staff also collected hotel guest satisfaction surveys during the experiment. Hotel management found that customers had a higher degree of satisfaction in the "green" floor than on other floors of the hotel.[5]

As a result of the "green" experiment, DoubleTree hotels expanded the use of these green practices to its other hotels. Similar practices have caught on at many other large hotel chains that now leave small placards in the hotel room asking visitors to reuse their towels and linens. Not only does this practice save water and energy for laundering, but also saves on the hotel's cost.

In many cases, what is good for the environment is also good for the organization. IKEA, a global furniture retailer, saves about £400,000 (approximately $590,000 in U.S. dollars) each year by removing plastic bags from the checkout.[6] IKEA also bales the cardboard and plastics from packaging and sells those materials. This practice has generated a new revenue stream for the company while at the same time keeping cardboards and plastics out of landfills. Many companies are finding that costs incurred for waste removal can be minimized, and new revenue streams generated, by recycling physical materials that in the past were sent to landfills.

[5]Langenwalter, Gary (2010). "Business Sustainability: Keeping Lean but with More Green for the Company's Long Haul," American Institute of Certified Public Accountants, Lewisville, Texas.
[6]Ibid.

Smith/MCT/Newscom

Regulatory Compliance

In many cases, companies must commit to environmental sustainability to assure regulatory compliance. Currently, many European countries and the United States have laws and regulations pertaining to air quality, emissions standards, hazardous substances, water quality, and waste management. Environmental regulations are continually increasing and becoming more stringent for organizations throughout the world. In the United Kingdom, the Climate Change Act (2008) commits the U.K. to an 80% reduction in carbon emissions by 2050. Since many U.S. companies have foreign operations, they need to be aware of the environmental regulation in each geographic location in which they operate. For example, Red Bull, the energy drink manufacturer, was penalized over £270,000 (approximately $412,000 U.S. dollars) for breaking recycling laws with its manufacturing process in the U.K.[7]

In addition, companies can often decrease the cost of implementing sustainability initiatives by taking advantage of available government grants and tax credits. For example, the Oregon Department of Energy has recently offered tax credits to businesses with their Business Energy Tax Credit (BETC) program. Under this program, a business could receive between $500,000 and $6 million for renewal energy projects.

Finally, companies that implement sustainable practices may find themselves reaping new revenue streams as a result of regulatory compliance. In anticipation of more stringent government regulations, DuPont systematically reduced its greenhouse gas emissions ahead of most other companies in the industry. Not only did DuPont save energy and emission-related costs, but the company was also able to sell emission reduction credits on the London Climate Exchange.[8]

Stakeholder Influence

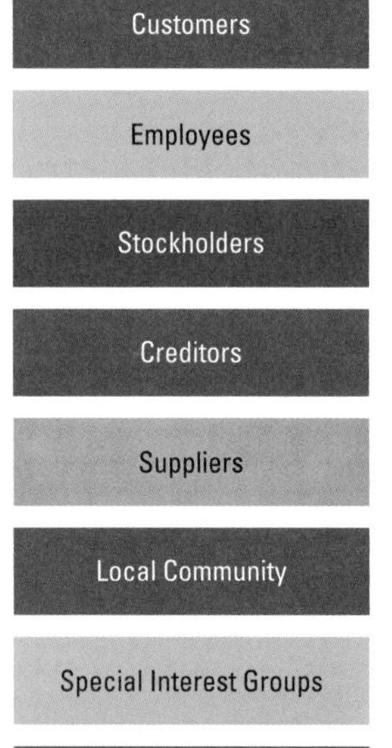

Companies often increase their commitment to environmental sustainability because of stakeholder influence. Stakeholders may include stockholders, bankers, special interest groups, employees, policy makers, customers, suppliers, or community members. Many investors seek to invest in corporations that are environmentally proactive. The growth of socially responsible investment indices, such as the Global LAMP 60 Index, FTSE4Good Index, and the Dow Jones Sustainability Index, has put increasing pressure on corporations to pay attention to sustainability. To help meet investor interest in sustainability, over 80% of the world's largest 250 companies voluntarily produce sustainability reports.[9]

Bankers are increasingly taking into account an organization's environmental performance when making credit decisions. Companies that do not adhere to sustainable practices may be at greater risk of defaulting on future loan payments and loan covenants. Why? Because they may be subject to future liabilities related to their negative impact on the environment.

Employees, customers, and suppliers are also putting pressure on companies to become more environmentally sustainable. Companies are finding that that they are better able to recruit and retain employees when their organization is actively pursuing environmental sustainability. Customers are increasingly selecting products not only on the basis of price and quality, but also on the basis of environmental impact. For example, many consumers now demand environmentally sensitive packaging, such as recyclable containers or the use of only post-consumer packaging materials. Suppliers can, and do, refuse to do business with organizations that do not meet strict environmental criteria.

In addition to the above stakeholders, community members and special interest groups can also place environmental demands on an organization by boycotting or picketing

[7]GreenBiz.com, "Red Bull Runs Afoul of U.K. Recycling Laws," July 31, 2009, retrieved at http://www.greenbiz.com/news/2009/07/31/red-bull-runs-afoul-uk-recycling-laws on July 7, 2010.

[8]Laszlo, Chris. *Sustainable Value: How the World's Leading Companies Are Doing Well by Doing Good.* Greenleaf Publishing.

[9]KPMG. *KPMG International Survey of Corporate Responsibility Reporting 2008.* The Netherlands: KPMG International, 2008.

an organization that is engaging in environmentally damaging actions. For example, in 2004, Walmart started a "green" campaign because of bad publicity it had received regarding its impact on the environment. Since that time, Walmart has saved $26 million per year in reduced fuel costs by installing auxiliary power units in its fleet of 7,200 trucks that allow the drivers to shut the trucks off during their mandatory ten-hour breaks. Walmart has also diverted over 1,100 tons of plastics from landfills since 2004 by baling and selling plastics that its stores used to discard.[10]

Why is this important?

"In order to **grow** the company, **managers** must listen to what their **customers**, stockholders, employees, and creditors want. Increasingly, these stakeholders want **"greener"** operations."

Competitive Strategy

Integrating sustainable practices can also provide companies with a competitive advantage that results from generating new revenue streams and cutting costs. For example, organizations potentially increase their market share and reputation by offering environmentally conscious products which are manufactured with environmentally sustainable processes. In addition to other features, these products use reduced packaging and have minimal disposal impact. For example, GE has a line of energy-efficient products marketed under the Ecomagination brand. Under Armour produces a line of athletic sportswear made out of recycled plastic bottles. Starbucks encourages customers to take home coffee grounds to use as soil amendment in their gardens.

Companies that become the "first mover" in an industry or societal trend often have a long-term competitive advantage because they are viewed by stakeholders as innovators, rather than followers. The development of greener products, packaging, and services gives these companies a distinct advantage as a result of product differentiation. As society's expectations for corporate responsibility continue to rise, first-movers are poised to reap huge competitive advantages. These product offerings and waste reduction practices have become part of these companies' competitive strategy.

A sustainability strategy is often implemented in the design stage of the value chain. For maximum impact, organizations should focus on initially designing the product or process with sustainability as the driving force, rather than simply focusing on pollution control and cleanup after the process has already taken place. By doing so, product quality and efficiency can be increased, and waste reduced. For example, by designing a handle-free plastic bottle for its milk, a dairy company has reduced its use of plastic by 10% and its generation of packaging waste by 5,000 tons each year.

Hasentree™ golf course community in Raleigh, NC, is another example of how sustainability can be designed into the entire competitive strategy of a business. Hasentree has partnered with Audubon International to create an environmentally based community that is a model of sustainable planning, design, construction and management. The golf course and surrounding community was developed and is marketed with environmental preservation at its core. All builders must adhere to strict "green" guidelines with respect to site clearing, home construction, and site preservation. All wastewater within the development is recycled and used to irrigate the golf course that winds through the community. As a result, the development has been awarded the Gold Signature Certification for excellence in sustainable development by Audubon International.[11] Hasentree's unique commitment to sustainability has given the housing development a competitive advantage over other golf course communities in attracting new homeowners and golfers.

[10]Walmart Corporate website, retrieved at http://walmartstores.com/Sustainability/7762.aspx on July 7, 2010.
[11]Hasentree™ Going Green, The Builder's Guide to Building Green, November, 2007.

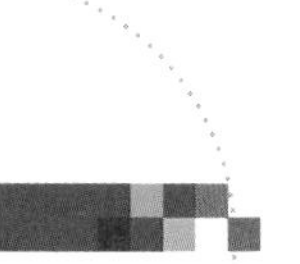

2 Describe the role of management accounting in supporting sustainability

Information Used to Support Sustainability

To support sustainability, organizations use environmental management accounting.[12] **Environmental management accounting** (EMA) is a system used for the identification, collection, analysis, and use of two types of information for internal decision making.[13] These two types of information include monetary and physical information. We'll discuss each type of information next.

Monetary Information

Monetary information is the type of information traditionally used in accounting systems. Though presented in monetary terms, the categories of costs are quite different than what has traditionally been collected and reported by financial and management accounting systems. For example, the monetary information reported in an EMA system may include:[14]

1. *Materials costs of product outputs*: These costs include the purchase costs of natural resources that are converted into products. An example would be the purchase cost of lumber for the manufacture of picnic tables. This category is similar to direct materials, since these materials become part of the final product.
2. *Materials costs of non-product outputs*: These costs include the costs of water and energy that become non-product output, such as air emissions and waste. An example would be the cost of water used as a coolant in a plant's manufacturing system.
3. *Waste and emission control costs*: These costs include the costs for handling, treating, and disposing of all forms of waste and emissions, including solid waste, hazardous waste, wastewater, and air emissions. An example would be the cost associated with treatment and disposal of hazardous by-products at a chemical production facility.
4. *Prevention costs*: These costs are incurred to prevent environmental costs. An example would be the costs of monitoring water output for contaminants.
5. *Research and development costs*: These costs include the costs of R&D projects related to environmental issues. An example would be the costs of running a laboratory aimed at developing biodegradable products.
6. *Intangible costs*: These costs include the costs of future liabilities, future regulations, productivity, company image, and stakeholder relations. An example would be the cost of a future lawsuit filed for an infringement of environmental regulations.

Physical Information

Physical information has not traditionally been part of managerial accounting systems but is a vital part of EMA systems. Examples of physical information include the following:

1. Quantity of air emissions
2. Tons of solid waste generated
3. Gallons of wastewater generated
4. Pounds of packaging recycled
5. Total amount of water consumed

By collecting and measuring physical information, such as tons of waste sent to landfills, EMA systems provide managers with a clearer view of the company's physical impact on the environment. The adage, "You can't manage what you don't measure" applies. If a company doesn't measure physical impact information, management has little chance of trying to reduce it.

[12]Environmental management accounting can also be known as "green accounting," "sustainability accounting," or "environmental accounting."

[13]United Nations Division for Sustainable Development, *Environmental Management Accounting, Procedures and Principles, 2001.*

[14]International Federation of Accountants (IFAC), 2005. *International Guidance Document of EMA*. New York: IFAC.

Materials Flow Accounting

To track their environmental inputs and outputs, organizations can use **materials flow accounting**, or MFA. As shown in Exhibit 15-2, MFA involves tracking all of the physical inputs (materials, energy, water, and so forth) and reconciling these with the output generated (including product units, wastewater generated, air emissions, packaging, and by-products). The goal is to track where everything is going; once it is visible, steps can be taken to reduce usage or to increase efficiencies. Essentially, MFA calculates the amount of waste and emissions from a manufacturing system by tracing materials (including energy) to the finished product. Identifying the processes that lead to waste and emissions can highlight opportunities for improvement.

EXHIBIT 15-2 Materials Flow Accounting: Equating Inputs with the Company's Outputs

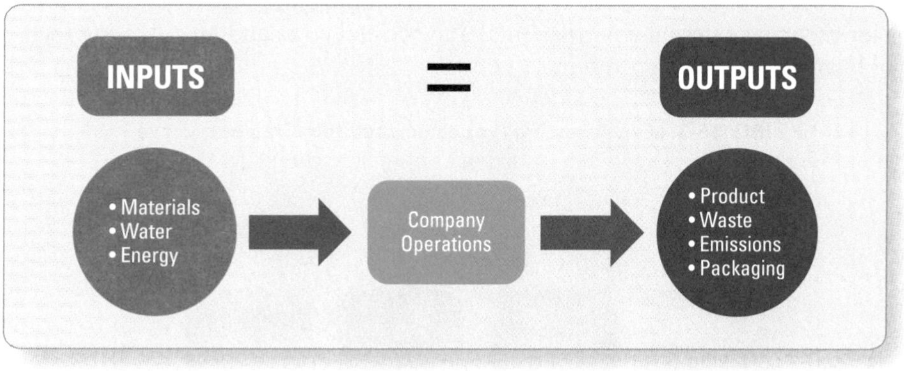

Uses of Environmental Management Accounting Information

The information contained in and produced by an organization's EMA system is designed to help support managers' primary responsibilities: planning, directing, controlling, and decision-making. Specific operational and decision-making situations where management accountants can support sustainability efforts include compliance, strategy development, systems and information flow, costing, investment appraisal, performance management, and reporting. We'll discuss each of these areas next.

Compliance

Companies are confronted with many environmental laws and regulations that can impact their operations. An EMA system gathers the information necessary to ensure that the organization complies with these laws and regulations. Management accountants also use this information to help managers understand the potential financial implications of pending environmental legislation and of past practices which may have caused environmental damage.

For example, in Chapter 3 we introduced you to Extended Producer Responsibility (EPR) laws that require manufacturers of electronic products to "take-back" a large percentage of those products at the end of the products' life in order to reduce the amount of toxic e-waste ending up in landfills. The EMA system would help gather the physical information required of these laws as well as provide managers with the costs of both compliance and non-compliance. The financial ramifications should drive product engineers to develop ways of shredding and recycling, or reusing e-waste components.

Strategy Development

In order to succeed in the long-term, organizations need to integrate sustainability into their business strategy. Management accountants can use the information from the EMA system to help identify the environmental impact of a potential strategic decision, identify opportunities to make more efficient use of resources, and take advantage of the organization's strengths. Additionally, they can help to assess the potential costs of *not* undertaking particular environmental initiatives.

Companies that imbed sustainability in their strategy take a systems thinking approach. Rather than concerning themselves with only internal costs (those costs that are incurred and paid for by the organization), managers and accountants are now considering the external costs that may not be directly or intentionally created as a result of the products and services sold by the company. These internal and external costs can be illuminated through the use of life cycle assessment (LCA).

As shown in Exhibit 15-3, LCA involves studying the environmental and societal impact of each product or service over the course of its life, from cradle-to-grave (all the way from sourcing to disposal). External costs, while not traditionally captured by GAAP-based accounting systems, can be captured by EMA systems. Both internal and external costs are considered in management's strategic decisions. Through partnership and collaboration with various stakeholders, such as suppliers, distributors, recyclers, and NGOs (non-government organizations), companies are finding innovative and cost-effective means for reducing external environmental and societal costs and are adapting their own internal business strategy as a result.

EXHIBIT 15-3 LCA: Assessing Product Impact from Cradle-to-Grave

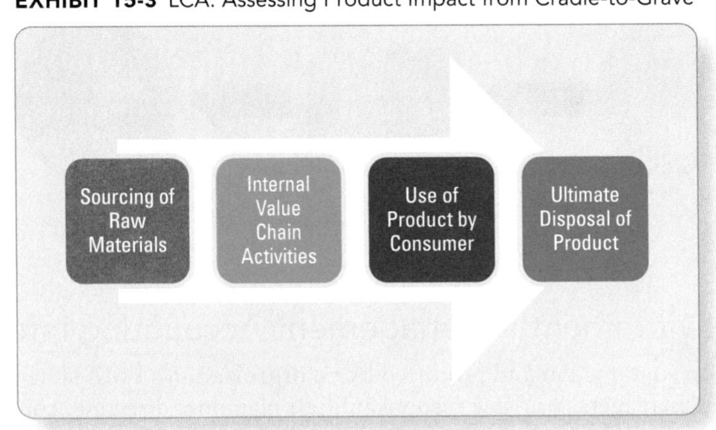

Part of the systems thinking approach to sustainability is management's ability to think beyond the impact of business activities solely on the company's profits. The triple bottom line expands on traditional financial reporting by reporting on three factors: profit, people, and planet. Traditional accounting has focused on the first bottom line: "profit." However, the second bottom line, "people," recognizes that communities and people must also thrive if businesses are to succeed. Finally, the third bottom line, "planet," recognizes that in the long-run, the survival of all people and businesses depend on the health of our planet. EMA systems support a triple bottom line approach to management.

"Management **accountants** are increasingly called upon to incorporate **environmental impact** information in the **analyses** they **provide** to management."

Systems and Information Flow

Management accountants can help to assess the need for new information systems. They can also help to implement new systems and suggest system modifications as the organization's information needs change. New environmental laws, new products, new processes, and new technologies all create demand for new or updated information systems.

Costing

Management accountants can help to make environmental costs more visible. Methods can be improved for allocating environmental costs (such as waste removal, water, and energy costs) to specific products, activities, or departments. Management accountants can also help to identify and estimate potential future environmental costs that should be recognized as potential liabilities in current periods.

Investment Appraisal

Management accountants can help to ensure that environmental costs and savings are included in capital investment analysis. In addition to the traditional methods described in Chapter 12, new capital investment tools are being developed that do a better job of incorporating environmental impact into the analysis. LCA not only helps organizations to evaluate the cradle-to-grave environmental impact of potential investments, but also provides rationale for making new investments. For example, Proctor & Gamble used LCA to justify research into developing a cool-water detergent once it determined that the majority of energy used in doing laundry was the cost of using hot water.[15] Investment appraisals for environmental projects should also consider traditionally ignored factors, such as enhanced reputation and stakeholder satisfaction gained through implementing sustainable practices.

Performance Management

Management accountants can help expand the traditional performance management systems to include environmental costs and savings, and potential environmental liabilities. Management accountants can help to identify best practices and to develop benchmarks for performance measurement.

For example, environmental sustainability measures could be included on the balanced scorecard. Recall from Chapter 10 that the balanced scorecard includes four perspectives. Some possible examples of key performance indicators for each of these perspectives might include the following:

1. *Financial perspective:* energy costs; recycling revenues
2. *Customer perspective:* number of "green" products; percent of products reclaimed after use
3. *Internal business perspective:* number of gallons of water used; amount of energy consumed
4. *Learning and growth perspective:* number of employees participating in sustainability education; number of "green" employee suggestions implemented; percent of employees with environmental responsibilities

Rather than being integrated into the original four perspectives of the balanced scorecard, sustainability has also been suggested as a new fifth perspective.

Many companies are now beginning to disclose their performance with respect to their carbon and water footprints. A **carbon footprint** is a measure of the total emissions of carbon dioxide and other greenhouse gases (GHGs), often expressed for simplicity as tons of equivalent carbon dioxide. It can be calculated for individual products, individual processes, or for the organization as a whole. Once the carbon footprint has been measured, managers can work towards reducing it.

© Christopher Steer / iStockphoto.com

Some companies, such as Timberland, Disney, and BP, are investing in reforestation projects to offset their carbon footprints in an effort to become more carbon neutral. Other companies provide customers with the opportunity to purchase carbon offsets. For example, Continental Airlines has partnered with Sustainable Travel International to provide a carbon offset program for its customers. At Continental's website, travelers have the option to calculate the carbon emissions associated with their travel and then purchase enough carbon offsets to make their travel carbon neutral. The carbon offsets are typically invested in reforestation and renewable energy projects.[16]

Similarly, a **water footprint** is the total volume of water use associated with the processes and products of a business. Some companies, such as Coca-Cola, measure their water footprint, thus enabling production engineers to consider means for reducing the footprint. For example, Rejuvenation, a manufacturer of period reproduction lighting, recently redesigned its brass antiquing processes to eliminate the discharge of selenium into the sewer

[15] P & G Global Sustainability Report 2007, retrieved July 7, 2010, at http://www.pg.com/en_US/downloads/sustainability/reports/gsr07_Web.pdf.

[16] http://www.continental.com/web/en-US/content/company/globalcitizenship/offset.aspx

system. The company's old system discharged 31,000 gallons of water per year and cost $21,655 per year to operate. The new system, which cost $8,100 to install, has no water discharge, costs $7,500 per year to operate, and discharges no selenium into the sewer system.[17]

Reporting

Environmental performance reporting is required or recommended by several agencies. The SEC requires, for example, that publicly-held companies disclose the following environment-related issues:

1. Significant costs of complying with environmental regulations in the future;
2. Costs of remediating contaminated sites;
3. Other contingent liabilities related to environmental issues; and
4. Any known trend or uncertainty about environmental issues impacting the organization.

Corporations with a global presence must also do environmental reporting for each country or locale in which they operate. For example, BP (British Petroleum) will need to disclose the estimated liability associated with its 2010 oil spill in the Gulf of Mexico. These costs include clean-up, reimbursements to neighboring states, support funds to businesses tragically affected by the spill, and so forth. These costs are estimated to be billions of dollars.

Although external environmental reporting has not yet been standardized, several organizations have been working to develop standards. Some of these organizations and their work in this area include the following:

- The Global Reporting Initiative (GRI) framework and guidelines provide standards for reporting on sustainability-related performance for organizations, including specific countries and specific sectors.
- The International Accounting Standards Board (IASB) has covered some environmental accounting reporting and disclosure standards in its international financial reporting standards.
- The Carbon Disclosure Project (CDP) involves an annual Information Request survey in which environment impact information is disclosed. The information provided through this survey is provided to institutional investors and purchasing organizations.
- The Accounting for Sustainability (A4S) Project has developed a Connected Reporting Framework (CRF) to provide information for internal and external use. A key idea behind the A4S Project is that sustainability should be integrated into an organization's overall strategy. A balanced picture of the organization should be provided to users by combining traditional financial information with environmental information.
- The International Organization for Standardization (ISO) has developed the ISO 14000 series, which address various aspects of environmental management systems. The ISO 14000 series has more than 20 voluntary standards and guides pertaining to environmental sustainability.

These organizations are not the only ones creating environmental reporting standards. Right now, environmental reporting is a field in its infancy and is constantly evolving. Management accountants can help to develop sustainability reporting that goes beyond the minimum required by law and allows the organization to take a proactive stance in managing its impact on the environment and society. By preparing internal reports that make environmental costs, savings, and other environmental issues more visible, management will be in a position to make better decisions.

Challenges to Implementing Environmental Management Accounting

3 Describe the challenges to implementing and using an environmental management accounting system

There are several challenges inherent in implementing and using an EMA system within an organization. Communication issues, hidden costs, aggregated accounting information, the historical orientation of accounting, and the newness of environmental management accounting are all potentially challenging areas.

[17]Langenwalter, Gary (2010). "Business Sustainability: Keeping Lean but with More Green for the Company's Long Haul," American Institute of Certified Public Accountants, Lewisville, Texas.

Communication Issues

For an EMA system to work effectively, many different employees within the organization need to communicate and work together. For example, members of environmental staff possess knowledge about environmental issues impacting the organization. Technical and production engineers have experience with the flow of materials, energy, and water throughout the company operations. Management accountants have expertise in accounting, cost assignment, and regulatory reporting. In reality, all areas of the value chain will need to coordinate efforts if sustainability is to be imbedded within the fabric of the organization. Communication and coordination can sometimes be challenging, yet it is necessary in order to provide the information needed to strategically manage the organization's journey towards sustainability.

Hidden Costs

In a traditional accounting system, many indirect costs are assigned to overhead because they are difficult to trace directly to a product or process. As a result, many environmental costs may get buried in the overhead account. Making environmental costs visible is a vital step in managing environmental costs.

Aggregated Accounting Information and Archaic Information Systems

Depending on the sophistication of the company's information system, accounting data is often aggregated into a limited number of accounts. For example, some companies still post material purchases into one "Purchases" account. Such a basic system does not allow management to identify the specific types and quantities of materials purchased (for example, hazardous and non-hazardous), the cost per unit for the material, nor the product for which it was purchased. If this specific information is tracked on the production floor, it is often not connected to the general ledger accounting data. In a similar vein, labor costs are often simply recorded as payroll expense or part of manufacturing overhead, rather than specifying whether the labor was related to product output, waste management, or environmental damage prevention. For an EMA system to be effective, accounting information will need to be tagged with multiple identifiers to serve various information needs.

Historical Orientation of Accounting

Financial accounting information focuses on historical transactions that are measurable, and rarely includes future-oriented costs. For an EMA system to be effective in helping management make good decisions, it will need to include a more open-minded and forward-looking definition of cost. For example, an EMA system might include an estimate of the cost of lost sales resulting from poor environmental performance. Or, it might include an estimate of the cost of losing access to markets with environment-related product restrictions. Both accountants and management will need to expand their view of what constitutes a "cost" as they develop EMA systems for their companies.

Why is this important?

"In order to provide managers with relevant **environmental information,** accountants will need to rethink their **traditional views** on what constitutes a **"cost"** and expand their costing systems to provide more **detailed information."**

Undeveloped field

Environmental management accounting is a relatively new, undeveloped field. Tools for providing environmental management accounting information are being developed and refined constantly as the field evolves. Organizations are still working to discover what information they need and how it can be reported in an accurate, timely, and relevant manner.

Future of Environmental Management Accounting

This chapter has briefly summarized the state of environmental management accounting as it exists today. There has been an increasing public interest in sustainability and "green" practices. There are a number of reasons for organizations to commit to these practices, including cost reduction, regulatory compliance, stakeholder influence, and competitive strategy. Organizations can use environmental management accounting, utilizing both monetary and physical information, to support these efforts. Accountants involved in these efforts can contribute to compliance, strategy development, systems and information flow, costing, investment appraisal, performance management, and reporting. However, sustainability practices present many challenges, including communication issues, hidden costs, aggregated accounting information, and the historical orientation of accounting information. Additionally, the field of environmental management accounting is new and is constantly evolving and changing.

Advancements in the development of managerial accounting tools to support sustainability are being made every day. Globally, sustainability is a major concern and its importance to organizations is increasing. There is a critical responsibility and opportunity for management accountants to assist their organizations in supporting sustainability through the use of environmental management accounting information which is accurate, timely, and relevant.

Decision Guidelines

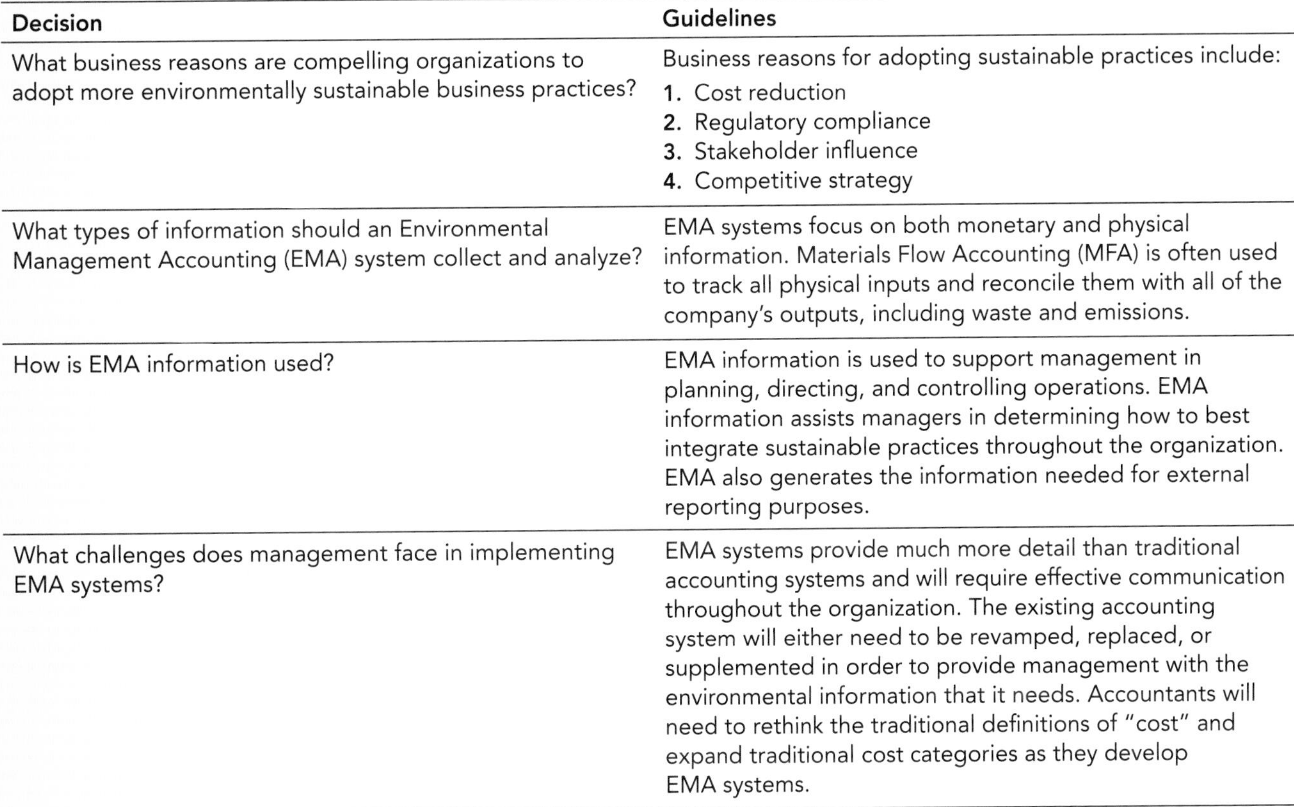

Decision	Guidelines
What business reasons are compelling organizations to adopt more environmentally sustainable business practices?	Business reasons for adopting sustainable practices include: **1.** Cost reduction **2.** Regulatory compliance **3.** Stakeholder influence **4.** Competitive strategy
What types of information should an Environmental Management Accounting (EMA) system collect and analyze?	EMA systems focus on both monetary and physical information. Materials Flow Accounting (MFA) is often used to track all physical inputs and reconcile them with all of the company's outputs, including waste and emissions.
How is EMA information used?	EMA information is used to support management in planning, directing, and controlling operations. EMA information assists managers in determining how to best integrate sustainable practices throughout the organization. EMA also generates the information needed for external reporting purposes.
What challenges does management face in implementing EMA systems?	EMA systems provide much more detail than traditional accounting systems and will require effective communication throughout the organization. The existing accounting system will either need to be revamped, replaced, or supplemented in order to provide management with the environmental information that it needs. Accountants will need to rethink the traditional definitions of "cost" and expand traditional cost categories as they develop EMA systems.

END OF CHAPTER

Learning Objectives

- 1 Describe why sustainability is important to today's organizations
- 2 Describe the role of management accounting in supporting sustainability
- 3 Describe the challenges to implementing and using an environmental management accounting system

Accounting Vocabulary

Carbon footprint. (p. 893) A measure of the total emissions of carbon dioxide and other greenhouse gases (GHGs), often expressed for simplicity as tons of equivalent carbon dioxide.

Environmental management accounting (EMA). (p. 890) A system used for the identification, collection, analysis and use of two types of information for internal decision making. These two types of information include monetary and physical information.

Materials Flow Accounting (MFA). (p. 891) An accounting system in which all physical inputs to an organization's operations are reconciled with output generated. The goal is to track where all physical inputs are going.

Monetary information. (p. 890) The type of information traditionally used in accounting systems.

Physical information. (p. 890) A vital part of environmental management accounting systems. Examples include: quantity of air emissions, tons of solid waste generated, gallons of wastewater generated, pounds of packaging recycled, and total amount of water consumed.

Sustainability. (p. 886) The ability to meet the needs of the present without compromising the ability of future generations to meet their own needs.

Triple bottom line. (p. 886) Evaluating a company's performance not only by its ability to generate economic profits, but also by its impact on people and the planet.

Water footprint. (p. 893) The total volume of water use associated with the processes and products of a business.

MyAccountingLab **Go to http://myaccountinglab.com/ for the following Quick Check, Short Exercises, Exercises, and Problems. They are available with immediate grading, explanations of correct and incorrect answers, and interactive media that acts as your own online tutor.**

Quick Check

1. (*Learning Objective 1*) All of the following are reasons a company may choose to become more sustainable *except*:
   a. State and local recycling and reclamation laws
   b. Pressure from employees
   c. Cost reduction
   d. Higher quality guarantee
2. (*Learning Objective 1*) A common definition of ***sustainability*** (from the Brundtland Report, 1987) is:
   a. The practice of conservation and the use of alternative energy sources to preserve the planet and its resources
   b. The ability to meet the needs of the present without compromising the ability of future generations to meet their own needs
   c. Doing the right thing now for the future
   d. Taking care of the planet today so that it will exist for future generations
3. (*Learning Objective 1*) Environmental sustainability is important to:
   a. Manufacturers
   b. Service organizations
   c. Retailers
   d. All of the listed choices are correct.
4. (*Learning Objective 2*) All of the following are examples of *monetary information* in an environmental management accounting system *except*:
   a. Tons of solid waste generated
   b. Cost of woods used to build chairs
   c. Dollars used for research into developing pharmaceutical products from natural ingredients
   d. Handling cost of wastewater
5. (*Learning Objective 2*) Which of the following measures is *not* an example of physical information that might be included in an environmental management accounting system?
   a. Tons of solid waste generated
   b. Cost of handling hazardous waste
   c. Gallons of wastewater generated
   d. Pounds of cardboard recycled
6. (*Learning Objective 2*) Which of the following situations is an example of a key performance indicator (KPI) for the internal business perspective?
   a. Amount of recycling revenues
   b. Number of employee sustainability training hours
   c. Amount of electricity used
   d. Percent of products reclaimed after use

7. (*Learning Objective 2*) Environmental management accounting systems should focus on what type(s) of information?
   a. Physical only
   b. Monetary only
   c. Both physical and monetary
   d. Neither physical or monetary
8. (*Learning Objective 3*) Which of the following is *not* a challenge to implementing and using an environmental management accounting system?
   a. Hidden costs
   b. Historical orientation of accounting
   c. Communication issues
   d. All of the listed items are challenges.
9. The triple bottom line consists of
   a. Profit, people, planet
   b. Product, people, place
   c. Process, planet, product
   d. People, planet, process
10. All of the following are organizations working to develop environmental reporting standards *except*:
    a. ERS
    b. IASB
    c. GRI
    d. ISO

Quick Check Answers

1. d 2. b 3. d 4. a 5. b 6. c 7. c 8. d 9. a 10. a

Short Exercises

S15-1 Identifying reasons to pursue sustainability (*Learning Objective 1*)

Listed below are several reasons an organization might pursue sustainability initiatives. Classify each reason as either: *Cost Reduction, Regulatory Compliance, Stakeholder Influence*, or *Competitive Strategy*.

a. Increasing pressure from customers has pushed Duke Energy to maintain regulated average retail rates for electricity that are lower than the U.S. average in South Carolina, North Carolina, Indiana, and Kentucky.
b. In light of rising food costs, The J.M. Smucker Company has reduced the amount of plastic used in each peanut butter jar, which helps to keep down the cost of raw materials (plastics) for the company. The drop in plastic usage also reduces the amount of plastic sent to the landfill after consumer use.
c. The Cell Phone Recycling Act (SB 20) was enacted in California to require retailers to take back old cell phones for recycling or reuse.
d. Employees at the DoubleTree Hotel in Portland, Oregon, approached management about implementing green practices throughout the hotel; as a result, the DoubleTree in Portland became the first lodging property in Oregon to earn the Green Seal certification.
e. The Ford Motor Company has committed to being the market leader in fuel economy with every new vehicle.
f. Johnson & Johnson experienced a significant increase in the number of non-compliance notices it received in a recent year. As a result, J&J has increased sustainability training throughout the company and has increased management attention on sustainability processes.
g. The DoubleTree Hotel in Portland, Oregon, instituted a paper-saving program that has reduced the cost of office paper purchased by 20% annually.

S15-2 Classifying sustainability costs (*Learning Objective 2*)

As discussed in the chapter, there are at least six categories of costs (monetary information) associated with sustainability efforts. In the table to follow, identify the proper sustainability cost category for each of the costs listed.

Cost	Sustainability cost category
Cost to the company's image and goodwill resulting from a large chemical spill	
Cost of installing scrubbers to control air pollution at an electricity-generation plant	
Cost of canvas used in producing tote bags	
Cost to develop ways to reduce greenhouse gases (GHGs) from products and processes	
Cost of air-monitoring equipment to ensure that scrubbers are functioning properly (scrubbers are air-pollution control equipment)	
Cost of water used to cool extruded products in a manufacturing plant	

S15-3 Distinguish between monetary and physical information (*Learning Objective 2*)

For each of the following examples of information, specify whether it would be included in an environmental management accounting system as monetary information (M), physical information (P), or not included in the environmental management accounting system (NA).

1. Costs of running a laboratory to develop alternative energy sources
2. Cost of the CEO's salary
3. Pounds of cardboard recycled
4. Cost of shipping raw materials between company plants
5. Cost to upgrade factory equipment to reduce emissions
6. Cost of wages for quality control inspector
7. Gallons of toxic waste generated
8. Wages of workers to comply with new EPA standards
9. Cost of electricity used to power manufacturing facilities
10. Total kilowatt hours of electricity used
11. Gallons of lubricants used in machinery
12. Tons of scrap metal recycled
13. Cost of sulfur used in erasers
14. Cost of wages for plant manager
15. Cost of materials used in lab to neutralize toxins

S15-4 Identify implementation challenges (*Learning Objective 3*)

Implementing an environmental management accounting (EMA) system can have several challenges. To follow are several implementation scenarios. For each scenario, identify which type of implementation challenge it represents (a. communication issue; b. hidden cost; c. aggregated accounting information; d. historical orientation of accounting; or e. newness of EMA.)

1. The costs of handling hazardous materials are included with the cost of handling all materials.
2. The production staff does not interact or share information with the accounting staff.
3. Company accountants can find little guidance on how to develop a sound environmental management accounting system.
4. The cost of future lost sales resulting from the poor publicity generated by a large chemical spill are not included in the results of operations provided to management even though the lost sales are significant.
5. The costs of handling hazardous materials are included with the material handling costs for all materials.

S15-5 Define key sustainability terms (*Learning Objectives 1, 2, & 3*)

Complete the following statements with one of the terms listed. You may use a term more than once. Some terms may not be used at all.

Carbon footprint	Environmental management accounting (EMA)	Monetary information
Physical information	Sustainability	Triple bottom line
Water footprint	Regulatory compliance	Materials Flow Accounting

1. The measurement of total greenhouse gas emissions (GHGs) is an organization's ____________________.
2. The number of tons of solid waste generated would be considered ____________________.
3. ____________________ involves tracking all of the physical inputs and reconciling the inputs with the output generated.
4. ____________________ is often defined as the ability to meet the needs of the present without compromising the ability of future generations to meet their own needs.
5. ____________________is a system used for the identification, collection, analysis, and use of two types of information for decision-making.

6. The type of information traditionally used in accounting systems is ________________.
7. The total volume of water use associated with the processes and products of an organization is its ________________.
8. Measuring the impact of operations on people, planet, and profit is the goal of the ________________.

EXERCISES Group A

E15-6A Identify impact of sustainability efforts (*Learning Objective 2*)

Sustainability involves more than just the impact of actions on the environment. The triple bottom line recognizes that a company has to measure its impact on people, planet, and profit for its long-term economic and social viability. To follow are examples of green initiatives recently undertaken at The Ford Motor Company. For each example, indicate whether this initiative would primarily impact people, planet, or profit.

Initiative at The Ford Motor Company	People, planet, or profit?
a. Founded Ford Volunteer Corps in response to natural disasters	
b. During the annual Global Week of Caring, 46,000 hours were contributed to volunteer projects like cleaning up highways	
c. National sponsor of the Susan G. Komen Race for the Cure	
d. Plan to aggressively restructure in order to operate profitably at the current rate of consumer demand in light of the difficult economic times and the rising costs of fuel commodities	
e. Product strategy includes advancement of technology in order to reduce greenhouse gas emissions and improved fuel economy	
f. Introduced Ford Driving Skills for Life, which educates teens about safe driving practices	
g. Expanded global markets to gain market share in more international countries	
h. Planning to focus on increasing repertoire of small-to-midsize vehicles to respond to consumer demands in an effort to gain market share	
i. Plan to introduce plug-in hybrid electric vehicles that run on advanced lithium ion batteries in 2011	
j. In 2010, Ford earned its highest net income in a decade at $6.6 billion	
k. Trained suppliers' workers in human rights via outreach programs, and as a result, was ranked first in *CRO Magazine*'s Best Citizens List	
l. Made goal to reduce CO_2 emissions in new vehicles by 30%	
m. In 2010, affiliates of the Ford Volunteer Corps gave over 112,000 volunteer hours to the community, targeting everything from schools to soup kitchens	

E15-7A Sustainability and the value chain (*Learning Objective 1*)

Each of the scenarios to follow describes a sustainability-related cost item for organizations. For each scenario, identify which function of the value chain that cost would represent (R&D, design, purchasing/producing, marketing, distributing, or customer service.) *Note: The companies and products used in this exercise are real companies with a strong sustainable practices commitment.*

a. Engineered Plastic Systems, LLC, a company that manufactures outdoor furniture, uses plastic lumber that is composed of recycled materials as a wood alternative for building its products. The plastic used is not only eco-friendly, but is also 50% recycled, 10% of which is post-consumer material. In promoting these eco-friendly features, the company is careful to make the distinction that it is not like other companies that falsely inflate their green efforts, stating specifically that it will always back up each of its claims with facts, and never mislead the customer about the actual amount of recycled plastic in its products. The cost of such promotions would fall into which function in the value chain?

b. The Hewlett-Packard Company, a manufacturer of computers and related products, established its own R&R program in 1987. This program enables consumers to return any defective or used electronic goods and ink cartridges, which helps decrease the company's impact on the environment by avoiding landfills and allows the company to recycle the plastics and metals used in these products. The cost of recycling used computer products for consumers would fall into which function in the value chain?

c. The Coca Cola Company is currently spotlighting one of its newest innovations in packaging: the PlantBottle. In one of its promotion ads, it is hailed as, "The **first ever** recyclable PET plastic beverage bottle made partially from plants... and recycles just like traditional PET plastic, but does so with a *lighter footprint* on the planet and its scarce resources." The cost of the research necessary for the Coca-Cola Company's newest foray into greener packaging would fall into which function in the value chain?

d. Able Plastics, a plastics production company, has very stringent audits on its carbon emissions, and puts a lot of effort into offsetting its carbon emissions. For instance, not only does Able Plastics invest in the Strzelecki Ranges replanting site, but Able Plastics also endeavors to cut emissions by requiring that all electronic devices be fully turned off at night in all company buildings. Able Plastics also uses carbon offsets for its delivery vehicles. The cost of these carbon offsets for delivery vehicles would fall into which function in the value chain?

e. GenPak, LLC, manufactures food packaging, and uses plastic in its products that is very conducive to recycling. In fact, much of its products are created from recycled plastic, much of which comes from GenPak's own products' post-consumer usage at the end of the products' life cycle. The cost of designing the process for continuing the life cycle of these products would fall into which function in the value chain?

f. The Sharp Corporation manufactures electronics. Sharp purchases recycled plastic parts to use in its products. The costs of this practice would fall into which function in the value chain?

E15-8A Sustainability and job costing (*Learning Objective 2*)

Anderson Plastics manufactures custom park furniture and signage from recycled plastics (primarily shredded milk jugs). Many of the company's customers are municipalities that are required by law to purchase goods that meet certain recycled-content guidelines. (Recycled content can include post-consumer waste materials, pre-consumer waste materials, and recovered materials.) As a result, Anderson Plastics includes two types of direct material charges in its job cost for each job: 1) Virgin materials (non-recycled); and 2) Recycled-content materials. Anderson Plastics also keeps track of the pounds of each type of direct material so that the final recycled-content percentage for the job can be reported to the customer. The company also reports on the percentage of recycled content to total plastic used each month on its own internal reporting system to help to encourage managers to use recycled content whenever possible.

Anderson Plastics uses a predetermined manufacturing overhead rate of $8.50 per direct labor hour. Here is a summary of the materials and labor used on a recent job for Delaware County:

Description	Quantity	Cost
Virgin materials	210 pounds	$ 5.00 per pound
Recycled-content materials	490 pounds	$ 5.50 per pound
Direct labor	15 hours	$16.00 per hour

Requirements

1. Calculate the total cost of the Delaware County job.
2. Calculate the percentage of recycled content used in the Delaware County job (using pounds). If items purchased by Delaware County are required by county charter to contain at least 50% recycled content, does this job meet that requirement?

E15-9A Sustainability and activity-based costing (*Learning Objective 2*)

Victor Industries manufactures a variety of custom widgets. The company has traditionally used a plantwide manufacturing overhead rate based on machine hours to allocate manufacturing overhead to its products. The company estimates that it will incur $790,000 in total manufacturing overhead costs in the upcoming year and will use 10,000 machine hours.

Up to this point, hazardous waste disposal fees have been absorbed into the plantwide manufacturing overhead rate and allocated to all products as part of the manufacturing overhead process. Recently the company has been experiencing significantly increased waste disposal fees for hazardous waste generated by certain products and, as a result, profit margins on all products have been negatively impacted. Company management wants to implement an activity-based costing system so that managers know the cost of each product, including its hazard waste disposal costs.

Expected usage and costs for manufacturing overhead activities for the upcoming year are as follows:

Description of cost pool	Estimated cost	Cost driver	Estimated activity for the year
Machine maintenance costs	$ 350,000	Number of machine hours	10,000
Engineering change orders	$ 50,000	Number of change orders	500
Hazardous waste disposal	$ 450,000	Pounds of hazardous material generated	1,000
Total overhead cost	$ 850,000		

During the year, Job 356 is started and completed. Usage data for this job follows:

200 pounds of direct material at $60 per pound
45 direct labor hours used at $18 per labor hour
100 machine hours used
4 change orders
52 pounds of hazardous waste generated

Requirements

1. Calculate the cost of Job 356 using the traditional plantwide manufacturing overhead rate based on machine hours.
2. Calculate the cost of Job 356 using activity-based costing.
3. If you were a manager, which cost estimate would provide you more useful information? How might you use this information?

E15-10A Sustainability and process costing (*Learning Objective 2*)

Keen Industries manufactures plastic bottles for the food industry. On average, Keen pays $65 per ton for its plastics. Keen's waste disposal company has increased its waste disposal charge to $45 per ton for solid and inert waste. Keen generates a total of 500 tons of waste per month.

Keen's managers have been evaluating the production processes for areas to cut waste. In the process of making plastic bottles, a certain amount of machine "drool" occurs. Machine drool is the excess plastic that "drips" off the machine between molds. In the past, Keen has discarded the machine drool. In an average month, 150 tons of machine drool are generated.

Management has arrived at three possible courses of action for the machine drool issue:

1. Do nothing and pay the increased waste disposal charge.
2. Sell the machine drool waste to a local recycler for $15 per ton.
3. Re-engineer the production process at an annual cost of $42,000. This change in the production process would cause the amount of machine drool generated to be reduced by 50% each month. The remaining machine drool would then be sold to a local recycler for $15 per ton.

Requirements

1. What is the annual cost of the machine drool currently? Include both the original plastics cost and the waste disposal cost.
2. How much would the company save per year (net) if the machine drool were to be sold to the local recycler?
3. How much would the company save per year (net) if the production process were to be re-engineered?
4. What do you think the company should do? Explain your rationale.

E15-11A Sustainability and cost behavior (*Learning Objective 2*)

Dazzle Entertainment is a provider of cable, internet, and on-demand video services. Dazzle currently sends monthly bills to its customers via the postal service. Because of a concern for the environment and recent increases in postal rates, Dazzle management is considering offering an option to its customers for paperless billing. In addition to saving printing, paper, and postal costs, paperless billing will save energy and water (through reduced paper needs, reduced waste disposal, and reduced transportation needs). While Dazzle would like to switch to 100% paperless billing, many of its customers are not comfortable with paperless billing or may not have web access so the paper billing option will remain regardless of whether Dazzle adopts a paperless billing system or not.

The cost of the paperless billing system would be $165,000 per quarter with no variable costs since the costs of the system are the salaries of the clerks and the cost of leasing the computer system. The paperless billing system being proposed would be able to handle up to 900,000 bills per quarter (more than 900,000 bills per quarter would require a different computer system and is outside the scope of the current situation at Dazzle).

Dazzle has gathered its cost data for the past year by quarter for paper, toner cartridges, printer maintenance costs, and postage costs for the billing department. The cost data is as follows:

	Quarter 1	Quarter 2	Quarter 3	Quarter 4
Total paper, toner, printer maintenance, and postage costs	$627,500	$635,000	$792,500	$650,000
Total number of bills mailed	575,000	605,000	725,000	625,000

Requirements

1. Calculate the variable cost per bill mailed under the current paper-based billing system.
2. Assume that the company projects that it will have a total of 700,000 bills to mail in the upcoming quarter. If enough customers choose the paperless billing option so that 25% of the mailings can be converted to paperless, how much would the company save from the paperless billing system (be sure to consider the cost of the paperless billing system)?
3. What if only 20% of the mailings are converted to the paperless option (assume a total of 700,000 bills)? Should the company still offer the paperless billing system? Explain your rationale.

E15-12A Sustainability and CVP concepts (*Learning Objective 2*)

Erks Garage Doors manufactures a premium garage door. Currently, the price and cost data associated with the premium garage door is as follows:

Average selling price per premium garage door	$ 1,600
Average variable manufacturing cost per door	$ 600
Average variable selling cost per door	$ 150
Total annual fixed costs	$297,500

Erks Garage Doors has undertaken several sustainability projects over the past few years. Management is currently evaluating whether to develop a comprehensive software control system for its manufacturing operations that would significantly reduce scrap and waste generated during the manufacturing process. If the company were to implement this software control system in its manufacturing operations, the use of the software control system would result in an increase of $62,500 in its annual fixed costs while the average variable manufacturing cost per door would drop by $50.

Requirements

1. What is the company's current breakeven in units and in dollars?
2. If the company expects to sell 500 premium garage doors in the upcoming year, and it does not develop the software control system, what is its expected operating income from premium garage doors?
3. If the software control system were to be developed and implemented, what would be the company's new breakeven point in units and in dollars?
4. If the company expects to sell 500 premium garage doors in the upcoming year, and it develops the software control system, what is its expected operating income from premium garage doors?
5. If the company expects to sell 500 premium garage doors in the upcoming year, do you think the company should implement the software control system? Why or why not? What factors should the company consider?

E15-13A Sustainability and short-term decision-making (*Learning Objective 2*)

Over the past several years, decommissioned U.S. warships have been turned into artificial reefs in the ocean by towing them out to sea and sinking them. The thinking was that sinking the ship would conveniently dispose of it while providing an artificial reef environment for aquatic life. In reality, some of the sunken ships have released toxins into the ocean and have been costly to decontaminate. Now the U.S. government is taking bids to instead dismantle and recycle ships that have recently been decommissioned (but have not been sunk yet).

Assume that a recently decommissioned aircraft, the USS *Hudak*, is estimated to contain approximately 40 tons of recyclable materials able to be sold for approximately $33.1 million. The low bid for dismantling and transporting the ship materials to appropriate facilities is $34.5 million. Recycling and dismantling the ship would create about 500 jobs for about a year in the Rust Belt. This geographic area has been experiencing record-high unemployment rates in recent years.

Requirements

1. Is it more financially advantageous to sink the ship (assume that it costs approximately $1.2 million to tow a ship out to sea and sink it) or to dismantle and recycle it? Show your calculations.
2. From a sustainability standpoint, what should be done with the decommissioned aircraft carrier? List some of the qualitative factors that should enter into this analysis.
3. As a taxpayer, which action would you prefer (sink or recycle)? Defend your answer.

E15-14A Sustainability and budgeting (*Learning Objective 2*)

Sparkle Beverages manufactures its own soda pop bottles. The bottles are made from polyethylene terephthalate (PET), a lightweight yet strong plastic. Sparkle uses as much PET recycled resin pellets in its bottles as it can, both because using recycled PET helps Sparkle to meet its sustainability goals and because recycled PET is less expensive than virgin PET.

Sparkle is continuing to search for ways to reduce its costs and its impact on the environment. PET plastic is melted and blown over soda bottle molds to produce the bottles. One idea Sparkle's engineers have suggested is to retrofit the soda bottle molds and change the plastic formulation slightly so that 20% less PET plastic is used for each bottle. The average kilograms of PET per soda bottle before any redesign is 0.005 kg. The cost of retrofitting the soda bottle molds will result a one-time charge of $18,000, while the plastic reformulation will cause the average cost per kilogram of PET plastic to change from $2.40 to $2.80.

Sparkle's management is analyzing whether the change to the bottle molds to reduce PET plastic usage should be made. Management expects the following number of soda bottles to be used in the upcoming year:

	Quarter 1	Quarter 2	Quarter 3	Quarter 4
Number of bottles to be produced	2,400,000	2,800,000	3,000,000	2,300,000

For the upcoming year, management expects the beginning inventory of PET to be 1,200 kilograms, while ending inventory is expected to be 1,600 kilograms. During the first three quarters of the year, management wants to keep the ending inventory of PET at the end of each quarter equal to 10% of the following quarter's PET needs.

Requirements

1. Using the original data (before any redesign of soda bottles), prepare a direct materials budget to calculate the cost of PET purchases in each quarter for the upcoming year and for the year in total.
2. Assume that the company retrofits the soda bottle molds and changes the plastic formulation slightly so that less PET plastic is used in each bottle. Now prepare a direct materials budget to calculate the cost of PET purchases in each quarter for the upcoming year and for the year in total for this possible scenario.
3. Compare the cost of PET plastic for Requirement 1 (original data) and for Requirement 2 (making change to using less PET). What is the direct material cost savings from making the change to using less PET? Compare the total of those savings to the cost of retrofitting the soda bottle molds. Should the company make the change? Explain your rationale.

E15-15A Sustainability and the balanced scorecard (*Learning Objective 2*)

Classify each of the following sustainability key performance indicators (KPIs) according to the balanced scorecard perspective it addresses. Choose from the following five perspectives:

- Financial perspective
- Customer perspective
- Internal business perspective
- Learning and growth perspective
- Community perspective

KPI		Perspective
a.	Water use per ton of production	
b.	Percent of packaging from products reclaimed and/or recycled	
c.	Global charitable contributions as a percent of income	
d.	Percentage of management with sustainability training	
e.	Energy use per ton of production	
f.	Revenue generated through sale of recycled goods	
g.	Environmental fines paid (expense item on income statement)	
h.	Wastewater per ton of production	
i.	Percentage of total income donated to aid during natural disasters	
j.	Safety fines paid	
k.	Energy use efficiency percentage	
l.	Number of green products	
m.	Percentage of general staff with sustainability training	
n.	Number of green products	
o.	Global in-kind donations as a percentage of total income	
p.	CO_2 in metric tons	
q.	Product safety ratings	
r.	Waste disposal costs	

E15-16A Sustainability and standard costing (*Learning Objective 2*)

Arness Containers currently uses a recycled plastic to make bottles for the food industry.

Current bottle production information:

The cost and time standards per batch of 10,000 bottles are as follows:

Plastic 300 kilograms at $8.00 per kg
Direct labor 4.0 hours at $30.00 per hour

The variable manufacturing overhead rate is based on total estimated variable manufacturing overhead of $500,000 and estimated total direct labor hours (DLH) of 10,000. Arness allocates its variable manufacturing overhead based on direct labor hours.

Proposed changes to bottle design and production process:

The container division manager is considering having both the bottle redesigned and the bottle production process reengineered so that the plastic usage would drop by 20% overall due both to generating less scrap in the manufacturing process and using less plastic in each bottle. In addition to decreasing the amount of plastic used in producing the bottles, the additional following benefits would be realized:

a. Direct labor hours would be reduced by 10% because less scrap would be handled in the production process.
b. Total estimated variable manufacturing overhead would be reduced by 5% because less scrap would need to be hauled away, less electricity would be used in the production process, and less inventory would need to be stocked.

Requirements

1. Calculate the standard cost per batch of 10,000 bottles using the current data (before the company makes any changes). Include direct materials, direct labor, and variable manufacturing overhead in the standard cost per unit.
2. Calculate the standard cost per batch of 10,000 bottles if the company makes the changes to the bottle design and production process so that less plastic is used. Include direct materials, direct labor, and variable manufacturing overhead in the standard cost per unit.

3. Calculate the cost savings per batch by comparing the standard cost per batch under each scenario (current versus prosed change). Assume that the total cost to implement the changes would be $175,700. How many batches of bottles would need to be produced after the change to have the cost savings total equal the cost to make the changes?
4. What other benefits might arise from making this change to using less plastic in the manufacture of the bottles? Are there any risks? What would you recommend the company do?

E15-17A Sustainability and capital investments (*Learning Objective 2*)

Gregg Industries is evaluating investing in solar panels to provide some of the electrical needs of its main office building in Scottsdale, Arizona. The solar panel project would cost $468,000 and would provide cost savings in its utility bills of $72,000 per year. It is anticipated that the solar panels would have a life of 20 years and would have no residual value.

Requirements

1. Calculate the payback period in years of the solar panel project.
2. If the company uses a discount rate of 8%, what is the net present value of this project?
3. If the company has a rule that no projects will be undertaken that have a payback period of more than five years, would this investment be accepted? If not, what arguments could managers make to get approval for the solar panel project?
4. What would you do if you were in charge of approving capital investment proposals?

E15-18A Sustainability and the statement of cash flows (*Learning Objectives 1 & 2*)

Renew-it Plastics is a manufacturer that takes in post-consumer plastics (i.e., empty milk jugs) and recycles those plastics into a variety of building materials. Because Renew-it has a strong focus on sustainability, the company managers try, whenever possible, to use recycled materials and to invest in sustainable projects.

Last year, the company engaged in several sustainable practices that had an impact on their cash flows. For each of the transactions listed below, indicate whether the transaction would have affected the operating, investing, or financing cash flows of the company. Additionally, indicate whether each transaction would have increased (+) or decreased (–) cash.

Transactions:

1. Throughout the year, Renew-it participated in several trade shows that featured green products for use by the housing construction industry. For each trade show, Renew-it incurred cash expenses for transportation, registration, meals and lodging, and booth setup.
2. Renew-it paid off long-term bonds during the year using excess funds.
3. Renew-it installed a "living roof" on its manufacturing facility. This roof is made mostly from sedum, a drought-resistant perennial grass-like groundcover. The plants help to reduce storm-water runoff and double the expected life of the roof over a conventional roof. The plants also reduce heating and cooling needs by providing an extra layer of insulation. Additionally, the plants absorb carbon dioxide to help to reduce greenhouse gases. The living roof was paid for with cash.
4. A fleet of plug-in electric cars was purchased for the sales staff.
5. New production equipment that is 40% more energy efficient than the old equipment was purchased for cash.
6. Engineers at Renew-it performed research into a new process that injects tiny air bubbles into the plastic to reduce the usage of raw materials (plastics) and to reduce the weight of the finished products.

7. When the plastic wood is cut into the lengths needed to make trellises, the end pieces cut off are scrap. Renew-it sold this cutting scrap to another recycler.
8. A wind-turbine was built to power part of Renew-it's operations.
9. A Honda Civic Hybrid automobile was purchased for use by the sales manager of Renew-it while on company business.
10. Renew-it became a minority partner in a biofuel project by investing $2 million in cash in the project.

E15-19A Sustainability and external financial reporting (*Learning Objective 2*)

In its 2010 Responsibility Report about sustainability, Johnson & Johnson (J&J) lists several sustainability goals and commitments it has made. In the following list from J&J's 2010 Responsibility Report, categorize each goal (or measurement) as to whether it is oriented towards the people, planet, or profit component of the triple bottom line.

Johnson & Johnson 2010 Responsibility Report—Selected Stated Goals and Commitments	People, profit, or planet?
a. Achieve an absolute reduction in water use of 10 percent compared to the 2005 baseline.	
b. Foster the most engaged, health-conscious, and safe employees in the world by improving upon our global culture of health and safety in our workplace, and by striving to make Johnson & Johnson a place where our employees are proud and excited to work.	
c. Zero accidental environmental releases; zero environmental violations.	
d. Maintain our financial discipline and strength in a tough global economy.	
e. Implement an electronics take-back program in all regions to ensure that 100 percent of electronic-based waste products can be taken back for remanufacturing or reuse.	
f. Advance community wellness by launching health initiatives to help people gain access to timely, easy-to-understand health-related information.	
g. Partner with suppliers that embrace sustainability and demonstrate a similar commitment to ours through their practices and goal-setting and the positive impacts they seek to achieve.	
h. Continue launching many new products and growing our market leadership.	
i. Enhance outcome measurement in philanthropy by working with our philanthropic partners to improve program measurements.	
j. 100 percent of manufacturing and research and development facilities will provide facility- or company-specific environmental sustainability information to the public.	

Source: Johnson & Johnson 2010 Responsibility Report (Retrieved from http://www.jnj.com/connect/caring/environment-protection/ *on June 21, 2011)*

EXERCISES Group B

E15-20B Identify sustainability efforts as impacting people, planet, or profit (*Learning Objective 2*)

Sustainability involves more than just the impact of actions on the environment. The triple bottom line recognizes that a company has to measure its impact on people, planet, and profit for its long-term economic and social viability. To follow are examples of green initiatives recently undertaken at Proctor and Gamble (P&G). For each example, indicate whether this initiative would primarily impact people, planet, or profit.

Initiative at Proctor and Gamble (P&G)	People, planet, or profit?
a. Total shareholder return has increased in the past fiscal year	
b. Long-term goals include integrating 100% renewable or recycled materials into product lines and packaging	
c. Aided 60 countries and saved thousands of lives by developing and providing PUR water filtration packets via the Children's Safe Drinking Water (CSDW) Program	
d. Partnered with Feeding America to help fight hunger	
e. Plans to eliminate manufacturing waste that is currently sent to landfills	
f. Shareholder's equity decreased from 2009 to 2010	
g. Provided disaster relief to Haiti, donating PUR packets and various hygiene products	
h. Within the past year, P&G has decreased the amount of company printed pages by 11 million through combined efforts with Xerox	
i. Working to improve and preserve the quality of water within regions and communities where operations take place to avoid contributing to water scarcity	
j. Moving toward 100% renewable energy to power plants to completely eliminate petroleum-based CO_2 emissions	
k. Partnered with UNICEF to provide vaccinations to women and children at risk for maternal and neonatal tetanus	
l. Funds NGO efforts to educate children in India through Project Shiksha	
m. Planning to create products and packaging in such a way that consumer waste goes to recycling, compost, or waste-to-energy rather than landfills	

E15-21B Sustainability and the value chain (*Learning Objective 1*)

Each of the scenarios to follow describes a sustainability-related cost item for organizations in recent years. For each scenario, identify which function of the value chain that cost would represent (R&D, design, purchasing/producing, marketing, distributing, or customer service.) *Note: The companies and products used in this exercise are real companies with a strong sustainable practices commitment.*

a. Bert's Bees, a manufacturer of products such as lip balm, has developed a new soap label called TerraSkin(TM) Wraps that is "treeless" and "bleach-free"(it is a paper-label alternative). The cost of researching the proper process and combinations of components for this new label would fall into which function in the value chain?

b. The Kellogg Company, known for its breakfast cereals, has successfully switched the majority of its packaging over to 100% recycled materials, 35% of which is consumer-recycled. According to the company's analysis, the impact of this achievement can be found in the decreased overall carbon footprint left by the company, as well as increased recyclability of this packaging. The cost of designing the life cycle of Kellogg's packaging would fall into which function in the value chain?

c. Patagonia, a clothing manufacturer, launched a program in 2005 called the Common Threads Initiative. In an effort to prevent clothing from going to landfills, the company collects used and damaged garments from consumers. These textiles are then salvaged and recycled as new products. The costs involved in running this program to take back used garments would fall into which function in the value chain?

d. General Mills produces a variety of different foods. The company recognizes the importance of encouraging good nutrition among the youth of America and has taken special initiative to ensure that its marketing strategies promote healthy lifestyles. It avoids targeting children under twelve with advertisements for foods that are high in sugar. The cost of these marketing campaigns would fall into which function in the value chain?

e. The Target Corporation, a retailing company, offers a line of garments that have been treated for stain management. However, such treatments usually include a chemical (PFOA) that has been found to be potentially harmful to humans, so Target only purchases from manufacturers that offer PFOA-free alternatives. The cost of the garments treated with the PFOA-alternatives would fall into which function in the value chain?

f. To help offset carbon emissions, U-Haul, a moving truck rental company, gives its consumers an option to donate $1 - $5 at the time of a transaction. Just two years after its launch in 2007, $1,000,000 was raised and 133,000 trees were planted with the proceeds. The cost of these carbon offsets purchased for the delivery vehicles rented by U-Haul would fall into which function in the value chain?

E15-22B Sustainability and job costing (*Learning Objective 2*)

Walton Plastics manufactures custom park furniture and signage from recycled plastics (primarily shredded milk jugs.) Many of the company's customers are municipalities that are required by law to purchase goods that meet certain recycled-content guidelines. (Recycled content can include post-consumer waste materials, pre-consumer waste materials, and recovered materials.) As a result, Walton Plastics includes two types of direct material charges in its job cost for each job: 1) Virgin materials (non-recycled); and 2) Recycled-content materials. The company also keeps track of the pounds of each type of direct material so that the final recycled-content percentage for the job can be reported to the customer. The company also reports on the percentage of recycled content to total plastic used each month on its own internal reporting system to help encourage managers to use recycled content whenever possible.

The company uses a predetermined manufacturing overhead rate of $10.00 per direct labor hour. Here is a summary of the materials and labor used on a recent job for Mission County:

Description	Quantity	Cost
Virgin materials	320 pounds	$ 4.00 per pound
Recycled-content materials	480 pounds	$ 5.00 per pound
Direct labor	12 hours	$20.00 per hour

Requirements

1. Calculate the total cost of the Mission County job.
2. Calculate the percentage of recycled content used in the Mission County job (using pounds). If items purchased by Mission County are required by county charter to contain at least 50% recycled content, does this job meet that requirement?

E15-23B Sustainability and activity-based costing (*Learning Objective 2*)

Benedict Industries manufactures a variety of custom widgets. The company has traditionally used a plantwide manufacturing overhead rate based on machine hours to allocate manufacturing overhead to its products. The company estimates that it will incur $790,000 in total manufacturing overhead costs in the upcoming year and will use 10,000 machine hours.

Up to this point, hazardous waste disposal fees have been absorbed into the plantwide manufacturing overhead rate and allocated to all products as part of the manufacturing overhead process. Recently the company has been experiencing significantly increased waste disposal fees for hazardous waste generated by certain products and, as a result, profit margins on all products have been negatively impacted. Company management wants to implement an activity-based costing system so that managers know the cost of each product, including its hazard waste disposal costs.

Expected usage and costs for manufacturing overhead activities for the upcoming year are as follows:

Description of cost pool	Estimated cost	Cost driver	Estimated activity for the year
Machine maintenance costs	$350,000	Number of machine hours	10,000
Engineering change orders	$100,000	Number of change orders	1,000
Hazardous waste disposal	$400,000	Pounds of hazardous material generated	2,000
Total overhead cost	$850,000		

During the year, Job 356 is started and completed. Usage data for this job follows:

150 pounds of direct material at $75 per pound
50 direct labor hours used at $20 per labor hour
110 machine hours used
6 change orders
73 pounds of hazardous waste generated

Requirements

1. Calculate the cost of Job 356 using the traditional plantwide manufacturing overhead rate based on machine hours.
2. Calculate the cost of Job 356 using activity-based costing.
3. If you were a manager, which cost estimate would provide you more useful information? How might you use this information?

E15-24B Sustainability and process costing (*Learning Objective 2*)

Sabatini Industries manufactures plastic bottles for the food industry. On average, Sabatini pays $65 per ton for its plastics. Sabatini's waste disposal company has increased its waste disposal charge to $25 per ton for solid and inert waste. Sabatini generates a total of 500 tons of waste per month.

Sabatini's managers have been evaluating the production processes for areas to cut waste. In the process of making plastic bottles, a certain amount of machine "drool" occurs. Machine drool is the excess plastic that drips off the machine between molds. In the past, Sabatini has discarded the machine drool. In an average month, 150 tons of machine drool are generated.

Management has arrived at three possible courses of action for the machine drool issue:

1. Do nothing and pay the increased waste disposal charge.
2. Sell the machine drool waste to a local recycler for $20 per ton.
3. Re-engineer the production process at an annual cost of $90,000. This change in the production process would cause the amount of machine drool generated to be reduced by 50% each month. The remaining machine drool would then be sold to a local recycler for $20 per ton.

Requirements

1. What is the annual cost of the machine drool currently? Include both the original plastics cost and the waste disposal cost.
2. How much would the company save per year (net) if the machine drool were to be sold to the local recycler?
3. How much would the company save per year (net) if the production process were to be re-engineered?
4. What do you think the company should do? Explain your rationale.

E15-25B Sustainability and cost behavior (*Learning Objective 2*)

Meriweather Entertainment is a provider of cable, internet, and on-demand video services. Meriweather currently sends monthly bills to its customers via the postal service. Because of a concern for the environment and recent increases in postal rates, Meriweather management is considering offering an option to its customers for paperless billing. In addition to saving printing, paper, and postal costs, paperless billing will save energy and water (through reduced paper needs, reduced waste disposal, and reduced transportation needs). While Meriweather would like to switch to 100% paperless billing, many of its customers are not comfortable with paperless billing or may not have web access so the paper billing option will remain regardless of whether Meriweather adopts a paperless billing system or not.

The cost of the paperless billing system would be $215,000 per quarter with no variable costs since the costs of the system are the salaries of the clerks and the cost of leasing the computer system. The paperless billing system being proposed would be able to handle up to 800,000 bills per quarter (more than 800,000 bills per quarter would require a different computer system and is outside the scope of the current situation at Meriweather).

Meriweather has gathered its cost data for the past year by quarter for paper, toner cartridges, printer maintenance costs, and postage costs for the billing department. The cost data is as follows:

	Quarter 1	Quarter 2	Quarter 3	Quarter 4
Total paper, toner, printer maintenance, and postage costs	$627,500	$645,000	$822,500	$678,000
Total number of bills mailed	575,000	655,000	725,000	665,000

Requirements

1. Calculate the variable cost per bill mailed under the current paper-based billing system.
2. Assume that the company projects that it will have a total of 600,000 bills to mail in the upcoming quarter. If enough customers choose the paperless billing option so that 45% of the mailings can be converted to paperless, how much would the company save from the paperless billing system (be sure to consider the cost of the paperless billing system)?
3. What if only 30% of the mailings are converted to the paperless option (assume a total of 600,000 bills)? Should the company still offer the paperless billing system? Explain your rationale.

E15-26B Sustainability and CVP concepts (*Learning Objective 2*)

Janasko Garage Doors manufactures a premium garage door. Currently, the price and cost data associated with the premium garage door is as follows:

Average selling price per premium garage door	$ 1,800
Average variable manufacturing cost per door	$ 700
Average variable selling cost per door	$ 150
Total annual fixed costs	$356,250

Janasko Garage Doors has undertaken several sustainability projects over the past few years. Management is currently evaluating whether to develop a comprehensive software control system for its manufacturing operations that would significantly reduce scrap and waste generated during the manufacturing process. If the company were to implement this software control system in its manufacturing operations, the use of the software control system would result in an increase of $33,750 in its annual fixed costs, while the average variable manufacturing cost per door would drop by $25.

Requirements

1. What is the company's current breakeven in units and in dollars?
2. If the company expects to sell 500 premium garage doors in the upcoming year, and it does not develop the software control system, what is its expected operating income from premium garage doors?
3. If the software control system were to be developed and implemented, what would be the company's new breakeven point in units and in dollars?
4. If the company expects to sell 500 premium garage doors in the upcoming year, and it develops the software control system, what is its expected operating income from premium garage doors?
5. If the company expects to sell 500 premium garage doors in the upcoming year, do you think the company should implement the software control system? Why or why not? What factors should the company consider?

E15-27B Sustainability and short-term decision-making (*Learning Objective 2*)

Over the past several years, decommissioned U.S. warships have been turned into artificial reefs in the ocean by towing them out to sea and sinking them. The thinking was that sinking the ship would conveniently dispose of it while providing an artificial reef environment for aquatic life. In reality, some of the sunken ships have released toxins into the ocean and have been costly to decontaminate. Now the U.S. government is taking bids to instead dismantle and recycle ships that have recently been decommissioned (but have not been sunk yet).

Assume that a recently decommissioned aircraft, the USS *Blaze*, is estimated to contain approximately 40 tons of recyclable materials able to be sold for approximately $32.9 million. The low bid for dismantling and transporting the ship materials to appropriate facilities is $34.7 million. Recycling and dismantling the ship would create about 500 jobs for about a year in the Rust Belt. This geographic area has been experiencing record-high unemployment rates in recent years.

Requirements

1. Is it more financially advantageous to sink the ship (assume that it costs approximately $1.45 million to tow a ship out to sea and sink it) or to dismantle and recycle it? Show your calculations.
2. From a sustainability standpoint, what should be done with the decommissioned aircraft carrier? List some of the qualitative factors that should enter into this analysis.
3. As a taxpayer, which action would you prefer (sink or recycle)? Defend your answer.

E15-28B Sustainability and budgeting (*Learning Objective 2*)

Tongish Beverages manufactures its own soda pop bottles. The bottles are made from polyethylene terephthalate (PET), a lightweight yet strong plastic. Tongish uses as much PET recycled resin pellets in its bottles as it can, both because using recycled PET helps Tongish to meet its sustainability goals and because recycled PET is less expensive than virgin PET.

Tongish is continuing to search for ways to reduce its costs and its impact on the environment. PET plastic is melted and blown over soda bottle molds to produce the bottles. One idea Tongish's engineers have suggested is to retrofit the soda bottle molds and change the plastic formulation slightly so that 20% less PET plastic is used for each bottle. The average kilograms of PET per soda bottle before any redesign is 0.005 kg. The cost of retrofitting the soda bottle molds will result a one-time charge of $15,000, while the plastic reformulation will cause the average cost per kilogram of PET plastic to change from $2.50 to $2.70.

Tongish's management is analyzing whether the change to the bottle molds to reduce PET plastic usage should be made. Management expects the following number of soda bottles to be used in the upcoming year:

	Quarter 1	Quarter 2	Quarter 3	Quarter 4
Number of bottles to be produced	2,400,000	2,900,000	2,700,000	2,300,000

For the upcoming year, management expects the beginning inventory of PET to be 1,200 kilograms, while ending inventory is expected to be 1,400 kilograms. During the first three quarters of the year, management wants to keep the ending inventory of PET at the end of each quarter equal to 10% of the following quarter's PET needs.

Requirements

1. Using the original data (before any redesign of soda bottles), prepare a direct materials budget to calculate the cost of PET purchases in each quarter for the upcoming year and for the year in total.
2. Assume that the company retrofits the soda bottle molds and changes the plastic formulation slightly so that less PET plastic is used in each bottle. Now prepare a direct materials budget to calculate the cost of PET purchases in each quarter for the upcoming year and for the year in total for this possible scenario.
3. Compare the cost of PET plastic for Requirement 1 (original data) and for Requirement 2 (making change to using less PET). What is the direct material cost savings from making the change to using less PET? Compare the total of those savings to the cost of retrofitting the soda bottle molds. Should the company make the change? Explain your rationale.

E15-29B Sustainability and the balanced scorecard (*Learning Objective 2*)

Classify each of the following sustainability key performance indicators (KPIs) according to the balanced scorecard perspective it addresses. Choose from the following five perspectives:

- Financial perspective
- Customer perspective
- Internal business perspective
- Learning and growth perspective
- Community perspective

KPI		Perspective
a.	Excessive overtime	
b.	Megawatts of energy consumed	
c.	Water reclamation costs	
d.	Number of departments integrating sustainable practices	
e.	Percentage of income donated to homeless shelters and food distribution units	
f.	Percentage of packaging utilizing recycled materials	
g.	Waste removal expense	
h.	Waste pounds generated per ton of production	
i.	Number of employee hours devoted to volunteering for Feeding America	
j.	Gas used per ton of production	
k.	Number of green products available	
l.	Refining costs for recycled goods	
m.	CO_2 emissions per ton of production	
n.	Revenue from recycled goods	
o.	Percentage of resources purchased from local vendors	
p.	Percentage of income donated to local after-school programs	
q.	Number of sustainability training hours	
r.	Percentage of packaging reclaimed or recycled after use	

E15-30B Sustainability and standard costing (*Learning Objective 2*)

Falcon Containers currently uses a recycled plastic to make bottles for the food industry.

Current bottle production information:

The cost and time standards per batch of 10,000 bottles are as follows:

Plastic 250 kilograms at $12.00 per kg
Direct labor 6.0 hours at $25.00 per hour

The variable manufacturing overhead rate is based on total estimated variable manufacturing overhead of $400,000 and estimated total direct labor hours (DLH) of 20,000. Falcon allocates its variable manufacturing overhead based on direct labor hours.

Proposed changes to bottle design and production process:

The container division manager is considering having both the bottle redesigned and the bottle production process reengineered so that the plastic usage would drop by 20% overall due both to generating less scrap in the manufacturing process and using less plastic in each bottle. In addition to decreasing the amount of plastic used in producing the bottles, the additional following benefits would be realized:

a. Direct labor hours would be reduced by 10% because less scrap would be handled in the production process.
b. Total estimated variable manufacturing overhead would be reduced by 5% because less scrap would need to be hauled away, less electricity would be used in the production process, and less inventory would need to be stocked.

Requirements

1. Calculate the standard cost per batch of 10,000 bottles using the current data (before the company makes any changes). Include direct materials, direct labor, and variable manufacturing overhead in the standard cost per unit.
2. Calculate the standard cost per batch of 10,000 bottles if the company makes the changes to the bottle design and production process so that less plastic is used. Include direct materials, direct labor, and variable manufacturing overhead in the standard cost per unit.

3. Calculate the cost savings per batch by comparing the standard cost per batch under each scenario (current versus prosed change). Assume that the total cost to implement the changes would be $248,400. How many batches of bottles would need to be produced after the change to have the cost savings total equal the cost to make the changes?
4. What other benefits might arise from making this change to using less plastic in the manufacture of the bottles? Are there any risks? What would you recommend the company do?

E15-31B Sustainability and capital investments (*Learning Objective 2*)

Thomas Industries is evaluating investing in solar panels to provide some of the electrical needs of its main office building in Phoenix, Arizona. The solar panel project would cost $490,000 and would provide cost savings in its utility bills of $70,000 per year. It is anticipated that the solar panels would have a life of 20 years and would have no residual value.

Requirements

1. Calculate the payback period in years for the solar panel project.
2. If the company uses a discount rate of 10%, what is the net present value of this project?
3. If the company has a rule that no projects will be undertaken that have a payback period of more than five years, would this investment be accepted? If not, what arguments could managers make to get approval for the solar panel project?
4. What would you do if you were in charge of approving capital investment proposals?

E15-32B Sustainability and the statement of cash flows (*Learning Objectives 1 & 2*)

The Plastic Lumber Company, Inc., (PLC) is a manufacturer that takes in post-consumer plastics (i.e., empty milk jugs) and recycles those plastics into a "plastic lumber" that can be used to build furniture, decking, and a variety of other items. Because Plastic Lumber has a strong focus on sustainability, the company managers try, whenever possible, to use recycled materials and to invest in sustainable projects.

Last year, the company engaged in several sustainable practices that had an impact on their cash flows. For each of the transactions listed below, indicate whether the transaction would have affected the operating, investing, or financing cash flows of the company. Additionally, indicate whether each transaction would have increased (+) or decreased (–) cash.

Transactions:

1. New production equipment that is 25% more energy efficient than the old equipment was purchased for cash.
2. A fleet of Toyota Prius hybrid automobiles were purchased for the use of the sales staff.
3. Throughout the year, PLC participated in several trade shows that featured green products for use by parks and recreation facilities. For each trade show, PLC incurred cash expenses for transportation, registration, meals and lodging, and booth setup.
4. A new delivery truck that uses biofuel was purchased for cash.
5. PLC built a new office building as its administrative headquarters. The new building is LEED certified and was paid for with cash.
6. PLC became a minority partner in a wind-turbine project by investing $1 million in cash in the project.
7. PLC sold plastic scrap generated by its manufacturing process.
8. Scientists at PLC performed research into whether another kind of post-consumer plastic not currently used in its plastics extrusion process could be used.
9. Solar panels were installed on the roof of the PLC manufacturing facility to supply part of the electricity needed for its operations.
10. PLC bought its own stock back to use for the company's 401K plan.

E15-33B Sustainability and external financial reporting (*Learning Objective 2*)

In its 2007–2009 Corporate Responsibility Report, Nike, Inc., lists several sustainability goals and commitments it has made. In the following list from Nike's CR Report, categorize each goal (or measurement) as to whether it is oriented toward the people, planet, or profit component of the triple bottom line.

Nike, Inc., CR Report for 2007–2009—Selected Stated Goals and Commitments	People, profit or planet?
a. Build an advocacy agenda to push for large-scale policies to help achieve global economic competitiveness for Nike.	
b. Achieve 17 percent reduction in waste generated by footwear production from a 2006 baseline by 2011.	
c. Develop scalable solutions to enable Nike's evolution to a closed-loop business model in the current economy to maximize profits.	
d. Maintain current amount of petroleum-derived solvents grams per pair of shoes (maintain the 95 percent reduction from the 1995 baseline).	
e. Implement Human Resources Management program in all factories.	
f. Increase use of Environmentally Preferred Methods in the production of footwear by 22 percent.	
g. Promote multi-brand collaboration on improving working conditions in the global supply chain, covering 30 percent of factory locations.	
h. Deliver 30 percent absolute reduction in CO_2 emissions from 2003 by 2020.	
i. Nike brand facilities and business travel are to be climate neutral by 2011.	
j. Make investing in environmentally-sustainable (green) ventures a priority.	

Source: Nike, Inc., Corporate Responsibility Report FY 07 08 09 (Retrieved from http://www.nikebiz.com/crreport/ *on June 21, 2011)*

PROBLEMS Group A

P15-34A Sustainability and cost behavior (*Learning Objective 2*)

Sparkling Spring Luxury Resorts has been evaluating how it might expand its sustainability efforts in its hotels. In any given month, an average of 109,500 room days are available in total (this total capacity figure is roughly estimated by taking the total number of hotel rooms in the hotels owned by Sparkling Spring and multiplying by 30 days per month). Management is currently targeting two areas for sustainability projects: Laundry and Housekeeping.

Laundry: Currently, in each hotel room, a small sign is placed beside the bed that informs the hotel guest that the environment will benefit if the guest reuses the linens. The company has experienced some success with the signs; the cost of laundry has decreased slightly over the past several years that the program has been in place. Management is now considering the possibility of giving guests a $0.40 credit on their hotel bill for each day of the stay that the linens in the room are reused rather than laundered.

Housekeeping: Management is also evaluating the possibility of expanding sustainability efforts in housekeeping by providing an incentive of a $1.50 credit on the hotel bill for each day the guest opts to skip a daily room cleaning.

To evaluate these options, management has gathered data for the past year for its laundry costs and housekeeping costs. The costs and occupancy data include:

Month	Monthly Occupancy Percentage	Total Laundry Costs	Total Housekeeping Costs
January	83%	$41,470	$150,051
February	81%	$41,032	$144,096
March	72%	$36,814	$141,097
April	66%	$31,435	$127,202
May	55%	$27,449	$109,858
June	51%	$26,943	$ 96,271
July	59%	$29,745	$113,977
August	53%	$26,739	$ 91,000
September	48%	$25,797	$ 83,891
October	39%	$19,700	$ 81,500
November	55%	$28,336	$111,099
December	64%	$33,572	$118,646

To satisfy investors, management only wants to implement programs which are cost effective; that is, the benefits of the program must exceed the costs of the program. Sustainability projects are expected to be cost effective.

Requirements

1. Using the high-low method, calculate the cost per guest of laundry per day. (The volume should be the number of room days, which you will have to calculate for each month.)
2. Using the high-low method, calculate the cost per guest of housekeeping per day. (Again, the volume should be the number of room days, which you would have calculated for Requirement 1.)
3. Using the high-low method, evaluate the proposal to give guests a $0.40 per day credit for reusing their room linens. Does it appear to be cost effective to offer this program?
4. Using the high-low method, evaluate the proposal to give guests a $1.50 per day credit for skipping housekeeping services. Does it appear to be cost effective to offer this program?
5. Using regression analysis, calculate the cost per guest of laundry per day. (Again, the volume should be the number of room days, which you would have calculated for Requirement 1.)
6. Using regression analysis, calculate the cost per guest of housekeeping per day. (Again, the volume should be the number of room days, which you would have calculated for Requirement 1.)
7. Using regression analysis, evaluate the proposal to give guests a $0.40 per day credit for skipping housekeeping services. Does it appear to be cost effective to offer this program?
8. Using regression analysis, evaluate the proposal to give guests a $1.50 per day credit for skipping housekeeping services. Does it appear to be cost effective to offer this program?
9. Regarding the two programs, what is your recommendation to management about which program(s) to implement? Provide rationale for your recommendation.

P15-35A Sustainability and capital investments (*Learning Objectives 1 & 2*)

A *living roof* is a roof of a building that is completely covered with grass or other vegetation planted over a waterproof layer (to protect the building interior). The Ford Motor Company's Rouge Plant in Dearborn, Michigan, is an example of a successful implementation of a living roof.

There are several benefits associated with a living roof including the following:

1. Reduce heating and cooling costs for the building.
2. Reduce storm water runoff.
3. Filter pollution out of air and water.
4. Help to insulate building for sound.
5. Create a habitat for various wildlife.
6. Increase life of roof (as compared to a typical traditional roof).

Royalton Consultants, Inc., is investigating whether it should replace its current roof with a long-lasting composite roof or a living roof. A long-lasting composite roof would cost the company $1,200,000 and would last approximately 30 years. The annual maintenance costs on this composite roof would be approximately $16,000 per year. At the end of its useful life of 30 years, various components of the composite roof could be recycled and sold for $60,000.

The other roofing alternative is a living roof. The costs associated with constructing the living roof total $1,385,000 and include the following: Vegetation $300,000, waterproof membrane $125,000, growing medium (dirt) $200,000, living roof expert consultant fee $25,000, construction costs $700,000, and other miscellaneous fees $35,000. Maintenance on the living roof is estimated to be $54,000 per year.

Management estimates that this living roof will last for 30 years. The following savings should result from the living roof:

- Heating and cooling costs will be reduced by $50,000 per year
- Storm water treatment costs will be reduced by $4,000 per year
- Filtering system costs will be reduced by $2,000 per year

The living roof would have no recyclable components to be sold at the end of its life. The company uses a 10% discount rate in evaluating capital investments.

Requirements

1. Calculate the present value of the composite roof.
2. Calculate the present value of the living roof.
3. From a purely quantitative standpoint, which roof would you recommend?
4. Are there qualitative factors to consider in this decision? What other factors besides financial should be considered in this situation?

P15-36B Sustainability and cost behavior (*Learning Objective 2*)

Cool Springs Luxury Resorts has been evaluating how it might expand its sustainability efforts in its hotels. In any given month, an average of 73,000 room days are available in total (this total capacity figure is roughly estimated by taking the total number of hotel rooms in the hotels owned by Cool Springs and multiplying by 30 days per month). Management is currently targeting two areas for sustainability projects: Laundry and Housekeeping.

Laundry: Currently, in each hotel room, a small sign is placed beside the bed that informs the hotel guest that the environment will benefit if the guest reuses the linens. The company has experienced some success with the signs; the cost of laundry has decreased slightly over the past several years that the program has been in place. Management is now considering the possibility of giving guests a $0.50 credit on their hotel bill for each day of the stay that the linens in the room are reused rather than laundered.

Housekeeping: Management is also evaluating the possibility of expanding sustainability efforts in housekeeping by providing an incentive of a $1.20 credit on the hotel bill for each day the guest opts to skip a daily room cleaning.

To evaluate these options, management has gathered data for the past year for its laundry costs and housekeeping costs. The costs and occupancy data include:

	Monthly Occupancy Percentage	Total Laundry Costs	Total Housekeeping Costs
January	73%	$ 29,544	$ 70,449
February	80%	$ 32,391	$ 84,852
March	71%	$ 29,403	$ 78,049
April	60%	$ 24,987	$ 64,511
May	50%	$ 20,318	$ 54,913
June	53%	$ 21,661	$ 57,524
July	58%	$ 25,011	$ 56,092
August	57%	$ 24,929	$ 54,679
September	39%	$ 17,100	$ 46,800
October	51%	$ 21,185	$ 50,422
November	54%	$ 23,632	$ 55,385
December	61%	$ 25,636	$ 65,910

To satisfy investors, management only wants to implement programs which are cost effective; that is, the benefits of the program must exceed the costs of the program. Sustainability projects are expected to be cost effective.

Requirements

1. Using the high-low method, calculate the cost per guest of laundry per day. (The volume should be the number of room days, which you will have to calculate for each month.)
2. Using the high-low method, calculate the cost per guest of housekeeping per day. (Again, the volume should be the number of room days, which you would have calculated for Requirement 1.)
3. Using the high-low method, evaluate the proposal to give guests a $0.50 per day credit for reusing their room linens. Does it appear to be cost effective to offer this program?
4. Using the high-low method, evaluate the proposal to give guests a $1.20 per day credit for skipping housekeeping services. Does it appear to be cost effective to offer this program?
5. Using regression analysis, calculate the cost per guest of laundry per day. (Again, the volume should be the number of room days, which you would have calculated for Requirement 1.)
6. Using regression analysis, calculate the cost per guest of housekeeping per day. (Again, the volume should be the number of room days, which you would have calculated for Requirement 1.)
7. Using regression analysis, evaluate the proposal to give guests a $0.50 per day credit for skipping housekeeping services. Does it appear to be cost effective to offer this program?
8. Using regression analysis, evaluate the proposal to give guests a $1.20 per day credit for skipping housekeeping services. Does it appear to be cost effective to offer this program?
9. Regarding the two programs, what is your recommendation to management about which program(s) to implement? Provide rationale for your recommendation.

P15-37B Sustainability and capital investments (*Learning Objectives 1 & 2*)

A *living roof* is a roof of a building that is completely covered with grass or other vegetation planted over a waterproof layer (to protect the building interior). The Ford Motor Company's Rouge Plant in Dearborn, Michigan, is an example of a successful implementation of a living roof.

There are several benefits associated with a living roof including the following:

1. Reduce heating and cooling costs for the building
2. Reduce storm water runoff
3. Filter pollution out of air and water
4. Help to insulate building for sound
5. Create a habitat for various wildlife
6. Increase life of roof (as compared to a typical traditional roof)

Brandleton Consultants, Inc., is investigating whether it should replace its current roof with a long-lasting composite roof or a living roof. A long-lasting composite roof would cost the company $1,100,000 and would last approximately 30 years. The annual maintenance costs on this composite roof would be approximately $18,000 per year. At the end of its useful life of 30 years, various components of the composite roof could be recycled and sold for $65,000.

The other roofing alternative is a living roof. The costs associated with constructing the living roof total $1,413,000 and include the following: Vegetation $350,000, waterproof membrane $140,000, growing medium (dirt) $220,000, living roof expert consultant fee $24,000, construction costs $650,000, and other miscellaneous fees $29,000. Maintenance on the living roof is estimated to be $49,000 per year.

Management estimates that this living roof will last for 30 years. The following savings should result from the living roof:

- Heating and cooling costs will be reduced by $50,000 per year
- Storm water treatment costs will be reduced by $4,000 per year
- Filtering system costs will be reduced by $2,000 per year

The living roof would have no recyclable components to be sold at the end of its life.

The company uses an 8% discount rate in evaluating capital investments.

Requirements

1. Calculate the present value of the composite roof.
2. Calculate the present value of the living roof.
3. From a purely quantitative standpoint, which roof would you recommend?
4. Are there qualitative factors to consider in this decision? What other factors besides financial should be considered in this situation?

CRITICAL THINKING

Discussion & Analysis

A15-38 Discussion Questions

1. Pressure to become more sustainable can usually be categorized into four main reasons: cost reduction, regulatory compliance, stakeholder influence, and competitive strategy. Think of an organization with which you are familiar. Which reason(s) do you think is(are) strongest in this organization? Which reason do you think is least relevant to this organization?
2. Adding a fifth perspective of "community" to the traditional four balanced scorecard perspectives (financial, customer, internal business, and learning and growth) is sometimes advocated as a way to measure a company's performance in sustainability. Do you think the fifth perspective should be added, or do you think sustainability measures should be integrated into the traditional four perspectives? Provide rationale for your answer.
3. Information from an environmental management accounting (EMA) system can be used to support managers and their primary responsibilities of planning, directing, and controlling. Think of an organization with which you are familiar. Give an example of information from an EMA system that could be useful to a manager in each of these three primary responsibility areas.
4. Find a recent annual report for a publicly-held company in which you are interested. Summarize what sustainability information is provided in that annual report. Based on the sustainability information provided in the annual report, what measurements do you think the company might use to track its sustainability efforts? (You can use your imagination here; the actual sustainability measures are unlikely to be in the annual report.)
5. There are three components in the triple bottom line: people, planet, and profit. Which component do you think is most important? Why?
6. The effect of sustainability on the planet (environment) is probably the most visible component of the triple bottom line. For a company with which you are familiar, list two examples of its sustainability efforts related to the planet.
7. One controversial area regarding sustainability is whether organizations should use their sustainability progress and activities in their advertising. Do you think a company should publicize their sustainability efforts? Why or why not?
8. Perform a web search on the terms "carbon offset" and "carbon footprint." What is a carbon footprint? What is a carbon offset? Why would carbon offsets be of interest to a company? What are some companies that offer (sell) carbon offsets?
9. Oftentimes, an investment in sustainable technology is more costly than a comparable investment in traditional technology. What arguments can you make for the investment in sustainable technology? What arguments can you make for the investment in traditional technology? You can use a specific technology or product in your arguments. For example, the hybrid model of a car is usually more expensive to purchase than the comparable gas-engine model.
10. Stakeholders are frequently the reason that companies adopt sustainable practices. Think of an organization with which you are familiar. List as many stakeholders as you can think of for this organization. For each stakeholder listed, describe why that stakeholder would have an interest in the company adopting sustainable practices.
11. In the chapter, five challenges to implementing an environmental management accounting (EMA) system within an organization were discussed. From your viewpoint, which of these challenges seems to be the biggest obstacle to successful implementation? Which challenge is most likely to be easiest to overcome? Provide your rationale for your answers.
12. Where do you think sustainability reporting is heading in the future? Will companies become more transparent or is sustainability reporting going to be mostly on internal reports? How important do you think this issue is?

Application & Analysis

A15-39 Corporate Sustainability Reports

Note: In the following activity, the word "sustainability" is used. You may need to search for "green" or "environmental accounting" or other similar terms, depending on the organization and the industry.

Locate an annual report for a company in which you are interested. Look through the annual report for a report on "Corporate Social Responsibility," "Sustainability," "Green," or other similar heading. Also skim the "Chairperson's Letter" or "Letter to Shareholders" for additional information on the organization's sustainability efforts. Additionally, many firms issue Corporate Responsibility (CR) reports; you may use that report if you find that there is a CR available.

Basic Discussion Questions

1. What environmental accounting information does this company report?
2. What environmental goals does this company have for the upcoming five to ten years?
3. Judging from the information in the report(s) from the company, does the company appear to emphasize people, planet, or profit? Or does the company appear to give equal emphasis to each component of the triple bottom line? Justify your answer.
4. What types of EMA information might be reported internally by this company? Make reasonable "guesses;" the annual report will not give this information directly. Use your imagination.
5. Perform a web search to find other sources of information about this company's sustainability efforts other than its own publications. What news articles can you find? Summarize the sustainability news about this company.
6. Perform a web search for sustainability issues in the industry in which this organization operates. Does the company appear to be addressing the sustainability issues of the industry?
7. What is your overall sense of the company's commitment to sustainability from everything you have seen? Be specific and give details to justify your response.

Team Project

A15-40 Sustainability and investment choices (*Learning Objectives 1 & 2*)

Increasingly, there are calls to manufacture hybrid or electric cars. Businesses and individuals purchase these cars to be environmentally friendly. However, there is an ongoing debate about whether these hybrid or electric cars are truly more environmentally friendly than the traditional gas-engine models and whether the additional upfront cost of the hybrid or electric model is offset by the fuel savings.

Requirements

1. Divide your team into two groups, the Traditional subgroup and the Hybrid subgroup. Select a car that comes in both a traditional gas-engine model and a hybrid model (for example, the Honda Civic comes in both a gas-engine model and a hybrid model). Make the assumption that the vehicle will be driven for five years and the annual miles driven will be 12,000 miles. Also, before going any further, as a group, decide upon an estimate for the cost per gallon of gas.
   a. The Traditional group should investigate the initial cost of the traditional gas-engine model. Include tax and title costs. This group should also estimate the annual fuel cost to operate this vehicle. Calculate the present value of the cost of this vehicle (include the initial cost and the annual fuel costs). Use a discount rate of 6%.
   b. The Hybrid group should investigate the initial cost of the hybrid model. Include tax and title costs. This group should also estimate the annual fuel cost to operate this vehicle. Calculate the present value of the cost of this vehicle (include the initial cost and the annual fuel costs). Use a discount rate of 6%.
2. The groups should compare costs of the two models. After comparing the costs, each group should:
   a. Research the environmental issues associated with the two car models. Formulate arguments to support your group's car model (either traditional gas-engine or hybrid).
   b. Debate which model is more desirable for businesses to purchase and why. Be specific in your reasoning. Cite your sources.

At the conclusion of the debate, as a team, make a recommendation as to which model of car (traditional gas-engine or hybrid) a typical organization today should purchase and why. Write up your conclusions in a one to two page paper.

COMPANY NAMES INDEX

Note: Company names in boldface indicate real companies.

A

B

C

D

T

U

V

W

Z

GLOSSARY/INDEX

A Combined Glossary/Subject Index

A

B

C

D

J

K

L

M

Q

R

S

T

U

V

Vertical analysis. Analysis of a financial statement that reveals the relationship of each statement item to a specified base, which is the 100% figure, 832, 836–839

Vertical integration. The practice of purchasing other companies within one's supply chain; predicated by the notion that a company's profits can be maximized by owning one's supplier, 603

Volume variance. The difference between the master budget and the flexible budget. The volume variance arises *only* because the volume of cases actually sold differs from the volume originally anticipated in the master budget, 610

W

Waste activities. Activities that neither enhance the customer's image of the product nor provide a competitive advantage; also known as non-value-added activities, 195

Water footprint. The total volume of water use associated with the processes and products of a business, 893

Weighted-average method of process costing. A process costing method that *combines* any beginning inventory units (and costs) with the current period's units (and costs) to get a weighted-average cost, 261

Wholesaler. Merchandising companies that buy in bulk from manufacturers, mark up the prices, and then sell those products to retailers, 48

Working capital. Current assets minus current liabilities; measures a business's ability to meet its short-term obligations with its current assets, 843

Work in process (WIP) inventory. Goods that are partway through the manufacturing process but not yet complete, 48–49, 106–107, 278–279

Z

Zero-based budgeting. A budgeting approach in which managers begin with a budget of zero and must justify every dollar put into the budget, 517